CODE OF FEDERAL REGULATIONS

Title 17
Commodity and Securities Exchanges

Part 240

Revised as of April 1, 2023

Containing a codification of documents
of general applicability and future effect

As of April 1, 2023

Published by the Office of the Federal Register
National Archives and Records Administration
as a Special Edition of the Federal Register

Table of Contents

	Page
Explanation	v

Title 17:

Chapter II—Securities and Exchange Commission (Continued)	3

Finding Aids:

Table of CFR Titles and Chapters	829
Alphabetical List of Agencies Appearing in the CFR	849
Table of OMB Control Numbers	859
List of CFR Sections Affected	865

Cite this Code: CFR

To cite the regulations in this volume use title, part and section number. Thus, 17 CFR 240.0–1 *refers to title 17, part 240, section 0–1.*

Explanation

The Code of Federal Regulations is a codification of the general and permanent rules published in the Federal Register by the Executive departments and agencies of the Federal Government. The Code is divided into 50 titles which represent broad areas subject to Federal regulation. Each title is divided into chapters which usually bear the name of the issuing agency. Each chapter is further subdivided into parts covering specific regulatory areas.

Each volume of the Code is revised at least once each calendar year and issued on a quarterly basis approximately as follows:

Title 1 through Title 16..as of January 1
Title 17 through Title 27..as of April 1
Title 28 through Title 41..as of July 1
Title 42 through Title 50..as of October 1

The appropriate revision date is printed on the cover of each volume.

LEGAL STATUS

The contents of the Federal Register are required to be judicially noticed (44 U.S.C. 1507). The Code of Federal Regulations is prima facie evidence of the text of the original documents (44 U.S.C. 1510).

HOW TO USE THE CODE OF FEDERAL REGULATIONS

The Code of Federal Regulations is kept up to date by the individual issues of the Federal Register. These two publications must be used together to determine the latest version of any given rule.

To determine whether a Code volume has been amended since its revision date (in this case, April 1, 2023), consult the "List of CFR Sections Affected (LSA)," which is issued monthly, and the "Cumulative List of Parts Affected," which appears in the Reader Aids section of the daily Federal Register. These two lists will identify the Federal Register page number of the latest amendment of any given rule.

EFFECTIVE AND EXPIRATION DATES

Each volume of the Code contains amendments published in the Federal Register since the last revision of that volume of the Code. Source citations for the regulations are referred to by volume number and page number of the Federal Register and date of publication. Publication dates and effective dates are usually not the same and care must be exercised by the user in determining the actual effective date. In instances where the effective date is beyond the cut-off date for the Code a note has been inserted to reflect the future effective date. In those instances where a regulation published in the Federal Register states a date certain for expiration, an appropriate note will be inserted following the text.

OMB CONTROL NUMBERS

The Paperwork Reduction Act of 1980 (Pub. L. 96-511) requires Federal agencies to display an OMB control number with their information collection request.

Many agencies have begun publishing numerous OMB control numbers as amendments to existing regulations in the CFR. These OMB numbers are placed as close as possible to the applicable recordkeeping or reporting requirements.

PAST PROVISIONS OF THE CODE

Provisions of the Code that are no longer in force and effect as of the revision date stated on the cover of each volume are not carried. Code users may find the text of provisions in effect on any given date in the past by using the appropriate List of CFR Sections Affected (LSA). For the convenience of the reader, a "List of CFR Sections Affected" is published at the end of each CFR volume. For changes to the Code prior to the LSA listings at the end of the volume, consult previous annual editions of the LSA. For changes to the Code prior to 2001, consult the List of CFR Sections Affected compilations, published for 1949-1963, 1964-1972, 1973-1985, and 1986-2000.

"[RESERVED]" TERMINOLOGY

The term "[Reserved]" is used as a place holder within the Code of Federal Regulations. An agency may add regulatory information at a "[Reserved]" location at any time. Occasionally "[Reserved]" is used editorially to indicate that a portion of the CFR was left vacant and not dropped in error.

INCORPORATION BY REFERENCE

What is incorporation by reference? Incorporation by reference was established by statute and allows Federal agencies to meet the requirement to publish regulations in the Federal Register by referring to materials already published elsewhere. For an incorporation to be valid, the Director of the Federal Register must approve it. The legal effect of incorporation by reference is that the material is treated as if it were published in full in the Federal Register (5 U.S.C. 552(a)). This material, like any other properly issued regulation, has the force of law.

What is a proper incorporation by reference? The Director of the Federal Register will approve an incorporation by reference only when the requirements of 1 CFR part 51 are met. Some of the elements on which approval is based are:

(a) The incorporation will substantially reduce the volume of material published in the Federal Register.

(b) The matter incorporated is in fact available to the extent necessary to afford fairness and uniformity in the administrative process.

(c) The incorporating document is drafted and submitted for publication in accordance with 1 CFR part 51.

What if the material incorporated by reference cannot be found? If you have any problem locating or obtaining a copy of material listed as an approved incorporation by reference, please contact the agency that issued the regulation containing that incorporation. If, after contacting the agency, you find the material is not available, please notify the Director of the Federal Register, National Archives and Records Administration, 8601 Adelphi Road, College Park, MD 20740-6001, or call 202-741-6010.

CFR INDEXES AND TABULAR GUIDES

A subject index to the Code of Federal Regulations is contained in a separate volume, revised annually as of January 1, entitled CFR INDEX AND FINDING AIDS. This volume contains the Parallel Table of Authorities and Rules. A list of CFR titles, chapters, subchapters, and parts and an alphabetical list of agencies publishing in the CFR are also included in this volume.

An index to the text of "Title 3—The President" is carried within that volume.

The Federal Register Index is issued monthly in cumulative form. This index is based on a consolidation of the "Contents" entries in the daily Federal Register.

A List of CFR Sections Affected (LSA) is published monthly, keyed to the revision dates of the 50 CFR titles.

REPUBLICATION OF MATERIAL

There are no restrictions on the republication of material appearing in the Code of Federal Regulations.

INQUIRIES

For a legal interpretation or explanation of any regulation in this volume, contact the issuing agency. The issuing agency's name appears at the top of odd-numbered pages.

For inquiries concerning CFR reference assistance, call 202-741-6000 or write to the Director, Office of the Federal Register, National Archives and Records Administration, 8601 Adelphi Road, College Park, MD 20740-6001 or e-mail *fedreg.info@nara.gov*.

THIS TITLE

Title 17—COMMODITY AND SECURITIES EXCHANGES is composed of five volumes. The first two volumes, containing parts 1–40 and 41–199, comprise Chapter I—Commodity Futures Trading Commission. The third volume contains Chapter II—Securities and Exchange Commission, parts 200–239. The fourth volume, comprising part 240, contains additional regulations of the Securities and Exchange Commission. The fifth volume, comprising part 241 to end, contains the remaining regulations of the Securities and Exchange Commission and Chapter IV—Department of the Treasury. The contents of these volumes represent all current regulations codified under this title by the Commodity Futures Trading Commission, the Securities and Exchange Commission, and the Department of the Treasury as of April 1, 2023.

The OMB control numbers for the Securities and Exchange Commission appear in §200.800 of chapter II. For the convenience of the user, §200.800 is reprinted in the Finding Aids sections of volume 4, containing part 240, and volume 5, containing part 241 to end.

For this volume, Robert J. Sheehan, III was Chief Editor. The Code of Federal Regulations publication program is under the direction of John Hyrum Martinez, assisted by Stephen J. Frattini.

Title 17—Commodity and Securities Exchanges

(This book contains part 240)

	Part
CHAPTER II—Securities and Exchange Commission (Continued)	240

CHAPTER II—SECURITIES AND EXCHANGE COMMISSION (CONTINUED)

Part		Page
240	General rules and regulations, Securities Exchange Act of 1934	5

PART 240—GENERAL RULES AND REGULATIONS, SECURITIES EXCHANGE ACT OF 1934

Subpart A—Rules and Regulations Under the Securities Exchange Act of 1934

RULES OF GENERAL APPLICATION

Sec.
240.0-1 Definitions.
240.0-2 Business hours of the Commission.
240.0-3 Filing of material with the Commission.
240.0-4 Nondisclosure of information obtained in examinations and investigations.
240.0-5 Reference to rule by obsolete designation.
240.0-6 Disclosure detrimental to the national defense or foreign policy.
240.0-8 Application of rules to registered broker-dealers.
240.0-9 Payment of filing fees.
240.0-10 Small entities under the Securities Exchange Act for purposes of the Regulatory Flexibility Act.
240.0-11 Filing fees for certain acquisitions, dispositions and similar transactions.
240.0-12 Commission procedures for filing applications for orders for exemptive relief under Section 36 of the Exchange Act.
240.0-13 Commission procedures for filing applications to request a substituted compliance or listed jurisdiction order under the Exchange Act.
240.3a1-1 Exemption from the definition of "Exchange" under Section 3(a)(1) of the Act.
240.3a4-1 Associated persons of an issuer deemed not to be brokers.
240.3a4-2—240.3a4-6 [Reserved]
240.3a5-1 Exemption from the definition of "dealer" for a bank engaged in riskless principal transactions.
240.3a5-2 Exemption from the definition of "dealer" for banks effecting transactions in securities issued pursuant to Regulation S.
240.3a5-3 Exemption from the definition of "dealer" for banks engaging in securities lending transactions.

DEFINITION OF "EQUITY SECURITY" AS USED IN SECTIONS 12(g) AND 16

240.3a11-1 Definition of the term "equity security".

MISCELLANEOUS EXEMPTIONS

240.3a12-1 Exemption of certain mortgages and interests in mortgages.
240.3a12-2 [Reserved]
240.3a12-3 Exemption from sections 14(a), 14(b), 14(c), 14(f), and 16 for securities of certain foreign issuers.
240.3a12-4 Exemptions from sections 15(a) and 15(c)(3) for certain mortgage securities.
240.3a12-5 Exemption of certain investment contract securities from sections 7(c) and 11(d)(1).
240.3a12-6 Definition of "common trust fund" as used in section 3(a)(12) of the Act.
240.3a12-7 Exemption for certain derivative securities traded otherwise than on a national securities exchange.
240.3a12-8 Exemption for designated foreign government securities for purposes of futures trading.
240.3a12-9 Exemption of certain direct participation program securities from the arranging provisions of sections 7(c) and 11(d)(1).
240.3a12-10 Exemption of certain securities issued by the Resolution Funding Corporation.
240.3a12-11 Exemption from sections 8(a), 14(a), 14(b), and 14(c) for debt securities listed on a national securities exchange.
240.3a12-12 Exemption from certain provisions of section 16 of the Act for asset-backed securities.
240.3a40-1 Designation of financial responsibility rules.
240.3a43-1 Customer-related government securities activities incidental to the futures-related business of a futures commission merchant registered with the Commodity Futures Trading Commission.
240.3a44-1 Proprietary government securities transactions incidental to the futures-related business of a CFTC-regulated person.
240.3a51-1 Definition of "penny stock".
240.3a55-1 Method for determining market capitalization and dollar value of average daily trading volume; application of the definition of narrow-based security index.
240.3a55-2 Indexes underlying futures contracts trading for fewer than 30 days.
240.3a55-3 Futures contracts on security indexes trading on or subject to the rules of a foreign board of trade.
240.3a55-4 Exclusion from definition of narrow-based security index for indexes composed of debt securities.

SECURITY-BASED SWAP DEALER AND PARTICIPANT DEFINITIONS

240.3a67-1 Definition of "major security-based swap participant."
240.3a67-2 Categories of security-based swaps.
240.3a67-3 Definition of "substantial position."
240.3a67-4 Definition of "hedging or mitigating commercial risk."
240.3a67-5 Definition of "substantial counterparty exposure."

240.3a67-6 Definition of "financial entity."
240.3a67-7 Definition of "highly leveraged."
240.3a67-8 Timing requirements, reevaluation period and termination of status.
240.3a67-9 Calculation of major participant status by certain persons.
240.3a67-10 Foreign major security-based swap participants.

FURTHER DEFINITION OF SWAP, SECURITY-BASED SWAP, AND SECURITY-BASED SWAP AGREEMENT; MIXED SWAPS; SECURITY-BASED SWAP AGREEMENT RECORDKEEPING

240.3a68-1a Meaning of "issuers of securities in a narrow-based security index" as used in section 3(a)(68)(A)(ii)(III) of the Act.
240.3a68-1b Meaning of "narrow-based security index" as used in section 3(a)(68)(A)(ii)(I) of the Act.
240.3a68-2 Requests for interpretation of swaps, security-based swaps, and mixed swaps.
240.3a68-3 Meaning of "narrow-based security index" as used in the definition of "security-based swap."
240.3a68-4 Regulation of mixed swaps.
240.3a68-5 Regulation of certain futures contracts on foreign sovereign debt.
240.3a69-1 Safe Harbor Definition of "security-based swap" and "swap" as used in sections 3(a)(68) and 3(a)(69) of the Act—insurance.
240.3a69-2 Definition of "swap" as used in section 3(a)(69) of the Act—additional products.
240.3a69-3 Books and records requirements for security-based swap agreements.
240.3a71-1 Definition of "security-based swap dealer."
240.3a71-2 *De minimis* exception.
240.3a71-2A Report regarding the "security-based swap dealer" and "major security-based swap participant" definitions (Appendix A to 17 CFR 240.3a71-2)
240.3a71-3 Cross-border security-based swap dealing activity.
240.3a71-4 Exception from aggregation for affiliated groups with registered security-based swap dealers.
240.3a71-5 Substituted compliance for foreign security-based swap dealers.
240.3a71-6 Substituted compliance for security-based swap dealers and major security-based swap participants.

DEFINITIONS

240.3b-1 Definition of "listed".
240.3b-2 Definition of "officer".
240.3b-3 [Reserved]
240.3b-4 Definition of "foreign government," "foreign issuer" and "foreign private issuer."
240.3b-5 Non-exempt securities issued under governmental obligations.
240.3b-6 Liability for certain statements by issuers.
240.3b-7 Definition of "executive officer".
240.3b-8 Definitions of "Qualified OTC Market Maker, Qualified Third Market Maker" and "Qualified Block Positioner".
240.3b-9—240.3b-10 [Reserved]
240.3b-11 Definitions relating to limited partnership roll-up transactions for purposes of sections 6(b)(9), 14(h) and 15A(b)(12)–(13).
240.3b-12 Definition of OTC derivatives dealer.
240.3b-13 Definition of eligible OTC derivative instrument.
240.3b-14 Definition of cash management securities activities.
240.3b-15 Definition of ancillary portfolio management securities activities.
240.3b-16 Definitions of terms used in Section 3(a)(1) of the Act.
240.3b-17 [Reserved]
240.3b-18 Definitions of terms used in Section 3(a)(5) of the Act.
240.3b-19 Definition of "issuer" in section 3(a)(8) of the Act in relation to asset-backed securities.

CLEARING OF SECURITY-BASED SWAPS

240.3Ca-1 Stay of clearing requirement and review by the Commission.
240.3Ca-2 Submission of security-based swaps for clearing.

REGISTRATION AND EXEMPTION OF EXCHANGES

240.6a-1 Application for registration as a national securities exchange or exemption from registration based on limited volume.
240.6a-2 Amendments to application.
240.6a-3 Supplemental material to be filed by exchanges.
240.6a-4 Notice of registration under Section 6(g) of the Act, amendment to such notice, and supplemental materials to be filed by exchanges registered under Section 6(g) of the Act.
240.6h-1 Settlement and regulatory halt requirements for security futures products.
240.6h-2 Security future based on note, bond, debenture, or evidence of indebtedness.
240.7c2-1 [Reserved]

HYPOTHECATION OF CUSTOMERS' SECURITIES

240.8c-1 Hypothecation of customers' securities.
240.9b-1 Options disclosure document.
240.10a-1—240.10a-2 [Reserved]

MANIPULATIVE AND DECEPTIVE DEVICES AND CONTRIVANCES

240.10b-1 Prohibition of use of manipulative or deceptive devices or contrivances with respect to certain securities exempted from registration.
240.10b-2 [Reserved]

Securities and Exchange Commission

Pt. 240

240.10b-3 Employment of manipulative and deceptive devices by brokers or dealers.
240.10b-4 [Reserved]
240.10b-5 Employment of manipulative and deceptive devices.
240.10b5-1 Trading "on the basis of" material nonpublic information in insider trading cases.
240.10b5-2 Duties of trust or confidence in misappropriation insider trading cases.
240.10b-6—240.10b-8 [Reserved]
240.10b-9 Prohibited representations in connection with certain offerings.
240.10b-10 Confirmation of transactions.
240.10b-13 [Reserved]
240.10b-16 Disclosure of credit terms in margin transactions.
240.10b-17 Untimely announcements of record dates.
240.10b-18 Purchases of certain equity securities by the issuer and others.
240.10b-21 Deception in connection with a seller's ability or intent to deliver securities on the date delivery is due.

REPORTS UNDER SECTION 10A

240.10A-1 Notice to the Commission Pursuant to Section 10A of the Act.
240.10A-2 Auditor independence.
240.10A-3 Listing standards relating to audit committees.

REQUIREMENTS UNDER SECTION 10C

240.10C-1 Listing standards relating to compensation committees.

REQUIREMENTS UNDER SECTION 10D

240.10D-1 Listing standards relating to recovery of erroneously awarded compensation.

ADOPTION OF FLOOR TRADING REGULATION (RULE 11A-1)

240.11a-1 Regulation of floor trading.
240.11a1-1(T) Transactions yielding priority, parity, and precedence.
240.11a1-2 Transactions for certain accounts of associated persons of members.
240.11a1-3(T) Bona fide hedge transactions in certain securities.
240.11a1-4(T) Bond transactions on national securities exchanges.
240.11a1-5 Transactions by registered competitive market makers and registered equity market makers.
240.11a1-6 Transactions for certain accounts of OTC derivatives dealers.
240.11a2-2(T) Transactions effected by exchange members through other members.

ADOPTION OF REGULATION ON CONDUCT OF SPECIALISTS

240.11b-1 Regulation of specialists.

EXEMPTION OF CERTAIN SECURITIES FROM SECTION 11(d)(1)

240.11d1-1 Exemption of certain securities from section 11(d)(1).
240.11d1-2 Exemption from section 11(d)(1) for certain investment company securities held by broker-dealers as collateral in margin accounts.
240.11d2-1 Exemption from Section 11(d)(2) for certain broker-dealers effecting transactions for customers security futures products in futures accounts.

SECURITIES EXEMPTED FROM REGISTRATION

240.12a-4 Exemption of certain warrants from section 12(a).
240.12a-5 Temporary exemption of substituted or additional securities.
240.12g-6 Exemption for securities issued pursuant to section 4(a)(6) of the Securities Act of 1933 or Regulation Crowdfunding.
240.12a-7 Exemption of stock contained in standardized market baskets from section 12(a) of the Act.
240.12a-8 Exemption of depositary shares.
240.12a-9 Exemption of standardized options from section 12(a) of the Act.
240.12a-10 Exemption of security-based swaps from section 12(a) of the Act.
240.12a-11 Exemption of security-based swaps sold in reliance on Securities Act of 1933 Rule 240 (§ 230.240) from section 12(a) of the Act.

REGULATION 12B: REGISTRATION AND REPORTING

GENERAL

240.12b-1 Scope of regulation.
240.12b-2 Definitions.
240.12b-3 Title of securities.
240.12b-4 Supplemental information.
240.12b-5 Determination of affiliates of banks.
240.12b-6 When securities are deemed to be registered.
240.12b-7 [Reserved]

FORMAL REQUIREMENTS

240.12b-10 Requirements as to proper form.
240.12b-11 Number of copies; signatures; binding.
240.12b-12 Requirements as to paper, printing and language.
240.12b-13 Preparation of statement or report.
240.12b-14 Riders; inserts.
240.12b-15 Amendments.

GENERAL REQUIREMENTS AS TO CONTENTS

240.12b-20 Additional information.
240.12b-21 Information unknown or not available.
240.12b-22 Disclaimer of control.
240.12b-23 Incorporation by reference.

Pt. 240

240.12b-24 [Reserved]
240.12b-25 Notification of inability to timely file all or any required portion of a Form 10-K, 20-F, 11-K, N-CEN, N-CSR, 10-Q, or 10-D.

EXHIBITS

240.12b-30 Additional exhibits.
240.12b-31 Omission of substantially identical documents.
240.12b-32 [Reserved]
240.12b-33 Annual reports to other Federal agencies.

SPECIAL PROVISIONS

240.12b-35 [Reserved]
240.12b-36 Use of financial statements filed under other acts.
240.12b-37 Satisfaction of filing requirements.

CERTIFICATION BY EXCHANGES AND EFFECTIVENESS OF REGISTRATION

240.12d1-1 Registration effective as to class or series.
240.12d1-2 Effectiveness of registration.
240.12d1-3 Requirements as to certification.
240.12d1-4 Date of receipt of certification by Commission.
240.12d1-5 Operation of certification on subsequent amendments.
240.12d1-6 Withdrawal of certification.

SUSPENSION OF TRADING, WITHDRAWAL, AND STRIKING FROM LISTING AND REGISTRATION

240.12d2-1 Suspension of trading.
240.12d2-2 Removal from listing and registration.

UNLISTED TRADING

240.12f-1 Applications for permission to reinstate unlisted trading privileges.
240.12f-2 Extending unlisted trading privileges to a security that is the subject of an initial public offering.
240.12f-3 Termination or suspension of unlisted trading privileges.
240.12f-4 Exemption of securities admitted to unlisted trading privileges from sections 13, 14, and 16.
240.12f-5 Exchange rules for securities to which unlisted trading privileges are extended.
240.12f-6 [Reserved]

EXTENSIONS AND TEMPORARY EXEMPTIONS; DEFINITIONS

240.12g-1 Exemption from section 12(g).
240.12g-2 Securities deemed to be registered pursuant to section 12(g)(1) upon termination of exemption pursuant to section 12(g)(2) (A) or (B).
240.12g-3 Registration of securities of successor issuers under section 12(b) or 12(g).
240.12g-4 Certifications of termination of registration under section 12(g).

17 CFR Ch. II (4-1-23 Edition)

240.12g-6 Exemption for securities issued pursuant to section 4(a)(6) of the Securities Act of 1933.
240.12g3-2 Exemptions for American depositary receipts and certain foreign securities.
240.12g5-1 Definition of securities "held of record".
240.12g5-2 Definition of "total assets".
240.12h-1 Exemptions from registration under section 12(g) of the Act.
240.12h-2 [Reserved]
240.12h-3 Suspension of duty to file reports under section 15(d).
240.12h-4 Exemption from duty to file reports under section 15(d).
240.12h-5 Exemption for subsidiary issuers of guaranteed securities and subsidiary guarantors.
240.12h-6 Certification by a foreign private issuer regarding the termination of registration of a class of securities under section 12(g) or the duty to file reports under section 13(a) or section 15(d).
240.12h-7 Exemption for issuers of securities that are subject to insurance regulation.

REGULATION 13A: REPORTS OF ISSUERS OF SECURITIES REGISTERED PURSUANT TO SECTION 12

ANNUAL REPORTS

240.13a-1 Requirements of annual reports.
240.13a-2 [Reserved]
240.13a-3 Reporting by Form 40-F registrant.

OTHER REPORTS

240.13a-10 Transition reports.
240.13a-11 Current reports on Form 8-K (§ 249.308 of this chapter).
240.13a-13 Quarterly reports on Form 10-Q (§ 249.308a of this chapter).
240.13a-14 Certification of disclosure in annual and quarterly reports.
240.13a-15 Controls and procedures.
240.13a-16 Reports of foreign private issuers on Form 6-K (17 CFR 249.306).
240.13a-17 Reports of asset-backed issuers on Form 10-D (§ 249.312 of this chapter).
240.13a-18 Compliance with servicing criteria for asset-backed securities.
240.13a-19 Reports by shell companies on Form 20-F.
240.13a-20 Plain English presentation of specified information.

REGULATION 13B-2: MAINTENANCE OF RECORDS AND PREPARATION OF REQUIRED REPORTS

240.13b2-1 Falsification of accounting records.
240.13b2-2 Representations and conduct in connection with the preparation of required reports and documents.

Securities and Exchange Commission

Pt. 240

REGULATION 13D–G

240.13d–1 Filing of Schedules 13D and 13G.
240.13d–2 Filing of amendments to Schedules 13D or 13G.
240.13d–3 Determination of beneficial owner.
240.13d–4 Disclaimer of beneficial ownership.
240.13d–5 Acquisition of securities.
240.13d–6 Exemption of certain acquisitions.
240.13d–7 Dissemination.
240.13d–101 Schedule 13D—Information to be included in statements filed pursuant to §240.13d–1(a) and amendments thereto filed pursuant to §240.13d–2(a).
240.13d–102 Schedule 13G—Information to be included in statements filed pursuant to §240.13d–1(b), (c), and (d) and amendments thereto filed pursuant to §240.13d–2(b).
240.13e–1 Purchase of securities by the issuer during a third-party tender offer.
240.13e–2 [Reserved]
240.13e–3 Going private transactions by certain issuers or their affiliates.
240.13e–4 Tender offers by issuers.
240.13e–100 Schedule 13E–3, Transaction statement under section 13(e) of the Securities Exchange Act of 1934 and Rule 13e–3 (§240.13e–3) thereunder.
240.13e–101 [Reserved]
240.13e–102 Schedule 13E–4F. Tender offer statement pursuant to section 13(e) (1) of the Securities Exchange Act of 1934 and §240.13e–4 thereunder.
240.13f–1 Reporting by institutional investment managers of information with respect to accounts over which they exercise investment discretion.
240.13h–1 Large trader reporting.
240.13k–1 Foreign bank exemption from the insider lending prohibition under section 13(k).
240.13n–1 Registration of security-based swap data repository.
240.13n–2 Withdrawal from registration; revocation and cancellation.
240.13n–3 Registration of successor to registered security-based swap data repository.
240.13n–4 Duties and core principles of security-based swap data repository.
240.13n–5 Data collection and maintenance.
240.13n–6 Automated systems.
240.13n–7 Recordkeeping of security-based swap data repository.
240.13n–8 Reports to be provided to the Commission.
240.13n–9 Privacy requirements of security-based swap data repository.
240.13n–10 Disclosure requirements of security-based swap data repository.
240.13n–11 Chief compliance officer of security-based swap data repository; compliance reports and financial reports.
240.13n–12 Exemption from requirements governing security-based swap data repositories for certain non-U.S. persons.
240.13p–1 Requirement of report regarding disclosure of registrant's supply chain information regarding conflict minerals.
240.13q–1 Disclosure of payments made by resource extraction issuers.

REGULATION 14A: SOLICITATIONS OF PROXIES

240.14a–1 Definitions.
240.14a–2 Solicitations to which §240.14a–3 to §240.14a–15 apply.
240.14a–3 Information to be furnished to security holders.
240.14a–4 Requirements as to proxy.
240.14a–5 Presentation of information in proxy statement.
240.14a–6 Filing requirements.
240.14a–7 Obligations of registrants to provide a list of, or mail soliciting material to, security holders.
240.14a–8 Shareholder proposals.
240.14a–9 False or misleading statements.
240.14a–10 Prohibition of certain solicitations.
240.14a–12 Solicitation before furnishing a proxy statement.
240.14a–13 Obligation of registrants in communicating with beneficial owners.
240.14a–14 Modified or superseded documents.
240.14a–15 Differential and contingent compensation in connection with roll-up transactions.
240.14a–16 Internet availability of proxy materials.
240.14a–17 Electronic shareholder forums.
240.14a–18 Disclosure regarding nominating shareholders and nominees submitted for inclusion in a registrant's proxy materials pursuant to applicable state or foreign law, or a registrant's governing documents.
240.14a–19 Solicitation of proxies in support of director nominees other than the registrant's nominees.
240.14a–20 Shareholder approval of executive compensation of TARP recipients.
240.14a–21 Shareholder approval of executive compensation, frequency of votes for approval of executive compensation and shareholder approval of golden parachute compensation.
240.14a–101 Schedule 14A. Information required in proxy statement.
240.14a–102 [Reserved]
240.14a–103 Notice of Exempt Solicitation. Information to be included in statements submitted by or on behalf of a person pursuant to §240.14a–6(g).
240.14a–104 Notice of Exempt Preliminary Roll-up Communication. Information regarding ownership interests and any potential conflicts of interest to be included in statements submitted by or on behalf of a person pursuant to §240.14a–2(b)(4) and §240.14a–6(n).
240.14Ad–1 Report of proxy voting record.

240.14b-1 Obligation of registered brokers and dealers in connection with the prompt forwarding of certain communications to beneficial owners.
240.14b-2 Obligation of banks, associations and other entities that exercise fiduciary powers in connection with the prompt forwarding of certain communications to beneficial owners.

REGULATION 14C: DISTRIBUTION OF INFORMATION PURSUANT TO SECTION 14(c)

240.14c-1 Definitions.
240.14c-2 Distribution of information statement.
240.14c-3 Annual report to be furnished security holders.
240.14c-4 Presentation of information in information statement.
240.14c-5 Filing requirements.
240.14c-6 False or misleading statements.
240.14c-7 Providing copies of material for certain beneficial owners.
240.14c-101 Schedule 14C. Information required in information statement.

REGULATION 14D

240.14d-1 Scope of and definitions applicable to Regulations 14D and 14E.
240.14d-2 Commencement of a tender offer.
240.14d-3 Filing and transmission of tender offer statement.
240.14d-4 Dissemination of tender offers to security holders.
240.14d-5 Dissemination of certain tender offers by the use of stockholder lists and security position listings.
240.14d-6 Disclosure of tender offer information to security holders.
240.14d-7 Additional withdrawal rights.
240.14d-8 Exemption from statutory pro rata requirements.
240.14d-9 Recommendation or solicitation by the subject company and others.
240.14d-10 Equal treatment of security holders.
240.14d-11 Subsequent offering period.
240.14d-100 Schedule TO. Tender offer statement under section 14(d)(1) or 13(e)(1) of the Securities Exchange Act of 1934.
240.14d-101 Schedule 14D-9.
240.14d-102 Schedule 14D-1F. Tender offer statement pursuant to rule 14d-1(b) under the Securities Exchange Act of 1934.
240.14d-103 Schedule 14D-9F. Solicitation/recommendation statement pursuant to section 14(d)(4) of the Securities Exchange Act of 1934 and rules 14d-1(b) and 14e-2(c) thereunder.

REGULATION 14E

240.14e-1 Unlawful tender offer practices.
240.14e-2 Position of subject company with respect to a tender offer.
240.14e-3 Transactions in securities on the basis of material, nonpublic information in the context of tender offers.
240.14e-4 Prohibited transactions in connection with partial tender offers.
240.14e-5 Prohibiting purchases outside of a tender offer.
240.14e-6 Repurchase offers by certain closed-end registered investment companies.
240.14e-7 Unlawful tender offer practices in connection with roll-ups.
240.14e-8 Prohibited conduct in connection with pre-commencement communications.
240.14f-1 Change in majority of directors.

REGULATION 14N: FILINGS REQUIRED BY CERTAIN NOMINATING SHAREHOLDERS

240.14n-1 Filing of Schedule 14N.
240.14n-2 Filing of amendments to Schedule 14N.
240.14n-3 Dissemination.
240.14n-101 Schedule 14N—Information to be included in statements filed pursuant to §240.14n-1 and amendments thereto filed pursuant to §240.14n-2.

EXEMPTION OF CERTAIN OTC DERIVATIVES DEALERS

240.15a-1 Securities activities of OTC derivatives dealers.

EXEMPTION OF CERTAIN SECURITIES FROM SECTION 15(a)

240.15a-2 Exemption of certain securities of cooperative apartment houses from section 15(a).
240.15a-3 [Reserved]
240.15a-4 Forty-five day exemption from registration for certain members of national securities exchanges.
240.15a-5 Exemption of certain nonbank lenders.

REGISTRATION OF BROKERS AND DEALERS

240.15a-6 Exemption of certain foreign brokers or dealers.
240.15a-7—240.15a-9 [Reserved]
240.15a-10 Exemption of certain brokers or dealers with respect to security futures products.
240.15a-11 [Reserved]
240.15b1-1 Application for registration of brokers or dealers.
240.15b1-2 [Reserved]
240.15b1-3 Registration of successor to registered broker or dealer.
240.15b1-4 Registration of fiduciaries.
240.15b1-5 Consent to service of process to be furnished by nonresident brokers or dealers and by nonresident general partners or managing agents of brokers or dealers.

Securities and Exchange Commission

Pt. 240

240.15b1-6 Notice to brokers and dealers of requirements regarding lost securityholders and unresponsive payees.
240.15b2-2 Inspection of newly registered brokers and dealers.
240.15b3-1 Amendments to application.
240.15b5-1 Extension of registration for purposes of the Securities Investor Protection Act of 1970 after cancellation or revocation.
240.15b6-1 Withdrawal from registration.
240.15b7-1 Compliance with qualification requirements of self-regulatory organizations.
240.15b7-3T Operational capability in a Year 2000 environment.
240.15b9-1 Exemption for certain exchange members.
240.15b9-2 Exemption from SRO membership for OTC derivatives dealers.
240.15b11-1 Registration by notice of security futures product broker-dealers.

Rules Relating to Over-the-Counter Markets

240.15c1-1 Definitions.
240.15c1-2 Fraud and misrepresentation.
240.15c1-3 Misrepresentation by brokers, dealers and municipal securities dealers as to registration.
240.15c1-4 [Reserved]
240.15c1-5 Disclosure of control.
240.15c1-6 Disclosure of interest in distribution.
240.15c1-7 Discretionary accounts.
240.15c1-8 Sales at the market.
240.15c1-9 Use of pro forma balance sheets.
240.15c2-1 Hypothecation of customers' securities.
240.15c2-3 [Reserved]
240.15c2-4 Transmission or maintenance of payments received in connection with underwritings.
240.15c2-5 Disclosure and other requirements when extending or arranging credit in certain transactions.
240.15c2-6 [Reserved]
240.15c2-7 Identification of quotations.
240.15c2-8 Delivery of prospectus.
240.15c2-11 Publication or submission of quotations without specified information.
240.15c2-12 Municipal securities disclosure.
240.15c3-1 Net capital requirements for brokers or dealers.
240.15c3-1a Options (Appendix A to 17 CFR 240.15c3-1).
240.15c3-1b Adjustments to net worth and aggregate indebtedness for certain commodities transactions (Appendix B to 17 CFR 240.15c3-1).
240.15c3-1c Consolidated computations of net capital and aggregate indebtedness for certain subsidiaries and affiliates (Appendix C to 17 CFR 240.15c3-1).
240.15c3-1d Satisfactory Subordination Agreements (Appendix D to 17 CFR 240.15c3-1).
240.15c3-1e Deductions for market and credit risk for certain brokers or dealers (Appendix E to 17 CFR 240.15c3-1).
240.15c3-1f Optional market and credit risk requirements for OTC derivatives dealers (Appendix F to 17 CFR 240.15c3-1)
240.15c3-1g Conditions for ultimate holding companies of certain brokers or dealers (Appendix G to 17 CFR 240.15c3-1).
240.15c3-2 [Reserved]
240.15c3-3 Customer protection—reserves and custody of securities.
240.15c3-3a Exhibit A—formula for determination reserve requirement of brokers and dealers under §240.15c3-3.
240.15c3-3b Exhibit B—Formula for determination of security-based swap customer reserve requirements of brokers and dealers under §240.15c3-3.
240.15c3-4 Internal risk management control systems for OTC derivatives dealers.
240.15c3-5 Risk management controls for brokers or dealers with market access.
240.15c6-1 Settlement cycle.
240.15c6-2 Same-day allocation, confirmation, and affirmation.

Regulation 15D: Reports of Registrants Under the Securities Act of 1933

Annual Reports

240.15d-1 Requirement of annual reports.
240.15d-2 Special financial report.
240.15d-3 Reports for depositary shares registered on Form F-6.
240.15d-4 Reporting by Form 40-F Registrants.
240.15d-5 Reporting by successor issuers.
240.15d-6 Suspension of duty to file reports.

Other Reports

240.15d-10 Transition reports.
240.15d-11 Current reports on Form 8-K (§249.308 of this chapter).
240.15d-13 Quarterly reports on Form 10-Q (§249.308 of this chapter).
240.15d-14 Certification of disclosure in annual and quarterly reports.
240.15d-15 Controls and procedures.
240.15d-16 Reports of foreign private issuers on Form 6-K [17 CFR 249.306].
240.15d-17 Reports of asset-backed issuers on Form 10-D (§249.312 of this chapter).
240.15d-18 Compliance with servicing criteria for asset-backed securities.
240.15d-19 Reports by shell companies on Form 20-F.
240.15d-20 Plain English presentation of specified information.

Exemption of Certain Issuers From Section 15(d) of the Act

240.15d-21 Reports for employee stock purchase, savings and similar plans.

Pt. 240

240.15d-22 Reporting regarding asset-backed securities under section 15(d) of the Act.
240.15d-23 Reporting regarding certain securities underlying asset-backed securities under section 15(d) of the Act.
240.15g-1 Exemptions for certain transactions.
240.15g-2 Penny stock disclosure document relating to the penny stock market.
240.15g-3 Broker or dealer disclosure of quotations and other information relating to the penny stock market.
240.15g-4 Disclosure of compensation to brokers or dealers.
240.15g-5 Disclosure of compensation of associated persons in connection with penny stock transactions.
240.15g-6 Account statements for penny stock customers.
240.15g-8 Sales of escrowed securities of blank check companies.
240.15g-9 Sales practice requirements for certain low-priced securities.
240.15g-100 Schedule 15G—Information to be included in the document distributed pursuant to 17 CFR 240.15g-2.
240.15l-1 Regulation best interest.

NATIONAL AND AFFILIATED SECURITIES ASSOCIATIONS

240.15Aa-1 Registration of a national or an affiliated securities association.
240.15Aj-1 Amendments and supplements to registration statements of securities associations.
240.15Al2-1 [Reserved]
240.15Ba1-1 Definitions.
240.15Ba1-2 Registration of municipal advisors and information regarding certain natural persons.
240.15Ba1-3 Exemption of certain natural persons from registration under section 15B(a)(1)(B) of the Act.
240.15Ba1-4 Withdrawal from municipal advisor registration.
240.15Ba1-5 Amendments to Form MA and Form MA-I.
240.15Ba1-6 Consent to service of process to be filed by non-resident municipal advisors; legal opinion to be provided by non-resident municipal advisors.
240.15Ba1-7 Registration of successor to municipal advisor.
240.15Ba1-8 Books and records to be made and maintained by municipal advisors.
240.15Ba2-1 Application for registration of municipal securities dealers which are banks or separately identifiable departments or divisions of banks.
240.15Ba2-2 Application for registration of non-bank municipal securities dealers whose business is exclusively intrastate.
240.15Ba2-4 Registration of successor to registered municipal securities dealer.
240.15Ba2-5 Registration of fiduciaries.
240.15Ba2-6 [Reserved]

17 CFR Ch. II (4-1-23 Edition)

240.15Ba2-6T Temporary registration as a municipal advisor; required amendments; and withdrawal from temporary registration.
240.15Bc3-1 Withdrawal from registration of municipal securities dealers.
240.15Bc4-1 Persons associated with municipal advisors.
240.15Bc7-1 Availability of examination reports.

REGISTRATION OF GOVERNMENT SECURITIES BROKERS AND GOVERNMENT SECURITIES DEALERS

240.15Ca1-1 Notice of government securities broker-dealer activities.
240.15Ca2-1 Application for registration as a government securities broker or government securities dealer.
240.15Ca2-2 [Reserved]
240.15Ca2-3 Registration of successor to registered government securities broker or government securities dealer.
240.15Ca2-4 Registration of fiduciaries.
240.15Ca2-5 Consent to service of process to be furnished by non-resident government securities brokers or government securities dealers and by non-resident general partners or managing agents of government securities brokers or government securities dealers.
240.15Cc1-1 Withdrawal from registration of government securities brokers or government securities dealers.

REGISTRATION AND REGULATION OF SECURITY-BASED SWAP DEALERS AND MAJOR SECURITY-BASED SWAP PARTICIPANTS

240.15Fb1-1 Signatures.
240.15Fb2-1 Registration of security-based swap dealers and major security-based swap participants.
240.15Fb2-3 Amendments to Form SBSE, Form SBSE-A, and Form SBSE-BD.
240.15Fb2-4 Nonresident security-based swap dealers and major security-based swap participants.
240.15Fb2-5 Registration of successor to registered security-based swap dealer or major security-based swap participant.
240.15Fb2-6 Registration of fiduciaries.
240.15Fb3-1 Duration of registration.
240.15Fb3-2 Withdrawal from registration.
240.15Fb3-3 Cancellation or revocation from registration.
240.15Fb6-1 [Reserved]
240.15Fb6-2 Associated person certification.
240.15Fh-1 Scope and reliance on representations.
240.15Fh-2 Definitions.
240.15Fh-3 Business conduct requirements.
240.15Fh-4 Antifraud provisions for security-based swap dealers and major security-based swap participants; special requirements for security-based swap dealers acting as advisors to special entities.

Securities and Exchange Commission

240.15Fh–5 Special requirements for security-based swap dealers and major security-based swap participants acting as counterparties to special entities.
240.15Fh–6 Political contributions by certain security-based swap dealers.
240.15Fi–1 Definitions.
240.15Fi–2 Acknowledgment and verification of security-based swap transactions.
240.15Fi–3 Security-based swap portfolio reconciliation.
240.15Fi–4 Security-based swap portfolio compression.
240.15Fi–5 Security-based swap trading relationship documentation.
240.15Fk–1 Designation of chief compliance officer for security-based swap dealers and major security-based swap participants.
240.15Ga–1 Repurchases and replacements relating to asset-backed securities.
240.15Ga–2 Findings and conclusions of third-party due diligence reports.

REPORTS OF DIRECTORS, OFFICERS, AND PRINCIPAL SHAREHOLDERS

240.16a–1 Definition of terms.
240.16a–2 Persons and transactions subject to section 16.
240.16a–3 Reporting transactions and holdings.
240.16a–4 Derivative securities.
240.16a–5 Odd-lot dealers.
240.16a–6 Small acquisitions.
240.16a–7 Transactions effected in connection with a distribution.
240.16a–8 Trusts.
240.16a–9 Stock splits, stock dividends, and pro rata rights.
240.16a–10 Exemptions under section 16(a).
240.16a–11 Dividend or interest reinvestment plans.
240.16a–12 Domestic relations orders.
240.16a–13 Change in form of beneficial ownership.

EXEMPTION OF CERTAIN TRANSACTIONS FROM SECTION 16(b)

240.16b–1 Transactions approved by a regulatory authority.
240.16b–2 [Reserved]
240.16b–3 Transactions between an issuer and its officers or directors.
240.16b–4 [Reserved]
240.16b–5 Bona fide gifts and inheritance.
240.16b–6 Derivative securities.
240.16b–7 Mergers, reclassifications, and consolidations.
240.16b–8 Voting trusts.

EXEMPTION OF CERTAIN TRANSACTIONS FROM SECTION 16(c)

240.16c–1 Brokers.
240.16c–2 Transactions effected in connection with a distribution.
240.16c–3 Exemption of sales of securities to be acquired.
240.16c–4 Derivative securities.

ARBITRAGE TRANSACTIONS

240.16e–1 Arbitrage transactions under section 16.

PRESERVATION OF RECORDS AND REPORTS OF CERTAIN STABILIZING ACTIVITIES

240.17a–1 Recordkeeping rule for national securities exchanges, national securities associations, registered clearing agencies and the Municipal Securities Rulemaking Board.
240.17a–2 Recordkeeping requirements relating to stabilizing activities.
240.17a–3 Records to be made by certain exchange members, brokers and dealers.
240.17a–4 Records to be preserved by certain exchange members, brokers and dealers.
240.17a–5 Reports to be made by certain brokers and dealers.
240.17a–6 Right of national securities exchange, national securities association, registered clearing agency or the Municipal Securities Rulemaking Board to destroy or dispose of documents.
240.17a–7 Records of non-resident brokers and dealers.
240.17a–8 Financial recordkeeping and reporting of currency and foreign transactions.
240.17a–9T Records to be made and retained by certain exchange members, brokers and dealers.
240.17a–10 Report of revenue and expenses.
240.17a–11 Notification provisions for brokers and dealers.
240.17a–12 Reports to be made by certain OTC derivatives dealers.
240.17a–13 Quarterly security counts to be made by certain exchange members, brokers, and dealers.
240.17a–14 Form CRS, for preparation, filing and delivery of Form CRS.
240.17a–18 [Reserved]
240.17a–19 Form X–17A–19 Report by national securities exchanges and registered national securities associations of changes in the membership status of any of their members.
240.17a–21 Reports of the Municipal Securities Rulemaking Board.
240.17a–22 Supplemental material of registered clearing agencies.
240.17a–25 Electronic submission of securities transaction information by exchange members, brokers, and dealers.
240.17d–1 Examination for compliance with applicable financial responsibility rules.
240.17d–2 Program for allocation of regulatory responsibility.
240.17f–1 Requirements for reporting and inquiry with respect to missing, lost, counterfeit or stolen securities.

240.17f-2 Fingerprinting of securities industry personnel.

NATIONALLY RECOGNIZED STATISTICAL RATING ORGANIZATIONS

240.17g-1 Application for registration as a nationally recognized statistical rating organization.
240.17g-2 Records to be made and retained by nationally recognized statistical rating organizations.
240.17g-3 Annual financial and other reports to be filed or furnished by nationally recognized statistical rating organizations.
240.17g-4 Prevention of misuse of material nonpublic information.
240.17g-5 Conflicts of interest.
240.17g-6 Prohibited acts and practices.
240.17g-7 Disclosure requirements.
240.17g-8 Policies, procedures, and internal controls.
240.17g-9 Standards of training, experience, and competence for credit analysts.
240.17g-10 Certification of providers of third-party due diligence services in connection with asset-backed securities.
240.17h-1T Risk assessment recordkeeping requirements for associated persons of brokers and dealers.
240.17h-2T Risk assessment reporting requirements for brokers and dealers.
240.17Ab2-1 Registration of clearing agencies.
240.17Ab2-2 Determinations affecting covered clearing agencies.
240.17Ac2-1 Application for registration of transfer agents.
240.17Ac2-2 Annual reporting requirement for registered transfer agents.
240.17Ac3-1 Withdrawal from registration with the Commission.
240.17Ad-1 Definitions.
240.17Ad-2 Turnaround, processing, and forwarding of items.
240.17Ad-3 Limitations on expansion.
240.17Ad-4 Applicability of §§ 240.17Ad-2, 240.17Ad-3 and 240.17Ad-6(a) (1) through (7) and (11).
240.17Ad-5 Written inquiries and requests.
240.17Ad-6 Recordkeeping.
240.17Ad-7 Record retention.
240.17Ad-8 Securities position listings.
240.17Ad-9 Definitions.
240.17Ad-10 Prompt posting of certificate detail to master securityholder files, maintenance of accurate securityholder files, communications between co-transfer agents and recordkeeping transfer agents, maintenance of current control book, retention of certificate detail and "buy-in" of physical over-issuance.
240.17Ad-11 Reports regarding aged record differences, buy-ins and failure to post certificate detail to master securityholder and subsidiary files.
240.17Ad-12 Safeguarding of funds and securities.
240.17Ad-13 Annual study and evaluation of internal accounting control.
240.17Ad-14 Tender agents.
240.17Ad-15 Signature guarantees.
240.17Ad-16 Notice of assumption or termination of transfer agent services.
240.17Ad-17 Lost securityholders and unresponsive payees.
240.17Ad-18 Year 2000 Reports to be made by certain transfer agents.
240.17Ad-19 Requirements for cancellation, processing, storage, transportation, and destruction or other disposition of securities certificates.
240.17Ad-20 Issuer restrictions or prohibitions on ownership by securities intermediaries.
240.17Ad-21T Operational capability in a Year 2000 environment.
240.17Ad-22 Standards for clearing agencies.
§ 240.17Ad-24 Exemption from clearing agency definition for certain registered security-based swap dealers, registered security-based swap execution facilities, and entities engaging in dealing activity in security-based swaps that are eligible for an exception under § 240.3a71-2(a) (or subject to the period set forth in § 240.3a71-2(b)).
240.17Ad-27 Straight-through processing by clearing agencies that provide a central matching service.

CAPITAL, MARGIN AND SEGREGATION REQUIREMENTS FOR SECURITY-BASED SWAP DEALERS AND MAJOR SECURITY-BASED SWAP PARTICIPANTS

240.18a-1 Net capital requirements for security-based swap dealers for which there is not a prudential regulator.
240.18a-1a Options.
240.18a-1b Adjustments to net worth for certain commodities transactions.
240.18a-1c Consolidated computations of net capital for certain subsidiaries and affiliates of security-based swap dealers.
240.18a-1d Satisfactory subordinated loan agreements.
240.18a-2 Capital requirements for major security-based swap participants for which there is not a prudential regulator.
240.18a-3 Non-cleared security-based swap margin requirements for security-based swap dealers and major security-based swap participants for which there is not a prudential regulator.
240.18a-4 Segregation requirements for security-based swap dealers and major security-based swap participants.
240.18a-4a Exhibit A—Formula for determination of security-based swap customer reserve requirements under § 240.18a-4.
240.18a-5 Records to be made by certain security-based swap dealers and major security-based swap participants.

Securities and Exchange Commission

240.18a-6 Records to be preserved by certain security-based swap dealers and major security-based swap participants.
240.18a-7 Reports to be made by certain security-based swap dealers and major security-based swap participants.
240.18a-8 Notification provisions for security-based swap dealers and major security-based swap participants.
240.18a-9 Quarterly security counts to be made by certain security-based swap dealers.
240.18a-10 Alternative compliance mechanism for security-based swap dealers that are registered as swap dealers and have limited security-based swap activities.

SUSPENSION AND EXPULSION OF EXCHANGE MEMBERS

240.19a3-1 [Reserved]
240.19b-3 [Reserved]
240.19b-4 Filings with respect to proposed rule changes by self-regulatory organizations.
240.19b-5 Temporary exemption from the filing requirements of Section 19(b) of the Act.
240.19b-7 Filings with respect to proposed rule changes submitted pursuant to Section 19(b)(7) of the Act.
240.19c-1 Governing certain off-board agency transactions by members of national securities exchanges.
240.19c-3 Governing off-board trading by members of national securities exchanges.
240.19c-4 Governing certain listing or authorization determinations by national securities exchanges and associations.
240.19c-5 Governing the multiple listing of options on national securities exchanges.
240.19d-1 Notices by self-regulatory organizations of final disciplinary actions, denials, bars, or limitations respecting membership, association, participation, or access to services, and summary suspensions.
240.19d-2 Applications for stays of disciplinary sanctions or summary suspensions by a self-regulatory organization.
240.19d-3 Applications for review of final disciplinary sanctions, denials of membership, participation or association, or prohibitions or limitations of access to services imposed by self-regulatory organizations.
240.19d-4 Notice by the Public Company Accounting Oversight Board of disapproval of registration or of disciplinary action.
240.19g2-1 Enforcement of compliance by national securities exchanges and registered securities associations with the Act and rules and regulations thereunder.
240.19h-1 Notice by a self-regulatory organization of proposed admission to or continuance in membership or participation

or association with a member of any person subject to a statutory disqualification, and applications to the Commission for relief therefrom.

SECURITIES WHISTLEBLOWER INCENTIVES AND PROTECTIONS

240.21F-1 General.
240.21F-2 Whistleblower status, award eligibility, confidentiality, and retaliation protections.
240.21F-3 Payment of award.
240.21F-4 Other definitions.
240.21F-5 Amount of award.
240.21F-6 Criteria for determining amount of award.
240.21F-7 Confidentiality of submissions.
240.21F-8 Eligibility and forms.
240.21F-9 Procedures for submitting original information.
240.21F-10 Procedures for making a claim for a whistleblower award in SEC actions that result in monetary sanctions in excess of $1,000,000
240.21F-11 Procedures for determining awards based upon a related action.
240.21F-12 Materials that may be used as the basis for an award determination and that may comprise the record on appeal.
240.21F-13 Appeals.
240.21F-14 Procedures applicable to the payment of awards.
240.21F-15 No amnesty.
240.21F-16 Awards to whistleblowers who engage in culpable conduct.
240.21F-17 Staff communications with individuals reporting possible securities law violations.
240.21F-18 Summary disposition.

INSPECTION AND PUBLICATION OF INFORMATION FILED UNDER THE ACT

240.24b-1 Documents to be kept public by exchanges.
240.24b-2 Nondisclosure of information filed with the Commission and with any exchange.
240.24b-3 Information filed by issuers and others under sections 12, 13, 14, and 16.
240.24c-1 Access to nonpublic information.
240.31 Section 31 transaction fees.
240.31T Temporary rule regarding fiscal year 2004.
240.36a1-1 Exemption from Section 7 for OTC derivatives dealers.
240.36a1-2 Exemption from SIPA for OTC derivatives dealers.

Subpart B—Rules and Regulations Under the Securities Investor Protection Act of 1970 [Reserved]

AUTHORITY: 15 U.S.C. 77c, 77d, 77g, 77j, 77s, 77z-2, 77z-3, 77eee, 77ggg, 77nnn, 77sss, 77ttt, 78c, 78c-3, 78c-5,78d, 78e, 78f, 78g, 78i, 78j, 78j-1, 78j-4, 78k, 78k-1, 78l, 78m, 78n, 78n-1, 78o,

78*o*–4, 78*o*–10, 78p, 78q, 78q–1, 78s, 78u–5, 78w, 78x, 78dd, 78*ll*, 78mm, 80a–20, 80a–23, 80a–29, 80a–37, 80b–3, 80b–4, 80b–11, 7201 *et seq.*, and 8302; 7 U.S.C. 2(c)(2)(E); 12 U.S.C.5221(e)(3); 18 U.S.C. 1350; and Pub. L. 111–203, 939A, 124 Stat.1376 (2010); and Pub. L. 112–106, sec. 503 and 602, 126 Stat. 326 (2012), unless otherwise noted.

Section 240.3a4–1 also issued under secs. 3 and 15, 89 Stat. 97, as amended, 89 Stat. 121 as amended;

Section 240.3a12–8 also issued under 15 U.S.C. 78a *et seq.*, particularly secs. 3(a)(12), 15 U.S.C. 78c(a)(12), and 23(a), 15 U.S.C. 78w(a);

Section 240.3a12–10 also issued under 15 U.S.C. 78b and c;

Section 240.3a12–9 also issued under secs. 3(a)(12), 7(c), 11(d)(1), 15 U.S.C. 78c(a)(12), 78g(c), 78k(d)(1));

Sections 240.3a43–1 and 240.3a44–1 also issued under sec. 3; 15 U.S.C. 78c;

Sections 3a67–1 through 3a67–9 and 3a71–1 and 3a71–2 are also issued under Pub. L. 111–203, §§ 712, 761(b), 124 Stat. 1841 (2010).

Sections 240.3a67–10, 240.3a71–3, 240.3a71–4, and 240.3a71–5 are also issued under Pub. L. 111–203, section 761(b), 124 Stat. 1754 (2010), and 15 U.S.C. 78dd(c).

Sections 240.3a71–3 and 240.3a71–5 are also issued under Pub. L. 111–203, sec. 761(b), 124 Stat. 1754 (2010), and 15 U.S.C. 78dd(c).

Section 240.3b–6 is also issued under 15 U.S.C. 77f, 77g, 77h, 77j, 77s(a).

Section 240.3b–9 also issued under secs. 2, 3 and 15, 89 Stat. 97, as amended, 89 Stat. 121, as amended (15 U.S.C. 78b, 78c, and 78o);

Section 240.9b–1 is also issued under sec. 2, 7, 10, 19(a), 48 Stat. 74, 78, 81, 85; secs. 201, 205, 209, 120, 48 Stat. 905, 906, 908; secs. 1–4, 8, 68 Stat. 683, 685; sec. 12(a), 73 Stat. 143; sec. 7(a), 74 Stat. 412; sec. 27(a), 84 Stat. 1433; sec. 308(a)(2), 90 Stat. 57; sec. 505, 94 Stat. 2292; secs. 9, 15, 23(a), 48 Stat. 889, 895, 901; sec. 230(a), 49 Stat. 704; secs. 3, 8, 49 Stat. 1377, 1379; sec. 2, 52 Stat. 1075; secs. 6, 10, 78 Stat. 570–574, 580; sec. 11(d), 84 Stat. 121; sec. 18, 89 Stat. 155; sec. 204, 91 Stat. 1500; 15 U.S.C. 77b, 77g, 77j, 77s(a), 78i, 78o, 78w(a);

Section 240.10b–10 is also issued under secs. 2, 3, 9, 10, 11, 11A, 15, 17, 23, 48 Stat. 891, 89 Stat. 97, 121, 137, 156, (15 U.S.C. 78b, 78c, 78i, 78j, 78k, 78k–1, 78o, 78q);

Section 240.12a–7 also issued under 15 U.S.C. 78a *et seq.*, particularly secs. 3(a)(12), 15 U.S.C. 78c(a)(12), 6, 15 U.S.C. 78(f), 11A, 15 U.S.C. 78k, 12, 15 U.S.C. 78(l), and 23(a)(1), 15 U.S.C. 78(w)(a)(1).

Sections 240.12b–1 to 240.12b–36 also issued under secs. 3, 12, 13, 15, 48 Stat. 892, as amended, 894, 895, as amended; 15 U.S.C. 78c, 78*l*, 78m, 78o;

Section 240.12b–15 is also issued under secs. 3(a) and 302, Pub.L. No. 107–204, 116 Stat. 745.

Section 240.12b–25 is also issued under 15 U.S.C. 80a–8, 80a–24(a), 80a–29, and 80a–37.

Section 240.12g–3 is also issued under 15 U.S.C. 77f, 77g, 77h, 77j, 77s(a).

Section 240.12g3–2 is also issued under 15 U.S.C. 77f, 77g, 77h, 77j, 77s(a).

Section 240.13a–10 is also issued under secs. 3(a) and 302, Pub.L. No. 107–204, 116 Stat. 745.

Section 240.13a–11 is also issued under secs. 3(a) and 306(a), Pub. L. 107–204, 116 Stat. 745.

Section 240.13a–14 is also issued under secs. 3(a) and 302, Pub.L. No. 107–204, 116 Stat. 745.

Section 240.13a–15 is also issued under secs. 3(a) and 302, Pub. L. No. 107–204, 116 Stat. 745.

Section 240.13d–3 is also issued under Public Law 111–203 § 766, 124 Stat. 1799 (2010).

Sections 240.13e–4, 240.14d–7, 240.14d–10 and 240.14e–1 also issued under secs. 3(b), 9(a)(6), 10(b), 13(e), 14(d) and 14(e), 15 U.S.C. 78c(b), 78i(a)(6), 78j(b), 78m(e), 78n(d) and 78n(e) and sec. 23(c) of the Investment Company Act of 1940, 15 U.S.C 80a–23(c);

Sections 240.13e–4 to 240.13e–101 also issued under secs. 3(b), 9(a)(6), 10(b), 13(e), 14(e), 15(c)(1), 48 Stat. 882, 889, 891, 894, 895, 901, sec. 8, 49 Stat. 1379, sec. 5, 78 Stat. 569, 570, secs. 2, 3, 82 Stat. 454, 455, secs. 1, 2, 3–5, 84 Stat. 1497, secs. 3, 18, 89 Stat. 97, 155; 15 U.S.C. 78c(b), 78i(a)(6), 78j(b), 78m(e), 78n(e), 78o(c); sec. 23(c) of the Investment Company Act of 1940; 54 Stat. 825; 15 U.S.C. 80a–23(c);

Section 240.13f-2(T) also issued under sec. 13(f)(1) (15 U.S.C. 78m(f)(1));

Section 240.13p–1 is also issued under sec. 1502, Pub. L. 111–203, 124 Stat. 1376.

Section 240.13q–1 is also issued under sec. 1504, Pub. L. 111–203, 124 Stat. 2220.

Sections 240.14a–1, 240.14a–3, 240.14a–13, 240.14b–1, 240.14b–2, 240.14c–1, and 240.14c–7 also issued under secs. 12, 15 U.S.C. 78*l*, and 14, Pub. L. 99–222, 99 Stat. 1737, 15 U.S.C. 78n;

Sections 240.14a–3, 240.14a–13, 240.14b–1 and 240.14c–7 also issued under secs. 12, 14 and 17, 15 U.S.C. 78*l*, 78n and 78g;

Sections 240.14c–1 to 240.14c–101 also issued under sec. 14, 48 Stat. 895; 15 U.S.C. 78n;

Section 240.14d–1 is also issued under 15 U.S.C. 77g, 77j, 77s(a), 77ttt(a), 80a–37.

Section 240.14e–2 is also issued under 15 U.S.C. 77g, 77h, 77s(a), 77sss, 80a–37(a).

Section 240.14e-4 also issued under the Exchange Act, 15 U.S.C. 78a *et seq.*, and particularly sections 3(b), 10(a), 10(b), 14(e), 15(c), and 23(a) of the Exchange Act (15 U.S.C. 78c(b), 78j(a), 78j(b), 78n(e), 78*o*(c), and 78w(a)).

Section 240.15a–6, also issued under secs. 3, 10, 15, and 17, 15 U.S.C. 78c, 78j, 78*o*, and 78q;

Section 240.15b1–3 also issued under sec. 15, 17; 15 U.S.C. 78*o* 78q;

Sections 240.15b1–3 and 240.15b2–1 also issued under 15 U.S.C. 78*o*, 78q;

Section 240.15b2–2 also issued under secs. 3, 15; 15 U.S.C. 78c, 78*o*;

Sections 240.15b10–1 to 240.15b10–9 also issued under secs. 15, 17, 48 Stat. 895, 897, sec. 203, 49 Stat. 704, secs. 4, 8, 49 Stat. 1379, sec. 5, 52 Stat. 1076, sec. 6, 78 Stat. 570; 15 U.S.C. 78*o*, 78q, 12 U.S.C. 241 nt.;

Securities and Exchange Commission   Pt. 240

Section 240.15c2–6, also issued under secs. 3, 10, and 15, 15 U.S.C. 78c, 78j, and 78o.

Section 240.15c2–11 also issued under 15 U.S.C. 78j(b), 78o(c), 78q(a), and 78w(a).

Section 240.15c2–12 also issued under 15 U.S.C. 78b, 78c, 78j, 78o, 78o–4 and 78q.

Section 240.15c3–1 is also issued under 15 U.S.C. 78o(c)(3), 78o–10(d), and 78o–10(e).

Sections 240.15c3–1a, 240.15c3–1e, 240.15c3–1f, 240.15c3–1g are also issued under Pub. L. 111–203, secs. 939, 939A, 124. Stat. 1376 (2010) (15 U.S.C. 78c, 15 U.S.C. 78o–7 note).

Section 240.15c3–3 is also issued under 15 U.S.C. 78c–5, 78o(c)(2), 78(c)(3), 78q(a), 78w(a); sec. 6(c), 84 Stat. 1652; 15 U.S.C. 78fff.

Section 240.15c3–3(o) is also issued under Pub. L. 106–554, 114 Stat. 2763, section 203.

Section 240.15c3–3a is also issued under Pub. L. 111–203, §§ 939, 939A, 124. Stat. 1376 (2010) (15 U.S.C. 78c, 15 U.S.C. 78o–7 note).

Section 240.15d–5 is also issued under 15 U.S.C. 77f, 77g, 77h, 77j, 77s(a).

Section 240.15d–10 is also issued under 15 U.S.C. 80a–20(a) and 80a–37(a), and secs. 3(a) and 302, Pub. L. No. 107–204, 116 Stat. 745.

Section 240.15d–11 is also issued under secs. 3(a) and 306(a), Pub. L. 107–204, 116 Stat. 745.

Section 240.15d–14 is also issued under secs. 3(a) and 302, Pub. L. No. 107–204, 116 Stat. 745.

Section 240.15d–15 is also issued under secs. 3(a) and 302, Pub. L. No. 107–204, 116 Stat. 745.

Section 240.15*l*–1 is also issued under Pub. L. 111–203, sec. 913, 124 Stat. 1376, 1827 (2010).

Sections 240.15Ba1–1 through 240.15Ba1–8 are also issued under sec. 975, Public Law 111–203, 124 Stat. 1376 (2010).

Section 240.15Bc4–1 is also issued under sec. 975, Public Law 111–203, 124 Stat. 1376 (2010).

Sections 240.15Ca1–1, 240.15Ca2–1, 240.15Ca2–2, 240.15Ca2–3, 240.15Ca2–4, 240.15Ca2–5, 240.15Cc1–1 also issued under secs. 3, 15C; 15 U.S.C. 78c, 78o–5;

Sections 240.15Fh–1 through 240.15Fh–6 and 240.15Fk–1 are also issued under sec. 943, Pub. L. 111–203, 124 Stat. 1376.

Section 240.15Ga–1 is also issued under sec. 943, Pub. L. 111–203, 124 Stat. 1376.

Section 240.15Ga–2 is also issued under sec. 943, Pub. L. 111–203, 124 Stat. 1376.

Section 240.16a–1(a) is also issued under Public Law 111–203 § 766, 124 Stat. 1799 (2010).

Section 240.17a–3 also issued under secs. 2, 17, 23a, 48 Stat. 897, as amended; 15 U.S.C. 78d–1, 78d–2, 78q; secs. 12, 14, 17, 23(a), 48 Stat. 892, 895, 897, 901; secs. 1, 4, 8, 49 Stat. 1375, 1379; sec. 203(a), 49 Stat. 704; sec. 5, 52 Stat. 1076; sec. 202, 68 Stat. 686; secs. 3, 5, 10, 78 Stat. 565–568, 569, 570, 580; secs. 1, 3, 82 Stat. 454, 455; secs. 28(c), 3–5, 84 Stat. 1435, 1497; sec. 105(b), 88 Stat. 1503; secs. 8, 9, 14, 18, 89 Stat. 117, 118, 137, 155; 15 U.S.C. 78l, 78n, 78q, 78w(a).

Section 240.17a–4 also issued under secs. 2, 17, 23(a), 48 Stat. 897, as amended; 15 U.S.C. 78a, 78d–1, 78d–2; sec. 14, Pub. L. 94–29, 89 Stat. 137 (15 U.S.C. 78a); sec. 18, Pub. L. 94–29, 89 Stat. 155 (15 U.S.C. 78w).

Section 240.17a–14 is also issued under Public Law 111–203, sec. 913, 124 Stat. 1376 (2010).

Section 240.17a–23 also issued under 15 U.S.C. 78b, 78c, 78o, 78q, and 78w(a).

Section 240.17f–1 is also authorized under sections 2, 17 and 17A, 48 Stat. 891, 89 Stat. 137, 141 (15 U.S.C. 78b, 78q, 78q–1);

Section 240.17g–7 is also issued under sec. 943, Pub. L. 111–203, 124 Stat. 1376.

Section 240.17g–8 is also issued under sec. 938, Pub. L. 111–203, 124 Stat. 1376.

Section 240.17g–9 is also issued under sec. 936, Pub. L. 111–203, 124 Stat. 1376.

Section 240.17h–1T also issued under 15 U.S.C. 78q.

Sections 240.17Ac2–1(c) and 240.17Ac2–2 also issued under secs. 17, 17A and 23(a); 48 Stat. 897, as amended, 89 Stat. 137, 141 and 48 Stat. 901 (15 U.S.C. 78q, 78q–1, 78w(a));

Section 240.17Ad–1 is also issued under secs. 2, 17, 17A and 23(a); 48 Stat. 841 as amended, 48 Stat. 897, as amended, 89 Stat. 137, 141, and 48 Stat. 901 (15 U.S.C. 78b, 78q, 78q–1, 78w);

Sections 240.17Ad–5 and 240.17Ad–10 are also issued under secs. 3 and 17A; 48 Stat. 882, as amended, and 89 Stat. (15 U.S.C. 78c and 78q–1);

Section 240.17Ad–7 also issued under 15 U.S.C. 78b, 78q, and 78q–1.

Section 240.17Ad–17 is also issued under Pub. L. 111–203, section 929W, 124 Stat. 1869 (2010).

Section 240.17Ad–22 is also issued under 12 U.S.C. 5461 et seq.

Sections 240.18a–1, 240.18a–1a, 240.18a–1b, 240.18a–1c, 240.18a–1d, 240.18a–2, 240.18a–3, and 240.18a–10 are also issued under 15 U.S.C. 78o–10(d) and 78o–10(e).

Section 240.18a–4 is also issued under 15 U.S.C. 78c–5(f).

Section 240.19b–4 is also issued under 12 U.S.C. 5465(e).

Sections 240.19c–4 also issued under secs. 6, 11A, 14, 15A, 19 and 23 of the Securities Exchange Act of 1934 (15 U.S.C. 78o–3, and 78s);

Section 240.19c–5 also issued under Sections 6, 11A, and 19 of the Securities Exchange Act of 1934, 48 Stat. 885, as amended, 89 Stat. 111, as amended, and 48 Stat. 898, as amended, 15 U.S.C. 78f, 78k–1, and 78s.

Section 240.21F is also issued under Pub. L. 111–203, § 922(a), 124 Stat. 1841 (2010).

Section 240.31–1 is also issued under sec. 31, 48 Stat. 904, as amended (15 U.S.C. 78ee).

EDITORIAL NOTE: Nomenclature changes to part 240 appear at 57 FR 36501, Aug. 13, 1992, and 57 FR 47409, Oct. 16, 1992.

NOTE: In §§ 240.0–1 to 240.24b–3, the numbers to the right of the decimal point correspond with the respective rule numbers of the rules and regulations under the Securities Exchange Act of 1934.

ATTENTION ELECTRONIC FILERS

§ 240.0-1

THIS REGULATION SHOULD BE READ IN CONJUNCTION WITH REGULATION S-T (PART 232 OF THIS CHAPTER), WHICH GOVERNS THE PREPARATION AND SUBMISSION OF DOCUMENTS IN ELECTRONIC FORMAT. MANY PROVISIONS RELATING TO THE PREPARATION AND SUBMISSION OF DOCUMENTS IN PAPER FORMAT CONTAINED IN THIS REGULATION ARE SUPERSEDED BY THE PROVISIONS OF REGULATION S-T FOR DOCUMENTS REQUIRED TO BE FILED IN ELECTRONIC FORMAT.

Subpart A—Rules and Regulations Under the Securities Exchange Act of 1934

RULES OF GENERAL APPLICATION

§ 240.0-1 Definitions.

(a) As used in the rules and regulations in this part, prescribed by the Commission pursuant to Title I of the Securities Exchange Act of 1934 (48 Stat. 881–905; 15 U.S.C. chapter 2B), unless the context otherwise specifically requires:

(1) The term *Commission* means the Securities and Exchange Commission.

(2) The term *act* means Title I of the Securities Exchange Act of 1934.

(3) The term *section* refers to a section of the Securities Exchange Act of 1934.[1]

(4) The term *rules and regulations* refers to all rules and regulations adopted by the Commission pursuant to the act, including the forms for registration and reports and the accompanying instructions thereto.

(5) The term *electronic filer* means a person or an entity that submits filings electronically pursuant to Rules 100 and 101 of Regulation S-T (§§ 232.100 and 232.101 of this chapter, respectively).

(6) The term *electronic filing* means a document under the federal securities laws that is transmitted or delivered to the Commission in electronic format.

---

[1] The provisions of paragraph (a)(3) of 17 CFR 240.0-1 relate to the terminology of rules and regulations as published by the Securities and Exchange Commission and are inapplicable to the terminology appearing in the Code of Federal Regulations.

(b) Unless otherwise specifically stated, the terms used in this part shall have the meaning defined in the act.

(c) A rule or regulation which defines a term without express reference to the act or to the rules and regulations, or to a portion thereof, defines such term for all purposes as used both in the act and in the rules and regulations, unless the context otherwise specifically requires.

(d) Unless otherwise specified or the context otherwise requires, the term *prospectus* means a prospectus meeting the requirements of section 10(a) of the Securities Act of 1933 as amended.

CROSS REFERENCES: For definition of "listed", see § 240.3b–1; "officer", § 240.3b–2; "short sale", § 240.3b–3. For additional definitions, see § 240.15c1–1.

[13 FR 8178, Dec. 22, 1948, as amended at 13 FR 9321, Dec. 31, 1948; 19 FR 6730, Oct. 20, 1954; 58 FR 14682, Mar. 18, 1993; 62 FR 36459, July 8, 1997]

§ 240.0-2 Business hours of the Commission.

(a) The principal office of the Commission, at 100 F Street, NE, Washington, DC 20549, is open each day, except Saturdays, Sundays, and Federal holidays, from 9 a.m. to 5:30 p.m., Eastern Standard Time or Eastern Daylight Saving Time, whichever currently is in effect in Washington, DC, *provided that* hours for the filing of documents pursuant to the Act or the rules and regulations thereunder are as set forth in paragraphs (b) and (c) of this section.

(b) *Submissions made in paper.* Paper documents filed with or otherwise furnished to the Commission may be submitted to the Commission each day, except Saturdays, Sundays and federal holidays, from 8 a.m. to 5:30 p.m., Eastern Standard Time or Eastern Daylight Saving Time, whichever is currently in effect.

(c) *Electronic filings.* Filings made by direct transmission may be submitted to the Commission each day, except Saturdays, Sundays, and Federal holidays, from 6 a.m. to 10 p.m., Eastern Standard Time or Eastern Daylight Saving Time, whichever is currently in effect.

CROSS REFERENCES: For registration and exemption of exchanges, see §§ 240.6a–1 to

Securities and Exchange Commission § 240.0-5

240.6a-3. For forms for permanent registration of securities, see § 240.12b-1. For regulations relating to registration of securities, see §§ 240.12b-1 to 240.12b-36. For forms for applications for registration of brokers and dealers, see §§ 240.15b1-1 to 240.15b9-1.

[58 FR 14682, Mar. 18, 1993, as amended at 65 FR 24801, Apr. 27, 2000; 68 FR 25799, May 13, 2003; 73 FR 973, Jan. 4, 2008; 88 FR 12209, Feb. 27, 2023]

§ 240.0-3 Filing of material with the Commission.

(a) All papers required to be filed with the Commission pursuant to the Act or the rules and regulations thereunder shall be filed at the principal office in Washington, DC. Material may be filed by delivery to the Commission, through the mails or otherwise. The date on which papers are actually received by the Commission shall be the date of filing thereof if all of the requirements with respect to the filing have been complied with, except that if the last day on which papers can be accepted as timely filed falls on a Saturday, Sunday or holiday, such papers may be filed on the first business day following.

(b) The manually signed original (or in the case of duplicate originals, one duplicate original) of all registrations, applications, statements, reports, or other documents filed under the Securities Exchange Act of 1934, as amended, shall be numbered sequentially (in addition to any internal numbering which otherwise may be present) by handwritten, typed, printed, or other legible form of notation from the facing page of the document through the last page of that document and any exhibits or attachments thereto. Further, the total number of pages contained in a numbered original shall be set forth on the first page of the document.

(c) Each document filed shall contain an exhibit index, which should immediately precede the exhibits filed with such document. The index shall list each exhibit filed and identify by handwritten, typed, printed, or other legible form of notation in the manually signed original, the page number in the sequential numbering system described in paragraph (b) of this section where such exhibit can be found or where it is stated that the exhibit is incorporated by reference. Further, the first page of the manually signed document shall list the page in the filing where the exhibit index is located.

[44 FR 4666, Jan. 23, 1979, as amended at 45 FR 58828, Sept. 5, 1980]

§ 240.0-4 Nondisclosure of information obtained in examinations and investigations.

Information or documents obtained by officers or employees of the Commission in the course of any examination or investigation pursuant to section 17(a) (48 Stat. 897, section 4, 49 Stat. 1379; 15 U.S.C. 78q(a)) or 21(a) (48 Stat. 899; 15 U.S.C. 78u(a)) shall, unless made a matter of public record, be deemed confidential. Except as provided by 17 CFR 203.2, officers and employees are hereby prohibited from making such confidential information or documents or any other non-public records of the Commission available to anyone other than a member, officer or employee of the Commission, unless the Commission or the General Counsel, pursuant to delegated authority, authorizes the disclosure of such information or the production of such documents as not being contrary to the public interest. Any officer or employee who is served with a subpoena requiring the disclosure of such information or the production of such documents shall appear in court and, unless the authorization described in the preceding sentence shall have been given, shall respectfully decline to disclose the information or produce the documents called for, basing his or her refusal upon this section. Any officer or employee who is served with such a subpoena shall promptly advise the General Counsel of the service of such subpoena, the nature of the information or documents sought, and any circumstances which may bear upon the desirability of making available such information or documents.

[44 FR 50836, Aug. 30, 1979, as amended at 53 FR 17459, May 17, 1988; 76 FR 71876, Nov. 21, 2011]

§ 240.0-5 Reference to rule by obsolete designation.

Wherever in any rule, form, or instruction book specific reference is made to a rule by number or other designation which is now obsolete, such

§ 240.0–6

reference shall be deemed to be made to the corresponding rule or rules in the existing general rules and regulations.

[13 FR 8179, Dec. 22, 1948]

§ 240.0–6 Disclosure detrimental to the national defense or foreign policy.

(a) Any requirement to the contrary notwithstanding, no registration statement, report, proxy statement or other document filed with the Commission or any securities exchange shall contain any document or information which, pursuant to Executive order, has been classified by an appropriate department or agency of the United States for protection in the interests of national defense or foreign policy.

(b) Where a document or information is omitted pursuant to paragraph (a) of this section, there shall be filed, in lieu of such document or information, a statement from an appropriate department or agency of the United States to the effect that such document or information has been classified or that the status thereof is awaiting determination. Where a document is omitted pursuant to paragraph (a) of this section, but information relating to the subject matter of such document is nevertheless included in material filed with the Commission pursuant to a determination of an appropriate department or agency of the United States that disclosure of such information would not be contrary to the interests of national defense or foreign policy, a statement from such department or agency to that effect shall be submitted for the information of the Commission. A registrant may rely upon any such statement in filing or omitting any document or information to which the statement relates.

(c) The Commission may protect any information in its possession which may require classification in the interests of national defense or foreign policy pending determination by an appropriate department or agency as to whether such information should be classified.

(d) It shall be the duty of the registrant to submit the documents or information referred to in paragraph (a) of this section to the appropriate department or agency of the United States prior to filing them with the Commission and to obtain and submit to the Commission, at the time of filing such documents or information, or in lieu thereof, as the case may be, the statements from such department or agency required by paragraph (b) of this section. All such statements shall be in writing.

[33 FR 7682, May 24, 1968]

§ 240.0–8 Application of rules to registered broker-dealers.

Any provision of any rule or regulation under the Act which prohibits any act, practice, or course of business by any person if the mails or any means or instrumentality of interstate commerce are used in connection therewith, shall also prohibit any such act, practice, or course of business by any broker or dealer registered pursuant to section 15(b) of the Act, or any person acting on behalf of such a broker or dealer, irrespective of any use of the mails or any means or instrumentality of interstate commerce.

[29 FR 12555, Sept. 3, 1964]

§ 240.0–9 Payment of filing fees.

All payment of filing fees shall be made by wire transfer, debit card, or credit card or via the Automated Clearing House Network. Payment of filing fees required by this section shall be made in accordance with the directions set forth in § 202.3a of this chapter.

[86 FR 70251, Dec. 9, 2021]

§ 240.0–10 Small entities under the Securities Exchange Act for purposes of the Regulatory Flexibility Act.

For purposes of Commission rulemaking in accordance with the provisions of Chapter Six of the Administrative Procedure Act (5 U.S.C. 601 *et seq.*), and unless otherwise defined for purposes of a particular rulemaking proceeding, the term *small business* or *small organization* shall:

(a) When used with reference to an ''issuer'' or a ''person,'' other than an investment company, mean an ''issuer'' or ''person'' that, on the last day of its most recent fiscal year, had total assets of $5 million or less;

Securities and Exchange Commission § 240.0-10

(b) When used with reference to an "issuer" or "person" that is an investment company, have the meaning ascribed to those terms by § 270.0-10 of this chapter;

(c) When used with reference to a broker or dealer, mean a broker or dealer that:

(1) Had total capital (net worth plus subordinated liabilities) of less than $500,000 on the date in the prior fiscal year as of which its audited financial statements were prepared pursuant to § 240.17a-5(d) or, if not required to file such statements, a broker or dealer that had total capital (net worth plus subordinated liabilities) of less than $500,000 on the last business day of the preceding fiscal year (or in the time that it has been in business, if shorter); and

(2) Is not affiliated with any person (other than a natural person) that is not a small business or small organization as defined in this section;

(d) When used with reference to a clearing agency, mean a clearing agency that:

(1) Compared, cleared and settled less than $500 million in securities transactions during the preceding fiscal year (or in the time that it has been in business, if shorter);

(2) Had less than $200 million of funds and securities in its custody or control at all times during the preceding fiscal year (or in the time that it has been in business, if shorter); and

(3) Is not affiliated with any person (other than a natural person) that is not a small business or small organization as defined in this section;

(e) When used with reference to an exchange, mean any exchange that:

(1) Has been exempted from the reporting requirements of § 242.601 of this chapter; and

(2) Is not affiliated with any person (other than a natural person) that is not a small business or small organization as defined in this section;

(f) When used with reference to a municipal securities dealer that is a bank (including any separately identifiable department or division of a bank), mean any such municipal securities dealer that:

(1) Had, or is a department of a bank that had, total assets of less than $10 million at all times during the preceding fiscal year (or in the time that it has been in business, if shorter);

(2) Had an average monthly volume of municipal securities transactions in the preceding fiscal year (or in the time it has been registered, if shorter) of less than $100,000; and

(3) Is not affiliated with any person (other than a natural person) that is not a small business or small organization as defined in this section;

(g) When used with reference to a securities information processor, mean a securities information processor that:

(1) Had gross revenues of less than $10 million during the preceding fiscal year (or in the time it has been in business, if shorter);

(2) Provided service to fewer than 100 interrogation devices or moving tickers at all times during the preceding fiscal year (or in the time that it has been in business, if shorter); and

(3) Is not affiliated with any person (other than a natural person) that is not a small business or small organization under this section; and

(h) When used with reference to a transfer agent, mean a transfer agent that:

(1) Received less than 500 items for transfer and less than 500 items for processing during the preceding six months (or in the time that it has been in business, if shorter);

(2) Transferred items only of issuers that would be deemed "small businesses" or "small organizations" as defined in this section; and

(3) Maintained master shareholder files that in the aggregate contained less than 1,000 shareholder accounts or was the named transfer agent for less than 1,000 shareholder accounts at all times during the preceding fiscal year (or in the time that it has been in business, if shorter); and

(4) Is not affiliated with any person (other than a natural person) that is not a small business or small organization under this section.

(i) For purposes of paragraph (c) of this section, a broker or dealer is affiliated with another person if:

(1) Such broker or dealer controls, is controlled by, or is under common control with such other person; a person

shall be deemed to control another person if that person has the right to vote 25 percent or more of the voting securities of such other person or is entitled to receive 25 percent or more of the net profits of such other person or is otherwise able to direct or cause the direction of the management or policies of such other person; or

(2) Such broker or dealer introduces transactions in securities, other than registered investment company securities or interests or participations in insurance company separate accounts, to such other person, or introduces accounts of customers or other brokers or dealers, other than accounts that hold only registered investment company securities or interests or participations in insurance company separate accounts, to such other person that carries such accounts on a fully disclosed basis.

(j) For purposes of paragraphs (d) through (h) of this section, a person is affiliated with another person if that person controls, is controlled by, or is under common control with such other person; a person shall be deemed to control another person if that person has the right to vote 25 percent or more of the voting securities of such other person or is entitled to receive 25 percent or more of the net profits of such other person or is otherwise able to direct or cause the direction of the management or policies of such other person.

(k) For purposes of paragraph (g) of this section, "interrogation device" shall refer to any device that may be used to read or receive securities information, including quotations, indications of interest, last sale data and transaction reports, and shall include proprietary terminals or personal computers that receive securities information via computer-to-computer interfaces or gateway access.

[47 FR 5222, Feb. 4, 1982, as amended at 51 FR 25362, July 14, 1986; 63 FR 35514, June 30, 1998; 70 FR 37617, June 29, 2005]

§ 240.0-11 Filing fees for certain acquisitions, dispositions and similar transactions.

(a) *General.* (1) At the time of filing a disclosure document described in paragraphs (b) through (d) of this section relating to certain acquisitions, dispositions, business combinations, consolidations or similar transactions, the person filing the specified document shall pay a fee payable to the Commission to be calculated as set forth in paragraphs (b) through (d) of this section.

(2) A required fee shall be reduced in an amount equal to any fee paid with respect to such transaction pursuant to either section 6(b) of the Securities Act of 1933 or any applicable provision of this section; the fee requirements under section 6(b) shall be reduced in an amount equal to the fee paid the Commission with respect to a transaction under this section. No part of a filing fee is refundable.

(3) If at any time after the initial payment the aggregate consideration offered is increased, an additional filing fee based upon such increase shall be paid with the required amended filing.

(4) When the fee is based upon the market value of securities, such market value shall be established by either the average of the high and low prices reported in the consolidated reporting system (for exchange traded securities and last sale reported over-the-counter securities) or the average of the bid and asked price (for other over-the-counter securities) as of a specified date within 5 business days prior to the date of the filing. If there is no market for the securities, the value shall be based upon the book value of the securities computed as of the latest practicable date prior to the date of the filing, unless the issuer of the securities is in bankruptcy or receivership or has an accumulated capital deficit, in which case one-third of the principal amount, par value or stated value of the securities shall be used.

(5) An exhibit to the filing shall set forth the calculation of the fee in tabular format, as well as the amount offset by a previous filing and the identification of such filing, if applicable.

(b) *Section 13(e)(1) filings.* At the time of filing such statement as the Commission may require pursuant to section 13(e)(1) of the Exchange Act, a fee equal to the product of the rate applicable under section 13(e) of the Exchange Act multiplied by the value of the securities proposed to be acquired by the acquiring person. The value of the securities proposed to be acquired shall be determined as follows:

(1) The value of the securities to be acquired solely for cash shall be the amount of cash to be paid for them:

(2) The value of the securities to be acquired with securities or other non-cash consideration, whether or not in combination with a cash payment for the same securities, shall be based upon the market value of the securities to be received by the acquiring person as established in accordance with paragraph (a)(4) of this section.

(c) *Proxy and information statement filings.* At the time of filing a preliminary proxy statement pursuant to Rule 14a-6(a) or preliminary information statement pursuant to Rule 14c-5(a) that concerns a merger, consolidation, acquisition of a company, or proposed sale or other disposition of substantially all the assets of the registrant (including a liquidation), the following fee:

(1) For preliminary material involving a vote upon a merger, consolidation or acquisition of a company, a fee equal to the product of the rate applicable under section 14(g) of the Exchange Act multiplied by the proposed cash payment or, if the consideration does not consistent entirely of cash, the value of the securities and other property to be transferred to security holders in the transaction. The fee is payable whether the registrant is acquiring another company or being acquired.

(i) The value of securities or other property to be transferred to security holders, whether or not in combination with a cash payment for the same securities, shall be based upon the market value of the securities to be received by the acquiring person as established in accordance with paragraph (a)(4) of this section.

(ii) Notwithstanding the above, where the acquisition, merger or consolidation is for the sole purpose of changing the registrant's domicile, no filing fee is required to be paid.

(2) For preliminary material involving a vote upon a proposed sale or other disposition of substantially all the assets of the registrant, a fee equal to the product of the rate applicable under section 14(g) of the Exchange Act multiplied by the aggregate of, as applicable, the cash and the value of the securities (other than its own) and other property to be received by the registrant. In the case of a disposition in which the registrant will not receive any property, such as at liquidation or spin-off, the fee shall be equal to the product of the rate applicable under section 14(g) of the Exchange Act multiplied by the aggregate of, as applicable, the cash and the value of the securities and other property to be distributed to security holders.

(i) The value of the securities to be received (or distributed in the case of a spin-off or liquidation) shall be based upon the market value of such securities as established in accordance with paragraph (a)(4) of this section.

(ii) The value of other property shall be a bona fide estimate of the fair market value of such property.

(3) Where two or more companies are involved in the transaction, each shall pay a proportionate share of such fee, determined by the persons involved.

(4) Notwithstanding the above, the fee required by this paragraph (c) shall not be payable for a proxy statement filed by a company registered under the Investment Company Act of 1940.

(d) *Section 14(d)(1) filings.* At the time of filing such statement as the Commission may require pursuant to section 14(d)(1) of the Act, a fee equal to the product of the rate applicable under section 14(g) of the Exchange Act multiplied by the cash or, if the consideration does not consist entirely of cash, the value of the securities and other property offered by the bidder. Where the bidder is offering securities or other non-cash consideration for some or all of the securities to be acquired, whether or not in combination with a cash payment for the same securities, the value of the consideration to be offered for such securities shall be based upon the market value of the securities to be received by the bidder as established in accordance with paragraph (a)(4) of this section.

[51 FR 2476, Jan. 17, 1986, as amended at 58 FR 14682, Mar. 18, 1993; 61 FR 49959, Sept. 24, 1996; 73 FR 17813, Apr. 1, 2008; 86 FR 70251, Dec. 9, 2021]

§ 240.0–12 Commission procedures for filing applications for orders for exemptive relief under Section 36 of the Exchange Act.

(a) The application shall be in writing in the form of a letter, must include any supporting documents necessary to make the application complete, and otherwise must comply with § 240.0–3. All applications must be submitted to the Office of the Secretary of the Commission. Requestors may seek confidential treatment of their applications to the extent provided under § 200.81 of this chapter. If an application is incomplete, the Commission, through the Division handling the application, may request that the application be withdrawn unless the applicant can justify, based on all the facts and circumstances, why supporting materials have not been submitted and undertakes to submit the omitted materials promptly.

(b) An applicant may submit a request electronically. The electronic mailbox to use for these applications is described on the Commission's Web site at *http://www.sec.gov* in the "Exchange Act Exemptive Applications" section. In the event the electronic mailbox is revised in the future, applicants can find the appropriate mailbox by accessing the "Electronic Mailboxes at the Commission" section.

(c) An applicant also may submit a request in paper format. Five copies of every paper application and every amendment to such an application must be submitted to the Office of the Secretary at 100 F Street, NE., Washington, DC 20549–1090. Applications must be on white paper no larger than 8½ by 11 inches in size. The left margin of applications must be at least 1½ inches wide, and if the application is bound, it must be bound on the left side. All typewritten or printed material must be on one side of the paper only and must be set forth in black ink so as to permit photocopying.

(d) Every application (electronic or paper) must contain the name, address and telephone number of each applicant and the name, address, and telephone number of a person to whom any questions regarding the application should be directed. The Commission will not consider hypothetical or anonymous requests for exemptive relief. Each applicant shall state the basis for the relief sought, and identify the anticipated benefits for investors and any conditions or limitations the applicant believes would be appropriate for the protection of investors. Applicants should also cite to and discuss applicable precedent.

(e) Amendments to the application should be prepared and submitted as set forth in these procedures and should be marked to show what changes have been made.

(f) After the filing is complete, the applicable Division will review the application. Once all questions and issues have been answered to the satisfaction of the Division, the staff will make an appropriate recommendation to the Commission. After consideration of the recommendation by the Commission, the Commission's Office of the Secretary will issue an appropriate response and will notify the applicant. If the application pertains to a section of the Exchange Act pursuant to which the Commission has delegated its authority to the appropriate Division, the Division Director or his or her designee will issue an appropriate response and notify the applicant.

(g) The Commission, in its sole discretion, may choose to publish in the FEDERAL REGISTER a notice that the application has been submitted. The notice would provide that any person may, within the period specified therein, submit to the Commission any information that relates to the Commission action requested in the application. The notice also would indicate the earliest date on which the Commission would take final action on the application, but in no event would such action be taken earlier than 25 days following publication of the notice in the FEDERAL REGISTER.

(h) The Commission may, in its sole discretion, schedule a hearing on the matter addressed by the application.

[63 FR 8102, Feb. 18, 1998, as amended at 73 FR 973, Jan. 4, 2008; 76 FR 43891, July 22, 2011]

Securities and Exchange Commission § 240.0–13

§ 240.0–13 Commission procedures for filing applications to request a substituted compliance or listed jurisdiction order under the Exchange Act.

(a) The application shall be in writing in the form of a letter, must include any supporting documents necessary to make the application complete, and otherwise must comply with § 240.0–3. All applications must be submitted to the Office of the Secretary of the Commission, by a party that potentially would comply with requirements under the Exchange Act pursuant to a substituted compliance or listed jurisdiction order, or by the relevant foreign financial regulatory authority or authorities. If an application is incomplete, the Commission may request that the application be withdrawn unless the applicant can justify, based on all the facts and circumstances, why supporting materials have not been submitted and undertakes to submit the omitted materials promptly.

(b) An applicant may submit a request electronically. The electronic mailbox to use for these applications is described on the Commission's website at *www.sec.gov* in the "Exchange Act Substituted Compliance and Listed Jurisdiction Applications" section. In the event electronic mailboxes are revised in the future, applicants can find the appropriate mailbox by accessing the "Electronic Mailboxes at the Commission" section.

(c) All filings and submissions filed pursuant to this rule must be in the English language. If a filing or submission filed pursuant to this rule requires the inclusion of a document that is in a foreign language, a party must submit instead a fair and accurate English translation of the entire foreign language document. A party may submit a copy of the unabridged foreign language document when including an English translation of a foreign language document in a filing or submission filed pursuant to this rule. A party must provide a copy of any foreign language document upon the request of Commission staff.

(d) An applicant also may submit a request in paper format. Five copies of every paper application and every amendment to such an application must be submitted to the Office of the Secretary at 100 F Street NE., Washington, DC 20549–1090. Applications must be on white paper no larger than 8½ by 11 inches in size. The left margin of applications must be at least 1½ inches wide, and if the application is bound, it must be bound on the left side. All typewritten or printed material must be set forth in black ink so as to permit photocopying.

(e) Every application (electronic or paper) must contain the name, address, telephone number, and email address of each applicant and the name, address, telephone number, and email address of a person to whom any questions regarding the application should be directed. The Commission will not consider hypothetical or anonymous requests for a substituted compliance or listed jurisdiction order. Each applicant shall provide the Commission with any supporting documentation it believes necessary for the Commission to make such determination, including information regarding applicable requirements established by the foreign financial regulatory authority or authorities, as well as the methods used by the foreign financial regulatory authority or authorities to monitor and enforce compliance with such rules. Applicants should also cite to and discuss applicable precedent.

(f) Amendments to the application should be prepared and submitted as set forth in these procedures and should be marked to show what changes have been made.

(g) After the filing is complete, the staff will review the application. Once all questions and issues have been answered to the satisfaction of the staff, the staff will make an appropriate recommendation to the Commission. After consideration of the recommendation and a vote by the Commission, the Commission's Office of the Secretary will issue an appropriate response and will notify the applicant.

(h) The Commission shall publish in the FEDERAL REGISTER a notice that a complete application has been submitted. The notice will provide that any person may, within the period specified therein, submit to the Commission any information that relates to the Commission action requested in

§ 240.3a1-1

the application. The notice also will indicate the earliest date on which the Commission would take final action on the application, but in no event would such action be taken earlier than 25 days following publication of the notice in the FEDERAL REGISTER.

(i) The Commission may, in its sole discretion, schedule a hearing on the matter addressed by the application.

[79 FR 47369, Aug. 12, 2014, as amended at 85 FR 6350, Feb. 4, 2020]

§ 240.3a1-1 Exemption from the definition of "Exchange" under Section 3(a)(1) of the Act.

(a) An organization, association, or group of persons shall be exempt from the definition of the term "exchange" under section 3(a)(1) of the Act, (15 U.S.C. 78c(a)(1)), if such organization, association, or group of persons:

(1) Is operated by a national securities association;

(2) Is in compliance with Regulation ATS, 17 CFR 242.300 through 242.304; or

(3) Pursuant to paragraph (a) of § 242.301 of Regulation ATS, 17 CFR 242.301(a), is not required to comply with Regulation ATS, 17 CFR 242.300 through 242.304.

(b) Notwithstanding paragraph (a) of this section, an organization, association, or group of persons shall not be exempt under this section from the definition of "exchange," if:

(1) During three of the preceding four calendar quarters such organization, association, or group of persons had:

(i) Fifty percent or more of the average daily dollar trading volume in any security and five percent or more of the average daily dollar trading volume in any class of securities; or

(ii) Forty percent or more of the average daily dollar trading volume in any class of securities; and

(2) The Commission determines, after notice to the organization, association, or group of persons, and an opportunity for such organization, association, or group of persons to respond, that such an exemption would not be necessary or appropriate in the public interest or consistent with the protection of investors taking into account the requirements for exchange registration under section 6 of the Act, (15 U.S.C. 78f), and the objectives of the national market system under section 11A of the Act, (15 U.S.C 78k-1).

(3) For purposes of paragraph (b) of this section, each of the following shall be considered a "class of securities":

(i) Equity securities, which shall have the same meaning as in § 240.3a11-1;

(ii) Listed options, which shall mean any options traded on a national securities exchange or automated facility of a national securities exchange;

(iii) Unlisted options, which shall mean any options other than those traded on a national securities exchange or automated facility of a national securities association;

(iv) Municipal securities, which shall have the same meaning as in section 3(a)(29) of the Act, (15 U.S.C. 78c(a)(29));

(v) Corporate debt securities, which shall mean any securities that:

(A) Evidence a liability of the issuer of such securities;

(B) Have a fixed maturity date that is at least one year following the date of issuance; and

(C) Are not exempted securities, as defined in section 3(a)(12) of the Act, (15 U.S.C. 78c(a)(12));

(vi) Foreign corporate debt securities, which shall mean any securities that:

(A) Evidence a liability of the issuer of such debt securities;

(B) Are issued by a corporation or other organization incorporated or organized under the laws of any foreign country; and

(C) Have a fixed maturity date that is at least one year following the date of issuance; and

(vii) Foreign sovereign debt securities, which shall mean any securities that:

(A) Evidence a liability of the issuer of such debt securities;

(B) Are issued or guaranteed by the government of a foreign country, any political subdivision of a foreign country or any supranational entity; and

(C) Do not have a maturity date of a year or less following the date of issuance.

[63 FR 70917, Dec. 22, 1998, as amended at 74 FR 52372, Oct. 9, 2009; 83 FR 38911, Aug. 7, 2018]

Securities and Exchange Commission § 240.3a4-1

§ 240.3a4-1 Associated persons of an issuer deemed not to be brokers.

(a) An associated person of an issuer of securities shall not be deemed to be a broker solely by reason of his participation in the sale of the securities of such issuer if the associated person:

(1) Is not subject to a statutory disqualification, as that term is defined in section 3(a)(39) of the Act, at the time of his participation; and

(2) Is not compensated in connection with his participation by the payment of commissions or other remuneration based either directly or indirectly on transactions in securities; and

(3) Is not at the time of his participation an associated person of a broker or dealer; and

(4) Meets the conditions of any one of paragraph (a)(4) (i), (ii), or (iii) of this section.

(i) The associated person restricts his participation to transactions involving offers and sales of securities:

(A) To a registered broker or dealer; a registered investment company (or registered separate account); an insurance company; a bank; a savings and loan association; a trust company or similar institution supervised by a state or federal banking authority; or a trust for which a bank, a savings and loan association, a trust company, or a registered investment adviser either is the trustee or is authorized in writing to make investment decisions; or

(B) That are exempted by reason of section 3(a)(7), 3(a)(9) or 3(a)(10) of the Securities Act of 1933 from the registration provisions of that Act; or

(C) That are made pursuant to a plan or agreement submitted for the vote or consent of the security holders who will receive securities of the issuer in connection with a reclassification of securities of the issuer, a merger or consolidation or a similar plan of acquisition involving an exchange of securities, or a transfer of assets of any other person to the issuer in exchange for securities of the issuer; or

(D) That are made pursuant to a bonus, profit-sharing, pension, retirement, thrift, savings, incentive, stock purchase, stock ownership, stock appreciation, stock option, dividend reinvestment or similar plan for employees of an issuer or a subsidiary of the issuer;

(ii) The associated person meets all of the following conditions:

(A) The associated person primarily performs, or is intended primarily to perform at the end of the offering, substantial duties for or on behalf of the issuer otherwise than in connection with transactions in securities; and

(B) The associated person was not a broker or dealer, or an associated person of a broker or dealer, within the preceding 12 months; and

(C) The associated person does not participate in selling an offering of securities for any issuer more than once every 12 months other than in reliance on paragraph (a)(4)(i) or (iii) of this section, except that for securities issued pursuant to rule 415 under the Securities Act of 1933, the 12 months shall begin with the last sale of any security included within one rule 415 registration.

(iii) The associated person restricts his participation to any one or more of the following activities:

(A) Preparing any written communication or delivering such communication through the mails or other means that does not involve oral solicitation by the associated person of a potential purchaser; *Provided, however,* that the content of such communication is approved by a partner, officer or director of the issuer;

(B) Responding to inquiries of a potential purchaser in a communication initiated by the potential purchaser; *Provided, however,* That the content of such responses are limited to information contained in a registration statement filed under the Securities Act of 1933 or other offering document; or

(C) Performing ministerial and clerical work involved in effecting any transaction.

(b) No presumption shall arise that an associated person of an issuer has violated section 15(a) of the Act solely by reason of his participation in the sale of securities of the issuer if he does not meet the conditions specified in paragraph (a) of this section.

(c) *Definitions.* When used in this section:

(1) The term *associated person of an issuer* means any natural person who is

§§ 240.3a4-2—240.3a4-6

a partner, officer, director, or employee of:
(i) The issuer;
(ii) A corporate general partner of a limited partnership that is the issuer;
(iii) A company or partnership that controls, is controlled by, or is under common control with, the issuer; or
(iv) An investment adviser registered under the Investment Advisers Act of 1940 to an investment company registered under the Investment Company Act of 1940 which is the issuer.

(2) The term *associated person of a broker or dealer* means any partner, officer, director, or branch manager of such broker or dealer (or any person occupying a similar status or performing similar functions), any person directly or indirectly controlling, controlled by, or under common control with such broker or dealer, or any employee of such broker or dealer, except that any person associated with a broker or dealer whose functions are solely clerical or ministerial and any person who is required under the laws of any State to register as a broker or dealer in that State solely because such person is an issuer of securities or associated person of an issuer of securities shall not be included in the meaning of such term for purposes of this section.

[50 FR 27946, July 9, 1985]

§§ 240.3a4-2—240.3a4-6 [Reserved]

§ 240.3a5-1 Exemption from the definition of "dealer" for a bank engaged in riskless principal transactions.

(a) A bank is exempt from the definition of the term "dealer" to the extent that it engages in or effects riskless principal transactions if the number of such riskless principal transactions during a calendar year combined with transactions in which the bank is acting as an agent for a customer pursuant to section 3(a)(4)(B)(xi) of the Act (15 U.S.C. 78c(a)(4)(B)(xi)) during that same year does not exceed 500.

(b) For purposes of this section, the term riskless principal transaction means a transaction in which, after having received an order to buy from a customer, the bank purchased the security from another person to offset a contemporaneous sale to such customer or, after having received an order to sell from a customer, the bank sold the security to another person to offset a contemporaneous purchase from such customer.

[68 FR 8700, Feb. 24, 2003]

§ 240.3a5-2 Exemption from the definition of "dealer" for banks effecting transactions in securities issued pursuant to Regulation S.

(a) A bank is exempt from the definition of the term "dealer" under section 3(a)(5) of the Act (15 U.S.C. 78c(a)(5)), to the extent that, in a riskless principal transaction, the bank:

(1) Purchases an eligible security from an issuer or a broker-dealer and sells that security in compliance with the requirements of 17 CFR 230.903 to a purchaser who is not in the United States;

(2) Purchases from a person who is not a U.S. person under 17 CFR 230.902(k) an eligible security after its initial sale with a reasonable belief that the eligible security was initially sold outside of the United States within the meaning of and in compliance with the requirements of 17 CFR 230.903, and resells that security to a purchaser who is not in the United States or to a registered broker or dealer, provided that if the resale is made prior to the expiration of any applicable distribution compliance period specified in 17 CFR 230.903(b)(2) or (b)(3), the resale is made in compliance with the requirements of 17 CFR 230.904; or

(3) Purchases from a registered broker or dealer an eligible security after its initial sale with a reasonable belief that the eligible security was initially sold outside of the United States within the meaning of and in compliance with the requirements of 17 CFR 230.903, and resells that security to a purchaser who is not in the United States, provided that if the resale is made prior to the expiration of any applicable distribution compliance period specified in 17 CFR 230.903(b)(2) or (b)(3), the resale is made in compliance with the requirements of 17 CFR 230.904.

(b) *Definitions.* For purposes of this section:

Securities and Exchange Commission § 240.3a11-1

(1) *Distributor* has the same meaning as in 17 CFR 230.902(d).

(2) *Eligible security* means a security that:

(i) Is not being sold from the inventory of the bank or an affiliate of the bank; and

(ii) Is not being underwritten by the bank or an affiliate of the bank on a firm-commitment basis, unless the bank acquired the security from an unaffiliated distributor that did not purchase the security from the bank or an affiliate of the bank.

(3) *Purchaser* means a person who purchases an eligible security and who is not a U.S. person under 17 CFR 230.902(k).

(4) *Riskless principal transaction* means a transaction in which, after having received an order to buy from a customer, the bank purchased the security from another person to offset a contemporaneous sale to such customer or, after having received an order to sell from a customer, the bank sold the security to another person to offset a contemporaneous purchase from such customer.

[72 FR 56567, Oct. 3, 2007]

§ 240.3a5-3 Exemption from the definition of "dealer" for banks engaging in securities lending transactions.

(a) A bank is exempt from the definition of the term "dealer" under section 3(a)(5) of the Act (15 U.S.C. 78c(a)(5)), to the extent that, as a conduit lender, it engages in or effects securities lending transactions, and any securities lending services in connection with such transactions, with or on behalf of a person the bank reasonably believes to be:

(1) A qualified investor as defined in section 3(a)(54)(A) of the Act (15 U.S.C. 78c(a)(54)(A)); or

(2) Any employee benefit plan that owns and invests, on a discretionary basis, not less than $25,000,000 in investments.

(b) *Securities lending transaction* means a transaction in which the owner of a security lends the security temporarily to another party pursuant to a written securities lending agreement under which the lender retains the economic interests of an owner of such securities, and has the right to terminate the transaction and to recall the loaned securities on terms agreed by the parties.

(c) *Securities lending services* means:

(1) Selecting and negotiating with a borrower and executing, or directing the execution of the loan with the borrower;

(2) Receiving, delivering, or directing the receipt or delivery of loaned securities;

(3) Receiving, delivering, or directing the receipt or delivery of collateral;

(4) Providing mark-to-market, corporate action, recordkeeping or other services incidental to the administration of the securities lending transaction;

(5) Investing, or directing the investment of, cash collateral; or

(6) Indemnifying the lender of securities with respect to various matters.

(d) For the purposes of this section, the term *conduit lender* means a bank that borrows or loans securities, as principal, for its own account, and contemporaneously loans or borrows the same securities, as principal, for its own account. A bank that qualifies under this definition as a conduit lender at the commencement of a transaction will continue to qualify, notwithstanding whether:

(1) The lending or borrowing transaction terminates and so long as the transaction is replaced within one business day by another lending or borrowing transaction involving the same securities; and

(2) Any substitutions of collateral occur.

[72 FR 56567, Oct. 3, 2007]

DEFINITION OF "EQUITY SECURITY" AS USED IN SECTIONS 12(g) AND 16

§ 240.3a11-1 Definition of the term "equity security."

The term *equity security* is hereby defined to include any stock or similar security, certificate of interest or participation in any profit sharing agreement, preorganization certificate or subscription, transferable share, voting trust certificate or certificate of deposit for an equity security, limited partnership interest, interest in a joint venture, or certificate of interest in a business trust; any security future on

§ 240.3a12–1

any such security; or any security convertible, with or without consideration into such a security, or carrying any warrant or right to subscribe to or purchase such a security; or any such warrant or right; or any put, call, straddle, or other option or privilege of buying such a security from or selling such a security to another without being bound to do so.

[67 FR 19673, Apr. 23, 2002]

MISCELLANEOUS EXEMPTIONS

§ 240.3a12–1 Exemption of certain mortgages and interests in mortgages.

Mortgages, as defined in section 302(d) of the Emergency Home Finance Act of 1970, which are or have been sold by the Federal Home Loan Mortgage Corporation are hereby exempted from the operation of such provisions of the Act as by their terms do not apply to an "exempted security" or to "exempted securities".

(Sec. 3(a)(12), 48 Stat. 882, 15 U.S.C. 78(c))

[37 FR 25167, Nov. 28, 1972]

§ 240.3a12–2 [Reserved]

§ 240.3a12–3 Exemption from sections 14(a), 14(b), 14(c), 14(f) and 16 for securities of certain foreign issuers.

(a) Securities for which the filing of registration statements on Form 18 [17 CFR 249.218] are authorized shall be exempt from the operation of sections 14 and 16 of the Act.

(b) Securities registered by a foreign private issuer, as defined in Rule 3b–4 (§ 240.3b–4 of this chapter), shall be exempt from sections 14(a), 14(b), 14(c), 14(f) and 16 of the Act.

[44 FR 70137, Dec. 6, 1979, as amended at 47 FR 54780, Dec. 6, 1982; 56 FR 30067, July 1, 1991]

§ 240.3a12–4 Exemptions from sections 15(a) and 15(c)(3) for certain mortgage securities.

(a) When used in this Rule the following terms shall have the meanings indicated:

(1) The term *whole loan mortgage* means an evidence of indebtedness secured by mortgage, deed of trust, or other lien upon real estate or upon leasehold interests therein where the entire mortgage, deed or other lien is transferred with the entire evidence of indebtedness.

(2) The term *aggregated whole loan mortgage* means two or more whole loan mortgages that are grouped together and sold to one person in one transaction.

(3) The term *participation interest* means an undivided interest representing one of only two such interests in a whole loan mortgage or in an aggregated whole loan mortgage, provided that the other interest is retained by the originator of such participation interest.

(4) The term *commitment* means a contract to purchase a whole loan mortgage, an aggregated whole loan mortgage or a participation interest which by its terms requires that the contract be fully executed within 2 years.

(5) The term *mortgage security* means a whole loan mortgage, an aggregated whole loan mortgage, a participation interest, or a commitment.

(b) A mortgage security shall be deemed an "exempted security" for purposes of subsections (a) and (c)(3) of section 15 of the Act provided that, in the case of and at the time of any sale of the mortgage security by a broker or dealer, such mortgage security is not in default and has an unpaid principal amount of at least $50,000.

[39 FR 19945, June 5, 1974]

§ 240.3a12–5 Exemption of certain investment contract securities from sections 7(c) and 11(d)(1).

(a) An investment contract security involving the direct ownership of specified residential real property shall be exempted from the provisions of sections 7(c) and 11(d)(1) of the Act with respect to any transaction by a broker or dealer who, directly or indirectly, arranges for the extension or maintenance of credit on the security to or from a customer, if the credit:

(1) Is secured by a lien, mortgage, deed of trust, or any other similar security interest related only to real property: *Provided, however,* That this provision shall not prevent a lender from requiring (i) a security interest in the common areas and recreational facilities or furniture and fixtures incidental to the investment contract if

the purchase of such furniture and fixtures is required by, or subject to the approval of, the issuer, as a condition of purchase; or (ii) an assignment of future rentals in the event of default by the purchaser or a co-signer or guarantor on the debt obligation other than the issuer, its affiliates, or any broker or dealer offering such securities;

(2) Is to be repaid by periodic payments of principal and interest pursuant to an amortization schedule established by the governing instruments: *Provided, however,* That this provision shall not prevent the extension of credit on terms which require the payment of interest only, if extended in compliance with the other provisions of this rule; and

(3) Is extended by a lender which is not, directly or indirectly controlling, controlled by, or under common control with the broker or dealer or the issuer of the securities or affiliates thereof.

(b) For purposes of this rule:

(1) *Residential real property* shall mean real property containing living accommodations, whether used on a permanent or transient basis, and may include furniture or fixtures if required as a condition of purchase of the investment contract or if subject to the approval of the issuer.

(2) *Direct ownership* shall mean ownership of a fee or leasehold estate or a beneficial interest in a trust the purchase of which, under applicable local law, is financed and secured by a security interest therein similar to a mortgage or deed of trust, but it shall not include an interest in a real estate investment trust, an interest in a general or limited partnership, or similar indirect interest in the ownership of real property.

(Sec. 3(a)(12), 48 Stat. 882, as amended 84 Stat. 718, 1435, 1499 (15 U.S.C. 78c(12)); sec. 7(c), 48 Stat. 886, as amended 82 Stat. 452 (15 U.S.C. 78g(c)); sec. 11(d)(1), 48 Stat. 891 as amended 68 Stat. 636 (15 U.S.C. 78k(d)(1)); sec. 15(c), 48 Stat. 895, as amended 52 Stat. 1075, 84 Stat. 1653 (15 U.S.C. 78o(c)); sec. 23(a), 48 Stat. 901, as amended 49 Stat. 704, 1379 (15 U.S.C. 78w(a)))

[40 FR 6646, Feb. 13, 1975]

§ 240.3a12-6 Definition of "common trust fund" as used in section 3(a)(12) of the Act.

The term *common trust fund* as used in section 3(a)(12) of the Act (15 U.S.C. 78c(a)(12)) shall include a common trust fund which is maintained by a bank which is a member of an affiliated group, as defined in section 1504(a) of the Internal Revenue Code of 1954 (26 U.S.C. 1504(a)), and which is maintained exclusively for the collective investment and reinvestment of monies contributed thereto by one or more bank members of such affiliated group in the capacity of trustee, executor, administrator, or guardian; *Provided,* That:

(a) The common trust fund is operated in compliance with the same state and federal regulatory requirements as would apply if the bank maintaining such fund and any other contributing banks were the same entity; and

(b) The rights of persons for whose benefit a contributing bank acts as trustee, executor, administrator, or guardian would not be diminished by reason of the maintenance of such common trust fund by another bank member of the affiliated group.

(15 U.S.C. 78c(b))

[43 FR 2392, Jan. 17, 1978]

§ 240.3a12-7 Exemption for certain derivative securities traded otherwise than on a national securities exchange.

Any put, call, straddle, option, or privilege traded exclusively otherwise than on a national securities exchange and for which quotations are not disseminated through an automated quotation system of a registered securities association, which relates to any securities which are direct obligations of, or obligations guaranteed as to principal or interest by, the United States, or securities issued or guaranteed by a corporation in which the United States has a direct or indirect interest as shall be designated for exemption by the Secretary of the Treasury pursuant to section 3(a)(12) of the Act, shall be exempt from all provisions of the Act which by their terms

§ 240.3a12–8

do not apply to any "exempted security" or "exempted securities," provided that the securities underlying such put, call, straddle, option or privilege represent an obligation equal to or exceeding $250,000 principal amount.

(15 U.S.C. 78a *et seq.*, and particularly secs. 3(a)(12), 15(a)(2) and 23(a) (15 U.S.C. 78c(a)(12), 78*o*(a)(2) and 78w(a)))

[49 FR 5073, Feb. 10, 1984]

§ 240.3a12–8 Exemption for designated foreign government securities for purposes of futures trading.

(a) When used in this Rule, the following terms shall have the meaning indicated:

(1) The term *designated foreign government security* shall mean a security not registered under the Securities Act of 1933 nor the subject of any American depositary receipt so registered, and representing a debt obligation of the government of

(i) The United Kingdom of Great Britain and Northern Ireland;
(ii) Canada;
(iii) Japan;
(iv) The Commonwealth of Australia;
(v) The Republic of France;
(vi) New Zealand;
(vii) The Republic of Austria;
(viii) The Kingdom of Denmark;
(ix) The Republic of Finland;
(x) The Kingdom of the Netherlands;
(xi) Switzerland;
(xii) The Federal Republic of Germany;
(xiii) The Republic of Ireland;
(xiv) The Republic of Italy;
(xv) The Kingdom of Spain;
(xvi) The United Mexican States;
(xvii) The Federative Republic of Brazil;
(xviii) The Republic of Argentina;
(xix) The Republic of Venezuela;
(xx) The Kingdom of Belgium; or
(xxi) The Kingdom of Sweden.

(2) The term *qualifying foreign futures contracts* shall mean any contracts for the purchase or sale of a designated foreign government security for future delivery, as "future delivery" is defined in 7 U.S.C. 2, provided such contracts require delivery outside the United States, any of its possessions or territories, and are traded on or through a board of trade, as defined at 7 U.S.C. 2.

(b) Any designated foreign government security shall, for purposes only of the offer, sale or confirmation of sale of qualifying foreign futures contracts, be exempted from all provisions of the Act which by their terms do not apply to an "exempted security" or "exempted securities."

(15 U.S.C. 78a *et seq.*, and particularly secs. 3(a)(12), and 23(a) 15 U.S.C. 78c(a)(12), and 78w(a))

[49 FR 8599, Mar. 8, 1984, as amended at 51 FR 25998, July 18, 1986; 52 FR 8877, Mar. 20, 1987; 52 FR 42279, Nov. 4, 1987; 53 FR 43863, Oct. 31, 1988; 57 FR 1378, Jan. 14, 1992; 59 FR 54815, Nov. 2, 1994; 60 FR 62326, Dec. 6, 1995; 61 FR 10274, Mar. 13, 1996; 64 FR 10567, Mar. 5, 1999; 64 FR 29553, June 2, 1999]

§ 240.3a12–9 Exemption of certain direct participation program securities from the arranging provisions of sections 7(c) and 11(d)(1).

(a) Direct participation program securities sold on a basis whereby the purchase price is paid to the issuer in one or more mandatory deferred payments shall be deemed to be exempted securities for purposes of the arranging provisions of sections 7(c) and 11(d)(1) of the Act, provided that:

(1) The securities are registered under the Securities Act of 1933 or are sold or offered exclusively on an intrastate basis in reliance upon section 3(a)(11) of that Act;

(2) The mandatory deferred payments bear a reasonable relationship to the capital needs and program objectives described in a business development plan disclosed to investors in a registration statement filed with the Commission under the Securities Act of 1933 or, where no registration statement is required to be filed with the Commission, as part of a statement filed with the relevant state securities administrator;

(3) Not less than 50 percent of the purchase price of the direct participation program security is paid by the investor at the time of sale;

(4) The total purchase price of the direct participation program security is due within three years in specified property programs or two years in non-specified property programs. Such pay-in periods are to be measured from the

Securities and Exchange Commission

§ 240.3a40–1

earlier of the completion of the offering or one year following the effective date of the offering.

(b) For purposes of this rule:

(1) *Direct participation program* shall mean a program financed through the sale of securities, other than securities that are listed on an exchange, quoted on NASDAQ, or will otherwise be actively traded during the pay-in period as a result of efforts by the issuer, underwriter, or other participants in the initial distribution of such securities, that provides for flow-through tax consequences to its investors; *Provided, however,* That the term "direct participation program" does not include real estate investment trusts, Subchapter S corporate offerings, tax qualified pension and profit sharing plans under sections 401 and 403(a) of the Internal Revenue Code ("Code"), tax shelter annuities under section 403(b) of the Code, individual retirement plans under section 408 of the Code, and any issuer, including a separate account, that is registered under the Investment Company Act of 1940.

(2) *Business development plan* shall mean a specific plan describing the program's anticipated economic development and the amounts of future capital contributions, in the form of mandatory deferred payments, to be required at specified times or upon the occurrence of certain events.

(3) *Specified property program* shall mean a direct participation program in which, at the date of effectiveness, more than 75 percent of the net proceeds from the sale of program securities are committed to specific purchases or expenditures. *Non-specified property program* shall mean any other direct participation program.

[51 FR 8801, Mar. 14, 1986]

§ 240.3a12–10 Exemption of certain securities issued by the Resolution Funding Corporation.

Securities that are issued by the Resolution Funding Corporation pursuant to section 21B(f) of the Federal Home Loan Bank Act (12 U.S.C. 1421 *et seq.*) are exempt from the operation of all provisions of the Act that by their terms do not apply to any "exempted security" or to "exempted securities."

[54 FR 37789, Sept. 13, 1989]

§ 240.3a12–11 Exemption from sections 8(a), 14(a), 14(b), and 14(c) for debt securities listed on a national securities exchange.

(a) Debt securities that are listed for trading on a national securities exchange shall be exempt from the restrictions on borrowing of section 8(a) of the Act (15 U.S.C. 78h(a)).

(b) Debt securities registered pursuant to the provisions of section 12(b) of the Act (15 U.S.C. 78*l*(b)) shall be exempt from sections 14(a), 14(b), and 14(c) of the Act (15 U.S.C. 78n(a), (b), and (c)), *except that* §§ 240.14a-1, 240.14a-2(a), 240.14a-9, 240.14a-13, 240.14b-1, 240.14b-2, 240.14c-1, 240.14c-6 and 240.14c-7 shall continue to apply.

(c) For purposes of this section, *debt securities* is defined to mean any securities that are not "equity securities" as defined in section 3(a)(11) of the Act (15 U.S.C. 78c(a)(11)) and § 240.3a11–1 thereunder.

[59 FR 55347, Nov. 7, 1994]

§ 240.3a12–12 Exemption from certain provisions of section 16 of the Act for asset-backed securities.

Asset-backed securities, as defined in § 229.1101 of this chapter, are exempt from section 16 of the Act (15 U.S.C. 78p).

[70 FR 1620, Jan. 7, 2005]

§ 240.3a40–1 Designation of financial responsibility rules.

The term *financial responsibility rules* for purposes of the Securities Investor Protection Act of 1970 shall include:

(a) Any rule adopted by the Commission pursuant to sections 8, 15(c)(3), 17(a) or 17(e)(1)(A) of the Securities Exchange Act of 1934;

(b) Any rule adopted by the Commission relating to hypothecation or lending of customer securities;

(c) Any rule adopted by any self-regulatory organization relating to capital, margin, recordkeeping, hypothecation or lending requirements; and

§ 240.3a43-1

(d) Any other rule adopted by the Commission or any self-regulatory organization relating to the protection of funds or securities.

(Secs. 3, 15(c)(3), 17(a) and 23 (15 U.S.C. 78c, 78o, 78q(a) and 78u))

[44 FR 28318, May 15, 1979]

§ 240.3a43-1 Customer-related government securities activities incidental to the futures-related business of a futures commission merchant registered with the Commodity Futures Trading Commission.

(a) A futures commission merchant registered with the Commodity Futures Trading Commission ("CFTC") is not a government securities broker or government securities dealer solely because such futures commission merchant effects transactions in government securities that are defined in paragraph (b) of this section as incidental to such person's futures-related business.

(b) Provided that the futures commission merchant maintains in a regulated account all funds and securities associated with such government securities transactions (except funds and securities associated with transactions under paragraph (b)(1)(i) of this section and does not advertise that it is in the business of effecting transactions in government securities otherwise than in connection with futures or options on futures trading or the investment of margin or excess funds related to such trading or the trading of any other instrument subject to CFTC jurisdiction, the following transactions in government securities are incidental to the futures-related business of such a futures commission merchant:

(1) Transactions as agent for a customer—

(i) To effect delivery pursuant to a futures contract; or

(ii) For risk reduction or arbitrage of existing or contemporaneously created postions in futures or options on futures;

(2) Transactions as agent for a customer for investment of margin and excess funds related to futures or options on futures trading or the trading of other instruments subject to CFTC jurisdiction, provided further that,

(i) Such transactions involve Treasury securities with a maturity of less than 93 days at the time of the transation.

(ii) Such transactions generate no monetary profit for the futures commission merchant in excess of the costs of executing such transactions, or

(iii) Such transactions are unsolicited, and commissions and other income generated on transactions pursuant to this paragraph (b)(2)(iii) (including transactional fees paid by the futures commission merchant and charged to its customer) do not exceed 2% of such futures commission merchant's total commission revenues;

(3) Exchange of futures for physicals transactions as agent for or as principal with a customer; and

(4) Any transaction or transactions that the Commission exempts, either unconditionally or on specified terms and conditions, as incidental to the futures-related business of a specified futures commission merchant, a specified category of futures commission merchants, or futures commission merchants generally.

(c) Definitions. (1) *Customer* means any person for whom the futures commission merchant effects or intends to effect transactions in futures, options on futures, or any other instruments subject to CFTC jurisdiction.

(2) *Regulated account* means a customer segregation account subject to the regulations of the CFTC; provided, however, that, where such regulations do not permit to be maintained in such an account or require to be maintained in a separate regulated account funds or securities in proprietary accounts or funds or securities used as margin for or excess funds related to futures contracts, options on futures or any other instruments subject to CFTC jurisdiction that trade outside the United States, its territories, or possessions, the term *regulated account* means such separate regulated account or any other account subject to record-keeping regulations of the CFTC.

(3) *Unsolicited transaction* means a transaction that is not effected in a discretionary account or recommended to a customer by the futures commission merchant, an associated person of

Securities and Exchange Commission

§ 240.3a44–1

a futures commission merchant, a business affiliate that is controlled by, controlling, or under common control with the futures commission merchant, or an introducing broker that is guaranteed by the futures commission merchant.

(4) *Futures* and *futures contracts* mean contracts of sale of a commodity for future delivery traded on or subject to the rules of a contract market designated by the CFTC or traded on or subject to the rules of any board of trade located outside the United States, its territories, or possessions.

(5) *Options on futures* means puts or calls on a futures contract traded on or subject to the rules of a contract market designated by the CFTC or traded or subject to the rules of any board of trade located outside the United States, its territories, or possessions.

[52 FR 27969, July 24, 1987]

§ 240.3a44–1 Proprietary government securities transactions incidental to the futures-related business of a CFTC-regulated person.

(a) A person registered with the Commodity Futures Trading Commission ("CFTC"), a contract market designated by the CFTC, such a contract market's affiliated clearing organization, or any floor trader or such a contract market (hereinafter referred to collectively as a "CFTC-regulated person") is not a government securities dealer solely because such person effects transactions for its own account in government securities that are defined in paragraph (b) of this section as incidental to such person's futures-related business.

(b) Provided that a CFTC-regulated person does not advertise or otherwise hold itself out as a government securities dealer except as permitted under rule 3a43–1 (§ 240.3a43–1) the following transactions in government securities for its own account are incidental to the futures-related business of such a CFTC-regulated person:

(1) Transactions to effect delivery of a government security pursuant to a futures contract;

(2) Exchange of futures for physicals transactions with (i) a government securities broker or government securities dealer that has registered with the Commission or filed notice pursuant to section 15C(a) of the Act or (ii) a CFTC-regulated person;

(3) Transactions (including repurchase agreements and reverse repurchase agreements) involving segregated customer funds and securities or funds and securities held by a clearing organization with (i) a government securities broker or government securities dealer that has registered with the Commission of filed notice pursuant to section 15C(a) of the Act or (ii) a bank;

(4) Transactions for risk reduction or arbitrage of existing or contemporaneously created positions in futures or options on futures with (i) a government securities broker or government securities dealer that has registered with the Commission or filed notice pursuant to section 15C(a) of the Act or (ii) a CFTC-regulated person;

(5) Repurchase and reverse repurchase agreement transactions between a futures commission merchant acting in a proprietary capacity and another CFTC-regulated person acting in a proprietary capacity and contemporaneous offsetting transactions between such a futures commission merchant and (i) a government securities broker or government securities dealer that has registered with the Commission or filed notice pursuant to section 15C(a) of the Act, (ii) a bank, or (iii) a CFTC-regulated person acting in a proprietary capacity; and

(6) Any transaction or transactions that the Commission exempts, either unconditionally or on specified terms and conditions, as incidental to the futures related business of a specified CFTC-regulated person, a specified category of CFTC-regulated persons, or CFTC-regulated persons generally.

(c) *Definitions*—(1) *Segregated customer funds* means funds subject to CFTC segregation requirements.

(2) *Futures* and *futures contracts* means contracts of sale of a commodity for future delivery traded on or subject to the rules of a contract market designated by the CFTC or traded on or subject to the rules of any board of trade located outside the United States, its territories, or possessions.

(3) *Options on futures* means puts or calls on a futures contract traded on or

§ 240.3a51-1

subject to the rules of a contract market designated by the CFTC or traded on or subject to the rules of any board of trade located outside the United States, its territories, or possessions.

[52 FR 27970, July 24, 1987]

§ 240.3a51-1 Definition of "penny stock".

For purposes of section 3(a)(51) of the Act, the term "penny stock" shall mean any equity security other than a security:

(a) That is an NMS stock, as defined in § 242.600(b)(55) of this chapter, provided that:

(1) The security is registered, or approved for registration upon notice of issuance, on a national securities exchange that has been continuously registered as a national securities exchange since April 20, 1992 (the date of the adoption of Rule 3a51-1 (§ 240.3a51-1) by the Commission); and the national securities exchange has maintained quantitative listing standards that are substantially similar to or stricter than those listing standards that were in place on that exchange on January 8, 2004; or

(2) The security is registered, or approved for registration upon notice of issuance, on a national securities exchange, or is listed, or approved for listing upon notice of issuance on, an automated quotation system sponsored by a registered national securities association, that:

(i) Has established initial listing standards that meet or exceed the following criteria:

(A) The issuer shall have:

(*1*) Stockholders' equity of $5,000,000;

(*2*) Market value of listed securities of $50 million for 90 consecutive days prior to applying for the listing (market value means the closing bid price multiplied by the number of securities listed); or

(*3*) Net income of $750,000 (excluding non-recurring items) in the most recently completed fiscal year or in two of the last three most recently completed fiscal years;

(B) The issuer shall have an operating history of at least one year or a market value of listed securities of $50 million (market value means the closing bid price multiplied by the number of securities listed);

(C) The issuer's stock, common or preferred, shall have a minimum bid price of $4 per share;

(D) In the case of common stock, there shall be at least 300 round lot holders of the security (a round lot holder means a holder of a normal unit of trading);

(E) In the case of common stock, there shall be at least 1,000,000 publicly held shares and such shares shall have a market value of at least $5 million (market value means the closing bid price multiplied by number of publicly held shares, and shares held directly or indirectly by an officer or director of the issuer and by any person who is the beneficial owner of more than 10 percent of the total shares outstanding are not considered to be publicly held);

(F) In the case of a convertible debt security, there shall be a principal amount outstanding of at least $10 million;

(G) In the case of rights and warrants, there shall be at least 100,000 issued and the underlying security shall be registered on a national securities exchange or listed on an automated quotation system sponsored by a registered national securities association and shall satisfy the requirements of paragraph (a) or (e) of this section;

(H) In the case of put warrants (that is, instruments that grant the holder the right to sell to the issuing company a specified number of shares of the company's common stock, at a specified price until a specified period of time), there shall be at least 100,000 issued and the underlying security shall be registered on a national securities exchange or listed on an automated quotation system sponsored by a registered national securities association and shall satisfy the requirements of paragraph (a) or (e) of this section;

(I) In the case of units (that is, two or more securities traded together), all component parts shall be registered on a national securities exchange or listed on an automated quotation system sponsored by a registered national securities association and shall satisfy the requirements of paragraph (a) or (e) of this section; and

Securities and Exchange Commission § 240.3a51–1

(J) In the case of equity securities (other than common and preferred stock, convertible debt securities, rights and warrants, put warrants, or units), including hybrid products and derivative securities products, the national securities exchange or registered national securities association shall establish quantitative listing standards that are substantially similar to those found in paragraphs (a)(2)(i)(A) through (a)(2)(i)(I) of this section; and

(ii) Has established quantitative continued listing standards that are reasonably related to the initial listing standards set forth in paragraph (a)(2)(i) of this section, and that are consistent with the maintenance of fair and orderly markets;

(b) That is issued by an investment company registered under the Investment Company Act of 1940;

(c) That is a put or call option issued by the Options Clearing Corporation;

(d) Except for purposes of section 7(b) of the Securities Act and Rule 419 (17 CFR 230.419), that has a price of five dollars or more;

(1) For purposes of paragraph (d) of this section:

(i) A security has a price of five dollars or more for a particular transaction if the security is purchased or sold in that transaction at a price of five dollars or more, excluding any broker or dealer commission, commission equivalent, mark-up, or markdown; and

(ii) Other than in connection with a particular transaction, a security has a price of five dollars or more at a given time if the inside bid quotation is five dollars or more; *provided, however*, that if there is no such inside bid quotation, a security has a price of five dollars or more at a given time if the average of three or more interdealer bid quotations at specified prices displayed at that time in an interdealer quotation system, as defined in 17 CFR 240.15c2–7(c)(1), by three or more market makers in the security, is five dollars or more.

(iii) The term "inside bid quotation" shall mean the highest bid quotation for the security displayed by a market maker in the security on an automated interdealer quotation system that has the characteristics set forth in section 17B(b)(2) of the Act, or such other automated interdealer quotation system designated by the Commission for purposes of this section, at any time in which at least two market makers are contemporaneously displaying on such system bid and offer quotations for the security at specified prices.

(2) If a security is a unit composed of one or more securities, the unit price divided by the number of shares of the unit that are not warrants, options, rights, or similar securities must be five dollars or more, as determined in accordance with paragraph (d)(1) of this section, and any share of the unit that is a warrant, option, right, or similar security, or a convertible security, must have an exercise price or conversion price of five dollars or more;

(e)(1) That is registered, or approved for registration upon notice of issuance, on a national securities exchange that makes transaction reports available pursuant to § 242.601, provided that:

(i) Price and volume information with respect to transactions in that security is required to be reported on a current and continuing basis and is made available to vendors of market information pursuant to the rules of the national securities exchange;

(ii) The security is purchased or sold in a transaction that is effected on or through the facilities of the national securities exchange, or that is part of the distribution of the security; and

(iii) The security satisfies the requirements of paragraph (a)(1) or (a)(2) of this section;

(2) A security that satisfies the requirements of this paragraph (e), but does not otherwise satisfy the requirements of paragraph (a), (b), (c), (d), (f), or (g) of this section, shall be a penny stock for purposes of section 15(b)(6) of the Act (15 U.S.C. 78o(b)(6));

(f) That is a security futures product listed on a national securities exchange or an automated quotation system sponsored by a registered national securities association; or

(g) Whose issuer has:

(1) Net tangible assets (i.e., total assets less intangible assets and liabilities) in excess of $2,000,000, if the issuer has been in continuous operation

§ 240.3a55–1

for at least three years, or $5,000,000, if the issuer has been in continuous operation for less than three years; or

(2) Average revenue of at least $6,000,000 for the last three years.

(3) For purposes of paragraph (g) of this section, net tangible assets or average revenues must be demonstrated by financial statements dated less than fifteen months prior to the date of the transaction that the broker or dealer has reviewed and has a reasonable basis for believing are accurate in relation to the date of the transaction, and:

(i) If the issuer is other than a foreign private issuer, are the most recent financial statements for the issuer that have been audited and reported on by an independent public accountant in accordance with the provisions of 17 CFR 210.2–02; or

(ii) If the issuer is a foreign private issuer, are the most recent financial statements for the issuer that have been filed with the Commission or furnished to the Commission pursuant to 17 CFR 240.12g3–2(b); *provided, however,* that if financial statements for the issuer dated less than fifteen months prior to the date of the transaction have not been filed with or furnished to the Commission, financial statements dated within fifteen months prior to the transaction shall be prepared in accordance with generally accepted accounting principles in the country of incorporation, audited in compliance with the requirements of that jurisdiction, and reported on by an accountant duly registered and in good standing in accordance with the regulations of that jurisdiction.

(4) The broker or dealer shall preserve, as part of its records, copies of the financial statements required by paragraph (g)(3) of this section for the period specified in 17 CFR 240.17a–4(b).

[57 FR 18032, Apr. 28, 1992, as amended at 58 FR 58101, Oct. 29, 1993; 70 FR 40631, July 13, 2005; 70 FR 46090, Aug. 9, 2005; 83 FR 50221, Oct. 4, 2018; 83 FR 58427, Nov. 19, 2018; 86 FR 18809, Apr. 9, 2021]

§ 240.3a55–1 Method for determining market capitalization and dollar value of average daily trading volume; application of the definition of narrow-based security index.

(a) *Market capitalization.* For purposes of Section 3(a)(55)(C)(i)(III)(bb) of the Act (15 U.S.C. 78c(a)(55)(C)(i)(III)(bb)):

(1) On a particular day, a security shall be 1 of 750 securities with the largest market capitalization as of the preceding 6 full calendar months when it is included on a list of such securities designated by the Commission and the CFTC as applicable for that day.

(2) In the event that the Commission and the CFTC have not designated a list under paragraph (a)(1) of this section:

(i) The method to be used to determine market capitalization of a security as of the preceding 6 full calendar months is to sum the values of the market capitalization of such security for each U.S. trading day of the preceding 6 full calendar months, and to divide this sum by the total number of such trading days.

(ii) The 750 securities with the largest market capitalization shall be identified from the universe of all NMS securities as defined in § 242.600 of this chapter that are common stock or depositary shares.

(b) *Dollar value of ADTV.* (1) For purposes of Section 3(a)(55)(B) of the Act (15 U.S.C. 78c(a)(55)(B)):

(i)(A) The method to be used to determine the dollar value of ADTV of a security is to sum the dollar value of ADTV of all reported transactions in such security in each jurisdiction as calculated pursuant to paragraphs (b)(1)(ii) and (iii).

(B) The dollar value of ADTV of a security shall include the value of all reported transactions for such security and for any depositary share that represents such security.

(C) The dollar value of ADTV of a depositary share shall include the value of all reported transactions for such depositary share and for the security that is represented by such depositary share.

(ii) For trading in a security in the United States, the method to be used to determine the dollar value of ADTV as of the preceding 6 full calendar

Securities and Exchange Commission § 240.3a55-1

months is to sum the value of all reported transactions in such security for each U.S. trading day during the preceding 6 full calendar months, and to divide this sum by the total number of such trading days.

(iii)(A) For trading in a security in a jurisdiction other than the United States, the method to be used to determine the dollar value of ADTV as of the preceding 6 full calendar months is to sum the value in U.S. dollars of all reported transactions in such security in such jurisdiction for each trading day during the preceding 6 full calendar months, and to divide this sum by the total number of trading days in such jurisdiction during the preceding 6 full calendar months.

(B) If the value of reported transactions used in calculating the ADTV of securities under paragraph (b)(1)(iii)(A) is reported in a currency other than U.S. dollars, the total value of each day's transactions in such currency shall be converted into U.S. dollars on the basis of a spot rate of exchange for that day obtained from at least one independent entity that provides or disseminates foreign exchange quotations in the ordinary course of its business.

(iv) The dollar value of ADTV of the lowest weighted 25% of an index is the sum of the dollar value of ADTV of each of the component securities comprising the lowest weighted 25% of such index.

(2) For purposes of Section 3(a)(55)(C)(i)(III)(cc) of the Act (15 U.S.C. 78c(a)(55)(C)(i)(III)(cc)):

(i) On a particular day, a security shall be 1 of 675 securities with the largest dollar value of ADTV as of the preceding 6 full calendar months when it is included on a list of such securities designated by the Commission and the CFTC as applicable for that day.

(ii) In the event that the Commission and the CFTC have not designated a list under paragraph (b)(2) of this section:

(A) The method to be used to determine the dollar value of ADTV of a security as of the preceding 6 full calendar months is to sum the value of all reported transactions in such security in the United States for each U.S. trading day during the preceding 6 full calendar months, and to divide this sum by the total number of such trading days.

(B) The 675 securities with the largest dollar value of ADTV shall be identified from the universe of all NMS securities as defined in § 242.600 of this chapter that are common stock or depositary shares.

(c) *Depositary Shares and Section 12 Registration.* For purposes of Section 3(a)(55)(C) of the Act (15 U.S.C. 78c(a)(55)(C)), the requirement that each component security of an index be registered pursuant to Section 12 of the Act (15 U.S.C. 78*l*) shall be satisfied with respect to any security that is a depositary share if the deposited securities underlying the depositary share are registered pursuant to Section 12 of the Act and the depositary share is registered under the Securities Act of 1933 (15 U.S.C. 77a *et seq.*) on Form F-6 (17 CFR 239.36).

(d) *Definitions.* For purposes of this section:

(1) *CFTC* means Commodity Futures Trading Commission.

(2) *Closing price* of a security means:

(i) If reported transactions in the security have taken place in the United States, the price at which the last transaction in such security took place in the regular trading session of the principal market for the security in the United States.

(ii) If no reported transactions in a security have taken place in the United States, the closing price of such security shall be the closing price of any depositary share representing such security divided by the number of shares represented by such depositary share.

(iii) If no reported transactions in a security or in a depositary share representing such security have taken place in the United States, the closing price of such security shall be the price at which the last transaction in such security took place in the regular trading session of the principal market for the security. If such price is reported in a currency other than U.S. dollars, such price shall be converted into U.S. dollars on the basis of a spot rate of exchange relevant for the time of the transaction obtained from at least one independent entity that provides or disseminates foreign exchange

§ 240.3a55–2

quotations in the ordinary course of its business.

(3) *Depositary share* has the same meaning as in § 240.12b–2.

(4) *Foreign financial regulatory authority* has the same meaning as in Section 3(a)(52) of the Act (15 U.S.C. 78c(a)(52)).

(5) *Lowest weighted 25% of an index.* With respect to any particular day, the lowest weighted component securities comprising, in the aggregate, 25% of an index's weighting for purposes of Section 3(a)(55)(B)(iv) of the Act (15 U.S.C. 78c(a)(55)(B)(iv)) ("lowest weighted 25% of an index") means those securities:

(i) That are the lowest weighted securities when all the securities in such index are ranked from lowest to highest based on the index's weighting methodology; and

(ii) For which the sum of the weight of such securities is equal to, or less than, 25% of the index's total weighting.

(6) *Market capitalization* of a security on a particular day:

(i) If the security is not a depositary share, is the product of:

(A) The closing price of such security on that same day; and

(B) The number of outstanding shares of such security on that same day.

(ii) If the security is a depositary share, is the product of:

(A) The closing price of the depositary share on that same day divided by the number of deposited securities represented by such depositary share; and

(B) The number of outstanding shares of the security represented by the depositary share on that same day.

(7) *Outstanding shares* of a security means the number of outstanding shares of such security as reported on the most recent Form 10–K, Form 10–Q, Form 10–KSB, Form 10–QSB, or Form 20–F (17 CFR 249.310, 249.308a, 249.310b, 249.308b, or 249.220f) filed with the Commission by the issuer of such security, including any change to such number of outstanding shares subsequently reported by the issuer on a Form 8–K (17 CFR 249.308).

(8) *Preceding 6 full calendar months* means, with respect to a particular day, the period of time beginning on the same day of the month 6 months before and ending on the day prior to such day.

(9) *Principal market* for a security means the single securities market with the largest reported trading volume for the security during the preceding 6 full calendar months.

(10) *Reported transaction* means:

(i) With respect to securities transactions in the United States, any transaction for which a transaction report is collected, processed, and made available pursuant to an effective transaction reporting plan, or for which a transaction report, last sale data, or quotation information is disseminated through an automated quotation system as described in Section 3(a)(51)(A)(ii) of the Act (15 U.S.C. 78c(a)(51)(A)(ii); and

(ii) With respect to securities transactions outside the United States, any transaction that has been reported to a foreign financial regulatory authority in the jurisdiction where such transaction has taken place.

(11) *U.S. trading day* means any day on which a national securities exchange is open for trading.

(12) *Weighting* of a component security of an index means the percentage of such index's value represented, or accounted for, by such component security.

[66 FR 44514, Aug. 23, 2001, as amended at 70 FR 43750, July 29, 2005]

§ 240.3a55–2 Indexes underlying futures contracts trading for fewer than 30 days.

(a) An index on which a contract of sale for future delivery is trading on a designated contract market, registered derivatives transaction execution facility, or foreign board of trade is not a narrow-based security index under Section 3(a)(55) of the Act (15 U.S.C. 78c(a)(55)) for the first 30 days of trading, if:

(1) Such index would not have been a narrow-based security index on each trading day of the preceding 6 full calendar months with respect to a date no earlier than 30 days prior to the commencement of trading of such contract;

(2) On each trading day of the preceding 6 full calendar months with respect to a date no earlier than 30 days prior to the commencement of trading such contract:

Securities and Exchange Commission

§ 240.3a55–4

(i) Such index had more than 9 component securities;
(ii) No component security in such index comprised more than 30 percent of the index's weighting;
(iii) The 5 highest weighted component securities in such index did not comprise, in the aggregate, more than 60 percent of the index's weighting; and
(iv) The dollar value of the trading volume of the lowest weighted 25% of such index was not less than $50 million (or in the case of an index with 15 or more component securities, $30 million); or

(3) On each trading day of the preceding 6 full calendar months, with respect to a date no earlier than 30 days prior to the commencement of trading such contract:
(i) Such index had at least 9 component securities;
(ii) No component security in such index comprised more than 30 percent of the index's weighting; and
(iii) Each component security in such index was:
(A) Registered pursuant to Section 12 of the Act (15 U.S.C. 78) or was a depositary share representing a security registered pursuant to Section 12 of the Act;
(B) 1 of 750 securities with the largest market capitalization that day; and
(C) 1 of 675 securities with the largest dollar value of trading volume that day.

(b) An index that is not a narrow-based security index for the first 30 days of trading pursuant to paragraph (a) of this section, shall become a narrow-based security index if such index has been a narrow-based security index for more than 45 business days over 3 consecutive calendar months.

(c) An index that becomes a narrow-based security index solely because it was a narrow-based security index for more than 45 business days over 3 consecutive calendar months pursuant to paragraph (b) of this section shall not be a narrow-based security index for the following 3 calendar months.

(d) *Definitions.* For purposes of this section:
(1) *Market capitalization* has the same meaning as in § 240.3a55–1(d)(6).
(2) *Dollar value of trading volume* of a security on a particular day is the value in U.S. dollars of all reported transactions in such security on that day. If the value of reported transactions used in calculating dollar value of trading volume is reported in a currency other than U.S. dollars, the total value of each day's transactions shall be converted into U.S. dollars on the basis of a spot rate of exchange for that day obtained from at least one independent entity that provides or disseminates foreign exchange quotations in the ordinary course of its business.
(3) *Lowest weighted 25% of an index* has the same meaning as in § 240.3a55–1(d)(5).
(4) *Preceding 6 full calendar months* has the same meaning as in § 240.3a55–1(d)(8).
(5) *Reported transaction* has the same meaning as in § 240.3a55–1(d)(10).

[66 FR 44514, Aug. 23, 2001]

§ 240.3a55–3 Futures contracts on security indexes trading on or subject to the rules of a foreign board of trade.

When a contract of sale for future delivery on a security index is traded on or subject to the rules of a foreign board of trade, such index shall not be a narrow-based security index if it would not be a narrow-based security index if a futures contract on such index were traded on a designated contract market or registered derivatives transaction execution facility.

[66 FR 44514, Aug. 23, 2001]

§ 240.3a55–4 Exclusion from definition of narrow-based security index for indexes composed of debt securities.

(a) An index is not a narrow-based security index if:
(1)(i) Each of the securities of an issuer included in the index is a security, as defined in section 2(a)(1) of the Securities Act of 1933 (15 U.S.C. 77b(a)(1)) and section 3(a)(10) of the Act (15 U.S.C. 78c(a)(10)) and the respective rules promulgated thereunder, that is a note, bond, debenture, or evidence of indebtedness;
(ii) None of the securities of an issuer included in the index is an equity security, as defined in section 3(a)(11) of the Act (15 U.S.C. 78c(a)(11)) and the rules promulgated thereunder;

§ 240.3a67-1

(iii) The index is comprised of more than nine securities that are issued by more than nine non-affiliated issuers;

(iv) The securities of any issuer included in the index do not comprise more than 30 percent of the index's weighting;

(v) The securities of any five non-affiliated issuers included in the index do not comprise more than 60 percent of the index's weighting;

(vi) Except as provided in paragraph (a)(1)(viii) of this section, for each security of an issuer included in the index one of the following criteria is satisfied:

(A) The issuer of the security is required to file reports pursuant to section 13 or section 15(d) of the Act (15 U.S.C. 78m and 78o(d));

(B) The issuer of the security has a [Worldwide market value of its outstanding common equity held by non-affiliates of $71 million or more;

(C) The issuer of the security has outstanding securities that are notes, bonds, debentures, or evidences of indebtedness having a total remaining principal amount of at least $1 billion;

(D) The security is an exempted security as defined in section 3(a)(12) of the Act (15 U.S.C. 78c(a)(12)) and the rules promulgated thereunder; or

(E) The issuer of the security is a government of a foreign country or a political subdivision of a foreign country;

(vii) Except as provided in paragraph (a)(1)(viii) of this section, for each security of an issuer included in the index one of the following criteria is satisfied

(A) The security has a total remaining principal amount of at least $250,000,000; or

(B) The security is a municipal security, as defined in section 3(a)(29) of the Act (15 U.S.C. 78c(a)(29)) and the rules promulgated thereunder that has a total remaining principal amount of at least $200,000,000 and the issuer of such municipal security has outstanding securities that are notes, bonds, debentures, or evidences of indebtedness having a total remaining principal amount of at least $1 billion; and

(viii) Paragraphs (a)(1)(vi) and (a)(1)(vii) of this section will not apply to securities of an issuer included in the index if:

(A) All securities of such issuer included in the index represent less than 5 percent of the index's weighting; and

(B) Securities comprising at least 80 percent of the index's weighting satisfy the provisions of paragraphs (a)(1)(vi) and (a)(1)(vii) of this section; or

(2)(i) The index includes exempted securities, other than municipal securities, as defined in section 3(a)(29) of the Act and the rules promulgated thereunder, that are:

(A) Notes, bonds, debentures, or evidences of indebtedness; and

(B) Not equity securities, as defined in section 3(a)(11) of the Act (15 U.S.C. 78c(a)(11)) and the rules promulgated thereunder; and

(ii) Without taking into account any portion of the index composed of such exempted securities, other than municipal securities, the remaining portion of the index would not be a narrow-based security index: meeting all the conditions under paragraph (a)(1) of this section.

(b) For purposes of this section:

(1) An issuer is affiliated with another issuer if it controls, is controlled by, or is under common control with, that issuer.

(2) For purposes of this section, *control* means ownership of 20 percent or more of an issuer's equity, or the ability to direct the voting of 20 percent or more of the issuer's voting equity.

(3) The term *issuer* includes a single issuer or group of affiliated issuers.

[71 FR 39542, July 13, 2006]

SECURITY-BASED SWAP DEALER AND PARTICIPANT DEFINITIONS

SOURCE: 77 FR 30751, May 23, 2012, unless otherwise noted.

§ 240.3a67-1 Definition of "major security-based swap participant."

(a) *General. Major security-based swap participant* means any person:

(1) That is not a security-based swap dealer; and

(2)(i) That maintains a substantial position in security-based swaps for any of the major security-based swap categories, excluding both positions

Securities and Exchange Commission

§ 240.3a67-3

held for hedging or mitigating commercial risk, and positions maintained by any employee benefit plan (or any contract held by such a plan) as defined in paragraphs (3) and (32) of section 3 of the Employee Retirement Income Security Act of 1974 (29 U.S.C. 1002) for the primary purpose of hedging or mitigating any risk directly associated with the operation of the plan;

(ii) Whose outstanding security-based swaps create substantial counterparty exposure that could have serious adverse effects on the financial stability of the United States banking system or financial markets; or

(iii) That is a financial entity that:

(A) Is highly leveraged relative to the amount of capital such entity holds and that is not subject to capital requirements established by an appropriate Federal banking agency (as defined in 15 U.S.C. 78c(a)(72)); and

(B) Maintains a substantial position in outstanding security-based swaps in any major security-based swap category.

(b) *Scope of designation.* A person that is a major security-based swap participant in general shall be deemed to be a major security-based swap participant with respect to each security-based swap it enters into, regardless of the category of the security-based swap or the person's activities in connection with the security-based swap, unless the Commission limits the person's designation as a major security-based swap participant to specified categories of security-based swaps.

§ 240.3a67-2 Categories of security-based swaps.

For purposes of section 3(a)(67) of the Act, 15 U.S.C. 78c(a)(67), and the rules thereunder, the terms *major security-based swap category, category of security-based swaps* and any similar terms mean either of the following categories of security-based swaps:

(a) *Debt security-based swaps.* Any security-based swap that is based, in whole or in part, on one or more instruments of indebtedness (including loans), or on a credit event relating to one or more issuers or securities, including but not limited to any security-based swap that is a credit default swap, total return swap on one or more debt instruments, debt swap, debt index swap, or credit spread.

(b) *Other security-based swaps.* Any security-based swap not described in paragraph (a) of this section.

§ 240.3a67-3 Definition of "substantial position."

(a) *General.* For purposes of section 3(a)(67) of the Act, 15 U.S.C. 78c(a)(67), and § 240.3a67-1, the term *substantial position* means security-based swap positions that equal or exceed either of the following thresholds in any major category of security-based swaps:

(1) $1 billion in daily average aggregate uncollateralized outward exposure; or

(2) $2 billion in:

(i) Daily average aggregate uncollateralized outward exposure; plus

(ii) Daily average aggregate potential outward exposure.

(b) *Aggregate uncollateralized outward exposure*—(1) *General.* Aggregate uncollateralized outward exposure in general means the sum of the current exposure, obtained by marking-to-market using industry standard practices, of each of the person's security-based swap positions with negative value in a major security-based swap category, less the value of the collateral the person has posted in connection with those positions.

(2) *Calculation of aggregate uncollateralized outward exposure.* In calculating this amount the person shall, with respect to each of its security-based swap counterparties in a given major security-based swap category:

(i) Determine the dollar value of the aggregate current exposure arising from each of its security-based swap positions with negative value (subject to the netting provisions described below) in that major category by marking-to-market using industry standard practices; and

(ii) Deduct from that dollar amount the aggregate value of the collateral the person has posted with respect to the security-based swap positions.

(iii) The aggregate uncollateralized outward exposure shall be the sum of those uncollateralized amounts across all of the person's security-based swap

43

§ 240.3a67-3

counterparties in the applicable major category.

(3) *Relevance of netting agreements.* (i) If a person has one or more master netting agreements with a counterparty, the person may measure the current exposure arising from its security-based swaps in any major category on a net basis, applying the terms of those agreements. Calculation of current exposure may take into account offsetting positions entered into with that particular counterparty involving security-based swaps (in any security-based swap category) as well as swaps and securities financing transactions (consisting of securities lending and borrowing, securities margin lending and repurchase and reverse repurchase agreements), and other financial instruments that are subject to netting offsets for purposes of applicable bankruptcy law, to the extent these are consistent with the offsets permitted by the master netting agreements.

(ii) Such adjustments may not take into account any offset associated with positions that the person has with separate counterparties.

(4) *Allocation of uncollateralized outward exposure.* If a person calculates current exposure with a particular counterparty on a net basis, as provided by paragraph (b)(3) of this section, the amount of current uncollateralized exposure attributable to each "major" category of security-based swaps should be calculated according to the following formula:

$$E_{SBS(MC)} = E_{net\ total} \cdot \frac{OTM_{SBS(MC)}}{OTM_{SBS(MC)} + OTM_{SBS(O)} + OTM_{non-SBS}}$$

NOTE TO PARAGRAPH (b)(4). Where: $E_{SBS(MC)}$ equals the amount of aggregate current exposure attributable to the entity's security-based swap positions in the "major" category at issue (either security-based credit derivatives or other security-based swaps); $E_{net\ total}$ equals the entity's aggregate current exposure to the counterparty at issue, after accounting for the netting of positions and the posting of collateral; $OTM_{SBS(MC)}$ equals the current exposure associated with the entity's out-of-the-money positions in security-based swaps in the "major" category at issue, subject to those netting arrangements; and $OTM_{SBS(O)}$ equals the current exposure associated with the entity's out-of-the-money positions in the other "major" category of security-based swaps, subject to those netting arrangements; and $OTM_{non-SBS}$ equals the current exposure associated with the entity's out-of-the-money positions associated with instruments, other than security-based swaps, that are subject to those netting arrangements.

(c) *Aggregate potential outward exposure*—(1) *General. Aggregate potential outward exposure* means the sum of:

(i) The aggregate potential outward exposure for each of the person's security-based swap positions in a major security-based swap category that are neither cleared by a registered or exempt clearing agency nor subject to daily mark-to-market margining, as calculated in accordance with paragraph (c)(2) of this section; and

(ii) The aggregate potential outward exposure for each of the person's security-based swap positions in a major security-based swap category that are either cleared by a registered or exempt clearing agency or subject to daily mark-to-market margining, as calculated in accordance with paragraph (c)(3) of this section.

(2) *Calculation of potential outward exposure for security-based swaps that are not cleared by a registered or exempt clearing agency or subject to daily mark-to-market margining*—(i) *General*—(A)(*1*) For positions in security-based swaps that are not cleared by a registered or exempt clearing agency or subject to daily mark-to-market margining, potential outward exposure equals the total notional principal amount of those positions, multiplied by the following factors on a position-by-position basis reflecting the type of security-based swap. For any security-based swap that is not of the "debt" type, the "equity and other" conversion factors are to be used:

Securities and Exchange Commission § 240.3a67-3

Residual maturity	Debt	Equity and other
One year or less	0.10	0.06
Over one to five years	0.10	0.08
Over five years	0.10	0.10

(2) If a security-based swap is structured such that on specified dates any outstanding exposure is settled and the terms are reset so that the market value of the security-based swap is zero, the remaining maturity equals the time until the next reset date.

(B) *Use of effective notional amounts.* If the stated notional amount on a position is leveraged or enhanced by the structure of the position, the calculation in paragraph (c)(2)(i)(A) of this section shall be based on the effective notional amount of the position rather than on the stated notional amount.

(C) *Exclusion of certain positions.* The calculation in paragraph (c)(2)(i)(A) of this section shall exclude:

(1) Positions that constitute the purchase of an option, such that the person has no additional payment obligations under the position;

(2) Other positions for which the person has prepaid or otherwise satisfied all of its payment obligations; and

(3) Positions for which, pursuant to regulatory requirement, the person has assigned an amount of cash or U.S. Treasury securities that is sufficient to pay the person's maximum possible liability under the position, and the person may not use that cash or those Treasury securities for other purposes.

(D) *Adjustment for certain positions.* Notwithstanding paragraph (c)(2)(i)(A) of this section, the potential outward exposure associated with a position by which a person buys credit protection using a credit default swap, or associated with a position by which a person purchases an option for which the person retains additional payment obligations under the position, is capped at the net present value of the unpaid premiums.

(ii) *Adjustment for netting agreements.* Notwithstanding paragraph (c)(2)(i) of this section, for positions subject to master netting agreements the potential outward exposure associated with the person's security-based swaps with each counterparty equals a weighted average of the potential outward exposure for the person's security-based swaps with that counterparty as calculated under paragraph (c)(2)(i) of this section, and that amount reduced by the ratio of net current exposure to gross current exposure, consistent with the following equation as calculated on a counterparty-by-counterparty basis:

$$P_{Net} = 0.4 \times P_{Gross} + 0.6 \times NGR \times P_{Gross}$$

NOTE TO PARAGRAPH (c)(2)(ii): *Where*: P_{Net} is the potential outward exposure, adjusted for bilateral netting, of the person's security-based swaps with a particular counterparty; P_{Gross} is the potential outward exposure without adjustment for bilateral netting, as calculated pursuant to paragraph (c)(2)(i) of this section; and *NGR* is the ratio of:

1. The current exposure arising from its security-based swaps in the major category as calculated on a net basis according to paragraphs (b)(3) and (4) of this section, divided by

2. The current exposure arising from its security-based swaps in the major category as calculated in the absence of those netting procedures.

(3) *Calculation of potential outward exposure for security-based swaps that are either cleared by a registered or exempt clearing agency or subject to daily mark-to-market margining.* For positions in security-based swaps that are cleared by a registered or exempt clearing agency or subject to daily mark-to-market margining:

(i) Potential outward exposure equals the potential outward exposure that would be attributed to such positions using the procedures in paragraph (c)(2) of this section, multiplied by:

(A) 0.1, in the case of positions cleared by a registered or exempt clearing agency; or

(B) 0.2, in the case of positions that are subject to daily mark-to-market margining but that are not cleared by a registered or exempt clearing agency.

(ii) Solely for purposes of calculating potential outward exposure:

(A) A security-based swap shall be considered to be subject to daily mark-to-market margining if, and for as long as, the counterparties follow the daily practice of exchanging collateral to reflect changes in the current exposure arising from the security-based swap (after taking into account any other financial positions addressed by a netting agreement between the counterparties).

§ 240.3a67-4

(B) If the person is permitted by agreement to maintain a threshold for which it is not required to post collateral, the position still will be considered to be subject to daily mark-to-market margining for purposes of calculating potential outward exposure, but the total amount of that threshold (regardless of the actual exposure at any time) less any initial margin posted up to the amount of that threshold, shall be added to the person's aggregate uncollateralized outward exposure for purposes of paragraph (a)(2) of this section.

(C) If the minimum transfer amount under the agreement is in excess of $1 million, the position still will be considered to be subject to daily mark-to-market margining for purposes of calculating potential outward exposure, but the entirety of the minimum transfer amount shall be added to the person's aggregate uncollateralized outward exposure for purposes of paragraph (a)(2) of this section.

(D) A person may, at its discretion, calculate the potential outward exposure of positions in security-based swaps that are subject to daily mark-to-market margining in accordance with paragraph (c)(2) of this section in lieu of calculating the potential outward exposure of such positions in accordance with this paragraph (c)(3).

(d) *Calculation of daily average.* Measures of daily average aggregate uncollateralized outward exposure and daily average aggregate potential outward exposure shall equal the arithmetic mean of the applicable measure of exposure at the close of each business day, beginning the first business day of each calendar quarter and continuing through the last business day of that quarter.

(e) *Inter-affiliate activities.* In calculating its aggregate uncollateralized outward exposure and its aggregate potential outward exposure, a person shall not consider its security-based swap positions with counterparties that are majority-owned affiliates. For these purposes the parties are majority-owned affiliates if one party directly or indirectly owns a majority interest in the other, or if a third party directly or indirectly owns a majority interest in both counterparties to the security-based swap, where "majority interest" is the right to vote or direct the vote of a majority of a class of voting securities of an entity, the power to sell or direct the sale of a majority of a class of voting securities of an entity, or the right to receive upon dissolution or the contribution of a majority of the capital of a partnership.

§ 240.3a67-4 Definition of "hedging or mitigating commercial risk."

For purposes of section 3(a)(67) of the Act, 15 U.S.C. 78c(a)(67), and § 240.3a67-1, a security-based swap position shall be deemed to be held for the purpose of hedging or mitigating commercial risk when:

(a)(1) Such position is economically appropriate to the reduction of risks that are associated with the present conduct and management of a commercial enterprise (or of a majority owned affiliate of the enterprise), or are reasonably expected to arise in the future conduct and management of the commercial enterprise, where such risks arise from:

(i) The potential change in the value of assets that a person owns, produces, manufactures, processes, or merchandises or reasonably anticipates owning, producing, manufacturing, processing, or merchandising in the ordinary course of business of the enterprise (or of an affiliate under common control with the enterprise);

(ii) The potential change in the value of liabilities that a person has incurred or reasonably anticipates incurring in the ordinary course of business of the enterprise (or of an affiliate under common control with the enterprise); or

(iii) The potential change in the value of services that a person provides, purchases, or reasonably anticipates providing or purchasing in the ordinary course of business of the enterprise (or of an affiliate under common control with the enterprise);

(2) Depending on the applicable facts and circumstances, the security-based swap positions described in paragraph (a)(1) of this section may be expected to encompass, among other positions:

Securities and Exchange Commission § 240.3a67–6

(i) Positions established to manage the risk posed by a customer's, supplier's or counterparty's potential default in connection with: Financing provided to a customer in connection with the sale of real property or a good, product or service; a customer's lease of real property or a good, product or service; a customer's agreement to purchase real property or a good, product or service in the future; or a supplier's commitment to provide or sell a good, product or service in the future;

(ii) Positions established to manage the default risk posed by a financial counterparty (different from the counterparty to the hedging position at issue) in connection with a separate transaction (including a position involving a credit derivative, equity swap, other security-based swap, interest rate swap, commodity swap, foreign exchange swap or other swap, option, or future that itself is for the purpose of hedging or mitigating commercial risk pursuant to this section or 17 CFR 1.3(kkk));

(iii) Positions established to manage equity or market risk associated with certain employee compensation plans, including the risk associated with market price variations in connection with stock-based compensation plans, such as deferred compensation plans and stock appreciation rights;

(iv) Positions established to manage equity market price risks connected with certain business combinations, such as a corporate merger or consolidation or similar plan or acquisition in which securities of a person are exchanged for securities of any other person (unless the sole purpose of the transaction is to change an issuer's domicile solely within the United States), or a transfer of assets of a person to another person in consideration of the issuance of securities of such other person or any of its affiliates;

(v) Positions established by a bank to manage counterparty risks in connection with loans the bank has made; and

(vi) Positions to close out or reduce any of the positions described in paragraphs (a)(2)(i) through (a)(2)(v) of this section; and

(b) Such position is:

(1) Not held for a purpose that is in the nature of speculation or trading; and

(2) Not held to hedge or mitigate the risk of another security-based swap position or swap position, unless that other position itself is held for the purpose of hedging or mitigating commercial risk as defined by this section or 17 CFR 1.3(kkk).

§ 240.3a67–5 Definition of "substantial counterparty exposure."

(a) *General.* For purposes of section 3(a)(67) of the Act, 15 U.S.C. 78c(a)(67), and § 240.3a67–1, the term *substantial counterparty exposure that could have serious adverse effects on the financial stability of the United States banking system or financial markets* means a security-based swap position that satisfies either of the following thresholds:

(1) $2 billion in daily average aggregate uncollateralized outward exposure; or

(2) $4 billion in:

(i) Daily average aggregate uncollateralized outward exposure; plus

(ii) Daily average aggregate potential outward exposure.

(b) *Calculation.* For these purposes, daily average *aggregate uncollateralized outward exposure* and daily average *aggregate potential outward exposure* shall be calculated the same way as is prescribed in § 240.3a67–3, except that these amounts shall be calculated by reference to all of the person's security-based swap positions, rather than by reference to a specific major security-based swap category.

§ 240.3a67–6 Definition of "financial entity."

(a) *General.* For purposes of section 3(a)(67) of the Act, 15 U.S.C. 78c(a)(67), and § 240.3a67–1, the term *financial entity* means:

(1) A swap dealer;

(2) A major swap participant;

(3) A commodity pool as defined in section 1a(10) of the Commodity Exchange Act (7 U.S.C. 1a(10));

(4) A private fund as defined in section 202(a) of the Investment Advisers Act of 1940 (15 U.S.C. 80b–2(a));

§ 240.3a67-7

(5) An employee benefit plan as defined in paragraphs (3) and (32) of section 3 of the Employee Retirement Income Security Act of 1974 (29 U.S.C. 1002); and

(6) A person predominantly engaged in activities that are in the business of banking or financial in nature, as defined in section 4(k) of the Bank Holding Company Act of 1956 (12 U.S.C. 1843k).

(b) *Exclusion for centralized hedging facilities*—(1) *General.* Notwithstanding paragraph (a) of this section, for purposes of this section the term *financial entity* shall not encompass a person that would be a financial entity solely as a result of the person's activities that facilitate hedging and/or treasury functions on behalf of one or more majority-owned affiliates that themselves do not constitute a financial entity.

(2) *Meaning of majority-owned.* For these purposes the counterparties to a security-based swap are majority-owned affiliates if one counterparty directly or indirectly owns a majority interest in the other, or if a third party directly or indirectly owns a majority interest in both counterparties to the security-based swap, where "majority interest" includes, but is not limited to, the right to vote or direct the vote of a majority of a class of voting securities of an entity, the power to sell or direct the sale of a majority of a class of voting securities of an entity, or the right to receive upon dissolution or the contribution of a majority of the capital of a partnership.

§ 240.3a67-7 **Definition of "highly leveraged."**

(a) *General.* For purposes of section 3(a)(67) of the Act, 15 U.S.C. 78c(a)(67), and § 240.3a67-1, the term *highly leveraged* means the existence of a ratio of an entity's total liabilities to equity in excess of 12 to 1 as measured at the close of business on the last business day of the applicable fiscal quarter.

(b) *Measurement of liabilities and equity.* For purposes of this section, liabilities and equity generally should each be determined in accordance with U.S. generally accepted accounting principles; provided, however, that a person that is an employee benefit plan, as defined in paragraphs (3) and

17 CFR Ch. II (4-1-23 Edition)

(32) of section 3 of the Employee Retirement Income Security Act of 1974 (29 U.S.C. 1002), may, for purposes of this paragraph (b):

(1) Exclude obligations to pay benefits to plan participants from the calculation of liabilities; and

(2) Substitute the total value of plan assets for equity.

§ 240.3a67-8 **Timing requirements, reevaluation period, and termination of status.**

(a) *Timing requirements.* A person that is not registered as a major security-based swap participant, but that meets the criteria in § 240.3a67-1 to be a major security-based swap participant as a result of its security-based swap activities in a fiscal quarter, will not be deemed to be a major security-based swap participant until the earlier of the date on which it submits a complete application for registration pursuant to section 15F of the Act (15 U.S.C. 78o-10) or two months after the end of that quarter.

(b) *Reevaluation period.* Notwithstanding paragraph (a) of this section, if a person that is not registered as a major security-based swap participant meets the criteria in § 240.3a67-1 to be a major security-based swap participant in a fiscal quarter, but does not exceed any applicable threshold by more than twenty percent in that quarter:

(1) That person will not immediately be deemed a major security-based swap participant pursuant to the timing requirements specified in paragraph (a) of this section; but

(2) That person will be deemed a major security-based swap participant pursuant to the timing requirements specified in paragraph (a) of this section at the end of the next fiscal quarter if the person exceeds any of the applicable daily average thresholds in that next fiscal quarter.

(c) *Termination of status.* A person that is deemed to be a major security-based swap participant shall continue to be deemed a major security-based swap participant until such time that its security-based swap activities do not exceed any of the daily average thresholds set forth within § 240.3a67-1 for four consecutive fiscal quarters

Securities and Exchange Commission

§ 240.3a67–9

after the date on which the person becomes registered as a major security-based swap participant.

§ 240.3a67–9 Calculation of major participant status by certain persons.

A person shall not be deemed to be a major security-based swap participant, regardless of whether the criteria in § 240.3a67–1 otherwise would cause the person to be a major security-based swap participant, provided the person meets the conditions set forth in paragraph (a) of this section.

(a) *Conditions*—(1) *Caps on uncollateralized exposure and notional positions*—(i) *Maximum potential uncollateralized exposure.* The express terms of the person's agreements or arrangements relating to security-based swaps with its counterparties at no time would permit the person to maintain a total uncollateralized exposure of more than $100 million to all such counterparties, including any exposure that may result from thresholds or minimum transfer amounts established by credit support annexes or similar arrangements; and

(ii) *Maximum notional amount of security-based swap positions.* The person does not maintain security-based swap positions in an effective notional amount of more than $2 billion in any major category of security-based swaps, or more than $4 billion in aggregate; or

(2) *Caps on uncollateralized exposure plus monthly calculation*—(i) *Maximum potential uncollateralized exposure.* The express terms of the person's agreements or arrangements relating to security-based swaps with its counterparties at no time would permit the person to maintain a total uncollateralized exposure of more than $200 million to all such counterparties (with regard to security-based swaps and any other instruments by which the person may have exposure to those counterparties), including any exposure that may result from thresholds or minimum transfer amounts established by credit support annexes or similar arrangements; and

(ii) *Calculation of positions.* (A) At the end of each month, the person performs the calculations prescribed by §§ 240.3a67–3 and 240.3a67–5 with regard to whether the aggregate uncollateralized outward exposure plus aggregate potential outward exposure as of that day constitute a substantial position in a major category of security-based swaps, or pose substantial counterparty exposure that could have serious adverse effects on the financial stability of the United States banking system or financial markets; these calculations shall disregard provisions of those rules that provide for the analyses to be determined based on a daily average over a calendar quarter; and

(B) Each such analysis produces thresholds of no more than:

(*1*) $1 billion in aggregate uncollateralized outward exposure plus aggregate potential outward exposure in any major category of security-based swaps; if the person is subject to § 240.3a67–3(a)(2)(iii), by virtue of being a highly leveraged financial entity that is not subject to capital requirements established by an appropriate Federal banking agency, this analysis shall account for all of the person's security-based swap positions in that major category (without excluding hedging positions), otherwise this analysis shall exclude the same hedging and related positions that are excluded from consideration pursuant to § 240.3a67–3(a)(2)(i); or

(*2*) $2 billion in aggregate uncollateralized outward exposure plus aggregate potential outward exposure (without any positions excluded from the analysis) with regard to all of the person's security-based swap positions.

(3) *Calculations based on certain information.* (i) At the end of each month:

(A)(*1*) The person's aggregate uncollateralized outward exposure with respect to its security-based swap positions is less than $500 million with respect to each of the major security-based swap categories; and

(*2*) The sum of the amount calculated under paragraph (a)(3)(i)(A)(*1*) of this section with respect to each major security-based swap category and the total notional principal amount of the person's security-based swap positions in each such major security-based swap category, adjusted by the multipliers set forth in § 240.3a67–3(c)(2)(i)(A) on a position-by-position basis reflecting the type of security-based swap, is less

49

§ 240.3a67–10

than $1 billion with respect to each of the major security-based swap categories; or

(B)(*1*) The person's aggregate uncollateralized outward exposure with respect to its security-based swap positions across all major security-based swap categories is less than $500 million; and

(*2*) The sum of the amount calculated under paragraph (a)(3)(i)(B)(*1*) of this section and the product of the total effective notional principal amount of the person's security-based swap positions in all major security-based swap categories multiplied by 0.10 is less than $1 billion.

(ii) For purposes of the calculations set forth in paragraph (a)(3)(i) of this section:

(A) The person's aggregate uncollateralized outward exposure for positions held with security-based swap dealers shall be equal to such exposure reported on the most recent reports of such exposure received from such security-based swap dealers; and

(B) The person's aggregate uncollateralized outward exposure for positions that are not reflected in any report of exposure from a security-based swap dealer (including all security-based swap positions it holds with persons other than security-based swap dealers) shall be calculated in accordance with § 240.3a67–3(b)(2).

(b) For purposes of the calculations set forth by this section, the person shall use the effective notional amount of a position rather than the stated notional amount of the position if the stated notional amount is leveraged or enhanced by the structure of the position.

(c) No presumption shall arise that a person is required to perform the calculations needed to determine if it is a major security-based swap participant, solely by reason that the person does not meet the conditions specified in paragraph (a) of this section.

§ 240.3a67–10 Foreign major security-based swap participants.

(a) *Definitions.* As used in this section, the following terms shall have the meanings indicated:

(1) *Conduit affiliate* has the meaning set forth in § 240.3a71–3(a)(1).

17 CFR Ch. II (4–1–23 Edition)

(2) *Foreign branch* has the meaning set forth in § 240.3a71–3(a)(2).

(3) *Transaction conducted through a foreign branch* has the meaning set forth in § 240.3a71–3(a)(3).

(4) *U.S. person* has the meaning set forth in § 240.3a71–3(a)(4).

(5) *U.S. major security-based swap participant* means a major security-based swap participant, as defined in section 3(a)(67) of the Act (15 U.S.C. 78c(a)(67)), and the rules and regulations thereunder, that is a U.S. person.

(6) *Foreign major security-based swap participant* means a major security-based swap participant, as defined in section 3(a)(67) of the Act (15 U.S.C. 78c(a)(67)), and the rules and regulations thereunder, that is not a U.S. person.

(b) *Application of major security-based swap participant tests in the cross-border context.* For purposes of calculating a person's status as a major security-based swap participant as defined in section 3(a)(67) of the Act (15 U.S.C. 78c(a)(67)), and the rules and regulations thereunder, a person shall include the following security-based swap positions:

(1) If such person is a U.S. person, all security-based swap positions that are entered into by the person, including positions entered into through a foreign branch;

(2) If such person is a conduit affiliate, all security-based swap positions that are entered into by the person; and

(3) If such person is a non-U.S. person other than a conduit affiliate, all of the following types of security-based swap positions that are entered into by the person:

(i) Security-based swap positions that are entered into with a U.S. person; provided, however, that this paragraph (b)(3)(i) shall not apply to:

(A) Positions with a U.S. person counterparty that arise from transactions conducted through a foreign branch of the counterparty, when the counterparty is a registered security-based swap dealer; and

(B) Positions with a U.S. person counterparty that arise from transactions conducted through a foreign branch of the counterparty, when the transaction is entered into prior to 60

Securities and Exchange Commission § 240.3a67–10

days following the earliest date on which the registration of security-based swap dealers is first required pursuant to the applicable final rules and regulations; and

(ii) Security-based swap positions for which the non-U.S. person's counterparty to the security-based swap has rights of recourse against a U.S. person; for these purposes a counterparty has rights of recourse against the U.S. person if the counterparty has a conditional or unconditional legally enforceable right, in whole or in part, to receive payments from, or otherwise collect from, the U.S. person in connection with the security-based swap.

(c) *Attributed positions*—(1) *In general.* For purposes of calculating a person's status as a major security-based swap participant as defined in section 3(a)(67) of the Act (15 U.S.C. 78c(a)(67)), and the rules and regulations thereunder, a person also shall include the following security-based swap positions:

(i) If such person is a U.S. person, any security-based swap position of a non-U.S. person for which the non-U.S. person's counterparty to the security-based swap has rights of recourse against that U.S. person.

NOTE TO PARAGRAPH (c)(1)(i). This paragraph describes attribution requirements for a U.S. person solely with respect to the guarantee of the obligations of a non-U.S. person under a security-based swap. The Commission and the Commodity Futures Trading Commission previously provided an interpretation about attribution to a U.S. parent, other affiliate, or guarantor to the extent that the counterparties to those positions have recourse against that parent, other affiliate, or guarantor in connection with the position. *See* Intermediary Definitions Adopting Release, *http://www.gpo.gov/fdsys/pkg/FR–2012–08–13/pdf/2012–18003.pdf*. The Commission explained that it intended to issue separate releases addressing the application of the major participant definition, and Title VII generally, to non-U.S. persons. *See id.* at note 1041.

(ii) If such person is a non-U.S. person:

(A) Any security-based swap position of a U.S. person for which that person's counterparty has rights of recourse against the non-U.S. person; and

(B) Any security-based swap position of another non-U.S. person entered into with a U.S. person counterparty who has rights of recourse against the first non-U.S. person, provided, however, that this paragraph (c)(1)(ii)(B) shall not apply to positions described in § 240.3a67–10(b)(3)(i)(A) and (B).

(2) *Exceptions.* Notwithstanding paragraph (c)(1) of this section, a person shall not include such security-based swap positions if the person whose performance is guaranteed in connection with the security-based swap is:

(i) Subject to capital regulation by the Commission or the Commodity Futures Trading Commission (including, but not limited to regulation as a swap dealer, major swap participant, security-based swap dealer, major security-based swap participant, futures commission merchant, broker, or dealer);

(ii) Regulated as a bank in the United States;

(iii) Subject to capital standards, adopted by the person's home country supervisor, that are consistent in all respects with the Capital Accord of the Basel Committee on Banking Supervision; or

(iv) Deemed not to be a major security-based swap participant pursuant to § 240.3a67–8(a).

(d) *Application of customer protection requirements.* (1) A registered foreign major security-based swap participant shall not be subject to the requirements relating to business conduct standards described in section 15F(h) of the Act (15 U.S.C. 78o–10(h)), and the rules and regulations thereunder, other than rules and regulations prescribed by the Commission pursuant to section 15F(h)(1)(B) of the Act (15 U.S.C. 78o–10(h)(1)(B)), with respect to a security-based swap transaction with a counterparty that is not a U.S. person or with a counterparty that is a U.S. person in a transaction conducted through a foreign branch of the U.S. person.

(2) A registered U.S. major security-based swap participant shall not be subject to the requirements relating to business conduct standards described in section 15F(h) of the Act (15 U.S.C. 78o–10(h)), and the rules and regulations thereunder, other than rules and

§ 240.3a68–1a

regulations prescribed by the Commission pursuant to section 15F(h)(1)(B) of the Act (15 U.S.C. 78o–10(h)(1)(B)), with respect to a security-based swap transaction that constitutes a transaction conducted through a foreign branch of the registered U.S. major security-based swap participant with a non-U.S. person or with a U.S.-person counterparty that constitutes a transaction conducted through a foreign branch of that U.S.-person counterparty.

[79 FR 47369, Aug. 12, 2014, as amended at 81 FR 30142, May 13, 2016]

FURTHER DEFINITION OF SWAP, SECURITY-BASED SWAP, AND SECURITY-BASED SWAP AGREEMENT; MIXED SWAPS; SECURITY-BASED SWAP AGREEMENT RECORDKEEPING

§ 240.3a68–1a Meaning of "issuers of securities in a narrow-based security index" as used in section 3(a)(68)(A)(ii)(III) of the Act.

(a) Notwithstanding § 240.3a68–3(a), and solely for purposes of determining whether a credit default swap is a security-based swap under section 3(a)(68)(A)(ii)(III) of the Act (15 U.S.C. 78c(a)(68)(A)(ii)(III)), the term *issuers of securities in a narrow-based security index* as used in section 3(a)(68)(A)(ii)(III) of the Act means issuers of securities included in an index (including an index referencing loan borrowers or loans of such borrowers) in which:

(1)(i) There are nine or fewer non-affiliated issuers of securities that are reference entities included in the index, provided that an issuer of securities shall not be deemed a reference entity included in the index for purposes of this section unless:

(A) A credit event with respect to such reference entity would result in a payment by the credit protection seller to the credit protection buyer under the credit default swap based on the related notional amount allocated to such reference entity; or

(B) The fact of such credit event or the calculation in accordance with paragraph (a)(1)(i)(A) of this section of the amount owed with respect to such credit event is taken into account in determining whether to make any future payments under the credit default swap with respect to any future credit events;

(ii) The effective notional amount allocated to any reference entity included in the index comprises more than 30 percent of the index's weighting;

(iii) The effective notional amount allocated to any five non-affiliated reference entities included in the index comprises more than 60 percent of the index's weighting; or

(iv) Except as provided in paragraph (b) of this section, for each reference entity included in the index, none of the criteria in paragraphs (a)(1)(iv)(A) through (a)(1)(iv)(H) of this section is satisfied:

(A) The reference entity included in the index is required to file reports pursuant to section 13 or section 15(d) of the Act (15 U.S.C. 78m or 78o(d));

(B) The reference entity included in the index is eligible to rely on the exemption provided in § 240.12g3–2(b);

(C) The reference entity included in the index has a worldwide market value of its outstanding common equity held by non-affiliates of $700 million or more;

(D) The reference entity included in the index (other than a reference entity included in the index that is an issuing entity of an asset-backed security as defined in section 3(a)(79) of the Act (15 U.S.C. 78c(a)(79))) has outstanding notes, bonds, debentures, loans, or evidences of indebtedness (other than revolving credit facilities) having a total remaining principal amount of at least $1 billion;

(E) The reference entity included in the index is the issuer of an exempted security as defined in section 3(a)(12) of the Act (15 U.S.C. 78c(a)(12)) (other than any municipal security as defined in section 3(a)(29) of the Act (15 U.S.C. 78c(a)(29)));

(F) The reference entity included in the index is a government of a foreign country or a political subdivision of a foreign country;

(G) If the reference entity included in the index is an issuing entity of an asset-backed security as defined in section 3(a)(79) of the Act (15 U.S.C. 78c(a)(79)), such asset-backed security was issued in a transaction registered

Securities and Exchange Commission

§ 240.3a68-1a

under the Securities Act of 1933 (15 U.S.C. 77a *et seq.*) and has publicly available distribution reports; and

(H) For a credit default swap entered into solely between eligible contract participants as defined in section 3(a)(65) of the Act (15 U.S.C. 78c(a)(65)):

(*1*) The reference entity included in the index (other than a reference entity included in the index that is an issuing entity of an asset-backed security as defined in section 3(a)(79) of the Act (15 U.S.C. 78c(a)(79))) makes available to the public or otherwise makes available to such eligible contract participant information about the reference entity included in the index pursuant to § 230.144A(d)(4)) of this chapter;

(*2*) Financial information about the reference entity included in the index (other than a reference entity included in the index that is an issuing entity of an asset-backed security as defined in section 3(a)(79) of the Act (15 U.S.C. 78c(a)(79))) is otherwise publicly available; or

(*3*) In the case of a reference entity included in the index that is an issuing entity of an asset-backed security as defined in section 3(a)(79) of the Act (15 U.S.C. 78c(a)(79)), information of the type and level included in publicly available distribution reports for similar asset-backed securities is publicly available about both the reference entity included in the index and such asset-backed security; and

(2)(i) The index is not composed solely of reference entities that are issuers of exempted securities as defined in section 3(a)(12) of the Act (15 U.S.C. 78c(a)(12)), as in effect on the date of enactment of the Futures Trading Act of 1982 (other than any municipal security as defined in section 3(a)(29) of the Act (15 U.S.C. 78c(a)(29))), as in effect on the date of enactment of the Futures Trading Act of 1982); and

(ii) Without taking into account any portion of the index composed of reference entities that are issuers of exempted securities as defined in section 3(a)(12) of the Act (15 U.S.C. 78c(a)(12)), as in effect on the date of enactment of the Futures Trading Act of 1982 (other than any municipal security as defined in section 3(a)(29) of the Act (15 U.S.C. 78c(a)(29))), the remaining portion of the index would be within the term "issuer of securities in a narrow-based security index" under paragraph (a)(1) of this section.

(b) Paragraph (a)(1)(iv) of this section will not apply with respect to a reference entity included in the index if:

(1) The effective notional amounts allocated to such reference entity comprise less than five percent of the index's weighting; and

(2) The effective notional amounts allocated to reference entities included in the index that satisfy paragraph (a)(1)(iv) of this section comprise at least 80 percent of the index's weighting.

(c) For purposes of this section:

(1) A reference entity included in the index is affiliated with another reference entity included in the index (for purposes of paragraph (c)(4) of this section) or another entity (for purposes of paragraph (c)(5) of this section) if it controls, is controlled by, or is under common control with, that other reference entity included in the index or other entity, as applicable; provided that each reference entity included in the index that is an issuing entity of an asset-backed security as defined in section 3(a)(79) of the Act (15 U.S.C. 78c(a)(79)) will not be considered affiliated with any other reference entity included in the index or any other entity that is an issuing entity of an asset-backed security.

(2) Control for purposes of this section means ownership of more than 50 percent of the equity of a reference entity included in the index (for purposes of paragraph (c)(4) of this section) or another entity (for purposes of paragraph (c)(5) of this section), or the ability to direct the voting of more than 50 percent of the voting equity of a reference entity included in the index (for purposes of paragraph (c)(4) of this section) or another entity (for purposes of paragraph (c)(5) of this section).

(3) In identifying a reference entity included in the index for purposes of this section, the term *reference entity* includes:

(i) An issuer of securities;

(ii) An issuer of securities that is an issuing entity of an asset-backed security as defined in section 3(a)(79) of the Act (15 U.S.C. 78c(a)(79)); and

§ 240.3a68-1b

(iii) An issuer of securities that is a borrower with respect to any loan identified in an index of borrowers or loans.

(4) For purposes of calculating the thresholds in paragraphs (a)(1)(i) through (a)(1)(iii) of this section, the term *reference entity included in the index* includes a single reference entity included in the index or a group of affiliated reference entities included in the index as determined in accordance with paragraph (c)(1) of this section (with each reference entity included in the index that is an issuing entity of an asset-backed security as defined in section 3(a)(79) of the Act (15 U.S.C. 78c(a)(79)) being considered a separate reference entity included in the index).

(5) For purposes of determining whether one of the criterion in either paragraphs (a)(1)(iv)(A) through (a)(1)(iv)(D) of this section or paragraphs (a)(1)(iv)(H)(*1*) and (a)(1)(iv)(H)(*2*) of this section is met, the term *reference entity included in the index* includes a single reference entity included in the index or a group of affiliated entities as determined in accordance with paragraph (c)(1) of this section (with each issuing entity of an asset-backed security as defined in section 3(a)(79) of the Act (15 U.S.C. 78c(a)(79)) being considered a separate entity).

[77 FR 48356, Aug. 13, 2012, as amended at 79 FR 57344, Sept. 24, 2014]

§ 240.3a68-1b Meaning of "narrow-based security index" as used in section 3(a)(68)(A)(ii)(I) of the Act.

(a) Notwithstanding § 240.3a68-3(a), and solely for purposes of determining whether a credit default swap is a security-based swap under section 3(a)(68)(A)(ii)(I) of the Act (15 U.S.C. 78c(a)(68)(A)(ii)(I)), the term *narrow-based security index* as used in section 3(a)(68)(A)(ii)(I) of the Act means an index in which:

(1)(i) The index is composed of nine or fewer securities or securities that are issued by nine or fewer non-affiliated issuers, provided that a security shall not be deemed a component of the index for purposes of this section unless:

(A) A credit event with respect to the issuer of such security or a credit event with respect to such security would result in a payment by the credit protection seller to the credit protection buyer under the credit default swap based on the related notional amount allocated to such security; or

(B) The fact of such credit event or the calculation in accordance with paragraph (a)(1)(i)(A) of this section of the amount owed with respect to such credit event is taken into account in determining whether to make any future payments under the credit default swap with respect to any future credit events;

(ii) The effective notional amount allocated to the securities of any issuer included in the index comprises more than 30 percent of the index's weighting;

(iii) The effective notional amount allocated to the securities of any five non-affiliated issuers included in the index comprises more than 60 percent of the index's weighting; or

(iv) Except as provided in paragraph (b) of this section, for each security included in the index none of the criteria in paragraphs (a)(1)(iv)(A) through (a)(1)(iv)(H) of this section is satisfied:

(A) The issuer of the security included in the index is required to file reports pursuant to section 13 or section 15(d) of the Act (15 U.S.C. 78m or 78o(d));

(B) The issuer of the security included in the index is eligible to rely on the exemption provided in § 240.12g3-2(b);

(C) The issuer of the security included in the index has a worldwide market value of its outstanding common equity held by non-affiliates of $700 million or more;

(D) The issuer of the security included in the index (other than an issuer of the security that is an issuing entity of an asset-backed security as defined in section 3(a)(79) of the Act (15 U.S.C. 78c(a)(79))) has outstanding notes, bonds, debentures, loans, or evidences of indebtedness (other than revolving credit facilities) having a total remaining principal amount of at least $1 billion;

(E) The security included in the index is an exempted security as defined in section 3(a)(12) of the Act (15

Securities and Exchange Commission § 240.3a68–1b

U.S.C. 78c(a)(12)) (other than any municipal security as defined in section 3(a)(29) of the Act (15 U.S.C. 78c(a)(29)));

(F) The issuer of the security included in the index is a government of a foreign country or a political subdivision of a foreign country;

(G) If the security included in the index is an asset-backed security as defined in section 3(a)(79) of the Act (15 U.S.C. 78c(a)(79)), the security was issued in a transaction registered under the Securities Act of 1933 (15 U.S.C. 77a *et seq.*) and has publicly available distribution reports; and

(H) For a credit default swap entered into solely between eligible contract participants as defined in section 3(a)(65) of the Act (15 U.S.C. 78c(a)(65)):

(*1*) The issuer of the security included in the index (other than an issuer of the security that is an issuing entity of an asset-backed security as defined in section 3(a)(79) of the Act (15 U.S.C. 78c(a)(79))) makes available to the public or otherwise makes available to such eligible contract participant information about such issuer pursuant to § 230.144A(d)(4)) of this chapter;

(*2*) Financial information about the issuer of the security included in the index (other than an issuer of the security that is an issuing entity of an asset-backed security as defined in section 3(a)(79) of the Act (15 U.S.C. 78c(a)(79))) is otherwise publicly available; or

(*3*) In the case of an asset-backed security as defined in section 3(a)(79) of the Act (15 U.S.C. 78c(a)(79)), information of the type and level included in public distribution reports for similar asset-backed securities is publicly available about both the issuing entity and such asset-backed security; and

(2)(i) The index is not composed solely of exempted securities as defined in section 3(a)(12) of the Act (15 U.S.C. 78c(a)(12)), as in effect on the date of enactment of the Futures Trading Act of 1982 (other than any municipal security as defined in section 3(a)(29) of the Act (15 U.S.C. 78c(a)(29))), as in effect on the date of enactment of the Futures Trading Act of 1982; and

(ii) Without taking into account any portion of the index composed of exempted securities as defined in section 3(a)(12) of the Act (15 U.S.C. 78c(a)(12)), as in effect on the date of enactment of the Futures Trading Act of 1982 (other than any municipal security as defined in section 3(a)(29) of the Act (15 U.S.C. 78c(a)(29))), the remaining portion of the index would be within the term "narrow-based security index" under paragraph (a)(1) of this section.

(b) Paragraph (a)(1)(iv) of this section will not apply with respect to securities of an issuer included in the index if:

(1) The effective notional amounts allocated to all securities of such issuer included in the index comprise less than five percent of the index's weighting; and

(2) The securities that satisfy paragraph (a)(1)(iv) of this section comprise at least 80 percent of the index's weighting.

(c) For purposes of this section:

(1) An issuer of securities included in the index is affiliated with another issuer of securities included in the index (for purposes of paragraph (c)(4) of this section) or another entity (for purposes of paragraph (c)(5) of this section) if it controls, is controlled by, or is under common control with, that other issuer or other entity, as applicable; provided that each issuer of securities included in the index that is an issuing entity of an asset-backed security as defined in section 3(a)(79) of the Act (15 U.S.C. 78c(a)(79)) will not be considered affiliated with any other issuer of securities included in the index or any other entity that is an issuing entity of an asset-backed security.

(2) Control for purposes of this section means ownership of more than 50 percent of the equity of an issuer of securities included in the index (for purposes of paragraph (c)(4) of this section) or another entity (for purposes of paragraph (c)(5) of this section), or the ability to direct the voting of more than 50 percent of the voting equity an issuer of securities included in the index (for purposes of paragraph (c)(4) of this section) or another entity (for purposes of paragraph (c)(5) of this section).

(3) In identifying an issuer of securities included in the index for purposes of this section, the term *issuer* includes:

§ 240.3a68-2

(i) An issuer of securities; and
(ii) An issuer of securities that is an issuing entity of an asset-backed security as defined in section 3(a)(79) of the Act (15 U.S.C. 78c(a)(79)).

(4) For purposes of calculating the thresholds in paragraphs (a)(1)(i) through (a)(1)(iii) of this section, the term *issuer of the security included in the index* includes a single issuer of securities included in the index or a group of affiliated issuers of securities included in the index as determined in accordance with paragraph (c)(1) of this section (with each issuer of securities included in the index that is an issuing entity of an asset-backed security as defined in section 3(a)(79) of the Act (15 U.S.C. 78c(a)(79)) being considered a separate issuer of securities included in the index).

(5) For purposes of determining whether one of the criterion in either paragraphs (a)(1)(iv)(A) through (a)(1)(iv)(D) of this section or paragraphs (a)(1)(iv)(H)(*1*) and (a)(1)(iv)(H)(*2*) of this section is met, the term *issuer of the security included in the index* includes a single issuer of securities included in the index or a group affiliated entities as determined in accordance with paragraph (c)(1) of this section (with each issuing entity of an asset-backed security as defined in section 3(a)(79) of the Act (15 U.S.C. 78c(a)(79)) being considered a separate entity).

[77 FR 48356, Aug. 13, 2012, as amended at 79 FR 57344, Sept. 24, 2014]

§ 240.3a68-2 Requests for interpretation of swaps, security-based swaps, and mixed swaps.

(a) *In general.* Any person may submit a request to the Commission and the Commodity Futures Trading Commission to provide a joint interpretation of whether a particular agreement, contract, or transaction (or class thereof) is:

(1) A swap, as that term is defined in section 3(a)(69) of the Act (15 U.S.C. 78c(a)(69)) and the rules and regulations promulgated thereunder;

(2) A security-based swap, as that term is defined in section 3(a)(68) of the Act (15 U.S.C. 78c(a)(68)) and the rules and regulations promulgated thereunder; or

(3) A mixed swap, as that term is defined in section 3(a)(68)(D) of the Act and the rules and regulations promulgated thereunder.

(b) *Request process.* In making a request pursuant to paragraph (a) of this section, the requesting person must provide the Commission and the Commodity Futures Trading Commission with the following:

(1) All material information regarding the terms of the agreement, contract, or transaction (or class thereof);

(2) A statement of the economic characteristics and purpose of the agreement, contract, or transaction (or class thereof);

(3) The requesting person's determination as to whether the agreement, contract, or transaction (or class thereof) should be characterized as a swap, a security-based swap, or both (i.e., a mixed swap), including the basis for such determination; and

(4) Such other information as may be requested by the Commission or the Commodity Futures Trading Commission.

(c) *Request withdrawal.* A person may withdraw a request made pursuant to paragraph (a) of this section at any time prior to the issuance of a joint interpretation or joint proposed rule by the Commission and the Commodity Futures Trading Commission in response to the request; provided, however, that notwithstanding such withdrawal, the Commission and the Commodity Futures Trading Commission may provide a joint interpretation of whether the agreement, contract, or transaction (or class thereof) is a swap, a security-based swap, or both (i.e., a mixed swap).

(d) *Request by the Commission or the Commodity Futures Trading Commission.* In the absence of a request for a joint interpretation under paragraph (a) of this section:

(1) If the Commission or the Commodity Futures Trading Commission receives a proposal to list, trade, or clear an agreement, contract, or transaction (or class thereof) that raises questions as to the appropriate characterization of such agreement, contract, or transaction (or class thereof) as a swap, a security-based swap, or both (i.e., a mixed swap), the Commission or

Securities and Exchange Commission § 240.3a68-3

the Commodity Futures Trading Commission, as applicable, promptly shall notify the other of the agreement, contract, or transaction (or class thereof); and

(2) The Commission or the Commodity Futures Trading Commission, or their Chairmen jointly, may submit a request for a joint interpretation as described in paragraph (a) of this section; such submission shall be made pursuant to paragraph (b) of this section, and may be withdrawn pursuant to paragraph (c) of this section.

(e) *Timeframe for joint interpretation.* (1) If the Commission and the Commodity Futures Trading Commission determine to issue a joint interpretation as described in paragraph (a) of this section, such joint interpretation shall be issued within 120 days after receipt of a complete submission requesting a joint interpretation under paragraph (a) or (d) of this section.

(2) The Commission and the Commodity Futures Trading Commission shall consult with the Board of Governors of the Federal Reserve System prior to issuing any joint interpretation as described in paragraph (a) of this section.

(3) If the Commission and the Commodity Futures Trading Commission seek public comment with respect to a joint interpretation regarding an agreement, contract, or transaction (or class thereof), the 120-day period described in paragraph (e)(1) of this section shall be stayed during the pendency of the comment period, but shall recommence with the business day after the public comment period ends.

(4) Nothing in this section shall require the Commission and the Commodity Futures Trading Commission to issue any joint interpretation.

(5) If the Commission and the Commodity Futures Trading Commission do not issue a joint interpretation within the time period described in paragraph (e)(1) or (e)(3) of this section, each of the Commission and the Commodity Futures Trading Commission shall publicly provide the reasons for not issuing such a joint interpretation within the applicable timeframes.

(f) *Joint proposed rule.* (1) Rather than issue a joint interpretation pursuant to paragraph (a) of this section, the Commission and the Commodity Futures Trading Commission may issue a joint proposed rule, in consultation with the Board of Governors of the Federal Reserve System, to further define one or more of the terms swap, security-based swap, or mixed swap.

(2) A joint proposed rule described in paragraph (f)(1) of this section shall be issued within the timeframe for issuing a joint interpretation set forth in paragraph (e) of this section.

[77 FR 48356, Aug. 13, 2012]

§ 240.3a68-3 Meaning of "narrow-based security index" as used in the definition of "security-based swap."

(a) *In general.* Except as otherwise provided in § 240.3a68-1a and § 240.3a68-1b, for purposes of section 3(a)(68) of the Act (15 U.S.C. 78c(a)(68)), the term *narrow-based security index* has the meaning set forth in section 3(a)(55) of the Act (15 U.S.C. 78c(a)(55)), and the rules, regulations, and orders of the Commission thereunder.

(b) *Tolerance period for swaps traded on designated contract markets, swap execution facilities and foreign boards of trade.* Notwithstanding paragraph (a) of this section, solely for purposes of swaps traded on or subject to the rules of a designated contract market, swap execution facility, or foreign board of trade pursuant to the Commodity Exchange Act (7 U.S.C. 1 et seq.), a security index underlying such swaps shall not be considered a narrow-based security index if:

(1)(i) A swap on the index is traded on or subject to the rules of a designated contract market, swap execution facility, or foreign board of trade pursuant to the Commodity Exchange Act (7 U.S.C. 1 et seq.) for at least 30 days as a swap on an index that was not a narrow-based security index; or

(ii) Such index was not a narrow-based security index during every trading day of the six full calendar months preceding a date no earlier than 30 days prior to the commencement of trading of a swap on such index on a market described in paragraph (b)(1)(i) of this section; and

(2) The index has been a narrow-based security index for no more than 45 business days over three consecutive calendar months.

57

§ 240.3a68-4

(c) *Tolerance period for security-based swaps traded on national securities exchanges or security-based swap execution facilities.* Notwithstanding paragraph (a) of this section, solely for purposes of security-based swaps traded on a national securities exchange or security-based swap execution facility, a security index underlying such security-based swaps shall be considered a narrow-based security index if:

(1)(i) A security-based swap on the index is traded on a national securities exchange or security-based swap execution facility for at least 30 days as a security-based swap on a narrow-based security index; or

(ii) Such index was a narrow-based security index during every trading day of the six full calendar months preceding a date no earlier than 30 days prior to the commencement of trading of a security-based swap on such index on a market described in paragraph (c)(1)(i) of this section; and

(2) The index has been a security index that is not a narrow-based security index for no more than 45 business days over three consecutive calendar months.

(d) *Grace period.* (1) Solely with respect to a swap that is traded on or subject to the rules of a designated contract market, swap execution facility or foreign board of trade pursuant to the Commodity Exchange Act (7 U.S.C. 1 *et seq.*), an index that becomes a narrow-based security index under paragraph (b) of this section solely because it was a narrow-based security index for more than 45 business days over three consecutive calendar months shall not be a narrow-based security index for the following three calendar months.

(2) Solely with respect to a security-based swap that is traded on a national securities exchange or security-based swap execution facility, an index that becomes a security index that is not a narrow-based security index under paragraph (c) of this section solely because it was not a narrow-based security index for more than 45 business days over three consecutive calendar months shall be a narrow-based security index for the following three calendar months.

[77 FR 48356, Aug. 13, 2012]

§ 240.3a68-4 Regulation of mixed swaps.

(a) *In general.* The term mixed swap has the meaning set forth in section 3(a)(68)(D) of the Act (15 U.S.C. 78c(a)(68)(D)).

(b) *Regulation of bilateral uncleared mixed swaps entered into by dually-registered dealers or major participants.* A mixed swap:

(1) That is neither executed on nor subject to the rules of a designated contract market, national securities exchange, swap execution facility, security-based swap execution facility, or foreign board of trade;

(2) That will not be submitted to a derivatives clearing organization or registered or exempt clearing agency to be cleared; and

(3) Where at least one party is registered with the Commission as a security-based swap dealer or major security-based swap participant and also with the Commodity Futures Trading Commission as a swap dealer or major swap participant, shall be subject to:

(i) The following provisions of the Commodity Exchange Act (7 U.S.C. 1 *et seq.*), and the rules and regulations promulgated thereunder, set forth in the rules and regulations of the Commodity Futures Trading Commission:

(A) Examinations and information sharing: 7 U.S.C. 6s(f) and 12;

(B) Enforcement: 7 U.S.C. 2(a)(1)(B), 6(b), 6b, 6c, 6s(h)(1)(A), 6s(h)(4)(A), 9, 13b, 13a-1, 13a-2, 13, 13c(a), 13c(b), 15 and 26;

(C) Reporting to a swap data repository: 7 U.S.C. 6r;

(D) Real-time reporting: 7 U.S.C. 2(a)(13);

(E) Capital: 7 U.S.C. 6s(e); and

(F) Position Limits: 7 U.S.C. 6a; and

(ii) The provisions of the Federal securities laws, as defined in section 3(a)(47) of the Act (15 U.S.C. 78c(a)(47)), and the rules and regulations promulgated thereunder.

(c) *Process for determining regulatory treatment for other mixed swaps*—(1) *In general.* Any person who desires or intends to list, trade, or clear a mixed swap (or class thereof) that is not subject to paragraph (b) of this section may request the Commission and the Commodity Futures Trading Commission to issue a joint order permitting

Securities and Exchange Commission § 240.3a68–4

the requesting person (and any other person or persons that subsequently lists, trades, or clears that mixed swap) to comply, as to parallel provisions only, with specified parallel provisions of either the Act (15 U.S.C. 78a *et seq.*) or the Commodity Exchange Act (7 U.S.C. 1 *et seq.*), and the rules and regulations thereunder (collectively, *specified parallel provisions*), instead of being required to comply with parallel provisions of both the Act and the Commodity Exchange Act. For purposes of this paragraph (c), *parallel provisions* means comparable provisions of the Act and the Commodity Exchange Act that were added or amended by the Wall Street Transparency and Accountability Act of 2010 with respect to security-based swaps and swaps, and the rules and regulations thereunder.

(2) *Request process.* A person submitting a request pursuant to paragraph (c)(1) of this section must provide the Commission and the Commodity Futures Trading Commission with the following:

(i) All material information regarding the terms of the specified, or specified class of, mixed swap;

(ii) The economic characteristics and purpose of the specified, or specified class of, mixed swap;

(iii) The specified parallel provisions, and the reasons the person believes such specified parallel provisions would be appropriate for the mixed swap (or class thereof); and

(iv) An analysis of:

(A) The nature and purposes of the parallel provisions that are the subject of the request;

(B) The comparability of such parallel provisions;

(C) The extent of any conflicts or differences between such parallel provisions; and

(D) Such other information as may be requested by the Commission or the Commodity Futures Trading Commission.

(3) *Request withdrawal.* A person may withdraw a request made pursuant to paragraph (c)(1) of this section at any time prior to the issuance of a joint order under paragraph (c)(4) of this section by the Commission and the Commodity Futures Trading Commission in response to the request.

(4) *Issuance of orders.* In response to a request under paragraph (c)(1) of this section, the Commission and the Commodity Futures Trading Commission, as necessary to carry out the purposes of the Wall Street Transparency and Accountability Act of 2010, may issue a joint order, after notice and opportunity for comment, permitting the requesting person (and any other person or persons that subsequently lists, trades, or clears that mixed swap) to comply, as to parallel provisions only, with the specified parallel provisions (or another subset of the parallel provisions that are the subject of the request, as the Commissions determine is appropriate), instead of being required to comply with parallel provisions of both the Act (15 U.S.C. 78a *et seq.*) and the Commodity Exchange Act (7 U.S.C. 1 *et seq.*). In determining the contents of such joint order, the Commission and the Commodity Futures Trading Commission may consider, among other things:

(i) The nature and purposes of the parallel provisions that are the subject of the request;

(ii) The comparability of such parallel provisions; and

(iii) The extent of any conflicts or differences between such parallel provisions.

(5) *Timeframe.* (i) If the Commission and the Commodity Futures Trading Commission determine to issue a joint order as described in paragraph (c)(4) of this section, such joint order shall be issued within 120 days after receipt of a complete request for a joint order under paragraph (c)(1) of this section, which time period shall be stayed during the pendency of the public comment period provided for in paragraph (c)(4) of this section and shall recommence with the business day after the public comment period ends.

(ii) Nothing in this section shall require the Commission and the Commodity Futures Trading Commission to issue any joint order.

(iii) If the Commission and the Commodity Futures Trading Commission do not issue a joint order within the time period described in paragraph (c)(5)(i) of this section, each of the

§ 240.3a68–5

Commission and the Commodity Futures Trading Commission shall publicly provide the reasons for not issuing such a joint order within that timeframe.

[77 FR 48356, Aug. 13, 2012]

§ 240.3a68–5 Regulation of certain futures contracts on foreign sovereign debt.

The term *security-based swap* as used in section 3(a)(68) of the Act (15 U.S.C. 78c(a)(68)) does not include an agreement, contract, or transaction that is based on or references a qualifying foreign futures contract (as defined in § 240.3a12–8 on the debt securities of any one or more of the foreign governments enumerated in § 240.3a12–8, provided that such agreement, contract, or transaction satisfies the following conditions:

(a) The futures contract that the agreement, contract, or transaction references or upon which the agreement, contract, or transaction is based is a qualifying foreign futures contract that satisfies the conditions of § 240.3a12–8 applicable to qualifying foreign futures contracts;

(b) The agreement, contract, or transaction is traded on or through a board of trade (as defined in 7 U.S.C. 2);

(c) The debt securities upon which the qualifying foreign futures contract is based or referenced and any security used to determine the cash settlement amount pursuant to paragraph (d) of this section were not registered under the Securities Act of 1933 (15 U.S.C. 77 *et seq.*) or the subject of any American depositary receipt registered under the Securities Act of 1933;

(d) The agreement, contract, or transaction may only be cash settled; and

(e) The agreement, contract or transaction is not entered into by the issuer of the debt securities upon which the qualifying foreign futures contract is based or referenced (including any security used to determine the cash payment due on settlement of such agreement, contract or transaction), an affiliate (as defined in the Securities Act of 1933 (15 U.S.C. 77 *et seq.*) and the rules and regulations thereunder) of the issuer, or an underwriter of such issuer's debt securities.

[77 FR 48356, Aug. 13, 2012]

§ 240.3a69–1 Safe Harbor Definition of "security-based swap" and "swap" as used in sections 3(a)(68) and 3(a)(69) of the Act—insurance.

(a) This paragraph is a non-exclusive safe harbor. The terms *security-based swap* as used in section 3(a)(68) of the Act (15 U.S.C. 78c(a)(68)) and *swap* as used in section 3(a)(69) of the Act (15 U.S.C. 78c(a)(69)) do not include an agreement, contract, or transaction that:

(1) By its terms or by law, as a condition of performance on the agreement, contract, or transaction:

(i) Requires the beneficiary of the agreement, contract, or transaction to have an insurable interest that is the subject of the agreement, contract, or transaction and thereby carry the risk of loss with respect to that interest continuously throughout the duration of the agreement, contract, or transaction;

(ii) Requires that loss to occur and to be proved, and that any payment or indemnification therefor be limited to the value of the insurable interest;

(iii) Is not traded, separately from the insured interest, on an organized market or over the counter; and

(iv) With respect to financial guaranty insurance only, in the event of payment default or insolvency of the obligor, any acceleration of payments under the policy is at the sole discretion of the insurer; and

(2) Is provided:

(i)(A) By a person that is subject to supervision by the insurance commissioner (or similar official or agency) of any State, as defined in section 3(a)(16) of the Act (15 U.S.C. 78c(a)(16)), or by the United States or an agency or instrumentality thereof; and

(B) Such agreement, contract, or transaction is regulated as insurance under applicable State law or the laws of the United States;

(ii)(A) Directly or indirectly by the United States, any State or any of their respective agencies or instrumentalities; or

(B) Pursuant to a statutorily authorized program thereof; or

Securities and Exchange Commission § 240.3a69–2

(iii) In the case of reinsurance only by a person to another person that satisfies the conditions set forth in paragraph (a)(2) of this section, provided that:

(A) Such person is not prohibited by applicable State law or the laws of the United States from offering such agreement, contract, or transaction to such person that satisfies the conditions set forth in paragraph (a)(2) of this section;

(B) The agreement, contract, or transaction to be reinsured satisfies the conditions set forth in paragraph (a)(1) or (3) of this section; and

(C) Except as otherwise permitted under applicable State law, the total amount reimbursable by all reinsurers for such agreement, contract, or transaction may not exceed the claims or losses paid by the person writing the risk being ceded or transferred by such person; or

(iv) In the case of non-admitted insurance by a person who:

(A) Is located outside of the United States and listed on the Quarterly Listing of Alien Insurers as maintained by the International Insurers Department of the National Association of Insurance Commissioners; or

(B) Meets the eligibility criteria for non-admitted insurers under applicable State law; or

(3) Is provided in accordance with the conditions set forth in paragraph (a)(2) of this section and is one of the following types of products:

(i) Surety bond;
(ii) Fidelity bond;
(iii) Life insurance;
(iv) Health insurance;
(v) Long term care insurance;
(vi) Title insurance;
(vii) Property and casualty insurance;
(viii) Annuity;
(ix) Disability insurance;
(x) Insurance against default on individual residential mortgages; and
(xi) Reinsurance of any of the foregoing products identified in paragraphs (i) through (x) of this section.

(b) The terms security-based swap as used in section 3(a)(68) of the Act (15 U.S.C. 78c(a)(68)) and swap as used in section 3(a)(69) of the Act (15 U.S.C. 78c(a)(69)) do not include an agreement, contract, or transaction that was entered into on or before the effective date of this section and that, at such time that it was entered into, was provided in accordance with the conditions set forth in paragraph (a)(2) of this section.

[77 FR 48356, Aug. 13, 2012]

§ 240.3a69–2 Definition of "swap" as used in section 3(a)(69) of the Act—additional products.

(a) *In general.* The term *swap* has the meaning set forth in section 3(a)(69) of the Act (15 U.S.C. 78c(a)(69)).

(b) *Inclusion of particular products.* (1) The term *swap* includes, without limiting the meaning set forth in section 3(a)(69) of the Act (15 U.S.C. 78c(a)(69)), the following agreements, contracts, and transactions:

(i) A cross-currency swap;
(ii) A currency option, foreign currency option, foreign exchange option and foreign exchange rate option;
(iii) A foreign exchange forward;
(iv) A foreign exchange swap;
(v) A forward rate agreement; and
(vi) A non-deliverable forward involving foreign exchange.

(2) The term *swap* does not include an agreement, contract, or transaction described in paragraph (b)(1) of this section that is otherwise excluded by section 1a(47)(B) of the Commodity Exchange Act (7 U.S.C. 1a(47)(B)).

(c) *Foreign exchange forwards and foreign exchange swaps.* Notwithstanding paragraph (b)(2) of this section:

(1) A foreign exchange forward or a foreign exchange swap shall not be considered a swap if the Secretary of the Treasury makes a determination described in section 1a(47)(E)(i) of the Commodity Exchange Act (7 U.S.C. 1a(47)(E)(i)).

(2) Notwithstanding paragraph (c)(1) of this section:

(i) The reporting requirements set forth in section 4r of the Commodity Exchange Act (7 U.S.C. 6r) and regulations promulgated thereunder shall apply to a foreign exchange forward or foreign exchange swap; and

(ii) The business conduct standards set forth in section 4s(h) of the Commodity Exchange Act (7 U.S.C. 6s) and regulations promulgated thereunder shall apply to a swap dealer or major swap participant that is a party to a

§ 240.3a69–3

foreign exchange forward or foreign exchange swap.

(3) For purposes of section 1a(47)(E) of the Commodity Exchange Act (7 U.S.C. 1a(47)(E)) and this section, the term *foreign exchange forward* has the meaning set forth in section 1a(24) of the Commodity Exchange Act (7 U.S.C. 1a(24)).

(4) For purposes of section 1a(47)(E) of the Commodity Exchange Act (7 U.S.C. 1a(47)(E)) and this section, the term *foreign exchange swap* has the meaning set forth in section 1a(25) of the Commodity Exchange Act (7 U.S.C. 1a(25)).

(5) For purposes of sections 1a(24) and 1a(25) of the Commodity Exchange Act (7 U.S.C. 1a(24) and (25)) and this section, the following transactions are not foreign exchange forwards or foreign exchange swaps:

(i) A currency swap or a cross-currency swap;

(ii) A currency option, foreign currency option, foreign exchange option, or foreign exchange rate option; and

(iii) A non-deliverable forward involving foreign exchange.

[77 FR 48356, Aug. 13, 2012]

§ 240.3a69–3 Books and records requirements for security-based swap agreements.

(a) A person registered as a swap data repository under section 21 of the Commodity Exchange Act (7 U.S.C. 24a) and the rules and regulations thereunder:

(1) Shall not be required to keep and maintain additional books and records regarding security-based swap agreements other than the books and records regarding swaps required to be kept and maintained pursuant to section 21 of the Commodity Exchange Act (7 U.S.C. 24a) and the rules and regulations thereunder; and

(2) Shall not be required to collect and maintain additional data regarding security-based swap agreements other than the data regarding swaps required to be collected and maintained by such persons pursuant to section 21 of the Commodity Exchange Act (7 U.S.C. 24a) and the rules and regulations thereunder.

(b) A person shall not be required to keep and maintain additional books and records, including daily trading records, regarding security-based swap agreements other than the books and records regarding swaps required to be kept and maintained by such persons pursuant to section 4s of the Commodity Exchange Act (7 U.S.C. 6s) and the rules and regulations thereunder if such person is registered as:

(1) A swap dealer under section 4s(a)(1) of the Commodity Exchange Act (7 U.S.C. 6s(a)(1)) and the rules and regulations thereunder;

(2) A major swap participant under section 4s(a)(2) of the Commodity Exchange Act (7 U.S.C. 6s(a)(2)) and the rules and regulations thereunder;

(3) A security-based swap dealer under section 15F(a)(1) of the Act (15 U.S.C. 78o–10(a)(1)) and the rules and regulations thereunder; or

(4) A major security-based swap participant under section 15F(a)(2) of the Act (15 U.S.C. 78o–10(a)(2)) and the rules and regulations thereunder.

(c) The term *security-based swap agreement* has the meaning set forth in section 3(a)(78) of the Act (15 U.S.C. 78c(a)(78)).

[77 FR 48356, Aug. 13, 2012]

§ 240.3a71–1 Definition of "security-based swap dealer."

(a) *General.* The term *security-based swap dealer* in general means any person who:

(1) Holds itself out as a dealer in security-based swaps;

(2) Makes a market in security-based swaps;

(3) Regularly enters into security-based swaps with counterparties as an ordinary course of business for its own account; or

(4) Engages in any activity causing it to be commonly known in the trade as a dealer or market maker in security-based swaps.

(b) *Exception.* The term *security-based swap dealer* does not include a person that enters into security-based swaps for such person's own account, either individually or in a fiduciary capacity, but not as a part of regular business.

(c) *Scope of designation.* A person that is a security-based swap dealer in general shall be deemed to be a security-based swap dealer with respect to each security-based swap it enters into, regardless of the type, class, or category

Securities and Exchange Commission

§ 240.3a71-2

of the security-based swap or the person's activities in connection with the security-based swap, unless the Commission limits the person's designation as a security-based swap dealer to specified types, classes, or categories of security-based swaps or specified activities of the person in connection with security-based swaps.

(d) *Inter-affiliate activities*—(1) *General.* In determining whether a person is a security-based swap dealer, that person's security-based swaps with majority-owned affiliates shall not be considered.

(2) *Meaning of majority-owned.* For these purposes the counterparties to a security-based swap are majority-owned affiliates if one counterparty directly or indirectly owns a majority interest in the other, or if a third party directly or indirectly owns a majority interest in both counterparties to the security-based swap, where "majority interest" is the right to vote or direct the vote of a majority of a class of voting securities of an entity, the power to sell or direct the sale of a majority of a class of voting securities of an entity, or the right to receive upon dissolution or the contribution of a majority of the capital of a partnership.

[78 FR 30751, May 23, 2013]

§ 240.3a71-2 *De minimis* exception.

(a) *Requirements.* For purposes of section 3(a)(71) of the Act (15 U.S.C. 78c(a)(71)) and § 240.3a71-1, a person that is not currently registered as a security-based swap dealer shall be deemed not to be a security-based swap dealer, and, therefore, shall not be subject to section 15F of the Act (15 U.S.C. 78o-10) and the rules, regulations and interpretations issued thereunder, as a result of security-based swap dealing activity that meets the following conditions:

(1) *Notional thresholds.* The security-based swap positions connected with the dealing activity in which the person—or any other entity controlling, controlled by or under common control with the person—engages over the course of the immediately preceding 12 months (or following the effective date of final rules implementing section 3(a)(68) of the Act (15 U.S.C. 78c(a)(68)) if that period is less than 12 months) have:

(i) An aggregate gross notional amount of no more than $3 billion, subject to a phase-in level of an aggregate gross notional amount of no more than $8 billion applied in accordance with paragraph (a)(2)(i) of this section, with regard to credit default swaps that constitute security-based swaps;

(ii) An aggregate gross notional amount of no more than $150 million, subject to a phase-in level of an aggregate gross notional amount of no more than $400 million applied in accordance with paragraph (a)(2)(i) of this section, with regard to security-based swaps not described in paragraph (a)(1)(i) of this section; and

(iii) An aggregate gross notional amount of no more than $25 million with regard to all security-based swaps in which the counterparty is a special entity (as that term is defined in section 15F(h)(2)(C) of the Act (15 U.S.C. 78o-10(h)(2)(C)).

(2) *Phase-in procedure*—(i) *Phase-in period.* For purposes of paragraphs (a)(1)(i) and (ii) of this section, a person that engages in security-based swap dealing activity that does not exceed either of the phase-in levels set forth in paragraphs (a)(1)(i) and (ii) of this section, as applicable, shall be deemed not to be a security-based swap dealer, and, therefore, shall not be subject to Section 15F of the Act (15 U.S.C. 78o-10) and the rules, regulations and interpretations issued thereunder, as a result of its security-based swap dealing activity, until the "phase-in termination date" established as provided in paragraph (a)(2)(ii) of this section; provided, however, that this phase-in period shall not be available to the extent that a person engages in security-based swap dealing activity with counterparties that are natural persons, other than natural persons who qualify as eligible contract participants by virtue of section 1a(18)(A)(xi)(II) of the Commodity Exchange Act, (7 U.S.C. 1a(18)(A)(xi)(II)). The Commission shall announce the phase-in termination date on the Commission Web site and publish such date in the FEDERAL REGISTER.

(ii) *Establishment of phase-in termination date.* (A) Nine months after the publication of the staff report described in Appendix A of this section,

§ 240.3a71-2

and after giving due consideration to that report and any associated public comment, the Commission may either:

(1) Terminate the phase-in period set forth in paragraph (a)(2)(i) of this section, in which case the phase-in termination date shall be established by the Commission by order published in the FEDERAL REGISTER; or

(2) Determine that it is necessary or appropriate in the public interest to propose through rulemaking an alternative to the $3 billion and $150 million amounts set forth in paragraphs (a)(1)(i) and (ii) of this section, as applicable, that would constitute a *de minimis* quantity of security-based swap dealing in connection with transactions with or on behalf of customers within the meaning of section 3(a)(71)(D) of the Act, (15 U.S.C. 78c(a)(71)(D)), in which case the Commission shall by order published in the FEDERAL REGISTER provide notice of such determination to propose through rulemaking an alternative, which order shall also establish the phase-in termination date.

(B) If the phase-in termination date has not been previously established pursuant to paragraph (a)(2)(ii)(A) of this section, then in any event the phase-in termination date shall occur five years after the data collection initiation date defined in paragraph (a)(2)(iii) of this section.

(iii) *Data collection initiation date.* The term "*data collection initiation date*" shall mean the date that is the later of: the last compliance date for the registration and regulatory requirements for security-based swap dealers and major security-based swap participants under Section 15F of the Act (15 U.S.C. 78o-10); or the first date on which compliance with the trade-by-trade reporting rules for credit-related and equity-related security-based swaps to a registered security-based swap data repository is required. The Commission shall announce the data collection initiation date on the Commission Web site and publish such date in the FEDERAL REGISTER.

(3) *Use of effective notional amounts.* For purposes of paragraph (a)(1) of this section, if the stated notional amount of a security-based swap is leveraged or enhanced by the structure of the security-based swap, the calculation shall be based on the effective notional amount of the security-based swap rather than on the stated notional amount.

(b) *Registration period for persons that no longer can take advantage of the exception.* A person that has not registered as a security-based swap dealer by virtue of satisfying the requirements of paragraph (a) of this section, but that no longer can take advantage of the *de minimis* exception provided for in paragraph (a) of this section, will be deemed not to be a security-based swap dealer under section 3(a)(71) of the Act (15 U.S.C. 78c(a)(71)) and subject to the requirements of section 15F of the Act (15 U.S.C. 78o-10) and the rules, regulations and interpretations issued thereunder until the earlier of the date on which it submits a complete application for registration pursuant to section 15F(b) (15 U.S.C. 78o-10(b)) or two months after the end of the month in which that person becomes no longer able to take advantage of the exception.

(c) *Applicability to registered security-based swap dealers.* A person who currently is registered as a security-based swap dealer may apply to withdraw that registration, while continuing to engage in security-based swap dealing activity in reliance on this section, so long as that person has been registered as a security-based swap dealer for at least 12 months and satisfies the conditions of paragraph (a) of this section.

(d) *Future adjustments to scope of the de minimis exception.* The Commission may by rule or regulation change the requirements of the *de minimis* exception described in paragraphs (a) through (c) of this section.

(e) *Voluntary registration.* Notwithstanding paragraph (a) of this section, a person that chooses to register with the Commission as a security-based swap dealer shall be deemed to be a security-based swap dealer, and, therefore, shall be subject to Section 15F of the Act (15 U.S.C 78o-10) and the rules, regulations and interpretations issued thereunder.

[78 FR 30751, May 23, 2013]

Securities and Exchange Commission

§ 240.3a71-2A

§ 240.3a71-2A Report regarding the "security-based swap dealer" and "major security-based swap participant" definitions (Appendix A to 17 CFR 240.3a71-2).

Appendix A to § 240.3a71-2 sets forth guidelines applicable to a report that the Commission has directed its staff to make in connection with the rules and interpretations further defining the Act's definitions of the terms "security-based swap dealer" (including the *de minimis* exception to that definition) and "major security-based swap participant." The Commission intends to consider this report in reviewing the effect and application of these rules based on the evolution of the security-based swap market following the implementation of the registration and regulatory requirements of Section 15F of the Act (15 U.S.C. 78o–10). The report may also be informative as to potential changes to the rules further defining those terms. In producing this report, the staff shall consider security-based swap data collected by the Commission pursuant to other Title VII rules, as well as any other applicable information as the staff may determine to be appropriate for its analysis.

(a) *Report topics.* As appropriate, based on the availability of data and information, the report should address the following topics:

(1) *De minimis exception.* In connection with the *de minimis* exception to the definition of "security-based swap dealer," the report generally should assess whether any of the *de minimis* thresholds set forth in paragraph (a)(1) of § 240.3a71-2 should be increased or decreased;

(2) *General security-based swap dealer analysis.* In connection with the definition of "security-based swap dealer," the report generally should consider the factors that are useful for identifying security-based swap dealing activity, including the application of the dealer-trader distinction for that purpose, and the potential use of more objective tests or safe harbors as part of the analysis;

(3) *General major security-based swap participant analysis.* In connection with the definition of "major security-based swap participant," the report generally should consider the tests used to identify the presence of a "substantial position" in a major category of security-based swaps, and the tests used to identify persons whose security-based swap positions create "substantial counterparty exposure," including the potential use of alternative tests or thresholds;

(4) *Commercial risk hedging exclusion.* In connection with the definition of "major security-based swap participant," the report generally should consider the definition of "hedging or mitigating commercial risk," including whether that latter definition inappropriately permits certain positions to be excluded from the "substantial position" analysis, and whether the continued availability of the exclusion for such hedging positions should be conditioned on a person assessing and documenting the hedging effectiveness of those positions;

(5) *Highly leveraged financial entities.* In connection with the definition of "major security-based swap participant," the report generally should consider the definition of "highly leveraged," including whether alternative approaches should be used to identify highly leveraged financial entities;

(6) *Inter-affiliate exclusions.* In connection with the definitions of "security-based swap dealer" and "major security-based swap participant," the report generally should consider the impact of rule provisions excluding inter-affiliate transactions from the relevant analyses, and should assess potential alternative approaches for such exclusions; and

(7) *Other topics.* Any other analysis of security-based swap data and information the Commission or the staff deem relevant to this rule.

(b) *Timing of report.* The report shall be completed no later than three years following the data collection initiation date, established pursuant to § 240.3a71-2(a)(2)(iii).

(c) *Public comment on the report.* Following completion of the report, the report shall be published in the FEDERAL REGISTER for public comment.

§ 240.3a71-3 Cross-border security-based swap dealing activity.

(a) *Definitions.* As used in this section, the following terms shall have the meanings indicated:

(1) *Conduit affiliate*—(i) *Definition.* Conduit affiliate means a person, other than a U.S. person, that:

(A) Is directly or indirectly majority-owned by one or more U.S. persons; and

(B) In the regular course of business enters into security-based swaps with one or more other non-U.S. persons, or with foreign branches of U.S. banks that are registered as security-based swap dealers, for the purpose of hedging or mitigating risks faced by, or otherwise taking positions on behalf of, one or more U.S. persons (other than U.S. persons that are registered as security-based swap dealers or major security-based swap participants) who are controlling, controlled by, or under common control with the person, and enters into offsetting security-based swaps or other arrangements with such U.S. persons to transfer risks and benefits of those security-based swaps.

(ii) *Majority-ownership standard.* The majority-ownership standard in paragraph (a)(1)(i)(A) of this section is satisfied if one or more persons described in § 240.3a71-3(a)(4)(i)(B) directly or indirectly own a majority interest in the non-U.S. person, where "majority interest" is the right to vote or direct the vote of a majority of a class of voting securities of an entity, the power to sell or direct the sale of a majority of a class of voting securities of an entity, or the right to receive upon dissolution, or the contribution of, a majority of the capital of a partnership.

(2) *Foreign branch* means any branch of a U.S. bank if:

(i) The branch is located outside the United States;

(ii) The branch operates for valid business reasons; and

(iii) The branch is engaged in the business of banking and is subject to substantive banking regulation in the jurisdiction where located.

(3) *Transaction conducted through a foreign branch*—(i) *Definition.* Transaction conducted through a foreign branch means a security-based swap transaction that is arranged, negotiated, and executed by a U.S. person through a foreign branch of such U.S. person if:

(A) The foreign branch is the counterparty to such security-based swap transaction; and

(B) The security-based swap transaction is arranged, negotiated, and executed on behalf of the foreign branch solely by persons located outside the United States.

(ii) *Representations.* A person shall not be required to consider its counterparty's activity in connection with paragraph (a)(3)(i)(B) of this section in determining whether a security-based swap transaction is a transaction conducted through a foreign branch if such person receives a representation from its counterparty that the security-based swap transaction is arranged, negotiated, and executed on behalf of the foreign branch solely by persons located outside the United States, unless such person knows or has reason to know that the representation is not accurate; for the purposes of this final rule a person would have reason to know the representation is not accurate if a reasonable person should know, under all of the facts of which the person is aware, that it is not accurate.

(4) *U.S. person.* (i) Except as provided in paragraph (a)(4)(iii) of this section, *U.S. person* means any person that is:

(A) A natural person resident in the United States;

(B) A partnership, corporation, trust, investment vehicle, or other legal person organized, incorporated, or established under the laws of the United States or having its principal place of business in the United States;

(C) An account (whether discretionary or non-discretionary) of a U.S. person; or

(D) An estate of a decedent who was a resident of the United States at the time of death.

(ii) For purposes of this section, *principal place of business* means the location from which the officers, partners, or managers of the legal person primarily direct, control, and coordinate the activities of the legal person. With respect to an externally managed investment vehicle, this location is the office from which the manager of the vehicle primarily directs, controls, and

Securities and Exchange Commission § 240.3a71–3

coordinates the investment activities of the vehicle.

(iii) The term *U.S. person* does not include the International Monetary Fund, the International Bank for Reconstruction and Development, the Inter-American Development Bank, the Asian Development Bank, the African Development Bank, the United Nations, and their agencies and pension plans, and any other similar international organizations, their agencies and pension plans.

(iv) A person shall not be required to consider its counterparty to a security-based swap to be a U.S. person if such person receives a representation from the counterparty that the counterparty does not satisfy the criteria set forth in paragraph (a)(4)(i) of this section, unless such person knows or has reason to know that the representation is not accurate; for the purposes of this final rule a person would have reason to know the representation is not accurate if a reasonable person should know, under all of the facts of which the person is aware, that it is not accurate.

(5) *United States* means the United States of America, its territories and possessions, any State of the United States, and the District of Columbia.

(6) *U.S. security-based swap dealer* means a security-based swap dealer, as defined in section 3(a)(71) of the Act (15 U.S.C. 78c(a)(71)), and the rules and regulations thereunder, that is a U.S. person.

(7) *Foreign security-based swap dealer* means a security-based swap dealer, as defined in section 3(a)(71) of the Act (15 U.S.C. 78c(a)(71)), and the rules and regulations thereunder, that is not a U.S. person.

(8) *U.S. business* means:

(i) With respect to a foreign security-based swap dealer:

(A) Any security-based swap transaction entered into, or offered to be entered into, by or on behalf of such foreign security-based swap dealer, with a U.S. person (other than a transaction conducted through a foreign branch of that person); or

(B) Any security-based swap transaction arranged, negotiated, or executed by personnel of the foreign security-based swap dealer located in a U.S. branch or office, or by personnel of an agent of the foreign security-based swap dealer located in a U.S. branch or office; and

(ii) With respect to a U.S. security-based swap dealer, any transaction entered into or offered to be entered into by or on behalf of such U.S. security-based swap dealer, other than a transaction conducted through a foreign branch with a non-U.S. person or with a U.S.-person counterparty that constitutes a transaction conducted through a foreign branch of the counterparty.

(9) *Foreign business* means security-based swap transactions entered into, or offered to be entered into, by or on behalf of a security-based swap dealer, other than the U.S. business of such person.

(10) An entity is a *majority-owned affiliate* of another entity if the entity directly or indirectly owns a majority interest in the other, or if a third party directly or indirectly owns a majority interest in both entities, where "majority interest" is the right to vote or direct the vote of a majority of a class of voting securities of an entity, the power to sell or direct the sale of a majority of a class of voting securities of an entity, or the right to receive upon dissolution, or the contribution of, a majority of the capital of a partnership.

(11) *Foreign associated person* means a natural person domiciled outside the United States who—with respect to a non-U.S. person relying on the exception set forth in paragraph (d) of this section—is a partner, officer, director, or branch manager of such non-U.S. person (or any person occupying a similar status or performing similar functions), any person directly or indirectly controlling, controlled by, or under common control with such non-U.S. person, or any employee of such non-U.S. person.

(12) *Listed jurisdiction* means any jurisdiction that the Commission by order has designated as a listed jurisdiction for purposes of the exception specified in paragraph (d) of this section.

(13) *Covered inter-dealer security-based swap* means any security-based swap between:

§ 240.3a71-3

(i) A non-U.S. person relying on the exception in paragraph (d) of this section; and

(ii) A non-U.S. person that is, or is an affiliate of, a registered security-based swap dealer or registered broker that has filed with the Commission a notice pursuant to paragraph (d)(1)(vi) of this section; *provided, however,* that a covered inter-dealer security-based swap does not include a security-based swap with a non-U.S. person that the non-U.S. person relying on the exception in paragraph (d) of this section reasonably determines at the time of execution of the security-based swap is neither a registered security-based swap dealer or registered broker that has filed with the Commission a notice pursuant to paragraph (d)(1)(vi) of this section nor an affiliate of such a registered security-based swap dealer or registered broker.

(b) *Application of de minimis exception to cross-border dealing activity.* For purposes of calculating the amount of security-based swap positions connected with dealing activity under § 240.3a71-2(a)(1), except as provided in § 240.3a71-5, a person shall include the following security-based swap transactions:

(1)(i) If such person is a U.S. person, all security-based swap transactions connected with the dealing activity in which such person engages, including transactions conducted through a foreign branch;

(ii) If such person is a conduit affiliate, all security-based swap transactions connected with the dealing activity in which such person engages; and

(iii) If such person is a non-U.S. person other than a conduit affiliate, all of the following types of transactions:

(A) Security-based swap transactions connected with the dealing activity in which such person engages that are entered into with a U.S. person; provided, however, that this paragraph (b)(1)(iii)(A) shall not apply to:

(*1*) Transactions with a U.S. person counterparty that constitute transactions conducted through a foreign branch of the counterparty, when the counterparty is a registered security-based swap dealer; and

(*2*) Transactions with a U.S. person counterparty that constitute transactions conducted through a foreign branch of the counterparty, when the transaction is entered into prior to 60 days following the earliest date on which the registration of security-based swap dealers is first required pursuant to the applicable final rules and regulations; and

(B) Security-based swap transactions connected with the dealing activity in which such person engages for which the counterparty to the security-based swap has rights of recourse against a U.S. person that is controlling, controlled by, or under common control with the non-U.S. person; for these purposes a counterparty has rights of recourse against the U.S. person if the counterparty has a conditional or unconditional legally enforceable right, in whole or in part, to receive payments from, or otherwise collect from, the U.S. person in connection with the security-based swap; and

(C) Except as provided in paragraph (d) of this section, or unless such person is a person described in paragraph (a)(4)(iii) of this section, security-based swap transactions connected with such person's security-based swap dealing activity that are arranged, negotiated, or executed by personnel of such non-U.S. person located in a U.S. branch or office, or by personnel of an agent of such non-U.S. person located in a U.S. branch or office; and

(2) If such person engages in transactions described in paragraph (b)(1) of this section, except as provided in § 240.3a71-4, all of the following types of security-based swap transactions:

(i) Security-based swap transactions connected with the dealing activity in which any U.S. person controlling, controlled by, or under common control with such person engages, including transactions conducted through a foreign branch;

(ii) Security-based swap transactions connected with the dealing activity in which any conduit affiliate controlling, controlled by, or under common control with such person engages; and

(iii) Security-based swap transactions connected with the dealing activity of any non-U.S. person, other than a conduit affiliate, that is controlling, controlled by, or under common control with such person, that are

Securities and Exchange Commission § 240.3a71–3

described in paragraph (b)(1)(iii) of this section.

(c) *Application of customer protection requirements.* A registered security-based swap dealer, with respect to its foreign business, shall not be subject to the requirements relating to business conduct standards described in section 15F(h) of the Act (15 U.S.C. 78o–10(h)), and the rules and regulations thereunder, other than the rules and regulations prescribed by the Commission pursuant to section 15F(h)(1)(B) of the Act (15 U.S.C. 78o–10(h)(1)(B)).

(d) *Exception from counting certain transactions.* The counting requirement described by paragraph (b)(1)(iii)(C) of this section will not apply to the security-based swap dealing transactions of a non-U.S. person if the conditions of paragraph (d)(1) of this section have been satisfied.

(1) *Conditions*—(i) *Entity conducting U.S. activity.* All activity that otherwise would cause a security-based swap transaction to be described by paragraph (b)(1)(iii)(C) of this section—namely, all arranging, negotiating or executing activity that is conducted by personnel of the entity (or its agent) located in a branch or office in the United States—is conducted by such U.S. personnel in their capacity as persons associated with an entity that:

(A) Is registered with the Commission as:

(*1*) A broker registered under section 15 of the Act (15 U.S.C. 78o) that is subject to and complies with § 240.15c3–1(a)(7);

(*2*) A broker registered under section 15 of the Act (15 U.S.C. 78o), other than a broker that is subject to § 240.15c3–1(a)(7), that complies with § 240.15c3–1(a)(10), as if that entity were registered with the Commission as a security-based swap dealer, if it is not so registered; or

(*3*) A security-based swap dealer; and

(B) Is a majority-owned affiliate of the non-U.S. person relying on this exception.

(ii) *Compliance with specified security-based swap dealer requirements*—(A) *Compliance required.* In connection with such transactions, the registered entity described in paragraph (d)(1)(i) of this section complies with the requirements described in paragraph (d)(1)(ii)(B) of this section

(*1*) As if the counterparties to the non-U.S. person relying on this exception also were counterparties to that entity; and

(*2*) As if that entity were registered with the Commission as a security-based swap dealer, if it is not so registered.

(B) *Applicable requirements.* The compliance obligation described in paragraph (d)(1)(ii)(A) of this section applies to the following provisions of the Act and the rules and regulations thereunder:

(*1*) Section 15F(h)(3)(B)(i), (ii) and § 240.15Fh–3(b), including in connection with material incentives and conflicts of interest associated with the non-U.S. person relying on the exception;

(*2*) Section 240.15Fh–3(f)(1); *provided, however,* that if the registered entity described in paragraph (d)(1)(i) of this section reasonably determines that the counterparty to whom it recommends a security-based swap or trading strategy involving a security-based swap is an "institutional counterparty" as defined in § 240.15Fh–3(f)(4), the registered entity instead may fulfill its obligations under § 240.15Fh–3(f)(1)(ii) if it discloses to the counterparty that it is not undertaking to assess the suitability of the security-based swap or trading strategy involving a security-based swap for the counterparty;

(*3*) Section 15F(h)(3)(C) of the Act and § 240.15Fh–3(g); and

(*4*) Sections 240.15Fi–1 and 240.15Fi–2.

(iii) *Commission access to books, records and testimony.* (A) The non-U.S. person relying on this exception promptly provides representatives of the Commission (upon request of the Commission or its representatives or pursuant to a supervisory or enforcement memorandum of understanding or other arrangement or agreement reached between any foreign securities authority, including any foreign government, as specified in section 3(a)(50) of the Act, and the Commission or the U.S. Government) with any information or documents within the non-U.S. person's possession, custody, or control, promptly makes its foreign associated persons available for testimony, and provides any assistance in taking the

§ 240.3a71–3

evidence of other persons, wherever located, that the Commission or its representatives requests and that relates to transactions subject to this exception; *provided, however,* that if, after exercising its best efforts, the non-U.S. person is prohibited by applicable foreign law or regulations from providing such information, documents, testimony, or assistance, the non-U.S. person may continue to rely on this exception until the Commission issues an order modifying or withdrawing an associated "listed jurisdiction" determination pursuant to paragraph (d)(2)(iii) of this section.

(B) The registered entity described in paragraph (d)(1)(i) of this section:

(*1*) Creates and maintains books and records relating to the transactions subject to this exception that are required, as applicable, by §§ 240.17a–3 and 240.17a–4, or by §§ 240.18a–5 and 240.18a–6, including any books and records requirements relating to the provisions specified in paragraph (d)(1)(ii)(B) of this section;

(*2*) Obtains from the non-U.S. person relying on the exception, and maintains for not less than three years following the activity described in paragraph (d)(1)(i) of this section, the first two years in an easily accessible place, documentation regarding such non-U.S. person's compliance with the condition in paragraph (d)(1)(vii) of this section;

(*3*) Obtains from the non-U.S. person relying on the exception, and maintains for not less than three years following the activity described in paragraph (d)(1)(i) of this section, the first two years in an easily accessible place, documentation encompassing all terms governing the trading relationship between the non-U.S. person and its counterparty relating to the transactions subject to this exception, including, without limitation, terms addressing payment obligations, netting of payments, events of default or other termination events, calculation and netting of obligations upon termination, transfer of rights and obligations, allocation of any applicable regulatory reporting obligations, governing law, valuation, and dispute resolution; and

(*4*) Obtains from the non-U.S. person relying on this exception, and maintains for not less than three years following the activity described in paragraph (d)(1)(i) of this section, the first two years in an easily accessible place, written consent to service of process for any civil action brought by or proceeding before the Commission, providing that process may be served on the non-U.S. person by service on the registered entity in the manner set forth in the registered entity's current Form BD, SBSE, SBSE–A or SBSE–BD, as applicable.

(iv) *Counterparty notification* In connection with the transaction, the registered entity described in paragraph (d)(1)(i) of this section notifies the counterparties of the non-U.S. person relying on this exception that the non-U.S. person is not registered with the Commission as a security-based swap dealer, and that certain Exchange Act provisions or rules addressing the regulation of security-based swaps would not be applicable in connection with the transaction, including provisions affording clearing rights to counterparties. Such notice shall be provided contemporaneously with, and in the same manner as, the arranging, negotiating, or executing activity at issue; *provided, however,* that during a period in which a counterparty is neither a customer (as such term is defined in § 240.15c3–3) of the registered entity described in paragraph (d)(1)(i) of this section (if such registered entity is a registered broker or dealer) nor a counterparty to a security-based swap with the registered entity described in paragraph (d)(1)(i) of this section, such notice need only be provided contemporaneously with, and in the same manner as, the first such arranging, negotiating, or executing activity during such period. This disclosure will not be required if the identity of that counterparty is not known to that registered entity at a reasonably sufficient time prior to the execution of the transaction to permit such disclosure.

(v) *Subject to regulation of a listed jurisdiction.* The non-U.S. person relying on this exception is subject to the margin and capital requirements of a listed jurisdiction when engaging in the transactions subject to this exception.

Securities and Exchange Commission § 240.3a71–3

(vi) *Notice by registered entity.* Before an associated person of the registered entity described in paragraph (d)(1)(i) of this section commences the activity described in paragraph (d)(1)(i) of this section, such registered entity shall file with the Commission a notice that its associated persons may conduct such activity. Such registered entity shall file this notice by submitting it to the electronic mailbox described on the Commission's website at *www.sec.gov* at the "ANE Exception Notices" section. The Commission shall publicly post such notice on the same section of its website.

(vii) *Limitation for covered inter-dealer security-based swaps.* The aggregate gross notional amount of covered interdealer security-based swap positions connected with dealing activity subject to the exception in this paragraph (d) engaged in by persons described in paragraph (d)(6)(i) of this section over the course of the immediately preceding 12 months does not exceed $50 billion.

(2) *Order for listed jurisdiction designation.* The Commission by order, may conditionally or unconditionally determine that a foreign jurisdiction is a listed jurisdiction for purposes of this section. The Commission may make listed jurisdiction determinations in response to applications, or upon the Commission's own initiative.

(i) *Applications.* Applications for an order requesting listed jurisdiction status may be made by a party or group of parties that potentially would seek to rely on the exception provided by paragraph (d) of this section, or by any foreign financial regulatory authority or authorities supervising such a party or its security-based swap activities. Applications must be filed pursuant to the procedures set forth in § 240.0–13.

(ii) *Criteria considered.* In considering a foreign jurisdiction's potential status as a listed jurisdiction, the Commission may consider factors relevant for purposes of assessing whether such an order would be in the public interest, including:

(A) Applicable margin and capital requirements of the foreign financial regulatory system; and

(B) The effectiveness of the supervisory compliance program adminis-tered by, and the enforcement authority exercised by, the foreign financial regulatory authority in connection with such requirements, including the application of those requirements in connection with an entity's cross-border business.

(iii) *Withdrawal or modification of listed jurisdiction status.* The Commission may, on its own initiative, by order after notice and opportunity for comment, modify or withdraw a jurisdiction's status as a listed jurisdiction, if the Commission determines that continued listed jurisdiction status no longer would be in the public interest, based on:

(A) The criteria set forth in paragraph (d)(2)(ii) of this section;

(B) Any laws or regulations that have had the effect of preventing the Commission or its representatives, on request, to promptly access information or documents regarding the activities of persons relying on the exception provided by this paragraph (d), to obtain the testimony of their foreign associated persons, and to obtain the assistance of persons relying on this exception in taking the evidence of other persons, wherever located, as described in paragraph (d)(1)(iii)(A) of this section; and

(C) Any other factor the Commission determines to be relevant to whether continued status as a listed jurisdiction would be in the public interest.

(3) *Exception for person that engages in arranging, negotiating, or executing activity as agent.* The registered entity described in paragraph (d)(1)(i) of this section need not count, against the *de minimis* thresholds described in § 240.3a71–2(a)(1), the transactions described by paragraph (d) of this section.

(4) *Limited exemption from registration as a broker.* A registered security-based swap dealer and its associated persons who conduct the activities described in paragraph (d)(1)(i) of this section shall not be subject to registration as a broker pursuant to section 15(a)(1) of the Act solely because the registered entity or the associated person conducts any activity described in paragraph (d)(1)(i) of this section with or for a person that is an eligible contract participant, *provided* that:

§ 240.3a71-4

(i) The conditions of paragraph (d)(1) of this section are satisfied in connection with such activities; and

(ii) If § 240.10b–10 would apply to an activity subject to the exception in paragraph (d)(1)(i), such registered security-based swap dealer provides to the customer the disclosures required by § 240.10b–10(a)(2) (excluding § 240.10b–10(a)(2)(i) and (ii)) and § 240.10b–10(a)(8) in accordance with the time and form requirements set forth in § 240.15Fi–2(b) and (c) or, alternatively, promptly after discovery of any defect in the registered security-based swap dealer's good faith effort to comply with such requirements.

(5) *Exemption from* § 240.10b–10. A broker or dealer that is also a registered security-based swap dealer or registered broker described in paragraph (d)(1)(i) of this section shall be exempt from the requirements of § 240.10b–10 with respect to activity described in paragraph (d)(1)(i) of this section, *provided* that such broker or dealer:

(i) Complies with paragraph (d)(1)(ii)(B)(*4*) of this section in connection with such activity; and

(ii) Provides to the customer the disclosures required by § 240.10b–10(a)(2) (excluding § 240.10b–10(a)(2)(i) and (ii)) and § 240.10b–10(a)(8) in accordance with the time and form requirements set forth in § 240.15Fi–2(b) and (c) or, alternatively, promptly after discovery of any defect in the broker or dealer's good faith effort to comply with such requirements.

(6) *Limitation for covered inter-dealer security-based swaps*—(i) *Scope of limitation for covered inter-dealer security-based swaps.* The threshold described in paragraph (d)(1)(vii) of this section applies to covered inter-dealer security-based swap positions connected with dealing activity subject to the exception in this paragraph (d) engaged in by any of the following persons:

(A) The non-U.S. person relying on the exception in this paragraph (d); and

(B) Any affiliate of such person, except for an affiliate that is deemed not to be a security-based swap dealer pursuant to Rule 3a71–2(b).

(ii) *Impact of exceeding exception threshold.* If the threshold described in

17 CFR Ch. II (4–1–23 Edition)

paragraph (d)(1)(vii) of this section is exceeded, then

(A) As of the date the condition in paragraph (d)(1)(vii) of this section is no longer satisfied, the non-U.S. person that is no longer able to satisfy that condition may not rely on the exception in this paragraph (d) for future security-based swap transactions.

(B) For purposes of calculating the amount of security-based swap positions connected with dealing activity under § 240.3a71–2(a)(1), the non-U.S. person that is no longer able to satisfy the condition in paragraph (d)(1)(vii) of this section shall include all covered inter-dealer security-based swap positions connected with dealing activity subject to the exception in this paragraph (d) engaged in by persons described in paragraph (d)(6)(i) of this section over the course of the immediately preceding 12 months, such positions to be included in such calculation as of the date that the condition in paragraph (d)(1)(vii) of this section is no longer satisfied.

[79 FR 47370, Aug. 12, 2014, as amended at 81 FR 8637, Feb. 19, 2016, 81 FR 30142, May 13, 2016; 85 FR 6350, Feb. 4, 2020]

§ 240.3a71–4 Exception from aggregation for affiliated groups with registered security-based swap dealers.

Notwithstanding §§ 240.3a71–2(a)(1) and 240.3a71–3(b)(2), a person shall not include the security-based swap transactions of another person (an "affiliate") controlling, controlled by, or under common control with such person where such affiliate either is:

(a) Registered with the Commission as a security-based swap dealer; or

(b) Deemed not to be a security-based swap dealer pursuant to § 240.3a71–2(b).

[79 FR 47370, Aug. 12, 2014]

§ 240.3a71–5 Exception for cleared transactions executed on a swap execution facility.

(a) For purposes of § 240.3a71–3(b)(1), a non-U.S. person, other than a conduit affiliate, shall not include its security-based swap transactions that are entered into anonymously on an execution facility or national securities exchange and are cleared through a clearing agency; and

Securities and Exchange Commission § 240.3a71–6

(b) For purposes of §240.3a71–3(b)(2), a person shall not include security-based swap transactions of an affiliated non-U.S. person, other than a conduit affiliate, when such transactions are entered into anonymously on an execution facility or national securities exchange and are cleared through a clearing agency.

(c) The exceptions in paragraphs (a) and (b) of this section shall not apply to any security-based swap transactions of a non-U.S. person or of an affiliated non-U.S. person connected with the person's security-based swap dealing activity that are arranged, negotiated, or executed by personnel of such non-U.S. person located in a U.S. branch or office, or by personnel of an agent of such non-U.S. person located in a U.S. branch or office.

[79 FR 47370, Aug. 12, 2014, as amended at 81 FR 8637, Feb. 19, 2016]

§ 240.3a71–6 Substituted compliance for security-based swap dealers and major security-based swap participants.

(a) *Determinations*—(1) *In general.* Subject to paragraph (a)(2) of this section, the Commission may, conditionally or unconditionally, by order, make a determination with respect to a foreign financial regulatory system that compliance with specified requirements under such foreign financial regulatory system by a registered security-based swap dealer and/or by a registered major security-based swap participant (each a "security-based swap entity"), or class thereof, may satisfy the corresponding requirements identified in paragraph (d) of this section that would otherwise apply to such security-based swap entity (or class thereof).

(2) *Standard.* The Commission shall not make a substituted compliance determination under paragraph (a)(1) of this section unless the Commission:

(i) Determines that the requirements of such foreign financial regulatory system applicable to such security-based swap entity (or class thereof) or to the activities of such security-based swap entity (or class thereof) are comparable to otherwise applicable requirements, after taking into account such factors as the Commission determines are appropriate, such as the scope and objectives of the relevant foreign regulatory requirements (taking into account the applicable criteria set forth in paragraph (d) of this section), as well as the effectiveness of the supervisory compliance program administered, and the enforcement authority exercised, by a foreign financial regulatory authority or authorities in such system to support its oversight of such security-based swap entity (or class thereof) or of the activities of such security-based swap entity (or class thereof); and

(ii) Has entered into a supervisory and enforcement memorandum of understanding and/or other arrangement with the relevant foreign financial regulatory authority or authorities under such foreign financial regulatory system addressing supervisory and enforcement cooperation and other matters arising under the substituted compliance determination.

(3) *Withdrawal or modification.* The Commission may, on its own initiative, by order, modify or withdraw a substituted compliance determination under paragraph (a)(1) of this section, after appropriate notice and opportunity for comment.

(b) *Reliance by security-based swap entities.* A registered security-based swap entity may satisfy the requirements described in paragraph (d) of this section by complying with corresponding law, rules and regulations under a foreign financial regulatory system, provided:

(1) The Commission has made a substituted compliance determination pursuant to paragraph (a)(1) of this section regarding such foreign financial regulatory system providing that compliance with specified requirements under such foreign financial regulatory system by such registered security-based swap entity (or class thereof) may satisfy the corresponding requirements described in paragraph (d) of this section; and

(2) Such registered security-based swap entity satisfies any conditions set forth in a substituted compliance determination made by the Commission pursuant to paragraph (a)(1) of this section.

73

(c) *Requests for determinations.* (1) A party or group of parties that potentially would comply with specified requirements pursuant to paragraph (a)(1), or any foreign financial regulatory authority or authorities supervising such a party or its security-based swap activities, may file an application, pursuant to the procedures set forth in § 240.0–13, requesting that the Commission make a substituted compliance determination pursuant to paragraph (a)(1) of this section, with respect to one or more requirements described in paragraph (d) of this section.

(2) Such a party or group of parties may make a request under paragraph (c)(1) of this section only if:

(i) Each such party, or the party's activities, is directly supervised by the foreign financial regulatory authority or authorities with respect to the foreign regulatory requirements relating to the applicable requirements described in paragraph (d) of this section; and

(ii) Each such party provides the certification and opinion of counsel as described in § 240.15Fb2–4(c), as if the party were subject to that requirement at the time of the request.

(3) Such foreign financial authority or authorities may make a request under paragraph (c)(1) of this section only if each such authority provides adequate assurances that no law or policy of any relevant foreign jurisdiction would impede the ability of any entity that is directly supervised by the foreign financial regulatory authority and that may register with the Commission as a security-based swap dealer or major security-based swap participant to provide prompt access to the Commission to such entity's books and records or to submit to onsite inspection or examination by the Commission.

(d) *Eligible requirements.* The Commission may make a substituted compliance determination under paragraph (a)(1) of this section to permit security-based swap entities that are not U.S. persons (as defined in § 240.3a71–3(a)(4)), but not security-based swap entities that are U.S. persons, to satisfy the following requirements by complying with comparable foreign requirements:

(1) *Business conduct and supervision.* The business conduct and supervision requirements of sections 15F(h) and (j) of the Act (15 U.S.C. 78o–10(h) and (j)) and §§ 240.15Fh–3 through 15Fh–6, other than the antifraud provisions of section 15F(h)(4)(A) of the Act and § 240.15Fh–4(a), and other than the provisions of sections 15F(j)(3) and 15F(j)(4)(B) of the Act; provided, however, that prior to making such a substituted compliance determination the Commission intends to consider whether the information that is required to be provided to counterparties pursuant to the requirements of the foreign financial regulatory system, the counterparty protections under the requirements of the foreign financial regulatory system, the mandates for supervisory systems under the requirements of the foreign financial regulatory system, and the duties imposed by the foreign financial regulatory system, are comparable to those associated with the applicable provisions arising under the Act and its rules and regulations.

(2) *Chief compliance officer.* The chief compliance officer requirements of section 15F(k) of the Act (15 U.S.C. 78o–10(k)) and § 240.15Fk–1; provided, however, that prior to making such a substituted compliance determination the Commission intends to consider whether the requirements of the foreign financial regulatory system regarding chief compliance officer obligations are comparable to those required pursuant to the applicable provisions arising under the Act and its rules and regulations.

(3) *Trade acknowledgment and verification.* The trade acknowledgment and verification requirements of section 15F(i) of the Act (15 U.S.C. 78o–10(i)) and § 240.15Fi–2; provided, however, that prior to making such a substituted compliance determination the Commission intends to consider whether the information that is required to be provided pursuant to the requirements of the foreign financial regulatory system, and the manner and timeframe by which that information must be provided, are comparable to those required pursuant to the applicable provisions arising under the Act and its rules and regulations.

Securities and Exchange Commission

§ 240.3b–1

(4) *Capital*—(i) *Security-based swap dealers.* The capital requirements of section 15F(e) of the Act (15 U.S.C. 78o–10(e)) and §240.18a–1; provided, however, that prior to making such substituted compliance determination, the Commission intends to consider (in addition to any conditions imposed) whether the capital requirements of the foreign financial regulatory system are designed to help ensure the safety and soundness of registrants in a manner that is comparable to the applicable provisions arising under the Act and its rules and regulations.

(ii) *Major security-based swap participants.* The capital requirements of section 15F(e) of the Act (15 U.S.C. 78o–10(e)) and §240.18a–2; provided, however, that prior to making such substituted compliance determination, the Commission intends to consider (in addition to any conditions imposed) whether the capital requirements of the foreign financial regulatory system are comparable to the applicable provisions arising under the Act and its rules and regulations.

(5) *Margin*—(i) *Security-based swap dealers.* The margin requirements of section 15F(e) of the Act (15 U.S.C. 78o–10(e)) and §240.18a–3; provided, however, that prior to making such substituted compliance determination, the Commission intends to consider (in addition to any conditions imposed) whether the foreign financial regulatory system requires registrants to adequately cover their current and potential future exposure to over-the-counter derivatives counterparties, and ensures registrants' safety and soundness, in a manner comparable to the applicable provisions arising under the Act and its rules and regulations.

(ii) *Major security-based swap participants.* The margin requirements of section 15F(e) of the Act (15 U.S.C. 78o–10(e)) and §240.18a–3; provided, however, that prior to making such substituted compliance determination, the Commission intends to consider (in addition to any conditions imposed) whether the foreign financial regulatory system requires registrants to adequately cover their current exposure to over-the-counter derivatives counterparties, and ensures registrants' safety and soundness, in a manner comparable to the applicable provisions arising under the Act and its rules and regulations.

(6) *Recordkeeping and reporting.* The recordkeeping and reporting requirements of Section 15F of the Act (15 U.S.C. 78o–10) and §§240.18a–5 through 240.18a–9; provided, however, that prior to making such a substituted compliance determination the Commission intends to consider (in addition to any conditions imposed), whether the foreign financial regulatory system's required records and reports, the timeframes for recording or reporting information, the accounting standards governing the records and reports, and the required format of the records and reports are comparable to applicable provisions arising under the Act and its rules and regulations and would permit the Commission to examine and inspect regulated firms' compliance with the applicable securities laws.

(7) *Portfolio reconciliation, portfolio compression, and trading relationship documentation requirements.* The portfolio reconciliation, portfolio compression, and trading relationship documentation requirements of section 15F(i) of the Act (15 U.S.C. 78o–10(i)) and §§240.15Fi–3 through 240.15Fi–5; provided, however, that prior to making such a substituted compliance determination the Commission intends to consider whether the requirements of the foreign financial regulatory system for engaging in portfolio reconciliation and portfolio compression and for executing trading relationship documentation with counterparties, the duties imposed by the foreign financial regulatory system, and the information that is required to be provided to counterparties pursuant to the requirements of the foreign financial regulatory system, are comparable to those required pursuant to the applicable provisions arising under the Act and its rules and regulations.

[81 FR 30143, May 13, 2016, as amended at 81 FR 39844, June 17, 2016; 84 FR 44041, Aug. 22, 2019; 84 FR 68646, Dec. 16, 2019; 85 FR 6412, Feb. 4, 2020]

Definitions

§ 240.3b–1 Definition of "listed".

The term *listed* means admitted to full trading privileges upon application

§ 240.3b-2

by the issuer or its fiscal agent or, in the case of the securities of a foreign corporation, upon application by a banker engaged in distributing them; and includes securities for which authority to add to the list on official notice of issuance has been granted.

(Sec. 3, 48 Stat. 884; 15 U.S.C. 78c)

[13 FR 8179, Dec. 22, 1948]

§ 240.3b-2 Definition of "officer".

The term *officer* means a president, vice president, secretary, treasury or principal financial officer, comptroller or principal accounting officer, and any person routinely performing corresponding functions with respect to any organization whether incorporated or unincorporated.

[47 FR 11464, Mar. 16, 1982; 47 FR 11819, Mar. 19, 1982]

§ 240.3b-3 [Reserved]

§ 240.3b-4 Definition of "foreign government," "foreign issuer" and "foreign private issuer".

(a) The term *foreign government* means the government of any foreign country or of any political subdivision of a foreign country.

(b) The term *foreign issuer* means any issuer which is a foreign government, a national of any foreign country or a corporation or other organization incorporated or organized under the laws of any foreign country.

(c) The term *foreign private issuer* means any foreign issuer other than a foreign government except for an issuer meeting the following conditions as of the last business day of its most recently completed second fiscal quarter:

(1) More than 50 percent of the issuer's outstanding voting securities are directly or indirectly held of record by residents of the United States; and

(2) Any of the following:

(i) The majority of the executive officers or directors are United States citizens or residents;

(ii) More than 50 percent of the assets of the issuer are located in the United States; or

(iii) The business of the issuer is administered principally in the United States.

17 CFR Ch. II (4-1-23 Edition)

NOTE TO PARAGRAPH (c)(1): To determine the percentage of outstanding voting securities held by U.S. residents:

A. Use the method of calculating record ownership in § 240.12g3-2(a), except that:

(1) Your inquiry as to the amount of shares represented by accounts of customers resident in the United States may be limited to brokers, dealers, banks and other nominees located in:

(i) The United States,

(ii) Your jurisdiction of incorporation, and

(iii) The jurisdiction that is the primary trading market for your voting securities, if different than your jurisdiction of incorporation; and

(2) Notwithstanding § 240.12g5-1(a)(8) of this chapter, you shall not exclude securities held by persons who received the securities pursuant to an employee compensation plan.

B. If, after reasonable inquiry, you are unable to obtain information about the amount of shares represented by accounts of customers resident in the United States, you may assume, for purposes of this definition, that the customers are residents of the jurisdiction in which the nominee has its principal place of business.

C. Count shares of voting securities beneficially owned by residents of the United States as reported on reports of beneficial ownership provided to you or filed publicly and based on information otherwise provided to you.

(d) Notwithstanding paragraph (c) of this section, in the case of a new registrant with the Commission, the determination of whether an issuer is a foreign private issuer will be made as of a date within 30 days prior to the issuer's filing of an initial registration statement under either the Act or the Securities Act of 1933.

(e) Once an issuer qualifies as a foreign private issuer, it will immediately be able to use the forms and rules designated for foreign private issuers until it fails to qualify for this status at the end of its most recently completed second fiscal quarter. An issuer's determination that it fails to qualify as a foreign private issuer governs its eligibility to use the forms and rules designated for foreign private issuers beginning on the first day of the fiscal year following the determination date. Once an issuer fails to qualify for foreign private issuer status, it will remain unqualified unless it meets the requirements for foreign private issuer

Securities and Exchange Commission

§ 240.3b-6

status as of the last business day of its second fiscal quarter.

[32 FR 7848, May 30, 1967, as amended at 48 FR 46739, Oct. 14, 1983; 64 FR 53912, Oct. 5, 1999; 73 FR 58323, Oct. 6, 2008; 81 FR 28705, May 10, 2016]

§ 240.3b-5 Non-exempt securities issued under governmental obligations.

(a) Any part of an obligation evidenced by any bond, note, debenture, or other evidence of indebtedness issued by any governmental unit specified in section 3(a)(12) of the Act which is payable from payments to be made in respect of property or money which is or will be used, under a lease, sale, or loan arrangement, by or for industrial or commercial enterprise, shall be deemed to be a separate "security" within the meaning of section 3(a)(10) of the Act, issued by the lessee or obligor under the lease, sale or loan arrangement.

(b) An obligation shall not be deemed a separate "security" as defined in paragraph (a) of this section if, (1) the obligation is payable from the general revenues of a governmental unit, specified in section 3(a)(12) of the Act, having other resources which may be used for the payment of the obligation, or (2) the obligation relates to a public project or facility owned and operated by or on behalf of and under the control of a governmental unit specified in such section, or (3) the obligation relates to a facility which is leased to and under the control of an industrial or commercial enterprise but is a part of a public project which, as a whole, is owned by and under the general control of a governmental unit specified in such section, or an instrumentality thereof.

(c) This rule shall apply to transactions of the character described in paragraph (a) of this section only with respect to bonds, notes, debentures or other evidences of indebtedness sold after December 31, 1968.

(Sec. 3, 48 Stat. 882; 15 U.S.C. 78c, 77s)

[33 FR 12648, Sept. 6, 1968, as amended at 35 FR 6000, Apr. 11, 1970]

§ 240.3b-6 Liability for certain statements by issuers.

(a) A statement within the coverage of paragraph (b) of this section which is made by or on behalf of an issuer or by an outside reviewer retained by the issuer shall be deemed not to be a fraudulent statement (as defined in paragraph (d) of this section), unless it is shown that such statement was made or reaffirmed without a reasonable basis or was disclosed other than in good faith.

(b) This rule applies to the following statements:

(1) A forward-looking statement (as defined in paragraph (c) of this section) made in a document filed with the Commission, in Part I of a quarterly report on Form 10-Q, § 249.308a of this chapter, or in an annual report to security holders meeting the requirements of Rules 14a-3(b) and (c) or 14c-3(a) and (b) (§ 240.14a-3(b) and (c) or § 240.14c-3(a) and (b)), a statement reaffirming such forward-looking statement after the date the document was filed or the annual report was made publicly available, or a forward-looking statement made before the date the document was filed or the date the annual report was made publicly available if such statement is reaffirmed in a filed document, in Part I of a quarterly report on Form 10-Q, or in an annual report made publicly available within a reasonable time after the making of such forward-looking statement; *Provided,* that:

(i) At the time such statements are made or reaffirmed, either the issuer is subject to the reporting requirements of Section 13(a) or 15(d) of the Act and has complied with the requirements of Rule 13a-1 or 15d-1 thereunder, if applicable, to file its most recent annual report on Form 10-K, Form 20-F or Form 40-F; or if the issuer is not subject to the reporting requirements of Section 13(a) or 15(d) of the Act, the statements are made in a registration statement filed under the Securities Act of 1933 offering statement or solicitation of interest, written document or broadcast script under Regulation A or pursuant to Section 12(b) or (g) of the Securities Exchange Act of 1934; and

(ii) The statements are not made by or on behalf of an issuer that is an investment company registered under

§ 240.3b–7

the Investment Company Act of 1940; and

(2) Information that is disclosed in a document filed with the Commission in Part I of a quarterly report on Form 10–Q (§ 249.308a of this chapter) or in an annual report to security holders meeting the requirements of Rules 14a–3(b) and (c) or 14c–3(a) and (b) under the Act (§ 240.14a–3(b) and (c) or § 240.14c–3(a) and (b) of this chapter) and that relates to:

(i) The effects of changing prices on the business enterprise, presented voluntarily or pursuant to Item 303 of Regulation S–K (§ 229.303 of this chapter), "Management's Discussion and Analysis of Financial Condition and Results of Operations," Item 5 of Form 20–F (§ 240.220(f) of this chapter), "Operating and Financial Review and Prospects," Item 302 of Regulation S–K (§ 229.302 of this chapter) "Supplementary Financial Information," or Rule 3–20(c) of Regulation S–X (§ 210.3–20(c) of this chapter); or

(ii) The value of proved oil and gas reserves (such as a standardized measure of discounted future net cash flows relating to proved oil and gas reserves as set forth in FASB ASC paragraphs 932–235–50–29 through 932–235–50–36 (Extractive Activities—Oil and Gas Topic)), presented voluntarily or pursuant to Item 302 of Regulation S–K (§ 229.302 of this chapter).

(c) For the purpose of this rule, the term *forward-looking statement* shall mean and shall be limited to:

(1) A statement containing a projection of revenues, income (loss), earnings (loss) per share, capital expenditures, dividends, capital structure or other financial items;

(2) A statement of management's plans and objectives for future operations;

(3) A statement of future economic performance contained in management's discussion and analysis of financial condition and results of operations included pursuant to Item 303 of Regulation S–K (§ 229.303 of this chapter) or Item 5 of Form 20–F or

(4) Disclosed statements of the assumptions underlying or relating to any of the statements described in paragraphs (c) (1), (2), or (3) of this section.

(d) For the purpose of this rule the term *fraudulent statement* shall mean a statement which is an untrue statement of a material fact, a statement false or misleading with respect to any material fact, an omission to state a material fact necessary to make a statement not misleading, or which constitutes the employment of a manipulative, deceptive, or fraudulent device, contrivance, scheme, transaction, act, practice, course of business, or an artifice to defraud, as those terms are used in the Securities Exchange Act of 1934 or the rules or regulations promulgated thereunder.

[46 FR 13990, Feb. 25, 1981, as amended at 46 FR 19457, Mar. 31, 1981; 47 FR 11464, Mar. 16, 1982; 47 FR 54780, Dec. 6, 1982; 47 FR 57915, Dec. 29, 1982; 48 FR 19876, May 3, 1983; 56 FR 30067, July 1, 1991; 57 FR 36494, Aug. 13, 1992; 64 FR 53912, Oct. 5, 1999; 73 FR 973, Jan. 4, 2008; 76 FR 50122, Aug. 12, 2011]

§ 240.3b–7 Definition of "executive officer".

The term *executive officer*, when used with reference to a registrant, means its president, any vice president of the registrant in charge of a principal business unit, division or function (such as sales, administration or finance), any other officer who performs a policy making function or any other person who performs similar policy making functions for the registrant. Executive officers of subsidiaries may be deemed executive officers of the registrant if they perform such policy making functions for the registrant.

[47 FR 11464, Mar. 16, 1982, as amended at 56 FR 7265, Feb. 21, 1991]

§ 240.3b–8 Definitions of "Qualified OTC Market Maker, Qualified Third Market Maker" and "Qualified Block Positioner".

For the purposes of Regulation U under the Act (12 CFR part 221):

(a) The term *Qualified OTC Market Maker* in an over-the-counter ("OTC") margin security means a dealer in any "OTC Margin Security" (as that term is defined in section 2(j) of Regulation U (12 CFR 221.2(j)) who (1) is a broker or dealer registered pursuant to section 15 of the Act, (2) is subject to and is in compliance with Rule 15c3–1 (17 CFR

Securities and Exchange Commission § 240.3b-12

240.15c3-1), (3) has and maintains minimum net capital, as defined in Rule 15c3-1, of the lesser of (i) $250,000 or (ii) $25,000 plus $5,000 for each security in excess of five with regard to which the broker or dealer is, or is seeking to become a Qualified OTC Market Maker, and (4) except when such activity is unlawful, meets all of the following conditions with respect to such security: (i) He regularly publishes bona fide, competitive bid and offer quotations in a recognized inter-dealer quotation system, (ii) he furnishes bona fide, competitive bid and offer quotations to other brokers and dealers on request, (iii) he is ready, willing and able to effect transactions in reasonable amounts, and at his quoted prices, with other brokers and dealers, and (iv) he has a reasonable average rate of inventory turnover in such security.

(b) The term *Qualified Third Market Maker* means a dealer in any stock registered on a national securities exchange ("exchange") who (1) is a broker or dealer registered pursuant to section 15 of the Act, (2) is subject to and is in compliance with Rule 15c3-1 (17 CFR 240.15c3-1), (3) has and maintains minimum net capital, as defined in Rule 15c3-1, of the lesser of (i) $500,000 or (ii) $100,000 plus $20,000 for each security in excess of five with regard to which the broker or dealer is, or is seeking to become, a Qualified Third Market Maker, and (4) except when such activity is unlawful, meets all of the following conditions with respect to such security: (i) He furnishes bona fide, competitive bid and offer quotations at all times to other brokers and dealers on request, (ii) he is ready, willing and able to effect transactions for his own account in reasonable amounts, and at his quoted prices with other brokers and dealers, and (iii) he has a reasonable average rate of inventory turnover in such security.

(c) The term *Qualified Block Positioner* means a dealer who (1) is a broker or dealer registered pursuant to section 15 of the Act, (2) is subject to and in compliance with Rule 15c3-1 (17 CFR 240.15c3-1), (3) has and maintains minimum net capital, as defined in Rule 15c3-1 of $1,000,000 and (4) except when such activity is unlawful, meets all of the following conditions: (i) He engages in the activity of purchasing long or selling short, from time to time, from or to a customer (other than a partner or a joint venture or other entity in which a partner, the dealer, or a person associated with such dealer, as defined in section 3(a) (18) of the Act, participates) a block of stock with a current market value of $200,000 or more in a single transaction, or in several transactions at approximately the same time, from a single source to facilitate a sale or purchase by such customer, (ii) he has determined in the exercise of reasonable diligence that the block could not be sold to or purchased from others on equivalent or better terms, and (iii) he sells the shares comprising the block as rapidly as possible commensurate with the circumstances.

(15 U.S.C. 78a *et seq.*, as amended by Pub. L. 94-29 (June 4, 1975), particularly secs. 2, 3, 11, 15, 17 and 23 thereof (15 U.S.C. 78b, 78c, 78k, 78o, 78q and 78w))

[48 FR 39606, Sept. 1, 1983]

§§ 240.3b-9—240.3b-10 [Reserved]

§ 240.3b-11 Definitions relating to limited partnership roll-up transactions for purposes of sections 6(b)(9), 14(h) and 15A(b)(12)–(13).

For purposes of sections 6(b)(9), 14(h) and 15A(b)(12)–(13) of the Act (15 U.S.C. 78f(b)(9), 78n(h) and 78o–3(b)(12)–(13)):

(a) The term *limited partnership roll-up transaction* does not include a transaction involving only entities that are not "finite-life" as defined in Item 901(b)(2) of Regulation S-K (§ 229.901(b)(2) of this chapter).

(b) The term *limited partnership roll-up transaction* does not include a transaction involving only entities registered under the Investment Company Act of 1940 (15 U.S.C. 80a–1 *et seq.*) or any Business Development Company as defined in section 2(a)(48) of that Act (15 U.S.C. 80a–2(a)(48)).

(c) The term *regularly traded* shall be defined as in Item 901(c)(2)(v)(C) of Regulation S-K (§ 229.901(c)(2)(v)(C) of this chapter).

[59 FR 63684, Dec. 8, 1994]

§ 240.3b-12 Definition of OTC derivatives dealer.

The term *OTC derivatives dealer* means any dealer that is affiliated with

§ 240.3b-13

a registered broker or dealer (other than an OTC derivatives dealer), and whose securities activities:

(a) Are limited to:

(1) Engaging in dealer activities in eligible OTC derivative instruments that are securities;

(2) Issuing and reacquiring securities that are issued by the dealer, including warrants on securities, hybrid securities, and structured notes;

(3) Engaging in cash management securities activities;

(4) Engaging in ancillary portfolio management securities activities; and

(5) Engaging in such other securities activities that the Commission designates by order pursuant to § 240.15a–1(b)(1); and

(b) Consist primarily of the activities described in paragraphs (a)(1), (a)(2), and (a)(3) of this section; and

(c) Do not consist of any other securities activities, including engaging in any transaction in any security that is not an eligible OTC derivative instrument, except as permitted under paragraphs (a)(3), (a)(4), and (a)(5) of this section.

(d) For purposes of this section, the term *hybrid security* means a security that incorporates payment features economically similar to options, forwards, futures, swap agreements, or collars involving currencies, interest or other rates, commodities, securities, indices, quantitative measures, or other financial or economic interests or property of any kind, or any payment or delivery that is dependent on the occurrence or nonoccurrence of any event associated with a potential financial, economic, or commercial consequence (or any combination, permutation, or derivative of such contract or underlying interest).

[63 FR 59394, Nov. 3, 1998]

§ 240.3b-13 Definition of eligible OTC derivative instrument.

(a) Except as otherwise provided in paragraph (b) of this section, the term *eligible OTC derivative instrument* means any contract, agreement, or transaction that:

(1) Provides, in whole or in part, on a firm or contingent basis, for the purchase or sale of, or is based on the value of, or any interest in, one or more commodities, securities, currencies, interest or other rates, indices, quantitative measures, or other financial or economic interests or property of any kind; or

(2) Involves any payment or delivery that is dependent on the occurrence or nonoccurrence of any event associated with a potential financial, economic, or commercial consequence; or

(3) Involves any combination or permutation of any contract, agreement, or transaction or underlying interest, property, or event described in paragraphs (a)(1) or (a)(2) of this section.

(b) The term *eligible OTC derivative instrument* does not include any contract, agreement, or transaction that:

(1) Provides for the purchase or sale of a security, on a firm basis, unless:

(i) The settlement date for such purchase or sale occurs at least one year following the trade date or, in the case of an eligible forward contract, at least four months following the trade date; or

(ii) The material economic features of the contract, agreement, or transaction consist primarily of features of a type described in paragraph (a) of this section other than the provision for the purchase or sale of a security on a firm basis; or

(2) Provides, in whole or in part, on a firm or contingent basis, for the purchase or sale of, or is based on the value of, or any interest in, any security (or group or index of securities), and is:

(i) Listed on, or traded on or through, a national securities exchange or registered national securities association, or facility or market thereof; or

(ii) Except as otherwise determined by the Commission by order pursuant to § 240.15a–1(b)(2), one of a class of fungible instruments that are standardized as to their material economic terms.

(c) The Commission may issue an order pursuant to § 240.15a–1(b)(3) clarifying whether certain contracts, agreements, or transactions are within the scope of eligible OTC derivative instrument.

(d) For purposes of this section, the term *eligible forward contract* means a forward contract that provides for the purchase or sale of a security other than a government security, provided that, if such contract provides for the purchase or sale of margin stock (as defined in Regulation U of the Regulations of the Board of Governors of the Federal Reserve System, 12 CFR Part 221), such contract either:

(1) Provides for the purchase or sale of such stock by the issuer thereof (or an affiliate that is not a bank or a broker or dealer); or

(2) Provides for the transfer of transaction collateral in an amount that would satisfy the requirements, if any, that would be applicable assuming the OTC derivatives dealer party to such transaction were not eligible for the exemption from Regulation T of the Regulations of the Board of Governors of the Federal Reserve System, 12 CFR part 220, set forth in § 240.36a1–1.

[63 FR 59395, Nov. 3, 1998]

§ 240.3b–14 Definition of cash management securities activities.

The term *cash management securities activities* means securities activities that are limited to transactions involving:

(a) Any taking possession of, and any subsequent sale or disposition of, collateral provided by a counterparty, or any acquisition of, and any subsequent sale or disposition of, collateral to be provided to a counterparty, in connection with any securities activities of the dealer permitted under § 240.15a–1 or any non-securities activities of the dealer that involve eligible OTC derivative instruments or other financial instruments;

(b) Cash management, in connection with any securities activities of the dealer permitted under § 240.15a–1 or any non-securities activities of the dealer that involve eligible OTC derivative instruments or other financial instruments; or

(c) Financing of positions of the dealer acquired in connection with any securities activities of the dealer permitted under § 240.15a–1 or any non-securities activities that involve eligible OTC derivative instruments or other financial instruments.

[63 FR 59395, Nov. 3, 1998]

§ 240.3b–15 Definition of ancillary portfolio management securities activities.

(a) The term *ancillary portfolio management securities activities* means securities activities that:

(1) Are limited to transactions in connection with:

(i) Dealer activities in eligible OTC derivative instruments;

(ii) The issuance of securities by the dealer; or

(iii) Such other securities activities that the Commission designates by order pursuant to § 240.15a–1(b)(1); and

(2) Are conducted for the purpose of reducing the market or credit risk of the dealer or consist of incidental trading activities for portfolio management purposes; and

(3) Are limited to risk exposures within the market, credit, leverage, and liquidity risk parameters set forth in:

(i) The trading authorizations granted to the associated person (or to the supervisor of such associated person) who executes a particular transaction for, or on behalf of, the dealer; and

(ii) The written guidelines approved by the governing body of the dealer and included in the internal risk management control system for the dealer pursuant to § 240.15c3–4; and

(4) Are conducted solely by one or more associated persons of the dealer who perform substantial duties for, or on behalf of, the dealer in connection with its dealer activities in eligible OTC derivative instruments.

(b) The Commission may issue an order pursuant to § 240.15a–1(b)(4) clarifying whether certain securities activities are within the scope of ancillary portfolio management securities activities.

[63 FR 59395, Nov. 3, 1998]

§ 240.3b–16 Definitions of terms used in Section 3(a)(1) of the Act.

(a) An organization, association, or group of persons shall be considered to constitute, maintain, or provide "a market place or facilities for bringing together purchasers and sellers of securities or for otherwise performing with respect to securities the functions commonly performed by a stock exchange," as those terms are used in

§ 240.3b–17

section 3(a)(1) of the Act, (15 U.S.C. 78c(a)(1)), if such organization, association, or group of persons:

(1) Brings together the orders for securities of multiple buyers and sellers; and

(2) Uses established, non-discretionary methods (whether by providing a trading facility or by setting rules) under which such orders interact with each other, and the buyers and sellers entering such orders agree to the terms of a trade.

(b) An organization, association, or group of persons shall not be considered to constitute, maintain, or provide "a market place or facilities for bringing together purchasers and sellers of securities or for otherwise performing with respect to securities the functions commonly performed by a stock exchange," solely because such organization, association, or group of persons engages in one or more of the following activities:

(1) Routes orders to a national securities exchange, a market operated by a national securities association, or a broker-dealer for execution; or

(2) Allows persons to enter orders for execution against the bids and offers of a single dealer; and

(i) As an incidental part of these activities, matches orders that are not displayed to any person other than the dealer and its employees; or

(ii) In the course of acting as a market maker registered with a self-regulatory organization, displays the limit orders of such market maker's, or other broker-dealer's, customers; and

(A) Matches customer orders with such displayed limit orders; and

(B) As an incidental part of its market making activities, crosses or matches orders that are not displayed to any person other than the market maker and its employees.

(c) For purposes of this section the term *order* means any firm indication of a willingness to buy or sell a security, as either principal or agent, including any bid or offer quotation, market order, limit order, or other priced order.

(d) For the purposes of this section, the terms *bid* and *offer* shall have the same meaning as under § 242.600 of this chapter.

(e) The Commission may conditionally or unconditionally exempt any organization, association, or group of persons from the definition in paragraph (a) of this section.

[63 FR 70918, Dec. 22, 1998, as amended at 70 FR 37617, June 29, 2005]

§ 240.3b–17 [Reserved]

§ 240.3b–18 Definitions of terms used in Section 3(a)(5) of the Act.

For the purposes of section 3(a)(5)(C) of the Act (15 U.S.C. 78c(a)(5)(C)):

(a) The term *affiliate* means any company that controls, is controlled by, or is under common control with another company.

(b) The term *consumer-related receivable* means any obligation incurred by any natural person to pay money arising out of a transaction in which the money, property, insurance, or services (being purchased) are primarily for personal, family, or household purposes.

(c) The term *member* as it relates to the term "syndicate of banks" means a bank that is a participant in a syndicate of banks and together with its affiliates, other than its broker or dealer affiliates, originates no less than 10% of the value of the obligations in a pool of obligations used to back the securities issued through a grantor trust or other separate entity.

(d) The term *obligation* means any note, draft, acceptance, loan, lease, receivable, or other evidence of indebtedness that is not a security issued by a person other than the bank.

(e) The term *originated* means:

(1) Funding an obligation at the time that the obligation is created; or

(2) Initially approving and underwriting the obligation, or initially agreeing to purchase the obligation, provided that:

(i) The obligation conforms to the underwriting standards or is evidenced by the loan documents of the bank or its affiliates, other than its broker or dealer affiliates; and

(ii) The bank or its affiliates, other than its broker or dealer affiliates, fund the obligation in a timely manner, not to exceed six months after the obligation is created.

(f) The term *pool* means more than one obligation or type of obligation

Securities and Exchange Commission § 240.3Ca–1

grouped together to provide collateral for a securities offering.

(g) The term *predominantly originated* means that no less than 85% of the value of the obligations in any pool were originated by:

(1) The bank or its affiliates, other than its broker or dealer affiliates; or

(2) Banks that are members of a syndicate of banks and affiliates of such banks, other than their broker or dealer affiliates, if the obligations or pool of obligations consist of mortgage obligations or consumer-related receivables.

(3) For this purpose, the bank and its affiliates include any financial institution with which the bank or its affiliates have merged but does not include the purchase of a pool of obligations or the purchase of a line of business.

(h) The term *syndicate of banks* means a group of banks that acts jointly, on a temporary basis, to issue through a grantor trust or other separate entity, securities backed by obligations originated by each of the individual banks or their affiliates, other than their broker or dealer affiliates.

[68 FR 8700, Feb. 24, 2003]

§ 240.3b–19 Definition of "issuer" in section 3(a)(8) of the Act in relation to asset-backed securities.

The following applies with respect to asset-backed securities under the Act. Terms used in this section have the same meaning as in Item 1101 of Regulation AB (§ 229.1101 of this chapter).

(a) The depositor for the asset-backed securities acting solely in its capacity as depositor to the issuing entity is the "issuer" for purposes of the asset-backed securities of that issuing entity.

(b) The person acting in the capacity as the depositor specified in paragraph (a) of this section is a different "issuer" from that same person acting as a depositor for another issuing entity or for purposes of that person's own securities.

[70 FR 1620, Jan. 7, 2005]

CLEARING OF SECURITY-BASED SWAPS

§ 240.3Ca–1 Stay of clearing requirement and review by the Commission.

(a) After making a determination pursuant to a clearing agency's security-based swap submission that a security-based swap, or any group, category, type or class of security-based swaps, is required to be cleared, the Commission, on application of a counterparty to a security-based swap or on the Commission's own initiative, may stay the clearing requirement until the Commission completes a review of the terms of the security-based swap (or group, category, type, or class of security-based swaps) and the clearing of the security-based swap (or group, category, type, or class of security-based swaps) by the clearing agency that has accepted it for clearing.

(b) A counterparty to a security-based swap applying for a stay of the clearing requirement for a security-based swap (or group, category, type, or class of security-based swaps) shall submit a written statement to the Commission that includes:

(1) A request for a stay of the clearing requirement;

(2) The identity of the counterparties to the security-based swap and a contact at the counterparty requesting the stay;

(3) The identity of the clearing agency clearing the security-based swap;

(4) The terms of the security-based swap subject to the clearing requirement and a description of the clearing arrangement; and

(5) Reasons why such stay should be granted and why the security-based swap should not be subject to a clearing requirement, specifically addressing the same factors a clearing agency must address in its security-based-swap submission pursuant to § 240.19b–4(o)(3).

(c) A stay of the clearing requirement may be granted with respect to a security-based swap, or the group, category, type, or class of security-based swaps, as determined by the Commission.

(d) The Commission's review shall include a quantitative and qualitative assessment of the factors specified in § 240.19b–4(o)(3). Any clearing agency

§ 240.3Ca-2

that has accepted for clearing a security-based swap, or any group, category, type or class of security-based swaps, that is subject to the stay of the clearing requirement shall provide information requested by the Commission as necessary to assess any of the factors it determines to be appropriate in the course of its review.

(e) Upon completion of its review, the Commission may:

(1) Determine, subject to any terms and conditions that the Commission determines to be appropriate in the public interest, that the security-based swap, or group, category, type, or class of security-based swaps must be cleared; or

(2) Determine that the clearing requirement will not apply to the security-based swap, or group, category, type, or class of security-based swaps, but clearing may continue on a nonmandatory basis.

[77 FR 41647, July 13, 2012]

§ 240.3Ca-2 Submission of security-based swaps for clearing.

Pursuant to section 3C(a)(1) of the Act (15 U.S.C. 78c-3(a)(1)), it shall be unlawful for any person to engage in a security-based swap unless that person submits such security-based swap for clearing to a clearing agency that is registered under this Act or a clearing agency that is exempt from registration under the Act if the security-based swap is required to be cleared. The phrase *submits such security-based swap for clearing to a clearing agency* in the clearing requirement of Section 3C(a)(1) of the Act shall mean that the security-based swap will be submitted for central clearing to a clearing agency that functions as a central counterparty.

[77 FR 41647, July 13, 2012]

REGISTRATION AND EXEMPTION OF EXCHANGES

§ 240.6a-1 Application for registration as a national securities exchange or exemption from registration based on limited volume.

(a) An application for registration as a national securities exchange, or for exemption from such registration based on limited volume, shall be filed on Form 1 (§ 249.1 of this chapter), in accordance with the instructions contained therein.

(b) Promptly after the discovery that any information filed on Form 1 was inaccurate when filed, the exchange shall file with the Commission an amendment correcting such inaccuracy.

(c) Promptly after the discovery that any information in the statement, any exhibit, or any amendment was inaccurate when filed, the exchange shall file with the Commission an amendment correcting such inaccuracy.

(d) Whenever the number of changes to be reported in an amendment, or the number of amendments filed, are so great that the purpose of clarity will be promoted by the filing of a new complete statement and exhibits, an exchange may, at its election, or shall, upon request of the Commission, file as an amendment a complete new statement together with all exhibits which are prescribed to be filed in connection with Form 1.

(Secs. 5, 6, 17, 48 Stat. 885, 897, as amended; 15 U.S.C. 78e, 78f, 78q)

[14 FR 7759, Dec. 29, 1949, as amended at 63 FR 70918, Dec. 22, 1998]

§ 240.6a-2 Amendments to application.

(a) A national securities exchange, or an exchange exempted from such registration based on limited volume, shall file an amendment to Form 1, (§ 249.1 of this chapter), which shall set forth the nature and effective date of the action taken and shall provide any new information and correct any information rendered inaccurate, on Form 1, (§ 249.1 of this chapter), within 10 days after any action is taken that renders inaccurate, or that causes to be incomplete, any of the following:

(1) Information filed on the Execution Page of Form 1, or amendment thereto; or

(2) Information filed as part of Exhibits C, F, G, H, J, K or M, or any amendments thereto.

(b) On or before June 30 of each year, a national securities exchange, or an exchange exempted from such registration based on limited volume, shall file, as an amendment to Form 1, the following:

Securities and Exchange Commission § 240.6a–3

(1) Exhibits D and I as of the end of the latest fiscal year of the exchange; and

(2) Exhibits K, M, and N, which shall be up to date as of the latest date practicable within 3 months of the date the amendment is filed.

(c) On or before June 30, 2001 and every 3 years thereafter, a national securities exchange, or an exchange exempted from such registration based on limited volume, shall file, as an amendment to Form 1, complete Exhibits A, B, C and J. The information filed under this paragraph (c) shall be current as of the latest practicable date, but shall, at a minimum, be up to date within 3 months as of the date the amendment is filed.

(d)(1) If an exchange, on an annual or more frequent basis, publishes, or co-operates in the publication of, any of the information required to be filed by paragraphs (b)(2) and (c) of this section, in lieu of filing such information, an exchange may:

(i) Identify the publication in which such information is available, the name, address, and telephone number of the person from whom such publication may be obtained, and the price of such publication; and

(ii) Certify to the accuracy of such information as of its publication date.

(2) If an exchange keeps the information required under paragraphs (b)(2) and (c) of this section up to date and makes it available to the Commission and the public upon request, in lieu of filing such information, an exchange may certify that the information is kept up to date and is available to the Commission and the public upon request.

(3) If the information required to be filed under paragraphs (b)(2) and (c) of this section is available continuously on an Internet web site controlled by an exchange, in lieu of filing such information with the Commission, such exchange may:

(i) Indicate the location of the Internet web site where such information may be found; and

(ii) Certify that the information available at such location is accurate as of its date.

(e) The Commission may exempt a national securities exchange, or an exchange exempted from such registration based on limited volume, from filing the amendment required by this section for any affiliate or subsidiary listed in Exhibit C of the exchange's application for registration, as amended, that either:

(1) Is listed in Exhibit C of the application for registration or notice of registration, as amended, of one or more other national securities exchanges; or

(2) Was an inactive subsidiary throughout the subsidiary's latest fiscal year. Any such exemption may be granted upon terms and conditions the Commission deems necessary or appropriate in the public interest or for the protection of investors, provided however, that at least one national securities exchange shall be required to file the amendments required by this section for an affiliate or subsidiary described in paragraph (e)(1) of this section.

(f) A national securities exchange registered pursuant to Section 6(g)(1) of the Act (15 U.S.C. 78f(g)(1)) shall be exempt from the requirements of this section.

[63 FR 70918, Dec. 22, 1998, as amended at 66 FR 43741, Aug. 20, 2001]

§ 240.6a–3 Supplemental material to be filed by exchanges.

(a)(1) A national securities exchange, or an exchange exempted from such registration based on limited volume, shall file with the Commission any material (including notices, circulars, bulletins, lists, and periodicals) issued or made generally available to members of, or participants or subscribers to, the exchange. Such material shall be filed with the Commission within 10 days after issuing or making such material available to members, participants or subscribers.

(2) If the information required to be filed under paragraph (a)(1) of this section is available continuously on an Internet web site controlled by an exchange, in lieu of filing such information with the Commission, such exchange may:

(i) Indicate the location of the Internet web site where such information may be found; and

§ 240.6a–4

(ii) Certify that the information available at such location is accurate as of its date.

(b) Within 15 days after the end of each calendar month, a national securities exchange or an exchange exempted from such registration based on limited volume, shall file a report concerning the securities sold on such exchange during the calendar month. Such report shall set forth:

(1) The number of shares of stock sold and the aggregate dollar amount of such stock sold;

(2) The principal amount of bonds sold and the aggregate dollar amount of such bonds sold; and

(3) The number of rights and warrants sold and the aggregate dollar amount of such rights and warrants sold.

(c) A national securities exchange registered pursuant to Section 6(g)(1) of the Act (15 U.S.C. 78f(g)(1)) shall be exempt from the requirements of this section.

[63 FR 70919, Dec. 22, 1998, as amended at 66 FR 43741, Aug. 20, 2001]

§ 240.6a–4 Notice of registration under Section 6(g) of the Act, amendment to such notice, and supplemental materials to be filed by exchanges registered under Section 6(g) of the Act.

(a) *Notice of registration.* (1) An exchange may register as a national securities exchange solely for the purposes of trading security futures products by filing Form 1–N (§ 249.10 of this chapter) ("notice of registration"), in accordance with the instructions contained therein, if:

(i) The exchange is a board of trade, as that term in defined in the Commodity Exchange Act (7 U.S.C. 1a(2)), that:

(A) Has been designated a contract market by the Commodity Futures Trading Commission and such designation is not suspended by order of the Commodity Futures Trading Commission; or

(B) Is registered as a derivative transaction execution facility under Section 5a of the Commodity Exchange Act (7 U.S.C. 7a) and such registration is not suspended by the Commodity Futures Trading Commission; and

(ii) Such exchange does not serve as a market place for transactions in securities other than:

(A) Security futures products; or

(B) Futures on exempted securities or on groups or indexes of securities or options thereon that have been authorized under Section 2(a)(1)(C) of the Commodity Exchange Act (7 U.S.C. 2a).

(2) Promptly after the discovery that any information filed on Form 1–N (§ 249.10 of this chapter) was inaccurate when filed, the exchange shall file with the Commission an amendment correcting such inaccuracy.

(b) *Amendment to notice of registration.* (1) A national securities exchange registered pursuant to Section 6(g)(1) of the Act (15 U.S.C. 78f(g)(1)) ("Security Futures Product Exchange") shall file an amendment to Form 1–N (§ 249.10 of this chapter), which shall set forth the nature and effective date of the action taken and shall provide any new information and correct any information rendered inaccurate, on Form 1–N (§ 249.10 of this chapter), within:

(i) Ten days after any action is taken that renders inaccurate, or that causes to be incomplete, any information filed on the Execution Page of Form 1–N (§ 249.10 of this chapter), or amendment thereto; or

(ii) 30 days after any action is taken that renders inaccurate, or that causes to be incomplete, any information filed as part of Exhibit F to Form 1–N (§ 249.10 of this chapter), or any amendments thereto.

(2) A Security Futures Product Exchange shall maintain records relating to changes in information required in Exhibits C and E to Form 1–N (§ 249.10 of this chapter) which shall be current of as of the latest practicable date, but shall, at a minimum, be up-to-date within 30 days. A Security Futures Product Exchange shall make such records available to the Commission and the public upon request.

(3) On or before June 30, 2002, and by June 30 every year thereafter, a Security Futures Product Exchange shall file, as an amendment to Form 1–N (§ 249.10 of this chapter), Exhibits F, H, and I, which shall be current of as of the latest practicable date, but shall, at a minimum, be up-to-date within

Securities and Exchange Commission § 240.6a–4

three months as of the date the amendment is filed.

(4) On or before June 30, 2004, and by June 30 every three years thereafter, a Security Futures Product Exchange shall file, as an amendment to Form 1–N (§ 249.10 of this chapter), complete Exhibits A, B, C, and E, which shall be current of as of the latest practicable date, but shall, at a minimum, be up-to-date within three months as of the date the amendment is filed.

(5)(i) If a Security Futures Product Exchange, on an annual or more frequent basis, publishes, or cooperates in the publication of, any of the information required to be filed by paragraphs (b)(3) and (b)(4) of this section, in lieu of filing such information, a Security Futures Product Exchange may satisfy this filing requirement by:

(A) Identifying the publication in which such information is available, the name, address, and telephone number of the person from whom such publication may be obtained, and the price of such publication; and

(B) Certifying to the accuracy of such information as of its publication date.

(ii) If a Security Futures Product Exchange keeps the information required under paragraphs (b)(3) and (b)(4) of this section up-to-date and makes it available to the Commission and the public upon request, in lieu of filing such information, a Security Futures Product Exchange may satisfy this filing requirement by certifying that the information is kept up-to-date and is available to the Commission and the public upon request.

(iii) If the information required to be filed under paragraphs (b)(3) and (b)(4) of this section is available continuously on an Internet web site controlled by a Security Futures Product Exchange, in lieu of filing such information with the Commission, such Security Futures Product Exchange may satisfy this filing requirement by:

(A) Indicating the location of the Internet web site where such information may be found; and

(B) Certifying that the information available at such location is accurate as of its date.

(6)(i) The Commission may exempt a Security Futures Product Exchange from filing the amendment required by this section for any affiliate or subsidiary listed in Exhibit C to Form 1–N (§ 249.10 of this chapter), as amended, that either:

(A) Is listed in Exhibit C to Form 1 (§ 249.1 of this chapter) or to Form 1–N (§ 249.10 of this chapter), as amended, of one or more other national securities exchanges; or

(B) Was an inactive affiliate or subsidiary throughout the affiliate's or subsidiary's latest fiscal year.

(ii) Any such exemption may be granted upon terms and conditions the Commission deems necessary or appropriate in the public interest or for the protection of investors, provided however, that at least one national securities exchange shall be required to file the amendments required by this section for an affiliate or subsidiary described in paragraph (b)(6)(i) of this section.

(7) If a Security Futures Product Exchange has filed documents with the Commodity Futures Trading Commission, to the extent that such documents contain information satisfying the Commission's informational requirements, copies of such documents may be filed with the Commission in lieu of the required written notice.

(c) *Supplemental material to be filed by Security Futures Product Exchanges.* (1)(i) A Security Futures Product Exchange shall file with the Commission any material related to the trading of security futures products (including notices, circulars, bulletins, lists, and periodicals) issued or made generally available to members of, participants in, or subscribers to, the exchange. Such material shall be filed with the Commission within ten days after issuing or making such material available to members, participants, or subscribers.

(ii) If the information required to be filed under paragraph (c)(1)(i) of this section is available continuously on an Internet web site controlled by an exchange, in lieu of filing such information with the Commission, such exchange may:

(A) Indicate the location of the Internet web site where such information may be found; and

§ 240.6h-1

(B) Certify that the information available at such location is accurate as of its date.

(2) Within 15 days after the end of each calendar month, a Security Futures Product Exchange shall file a report concerning the security futures products traded on such exchange during the previous calendar month. Such a report shall:

(i) For each contract of sale for future delivery of a single security, the number of contracts traded on such exchange during the relevant calendar month and the total number of shares underlying such contracts traded; and

(ii) For each contract of sale for future delivery of a narrow-based security index, the number of contracts traded on such exchange during the relevant calendar month and the total number of shares represented by the index underlying such contracts traded.

[66 FR 43741, Aug. 20, 2001]

§ 240.6h-1 Settlement and regulatory halt requirements for security futures products.

(a) For the purposes of this section:

(1) *Opening price* means the price at which a security opened for trading, or a price that fairly reflects the price at which a security opened for trading, during the regular trading session of the national securities exchange or national securities association that lists the security. If the security is not listed on a national securities exchange or a national securities association, then *opening price* shall mean the price at which a security opened for trading, or a price that fairly reflects the price at which a security opened for trading, on the primary market for the security.

(2) *Regular trading session* of a security means the normal hours for business of a national securities exchange or national securities association that lists the security.

(3) *Regulatory halt* means a delay, halt, or suspension in the trading of a security, that is instituted by the national securities exchange or national securities association that lists the security, as a result of:

(i) A determination that there are matters relating to the security or issuer that have not been adequately disclosed to the public, or that there are regulatory problems relating to the security which should be clarified before trading is permitted to continue; or

(ii) The operation of circuit breaker procedures to halt or suspend trading in all equity securities trading on that national securities exchange or national securities association.

(b) *Final settlement prices for security futures products.* (1) The final settlement price of a cash-settled security futures product must fairly reflect the opening price of the underlying security or securities.

(2) Notwithstanding paragraph (b)(1) of this section, if an opening price for one or more securities underlying a security futures product is not readily available, the final settlement price of the security futures product shall fairly reflect:

(i) The price of the underlying security or securities during the most recent regular trading session for such security or securities; or

(ii) The next available opening price of the underlying security or securities.

(3) Notwithstanding paragraph (b)(1) or (b)(2) of this section, if a clearing agency registered under Section 17A of the Act (15 U.S.C. 78q-1), or exempt from registration pursuant to Section 17A(b)(7) of the Act (15 U.S.C. 78q-1(b)(7)), to which the final settlement price of a security futures product is or would be reported determines, pursuant to its rules, that such final settlement price is not consistent with the protection of investors and the public interest, taking into account such factors as fairness to buyers and sellers of the affected security futures product, the maintenance of a fair and orderly market in such security futures product, and consistency of interpretation and practice, the clearing agency shall have the authority to determine, under its rules, a final settlement price for such security futures product.

(c) *Regulatory trading halts.* The rules of a national securities exchange or national securities association registered pursuant to Section 15A(a) of the Act (15 U.S.C. 78o-3(a)) that lists or trades one or more security futures products must include the following provisions:

Securities and Exchange Commission § 240.8c–1

(1) Trading of a security futures product based on a single security shall be halted at all times that a regulatory halt has been instituted for the underlying security; and

(2) Trading of a security futures product based on a narrow-based security index shall be halted at all times that a regulatory halt has been instituted for one or more underlying securities that constitute 50 percent or more of the market capitalization of the narrow-based security index.

(d) The Commission may exempt from the requirements of this section, either unconditionally or on specified terms and conditions, any national securities exchange or national securities association, if the Commission determines that such exemption is necessary or appropriate in the public interest and consistent with the protection of investors. An exemption granted pursuant to this paragraph shall not operate as an exemption from any Commodity Futures Trading Commission rules. Any exemption that may be required from such rules must be obtained separately from the Commodity Futures Trading Commission.

[67 FR 36762, May 24, 2002]

§ 240.6h–2 Security future based on note, bond, debenture, or evidence of indebtedness.

A security future may be based upon a security that is a note, bond, debenture, or evidence of indebtedness or a narrow-based security index composed of such securities.

[71 FR 39543, July 13, 2006]

§ 240.7c2–1 [Reserved]

HYPOTHECATION OF CUSTOMERS' SECURITIES

§ 240.8c–1 Hypothecation of customers' securities.

(a) *General provisions.* No member of a national securities exchange, and no broker or dealer who transacts a business in securities through the medium of any such member shall, directly or indirectly, hypothecate or arrange for or permit the continued hypothecation of any securities carried for the account of any customer under circumstances:

(1) That will permit the commingling of securities carried for the account of any such customer with securities carried for the account of any other customer, without first obtaining the written consent of each such customer to such hypothecation;

(2) That will permit such securities to be commingled with securities carried for the account of any person other than a bona fide customer of such member, broker or dealer under a lien for a loan made to such member, broker or dealer; or

(3) That will permit securities carried for the account of customers to be hypothecated or subjected to any lien or liens or claim or claims of the pledges or pledgees, for a sum which exceeds the aggregate indebtedness of all customers in respect of securities carried for their accounts; except that this clause shall not be deemed to be violated by reason of an excess arising on any day through the reduction of the aggregate indebtedness of customers on such day, provided that funds or securities in an amount sufficient to eliminate such excess are paid or placed in transfer to pledgees for the purpose of reducing the sum of the liens or claims to which securities carried for the account of customers are subjected as promptly as practicable after such reduction occurs, but before the lapse of one-half hour after the commencement of banking hours on the next banking day at the place where the largest principal amount of loans of such member, broker or dealer are payable and, in any event, before such member, broker or dealer on such day has obtained or increased any bank loan collateralized by securities carried for the account of customers.

(b) *Definitions.* For the purposes of this section:

(1) The term *customer* shall not include any general or special partner or any director or officer of such member, broker or dealer, or any participant, as such, in any joint, group or syndicate account with such member, broker or dealer or with any partner, officer or director thereof. The term also shall not include any counterparty who has delivered collateral to an OTC derivatives dealer pursuant to a transaction

§ 240.8c-1

in an eligible OTC derivative instrument, or pursuant to the OTC derivatives dealer's cash management securities activities or ancillary portfolio management securities activities, and who has received a prominent written notice from the OTC derivatives dealer that:

(i) Except as otherwise agreed in writing by the OTC derivatives dealer and the counterparty, the dealer may repledge or otherwise use the collateral in its business;

(ii) In the event of the OTC derivatives dealer's failure, the counterparty will likely be considered an unsecured creditor of the dealer as to that collateral;

(iii) The Securities Investor Protection Act of 1970 (15 U.S.C. 78aaa through 78lll) does not protect the counterparty; and

(iv) The collateral will not be subject to the requirements of § 240.8c-1, § 240.15c2-1, § 240.15c3-2, or § 240.15c3-3;

(2) The term *securities carried for the account of any customer* shall be deemed to mean:

(i) Securities received by or on behalf of such member, broker or dealer for the account of any customer;

(ii) Securities sold and appropriated by such member, broker or dealer to a customer, except that if such securities were subject to a lien when appropriated to a customer they shall not be deemed to be "securities carried for the account of any customer" pending their release from such lien as promptly as practicable;

(iii) Securities sold, but not appropriated, by such member, broker or dealer to a customer who has made any payment therefor, to the extent that such member, broker or dealer owns and has received delivery of securities of like kind, except that if such securities were subject to a lien when such payment was made they shall not be deemed to be "securities carried for the account of any customer" pending their release from such lien as promptly as practicable:

(3) "Aggregate indebtedness" shall not be deemed to be reduced by reason of uncollected items. In computing aggregate indebtedness, related guaranteed and guarantor accounts shall be treated as a single account and considered on a consolidated basis, and balances in accounts carrying both long and short positions shall be adjusted by treating the market value of the securities required to cover such short positions as though such market value were a debit; and

(4) In computing the sum of the liens or claims to which securities carried for the account of customers of a member, broker or dealer are subject, any rehypothecation of such securities by another member, broker or dealer who is subject to this section or to § 240.15c2-1 shall be disregarded.

(c) *Exemption for cash accounts.* The provisions of paragraph (a)(1) of this section shall not apply to any hypothecation of securities carried for the account of a customer in a special cash account within the meaning of 12 CFR 220.4(c): *Provided,* That at or before the completion of the transaction of purchase of such securities for, or of sale of such securities to, such customer, written notice is given or sent to such customer disclosing that such securities are or may be hypothecated under circumstances which will permit the commingling thereof with securities carried for the account of other customers. The term *the completion of the transaction* shall have the meaning given to such term by § 240.15c1-1(b).

(d) *Exemption for clearinghouse liens.* The provisions of paragraphs (a)(2), (a)(3), and (f) of this section shall not apply to any lien or claim of the clearing corporation, or similar department or association, of a national securities exchange or a registered national securities association for a loan made and to be repaid on the same calendar day, which is incidental to the clearing of transactions in securities or loans through such corporation, department, or association: *Provided, however,* That for the purpose of paragraph (a)(3) of this section, "aggregate indebtedness of all customers in respect of securities carried for their accounts" shall not include indebtedness in respect of any securities subject to any lien or claim exempted by this paragraph.

(e) *Exemption for certain liens on securities of noncustomers.* The provisions of paragraph (a)(2) of this section shall not be deemed to prevent such member,

Securities and Exchange Commission § 240.8c–1

broker or dealer from permitting securities not carried for the account of a customer to be subjected (1) to a lien for a loan made against securities carried for the account of customers, or (2) to a lien for a loan made and to be repaid on the same calendar day. For the purpose of this exemption, a loan shall be deemed to be "made against securities carried for the account of customers" if only securities carried for the account of customers are used to obtain or to increase such loan or as substitutes for other securities carried for the account of customers.

(f) *Notice and certification requirements.* No person subject to this section shall hypothecate any security carried for the account of a customer unless at or prior to the time of each such hypothecation, he gives written notice to the pledgee that the security pledged is carried for the account of a customer and that such hypothecation does not contravene any provision of this section, except that in the case of an omnibus account the members, broker or dealer for whom such account is carried may furnish a signed statement to the person carrying such account that all securities carried therein by such member, broker or dealer will be securities carried for the account of his customers and that the hypothecation thereof by such member, broker or dealer will not contravene any provision of this section. The provisions of this paragraph shall not apply to any hypothecation of securities under any lien or claim of a pledgee securing a loan made and to be repaid on the same calendar day.

(g) The fact that securities carried for the accounts of customers and securities carried for the accounts of others are represented by one or more certificates in the custody of a clearing corporation or other subsidiary organization of either a national securities exchange or of a registered national securities association, or of a custodian bank, in accordance with a system for the central handling of securities established by a national securities exchange or a registered national securities association, pursuant to which system the hypothecation of such securities is effected by bookkeeping entries without physical delivery of such securities, shall not, in and of itself, result in a commingling of securities prohibited by paragraph (a)(1) or (a)(2) of this section, whenever a participating member, broker or dealer hypothecates securities in accordance with such system: *Provided, however,* That (1) any such custodian of any securities held by or for such system shall agree that it will not for any reason, including the assertion of any claim, right or lien of any kind, refuse to refrain from promptly delivering any such securities (other than securities then hypothecated in accordance with such system) to such clearing corporation or other subsidiary organization or as directed by it, except that nothing in such agreement shall be deemed to require the custodian to deliver any securities in contravention of any notice of levy, seizure or similar notice, or order or judgment, issued or directed by a governmental agency or court, or officer thereof, having jurisdiction over such custodian, which on its face affects such securities; (2) such systems shall have safeguards in the handling, transfer and delivery of securities and provisions for fidelity bond coverage of the employees and agents of the clearing corporation or other subsidiary organization and for periodic examinations by independent public accountants; and (3) the provisions of this paragraph shall not be effective with respect to any particular system unless the agreement required by paragraph (g)(1) of this section and the safeguards and provisions required by paragraph (g)(2) of this section shall have been deemed adequate by the Commission for the protection of investors, and unless any subsequent amendments to such agreement, safeguards or provisions shall have been deemed adequate by the Commission for the protection of investors.

(Secs. 3, 8, 15, 48 Stat. 882, 888, 895; 15 U.S.C. 78c, 78h, 78o)

CROSS REFERENCE: For interpretative releases applicable to §240.8c–1, see Nos. 2690 and 2822 in tabulation, part 241 of this chapter.

[13 FR 8180, Dec. 22, 1948, as amended at 31 FR 7740, June 1, 1966; 37 FR 73, Jan. 5, 1973; 63 FR 59395, Nov. 3, 1998]

§ 240.9b-1 Options disclosure document.

(a) *Definitions.* The following definitions shall apply for the purpose of this rule.

(1) *Options market* means a national securities exchange, an automated quotation system of a registered securities association or a foreign securities exchange on which standardized options are traded.

(2) *Options class* means all options contracts covering the same underlying instrument.

(3) *Options disclosure document* means a document, including all amendments and supplements thereto, prepared by one or more options markets which has been filed with the Commission or distributed in accordance with paragraph (b) of this section. *Definitive options disclosure document* or *document* means an options disclosure document furnished to customers in accordance with paragraph (b) of this section.

(4) *Standardized options* are options contracts trading on a national securities exchange, an automated quotation system of a registered securities association, or a foreign securities exchange which relate to options classes the terms of which are limited to specific expiration dates and exercise prices, or such other securities as the Commission may, by order, designate.

(b)(1) Five preliminary copies of an options disclosure document containing the information specified in paragraph (c) of this section shall be filed with the Commission by an options market at least 60 days prior to the date definitive copies are furnished to customers, unless the commission determines otherwise having due regard to the adequacy of the information disclosed and the public interest and protection of investors. Five copies of the definitive options disclosure document shall be filed with the Commission not later than the date the options disclosure document is furnished to customers. Notwithstanding the above, the use of an options disclosure document shall not be permitted unless the options class to which such document relates is the subject of an effective registration statement on Form S-20 under the Securities Act of 1933, or is exempt from registration under the Securities Act of 1933 (15 U.S.C. 77a *et seq.*).

(2)(i) If the information contained in the options disclosure document becomes or will become materially inaccurate or incomplete or there is or will be an omission of material information necessary to make the options disclosure document not misleading, the options market shall amend or supplement its options disclosure document by filing five copies of an amendment or supplement to such options disclosure document with the Commission at least 30 days prior to the date definitive copies are furnished to customers, unless the Commission determines otherwise having due regard to the adequacy of the information disclosed and the public interest and protection of investors. Five copies of the definitive options disclosure document, as amended or supplemented, shall be filed with the Commission not later than the date the amendment or supplement, or the amended options disclosure document, is furnished to customers.

(ii) Notwithstanding paragraph (b)(2)(i) of this section, an options market may distribute an amendment or supplement to an options disclosure document prior to such 30 day period if it determines, in good faith, that such delivery is necessary to ensure timely and accurate disclosure with respect to one or more of the options classes covered by the document. Five copies of any amendment or supplement distributed pursuant to this paragraph shall be filed with the Commission at the time of distribution. In that instance, if the Commission determines, having given due regard to the adequacy of the information disclosed and the public interest and the protection of investors, it may require refiling of the amendment pursuant to paragraph (b)(2)(i) of this section.

(c) *Information required in an options disclosure document.* An options disclosure document shall contain the following information, unless otherwise provided by the Commission, with respect to the options classes covered by the document:

(1) A glossary of terms;

(2) A discussion of the mechanics of exercising the options;

Securities and Exchange Commission § 240.10b–3

(3) A discussion of the risks of being a holder or writer of the options;

(4) The identification of the market or markets in which the options are traded;

(5) A brief reference to the transaction costs, margin requirements and tax consequences of options trading;

(6) The identification of the issuer of the options;

(7) A general identification of the type of instrument or instruments underlying the options class or classes covered by the document;

(8) If the options are not exempt from registration under the Securities Act of 1933 (15 U.S.C. 77a *et seq.*), the registration of the options on form S–20 (17 CFR 239.20) and the availability of the prospectus and the information in part II of the registration statement; and

(9) Such other information as the Commission may specify.

(d) *Broker-dealer obligations.* (1) No broker or dealer shall accept an order from a customer to purchase or sell an option contract relating to an options class that is the subject of a definitive options disclosure document, or approve the customer's account for the trading of such option, unless the broker or dealer furnishes or has furnished to the customer a copy of the definitive options disclosure document.

(2) If a definitive options disclosure document relating to an options class is amended or supplemented, each broker and dealer shall promptly send a copy of the definitive amendment or supplement or a copy of the definitive options disclosure document as amended to each customer whose account is approved for trading the options class or classes to which the amendment or supplement relates.

[47 FR 41956, Sept. 23, 1982, as amended at 51 FR 14982, Apr. 22, 1986; 65 FR 64139, Oct. 26, 2000; 68 FR 192, Jan. 2, 2003]

§§ 240.10a–1—240.10a–2 [Reserved]

MANIPULATIVE AND DECEPTIVE DEVICES AND CONTRIVANCES

§ 240.10b–1 Prohibition of use of manipulative or deceptive devices or contrivances with respect to certain securities exempted from registration.

The term *manipulative or deceptive device or contrivance,* as used in section 10(b) (48 Stat. 891; 15 U.S.C. 78j(b)), is hereby defined to include any act or omission to act with respect to any security exempted from the operation of section 12(a) (48 Stat. 892; 15 U.S.C. 78*l*(a)) pursuant to any section in this part which specifically provides that this section shall be applicable to such security if such act or omission to act would have been unlawful under section 9(a) (48 Stat. 889; 15 U.S.C. 78i(a)), or any rule or regulation heretofore or hereafter prescribed thereunder, if done or omitted to be done with respect to a security registered on a national securities exchange, and the use of any means or instrumentality of interstate commerce or of the mails or of any facility of any national securities exchange to use or employ any such device or contrivance in connection with the purchase or sale of any such security is hereby prohibited.

(Secs. 10, 12, 48 Stat. 891, 892; 15 U.S.C. 78j, 78*l*)

CROSS REFERENCES: For applicability of this section, see §§ 240.12a–4 and 240.12a–5. For regulations relating to employment of manipulative and deceptive devices, see §§ 240.10b–3 and 240.10b–5.

[13 FR 8183, Dec. 22, 1948]

§ 240.10b–2 [Reserved]

§ 240.10b–3 Employment of manipulative and deceptive devices by brokers or dealers.

(a) It shall be unlawful for any broker or dealer, directly or indirectly, by the use of any means or instrumentality of interstate commerce, or of the mails, or of any facility of any national securities exchange, to use or employ, in connection with the purchase or sale of any security otherwise than on a national securities exchange, any act, practice, or course of business defined

§ 240.10b-4

by the Commission to be included within the term "manipulative, deceptive, or other fraudulent device or contrivance", as such term is used in section 15(c)(1) of the act.

(b) It shall be unlawful for any municipal securities dealer directly or indirectly, by the use of any means or instrumentality of interstate commerce, or of the mails, or of any facility of any national securities exchange, to use or employ, in connection with the purchase or sale of any municipal security, any act, practice, or course of business defined by the Commission to be included within the term "manipulative, deceptive, or other fraudulent device or contrivance," as such term is used in section 15(c)(1) of the act.

(Secs. 10, 12, 48 Stat. 891, 892, as amended; 15 U.S.C. 78j, 78*l*)

CROSS REFERENCES: See also § 240.10b-5. For regulation relating to prohibition of manipulative or deceptive devices, see § 240.10b-1. For the term "manipulative, deceptive, or other fraudulent device or contrivance", as used in section 15(c)(1) of the act, see §§ 240.15c1-2 to 240.15c1-9.

[13 FR 8183, Dec. 22, 1948, as amended at 19 FR 8017, Dec. 4, 1954; 41 FR 22824, June 7, 1976]

§ 240.10b-4 [Reserved]

§ 240.10b-5 Employment of manipulative and deceptive devices.

It shall be unlawful for any person, directly or indirectly, by the use of any means or instrumentality of interstate commerce, or of the mails or of any facility of any national securities exchange,

(a) To employ any device, scheme, or artifice to defraud,

(b) To make any untrue statement of a material fact or to omit to state a material fact necessary in order to make the statements made, in the light of the circumstances under which they were made, not misleading, or

(c) To engage in any act, practice, or course of business which operates or would operate as a fraud or deceit upon any person,

in connection with the purchase or sale of any security.

(Sec. 10; 48 Stat. 891; 15 U.S.C. 78j)

[13 FR 8183, Dec. 22, 1948, as amended at 16 FR 7928, Aug. 11, 1951]

§ 240.10b5-1 Trading "on the basis of" material nonpublic information in insider trading cases.

(a) *Manipulative or deceptive devices.* The "manipulative or deceptive device[s] or contrivance[s]" prohibited by Section 10(b) of the Act (15 U.S.C. 78j) and § 240.10b-5 (Rule 10b-5) thereunder include, among other things, the purchase or sale of a security of any issuer, on the basis of material nonpublic information about that security or issuer, in breach of a duty of trust or confidence that is owed directly, indirectly, or derivatively, to the issuer of that security or the shareholders of that issuer, or to any other person who is the source of the material nonpublic information.

(b) *Awareness of material nonpublic information.* Subject to the affirmative defenses in paragraph (c) of this section, a purchase or sale of a security of an issuer is on the basis of material nonpublic information for purposes of Section 10(b) and Rule 10b-5 if the person making the purchase or sale was aware of the material nonpublic information when the person made the purchase or sale. The law of insider trading is otherwise defined by judicial opinions construing Rule 10b-5, and Rule 10b5-1 does not modify the scope of insider trading law in any other respect.

(c) *Affirmative defenses.* (1)(i) Subject to paragraph (1)(ii) of this section, a person's purchase or sale is not on the basis of material nonpublic information if the person making the purchase or sale demonstrates that:

(A) Before becoming aware of the information, the person had:

(*1*) Entered into a binding contract to purchase or sell the security,

(*2*) Instructed another person to purchase or sell the security for the instructing person's account, or

(*3*) Adopted a written plan for trading securities;

(B) The contract, instruction, or plan described in paragraph (c)(1)(i)(A) of this section:

(*1*) Specified the amount of securities to be purchased or sold and the price at which and the date on which the securities were to be purchased or sold;

Securities and Exchange Commission § 240.10b5-1

(2) Included a written formula or algorithm, or computer program, for determining the amount of securities to be purchased or sold and the price at which and the date on which the securities were to be purchased or sold; or

(3) Did not permit the person to exercise any subsequent influence over how, when, or whether to effect purchases or sales; provided, in addition, that any other person who, pursuant to the contract, instruction, or plan, did exercise such influence must not have been aware of the material nonpublic information when doing so; and

(C) The purchase or sale that occurred was pursuant to the contract, instruction, or plan. A purchase or sale is not "pursuant to a contract, instruction, or plan" if, among other things, the person who entered into the contract, instruction, or plan altered or deviated from the contract, instruction, or plan to purchase or sell securities (whether by changing the amount, price, or timing of the purchase or sale), or entered into or altered a corresponding or hedging transaction or position with respect to those securities.

(ii) Paragraph (c)(1)(i) of this section is applicable only when:

(A) The contract, instruction, or plan to purchase or sell securities was given or entered into in good faith and not as part of a plan or scheme to evade the prohibitions of this section, and the person who entered into the contract, instruction, or plan has acted in good faith with respect to the contract, instruction or plan;

(B) If the person who entered into the contract, instruction, or plan is:

(1) A director or officer (as defined in §240.16a-1(f) (Rule 16a-1(f)) of the issuer, no purchases or sales occur until expiration of a cooling-off period consisting of the later of:

(i) Ninety days after the adoption of the contract, instruction, or plan or

(ii) Two business days following the disclosure of the issuer's financial results in a Form 10-Q (§249.308a of this chapter) or Form 10-K (§249.310 of this chapter) for the completed fiscal quarter in which the plan was adopted or, for foreign private issuers, in a Form 20-F (§249.220f of this chapter) or Form 6-K (§249.306 of this chapter) that discloses the issuer's financial results (but, in any event, this required cooling-off period is subject to a maximum of 120 days after adoption of the contract, instruction, or plan); or

(2) Not the issuer and not a director or officer (as defined in §240.16a-1(f) (Rule 16a-1(f)) of the issuer, no purchases or sales occur until the expiration of a cooling-off period that is 30 days after the adoption of the contract, instruction or plan;

(C) If the person who entered into a plan as described in paragraph (c)(1)(i)(A)(3) of this section is a director or officer (as defined in Rule 16a-1(f) (§240.16a-1(f)) of the issuer of the securities, such director or officer included a representation in the plan certifying that, on the date of adoption of the plan:

(1) The individual director or officer is not aware of any material nonpublic information about the security or issuer; and

(2) The individual director or officer is adopting the plan in good faith and not as part of a plan or scheme to evade the prohibitions of this section;

(D) The person (other than the issuer) who entered into the contract, instruction, or plan has no outstanding (and does not subsequently enter into any additional) contract, instruction, or plan that would qualify for the affirmative defense under paragraph (c)(1) of this section for purchases or sales of the issuer's securities on the open market; except that:

(1) For purposes of this paragraph (c)(1)(ii)(D), a series of separate contracts with different broker-dealers or other agents acting on behalf of the person (other than the issuer) to execute trades thereunder may be treated as a single "plan," provided that the individual constituent contracts with each broker-dealer or other agent, when taken together as a whole, meet all of the applicable conditions of and remain collectively subject to the provisions of this rule, including that a modification of any individual contract acts as modification of the whole contract, instruction of plan, as defined in paragraph (c)(1)(iv) of this section. The substitution of a broker-dealer or other agent acting on behalf of the person (other than the issuer) for another

§ 240.10b5–1

broker-dealer that is executing trades pursuant to a contract, instruction or plan shall not be a modification of the contract, instruction, or plan (as defined in paragraph (c)(1)(iv) of this section) as long as the purchase or sales instructions applicable to the substitute and substituted broker are identical with respect to the prices of securities to be purchased or sold, dates of the purchases or sales to be executed, and amount of securities to be purchased or sold; and

(*2*) The person (other than the issuer) may have one later-commencing contract, instruction, or plan for purchases or sales of any securities of the issuer on the open market under which trading is not authorized to begin until after all trades under the earlier-commencing contract, instruction, or plan are completed or expired without execution; provided, however, that if the first trade under the later-commencing contract, instruction, or plan is scheduled during the Effective Cooling-Off Period, the later-commencing contract, instruction, or plan may not rely on this paragraph (c)(1)(ii)(D)(*2*). For purposes of this paragraph (c)(1)(ii)(D)(*2*), "Effective Cooling-Off Period" means the cooling-off period that would be applicable under paragraph (c)(1)(ii)(B) of this section with respect to the later-commencing contract, instruction, or plan if the date of adoption of the later-commencing contract, instruction, or plan were deemed to be the date of termination of the earlier-commencing contract, instruction, or plan; and

(*3*) A contract, instruction, or plan providing for an eligible sell-to-cover transaction shall not be considered an outstanding or additional contract, instruction, or plan under paragraph (c)(1)(ii)(D) of this section, and such eligible sell-to-cover transaction shall not be subject to the limitation under paragraph (c)(1)(ii)(D) of this section. A contract, instruction, or plan provides for an eligible sell-to-cover transaction where the contract, instruction, or plan authorizes an agent to sell only such securities as are necessary to satisfy tax withholding obligations arising exclusively from the vesting of a compensatory award, such as restricted stock or stock appreciation rights, and

17 CFR Ch. II (4–1–23 Edition)

the insider does not otherwise exercise control over the timing of such sales; and

(E) With respect to persons (other than the issuer), if the contract, instruction, or plan does not provide for an eligible sell-to-cover transaction as described in paragraph (c)(1)(ii)(D)(*3*) of this section and is designed to effect the open-market purchase or sale of the total amount of securities as a single transaction, the person who entered into the contract, instruction, or plan has not during the prior 12-month period adopted a contract, instruction, or plan that:

(*1*) was designed to effect the open-market purchase or sale of all of the securities covered by such prior contract, instruction or plan, in a single transaction; and

(*2*) Would otherwise qualify for the affirmative defense under paragraph (c)(1) of this section.

(iii) This paragraph (c)(1)(iii) defines certain terms as used in paragraph (c) of this Section.

(A) *Amount.* "Amount" means either a specified number of shares or other securities or a specified dollar value of securities.

(B) *Price.* "Price" means the market price on a particular date or a limit price, or a particular dollar price.

(C) *Date.* "Date" means, in the case of a market order, the specific day of the year on which the order is to be executed (or as soon thereafter as is practicable under ordinary principles of best execution). "Date" means, in the case of a limit order, a day of the year on which the limit order is in force.

(iv) Any modification or change to the amount, price, or timing of the purchase or sale of the securities underlying a contract, instruction, or written plan as described in paragraph (c)(1)(i)(A) of this section is a termination of such contract, instruction, or written plan, and the adoption of a new contract, instruction, or written plan. A plan modification, such as the substitution or removal of a broker that is executing trades pursuant to a Rule 10b5–1 arrangement on behalf of the person, that changes the price or date on which purchases or sales are to be executed, is a termination of such plan and the adoption of a new plan.

Securities and Exchange Commission § 240.10b–9

(2) A person other than a natural person also may demonstrate that a purchase or sale of securities is not "on the basis of" material nonpublic information if the person demonstrates that:

(i) The individual making the investment decision on behalf of the person to purchase or sell the securities was not aware of the information; and

(ii) The person had implemented reasonable policies and procedures, taking into consideration the nature of the person's business, to ensure that individuals making investment decisions would not violate the laws prohibiting trading on the basis of material nonpublic information. These policies and procedures may include those that restrict any purchase, sale, and causing any purchase or sale of any security as to which the person has material nonpublic information, or those that prevent such individuals from becoming aware of such information.

[65 FR 51737, Aug. 24, 2000, as amended at 87 FR 80429, Dec. 29, 2022]

§ 240.10b5–2 Duties of trust or confidence in misappropriation insider trading cases.

PRELIMINARY NOTE TO § 240.10b5–2: This section provides a non-exclusive definition of circumstances in which a person has a duty of trust or confidence for purposes of the "misappropriation" theory of insider trading under Section 10(b) of the Act and Rule 10b–5. The law of insider trading is otherwise defined by judicial opinions construing Rule 10b–5, and Rule 10b5–2 does not modify the scope of insider trading law in any other respect.

(a) *Scope of Rule.* This section shall apply to any violation of Section 10(b) of the Act (15 U.S.C. 78j(b)) and § 240.10b–5 thereunder that is based on the purchase or sale of securities on the basis of, or the communication of, material nonpublic information misappropriated in breach of a duty of trust or confidence.

(b) *Enumerated "duties of trust or confidence."* For purposes of this section, a "duty of trust or confidence" exists in the following circumstances, among others:

(1) Whenever a person agrees to maintain information in confidence;

(2) Whenever the person communicating the material nonpublic information and the person to whom it is communicated have a history, pattern, or practice of sharing confidences, such that the recipient of the information knows or reasonably should know that the person communicating the material nonpublic information expects that the recipient will maintain its confidentiality; or

(3) Whenever a person receives or obtains material nonpublic information from his or her spouse, parent, child, or sibling; *provided,* however, that the person receiving or obtaining the information may demonstrate that no duty of trust or confidence existed with respect to the information, by establishing that he or she neither knew nor reasonably should have known that the person who was the source of the information expected that the person would keep the information confidential, because of the parties' history, pattern, or practice of sharing and maintaining confidences, and because there was no agreement or understanding to maintain the confidentiality of the information.

[65 FR 51738, Aug. 24, 2000]

§§ 240.10b–6—240.10b–8 [Reserved]

§ 240.10b–9 Prohibited representations in connection with certain offerings.

(a) It shall constitute a *manipulative or deception device or contrivance,* as used in section 10(b) of the Act, for any person, directly or indirectly, in connection with the offer or sale of any security, to make any representation:

(1) To the effect that the security is being offered or sold on an "all-or-none" basis, unless the security is part of an offering or distribution being made on the condition that all or a specified amount of the consideration paid for such security will be promptly refunded to the purchaser unless (i) all of the securities being offered are sold at a specified price within a specified time, and (ii) the total amount due to the seller is received by him by a specified date; or

(2) To the effect that the security is being offered or sold on any other basis whereby all or part of the consideration paid for any such security will be refunded to the purchaser if all or some

§ 240.10b-10

of the securities are not sold, unless the security is part of an offering or distribution being made on the condition that all or a specified part of the consideration paid for such security will be promptly refunded to the purchaser unless (i) a specified number of units of the security are sold at a specified price within a specified time, and (ii) the total amount due to the seller is received by him by a specified date.

(b) This rule shall not apply to any offer or sale of securities as to which the seller has a firm commitment from underwriters or others (subject only to customary conditions precedent, including "market outs") for the purchase of all the securities being offered.

(Sec. 10, 48 Stat. 891, as amended; 15 U.S.C. 78j)

[27 FR 9943, Oct. 10, 1962]

§ 240.10b-10 Confirmation of transactions.

PRELIMINARY NOTE. This section requires broker-dealers to disclose specified information in writing to customers at or before completion of a transaction. The requirements under this section that particular information be disclosed is not determinative of a broker-dealer's obligation under the general antifraud provisions of the federal securities laws to disclose additional information to a customer at the time of the customer's investment decision.

(a) *Disclosure requirement.* It shall be unlawful for any broker or dealer to effect for or with an account of a customer any transaction in, or to induce the purchase or sale by such customer of, any security (other than U.S. Savings Bonds or municipal securities) unless such broker or dealer, at or before completion of such transaction, gives or sends to such customer written notification disclosing:

(1) The date and time of the transaction (or the fact that the time of the transaction will be furnished upon written request to such customer) and the identity, price, and number of shares or units (or principal amount) of such security purchased or sold by such customer; and

(2) Whether the broker or dealer is acting as agent for such customer, as agent for some other person, as agent for both such customer and some other person, or as principal for its own account; and if the broker or dealer is acting as principal, whether it is a market maker in the security (other than by reason of acting as a block positioner); and

(i) If the broker or dealer is acting as agent for such customer, for some other person, or for both such customer and some other person:

(A) The name of the person from whom the security was purchased, or to whom it was sold, for such customer or the fact that the information will be furnished upon written request of such customer; and

(B) The amount of any remuneration received or to be received by the broker from such customer in connection with the transaction unless remuneration paid by such customer is determined pursuant to written agreement with such customer, otherwise than on a transaction basis; and

(C) For a transaction in any NMS stock as defined in § 242.600 of this chapter or a security authorized for quotation on an automated interdealer quotation system that has the characteristics set forth in section 17B of the Act (15 U.S.C. 78q–2), a statement whether payment for order flow is received by the broker or dealer for transactions in such securities and the fact that the source and nature of the compensation received in connection with the particular transaction will be furnished upon written request of the customer; *provided, however,* that brokers or dealers that do not receive payment for order flow in connection with any transaction have no disclosure obligations under this paragraph; and

(D) The source and amount of any other remuneration received or to be received by the broker in connection with the transaction: *Provided, however,* that if, in the case of a purchase, the broker was not participating in a distribution, or in the case of a sale, was not participating in a tender offer, the written notification may state whether any other remuneration has been or will be received and the fact that the source and amount of such other remuneration will be furnished upon written request of such customer; or

Securities and Exchange Commission § 240.10b-10

(ii) If the broker or dealer is acting as principal for its own account:

(A) In the case where such broker or dealer is not a market maker in an equity security and, if, after having received an order to buy from a customer, the broker or dealer purchased the equity security from another person to offset a contemporaneous sale to such customer or, after having received an order to sell from a customer, the broker or dealer sold the security to another person to offset a contemporaneous purchase from such customer, the difference between the price to the customer and the dealer's contemporaneous purchase (for customer purchases) or sale price (for customer sales); or

(B) In the case of any other transaction in an NMS stock as defined by § 242.600 of this chapter, or an equity security that is traded on a national securities exchange and that is subject to last sale reporting, the reported trade price, the price to the customer in the transaction, and the difference, if any, between the reported trade price and the price to the customer.

(3) Whether any odd-lot differential or equivalent fee has been paid by such customer in connection with the execution of an order for an odd-lot number of shares or units (or principal amount) of a security and the fact that the amount of any such differential or fee will be furnished upon oral or written request: *Provided, however*, that such disclosure need not be made if the differential or fee is included in the remuneration disclosure, or exempted from disclosure, pursuant to paragraph (a)(2)(i)(B) of this section; and

(4) In the case of any transaction in a debt security subject to redemption before maturity, a statement to the effect that such debt security may be redeemed in whole or in part before maturity, that such a redemption could affect the yield represented and the fact that additional information is available upon request; and

(5) In the case of a transaction in a debt security effected exclusively on the basis of a dollar price:

(i) The dollar price at which the transaction was effected, and

(ii) The yield to maturity calculated from the dollar price: *Provided, however*, that this paragraph (a)(5)(ii) shall not apply to a transaction in a debt security that either:

(A) Has a maturity date that may be extended by the issuer thereof, with a variable interest payable thereon; or

(B) Is an asset-backed security, that represents an interest in or is secured by a pool of receivables or other financial assets that are subject continuously to prepayment; and

(6) In the case of a transaction in a debt security effected on the basis of yield:

(i) The yield at which the transaction was effected, including the percentage amount and its characterization (e.g., current yield, yield to maturity, or yield to call) and if effected at yield to call, the type of call, the call date and call price; and

(ii) The dollar price calculated from the yield at which the transaction was effected; and

(iii) If effected on a basis other than yield to maturity and the yield to maturity is lower than the represented yield, the yield to maturity as well as the represented yield; *Provided, however*, that this paragraph (a)(6)(iii) shall not apply to a transaction in a debt security that either:

(A) Has a maturity date that may be extended by the issuer thereof, with a variable interest rate payable thereon; or

(B) Is an asset-backed security, that represents an interest in or is secured by a pool of receivables or other financial assets that are subject continuously to prepayment; and

(7) In the case of a transaction in a debt security that is an asset-backed security, which represents an interest in or is secured by a pool of receivables or other financial assets that are subject continuously to prepayment, a statement indicating that the actual yield of such asset-backed security may vary according to the rate at which the underlying receivables or other financial assets are prepaid and a statement of the fact that information concerning the factors that affect yield (including at a minimum estimated yield, weighted average life, and the prepayment assumptions underlying yield) will be furnished upon written request of such customer; and

§ 240.10b–10

(8) That the broker or dealer is not a member of the Securities Investor Protection Corporation (SIPC), or that the broker or dealer clearing or carrying the customer account is not a member of SIPC, if such is the case: *Provided, however,* that this paragraph (a)(9) shall not apply in the case of a transaction in shares of a registered open-end investment company or unit investment trust if:

(i) The customer sends funds or securities directly to, or receives funds or securities directly from, the registered open-end investment company or unit investment trust, its transfer agent, its custodian, or other designated agent, and such person is not an associated person of the broker or dealer required by paragraph (a) of this section to send written notification to the customer; and

(ii) The written notification required by paragraph (a) of this section is sent on behalf of the broker or dealer to the customer by a person described in paragraph (a)(9)(i) of this section.

(b) *Alternative periodic reporting.* A broker or dealer may effect transactions for or with the account of a customer without giving or sending to such customer the written notification described in paragraph (a) of this section if:

(1) Such transactions are effected pursuant to a periodic plan or an investment company plan, or effected in shares of any open-end management investment company registered under the Investment Company Act of 1940 that holds itself out as a money market fund and attempts to maintain a stable net asset value per share: *Provided, however,* that no sales load is deducted upon the purchase or redemption of shares in the money market fund; and

(2) Such broker or dealer gives or sends to such customer within five business days after the end of each *quarterly* period, for transactions involving investment company and periodic plans, and after the end of each *monthly* period, for other transactions described in paragraph (b)(1) of this section, a written statement disclosing each purchase or redemption, effected for or with, and each dividend or distribution credited to or reinvested for, the account of such customer during the month; the date of such transaction; the identity, number, and price of any securities purchased or redeemed by such customer in each such transaction; the total number of shares of such securities in such customer's account; any remuneration received or to be received by the broker or dealer in connection therewith; and that any other information required by paragraph (a) of this section will be furnished upon written request: *Provided, however,* that the written statement may be delivered to some other person designated by the customer for distribution to the customer; and

(3) Such customer is provided with prior notification in writing disclosing the intention to send the written information referred to in paragraph (b)(1) of this section in lieu of an immediate confirmation.

(c) A broker or dealer shall give or send to a customer information requested pursuant to this rule within 5 business days of receipt of the request: *Provided, however,* That in the case of information pertaining to a transaction effected more than 30 days prior to receipt of the request, the information shall be given or sent to the customer within 15 business days.

(d) *Definitions.* For the purposes of this section:

(1) *Customer* shall not include a broker or dealer;

(2) *Completion of the transaction* shall have the meaning provided in rule 15c1–1 under the Act;

(3) *Time of the transaction* means the time of execution, to the extent feasible, of the customer's order;

(4) *Debt security* as used in paragraphs (a)(3), (4), and (5) only, means any security, such as a bond, debenture, note, or any other similar instrument which evidences a liability of the issuer (including any such security that is convertible into stock or a similar security) and fractional or participation interests in one or more of any of the foregoing: *Provided, however,* That securities issued by an investment company registered under the Investment Company Act of 1940 shall not be included in this definition;

(5) *Periodic plan* means any written authorization for a broker acting as

Securities and Exchange Commission

§ 240.10b-10

agent to purchase or sell for a customer a specific security or securities (other than securities issued by an open end investment company or unit investment trust registered under the Investment Company Act of 1940), in specific amounts (calculated in security units or dollars), at specific time intervals and setting forth the commissions or charges to be paid by the customer in connection therewith (or the manner of calculating them); and

(6) *Investment company plan* means any plan under which securities issued by an open-end investment company or unit investment trust registered under the Investment Company Act of 1940 are purchased by a customer (the payments being made directly to, or made payable to, the registered investment company, or the principal underwriter, custodian, trustee, or other designated agent of the registered investment company), or sold by a customer pursuant to:

(i) An individual retirement or individual pension plan qualified under the Internal Revenue Code;

(ii) A contractual or systematic agreement under which the customer purchases at the applicable public offering price, or redeems at the applicable redemption price, such securities in specified amounts (calculated in security units or dollars) at specified time intervals and setting forth the commissions or charges to be paid by such customer in connection therewith (or the manner of calculating them; or

(iii) Any other arrangement involving a group of two or more customers and contemplating periodic purchases of such securities by each customer through a person designated by the group: *Provided,* That such arrangement requires the registered investment company or its agent—

(A) To give or send to the designated person, at or before the completion of the transaction for the purchase of such securities, a written notification of the receipt of the total amount paid by the group;

(B) To send to anyone in the group who was a customer in the prior quarter and on whose behalf payment has not been received in the current quarter a quarterly written statement reflecting that a payment was not received on his behalf; and

(C) To advise each customer in the group if a payment is not received from the designated person on behalf of the group within 10 days of a date certain specified in the arrangement for delivery of that payment by the designated person and thereafter to send to each such customer the written notification described in paragraph (a) of this section for the next three succeeding payments.

(7) *NMS stock* shall have the meaning provided in § 242.600 of this chapter.

(8) *Payment for order flow* shall mean any monetary payment, service, property, or other benefit that results in remuneration, compensation, or consideration to a broker or dealer from any broker or dealer, national securities exchange, registered securities association, or exchange member in return for the routing of customer orders by such broker or dealer to any broker or dealer, national securities exchange, registered securities association, or exchange member for execution, including but not limited to: research, clearance, custody, products or services; reciprocal agreements for the provision of order flow; adjustment of a broker or dealer's unfavorable trading errors; offers to participate as underwriter in public offerings; stock loans or shared interest accrued thereon; discounts, rebates, or any other reductions of or credits against any fee to, or expense or other financial obligation of, the broker or dealer routing a customer order that exceeds that fee, expense or financial obligation.

(9) *Asset-backed security* means a security that is primarily serviced by the cashflows of a discrete pool of receivables or other financial assets, either fixed or revolving, that by their terms convert into cash within a finite time period plus any rights or other assets designed to assure the servicing or timely distribution of proceeds to the security holders.

(e) *Security futures products.* The provisions of paragraphs (a) and (b) of this section shall not apply to a broker or dealer registered pursuant to section 15(b)(11)(A) of the Act (15 U.S.C.

§ 240.10b-13

78o(b)(11)(A)) to the extent that it effects transactions for customers in security futures products in a futures account (as that term is defined in § 240.15c3–3(a)(15)) and a broker or dealer registered pursuant to section 15(b)(1) of the Act (15 U.S.C. 78o(b)(1)) that is also a futures commission merchant registered pursuant to section 4f(a)(1) of the Commodity Exchange Act (7 U.S.C. 6f(a)(1)), to the extent that it effects transactions for customers in security futures products in a futures account (as that term is defined in § 240.15c3–3(a)(15)), *Provided* that:

(1) The broker or dealer that effects any transaction for a customer in security futures products in a futures account gives or sends to the customer no later than the next business day after execution of any futures securities product transaction, written notification disclosing:

(i) The date the transaction was executed, the identity of the single security or narrow-based security index underlying the contract for the security futures product, the number of contracts of such security futures product purchased or sold, the price, and the delivery month;

(ii) The source and amount of any remuneration received or to be received by the broker or dealer in connection with the transaction, including, but not limited to, markups, commissions, costs, fees, and other charges incurred in connection with the transaction, provided, however, that if no remuneration is to be paid for an initiating transaction until the occurrence of the corresponding liquidating transaction, that the broker or dealer may disclose the amount of remuneration only on the confirmation for the liquidating transaction;

(iii) The fact that information about the time of the execution of the transaction, the identity of the other party to the contract, and whether the broker or dealer is acting as agent for such customer, as agent for some other person, as agent for both such customer and some other person, or as principal for its own account, and if the broker or dealer is acting as principal, whether it is engaging in a block transaction or an exchange of security futures products for physical securities, will be available upon written request of the customer; and

(iv) Whether payment for order flow is received by the broker or dealer for such transactions, the amount of this payment and the fact that the source and nature of the compensation received in connection with the particular transaction will be furnished upon written request of the customer; provided, however, that brokers or dealers that do not receive payment for order flow have no disclosure obligation under this paragraph.

(2) *Transitional provision.* (i) Broker-dealers are not required to comply with paragraph (e)(1)(iii) of this section until June 1, 2003, *Provided* that, if, not withstanding the absence of the disclosure required in that paragraph, the broker-dealer receives a written request from a customer for the information described in paragraph (e)(1)(iii) of this section, the broker-dealer must make the information available to the customer; and

(ii) Broker-dealers are not required to comply with paragraph (e)(1)(iv) of this section until June 1, 2003.

(f) The Commission may exempt any broker or dealer from the requirements of paragraphs (a) and (b) of this section with regard to specific transactions of specific classes of transactions for which the broker or dealer will provide alternative procedures to effect the purposes of this section; any such exemption may be granted subject to compliance with such alternative procedures and upon such other stated terms and conditions as the Commission may impose.

[43 FR 47503, Oct. 16, 1978, as amended at 48 FR 17585, Apr. 25, 1983; 50 FR 37654, Sept. 17, 1985; 53 FR 40721, Oct. 18, 1988; 59 FR 55012, Nov. 2, 1994; 59 FR 59620, Nov. 17, 1994; 59 FR 60555, Nov. 25, 1994; 67 FR 58312, Sept. 13, 2002; 70 FR 37618, June 29, 2005; 79 FR 1549, Jan. 8, 2014]

§ 240.10b-13 [Reserved]

§ 240.10b-16 Disclosure of credit terms in margin transactions.

(a) It shall be unlawful for any broker or dealer to extend credit, directly or indirectly, to any customer in connection with any securities transaction unless such broker or dealer has

Securities and Exchange Commission § 240.10b-16

established procedures to assure that each customer:

(1) Is given or sent at the time of opening the account, a written statement or statements disclosing (i) the conditions under which an interest charge will be imposed; (ii) the annual rate or rates of interest that can be imposed; (iii) the method of computing interest; (iv) if rates of interest are subject to change without prior notice, the specific conditions under which they can be changed; (v) the method of determining the debit balance or balances on which interest is to be charged and whether credit is to be given for credit balances in cash accounts; (vi) what other charges resulting from the extension of credit, if any, will be made and under what conditions; and (vii) the nature of any interest or lien retained by the broker or dealer in the security or other property held as collateral and the conditions under which additional collateral can be required: *Provided, however,* That the requirements of this subparagraph will be met in any case where the account is opened by telephone if the information required to be disclosed is orally communicated to the customer at that time and the required written statement or statements are sent to the customer immediately thereafter: *And provided, further,* That in the case of customers to whom credit is already being extended on the effective date of this section, the written statement or statements required hereunder must be given or sent to said customers within 90 days after the effective date of this section; and

(2) Is given or sent a written statement or statements, at least quarterly, for each account in which credit was extended, disclosing (i) the balance at the beginning of the period; the date, amount and a brief description of each debit and credit entered during such period; the closing balance; and, if interest is charged for a period different from the period covered by the statement, the balance as of the last day of the interest period; (ii) the total interest charge for the period during which interest is charged (or, if interest is charged separately for separate accounts, the total interest charge for each such account), itemized to show the dates on which the interest period began and ended; the annual rate or rates of interest charged and the interest charge for each such different annual rate of interest; and either each different debit balance on which an interest calculation was based or the average debit balance for the interest period, except that if an average debit balance is used, a separate average debit balance must be disclosed for each interest rate applied; and (iii) all other charges resulting from the extension of credit in that account: *Provided, however,* That if the interest charge disclosed on a statement is for a period different from the period covered by the statement, there must be printed on the statement appropriate language to the effect that it should be retained for use in conjunction with the next statement containing the remainder of the required information: *And provided further,* That in the case of "equity funding programs" registered under the Securities Act of 1933, the requirements of this paragraph will be met if the broker or dealer furnishes to the customer, within 1 month after each extension of credit, a written statement or statements containing the information required to be disclosed under this paragraph.

(b) It shall be unlawful for any broker or dealer to make any changes in the terms and conditions under which credit charges will be made (as described in the initial statement made under paragraph (a) of this section), unless the customer shall have been given not less than thirty (30) days written notice of such changes, except that no such prior notice shall be necessary where such changes are required by law: *Provided, however,* That if any change for which prior notice would otherwise be required under this paragraph results in a lower interest charge to the customer than would have been imposed before the change, notice of such change may be given within a reasonable time after the effective date of the change.

(15 U.S.C. 78j)

[34 FR 19718, Dec. 16, 1969]

§ 240.10b-17 Untimely announcements of record dates.

(a) It shall constitute a "manipulative or deceptive device or contrivance" as used in section 10(b) of the Act for any issuer of a class of securities publicly traded by the use of any means or instrumentality of interstate commerce or of the mails or of any facility of any national securities exchange to fail to give notice in accordance with paragraph (b) of this section of the following actions relating to such class of securities:

(1) A dividend or other distribution in cash or in kind, except an ordinary interest payment on a debt security, but including a dividend or distribution of any security of the same or another issuer;

(2) A stock split or reverse split; or

(3) A rights or other subscription offering.

(b) Notice shall be deemed to have been given in accordance with this section only if:

(1) Given to the National Association of Securities Dealers, Inc., no later than 10 days prior to the record date involved or, in case of a rights subscription or other offering if such 10 days advance notice is not practical, on or before the record date and in no event later than the effective date of the registration statement to which the offering relates, and such notice includes:

(i) Title of the security to which the declaration relates;

(ii) Date of declaration;

(iii) Date of record for determining holders entitled to receive the dividend or other distribution or to participate in the stock or reverse split;

(iv) Date of payment or distribution or, in the case of a stock or reverse split or rights or other subscription offering, the date of delivery;

(v) For a dividend or other distribution including a stock or reverse split or rights or other subscription offering:

(a) In cash, the amount of cash to be paid or distributed per share, except if exact per share cash distributions cannot be given because of existing conversion rights which may be exercised during the notice period and which may affect the per share cash distribution, then a reasonable approximation of the per share distribution may be provided so long as the actual per share distribution is subsequently provided on the record date,

(b) In the same security, the amount of the security outstanding immediately prior to and immediately following the dividend or distribution and the rate of the dividend or distribution,

(c) In any other security of the same issuer, the amount to be paid or distributed and the rate of the dividend or distribution,

(d) In any security of another issuer, the name of the issuer and title of that security, the amount to be paid or distributed, and the rate of the dividend or distribution and if that security is a right or a warrant, the subscription price,

(e) In any other property (including securities not covered under paragraphs (b)(1)(v) (b) through (d) of this section) the identity of the property and its value and basis for assigning that value;

(vi) Method of settlement of fractional interests;

(vii) Details of any condition which must be satisfied or Government approval which must be secured to enable payment of distribution; and in

(viii) The case of stock or reverse split in addition to the aforementioned information;

(a) The name and address of the transfer or exchange agent; or

(2) The Commission, upon written request or upon its own motion, exempts the issuer from compliance with paragraph (b)(1) of this section either unconditionally or on specified terms or conditions, as not constituting a manipulative or deceptive device or contrivance comprehended within the purpose of this section; or

(3) Given in accordance with procedures of the national securities exchange or exchanges upon which a security of such issuer is registered pursuant to section 12 of the Act which contain requirements substantially comparable to those set forth in paragraph (b)(1) of this section.

(c) The provisions of this rule shall not apply, however, to redeemable securities issued by open-end investment companies and unit investment trusts

Securities and Exchange Commission § 240.10b-18

registered with the Commission under the Investment Company Act of 1940.

(Secs. 10(b), 23(a), 48 Stat. 891, as amended, 49 Stat. 1379, 15 U.S.C. 78j)

[36 FR 11514, June 15, 1971, as amended at 37 FR 4330, Mar. 2, 1972]

§ 240.10b-18 Purchases of certain equity securities by the issuer and others.

PRELIMINARY NOTES TO § 240.10b-18 1. Section 240.10b-18 provides an issuer (and its affiliated purchasers) with a "safe harbor" from liability for manipulation under sections 9(a)(2) of the Act and § 240.10b-5 under the Act *solely* by reason of the manner, timing, price, and volume of their repurchases when they repurchase the issuer's common stock in the market in accordance with the section's manner, timing, price, and volume conditions. As a safe harbor, compliance with § 240.10b-18 is voluntary. To come within the safe harbor, however, an issuer's repurchases must satisfy (on a daily basis) each of the section's four conditions. Failure to meet any one of the four conditions will remove all of the issuer's repurchases from the safe harbor for that day. The safe harbor, moreover, is not available for repurchases that, although made in technical compliance with the section, are part of a plan or scheme to evade the federal securities laws.

2. Regardless of whether the repurchases are effected in accordance with § 240.10b-18, reporting issuers must report their repurchasing activity as required by Item 703 of Regulations S-K and S-B (17 CFR 229.703 and 228.703) and Item 15(e) of Form 20-F (17 CFR 249.220f) (regarding foreign private issuers), and closed-end management investment companies that are registered under the Investment Company Act of 1940 must report their repurchasing activity as required by Item 8 of Form N-CSR (17 CFR 249.331; 17 CFR 274.128).

(a) *Definitions.* Unless otherwise provided, all terms used in this section shall have the same meaning as in the Act. In addition, the following definitions shall apply:

(1) *ADTV* means the average daily trading volume reported for the security during the four calendar weeks preceding the week in which the Rule 10b-18 purchase is to be effected.

(2) *Affiliate* means any person that directly or indirectly controls, is controlled by, or is under common control with, the issuer.

(3) *Affiliated purchaser* means:

(i) A person acting, directly or indirectly, in concert with the issuer for the purpose of acquiring the issuer's securities; or

(ii) An affiliate who, directly or indirectly, controls the issuer's purchases of such securities, whose purchases are controlled by the issuer, or whose purchases are under common control with those of the issuer; *Provided, however,* that "affiliated purchaser" shall not include a broker, dealer, or other person solely by reason of such broker, dealer, or other person effecting Rule 10b-18 purchases on behalf of the issuer or for its account, and shall not include an officer or director of the issuer solely by reason of that officer or director's participation in the decision to authorize Rule 10b-18 purchases by or on behalf of the issuer.

(4) *Agent independent of the issuer* has the meaning contained in § 242.100 of this chapter.

(5) *Block* means a quantity of stock that either:

(i) Has a purchase price of $200,000 or more; or

(ii) Is at least 5,000 shares and has a purchase price of at least $50,000; or

(iii) Is at least 20 round lots of the security and totals 150 percent or more of the trading volume for that security or, in the event that trading volume data are unavailable, is at least 20 round lots of the security and totals at least one-tenth of one percent (.001) of the outstanding shares of the security, exclusive of any shares owned by any affiliate; *Provided, however,* That a block under paragraph (a)(5)(i), (ii), and (iii) shall not include any amount a broker or dealer, acting as principal, has accumulated for the purpose of sale or resale to the issuer or to any affiliated purchaser of the issuer if the issuer or such affiliated purchaser knows or has reason to know that such amount was accumulated for such purpose, nor shall it include any amount that a broker or dealer has sold short to the issuer or to any affiliated purchaser of the issuer if the issuer or such affiliated purchaser knows or has reason to know that the sale was a short sale.

(6) *Consolidated system* means a consolidated transaction or quotation reporting system that collects and publicly disseminates on a current and continuous basis transaction or

105

§ 240.10b–18

quotation information in common equity securities pursuant to an effective transaction reporting plan or an effective national market system plan (as those terms are defined in § 242.600 of this chapter).

(7) *Market-wide trading suspension* means a market-wide trading halt of 30 minutes or more that is:

(i) Imposed pursuant to the rules of a national securities exchange or a national securities association in response to a market-wide decline during a single trading session; or

(ii) Declared by the Commission pursuant to its authority under section 12(k) of the Act (15 U.S.C. 78*l* (k)).

(8) *Plan* has the meaning contained in § 242.100 of this chapter.

(9) *Principal market* for a security means the single securities market with the largest reported trading volume for the security during the six full calendar months preceding the week in which the Rule 10b–18 purchase is to be effected.

(10) *Public float value* has the meaning contained in § 242.100 of this chapter.

(11) *Purchase price* means the price paid per share as reported, exclusive of any commission paid to a broker acting as agent, or commission equivalent, mark-up, or differential paid to a dealer.

(12) *Riskless principal transaction* means a transaction in which a broker or dealer after having received an order from an issuer to buy its security, buys the security as principal in the market at the same price to satisfy the issuer's buy order. The issuer's buy order must be effected at the same price per-share at which the broker or dealer bought the shares to satisfy the issuer's buy order, exclusive of any explicitly disclosed markup or markdown, commission equivalent, or other fee. In addition, only the first leg of the transaction, when the broker or dealer buys the security in the market as principal, is reported under the rules of a self-regulatory organization or under the Act. For purposes of this section, the broker or dealer must have written policies and procedures in place to assure that, at a minimum, the issuer's buy order was received prior to the offsetting transaction; the offsetting transaction is allocated to a riskless principal account or the issuer's account within 60 seconds of the execution; and the broker or dealer has supervisory systems in place to produce records that enable the broker or dealer to accurately and readily reconstruct, in a time-sequenced manner, all orders effected on a riskless principal basis.

(13) *Rule 10b–18 purchase* means a purchase (or any bid or limit order that would effect such purchase) of an issuer's common stock (or an equivalent interest, including a unit of beneficial interest in a trust or limited partnership or a depository share) by or for the issuer or any affiliated purchaser (including riskless principal transactions). However, it does *not* include any purchase of such security:

(i) Effected during the applicable restricted period of a distribution that is subject to § 242.102 of this chapter;

(ii) Effected by or for an issuer plan by an agent independent of the issuer;

(iii) Effected as a fractional share purchase (a fractional interest in a security) evidenced by a script certificate, order form, or similar document;

(iv) Effected during the period from the time of public announcement (as defined in § 230.165(f)) of a merger, acquisition, or similar transaction involving a recapitalization, until the earlier of the completion of such transaction or the completion of the vote by target shareholders. This exclusion does *not* apply to Rule 10b–18 purchases:

(A) Effected during such transaction in which the consideration is solely cash and there is no valuation period; or

(B) Where:

(*1*) The total volume of Rule 10b–18 purchases effected on any single day does not exceed the lesser of 25% of the security's four-week ADTV or the issuer's average daily Rule 10b–18 purchases during the three full calendar months preceding the date of the announcement of such transaction;

(*2*) The issuer's block purchases effected pursuant to paragraph (b)(4) of this section do not exceed the average size and frequency of the issuer's block purchases effected pursuant to paragraph (b)(4) of this section during the three full calendar months preceding

Securities and Exchange Commission § 240.10b-18

the date of the announcement of such transaction; and

(3) Such purchases are not otherwise restricted or prohibited;

(v) Effected pursuant to § 240.13e-1;

(vi) Effected pursuant to a tender offer that is subject to § 240.13e-4 or specifically excepted from § 240.13e-4; or

(vii) Effected pursuant to a tender offer that is subject to section 14(d) of the Act (15 U.S.C. 78n(d)) and the rules and regulations thereunder.

(b) *Conditions to be met.* Rule 10b–18 purchases shall not be deemed to have violated the anti-manipulation provisions of sections 9(a)(2) or 10(b) of the Act (15 U.S.C. 78i(a)(2) or 78j(b)), or § 240.10b–5 under the Act, solely by reason of the time, price, or amount of the Rule 10b–18 purchases, or the number of brokers or dealers used in connection with such purchases, if the issuer or affiliated purchaser of the issuer effects the Rule 10b–18 purchases according to each of the following conditions:

(1) *One broker or dealer.* Rule 10b–18 purchases must be effected from or through only one broker or dealer on any single day; *Provided, however,* that:

(i) The "one broker or dealer" condition shall not apply to Rule 10b–18 purchases that are not solicited by or on behalf of the issuer or its affiliated purchaser(s);

(ii) Where Rule 10b–18 purchases are effected by or on behalf of more than one affiliated purchaser of the issuer (or the issuer and one or more of its affiliated purchasers) on a single day, the issuer and all affiliated purchasers must use the same broker or dealer; and

(iii) Where Rule 10b–18 purchases are effected on behalf of the issuer by a broker-dealer that is not an electronic communication network (ECN) or other alternative trading system (ATS), that broker-dealer can access ECN or other ATS liquidity in order to execute repurchases on behalf of the issuer (or any affiliated purchaser of the issuer) on that day.

(2) *Time of purchases.* Rule 10b–18 purchases must not be:

(i) The opening (regular way) purchase reported in the consolidated system;

(ii) Effected during the 10 minutes before the scheduled close of the primary trading session in the principal market for the security, and the 10 minutes before the scheduled close of the primary trading session in the market where the purchase is effected, for a security that has an ADTV value of $1 million or more and a public float value of $150 million or more; and

(iii) Effected during the 30 minutes before the scheduled close of the primary trading session in the principal market for the security, and the 30 minutes before the scheduled close of the primary trading session in the market where the purchase is effected, for all other securities;

(iv) However, for purposes of this section, Rule 10b–18 purchases may be effected following the close of the primary trading session until the termination of the period in which last sale prices are reported in the consolidated system so long as such purchases are effected at prices that do not exceed the lower of the closing price of the primary trading session in the principal market for the security and any lower bids or sale prices subsequently reported in the consolidated system, and all of this section's conditions are met. However, for purposes of this section, the issuer may use one broker or dealer to effect Rule 10b–18 purchases during this period that may be different from the broker or dealer that it used during the primary trading session. However, the issuer's Rule 10b–18 purchase may not be the opening transaction of the session following the close of the primary trading session.

(3) *Price of purchases.* Rule 10b–18 purchases must be effected at a purchase price that:

(i) Does not exceed the highest independent bid or the last independent transaction price, whichever is higher, quoted or reported in the consolidated system at the time the Rule 10b–18 purchase is effected;

(ii) For securities for which bids and transaction prices are not quoted or reported in the consolidated system, Rule 10b–18 purchases must be effected at a purchase price that does not exceed the highest independent bid or the last independent transaction price, whichever is higher, displayed and disseminated on any national securities exchange or on any inter-dealer

§ 240.10b-21

quotation system (as defined in § 240.15c2-11) that displays at least two priced quotations for the security, at the time the Rule 10b-18 purchase is effected; and

(iii) For all other securities, Rule 10b-18 purchases must be effected at a price no higher than the highest independent bid obtained from three independent dealers.

(4) *Volume of purchases.* The total volume of Rule 10b-18 purchases effected by or for the issuer and any affiliated purchasers effected on any single day must not exceed 25 percent of the ADTV for that security; *However,* once each week, in lieu of purchasing under the 25 percent of ADTV limit for that day, the issuer or an affiliated purchaser of the issuer may effect one block purchase if:

(i) No other Rule 10b-18 purchases are effected that day, and

(ii) The block purchase is *not* included when calculating a security's four week ADTV under this section.

(c) *Alternative conditions.* The conditions of paragraph (b) of this section shall apply in connection with Rule 10b-18 purchases effected during a trading session following the imposition of a market-wide trading suspension, except:

(1) That the time of purchases condition in paragraph (b)(2) of this section shall not apply, either:

(i) From the reopening of trading until the scheduled close of trading on the day that the market-wide trading suspension is imposed; or

(ii) At the opening of trading on the next trading day until the scheduled close of trading that day, if a market-wide trading suspension was in effect at the close of trading on the preceding day; and

(2) The volume of purchases condition in paragraph (b)(4) of this section is modified so that the amount of Rule 10b-18 purchases must not exceed 100 percent of the ADTV for that security.

(d) *Other purchases.* No presumption shall arise that an issuer or an affiliated purchaser has violated the anti-manipulation provisions of sections 9(a)(2) or 10(b) of the Act (15 U.S.C. 78i(a)(2) or 78j(b)), or § 240.10b-5 under the Act, if the Rule 10b-18 purchases of such issuer or affiliated purchaser do not meet the conditions specified in paragraph (b) or (c) of this section.

[68 FR 64970, Nov. 17, 2003, as amended at 70 FR 37618, June 29, 2005]

§ 240.10b-21 Deception in connection with a seller's ability or intent to deliver securities on the date delivery is due.

PRELIMINARY NOTE TO § 240.10b-21: This rule is not intended to limit, or restrict, the applicability of the general antifraud provisions of the federal securities laws, such as section 10(b) of the Act and rule 10b-5 thereunder.

(a) It shall also constitute a "manipulative or deceptive device or contrivance" as used in section 10(b) of this Act for any person to submit an order to sell an equity security if such person deceives a broker or dealer, a participant of a registered clearing agency, or a purchaser about its intention or ability to deliver the security on or before the settlement date, and such person fails to deliver the security on or before the settlement date.

(b) For purposes of this rule, the term *settlement date* shall mean the business day on which delivery of a security and payment of money is to be made through the facilities of a registered clearing agency in connection with the sale of a security.

[73 FR 61677, Oct. 17, 2008]

REPORTS UNDER SECTION 10A

§ 240.10A-1 Notice to the Commission Pursuant to Section 10A of the Act.

(a)(1) If any issuer with a reporting obligation under the Act receives a report requiring a notice to the Commission in accordance with section 10A(b)(3) of the Act, 15 U.S.C. 78j-1(b)(3), the issuer shall submit such notice to the Commission's Office of the Chief Accountant within the time period prescribed in that section. The notice may be provided by facsimile, telegraph, personal delivery, or any other means, *provided* it is received by the Office of the Chief Accountant within the required time period.

(2) The notice specified in paragraph (a)(1) of this section shall be in writing and:

(i) Shall identify the issuer (including the issuer's name, address, phone

Securities and Exchange Commission

§ 240.10A–1

number, and file number assigned to the issuer's filings by the Commission) and the independent accountant (including the independent accountant's name and phone number, and the address of the independent accountant's principal office);

(ii) Shall state the date that the issuer received from the independent accountant the report specified in section 10A(b)(2) of the Act, 15 U.S.C. 78j–1(b)(2);

(iii) Shall provide, at the election of the issuer, either:

(A) A summary of the independent accountant's report, including a description of the act that the independent accountant has identified as a likely illegal act and the possible effect of that act on all affected financial statements of the issuer or those related to the most current three-year period, whichever is shorter; or

(B) A copy of the independent accountant's report; and

(iv) May provide additional information regarding the issuer's views of and response to the independent accountant's report.

(3) Reports of the independent accountant submitted by the issuer to the Commission's Office of the Chief Accountant in accordance with paragraph (a)(2)(iii)(B) of this section shall be deemed to have been made pursuant to section 10A(b)(3) or section 10A(b)(4) of the Act, 15 U.S.C. 78j–1(b)(3) or 78j–1(b)(4), for purposes of the safe harbor provided by section 10A(c) of the Act, 15 U.S.C. 78j–1(c).

(4) Submission of the notice in paragraphs (a)(1) and (a)(2) of this section shall not relieve the issuer from its obligations to comply fully with all other reporting requirements, including, without limitation:

(i) The filing requirements of Form 8–K, § 249.308 of this chapter, and Form N–CSR, § 274.128 of this chapter, regarding a change in the issuer's certifying accountant and

(ii) The disclosure requirements of Item 304 of Regulation S–K, § 229.304 of this chapter.

(b)(1) Any independent accountant furnishing to the Commission a copy of a report (or the documentation of any oral report) in accordance with section 10A(b)(3) or section 10A(b)(4) of the Act, 15 U.S.C. 78j–1(b)(3) or 78j–1(b)(4), shall submit that report (or documentation) to the Commission's Office of the Chief Accountant within the time period prescribed by the appropriate section of the Act. The report (or documentation) may be submitted to the Commission's Office of the Chief Accountant by facsimile, telegraph, personal delivery, or any other means, *provided* it is received by the Office of the Chief Accountant within the time period set forth in section 10A(b)(3) or 10A(b)(4) of the Act, 15 U.S.C. 78j–1(b)(3) or 78j–(b)(4), whichever is applicable in the circumstances.

(2) If the report (or documentation) submitted to the Office of the Chief Accountant in accordance with paragraph (b)(1) of this section does not clearly identify both the issuer (including the issuer's name, address, phone number, and file number assigned to the issuer's filings with the Commission) and the independent accountant (including the independent accountant's name and phone number, and the address of the independent accountant's principal office), then the independent accountant shall place that information in a prominent attachment to the report (or documentation) and shall submit that attachment to the Office of the Chief Accountant at the same time and in the same manner as the report (or documentation) is submitted to that Office.

(3) Submission of the report (or documentation) by the independent accountant as described in paragraphs (b)(1) and (2) of this section shall not replace, or otherwise satisfy the need for, the newly engaged and former accountants' letters under §§ 229.304(a)(2)(D) and 229.304(a)(3) of this chapter (Items 304(a)(2)(D) and 304(a)(3) of Regulation S–K, respectively) and shall not limit, reduce, or affect in any way the independent accountant's obligations to comply fully with all other legal and professional responsibilities, including, without limitation, those under the standards of the Public Company Accounting Oversight Board (United States) ("PCAOB") and the rules or interpretations of the Commission that modify or supplement those auditing standards.

(c) A notice or report submitted to the Office of the Chief Accountant in

§ 240.10A-2

accordance with paragraphs (a) and (b) of this section shall be deemed to be an investigative record and shall be nonpublic and exempt from disclosure pursuant to the Freedom of Information Act to the same extent and for the same periods of time that the Commission's investigative records are nonpublic and exempt from disclosure under, among other applicable provisions, 5 U.S.C. 552(b)(7). Nothing in this paragraph, however, shall relieve, limit, delay, or affect in any way, the obligation of any issuer or any independent accountant to make all public disclosures required by law, by any Commission disclosure item, rule, report, or form, or by any applicable accounting, auditing, or professional standard.

INSTRUCTION TO PARAGRAPH (c): Issuers and independent accountants may apply for additional bases for confidential treatment for a notice, report, or part thereof, in accordance with § 200.83 of this chapter. That section indicates, in part, that any person who, pursuant to any requirement of law, submits any information or causes or permits any information to be submitted to the Commission, may request that the Commission afford it confidential treatment by reason of personal privacy or business confidentiality, or for any other reason permitted by Federal law.

[62 FR 12749, Mar. 18, 1997, as amended at 73 FR 973, Jan. 4, 2008; 81 FR 82020, Nov. 18, 2016; 83 FR 50221, Oct. 4, 2018; 84 FR 50739, Sept. 26, 2019]

§ 240.10A-2 Auditor independence.

It shall be unlawful for an auditor not to be independent under § 210.2-01(c)(2)(iii)(B), (c)(4), (c)(6), (c)(7), and § 210.2-07.

[68 FR 6048, Feb. 5, 2003]

§ 240.10A-3 Listing standards relating to audit committees.

(a) Pursuant to section 10A(m) of the Act (15 U.S.C. 78j-1(m)) and section 3 of the Sarbanes-Oxley Act of 2002 (15 U.S.C. 7202):

(1) *National securities exchanges.* The rules of each national securities exchange registered pursuant to section 6 of the Act (15 U.S.C. 78f) must, in accordance with the provisions of this section, prohibit the initial or continued listing of any security of an issuer that is not in compliance with the requirements of any portion of paragraph (b) or (c) of this section.

(2) *National securities associations.* The rules of each national securities association registered pursuant to section 15A of the Act (15 U.S.C. 78o-3) must, in accordance with the provisions of this section, prohibit the initial or continued listing in an automated inter-dealer quotation system of any security of an issuer that is not in compliance with the requirements of any portion of paragraph (b) or (c) of this section.

(3) *Opportunity to cure defects.* The rules required by paragraphs (a)(1) and (a)(2) of this section must provide for appropriate procedures for a listed issuer to have an opportunity to cure any defects that would be the basis for a prohibition under paragraph (a) of this section, before the imposition of such prohibition. Such rules also may provide that if a member of an audit committee ceases to be independent in accordance with the requirements of this section for reasons outside the member's reasonable control, that person, with notice by the issuer to the applicable national securities exchange or national securities association, may remain an audit committee member of the listed issuer until the earlier of the next annual shareholders meeting of the listed issuer or one year from the occurrence of the event that caused the member to be no longer independent.

(4) *Notification of noncompliance.* The rules required by paragraphs (a)(1) and (a)(2) of this section must include a requirement that a listed issuer must notify the applicable national securities exchange or national securities association promptly after an executive officer of the listed issuer becomes aware of any material noncompliance by the listed issuer with the requirements of this section.

(5) *Implementation.* (i) The rules of each national securities exchange or national securities association meeting the requirements of this section must be operative, and listed issuers must be in compliance with those rules, by the following dates:

(A) July 31, 2005 for foreign private issuers and smaller reporting companies (as defined in § 240.12b-2); and

Securities and Exchange Commission

§ 240.10A-3

(B) For all other listed issuers, the earlier of the listed issuer's first annual shareholders meeting after January 15, 2004, or October 31, 2004.

(ii) Each national securities exchange and national securities association must provide to the Commission, no later than July 15, 2003, proposed rules or rule amendments that comply with this section.

(iii) Each national securities exchange and national securities association must have final rules or rule amendments that comply with this section approved by the Commission no later than December 1, 2003.

(b) *Required standards*—(1) *Independence.* (i) Each member of the audit committee must be a member of the board of directors of the listed issuer, and must otherwise be independent; provided that, where a listed issuer is one of two dual holding companies, those companies may designate one audit committee for both companies so long as each member of the audit committee is a member of the board of directors of at least one of such dual holding companies.

(ii) *Independence requirements for non-investment company issuers.* In order to be considered to be independent for purposes of this paragraph (b)(1), a member of an audit committee of a listed issuer that is not an investment company may not, other than in his or her capacity as a member of the audit committee, the board of directors, or any other board committee:

(A) Accept directly or indirectly any consulting, advisory, or other compensatory fee from the issuer or any subsidiary thereof, provided that, unless the rules of the national securities exchange or national securities association provide otherwise, compensatory fees do not include the receipt of fixed amounts of compensation under a retirement plan (including deferred compensation) for prior service with the listed issuer (provided that such compensation is not contingent in any way on continued service); or

(B) Be an affiliated person of the issuer or any subsidiary thereof.

(iii) *Independence requirements for investment company issuers.* In order to be considered to be independent for purposes of this paragraph (b)(1), a member of an audit committee of a listed issuer that is an investment company may not, other than in his or her capacity as a member of the audit committee, the board of directors, or any other board committee:

(A) Accept directly or indirectly any consulting, advisory, or other compensatory fee from the issuer or any subsidiary thereof, provided that, unless the rules of the national securities exchange or national securities association provide otherwise, compensatory fees do not include the receipt of fixed amounts of compensation under a retirement plan (including deferred compensation) for prior service with the listed issuer (provided that such compensation is not contingent in any way on continued service); or

(B) Be an "interested person" of the issuer as defined in section 2(a)(19) of the Investment Company Act of 1940 (15 U.S.C. 80a–2(a)(19)).

(iv) *Exemptions from the independence requirements.* (A) For an issuer listing securities pursuant to a registration statement under section 12 of the Act (15 U.S.C. 78l), or for an issuer that has a registration statement under the Securities Act of 1933 (15 U.S.C. 77a *et seq.*) covering an initial public offering of securities to be listed by the issuer, where in each case the listed issuer was not, immediately prior to the effective date of such registration statement, required to file reports with the Commission pursuant to section 13(a) or 15(d) of the Act (15 U.S.C. 78m(a) or 78o(d)):

(*1*) All but one of the members of the listed issuer's audit committee may be exempt from the independence requirements of paragraph (b)(1)(ii) of this section for 90 days from the date of effectiveness of such registration statement; and

(*2*) A minority of the members of the listed issuer's audit committee may be exempt from the independence requirements of paragraph (b)(1)(ii) of this section for one year from the date of effectiveness of such registration statement.

(B) An audit committee member that sits on the board of directors of a listed issuer and an affiliate of the listed issuer is exempt from the requirements of paragraph (b)(1)(ii)(B) of this section

§ 240.10A-3

if the member, except for being a director on each such board of directors, otherwise meets the independence requirements of paragraph (b)(1)(ii) of this section for each such entity, including the receipt of only ordinary-course compensation for serving as a member of the board of directors, audit committee or any other board committee of each such entity.

(C) An employee of a foreign private issuer who is not an executive officer of the foreign private issuer is exempt from the requirements of paragraph (b)(1)(ii) of this section if the employee is elected or named to the board of directors or audit committee of the foreign private issuer pursuant to the issuer's governing law or documents, an employee collective bargaining or similar agreement or other home country legal or listing requirements.

(D) An audit committee member of a foreign private issuer may be exempt from the requirements of paragraph (b)(1)(ii)(B) of this section if that member meets the following requirements:

(*1*) The member is an affiliate of the foreign private issuer or a representative of such an affiliate;

(*2*) The member has only observer status on, and is not a voting member or the chair of, the audit committee; and

(*3*) Neither the member nor the affiliate is an executive officer of the foreign private issuer.

(E) An audit committee member of a foreign private issuer may be exempt from the requirements of paragraph (b)(1)(ii)(B) of this section if that member meets the following requirements:

(*1*) The member is a representative or designee of a foreign government or foreign governmental entity that is an affiliate of the foreign private issuer; and

(*2*) The member is not an executive officer of the foreign private issuer.

(F) In addition to paragraphs (b)(1)(iv)(A) through (E) of this section, the Commission may exempt from the requirements of paragraphs (b)(1)(ii) or (b)(1)(iii) of this section a particular relationship with respect to audit committee members, as the Commission determines appropriate in light of the circumstances.

(2) *Responsibilities relating to registered public accounting firms.* The audit committee of each listed issuer, in its capacity as a committee of the board of directors, must be directly responsible for the appointment, compensation, retention and oversight of the work of any registered public accounting firm engaged (including resolution of disagreements between management and the auditor regarding financial reporting) for the purpose of preparing or issuing an audit report or performing other audit, review or attest services for the listed issuer, and each such registered public accounting firm must report directly to the audit committee.

(3) *Complaints.* Each audit committee must establish procedures for:

(i) The receipt, retention, and treatment of complaints received by the listed issuer regarding accounting, internal accounting controls, or auditing matters; and

(ii) The confidential, anonymous submission by employees of the listed issuer of concerns regarding questionable accounting or auditing matters.

(4) *Authority to engage advisers.* Each audit committee must have the authority to engage independent counsel and other advisers, as it determines necessary to carry out its duties.

(5) *Funding.* Each listed issuer must provide for appropriate funding, as determined by the audit committee, in its capacity as a committee of the board of directors, for payment of:

(i) Compensation to any registered public accounting firm engaged for the purpose of preparing or issuing an audit report or performing other audit, review or attest services for the listed issuer;

(ii) Compensation to any advisers employed by the audit committee under paragraph (b)(4) of this section; and

(iii) Ordinary administrative expenses of the audit committee that are necessary or appropriate in carrying out its duties.

(c) *General exemptions.* (1) At any time when an issuer has a class of securities that is listed on a national securities exchange or national securities association subject to the requirements of this section, the listing of other classes of securities of the listed issuer on a

Securities and Exchange Commission §240.10A-3

national securities exchange or national securities association is not subject to the requirements of this section.

(2) At any time when an issuer has a class of common equity securities (or similar securities) that is listed on a national securities exchange or national securities association subject to the requirements of this section, the listing of classes of securities of a direct or indirect consolidated subsidiary or an at least 50% beneficially owned subsidiary of the issuer (except classes of equity securities, other than nonconvertible, non-participating preferred securities, of such subsidiary) is not subject to the requirements of this section.

(3) The listing of securities of a foreign private issuer is not subject to the requirements of paragraphs (b)(1) through (b)(5) of this section if the foreign private issuer meets the following requirements:

(i) The foreign private issuer has a board of auditors (or similar body), or has statutory auditors, established and selected pursuant to home country legal or listing provisions expressly requiring or permitting such a board or similar body;

(ii) The board or body, or statutory auditors is required under home country legal or listing requirements to be either:

(A) Separate from the board of directors; or

(B) Composed of one or more members of the board of directors and one or more members that are not also members of the board of directors;

(iii) The board or body, or statutory auditors, are not elected by management of such issuer and no executive officer of the foreign private issuer is a member of such board or body, or statutory auditors;

(iv) Home country legal or listing provisions set forth or provide for standards for the independence of such board or body, or statutory auditors, from the foreign private issuer or the management of such issuer;

(v) Such board or body, or statutory auditors, in accordance with any applicable home country legal or listing requirements or the issuer's governing documents, are responsible, to the extent permitted by law, for the appointment, retention and oversight of the work of any registered public accounting firm engaged (including, to the extent permitted by law, the resolution of disagreements between management and the auditor regarding financial reporting) for the purpose of preparing or issuing an audit report or performing other audit, review or attest services for the issuer; and

(vi) The audit committee requirements of paragraphs (b)(3), (b)(4) and (b)(5) of this section apply to such board or body, or statutory auditors, to the extent permitted by law.

(4) The listing of a security futures product cleared by a clearing agency that is registered pursuant to section 17A of the Act (15 U.S.C. 78q-1) or that is exempt from the registration requirements of section 17A pursuant to paragraph (b)(7)(A) of such section is not subject to the requirements of this section.

(5) The listing of a standardized option, as defined in §240.9b-1(a)(4), issued by a clearing agency that is registered pursuant to section 17A of the Act (15 U.S.C. 78q-1) is not subject to the requirements of this section.

(6) The listing of securities of the following listed issuers are not subject to the requirements of this section:

(i) Asset-Backed Issuers (as defined in §229.1101 of this chapter);

(ii) Unit investment trusts (as defined in 15 U.S.C. 80a-4(2)); and

(iii) Foreign governments (as defined in §240.3b-4(a)).

(7) The listing of securities of a listed issuer is not subject to the requirements of this section if:

(i) The listed issuer, as reflected in the applicable listing application, is organized as a trust or other unincorporated association that does not have a board of directors or persons acting in a similar capacity; and

(ii) The activities of the listed issuer that is described in paragraph (c)(7)(i) of this section are limited to passively owning or holding (as well as administering and distributing amounts in respect of) securities, rights, collateral or other assets on behalf of or for the benefit of the holders of the listed securities.

§ 240.10A-3

(d) *Disclosure.* Any listed issuer availing itself of an exemption from the independence standards contained in paragraph (b)(1)(iv) of this section (except paragraph (b)(1)(iv)(B) of this section), the general exemption contained in paragraph (c)(3) of this section or the last sentence of paragraph (a)(3) of this section, must:

(1) Disclose its reliance on the exemption and its assessment of whether, and if so, how, such reliance would materially adversely affect the ability of the audit committee to act independently and to satisfy the other requirements of this section in any proxy or information statement for a meeting of shareholders at which directors are elected that is filed with the Commission pursuant to the requirements of section 14 of the Act (15 U.S.C. 78n); and

(2) Disclose the information specified in paragraph (d)(1) of this section in, or incorporate such information by reference from such proxy or information statement filed with the Commission into, its annual report filed with the Commission pursuant to the requirements of section 13(a) or 15(d) of the Act (15 U.S.C. 78m(a) or 78o(d)).

(e) *Definitions.* Unless the context otherwise requires, all terms used in this section have the same meaning as in the Act. In addition, unless the context otherwise requires, the following definitions apply for purposes of this section:

(1)(i) The term *affiliate* of, or a person *affiliated* with, a specified person, means a person that directly, or indirectly through one or more intermediaries, controls, or is controlled by, or is under common control with, the person specified.

(ii)(A) A person will be deemed not to be in control of a specified person for purposes of this section if the person:

(*1*) Is not the beneficial owner, directly or indirectly, of more than 10% of any class of voting equity securities of the specified person; and

(*2*) Is not an executive officer of the specified person.

(B) Paragraph (e)(1)(ii)(A) of this section only creates a safe harbor position that a person does not control a specified person. The existence of the safe harbor does not create a presumption in any way that a person exceeding the ownership requirement in paragraph (e)(1)(ii)(A)(*1*) of this section controls or is otherwise an affiliate of a specified person.

(iii) The following will be deemed to be affiliates:

(A) An executive officer of an affiliate;

(B) A director who also is an employee of an affiliate;

(C) A general partner of an affiliate; and

(D) A managing member of an affiliate.

(iv) For purposes of paragraph (e)(1)(i) of this section, dual holding companies will not be deemed to be affiliates of or persons affiliated with each other by virtue of their dual holding company arrangements with each other, including where directors of one dual holding company are also directors of the other dual holding company, or where directors of one or both dual holding companies are also directors of the businesses jointly controlled, directly or indirectly, by the dual holding companies (and, in each case, receive only ordinary-course compensation for serving as a member of the board of directors, audit committee or any other board committee of the dual holding companies or any entity that is jointly controlled, directly or indirectly, by the dual holding companies).

(2) In the case of foreign private issuers with a two-tier board system, the term *board of directors* means the supervisory or non-management board.

(3) In the case of a listed issuer that is a limited partnership or limited liability company where such entity does not have a board of directors or equivalent body, the term *board of directors* means the board of directors of the managing general partner, managing member or equivalent body.

(4) The term *control* (including the terms *controlling, controlled by* and under *common control with*) means the possession, direct or indirect, of the power to direct or cause the direction of the management and policies of a person, whether through the ownership of voting securities, by contract, or otherwise.

Securities and Exchange Commission § 240.10C-1

(5) The term *dual holding companies* means two foreign private issuers that:
(i) Are organized in different national jurisdictions;
(ii) Collectively own and supervise the management of one or more businesses which are conducted as a single economic enterprise; and
(iii) Do not conduct any business other than collectively owning and supervising such businesses and activities reasonably incidental thereto.

(6) The term *executive officer* has the meaning set forth in § 240.3b–7.

(7) The term *foreign private issuer* has the meaning set forth in § 240.3b–4(c).

(8) The term *indirect* acceptance by a member of an audit committee of any consulting, advisory or other compensatory fee includes acceptance of such a fee by a spouse, a minor child or stepchild or a child or stepchild sharing a home with the member or by an entity in which such member is a partner, member, an officer such as a managing director occupying a comparable position or executive officer, or occupies a similar position (except limited partners, non-managing members and those occupying similar positions who, in each case, have no active role in providing services to the entity) and which provides accounting, consulting, legal, investment banking or financial advisory services to the issuer or any subsidiary of the issuer.

(9) The terms *listed* and *listing* refer to securities listed on a national securities exchange or listed in an automated inter-dealer quotation system of a national securities association or to issuers of such securities.

INSTRUCTIONS TO § 240.10A–3: 1. The requirements in paragraphs (b)(2) through (b)(5), (c)(3)(v) and (c)(3)(vi) of this section do not conflict with, and do not affect the application of, any requirement or ability under a listed issuer's governing law or documents or other home country legal or listing provisions that requires or permits shareholders to ultimately vote on, approve or ratify such requirements. The requirements instead relate to the assignment of responsibility as between the audit committee and management. In such an instance, however, if the listed issuer provides a recommendation or nomination regarding such responsibilities to shareholders, the audit committee of the listed issuer, or body performing similar functions, must be responsible for making the recommendation or nomination.

2. The requirements in paragraphs (b)(2) through (b)(5), (c)(3)(v), (c)(3)(vi) and Instruction 1 of this section do not conflict with any legal or listing requirement in a listed issuer's home jurisdiction that prohibits the full board of directors from delegating such responsibilities to the listed issuer's audit committee or limits the degree of such delegation. In that case, the audit committee, or body performing similar functions, must be granted such responsibilities, which can include advisory powers, with respect to such matters to the extent permitted by law, including submitting nominations or recommendations to the full board.

3. The requirements in paragraphs (b)(2) through (b)(5), (c)(3)(v) and (c)(3)(vi) of this section do not conflict with any legal or listing requirement in a listed issuer's home jurisdiction that vests such responsibilities with a government entity or tribunal. In that case, the audit committee, or body performing similar functions, must be granted such responsibilities, which can include advisory powers, with respect to such matters to the extent permitted by law.

4. For purposes of this section, the determination of a person's beneficial ownership must be made in accordance with § 240.13d–3.

[68 FR 18818, Apr. 16, 2003, as amended at 70 FR 1620, Jan. 7, 2005; 73 FR 973, Jan. 4, 2008]

REQUIREMENTS UNDER SECTION 10C

§ 240.10C–1 Listing standards relating to compensation committees.

(a) Pursuant to section 10C(a) of the Act (15 U.S.C. 78j–3(a)) and section 952 of the Dodd-Frank Wall Street Reform and Consumer Protection Act of 2010 (Pub. L. 111–203, 124 Stat. 1900):

(1) *National securities exchanges.* The rules of each national securities exchange registered pursuant to section 6 of the Act (15 U.S.C. 78f), to the extent such national securities exchange lists equity securities, must, in accordance with the provisions of this section, prohibit the initial or continued listing of any equity security of an issuer that is not in compliance with the requirements of any portion of paragraph (b) or (c) of this section.

(2) *National securities associations.* The rules of each national securities association registered pursuant to section 15A of the Act (15 U.S.C. 78o–3), to the extent such national securities association lists equity securities in an automated inter-dealer quotation system,

§ 240.10C-1

must, in accordance with the provisions of this section, prohibit the initial or continued listing in an automated inter-dealer quotation system of any equity security of an issuer that is not in compliance with the requirements of any portion of paragraph (b) or (c) of this section.

(3) *Opportunity to cure defects.* The rules required by paragraphs (a)(1) and (a)(2) of this section must provide for appropriate procedures for a listed issuer to have a reasonable opportunity to cure any defects that would be the basis for a prohibition under paragraph (a) of this section, before the imposition of such prohibition. Such rules may provide that if a member of a compensation committee ceases to be independent in accordance with the requirements of this section for reasons outside the member's reasonable control, that person, with notice by the issuer to the applicable national securities exchange or national securities association, may remain a compensation committee member of the listed issuer until the earlier of the next annual shareholders meeting of the listed issuer or one year from the occurrence of the event that caused the member to be no longer independent.

(4) *Implementation.* (i) Each national securities exchange and national securities association that lists equity securities must provide to the Commission, no later than 90 days after publication of this section in the FEDERAL REGISTER, proposed rules or rule amendments that comply with this section. Each submission must include, in addition to any other information required under section 19(b) of the Act (15 U.S.C. 78s(b)) and the rules thereunder, a review of whether and how existing or proposed listing standards satisfy the requirements of this rule, a discussion of the consideration of factors relevant to compensation committee independence conducted by the national securities exchange or national securities association, and the definition of independence applicable to compensation committee members that the national securities exchange or national securities association proposes to adopt or retain in light of such review.

(ii) Each national securities exchange and national securities association that lists equity securities must have rules or rule amendments that comply with this section approved by the Commission no later than one year after publication of this section in the FEDERAL REGISTER.

(b) *Required standards.* The requirements of this section apply to the compensation committees of listed issuers.

(1) *Independence.* (i) Each member of the compensation committee must be a member of the board of directors of the listed issuer, and must otherwise be independent.

(ii) *Independence requirements.* In determining independence requirements for members of compensation committees, the national securities exchanges and national securities associations shall consider relevant factors, including, but not limited to:

(A) The source of compensation of a member of the board of directors of an issuer, including any consulting, advisory or other compensatory fee paid by the issuer to such member of the board of directors; and

(B) Whether a member of the board of directors of an issuer is affiliated with the issuer, a subsidiary of the issuer or an affiliate of a subsidiary of the issuer.

(iii) *Exemptions from the independence requirements.* (A) The listing of equity securities of the following categories of listed issuers is not subject to the requirements of paragraph (b)(1) of this section:

(*1*) Limited partnerships;

(*2*) Companies in bankruptcy proceedings;

(*3*) Open-end management investment companies registered under the Investment Company Act of 1940; and

(*4*) Any foreign private issuer that discloses in its annual report the reasons that the foreign private issuer does not have an independent compensation committee.

(B) In addition to the issuer exemptions set forth in paragraph (b)(1)(iii)(A) of this section, a national securities exchange or a national securities association, pursuant to section 19(b) of the Act (15 U.S.C. 78s(b)) and the rules thereunder, may exempt from the requirements of paragraph (b)(1) of

Securities and Exchange Commission § 240.10C-1

this section a particular relationship with respect to members of the compensation committee, as each national securities exchange or national securities association determines is appropriate, taking into consideration the size of an issuer and any other relevant factors.

(2) *Authority to retain compensation consultants, independent legal counsel and other compensation advisers.* (i) The compensation committee of a listed issuer, in its capacity as a committee of the board of directors, may, in its sole discretion, retain or obtain the advice of a compensation consultant, independent legal counsel or other adviser.

(ii) The compensation committee shall be directly responsible for the appointment, compensation and oversight of the work of any compensation consultant, independent legal counsel and other adviser retained by the compensation committee.

(iii) Nothing in this paragraph (b)(2) shall be construed:

(A) To require the compensation committee to implement or act consistently with the advice or recommendations of the compensation consultant, independent legal counsel or other adviser to the compensation committee; or

(B) To affect the ability or obligation of a compensation committee to exercise its own judgment in fulfillment of the duties of the compensation committee.

(3) *Funding.* Each listed issuer must provide for appropriate funding, as determined by the compensation committee, in its capacity as a committee of the board of directors, for payment of reasonable compensation to a compensation consultant, independent legal counsel or any other adviser retained by the compensation committee.

(4) *Independence of compensation consultants and other advisers.* The compensation committee of a listed issuer may select a compensation consultant, legal counsel or other adviser to the compensation committee only after taking into consideration the following factors, as well as any other factors identified by the relevant national securities exchange or national securities association in its listing standards:

(i) The provision of other services to the issuer by the person that employs the compensation consultant, legal counsel or other adviser;

(ii) The amount of fees received from the issuer by the person that employs the compensation consultant, legal counsel or other adviser, as a percentage of the total revenue of the person that employs the compensation consultant, legal counsel or other adviser;

(iii) The policies and procedures of the person that employs the compensation consultant, legal counsel or other adviser that are designed to prevent conflicts of interest;

(iv) Any business or personal relationship of the compensation consultant, legal counsel or other adviser with a member of the compensation committee;

(v) Any stock of the issuer owned by the compensation consultant, legal counsel or other adviser; and

(vi) Any business or personal relationship of the compensation consultant, legal counsel, other adviser or the person employing the adviser with an executive officer of the issuer.

INSTRUCTION TO PARAGRAPH (b)(4) OF THIS SECTION: A listed issuer's compensation committee is required to conduct the independence assessment outlined in paragraph (b)(4) *of this section* with respect to any compensation consultant, legal counsel or other adviser that provides advice to the compensation committee, other than in-house legal counsel.

(5) *General exemptions.* (i) The national securities exchanges and national securities associations, pursuant to section 19(b) of the Act (15 U.S.C. 78s(b)) and the rules thereunder, may exempt from the requirements of this section certain categories of issuers, as the national securities exchange or national securities association determines is appropriate, taking into consideration, among other relevant factors, the potential impact of such requirements on smaller reporting issuers.

(ii) The requirements of this section shall not apply to any controlled company or to any smaller reporting company.

§ 240.10D-1

(iii) The listing of a security futures product cleared by a clearing agency that is registered pursuant to section 17A of the Act (15 U.S.C. 78q–1) or that is exempt from the registration requirements of section 17A(b)(7)(A) (15 U.S.C. 78q–1(b)(7)(A)) is not subject to the requirements of this section.

(iv) The listing of a standardized option, as defined in §240.9b–1(a)(4), issued by a clearing agency that is registered pursuant to section 17A of the Act (15 U.S.C. 78q–1) is not subject to the requirements of this section.

(c) *Definitions.* Unless the context otherwise requires, all terms used in this section have the same meaning as in the Act and the rules and regulations thereunder. In addition, unless the context otherwise requires, the following definitions apply for purposes of this section:

(1) In the case of foreign private issuers with a two-tier board system, the term *board of directors* means the supervisory or non-management board.

(2) The term *compensation committee* means:

(i) A committee of the board of directors that is designated as the compensation committee; or

(ii) In the absence of a committee of the board of directors that is designated as the compensation committee, a committee of the board of directors performing functions typically performed by a compensation committee, including oversight of executive compensation, even if it is not designated as the compensation committee or also performs other functions; or

(iii) For purposes of this section other than paragraphs (b)(2)(i) and (b)(3), in the absence of a committee as described in paragraphs (c)(2)(i) or (ii) of this section, the members of the board of directors who oversee executive compensation matters on behalf of the board of directors.

(3) The term *controlled company* means an issuer:

(i) That is listed on a national securities exchange or by a national securities association; and

(ii) Of which more than 50 percent of the voting power for the election of directors is held by an individual, a group or another company.

(4) The terms *listed* and *listing* refer to equity securities listed on a national securities exchange or listed in an automated inter-dealer quotation system of a national securities association or to issuers of such securities.

(5) The term *open-end management investment company* means an open-end company, as defined by Section 5(a)(1) of the Investment Company Act of 1940 (15 U.S.C. 80a–5(a)(1)), that is registered under that Act.

[77 FR 38454, June 27, 2012]

REQUIREMENTS UNDER SECTION 10D

§ 240.10D–1 Listing standards relating to recovery of erroneously awarded compensation.

(a) Each national securities exchange registered pursuant to section 6 of the Act (15 U.S.C. 78f) and each national securities association registered pursuant to section 15A of the Act (15 U.S.C. 78o–3), to the extent such national securities exchange or association lists securities, must:

(1) In accordance with the provisions of this section, prohibit the initial or continued listing of any security of an issuer that is not in compliance with the requirements of any portion of this section;

(2) No later than February 27, 2023, propose rules or rule amendments that comply with this section. Such rules or rule amendments that comply with this section must be effective no later than one year after November 28, 2022;

(3) Require that each listed issuer:

(i) Adopt the recovery policy required by this section no later than 60 days following the effective date of the listing standard referenced in paragraph (a)(2) of this section to which the issuer is subject;

(ii) Comply with that recovery policy for all incentive-based compensation received (as defined in paragraph (d) of this section) by executive officers on or after the effective date of the applicable listing standard;

(iii) Provide the disclosures required by this section and in the applicable Commission filings required on or after the effective date of the listing standard referenced in paragraph (a)(2) of this section to which the issuer is subject.

Securities and Exchange Commission § 240.10D–1

(b) *Recovery of Erroneously Awarded Compensation.* The issuer must:

(1) Adopt and comply with a written policy providing that the issuer will recover reasonably promptly the amount of erroneously awarded incentive-based compensation in the event that the issuer is required to prepare an accounting restatement due to the material noncompliance of the issuer with any financial reporting requirement under the securities laws, including any required accounting restatement to correct an error in previously issued financial statements that is material to the previously issued financial statements, or that would result in a material misstatement if the error were corrected in the current period or left uncorrected in the current period.

(i) The issuer's recovery policy must apply to all incentive-based compensation received by a person:

(A) After beginning service as an executive officer;

(B) Who served as an executive officer at any time during the performance period for that incentive-based compensation;

(C) While the issuer has a class of securities listed on a national securities exchange or a national securities association; and

(D) During the three completed fiscal years immediately preceding the date that the issuer is required to prepare an accounting restatement as described in paragraph (b)(1) of this section. In addition to these last three completed fiscal years, the recovery policy must apply to any transition period (that results from a change in the issuer's fiscal year) within or immediately following those three completed fiscal years. However, a transition period between the last day of the issuer's previous fiscal year end and the first day of its new fiscal year that comprises a period of nine to 12 months would be deemed a completed fiscal year. An issuer's obligation to recover erroneously awarded compensation is not dependent on if or when the restated financial statements are filed.

(ii) For purposes of determining the relevant recovery period, the date that an issuer is required to prepare an accounting restatement as described in paragraph (b)(1) of this section is the earlier to occur of:

(A) The date the issuer's board of directors, a committee of the board of directors, or the officer or officers of the issuer authorized to take such action if board action is not required, concludes, or reasonably should have concluded, that the issuer is required to prepare an accounting restatement as described in paragraph (b)(1) of this section; or

(B) The date a court, regulator, or other legally authorized body directs the issuer to prepare an accounting restatement as described in paragraph (b)(1) of this section.

(iii) The amount of incentive-based compensation that must be subject to the issuer's recovery policy ("erroneously awarded compensation") is the amount of incentive-based compensation received that exceeds the amount of incentive-based compensation that otherwise would have been received had it been determined based on the restated amounts, and must be computed without regard to any taxes paid. For incentive-based compensation based on stock price or total shareholder return, where the amount of erroneously awarded compensation is not subject to mathematical recalculation directly from the information in an accounting restatement:

(A) The amount must be based on a reasonable estimate of the effect of the accounting restatement on the stock price or total shareholder return upon which the incentive-based compensation was received; and

(B) The issuer must maintain documentation of the determination of that reasonable estimate and provide such documentation to the exchange or association.

(iv) The issuer must recover erroneously awarded compensation in compliance with its recovery policy except to the extent that the conditions of paragraphs (b)(1)(iv)(A), (B), or (C) of this section are met, and the issuer's committee of independent directors responsible for executive compensation decisions, or in the absence of such a committee, a majority of the independent directors serving on the board, has made a determination that recovery would be impracticable.

§ 240.10D-1

(A) The direct expense paid to a third party to assist in enforcing the policy would exceed the amount to be recovered. Before concluding that it would be impracticable to recover any amount of erroneously awarded compensation based on expense of enforcement, the issuer must make a reasonable attempt to recover such erroneously awarded compensation, document such reasonable attempt(s) to recover, and provide that documentation to the exchange or association.

(B) Recovery would violate home country law where that law was adopted prior to November 28, 2022. Before concluding that it would be impracticable to recover any amount of erroneously awarded compensation based on violation of home country law, the issuer must obtain an opinion of home country counsel, acceptable to the applicable national securities exchange or association, that recovery would result in such a violation, and must provide such opinion to the exchange or association.

(C) Recovery would likely cause an otherwise tax-qualified retirement plan, under which benefits are broadly available to employees of the registrant, to fail to meet the requirements of 26 U.S.C. 401(a)(13) or 26 U.S.C. 411(a) and regulations thereunder.

(v) The issuer is prohibited from indemnifying any executive officer or former executive officer against the loss of erroneously awarded compensation.

(2) File all disclosures with respect to such recovery policy in accordance with the requirements of the Federal securities laws, including the disclosure required by the applicable Commission filings.

(c) *General Exemptions.* The requirements of this section do not apply to the listing of:

(1) A security futures product cleared by a clearing agency that is registered pursuant to section 17A of the Act (15 U.S.C. 78q-1) or that is exempt from the registration requirements of section 17A(b)(7)(A) (15 U.S.C. 78q-1(b)(7)(A));

(2) A standardized option, as defined in 17 CFR 240.9b-1(a)(4), issued by a clearing agency that is registered pursuant to section 17A of the Act (15 U.S.C. 78q-1);

(3) Any security issued by a unit investment trust, as defined in 15 U.S.C. 80a-4(2);

(4) Any security issued by a management company, as defined in 15 U.S.C. 80a-4(3), that is registered under section 8 of the Investment Company Act of 1940 (15 U.S.C. 80a-8), if such management company has not awarded incentive-based compensation to any executive officer of the company in any of the last three fiscal years, or in the case of a company that has been listed for less than three fiscal years, since the listing of the company.

(d) *Definitions.* Unless the context otherwise requires, the following definitions apply for purposes of this section:

Executive Officer. An *executive officer* is the issuer's president, principal financial officer, principal accounting officer (or if there is no such accounting officer, the controller), any vice-president of the issuer in charge of a principal business unit, division, or function (such as sales, administration, or finance), any other officer who performs a policy-making function, or any other person who performs similar policy-making functions for the issuer. Executive officers of the issuer's parent(s) or subsidiaries are deemed executive officers of the issuer if they perform such policy making functions for the issuer. In addition, when the issuer is a limited partnership, officers or employees of the general partner(s) who perform policy-making functions for the limited partnership are deemed officers of the limited partnership. When the issuer is a trust, officers, or employees of the trustee(s) who perform policy-making functions for the trust are deemed officers of the trust. Policy-making function is not intended to include policy-making functions that are not significant. Identification of an executive officer for purposes of this section would include at a minimum executive officers identified pursuant to 17 CFR 229.401(b).

Financial reporting measures. Financial reporting measures are measures that

Securities and Exchange Commission § 240.11a–1

are determined and presented in accordance with the accounting principles used in preparing the issuer's financial statements, and any measures that are derived wholly or in part from such measures. Stock price and total shareholder return are also financial reporting measures. A financial reporting measure need not be presented within the financial statements or included in a filing with the Commission.

Incentive-based compensation. Incentive-based compensation is any compensation that is granted, earned, or vested based wholly or in part upon the attainment of a financial reporting measure.

Received. Incentive-based compensation is deemed received in the issuer's fiscal period during which the financial reporting measure specified in the incentive-based compensation award is attained, even if the payment or grant of the incentive-based compensation occurs after the end of that period.

[87 FR 73138, Nov. 28, 2022]

ADOPTION OF FLOOR TRADING REGULATION (RULE 11A–1)

§ 240.11a–1 Regulation of floor trading.

(a) No member of a national securities exchange, while on the floor of such exchange, shall initiate, directly or indirectly, any transaction in any security admitted to trading on such exchange, for any account in which such member has an interest, or for any such account with respect to which such member has discretion as to the time of execution, the choice of security to be bought or sold, the total amount of any security to be bought or sold, or whether any such transaction shall be one of purchase or sale.

(b) The provisions of paragraph (a) of this section shall not apply to:

(1) Any transaction by a registered specialist in a security in which he is so registered on such exchange;

(2) Any transaction for the account of an odd-lot dealer in a security in which he is so registered on such exchange;

(3) Any stabilizing transaction effected in compliance with § 242.104 of this chapter to facilitate a distribution of such security in which such member is participating;

(4) Any bona fide arbitrage transaction;

(5) Any transaction made with the prior approval of a floor official of such exchange to permit such member to contribute to the maintenance of a fair and orderly market in such security, or any purchase or sale to reverse any such transaction;

(6) Any transaction to offset a transaction made in error; or

(7) Any transaction effected in conformity with a plan designed to eliminate floor trading activities which are not beneficial to the market and which plan has been adopted by an exchange and declared effective by the Commission. For the purpose of this rule, a plan filed with the Commission by a national securities exchange shall not become effective unless the Commission, having due regard for the maintenance of fair and orderly markets, for the public interest, and for the protection of investors, declares the plan to be effective.

(c) For the purpose of this rule the term "on the floor of such exchange" shall include the trading floor; the rooms, lobbies, and other premises immediately adjacent thereto for use of members generally; other rooms, lobbies and premises made available primarily for use by members generally; and the telephone and other facilities in any such place.

(d) Any national securities exchange may apply for an exemption from the provisions of this rule in compliance with the provisions of section 11(c) of the Act.

(Sec. 11, 48 Stat. 891; 15 U.S.C. 78k)

[29 FR 7381, June 6, 1964, as amended at 62 FR 544, Jan. 3, 1997]

NOTE 1: The Commission finding that the floor trading plan of the New York Stock Exchange filed on May 25, 1964 is designed to eliminate floor trading activities not beneficial to the market hereby declares such plan effective August 3, 1964 subject to suspension or termination on sixty days written notice from the Commission, 29 FR 7381, June 6, 1964.

NOTE 2: The text of the Commission's action declaring effective the amendments to the Floor Trading Plan of the American Stock Exchange (33 FR 1073, Jan. 27, 1968) is as follows:

The Securities and Exchange Commission acting pursuant to the Securities Exchange Act of 1934, particularly sections 11(a) and

§ 240.11a1-1(T)

23(a) thereof, and Rule 11a-1 (17 CFR 240.11a-1) under the Act, deeming it necessary for the exercise of the functions vested in it, and having due regard for the maintenance of fair and orderly markets, for the public interest, and for the protection of investors, hereby declares the Floor Trading Plan of the American Stock Exchange, as amended by amendments filed on May 11, 1967, effective January 31, 1968. If at any time it appears to the Commission to be necessary or appropriate in the public interest, for the protection of investors, or for the maintenance of fair and orderly markets, or that floor trading activities which are not beneficial to the market have not been eliminated by the Floor Trading Plan of the American Stock Exchange, the Commission may suspend or terminate the effectiveness of the plan by sending at least 60 days written notice to the American Stock Exchange. The American Stock Exchange shall have the opportunity to submit any written data, facts, arguments, or modifications in its plan within such 60-day period in such form as the Commission deems appropriate under the circumstances. The Commission has been informed that all persons subject to the Floor Trading Plan of the American Stock Exchange, as amended, have had actual notice thereof, and the Commission finds that notice and procedure pursuant to section 4 of the Administrative Procedure Act (5 U.S.C. section 553) are impracticable and unnecessary and that such Plan, as amended, may be, and is hereby, declared effective on January 31, 1968.

§ 240.11a1-1(T) Transactions yielding priority, parity, and precedence.

(a) A transaction effected on a national securities exchange for the account of a member which meets the requirements of section 11(a)(1)(G)(i) of the Act shall be deemed, in accordance with the requirements of section 11(a)(1)(G)(ii), to be not inconsistent with the maintenance of fair and orderly markets and to yield priority, parity, and precedence in execution to orders for the account of persons who are not members or associated with members of the exchange if such transaction is effected in compliance with each of the following requirements:

(1) A member shall disclose that a bid or offer for its account is for its account to any member with whom such bid or offer is placed or to whom it is communicated, and any such member through whom that bid or offer is communicated shall disclose to others participating in effecting the order that it is for the account of a member.

(2) Immediately before executing the order, a member (other than the specialist in such security) presenting any order for the account of a member on the exchange shall clearly announce or otherwise indicate to the specialist and to other members then present for the trading in such security on the exchange that he is presenting an order for the account of a member.

(3) Notwithstanding rules of priority, parity, and precedence otherwise applicable, any member presenting for execution a bid or offer for its own account or for the account of another member shall grant priority to any bid or offer at the same price for the account of a person who is not, or is not associated with, a member, irrespective of the size of any such bid or offer or the time when entered.

(b) A member shall be deemed to meet the requirements of section 11(a)(1)(G)(i) of the Act if during its preceding fiscal year more than 50 percent of its gross revenues was derived from one or more of the sources specified in that section. In addition to any revenue which independently meets the requirements of section 11(a)(1)(G)(i), revenue derived from any transaction specified in paragraph (A), (B), or (D) of section 11(a)(1) of the Act or specified in 17 CFR 240.11a1-4(T) shall be deemed to be revenue derived from one or more of the sources specified in section 11(a)(1)(G)(i). A member may rely on a list of members which are stated to meet the requirements of section 11(a)(1)(G)(i) if such list is prepared, and updated at least annually, by the exchange. In preparing any such list, an exchange may rely on a report which sets forth a statement of gross revenues of a member if covered by a report of independent accountants for such member to the effect that such report has been prepared in accordance with generally accepted accounting principles.

(Secs. 2, 3, 6, 11, 11A, and 23, 89 Stat. 97, 104, 110, 111, 156 (15 U.S.C. 78b, 78c, 78f, 78k, 78k-1, 78w); secs. 2, 3, 11, 23, 48 Stat. 881, 882, 885, 891, 901, as amended)

[43 FR 11553, Mar. 17, 1978, as amended at 43 FR 18562, May 1, 1978; 44 FR 6093, Jan. 31, 1979]

Securities and Exchange Commission

§ 240.11a1-6

§ 240.11a1-2 Transactions for certain accounts of associated persons of members.

A transaction effected by a member of a national securities exchange for the account of an associated person thereof shall be deemed to be of a kind which is consistent with the purposes of section 11(a)(1) of the Act, the protection of investors, and the maintenance of fair and orderly markets if the transaction is effected:

(a) For the account of and for the benefit of an associated person, if, assuming such transaction were for the account of a member, or

(b) For the account of an associated person but for the benefit of an account carried by such associated person, if, assuming such account were carried on the same basis by a member.

The member would have been permitted, under section 11(a) of the Act and the other rules thereunder, to effect the transaction: *Provided, however,* That a transaction may not be effected by a member for the account of and for the benefit of an associated person under section 11(a)(1)(G) of the Act and Rule 11a1–1(T) thereunder unless the associated person derived, during its preceding fiscal year, more than 50 percent of its gross revenues from one or more of the sources specified in section 11(a)(1)(G)(i) of the Act.

(Secs. 2, 3, 4, 6, 7, 11, 18, 89 Stat. 97, 104, 110, 111, 121, 155 (15 U.S.C. 78b, 78c, 78f, 78k, 78k–1, 78o, 78w); secs. 2, 3, 10, 23, 48 Stat. 881, 882, 891, 901, as amended (15 U.S.C. 78j))

[43 FR 11553, Mar. 17, 1978; 43 FR 14451, Apr. 6, 1978]

§ 240.11a1-3(T) Bona fide hedge transactions in certain securities.

A bona fide hedge transaction effected on a national securities exchange by a member for its own account or an account of an associated person thereof and involving a long or short position in a security entitling the holder to acquire or sell an equity security, and a long or short position in one or more other securities entitling the holder to acquire or sell such equity security, shall be deemed to be of a kind which is consistent with the purposes of section 11(a)(1) of the Act, the protection of investors, and the maintenance of fair and orderly markets.

(Secs. 2, 3, 6, 11, 11A, and 23, 89 Stat. 97, 104, 110, 111, 156 (15 U.S.C. 78b, 78c, 78f, 78k, 78k–1, 78w); secs. 2, 3, 11, 23, 48 Stat. 881, 882, 885, 891, 901, as amended)

[44 FR 6093, Jan. 31, 1979]

§ 240.11a1-4(T) Bond transactions on national securities exchanges.

A transaction in a bond, note, debenture, or other form of indebtedness effected on a national securities exchange by a member for its own account or the account of an associated person thereof shall be deemed to be of a kind which is consistent with the purposes of section 11(a)(1) of the Act, the protection of investors, and the maintenance of fair and orderly markets.

(Secs. 2, 3, 6, 10, 11, 11A, 15 and 23 of the Securities Exchange Act of 1934 (15 U.S.C. 78b, 78c, 78f, 78j, 78k, 78k–1, 78o, and 78w))

[43 FR 18562, May 1, 1978]

§ 240.11a1-5 Transactions by registered competitive market makers and registered equity market makers.

Any transaction by a New York Stock Exchange registered competitive market maker or an American Stock Exchange registered equity market maker effected in compliance with their respective governing rules shall be deemed to be of a kind which is consistent with the purposes of section 11(a)(1) of the Act, the protection of investors, and the maintenance of fair and orderly markets.

[46 FR 14889, Mar. 3, 1981]

§ 240.11a1-6 Transactions for certain accounts of OTC derivatives dealers.

A transaction effected by a member of a national securities exchange for the account of an OTC derivatives dealer that is an associated person of that member shall be deemed to be of a kind that is consistent with the purposes of section 11(a)(1) of the Act (15 U.S.C. 78k(a)(1)), the protection of investors,

§ 240.11a2-2(T)

and the maintenance of fair and orderly markets if, assuming such transaction were for the account of a member, the member would have been permitted, under section 11(a) of the Act and the other rules thereunder (with the exception of § 240.11a1-2), to effect the transaction.

[63 FR 59396, Nov. 3, 1998]

§ 240.11a2-2(T) Transactions effected by exchange members through other members.

(a) A member of a national securities exchange (the "initiating member") may not effect a transaction on that exchange for its own account, the account of an associated person, or an account with respect to which it or an associated person thereof exercises investment discretion unless:

(1) The transaction is of a kind described in paragraphs A through H of section 11(a)(1) of the Act and is effected in accordance with applicable rules and regulations thereunder; or

(2) The transaction is effected in compliance with each of the following conditions:

(i) The transaction is executed on the floor, or through use of the facilities, of the exchange by a member (the "executing member") which is not an associated person of the initiating member;

(ii) The order for the transaction is transmitted from off the exchange floor;

(iii) Neither the initiating member nor an associated person of the initiating member participates in the execution of the transaction at any time after the order for the transaction has been so transmitted; and

(iv) In the case of a transaction effected for an account with respect to which the initiating member or an associated person thereof exercises investment discretion, neither the initiating member nor any associated person thereof retains any compensation in connection with effecting the transaction: *Provided, however,* That this condition shall not apply to the extent that the person or persons authorized to transact business for the account have expressly provided otherwise by written contract referring to section 11(a) of the Act and this section executed on or after March 15, 1978, by each of them and by such exchange member or associated person exercising investment discretion.

(b) For purposes of this section, a member "effects" a securities transaction when it performs any function in connection with the processing of that transaction, including, but not limited to, (1) transmission of an order for execution, (2) execution of the order, (3) clearance and settlement of the transaction, and (4) arranging for the performance of any such function.

(c) For purposes of this section, the term "compensation in connection with effecting the transaction" refers to compensation directly or indirectly received or calculated on a transaction-related basis for the performance of any function involved in effecting a securities transaction.

(d) A member, or an associated person of a member, authorized by written contract to retain compensation in connection with effecting transactions pursuant to paragraph (a)(2)(iv) of this section shall furnish at least annually to the person or persons authorized to transact business for the account a statement setting forth the total amount of all compensation retained by the member or any associated person thereof in connection with effecting transactions for that account during the period covered by the statement, which amount shall be exclusive of all amounts paid to others during that period for services rendered in effecting such transactions.

(e) A transaction effected in compliance with the requirements of this section shall be deemed to be of a kind which is consistent with the purposes of section 11(a)(1) of the Act, the protection of investors, and the maintenance of fair and orderly markets.

(f) The provisions of this section shall not apply to transactions by exchange members to which, by operation of section 11(a)(3) of the Act, section 11(a)(1) of the Act is not effective.

(Secs. 2, 3, 4, 6, 7, 11, 18, 89 Stat. 97, 104, 110, 111, 121, 155 (15 U.S.C. 78b, 78c, 78f, 78k, 78k-1, 78*o*, 78w); secs. 2, 3, 10, 23, 48 Stat. 881, 882, 891, 901, as amended (15 U.S.C. 78j))

[43 FR 11554, Mar. 17, 1978, as amended at 43 FR 18562, May 1, 1978]

Securities and Exchange Commission

Adoption of Regulation on Conduct of Specialists

§ 240.11b-1 Regulation of specialists.

(a)(1) The rules of a national securities exchange may permit a member of such exchange to register as a specialist and to act as a dealer.

(2) The rules of a national securities exchange permitting a member of such exchange to register as a specialist and to act as a dealer shall include:

(i) Adequate minimum capital requirements in view of the markets for securities on such exchange;

(ii) Requirements, as a condition of a specialist's registration, that a specialist engage in a course of dealings for his own account to assist in the maintenance, so far as practicable, of a fair and orderly market, and that a finding by the exchange of any substantial or continued failure by a specialist to engage in such a course of dealings will result in the suspension or cancellation of such specialist's registration in one or more of the securities in which such specialist is registered;

(iii) Provisions restricting his dealings so far as practicable to those reasonably necessary to permit him to maintain a fair and orderly market or necessary to permit him to act as an odd-lot dealer;

(iv) Provisions stating the responsibilities of a specialist acting as a broker in securities in which he is registered; and

(v) Procedures to provide for the effective and systematic surveillance of the activities of specialists.

(b) If after appropriate notice and opportunity for hearing the Commission finds that a member of a national securities exchange registered with such exchange as a specialist in specified securities has, for any account in which he, his member organization, or any participant therein has any beneficial interest, direct or indirect, effected transactions in such securities which were not part of a course of dealings reasonably necessary to permit such specialist to maintain a fair and orderly market, or to act as an odd-lot dealer, in the securities in which he is registered and were not effected in a manner consistent with the rules adopted by such exchange pursuant to paragraph (a)(2)(iii) of this section, the Commission may by order direct such exchange to cancel, or to suspend for such period as the Commission may determine, such specialist's registration in one or more of the securities in which such specialist is registered: *Provided, however,* If such exchange has itself suspended or cancelled such specialist's registration in one or more of the securities in which such specialist is registered, no further sanction shall be imposed pursuant to this paragraph (b) except in a case where the Commission finds substantial or continued misconduct by a specialist: *And provided, further,* That the provisions of this paragraph (b) shall not apply to a member of a national securities exchange exempted pursuant to the provisions of paragraph (d) of this section.

(c) For the purposes of this section, the term *rules* of an exchange shall mean its constitution, articles of incorporation, by-laws, or rules or instruments corresponding thereto, whatever the name, and its stated policies.

(d) Any national securities exchange may apply for an exemption from the provisions of this section in compliance with the provisions of section 11(c) of the Act.

(Sec. 11, 48 Stat. 891, 892; 15 U.S.C. 78k)

[29 FR 15863, Nov. 26, 1964, as amended at 46 FR 15135, Mar. 4, 1981]

Exemption of Certain Securities from Section 11(d)(1)

§ 240.11d1-1 Exemption of certain securities from section 11(d)(1).

A security shall be exempt from the provisions of section 11(d)(1) with respect to any transaction by a broker and dealer who, directly or indirectly extends or maintains or arranges for the extension or maintenance of credit on the security to or for a customer if:

(a) The broker and dealer has not sold the security to the customer or bought the security for the customer's account; or

(b) The security is acquired by the customer in exchange with the issuer thereof for an outstanding security of the same issuer on which credit was lawfully maintained for the customer at the time of the exchange; or

§ 240.11d1-2

(c) The customer is a broker or dealer or bank; or

(d) The security is acquired by the customer through the exercise of a right evidenced by a warrant or certificate expiring within 90 days after issuance, provided such right was originally issued to the customer as a stockholder of the corporation issuing the security upon which credit is to be extended. The right shall be deemed to be issued to the customer as a stockholder if he actually owned the stock giving rise to the right when such right accrued, even though such stock was not registered in his name; and in determining such fact the broker and dealer may rely upon a signed statement of the customer which the broker and dealer accepts in good faith; or

(e) Such broker and dealer would otherwise be subject to the prohibition of section 11(d)(1) with respect to 50 percent or less of all the securities of the same class which are outstanding or currently being distributed, and such broker and dealer sold the security to the customer or bought the security for the customer's account on a day when he was not participating in the distribution of any new issue of such security. A brokerdealer shall be deemed to be participating in a distribution of a new issue if (1) he owns, directly or indirectly, any undistributed security of such issue, or (2) he is engaged in any stabilizing activities to facilitate a distribution of such issue, or (3) he is a party to any syndicate agreement under which such stabilizing activities are being or may be undertaken, or (4) he is a party to an executory agreement to purchase or distribute such issue.

[13 FR 8184, Dec. 22, 1948, as amended at 76 FR 71876, Nov. 21, 2011]

§ 240.11d1-2 Exemption from section 11(d)(1) for certain investment company securities held by broker-dealers as collateral in margin accounts.

Any securities issued by a registered open-end investment company or unit investment trust as defined in the Investment Company Act of 1940 shall be exempted from the provisions of section 11(d)(1) with respect to any transaction by a person who is a broker and a dealer who, directly or indirectly, extends or maintains or arranges for the extension or maintenance of credit on such security, provided such security has been owned by the person to whom credit would be provided for more than 30 days, or purchased by such person pursuant to a plan for the automatic reinvestment of the dividends of such company or trust.

(Secs. 2, 3, 11, and 23, Exchange Act, 15 U.S.C. 78b, 78c, 78k and 78w)

[49 FR 50174, Dec. 27, 1984]

§ 240.11d2-1 Exemption from Section 11(d)(2) for certain broker-dealers effecting transactions for customers security futures products in futures accounts.

A broker or dealer registered pursuant to section 15(b)(1) of the Act (15 U.S.C. 78*o*(b)(1)) that is also a futures commission merchant registered pursuant to section 4f(a)(1) of the Commodity Exchange Act (7 U.S.C. 6f(a)(1)), to the extent that it effects transactions for customers in security futures products in a futures account (as that term is defined in § 240.15c3-3(a)(15)), is exempt from section 11(d)(2) of the Act (15 U.S.C. 78k(d)(2)).

[67 FR 58313, Sept. 13, 2002]

SECURITIES EXEMPTED FROM REGISTRATION

§ 240.12a-4 Exemption of certain warrants from section 12(a).

(a) When used in this section, the following terms shall have the meaning indicated unless the context otherwise requires:

(1) The term *warrant* means any warrant or certificate evidencing a right to subscribe to or otherwise acquire another security, issued or unissued.

(2) The term *beneficiary security* means a security to the holders of which a warrant or right to subscribe to or otherwise acquire another security is granted.

(3) The term *subject security* means a security which is the subject of a warrant or right to subscribe to or otherwise acquire such security.

(4) The term *in the process of admission to dealing*, in respect of a specified security means that (i) an application has been filed pursuant to section 12 (b)

Securities and Exchange Commission § 240.12a-4

and (c) of the Act for the registration of such security on a national securities exchange; or (ii) the Commission has granted an application made pursuant to section 12(f) of the Act to continue or extend unlisted trading privileges to such security on a national securities exchange; or (iii) written notice has been filed with the Commission by a national securities exchange to the effect that such security has been approved for admission to dealing as a security exempted from the operation of section 12(a) of the Act.

(b) Any issued or unissued warrant granted to the holders of a security admitted to dealing on a national securities exchange, shall be exempt from the operation of section 12(a) of the Act to the extent necessary to render lawful the effecting of transactions therein on any national securities exchange (i) on which the beneficiary security is admitted to dealing or (ii) on which the subject security is admitted to dealing or is in the process of admission to dealing, subject to the following terms and conditions:

(1) Such warrant by its terms expires within 90 days after the issuance thereof;

(2) A registration statement under the Securities Act of 1933 is in effect as to such warrant and as to each subject security, or the applicable terms of any exemption from such registration have been met in respect to such warrant and each subject security; and

(3) Within five days after the exchange has taken official action to admit such warrant to dealing, it shall notify the Commission of such action.

(c) Notwithstanding paragraph (b) of this section, no exemption pursuant to this section shall be available for transactions in any such warrant on any exchange on which the beneficiary security is admitted to dealing unless:

(1) Each subject security is admitted to dealing or is in process of admission to dealing on a national securities exchange; or

(2) There is available from a registration statement and periodic reports or other data filed by the issuer of the subject security, pursuant to any act administered by the Commission, information substantially equivalent to that available with respect to a security listed and registered on a national securities exchange.

(d) Notwithstanding the foregoing, an unissued warrant shall not be exempt pursuant to this section unless:

(1) Formal or official announcement has been made by the issuer specifying (i) the terms upon which such warrant and each subject security is to be issued, (ii) the date, if any, as of which the security holders entitled to receive such warrant will be determined, (iii) the approximate date of the issuance of such warrant, and (iv) the approximate date of the issuance of each subject security; and,

(2) The members of the exchange are subject to rules which provide that the performance of the contract to purchase and sell an unissued warrant shall be conditioned upon the issuance of such warrant.

(e) The Commission may by order deny or revoke the exemption of a warrant under this section, if, after appropriate notice and opportunity for hearing to the issuer of such warrant and to the exchange or exchanges on which such warrant is admitted to dealing as an exempted security, it finds that:

(1) Any of the terms or conditions of this section have not been met with respect to such exemption, or

(2) At any time during the period of such exemption transactions have been effected on any such exchanges in such warrant which (i) create or induce a false, misleading or artificial appearance of activity, (ii) unduly or improperly influence the market price, or (iii) make a price which does not reflect the true state of the market; or

(3) Any other facts exist which make such denial or revocation necessary or appropriate in the public interest or for the protection of investors.

(f) If it appears necessary or appropriate in the public interest or for the protection of investors, the Commission may summarily suspend the exemption of such warrant pending the determination by the Commission whether such exemption shall be denied or revoked.

§ 240.12a-5

(g) Section 240.10b-1 shall be applicable to any warrant exempted by this section.

(Secs. 3, 12, 48 Stat. 882, as amended, 892; 15 U.S.C. 78c, 78*l*)

[15 FR 3450, June 2, 1950, as amended at 18 FR 128, Jan. 7, 1953]

§ 240.12a-5 Temporary exemption of substituted or additional securities.

(a)(1) Subject to the conditions of paragraph (a)(2) of this section, whenever the holders of a security admitted to trading on a national securities exchange (hereinafter called the original security) obtain the right, by operation of law or otherwise, to acquire all or any part of a class of another or substitute security of the same or another issuer, or an additional amount of the original security, then:

(i) All or any part of the class of such other or substituted security shall be temporarily exempted from the operation of section 12(a) to the extent necessary to render lawful transactions therein on an issued or "when-issued" basis on any national securities exchange on which the original, the other or the substituted security is lawfully admitted to trading; and

(ii) The additional amount of the original security shall be temporarily exempted from the operation of section 12(a) to the extent necessary to render lawful transactions therein on a "when-issued" basis on any national securities exchange on which the original security is lawfully admitted to trading.

(2) The exemptions provided by paragraph (a)(1) of this section shall be available only if the following conditions are met:

(i) A registration statement is in effect under the Securities Act of 1933 to the extent required as to the security which is the subject of such exemption, or the terms of any applicable exemption from registration under such act have been complied with, if required;

(ii) Any stockholder approval necessary to the issuance of the security which is the subject of the exemption, has been obtained; and

(iii) All other necessary official action, other than the filing or recording of charter amendments or other documents with the appropriate State authorities, has been taken to authorize and assure the issuance of the security which is the subject of such exemption.

(b) The exemption provided by this section shall terminate on the earliest of the following dates:

(1) When registration of the exempt security on the exchange become effective;

(2) When the exempt security is granted unlisted trading privileges on the exchange;

(3) The close of business on the tenth day after (i) withdrawal of an application for registration of the exempt security on the exchange; (ii) withdrawal by the exchange of its certification of approval of the exempt security for listing and registration; (iii) withdrawal of an application for admission of the exempt security to unlisted trading privileges on the exchange; or (iv) the sending to the exchange of notice of the entry of an order by the Commission denying any application for admission of the exempt security to unlisted trading privileges on the exchange;

(4) The close of business on the one hundred and twentieth day after the date on which the exempt security was admitted by action of the exchange to trading thereon as a security exempted from the operation of section 12 (a) by this section, unless prior thereto an application for registration of the exempt security or for admission of the exempt security to unlisted trading privileges on the exchange has been filed.

(c) Notwithstanding paragraph (b) of this section, the Commission, having due regard for the public interest and the protection of investors, may at any time extend the period of exemption of any security by this rule or may sooner terminate the exemption upon notice to the exchange and to the issuer of the extension or termination thereof.

(d) The Exchange shall file with the Commission a notification on Form 26[1] promptly after taking action to admit any security to trading under this section: *Provided, however,* That no notification need be filed under this section concerning the admission or proposed admission to trading of additional

---

[1] Copy filed with the Federal Register Division.

Securities and Exchange Commission

§ 240.12a–8

amounts of a class of security admitted to trading on such exchange.

(e) Section 240.10b–1 shall be applicable to all securities exempted from the operation of section 12(a) of the act by this section.

(Secs. 3, 12, 48 Stat. 882, 892; 15 U.S.C. 78c (12), 78*l*)

[13 FR 8185, Dec. 22, 1948, as amended at 19 FR 669, Feb. 5, 1954; 20 FR 2081, Apr. 2, 1955; 53 FR 41206, Oct. 20, 1988]

§ 240.12a–6 Exemption of securities underlying certain options from section 12(a).

(a) When used in this rule, the following terms shall have the meanings indicated unless the context otherwise requires:

(1) The term *option* shall include any put, call, spread, straddle, or other option or privilege of buying a security from or selling a security to another without being bound to do so, but such term shall not include any such option where the writer is: The issuer of the security which may be purchased or sold upon exercise of the option, or is a person that directly, or indirectly, through one or more intermediaries, controls, or is controlled by, or is under common control with such issuer;

(2) The term *underlying security* means a security which relates to or is the subject of an option.

(b) Any underlying security shall be exempt from the operation of section 12(a) of the Act if all of the following terms and conditions are met:

(1) The related option is duly listed and registered on a national securities exchange;

(2) The only transactions on such exchange with respect to such underlying securities consist of the delivery of and payment for such underlying securities pursuant to the terms of such options relating to the exercise thereof; and

(3) Such underlying security is (i) duly listed and registered on another national securities exchange at the time the option is issued; or (ii) duly quoted on the National Association of Securities Dealers Automated Quotation System ("NASDAQ") at the time the option is issued.

(Secs. 3(a)(12); 48 Stat. 882, 84 Stat. 718, 1435, 1499 (15 U.S.C. 78(c)))

[38 FR 11449, May 8, 1973, as amended at 50 FR 20203, May 15, 1985]

§ 240.12a–7 Exemption of stock contained in standardized market baskets from section 12(a) of the Act.

(a) Any component stock of a standardized market basket shall be exempt from the registration requirement of section 12(a) of the Act, solely for the purpose of inclusion in a standardized market basket, provided that all of the following terms and conditions are met:

(1) The standardized market basket has been duly approved by the Commission for listing on a national securities exchange pursuant to the requirements of section 19(b) of the Act; and

(2) The stock is an NMS stock as defined in § 242.600 of this chapter and is either:

(i) Listed and registered for trading on a national securities exchange by the issuer or

(ii) Quoted on the National Association of Securities Dealers Automated Quotation System;

(b) When used in this rule, the term standardized market basket means a group of at least 100 stocks purchased or sold in a single execution and at a single trading location with physical delivery and transfer of ownership of each component stock resulting from such execution.

[56 FR 28322, June 20, 1991, as amended at 70 FR 37618, June 29, 2005]

§ 240.12a–8 Exemption of depositary shares.

Depositary shares (as that term is defined in § 240.12b–2) registered on Form F–6 (§ 239.36 of this chapter), but not the underlying deposited securities, shall be exempt from the operation of section 12(a) of the Act (15 U.S.C. 78*l*(a)).

[62 FR 39766, July 24, 1997]

§ 240.12a-9 Exemption of standardized options from section 12(a) of the Act.

The provisions of section 12(a) of the Act (15 U.S.C. 78l(a)) do not apply in respect of any standardized option, as defined by section 240.9b-1(a)(4), issued by a clearing agency registered under section 17A of the Act (15 U.S.C. 78q-1) and traded on a national securities exchange registered pursuant to section 6(a) of the Act (15 U.S.C. 78f(a)).

[68 FR 192, Jan. 2, 2003]

§ 240.12a-10 Exemption of security-based swaps from section 12(a) of the Act.

The provisions of Section 12(a) of the Act (15 U.S.C. 78l(a)) do not apply to any security-based swap that:

(a) Is issued or will be issued by a clearing agency registered as a clearing agency under Section 17A of the Act (15 U.S.C. 78q-1) or exempt from registration under Section 17A of the Act pursuant to a rule, regulation, or order of the Commission, in its function as a central counterparty with respect to the security-based swap;

(b) The Commission has determined is required to be cleared or that is permitted to be cleared pursuant to the clearing agency's rules;

(c) Is sold to an eligible contract participant (as defined in Section 1a(18) of the Commodity Exchange Act (7 U.S.C. 1a(18))) in reliance on Rule 239 under the Securities Act of 1933 (17 CFR 230.239); and

(d) Is traded on a national securities exchange registered pursuant to Section 6(a) of the Act (15 U.S.C. 78f(a)).

[77 FR 20549, Apr. 5, 2012]

§ 240.12a-11 Exemption of security-based swaps sold in reliance on Securities Act of 1933 Rule 240 (§ 230.240) from section 12(a) of the Act.

(a) The provisions of Section 12(a) of the Act (15 U.S.C. 78l(a)) do not apply to any security-based swap offered and sold in reliance on § 230.240 of this chapter.

(b) This section will expire on February 11, 2018.

[82 FR 10707, Feb. 15, 2017]

REGULATION 12B: REGISTRATION AND REPORTING

SOURCE: Sections 240.12b-1 through 240.12b-36 appear at 13 FR 9321, Dec. 31, 1948, unless otherwise noted.

ATTENTION ELECTRONIC FILERS

THIS REGULATION SHOULD BE READ IN CONJUNCTION WITH REGULATION S-T (PART 232 OF THIS CHAPTER), WHICH GOVERNS THE PREPARATION AND SUBMISSION OF DOCUMENTS IN ELECTRONIC FORMAT. MANY PROVISIONS RELATING TO THE PREPARATION AND SUBMISSION OF DOCUMENTS IN PAPER FORMAT CONTAINED IN THIS REGULATION ARE SUPERSEDED BY THE PROVISIONS OF REGULATION S-T FOR DOCUMENTS REQUIRED TO BE FILED IN ELECTRONIC FORMAT.

GENERAL

§ 240.12b-1 Scope of regulation.

The rules contained in this regulation shall govern all registration statements pursuant to sections 12(b) and 12(g) of the Act and all reports filed pursuant to sections 13 and 15(d) of the Act, including all amendments to such statements and reports, except that any provision in a form covering the same subject matter as any such rule shall be controlling.

[47 FR 11464, Mar. 16, 1982]

§ 240.12b-2 Definitions.

Unless the context otherwise requires, the following terms, when used in the rules contained in this regulation or in Regulation 13A or 15D or in the forms for statements and reports filed pursuant to sections 12, 13 or 15(d) of the act, shall have the respective meanings indicated in this rule:

Accelerated filer and large accelerated filer—(1) *Accelerated filer.* The term *accelerated filer* means an issuer after it first meets the following conditions as of the end of its fiscal year:

(i) The issuer had an aggregate worldwide market value of the voting and non-voting common equity held by its non-affiliates of $75 million or more, but less than $700 million, as of the last business day of the issuer's most recently completed second fiscal quarter;

Securities and Exchange Commission § 240.12b-2

(ii) The issuer has been subject to the requirements of section 13(a) or 15(d) of the Act (15 U.S.C. 78m or 78o(d)) for a period of at least twelve calendar months; and

(iii) The issuer has filed at least one annual report pursuant to section 13(a) or 15(d) of the Act; and

(iv) The issuer is not eligible to use the requirements for smaller reporting companies under the revenue test in paragraph (2) or (3)(iii)(B) of the "smaller reporting company" definition in this section, as applicable.

(2) *Large accelerated filer.* The term *large accelerated filer* means an issuer after it first meets the following conditions as of the end of its fiscal year:

(i) The issuer had an aggregate worldwide market value of the voting and non-voting common equity held by its non-affiliates of $700 million or more, as of the last business day of the issuer's most recently completed second fiscal quarter;

(ii) The issuer has been subject to the requirements of section 13(a) or 15(d) of the Act for a period of at least twelve calendar months; and

(iii) The issuer has filed at least one annual report pursuant to section 13(a) or 15(d) of the Act; and

(iv) The issuer is not eligible to use the requirements for smaller reporting companies under the revenue test in paragraph (2) or (3)(iii)(B) of the "smaller reporting company" definition in this section, as applicable.

(3) *Entering and exiting accelerated filer and large accelerated filer status.*

(i) The determination at the end of the issuer's fiscal year for whether a non-accelerated filer becomes an accelerated filer, or whether a non-accelerated filer or accelerated filer becomes a large accelerated filer, governs the deadlines for the annual report to be filed for that fiscal year, the quarterly and annual reports to be filed for the subsequent fiscal year and all annual and quarterly reports to be filed thereafter while the issuer remains an accelerated filer or large accelerated filer.

(ii) Once an issuer becomes an accelerated filer, it will remain an accelerated filer unless: The issuer determines, at the end of a fiscal year, that the aggregate worldwide market value of the voting and non-voting common equity held by its non-affiliates was less than $60 million, as of the last business day of the issuer's most recently completed second fiscal quarter; or it determines that it is eligible to use the requirements for smaller reporting companies under the revenue test in paragraph (2) or (3)(iii)(B) of the "smaller reporting company" definition in this section, as applicable. An issuer that makes either of these determinations becomes a non-accelerated filer. The issuer will not become an accelerated filer again unless it subsequently meets the conditions in paragraph (1) of this definition.

(iii) Once an issuer becomes a large accelerated filer, it will remain a large accelerated filer unless: It determines, at the end of a fiscal year, that the aggregate worldwide market value of the voting and non-voting common equity held by its non-affiliates ("aggregate worldwide market value") was less than $560 million, as of the last business day of the issuer's most recently completed second fiscal quarter or it determines that it is eligible to use the requirements for smaller reporting companies under the revenue test in paragraph (2) or (3)(iii)(B) of the "smaller reporting company" definition in this section, as applicable. If the issuer's aggregate worldwide market value was $60 million or more, but less than $560 million, as of the last business day of the issuer's most recently completed second fiscal quarter, and it is not eligible to use the requirements for smaller reporting companies under the revenue test in paragraph (2) or (3)(iii)(B) of the "smaller reporting company" definition in this section, as applicable, it becomes an accelerated filer. If the issuer's aggregate worldwide market value was less than $60 million, as of the last business day of the issuer's most recently completed second fiscal quarter, or it is eligible to use the requirements for smaller reporting companies under the revenue test in paragraph (2) or (3)(iii)(B) of the "smaller reporting company" definition in this section, it becomes a non-accelerated filer. An issuer will not become a large accelerated filer again unless it subsequently meets the conditions in paragraph (2) of this definition.

§ 240.12b–2

(iv) The determination at the end of the issuer's fiscal year for whether an accelerated filer becomes a non-accelerated filer, or a large accelerated filer becomes an accelerated filer or a non-accelerated filer, governs the deadlines for the annual report to be filed for that fiscal year, the quarterly and annual reports to be filed for the subsequent fiscal year and all annual and quarterly reports to be filed thereafter while the issuer remains an accelerated filer or non-accelerated filer.

NOTE TO PARAGRAPHS (1), (2) AND (3): The aggregate worldwide market value of the issuer's outstanding voting and non-voting common equity shall be computed by use of the price at which the common equity was last sold, or the average of the bid and asked prices of such common equity, in the principal market for such common equity.

(4) For purposes of paragraphs (1), (2), and (3) of this definition only, a business development company is considered to be eligible to use the requirements for smaller reporting companies under the revenue test in paragraph (2) or (3)(iii)(B) of the "smaller reporting company" definition in this section, provided that the business development company meets the requirements of the test using annual investment income under Rule 6–07.1 of Regulation S–X (17 CFR 210.6–07.1) as the measure of its "annual revenues" for purposes of the test.

Affiliate. An "affiliate" of, or a person "affiliated" with, a specified person, is a person that directly, or indirectly through one or more intermediaries, controls, or is controlled by, or is under common control with, the person specified.

Amount. The term "amount," when used in regard to securities, means the principal amount if relating to evidences of indebtedness, the number of shares if relating to shares, and the number of units if relating to any other kind of security.

Associate. The term "associate" used to indicate a relationship with any person, means (1) any corporation or organization (other than the registrant or a majority-owned subsidiary of the registrant) of which such person is an officer or partner or is, directly or indirectly, the beneficial owner of 10 percent or more of any class of equity securities, (2) any trust or other estate in which such person has a substantial beneficial interest or as to which such person serves as trustee or in a similar fiduciary capacity, and (3) any relative or spouse of such person, or any relative of such spouse, who has the same home as such person or who is a director or officer of the registrant or any of its parents or subsidiaries.

Business combination related shell company: The term *business combination related shell company* means a shell company (as defined in § 240.12b–2) that is:

(1) Formed by an entity that is not a shell company solely for the purpose of changing the corporate domicile of that entity solely within the United States; or

(2) Formed by an entity that is not a shell company solely for the purpose of completing a business combination transaction (as defined in § 230.165(f) of this chapter) among one or more entities other than the shell company, none of which is a shell company.

Certified. The term "certified," when used in regard to financial statements, means examined and reported upon with an opinion expressed by an independent public or certified public accountant.

Charter. The term "charter" includes articles of incorporation, declarations of trust, articles of association or partnership, or any similar instrument, as amended, effecting (either with or without filing with any governmental agency) the organization or creation of an incorporated or unincorporated person.

Common equity. The term "common equity" means any class of common stock or an equivalent interest, including but not limited to a unit of beneficial interest in a trust or a limited partnership interest.

Control. The term "control" (including the terms "controlling," "controlled by" and "under common control with") means the possession, direct or indirect, of the power to direct or cause the direction of the management and policies of a person, whether through the ownership of voting securities, by contract, or otherwise.

Securities and Exchange Commission § 240.12b-2

Depositary share. The term "depositary share" means a security, evidenced by an American Depositary Receipt, that represents a foreign security or a multiple of or fraction thereof deposited with a depositary.

Emerging growth company. (1) The term *emerging growth company* means an issuer that had total annual gross revenues of less than $1,235,000,000 during its most recently completed fiscal year.

(2) An issuer that is an emerging growth company as of the first day of that fiscal year shall continue to be deemed an emerging growth company until the earliest of:

(i) The last day of the fiscal year of the issuer during which it had total annual gross revenues of $1,235,000,000 or more;

(ii) The last day of the fiscal year of the issuer following the fifth anniversary of the date of the first sale of common equity securities of the issuer pursuant to an effective registration statement under the Securities Act of 1933;

(iii) The date on which such issuer has, during the previous three year period, issued more than $1,000,000,000 in non-convertible debt; or

(iv) The date on which such issuer is deemed to be a large accelerated filer, as defined in Rule 12b-2 (§ 240.12b-2 of this chapter).

Employee. The term "employee" does not include a director, trustee, or officer.

Fiscal year. The term "fiscal year" means the annual accounting period or, if no closing date has been adopted, the calendar year ending on December 31.

Majority-owned subsidiary. The term "majority-owned subsidiary" means a subsidiary more than 50 percent of whose outstanding securities representing the right, other than as affected by events of default, to vote for the election of directors, is owned by the subsidiary's parent and/or one or more of the parent's other majority-owned subsidiaries.

Managing underwriter. The term "managing underwriter" includes an underwriter (or underwriters) who, by contract or otherwise, deals with the registrant; organizes the selling effort; receives some benefit directly or indirectly in which all other underwriters similarly situated do not share in proportion to their respective interests in the underwriting; or represents any other underwriters in such matters as maintaining the records of the distribution, arranging the allotments of securities offered or arranging for appropriate stabilization activities, if any.

Material. The term "material," when used to qualify a requirement for the furnishing of information as to any subject, limits the information required to those matters to which there is a substantial likelihood that a reasonable investor would attach importance in determining whether to buy or sell the securities registered.

Material weakness. The term *material weakness* is a deficiency, or a combination of deficiencies, in internal control over financial reporting such that there is a reasonable possibility that a material misstatement of the registrant's annual or interim financial statements will not be prevented or detected on a timely basis.

Parent. A "parent" of a specified person is an affiliate controlling such person directly, or indirectly through one or more intermediaries.

Predecessor. The term "predecessor" means a person the major portion of the business and assets of which another person acquired in a single succession or in a series of related successions in each of which the acquiring person acquired the major portion of the business and assets of the acquired person.

Previously filed or reported. The terms "previously filed" and "previously reported" mean previously filed with, or reported in, a statement under section 12, a report under section 13 or 15(d), a definitive proxy statement or information statement under section 14 of the act, or a registration statement under the Securities Act of 1933: *Provided,* That information contained in any such document shall be deemed to have been previously filed with, or reported to, an exchange only if such document is filed with such exchange.

Principal underwriter. The term "principal underwriter" means an underwriter in privity of contract with the issuer of the securities as to which he is underwriter.

§ 240.12b-2   17 CFR Ch. II (4-1-23 Edition)

Promoter. (1) The term "promoter" includes:

(i) Any person who, acting alone or in conjunction with one or more other persons, directly or indirectly takes initiative in founding and organizing the business or enterprise of an issuer; or

(ii) Any person who, in connection with the founding and organizing of the business or enterprise of an issuer, directly or indirectly receives in consideration of services or property, or both services and property, 10 percent or more of any class of securities of the issuer or 10 percent or more of the proceeds from the sale of any class of such securities. However, a person who receives such securities or proceeds either solely as underwriting commissions or solely in consideration of property shall not be deemed a promoter within the meaning of this paragraph if such person does not otherwise take part in founding and organizing the enterprise.

(2) All persons coming within the definition of "promoter" in paragraph (1) of this definition may be referred to as "founders" or "organizers" or by another term provided that such term is reasonably descriptive of those persons' activities with respect to the issuer.

Prospectus. Unless otherwise specified or the context otherwise requires, the term "prospectus" means a prospectus meeting the requirements of section 10(a) of the Securities Act of 1933 as amended.

Registrant. The term "registrant" means an issuer of securities with respect to which a registration statement or report is to be filed.

Registration statement. The term "registration statement" or "statement", when used with reference to registration pursuant to section 12 of the act, includes both an application for registration of securities on a national securities exchange pursuant to section 12(b) of the act and a registration statement filed pursuant to section 12(g) of the act.

Share. The term "share" means a share of stock in a corporation or unit of interest in an unincorporated person.

Shell company: The term *shell company* means a registrant, other than an asset-backed issuer as defined in Item 1101(b) of Regulation AB (§ 229.1101(b) of this chapter), that has:

(1) No or nominal operations; and
(2) Either:
(i) No or nominal assets;
(ii) Assets consisting solely of cash and cash equivalents; or
(iii) Assets consisting of any amount of cash and cash equivalents and nominal other assets.

NOTE: For purposes of this definition, the determination of a registrant's assets (including cash and cash equivalents) is based solely on the amount of assets that would be reflected on the registrant's balance sheet prepared in accordance with generally accepted accounting principles on the date of that determination.

Significant deficiency. The term *significant deficiency* is a deficiency, or a combination of deficiencies, in internal control over financial reporting that is less severe than a material weakness, yet important enough to merit attention by those responsible for oversight of the registrant's financial reporting.

Significant subsidiary. The term *significant subsidiary* means a subsidiary, including its subsidiaries, which meets any of the conditions in paragraph (1), (2), or (3) of this definition; however, if the registrant is a registered investment company or a business development company, the tested subsidiary meets any of the conditions in paragraph (4) of this definition instead of any of the conditions in paragraph (1), (2), or (3) of this definition. A registrant that files its financial statements in accordance with or provides a reconciliation to U.S. Generally Accepted Accounting Principles (U.S. GAAP) must use amounts determined under U.S. GAAP. A foreign private issuer that files its financial statements in accordance with International Financial Reporting Standards as issued by the International Accounting Standards Board (IFRS-IASB) must use amounts determined under IFRS-IASB.

(1) *Investment test.* (i) For acquisitions, other than those described in paragraph (1)(ii) of this definition, and dispositions this test is met when the registrant's and its other subsidiaries'

Securities and Exchange Commission § 240.12b-2

investments in and advances to the tested subsidiary exceed 10 percent of the aggregate worldwide market value of the registrant's voting and non-voting common equity, or if the registrant has no such aggregate worldwide market value, the total assets of the registrant and its subsidiaries consolidated as of the end of the most recently completed fiscal year.

(A) For acquisitions, the "investments in" the tested subsidiary is the consideration transferred, adjusted to exclude the registrant's and its subsidiaries' proportionate interest in the carrying value of assets transferred by the registrant and its subsidiaries consolidated to the tested subsidiary that will remain with the combined entity after the acquisition. It must include the fair value of contingent consideration if required to be recognized at fair value by the registrant at the acquisition date under U.S. GAAP or IFRS–IASB, as applicable; however if recognition at fair value is not required, it must include all contingent consideration, except contingent consideration for which the likelihood of payment is remote.

(B) For dispositions, the "investments in" the tested subsidiary is the fair value of the consideration, including contingent consideration, for the disposed subsidiary when comparing to the aggregate worldwide market value of the registrant's voting and non-voting common equity, or, when the registrant has no such aggregate worldwide market value, the carrying value of the disposed subsidiary when comparing to total assets of the registrant.

(C) When determining the aggregate worldwide market value of the registrant's voting and non-voting common equity, use the average of such aggregate worldwide market value calculated daily for the last five trading days of the registrant's most recently completed month ending prior to the earlier of the registrant's announcement date or agreement date of the acquisition or disposition.

(ii) For a combination between entities or businesses under common control, this test is met when either the net book value of the tested subsidiary exceeds 10 percent of the registrant's and its subsidiaries' consolidated total assets or the number of common shares exchanged or to be exchanged by the registrant exceeds 10 percent of its total common shares outstanding at the date the combination is initiated.

(iii) In all other cases, this test is met when the registrant's and its other subsidiaries' investments in and advances to the tested subsidiary exceed 10 percent of the total assets of the registrant and its subsidiaries consolidated as of the end of the most recently completed fiscal year.

(2) *Asset test.* This test is met when the registrant's and its other subsidiaries' proportionate share of the tested subsidiary's consolidated total assets (after intercompany eliminations) exceeds 10 percent of such total assets of the registrant and its subsidiaries consolidated as of the end of the most recently completed fiscal year.

(3) *Income test.* (i) This test is met when:

(A) The absolute value of the registrant's and its other subsidiaries' equity in the tested subsidiary's consolidated income or loss from continuing operations before income taxes (after intercompany eliminations) attributable to the controlling interests exceeds 10 percent of the absolute value of such income or loss of the registrant and its subsidiaries consolidated for the most recently completed fiscal year; and

(B) The registrant's and its other subsidiaries' proportionate share of the tested subsidiary's consolidated total revenue from continuing operations (after intercompany eliminations) exceeds 10 percent of such total revenue of the registrant and its subsidiaries consolidated for the most recently completed fiscal year. This paragraph (3)(i)(B) does not apply if either the registrant and its subsidiaries consolidated or the tested subsidiary did not have material revenue in each of the two most recently completed fiscal years.

(ii) When determining the income component in paragraph (3)(i)(A) of this definition:

(A) If a net loss from continuing operations before income taxes (after intercompany eliminations) attributable to the controlling interest has been incurred by either the registrant

§ 240.12b–2

and its subsidiaries consolidated or the tested subsidiary, but not both, exclude the equity in the income or loss from continuing operations before income taxes (after intercompany eliminations) of the tested subsidiary attributable to the controlling interest from such income or loss of the registrant and its subsidiaries consolidated for purposes of the computation;

(B) Compute the test using the average described in this paragraph (3)(ii)(B) if the revenue component in paragraph (3)(i)(B) in this definition does not apply and the absolute value of the registrant's and its subsidiaries' consolidated income or loss from continuing operations before income taxes (after intercompany eliminations) attributable to the controlling interests for the most recent fiscal year is at least 10 percent lower than the average of the absolute value of such amounts for each of its last five fiscal years; and

(C) Entities reporting losses must not be aggregated with entities reporting income where the test involves combined entities, as in the case of determining whether summarized financial data must be presented or whether the aggregate impact specified in §§ 210.3–05(b)(2)(iv) and 210.3–14(b)(2)(i)(C) of this chapter is met, except when determining whether related businesses meet this test for purposes of §§ 210.3–05 and 210.8–04 of this chapter.

(4) *Registered investment company or business development company.* For a registrant that is a registered investment company or a business development company, the term *significant subsidiary* means a subsidiary, including its subsidiaries, which meets any of the following conditions using amounts determined under U.S. GAAP and, if applicable, section 2(a)(41) of the Investment Company Act of 1940 (15 U.S.C. 80a–2(a)(41)):

(i) *Investment test.* The value of the registrant's and its other subsidiaries' investments in and advances to the tested subsidiary exceed 10 percent of the value of the total investments of the registrant and its subsidiaries consolidated as of the end of the most recently completed fiscal year; or

(ii) *Income test.* The absolute value of the sum of combined investment income from dividends, interest, and other income, the net realized gains and losses on investments, and the net change in unrealized gains and losses on investments from the tested subsidiary (except, for purposes of § 210.6–11 of this chapter, the absolute value of the change in net assets resulting from operations of the tested subsidiary), for the most recently completed fiscal year exceeds:

(A) 80 percent of the absolute value of the change in net assets resulting from operations of the registrant and its subsidiaries consolidated for the most recently completed fiscal year; or

(B) 10 percent of the absolute value of the change in net assets resulting from operations of the registrant and its subsidiaries consolidated for the most recently completed fiscal year and the investment test (paragraph (4)(i) of this definition) condition exceeds 5 percent. However, if the absolute value of the change in net assets resulting from operations of the registrant and its subsidiaries consolidated is at least 10 percent lower than the average of the absolute value of such amounts for each of its last five fiscal years, then the registrant may compute both conditions of the income test using the average of the absolute value of such amounts for the registrant and its subsidiaries consolidated for each of its last five fiscal years.

Smaller reporting company. As used in this part, the term *smaller reporting company* means an issuer that is not an investment company, an asset-backed issuer (as defined in § 229.1101 of this chapter), or a majority-owned subsidiary of a parent that is not a smaller reporting company and that:

(1) Had a public float of less than $250 million; or

(2) Had annual revenues of less than $100 million and either:

(i) No public float; or

(ii) A public float of less than $700 million.

(3) Whether an issuer is a smaller reporting company is determined on an annual basis.

(i) For issuers that are required to file reports under section 13(a) or 15(d) of the Exchange Act:

(A) Public float is measured as of the last business day of the issuer's most recently completed second fiscal quarter and computed by multiplying the aggregate worldwide number of shares of its voting and non-voting common equity held by non-affiliates by the price at which the common equity was last sold, or the average of the bid and asked prices of common equity, in the principal market for the common equity;

(B) Annual revenues are as of the most recently completed fiscal year for which audited financial statements are available; and

(C) An issuer must reflect the determination of whether it came within the definition of smaller reporting company in its quarterly report on Form 10–Q for the first fiscal quarter of the next year, indicating on the cover page of that filing, and in subsequent filings for that fiscal year, whether it is a smaller reporting company, except that, if a determination based on public float indicates that the issuer is newly eligible to be a smaller reporting company, the issuer may choose to reflect this determination beginning with its first quarterly report on Form 10–Q following the determination, rather than waiting until the first fiscal quarter of the next year.

(ii) For determinations based on an initial registration statement under the Securities Act or Exchange Act for shares of its common equity:

(A) Public float is measured as of a date within 30 days of the date of the filing of the registration statement and computed by multiplying the aggregate worldwide number of shares of its voting and non-voting common equity held by non-affiliates before the registration plus, in the case of a Securities Act registration statement, the number of shares of its voting and non-voting common equity included in the registration statement by the estimated public offering price of the shares;

(B) Annual revenues are as of the most recently completed fiscal year for which audited financial statements are available; and

(C) The issuer must reflect the determination of whether it came within the definition of smaller reporting company in the registration statement and must appropriately indicate on the cover page of the filing, and subsequent filings for the fiscal year in which the filing is made, whether it is a smaller reporting company. The issuer must re-determine its status at the end of its second fiscal quarter and then reflect any change in status as provided in paragraph (3)(i)(C) of this definition. In the case of a determination based on an initial Securities Act registration statement, an issuer that was not determined to be a smaller reporting company has the option to re-determine its status at the conclusion of the offering covered by the registration statement based on the actual offering price and number of shares sold.

(iii) Once an issuer determines that it does not qualify for smaller reporting company status because it exceeded one or more of the current thresholds, it will remain unqualified unless when making its annual determination either:

(A) It determines that its public float was less than $200 million; or

(B) It determines that its public float and its annual revenues meet the requirements for subsequent qualification included in the following chart:

Prior annual revenues	Prior public float	
	None or less than $700 million	$700 million or more
Less than $100 million	Neither threshold exceeded	Public float—Less than $560 million; and Revenues—Less than $100 million.
$100 million or more	Public float—None or less than $700 million; and. Revenues—Less than $80 million	Public float—Less than $560 million; and Revenues—Less than $80 million.

INSTRUCTION 1 TO DEFINITION OF "SMALLER REPORTING COMPANY": A registrant that qualifies as a smaller reporting company under the public float thresholds identified in paragraphs (1) and (3)(iii)(A) of this definition will qualify as a smaller reporting company regardless of its revenues.

Instruction 2 to definition of "smaller reporting company": A foreign private issuer is not eligible to use the requirements for

§ 240.12b-3

smaller reporting companies unless it uses the forms and rules designated for domestic issuers and provides financial statements prepared in accordance with U.S. Generally Accepted Accounting Principles.

Succession: The term *succession* means the direct acquisition of the assets comprising a going business, whether by merger, consolidation, purchase, or other direct transfer; or the acquisition of control of a shell company in a transaction required to be reported on Form 8-K (§ 249.308 of this chapter) in compliance with Item 5.01 of that Form or on Form 20-F (§ 249.220f of this chapter) in compliance with Rule 13a-19 (§ 240.13a-19) or Rule 15d-19 (§ 240.15d-19). Except for an acquisition of control of a shell company, the term does not include the acquisition of control of a business unless followed by the direct acquisition of its assets. The terms *succeed* and *successor* have meanings correlative to the foregoing.

Totally held subsidiary. The term "totally held subsidiary" means a subsidiary (1) substantially all of whose outstanding securities are owned by its parent and/or the parent's other totally held subsidiaries, and (2) which is not indebted to any person other than its parent and/or the parent's other totally held subsidiaries in an amount which is material in relation to the particular subsidiary, excepting indebtedness incurred in the ordinary course of business which is not overdue and which matures within one year from the date of its creation, whether evidenced by securities or not.

Voting securities. The term "voting securities" means securities the holders of which are presently entitled to vote for the election of directors.

Wholly-owned subsidiary. The term "wholly-owned subsidiary" means a subsidiary substantially all of whose outstanding voting securities are owned by its parent and/or the parent's other wholly-owned subsidiaries.

[13 FR 9321, Dec. 31, 1948]

EDITORIAL NOTE: For FEDERAL REGISTER citations affecting § 240.12b-2, see the List of CFR Sections Affected, which appears in the Finding Aids section of the printed volume and at *www.govinfo.gov*.

§ 240.12b-3 Title of securities.

Wherever the title of securities is required to be stated there shall be given such information as will indicate the type and general character of the securities, including the following:

(a) In the case of shares, the par or stated value, if any; the rate of dividends, if fixed, and whether cumulative or noncumulative; a brief indication of the preference, if any; and if convertible, a statement to that effect.

(b) In the case of funded debt, the rate of interest; the date of maturity, or if the issue matures serially, a brief indication of the serial maturities, such as "maturing serially from 1950 to 1960"; if the payment of principal or interest is contingent, an appropriate indication of such contingency; a brief indication of the priority of the issue; and if convertible, a statement to that effect.

(c) In the case of any other kind of security, appropriate information of comparable character.

§ 240.12b-4 Supplemental information.

The Commission or its staff may, where it is deemed appropriate, request supplemental information concerning the registrant, a registration statement or a periodic or other report under the Act. This information shall not be required to be filed with or deemed part of the registration statement or report. The information shall be returned to the registrant upon request, provided that:

(a) Such request is made at the time such information is furnished to the staff;

(b) The return of such information is consistent with the protection of investors; and

(c) The return of such information is consistent with the provisions of the Freedom of Information Act (5 U.S.C. 552).

[47 FR 11465, Mar. 16, 1982]

§ 240.12b-5 Determination of affiliates of banks.

In determining whether a person is an "affiliate" or "parent" of a bank or whether a bank is a "subsidiary" or "majority-owner subsidiary" of a person within the meaning of those terms

Securities and Exchange Commission § 240.12b-12

as defined in § 240.12b-2, voting securities of the bank held by a corporation all of the stock of which is directly owned by the United States Government shall not be taken into consideration.

§ 240.12b-6 When securities are deemed to be registered.

A class of securities with respect to which a registration statement has been filed pursuant to section 12 of the act shall be deemed to be registered for the purposes of sections 13, 14, 15(d) and 16 of the act and the rules and regulations thereunder only when such statement has become effective as provided in section 12, and securities of said class shall not be subject to sections 13, 14 and 16 of the act until such statement has become effective as provided in section 12.

(Secs. 3, 14, 16, 48 Stat. 882, 895, 896, sec. 3(d), 78 Stat. 568; 15 U.S.C. 78c, 78n, 78p, 78*l*)

[30 FR 482, Jan. 14, 1965]

§ 240.12b-7 [Reserved]

FORMAL REQUIREMENTS

§ 240.12b-10 Requirements as to proper form.

Every statement or report shall be on the form prescribed therefor by the Commission, as in effect on the date of filing. Any statement or report shall be deemed to be filed on the proper form unless objection to the form is made by the Commission within thirty days after the date of filing.

(Secs. 4, 16, 19, 24, 48 Stat. 77, 896, 85, as amended, 901; 15 U.S.C. 77d, 78p, 77s, 78x)

[30 FR 2022, Feb. 13, 1965]

§ 240.12b-11 Number of copies; signatures; binding.

(a) Except as provided in a particular form, three complete copies of each statement or report, including exhibits and all other papers and documents filed as a part thereof, shall be filed with the Commission. At least one complete copy of each statement shall be filed with each exchange on which the securities covered thereby are to be registered. At least one complete copy of each report under section 13 of the Act shall be filed with each exchange on which the registrant has securities registered.

(b) At least one copy of each statement or report filed with the Commission and one copy thereof filed with each exchange shall be signed in the manner prescribed by the appropriate form.

(c) Each copy of a statement or report filed with the Commission or with an exchange shall be bound in one or more parts. Copies filed with the Commission shall be bound without stiff covers. The statement or report shall be bound on the left side in such a manner as to leave the reading matter legible.

(d) *Signatures.* Where the Act or the rules, forms, reports or schedules thereunder, including paragraph (b) of this section, require a document filed with or furnished to the Commission to be signed, such document shall be manually signed, or signed using either typed signatures or duplicated or facsimile versions of manual signatures. Where typed, duplicated, or facsimile signatures are used, each signatory to the filing shall manually or electronically sign a signature page or other document authenticating, acknowledging, or otherwise adopting his or her signature that appears in the filing ("authentication document"). Such authentication document shall be executed before or at the time the filing is made and shall be retained by the filer for a period of five years. The requirements set forth in § 232.302(b) must be met with regards to the use of an electronically signed authentication document pursuant to this paragraph (d). Upon request, the filer shall furnish to the Commission or its staff a copy of any or all documents retained pursuant to this section.

[47 FR 11465, Mar. 16, 1982, as amended at 60 FR 26622, May 17, 1995; 61 FR 30403, June 14, 1996; 85 FR 78229, Dec. 4, 2020]

§ 240.12b-12 Requirements as to paper, printing and language.

(a) Statements and reports shall be filed on good quality, unglazed white paper, no larger than 8½ × 11 inches in size, insofar as practicable. To the extent that the reduction of larger documents would render them illegible,

§ 240.12b–12

such documents may be filed on paper larger than 8½ × 11 inches in size.

(b) The statement or report and, insofar as practicable, all papers and documents filed as a part thereof, shall be printed, lithographed, mimeographed, or typewritten. However, the statement or report or any portion thereof may be prepared by any similar process which, in the opinion of the Commission, produces copies suitable for a permanent record and microfilming. Irrespective of the process used, all copies of any such material shall be clear, easily readable and suitable for repeated photocopying. Debits in credit categories and credits in debit categories shall be designated so as to be clearly distinguishable as such on photocopies.

(c) The body of all printed statements and reports and all notes to financial statements and other tabular data included therein shall be in roman type at least as large and as legible as 10-point modern type. However, to the extent necessary for convenient presentation, financial statements and other tabular data, including tabular data in notes, may be in roman type at least as large and as legible as 8-point modern type. All such type shall be leaded at least 2 points.

(d)(1) All Exchange Act filings and submissions must be in the English language, except as otherwise provided by this section. If a filing or submission requires the inclusion of a document that is in a foreign language, a party must submit instead a fair and accurate English translation of the entire foreign language document, except as provided by paragraph (d)(3) of this section.

(2) If a filing or submission subject to review by the Division of Corporation Finance requires the inclusion of a foreign language document as an exhibit or attachment, a party must submit a fair and accurate English translation of the foreign language document if consisting of any of the following, or an amendment of any of the following:

(i) Articles of incorporation, memoranda of association, bylaws, and other comparable documents, whether original or restated;

(ii) Instruments defining the rights of security holders, including indentures qualified or to be qualified under the Trust Indenture Act of 1939;

(iii) Voting agreements, including voting trust agreements;

(iv) Contracts to which directors, officers, promoters, voting trustees or security holders named in a registration statement, report or other document are parties;

(v) Contracts upon which a filer's business is substantially dependent;

(vi) Audited annual and interim consolidated financial information; and

(vii) Any document that is or will be the subject of a confidential treatment request under § 240.24b–2 or § 230.406 of this chapter.

(3)(i) A party may submit an English summary instead of an English translation of a foreign language document as an exhibit or attachment to a filing or submission subject to review by the Division of Corporation Finance, as long as:

(A) The foreign language document does not consist of any of the subject matter enumerated in paragraph (d)(2) of this section; or

(B) The applicable form permits the use of an English summary.

(ii) Any English summary submitted under paragraph (d)(3) of this section must:

(A) Fairly and accurately summarize the terms of each material provision of the foreign language document; and

(B) Fairly and accurately describe the terms that have been omitted or abridged.

(4) When submitting an English summary or English translation of a foreign language document under this section, a party must identify the submission as either an English summary or English translation. A party may submit a copy of the unabridged foreign language document when including an English summary or English translation of a foreign language document in a filing or submission. A party must provide a copy of any foreign language document upon the request of Commission staff.

(5) A foreign government or its political subdivision must provide a fair and accurate English translation of its latest annual budget submitted as Exhibit B to Form 18 (§ 249.218 of this chapter) or Exhibit (c) to Form 18–K (§ 249.318 of

Securities and Exchange Commission § 240.12b–15

this chapter) only if one is available. If no English translation is available, a filer must provide a copy of the foreign language version of its latest annual budget as an exhibit.

(6) A Canadian issuer may file an exhibit, attachment or other part of a Form 40–F registration statement or annual report (§ 249.240f of this chapter), Schedule 13E–4F (§ 240.13e–102), Schedule 14D–1F (§ 240.14d–102), or Schedule 14D–9F (§ 240.14d–103), that contains text in both French and English if the issuer included the French text to comply with the requirements of the Canadian securities administrator or other Canadian authority and, for an electronic filing, if the filing is an HTML document, as defined in Regulation S-T Rule 11 (17 CFR 232.11).

(e) Where a statement or report is distributed to investors through an electronic medium, issuers may satisfy legibility requirements applicable to printed documents, such as paper size and type size and font, by presenting all required information in a format readily communicated to investors.

[47 FR 11466, Mar. 16, 1982, as amended at 47 FR 58238, Dec. 30, 1982; 61 FR 24656, May 15, 1996; 67 FR 36704, May 24, 2002]

§ 240.12b–13 Preparation of statement or report.

The statement or report shall contain the numbers and captions of all items of the appropriate form, but the text of the items may be omitted provided the answers thereto are so prepared as to indicate to the reader the coverage of the items without the necessity of his referring to the text of the items or instructions thereto. However, where any item requires information to be given in tabular form, it shall be given in substantially the tabular form specified in the item. All instructions, whether appearing under the items of the form or elsewhere therein, are to be omitted. Unless expressly provided otherwise, if any item is inapplicable or the answer thereto is in the negative, an appropriate statement to that effect shall be made.

(Secs. 4, 16, 19, 24, 48 Stat. 77, 896, 85, as amended, 901; 15 U.S.C. 77d, 78p, 77s, 78x)

[30 FR 2023, Feb. 13, 1965]

§ 240.12b–14 Riders; inserts.

Riders shall not be used. If the statement or report is typed on a printed form, and the space provided for the answer to any given item is insufficient, reference shall be made in such space to a full insert page or pages on which the item number and caption and the complete answer are given.

(Secs. 4, 16, 19, 24, 48 Stat. 77, 896, 85, as amended, 901; 15 U.S.C. 77d, 78p, 77s, 78x)

[30 FR 2023, Feb. 13, 1965]

§ 240.12b–15 Amendments.

All amendments must be filed under cover of the form amended, marked with the letter "A" to designate the document as an amendment, e.g., "10–K/A," and in compliance with pertinent requirements applicable to statements and reports. Amendments filed pursuant to this section must set forth the complete text of each item as amended. Amendments must be numbered sequentially and be filed separately for each statement or report amended. Amendments to a statement may be filed either before or after registration becomes effective. Amendments must be signed on behalf of the registrant by a duly authorized representative of the registrant. An amendment to any report required to include the certifications as specified in § 240.13a–14(a) or § 240.15d–14(a) must include new certifications by each principal executive and principal financial officer of the registrant, and an amendment to any report required to be accompanied by the certifications as specified in § 240.13a–14(b) or § 240.15d–14(b) must be accompanied by new certifications by each principal executive and principal financial officer of the registrant. An amendment to any report required to include the certifications as specified in § 240.13a–14(d) or § 240.15d–14(d) must include a new certification by an individual specified in § 240.13a–14(e) or § 240.15d–14(e), as applicable. The requirements of the form being amended will govern the number of copies to be filed in connection with a paper format amendment. Electronic filers satisfy the provisions dictating the number of copies by filing one copy of the amendment in electronic format. See § 232.309

§ 240.12b-20

of this chapter (Rule 309 of Regulation S-T).

[68 FR 36665, June 18, 2003, as amended at 70 FR 1620, Jan. 7, 2005]

GENERAL REQUIREMENTS AS TO CONTENTS

§ 240.12b-20 Additional information.

In addition to the information expressly required to be included in a statement or report, there shall be added such further material information, if any, as may be necessary to make the required statements, in the light of the circumstances under which they are made not misleading.

(Secs. 4, 16, 19, 24, 48 Stat. 77, 896, 85, as amended, 901; 15 U.S.C. 77d, 78p, 77s, 78x)

[30 FR 2023, Feb. 13, 1965]

§ 240.12b-21 Information unknown or not available.

Information required need be given only insofar as it is known or reasonably available to the registrant. If any required information is unknown and not reasonably available to the registrant, either because the obtaining thereof would involve unreasonable effort or expense, or because it rests peculiarly within the knowledge of another person not affiliated with the registrant, the information may be omitted, subject to the following conditions.

(a) The registrant shall give such information on the subject as it possesses or can acquire without unreasonable effort or expense, together with the sources thereof.

(b) The registrant shall include a statement either showing that unreasonable effort or expense would be involved or indicating the absence of any affiliation with the person within whose knowledge the information rests and stating the result of a request made to such person for the information.

§ 240.12b-22 Disclaimer of control.

If the existence of control is open to reasonable doubt in any instance, the registrant may disclaim the existence of control and any admission thereof; in such case, however, the registrant shall state the material facts pertinent to the possible existence of control.

§ 240.12b-23 Incorporation by reference.

(a) *Registration statement or report.* Except as provided by this section or in the appropriate form, information may be incorporated by reference in answer, or partial answer, to any item of a registration statement or report.

(b) *Financial information.* Except as provided in the Commission's rules, financial information required to be given in comparative form for two or more fiscal years or periods must not be incorporated by reference unless the information incorporated by reference includes the entire period for which the comparative data is given. In the financial statements, incorporating by reference, or cross-referencing to, information outside of the financial statements is not permitted unless otherwise specifically permitted or required by the Commission's rules or by U.S. Generally Accepted Accounting Principles or International Financial Reporting Standards as issued by the International Accounting Standards Board, whichever is applicable.

(c) *Exhibits.* Any document or part thereof filed with the Commission pursuant to any Act administered by the Commission may be incorporated by reference as an exhibit to any statement or report filed with the Commission by the same or any other person. Any document or part thereof filed with an exchange pursuant to the Act may be incorporated by reference as an exhibit to any statement or report filed with the exchange by the same or any other person. If any modification has occurred in the text of any document incorporated by reference since the filing thereof, the registrant must file with the reference a statement containing the text of any such modification and the date thereof.

(d) *Hyperlinks.* You must include an active hyperlink to information incorporated into a registration statement or report by reference if such information is publicly available on the Commission's Electronic Data Gathering, Analysis and Retrieval System ("EDGAR") at the time the registration statement or form is filed. For

Securities and Exchange Commission § 240.12b-25

hyperlinking to exhibits, please refer to Item 601 of Regulation S-K (§ 229.601 of this chapter) or the appropriate form.

(e) *General.* Include an express statement clearly describing the specific location of the information you are incorporating by reference. The statement must identify the document where the information was originally filed or submitted and the location of the information within that document. The statement must be made at the particular place where the information is required, if applicable. Information must not be incorporated by reference in any case where such incorporation would render the disclosure incomplete, unclear, or confusing. For example, unless expressly permitted or required, disclosure must not be incorporated by reference from a second document if that second document incorporates information pertinent to such disclosure by reference to a third document.

[84 FR 12727, Apr. 2, 2019]

§ 240.12b-24 [Reserved]

§ 240.12b-25 Notification of inability to timely file all or any required portion of a Form 10-K, 20-F, 11-K, N-CEN, N-CSR, 10-Q, or 10-D.

(a) If all or any required portion of an annual or transition report on Form 10-K, 20-F or 11-K (17 CFR 249.310, 249.220f or 249.311), a quarterly or transition report on Form 10-Q (17 CFR 249.308a), or a distribution report on Form 10-D (17 CFR 249.312) required to be filed pursuant to Section 13 or 15(d) of the Act (15 U.S.C. 78m or 78o(d)) and rules thereunder, or if all or any required portion of a semi-annual, annual or transition report on Form N-CSR (17 CFR 249.331; 17 CFR 274.128) or Form N-CEN (17 CFR 249.330; 17 CFR 274.101) required to be filed pursuant to Section 13 or 15(d) of the Act or section 30 of the Investment Company Act of 1940 (15 U.S.C. 80a-29) and the rules thereunder, is not filed within the time period prescribed for such report, the registrant, no later than one business day after the due date for such report, shall file a Form 12b-25 (17 CFR 249.322) with the Commission which shall contain disclosure of its inability to file the report timely and the reasons therefore in reasonable detail.

(b) With respect to any report or portion of any report described in paragraph (a) of this section which is not timely filed because the registrant is unable to do so without unreasonable effort or expense, such report shall be deemed to be filed on the prescribed due date for such report if:

(1) The registrant files the Form 12b-25 in compliance with paragraph (a) of this section and, when applicable, furnishes the exhibit required by paragraph (c) of this section;

(2) The registrant represents in the Form 12b-25 that:

(i) The reason(s) causing the inability to file timely could not be eliminated by the registrant without unreasonable effort or expense; and

(ii) The subject annual report, semi-annual report or transition report on Form 10-K, 20-F, 11-K, N-CEN, or N-CSR, or portion thereof, will be filed no later than the fifteenth calendar day following the prescribed due date; or the subject quarterly report or transition report on Form 10-Q or distribution report on Form 10-D, or portion thereof, will be filed no later than the fifth calendar day following the prescribed due date; and

(3) The report/portion thereof is actually filed within the period specified by paragraph (b)(2)(ii) of this section.

(c) If paragraph (b) of this section is applicable and the reason the subject report/portion thereof cannot be filed timely without unreasonable effort or expense relates to the inability of any person, other than the registrant, to furnish any required opinion, report or certification, the Form 12b-25 shall have attached as an exhibit a statement signed by such person stating the specific reasons why such person is unable to furnish the required opinion, report or certification on or before the date such report must be filed.

(d) Notwithstanding paragraph (b) of this section, a registrant will not be eligible to use any registration statement form under the Securities Act of 1933 the use of which is predicated on timely filed reports until the subject report is actually filed pursuant to paragraph (b)(3) of this section.

§ 240.12b–30

(e) If a Form 12b–25 filed pursuant to paragraph (a) of this sectin relates only to a portion of a subject report, the registrant shall:

(1) File the balance of such report and indicate on the cover page thereof which disclosure items are omitted; and

(2) Include, on the upper right corner of the amendment to the report which includes the previously omitted information, the following statement:

The following items were the subject of a Form 12b–25 and are included herein: (*List Item Numbers*)

(f) The provisions of this section shall not apply to financial statements to be filed by amendment to a form 10–K as provided for by paragraph (a) of § 210.3–09 or schedules to be filed by amendment in accordance with General Instruction A to form 10–K.

(g) *Electronic filings.* The provisions of this section shall not apply to reports required to be filed in electronic format if the sole reason the report is not filed within the time period prescribed is that the filer is unable to file the report in electronic format. Filers unable to submit a report in electronic format within the time period prescribed solely due to difficulties with electronic filing should comply with either Rule 201 or 202 of Regulation S-T (§§ 232.201 and 232.202 of this chapter), or apply for an adjustment of filing date pursuant to Rule 13(b) of Regulation S-T (§ 232.13(c) of this chapter).

(h) *Interactive data submissions.* The provisions of this section shall not apply to the submission or posting of an Interactive Data File (§ 232.11 of this chapter). Filers unable to submit or post an Interactive Data File within the time period prescribed should comply with either Rule 201 or 202 of Regulation S–T (§§ 232.201 and 232.202 of this chapter).

[45 FR 23652, Apr. 8, 1980, as amended at 50 FR 1449, Jan. 11, 1985; 50 FR 2957, Jan. 23, 1985; 54 FR 10316, Mar. 13, 1989; 58 FR 14683, Mar. 18, 1993; 58 FR 21349, Apr. 21, 1993; 59 FR 67764, Dec. 30, 1994; 68 FR 5364, Feb. 3, 2003; 70 FR 1620, Jan. 7, 2005; 73 FR 974, Jan. 4, 2008; 74 FR 6818, Feb. 10, 2009; 81 82020, Nov. 18, 2016]

EXHIBITS

§ 240.12b–30 Additional exhibits.

The registrant may file such exhibits as it may desire, in addition to those required by the appropriate form. Such exhibits shall be so marked as to indicate clearly the subject matters to which they refer.

§ 240.12b–31 Omission of substantially identical documents.

In any case where two or more indentures, contracts, franchises, or other documents required to be filed as exhibits are substantially identical in all material respects except as to the parties thereto, the dates of execution, or other details, the registrant need file a copy of only one of such documents, with a schedule identifying the other documents omitted and setting forth the material details in which such documents differ from the document of which a copy is filed. The Commission may at any time in its discretion require the filing of copies of any documents so omitted.

§ 240.12b–32 [Reserved]

§ 240.12b–33 Annual reports to other Federal agencies.

Notwithstanding any rule or other requirement to the contrary, whenever copies of an annual report by a registrant to any other Federal agency are required or permitted to be filed as an exhibit to an application or report filed by such registrant with the Commission or with a securities exchange, only one copy of such annual report need be filed with the Commission and one copy thereof with each such exchange, provided appropriate reference to such copy is made in each copy of the application or report filed with the Commission or with such exchange.

[18 FR 1441, Mar. 13, 1953]

SPECIAL PROVISIONS

§ 240.12b–35 [Reserved]

§ 240.12b–36 Use of financial statements filed under other acts.

Where copies of certified financial statements filed under other acts administered by the Commission are filed

Securities and Exchange Commission

§ 240.12d1-2

with a statement or report, the accountant's certificate shall be manually signed or manually signed copies of the certificate shall be filed with the financial statements. Where such financial statements are incorporated by reference in a statement or report, the written consent of the accountant to such incorporation by reference shall be filed with the statement or report. Such consent shall be dated and signed manually.

(Secs. 4, 16, 19, 24, 48 Stat. 77, 896, 85, as amended, 901; 15 U.S.C. 77d, 78p, 77s, 78x)

[30 FR 2023, Feb. 13, 1965]

§ 240.12b-37 Satisfaction of filing requirements.

With regard to issuers eligible to rely on Release No. 34-45589 (March 18, 2002) or Release No. IC-25463 (March 18, 2002) (each of which may be viewed on the Commission's website at *www.sec.gov*), filings made in accordance with the provisions of those Releases shall satisfy the issuer's requirement to make such a filing under Section 13(a), 14 or 15(d) of the Act (15 U.S.C. 77m(a), 78n or 78o(d)), as applicable, and the Commission's rules and regulations thereunder.

[67 FR 13537, Mar. 22, 2002]

CERTIFICATION BY EXCHANGES AND EFFECTIVENESS OF REGISTRATION

SOURCE: Sections 240.12d1-1 through 240.12d-6 appear at 19 FR 670, Feb. 5, 1954, unless otherwise noted.

§ 240.12d1-1 Registration effective as to class or series.

(a) An application filed pursuant to section 12 (b) and (c) of the act for registration of a security on a national securities exchange shall be deemed to apply for registration of the entire class of such security. Registration shall become effective, as provided in section 12(d) of the act, (1) as to the shares or amounts of such class then issued, and (2), without further application for registration, upon issuance as to additional shares or amounts of such class then or thereafter authorized.

(b) This section shall apply to classes of securities of which a specified number of shares or amounts was registered or registered upon notice of issuance, and to applications for registration filed, prior to the close of business on January 28, 1954, as well as to classes registered, or applications filed, thereafter.

(c) This section shall not affect the right of a national securities exchange to require the issuer of a registered security to file documents with or pay fees to the exchange in connection with the modification of such security or the issuance of additional shares or amounts.

(d) If a class of security is issuable in two or more series with different terms, each such series shall be deemed a separate class for the purposes of this section.

(Sec. 12, 48 Stat. 892, as amended; 15 U.S.C. 78*l*)

§ 240.12d1-2 Effectiveness of registration.

(a) A request for acceleration of the effective date of registration pursuant to section 12(d) of the act and § 240.12d1-1 shall be made in writing by either the registrant, the exchange, or both and shall briefly describe the reasons therefor.

(b) A registration statement on Form 8-A (17 CFR 249.208a) for the registration of a class of securities under Section 12(b) of the Act (15 U.S.C. 78*l*(b)) shall become effective:

(1) If a class of securities is not concurrently being registered under the Securities Act of 1933 ("Securities Act"), upon the later of receipt by the Commission of certification from the national securities exchange or the filing of the Form 8-A with the Commission; or

(2) If a class of securities is concurrently being registered under the Securities Act, upon the later of the filing of the Form 8-A with the Commission, receipt by the Commission of certification from the national securities exchange listed on the Form 8-A or effectiveness of the Securities Act registration statement relating to the class of securities.

(c) A registration statement on Form 8-A (17 CFR 249.208a) for the registration of a class of securities under Section 12(g) of the Act (15 U.S.C. 78*l*(g)) shall become effective:

§ 240.12d1-3

(1) If a class of securities is not concurrently being registered under the Securities Act, upon the filing of the Form 8-A with the Commission; or

(2) If class of securities is concurrently being registered under the Securities Act, upon the later of the filing of the Form 8-A with the Commission or the effectiveness of the Securities Act registration statement relating to the class of securities.

(Sec. 12, 48 Stat. 892, as amended; 15 U.S.C. 78*l*)

[19 FR 670, Feb. 5, 1954, as amended at 59 FR 55347, Nov. 7, 1994; 62 FR 39766, July 24, 1997]

§ 240.12d1-3 Requirements as to certification.

(a) Certification that a security has been approved by an exchange for listing and registration pursuant to section 12(d) of the act and § 240.12d1-1 shall be made by the governing committee or other corresponding authority of the exchange.

(b) The certification shall specify (1) the approval of the exchange for listing and registration; (2) the title of the security so approved; (3) the date of filing with the exchange of the application for registration and of any amendments thereto; and (4) any conditions imposed on such certification. The exchange shall promptly notify the Commission of the partial or complete satisfaction of any such conditions.

(c) The certification must be filed in electronic format via the Commission's Electronic Data Gathering, Analysis, and Retrieval (EDGAR) system in accordance with the EDGAR rules set forth in § 232 of this chapter (Regulation S-T).

(Sec. 12, 48 Stat. 892, as amended; 15 U.S.C. 78*l*)

[19 FR 670, Feb. 5, 1954, as amended at 87 FR 35413, June 10, 2022]

§ 240.12d1-4 Date of receipt of certification by Commission.

The date of receipt by the Commission of the certification approving a security for listing and registration shall be the date on which the certification is actually received by the Commission or the date on which the application for registration to which the certification relates is actually received by the Commission, whichever date is later.

(Sec. 12, 48 Stat. 892, as amended; 15 U.S.C. 78*l*)

§ 240.12d1-5 Operation of certification on subsequent amendments.

If an amendment to the application for registration of a security is filed with the exchange and with the Commission after the receipt by the Commission of the certification of the exchange approving the security for listing and registration, the certification, unless withdrawn, shall be deemed made with reference to the application as amended.

(Sec. 12, 48 Stat. 892, as amended; 15 U.S.C. 78*l*)

§ 240.12d1-6 Withdrawal of certification.

An exchange may, by notice to the Commission, withdraw its certification prior to the time that the registration to which it relates first becomes effective pursuant to § 240.12d1-1.

(Sec. 12, 48 Stat. 892, as amended; 15 U.S.C. 78*l*)

SUSPENSION OF TRADING, WITHDRAWAL, AND STRIKING FROM LISTING AND REGISTRATION

§ 240.12d2-1 Suspension of trading.

(a) A national securities exchange may suspend from trading a security listed and registered thereon in accordance with its rules. Such exchange shall promptly notify the Commission of any such suspension, the effective date thereof, and the reasons therefor.

(b) Any such suspension may be continued until such time as it shall appear to the Commission that such suspension is designed to evade the provisions of section 12(d) and the rules and regulations thereunder relating to the withdrawal and striking of a security from listing and registration. During the continuance of such suspension the exchange shall notify the Commission promptly of any change in the reasons for the suspension. Upon the restoration to trading of any security suspended under this rule, the exchange shall notify the Commission promptly of the effective date thereof.

Securities and Exchange Commission § 240.12d2-2

(c) Suspension of trading shall not terminate the registration of any security.

(Sec. 12, 48 Stat. 892, as amended; 15 U.S.C. 78*l*)

[28 FR 1506, Feb. 16, 1963]

§ 240.12d2-2 Removal from listing and registration.

PRELIMINARY NOTES: 1. The filing of the Form 25 (Sec. 249.25 of this chapter) by an issuer relates solely to the withdrawal of a class of securities from listing on a national securities exchange and/or from registration under section 12(b) of the Act (15 U.S.C. 78*l*(b)), and shall not affect its obligation to be registered under section 12(g) of the Act and/or reporting obligations under section 15(d) of the Act (15 U.S.C. 78o(d)).

2. Implementation. The rules of each national securities exchange must be designed to meet the requirements of this section and must be operative no later than April 24, 2006. Each national securities exchange must submit to the Commission a proposed rule change that complies with section 19(b) of the Act (15 U.S.C. 78s) and Rule 19b–4 (17 CFR 240.19b–4) thereunder, and this section no later than October 24, 2005.

(a) A national securities exchange must file with the Commission an application on Form 25 (17 CFR 249.25) to strike a class of securities from listing on a national securities exchange and/or registration under section 12(b) of the Act within a reasonable time after the national securities exchange is reliably informed that any of the following conditions exist with respect to such a security:

(1) The entire class of the security has been called for redemption, maturity or retirement; appropriate notice thereof has been given; funds sufficient for the payment of all such securities have been deposited with an agency authorized to make such payments; and such funds have been made available to security holders.

(2) The entire class of the security has been redeemed or paid at maturity or retirement.

(3) The instruments representing the securities comprising the entire class have come to evidence, by operation of law or otherwise, other securities in substitution therefor and represent no other right, except, if such be the fact, the right to receive an immediate cash payment (the right of dissenters to receive the appraised or fair value of their holdings shall not prevent the application of this provision).

(4) All rights pertaining to the entire class of the security have been extinguished; provided, however, that where such an event occurs as a result of an order of a court or other governmental authority, the order shall be final, all applicable appeal periods shall have expired, and no appeals shall be pending.

EFFECTIVE DATE: Such an application shall be deemed to be granted and shall become effective at the opening of business on such date as the exchange shall specify in said application, but not less than 10 days following the date on which said application is filed with the Commission; *Provided, however,* That in the event removal is being effected under paragraph (a)(3) of this section and the exchange has admitted or intends to admit a successor security to trading under the temporary exemption provided for by §240.12a–5, such date shall not be earlier than the date on which the successor security is removed from its exempt status.

(b)(1) In cases not provided for in paragraph (a) of this section, a national securities exchange may file an application on Form 25 to strike a class of securities from listing and/or withdraw the registration of such securities, in accordance with its rules, if the rules of such exchange, at a minimum, provide for:

(i) Notice to the issuer of the exchange's decision to delist its securities;

(ii) An opportunity for appeal to the national securities exchange's board of directors, or to a committee designated by the board; and

(iii) Public notice of the national securities exchange's final determination to remove the security from listing and/or registration, by issuing a press release and posting notice on its Web site. Public notice under this paragraph shall be disseminated no fewer than 10 days before the delisting becomes effective pursuant to paragraph (d)(1) of this section, and must remain posted on its Web site until the delisting is effective.

(2) A national securities exchange must promptly deliver a copy of the application on Form 25 to the issuer.

(c)(1) The issuer of a class of securities listed on a national securities exchange and/or registered under section

147

§ 240.12d2-2

12(b) of the Act may file an application on Form 25 to notify the Commission of its withdrawal of such securities from listing on such national securities exchange and its intention to withdraw the securities from registration under section 12(b) of the Act.

(2) An issuer filing Form 25 under this paragraph must satisfy the requirements in paragraph (c)(2) of this section and represent on the Form 25 that such requirements have been met:

(i) The issuer must comply with all applicable laws in effect in the state in which it is incorporated and with the national securities exchange's rules governing an issuer's voluntary withdrawal of a class of securities from listing and/or registration.

(ii) No fewer than 10 days before the issuer files an application on Form 25 with the Commission, the issuer must provide written notice to the national securities exchange of its determination to withdraw the class of securities from listing and/or registration on such exchange. Such written notice must set forth a description of the security involved, together with a statement of all material facts relating to the reasons for withdrawal from listing and/or registration.

(iii) Contemporaneous with providing written notice to the exchange of its intent to withdraw a class of securities from listing and/or registration, the issuer must publish notice of such intention, along with its reasons for such withdrawal, via a press release and, if it has a publicly accessible Web site, posting such notice on that Web site. Any notice provided on an issuer's Web site under this paragraph shall remain available until the delisting on Form 25 has become effective pursuant to paragraph (d)(1) of this section. If the issuer has not arranged for listing and/or registration on another national securities exchange or for quotation of its security in a quotation medium (as defined in § 240.15c2-11), then the press release and posting on the Web site must contain this information.

(3) A national securities exchange, that receives, pursuant to paragraph (c)(2)(ii) of this section, written notice from an issuer that such issuer has determined to withdraw a class of securities from listing and/or registration on

17 CFR Ch. II (4-1-23 Edition)

such exchange, must provide notice on its Web site of the issuer's intent to delist and/or withdraw from registration its securities by the next business day. Such notice must remain posted on the exchange's Web site until the delisting on Form 25 is effective pursuant to paragraph (d)(1) of this section.

(d)(1) An application on Form 25 to strike a class of securities from listing on a national securities exchange will be effective 10 days after Form 25 is filed with the Commission.

(2) An application on Form 25 to withdraw the registration of a class of securities under section 12(b) of the Act will be effective 90 days, or such shorter period as the Commission may determine, after filing with the Commission.

(3) Notwithstanding paragraphs (d)(1) and (d)(2) of this section, the Commission may, by written notice to the exchange and issuer, postpone the effectiveness of an application to delist and/or to deregister to determine whether the application on Form 25 to strike the security from registration under section 12(b) of the Act has been made in accordance with the rules of the exchange, or what terms should be imposed by the Commission for the protection of investors.

(4) Notwithstanding paragraph (d)(2) of this section, whenever the Commission commences a proceeding against an issuer under section 12 of the Act prior to the withdrawal of the registration of a class of securities, such security will remain registered under section 12(b) of the Act until the final decision of such proceeding or until the Commission otherwise determines to suspend the effective date of, or revoke, the registration of a class of securities.

(5) An issuer's duty to file any reports under section 13(a) of the Act (15 U.S.C. 78m(a)) and the rules and regulations thereunder solely because of such security's registration under section 12(b) of the Act will be suspended upon the effective date for the delisting pursuant to paragraph (d)(1) of this section. If, following the effective date of delisting on Form 25, the Commission, an exchange, or an issuer delays the withdrawal of a security's registration under section 12(b) of the Act, an issuer

Securities and Exchange Commission § 240.12f–1

shall, within 60 days of such delay, file any reports that would have been required under section 13(a) of the Act and the rules and regulations thereunder, had the Form 25 not been filed. The issuer also shall timely file any subsequent reports required under section 13(a) of the Act for the duration of the delay.

(6) An issuer whose reporting responsibilities under section 13(a) of the Act are suspended for a class of securities under paragraph (d)(5) of this section is, nevertheless, required to file any reports that an issuer with such a class of securities registered under section 12 of the Act would be required to file under section 13(a) of the Act if such class of securities:

(i) Is registered under section 12(g) of the Act; or

(ii) Would be registered, or would be required to be registered, under section 12(g) of the Act but for the exemption from registration under section 12(g) of the Act provided by section 12(g)(2)(A) of the Act.

(7)(i) An issuer whose reporting responsibilities under section 13(a) of the Act are suspended under paragraph (d)(5) of this section is, nevertheless, required to file any reports that would be required under section 15(d) of the Act but for the fact that the reporting obligations are:

(A) Suspended for a class of securities under paragraph (d)(5) of this section; and

(B) Suspended, terminated, or otherwise absent under section 12(g) of the Act.

(ii) The reporting responsibilities of an issuer under section 15(d) of the Act shall continue until the issuer is required to file reports under section 13(a) of the Act or the issuer's reporting responsibilities under section 15(d) of the Act are otherwise suspended.

(8) In the event removal is being effected under paragraph (a)(3) of this section and the national securities exchange has admitted or intends to admit a successor security to trading under the temporary exemption provided for by §240.12a–5, the effective date of the Form 25, as set forth in paragraph (d)(1) of this section, shall not be earlier than the date the successor security is removed from its exempt status.

(e) The following are exempt from section 12(d) of the Act and the provisions of this section:

(1) Any standardized option, as defined in §240.9b–1, that is:

(i) Issued by a clearing agency registered under section 17A of the Act (15 U.S.C. 78q–1); and

(ii) Traded on a national securities exchange registered pursuant to section 6(a) of the Act (15 U.S.C. 78f(a)); and

(2) Any security futures product that is:

(i) Traded on a national securities exchange registered under section 6(a) of the Act or on a national securities association registered pursuant to section 15A(a) of the Act (15 U.S.C. 78o–3(a)); and

(ii) Cleared by a clearing agency registered as a clearing agency pursuant to section 17A of the Act or is exempt from registration under section 17A(b)(7) of the Act.

[28 FR 1506, Feb. 16, 1963, as amended at 70 FR 42468, July 22, 2005]

UNLISTED TRADING

§ 240.12f–1 Applications for permission to reinstate unlisted trading privileges.

(a) An application to reinstate unlisted trading privileges may be made to the Commission by any national securities exchange for the extension of unlisted trading privileges to any security for which such unlisted trading privileges have been suspended by the Commission, pursuant to section 12(f)(2)(A) of the Act (15 U.S.C. 78l(2)(A)). One copy of such application, executed by a duly authorized officer of the exchange, shall be filed and shall set forth:

(1) Name of issuer;

(2) Title of security;

(3) The name of each national securities exchange, if any, on which such security is listed or admitted to unlisted trading privileges;

(4) Whether transaction information concerning such security is reported pursuant to an effective transaction reporting plan contemplated by §242.601 of this chapter;

§ 240.12f-2

(5) The date of the Commission's suspension of unlisted trading privileges in the security on the exchange;

(6) Any other information which is deemed pertinent to the question of whether the reinstatement of unlisted trading privileges in such security is consistent with the maintenance of fair and orderly markets and the protection of investors; and

(7) That a copy of the instant application has been mailed, or otherwise personally provided, to the issuer of the securities for which unlisted trading privileges are sought and to each exchange listed in item (3) of this section.

[44 FR 75134, Dec. 19, 1979, as amended at 45 FR 12390, Feb. 26, 1980; 45 FR 36076, May 29, 1980; 60 FR 20896, Apr. 28, 1995; 70 FR 37618, June 29, 2005]

§ 240.12f-2 Extending unlisted trading privileges to a security that is the subject of an initial public offering.

(a) *General provision.* A national securities exchange may extend unlisted trading privileges to a subject security when at least one transaction in the subject security has been effected on the national securities exchange upon which the security is listed and the transaction has been reported pursuant to an effective transaction reporting plan, as defined in § 242.600 of this chapter.

(b) The extension of unlisted trading privileges pursuant to this section shall be subject to all the provisions set forth in Section 12(f) of the Act (15 U.S.C. 78l(f)), as amended, and any rule or regulation promulgated thereunder, or which may be promulgated thereunder while the extension is in effect.

(c) *Definitions.* For the purposes of this section:

(1) The term *subject security* shall mean a security that is the subject of an initial public offering, as that term is defined in section 12(f)(1)(G)(i) of the Act (15 U.S.C. 78l(f)(1)(G)(i)), and

(2) An *initial public offering commences* at such time as is described in section 12(f)(1)(G)(ii) of the Act (15 U.S.C. 78l(f)(*I*)(G)(ii)).

[60 FR 20896, Apr. 28, 1995, as amended at 65 FR 53565, Sept. 5, 2000; 70 FR 37618, June 29, 2005]

17 CFR Ch. II (4-1-23 Edition)

§ 240.12f-3 Termination or suspension of unlisted trading privileges.

(a) The issuer of any security for which unlisted trading privileges on any exchange have been continued or extended, or any broker or dealer who makes or creates a market for such security, or any other person having a bona fide interest in the question of termination or suspension of such unlisted trading privileges, may make application to the Commission for the termination or suspension of such unlisted trading privileges. One duly executed copy of such application shall be filed, and it shall contain the following information:

(1) Name and address of applicant;

(2) A brief statement of the applicant's interest in the question of termination or suspension of such unlisted trading privileges;

(3) Title of security;

(4) Names of issuer;

(5) Amount of such security issued and outstanding (number of shares of stock or principal amount of bonds), stating source of information;

(6) Annual volume of public trading in such security (number of shares of stock or principal amount of bonds) on such exchange for each of the three calendar years immediately preceding the date of such application, and monthly volume of trading in such security for each of the twelve calendar months immediately preceding the date of such application;

(7) Price range on such exchange for each of the twelve calendar months immediately preceding the date of such application; and

(8) A brief statement of the information in the applicant's possession, and the source thereof, with respect to (i) the extent of public trading in such security on such exchange, and (ii) character of trading in such security on such exchange; and

(9) A brief statement that a copy of the instant application has been mailed, or otherwise personally provided, to the exchange from which the suspension or termination of unlisted trading privileges is sought, and to any other exchange on which such security is listed or traded pursuant to unlisted trading privileges.

Securities and Exchange Commission § 240.12g-1

(b) Unlisted trading privileges in any security on any national securities exchange may be suspended or terminated by such exchange in accordance with its rules.

(Secs. 12(f) and 23, 15 U.S.C. 78*l* and 78w)

[20 FR 6702, Sept. 13, 1955, as amended at 44 FR 75135, Dec. 19, 1979; 45 FR 36076, May 29, 1980; 60 FR 20896, Apr. 28, 1995]

§ 240.12f-4 Exemption of securities admitted to unlisted trading privileges from sections 13, 14 and 16.

(a) Any security for which unlisted trading privileges on any national securities exchange have been continued or extended pursuant to section 12(f) of the Act shall be exempt from section 13 of the Act unless (1) such security or another security of the same issuer is listed and registered on a national securities exchange or registered pursuant to section 12(g) of the Act, or (2) such issuer would be required to file information, documents and reports pursuant to section 15(d) of the Act but for the fact that securities of the issuer are deemed to be "registered on a national securities exchange" within the meaning of section 12(f)(6) of the Act.

(b) Any security for which unlisted trading privileges on any national securities exchange have been continued or extended pursuant to section 12(f) of the Act shall be exempt from section 14 of the Act unless such security is also listed and registered on a national securities exchange or registered pursuant to section 12(g) of the Act.

(c)(1) Any equity security for which unlisted trading privileges on any national securities exchange have been continued or extended pursuant to section 12(f) of the Act shall be exempt from section 16 of the act unless such security or another equity security of the same issuer is listed and registered on a national securities exchange or registered pursuant to section 12(g) of the Act.

(2) Any equity security for which unlisted trading privileges on any national securities exchange have been continued or extended pursuant to section 12(f) of the Act and which is not listed and registered on any other such exchange or registered pursuant to section 12(g) of the Act shall be exempt from section 16 of the Act insofar as that section would otherwise apply to any person who is directly or indirectly the beneficial owner of more than 10 percent of such security, unless another equity security of the issuer of such unlisted security is so listed or registered and such beneficial owner is a director or officer of such issuer or directly or indirectly the beneficial owner of more than 10 percent of any such listed security.

(d) Any reference in this section to a security registered pursuant to section 12(g) of the Act shall include, and any reference to a security not so registered shall exclude, any security as to which a registration statement pursuant to such section is at the time required to be effective.

(Sec. 3, 78 Stat. 565, 15 U.S.C. 78*l*)

[30 FR 482, Jan. 14, 1965]

§ 240.12f-5 Exchange rules for securities to which unlisted trading privileges are extended.

A national securities exchange shall not extend unlisted trading privileges to any security unless the national securities exchange has in effect a rule or rules providing for transactions in the class or type of security to which the exchange extends unlisted trading privileges.

[60 FR 20896, Apr. 28, 1995]

§ 240.12f-6 [Reserved]

EXTENSIONS AND TEMPORARY EXEMPTIONS; DEFINITIONS

§ 240.12g-1 Registration of securities; exemption from section 12(g).

An issuer is not required to register a class of equity securities pursuant to section 12(g)(1) of the Act (15 U.S.C. 78*l*(g)(1)) if on the last day of its most recent fiscal year:

(a) The issuer had total assets not exceeding $10 million; or

(b)(1) The class of equity securities was held of record by fewer than 2,000 persons and fewer than 500 of those persons were not accredited investors (as such term is defined in § 230.501(a) of this chapter, determined as of such day rather than at the time of the sale of the securities); or

§ 240.12g-2

(2) The class of equity securities was held of record by fewer than 2,000 persons in the case of a bank; a savings and loan holding company, as such term is defined in section 10 of the Home Owners' Loan Act (12 U.S.C. 1461); or a bank holding company, as such term is defined in section 2 of the Bank Holding Company Act of 1956 (12 U.S.C. 1841).

[81 FR 28705, May 10, 2016, as amended at 81 FR 95458, Dec. 28, 2016]

§ 240.12g-2 Securities deemed to be registered pursuant to section 12(g)(1) upon termination of exemption pursuant to section 12(g)(2)(A) or (B).

Any class of securities that would have been required to be registered pursuant to section 12(g)(1) of the Act (15 U.S.C. 78l(g)(1)) except for the fact that it was exempt from such registration by section 12(g)(2)(A) of the Act (15 U.S.C. 78l(g)(2)(A)) because it was listed and registered on a national securities exchange, or by section 12(g)(2)(B) of the Act (15 U.S.C. 78l(g)(2)(B)) because it was issued by an investment company registered pursuant to section 8 of the Investment Company Act of 1940 (15 U.S.C. 80a-8), shall upon the termination of the listing and registration of such class or the termination of the registration of such company and without the filing of an additional registration statement be deemed to be registered pursuant to section 12(g)(1) of the Act if at the time of such termination:

(a) The issuer of such class of securities has elected to be regulated as a business development company pursuant to sections 55 through 65 of the Investment Company Act of 1940 (15 U.S.C. 80a-54 through 64) and such election has not been withdrawn; or

(b) Securities of the class are not exempt from such registration pursuant to section 12 of the Act (15 U.S.C. 78l) or rules thereunder and all securities of such class are held of record by 300 or more persons, or 1,200 or more persons in the case of a bank; a savings and loan holding company, as such term is defined in section 10 of the Home Owners' Loan Act (12 U.S.C. 1461); or a bank holding company, as such term is defined in section 2 of the Bank Holding Company Act of 1956 (12 U.S.C. 1841).

[81 FR 28705, May 10, 2016]

§ 240.12g-3 Registration of securities of successor issuers under section 12(b) or 12(g).

(a) Where in connection with a succession by merger, consolidation, exchange of securities, acquisition of assets or otherwise, securities of an issuer that are not already registered pursuant to section 12 of the Act (15 U.S.C. 78l) are issued to the holders of any class of securities of another issuer that is registered pursuant to either section 12 (b) or (g) of the Act (15 U.S.C. 78l (b) or (g)), the class of securities so issued shall be deemed to be registered under the same paragraph of section 12 of the Act unless upon consummation of the succession:

(1) Such class is exempt from such registration other than by § 240.12g3-2;

(2) All securities of such class are held of record by fewer than 300 persons, or 1,200 persons in the case of a bank; a savings and loan holding company, as such term is defined in section 10 of the Home Owners' Loan Act (12 U.S.C. 1461); or a bank holding company, as such term is defined in section 2 of the Bank Holding Company Act of 1956 (12 U.S.C. 1841); or

(3) The securities issued in connection with the succession were registered on Form F-8 or Form F-80 (§ 239.38 or § 239.41 of this chapter) and following succession the successor would not be required to register such class of securities under section 12 of the Act (15 U.S.C. 78l) but for this section.

(b) Where in connection with a succession by merger, consolidation, exchange of securities, acquisition of assets or otherwise, securities of an issuer that are not already registered pursuant to section 12 of the Act (15 U.S.C. 78l) are issued to the holders of any class of securities of another issuer that is required to file a registration statement pursuant to either section 12(b) or (g) of the Act (15 U.S.C. 78l(b) or (g)) but has not yet done so, the duty to file such statement shall be deemed to have been assumed by the issuer of the class of securities so issued. The successor issuer shall file a

Securities and Exchange Commission § 240.12g–3

registration statement pursuant to the same paragraph of section 12 of the Act with respect to such class within the period of time the predecessor issuer would have been required to file such a statement unless upon consummation of the succession:

(1) Such class is exempt from such registration other than by § 240.12g3–2;

(2) All securities of such class are held of record by fewer than 300 persons, or 1,200 persons in the case of a bank; a savings and loan holding company, as such term is defined in section 10 of the Home Owners' Loan Act (12 U.S.C. 1461); or a bank holding company, as such term is defined in section 2 of the Bank Holding Company Act of 1956 (12 U.S.C. 1841); or

(3) The securities issued in connection with the succession were registered on Form F–8 or Form F–80 (§ 239.38 or § 239.41 of this chapter) and following the succession the successor would not be required to register such class of securities under section 12 of the Act (15 U.S.C. 78*l*) but for this section.

(c) Where in connection with a succession by merger, consolidation, exchange of securities, acquisition of assets or otherwise, securities of an issuer that are not already registered pursuant to section 12 of the Act (15 U.S.C. 78*l*) are issued to the holders of classes of securities of two or more other issuers that are each registered pursuant to section 12 of the Act, the class of securities so issued shall be deemed to be registered under section 12 of the Act unless upon consummation of the succession:

(1) Such class is exempt from such registration other than by § 240.12g3–2;

(2) All securities of such class are held of record by fewer than 300 persons, or 1,200 persons in the case of a bank; a savings and loan holding company, as such term is defined in section 10 of the Home Owners' Loan Act (12 U.S.C. 1461); or a bank holding company, as such term is defined in section 2 of the Bank Holding Company Act of 1956 (12 U.S.C. 1841); or

(3) The securities issued in connection with the succession were registered on Form F–8 or Form F–80 (§ 239.38 or § 239.41 of this chapter) and following succession the successor would not be required to register such class of securities under section 12 of the Act (15 U.S.C. 78*l*) but for this section.

(d) If the classes of securities issued by two or more predecessor issuers (as described in paragraph (c) of this section) are registered under the same paragraph of section 12 of the Act (15 U.S.C. 78*l*), the class of securities issued by the successor issuer shall be deemed registered under the same paragraph of section 12 of the Act. If the classes of securities issued by the predecessor issuers are not registered under the same paragraph of section 12 of the Act, the class of securities issued by the successor issuer shall be deemed registered under section 12(g) of the Act (15 U.S.C. 78*l*(g)).

(e) An issuer that is deemed to have a class of securities registered pursuant to section 12 of the Act (15 U.S.C. 78*l*) according to paragraph (a), (b), (c) or (d) of this section shall file reports on the same forms and such class of securities shall be subject to the provisions of sections 14 and 16 of the Act (15 U.S.C. 78n and 78p) to the same extent as the predecessor issuers, except as follows:

(1) An issuer that is not a foreign issuer shall not be eligible to file on Form 20–F (§ 249.220f of this chapter) or to use the exemption in § 240.3a12–3.

(2) A foreign private issuer shall be eligible to file on Form 20–F (§ 249.220f of this chapter) and to use the exemption in § 240.3a12–3.

(f) An issuer that is deemed to have a class of securities registered pursuant to section 12 of the Act (15 U.S.C. 78*l*) according to paragraphs (a), (b), (c) or (d) of this section shall indicate in the Form 8–K (§ 249.308 of this chapter) report filed with the Commission in connection with the succession, pursuant to the requirements of Form 8–K, the paragraph of section 12 of the Act under which the class of securities issued by the successor issuer is deemed registered by operation of paragraphs (a), (b), (c) or (d) of this section. If a successor issuer that is deemed registered under section 12(g) of the Act (15 U.S.C. 78*l*(g)) by paragraph (d) of this section intends to list

§ 240.12g-4

a class of securities on a national securities exchange, it must file a registration statement pursuant to section 12(b) of the Act (15 U.S.C. 78l(b)) with respect to that class of securities.

(g) An issuer that is deemed to have a class of securities registered pursuant to section 12 of the Act (15 U.S.C. 78l) according to paragraph (a), (b), (c) or (d) of this section shall file an annual report for each fiscal year beginning on or after the date as of which the succession occurred. Annual reports shall be filed within the period specified in the appropriate form. Each such issuer shall file an annual report for each of its predecessors that had securities registered pursuant to section 12 of the Act (15 U.S.C. 78l) covering the last full fiscal year of the predecessor before the registrant's succession, unless such report has been filed by the predecessor. Such annual report shall contain information that would be required if filed by the predecessor.

[62 FR 39767, July 24, 1997, as amended at 81 FR 28706, May 10, 2016; 83 FR 50221, Oct. 4, 2018]

§ 240.12g-4 Certifications of termination of registration under section 12(g).

(a) Termination of registration of a class of securities under section 12(g) of the Act (15 U.S.C. 78l(g)) shall take effect 90 days, or such shorter period as the Commission may determine, after the issuer certifies to the Commission on Form 15 (§ 249.323 of this chapter) that the class of securities is held of record by:

(1) Fewer than 300 persons, or in the case of a bank; a savings and loan holding company, as such term is defined in section 10 of the Home Owners' Loan Act (12 U.S.C. 1461); or a bank holding company, as such term is defined in section 2 of the Bank Holding Company Act of 1956 (12 U.S.C. 1841), 1,200 persons; or

(2) Fewer than 500 persons, where the total assets of the issuer have not exceeded $10 million on the last day of each of the issuer's most recent three fiscal years.

(b) The issuer's duty to file any reports required under section 13(a) shall be suspended immediately upon filing a certification on Form 15; *Provided, however,* That if the certification on Form 15 is subsequently withdrawn or denied, the issuer shall, within 60 days after the date of such withdrawal or denial, file with the Commission all reports which would have been required had the certification on Form 15 not been filed. If the suspension resulted from the issuer's merger into, or consolidation with, another issuer or issuers, the certification shall be filed by the successor issuer.

[49 FR 12689, Mar. 30, 1984, as amended at 51 FR 25362, July 14, 1986; 61 FR 21356, May 9, 1996; 72 FR 16956, Apr. 5, 2007; 81 FR 28706, May 10, 2016]

§ 240.12g-6 Exemption for securities issued pursuant to section 4(a)(6) of the Securities Act of 1933 or Regulation Crowdfunding.

(a) For purposes of determining whether an issuer is required to register a security with the Commission pursuant to section 12(g)(1) of the Act (15 U.S.C. 78l(g)(1)), the definition of held of record shall not include securities issued pursuant to the offering exemption under section 4(a)(6) of the Securities Act (15 U.S.C. 77d(a)(6)) or §§ 227.100 through 227.504 (Regulation Crowdfunding) by an issuer that:

(1) Is current in filing its ongoing annual reports required pursuant to § 227.202 of this chapter;

(2) Has total assets not in excess of $25 million as of the end of its most recently completed fiscal year; and

(3) Has engaged a transfer agent registered pursuant to Section 17A(c) of the Act to perform the function of a transfer agent with respect to such securities.

(b) An issuer that would be required to register a class of securities under Section 12(g) of the Act as a result of exceeding the asset threshold in paragraph (a)(2) of this section may continue to exclude the relevant securities from the definition of "held of record" for a transition period ending on the penultimate day of the fiscal year two years after the date it became ineligible. The transition period terminates immediately upon the failure of an issuer to timely file any periodic report due pursuant to § 227.202 at which time the issuer must file a registration statement that registers that class of

Securities and Exchange Commission § 240.12g3–2

securities under the Act within 120 days.

[80 FR 71750, Nov. 16, 2015, as amended at 86 FR 3601, Jan. 14, 2021]

§ 240.12g3–2 Exemptions for American depositary receipts and certain foreign securities.

(a) Securities of any class issued by any foreign private issuer shall be exempt from section 12(g) (15 U.S.C. 78*l*(g)) of the Act if the class has fewer than 300 holders resident in the United States. This exemption shall continue until the next fiscal year end at which the issuer has a class of equity securities held by 300 or more persons resident in the United States. For the purpose of determining whether a security is exempt pursuant to this paragraph:

(1) Securities held of record by persons resident in the United States shall be determined as provided in § 240.12g5–1 except that securities held of record by a broker, dealer, bank or nominee for any of them for the accounts of customers resident in the United States shall be counted as held in the United States by the number of separate accounts for which the securities are held. The issuer may rely in good faith on information as to the number of such separate accounts supplied by all owners of the class of its securities which are brokers, dealers, or banks or a nominee for any of them.

(2) Persons in the United States who hold the security only through a Canadian Retirement Account (as that term is defined in rule 237(a)(2) under the Securities Act of 1933 (§ 230.237(a)(2) of this chapter)), shall not be counted as holders resident in the United States.

(b)(1) A foreign private issuer shall be exempt from the requirement to register a class of equity securities under section 12(g) of the Act (15 U.S.C. 78*l*(g)) if:

(i) The issuer is not required to file or furnish reports under section 13(a) of the Act (15 U.S.C. 78m(a)) or section 15(d) of the Act (15 U.S.C. 78o(d));

(ii) The issuer currently maintains a listing of the subject class of securities on one or more exchanges in a foreign jurisdiction that, either singly or together with the trading of the same class of the issuer's securities in another foreign jurisdiction, constitutes the primary trading market for those securities; and

(iii) The issuer has published in English, on its Internet Web site or through an electronic information delivery system generally available to the public in its primary trading market, information that, since the first day of its most recently completed fiscal year, it:

(A) Has made public or been required to make public pursuant to the laws of the country of its incorporation, organization or domicile;

(B) Has filed or been required to file with the principal stock exchange in its primary trading market on which its securities are traded and which has been made public by that exchange; and

(C) Has distributed or been required to distribute to its security holders.

NOTE 1 TO PARAGRAPH (b)(1): For the purpose of paragraph (b) of this section, *primary trading market* means that at least 55 percent of the trading in the subject class of securities on a worldwide basis took place in, on or through the facilities of a securities market or markets in a single foreign jurisdiction or in no more than two foreign jurisdictions during the issuer's most recently completed fiscal year. If a foreign private issuer aggregates the trading of its subject class of securities in two foreign jurisdictions for the purpose of this paragraph, the trading for the issuer's securities in at least one of the two foreign jurisdictions must be larger than the trading in the United States for the same class of the issuer's securities. When determining an issuer's primary trading market under this paragraph, calculate average daily trading volume in the United States and on a worldwide basis as under Rule 12h–6 under the Act (§ 240.12h–6).

NOTE 2 TO PARAGRAPH (b)(1): Paragraph (b)(1)(iii) of this section does not apply to an issuer when claiming the exemption under paragraph (b) of this section upon the effectiveness of the termination of its registration of a class of securities under section 12(g) of the Act, or the termination of its obligation to file or furnish reports under section 15(d) of the Act.

NOTE 3 TO PARAGRAPH (b)(1): Compensatory stock options for which the underlying securities are in a class exempt under paragraph (b) of this section are also exempt under that paragraph.

(2)(i) In order to maintain the exemption under paragraph (b) of this section, a foreign private issuer shall publish, on an ongoing basis and for each

§ 240.12g5–1

subsequent fiscal year, in English, on its Internet Web site or through an electronic information delivery system generally available to the public in its primary trading market, the information specified in paragraph (b)(1)(iii) of this section.

(ii) An issuer must electronically publish the information required by paragraph (b)(2) of this section promptly after the information has been made public.

(3)(i) The information required to be published electronically under paragraph (b) of this section is information that is material to an investment decision regarding the subject securities, such as information concerning:

(A) Results of operations or financial condition;

(B) Changes in business;

(C) Acquisitions or dispositions of assets;

(D) The issuance, redemption or acquisition of securities;

(E) Changes in management or control;

(F) The granting of options or the payment of other remuneration to directors or officers; and

(G) Transactions with directors, officers or principal security holders.

(ii) At a minimum, a foreign private issuer shall electronically publish English translations of the following documents required to be published under paragraph (b) of this section if in a foreign language:

(A) Its annual report, including or accompanied by annual financial statements;

(B) Interim reports that include financial statements;

(C) Press releases; and

(D) All other communications and documents distributed directly to security holders of each class of securities to which the exemption relates.

(c) The exemption under paragraph (b) of this section shall remain in effect until:

(1) The issuer no longer satisfies the electronic publication condition of paragraph (b)(2) of this section;

(2) The issuer no longer maintains a listing of the subject class of securities on one or more exchanges in a primary trading market, as defined under paragraph (b)(1) of this section; or

(3) The issuer registers a class of securities under section 12 of the Act or incurs reporting obligations under section 15(d) of the Act.

(d) Depositary shares registered on Form F–6 (§ 239.36 of this chapter), but not the underlying deposited securities, are exempt from section 12(g) of the Act under this paragraph.

[48 FR 46739, Oct. 14, 1983, as amended at 49 FR 12689, Mar. 30, 1984; 56 FR 30068, July 1, 1991; 65 FR 37676, June 15, 2000; 72 FR 16955, Apr. 5, 2007; 73 FR 52768, Sept. 10, 2008]

§ 240.12g5–1 Definition of securities "held of record".

(a) For the purpose of determining whether an issuer is subject to the provisions of sections 12(g) and 15(d) of the Act, securities shall be deemed to be "held of record" by each person who is identified as the owner of such securities on records of security holders maintained by or on behalf of the issuer, subject to the following:

(1) In any case where the records of security holders have not been maintained in accordance with accepted practice, any additional person who would be identified as such an owner on such records if they had been maintained in accordance with accepted practice shall be included as a holder of record.

(2) Except as specified in paragraph (a)(9) of this section, securities identified as held of record by a corporation, a partnership, a trust whether or not the trustees are named, or other organization shall be included as so held by one person.

(3) Securities identified as held of record by one or more persons as trustees, executors, guardians, custodians or in other fiduciary capacities with respect to a single trust, estate or account shall be included as held of record by one person.

(4) Securities held by two or more persons as coowners shall be included as held by one person.

(5) Each outstanding unregistered or bearer certificate shall be included as held of record by a separate person, except to the extent that the issuer can establish that, if such securities were registered, they would be held of record, under the provisions of this rule, by a lesser number of persons.

156

Securities and Exchange Commission § 240.12g5–1

(6) Securities registered in substantially similar names where the issuer has reason to believe because of the address or other indications that such names represent the same person, may be included as held of record by one person.

(7) Other than when determining compliance with Rule 257(d)(2) of Regulation A (§ 230.257(d)(2) of this chapter), the definition of "held of record" shall not include securities issued in a Tier 2 offering pursuant to Regulation A by an issuer that:

(i) Is required to file reports pursuant to Rule 257(b) of Regulation A (§ 230.257(b) of this chapter);

(ii) Is current in filing annual, semiannual and special financial reports pursuant to such rule as of its most recently completed fiscal year end;

(iii) Has engaged a transfer agent registered pursuant to Section 17A(c) of the Act to perform the function of a transfer agent with respect to such securities; and

(iv) Had a public float of less than $75 million as of the last business day of its most recently completed semiannual period, computed by multiplying the aggregate worldwide number of shares of its common equity securities held by non-affiliates by the price at which such securities were last sold (or the average bid and asked prices of such securities) in the principal market for such securities or, in the event the result of such public float calculation was zero, had annual revenues of less than $50 million as of its most recently completed fiscal year. An issuer that would be required to register a class of securities under Section 12(g) of the Act as a result of exceeding the applicable threshold in this paragraph (a)(7)(iv), may continue to exclude the relevant securities from the definition of "held of record" for a transition period ending on the penultimate day of the fiscal year two years after the date it became ineligible. The transition period terminates immediately upon the failure of an issuer to timely file any periodic report due pursuant to Rule 257 (§ 230.257 of this chapter) at which time the issuer must file a registration statement that registers that class of securities under the Act within 120 days.

(8)(i) For purposes of determining whether an issuer is required to register a class of equity securities with the Commission pursuant to section 12(g)(1) of the Act (15 U.S.C. 78l(g)(1)), an issuer may exclude securities:

(A) Held by persons who received the securities pursuant to an employee compensation plan in transactions exempt from, or not subject to, the registration requirements of section 5 of the Securities Act of 1933 (15 U.S.C. 77e); and

(B) Held by persons who received the securities in a transaction exempt from, or not subject to, the registration requirements of section 5 of the Securities Act (15 U.S.C. 77e) from the issuer, a predecessor of the issuer or an acquired company in substitution or exchange for excludable securities under paragraph (a)(8)(i)(A) of this section, as long as the persons were eligible to receive securities pursuant to § 230.701(c) of this chapter at the time the excludable securities were originally issued to them.

(ii) As a non-exclusive safe harbor under this paragraph (a)(8):

(A) An issuer may deem a person to have received the securities pursuant to an employee compensation plan if such plan and the person who received the securities pursuant to the plan met the plan and participant conditions of § 230.701(c) of this chapter; and

(B) An issuer may, solely for the purposes of Section 12(g) of the Act (15 U.S.C. 78l(g)(1)), deem the securities to have been issued in a transaction exempt from, or not subject to, the registration requirements of Section 5 of the Securities Act (15 U.S.C. 77e) if the issuer had a reasonable belief at the time of the issuance that the securities were issued in such a transaction.

(9) For purposes of determining whether a crowdfunding issuer, as defined in § 270.3a–9(b)(1) of this chapter, or a crowdfunding vehicle, as defined in § 270.3a–9(b)(2) of this chapter, is required to register a class of equity securities with the Commission pursuant to section 12(g)(1) of the Act, both the crowdfunding issuer and the crowdfunding vehicle:

(i) May exclude securities issued by a crowdfunding vehicle, as defined in

§ 240.12g5-2

§ 270.3a–9(b)(2) of this chapter, in an offering under §§ 227.100 through 227.504 (Regulation Crowdfunding) in which the crowdfunding vehicle and the crowdfunding issuer are deemed to be co-issuers under the Securities Act (15 U.S.C. 77a *et seq.*) and that are held by natural persons; and

(ii) Shall include securities issued by a crowdfunding vehicle, as defined in § 270.3a–9(b)(2) of this chapter, in an offering under Regulation Crowdfunding in which the crowdfunding vehicle and the crowdfunding issuer are deemed to be co-issuers under the Securities Act and that are held by investors that are not natural persons.

(b) Notwithstanding paragraph (a) of this section:

(1) Securities held, to the knowledge of the issuer, subject to a voting trust, deposit agreement or similar arrangement shall be included as held of record by the record holders of the voting trust certificates, certificates of deposit, receipts or similar evidences of interest in such securities: *Provided, however,* That the issuer may rely in good faith on such information as is received in response to its request from a non-affiliated issuer of the certificates or evidences of interest.

(2) Whole or fractional securities issued by a savings and loan association, building and loan association, cooperative bank, homestead association, or similar institution for the sole purpose of qualifying a borrower for membership in the issuer, and which are to be redeemed or repurchased by the issuer when the borrower's loan is terminated, shall not be included as held of record by any person.

(3) If the issuer knows or has reason to know that the form of holding securities of record is used primarily to circumvent the provisions of section 12(g) or 15(d) of the Act, the beneficial owners of such securities shall be deemed to be the record owners thereof.

(Sec. 3, 48 Stat. 882, as amended, sec. 3, 78 Stat. 566; 15 U.S.C. 78c, 78*l*)

[30 FR 484, Jan. 14, 1965, as amended at 80 FR 21922, Apr. 20, 2015; 81 FR 28706, May 10, 2016; 86 FR 3601, Jan. 14, 2021]

§ 240.12g5-2 Definition of "total assets".

For the purpose of section 12(g)(1) of the Act, the term *total assets* shall mean the total assets as shown on the issuer's balance sheet or the balance sheet of the issuer and its subsidiaries consolidated, whichever is larger, as required to be filed on the form prescribed for registration under this section and prepared in accordance with the pertinent provisions of Regulation S–X (17 CFR part 210). Where the security is a certificate of deposit, voting trust certificate, or certificate or other evidence of interest in a similar trust or agreement, the "total assets" of the issuer of the security held under the trust or agreement shall be deemed to be the "total assets" of the issuer of such certificate or evidence of interest.

(Sec. 3, 48 Stat. 882, as amended, sec. 3, 78 Stat. 566; 15 U.S.C. 78c, 78*l*)

[30 FR 484, Jan. 14, 1965]

§ 240.12h-1 Exemptions from registration under section 12(g) of the Act.

Issuers shall be exempt from the provisions of section 12(g) of the Act with respect to the following securities:

(a) Any interest or participation in an employee stock bonus, stock purchase, profit sharing, pension, retirement, incentive, thrift, savings or similar plan which is not transferable by the holder except in the event of death or mental incompetency, or any security issued solely to fund such plans;

(b) Any interest or participation in any common trust fund or similar fund maintained by a bank exclusively for the collective investment and reinvestment of monies contributed thereto by the bank in its capacity as a trustee, executor, administrator, or guardian. For purposes of this paragraph (b), the term "common trust fund" shall include a common trust fund which is maintained by a bank which is a member of an affiliated group, as defined in section 1504(a) of the Internal Revenue Code of 1954 (26 U.S.C. 1504(a)), and which is maintained exclusively for the investment and reinvestment of monies contributed thereto by one or more bank members of such affilated group

Securities and Exchange Commission § 240.12h-1

in the capacity of trustee, executor, administrator, or guardian; *Provided,* That:

(1) The common trust fund is operated in compliance with the same state and Federal regulatory requirements as would apply if the bank maintaining such fund as any other contributing banks were the same entity; and

(2) The rights of persons for whose benefit a contributiong bank acts as trustee, executor, administrator or guardian would not be diminished by reason of the maintenance of such common trust furid by another bank member of the affiliated group;

(c) Any class of equity security which would not be outstanding 60 days after a registration statement would be required to be filed with respect thereto;

(d) Any standardized option, as that term is defined in section 240.9b-1(a)(4), that is issued by a clearing agency registered under section 17A of the Act (15 U.S.C. 78q-1) and traded on a national securities exchange registered pursuant to section 6(a) of the Act (15 U.S.C. 78f(a)) or on a national securities association registered pursuant to section 15A(a) of the Act (15 U.S.C. 78o-3(a));

(e) Any security futures product that is traded on a national securities exchange registered pursuant to section 6 of the Act (15 U.S.C. 78f) or on a national securities association registered pursuant to section 15A(a) of the Act (15 U.S.C. 78o-3(a)) and cleared by a clearing agency that is registered pursuant to section 17A of the Act (15 U.S.C. 78q-1) or is exempt from registration under section 17A(b)(7) of the Act (15 U.S.C. 78q-1(b)(7)).

(f)(1) Stock options issued under written compensatory stock option plans under the following conditions:

(i) The issuer of the equity security underlying the stock options does not have a class of security registered under section 12 of the Act and is not required to file reports pursuant to section 15(d) of the Act;

(ii) The stock options have been issued pursuant to one or more written compensatory stock option plans established by the issuer, its parents, its majority-owned subsidiaries or majority-owned subsidiaries of the issuer's parents;

NOTE TO PARAGRAPH (f)(1)(ii): All stock options issued under all written compensatory stock option plans on the same class of equity security of the issuer will be considered part of the same class of equity security for purposes of the provisions of paragraph (f) of this section.

(iii) The stock options are held only by those persons described in Rule 701(c) under the Securities Act (17 CFR 230.701(c)) or their permitted transferees as provided in paragraph (f)(1)(iv) of this section;

(iv) The stock options and, prior to exercise, the shares to be issued on exercise of the stock options are restricted as to transfer by the optionholder other than to persons who are family members (as defined in Rule 701(c)(3) under the Securities Act (17 CFR 230.701(c)(3)) through gifts or domestic relations orders, or to an executor or guardian of the optionholder upon the death or disability of the optionholder until the issuer becomes subject to the reporting requirements of section 13 or 15(d) of the Act or is no longer relying on the exemption pursuant to this section; provided that the optionholder may transfer the stock options to the issuer, or in connection with a change of control or other acquisition transaction involving the issuer, if after such transaction the stock options no longer will be outstanding and the issuer no longer will be relying on the exemption pursuant to this section;

NOTE TO PARAGRAPH (f)(1)(iv): For purposes of this section, optionholders may include any permitted transferee under paragraph (f)(1)(iv) of this section; provided that such permitted transferees may not further transfer the stock options.

(v) The stock options and the shares issuable upon exercise of such stock options are restricted as to any pledge, hypothecation, or other transfer, including any short position, any "put equivalent position" (as defined in § 240.16a-1(h) of this chapter), or any "call equivalent position" (as defined in § 240.16a-1(b) of this chapter) by the optionholder prior to exercise of an option, except in the circumstances permitted in paragraph (f)(1)(iv) of this section, until the issuer becomes subject to the reporting requirements of section 13 or 15(d) of the Act or is no

§ 240.12h-1

longer relying on the exemption pursuant paragraph (f)(1) of this section; and

NOTE TO PARAGRAPHS (f)(1)(iv) AND (f)(1)(v): The transferability restrictions in paragraphs (f)(1)(iv) and (f)(1)(v) of this section must be contained in a written compensatory stock option plan, individual written compensatory stock option agreement, other stock purchase or stockholder agreement to which the issuer and the optionholder are a signatory or party, other enforceable agreement by or against the issuer and the optionholder, or in the issuer's by-laws or certificate or articles of incorporation.

(vi) The issuer has agreed in the written compensatory stock option plan, the individual written compensatory stock option agreement, or another agreement enforceable against the issuer to provide the following information to optionholders once the issuer is relying on the exemption pursuant to paragraph (f)(1) of this section until the issuer becomes subject to the reporting requirements of section 13 or 15(d) of the Act or is no longer relying on the exemption pursuant paragraph (f)(1) of this section:

The information described in Rules 701(e)(3), (4), and (5) under the Securities Act (17 CFR 230.701(e)(3), (4), and (5)), every six months with the financial statements being not more than 180 days old and with such information provided either by physical or electronic delivery to the optionholders or by written notice to the optionholders of the availability of the information on an Internet site that may be password-protected and of any password needed to access the information.

NOTE TO PARAGRAPH (f)(1)(vi): The issuer may request that the optionholder agree to keep the information to be provided pursuant to this section confidential. If an optionholder does not agree to keep the information to be provided pursuant to this section confidential, then the issuer is not required to provide the information.

(2) If the exemption provided by paragraph (f)(1) of this section ceases to be available, the issuer of the stock options that is relying on the exemption provided by this section must file a registration statement to register the class of stock options under section 12 of the Act within 120 calendar days after the exemption provided by paragraph (f)(1) of this section ceases to be available; and

(g)(1) Stock options issued under written compensatory stock option plans under the following conditions:

(i) The issuer of the equity security underlying the stock options has registered a class of security under section 12 of the Act or is required to file periodic reports pursuant to section 15(d) of the Act;

(ii) The stock options have been issued pursuant to one or more written compensatory stock option plans established by the issuer, its parents, its majority-owned subsidiaries or majority-owned subsidiaries of the issuer's parents;

NOTE TO PARAGRAPH (g)(1)(ii): All stock options issued under all of the written compensatory stock option plans on the same class of equity security of the issuer will be considered part of the same class of equity security of the issuer for purposes of the provisions of paragraph (g) of this section.

(iii) The stock options are held only by those persons described in Rule 701(c) under the Securities Act (17 CFR 230.701(c)) or those persons specified in General Instruction A.1(a) of Form S-8 (17 CFR 239.16b); provided that an issuer can still rely on this exemption if there is an insignificant deviation from satisfaction of the condition in this paragraph (g)(1)(iii) and after December 7, 2007 the issuer has made a good faith and reasonable attempt to comply with the conditions of this paragraph (g)(1)(iii). For purposes of this paragraph (g)(1)(iii), an insignificant deviation exists if the number of optionholders that do not meet the condition in this paragraph (g)(1)(iii) are insignificant both as to the aggregate number of optionholders and number of outstanding stock options.

(2) If the exemption provided by paragraph (g)(1) of this section ceases to be available, the issuer of the stock options that is relying on the exemption provided by this section must file a registration statement to register the class of stock options or a class of security under section 12 of the Act within 60 calendar days after the exemption provided in paragraph (g)(1) of this section ceases to be available.

(h) Any security-based swap that is issued by a clearing agency registered

Securities and Exchange Commission § 240.12h–3

as a clearing agency under Section 17A of the Act (15 U.S.C. 78q–1) or exempt from registration under Section 17A of the Act pursuant to a rule, regulation, or order of the Commission in its function as a central counterparty that the Commission has determined must be cleared or that is permitted to be cleared pursuant to the clearing agency's rules, and that was sold to an eligible contract participant (as defined in Section 1a(18) of the Commodity Exchange Act (7 U.S.C. 1a(18))) in reliance on Rule 239 under the Securities Act of 1933 (17 CFR 230.239).

(i) Any security-based swap offered and sold in reliance on § 230.240 of this chapter. This section will expire on February 11, 2018.

[30 FR 6114, Apr. 30, 1965, as amended at 43 FR 2392, Jan. 17, 1978. Redesignated at 47 FR 17052, Apr. 21, 1982; 68 FR 192, Jan. 2, 2003; 72 FR 69566, Dec. 7, 2007; 76 FR 40612, July 11, 2011; 77 FR 20549, Apr. 5, 2012; 78 FR 7659, Feb. 4, 2013; 79 FR 7576, Feb. 10, 2014; 82 FR 10707, Feb. 15, 2017]

§ 240.12h–2 [Reserved]

§ 240.12h–3 Suspension of duty to file reports under section 15(d).

(a) Subject to paragraphs (c) and (d) of this section, the duty under section 15(d) to file reports required by section 13(a) of the Act with respect to a class of securities specified in paragraph (b) of this section shall be suspended for such class of securities immediately upon filing with the Commission a certification on Form 15 (17 CFR 249.323) if the issuer of such class has filed all reports required by section 13(a), without regard to Rule 12b–25 (17 CFR 249.322), for the shorter of its most recent three fiscal years and the portion of the current year preceding the date of filing Form 15, or the period since the issuer became subject to such reporting obligation. If the certification on Form 15 is subsequently withdrawn or denied, the issuer shall, within 60 days, file with the Commission all reports which would have been required if such certification had not been filed.

(b) The classes of securities eligible for the suspension provided in paragraph (a) of this section are:

(1) Any class of securities, other than any class of asset-backed securities, held of record by:

(i) Fewer than 300 persons, or in the case of a bank; a savings and loan holding company, as such term is defined in section 10 of the Home Owners' Loan Act (12 U.S.C. 1461); or a bank holding company, as such term is defined in section 2 of the Bank Holding Company Act of 1956 (12 U.S.C. 1841), 1,200 persons; or

(ii) Fewer than 500 persons, where the total assets of the issuer have not exceeded $10 million on the last day of each of the issuer's three most recent fiscal years; and

(2) Any class or securities deregistered pursuant to section 12(d) of the Act if such class would not thereupon be deemed registered under section 12(g) of the Act or the rules thereunder.

NOTE TO PARAGRAPH (b): The suspension of classes of asset-backed securities is addressed in § 240.15d–22.

(c) This section shall not be available for any class of securities for a fiscal year in which a registration statement relating to that class becomes effective under the Securities Act of 1933, or is required to be updated pursuant to section 10(a)(3) of the Act, and, in the case of paragraph (b)(1)(ii), the two succeeding fiscal years; *Provided, however,* That this paragraph shall not apply to the duty to file reports which arises solely from a registration statement filed by an issuer with no significant assets, for the reorganization of a non-reporting issuer into a one subsidiary holding company in which equity security holders receive the same proportional interest in the holding company as they held in the non-reporting issuer, except for changes resulting from the exercise of dissenting shareholder rights under state law.

(d) The suspension provided by this rule relates only to the reporting obligation under section 15(d) with respect to a class of securities, does not affect any other duties imposed on that class of securities, and shall continue as long as either criteria (i) or (ii) of paragraph (b)(1) is met on the first day of any subsequent fiscal year; *Provided, however,* That such criteria need not be met if the duty to file reports arises solely from a registration statement filed by an issuer with no significant assets in a reorganization of a non-reporting

§ 240.12h-4

company into a one subsidiary holding company in which equity security holders receive the same proportional interest in the holding company as they held in the non-reporting issuer except for changes resulting from the exercise of dissenting shareholder rights under state law.

(e) If the suspension provided by this section is discontinued because a class of securities does not meet the eligibility criteria of paragraph (b) of this section on the first day of an issuer's fiscal year, then the issuer shall resume periodic reporting pursuant to section 15(d) of the Act by filing an annual report on Form 10-K for its preceding fiscal year, not later than 120 days after the end of such fiscal year.

[49 FR 12689, Mar. 30, 1984, as amended at 51 FR 25362, July 14, 1986; 61 FR 21356, May 9, 1996; 72 FR 16956, Apr. 5, 2007; 73 FR 975, Jan. 4, 2008; 76 FR 52555, Aug. 23, 2011; 81 FR 28706, May 10, 2016]

§ 240.12h-4 Exemption from duty to file reports under section 15(d).

An issuer shall be exempt from the duty under section 15(d) of the Act to file reports required by section 13(a) of the Act with respect to securities registered under the Securities Act of 1933 on Form F-7, Form F-8 or Form F-80, provided that the issuer is exempt from the obligations of Section 12(g) of the Act pursuant to Rule 12g3-2(b).

[56 FR 30068, July 1, 1991]

§ 240.12h-5 Exemption for subsidiary issuers of guaranteed securities and subsidiary guarantors.

Any issuer of a guaranteed security, or guarantor of a security, that is permitted to omit financial statements by § 210.3-10 (Rule 3-10 of Regulation S-X) of this chapter is exempt from the requirements of 15 U.S.C. 78m(a) (Section 13(a) of the Act) or 78o(d) (Section 15(d) of the Act).

[85 FR 22006, Apr. 20, 2020]

§ 240.12h-6 Certification by a foreign private issuer regarding the termination of registration of a class of securities under section 12(g) or the duty to file reports under section 13(a) or section 15(d).

(a) A foreign private issuer may terminate the registration of a class of securities under section 12(g) of the Act (15 U.S.C. 78l(g)), or terminate the obligation under section 15(d) of the Act (15 U.S.C. 78o(d)) to file or furnish reports required by section 13(a) of the Act (15 U.S.C. 78m(a)) with respect to a class of equity securities, or both, after certifying to the Commission on Form 15F (17 CFR 249.324) that:

(1) The foreign private issuer has had reporting obligations under section 13(a) or section 15(d) of the Act for at least the 12 months preceding the filing of the Form 15F, has filed or furnished all reports required for this period, and has filed at least one annual report pursuant to section 13(a) of the Act;

(2) The foreign private issuer's securities have not been sold in the United States in a registered offering under the Securities Act of 1933 (15 U.S.C. 77a et seq.) during the 12 months preceding the filing of the Form 15F, other than securities issued:

(i) To the issuer's employees;

(ii) By selling security holders in non-underwritten offerings;

(iii) Upon the exercise of outstanding rights granted by the issuer if the rights are granted pro rata to all existing security holders of the class of the issuer's securities to which the rights attach;

(iv) Pursuant to a dividend or interest reinvestment plan; or

(v) Upon the conversion of outstanding convertible securities or upon the exercise of outstanding transferable warrants issued by the issuer;

NOTE TO PARAGRAPH (a)(2): The exceptions in paragraphs (a)(2)(iii) through (v) do not apply to securities issued pursuant to a standby underwritten offering or other similar arrangement in the United States.

(3) The foreign private issuer has maintained a listing of the subject class of securities for at least the 12 months preceding the filing of the Form 15F on one or more exchanges in a foreign jurisdiction that, either singly or together with the trading of the same class of the issuer's securities in another foreign jurisdiction, constitutes the primary trading market for those securities; and

(4)(i) The average daily trading volume of the subject class of securities in the United States for a recent 12-month period has been no greater than

Securities and Exchange Commission §240.12h-6

5 percent of the average daily trading volume of that class of securities on a worldwide basis for the same period; or

(ii) On a date within 120 days before the filing date of the Form 15F, a foreign private issuer's subject class of equity securities is either held of record by:

(A) Less than 300 persons on a worldwide basis; or

(B) Less than 300 persons resident in the United States.

NOTE TO PARAGRAPH (a)(4): If an issuer's equity securities trade in the form of American Depositary Receipts in the United States, for purposes of paragraph (a)(4)(i), it must calculate the trading volume of its American Depositary Receipts in terms of the number of securities represented by those American Depositary Receipts.

(b) A foreign private issuer must wait at least 12 months before it may file a Form 15F to terminate its section 13(a) or 15(d) reporting obligations in reliance on paragraph (a)(4)(i) of this section if:

(1) The issuer has delisted a class of equity securities from a national securities exchange or inter-dealer quotation system in the United States, and at the time of delisting, the average daily trading volume of that class of securities in the United States exceeded 5 percent of the average daily trading volume of that class of securities on a worldwide basis for the preceding 12 months; or

(2) The issuer has terminated a sponsored American Depositary Receipts facility, and at the time of termination the average daily trading volume in the United States of the American Depositary Receipts exceeded 5 percent of the average daily trading volume of the underlying class of securities on a worldwide basis for the preceding 12 months.

(c) A foreign private issuer may terminate its duty to file or furnish reports pursuant to section 13(a) or section 15(d) of the Act with respect to a class of debt securities after certifying to the Commission on Form 15F that:

(1) The foreign private issuer has filed or furnished all reports required by section 13(a) or section 15(d) of the Act, including at least one annual report pursuant to section 13(a) of the Act; and

(2) On a date within 120 days before the filing date of the Form 15F, the class of debt securities is either held of record by:

(i) Less than 300 persons on a worldwide basis; or

(ii) Less than 300 persons resident in the United States.

(d)(1) Following a merger, consolidation, exchange of securities, acquisition of assets or otherwise, a foreign private issuer that has succeeded to the registration of a class of securities under section 12(g) of the Act of another issuer pursuant to §240.12g-3, or to the reporting obligations of another issuer under section 15(d) of the Act pursuant to §240.15d-5, may file a Form 15F to terminate that registration or those reporting obligations if:

(i) Regarding a class of equity securities, the successor issuer meets the conditions under paragraph (a) of this section; or

(ii) Regarding a class of debt securities, the successor issuer meets the conditions under paragraph (c) of this section.

(2) When determining whether it meets the prior reporting requirement under paragraph (a)(1) or paragraph (c)(1) of this section, a successor issuer may take into account the reporting history of the issuer whose reporting obligations it has assumed pursuant to §240.12g-3 or §240.15d-5.

(e) *Counting method.* When determining under this section the number of United States residents holding a foreign private issuer's equity or debt securities:

(1)(i) Use the method for calculating record ownership §240.12g3-2(a), except that you may limit your inquiry regarding the amount of securities represented by accounts of customers resident in the United States to brokers, dealers, banks and other nominees located in:

(A) The United States;

(B) The foreign private issuer's jurisdiction of incorporation, legal organization or establishment; and

(C) The foreign private issuer's primary trading market, if different from the issuer's jurisdiction of incorporation, legal organization or establishment.

163

§ 240.12h–6

(ii) If you aggregate the trading volume of the issuer's securities in two foreign jurisdictions for the purpose of complying with paragraph (a)(3) of this section, you must include both of those foreign jurisdictions when conducting your inquiry under paragraph (e)(1)(i) of this section.

(2) If, after reasonable inquiry, you are unable without unreasonable effort to obtain information about the amount of securities represented by accounts of customers resident in the United States, for purposes of this section, you may assume that the customers are the residents of the jurisdiction in which the nominee has its principal place of business.

(3) You need count securities as owned by United States holders when publicly filed reports of beneficial ownership or other reliable information that is provided to you indicates that the securities are held by United States residents.

(4) When calculating under this section the number of your United States resident security holders, you may rely in good faith on the assistance of an independent information services provider that in the regular course of its business assists issuers in determining the number of, and collecting other information concerning, their security holders.

(f) *Definitions.* For the purpose of this section:

(1) *Debt security* means any security other than an equity security as defined under § 240.3a11–1, including:

(i) Non-participatory preferred stock, which is defined as non-convertible capital stock, the holders of which are entitled to a preference in payment of dividends and in distribution of assets on liquidation, dissolution, or winding up of the issuer, but are not entitled to participate in residual earnings or assets of the issuer; and

(ii) Notwithstanding § 240.3a11–1, any debt security described in paragraph (f)(3)(i) and (ii) of this section;

(2) *Employee* has the same meaning as the definition of employee provided in Form S–8 (§ 239.16b of this chapter).

(3) *Equity security* means the same as under § 240.3a11–1, but, for purposes of paragraphs (a)(3) and (a)(4)(i) of this section, does not include:

17 CFR Ch. II (4–1–23 Edition)

(i) Any debt security that is convertible into an equity security, with or without consideration;

(ii) Any debt security that includes a warrant or right to subscribe to or purchase an equity security;

(iii) Any such warrant or right; or

(iv) Any put, call, straddle, or other option or privilege that gives the holder the option of buying or selling a security but does not require the holder to do so.

(4) *Foreign private issuer* has the same meaning as under § 240.3b–4.

(5) *Primary trading market* means that:

(i) At least 55 percent of the trading in a foreign private issuer's class of securities that is the subject of Form 15F took place in, on or through the facilities of a securities market or markets in a single foreign jurisdiction or in no more than two foreign jurisdictions during a recent 12-month period; and

(ii) If a foreign private issuer aggregates the trading of its subject class of securities in two foreign jurisdictions for the purpose of paragraph (a)(3) of this section, the trading for the issuer's securities in at least one of the two foreign jurisdictions must be larger than the trading in the United States for the same class of the issuer's securities.

(6) *Recent 12-month period* means a 12-calendar-month period that ended no more than 60 days before the filing date of the Form 15F.

(g)(1) Suspension of a foreign private issuer's duty to file reports under section 13(a) or section 15(d) of the Act shall occur immediately upon filing the Form 15F with the Commission if filing pursuant to paragraph (a), (c) or (d) of this section. If there are no objections from the Commission, 90 days, or such shorter period as the Commission may determine, after the issuer has filed its Form 15F, the effectiveness of any of the following shall occur:

(i) The termination of registration of a class of securities under section 12(g); and

(ii) The termination of a foreign private issuer's duty to file reports under section 13(a) or section 15(d) of the Act.

(2) If the Form 15F is subsequently withdrawn or denied, the issuer shall, within 60 days after the date of the

Securities and Exchange Commission

§ 240.12h–7

withdrawal or denial, file with or submit to the Commission all reports that would have been required had the issuer not filed the Form 15F.

(h) As a condition to termination of registration or reporting under paragraph (a), (c) or (d) of this section, a foreign private issuer must, either before or on the date that it files its Form 15F, publish a notice in the United States that discloses its intent to terminate its registration of a class of securities under section 12(g) of the Act, or its reporting obligations under section 13(a) or section 15(d) of the Act, or both. The issuer must publish the notice through a means reasonably designed to provide broad dissemination of the information to the public in the United States. The issuer must also submit a copy of the notice to the Commission, either under cover of a Form 6–K (17 CFR 249.306) before or at the time of filing of the Form 15F, or as an exhibit to the Form 15F.

(i)(1) A foreign private issuer that, before the effective date of this section, terminated the registration of a class of securities under section 12(g) of the Act or suspended its reporting obligations regarding a class of equity or debt securities under section 15(d) of the Act may file a Form 15F in order to:

(i) Terminate under this section the registration of a class of equity securities that was the subject of a Form 15 (§ 249.323 of this chapter) filed by the issuer pursuant to § 240.12g–4; or

(ii) Terminate its reporting obligations under section 15(d) of the Act, which had been suspended by the terms of that section or by the issuer's filing of a Form 15 pursuant to § 240.12h–3, regarding a class of equity or debt securities.

(2) In order to be eligible to file a Form 15F under this paragraph:

(i) If a foreign private issuer terminated the registration of a class of securities pursuant to § 240.12g–4 or suspended its reporting obligations pursuant to § 240.12h–3 or section 15(d) of the Act regarding a class of equity securities, the issuer must meet the requirements under paragraph (a)(3) and paragraph (a)(4)(i) or (a)(4)(ii) of this section; or

(ii) If a foreign private issuer suspended its reporting obligations pursuant to § 240.12h–3 or section 15(d) of the Act regarding a class of debt securities, the issuer must meet the requirements under paragraph (c)(2) of this section.

(3)(i) If the Commission does not object, 90 days after the filing of a Form 15F under this paragraph, or such shorter period as the Commission may determine, the effectiveness of any of the following shall occur:

(A) The termination under this section of the registration of a class of equity securities, which was the subject of a Form 15 filed pursuant to § 240.12g–4, and the duty to file reports required by section 13(a) of the Act regarding that class of securities; or

(B) The termination of a foreign private issuer's reporting obligations under section 15(d) of the Act, which had previously been suspended by the terms of that section or by the issuer's filing of a Form 15 pursuant to § 240.12h–3, regarding a class of equity or debt securities.

(ii) If the Form 15F is subsequently withdrawn or denied, the foreign private issuer shall, within 60 days after the date of the withdrawal or denial, file with or submit to the Commission all reports that would have been required had the issuer not filed the Form 15F.

NOTE TO § 240.12h–6: The suspension of classes of asset-backed securities is addressed in § 240.15d–22.

[72 FR 16956, Apr. 5, 2007, as amended at 76 FR 52555, Aug. 23, 2011]

§ 240.12h–7 Exemption for issuers of securities that are subject to insurance regulation.

An issuer shall be exempt from the duty under section 15(d) of the Act (15 U.S.C. 78o(d)) to file reports required by section 13(a) of the Act (15 U.S.C. 78m(a)) with respect to securities registered under the Securities Act of 1933 (15 U.S.C. 77a et seq.), provided that:

(a) The issuer is a corporation subject to the supervision of the insurance commissioner, bank commissioner, or any agency or officer performing like functions, of any State;

(b) The securities do not constitute an equity interest in the issuer and are either subject to regulation under the

§ 240.13a-1

insurance laws of the domiciliary State of the issuer or are guarantees of securities that are subject to regulation under the insurance laws of that jurisdiction;

(c) The issuer files an annual statement of its financial condition with, and is supervised and its financial condition examined periodically by, the insurance commissioner, bank commissioner, or any agency or officer performing like functions, of the issuer's domiciliary State;

(d) The securities are not listed, traded, or quoted on an exchange, alternative trading system (as defined in § 242.300(a) of this chapter), inter-dealer quotation system (as defined in § 240.15c2–11(e)(2)), electronic communications network, or any other similar system, network, or publication for trading or quoting;

(e) The issuer takes steps reasonably designed to ensure that a trading market for the securities does not develop, including, except to the extent prohibited by the law of any State or by action of the insurance commissioner, bank commissioner, or any agency or officer performing like functions of any State, requiring written notice to, and acceptance by, the issuer prior to any assignment or other transfer of the securities and reserving the right to refuse assignments or other transfers at any time on a non-discriminatory basis; and

(f) The prospectus for the securities contains a statement indicating that the issuer is relying on the exemption provided by this rule.

[74 FR 3175, Jan. 16, 2009]

REGULATION 13A: REPORTS OF ISSUERS OF SECURITIES REGISTERED PURSUANT TO SECTION 12

ANNUAL REPORTS

§ 240.13a-1 Requirements of annual reports.

Every issuer having securities registered pursuant to section 12 of the Act (15 U.S.C. 78*l*) shall file an annual report on the appropriate form authorized or prescribed therefor for each fiscal year after the last full fiscal year for which financial statements were filed in its registration statement. Annual reports shall be filed within the period specified in the appropriate form.

[62 FR 39767, July 24, 1997]

§ 240.13a-2 [Reserved]

§ 240.13a-3 Reporting by Form 40–F registrant.

A registrant that is eligible to use Forms 40–F and 6–K and files reports in accordance therewith shall be deemed to satisfy the requirements of Regulation 13A (§§ 240.13a–1 through 240.13a–17 of this chapter).

[56 FR 30068, July 1, 1991]

OTHER REPORTS

§ 240.13a-10 Transition reports.

(a) Every issuer that changes its fiscal closing date shall file a report covering the resulting transition period between the closing date of its most recent fiscal year and the opening date of its new fiscal year; *Provided, however,* that an issuer shall file an annual report for any fiscal year that ended before the date on which the issuer determined to change its fiscal year end. In no event shall the transition report cover a period of 12 or more months.

(b) The report pursuant to this section shall be filed for the transition period not more than the number of days specified in paragraph (j) of this section after either the close of the transition period or the date of the determination to change the fiscal closing date, whichever is later. The report shall be filed on the form appropriate for annual reports of the issuer, shall cover the period from the close of the last fiscal year end and shall indicate clearly the period covered. The financial statements for the transition period filed therewith shall be audited. Financial statements, which may be unaudited, shall be filed for the comparable period of the prior year, or a footnote, which may be unaudited, shall state for the comparable period of the prior year, revenues, gross profits, income taxes, income or loss from continuing operations and net income or loss. The effects of any discontinued operations as classified under the provisions of generally accepted accounting principles also shall be shown, if

Securities and Exchange Commission § 240.13a–10

applicable. Per share data based upon such income or loss and net income or loss shall be presented in conformity with applicable accounting standards. Where called for by the time span to be covered, the comparable period financial statements or footnote shall be included in subsequent filings.

(c) If the transition period covers a period of less than six months, in lieu of the report required by paragraph (b) of this section, a report may be filed for the transition period on Form 10–Q (§ 249.308a of this chapter) not more than the number of days specified in paragraph (j) of this section after either the close of the transition period or the date of the determination to change the fiscal closing date, whichever is later. The report on Form 10–Q shall cover the period from the close of the last fiscal year end and shall indicate clearly the period covered. The financial statements filed therewith need not be audited but, if they are not audited, the issuer shall file with the first annual report for the newly adopted fiscal year separate audited statements of income and cash flows covering the transition period. The notes to financial statements for the transition period included in such first annual report may be integrated with the notes to financial statements for the full fiscal period. A separate audited balance sheet as of the end of the transition period shall be filed in the annual report only if the audited balance sheet as of the end of the fiscal year prior to the transition period is not filed. Schedules need not be filed in transition reports on Form 10–Q.

(d) Notwithstanding the foregoing in paragraphs (a), (b), and (c) of this section, if the transition period covers a period of one month or less, the issuer need not file a separate transition report if either:

(1) The first report required to be filed by the issuer for the newly adopted fiscal year after the date of the determination to change the fiscal year end is an annual report, and that report covers the transition period as well as the fiscal year; or

(2)(i) The issuer files with the first annual report for the newly adopted fiscal year separate audited statements of income and cash flows covering the transition period; and

(ii) The first report required to be filed by the issuer for the newly adopted fiscal year after the date of the determination to change the fiscal year end is a quarterly report on Form 10–Q; and

(iii) Information on the transition period is included in the issuer's quarterly report on Form 10–Q for the first quarterly period (except the fourth quarter) of the newly adopted fiscal year that ends after the date of the determination to change the fiscal year. The information covering the transition period required by Part II and Item 2 of Part I may be combined with the information regarding the quarter. However, the financial statements required by Part I, which may be unaudited, shall be furnished separately for the transition period.

(e) Every issuer required to file quarterly reports on Form 10–Q pursuant to § 240.13a–13 of this chapter that changes its fiscal year end shall:

(1) File a quarterly report on Form 10–Q within the time period specified in General Instruction A.1. to that form for any quarterly period (except the fourth quarter) of the old fiscal year that ends before the date on which the issuer determined to change its fiscal year end, except that the issuer need not file such quarterly report if the date on which the quarterly period ends also is the date on which the transition period ends;

(2) File a quarterly report on Form 10–Q within the time specified in General Instruction A.1. to that form for each quarterly period of the old fiscal year within the transition period. In lieu of a quarterly report for any quarter of the old fiscal year within the transition period, the issuer may file a quarterly report on Form 10–Q for any period of three months within the transition period that coincides with a quarter of the newly adopted fiscal year if the quarterly report is filed within the number of days specified in paragraph (j) of this section after the end of such three month period, provided the issuer thereafter continues filing quarterly reports on the basis of the quarters of the newly adopted fiscal year;

§ 240.13a-10

(3) Commence filing quarterly reports for the quarters of the new fiscal year no later than the quarterly report for the first quarter of the new fiscal year that ends after the date on which the issuer determined to change the fiscal year end; and

(4) Unless such information is or will be included in the transition report, or the first annual report on Form 10-K for the newly adopted fiscal year, include in the initial quarterly report on Form 10-Q for the newly adopted fiscal year information on any period beginning on the first day subsequent to the period covered by the issuer's final quarterly report on Form 10-Q or annual report on Form 10-K for the old fiscal year. The information covering such period required by Part II and Item 2 of Part I may be combined with the information regarding the quarter. However, the financial statements required by Part I, which may be unaudited, shall be furnished separately for such period.

NOTE TO PARAGRAPHS (c) AND (e): If it is not practicable or cannot be cost-justified to furnish in a transition report on Form 10-Q or a quarterly report for the newly adopted fiscal year financial statements for corresponding periods of the prior year where required, financial statements may be furnished for the quarters of the preceding fiscal year that most nearly are comparable if the issuer furnishes an adequate discussion of seasonal and other factors that could affect the comparability of information or trends reflected, an assessment of the comparability of the data, and a representation as to the reason recasting has not been undertaken.

(f) Every successor issuer with securities registered under Section 12 of this Act that has a different fiscal year from that of its predecessor(s) shall file a transition report pursuant to this section, containing the required information about each predecessor, for the transition period, if any, between the close of the fiscal year covered by the last annual report of each predecessor and the date of succession. The report shall be filed for the transition period on the form appropriate for annual reports of the issuer not more than the number of days specified in paragraph (j) of this section after the date of the succession, with financial statements in conformity with the requirements set forth in paragraph (b) of this section. If the transition period covers a period of less than six months, in lieu of a transition report on the form appropriate for the issuer's annual reports, the report may be filed for the transition period on Form 10-Q and Form 10-QSB not more than the number of days specified in paragraph (j) of this section after the date of the succession, with financial statements in conformity with the requirements set forth in paragraph (c) of this section. Notwithstanding the foregoing, if the transition period covers a period of one month or less, the successor issuer need not file a separate transition report if the information is reported by the successor issuer in conformity with the requirements set forth in paragraph (d) of this section.

(g)(1) Paragraphs (a) through (f) of this section shall not apply to foreign private issuers.

(2) Every foreign private issuer that changes its fiscal closing date shall file a report covering the resulting transition period between the closing date of its most recent fiscal year and the opening date of its new fiscal year. In no event shall a transition report cover a period longer than 12 months.

(3) The report for the transition period shall be filed on Form 20-F (§ 249.220f of this chapter) responding to all items to which such issuer is required to respond when Form 20-F is used as an annual report. The financial statements for the transition period filed therewith shall be audited. The report shall be filed within four months after either the close of the transition period or the date on which the issuer made the determination to change the fiscal closing date, whichever is later.

(4) If the transition period covers a period of six or fewer months, in lieu of the report required by paragraph (g)(3) of this section, a report for the transition period may be filed on Form 20-F responding to Items 5, 8.A.7., 13, 14, and 17 or 18 within three months after either the close of the transition period or the date on which the issuer made the determination to change the fiscal closing date, whichever is later. The financial statements required by either Item 17 or Item 18 shall be furnished

Securities and Exchange Commission

§ 240.13a–11

for the transition period. Such financial statements may be unaudited and condensed as permitted in Article 10 of Regulation S-X (§ 210.10–01 of this chapter), but if the financial statements are unaudited and condensed, the issuer shall file with the first annual report for the newly adopted fiscal year separate audited statements of income and cash flows covering the transition period.

(5) Notwithstanding the foregoing in paragraphs (g)(2), (g)(3), and (g)(4) of this section, if the transition period covers a period of one month or less, a foreign private issuer need not file a separate transition report if the first annual report for the newly adopted fiscal year covers the transition period as well as the fiscal year.

(h) The provisions of this rule shall not apply to investment companies required to file reports pursuant to Rule 30a–1 (§ 270.30a–1 of this chapter) under the Investment Company Act of 1940 (15 U.S.C. 80a–1 et seq.).

(i) No filing fee shall be required for a transition report filed pursuant to this section.

(j)(1) For transition reports to be filed on the form appropriate for annual reports of the issuer, the number of days shall be:

(i) 60 days (75 days for fiscal years ending before December 15, 2006) for large accelerated filers (as defined in § 240.12b–2);

(ii) 75 days for accelerated filers (as defined in § 240.12b–2); and

(iii) 90 days for all other issuers; and

(2) For transition reports to be filed on Form 10–Q (§ 249.308a of this chapter) the number of days shall be:

(i) 40 days for large accelerated filers and accelerated filers (as defined in § 240.12b–2); and

(ii) 45 days for all other issuers.

(k)(1) Paragraphs (a) through (g) of this section shall not apply to asset-backed issuers.

(2) Every asset-backed issuer that changes its fiscal closing date shall file a report covering the resulting transition period between the closing date of its most recent fiscal year and the opening date of its new fiscal year. In no event shall a transition report cover a period longer than 12 months.

(3) The report for the transition period shall be filed on Form 10–K (§ 249.310 of this chapter) responding to all items to which such asset-backed issuer is required to respond pursuant to General Instruction J. of Form 10–K. Such report shall be filed within 90 days after the later of either the close of the transition period or the date on which the issuer made the determination to change the fiscal closing date.

(4) Notwithstanding the foregoing in paragraphs (k)(2) and (k)(3) of this section, if the transition period covers a period of one month or less, an asset-backed issuer need not file a separate transition report if the first annual report for the newly adopted fiscal year covers the transition period as well as the fiscal year.

(5) Any obligation of the asset-backed issuer to file distribution reports pursuant to § 240.13a–17 will continue to apply regardless of a change in the asset-backed issuer's fiscal closing date.

NOTE 1: In addition to the report or reports required to be filed pursuant to this section, every issuer, except a foreign private issuer or an investment company required to file reports pursuant to § 270.30a–1 of this chapter, that changes its fiscal closing date is required to file a Form 8–K (§ 249.308 of this chapter) report that includes the information required by Item 5.03 of Form 8–K within the period specified in General Instruction B.1. to that form.

NOTE 2: The report or reports to be filed pursuant to this section must include the certification required by § 240.13a–14.

[54 FR 10316, Mar. 13, 1989, as amended at 56 FR 30068, July 1, 1991; 64 FR 53912, Oct. 5, 1999; 67 FR 57288, Sept. 9, 2002; 67 FR 58505, Sept. 16, 2002; 69 FR 15618, Mar. 25, 2004; 69 FR 68325, Nov. 23, 2004; 70 FR 1621, Jan. 7, 2005; 70 FR 76641, Dec. 27, 2005; 73 FR 975, Jan. 4, 2008; 73 FR 58323, Oct. 6, 2008; 81 FR 82020, Nov. 18, 2016; 83 FR 50221, Oct. 4, 2018]

§ 240.13a–11 Current reports on Form 8–K (§ 249.308 of this chapter).

(a) Except as provided in paragraph (b) of this section, every registrant subject to § 240.13a–1 shall file a current report on Form 8–K within the period specified in that form unless substantially the same information as that required by Form 8–K has been previously reported by the registrant.

(b) This section shall not apply to foreign governments, foreign private

169

§ 240.13a-13

issuers required to make reports on Form 6-K (17 CFR 249.306) pursuant to § 240.13a-16, issuers of American Depositary Receipts for securities of any foreign issuer, or investment companies required to file reports pursuant to § 270.30a-1 of this chapter under the Investment Company Act of 1940, except where such an investment company is required to file:

(1) Notice of a blackout period pursuant to § 245.104 of this chapter;

(2) Disclosure pursuant to Instruction 2 to § 240.14a-11(b)(1) of information concerning outstanding shares and voting; or

(3) Disclosure pursuant to Instruction 2 to § 240.14a-11(b)(10) of the date by which a nominating shareholder or nominating shareholder group must submit the notice required pursuant to § 240.14a-11(b)(10).

(c) No failure to file a report on Form 8-K that is required solely pursuant to Item 1.01, 1.02, 2.03, 2.04, 2.05, 2.06, 4.02(a), 5.02(e) or 6.03 of Form 8-K shall be deemed to be a violation of 15 U.S.C. 78j(b) and § 240.10b-5.

[42 FR 4428, Jan. 25, 1977, as amended at 50 FR 27939, July 9, 1985; 68 FR 4355, Jan. 28, 2003; 69 FR 15618, Mar. 25, 2004; 70 FR 1621, Jan. 7, 2005; 71 FR 53260, Sept. 8, 2006; 75 FR 56780, Sept. 16, 2010; 81 FR 82020, Nov. 18, 2016]

§ 240.13a-13 Quarterly reports on Form 10-Q (§ 249.308a of this chapter).

(a) Except as provided in paragraphs (b) and (c) of this section, every issuer that has securities registered pursuant to section 12 of the Act and is required to file annual reports pursuant to section 13 of the Act, and has filed or intends to file such reports on Form 10-K (§ 249.310 of this chapter), shall file a quarterly report on Form 10-Q (§ 249.308a of this chapter) within the period specified in General Instruction A.1. to that form for each of the first three quarters of each fiscal year of the issuer, commencing with the first fiscal quarter following the most recent fiscal year for which full financial statements were included in the registration statement, or, if the registration statement included financial statements for an interim period subsequent to the most recent fiscal year end meeting the requirements of Article 10 of Regulation S-X and Rule 8-03 of Regulation S-X for smaller reporting companies, for the first fiscal quarter subsequent to the quarter reported upon in the registration statement. The first quarterly report of the issuer shall be filed either within 45 days after the effective date of the registration statement or on or before the date on which such report would have been required to be filed if the issuer has been required to file reports on Form 10-Q as of its last fiscal quarter, whichever is later.

(b) The provisions of this rule shall not apply to the following issuers:

(1) Investment companies required to file reports pursuant to § 270.30a-1;

(2) Foreign private issuers required to file reports pursuant to § 240.13a-16; and

(3) Asset-backed issuers required to file reports pursuant to § 240.13a-17.

(c) Part I of the quarterly reports on Form 10-Q need not be filed by:

(1) Mutual life insurance companies; or

(2) Mining companies not in the production stage but engaged primarily in the exploration for the development of mineral deposits other than oil, gas or coal, if all of the following conditions are met:

(i) The registrant has not been in production during the current fiscal year or the two years immediately prior thereto; except that being in production for an aggregate period of not more than eight months over the three-year period shall not be a violation of this condition.

(ii) Receipts from the sale of mineral products or from the operations of mineral producing properties by the registrant and its subsidiaries combined have not exceeded $500,000 in any of the most recent six years and have not aggregated more than $1,500,000 in the most recent six fiscal years.

(d) Notwithstanding the foregoing provisions of this section, the financial information required by Part I of Form 10-Q shall not be deemed to be "filed" for the purpose of Section 18 of the Act or otherwise subject to the liabilities of that section of the Act, but shall be

Securities and Exchange Commission § 240.13a-15

subject to all other provisions of the Act.

[42 FR 24064, May 12, 1977, as amended at 48 FR 19877, May 3, 1983; 50 FR 27939, July 9, 1985; 54 FR 10317, Mar. 13, 1989; 57 FR 10615, Mar. 27, 1992; 61 FR 30403, June 14, 1996; 70 FR 1621, Jan. 7, 2005; 73 FR 975, Jan. 4, 2008; 81 FR 82020, Nov. 18, 2016]

§ 240.13a-14 Certification of disclosure in annual and quarterly reports.

(a) Each report, including transition reports, filed on Form 10-Q, Form 10-K, Form 20-F or Form 40-F (§ 249.308a, § 249.310, § 249.220f or § 249.240f of this chapter) under Section 13(a) of the Act (15 U.S.C. 78m(a)), other than a report filed by an Asset-Backed Issuer (as defined in § 229.1101 of this chapter) or a report on Form 20-F filed under § 240.13a-19, must include certifications in the form specified in the applicable exhibit filing requirements of such report and such certifications must be filed as an exhibit to such report. Each principal executive and principal financial officer of the issuer, or persons performing similar functions, at the time of filing of the report must sign a certification. The principal executive and principal financial officers of an issuer may omit the portion of the introductory language in paragraph 4 as well as language in paragraph 4(b) of the certification that refers to the certifying officers' responsibility for designing, establishing and maintaining internal control over financial reporting for the issuer until the issuer becomes subject to the internal control over financial reporting requirements in § 240.13a-15 or § 240.15d-15.

(b) Each periodic report containing financial statements filed by an issuer pursuant to section 13(a) of the Act (15 U.S.C. 78m(a)) must be accompanied by the certifications required by Section 1350 of Chapter 63 of Title 18 of the United States Code (18 U.S.C. 1350) and such certifications must be furnished as an exhibit to such report as specified in the applicable exhibit requirements for such report. Each principal executive and principal financial officer of the issuer (or equivalent thereof) must sign a certification. This requirement may be satisfied by a single certification signed by an issuer's principal executive and principal financial officers.

(c) A person required to provide a certification specified in paragraph (a), (b) or (d) of this section may not have the certification signed on his or her behalf pursuant to a power of attorney or other form of confirming authority.

(d) Each annual report and transition report filed on Form 10-K (§ 249.310 of this chapter) by an asset-backed issuer under section 13(a) of the Act (15 U.S.C. 78m(a)) must include a certification in the form specified in the applicable exhibit filing requirements of such report and such certification must be filed as an exhibit to such report. Terms used in paragraphs (d) and (e) of this section have the same meaning as in Item 1101 of Regulation AB (§ 229.1101 of this chapter).

(e) With respect to asset-backed issuers, the certification required by paragraph (d) of this section must be signed by either:

(1) The senior officer in charge of securitization of the depositor if the depositor is signing the report; or

(2) The senior officer in charge of the servicing function of the servicer if the servicer is signing the report on behalf of the issuing entity. If multiple servicers are involved in servicing the pool assets, the senior officer in charge of the servicing function of the master servicer (or entity performing the equivalent function) must sign if a representative of the servicer is to sign the report on behalf of the issuing entity.

(f) The certification requirements of this section do not apply to an Interactive Data File, as defined in § 232.11 of this chapter (Rule 11 of Regulation S-T).

[67 FR 57288, Sept. 9, 2002, as amended at 68 FR 36665, June 18, 2003; 70 FR 1621, Jan. 7, 2005; 70 FR 6572, Feb. 8, 2005; 70 FR 42247, July 21, 2005; 71 FR 76596, Dec. 21, 2006; 73 FR 976, Jan. 4, 2008; 74 FR 6818, Feb. 10, 2009; 83 FR 40878, Aug. 16, 2018]

§ 240.13a-15 Controls and procedures.

(a) Every issuer that has a class of securities registered pursuant to section 12 of the Act (15 U.S.C. 78*l*), other than an Asset-Backed Issuer (as defined in § 229.1101 of this chapter), a small business investment company

§ 240.13a-15

registered on Form N-5 (§§ 239.24 and 274.5 of this chapter), or a unit investment trust as defined in section 4(2) of the Investment Company Act of 1940 (15 U.S.C. 80a-4(2)), must maintain disclosure controls and procedures (as defined in paragraph (e) of this section) and, if the issuer either had been required to file an annual report pursuant to section 13(a) or 15(d) of the Act (15 U.S.C. 78m(a) or 78o(d)) for the prior fiscal year or had filed an annual report with the Commission for the prior fiscal year, internal control over financial reporting (as defined in paragraph (f) of this section).

(b) Each such issuer's management must evaluate, with the participation of the issuer's principal executive and principal financial officers, or persons performing similar functions, the effectiveness of the issuer's disclosure controls and procedures, as of the end of each fiscal quarter, except that management must perform this evaluation:

(1) In the case of a foreign private issuer (as defined in § 240.3b-4) as of the end of each fiscal year; and

(2) In the case of an investment company registered under section 8 of the Investment Company Act of 1940 (15 U.S.C. 80a-8), within the 90-day period prior to the filing date of each report requiring certification under § 270.30a-2 of this chapter.

(c) The management of each such issuer, that either had been required to file an annual report pursuant to section 13(a) or 15(d) of the Act (15 U.S.C. 78m(a) or 78o(d)) for the prior fiscal year or previously had filed an annual report with the Commission for the prior fiscal year, other than an investment company registered under section 8 of the Investment Company Act of 1940, must evaluate, with the participation of the issuer's principal executive and principal financial officers, or persons performing similar functions, the effectiveness, as of the end of each fiscal year, of the issuer's internal control over financial reporting. The framework on which management's evaluation of the issuer's internal control over financial reporting is based must be a suitable, recognized control framework that is established by a body or group that has followed due-process procedures, including the broad

17 CFR Ch. II (4-1-23 Edition)

distribution of the framework for public comment. Although there are many different ways to conduct an evaluation of the effectiveness of internal control over financial reporting to meet the requirements of this paragraph, an evaluation that is conducted in accordance with the interpretive guidance issued by the Commission in Release No. 34-55929 will satisfy the evaluation required by this paragraph.

(d) The management of each such issuer that either had been required to file an annual report pursuant to section 13(a) or 15(d) of the Act (15 U.S.C. 78m(a) or 78o(d) for the prior fiscal year or had filed an annual report with the Commission for the prior fiscal year, other than an investment company registered under section 8 of the Investment Company Act of 1940 (15 U.S.C. 80a-8), must evaluate, with the participation of the issuer's principal executive and principal financial officers, or persons performing similar functions, any change in the issuer's internal control over financial reporting, that occurred during each of the issuer's fiscal quarters, or fiscal year in the case of a foreign private issuer, that has materially affected, or is reasonably likely to materially affect, the issuer's internal control over financial reporting.

(e) For purposes of this section, the term *disclosure controls and procedures* means controls and other procedures of an issuer that are designed to ensure that information required to be disclosed by the issuer in the reports that it files or submits under the Act (15 U.S.C. 78a *et seq.*) is recorded, processed, summarized and reported, within the time periods specified in the Commission's rules and forms. Disclosure controls and procedures include, without limitation, controls and procedures designed to ensure that information required to be disclosed by an issuer in the reports that it files or submits under the Act is accumulated and communicated to the issuer's management, including its principal executive and principal financial officers, or persons performing similar functions, as appropriate to allow timely decisions regarding required disclosure.

(f) The term *internal control over financial reporting* is defined as a process

Securities and Exchange Commission § 240.13a–18

designed by, or under the supervision of, the issuer's principal executive and principal financial officers, or persons performing similar functions, and effected by the issuer's board of directors, management and other personnel, to provide reasonable assurance regarding the reliability of financial reporting and the preparation of financial statements for external purposes in accordance with generally accepted accounting principles and includes those policies and procedures that:

(1) Pertain to the maintenance of records that in reasonable detail accurately and fairly reflect the transactions and dispositions of the assets of the issuer;

(2) Provide reasonable assurance that transactions are recorded as necessary to permit preparation of financial statements in accordance with generally accepted accounting principles, and that receipts and expenditures of the issuer are being made only in accordance with authorizations of management and directors of the issuer; and

(3) Provide reasonable assurance regarding prevention or timely detection of unauthorized acquisition, use or disposition of the issuer's assets that could have a material effect on the financial statements.

[68 FR 36666, June 18, 2003, as amended at 70 FR 1621, Jan. 7, 2005; 71 FR 76596, Dec. 21, 2006; 72 FR 35321, June 27, 2007]

§ 240.13a–16 Reports of foreign private issuers on Form 6–K (17 CFR 249.306).

(a) Every foreign private issuer which is subject to Rule 13a–1 (17 CFR 240.13a–1) shall make reports on Form 6–K, except that this rule shall not apply to:

(1) Investment companies required to file reports pursuant to § 270.30a–1 of this chapter ;

(2) Issuers of American depositary receipts for securities of any foreign issuer;

(3) Issuers filing periodic reports on Form 10–K, Form 10–Q, and Form 8–K; or

(4) Asset-backed issuers, as defined in § 229.1101 of this chapter.

(b) Such reports shall be transmitted promptly after the information required by Form 6–K is made public by the issuer, by the country of its domicile or under the laws of which it was incorporated or organized, or by a foreign securities exchange with which the issuer has filed the information.

(c) Reports furnished pursuant to this rule shall not be deemed to be "filed" for the purpose of section 18 of the Act or otherwise subject to the liabilities of that section.

[32 FR 7849, May 30, 1967, as amended at 44 FR 70137, Dec. 6, 1979; 47 FR 54781, Dec. 6, 1982; 50 FR 27939, July 9, 1985; 57 FR 10615, Mar. 27, 1991; 70 FR 1621, Jan. 7, 2005; 73 FR 976, Jan. 4, 2008; 81 FR 82020, Nov. 18, 2016]

§ 240.13a–17 Reports of asset-backed issuers on Form 10–D (§ 249.312 of this chapter).

Every asset-backed issuer subject to § 240.13a–1 shall make reports on Form 10–D (§ 249.312 of this chapter). Such reports shall be filed within the period specified in Form 10–D.

[70 FR 1621, Jan. 7, 2005]

§ 240.13a–18 Compliance with servicing criteria for asset-backed securities.

(a) This section applies to every class of asset-backed securities subject to the reporting requirements of section 13(a) of the Act (15 U.S.C. 78m(a)). Terms used in this section have the same meaning as in Item 1101 of Regulation AB (§ 229.1101 of this chapter).

(b) *Reports on assessments of compliance with servicing criteria for asset-backed securities required.* With regard to a class of asset-backed securities subject to the reporting requirements of section 13(a) of the Act, the annual report on Form 10–K (§ 249.308 of this chapter) for such class must include from each party participating in the servicing function a report regarding its assessment of compliance with the servicing criteria specified in paragraph (d) of Item 1122 of Regulation AB (§ 229.1122(d) of this chapter), as of and for the period ending the end of each fiscal year, with respect to asset-backed securities transactions taken as a whole involving the party participating in the servicing function and that are backed by the same asset type

173

§ 240.13a-19

backing the class of asset-backed securities (including the asset-backed securities transaction that is to be the subject of the report on Form 10-K for that fiscal year).

(c) *Attestation reports on assessments of compliance with servicing criteria for asset-backed securities required.* With respect to each report included pursuant to paragraph (b) of this section, the annual report on Form 10-K must also include a report by a registered public accounting firm that attests to, and reports on, the assessment made by the asserting party. The attestation report on assessment of compliance with servicing criteria for asset-backed securities must be made in accordance with standards for attestation engagements issued or adopted by the Public Company Accounting Oversight Board.

NOTE TO § 240.13a-18. If multiple parties are participating in the servicing function, a separate assessment report and attestation report must be included for each party participating in the servicing function. A party participating in the servicing function means any entity (e.g., master servicer, primary servicers, trustees) that is performing activities that address the criteria in paragraph (d) of Item 1122 of Regulation AB (§ 229.1122(d) of this chapter), unless such entity's activities relate only to 5% or less of the pool assets.

[70 FR 1621, Jan. 7, 2005]

§ 240.13a-19 Reports by shell companies on Form 20-F.

Every foreign private issuer that was a shell company, other than a business combination related shell company, immediately before a transaction that causes it to cease to be a shell company shall, within four business days of completion of that transaction, file a report on Form 20-F (§ 249.220f of this chapter) containing the information that would be required if the issuer were filing a form for registration of securities on Form 20-F to register under the Act all classes of the issuer's securities subject to the reporting requirements of section 13 (15 U.S.C. 78m) or section 15(d) (15 U.S.C. 78o(d)) of the Act upon consummation of the transaction, with such information reflecting the registrant and its securities upon consummation of the transaction.

[70 FR 42247, July 21, 2005]

§ 240.13a-20 Plain English presentation of specified information.

(a) Any information included or incorporated by reference in a report filed under section 13(a) of the Act (15 U.S.C. 78m(a)) that is required to be disclosed pursuant to Item 402, 403, 404 or 407 of Regulation S-K (§ 229.402, § 229.403, § 229.404 or § 229.407 of this chapter) must be presented in a clear, concise and understandable manner. You must prepare the disclosure using the following standards:

(1) Present information in clear, concise sections, paragraphs and sentences;

(2) Use short sentences;

(3) Use definite, concrete, everyday words;

(4) Use the active voice;

(5) Avoid multiple negatives;

(6) Use descriptive headings and subheadings;

(7) Use a tabular presentation or bullet lists for complex material, wherever possible;

(8) Avoid legal jargon and highly technical business and other terminology;

(9) Avoid frequent reliance on glossaries or defined terms as the primary means of explaining information. Define terms in a glossary or other section of the document only if the meaning is unclear from the context. Use a glossary only if it facilitates understanding of the disclosure; and

(10) In designing the presentation of the information you may include pictures, logos, charts, graphs and other design elements so long as the design is not misleading and the required information is clear. You are encouraged to use tables, schedules, charts and graphic illustrations that present relevant data in an understandable manner, so long as such presentations are consistent with applicable disclosure requirements and consistent with other information in the document. You must draw graphs and charts to scale. Any information you provide must not be misleading.

(b) [Reserved]

NOTE TO § 240.13a-20: In drafting the disclosure to comply with this section, you should avoid the following:

Securities and Exchange Commission

§ 240.13b2-2

1. Legalistic or overly complex presentations that make the substance of the disclosure difficult to understand;
2. Vague "boilerplate" explanations that are imprecise and readily subject to different interpretations;
3. Complex information copied directly from legal documents without any clear and concise explanation of the provision(s); and
4. Disclosure repeated in different sections of the document that increases the size of the document but does not enhance the quality of the information.

[71 FR 53261, Sept. 8, 2006, as amended at 73 FR 976, Jan. 4, 2008]

REGULATION 13B-2: MAINTENANCE OF RECORDS AND PREPARATION OF REQUIRED REPORTS

§ 240.13b2-1 Falsification of accounting records.

No person shall directly or indirectly, falsify or cause to be falsified, any book, record or account subject to section 13(b)(2)(A) of the Securities Exchange Act.

(15 U.S.C. 78m(b)(2); 15 U.S.C. 78m(a), 78m(b)(1), 78o(d), 78j(b), 78n(a), 78t(b), 78t(c))

[44 FR 10970, Feb. 23, 1979]

§ 240.13b2-2 Representations and conduct in connection with the preparation of required reports and documents.

(a) No director or officer of an issuer shall, directly or indirectly:

(1) Make or cause to be made a materially false or misleading statement to an accountant in connection with; or

(2) Omit to state, or cause another person to omit to state, any material fact necessary in order to make statements made, in light of the circumstances under which such statements were made, not misleading, to an accountant in connection with:

(i) Any audit, review or examination of the financial statements of the issuer required to be made pursuant to this subpart; or

(ii) The preparation or filing of any document or report required to be filed with the Commission pursuant to this subpart or otherwise.

(b)(1) No officer or director of an issuer, or any other person acting under the direction thereof, shall directly or indirectly take any action to coerce, manipulate, mislead, or fraudulently influence any independent public or certified public accountant engaged in the performance of an audit or review of the financial statements of that issuer that are required to be filed with the Commission pursuant to this subpart or otherwise if that person knew or should have known that such action, if successful, could result in rendering the issuer's financial statements materially misleading.

(2) For purposes of paragraphs (b)(1) and (c)(2) of this section, actions that, "if successful, could result in rendering the issuer's financial statements materially misleading" include, but are not limited to, actions taken at any time with respect to the professional engagement period to coerce, manipulate, mislead, or fraudulently influence an auditor:

(i) To issue or reissue a report on an issuer's financial statements that is not warranted in the circumstances (due to material violations of generally accepted accounting principles, the standards of the PCAOB, or other professional or regulatory standards);

(ii) Not to perform audit, review or other procedures required by the standards of the PCAOB or other professional standards;

(iii) Not to withdraw an issued report; or

(iv) Not to communicate matters to an issuer's audit committee.

(c) In addition, in the case of an investment company registered under section 8 of the Investment Company Act of 1940 (15 U.S.C. 80a-8), or a business development company as defined in section 2(a)(48) of the Investment Company Act of 1940 (15 U.S.C. 80a-2(a)(48)), no officer or director of the company's investment adviser, sponsor, depositor, trustee, or administrator (or, in the case of paragraph (c)(2) of this section, any other person acting under the direction thereof) shall, directly or indirectly:

(1)(i) Make or cause to be made a materially false or misleading statement to an accountant in connection with; or

(ii) Omit to state, or cause another person to omit to state, any material

§ 240.13d-1

fact necessary in order to make statements made, in light of the circumstances under which such statements were made, not misleading to an accountant in connection with:

(A) Any audit, review, or examination of the financial statements of the investment company required to be made pursuant to this subpart; or

(B) The preparation or filing of any document or report required to be filed with the Commission pursuant to this subpart or otherwise; or

(2) Take any action to coerce, manipulate, mislead, or fraudulently influence any independent public or certified public accountant engaged in the performance of an audit or review of the financial statements of that investment company that are required to be filed with the Commission pursuant to this subpart or otherwise if that person knew or should have known that such action, if successful, could result in rendering the investment company's financial statements materially misleading.

[68 FR 31830, May 28, 2003, as amended at 83 FR 50222, Oct. 4, 2018]

REGULATION 13D-G

SOURCE: Sections 240.13d-1 through 240.13f-1 appear at 43 FR 18495, Apr. 28, 1978, unless otherwise noted.

ATTENTION ELECTRONIC FILERS

THIS REGULATION SHOULD BE READ IN CONJUNCTION WITH REGULATION S-T (PART 232 OF THIS CHAPTER), WHICH GOVERNS THE PREPARATION AND SUBMISSION OF DOCUMENTS IN ELECTRONIC FORMAT. MANY PROVISIONS RELATING TO THE PREPARATION AND SUBMISSION OF DOCUMENTS IN PAPER FORMAT CONTAINED IN THIS REGULATION ARE SUPERSEDED BY THE PROVISIONS OF REGULATION S-T FOR DOCUMENTS REQUIRED TO BE FILED IN ELECTRONIC FORMAT.

§ 240.13d-1 Filing of Schedules 13D and 13G.

(a) Any person who, after acquiring directly or indirectly the beneficial ownership of any equity security of a class which is specified in paragraph (i) of this section, is directly or indirectly the beneficial owner of more than five percent of the class shall, within 10 days after the acquisition, file with the Commission, a statement containing the information required by Schedule 13D (§ 240.13d-101).

(b)(1) A person who would otherwise be obligated under paragraph (a) of this section to file a statement on Schedule 13D (§ 240.13d-101) may, in lieu thereof, file with the Commission, a short-form statement on Schedule 13G (§ 240.13d-102), *Provided,* That:

(i) Such person has acquired such securities in the ordinary course of his business and not with the purpose nor with the effect of changing or influencing the control of the issuer, nor in connection with or as a participant in any transaction having such purpose or effect, including any transaction subject to § 240.13d-3(b), other than activities solely in connection with a nomination under § 240.14a-11; and

(ii) Such person is:

(A) A broker or dealer registered under section 15 of the Act (15 U.S.C. 78o);

(B) A bank as defined in section 3(a)(6) of the Act (15 U.S.C. 78c);

(C) An insurance company as defined in section 3(a)(19) of the Act (15 U.S.C. 78c);

(D) An investment company registered under section 8 of the Investment Company Act of 1940 (15 U.S.C. 80a-8);

(E) Any person registered as an investment adviser under Section 203 of the Investment Advisers Act of 1940 (15 U.S.C. 80b-3) or under the laws of any state;

(F) An employee benefit plan as defined in Section 3(3) of the Employee Retirement Income Security Act of 1974, as amended, 29 U.S.C. 1001 *et seq.* ("ERISA") that is subject to the provisions of ERISA, or any such plan that is not subject to ERISA that is maintained primarily for the benefit of the employees of a state or local government or instrumentality, or an endowment fund;

(G) A parent holding company or control person, provided the aggregate amount held directly by the parent or control person, and directly and indirectly by their subsidiaries or affiliates that are not persons specified in § 240.13d-1(b)(1)(ii)(A) through (J), does not exceed one percent of the securities of the subject class;

Securities and Exchange Commission § 240.13d-1

(H) A savings association as defined in Section 3(b) of the Federal Deposit Insurance Act (12 U.S.C. 1813);

(I) A church plan that is excluded from the definition of an investment company under section 3(c)(14) of the Investment Company Act of 1940 (15 U.S.C. 80a-3);

(J) A non-U.S. institution that is the functional equivalent of any of the institutions listed in § 240.13d-1(b)(1)(ii)(A) through (I), so long as the non-U.S. institution is subject to a regulatory scheme that is substantially comparable to the regulatory scheme applicable to the equivalent U.S. institution; and

(K) A group, provided that all the members are persons specified in § 240.13d-1(b)(1)(ii)(A) through (J).

(iii) Such person has promptly notified any other person (or group within the meaning of section 13(d)(3) of the Act) on whose behalf it holds, on a discretionary basis, securities exceeding five percent of the class, of any acquisition or transaction on behalf of such other person which might be reportable by that person under section 13(d) of the Act. This paragraph only requires notice to the account owner of information which the filing person reasonably should be expected to know and which would advise the account owner of an obligation he may have to file a statement pursuant to section 13(d) of the Act or an amendment thereto.

INSTRUCTION 1 TO PARAGRAPH (b)(1). For purposes of paragraph (b)(1)(i) of this section, the exception for activities solely in connection with a nomination under § 240.14a-11 will not be available after the election of directors.

(2) The Schedule 13G filed pursuant to paragraph (b)(1) of this section shall be filed within 45 days after the end of the calendar year in which the person became obligated under paragraph (b)(1) of this section to report the person's beneficial ownership as of the last day of the calendar year, *Provided*, That it shall not be necessary to file a Schedule 13G unless the percentage of the class of equity security specified in paragraph (i) of this section beneficially owned as of the end of the calendar year is more than five percent; *However*, if the person's direct or indirect beneficial ownership exceeds 10 percent of the class of equity securities prior to the end of the calendar year, the initial Schedule 13G shall be filed within 10 days after the end of the first month in which the person's direct or indirect beneficial ownership exceeds 10 percent of the class of equity securities, computed as of the last day of the month.

(c) A person who would otherwise be obligated under paragraph (a) of this section to file a statement on Schedule 13D (§ 240.13d-101) may, in lieu thereof, file with the Commission, within 10 days after an acquisition described in paragraph (a) of this section, a short-form statement on Schedule 13G (§ 240.13d-102). *Provided*, That the person:

(1) Has not acquired the securities with any purpose, or with the effect, of changing or influencing the control of the issuer, or in connection with or as a participant in any transaction having that purpose or effect, including any transaction subject to § 240.13d-3(b), other than activities solely in connection with a nomination under § 240.14a-11;

INSTRUCTION 1 TO PARAGRAPH (c)(1). For purposes of paragraph (c)(1) of this section, the exception for activities solely in connection with a nomination under § 240.14a-11 will not be available after the election of directors.

(2) Is not a person reporting pursuant to paragraph (b)(1) of this section; and

(3) Is not directly or indirectly the beneficial owner of 20 percent or more of the class.

(d) Any person who, as of the end of any calendar year, is or becomes directly or indirectly the beneficial owner of more than five percent of any equity security of a class specified in paragraph (i) of this section and who is not required to file a statement under paragraph (a) of this section by virtue of the exemption provided by Section 13(d)(6)(A) or (B) of the Act (15 U.S.C. 78m(d)(6)(A) or 78m(d)(6)(B)), or because the beneficial ownership was acquired prior to December 22, 1970, or because the person otherwise (except for the exemption provided by Section 13(d)(6)(C) of the Act (15 U.S.C. 78m(d)(6)(C))) is not required to file a statement, shall file with the Commission, within 45 days after the end of the calendar year

§ 240.13d-1

in which the person became obligated to report under this paragraph (d), a statement containing the information required by Schedule 13G (§ 240.13d-102).

(e)(1) Notwithstanding paragraphs (b) and (c) of this section and § 240.13d-2(b), a person that has reported that it is the beneficial owner of more than five percent of a class of equity securities in a statement on Schedule 13G (§ 240.13d-102) pursuant to paragraph (b) or (c) of this section, or is required to report the acquisition but has not yet filed the schedule, shall immediately become subject to §§ 240.13d-1(a) and 240.13d-2(a) and shall file a statement on Schedule 13D (§ 240.13d-101) within 10 days if, and shall remain subject to those requirements for so long as, the person:

(i) Has acquired or holds the securities with a purpose or effect of changing or influencing control of the issuer, or in connection with or as a participant in any transaction having that purpose or effect, including any transaction subject to § 240.13d-3(b); and

(ii) Is at that time the beneficial owner of more than five percent of a class of equity securities described in § 240.13d-1(i).

(2) From the time the person has acquired or holds the securities with a purpose or effect of changing or influencing control of the issuer, or in connection with or as a participant in any transaction having that purpose or effect until the expiration of the tenth day from the date of the filing of the Schedule 13D (§ 240.13d-101) pursuant to this section, that person shall not:

(i) Vote or direct the voting of the securities described therein; or

(ii) Acquire an additional beneficial ownership interest in any equity securities of the issuer of the securities, nor of any person controlling the issuer.

(f)(1) Notwithstanding paragraph (c) of this section and § 240.13d-2(b), persons reporting on Schedule 13G (§ 240.13d-102) pursuant to paragraph (c) of this section shall immediately become subject to §§ 240.13d-1(a) and 240.13d-2(a) and shall remain subject to those requirements for so long as, and shall file a statement on Schedule 13D (§ 240.13d-101) within 10 days of the date on which, the person's beneficial ownership equals or exceeds 20 percent of the class of equity securities.

(2) From the time of the acquisition of 20 percent or more of the class of equity securities until the expiration of the tenth day from the date of the filing of the Schedule 13D (§ 240.13d-101) pursuant to this section, the person shall not:

(i) Vote or direct the voting of the securities described therein, or

(ii) Acquire an additional beneficial ownership interest in any equity securities of the issuer of the securities, nor of any person controlling the issuer.

(g) Any person who has reported an acquisition of securities in a statement on Schedule 13G (§ 240.13d-102) pursuant to paragraph (b) of this section, or has become obligated to report on the Schedule 13G (§ 240.13d-102) but has not yet filed the Schedule, and thereafter ceases to be a person specified in paragraph (b)(1)(ii) of this section or determines that it no longer has acquired or holds the securities in the ordinary course of business shall immediately become subject to § 240.13d-1(a) or § 240.13d-1(c) (if the person satisfies the requirements specified in § 240.13d-1(c)), and §§ 240.13d-2 (a), (b) or (d), and shall file, within 10 days thereafter, a statement on Schedule 13D (§ 240.13d-101) or amendment to Schedule 13G, as applicable, if the person is a beneficial owner at that time of more than five percent of the class of equity securities.

(h) Any person who has filed a Schedule 13D (§ 240.13d-101) pursuant to paragraph (e), (f) or (g) of this section may again report its beneficial ownership on Schedule 13G (§ 240.13d-102) pursuant to paragraphs (b) or (c) of this section provided the person qualifies thereunder, as applicable, by filing a Schedule 13G (§ 240.13d-102) once the person determines that the provisions of paragraph (e), (f) or (g) of this section no longer apply.

(i) For the purpose of this regulation, the term "equity security" means any equity security of a class which is registered pursuant to section 12 of that Act, or any equity security of any insurance company which would have been required to be so registered except for the exemption contained in section

Securities and Exchange Commission § 240.13d-2

12(g)(2)(G) of the Act, or any equity security issued by a closed-end investment company registered under the Investment Company Act of 1940; *Provided,* Such term shall not include securities of a class of non-voting securities.

(j) For the purpose of sections 13(d) and 13(g), any person, in determining the amount of outstanding securities of a class of equity securities, may rely upon information set forth in the issuer's most recent quarterly or annual report, and any current report subsequent thereto, filed with the Commission pursuant to this Act, unless he knows or has reason to believe that the information contained therein is inaccurate.

(k)(1) Whenever two or more persons are required to file a statement containing the information required by Schedule 13D or Schedule 13G with respect to the same securities, only one statement need be filed: *Provided,* That:

(i) Each person on whose behalf the statement is filed is individually eligible to use the Schedule on which the information is filed;

(ii) Each person on whose behalf the statement is filed is responsible for the timely filing of such statement and any amendments thereto, and for the completeness and accuracy of the information concerning such person contained therein; such person is not responsible for the completeness or accuracy of the information concerning the other persons making the filing, unless such person knows or has reason to believe that such information is inaccurate; and

(iii) Such statement identifies all such persons, contains the required information with regard to each such person, indicates that such statement is filed on behalf of all such persons, and includes, as an exhibit, their agreement in writing that such a statement is filed on behalf of each of them.

(2) A group's filing obligation may be satisfied either by a single joint filing or by each of the group's members making an individual filing. If the group's members elect to make their own filings, each such filing should identify all members of the group but the information provided concerning the other persons making the filing need only reflect information which the filing person knows or has reason to know.

[43 FR 18495, Apr. 28, 1978, as amended at 43 FR 29768, July 11, 1978; 43 FR 55755, Nov. 29, 1978; 44 FR 10703, Feb. 23, 1979; 63 FR 2865, Jan. 16, 1998; 63 FR 15287, Mar. 31, 1998; 73 FR 60089, Oct. 9, 2008; 75 FR 56780, Sept. 16, 2010]

§ 240.13d-2 Filing of amendments to Schedules 13D or 13G.

(a) If any material change occurs in the facts set forth in the Schedule 13D (§ 240.13d-101) required by § 240.13d-1(a), including, but not limited to, any material increase or decrease in the percentage of the class beneficially owned, the person or persons who were required to file the statement shall promptly file or cause to be filed with the Commission an amendment disclosing that change. An acquisition or disposition of beneficial ownership of securities in an amount equal to one percent or more of the class of securities shall be deemed "material" for purposes of this section; acquisitions or dispositions of less than those amounts may be material, depending upon the facts and circumstances.

(b) Notwithstanding paragraph (a) of this section, and provided that the person filing a Schedule 13G (§ 240.13d-102) pursuant to § 240.13d-1(b) or § 240.13d-1(c) continues to meet the requirements set forth therein, any person who has filed a Schedule 13G (§ 240.13d-102) pursuant to § 240.13d-1(b), § 240.13d-1(c) or § 240.13d-1(d) shall amend the statement within forty-five days after the end of each calendar year if, as of the end of the calendar year, there are any changes in the information reported in the previous filing on that Schedule: *Provided, however,* That an amendment need not be filed with respect to a change in the percent of class outstanding previously reported if the change results solely from a change in the aggregate number of securities outstanding. Once an amendment has been filed reflecting beneficial ownership of five percent or less of the class of securities, no additional filings are required unless the person thereafter becomes the beneficial owner of more than five percent of the class and is required to file pursuant to § 240.13d-1.

§ 240.13d-3

(c) Any person relying on § 240.13d-1(b) that has filed its initial Schedule 13G (§ 240.13d-102) pursuant to that paragraph shall, in addition to filing any amendments pursuant to § 240.13d-2(b), file an amendment on Schedule 13G (§ 240.13d-102) within 10 days after the end of the first month in which the person's direct or indirect beneficial ownership, computed as of the last day of the month, exceeds 10 percent of the class of equity securities. Thereafter, that person shall, in addition to filing any amendments pursuant to § 240.13d-2(b), file an amendment on Schedule 13G (§ 240.13d-102) within 10 days after the end of the first month in which the person's direct or indirect beneficial ownership, computed as of the last day of the month, increases or decreases by more than five percent of the class of equity securities. Once an amendment has been filed reflecting beneficial ownership of five percent or less of the class of securities, no additional filings are required by this paragraph (c).

(d) Any person relying on § 240.13d-1(c) and has filed its initial Schedule 13G (§ 240.13d-102) pursuant to that paragraph shall, in addition to filing any amendments pursuant to § 240.13d-2(b), file an amendment on Schedule 13G (§ 240.13d-102) promptly upon acquiring, directly or indirectly, greater than 10 percent of a class of equity securities specified in § 240.13d-1(d), and thereafter promptly upon increasing or decreasing its beneficial ownership by more than five percent of the class of equity securities. Once an amendment has been filed reflecting beneficial ownership of five percent or less of the class of securities, no additional filings are required by this paragraph (d).

(e) The first electronic amendment to a paper format Schedule 13D (§ 240.13d-101 of this chapter) or Schedule 13G (§ 240.13d-102 of this chapter) shall restate the entire text of the Schedule 13D or 13G, but previously filed paper exhibits to such Schedules are not required to be restated electronically. *See* Rule 102 of Regulation S-T (§ 232.102 of this chapter) regarding amendments to exhibits previously filed in paper format. Notwithstanding the foregoing, if the sole purpose of filing the first electronic Schedule 13D or 13G amendment is to report a change in beneficial ownership that would terminate the filer's obligation to report, the amendment need not include a restatement of the entire text of the Schedule being amended.

NOTE TO § 240.13d-2: For persons filing a short-form statement pursuant to Rule 13d-1(b) or (c), see also Rules 13d-1(e), (f), and (g).

(Secs. 3(b), 13(d)(1), 13(d)(2), 13(d)(5), 13(d)(6), 14(d)(1), 23; 48 Stat. 882, 894, 895, 901; sec. 203(a), 49 Stat. 704, sec. 8, 49 Stat. 1379; sec. 10, 78 Stat. 88a; secs. 2, 3, 82 Stat. 454, 455; secs. 1, 2, 3-5, 84 Stat. 1497; secs. 3, 18, 89 Stat. 97, 155 (15 U.S.C. 78c(b), 78m(d)(1), 89m(d)(2), 78m(d)(5), 78m(d)(6), 78n(d)(1), 78w); sec. 23, 48 Stat. 901; sec. 203(a), 49 Stat. 704; sec. 8, 49 Stat. 1379; sec. 10, 78 Stat. 580; sec. 18, 89 Stat. 155; secs. 102, 202, 203, 91 Stat. 1494, 1498, 1499; 15 U.S.C. 78m(g), 78w(a))

[43 FR 18495, Apr. 28, 1978, as amended at 45 FR 81558, Dec. 11, 1980; 47 FR 49964, Nov. 4, 1982; 58 FR 14683, Mar. 18, 1993; 59 FR 67764, Dec. 30, 1994; 62 FR 36459, July 8, 1997; 63 FR 2866, Jan. 16, 1998]

§ 240.13d-3 Determination of beneficial owner.

(a) For the purposes of sections 13(d) and 13(g) of the Act a beneficial owner of a security includes any person who, directly or indirectly, through any contract, arrangement, understanding, relationship, or otherwise has or shares:

(1) Voting power which includes the power to vote, or to direct the voting of, such security; and/or,

(2) Investment power which includes the power to dispose, or to direct the disposition of, such security.

(b) Any person who, directly or indirectly, creates or uses a trust, proxy, power of attorney, pooling arrangement or any other contract, arrangement, or device with the purpose of effect of divesting such person of beneficial ownership of a security or preventing the vesting of such beneficial ownership as part of a plan or scheme to evade the reporting requirements of section 13(d) or (g) of the Act shall be deemed for purposes of such sections to be the beneficial owner of such security.

(c) All securities of the same class beneficially owned by a person, regardless of the form which such beneficial ownership takes, shall be aggregated in calculating the number of shares beneficially owned by such person.

Securities and Exchange Commission § 240.13d–3

(d) Notwithstanding the provisions of paragraphs (a) and (c) of this rule:

(1)(i) A person shall be deemed to be the beneficial owner of a security, subject to the provisions of paragraph (b) of this rule, if that person has the right to acquire beneficial ownership of such security, as defined in Rule 13d–3(a) (§ 240.13d–3(a)) within sixty days, including but not limited to any right to acquire: (A) Through the exercise of any option, warrant or right; (B) through the conversion of a security; (C) pursuant to the power to revoke a trust, discretionary account, or similar arrangement; or (D) pursuant to the automatic termination of a trust, discretionary account or similar arrangement; provided, however, any person who acquires a security or power specified in paragraphs (d)(1)(i)(A), (B) or (C), of this section, with the purpose or effect of changing or influencing the control of the issuer, or in connection with or as a participant in any transaction having such purpose or effect, immediately upon such acquisition shall be deemed to be the beneficial owner of the securities which may be acquired through the exercise or conversion of such security or power. Any securities not outstanding which are subject to such options, warrants, rights or conversion privileges shall be deemed to be outstanding for the purpose of computing the percentage of outstanding securities of the class owned by such person but shall not be deemed to be outstanding for the purpose of computing the percentage of the class by any other person.

(ii) Paragraph (d)(1)(i) of this section remains applicable for the purpose of determining the obligation to file with respect to the underlying security even though the option, warrant, right or convertible security is of a class of equity security, as defined in § 240.13d–1(i), and may therefore give rise to a separate obligation to file.

(2) A member of a national securities exchange shall not be deemed to be a beneficial owner of securities held directly or indirectly by it on behalf of another person solely because such member is the record holder of such securities and, pursuant to the rules of such exchange, may direct the vote of such securities, without instruction, on other than contested matters or matters that may affect substantially the rights or privileges of the holders of the securities to be voted, but is otherwise precluded by the rules of such exchange from voting without instruction.

(3) A person who in the ordinary course of his business is a pledgee of securities under a written pledge agreement shall not be deemed to be the beneficial owner of such pledged securities until the pledgee has taken all formal steps necessary which are required to declare a default and determines that the power to vote or to direct the vote or to dispose or to direct the disposition of such pledged securities will be exercised, provided, that:

(i) The pledgee agreement is bona fide and was not entered into with the purpose nor with the effect of changing or influencing the control of the issuer, nor in connection with any transaction having such purpose or effect, including any transaction subject to Rule 13d–3(b);

(ii) The pledgee is a person specified in Rule 13d–1(b)(ii), including persons meeting the conditions set forth in paragraph (G) thereof; and

(iii) The pledgee agreement, prior to default, does not grant to the pledgee:

(A) The power to vote or to direct the vote of the pledged securities; or

(B) The power to dispose or direct the disposition of the pledged securities, other than the grant of such power(s) pursuant to a pledge agreement under which credit is extended subject to regulation T (12 CFR 220.1 to 220.8) and in which the pledgee is a broker or dealer registered under section 15 of the act.

(4) A person engaged in business as an underwriter of securities who acquires securities through his participation in good faith in a firm commitment underwriting registered under the Securities Act of 1933 shall not be deemed to be the beneficial owner of such securities until the expiration of

§ 240.13d-4

forty days after the date of such acquisition.

(Secs. 3(b), 13(d)(1), 13(d)(2), 13(d)(5), 13(d)(6), 14(d)(1), 23; 48 Stat. 882, 894, 895, 901; sec. 203(a), 49 Stat. 704, sec. 8, 49 Stat. 1379; sec. 10, 78 Stat. 88a; secs. 2, 3, 82 Stat. 454, 455; secs. 1, 2, 3–5, 84 Stat. 1497; secs. 3, 18, 89 Stat. 97, 155 (15 U.S.C. 78c(b), 78m(d)(1), 89m(d)(2), 78m(d)(5), 78m(d)(6), 78n(d)(1), 78w)

[43 FR 18495, Apr. 28, 1978, as amended at 43 FR 29768, July 11, 1978; 63 FR 2867, Jan. 16, 1998]

§ 240.13d-4 Disclaimer of beneficial ownership.

Any person may expressly declare in any statement filed that the filing of such statement shall not be construed as an admission that such person is, for the purposes of sections 13(d) or 13(g) of the Act, the beneficial owner of any securities covered by the statement.

(Secs. 3(b), 13(d)(1), 13(d)(2), 13(d)(5), 13(d)(6), 14(d)(1), 23; 48 Stat. 882, 894, 895, 901; sec. 203(a), 49 Stat. 704, sec. 8, 49 Stat. 1379; sec. 10, 78 Stat. 88a; secs. 2, 3, 82 Stat. 454, 455; secs. 1, 2, 3–5, 84 Stat. 1497; secs. 3, 18, 89 Stat. 97, 155 (15 U.S.C. 78c(b), 78m(d)(1), 89m(d)(2), 78m(d)(5), 78m(d)(6), 78n(d)(1), 78w)

§ 240.13d-5 Acquisition of securities.

(a) A person who becomes a beneficial owner of securities shall be deemed to have acquired such securities for purposes of section 13(d)(1) of the Act, whether such acquisition was through purchase or otherwise. However, executors or administrators of a decedent's estate generally will be presumed not to have acquired beneficial ownership of the securities in the decedent's estate until such time as such executors or administrators are qualified under local law to perform their duties.

(b)(1) When two or more persons agree to act together for the purpose of acquiring, holding, voting or disposing of equity securities of an issuer, the group formed thereby shall be deemed to have acquired beneficial ownership, for purposes of sections 13(d) and (g) of the Act, as of the date of such agreement, of all equity securities of that issuer beneficially owned by any such persons.

(2) Notwithstanding the previous paragraph, a group shall be deemed not to have acquired any equity securities beneficially owned by the other members of the group solely by virtue of their concerted actions relating to the purchase of equity securities directly from an issuer in a transaction not involving a public offering: *Provided, That:*

(i) All the members of the group are persons specified in Rule 13d–1(b)(1)(ii);

(ii) The purchase is in the ordinary course of each member's business and not with the purpose nor with the effect of changing or influencing control of the issuer, nor in connection with or as a participant in any transaction having such purpose or effect, including any transaction subject to Rule 13d–3(b);

(iii) There is no agreement among, or between any members of the group to act together with respect to the issuer or its securities except for the purpose of facilitating the specific purchase involved; and

(iv) The only actions among or between any members of the group with respect to the issuer or its securities subsequent to the closing date of the non-public offering are those which are necessary to conclude ministerial matters directly related to the completion of the offer or sale of the securities.

(Secs. 3(b), 13(d)(1), 13(d)(2), 13(d)(5), 13(d)(6), 14(d)(1), 23; 48 Stat. 882, 894, 895, 901; sec. 203(a), 49 Stat. 704, sec. 8, 49 Stat. 1379; sec. 10, 78 Stat. 88a; secs. 2, 3, 82 Stat. 454, 455; secs. 1, 2, 3–5, 84 Stat. 1497; secs. 3, 18, 89 Stat. 97, 155 (15 U.S.C. 78c(b), 78m(d)(1), 89m(d)(2), 78m(d)(5), 78m(d)(6), 78n(d)(1), 78w))

§ 240.13d-6 Exemption of certain acquisitions.

The acquisition of securities of an issuer by a person who, prior to such acquisition, was a beneficial owner of more than five percent of the outstanding securities of the same class as those acquired shall be exempt from section 13(d) of the Act: *Provided, That:*

(a) The acquisition is made pursuant to preemptive subscription rights in an offering made to all holders of securities of the class to which the preemptive subscription rights pertain;

(b) Such person does not acquire additional securities except through the exercise of his pro rata share of the preemptive subscription rights; and

Securities and Exchange Commission § 240.13d–101

(c) The acquisition is duly reported, if required, pursuant to section 16(a) of the Act and the rules and regulations thereunder.

(Secs. 3(b), 13(d)(1), 13(d)(2), 13(d)(5), 13(d)(6), 14(d)(1), 23; 48 Stat. 882, 894, 895, 901; sec. 203(a), 49 Stat. 704, sec. 8, 49 Stat. 1379; sec. 10, 78 Stat. 88a; secs. 2, 3, 82 Stat. 454, 455; secs. 1, 2, 3–5, 84 Stat. 1497; secs. 3, 18, 89 Stat. 97, 155 (15 U.S.C. 78c(b), 78m(d)(1), 89m(d)(2), 78m(d)(5), 78m(d)(6), 78n(d)(1), 78w))

§ 240.13d–7 Dissemination.

One copy of the Schedule filed pursuant to §§ 240.13d–1 and 240.13d–2 shall be sent to the issuer of the security at its principal executive office by registered or certified mail. A copy of Schedules filed pursuant to §§ 240.13d–1(a) and 240.13d–2(a) shall also be sent to each national securities exchange where the security is traded.

[63 FR 2867, Jan. 16, 1998]

§ 240.13d–101 Schedule 13D—Information to be included in statements filed pursuant to § 240.13d–1(a) and amendments thereto filed pursuant to § 240.13d–2(a).

Securities and Exchange Commission, Washington, D.C. 20549

Schedule 13D

Under the Securities Exchange Act of 1934

(Amendment No.___)*

_____

(Name of Issuer)

_____

(Title of Class of Securities)

_____

(CUSIP Number)

_____

(Name, Address and Telephone Number of Person Authorized to Receive Notices and Communications)

_____

(Date of Event Which Requires Filing of This Statement)

If the filing person has previously filed a statement on Schedule 13G to report the acquisition that is the subject of this Schedule 13D, and is filing this schedule because of §§ 240.13d–1(e), 240.13d–1(f) or 240.13d–1(g), check the following box. ☐

NOTE: Schedules filed in paper format shall include a signed original and five copies of the schedule, including all exhibits. See Rule 13d–7 for other parties to whom copies are to be sent.

*The remainder of this cover page shall be filled out for a reporting person's initial filing on this form with respect to the subject class of securities, and for any subsequent amendment containing information which would alter disclosures provided in a prior cover page.

The information required on the remainder of this cover page shall not be deemed to be "filed" for the purpose of section 18 of the Securities Exchange Act of 1934 ("Act") or otherwise subject to the liabilities of that section of the Act but shall be subject to all other provisions of the Act (however, see the Notes).

CUSIP No._____

(1) Names of reporting persons.	
(2) Check the appropriate box if a member of a group (see instructions)	(a)
	(b)
(3) SEC use only.	
(4) Source of funds (see instructions).	
(5) Check if disclosure of legal proceedings is required pursuant to Items 2(d) or 2(e).	
(6) Citizenship or place of organization.	
Number of shares beneficially owned by each reporting person with:	
(7) Sole voting power.	
(8) Shared voting power.	
(9) Sole dispositive power.	
(10) Shared dispositive power.	
(11) Aggregate amount beneficially owned by each reporting person.	

§ 240.13d-101 17 CFR Ch. II (4-1-23 Edition)

(12) Check if the aggregate amount in Row (11) excludes certain shares (see instructions).	
(13) Percent of class represented by amount in Row (11).	
(14) Type of reporting person (see instructions).	

Page __ of __ Pages

Instructions for Cover Page

(1) *Names of Reporting Persons*—Furnish the full legal name of each person for whom the report is filed—i.e., each person required to sign the schedule itself—including each member of a group. Do not include the name of a person required to be identified in the report but who is not a reporting person.

(2) If any of the shares beneficially owned by a reporting person are held as a member of the group and the membership is expressly affirmed, please check row 2(a). If the reporting person disclaims membership in a group or describes a relationship with other person but does not affirm the existence of a group, please check row 2(b) (unless it is a joint filing pursuant to Rule 13d-1(k)(1) in which case it may not be necessary to check row 2(b)).

(3) The 3rd row is for SEC internal use; please leave blank.

(4) Classify the source of funds or other consideration used or to be used in making the purchases as required to be disclosed pursuant to Item 3 of Schedule 13D and insert the appropriate symbol (or symbols if more than one is necessary) in row (4):

Category of Source	Symbol
Subject Company (Company whose securities are being acquired).	SC
Bank	BK
Affiliate (of reporting person)	AF
Working Capital (of reporting person)	WC
Personal Funds (of reporting person)	PF
Other	OO

(5) If disclosure of legal proceedings or actions is required pursuant to either Items 2(d) or 2(e) of Schedule 13D, row 5 should be checked.

(6) *Citizenship or Place of Organization*—Furnish citizenship if the named reporting person is a natural person. Otherwise, Furnish place of organization. (See Item 2 of Schedule 13D).

(7)–(11) [Reserved]

(12) Check if the aggregate amount reported as beneficially owned in row (11) does not include shares which the reporting person discloses in the report but as to which beneficial ownership is disclaimed pursuant to Rule 13d-4 [17 CFR 240.13d-4] under the Securities Exchange Act of 1934.

(13) *Aggregate Amount Beneficially Owned by Each Reporting Person, Etc.*—Rows (7) through (11), inclusive, and (13) are to be completed in accordance with the provisions of Item 5 of Schedule 13D. All percentages are to be rounded off to nearest tenth (one place after decimal point).

(14) *Type of Reporting Person*—Please classify each "reporting person" according to the following breakdown and place the appropriate symbol (or symbols, i.e., if more than one is applicable, insert all applicable symbols) on the form:

Category	Symbol
Broker Dealer	BD
Bank	BK
Insurance Company	IC
Investment Company	IV
Investment Adviser	IA
Employee Benefit Plan or Endowment Fund	EP
Parent Holding Company/Control Person	HC
Savings Association	SA
Church Plan	CP
Corporation	CO
Partnership	PN
Individual	IN
Other	OO

NOTES: Attach as many copies of the second part of the cover page as are needed, one reporting person per page.

Filing persons may, in order to avoid unnecessary duplication, answer items on the schedules (Schedule 13D, 13G or TO) by appropriate cross references to an item or items on the cover page(s). This approach may only be used where the cover page item or items provide all the disclosure required by the schedule item. Moreover, such a use of a cover page item will result in the item becoming a part of the schedule and accordingly being considered as "filed" for purposes of section 18 of the Securities Exchange Act or otherwise subject to the liabilities of that section of the Act.

Reporting persons may comply with their cover page filing requirements by filing either completed copies of the blank forms available from the Commission, printed or typed facsimiles, or computer printed facsimiles, provided the documents filed have identical formats to the forms prescribed in the Commission's regulations and meet existing Securities Exchange Act rules as to such matters as clarity and size (Securities Exchange Act Rule 12b-12).

Securities and Exchange Commission §240.13d-101

SPECIAL INSTRUCTIONS FOR COMPLYING WITH SCHEDULE 13D

Under sections 13(d) and 23 of the Securities Exchange Act of 1934 and the rules and regulations thereunder, the Commission is authorized to solicit the information required to be supplied by this schedule by certain security holders of certain issuers.

Disclosure of the information specified in this schedule is mandatory. The information will be used for the primary purpose of determining and disclosing the holdings of certain beneficial owners of certain equity securities. This statement will be made a matter of public record. Therefore, any information given will be available for inspection by any member of the public.

Because of the public nature of the information, the Commission can use it for a variety of purposes, including referral to other governmental authorities or securities self-regulatory organizations for investigatory purposes or in connection with litigation involving the federal securities laws or other civil, criminal or regulatory statutes or provisions.

Failure to disclose the information requested by this schedule may result in civil or criminal action against the persons involved for violation of the federal securities laws and rules promulgated thereunder.

Instructions. A. The item numbers and captions of the items shall be included but the text of the items is to be omitted. The answers to the items shall be so prepared as to indicate clearly the coverage of the items without referring to the text of the items. Answer every item. If an item is inapplicable or the answer is in the negative, so state.

B. Information contained in exhibits to the statement may be incorporated by reference in answer or partial answer to any item or sub-item of the statement unless it would render such answer misleading, incomplete, unclear or confusing. Material incorporated by reference shall be clearly identified in the reference by page, paragraph, caption or otherwise. An express statement that the specified matter is incorporated by reference shall be made at the particular place in the statement where the information is required. A copy of any information or a copy of the pertinent pages of a document containing such information which is incorporated by reference shall be submitted with this statement as an exhibit and shall be deemed to be filed with the Commission for all purposes of the Act.

C. If the statement is filed by a general or limited partnership, syndicate, or other group, the information called for by Items 2–6, inclusive, shall be given with respect to (i) each partner of such general partnership; (ii) each partner who is denominated as a general partner or who functions as a general partner of such limited partnership; (iii) each member of such syndicate or group; and (iv) each person controlling such partner or member. If the statement is filed by a corporation or if a person referred to in (i), (ii), (iii) or (iv) of this Instruction is a corporation, the information called for by the above mentioned items shall be given with respect to (a) each executive officer and director of such corporation; (b) each person controlling such corporation; and (c) each executive officer and director of any corporation or other person ultimately in control of such corporation.

Item 1. Security and Issuer. State the title of the class of equity securities to which this statement relates and the name and address of the principal executive offices of the issuer of such securities.

Item 2. Identity and Background. If the person filing this statement or any person enumerated in Instruction C of this statement is a corporation, general partnership, limited partnership, syndicate or other group of persons, state its name, the state or other place of its organization, its principal business, the address of its principal office and the information required by (d) and (e) of this Item. If the person filing this statement or any person enumerated in Instruction C is a natural person, provide the information specified in (a) through (f) of this Item with respect to such person(s).

(a) Name;

(b) Residence or business address;

(c) Present principal occupation or employment and the name, principal business and address of any corporation or other organization in which such employment is conducted;

(d) Whether or not, during the last five years, such person has been convicted in a criminal proceeding (excluding traffic violations or similar misdemeanors) and, if so, give the dates, nature of conviction, name and location of court, any penalty imposed, or other disposition of the case;

(e) Whether or not, during the last five years, such person was a party to a civil proceeding of a judicial or administrative body of competent jurisdiction and as a result of such proceeding was or is subject to a judgment, decree or final order enjoining future violations of, or prohibiting or mandating activities subject to, federal or state securities laws or finding any violation with respect to such laws; and, if so, identify and describe such proceedings and summarize the terms of such judgment, decree or final order; and

(f) Citizenship.

Item 3. Source and Amount of Funds or Other Consideration. State the source and the amount of funds or other consideration used or to be used in making the purchases, and if any part of the purchase price is or will be represented by funds or other consideration

§ 240.13d-101

borrowed or otherwise obtained for the purpose of acquiring, holding, trading or voting the securities, a description of the transaction and the names of the parties thereto. Where material, such information should also be provided with respect to prior acquisitions not previously reported pursuant to this regulation. If the source of all or any part of the funds is a loan made in the ordinary course of business by a bank, as defined in section 3(a)(6) of the Act, the name of the bank shall not be made available to the public if the person at the time of filing the statement so requests in writing and files such request, naming such bank, with the Secretary of the Commission. If the securities were acquired other than by purchase, describe the method of acquisition.

Item 4. Purpose of Transaction. State the purpose or purposes of the acquisition of securities of the issuer. Describe any plans or proposals which the reporting persons may have which relate to or would result in:

(a) The acquisition by any person of additional securities of the issuer, or the disposition of securities of the issuer;

(b) An extraordinary corporate transaction, such as a merger, reorganization or liquidation, involving the issuer or any of its subsidiaries;

(c) A sale or transfer of a material amount of assets of the issuer or any of its subsidiaries;

(d) Any change in the present board of directors or management of the issuer, including any plans or proposals to change the number or term of directors or to fill any existing vacancies on the board;

(e) Any material change in the present capitalization or dividend policy of the issuer;

(f) Any other material change in the issuer's business or corporate structure, including but not limited to, if the issuer is a registered closed-end investment company, any plans or proposals to make any changes in its investment policy for which a vote is required by section 13 of the Investment Company Act of 1940;

(g) Changes in the issuer's charter, bylaws or instruments corresponding thereto or other actions which may impede the acquisition of control of the issuer by any person;

(h) Causing a class of securities of the issuer to be delisted from a national securities exchange or to cease to be authorized to be quoted in an inter-dealer quotation system of a registered national securities association;

(i) A class of equity securities of the issuer becoming eligible for termination of registration pursuant to section 12(g)(4) of the Act; or

(j) Any action similar to any of those enumerated above.

Item 5. Interest in Securities of the Issuer. (a) State the aggregate number and percentage of the class of securities identified pursuant to Item 1 (which may be based on the number of securities outstanding as contained in the most recently available filing with the Commission by the issuer unless the filing person has reason to believe such information is not current) beneficially owned (identifying those shares which there is a right to acquire) by each person named in Item 2. The above mentioned information should also be furnished with respect to persons who, together with any of the persons named in Item 2, comprise a group within the meaning of section 13(d)(3) of the Act;

(b) For each person named in response to paragraph (a), indicate the number of shares as to which there is sole power to vote or to direct the vote, sole power to dispose or to direct the disposition, or shared power to dispose or to direct the disposition. Provide the applicable information required by Item 2 with respect to each person with whom the power to vote or to direct the vote or to dispose or direct the disposition is shared;

(c) Describe any transactions in the class of securities reported on that were effected during the past sixty days or since the most recent filing of Schedule 13D (§ 240.13d–101), whichever is less, by the persons named in response to paragraph (a).

Instruction. The description of a transaction required by Item 5(c) shall include, but not necessarily be limited to: (1) The identity of the person covered by Item 5(c) who effected the transaction; (2) the date of transaction; (3) the amount of securities involved; (4) the price per share or unit; and (5) where and how the transaction was effected.

(d) If any other person is known to have the right to receive or the power to direct the receipt of dividends from, or the proceeds from the sale of, such securities, a statement to that effect should be included in response to this item and, if such interest relates to more than five percent of the class, such person should be identified. A listing of the shareholders of an investment company registered under the Investment Company Act of 1940 or the beneficiaries of an employee benefit plan, pension fund or endowment fund is not required.

(e) If applicable, state the date on which the reporting person ceased to be the beneficial owner of more than five percent of the class of securities.

Instruction. For computations regarding securities which represent a right to acquire an underlying security, see Rule 13d–3(d)(1) and the note thereto.

Item 6. Contracts, Arrangements, Understandings or Relationships With Respect to Securities of the Issuer. Describe any contracts, arrangements, understandings or relationships (legal or otherwise) among the persons named in Item 2 and between such persons and any person with respect to any securities of the issuer, including but not limited to transfer or voting of any of the securities,

Securities and Exchange Commission

§ 240.13d–102

finder's fees, joint ventures, loan or option arrangements, puts or calls, guarantees of profits, division of profits or loss, or the giving or withholding of proxies, naming the persons with whom such contracts, arrangements, understandings or relationships have been entered into. Include such information for any of the securities that are pledged or otherwise subject to a contingency the occurrence of which would give another person voting power or investment power over such securities except that disclosure of standard default and similar provisions contained in loan agreements need not be included.

Item 7. Material to be Filed as Exhibits. The following shall be filed as exhibits: Copies of written agreements relating to the filing of joint acquisition statements as required by Rule 13d–1(k) and copies of all written agreements, contracts, arrangements, understanding, plans or proposals relating to: (1) The borrowing of funds to finance the acquisition as disclosed in Item 3; (2) the acquisition of issuer control, liquidation, sale of assets, merger, or change in business or corporate structure, or any other matter as disclosed in Item 4; and (3) the transfer or voting of the securities, finder's fees, joint ventures, options, puts, calls, guarantees of loans, guarantees against loss or of profit, or the giving or withholding of any proxy as disclosed in Item 6.

Signature. After reasonable inquiry and to the best of my knowledge and belief, I certify that the information set forth in this statement is true, complete and correct.

Date _____
Signature _____
Name/Title _____

The original statement shall be signed by each person on whose behalf the statement is filed or his authorized representative. If the statement is signed on behalf of a person by his authorized representative (other than an executive officer or general partner of the filing person), evidence of the representative's authority to sign on behalf of such person shall be filed with the statement: *Provided, however,* That a power of attorney for this purpose which is already on file with the Commission may be incorporated by reference. The name and any title of each person who signs the statement shall be typed or printed beneath his signature.

ATTENTION—Intentional misstatements or omissions of fact constitute Federal criminal violations (See 18 U.S.C. 1001).

[44 FR 2145, Jan. 9, 1979; 44 FR 11751, Mar. 2, 1979; 44 FR 70340, Dec. 6, 1979; 47 FR 11466, Mar. 16, 1982; 61 FR 49959, Sept. 24, 1996; 62 FR 35340, July 1, 1997; 63 FR 2867, Jan. 16, 1998; 63 FR 15287, Mar. 31, 1998; 72 FR 45111, Aug. 10, 2007; 73 FR 17813, Apr. 1, 2008]

§ 240.13d–102 Schedule 13G—Information to be included in statements filed pursuant to § 240.13d–1(b), (c), and (d) and amendments thereto filed pursuant to § 240.13d–2.

Securities and Exchange Commission, Washington, D.C. 20549

Schedule 13G

Under the Securities Exchange Act of 1934

(Amendment No.__)*

_____
(Name of Issuer)

_____
(Title of Class of Securities)

_____
(CUSIP Number)

_____
(Date of Event Which Requires Filing of this Statement)

Check the appropriate box to designate the rule pursuant to which this Schedule is filed:

[ ] Rule 13d–1(b)
[ ] Rule 13d–1(c)
[ ] Rule 13d–1(d)

*The remainder of this cover page shall be filled out for a reporting person's initial filing on this form with respect to the subject class of securities, and for any subsequent amendment containing information which would alter the disclosures provided in a prior cover page.

The information required in the remainder of this cover page shall not be deemed to be "filed" for the purpose of Section 18 of the Securities Exchange Act of 1934 ("Act") or otherwise subject to the liabilities of that section of the Act but shall be subject to all other provisions of the Act (however, see the Notes).

	CUSIP No._____	
(1) Names of reporting persons. (2) Check the appropriate box if a member of a group (see instructions)	(a)	
	(b)	
(3) SEC use only.		
(4) Citizenship or place of organization.		

§ 240.13d–102

Number of shares beneficially owned by each reporting person with:	
(5) Sole voting power.	
(6) Shared voting power.	
(7) Sole dispositive power.	
(8) Shared dispositive power.	
(9) Aggregate amount beneficially owned by each reporting person.	
(10) Check if the aggregate amount in Row (9) excludes certain shares (see instructions).	
(11) Percent of class represented by amount in Row (9).	
(12) Type of reporting person (see instructions).	

Page __ of __ Pages

Instructions for Cover Page:

(1) *Names of Reporting Persons*—Furnish the full legal name of each person for whom the report is filed—i.e., each person required to sign the schedule itself—including each member of a group. Do not include the name of a person required to be identified in the report but who is not a reporting person.

(2) If any of the shares beneficially owned by a reporting person are held as a member of a group and that membership is expressly affirmed, please check row 2(a). If the reporting person disclaims membership in a group or describes a relationship with other person but does not affirm the existence of a group, please check row 2(b) [unless it is a joint filing pursuant to Rule 13d-1(k)(1) in which case it may not be necessary to check row 2(b)].

(3) The third row is for SEC internal use; please leave blank.

(4) *Citizenship or Place of Organization*—Furnish citizenship if the named reporting person is a natural person. Otherwise, furnish place of organization.

(5)–(9), (11) *Aggregated Amount Beneficially Owned By Each Reporting Person, etc.*—Rows (5) through (9) inclusive, and (11) are to be completed in accordance with the provisions of Item 4 of Schedule 13G. All percentages are to be rounded off to the nearest tenth (one place after decimal point).

(10) Check if the aggregate amount reported as beneficially owned in row (9) does not include shares as to which beneficial ownership is disclaimed pursuant to Rule 13d-4 [17 CFR 240.13d-4] under the Securities Exchange Act of 1934.

(12) *Type of Reporting Person*—Please classify each "reporting person" according to the following breakdown (see Item 3 of Schedule 13G) and place the appropriate Symbol on the form:

Category	Symbol
Broker Dealer	BD
Bank	BK
Insurance Company	IC
Investment Company	IV
Investment Adviser	IA
Employee Benefit Plan or Endowment Fund	EP
Parent Holding Company/Control Person	HC
Savings Association	SA
Church Plan	CP
Corporation	CO
Partnership	PN
Individual	IN
Non-U.S. Institution	FI
Other	OO

NOTES: Attach as many copies of the second part of the cover page as are needed, one reporting person per page.

Filing persons may, in order to avoid unnecessary duplication, answer items on the schedules (Schedule 13D, 13G or TO) by appropriate cross references to an item or items on the cover page(s). This approach may only be used where the cover page item or items provide all the disclosure required by the schedule item. Moreover, such a use of a cover page item will result in the item becoming a part of the schedule and accordingly being considered as "filed" for purposes of section 18 of the Securities Exchange Act or otherwise subject to the liabilities of that section of the Act.

Reporting persons may comply with their cover page filing requirements by filing either completed copies of the blank forms available from the Commission, printed or typed facsimiles, or computer printed facsimiles, provided the documents filed have identical formats to the forms prescribed in the Commission's regulations and meet existing Securities Exchange Act rules as to such matters as clarity and size (Securities Exchange Act Rule 12b-12).

Securities and Exchange Commission § 240.13d–102

SPECIAL INSTRUCTIONS FOR COMPLYING WITH SCHEDULE 13G

Under Sections 13(d), 13(g) and 23 of the Securities Exchange Act of 1934 and the rules and regulations thereunder, the Commission is authorized to solicit the information required to be supplied by this schedule by certain security holders of certain issuers.

Disclosure of the information specified in this schedule is mandatory. The information will be used for the primary purpose of determining and disclosing the holdings of certain beneficial owners of certain equity securities. This statement will be made a matter of public record. Therefore, any information given will be available for inspection by any member of the public.

Because of the public nature of the information, the Commission can use it for a variety of purposes, including referral to other governmental authorities or securities self-regulatory organizations for investigatory purposes or in connection with litigation involving the Federal securities laws or other civil, criminal or regulatory statutes or provisions.

Failure to disclose the information requested by this schedule may result in civil or criminal action against the persons involved for violation of the Federal securities laws and rules promulgated thereunder.

Instructions. A. Statements filed pursuant to Rule 13d–1(b) containing the information required by this schedule shall be filed not later than February 14 following the calendar year covered by the statement or within the time specified in Rules 13d–1(b)(2) and 13d–2(c). Statements filed pursuant to Rule 13d–1(d) shall be filed within the time specified in Rules 13d–1(c), 13d–2(b) and 13d–2(d). Statements filed pursuant to Rule 13d–1(c) shall be filed not later than February 14 following the calendar year covered by the statement pursuant to Rules 13d–1(d) and 13d–2(b).

B. Information contained in a form which is required to be filed by rules under section 13(f) (15 U.S.C. 78m(f)) for the same calendar year as that covered by a statement on this schedule may be incorporated by reference in response to any of the items of this schedule. If such information is incorporated by reference in this schedule, copies of the relevant pages of such form shall be filed as an exhibit to this schedule.

C. The item numbers and captions of the items shall be included but the text of the items is to be omitted. The answers to the items shall be so prepared as to indicate clearly the coverage of the items without referring to the text of the items. Answer every item. If an item is inapplicable or the answer is in the negative, so state.

Item 1(a) Name of issuer:_____

Item 1(b) Address of issuer's principal executive offices:_____

2(a) Name of person filing:

2(b) Address or principal business office or, if none, residence:

2(c) Citizenship:

2(d) Title of class of securities:

2(e) CUSIP No.:

Item 3. If this statement is filed pursuant to §§ 240.13d–1(b) or 240.13d–2(b) or (c), check whether the person filing is a:

(a) [ ] Broker or dealer registered under section 15 of the Act (15 U.S.C. 78o);

(b) [ ] Bank as defined in section 3(a)(6) of the Act (15 U.S.C. 78c);

(c) [ ] Insurance company as defined in section 3(a)(19) of the Act (15 U.S.C. 78c);

(d) [ ] Investment company registered under section 8 of the Investment Company Act of 1940 (15 U.S.C 80a–8);

(e) [ ] An investment adviser in accordance with § 240.13d–1(b)(1)(ii)(E);

(f) [ ] An employee benefit plan or endowment fund in accordance with § 240.13d–1(b)(1)(ii)(F);

(g) [ ] A parent holding company or control person in accordance with § 240.13d–1(b)(1)(ii)(G);

(h) [ ] A savings associations as defined in Section 3(b) of the Federal Deposit Insurance Act (12 U.S.C. 1813);

(i) [ ] A church plan that is excluded from the definition of an investment company under section 3(c)(14) of the Investment Company Act of 1940 (15 U.S.C. 80a–3);

(j) [ ] A non-U.S. institution in accordance with § 240.13d–1(b)(1)(ii)(J);

(k) [ ] Group, in accordance with § 240.13d–1(b)(1)(ii)(K). If filing as a non-U.S. institution in accordance with § 240.13d–1(b)(1)(ii)(J), please specify the type of institution: _____

Item 4. Ownership

Provide the following information regarding the aggregate number and percentage of the class of securities of the issuer identified in Item 1.

(a) Amount beneficially owned: _____.

(b) Percent of class: _____.

(c) Number of shares as to which the person has:

(i) Sole power to vote or to direct the vote _____.

(ii) Shared power to vote or to direct the vote _____.

(iii) Sole power to dispose or to direct the disposition of _____.

(iv) Shared power to dispose or to direct the disposition of _____.

Instruction. For computations regarding securities which represent a right to acquire an underlying security *see* § 240.13d–3(d)(1).

§ 240.13d-102

Item 5. Ownership of 5 Percent or Less of a Class. If this statement is being filed to report the fact that as of the date hereof the reporting person has ceased to be the beneficial owner of more than 5 percent of the class of securities, check the following [ ].

Instruction. Dissolution of a group requires a response to this item.

Item 6. Ownership of More than 5 Percent on Behalf of Another Person. If any other person is known to have the right to receive or the power to direct the receipt of dividends from, or the proceeds from the sale of, such securities, a statement to that effect should be included in response to this item and, if such interest relates to more than 5 percent of the class, such person should be identified. A listing of the shareholders of an investment company registered under the Investment Company Act of 1940 or the beneficiaries of employee benefit plan, pension fund or endowment fund is not required.

Item 7. Identification and Classification of the Subsidiary Which Acquired the Security Being Reported on by the Parent Holding Company or Control Person. If a parent holding company or control person has filed this schedule pursuant to Rule 13d-1(b)(1)(ii)(G), so indicate under Item 3(g) and attach an exhibit stating the identity and the Item 3 classification of the relevant subsidiary. If a parent holding company or control person has filed this schedule pursuant to Rule 13d-1(c) or Rule 13d-1(d), attach an exhibit stating the identification of the relevant subsidiary.

Item 8. Identification and Classification of Members of the Group

If a group has filed this schedule pursuant to § 240.13d-1(b)(1)(ii)(J), so indicate under Item 3(j) and attach an exhibit stating the identity and Item 3 classification of each member of the group. If a group has filed this schedule pursuant to Rule 13d-1(c) or Rule 13d-1(d), attach an exhibit stating the identity of each member of the group.

Item 9. Notice of Dissolution of Group. Notice of dissolution of a group may be furnished as an exhibit stating the date of the dissolution and that all further filings with respect to transactions in the security reported on will be filed, if required, by members of the group, in their individual capacity. See Item 5.

Item 10. Certifications

(a) The following certification shall be included if the statement is filed pursuant to § 240.13d-1(b):

By signing below I certify that, to the best of my knowledge and belief, the securities referred to above were acquired and are held in the ordinary course of business and were not acquired and are not held for the purpose of or with the effect of changing or influencing the control of the issuer of the securities and were not acquired and are not held in connection with or as a participant in any transaction having that purpose or effect, other than activities solely in connection with a nomination under § 240.14a-11.

(b) The following certification shall be included if the statement is filed pursuant to § 240.13d-1(b)(1)(ii)(J), or if the statement is filed pursuant to § 240.13d-1(b)(1)(ii)(K) and a member of the group is a non-U.S. institution eligible to file pursuant to § 240.13d-1(b)(1)(ii)(J):

By signing below I certify that, to the best of my knowledge and belief, the foreign regulatory scheme applicable to [insert particular category of institutional investor] is substantially comparable to the regulatory scheme applicable to the functionally equivalent U.S. institution(s). I also undertake to furnish to the Commission staff, upon request, information that would otherwise be disclosed in a Schedule 13D.

(c) The following certification shall be included if the statement is filed pursuant to § 240.13d-1(c):

By signing below I certify that, to the best of my knowledge and belief, the securities referred to above were not acquired and are not held for the purpose of or with the effect of changing or influencing the control of the issuer of the securities and were not acquired and are not held in connection with or as a participant in any transaction having that purpose or effect, other than activities solely in connection with a nomination under § 240.14a-11.

Signature. After reasonable inquiry and to the best of my knowledge and belief, I certify that the information set forth in this statement is true, complete and correct.

Dated:____

_____.
Signature.

_____.
Name/Title.

The original statement shall be signed by each person on whose behalf the statement is filed or his authorized representative. If the statement is signed on behalf of a person by his authorized representative other than an executive officer or general partner of the filing person, evidence of the representative's authority to sign on behalf of such person shall be filed with the statement, *Provided, however,* That a power of attorney for this purpose which is already on file with the Commission may be incorporated by reference. The name and any title of each person who signs the statement shall be typed or printed beneath his signature.

NOTE: Schedules filed in paper format shall include a signed original and five copies of the schedule, including all exhibits. See Rule 13d-7 for other parties for whom copies are to be sent.

Securities and Exchange Commission § 240.13e–1

ATTENTION: Intentional misstatements or omissions of fact constitute Federal criminal violations (see 18 U.S.C. 1001).

[43 FR 18499, Apr. 28, 1978, as amended at 43 FR 55756, Nov. 29, 1978; 44 FR 2148, Jan. 9, 1979; 44 FR 11751, Mar. 2, 1979; 61 FR 49959, Sept. 24, 1996; 62 FR 35340, July 1, 1997; 63 FR 2867, Jan. 16, 1998; 63 FR 15287, Mar. 31, 1998; 72 FR 45112, Aug. 10, 2007; 73 FR 17813, Apr. 1, 2008; 73 FR 60089, Oct. 9, 2008; 75 FR 56780, Sept. 16, 2010]

§ 240.13e–1 Purchase of securities by the issuer during a third-party tender offer.

An issuer that has received notice that it is the subject of a tender offer made under Section 14(d)(1) of the Act (15 U.S.C. 78n), that has commenced under § 240.14d–2 must not purchase any of its equity securities during the tender offer unless the issuer first:

(a) Files a statement with the Commission containing the following information:

(1) The title and number of securities to be purchased;

(2) The names of the persons or classes of persons from whom the issuer will purchase the securities;

(3) The name of any exchange, interdealer quotation system or any other market on or through which the securities will be purchased;

(4) The purpose of the purchase;

(5) Whether the issuer will retire the securities, hold the securities in its treasury, or dispose of the securities. If the issuer intends to dispose of the securities, describe how it intends to do so;

(6) The source and amount of funds or other consideration to be used to make the purchase. If the issuer borrows any funds or other consideration to make the purchase or enters any agreement for the purpose of acquiring, holding, or trading the securities, describe the transaction and agreement and identify the parties; and

(7) An exhibit to the statement that sets forth the transaction valuation, fee rate, amount of filing fee and, as applicable, information relating to reliance on § 240.0–11(a)(2) in the tabular form indicated in Tables 1 and 2 to this paragraph (a)(7) and as further specified in this paragraph (a)(7).

TABLE 1 TO PARAGRAPH (a)(7)

	Transaction valuation	Fee rate	Amount of filing fee
Fees to Be Paid	X	X	X
Fees Previously Paid	X		X
Total Transaction Valuation	X		
Total Fees Due for Filing			X
Total Fees Previously Paid			X
Total Fee Offsets			X
Net Fee Due			X

TABLE 2 TO PARAGRAPH (a)(7)

	Registrant or filer name	Form or filing type	File number	Initial filing date	Filing date	Fee offset claimed	Fee paid with fee offset source
Fee Offset Claims		X	X	X		X	
Fee Offset Sources	X	X	X		X		X

191

§ 240.13e-1

(i) *General requirements*—(A) *Applicable table requirements.* The "X" designation indicates the information required to be disclosed, as applicable, in tabular format. Add as many rows of each table as necessary.

(B) *Fee rate.* For the current fee rate, see https://www.sec.gov/ofm/Article/feeamt.html.

(C) *Explanations.* If not otherwise explained in response to this paragraph (a)(7), disclose specific details relating to the fee calculation as necessary to clarify the information presented in each table, including references to the applicable provisions of § 240.0–11 (Rule 0–11). All disclosure this paragraph (a)(7) requires that is not specifically required to be presented in tabular format must appear in narrative format immediately after the table(s) to which it corresponds.

(ii) *Table 1 to this paragraph (a)(7)*—(A) *Fees to be paid and fees previously paid*—(1) *Fees to be paid.* Provide the information Table 1 to this paragraph (a)(7) requires for the line item "Fees to Be Paid" as follows:

(i) *Initial filings.* For an initial filing on the statement, provide the required information for the total transaction valuation.

(ii) *Amendments with then-current total transaction valuation higher than highest total transaction valuation previously reported.* For amendments to the statement that reflect a then-current total transaction valuation higher than the highest total transaction valuation previously reported, provide the required information for the incremental increase.

(2) *Fees previously paid.* Provide the information Table 1 to this paragraph (a)(7) requires for the line item "Fees Previously Paid" for the prior initial filing or amendment to the statement that reflected a then-current total transaction valuation that was the highest total transaction valuation previously reported.

(B) *Other tabular information.* Provide the following information in Table 1 to this paragraph (a)(7) for the line items "Fees to be Paid" and "Fees Previously Paid", as applicable:

(1) The transaction valuation computed pursuant to Rule 0–11;

(2) The fee rate; and

17 CFR Ch. II (4–1–23 Edition)

(3) The filing fee due without regard to any previous payments or offsets.

(C) *Totals*—(1) *Total transaction valuation.* Provide the sum of the transaction valuations for the line items "Fees to be Paid" and "Fees Previously Paid".

(2) *Total fees due for filing.* Provide the sum of the fees due without regard to any previous payments or offsets for the line items "Fees to be Paid" and "Fees Previously Paid."

(3) *Total fees previously paid.* Provide the aggregate of filing fees previously paid with this filing.

(4) *Total fee offsets.* Provide the aggregate of the fee offsets that are claimed in Table 2 to this paragraph (a)(7) pursuant to paragraph (a)(7)(iii) of this section.

(5) *Net fee due.* Provide the difference between:

(i) The total fees due for the statement from the "Total Fees Due for Filing" row; and

(ii) The sum of the aggregate of filing fees previously paid from the "Total Fees Previously Paid" row; and the aggregate fee offsets claimed from the "Total Fee Offsets" row.

(D) *Narrative disclosure.* Explain how the transaction valuation was determined.

(iii) *Table 2 to this paragraph (a)(7)*—(A) *Terminology.* For purposes of this paragraph (a)(7)(iii) and Table 2 to this paragraph (a)(7):

(1) The term *submission* means any:

(i) Initial filing of, or amendment (pre-effective or post-effective), to a fee-bearing document; or

(ii) Fee-bearing form of prospectus filed under § 230.424 of this chapter (Rule 424 under the Securities Act), in all cases that was accompanied by a contemporaneous fee payment.

Note 1 to paragraph (a)(7)(iii)(A). For purposes of this paragraph (a)(7)(iii), a contemporaneous fee payment is the payment of a required fee that is satisfied through the actual transfer of funds, and does not include any amount of a required fee satisfied through a claimed fee offset. Paragraph (a)(7)(iii)(B)(2) of this section requires a filer that claims a fee offset under Rule 0–11(a)(2) to identify previous submissions with contemporaneous fee payments that are the original source to

Securities and Exchange Commission § 240.13e–3

which the fee offsets claimed on this filing can be traced. *See* Instruction 3.C to the Calculation of Filing Fee Tables in Item 16(b) of § 240.13e–100 (Schedule 13E–3) for an example.

(B) *Rule 0–11(a)(2)*. If relying on Rule 0–11(a)(2) to offset some or all of the filing fee due on the statement by amounts paid in connection with earlier filings (other than the statement) relating to the same transaction, provide the following information:

(1) Fee offset claims. For each earlier filed Securities Act registration statement or Exchange Act document relating to the same transaction from which a fee offset is being claimed, provide the information that Table 2 to this paragraph (a)(7) requires for the line item "Fee Offset Claims". The "Fee Offset Claimed" column requires the dollar amount of the previously paid filing fee to be offset against the currently due fee.

Note 2 to paragraph (a)(7)(iii)(B)(*1*). If claiming an offset from a Securities Act registration statement, provide a detailed explanation of the basis for the claimed offset.

(2) Fee offset sources. With respect to amounts claimed as an offset under Rule 0–11(a)(2), identify those submissions with contemporaneous fee payments that are the original source to which those amounts can be traced. For each submission identified, provide the information that Table 2 to this paragraph (a)(7) requires for the line item "Fee Offset Sources". The "Fee Paid with Fee Offset Source" column requires the dollar amount of the contemporaneous fee payment made with respect to each identified submission that is the source of the fee offset claimed pursuant to Rule 0–11(a)(2).

(b) Pays the fee required by § 240.0–11 when it files the initial statement and any amendment with respect to which an additional fee is due.

(c) Submits to the Commission the exhibit required by paragraph (a)(7) of this section as required by § 232.408 of this chapter (Rule 408 of Regulation S–T).

(d) This section does not apply to periodic repurchases in connection with an employee benefit plan or other similar plan of the issuer so long as the purchases are made in the ordinary course and not in response to the tender offer.

INSTRUCTION TO § 240.13e–1: File eight copies if paper filing is permitted.

[64 FR 61452, Nov. 10, 1999, as amended at 86 FR 70251, Dec. 9, 2021]

§ 240.13e–2 [Reserved]

§ 240.13e–3 Going private transactions by certain issuers or their affiliates.

(a) *Definitions.* Unless indicated otherwise or the context otherwise requires, all terms used in this section and in Schedule 13E–3 [§ 240.13e–100] shall have the same meaning as in the Act or elsewhere in the General Rules and Regulations thereunder. In addition, the following definitions apply:

(1) An *affiliate* of an issuer is a person that directly or indirectly through one or more intermediaries controls, is controlled by, or is under common control with such issuer. For the purposes of this section only, a person who is not an affiliate of an issuer at the commencement of such person's tender offer for a class of equity securities of such issuer will not be deemed an affiliate of such issuer prior to the stated termination of such tender offer and any extensions thereof;

(2) The term *purchase* means any acquisition for value including, but not limited to, (i) any acquisition pursuant to the dissolution of an issuer subsequent to the sale or other disposition of substantially all the assets of such issuer to its affiliate, (ii) any acquisition pursuant to a merger, (iii) any acquisition of fractional interests in connection with a reverse stock split, and (iv) any acquisition subject to the control of an issuer or an affiliate of such issuer;

(3) A *Rule 13e–3 transaction* is any transaction or series of transactions involving one or more of the transactions described in paragraph (a)(3)(i) of this section which has either a reasonable likelihood or a purpose of producing, either directly or indirectly, any of the effects described in paragraph (a)(3)(ii) of this section;

(i) The transactions referred to in paragraph (a)(3) of this section are:

(A) A purchase of any equity security by the issuer of such security or by an affiliate of such issuer;

193

§ 240.13e-3

(B) A tender offer for or request or invitation for tenders of any equity security made by the issuer of such class of securities or by an affiliate of such issuer; or

(C) A solicitation subject to Regulation 14A [§§ 240.14a-1 to 240.14b-1] of any proxy, consent or authorization of, or a distribution subject to Regulation 14C [§§ 240.14c-1 to 14c-101] of information statements to, any equity security holder by the issuer of the class of securities or by an affiliate of such issuer, in connection with: a merger, consolidation, reclassification, recapitalization, reorganization or similar corporate transaction of an issuer or between an issuer (or its subsidiaries) and its affiliate; a sale of substantially all the assets of an issuer to its affiliate or group of affiliates; or a reverse stock split of any class of equity securities of the issuer involving the purchase of fractional interests.

(ii) The effects referred to in paragraph (a)(3) of this section are:

(A) Causing any class of equity securities of the issuer which is subject to section 12(g) or section 15(d) of the Act to become eligible for termination of registration under Rule 12g-4 (§ 240.12g-4) or Rule 12h-6 (§ 240.12h-6), or causing the reporting obligations with respect to such class to become eligible for termination under Rule 12h-6 (§ 240.12h-6); or suspension under Rule 12h-3 (§ 240.12h-3) or section 15(d); or

(B) Causing any class of equity securities of the issuer which is either listed on a national securities exchange or authorized to be quoted in an inter-dealer quotation system of a registered national securities association to be neither listed on any national securities exchange nor authorized to be quoted on an inter-dealer quotation system of any registered national securities association.

(4) An *unaffiliated security holder* is any security holder of an equity security subject to a Rule 13e-3 transaction who is not an affiliate of the issuer of such security.

(b) *Application of section to an issuer (or an affiliate of such issuer) subject to section 12 of the Act.* (1) It shall be a fraudulent, deceptive or manipulative act or practice, in connection with a Rule 13e-3 transaction, for an issuer which has a class of equity securities registered pursuant to section 12 of the Act or which is a closed-end investment company registered under the Investment Company Act of 1940, or an affiliate of such issuer, directly or indirectly

(i) To employ any device, scheme or artifice to defraud any person;

(ii) To make any untrue statement of a material fact or to omit to state a material fact necessary in order to make the statements made, in light of the circumstances under which they were made, not misleading; or

(iii) To engage in any act, practice or course of business which operates or would operate as a fraud or deceit upon any person.

(2) As a means reasonably designed to prevent fraudulent, deceptive or manipulative acts or practices in connection with any Rule 13e-3 transaction, it shall be unlawful for an issuer which has a class of equity securities registered pursuant to section 12 of the Act, or an affiliate of such issuer, to engage, directly or indirectly, in a Rule 13e-3 transaction unless:

(i) Such issuer or affiliate complies with the requirements of paragraphs (d), (e) and (f) of this section; and

(ii) The Rule 13e-3 transaction is not in violation of paragraph (b)(1) of this section.

(c) *Application of section to an issuer (or an affiliate of such issuer) subject to section 15(d) of the Act.* (1) It shall be unlawful as a fraudulent, deceptive or manipulative act or practice for an issuer which is required to file periodic reports pursuant to Section 15(d) of the Act, or an affiliate of such issuer, to engage, directly or indirectly, in a Rule 13e-3 transaction unless such issuer or affiliate complies with the requirements of paragraphs (d), (e) and (f) of this section.

(2) An issuer or affiliate which is subject to paragraph (c)(1) of this section and which is soliciting proxies or distributing information statements in connection with a transaction described in paragraph (a)(3)(i)(A) of this section may elect to use the timing procedures for conducting a solicitation subject to Regulation 14A (§§ 240.14a-1 to 240.14b-1) or a distribution subject to Regulation 14C

Securities and Exchange Commission

§ 240.13e–3

(§§ 240.14c–1 to 240.14c–101) in complying with paragraphs (d), (e) and (f) of this section, provided that if an election is made, such solicitation or distribution is conducted in accordance with the requirements of the respective regulations, including the filing of preliminary copies of soliciting materials or an information statement at the time specified in Regulation 14A or 14C, respectively.

(d) *Material required to be filed.* The issuer or affiliate engaging in a Rule 13e–3 transaction must file with the Commission:

(1) A Schedule 13E–3 (§ 240.13e–100), including all exhibits;

(2) An amendment to Schedule 13E–3 reporting promptly any material changes in the information set forth in the schedule previously filed; and

(3) A final amendment to Schedule 13E–3 reporting promptly the results of the Rule 13e–3 transaction.

(e) *Disclosure of information to security holders.* (1) In addition to disclosing the information required by any other applicable rule or regulation under the federal securities laws, the issuer or affiliate engaging in a § 240.13e–3 transaction must disclose to security holders of the class that is the subject of the transaction, as specified in paragraph (f) of this section, the following:

(i) The information required by Item 1 of Schedule 13E–3 (§ 240.13e–100) (Summary Term Sheet);

(ii) The information required by Items 7, 8 and 9 of Schedule 13E–3, which must be prominently disclosed in a "Special Factors" section in the front of the disclosure document;

(iii) A prominent legend on the outside front cover page that indicates that neither the Securities and Exchange Commission nor any state securities commission has: approved or disapproved of the transaction; passed upon the merits or fairness of the transaction; or passed upon the adequacy or accuracy of the disclosure in the document. The legend also must make it clear that any representation to the contrary is a criminal offense;

(iv) The information concerning appraisal rights required by § 229.1016(f) of this chapter; and

(v) The information required by the remaining items of Schedule 13E–3, except for § 229.1016 of this chapter (exhibits), or a fair and adequate summary of the information.

INSTRUCTIONS TO PARAGRAPH (e)(1): 1. If the Rule 13e–3 transaction also is subject to Regulation 14A (§§ 240.14a–1 through 240.14b–2) or 14C (§§ 240.14c–1 through 240.14c–101), the registration provisions and rules of the Securities Act of 1933, Regulation 14D or § 240.13e–4, the information required by paragraph (e)(1) of this section must be combined with the proxy statement, information statement, prospectus or tender offer material sent or given to security holders.

2. If the Rule 13e–3 transaction involves a registered securities offering, the legend required by § 229.501(b)(7) of this chapter must be combined with the legend required by paragraph (e)(1)(iii) of this section.

3. The required legend must be written in clear, plain language.

(2) If there is any material change in the information previously disclosed to security holders, the issuer or affiliate must disclose the change promptly to security holders as specified in paragraph (f)(1)(iii) of this section.

(f) *Dissemination of information to security holders.* (1) If the Rule 13e–3 transaction involves a purchase as described in paragraph (a)(3)(i)(A) of this section or a vote, consent, authorization, or distribution of information statements as described in paragraph (a)(3)(i)(C) of this section, the issuer or affiliate engaging in the Rule 13e–3 transaction shall:

(i) Provide the information required by paragraph (e) of this section: (A) In accordance with the provisions of any applicable Federal or State law, but in no event later than 20 days prior to: any such purchase; any such vote, consent or authorization; or with respect to the distribution of information statements, the meeting date, or if corporate action is to be taken by means of the written authorization or consent of security holders, the earliest date on which corporate action may be taken: *Provided, however,* That if the purchase subject to this section is pursuant to a tender offer excepted from Rule 13e–4 by paragraph (g)(5) of Rule 13e–4, the information required by paragraph (e) of this section shall be disseminated in accordance with paragraph (e) of Rule 13e–4 no later than 10 business days prior to any purchase pursuant to such tender offer, (B) to each person who is

195

§ 240.13e-3

a record holder of a class of equity securities subject to the Rule 13e-3 transaction as of a date not more than 20 days prior to the date of dissemination of such information.

(ii) If the issuer or affiliate knows that securities of the class of securities subject to the Rule 13e-3 transaction are held of record by a broker, dealer, bank or voting trustee or their nominees, such issuer or affiliate shall (unless Rule 14a-13(a) [§ 240.14a-13(a)] or 14c-7 [§ 240.14c-7] is applicable) furnish the number of copies of the information required by paragraph (e) of this section that are requested by such persons (pursuant to inquiries by or on behalf of the issuer or affiliate), instruct such persons to forward such information to the beneficial owners of such securities in a timely manner and undertake to pay the reasonable expenses incurred by such persons in forwarding such information; and

(iii) Promptly disseminate disclosure of material changes to the information required by paragraph (d) of this section in a manner reasonably calculated to inform security holders.

(2) If the Rule 13e-3 transaction is a tender offer or a request or invitation for tenders of equity securities which is subject to Regulation 14D [§§ 240.14d-1 to 240.14d-101] or Rule 13e-4 [§ 240.13e-4], the tender offer containing the information required by paragraph (e) of this section, and any material change with respect thereto, shall be published, sent or given in accordance with Regulation 14D or Rule 13e-4, respectively, to security holders of the class of securities being sought by the issuer or affiliate.

(g) *Exceptions.* This section shall not apply to:

(1) Any Rule 13e-3 transaction by or on behalf of a person which occurs within one year of the date of termination of a tender offer in which such person was the bidder and became an affiliate of the issuer as a result of such tender offer: *Provided,* That the consideration offered to unaffiliated security holders in such Rule 13e-3 transaction is at least equal to the highest consideration offered during such tender offer and *Provided further,* That:

(i) If such tender offer was made for any or all securities of a class of the issuer;

(A) Such tender offer fully disclosed such person's intention to engage in a Rule 13e-3 transaction, the form and effect of such transaction and, to the extent known, the proposed terms thereof; and

(B) Such Rule 13e-3 transaction is substantially similar to that described in such tender offer; or

(ii) If such tender offer was made for less than all the securities of a class of the issuer:

(A) Such tender offer fully disclosed a plan of merger, a plan of liquidation or a similar binding agreement between such person and the issuer with respect to a Rule 13e-3 transaction; and

(B) Such Rule 13e-3 transaction occurs pursuant to the plan of merger, plan of liquidation or similar binding agreement disclosed in the bidder's tender offer.

(2) Any Rule 13e-3 transaction in which the security holders are offered or receive only an equity security *Provided,* That:

(i) Such equity security has substantially the same rights as the equity security which is the subject of the Rule 13e-3 transaction including, but not limited to, voting, dividends, redemption and liquidation rights except that this requirement shall be deemed to be satisfied if unaffiliated security holders are offered common stock;

(ii) Such equity security is registered pursuant to section 12 of the Act or reports are required to be filed by the issuer thereof pursuant to section 15(d) of the Act; and

(iii) If the security which is the subject of the Rule 13e-3 transaction was either listed on a national securities exchange or authorized to be quoted in an interdealer quotation system of a registered national securities association, such equity security is either listed on a national securities exchange or authorized to be quoted in an interdealer quotation system of a registered national securities association.

(3) [Reserved]

(4) Redemptions, calls or similar purchases of an equity security by an issuer pursuant to specific provisions set forth in the instrument(s) creating

Securities and Exchange Commission § 240.13e-4

or governing that class of equity securities; or

(5) Any solicitation by an issuer with respect to a plan of reorganization under Chapter XI of the Bankruptcy Act, as amended, if made after the entry of an order approving such plan pursuant to section 1125(b) of that Act and after, or concurrently with, the transmittal of information concerning such plan as required by section 1125(b) of that Act.

(6) Any tender offer or business combination made in compliance with § 230.802 of this chapter, § 240.13e–4(h)(8) or § 240.14d–1(c) or any other kind of transaction that otherwise meets the conditions for reliance on the cross-border exemptions set forth in § 240.13e–4(h)(8), § 240.14d–1(c) or § 230.802 of this chapter except for the fact that it is not technically subject to those rules.

INSTRUCTION TO § 240.13e–3(g)(6): To the extent applicable, the acquiror must comply with the conditions set forth in § 230.802 of this chapter, and §§ 240.13e–4(h)(8) and 14d–1(c). If the acquiror publishes or otherwise disseminates an informational document to the holders of the subject securities in connection with the transaction, the acquiror must furnish an English translation of that informational document, including any amendments thereto, to the Commission under cover of Form CB (§ 230.800 of this chapter) by the first business day after publication or dissemination. If the acquiror is a foreign entity, it must also file a Form F–X (§ 239.42 of this chapter) with the Commission at the same time as the submission of the Form CB to appoint an agent for service in the United States.

[44 FR 46741, Aug. 8, 1979, as amended at 47 FR 11466, Mar. 16, 1982; 48 FR 19877, May 3, 1983; 48 FR 34253, July 28, 1983; 51 FR 42059, Nov. 20, 1986; 61 FR 24656, May 15, 1996; 64 FR 61403, 64 FR 61452, Nov. 10, 1999; 73 FR 17813, Apr. 1, 2008; 73 FR 58323, Oct. 6, 2008; 73 FR 60090, Oct. 9, 2008]

§ 240.13e–4 Tender offers by issuers.

(a) *Definitions.* Unless the context otherwise requires, all terms used in this section and in Schedule TO (§ 240.14d–100) shall have the same meaning as in the Act or elsewhere in the General Rules and Regulations thereunder. In addition, the following definitions shall apply:

(1) The term *issuer* means any issuer which has a class of equity security registered pursuant to section 12 of the Act, or which is required to file periodic reports pursuant to section 15(d) of the Act, or which is a closed-end investment company registered under the Investment Company Act of 1940.

(2) The term *issuer tender offer* refers to a tender offer for, or a request or invitation for tenders of, any class of equity security, made by the issuer of such class of equity security or by an affiliate of such issuer.

(3) As used in this section and in Schedule TO (§ 240.14d–100), the term *business day* means any day, other than Saturday, Sunday, or a Federal holiday, and shall consist of the time period from 12:01 a.m. through 12:00 midnight Eastern Time. In computing any time period under this Rule or Schedule TO, the date of the event that begins the running of such time period shall be included *except that* if such event occurs on other than a business day such period shall begin to run on and shall include the first business day thereafter.

(4) The term *commencement* means 12:01 a.m. on the date that the issuer or affiliate has first published, sent or given the means to tender to security holders. For purposes of this section, the means to tender includes the transmittal form or a statement regarding how the transmittal form may be obtained.

(5) The term *termination* means the date after which securities may not be tendered pursuant to an issuer tender offer.

(6) The term *security holders* means holders of record and beneficial owners of securities of the class of equity security which is the subject of an issuer tender offer.

(7) The term *security position listing* means, with respect to the securities of any issuer held by a registered clearing agency in the name of the clearing agency or its nominee, a list of those participants in the clearing agency on whose behalf the clearing agency holds the issuer's securities and of the participants' respective positions in such securities as of a specified date.

(b) *Filing, disclosure and dissemination.* As soon as practicable on the date of commencement of the issuer tender offer, the issuer or affiliate making the issuer tender offer must comply with:

§ 240.13e-4

(1) The filing requirements of paragraph (c)(2) of this section;
(2) The disclosure requirements of paragraph (d)(1) of this section; and
(3) The dissemination requirements of paragraph (e) of this section.

(c) *Material required to be filed.* The issuer or affiliate making the issuer tender offer must file with the Commission:

(1) All written communications made by the issuer or affiliate relating to the issuer tender offer, from and including the first public announcement, as soon as practicable on the date of the communication;
(2) A Schedule TO (§ 240.14d–100), including all exhibits;
(3) An amendment to Schedule TO (§ 240.14d–100) reporting promptly any material changes in the information set forth in the schedule previously filed; and
(4) A final amendment to Schedule TO (§ 240.14d–100) reporting promptly the results of the issuer tender offer.

INSTRUCTIONS TO § 240.13e–4(C): 1. Pre-commencement communications must be filed under cover of Schedule TO (§ 240.14d–100) and the box on the cover page of the schedule must be marked.
2. Any communications made in connection with an exchange offer registered under the Securities Act of 1933 need only be filed under § 230.425 of this chapter and will be deemed filed under this section.
3. Each pre-commencement written communication must include a prominent legend in clear, plain language advising security holders to read the tender offer statement when it is available because it contains important information. The legend also must advise investors that they can get the tender offer statement and other filed documents for free at the Commission's web site and explain which documents are free from the issuer.
4. See §§ 230.135, 230.165 and 230.166 of this chapter for pre-commencement communications made in connection with registered exchange offers.
5. "Public announcement" is any oral or written communication by the issuer, affiliate or any person authorized to act on their behalf that is reasonably designed to, or has the effect of, informing the public or security holders in general about the issuer tender offer.

(d) *Disclosure of tender offer information to security holders.* (1) The issuer or affiliate making the issuer tender offer must disclose, in a manner prescribed by paragraph (e)(1) of this section, the following:

(i) The information required by Item 1 of Schedule TO (§ 240.14d–100) (summary term sheet); and
(ii) The information required by the remaining items of Schedule TO for issuer tender offers, except for Item 12 (exhibits), or a fair and adequate summary of the information.

(2) If there are any material changes in the information previously disclosed to security holders, the issuer or affiliate must disclose the changes promptly to security holders in a manner specified in paragraph (e)(3) of this section.

(3) If the issuer or affiliate disseminates the issuer tender offer by means of summary publication as described in paragraph (e)(1)(iii) of this section, the summary advertisement must not include a transmittal letter that would permit security holders to tender securities sought in the offer and must disclose at least the following information:

(i) The identity of the issuer or affiliate making the issuer tender offer;
(ii) The information required by § 229.1004(a)(1) and § 229.1006(a) of this chapter;
(iii) Instructions on how security holders can obtain promptly a copy of the statement required by paragraph (d)(1) of this section, at the issuer or affiliate's expense; and
(iv) A statement that the information contained in the statement required by paragraph (d)(1) of this section is incorporated by reference.

(e) *Dissemination of tender offers to security holders.* An issuer tender offer will be deemed to be published, sent or given to security holders if the issuer or affiliate making the issuer tender offer complies fully with one or more of the methods described in this section.

(1) For issuer tender offers in which the consideration offered consists solely of cash and/or securities exempt from registration under section 3 of the Securities Act of 1933 (15 U.S.C. 77c):

(i) Dissemination of cash issuer tender offers by long-form publication: By making adequate publication of the information required by paragraph (d)(1)

Securities and Exchange Commission § 240.13e–4

of this section in a newspaper or newspapers, on the date of commencement of the issuer tender offer.

(ii) Dissemination of any issuer tender offer by use of stockholder and other lists:

(A) By mailing or otherwise furnishing promptly a statement containing the information required by paragraph (d)(1) of this section to each security holder whose name appears on the most recent stockholder list of the issuer;

(B) By contacting each participant on the most recent security position listing of any clearing agency within the possession or access of the issuer or affiliate making the issuer tender offer, and making inquiry of each participant as to the approximate number of beneficial owners of the securities sought in the offer that are held by the participant;

(C) By furnishing to each participant a sufficient number of copies of the statement required by paragraph (d)(1) of this section for transmittal to the beneficial owners; and

(D) By agreeing to reimburse each participant promptly for its reasonable expenses incurred in forwarding the statement to beneficial owners.

(iii) Dissemination of certain cash issuer tender offers by summary publication:

(A) If the issuer tender offer is not subject to § 240.13e–3, by making adequate publication of a summary advertisement containing the information required by paragraph (d)(3) of this section in a newspaper or newspapers, on the date of commencement of the issuer tender offer; and

(B) By mailing or otherwise furnishing promptly the statement required by paragraph (d)(1) of this section and a transmittal letter to any security holder who requests a copy of the statement or transmittal letter.

INSTRUCTION TO PARAGRAPH (e)(1): For purposes of paragraphs (e)(1)(i) and (e)(1)(iii) of this section, adequate publication of the issuer tender offer may require publication in a newspaper with a national circulation, a newspaper with metropolitan or regional circulation, or a combination of the two, depending upon the facts and circumstances involved.

(2) For tender offers in which the consideration consists solely or partially of securities registered under the Securities Act of 1933, a registration statement containing all of the required information, including pricing information, has been filed and a preliminary prospectus or a prospectus that meets the requirements of Section 10(a) of the Securities Act (15 U.S.C. 77j(a)), including a letter of transmittal, is delivered to security holders. However, for going-private transactions (as defined by § 240.13e–3) and roll-up transactions (as described by Item 901 of Regulation S-K (§ 229.901 of this chapter)), a registration statement registering the securities to be offered must have become effective and only a prospectus that meets the requirements of Section 10(a) of the Securities Act may be delivered to security holders on the date of commencement.

INSTRUCTIONS TO PARAGRAPH (e)(2): 1. If the prospectus is being delivered by mail, mailing on the date of commencement is sufficient.

2. A preliminary prospectus used under this section may not omit information under § 230.430 or § 230.430A of this chapter.

3. If a preliminary prospectus is used under this section and the issuer must disseminate material changes, the tender offer must remain open for the period specified in paragraph (e)(3) of this section.

4. If a preliminary prospectus is used under this section, tenders may be requested in accordance with § 230.162(a) of this chapter.

(3) If a material change occurs in the information published, sent or given to security holders, the issuer or affiliate must disseminate promptly disclosure of the change in a manner reasonably calculated to inform security holders of the change. In a registered securities offer where the issuer or affiliate disseminates the preliminary prospectus as permitted by paragraph (e)(2) of this section, the offer must remain open from the date that material changes to the tender offer materials are disseminated to security holders, as follows:

(i) Five business days for a prospectus supplement containing a material change other than price or share levels;

(ii) Ten business days for a prospectus supplement containing a change in price, the amount of securities sought, the dealer's soliciting fee, or other similarly significant change;

(iii) Ten business days for a prospectus supplement included as part of a post-effective amendment; and

(iv) Twenty business days for a revised prospectus when the initial prospectus was materially deficient.

(f) *Manner of making tender offer.* (1) The issuer tender offer, unless withdrawn, shall remain open until the expiration of:

(i) At least twenty business days from its commencement; and

(ii) At least ten business days from the date that notice of an increase or decrease in the percentage of the class of securities being sought or the consideration offered or the dealer's soliciting fee to be given is first published, sent or given to security holders.

Provided, however, That, for purposes of this paragraph, the acceptance for payment by the issuer or affiliate of an additional amount of securities not to exceed two percent of the class of securities that is the subject of the tender offer shall not be deemed to be an increase. For purposes of this paragraph, the percentage of a class of securities shall be calculated in accordance with section 14(d)(3) of the Act.

(2) The issuer or affiliate making the issuer tender offer shall permit securities tendered pursuant to the issuer tender offer to be withdrawn:

(i) At any time during the period such issuer tender offer remains open; and

(ii) If not yet accepted for payment, after the expiration of forty business days from the commencement of the issuer tender offer.

(3) If the issuer or affiliate makes a tender offer for less than all of the outstanding equity securities of a class, and if a greater number of securities is tendered pursuant thereto than the issuer or affiliate is bound or willing to take up and pay for, the securities taken up and paid for shall be taken up and paid for as nearly as may be pro rata, disregarding fractions, according to the number of securities tendered by each security holder during the period such offer remains open; *Provided, however,* That this provision shall not prohibit the issuer or affiliate making the issuer tender offer from:

(i) Accepting all securities tendered by persons who own, beneficially or of record, an aggregate of not more than a specified number which is less than one hundred shares of such security and who tender all their securities, before prorating securities tendered by others; or

(ii) Accepting by lot securities tendered by security holders who tender all securities held by them and who, when tendering their securities, elect to have either all or none or at least a minimum amount or none accepted, if the issuer or affiliate first accepts all securities tendered by security holders who do not so elect;

(4) In the event the issuer or affiliate making the issuer tender increases the consideration offered after the issuer tender offer has commenced, such issuer or affiliate shall pay such increased consideration to all security holders whose tendered securities are accepted for payment by such issuer or affiliate.

(5) The issuer or affiliate making the tender offer shall either pay the consideration offered, or return the tendered securities, promptly after the termination or withdrawal of the tender offer.

(6) Until the expiration of at least ten business days after the date of termination of the issuer tender offer, neither the issuer nor any affiliate shall make any purchases, otherwise than pursuant to the tender offer, of:

(i) Any security which is the subject of the issuer tender offer, or any security of the same class and series, or any right to purchase any such securities; and

(ii) In the case of an issuer tender offer which is an exchange offer, any security being offered pursuant to such exchange offer, or any security of the same class and series, or any right to purchase any such security.

(7) The time periods for the minimum offering periods pursuant to this section shall be computed on a concurrent as opposed to a consecutive basis.

(8) No issuer or affiliate shall make a tender offer unless:

Securities and Exchange Commission § 240.13e-4

(i) The tender offer is open to all security holders of the class of securities subject to the tender offer; and

(ii) The consideration paid to any security holder for securities tendered in the tender offer is the highest consideration paid to any other security holder for securities tendered in the tender offer.

(9) Paragraph (f)(8)(i) of this section shall not:

(i) Affect dissemination under paragraph (e) of this section; or

(ii) Prohibit an issuer or affiliate from making a tender offer excluding all security holders in a state where the issuer or affiliate is prohibited from making the tender offer by administrative or judicial action pursuant to a state statute after a good faith effort by the issuer or affiliate to comply with such statute.

(10) Paragraph (f)(8)(ii) of this section shall not prohibit the offer of more than one type of consideration in a tender offer, provided that:

(i) Security holders are afforded equal right to elect among each of the types of consideration offered; and

(ii) The highest consideration of each type paid to any security holder is paid to any other security holder receiving that type of consideration.

(11) If the offer and sale of securities constituting consideration offered in an issuer tender offer is prohibited by the appropriate authority of a state after a good faith effort by the issuer or affiliate to register or qualify the offer and sale of such securities in such state:

(i) The issuer or affiliate may offer security holders in such state an alternative form of consideration; and

(ii) Paragraph (f)(10) of this section shall not operate to require the issuer or affiliate to offer or pay the alternative form of consideration to security holders in any other state.

(12)(i) Paragraph (f)(8)(ii) of this section shall not prohibit the negotiation, execution or amendment of an employment compensation, severance or other employee benefit arrangement, or payments made or to be made or benefits granted or to be granted according to such an arrangement, with respect to any security holder of the issuer, where the amount payable under the arrangement:

(A) Is being paid or granted as compensation for past services performed, future services to be performed, or future services to be refrained from performing, by the security holder (and matters incidental thereto); and

(B) Is not calculated based on the number of securities tendered or to be tendered in the tender offer by the security holder.

(ii) The provisions of paragraph (f)(12)(i) of this section shall be satisfied and, therefore, pursuant to this non-exclusive safe harbor, the negotiation, execution or amendment of an arrangement and any payments made or to be made or benefits granted or to be granted according to that arrangement shall not be prohibited by paragraph (f)(8)(ii) of this section, if the arrangement is approved as an employment compensation, severance or other employee benefit arrangement solely by independent directors as follows:

(A) The compensation committee or a committee of the board of directors that performs functions similar to a compensation committee of the issuer approves the arrangement, regardless of whether the issuer is a party to the arrangement, or, if an affiliate is a party to the arrangement, the compensation committee or a committee of the board of directors that performs functions similar to a compensation committee of the affiliate approves the arrangement; or

(B) If the issuer's or affiliate's board of directors, as applicable, does not have a compensation committee or a committee of the board of directors that performs functions similar to a compensation committee or if none of the members of the issuer's or affiliate's compensation committee or committee that performs functions similar to a compensation committee is independent, a special committee of the board of directors formed to consider and approve the arrangement approves the arrangement; or

(C) If the issuer or affiliate, as applicable, is a foreign private issuer, any or all members of the board of directors or any committee of the board of directors authorized to approve employment

§ 240.13e-4

compensation, severance or other employee benefit arrangements under the laws or regulations of the home country approves the arrangement.

INSTRUCTIONS TO PARAGRAPH (f)(12)(ii): For purposes of determining whether the members of the committee approving an arrangement in accordance with the provisions of paragraph (f)(12)(ii) of this section are independent, the following provisions shall apply:

1. If the issuer or affiliate, as applicable, is a listed issuer (as defined in § 240.10A-3 of this chapter) whose securities are listed either on a national securities exchange registered pursuant to section 6(a) of the Exchange Act (15 U.S.C. 78f(a)) or in an interdealer quotation system of a national securities association registered pursuant to section 15A(a) of the Exchange Act (15 U.S.C. 78o-3(a)) that has independence requirements for compensation committee members that have been approved by the Commission (as those requirements may be modified or supplemented), apply the issuer's or affiliate's definition of independence that it uses for determining that the members of the compensation committee are independent in compliance with the listing standards applicable to compensation committee members of the listed issuer.

2. If the issuer or affiliate, as applicable, is not a listed issuer (as defined in § 240.10A-3 of this chapter), apply the independence requirements for compensation committee members of a national securities exchange registered pursuant to section 6(a) of the Exchange Act (15 U.S.C. 78f(a)) or an inter-dealer quotation system of a national securities association registered pursuant to section 15A(a) of the Exchange Act (15 U.S.C. 78o-3(a)) that have been approved by the Commission (as those requirements may be modified or supplemented). Whatever definition the issuer or affiliate, as applicable, chooses, it must apply that definition consistently to all members of the committee approving the arrangement.

3. Notwithstanding Instructions 1 and 2 to paragraph (f)(12)(ii), if the issuer or affiliate, as applicable, is a closed-end investment company registered under the Investment Company Act of 1940, a director is considered to be independent if the director is not, other than in his or her capacity as a member of the board of directors or any board committee, an "interested person" of the investment company, as defined in section 2(a)(19) of the Investment Company Act of 1940 (15 U.S.C. 80a-2(a)(19)).

4. If the issuer or affiliate, as applicable, is a foreign private issuer, apply either the independence standards set forth in Instructions 1 and 2 to paragraph (f)(12)(ii) or the independence requirements of the laws, regulations, codes or standards of the home country of the issuer or affiliate, as applicable, for members of the board of directors or the committee of the board of directors approving the arrangement.

5. A determination by the issuer's or affiliate's board of directors, as applicable, that the members of the board of directors or the committee of the board of directors, as applicable, approving an arrangement in accordance with the provisions of paragraph (f)(12)(ii) are independent in accordance with the provisions of this instruction to paragraph (f)(12)(ii) shall satisfy the independence requirements of paragraph (f)(12)(ii).

INSTRUCTION TO PARAGRAPH (f)(12): The fact that the provisions of paragraph (f)(12) of this section extend only to employment compensation, severance and other employee benefit arrangements and not to other arrangements, such as commercial arrangements, does not raise any inference that a payment under any such other arrangement constitutes consideration paid for securities in a tender offer.

(13) *Electronic filings.* If the issuer or affiliate is an electronic filer, the minimum offering periods set forth in paragraph (f)(1) of this section shall be tolled for any period during which it fails to file in electronic format, absent a hardship exemption (§§ 232.201 and 232.202 of this chapter), the Schedule TO (§ 240.14d-100), the tender offer material specified in Item 1016(a)(1) of Regulation M-A (§ 229.1016(a)(1) of this chapter), and any amendments thereto. If such documents were filed in paper pursuant to a hardship exemption (*see* § 232.201 and § 232.202 of this chapter), the minimum offering periods shall be tolled for any period during which a required confirming electronic copy of such Schedule and tender offer material is delinquent.

(g) The requirements of section 13(e)(1) of the Act and Rule 13e-4 and Schedule TO (§ 240.14d-100) thereunder shall be deemed satisfied with respect to any issuer tender offer, including any exchange offer, where the issuer is incorporated or organized under the laws of Canada or any Canadian province or territory, is a foreign private issuer, and is not an investment company registered or required to be registered under the Investment Company Act of 1940, if less than 40 percent of the class of securities that is the subject of the tender offer is held by U. S. holders, and the tender offer is subject to, and

Securities and Exchange Commission § 240.13e–4

the issuer complies with, the laws, regulations and policies of Canada and/or any of its provinces or territories governing the conduct of the offer (unless the issuer has received an exemption(s) from, and the issuer tender offer does not comply with, requirements that otherwise would be prescribed by this section), *provided that:*

(1) Where the consideration for an issuer tender offer subject to this paragraph consists solely of cash, the entire disclosure document or documents required to be furnished to holders of the class of securities to be acquired shall be filed with the Commission on Schedule 13E–4F (§ 240.13e–102) and disseminated to shareholders residing in the United States in accordance with such Canadian laws, regulations and policies; or

(2) Where the consideration for an issuer tender offer subject to this paragraph includes securities to be issued pursuant to the offer, any registration statement and/or prospectus relating thereto shall be filed with the Commission along with the Schedule 13E–4F referred to in paragraph (g)(1) of this section, and shall be disseminated, together with the home jurisdiction document(s) accompanying such Schedule, to shareholders of the issuer residing in the United States in accordance with such Canadian laws, regulations and policies.

NOTE: Notwithstanding the grant of an exemption from one or more of the applicable Canadian regulatory provisions imposing requirements that otherwise would be prescribed by this section, the issuer tender offer will be eligible to proceed in accordance with the requirements of this section if the Commission by order determines that the applicable Canadian regulatory provisions are adequate to protect the interest of investors.

(h) This section shall not apply to:

(1) Calls or redemptions of any security in accordance with the terms and conditions of its governing instruments;

(2) Offers to purchase securities evidenced by a scrip certificate, order form or similar document which represents a fractional interest in a share of stock or similar security;

(3) Offers to purchase securities pursuant to a statutory procedure for the purchase of dissenting security holders' securities;

(4) Any tender offer which is subject to section 14(d) of the Act;

(5) Offers to purchase from security holders who own an aggregate of not more than a specified number of shares that is less than one hundred: *Provided, however,* That:

(i) The offer complies with paragraph (f)(8)(i) of this section with respect to security holders who own a number of shares equal to or less than the specified number of shares, except that an issuer can elect to exclude participants in a plan as that term is defined in § 242.100 of this chapter, or to exclude security holders who do not own their shares as of a specified date determined by the issuer; and

(ii) The offer complies with paragraph (f)(8)(ii) of this section or the consideration paid pursuant to the offer is determined on the basis of a uniformly applied formula based on the market price of the subject security;

(6) An issuer tender offer made solely to effect a rescission offer: *Provided, however,* That the offer is registered under the Securities Act of 1933 (15 U.S.C. 77a *et seq.*), and the consideration is equal to the price paid by each security holder, plus legal interest if the issuer elects to or is required to pay legal interest;

(7) Offers by closed-end management investment companies to repurchase equity securities pursuant to § 270.23c–3 of this chapter;

(8) *Cross-border tender offers (Tier I).* Any issuer tender offer (including any exchange offer) where the issuer is a foreign private issuer as defined in § 240.3b–4 if the following conditions are satisfied.

(i) Except in the case of an issuer tender offer that is commenced during the pendency of a tender offer made by a third party in reliance on § 240.14d–1(c), U.S. holders do not hold more than 10 percent of the subject class sought in the offer (as determined under Instructions 2 or 3 to paragraph (h)(8) and paragraph (i) of this section);

(ii) The issuer or affiliate must permit U.S. holders to participate in the offer on terms at least as favorable as those offered any other holder of the

203

§ 240.13e-4

same class of securities that is the subject of the offer; however:

(A) *Registered exchange offers.* If the issuer or affiliate offers securities registered under the Securities Act of 1933 (15 U.S.C. 77a *et seq.*), the issuer or affiliate need not extend the offer to security holders in those states or jurisdictions that prohibit the offer or sale of the securities after the issuer or affiliate has made a good faith effort to register or qualify the offer and sale of securities in that state or jurisdiction, except that the issuer or affiliate must offer the same cash alternative to security holders in any such state or jurisdiction that it has offered to security holders in any other state or jurisdiction.

(B) *Exempt exchange offers.* If the issuer or affiliate offers securities exempt from registration under § 230.802 of this chapter, the issuer or affiliate need not extend the offer to security holders in those states or jurisdictions that require registration or qualification, except that the issuer or affiliate must offer the same cash alternative to security holders in any such state or jurisdiction that it has offered to security holders in any other state or jurisdiction.

(C) *Cash only consideration.* The issuer or affiliate may offer U.S. holders cash only consideration for the tender of the subject securities, notwithstanding the fact that the issuer or affiliate is offering security holders outside the United States a consideration that consists in whole or in part of securities of the issuer or affiliate, if the issuer or affiliate has a reasonable basis for believing that the amount of cash is substantially equivalent to the value of the consideration offered to non-U.S. holders, and either of the following conditions are satisfied:

(*1*) The offered security is a "margin security" within the meaning of Regulation T (12 CFR 220.2) and the issuer or affiliate undertakes to provide, upon the request of any U.S. holder or the Commission staff, the closing price and daily trading volume of the security on the principal trading market for the security as of the last trading day of each of the six months preceding the announcement of the offer and each of the trading days thereafter; or

(*2*) If the offered security is not a "margin security" within the meaning of Regulation T (12 CFR 220.2), the issuer or affiliate undertakes to provide, upon the request of any U.S. holder or the Commission staff, an opinion of an independent expert stating that the cash consideration offered to U.S. holders is substantially equivalent to the value of the consideration offered security holders outside the United States.

(D) *Disparate tax treatment.* If the issuer or affiliate offers "loan notes" solely to offer sellers tax advantages not available in the United States and these notes are neither listed on any organized securities market nor registered under the Securities Act of 1933 (15 U.S.C. 77a *et seq.*), the loan notes need not be offered to U.S. holders.

(iii) *Informational documents.* (A) If the issuer or affiliate publishes or otherwise disseminates an informational document to the holders of the securities in connection with the issuer tender offer (including any exchange offer), the issuer or affiliate must furnish that informational document, including any amendments thereto, in English, to the Commission on Form CB (§ 249.480 of this chapter) by the first business day after publication or dissemination. If the issuer or affiliate is a foreign company, it must also file a Form F-X (§ 239.42 of this chapter) with the Commission at the same time as the submission of Form CB to appoint an agent for service in the United States.

(B) The issuer or affiliate must disseminate any informational document to U.S. holders, including any amendments thereto, in English, on a comparable basis to that provided to security holders in the home jurisdiction.

(C) If the issuer or affiliate disseminates by publication in its home jurisdiction, the issuer or affiliate must publish the information in the United States in a manner reasonably calculated to inform U.S. holders of the offer.

(iv) An investment company registered or required to be registered under the Investment Company Act of 1940 (15 U.S.C. 80a-1 *et seq.*), other than a registered closed-end investment

Securities and Exchange Commission § 240.13e-4

company, may not use this paragraph (h)(8); or

(9) Any other transaction or transactions, if the Commission, upon written request or upon its own motion, exempts such transaction or transactions, either unconditionally, or on specified terms and conditions, as not constituting a fraudulent, deceptive or manipulative act or practice comprehended within the purpose of this section.

(i) *Cross-border tender offers (Tier II).* Any issuer tender offer (including any exchange offer) that meets the conditions in paragraph (i)(1) of this section shall be entitled to the exemptive relief specified in paragraph (i)(2) of this section, provided that such issuer tender offer complies with all the requirements of this section other than those for which an exemption has been specifically provided in paragraph (i)(2) of this section. In addition, any issuer tender offer (including any exchange offer) subject only to the requirements of section 14(e) of the Act and Regulation 14E (§§ 240.14e–1 through 240.14e–8) thereunder that meets the conditions in paragraph (i)(1) of this section also shall be entitled to the exemptive relief specified in paragraph (i)(2) of this section, to the extent needed under the requirements of Regulation 14E, so long as the tender offer complies with all requirements of Regulation 14E other than those for which an exemption has been specifically provided in paragraph (i)(2) of this section:

(1) *Conditions.* (i) The issuer is a foreign private issuer as defined in § 240.3b–4 and is not an investment company registered or required to be registered under the Investment Company Act of 1940 (15 U.S.C. 80a–1 *et seq.*), other than a registered closed-end investment company; and

(ii) Except in the case of an issuer tender offer commenced during the pendency of a tender offer made by a third party in reliance on § 240.14d–1(d), U.S. holders do not hold more than 40 percent of the class of securities sought in the offer (as determined in accordance with Instructions 2 or 3 to paragraphs (h)(8) and (i) of this section).

(2) *Exemptions.* The issuer tender offer shall comply with all requirements of this section other than the following:

(i) *Equal treatment—loan notes.* If the issuer or affiliate offers loan notes solely to offer sellers tax advantages not available in the United States and these notes are neither listed on any organized securities market nor registered under the Securities Act (15 U.S.C. 77a *et seq.*), the loan notes need not be offered to U.S. holders, notwithstanding paragraph (f)(8) and (h)(9) of this section.

(ii) *Equal treatment—separate U.S. and foreign offers.* Notwithstanding the provisions of paragraph (f)(8) of this section, an issuer or affiliate conducting an issuer tender offer meeting the conditions of paragraph (i)(1) of this section may separate the offer into multiple offers: one offer made to U.S. holders, which also may include all holders of American Depositary Shares representing interests in the subject securities, and one or more offers made to non-U.S. holders. The U.S. offer must be made on terms at least as favorable as those offered any other holder of the same class of securities that is the subject of the tender offers. U.S. holders may be included in the foreign offer(s) only where the laws of the jurisdiction governing such foreign offer(s) expressly preclude the exclusion of U.S. holders from the foreign offer(s) and where the offer materials distributed to U.S. holders fully and adequately disclose the risks of participating in the foreign offer(s).

(iii) *Notice of extensions.* Notice of extensions made in accordance with the requirements of the home jurisdiction law or practice will satisfy the requirements of § 240.14e–1(d).

(iv) *Prompt payment.* Payment made in accordance with the requirements of the home jurisdiction law or practice will satisfy the requirements of § 240.14e–1(c).

(v) *Suspension of withdrawal rights during counting of tendered securities.* The issuer or affiliate may suspend withdrawal rights required under paragraph (f)(2) of this section at the end of the offer and during the period that securities tendered into the offer are being counted, provided that:

(A) The issuer or affiliate has provided an offer period, including withdrawal rights, for a period of at least 20 U.S. business days;

205

§ 240.13e-4

(B) At the time withdrawal rights are suspended, all offer conditions have been satisfied or waived, except to the extent that the issuer or affiliate is in the process of determining whether a minimum acceptance condition included in the terms of the offer has been satisfied by counting tendered securities; and

(C) Withdrawal rights are suspended only during the counting process and are reinstated immediately thereafter, except to the extent that they are terminated through the acceptance of tendered securities.

(vi) *Early termination of an initial offering period.* An issuer or affiliate conducting an issuer tender offer may terminate an initial offering period, including a voluntary extension of that period, if at the time the initial offering period and withdrawal rights terminate, the following conditions are met:

(A) The initial offering period has been open for at least 20 U.S. business days;

(B) The issuer or affiliate has adequately discussed the possibility of and the impact of the early termination in the original offer materials;

(C) The issuer or affiliate provides a subsequent offering period after the termination of the initial offering period;

(D) All offer conditions are satisfied as of the time when the initial offering period ends; and

(E) The issuer or affiliate does not terminate the initial offering period or any extension of that period during any mandatory extension required under U.S. tender offer rules.

INSTRUCTIONS TO PARAGRAPH (h)(8) AND (i) OF THIS SECTION: 1. *Home jurisdiction* means both the jurisdiction of the issuer's incorporation, organization or chartering and the principal foreign market where the issuer's securities are listed or quoted.

2. *U.S. holder* means any security holder resident in the United States. To determine the percentage of outstanding securities held by U.S. holders:

i. Calculate the U.S. ownership as of a date no more than 60 days before and no more than 30 days after the public announcement of the tender offer. If you are unable to calculate as of a date within these time frames, the calculation may be made as of the most recent practicable date before public announcement, but in no event earlier than 120 days before announcement;

ii. Include securities underlying American Depositary Shares convertible or exchangeable into the securities that are the subject of the tender offer when calculating the number of subject securities outstanding, as well as the number held by U.S. holders. Exclude from the calculations other types of securities that are convertible or exchangeable into the securities that are the subject of the tender offer, such as warrants, options and convertible securities;

iii. Use the method of calculating record ownership in § 240.12g3-2(a), except that your inquiry as to the amount of securities represented by accounts of customers resident in the United States may be limited to brokers, dealers, banks and other nominees located in the United States, your jurisdiction of incorporation, and the jurisdiction that is the primary trading market for the subject securities, if different than your jurisdiction of incorporation;

iv. If, after reasonable inquiry, you are unable to obtain information about the amount of securities represented by accounts of customers resident in the United States, you may assume, for purposes of this definition, that the customers are residents of the jurisdiction in which the nominee has its principal place of business; and

v. Count securities as beneficially owned by residents of the United States as reported on reports of beneficial ownership that are provided to you or publicly filed and based on information otherwise provided to you.

3. If you are unable to conduct the analysis of U.S. ownership set forth in Instruction 2 above, U.S. holders will be presumed to hold 10 percent or less of the outstanding subject securities (40 percent for Tier II) so long as there is a primary trading market outside the United States, as defined in § 240.12h-6(f)(5) of this chapter, unless:

i. Average daily trading volume of the subject securities in the United States for a recent twelve-month period ending on a date no more than 60 days before the public announcement of the tender offer exceeds 10 percent (or 40 percent) of the average daily trading volume of that class of securities on a worldwide basis for the same period; or

ii. The most recent annual report or annual information filed or submitted by the issuer with securities regulators of the home jurisdiction or with the Commission or any jurisdiction in which the subject securities trade before the public announcement of the offer indicates that U.S. holders hold more than 10 percent (or 40 percent) of the outstanding subject class of securities; or

iii. You know or have reason to know, before the public announcement of the offer, that the level of U.S. ownership of the subject securities exceeds 10 percent (or 40 percent) of such securities. As an example, you

Securities and Exchange Commission § 240.13e–100

are deemed to know information about U.S. ownership of the subject class of securities that is publicly available and that appears in any filing with the Commission or any regulatory body in the home jurisdiction and, if different, the non-U.S. jurisdiction in which the primary trading market for the subject class of securities is located. You are also deemed to know information obtained or readily available from any other source that is reasonably reliable, including from persons you have retained to advise you about the transaction, as well as from third-party information providers. These examples are not intended to be exclusive.

4. *United States* means the United States of America, its territories and possessions, any State of the United States, and the District of Columbia.

5. The exemptions provided by paragraphs (h)(8) and (i) of this section are not available for any securities transaction or series of transactions that technically complies with paragraph (h)(8) and (i) of this section but are part of a plan or scheme to evade the provisions of this section.

(j)(1) It shall be a fraudulent, deceptive or manipulative act or practice, in connection with an issuer tender offer, for an issuer or an affiliate of such issuer, in connection with an issuer tender offer:

(i) To employ any device, scheme or artifice to defraud any person;

(ii) To make any untrue statement of a material fact or to omit to state a material fact necessary in order to make the statements made, in the light of the circumstances under which they were made, not misleading; or

(iii) To engage in any act, practice or course of business which operates or would operate as a fraud or deceit upon any person.

(2) As a means reasonably designed to prevent fraudulent, deceptive or manipulative acts or practices in connection with any issuer tender offer, it shall be unlawful for an issuer or an affiliate of such issuer to make an issuer tender offer unless:

(i) Such issuer or affiliate complies with the requirements of paragraphs (b), (c), (d), (e) and (f) of this section; and

(ii) The issuer tender offer is not in violation of paragraph (j)(1) of this section.

[44 FR 49410, Aug. 22, 1979]

EDITORIAL NOTE: For FEDERAL REGISTER citations affecting § 240.13e–4, see the List of CFR Sections Affected, which appears in the Finding Aids section of the printed volume and at *www.govinfo.gov*.

§ 240.13e–100 Schedule 13E–3, Transaction statement under section 13(e) of the Securities Exchange Act of 1934 and Rule 13e–3 (§ 240.13e–3) thereunder.

Securities and Exchange Commission,
Washington, D.C. 20549

Rule 13e–3 Transaction Statement under Section 13(e) of the Securities Exchange Act of 1934 (Amendment No. __)

_____
(Name of the Issuer)

_____
(Names of Persons Filing Statement)

_____
(Title of Class of Securities)

_____
(CUSIP Number of Class of Securities)

_____
(Name, Address, and Telephone Numbers of Person Authorized to Receive Notices and Communications on Behalf of the Persons Filing Statement)

This statement is filed in connection with (check the appropriate box):

a. [ ] The filing of solicitation materials or an information statement subject to Regulation 14A (§§ 240.14a–1 through 240.14b–2), Regulation 14C (§§ 240.14c–1 through 240.14c–101) or Rule 13e–3(c) (§ 240.13e–3(c)) under the Securities Exchange Act of 1934 ("the Act").

b. [ ] The filing of a registration statement under the Securities Act of 1933.

c. [ ] A tender offer.

d. [ ] None of the above.

Check the following box if the soliciting materials or information statement referred to in checking box (a) are preliminary copies: [ ]

Check the following box if the filing is a final amendment reporting the results of the transaction [ ]

General Instructions:

A. File eight copies of the statement, including all exhibits, with the Commission if paper filing is permitted.

B. This filing must be accompanied by a fee payable to the Commission as required by § 240.0–11(b). The filing fee exhibit required by Item 16(b) of this schedule must be submitted as required by Rule 408 of Regulation S–T (§ 232.408 of this chapter).

C. If the statement is filed by a general or limited partnership, syndicate or other group, the information called for by Items 3, 5, 6, 10 and 11 must be given with respect to:
(i) Each partner of the general partnership;
(ii) each partner who is, or functions as, a general partner of the limited partnership;
(iii) each member of the syndicate or group;

§ 240.13e–100

and (iv) each person controlling the partner or member. If the statement is filed by a corporation or if a person referred to in (i), (ii), (iii) or (iv) of this Instruction is a corporation, the information called for by the items specified above must be given with respect to: (a) Each executive officer and director of the corporation; (b) each person controlling the corporation; and (c) each executive officer and director of any corporation or other person ultimately in control of the corporation.

D. Depending on the type of Rule 13e–3 transaction (§ 240.13e–3(a)(3)), this statement must be filed with the Commission:

1. At the same time as filing preliminary or definitive soliciting materials or an information statement under Regulations 14A or 14C of the Act;

2. At the same time as filing a registration statement under the Securities Act of 1933;

3. As soon as practicable on the date a tender offer is first published, sent or given to security holders; or

4. At least 30 days before any purchase of securities of the class of securities subject to the Rule 13e–3 transaction, if the transaction does not involve a solicitation, an information statement, the registration of securities or a tender offer, as described in paragraphs 1, 2 or 3 of this Instruction; and

5. If the Rule 13e–3 transaction involves a series of transactions, the issuer or affiliate must file this statement at the time indicated in paragraphs 1 through 4 of this Instruction for the first transaction and must amend the schedule promptly with respect to each subsequent transaction.

E. If an item is inapplicable or the answer is in the negative, so state. The statement published, sent or given to security holders may omit negative and not applicable responses, except that responses to Items 7, 8 and 9 of this schedule must be provided in full. If the schedule includes any information that is not published, sent or given to security holders, provide that information or specifically incorporate it by reference under the appropriate item number and heading in the schedule. Do not recite the text of disclosure requirements in the schedule or any document published, sent or given to security holders. Indicate clearly the coverage of the requirements without referring to the text of the items.

F. Information contained in exhibits to the statement may be incorporated by reference in answer or partial answer to any item unless it would render the answer misleading, incomplete, unclear or confusing. A copy of any information that is incorporated by reference or a copy of the pertinent pages of a document containing the information must be submitted with this statement as an exhibit, unless it was previously filed with the Commission electronically on EDGAR. If an exhibit contains information responding to more than one item in the schedule, all information in that exhibit may be incorporated by reference once in response to the several items in the schedule for which it provides an answer. Information incorporated by reference is deemed filed with the Commission for all purposes of the Act.

G. If the Rule 13e–3 transaction also involves a transaction subject to Regulation 14A (§§ 240.14a–1 through 240.14b–2) or 14C (§§ 240.14c–1 through 240.14c–101) of the Act, the registration of securities under the Securities Act of 1933 and the General Rules and Regulations of that Act, or a tender offer subject to Regulation 14D (§§ 240.14d–1 through 240.14d–101) or § 240.13e–4, this statement must incorporate by reference the information contained in the proxy, information, registration or tender offer statement in answer to the items of this statement.

H. The information required by the items of this statement is intended to be in addition to any disclosure requirements of any other form or schedule that may be filed with the Commission in connection with the Rule 13e–3 transaction. If those forms or schedules require less information on any topic than this statement, the requirements of this statement control.

I. If the Rule 13e–3 transaction involves a tender offer, then a combined statement on Schedules 13E–3 and TO may be filed with the Commission under cover of Schedule TO (§ 240.14d–100). See Instruction J of Schedule TO (§ 240.14d–100).

J. Amendments disclosing a material change in the information set forth in this statement may omit any information previously disclosed in this statement.

Item 1. Summary Term Sheet

Furnish the information required by Item 1001 of Regulation M-A (§ 229.1001 of this chapter) unless information is disclosed to security holders in a prospectus that meets the requirements of § 230.421(d) of this chapter.

Item 2. Subject Company Information

Furnish the information required by Item 1002 of Regulation M-A (§ 229.1002 of this chapter).

Item 3. Identity and Background of Filing Person

Furnish the information required by Item 1003(a) through (c) of Regulation M-A (§ 229.1003 of this chapter).

Item 4. Terms of the Transaction

Furnish the information required by Item 1004(a) and (c) through (f) of Regulation M-A (§ 229.1004 of this chapter).

Securities and Exchange Commission

§ 240.13e-100

Item 5. Past Contacts, Transactions, Negotiations and Agreements

Furnish the information required by Item 1005(a) through (c) and (e) of Regulation M-A (§ 229.1005 of this chapter).

Item 6. Purposes of the Transaction and Plans or Proposals

Furnish the information required by Item 1006(b) and (c)(1) through (8) of Regulation M-A (§ 229.1006 of this chapter).

Instruction to Item 6: In providing the information specified in Item 1006(c) for this item, discuss any activities or transactions that would occur after the Rule 13e-3 transaction.

Item 7. Purposes, Alternatives, Reasons and Effects

Furnish the information required by Item 1013 of Regulation M-A (§ 229.1013 of this chapter).

Item 8. Fairness of the Transaction

Furnish the information required by Item 1014 of Regulation M-A (§ 229.1014 of this chapter).

Item 9. Reports, Opinions, Appraisals and Negotiations

Furnish the information required by Item 1015 of Regulation M-A (§ 229.1015 of this chapter).

Item 10. Source and Amounts of Funds or Other Consideration

Furnish the information required by Item 1007 of Regulation M-A (§ 229.1007 of this chapter).

Item 11. Interest in Securities of the Subject Company

Furnish the information required by Item 1008 of Regulation M-A (§ 229.1008 of this chapter).

Item 12. The Solicitation or Recommendation

Furnish the information required by Item 1012(d) and (e) of Regulation M-A (§ 229.1012 of this chapter).

Item 13. Financial Statements

Furnish the information required by Item 1010(a) through (b) of Regulation M-A (§ 229.1010 of this chapter) for the issuer of the subject class of securities.

Instructions to Item 13: 1. The disclosure materials disseminated to security holders may contain the summarized financial information required by Item 1010(c) of Regulation M-A (§ 229.1010 of this chapter) instead of the financial information required by Item 1010(a) and (b). In that case, the financial information required by Item 1010(a) and (b) of Regulation M-A must be disclosed directly or incorporated by reference in the statement. If summarized financial information is disseminated to security holders, include appropriate instructions on how more complete financial information can be obtained. If the summarized financial information is prepared on the basis of a comprehensive body of accounting principles other than U.S. GAAP, the summarized financial information must be accompanied by a reconciliation as described in Instruction 2.

2. If the financial statements required by this Item are prepared on the basis of a comprehensive body of accounting principles other than U.S. GAAP, provide a reconciliation to U.S. GAAP in accordance with Item 17 of Form 20-F (§ 249.220f of this chapter).

3. The filing person may incorporate by reference financial statements contained in any document filed with the Commission, solely for the purposes of this schedule, if: (a) The financial statements substantially meet the requirements of this Item; (b) an express statement is made that the financial statements are incorporated by reference; (c) the matter incorporated by reference is clearly identified by page, paragraph, caption or otherwise; and (d) if the matter incorporated by reference is not filed with this Schedule, an indication is made where the information may be inspected and copies obtained. Financial statements that are required to be presented in comparative form for two or more fiscal years or periods may not be incorporated by reference unless the material incorporated by reference includes the entire period for which the comparative data is required to be given. *See* General Instruction F to this Schedule.

Item 14. Persons/Assets, Retained, Employed, Compensated or Used

Furnish the information required by Item 1009 of Regulation M-A (§ 229.1009 of this chapter).

Item 15. Additional Information

Furnish the information required by Item 1011(b) and (c) of Regulation M-A (§ 229.1011(b) and (c) of this chapter).

Item 16. Exhibits

File each of the following as an exhibit to the Schedule:

(a) All documents specified in Item 1016(a) through (d), (f) and (g) of Regulation M-A (§ 229.1016 of this chapter); and

(b) The transaction valuation, fee rate, amount of filing fee and, as applicable, information relating to reliance on § 240.0-11(a)(2) in the tabular form indicated.

CALCULATION OF FILING FEE TABLES

§ 240.13e-100   17 CFR Ch. II (4-1-23 Edition)

TABLE 1—TRANSACTION VALUATION

	Transaction valuation	Fee rate	Amount of filing fee
Fees to Be Paid	X	X	X
Fees Previously Paid	X		X
Total Transaction Valuation	X		
Total Fees Due for Filing			X
Total Fees Previously Paid			X
Total Fee Offsets			X
Net Fee Due			X

TABLE 2—FEE OFFSET CLAIMS AND SOURCES

	Registrant or filer name	Form or filing type	File number	Initial filing date	Filing date	Fee offset claimed	Fee paid with fee offset source
Fee Offset Claims		X	X	X		X	
Fee Offset Sources	X	X	X		X		X

Instructions to the Calculation of Filing Fee Tables and Related Disclosure ("Instructions"):
1. General Requirements.
A. Applicable Table Requirements.
The "X" designation indicates the information required to be disclosed, as applicable, in tabular format. Add as many rows of each table as necessary.
B. Fee Rate.
For the current fee rate, see https://www.sec.gov/ofm/Article/feeamt.html.
C. Explanations.
If not otherwise explained in response to these instructions, disclose specific details relating to the fee calculation as necessary to clarify the information presented in each table, including references to the applicable provisions of Rule 0–11 (§ 240.0–11 of this chapter). All disclosure these Instructions require that is not specifically required to be presented in tabular format must appear in narrative format immediately after the table(s) to which it corresponds.
2. Table 1: Transaction Valuation Table and Related Disclosure.
A. Fees to Be Paid and Fees Previously Paid.
i. Fees to Be Paid.
Provide the information Table 1 requires for the line item "Fees to Be Paid" as follows:
a. Initial Filings.
For an initial filing on this schedule, provide the required information for the total transaction valuation.

b. Amendments with Then-Current Total Transaction Valuation Higher than Highest Total Transaction Valuation Previously Reported.
For amendments to this schedule that reflect a then-current total transaction valuation higher than the highest total transaction valuation previously reported, provide the required information for the incremental increase.
ii. Fees Previously Paid.
Provide the information Table 1 requires for the line item "Fees Previously Paid" for the prior initial filing or amendment to this transaction statement that reflected a then-current total transaction valuation that was the highest total transaction valuation previously reported.
B. Other Tabular Information.
Provide the following information in the table for the line items "Fees to be Paid" and "Fees Previously Paid", as applicable:
i. The transaction valuation computed pursuant to Exchange Act Rule 0–11;
ii. The fee rate; and
iii. The filing fee due, without regard to any previous payments or offsets.
C. Totals.
i. Total Transaction Valuation.
Provide the sum of the transaction valuations for the line items "Fees to be Paid" and "Fees Previously Paid."
ii. Total Fees Due for Filing.
Provide the sum of the fees due without regard to any previous payments or offsets for

Securities and Exchange Commission § 240.13e-100

the line items "Fees to be Paid" and "Fees Previously Paid."

iii. Total Fees Previously Paid.

Provide the aggregate of filing fees previously paid with this filing.

iv. Total Fee Offsets.

Provide the aggregate of the fee offsets that are claimed in Table 2 pursuant to Instruction 3.

v. Net Fee Due.

Provide the difference between (a) the total fees due for this transaction statement from the Total Fees Due for Filing row; and (b) the sum of (i) the aggregate of filing fees previously paid from the Total Fees Previously Paid row; and (ii) the aggregate fee offsets claimed from the Total Fee Offsets row.

D. Narrative Disclosure

Explain how the transaction valuation was determined.

3. Table 2: Fee Offset Claims and Sources.

A. Terminology.

For purposes of this Instruction 3 and Table 2, the term "submission" means any (i) initial filing of, or amendment (pre-effective or post-effective), to a fee-bearing document; or (ii) fee-bearing form of prospectus filed under Rule 424 under the Securities Act (§ 230.424 of this chapter), in all cases that was accompanied by a contemporaneous fee payment. For purposes of these instructions to Table 2, a contemporaneous fee payment is the payment of a required fee that is satisfied through the actual transfer of funds, and does not include any amount of a required fee satisfied through a claimed fee offset. Instruction 3.B.ii requires a filer that claims a fee offset under Rule 0–11(a)(2) to identify previous submissions with contemporaneous fee payments that are the original source to which the fee offsets claimed on this filing can be traced. See Instruction 3.C for an example.

B. Rule 0–11(a)(2).

If relying on Rule 0–11(a)(2) to offset some or all of the filing fee due on this transaction statement by amounts paid in connection with earlier filings (other than this Schedule 13E–3) relating to the same transaction, provide the following information:

i. Fee Offset Claims.

For each earlier filed Securities Act registration statement or Exchange Act document relating to the same transaction from which a fee offset is being claimed, provide the information that Table 2 requires for the line item "Fee Offset Claims". The "Fee Offset Claimed" column requires the dollar amount of the previously paid filing fee to be offset against the currently due fee.

Note to Instruction 3.B.i.

If claiming an offset from a Securities Act registration statement, provide a detailed explanation of the basis for the claimed offset.

ii. Fee Offset Sources.

With respect to amounts claimed as an offset under Rule 0–11(a)(2), identify those submissions with contemporaneous fee payments that are the original source to which those amounts can be traced. For each submission identified, provide the information that Table 2 requires for the line item "Fee Offset Sources". The "Fee Paid with Fee Offset Source" column requires the dollar amount of the contemporaneous fee payment made with respect to each identified submission that is the source of the fee offset claimed pursuant to Rule 0–11(a)(2).

C. Fee Offset Source Submission Identification Example.

A filer:

• Initially files a registration statement on Form S–1 on 1/15/20X1 (assigned file number 333–123456) with a fee payment of $10,000;

• Files pre-effective amendment number 1 to the Form S–1 (333–123456) on 2/15/20X1 with a fee payment of $15,000 and the registration statement goes effective on 2/20/20X1;

• Initially files a registration statement on Form S–1 on 1/15/20X4 (assigned file number 333–123467) with a fee payment of $25,000 and relies on Rule 457(p) to claim an offset of $10,000 related to the unsold securities registered on the previously filed Form S–1 (333–123456) and apply it to the $35,000 filing fee due and the registration statement goes effective on 2/15/20X4.

• Initially files a registration statement related to a tender offer on Form S–4 (assigned file number 333–123478) on 1/15/20X7 with a fee payment of $15,000 and relies on Rule '457(p) to claim an offset of $30,000 related to the unsold securities registered on the most recently effective Form S–1 (333–123467) filed on 1/15/20X4 and apply it to the $45,000 filing fee due.

• Initially files a Schedule TO related to the same tender offer on 1/22/20X7 and relies on Rule 0–11(a)(2) to claim an offset of $45,000 from the fee paid directly and by offset claimed on the Form S–4 (333–123478) filed 1/15/20X7 and apply it to the $45,000 filing fee due.

For the Schedule TO filed on 1/22/20X7, the filer can satisfy the submission identification requirement when it claims the $45,000 fee offset from the Form S–4 (333–123478) filed on 1/15/20X7 by referencing any combination of the Form S–4 (333–123478) filed on 1/15/20X7, the Form S–1 (333–123467) filed on 1/15/20X4, the pre-effective amendment to the Form S–1 (333–123456) filed on 2/15/20X1 or the initial filing of the Form S–1 (333–123456) on 1/15/20X1 in relation to which contemporaneous fee payments were made equal to $45,000.

One example could be:

• The Form S–4 (333–123478) filed on 1/15/20X7 in relation to the payment of $15,000 made with that submission;

• the Form S–1 (333–123467) filed on 1/15/20X4 in relation to the payment of $25,000 made with that submission; and

§ 240.13e–101

- the pre-effective amendment to the Form S–1 (333–123456) filed on 2/15/20X1 in relation to the payment of $5,000 out of the payment of $15,000 made with that submission (it would not matter if the filer cited to this pre-effective amendment and/or the initial submission of this Form S–1 (333–123456) on 1/15/20X1 as long as singly or together they were cited as relating to a total of $5,000 in this example).

In this example, the filer could not satisfy the submission identification requirement solely by citing to the Form S–4 (333–123478) filed on 1/15/20X7 because even though the offset claimed and available from that filing was $45,000, the contemporaneous fee payment made with that filing ($15,000) was less than the offset being claimed. As a result, the filer must also identify a prior submission or submissions with an aggregate of contemporaneous fee payment(s) of $30,000 as the original source(s) to which the rest of the claimed offset can be traced.

Signature. After due inquiry and to the best of my knowledge and belief, I certify that the information set forth in this statement is true, complete and correct.

_____
(Signature)

_____
(Name and title)

_____
(Date)

Instruction to Signature: The statement must be signed by the filing person or that person's authorized representative. If the statement is signed on behalf of a person by an authorized representative (other than an executive officer of a corporation or general partner of a partnership), evidence of the representative's authority to sign on behalf of the person must be filed with the statement. The name and any title of each person who signs the statement must be typed or printed beneath the signature. See § 240.12b–11 with respect to signature requirements.

[64 FR 61454, Nov. 10, 1999, as amended at 76 FR 6045, Feb. 2, 2011; 86 FR 70253, Dec. 9, 2021]

§ 240.13e–101 [Reserved]

§ 240.13e–102 Schedule 13E–4F. Tender offer statement pursuant to section 13(e)(1) of the Securities Exchange Act of 1934 and § 240.13e–4 thereunder.

Securities and Exchange Commission
Washington, DC 20549
Schedule 13E–4F

Issuer Tender Offer Statement Pursuant to Section 13(e)(1) of the Securities Exchange Act of 1934
[Amendment No. ____]

_____
(Exact name of Issuer as specified in its charter)

_____
(Translation of Issuer's Name into English (if applicable))

_____
(Jurisdiction of Issuer's Incorporation or Organization)

_____
(Name(s) of Person(s) Filing Statement)

_____
(Title of Class of Securities)

_____
(CUSIP Number of Class of Securities) (if applicable)

_____
(Name, address (including zip code) and telephone number (including area code) of person authorized to receive notices and communications on behalf of the person(s) filing statement)

_____
(Date tender offer first published, sent or given to securityholders)

GENERAL INSTRUCTIONS

I. ELIGIBILITY REQUIREMENTS FOR USE OF SCHEDULE 13E–4F

A. Schedule 13E–4F may be used by any foreign private issuer if: (1) The issuer is incorporated or organized under the laws of Canada or any Canadian province or territory; (2) the issuer is making a cash tender or exchange offer for the issuer's own securities; and (3) less than 40 percent of the class of such issuer's securities outstanding that is the subject of the tender offer is held by U.S. holders. The calculation of securities held by U.S. holders shall be made as of the end of the issuer's last quarter or, if such quarter terminated within 60 days of the filing date, as of the end of the issuer's preceding quarter.

Instructions

1. For purposes of this Schedule, "foreign private issuer" shall be construed in accordance with Rule 405 under the Securities Act.
2. For purposes of this Schedule, the term "U.S. holder" shall mean any person whose address appears on the records of the issuer, any voting trustee, any depositary, any share transfer agent or any person acting in a similar capacity on behalf of the issuer as being located in the United States.
3. If this Schedule is filed during the pendency of one or more ongoing cash tender or exchange offers for securities of the class subject to this offer that was commenced or was eligible to be commenced on Schedule 14D–1F and/or Form F–8 or Form F–80, the

Securities and Exchange Commission § 240.13e-102

date for calculation of U.S. ownership for purposes of this Schedule shall be the same as that date used by the initial bidder or issuer.

4. For purposes of this Schedule, the class of subject securities shall not include any securities that may be converted into or are exchangeable for the subject securities.

B. Any issuer using this Schedule must extend the cash tender or exchange offer to U.S. holders of the class of securities subject to the offer upon terms and conditions not less favorable than those extended to any other holder of the same class of such securities, and must comply with the requirements of any Canadian federal, provincial and/or territorial law, regulation or policy relating to the terms and conditions of the offer.

C. This Schedule shall not be used if the issuer is an investment company registered or required to be registered under the Investment Company Act of 1940.

II. FILING INSTRUCTIONS AND FEES

A.(1) The issuer must file this Schedule and any amendment to the Schedule (*see* Part I, Item 1.(b)), including all exhibits and other documents filed as part of the Schedule or amendment, in electronic format via the Commission's Electronic Data Gathering, Analysis, and Retrieval (EDGAR) system in accordance with the EDGAR rules set forth in Regulation S–T (17 CFR part 232). The filing fee exhibit required by paragraph (4) under "Part II—Information Not Required To Be Sent to Shareholders" must be submitted as required by Rule 408 of Regulation S–T (§ 232.408 of this chapter). For assistance with technical questions about EDGAR or to request an access code, call the EDGAR Filer Support Office at (202) 551–8900. For assistance with the EDGAR rules, call EDGAR filer support at (202) 551–8900.

(2) If filing the Schedule in paper under a hardship exemption in 17 CFR 232.201 or 232.202 of Regulation S–T, or as otherwise permitted, the issuer must file with the Commission at its principal office five copies of the complete Schedule and any amendment, including exhibits and all other documents filed as a part of the Schedule or amendment. The issuer must bind, staple or otherwise compile each copy in one or more parts without stiff covers. The issuer must further bind the Schedule or amendment on the side or stitching margin in a manner that leaves the reading matter legible. The issuer must provide three additional copies of the Schedule or amendment without exhibits to the Commission.

B. An electronic filer must provide the signatures required for the Schedule or amendment in accordance with 17 CFR 232.302 of Regulation S–T. An issuer filing in paper must have the original and at least one copy of the Schedule and any amendment signed in accordance with Exchange Act Rule 12b–11(d) (17 CFR 12b–11(d)) by the persons whose signatures are required for this Schedule or amendment. The issuer must also conform the unsigned copies.

C. At the time of filing this Schedule with the Commission, the issuer shall pay to the Commission in accordance with Rule 0–11 of the Exchange Act, a fee in U.S. dollars in the amount prescribed by section 13(e)(3) of the Exchange Act. See also Rule 0–9 of the Exchange Act.

(1) The value of the securities to be acquired solely for cash shall be the amount of cash to be paid for them, calculated into U.S. dollars.

(2) The value of the securities to be acquired with securities or other non-cash consideration, whether or not in combination with a cash payment for the same securities, shall be based on the market value of the securities to be acquired by the issuer as established in accordance with paragraph (3) of this section.

(3) When the fee is based upon the market value of the securities, such market value shall be established by either the average of the high and low prices reported on the consolidated reporting system (for exchange-traded securities and last sale reported for over-the-counter securities) or the average of the bid and asked price (for other over-the-counter securities) as of a specified date within 5 business days prior to the date of filing the Schedule. If there is no market for the securities to be acquired by the issuer, the value shall be based upon the book value of such securities computed as of the latest practicable date prior to the date of filing of the Schedule, unless the issuer of the securities is in bankruptcy or receivership or has an accumulated capital deficit, in which case one-third of the principal amount, par value or stated value of such securities shall be used.

D. If at any time after the initial payment of the fee the aggregate consideration offered is increased, an additional filing fee based upon such increase shall be paid with the required amended filing.

E. The issuer must file the Schedule or amendment in electronic format in the English language in accordance with 17 CFR 232.306 of Regulation S–T. The issuer may file part of the Schedule or amendment, or exhibit or other attachment to the Schedule or amendment, in both French and English if the issuer included the French text to comply with the requirements of the Canadian securities administrator or other Canadian authority and, for an electronic filing, if the filing is an HTML document, as defined in 17 CFR 232.11 of Regulation S–T. For both an electronic filing and a paper filing, the issuer may provide an English translation or English summary of a foreign language document as an exhibit or other attachment to the Schedule or amendment as permitted by

§ 240.13e–102

the rules of the applicable Canadian securities administrator.

F. A paper filer must number sequentially the signed original of the Schedule or amendment (in addition to any internal numbering that otherwise may be present) by handwritten, typed, printed or other legible form of notation from the first page through the last page of the Schedule or amendment, including any exhibits or attachments. A paper filer must disclose the total number of pages on the first page of the sequentially numbered Schedule or amendment.

III. COMPLIANCE WITH THE EXCHANGE ACT

A. Pursuant to Rule 13e–4(g) under the Exchange Act, the issuer shall be deemed to comply with the requirements of section 13(e)(1) of the Exchange Act and Rule 13e–4 and Schedule TO thereunder in connection with a cash tender or exchange offer for securities that may be made pursuant to this Schedule, *provided that,* if an exemption has been granted from the requirements of Canadian federal, provincial and/or territorial laws, regulations or policies, and the tender offer does not comply with requirements that otherwise would be prescribed by Rule 13e–4, the issuer (absent an order from the Commission) shall comply with the provisions of section 13(e)(1) of the Exchange Act and Rule 13e–4 and Schedule TO thereunder.

B. Any cash tender or exchange offer made pursuant to this Schedule is not exempt from the antifraud provisions of section 10(b) of the Exchange Act and Rule 10b–5 thereunder, section 13(e)(1) of the Exchange Act and Rule 13e–4(b)(1) thereunder, and section 14(e) of the Exchange Act and Rule 14e–3 thereunder, and this Schedule shall be deemed "filed" for purposes of section 18 of the Exchange Act.

C. The issuer's attention is directed to Regulation M (§§ 242.100 through 242.105 of this chapter), in the case of an issuer exchange offer, and to Rule 14e–5 under the Exchange Act (§ 240.14e–5), in the case of an issuer cash tender offer or issuer exchange offer. [*See* Exchange Act Release No. 29355 (June 21, 1991) containing an exemption from Rule 10b–13, the predecessor to Rule 14e–5.]

Part I—Information Required To Be Sent to Shareholders

Item 1. Home Jurisdiction Documents

(a) This Schedule shall be accompanied by the entire disclosure document or documents required to be delivered to holders of securities to be acquired by the issuer in the proposed transaction pursuant to the laws, regulations or policies of the Canadian jurisdiction in which the issuer is incorporated or organized, and any other Canadian federal, provincial and/or territorial law, regulation or policy relating to the terms and conditions of the offer. The Schedule need not include any documents incorporated by reference into such disclosure document(s) and not distributed to offerees pursuant to any such law, regulation or policy.

(b) Any amendment made by the issuer to a home jurisdiction document or documents shall be filed with the Commission under cover of this Schedule, which must indicate on the cover page the number of the amendment.

(c) In an exchange offer where securities of the issuer have been or are to be offered or cancelled in the transaction, such securities shall be registered on forms promulgated by the Commission under the Securities Act of 1933 including, where available, the Commission's Form F–8 or F–80 providing for inclusion in that registration statement of the home jurisdiction prospectus.

Item 2. Informational Legends

The following legends, to the extent applicable, shall appear on the outside front cover page of the home jurisdiction document(s) in bold-face roman type at least as high as ten-point modern type and at least two-points leaded:

"This tender offer is made by a foreign issuer for its own securities, and while the offer is subject to disclosure requirements of the country in which the issuer is incorporated or organized, investors should be aware that these requirements are different from those of the United States. Financial statements included herein, if any, have been prepared in accordance with foreign generally accepted accounting principles and thus may not be comparable to financial statements of United States companies.

"The enforcement by investors of civil liabilities under the federal securities laws may be affected adversely by the fact that the issuer is located in a foreign country, and that some or all of its officers and directors are residents of a foreign country.

"Investors should be aware that the issuer or its affiliates, directly or indirectly, may bid for or make purchases of the securities of the issuer subject to the offer, or of its related securities, during the period of the issuer tender offer, as permitted by applicable Canadian laws or provincial laws or regulations."

NOTE TO ITEM 2. If the home jurisdiction document(s) are delivered through an electronic medium, the issuer may satisfy the legibility requirements for the required legends relating to type size and fonts by presenting the legend in any manner reasonably calculated to draw security holder attention to it.

Securities and Exchange Commission § 240.13e-102

Part II—Information Not Required To Be Sent to Shareholders

The exhibits specified below shall be filed as part of the Schedule, but are not required to be sent to shareholders unless so required pursuant to the laws, regulations or policies of Canada and/or any of its provinces or territories. Exhibits shall be lettered or numbered appropriately for convenient reference.

(1) File any reports or information that, in accordance with the requirements of the home jurisdiction(s), must be made publicly available by the issuer in connection with the transaction, but need not be disseminated to shareholders.

(2) File copies of any documents incorporated by reference into the home jurisdiction document(s).

(3) If any name is signed to the Schedule pursuant to power of attorney, manually signed copies of any such power of attorney shall be filed. If the name of any officer signing on behalf of the issuer is signed pursuant to a power of attorney, certified copies of a resolution of the issuer's board of directors authorizing such signature also shall be filed.

(4) File the following information: The transaction valuation, fee rate, amount of filing fee and, as applicable, information relating to reliance on § 240.0–11(a)(2) in the tabular form indicated.

CALCULATION OF FILING FEE TABLES

TABLE 1—TRANSACTION VALUATION

	Transaction valuation	Fee rate	Amount of filing fee
Fees to Be Paid	X	X	X
Fees Previously Paid	X		X
Total Transaction Valuation	X		
Total Fees Due for Filing			X
Total Fees Previously Paid			X
Total Fee Offsets			X
Net Fee Due			X

TABLE 2—FEE OFFSET CLAIMS AND SOURCES

	Registrant or filer name	Form or filing type	File number	Initial filing date	Filing date	Fee offset claimed	Fee paid with fee offset source
Fee Offset Claims		X	X	X		X	
Fee Offset Sources	X	X	X		X		X

Instructions to the Calculation of Filing Fee Tables and Related Disclosure ("Instructions"):

1. General Requirements.
A. Applicable Table Requirements.
The "X" designation indicates the information required to be disclosed, as applicable, in tabular format. Add as many rows of each table as necessary.
B. Fee Rate.
For the current fee rate, see https://www.sec.gov/ofm/Article/feeamt.html.
C. Additional Filing Fee Provisions.
See General Instructions II.C and D of this Schedule for additional provisions regarding filing fees.
D. Explanations.

If not otherwise explained in response to these instructions, disclose specific details relating to the fee calculation as necessary to clarify the information presented in each table, including references to the applicable provisions of Rule 0–11 (§ 240.0–11 of this chapter). All disclosure these Instructions require that is not specifically required to be presented in tabular format must appear in narrative format immediately after the table(s) to which it corresponds.

2. Table 1: Transaction Valuation Table and Related Disclosure.
A. Fees to Be Paid and Fees Previously Paid.
i. Fees to Be Paid.

215

§ 240.13e-102

Provide the information Table 1 requires for the line item "Fees to Be Paid" as follows:

a. Initial Filings.

For an initial filing on this schedule, provide the required information for the total transaction valuation.

b. Amendments with Then-Current Total Transaction Valuation Higher than Highest Total Transaction Valuation Previously Reported.

For amendments to this schedule that reflect a then-current total transaction valuation higher than the highest total transaction valuation previously reported, provide the required information for the incremental increase.

ii. Fees Previously Paid.

Provide the information Table 1 requires for the line item "Fees Previously Paid" for the prior initial filing or amendment to this schedule that reflected a then-current total transaction valuation that was the highest total transaction valuation previously reported.

B. Other Tabular Information.

Provide the following information in the table for the line items "Fees to be Paid" and "Fees Previously Paid", as applicable:

i. The transaction valuation computed pursuant to Exchange Act Rule 0–11;

ii. The fee rate; and

iii. The filing fee due without regard to any previous payments or offsets.

C. Totals.

1. Total Transaction Valuation.

Provide the sum of the transaction valuations for the line items "Fees to be Paid" and "Fees Previously Paid".

ii. Total Fees Due for Filing.

Provide the sum of the fees due without regard to any previous payments or offsets for the line items "Fees to be Paid" and "Fees Previously Paid."

iii. Total Fees Previously Paid.

Provide the aggregate of filing fees previously paid with this filing.

iv. Total Fee Offsets.

Provide the aggregate of the fee offsets that are claimed in Table 2 pursuant to Instruction 3.

v. Net Fee Due.

Provide the difference between (a) the total fees due for this tender offer statement from the Total Fees Due for Filing row; and (b) the sum of (i) the aggregate of filing fees previously paid from the Total Fees Previously Paid row; and (ii) the aggregate fee offsets claimed from the Total Fee Offsets row.

D. Narrative Disclosure

Explain how the transaction valuation was determined.

3. Table 2: Fee Offset Claims and Sources.

A. Terminology.

For purposes of this Instruction 3 and Table 2, the term "submission" means any (i) initial filing of, or amendment (pre-effective or post-effective), to a fee-bearing document; or (ii) fee-bearing form of prospectus filed under Rule 424 under the Securities Act (§ 230.424 of this chapter), in all cases that was accompanied by a contemporaneous fee payment. For purposes of these instructions to Table 2, a contemporaneous fee payment is the payment of a required fee that is satisfied through the actual transfer of funds, and does not include any amount of a required fee satisfied through a claimed fee offset. Instruction 3.B.ii requires a filer that claims a fee offset under Rule 0–11(a)(2) to identify previous submissions with contemporaneous fee payments that are the original source to which the fee offsets claimed on this filing can be traced. *See* Instruction 3.C for an example.

B. Rule 0–11(a)(2).

If relying on Rule 0–11(a)(2) to offset some or all of the filing fee due on this tender offer statement by amounts paid in connection with earlier filings (other than this Schedule 13E–4F) relating to the same transaction, provide the following information:

i. Fee Offset Claims.

For each earlier filed Securities Act registration statement or Exchange Act document relating to the same transaction from which a fee offset is being claimed, provide the information that Table 2 requires for the line item "Fee Offset Claims". The "Fee Offset Claimed" column requires the dollar amount of the previously paid filing fee to be offset against the currently due fee.

Note to Instruction 3.B.i.

If claiming an offset from a Securities Act registration statement, provide a detailed explanation of the basis for the claimed offset.

ii. Fee Offset Sources.

With respect to amounts claimed as an offset under Rule 0–11(a)(2), identify those submissions with contemporaneous fee payments that are the original source to which those amounts can be traced. For each submission identified, provide the information that Table 2 requires for the line item "Fee Offset Sources". The "Fee Paid with Fee Offset Source" column requires the dollar amount of the contemporaneous fee payment made with respect to each identified submission that is the source of the fee offset claimed pursuant to Rule 0–11(a)(2).

C. Fee Offset Source Submission Identification Example.

A filer:

• Initially files a registration statement on Form S–1 on 1/15/20X1 (assigned file number 333–123456) with a fee payment of $10,000;

• Files pre-effective amendment number 1 to the Form S–1 (333–123456) on 2/15/20X1 with a fee payment of $15,000 and the registration statement goes effective on 2/20/20X1;

Securities and Exchange Commission

§ 240.13e-102

- Initially files a registration statement on Form S-1 on 1/15/20X4 (assigned file number 333-123467) with a fee payment of $25,000 and relies on Rule 457(p) to claim an offset of $10,000 related to the unsold securities registered on the previously filed Form S-1 (333-123456) and apply it to the $35,000 filing fee due and the registration statement goes effective on 2/15/20X4.
- Initially files a registration statement related to a tender offer on Form S-4 (assigned file number 333-123478) on 1/15/20X7 with a fee payment of $15,000 and relies on Rule 457(p) to claim an offset of $30,000 related to the unsold securities registered on the most recently effective Form S-1 (333-123467) filed on 1/15/20X4 and apply it to the $45,000 filing fee due.
- Initially files a Schedule TO related to the same tender offer on 1/22/20X7 and relies on Rule 0-11(a)(2) to claim an offset of $45,000 from the fee paid directly and by offset claimed on the Form S-4 (333-123478) filed 1/15/20X7 and apply it to the $45,000 filing fee due.

For the Schedule TO filed on 1/22/20X7, the filer can satisfy the submission identification requirement when it claims the $45,000 fee offset from the Form S-4 (333-123478) filed on 1/15/20X7 by referencing any combination of the Form S-4 (333-123478) filed on 1/15/20X7, the Form S-1 (333-123467) filed on 1/15/20X4, the pre-effective amendment to the Form S-1 (333-123456) filed on 2/15/20X1 or the initial filing of the Form S-1 (333-123456) on 1/15/20X1 in relation to which contemporaneous fee payments were made equal to $45,000. One example could be:

- The Form S-4 (333-123478) filed on 1/15/20X7 in relation to the payment of $15,000 made with that submission;
- the Form S-1 (333-123467) filed on 1/15/20X4 in relation to the payment of $25,000 made with that submission; and
- the pre-effective amendment to the Form S-1 (333-123456) filed on 2/15/20X1 in relation to the payment of $5,000 out of the payment of $15,000 made with that submission (it would not matter if the filer cited to this pre-effective amendment and/or the initial submission of this Form S-1 (333-123456) on 1/15/20X1 as long as singly or together they were cited as relating to a total of $5,000 in this example).

In this example, the filer could not satisfy the submission identification requirement solely by citing to the Form S-4 (333-123478) filed on 1/15/20X7 because even though the offset claimed and available from that filing was $45,000, the contemporaneous fee payment made with that filing ($15,000) was less than the offset being claimed. As a result, the filer must also identify a prior submission or submissions with an aggregate of contemporaneous fee payment(s) of $30,000 as the original source(s) to which the rest of the claimed offset can be traced.

Part III—Undertakings and Consent to Service of Process

1. Undertakings

The Schedule shall set forth the following undertakings of the issuer:

(a) The issuer undertakes to make available, in person or by telephone, representatives to respond to inquiries made by the Commission staff, and to furnish promptly, when requested to do so by the Commission staff, information relating to this Schedule or to transactions in said securities.

(b) The issuer also undertakes to disclose in the United States, on the same basis as it is required to make such disclosure pursuant to applicable Canadian federal and/or provincial or territorial laws, regulations or policies, or otherwise discloses, information regarding purchases of the issuer's securities in connection with the cash tender or exchange offer covered by this Schedule. Such information shall be set forth in amendments to this Schedule.

2. Consent to Service of Process

(a) At the time of filing this Schedule, the issuer shall file with the Commission a written irrevocable consent and power of attorney on Form F-X.

(b) Any change to the name or address of a registrant's agent for service shall be communicated promptly to the Commission by amendment to Form F-X referencing the file number of the registrant.

Part IV—Signatures

A. The Schedule shall be signed by each person on whose behalf the Schedule is filed or its authorized representative. If the Schedule is signed on behalf of a person by his authorized representative (other than an executive officer or general partner of the company), evidence of the representative's authority shall be filed with the Schedule.

B. The name of each person who signs the Schedule shall be typed or printed beneath his signature.

C. By signing this Schedule, the person(s) filing the Schedule consents without power of revocation that any administrative subpoena may be served, or any administrative proceeding, civil suit or civil action where the cause of action arises out of or relates to or concerns any offering made or purported to be made in connection with the filing on Schedule 13E-4F or any purchases or sales of any security in connection therewith, may be commenced against it in any administrative tribunal or in any appropriate court in any place subject to the jurisdiction of any state or of the United States by service of said subpoena or process upon the registrant's designated agent.

§ 240.13f-1

After due inquiry and to the best of my knowledge and belief, I certify that the information set forth in this statement is true, complete and correct.

_____
(Signature)

_____
(Name and Title)

_____
(Date)

[56 FR 30069, July 1, 1991, as amended at 61 FR 24656, May 15, 1996; 62 FR 544, Jan. 3, 1997; 67 FR 36705, May 24, 2002; 73 FR 17814, Apr. 1, 2008; 86 FR 70255, Dec. 9, 2021]

§ 240.13f-1 Reporting by institutional investment managers of information with respect to accounts over which they exercise investment discretion.

(a)(1) Every institutional investment manager which exercises investment discretion with respect to accounts holding section 13(f) securities, as defined in paragraph (c) of this section, having an aggregate fair market value on the last trading day of any month of any calendar year of at least $100,000,000 shall file a report on Form 13F (§ 249.325 of this chapter) with the Commission within 45 days after the last day of such calendar year and within 45 days after the last day of each of the first three calendar quarters of the subsequent calendar year.

(2) An amendment to a Form 13F (§ 249.325 of this chapter) report, other than one reporting only holdings that were not previously reported in a public filing for the same period, must set forth the complete text of the Form 13F. Amendments must be numbered sequentially.

(b) For the purposes of this rule, "investment descretion" has the meaning set forth in section 3(a)(35) of the Act (15 U.S.C. 78c(a)(35)). An institutional investment manager shall also be deemed to exercise "investment discretion" with respect to all accounts over which any person under its control exercises investment discretion.

(c) For purposes of this rule "section 13(f) securities" shall mean equity securities of a class described in section 13(d)(1) of the Act that are admitted to trading on a national securities exchange or quoted on the automated quotation system of a registered securities association. In determining what classes of securities are section 13(f) securities, an institutional investment manager may rely on the most recent list of such securities published by the Commission pursuant to section 13(f)(4) of the Act (15 U.S.C. 78m(f)(4)). Only securities of a class on such list shall be counted in determining whether an institutional investment manager must file a report under this rule (§ 240.13f-1(a)) and only those securities shall be reported in such report. Where a person controls the issuer of a class of equity securities which are "section 13(f) securities" as defined in this rule, those securities shall not be deemed to be "section 13(f) securities" with respect to the controlling person, provided that such person does not otherwise exercise investment descretion with respect to accounts with fair market value of at least $100,000,000 within the meaning of paragraph (a) of this section.

(Secs. 3(b), 13(f) and 23 of the Exchange Act (15 U.S.C. 78c(b), 78m(f) and 78w))

[43 FR 26705, June 22, 1978, as amended at 44 FR 3034, Jan. 15, 1979; 64 FR 2849, Jan. 19, 1999; 76 FR 71876, Nov. 21, 2011]

§ 240.13h-1 Large trader reporting.

(a) *Definitions.* For purposes of this section:

(1) The term *large trader* means any person that:

(i) Directly or indirectly, including through other persons controlled by such person, exercises investment discretion over one or more accounts and effects transactions for the purchase or sale of any NMS security for or on behalf of such accounts, by or through one or more registered broker-dealers, in an aggregate amount equal to or greater than the identifying activity level; or

(ii) Voluntarily registers as a large trader by filing electronically with the Commission Form 13H (§ 249.327 of this chapter).

(2) The term *person* has the same meaning as in Section 13(h)(8)(E) of the Securities Exchange Act of 1934 (15 U.S.C. 78m(h)(8)(E)).

(3) The term *control* (including the terms *controlling, controlled by* and *under common control with*) means the possession, direct or indirect, of the power to direct or cause the direction of the management and policies of a

Securities and Exchange Commission § 240.13h-1

person, whether through the ownership of securities, by contract, or otherwise. For purposes of this section only, any person that directly or indirectly has the right to vote or direct the vote of 25% or more of a class of voting securities of an entity or has the power to sell or direct the sale of 25% or more of a class of voting securities of such entity, or in the case of a partnership, has the right to receive, upon dissolution, or has contributed, 25% or more of the capital, is presumed to control that entity.

(4) The term *investment discretion* has the same meaning as in Section 3(a)(35) of the Securities Exchange Act of 1934 (15 U.S.C. 78c(3)(a)(35)). A person's employees who exercise investment discretion within the scope of their employment are deemed to do so on behalf of such person.

(5) The term *NMS security* has the meaning provided for in § 242.600(b)(54) of this chapter.

(6) The term *transaction* or *transactions* means all transactions in NMS securities, excluding the purchase or sale of such securities pursuant to exercises or assignments of option contracts. For the sole purpose of determining whether a person is a large trader, the following transactions are excluded from this definition:

(i) Any journal or bookkeeping entry made to an account in order to record or memorialize the receipt or delivery of funds or securities pursuant to the settlement of a transaction;

(ii) Any transaction that is part of an offering of securities by or on behalf of an issuer, or by an underwriter on behalf of an issuer, or an agent for an issuer, whether or not such offering is subject to registration under the Securities Act of 1933 (15 U.S.C. 77a), provided, however, that this exemption shall not include an offering of securities effected through the facilities of a national securities exchange;

(iii) Any transaction that constitutes a gift;

(iv) Any transaction effected by a court appointed executor, administrator, or fiduciary pursuant to the distribution of a decedent's estate;

(v) Any transaction effected pursuant to a court order or judgment;

(vi) Any transaction effected pursuant to a rollover of qualified plan or trust assets subject to Section 402(a)(5) of the Internal Revenue Code (26 U.S.C. 1 *et seq.*);

(vii) Any transaction between an employer and its employees effected pursuant to the award, allocation, sale, grant, or exercise of a NMS security, option or other right to acquire securities at a pre-established price pursuant to a plan which is primarily for the purpose of an issuer benefit plan or compensatory arrangement; or

(viii) Any transaction to effect a business combination, including a reclassification, merger, consolidation, or tender offer subject to Section 14(d) of the Securities Exchange Act of 1934 (15 U.S.C. 78n(d)); an issuer tender offer or other stock buyback by an issuer; or a stock loan or equity repurchase agreement.

(7) The term *identifying activity level* means: aggregate transactions in NMS securities that are equal to or greater than:

(i) During a calendar day, either two million shares or shares with a fair market value of $20 million; or

(ii) During a calendar month, either twenty million shares or shares with a fair market value of $200 million.

(8) The term *reporting activity level* means:

(i) Each transaction in NMS securities, effected in a single account during a calendar day, that is equal to or greater than 100 shares;

(ii) Any transaction in NMS securities for fewer than 100 shares, effected in a single account during a calendar day, that a registered broker-dealer may deem appropriate; or

(iii) Such other amount that may be established by order of the Commission from time to time.

(9) The term *Unidentified Large Trader* means each person who has not complied with the identification requirements of paragraphs (b)(1) and (b)(2) of this section that a registered broker-dealer knows or has reason to know is a large trader. For purposes of determining under this section whether a registered broker-dealer has reason to know that a person is large trader, a registered broker-dealer need take into

§ 240.13h–1

account only transactions in NMS securities effected by or through such broker-dealer.

(b) *Identification requirements for large traders*—(1) *Form 13H.* Except as provided in paragraph (b)(3) of this section, each large trader shall file electronically Form 13H (17 CFR 249.327) with the Commission, in accordance with the instructions contained therein:

(i) Promptly after first effecting aggregate transactions, or after effecting aggregate transactions subsequent to becoming inactive pursuant to paragraph (b)(3) of this section, equal to or greater than the identifying activity level;

(ii) Within 45 days after the end of each full calendar year; and

(iii) Promptly following the end of a calendar quarter in the event that any of the information contained in a Form 13H filing becomes inaccurate for any reason.

(2) *Disclosure of large trader status.* Each large trader shall disclose to the registered broker-dealers effecting transactions on its behalf its large trader identification number and each account to which it applies. A large trader on Inactive Status pursuant to paragraph (b)(3) of this section must notify broker-dealers promptly after filing for reactivated status with the Commission.

(3) *Filing requirement*—(i) *Compliance by controlling person.* A large trader shall not be required to separately comply with the requirements of this paragraph (b) if a person who controls the large trader complies with all of the requirements under paragraphs (b)(1), (b)(2), and (b)(4) of this section applicable to such large trader with respect to all of its accounts.

(ii) *Compliance by controlled person.* A large trader shall not be required to separately comply with the requirements of this paragraph (b) if one or more persons controlled by such large trader collectively comply with all of the requirements under paragraphs (b)(1), (b)(2), and (b)(4) of this section applicable to such large trader with respect to all of its accounts.

(iii) *Inactive status.* A large trader that has not effected aggregate transactions at any time during the previous full calendar year in an amount equal to or greater than the identifying activity level shall become inactive upon filing a Form 13H (17 CFR 249.327) and thereafter shall not be required to file Form 13H or disclose its large trader status unless and until its transactions again are equal to or greater than the identifying activity level. A large trader that has ceased operations may elect to become inactive by filing an amended Form 13H to indicate its terminated status.

(4) *Other information.* Upon request, a large trader must promptly provide additional descriptive or clarifying information that would allow the Commission to further identify the large trader and all accounts through which the large trader effects transactions.

(c) *Aggregation*—(1) *Transactions.* For the purpose of determining whether a person is a large trader, the following shall apply:

(i) The volume or fair market value of transactions in equity securities and the volume or fair market value of the equity securities underlying transactions in options on equity securities, purchased and sold, shall be aggregated;

(ii) The fair market value of transactions in options on a group or index of equity securities (or based on the value thereof), purchased and sold, shall be aggregated; and

(iii) Under no circumstances shall a person subtract, offset, or net purchase and sale transactions, in equity securities or option contracts, and among or within accounts, when aggregating the volume or fair market value of transactions for purposes of this section.

(2) *Accounts.* Under no circumstances shall a person disaggregate accounts to avoid the identification requirements of this section.

(d) *Recordkeeping requirements for broker and dealers*—(1) *Generally.* Every registered broker-dealer shall maintain records of all information required under paragraphs (d)(2) and (d)(3) of this section for all transactions effected directly or indirectly by or through:

(i) An account such broker-dealer carries for a large trader or an Unidentified Large Trader, or

Securities and Exchange Commission § 240.13h–1

(ii) If the broker-dealer is a large trader, any proprietary or other account over which such broker-dealer exercises investment discretion.

(iii) Additionally, where a non-broker-dealer carries an account for a large trader or an Unidentified Large Trader, the broker-dealer effecting transactions directly or indirectly for such large trader or Unidentified Large Trader shall maintain records of all of the information required under paragraphs (d)(2) and (d)(3) of this section for those transactions.

(2) *Information.* The information required to be maintained for all transactions shall include:

(i) The clearing house number or alpha symbol of the broker or dealer submitting the information and the clearing house numbers or alpha symbols of the entities on the opposite side of the transaction;

(ii) Identifying symbol assigned to the security;

(iii) Date transaction was executed;

(iv) The number of shares or option contracts traded in each specific transaction; whether each transaction was a purchase, sale, or short sale; and, if an option contract, whether the transaction was a call or put option, an opening purchase or sale, a closing purchase or sale, or an exercise or assignment;

(v) Transaction price;

(vi) Account number;

(vii) Identity of the exchange or other market center where the transaction was executed.

(viii) A designation of whether the transaction was effected or caused to be effected for the account of a customer of such registered broker-dealer, or was a proprietary transaction effected or caused to be effected for the account of such broker-dealer;

(ix) If part or all of an account's transactions at the registered broker-dealer have been transferred or otherwise forwarded to one or more accounts at another registered broker-dealer, an identifier for this type of transaction; and if part or all of an account's transactions at the reporting broker-dealer have been transferred or otherwise received from one or more other registered broker-dealers, an identifier for this type of transaction;

(x) If part or all of an account's transactions at the reporting broker-dealer have been transferred or otherwise received from another account at the reporting broker-dealer, an identifier for this type of transaction; and if part or all of an account's transactions at the reporting broker-dealer have been transferred or otherwise forwarded to one or more other accounts at the reporting broker-dealer, an identifier for this type of transaction;

(xi) If a transaction was processed by a depository institution, the identifier assigned to the account by the depository institution;

(xii) The time that the transaction was executed; and

(xiii) The large trader identification number(s) associated with the account, unless the account is for an Unidentified Large Trader.

(3) *Information relating to Unidentified Large Traders.* With respect to transactions effected directly or indirectly by or through the account of an Unidentified Large Trader, the information required to be maintained for all transactions also shall include such Unidentified Large Trader's name, address, date the account was opened, and tax identification number(s).

(4) *Retention.* The records and information required to be made and kept pursuant to the provisions of this section shall be kept for such periods of time as provided in § 240.17a–4(b).

(5) *Availability of information.* The records and information required to be made and kept pursuant to the provisions of this rule shall be available on the morning after the day the transactions were effected (including Saturdays and holidays).

(e) *Reporting requirements for brokers and dealers.* Upon the request of the Commission, every registered broker-dealer who is itself a large trader or carries an account for a large trader or an Unidentified Large Trader shall electronically report to the Commission, using the infrastructure supporting § 240.17a–25, in machine-readable form and in accordance with instructions issued by the Commission, all information required under paragraphs (d)(2) and (d)(3) of this section for all transactions effected directly or

§ 240.13k-1

indirectly by or through accounts carried by such broker-dealer for large traders and Unidentified Large Traders, equal to or greater than the reporting activity level. Additionally, where a non-broker-dealer carries an account for a large trader or an Unidentified Large Trader, the broker-dealer effecting such transactions directly or indirectly for a large trader shall electronically report using the infrastructure supporting § 240.17a–25, in machine-readable form and in accordance with instructions issued by the Commission, all information required under paragraphs (d)(2) and (d)(3) of this section for such transactions equal to or greater than the reporting activity level. Such reports shall be submitted to the Commission no later than the day and time specified in the request for transaction information, which shall be no earlier than the opening of business of the day following such request, unless in unusual circumstances the same-day submission of information is requested.

(f) *Monitoring safe harbor.* For the purposes of this rule, a registered broker-dealer shall be deemed not to know or have reason to know that a person is a large trader if it does not have actual knowledge that a person is a large trader and it establishes policies and procedures reasonably designed to:

(1) Identify persons who have not complied with the identification requirements of paragraphs (b)(1) and (b)(2) of this section but whose transactions effected through an account or a group of accounts carried by such broker-dealer or through which such broker-dealer executes transactions, as applicable (and considering account name, tax identification number, or other identifying information available on the books and records of such broker-dealer) equal or exceed the identifying activity level;

(2) Treat any persons identified in paragraph (f)(1) of this section as an Unidentified Large Trader for purposes of this section; and

(3) Inform any person identified in paragraph (f)(1) of this section of its potential obligations under this section.

(g) *Exemptions.* Upon written application or upon its own motion, the Commission may by order exempt, upon specified terms and conditions or for stated periods, any person or class of persons or any transaction or class of transactions from the provisions of this section to the extent that such exemption is consistent with the purposes of the Securities Exchange Act of 1934 (15 U.S.C. 78a).

[76 FR 47002, Aug. 3, 2011, as amended at 83 FR 58427, Nov. 19, 2018; 86 FR 18809, Apr. 9, 2021]

§ 240.13k-1 Foreign bank exemption from the insider lending prohibition under section 13(k).

(a) For the purpose of this section:

(1) *Foreign bank* means an institution:

(i) The home jurisdiction of which is other than the United States;

(ii) That is regulated as a bank in its home jurisdiction; and

(iii) That engages directly in the business of banking.

(2) *Home jurisdiction* means the country, political subdivision or other place in which a foreign bank is incorporated or organized.

(3) *Engages directly in the business of banking* means that an institution engages directly in banking activities that are usual for the business of banking in its home jurisdiction.

(4) *Affiliate, parent* and *subsidiary* have the same meaning as under 17 CFR 240.12b–2.

(b) An issuer that is a foreign bank or the parent or other affiliate of a foreign bank is exempt from the prohibition of extending, maintaining, arranging for, or renewing credit in the form of a personal loan to or for any of its directors or executive officers under section 13(k) of the Act (15 U.S.C. 78m(k)) with respect to any such loan made by the foreign bank as long as:

(1) Either:

(i) The laws or regulations of the foreign bank's home jurisdiction require the bank to insure its deposits or be subject to a deposit guarantee or protection scheme; or

(ii) The Board of Governors of the Federal Reserve System has determined that the foreign bank or another bank organized in the foreign bank's home jurisdiction is subject to comprehensive supervision or regulation on a consolidated basis by the bank supervisor in its home jurisdiction under 12 CFR 211.24(c); and

(2) The loan by the foreign bank to any of its directors or executive officers or those of its parent or other affiliate:

(i) Is on substantially the same terms as those prevailing at the time for comparable transactions by the foreign bank with other persons who are not executive officers, directors or employees of the foreign bank, its parent or other affiliate; or

(ii) Is pursuant to a benefit or compensation program that is widely available to the employees of the foreign bank, its parent or other affiliate and does not give preference to any of the executive officers or directors of the foreign bank, its parent or other affiliate over any other employees of the foreign bank, its parent or other affiliate; or

(iii) Has received express approval by the bank supervisor in the foreign bank's home jurisdiction.

NOTES TO PARAGRAPH (b): 1. The exemption provided in paragraph (b) of this section applies to a loan by the subsidiary of a foreign bank to a director or executive officer of the foreign bank, its parent or other affiliate as long as the subsidiary is under the supervision or regulation of the bank supervisor in the foreign bank's home jurisdiction, the subsidiary's loan meets the requirements of paragraph (b)(2) of this section, and the foreign bank meets the requirements of paragraph (b)(1) of this section.

2. For the purpose of paragraph (b)(1)(ii) of this section, a foreign bank may rely on a determination by the Board of Governors of the Federal Reserve System that another bank in the foreign bank's home jurisdiction is subject to comprehensive supervision or regulation on a consolidated basis by the bank supervisor under 12 CFR 211.24(c) as long as the foreign bank is under substantially the same banking supervision or regulation as the other bank in their home jurisdiction.

(c) As used in paragraph (1) of section 13(k) of the Act (15 U.S.C. 78m(k)(1)), *issuer* does not include a foreign government, as defined under 17 CFR 230.405, that files a registration statement under the Securities Act of 1933 (15 U.S.C. 77a *et seq.*) on Schedule B.

[69 FR 24024, Apr. 30, 2004]

§ 240.13n-1 Registration of security-based swap data repository.

(a) *Definitions.* For purposes of this section —

(1) *Non-resident security-based swap data repository* means:

(i) In the case of an individual, one who resides in or has his principal place of business in any place not in the United States;

(ii) In the case of a corporation, one incorporated in or having its principal place of business in any place not in the United States; or

(iii) In the case of a partnership or other unincorporated organization or association, one having its principal place of business in any place not in the United States.

(2) *Tag* (including the term *tagged*) has the same meaning as set forth in Rule 11 of Regulation S-T (17 CFR 232.11).

(b) An application for the registration of a security-based swap data repository and all amendments thereto shall be filed electronically in a tagged data format on Form SDR (17 CFR 249.1500) with the Commission in accordance with the instructions contained therein. As part of the application process, each security-based swap data repository shall provide additional information to any representative of the Commission upon request.

(c) Within 90 days of the date of the publication of notice of the filing of such application (or within such longer period as to which the applicant consents), the Commission shall –

(1) By order grant registration; or

(2) Institute proceedings to determine whether registration should be granted or denied. Such proceedings shall include notice of the issues under consideration and opportunity for hearing on the record and shall be concluded within 180 days of the date of the publication of notice of the filing of the application for registration under paragraph (b) of this section. At the conclusion of such proceedings, the Commission, by order, shall grant or

§ 240.13n–2

deny such registration. The Commission may extend the time for conclusion of such proceedings for up to 90 days if it finds good cause for such extension and publishes its reasons for so finding or for such longer period as to which the applicant consents.

(3) The Commission shall grant the registration of a security-based swap data repository if the Commission finds that such security-based swap data repository is so organized, and has the capacity, to be able to assure the prompt, accurate, and reliable performance of its functions as a security-based swap data repository, comply with any applicable provision of the federal securities laws and the rules and regulations thereunder, and carry out its functions in a manner consistent with the purposes of section 13(n) of the Act (15 U.S.C. 78m(n)) and the rules and regulations thereunder. The Commission shall deny the registration of a security-based swap data repository if it does not make any such finding.

(d) If any information reported in items 1 through 17, 26, and 48 of Form SDR (17 CFR 249.1500) or in any amendment thereto is or becomes inaccurate for any reason, whether before or after the registration has been granted, the security-based swap data repository shall promptly file an amendment on Form SDR updating such information. In addition, the security-based swap data repository shall annually file an amendment on Form SDR within 60 days after the end of each fiscal year of such security-based swap data repository.

(e) Each security-based swap data repository shall designate and authorize on Form SDR an agent in the United States, other than a Commission member, official, or employee, who shall accept any notice or service of process, pleadings, or other documents in any action or proceedings brought against the security-based swap data repository to enforce the federal securities laws and the rules and regulations thereunder.

(f) Any non-resident security-based swap data repository applying for registration pursuant to this section shall:

(1) Certify on Form SDR that the security-based swap data repository can, as a matter of law, and will provide the Commission with prompt access to the books and records of such security-based swap data repository and can, as a matter of law, and will submit to onsite inspection and examination by the Commission, and

(2) Provide an opinion of counsel that the security-based swap data repository can, as a matter of law, provide the Commission with prompt access to the books and records of such security-based swap data repository and can, as a matter of law, submit to onsite inspection and examination by the Commission.

(g) An application for registration or any amendment thereto that is filed pursuant to this section shall be considered a "report" filed with the Commission for purposes of sections 18(a) and 32(a) of the Act (15 U.S.C. 78r(a) and 78ff(a)) and the rules and regulations thereunder and other applicable provisions of the United States Code and the rules and regulations thereunder.

[80 FR 14550, Mar. 19, 2015]

§ 240.13n–2 Withdrawal from registration; revocation and cancellation.

(a) *Definition.* For purposes of this section, *tag* (including the term *tagged*) has the same meaning as set forth in Rule 11 of Regulation S–T (17 CFR 232.11).

(b) A registered security-based swap data repository may withdraw from registration by filing a withdrawal from registration on Form SDR (17 CFR 249.1500) electronically in a tagged data format. The security-based swap data repository shall designate on Form SDR a person to serve as the custodian of the security-based swap data repository's books and records. When filing a withdrawal from registration on Form SDR, a security-based swap data repository shall update any inaccurate information.

(c) A withdrawal from registration filed by a security-based swap data repository shall become effective for all matters (except as provided in this paragraph (c)) on the 60th day after the filing thereof with the Commission, within such longer period of time as to which such security-based swap data repository consents or which the Commission, by order, may determine as necessary or appropriate in the public interest or for the protection of investors, or within such shorter period of time as the Commission may determine.

(d) A withdrawal from registration that is filed pursuant to this section shall be considered a "report" filed with the Commission for purposes of sections 18(a) and 32(a) of the Act (15 U.S.C. 78r(a) and 78ff(a)) and the rules and regulations thereunder and other applicable provisions of the United States Code and the rules and regulations thereunder.

(e) If the Commission finds, on the record after notice and opportunity for hearing, that any registered security-based swap data repository has obtained its registration by making any false and misleading statements with respect to any material fact or has violated or failed to comply with any provision of the federal securities laws and the rules and regulations thereunder, the Commission, by order, may revoke the registration. Pending final determination of whether any registration shall be revoked, the Commission, by order, may suspend such registration, if such suspension appears to the Commission, after notice and opportunity for hearing on the record, to be necessary or appropriate in the public interest or for the protection of investors.

(f) If the Commission finds that a registered security-based swap data repository is no longer in existence or has ceased to do business in the capacity specified in its application for registration, the Commission, by order, may cancel the registration.

[80 FR 14550, Mar. 19, 2015]

§ 240.13n-3 Registration of successor to registered security-based swap data repository.

(a) In the event that a security-based swap data repository succeeds to and continues the business of a security-based swap data repository registered pursuant to section 13(n) of the Act (15 U.S.C. 78m(n)), the registration of the predecessor shall be deemed to remain effective as the registration of the successor if, within 30 days after such succession, the successor files an application for registration on Form SDR (17 CFR 249.1500), and the predecessor files a withdrawal from registration on Form SDR; *provided, however,* that the registration of the predecessor security-based swap data repository shall cease to be effective 90 days after the publication of notice of the filing of the application for registration on Form SDR filed by the successor security-based swap data repository.

(b) Notwithstanding paragraph (a) of this section, if a security-based swap data repository succeeds to and continues the business of a registered predecessor security-based swap data repository, and the succession is based solely on a change in the predecessor's date or state of incorporation, form of organization, or composition of a partnership, the successor may, within 30 days after the succession, amend the registration of the predecessor security-based swap data repository on Form SDR (17 CFR 249.1500) to reflect these changes. This amendment shall be deemed an application for registration filed by the predecessor and adopted by the successor.

[80 FR 14550, Mar. 19, 2015]

§ 240.13n-4 Duties and core principles of security-based swap data repository.

(a) *Definitions.* For purposes of this section—

(1) *Affiliate* of a security-based swap data repository means a person that, directly or indirectly, controls, is controlled by, or is under common control with the security-based swap data repository.

(2) *Board* means the board of directors of the security-based swap data repository or a body performing a function similar to the board of directors of the security-based swap data repository.

(3) *Control* (including the terms *controlled by* and *under common control with*) means the possession, direct or indirect, of the power to direct or cause the direction of the management and policies of a person, whether through the ownership of voting securities, by contract, or otherwise. A person is presumed to control another person if the person:

§ 240.13n-4

(i) Is a director, general partner, or officer exercising executive responsibility (or having similar status or functions);

(ii) Directly or indirectly has the right to vote 25 percent or more of a class of voting securities or has the power to sell or direct the sale of 25 percent or more of a class of voting securities; or

(iii) In the case of a partnership, has the right to receive, upon dissolution, or has contributed, 25 percent or more of the capital.

(4) *Director* means any member of the board.

(5) *Direct electronic access* means access, which shall be in a form and manner acceptable to the Commission, to data stored by a security-based swap data repository in an electronic format and updated at the same time as the security-based swap data repository's data is updated so as to provide the Commission or any of its designees with the ability to query or analyze the data in the same manner that the security-based swap data repository can query or analyze the data.

(6) *Market participant* means any person participating in the security-based swap market, including, but not limited to, security-based swap dealers, major security-based swap participants, and any other counterparties to a security-based swap transaction.

(7) *Nonaffiliated third party* of a security-based swap data repository means any person except:

(i) The security-based swap data repository;

(ii) Any affiliate of the security-based swap data repository; or

(iii) A person employed by a security-based swap data repository and any entity that is not the security-based swap data repository's affiliate (and "nonaffiliated third party" includes such entity that jointly employs the person).

(8) *Person associated with a security-based swap data repository* means:

(i) Any partner, officer, or director of such security-based swap data repository (or any person occupying a similar status or performing similar functions);

(ii) Any person directly or indirectly controlling, controlled by, or under common control with such security-based swap data repository; or

(iii) Any employee of such security-based swap data repository.

(b) *Duties.* To be registered, and maintain registration, as a security-based swap data repository, a security-based swap data repository shall:

(1) Subject itself to inspection and examination by any representative of the Commission;

(2) Accept data as prescribed in Regulation SBSR (17 CFR 242.900 through 242.909) for each security-based swap;

(3) Confirm, as prescribed in Rule 13n–5 (§ 240.13n–5), with both counterparties to the security-based swap the accuracy of the data that was submitted;

(4) Maintain, as prescribed in Rule 13n–5, the data described in Regulation SBSR in such form, in such manner, and for such period as provided therein and in the Act and the rules and regulations thereunder;

(5) Provide direct electronic access to the Commission (or any designee of the Commission, including another registered entity);

(6) Provide the information described in Regulation SBSR in such form and at such frequency as prescribed in Regulation SBSR to comply with the public reporting requirements set forth in section 13(m) of the Act (15 U.S.C. 78m(m)) and the rules and regulations thereunder;

(7) At such time and in such manner as may be directed by the Commission, establish automated systems for monitoring, screening, and analyzing security-based swap data;

(8) Maintain the privacy of any and all security-based swap transaction information that the security-based swap data repository receives from a security-based swap dealer, counterparty, or any registered entity as prescribed in Rule 13n–9 (§ 240.13n–9);

(9) On a confidential basis, pursuant to section 24 of the Act (15 U.S.C. 78x), upon request, and after notifying the Commission of the request in a manner consistent with paragraph (d) of this section, make available security-based swap data obtained by the security-based swap data repository, including individual counterparty trade and position data, to the following:

Securities and Exchange Commission § 240.13n-4

(i) The Board of Governors of the Federal Reserve System and any Federal Reserve Bank;
(ii) The Office of the Comptroller of the Currency;
(iii) The Federal Deposit Insurance Corporation;
(iv) The Farm Credit Administration;
(v) The Federal Housing Finance Agency;
(vi) The Financial Stability Oversight Council;
(vii) The Commodity Futures Trading Commission;
(viii) The Department of Justice;
(ix) The Office of Financial Research; and
(x) Any other person that the Commission determines to be appropriate, conditionally or unconditionally, by order, including, but not limited to—
(A) Foreign financial supervisors (including foreign futures authorities);
(B) Foreign central banks;
(C) Foreign ministries; and
(D) Other foreign authorities;
(10) Before sharing information with any entity described in paragraph (b)(9) of this section, there shall be in effect an arrangement between the Commission and the entity (in the form of a memorandum of understanding or otherwise) to address the confidentiality of the security-based swap information made available to the entity; this arrangement shall be deemed to satisfy the requirement, set forth in section 13(n)(5)(H) of the Act (15 U.S.C. 78m(n)(5)(H)), that the security-based swap data repository receive a written agreement from the entity stating that the entity shall abide by the confidentiality requirements described in section 24 of the Act (15 U.S.C. 78x) relating to the information on security-based swap transactions that is provided; and
(11) Designate an individual to serve as a chief compliance officer.
(c) *Compliance with core principles.* A security-based swap data repository shall comply with the core principles as described in this paragraph.
(1) *Market access to services and data.* Unless necessary or appropriate to achieve the purposes of the Act and the rules and regulations thereunder, the security-based swap data repository shall not adopt any policies or procedures or take any action that results in an unreasonable restraint of trade or impose any material anticompetitive burden on the trading, clearing, or reporting of transactions. To comply with this core principle, each security-based swap data repository shall:
(i) Ensure that any dues, fees, or other charges imposed by, and any discounts or rebates offered by, a security-based swap data repository are fair and reasonable and not unreasonably discriminatory. Such dues, fees, other charges, discounts, or rebates shall be applied consistently across all similarly-situated users of such security-based swap data repository's services, including, but not limited to, market participants, market infrastructures (including central counterparties), venues from which data can be submitted to the security-based swap data repository (including exchanges, security-based swap execution facilities, electronic trading venues, and matching and confirmation platforms), and third party service providers;
(ii) Permit market participants to access specific services offered by the security-based swap data repository separately;
(iii) Establish, monitor on an ongoing basis, and enforce clearly stated objective criteria that would permit fair, open, and not unreasonably discriminatory access to services offered and data maintained by the security-based swap data repository as well as fair, open, and not unreasonably discriminatory participation by market participants, market infrastructures, venues from which data can be submitted to the security-based swap data repository, and third party service providers that seek to connect to or link with the security-based swap data repository; and
(iv) Establish, maintain, and enforce written policies and procedures reasonably designed to review any prohibition or limitation of any person with respect to access to services offered, directly or indirectly, or data maintained by the security-based swap data repository and to grant such person access to such services or data if such person has been discriminated against unfairly.
(2) *Governance arrangements.* Each security-based swap data repository shall

§ 240.13n–4

establish governance arrangements that are transparent to fulfill public interest requirements under the Act and the rules and regulations thereunder; to carry out functions consistent with the Act, the rules and regulations thereunder, and the purposes of the Act; and to support the objectives of the Federal Government, owners, and participants. To comply with this core principle, each security-based swap data repository shall:

(i) Establish governance arrangements that are well defined and include a clear organizational structure with effective internal controls;

(ii) Establish governance arrangements that provide for fair representation of market participants;

(iii) Provide representatives of market participants, including end-users, with the opportunity to participate in the process for nominating directors and with the right to petition for alternative candidates; and

(iv) Establish, maintain, and enforce written policies and procedures reasonably designed to ensure that the security-based swap data repository's senior management and each member of the board or committee that has the authority to act on behalf of the board possess requisite skills and expertise to fulfill their responsibilities in the management and governance of the security-based swap data repository, have a clear understanding of their responsibilities, and exercise sound judgment about the security-based swap data repository's affairs.

(3) *Conflicts of interest.* Each security-based swap data repository shall establish and enforce written policies and procedures reasonably designed to minimize conflicts of interest in the decision-making process of the security-based swap data repository and establish a process for resolving any such conflicts of interest. Such conflicts of interest include, but are not limited to: conflicts between the commercial interests of a security-based swap data repository and its statutory and regulatory responsibilities; conflicts in connection with the commercial interests of certain market participants or linked market infrastructures, third party service providers, and others; conflicts between, among, or with persons associated with the security-based swap data repository, market participants, affiliates of the security-based swap data repository, and nonaffiliated third parties; and misuse of confidential information, material, nonpublic information, and/or intellectual property. To comply with this core principle, each security-based swap data repository shall:

(i) Establish, maintain, and enforce written policies and procedures reasonably designed to identify and mitigate potential and existing conflicts of interest in the security-based swap data repository's decision-making process on an ongoing basis;

(ii) With respect to the decision-making process for resolving any conflicts of interest, require the recusal of any person involved in such conflict from such decision-making; and

(iii) Establish, maintain, and enforce reasonable written policies and procedures regarding the security-based swap data repository's non-commercial and/or commercial use of the security-based swap transaction information that it receives from a market participant, any registered entity, or any other person.

(d) *Notification requirement compliance.* To satisfy the notification requirement of the data access provisions of paragraph (b)(9) of this section, a security-based swap data repository shall inform the Commission upon its receipt of the first request for security-based swap data from a particular entity (which may include any request to be provided ongoing online or electronic access to the data), and the repository shall maintain records of all information related to the initial and all subsequent requests for data access from that entity, including records of all instances of online or electronic access, and records of all data provided in connection with such requests or access.

NOTE TO § 240.13N–4: This rule is not intended to limit, or restrict, the applicability of other provisions of the federal securities laws, including, but not limited to, section 13(m) of the Act (15 U.S.C. 78m(m)) and the rules and regulations thereunder.

[80 FR 14550, Mar. 19, 2015, as amended at 81 FR 60607, Nov. 1, 2016]

Securities and Exchange Commission § 240.13n–5

§ 240.13n–5 Data collection and maintenance.

(a) *Definitions.* For purposes of this section—

(1) *Asset class* means those security-based swaps in a particular broad category, including, but not limited to, credit derivatives and equity derivatives.

(2) *Position* means the gross and net notional amounts of open security-based swap transactions aggregated by one or more attributes, including, but not limited to, the:

(i) Underlying instrument, index, or reference entity;

(ii) Counterparty;

(iii) Asset class;

(iv) Long risk of the underlying instrument, index, or reference entity; and

(v) Short risk of the underlying instrument, index, or reference entity.

(3) *Transaction data* means all information reported to a security-based swap data repository pursuant to the Act and the rules and regulations thereunder, except for information provided pursuant to Rule 906(b) of Regulation SBSR (17 CFR 242.906(b)).

(b) *Requirements.* Every security-based swap data repository registered with the Commission shall comply with the following data collection and data maintenance standards:

(1) *Transaction data.* (i) Every security-based swap data repository shall establish, maintain, and enforce written policies and procedures reasonably designed for the reporting of complete and accurate transaction data to the security-based swap data repository and shall accept all transaction data that is reported in accordance with such policies and procedures.

(ii) If a security-based swap data repository accepts any security-based swap in a particular asset class, the security-based swap data repository shall accept all security-based swaps in that asset class that are reported to it in accordance with its policies and procedures required by paragraph (b)(1)(i) of this section.

(iii) Every security-based swap data repository shall establish, maintain, and enforce written policies and procedures reasonably designed to satisfy itself that the transaction data that has been submitted to the security-based swap data repository is complete and accurate, and clearly identifies the source for each trade side and the pairing method (if any) for each transaction in order to identify the level of quality of the transaction data.

(iv) Every security-based swap data repository shall promptly record the transaction data it receives.

(2) *Positions.* Every security-based swap data repository shall establish, maintain, and enforce written policies and procedures reasonably designed to calculate positions for all persons with open security-based swaps for which the security-based swap data repository maintains records.

(3) Every security-based swap data repository shall establish, maintain, and enforce written policies and procedures reasonably designed to ensure that the transaction data and positions that it maintains are complete and accurate.

(4) Every security-based swap data repository shall maintain transaction data and related identifying information for not less than five years after the applicable security-based swap expires and historical positions for not less than five years:

(i) In a place and format that is readily accessible and usable to the Commission and other persons with authority to access or view such information; and

(ii) In an electronic format that is non-rewriteable and non-erasable.

(5) Every security-based swap data repository shall establish, maintain, and enforce written policies and procedures reasonably designed to prevent any provision in a valid security-based swap from being invalidated or modified through the procedures or operations of the security-based swap data repository.

(6) Every security-based swap data repository shall establish procedures and provide facilities reasonably designed to effectively resolve disputes over the accuracy of the transaction data and positions that are recorded in the security-based swap data repository.

(7) If a security-based swap data repository ceases doing business, or

§ 240.13n-6

ceases to be registered pursuant to section 13(n) of the Act (15 U.S.C. 78m(n)) and the rules and regulations thereunder, it must continue to preserve, maintain, and make accessible the transaction data and historical positions required to be collected, maintained, and preserved by this section in the manner required by the Act and the rules and regulations thereunder and for the remainder of the period required by this section.

(8) Every security-based swap data repository shall make and keep current a plan to ensure that the transaction data and positions that are recorded in the security-based swap data repository continue to be maintained in accordance with Rule 13n-5(b)(7) (§ 240.13n-5(b)(7)), which shall include procedures for transferring the transaction data and positions to the Commission or its designee (including another registered security-based swap data repository).

[80 FR 14550, Mar. 19, 2015]

§ 240.13n-6 Automated systems.

Every security-based swap data repository, with respect to those systems that support or are integrally related to the performance of its activities, shall establish, maintain, and enforce written policies and procedures reasonably designed to ensure that its systems provide adequate levels of capacity, integrity, resiliency, availability, and security.

[80 FR 14550, Mar. 19, 2015]

§ 240.13n-7 Recordkeeping of security-based swap data repository.

(a) Every security-based swap data repository shall make and keep current the following books and records relating to its business:

(1) A record for each office listing, by name or title, each person at that office who, without delay, can explain the types of records the security-based swap data repository maintains at that office and the information contained in those records; and

(2) A record listing each officer, manager, or person performing similar functions of the security-based swap data repository responsible for establishing policies and procedures that are reasonably designed to ensure compliance with the Act and the rules and regulations thereunder.

(b) *Recordkeeping rule for security-based swap data repositories.* (1) Every security-based swap data repository shall keep and preserve at least one copy of all documents, including all documents and policies and procedures required by the Act and the rules and regulations thereunder, correspondence, memoranda, papers, books, notices, accounts, and other such records as shall be made or received by it in the course of its business as such.

(2) Every security-based swap data repository shall keep all such documents for a period of not less than five years, the first two years in a place that is immediately available to representatives of the Commission for inspection and examination.

(3) Every security-based swap data repository shall, upon request of any representative of the Commission, promptly furnish to the possession of such representative copies of any documents required to be kept and preserved by it pursuant to paragraphs (a) and (b) of this section.

(c) If a security-based swap data repository ceases doing business, or ceases to be registered pursuant to section 13(n) of the Act (15 U.S.C. 78m(n)) and the rules and regulations thereunder, it must continue to preserve, maintain, and make accessible the records and data required to be collected, maintained and preserved by this section in the manner required by this section and for the remainder of the period required by this section.

(d) This section does not apply to transaction data and positions collected and maintained pursuant to Rule 13n-5 (§ 240.13n-5).

[80 FR 14550, Mar. 19, 2015]

§ 240.13n-8 Reports to be provided to the Commission.

Every security-based swap data repository shall promptly report to the Commission, in a form and manner acceptable to the Commission, such information as the Commission determines to be necessary or appropriate for the Commission to perform the duties of the Commission under the Act

Securities and Exchange Commission § 240.13n-9

and the rules and regulations thereunder.

[80 FR 14550, Mar. 19, 2015]

§ 240.13n-9 Privacy requirements of security-based swap data repository.

(a) *Definitions.* For purposes of this section—

(1) *Affiliate* of a security-based swap data repository means a person that, directly or indirectly, controls, is controlled by, or is under common control with the security-based swap data repository.

(2) *Control* (including the terms *controlled by* and *under common control with*) means the possession, direct or indirect, of the power to direct or cause the direction of the management and policies of a person, whether through the ownership of voting securities, by contract, or otherwise. A person is presumed to control another person if the person:

(i) Is a director, general partner, or officer exercising executive responsibility (or having similar status or functions);

(ii) Directly or indirectly has the right to vote 25 percent or more of a class of voting securities or has the power to sell or direct the sale of 25 percent or more of a class of voting securities; or

(iii) In the case of a partnership, has the right to receive, upon dissolution, or has contributed, 25 percent or more of the capital.

(3) *Market participant* means any person participating in the security-based swap market, including, but not limited to, security-based swap dealers, major security-based swap participants, and any other counterparties to a security-based swap transaction.

(4) *Nonaffiliated third party* of a security-based swap data repository means any person except:

(i) The security-based swap data repository;

(ii) The security-based swap data repository's affiliate; or

(iii) A person employed by a security-based swap data repository and any entity that is not the security-based swap data repository's affiliate (and *nonaffiliated third party* includes such entity that jointly employs the person).

(5) *Nonpublic personal information* means:

(i) Personally identifiable information that is not publicly available information; and

(ii) Any list, description, or other grouping of market participants (and publicly available information pertaining to them) that is derived using personally identifiable information that is not publicly available information.

(6) *Personally identifiable information* means any information:

(i) A market participant provides to a security-based swap data repository to obtain service from the security-based swap data repository;

(ii) About a market participant resulting from any transaction involving a service between the security-based swap data repository and the market participant; or

(iii) The security-based swap data repository obtains about a market participant in connection with providing a service to that market participant.

(7) *Person associated with a security-based swap data repository* means:

(i) Any partner, officer, or director of such security-based swap data repository (or any person occupying a similar status or performing similar functions);

(ii) Any person directly or indirectly controlling, controlled by, or under common control with such security-based swap data repository; or

(iii) Any employee of such security-based swap data repository.

(b) Each security-based swap data repository shall:

(1) Establish, maintain, and enforce written policies and procedures reasonably designed to protect the privacy of any and all security-based swap transaction information that the security-based swap data repository receives from a security-based swap dealer, counterparty, or any registered entity. Such policies and procedures shall include, but are not limited to, policies and procedures to protect the privacy of any and all security-based swap transaction information that the security-based swap data repository shares with affiliates and nonaffiliated third parties; and

§ 240.13n-10

(2) Establish and maintain safeguards, policies, and procedures reasonably designed to prevent the misappropriation or misuse, directly or indirectly, of:

(i) Any confidential information received by the security-based swap data repository, including, but not limited to, trade data, position data, and any nonpublic personal information about a market participant or any of its customers;

(ii) Material, nonpublic information; and/or

(iii) Intellectual property, such as trading strategies or portfolio positions, by the security-based swap data repository or any person associated with the security-based swap data repository for their personal benefit or the benefit of others. Such safeguards, policies, and procedures shall address, without limitation:

(A) Limiting access to such confidential information, material, nonpublic information, and intellectual property;

(B) Standards pertaining to the trading by persons associated with the security-based swap data repository for their personal benefit or the benefit of others; and

(C) Adequate oversight to ensure compliance with this subparagraph.

[80 FR 14550, Mar. 19, 2015]

§ 240.13n-10 Disclosure requirements of security-based swap data repository.

(a) *Definition.* For purposes of this section, *market participant* means any person participating in the over-the-counter derivatives market, including, but not limited to, security-based swap dealers, major security-based swap participants, and any other counterparties to a security-based swap transaction.

(b) Before accepting any security-based swap data from a market participant or upon a market participant's request, a security-based swap data repository shall furnish to the market participant a disclosure document that contains the following written information, which must reasonably enable the market participant to identify and evaluate accurately the risks and costs associated with using the services of the security-based swap data repository:

(1) The security-based swap data repository's criteria for providing others with access to services offered and data maintained by the security-based swap data repository;

(2) The security-based swap data repository's criteria for those seeking to connect to or link with the security-based swap data repository;

(3) A description of the security-based swap data repository's policies and procedures regarding its safeguarding of data and operational reliability, as described in Rule 13n-6 (§ 240.13n-6);

(4) A description of the security-based swap data repository's policies and procedures reasonably designed to protect the privacy of any and all security-based swap transaction information that the security-based swap data repository receives from a security-based swap dealer, counterparty, or any registered entity, as described in Rule 13n-9(b)(1) (§ 240.13n-9(b)(1));

(5) A description of the security-based swap data repository's policies and procedures regarding its non-commercial and/or commercial use of the security-based swap transaction information that it receives from a market participant, any registered entity, or any other person;

(6) A description of the security-based swap data repository's dispute resolution procedures involving market participants, as described in Rule 13n-5(b)(6) (§ 240.13n-5(b)(6));

(7) A description of all the security-based swap data repository's services, including any ancillary services;

(8) The security-based swap data repository's updated schedule of any dues; unbundled prices, rates, or other fees for all of its services, including any ancillary services; any discounts or rebates offered; and the criteria to benefit from such discounts or rebates; and

(9) A description of the security-based swap data repository's governance arrangements.

[80 FR 14550, Mar. 19, 2015]

Securities and Exchange Commission § 240.13n–11

§ 240.13n–11 Chief compliance officer of security-based swap data repository; compliance reports and financial reports.

(a) *In general.* Each security-based swap data repository shall identify on Form SDR (17 CFR 249.1500) a person who has been designated by the board to serve as a chief compliance officer of the security-based swap data repository. The compensation, appointment, and removal of the chief compliance officer shall require the approval of a majority of the security-based swap data repository's board.

(b) *Definitions.* For purposes of this section—

(1) *Board* means the board of directors of the security-based swap data repository or a body performing a function similar to the board of directors of the security-based swap data repository.

(2) *Director* means any member of the board.

(3) *EDGAR Filer Manual* has the same meaning as set forth in Rule 11 of Regulation S–T (17 CFR 232.11).

(4) *Interactive Data Financial Report* has the same meaning as set forth in Rule 11 of Regulation S–T (17 CFR 232.11).

(5) *Material change* means a change that a chief compliance officer would reasonably need to know in order to oversee compliance of the security-based swap data repository.

(6) *Material compliance matter* means any compliance matter that the board would reasonably need to know to oversee the compliance of the security-based swap data repository and that involves, without limitation:

(i) A violation of the federal securities laws by the security-based swap data repository, its officers, directors, employees, or agents;

(ii) A violation of the policies and procedures of the security-based swap data repository by the security-based swap data repository, its officers, directors, employees, or agents; or

(iii) A weakness in the design or implementation of the policies and procedures of the security-based swap data repository.

(7) *Official filing* has the same meaning as set forth in Rule 11 of Regulation S–T (17 CFR 232.11).

(8) *Senior officer* means the chief executive officer or other equivalent officer.

(9) *Tag* (including the term *tagged*) has the same meaning as set forth in Rule 11 of Regulation S–T (17 CFR 232.11).

(c) *Duties.* Each chief compliance officer of a security-based swap data repository shall:

(1) Report directly to the board or to the senior officer of the security-based swap data repository;

(2) Review the compliance of the security-based swap data repository with respect to the requirements and core principles described in section 13(n) of the Act (15 U.S.C. 78m(n)) and the rules and regulations thereunder;

(3) In consultation with the board or the senior officer of the security-based swap data repository, take reasonable steps to resolve any material conflicts of interest that may arise;

(4) Be responsible for administering each policy and procedure that is required to be established pursuant to section 13 of the Act (15 U.S.C. 78m) and the rules and regulations thereunder;

(5) Take reasonable steps to ensure compliance with the Act and the rules and regulations thereunder relating to security-based swaps, including each rule prescribed by the Commission under section 13 of the Act (15 U.S.C. 78m);

(6) Establish procedures for the remediation of noncompliance issues identified by the chief compliance officer through any—

(i) Compliance office review;

(ii) Look-back;

(iii) Internal or external audit finding;

(iv) Self-reported error; or

(v) Validated complaint; and

(7) Establish and follow appropriate procedures for the handling, management response, remediation, retesting, and closing of noncompliance issues.

(d) *Compliance reports*—(1) *In general.* The chief compliance officer shall annually prepare and sign a report that contains a description of the compliance of the security-based swap data repository with respect to the Act and the rules and regulations thereunder and each policy and procedure of the security-based swap data repository (including the code of ethics and conflicts of interest policies of the security-based swap data repository). Each compliance report shall also contain, at a minimum, a description of:

(i) The security-based swap data repository's enforcement of its policies and procedures;

(ii) Any material changes to the policies and procedures since the date of the preceding compliance report;

(iii) Any recommendation for material changes to the policies and procedures as a result of the annual review, the rationale for such recommendation, and whether such policies and procedures were or will be modified by the security-based swap data repository to incorporate such recommendation; and

(iv) Any material compliance matters identified since the date of the preceding compliance report.

(2) *Requirements.* A financial report of the security-based swap data repository shall be filed with the Commission as described in paragraph (g) of this section and shall accompany a compliance report as described in paragraph (d)(1) of this section. The compliance report shall include a certification by the chief compliance officer that, to the best of his or her knowledge and reasonable belief, and under penalty of law, the compliance report is accurate and complete. The compliance report shall also be filed in a tagged data format in accordance with the instructions contained in the EDGAR Filer Manual, as described in Rule 301 of Regulation S–T (17 CFR 232.301).

(e) The chief compliance officer shall submit the annual compliance report to the board for its review prior to the filing of the report with the Commission.

(f) *Financial reports.* Each financial report filed with a compliance report shall:

(1) Be a complete set of financial statements of the security-based swap data repository that are prepared in accordance with U.S. generally accepted accounting principles for the most recent two fiscal years of the security-based swap data repository;

(2) Be audited in accordance with the standards of the Public Company Accounting Oversight Board by a registered public accounting firm that is qualified and independent in accordance with Rule 2–01 of Regulation S–X (17 CFR 210.2–01);

(3) Include a report of the registered public accounting firm that complies with paragraphs (a) through (d) of Rule 2–02 of Regulation S–X (17 CFR 210.2–02);

(4) If the security-based swap data repository's financial statements contain consolidated information of a subsidiary of the security-based swap data repository, provide condensed financial information, in a financial statement footnote, as to the financial position, changes in financial position and results of operations of the security-based swap data repository, as of the same dates and for the same periods for which audited consolidated financial statements are required. Such financial information need not be presented in greater detail than is required for condensed statements by Rules 10–01(a)(2), (3), and (4) of Regulation S–X (17 CFR 210.10–01). Detailed footnote disclosure that would normally be included with complete financial statements may be omitted with the exception of disclosures regarding material contingencies, long-term obligations, and guarantees. Descriptions of significant provisions of the security-based swap data repository's long-term obligations, mandatory dividend or redemption requirements of redeemable stocks, and guarantees of the security-based swap data repository shall be provided along with a five-year schedule of maturities of debt. If the material contingencies, long-term obligations, redeemable stock requirements, and guarantees of the security-based swap data repository have been separately disclosed in the consolidated statements, then they need not be repeated in this schedule; and

(5) Be provided as an official filing in accordance with the EDGAR Filer Manual and include, as part of the official filing, an Interactive Data Financial Report filed in accordance with Rule 407 of Regulation S–T (17 CFR 232.407).

(g) Reports filed pursuant to paragraphs (d) and (f) of this section shall

Securities and Exchange Commission

be filed within 60 days after the end of the fiscal year covered by such reports.

(h) No officer, director, or employee of a security-based swap data repository may directly or indirectly take any action to coerce, manipulate, mislead, or fraudulently influence the security-based swap data repository's chief compliance officer in the performance of his or her duties under this section.

[80 FR 14550, Mar. 19, 2015]

§ 240.13n-12 Exemption from requirements governing security-based swap data repositories for certain non-U.S. persons.

(a) *Definitions.* For purposes of this section—

(1) *Non-U.S. person* means a person that is not a U.S. person.

(2) *U.S. person* shall have the same meaning as set forth in Rule 3a71-3(a)(4)(i) (§ 240.3a71-3(a)(4)(i)).

(b) A non-U.S. person that performs the functions of a security-based swap data repository within the United States shall be exempt from the registration and other requirements set forth in section 13(n) of the Act (15 U.S.C. 78m(n)), and the rules and regulations thereunder, provided that each regulator with supervisory authority over such non-U.S. person has entered into a memorandum of understanding or other arrangement with the Commission that addresses the confidentiality of data collected and maintained by such non-U.S. person, access by the Commission to such data, and any other matters determined by the Commission.

[80 FR 14550, Mar. 19, 2015]

§ 240.13p-1 Requirement of report regarding disclosure of registrant's supply chain information regarding conflict minerals.

Every registrant that files reports with the Commission under Sections 13(a) (15 U.S.C. 78m(a)) or 15(d) (15 U.S.C. 78o(d)) of the Exchange Act, having conflict minerals that are necessary to the functionality or production of a product manufactured or contracted by that registrant to be manufactured, shall file a report on Form SD, within the period specified in that Form disclosing the information required by the applicable items of Form SD as specified in that Form (17 CFR 249b.400).

[77 FR 56362, Sept. 12, 2012]

§ 240.13q-1 Disclosure of payments made by resource extraction issuers.

(a) *Resource extraction issuers.* Every issuer that is required to file an annual report with the Commission on Form 10-K (17 CFR 249.310), Form 20-F (17 CFR 249.220f), or Form 40-F (17 CFR 249.240f) pursuant to Section 13 or 15(d) of the Exchange Act (15 U.S.C. 78m or 78o(d)) and engages in the commercial development of oil, natural gas, or minerals must furnish a report on Form SD (17 CFR 249b.400) within the period specified in that Form disclosing the information required by the applicable items of Form SD as specified in that Form.

(b) *Anti-evasion.* Disclosure is required under this section in circumstances in which an activity related to the commercial development of oil, natural gas, or minerals, or a payment or series of payments made by a resource extraction issuer to a foreign government or the Federal Government for the purpose of commercial development of oil, natural gas, or minerals, is not, in form or characterization, within one of the categories of activities or payments specified in Form SD, but is part of a plan or scheme to evade the disclosure required under this section.

(c) *Alternative reporting.* An application for recognition by the Commission that an alternative reporting regime requires disclosure that satisfies the transparency objectives of Section 13(q) (15 U.S.C. 78m(q)), for purposes of alternative reporting pursuant to Item 2.01(c) of Form SD, must be filed in accordance with the procedures set forth in § 240.0-13, except that, for purposes of this paragraph (c), applications may be submitted by resource extraction issuers, governments, industry groups, or trade associations.

(d) *Exemptions*—(1) *Conflicts of law.* A resource extraction issuer that is prohibited by the law of the jurisdiction where the project is located from providing the payment information required by Form SD may exclude such

§ 240.14a-1

disclosure, subject to the following conditions:

(i) The issuer has taken all reasonable steps to seek and use any exemptions or other relief under the applicable law of the foreign jurisdiction, and has been unable to obtain or use such an exemption or other relief;

(ii) The issuer must disclose on Form SD:

(A) The foreign jurisdiction for which it is omitting the disclosure pursuant to this paragraph (d)(1);

(B) The particular law of that jurisdiction that prevents the issuer from providing such disclosure; and

(C) The efforts the issuer has undertaken to seek and use exemptions or other relief under the applicable law of that jurisdiction, and the results of those efforts; and

(iii) The issuer must furnish as an exhibit to Form SD a legal opinion from counsel that opines on the issuer's inability to provide such disclosure without violating the foreign jurisdiction's law.

(2) *Conflicts with pre-existing contracts.* A resource extraction issuer that is unable to provide the payment information required by Form SD without violating one or more contract terms that were in effect prior to the effective date of this section may exclude such disclosure, subject to the following conditions:

(i) The issuer has taken all reasonable steps to obtain the consent of the relevant contractual parties, or to seek and use another contractual exception or other relief, to disclose the payment information, and has been unable to obtain such consent or other contractual exception or relief;

(ii) The issuer must disclose on Form SD:

(A) The jurisdiction for which it is omitting the disclosure pursuant to this paragraph (d)(2);

(B) The particular contract terms that prohibit the issuer from providing such disclosure; and

(C) The efforts the issuer has undertaken to obtain the consent of the contracting parties, or to seek and use another contractual exception or relief, to disclose the payment information, and the results of those efforts; and

(iii) The issuer must furnish as an exhibit to Form SD a legal opinion from counsel that opines on the issuer's inability to provide such disclosure without violating the contractual terms.

(3) *Exemption for emerging growth companies and smaller reporting companies.* An issuer that is an emerging growth company or a smaller reporting company, each as defined under § 240.12b-2, is exempt from, and need not comply with, the requirements of this section, unless it is subject to the resource extraction payment disclosure requirements of an alternative reporting regime, which has been deemed by the Commission to require disclosure that satisfies the transparency objectives of Section 13(q) (15 U.S.C. 78m(q)), pursuant to § 240.13q-1(c).

(4) *Case-by-case exemption.* A resource extraction issuer may file an application for exemptive relief under this section in accordance with the procedures set forth in § 240.0-12.

(e) *Compilation.* To the extent practicable, the staff will periodically make a compilation of the information required to be submitted under this section publicly available online. The staff may determine the form, manner and timing of the compilation, except that no information included therein may be anonymized (whether by redacting the names of the resource extraction issuers or otherwise).

[86 FR 4714, Jan. 15, 2021]

REGULATION 14A: SOLICITATION OF PROXIES

ATTENTION ELECTRONIC FILERS

THIS REGULATION SHOULD BE READ IN CONJUNCTION WITH REGULATION S-T (PART 232 OF THIS CHAPTER), WHICH GOVERNS THE PREPARATION AND SUBMISSION OF DOCUMENTS IN ELECTRONIC FORMAT. MANY PROVISIONS RELATING TO THE PREPARATION AND SUBMISSION OF DOCUMENTS IN PAPER FORMAT CONTAINED IN THIS REGULATION ARE SUPERSEDED BY THE PROVISIONS OF REGULATION S-T FOR DOCUMENTS REQUIRED TO BE FILED IN ELECTRONIC FORMAT.

§ 240.14a-1 Definitions.

Unless the context otherwise requires, all terms used in this regulation have the same meanings as in the

Securities and Exchange Commission § 240.14a–1

Act or elsewhere in the general rules and regulations thereunder. In addition, the following definitions apply unless the context otherwise requires:

(a) *Associate.* The term "associate," used to indicate a relationship with any person, means:

(1) Any corporation or organization (other than the registrant or a majority owned subsidiary of the registrant) of which such person is an officer or partner or is, directly or indirectly, the beneficial owner of 10 percent or more of any class of equity securities;

(2) Any trust or other estate in which such person has a substantial beneficial interest or as to which such person serves as trustee or in a similar fiduciary capacity; and

(3) Any relative or spouse of such person, or any relative of such spouse, who has the same home as such person or who is a director or officer of the registrant or any of its parents or subsidiaries.

(b) *Employee benefit plan.* For purposes of §§ 240.14a–13, 240.14b–1 and 240.14b–2, the term "employee benefit plan" means any purchase, savings, option, bonus, appreciation, profit sharing, thrift, incentive, pension or similar plan primarily for employees, directors, trustees or officers.

(c) *Entity that exercises fiduciary powers.* The term "entity that exercises fiduciary powers" means any entity that holds securities in nominee name or otherwise on behalf of a beneficial owner but does not include a clearing agency registered pursuant to section 17A of the Act or a broker or a dealer.

(d) *Exempt employee benefit plan securities.* For purposes of §§ 240.14a–13, 240.14b–1 and 240.14b–2, the term "exempt employee benefit plan securities" means:

(1) Securities of the registrant held by an employee benefit plan, as defined in paragraph (b) of this section, where such plan is established by the registrant; or

(2) If notice regarding the current solicitation has been given pursuant to § 240.14a–13(a)(1)(ii)(C) or if notice regarding the current request for a list of names, addresses and securities positions of beneficial owners has been given pursuant to § 240.14a–13(b)(3), securities of the registrant held by an employee benefit plan, as defined in paragraph (b) of this section, where such plan is established by an affiliate of the registrant.

(e) *Last fiscal year.* The term "last fiscal year" of the registrant means the last fiscal year of the registrant ending prior to the date of the meeting for which proxies are to be solicited or if the solicitation involves written authorizations or consents in lieu of a meeting, the earliest date they may be used to effect corporate action.

(f) *Proxy.* The term "proxy" includes every proxy, consent or authorization within the meaning of section 14(a) of the Act. The consent or authorization may take the form of failure to object or to dissent.

(g) *Proxy statement.* The term "proxy statement" means the statement required by § 240.14a–3(a) whether or not contained in a single document.

(h) *Record date.* The term "record date" means the date as of which the record holders of securities entitled to vote at a meeting or by written consent or authorization shall be determined.

(i) *Record holder.* For purposes of §§ 240.14a–13, 240.14b–1 and 240.14b–2, the term "record holder" means any broker, dealer, voting trustee, bank, association or other entity that exercises fiduciary powers which holds securities of record in nominee name or otherwise or as a participant in a clearing agency registered pursuant to section 17A of the Act.

(j) *Registrant.* The term "registrant" means the issuer of the securities in respect of which proxies are to be solicited.

(k) *Respondent bank.* For purposes of §§ 240.14a–13, 240.14b–1 and 240.14b–2, the term "respondent bank" means any bank, association or other entity that exercises fiduciary powers which holds securities on behalf of beneficial owners and deposits such securities for safekeeping with another bank, association or other entity that exercises fiduciary powers.

(l) *Solicitation.* (1) The terms "solicit" and "solicitation" include:

(i) Any request for a proxy whether or not accompanied by or included in a form of proxy;

§ 240.14a-2

(ii) Any request to execute or not to execute, or to revoke, a proxy; or

(iii) The furnishing of a form of proxy or other communication to security holders under circumstances reasonably calculated to result in the procurement, withholding or revocation of a proxy, including:

(A) Any proxy voting advice that makes a recommendation to a security holder as to its vote, consent, or authorization on a specific matter for which security holder approval is solicited, and that is furnished by a person that markets its expertise as a provider of such proxy voting advice, separately from other forms of investment advice, and sells such proxy voting advice for a fee.

(B) [Reserved]

(2) The terms do not apply, however, to:

(i) The furnishing of a form of proxy to a security holder upon the unsolicited request of such security holder;

(ii) The performance by the registrant of acts required by § 240.14a-7;

(iii) The performance by any person of ministerial acts on behalf of a person soliciting a proxy;

(iv) A communication by a security holder who does not otherwise engage in a proxy solicitation (other than a solicitation exempt under § 240.14a-2) stating how the security holder intends to vote and the reasons therefor, provided that the communication:

(A) Is made by means of speeches in public forums, press releases, published or broadcast opinions, statements, or advertisements appearing in a broadcast media, or newspaper, magazine or other bona fide publication disseminated on a regular basis;

(B) Is directed to persons to whom the security holder owes a fiduciary duty in connection with the voting of securities of a registrant held by the security holder, or

(C) Is made in response to unsolicited requests for additional information with respect to a prior communication by the security holder made pursuant to this paragraph (l)(2)(iv); or

(v) The furnishing of any proxy voting advice by a person who furnishes such advice only in response to an unprompted request.

[51 FR 44275, Dec. 9, 1986, as amended at 52 FR 23648, June 24, 1987; 53 FR 16405, May 9, 1988; 57 FR 48290, Oct. 22, 1992; 85 FR 55154, Sept. 3, 2020]

§ 240.14a-2 Solicitations to which § 240.14a-3 to § 240.14a-15 apply.

Sections 240.14a-3 to 240.14a-15, except as specified, apply to every solicitation of a proxy with respect to securities registered pursuant to section 12 of the Act (15 U.S.C. 78*l*), whether or not trading in such securities has been suspended. To the extent specified below, certain of these sections also apply to roll-up transactions that do not involve an entity with securities registered pursuant to section 12 of the Act.

(a) Sections 240.14a-3 to 240.14a-15 do not apply to the following:

(1) Any solicitation by a person in respect to securities carried in his name or in the name of his nominee (otherwise than as voting trustee) or held in his custody, if such person—

(i) Receives no commission or remuneration for such solicitation, directly or indirectly, other than reimbursement of reasonable expenses;

(ii) Furnishes promptly to the person solicited (or such person's household in accordance with § 240.14a-3(e)(1)) a copy of all soliciting material with respect to the same subject matter or meeting received from all persons who shall furnish copies thereof for such purpose and who shall, if requested, defray the reasonable expenses to be incurred in forwarding such material, and

(iii) In addition, does no more than impartially instruct the person solicited to forward a proxy to the person, if any, to whom the person solicited desires to give a proxy, or impartially request from the person solicited instructions as to the authority to be conferred by the proxy and state that a proxy will be given if no instructions are received by a certain date.

(2) Any solicitation by a person in respect of securities of which he is the beneficial owner;

(3) Any solicitation involved in the offer and sale of securities registered under the Securities Act of 1933: *Provided*, That this paragraph shall not

Securities and Exchange Commission

§ 240.14a–2

apply to securities to be issued in any transaction of the character specified in paragraph (a) of Rule 145 under that Act;

(4) Any solicitation with respect to a plan of reorganization under Chapter 11 of the Bankruptcy Reform Act of 1978, as amended, if made after the entry of an order approving the written disclosure statement concerning a plan of reorganization pursuant to section 1125 of said Act and after, or concurrently with, the transmittal of such disclosure statement as required by section 1125 of said Act;

(5) [Reserved]

(6) Any solicitation through the medium of a newspaper advertisement which informs security holders of a source from which they may obtain copies of a proxy statement, form of proxy and any other soliciting material and does no more than:

(i) Name the registrant,

(ii) State the reason for the advertisement, and

(iii) Identify the proposal or proposals to be acted upon by security holders.

(b) Sections 240.14a–3 through 240.14a–6 (other than § 240.14a–6(g) and (p)), 240.14a–8, 240.14a–10, 240.14a–12 through 240.14a–15, and 240.14a–19 do not apply to the following:

(1) Any solicitation by or on behalf of any person who does not, at any time during such solicitation, seek directly or indirectly, either on its own or another's behalf, the power to act as proxy for a security holder and does not furnish or otherwise request, or act on behalf of a person who furnishes or requests, a form of revocation, abstention, consent or authorization. *Provided, however,* That the exemption set forth in this paragraph shall not apply to:

(i) The registrant or an affiliate or associate of the registrant (other than an officer or director or any person serving in a similar capacity);

(ii) An officer or director of the registrant or any person serving in a similar capacity engaging in a solicitation financed directly or indirectly by the registrant;

(iii) An officer, director, affiliate or associate of a person that is ineligible to rely on the exemption set forth in this paragraph (other than persons specified in paragraph (b)(1)(i) of this section), or any person serving in a similar capacity;

(iv) Any nominee for whose election as a director proxies are solicited;

(v) Any person soliciting in opposition to a merger, recapitalization, reorganization, sale of assets or other extraordinary transaction recommended or approved by the board of directors of the registrant who is proposing or intends to propose an alternative transaction to which such person or one of its affiliates is a party;

(vi) Any person who is required to report beneficial ownership of the registrant's equity securities on a Schedule 13D (§ 240.13d–101), unless such person has filed a Schedule 13D and has not disclosed pursuant to Item 4 thereto an intent, or reserved the right, to engage in a control transaction, or any contested solicitation for the election of directors;

(vii) Any person who receives compensation from an ineligible person directly related to the solicitation of proxies, other than pursuant to § 240.14a–13;

(viii) Where the registrant is an investment company registered under the Investment Company Act of 1940 (15 U.S.C. 80a–1 *et seq.*), an "interested person" of that investment company, as that term is defined in section 2(a)(19) of the Investment Company Act (15 U.S.C. 80a–2);

(ix) Any person who, because of a substantial interest in the subject matter of the solicitation, is likely to receive a benefit from a successful solicitation that would not be shared pro rata by all other holders of the same class of securities, other than a benefit arising from the person's employment with the registrant; and

(x) Any person acting on behalf of any of the foregoing.

(2) Any solicitation made otherwise than on behalf of the registrant where the total number of persons solicited is not more than ten;

(3) The furnishing of proxy voting advice by any person (the "advisor") to any other person with whom the advisor has a business relationship, if:

§ 240.14a-2

(i) The advisor renders financial advice in the ordinary course of his business;

(ii) The advisor discloses to the recipient of the advice any significant relationship with the registrant or any of its affiliates, or a security holder proponent of the matter on which advice is given, as well as any material interests of the advisor in such matter;

(iii) The advisor receives no special commission or remuneration for furnishing the proxy voting advice from any person other than a recipient of the advice and other persons who receive similar advice under this subsection; and

(iv) The proxy voting advice is not furnished on behalf of any person soliciting proxies or on behalf of a participant in an election subject to the provisions of § 240.14a–12(c); and

(4) Any solicitation in connection with a roll-up transaction as defined in Item 901(c) of Regulation S-K (§ 229.901 of this chapter) in which the holder of a security that is the subject of a proposed roll-up transaction engages in preliminary communications with other holders of securities that are the subject of the same limited partnership roll-up transaction for the purpose of determining whether to solicit proxies, consents, or authorizations in opposition to the proposed limited partnership roll-up transaction; *provided, however*, that:

(i) This exemption shall not apply to a security holder who is an affiliate of the registrant or general partner or sponsor; and

(ii) This exemption shall not apply to a holder of five percent (5%) or more of the outstanding securities of a class that is the subject of the proposed roll-up transaction who engages in the business of buying and selling limited partnership interests in the secondary market unless that holder discloses to the persons to whom the communications are made such ownership interest and any relations of the holder to the parties of the transaction or to the transaction itself, as required by § 240.14a–6(n)(1) and specified in the Notice of Exempt Preliminary Roll-up Communication (§ 240.14a–104). If the communication is oral, this disclosure may be provided to the security holder orally. Whether the communication is written or oral, the notice required by § 240.14a–6(n) and § 240.14a–104 shall be furnished to the Commission.

(5) Publication or distribution by a broker or a dealer of a research report in accordance with Rule 138 (§ 230.138 of this chapter) or Rule 139 (§ 230.139 of this chapter) during a transaction in which the broker or dealer or its affiliate participates or acts in a an advisory role.

(6) Any solicitation by or on behalf of any person who does not seek directly or indirectly, either on its own or another's behalf, the power to act as proxy for a shareholder and does not furnish or otherwise request, or act on behalf of a person who furnishes or requests, a form of revocation, abstention, consent, or authorization in an electronic shareholder forum that is established, maintained or operated pursuant to the provisions of § 240.14a–17, provided that the solicitation is made more than 60 days prior to the date announced by a registrant for its next annual or special meeting of shareholders. If the registrant announces the date of its next annual or special meeting of shareholders less than 60 days before the meeting date, then the solicitation may not be made more than two days following the date of the registrant's announcement of the meeting date. Participation in an electronic shareholder forum does not eliminate a person's eligibility to solicit proxies after the date that this exemption is no longer available, or is no longer being relied upon, provided that any such solicitation is conducted in accordance with this regulation.

(7) Any solicitation by or on behalf of any shareholder in connection with the formation of a nominating shareholder group pursuant to § 240.14a–11, provided that:

(i) The soliciting shareholder is not holding the registrant's securities with the purpose, or with the effect, of changing control of the registrant or to gain a number of seats on the board of directors that exceeds the maximum number of nominees that the registrant could be required to include under § 240.14a–11(d);

(ii) Each written communication includes no more than:

Securities and Exchange Commission §240.14a-2

(A) A statement of each soliciting shareholder's intent to form a nominating shareholder group in order to nominate one or more directors under §240.14a-11;

(B) Identification of, and a brief statement regarding, the potential nominee or nominees or, where no nominee or nominees have been identified, the characteristics of the nominee or nominees that the shareholder intends to nominate, if any;

(C) The percentage of voting power of the registrant's securities that are entitled to be voted on the election of directors that each soliciting shareholder holds or the aggregate percentage held by any group to which the shareholder belongs; and

(D) The means by which shareholders may contact the soliciting party.

(iii) Any written soliciting material published, sent or given to shareholders in accordance with this paragraph must be filed by the shareholder with the Commission, under the registrant's Exchange Act file number, or, in the case of a registrant that is an investment company registered under the Investment Company Act of 1940 (15 U.S.C. 80a-1 *et seq.*), under the registrant's Investment Company Act file number, no later than the date the material is first published, sent or given to shareholders. Three copies of the material must at the same time be filed with, or mailed for filing to, each national securities exchange upon which any class of securities of the registrant is listed and registered. The soliciting material must include a cover page in the form set forth in Schedule 14N (§240.14n-101) and the appropriate box on the cover page must be marked.

(iv) In the case of an oral solicitation made in accordance with the terms of this section, the nominating shareholder must file a cover page in the form set forth in Schedule 14N (§240.14n-101), with the appropriate box on the cover page marked, under the registrant's Exchange Act file number (or in the case of an investment company registered under the Investment Company Act of 1940 (15 U.S.C. 80a-1 *et seq.*), under the registrant's Investment Company Act file number), no later than the date of the first such communication.

INSTRUCTION TO PARAGRAPH (b)(7). The exemption provided in paragraph (b)(7) of this section shall not apply to a shareholder that subsequently engages in soliciting or other nominating activities outside the scope of §240.14a-2(b)(8) and §240.14a-11 in connection with the subject election of directors or is or becomes a member of any other group, as determined under section 13(d)(3) of the Act (15 U.S.C. 78m(d)(3) and §240.13d-5(b)), or otherwise, with persons engaged in soliciting or other nominating activities in connection with the subject election of directors.

(8) Any solicitation by or on behalf of a nominating shareholder or nominating shareholder group in support of its nominee that is included or that will be included on the registrant's form of proxy in accordance with §240.14a-11 or for or against the registrant's nominee or nominees, provided that:

(i) The soliciting party does not, at any time during such solicitation, seek directly or indirectly, either on its own or another's behalf, the power to act as proxy for a shareholder and does not furnish or otherwise request, or act on behalf of a person who furnishes or requests, a form of revocation, abstention, consent or authorization;

(ii) Any written communication includes:

(A) The identity of each nominating shareholder and a description of his or her direct or indirect interests, by security holdings or otherwise;

(B) A prominent legend in clear, plain language advising shareholders that a shareholder nominee is or will be included in the registrant's proxy statement and that they should read the registrant's proxy statement when available because it includes important information (or, if the registrant's proxy statement is publicly available, advising shareholders of that fact and encouraging shareholders to read the registrant's proxy statement because it includes important information). The legend also must explain to shareholders that they can find the registrant's proxy statement, other soliciting material, and any other relevant documents at no charge on the Commission's Web site; and

(iii) Any written soliciting material published, sent or given to shareholders in accordance with this paragraph must be filed by the nominating

241

§ 240.14a-3

shareholder or nominating shareholder group with the Commission, under the registrant's Exchange Act file number, or, in the case of a registrant that is an investment company registered under the Investment Company Act of 1940 (15 U.S.C. 80a-1 *et seq.*), under the registrant's Investment Company Act file number, no later than the date the material is first published, sent or given to shareholders. Three copies of the material must at the same time be filed with, or mailed for filing to, each national securities exchange upon which any class of securities of the registrant is listed and registered. The soliciting material must include a cover page in the form set forth in Schedule 14N (§ 240.14n-101) and the appropriate box on the cover page must be marked.

INSTRUCTION 1 TO PARAGRAPH (b)(8). A nominating shareholder or nominating shareholder group may rely on the exemption provided in paragraph (b)(8) of this section only after receiving notice from the registrant in accordance with § 240.14a-11(g)(1) or § 240.14a-11(g)(3)(iv) that the registrant will include the nominating shareholder's or nominating shareholder group's nominee or nominees in its form of proxy.

INSTRUCTION 2 TO PARAGRAPH (b)(8). Any solicitation by or on behalf of a nominating shareholder or nominating shareholder group in support of its nominee included or to be included on the registrant's form of proxy in accordance with § 240.14a-11 or for or against the registrant's nominee or nominees must be made in reliance on the exemption provided in paragraph (b)(8) of this section and not on any other exemption.

INSTRUCTION 3 TO PARAGRAPH (b)(8). The exemption provided in paragraph (b)(8) of this section shall not apply to a person that subsequently engages in soliciting or other nominating activities outside the scope of § 240.14a-11 in connection with the subject election of directors or is or becomes a member of any other group, as determined under section 13(d)(3) of the Act (15 U.S.C. 78m(d)(3) and § 240.13d-5(b)), or otherwise, with persons engaged in soliciting or other nominating activities in connection with the subject election of directors.

(9) Paragraphs (b)(1) and (b)(3) of this section shall not be available to a person furnishing proxy voting advice covered by § 240.14a-1(l)(1)(iii)(A) ("proxy voting advice business") unless the proxy voting advice business includes in its proxy voting advice or in an electronic medium used to deliver the proxy voting advice prominent disclosure of:

(i) Any information regarding an interest, transaction, or relationship of the proxy voting advice business (or its affiliates) that is material to assessing the objectivity of the proxy voting advice in light of the circumstances of the particular interest, transaction, or relationship; and

(ii) Any policies and procedures used to identify, as well as the steps taken to address, any such material conflicts of interest arising from such interest, transaction, or relationship.

[44 FR 68769, Nov. 29, 1979, as amended at 51 FR 42059, Nov. 20, 1986; 52 FR 21936, June 10, 1987; 57 FR 48290, Oct. 22, 1992; 59 FR 63684, Dec. 8, 1994; 65 FR 65749, Nov. 2, 2000; 70 FR 44829, Aug. 3, 2005; 72 FR 4166, Jan. 29, 2007; 73 FR 4458, Jan. 25, 2008; 73 FR 17814, Apr. 1, 2008; 75 FR 56780, Sept. 16, 2010; 85 FR 55154, Sept. 3, 2020; 86 FR 68378, Dec. 1, 2021; 87 FR 43196, July 19, 2022]

§ 240.14a-3 Information to be furnished to security holders.

(a) No solicitation subject to this regulation shall be made unless each person solicited is concurrently furnished or has previously been furnished with:

(1) A publicly-filed preliminary or definitive proxy statement, in the form and manner described in § 240.14a-16, containing the information specified in Schedule 14A (§ 240.14a-101);

(2) A preliminary or definitive written proxy statement included in a registration statement filed under the Securities Act of 1933 on Form S-4 or F-4 (§ 239.25 or § 239.34 of this chapter) or Form N-14 (§ 239.23 of this chapter) and containing the information specified in such Form; or

(3) A publicly-filed preliminary or definitive proxy statement, not in the form and manner described in § 240.14a-16, containing the information specified in Schedule 14A (§ 240.14a-101), if:

(i) The solicitation relates to a business combination transaction as defined in § 230.165 of this chapter, as well as transactions for cash consideration requiring disclosure under Item 14 of § 240.14a-101; or

(ii) The solicitation may not follow the form and manner described in § 240.14a-16 pursuant to the laws of the

Securities and Exchange Commission

§ 240.14a–3

state of incorporation of the registrant.

(b) If the solicitation is made on behalf of the registrant, other than an investment company registered under the Investment Company Act of 1940, and relates to an annual (or special meeting in lieu of the annual) meeting of security holders, or written consent in lieu of such meeting, at which directors are to be elected, each proxy statement furnished pursuant to paragraph (a) of this section shall be accompanied or preceded by an annual report to security holders as follows:

(1) The report shall include, for the registrant and its subsidiaries, consolidated and audited balance sheets as of the end of the two most recent fiscal years and audited statements of income and cash flows for each of the three most recent fiscal years prepared in accordance with Regulation S–X (part 210 of this chapter), except that the provisions of Article 3 (other than §§ 210.3–03(e), 210.3–04 and 210.3–20) and Article 11 shall not apply. Any financial statement schedules or exhibits or separate financial statements which may otherwise be required in filings with the Commission may be omitted. If the financial statements of the registrant and its subsidiaries consolidated in the annual report filed or to be filed with the Commission are not required to be audited, the financial statements required by this paragraph may be unaudited. A smaller reporting company may provide the information in Article 8 of Regulation S–X (§ 210.8 of this chapter) in lieu of the financial information required by this paragraph 9(b)(1).

NOTE 1 TO PARAGRAPH (b)(1): If the financial statements for a period prior to the most recently completed fiscal year have been examined by a predecessor accountant, the separate report of the predecessor accountant may be omitted in the report to security holders, provided the registrant has obtained from the predecessor accountant a reissued report covering the prior period presented and the successor accountant clearly indicates in the scope paragraph of his or her report (a) that the financial statements of the prior period were examined by other accountants, (b) the date of their report, (c) the type of opinion expressed by the predecessor accountant and (d) the substantive reasons therefore, if it was other than unqualified. It should be noted, however, that the separate report of any predecessor accountant is required in filings with the Commission. If, for instance, the financial statements in the annual report to security holders are incorporated by reference in a Form 10–K, the separate report of a predecessor accountant shall be filed in Part II or in Part IV as a financial statement schedule.

NOTE 2 TO PARAGRAPH (b)(1): For purposes of complying with § 240.14a–3, if the registrant has changed its fiscal closing date, financial statements covering two years and one period of 9 to 12 months shall be deemed to satisfy the requirements for statements of income and cash flows for the three most recent fiscal years.

(2)(i) Financial statements and notes thereto shall be presented in roman type at least as large and as legible as 10-point modern type. If necessary for convenient presentation, the financial statements may be in roman type as large and as legible as 8-point modern type. All type shall be leaded at least 2 points.

(ii) Where the annual report to security holders is delivered through an electronic medium, issuers may satisfy legibility requirements applicable to printed documents, such as type size and font, by presenting all required information in a format readily communicated to investors.

(3) The report shall contain the supplementary financial information required by item 302 of Regulation S–K (§ 229.302 of this chapter).

(4) The report shall contain information concerning changes in and disagreements with accountants on accounting and financial disclosure required by Item 304 of Regulation S–K (§ 229.304 of this chapter).

(5)(i) [Reserved]

(ii) The report shall contain management's discussion and analysis of financial condition and results of operations required by Item 303 of Regulation S–K (§ 229.303 of this chapter).

(iii) The report shall contain the quantitative and qualitative disclosures about market risk required by Item 305 of Regulation S–K (§ 229.305 of this chapter).

(6) The report shall contain a brief description of the business done by the registrant and its subsidiaries during the most recent fiscal year which will, in the opinion of management, indicate the general nature and scope of the

§ 240.14a-3

business of the registrant and its subsidiaries.

(7) The report shall contain information relating to the registrant's industry segments, classes of similar products or services, foreign and domestic operations and exports sales required by paragraphs (b), (c)(1)(i) and (d) of Item 101 of Regulation S-K (§ 229.101 of this chapter).

(8) The report shall identify each of the registrant's directors and executive officers, and shall indicate the principal occupation or employment of each such person and the name and principal business of any organization by which such person is employed.

(9) The report shall contain the market price of and dividends on the registrant's common equity and related security holder matters required by Items 201(a), (b) and (c) of Regulation S-K (§ 229.201(a), (b) and (c) of this chapter). If the report precedes or accompanies a proxy statement or information statement relating to an annual meeting of security holders at which directors are to be elected (or special meeting or written consents in lieu of such meeting), furnish the performance graph required by Item 201(e) (§ 229.201(e) of this chapter).

(10) The registrant's proxy statement, or the report, shall contain an undertaking in bold face or otherwise reasonably prominent type to provide without charge to each person solicited upon the written request of any such person, a copy of the registrant's annual report on Form 10-K, including the financial statements and the financial statement schedules, required to be filed with the Commission pursuant to Rule 13a-1 (§ 240.13a-1 of this chapter) under the Act for the registrant's most recent fiscal year, and shall indicate the name and address (including title or department) of the person to whom such a written request is to be directed. In the discretion of management, a registrant need not undertake to furnish without charge copies of all exhibits to its Form 10-K, provided that the copy of the annual report on Form 10-K furnished without charge to requesting security holders is accompanied by a list briefly describing all the exhibits not contained therein and indicating that the registrant will furnish any exhibit upon the payment of a specified reasonable fee, which fee shall be limited to the registrant's reasonable expenses in furnishing such exhibit. If the registrant's annual report to security holders complies with all of the disclosure requirements of Form 10-K and is filed with the Commission in satisfaction of its Form 10-K filing requirements, such registrant need not furnish a separate Form 10-K to security holders who receive a copy of such annual report.

NOTE TO PARAGRAPH (b)(10): Pursuant to the undertaking required by paragraph (b)(10) of this section, a registrant shall furnish a copy of its annual report on Form 10-K (§ 249.310 of this chapter) to a beneficial owner of its securities upon receipt of a written request from such person. Each request must set forth a good faith representation that, as of the record date for the solicitation requiring the furnishing of the annual report to security holders pursuant to paragraph (b) of this section, the person making the request was a beneficial owner of securities entitled to vote.

(11) Subject to the foregoing requirements, the report may be in any form deemed suitable by management and the information required by paragraphs (b)(5) to (10) of this section may be presented in an appendix or other separate section of the report, provided that the attention of security holders is called to such presentation.

NOTE: Registrants are encouraged to utilize tables, schedules, charts and graphic illustrations of present financial information in an understandable manner. Any presentation of financial information must be consistent with the data in the financial statements contained in the report and, if appropriate, should refer to relevant portions of the financial statements and notes thereto.

(12) [Reserved]

(13) Paragraph (b) of this section shall not apply, however, to solicitations made on behalf of the registrant before the financial statements are available if a solicitation is being made at the same time in opposition to the registrant and if the registrant's proxy statement includes an undertaking in bold face type to furnish such annual report to security holders to all persons being solicited at least 20 calendar days before the date of the meeting or, if the solicitation refers to a written consent or authorization in lieu of a

Securities and Exchange Commission § 240.14a–3

meeting, at least 20 calendar days prior to the earliest date on which it may be used to effect corporate action.

(c) The report sent to security holders pursuant to this rule shall be submitted in electronic format, in accordance with the EDGAR Filer Manual, to the Commission, solely for its information, not later than the date on which such report is first sent or given to security holders or the date on which preliminary copies, or definitive copies, if preliminary filing was not required, of solicitation material are filed with the Commission pursuant to § 240.14a–6, whichever date is later. The report is not deemed to be "soliciting material" or to be "filed" with the Commission or subject to this regulation otherwise than as provided in this Rule, or to the liabilities of section 18 of the Act, except to the extent that the registrant specifically requests that it be treated as a part of the proxy soliciting material or incorporates it in the proxy statement or other filed report by reference.

(d) An annual report to security holders prepared on an integrated basis pursuant to General Instruction H to Form 10–K (§ 249.310 of this chapter) may also be submitted in satisfaction of this section. When filed as the annual report on Form 10–K, responses to the Items of that form are subject to section 18 of the Act notwithstanding paragraph (c) of this section.

(e)(1)(i) A registrant will be considered to have delivered an annual report to security holders, proxy statement or Notice of Internet Availability of Proxy Materials, as described in § 240.14a–16, to all security holders of record who share an address if:

(A) The registrant delivers one annual report to security holders, proxy statement or Notice of Internet Availability of Proxy Materials, as applicable, to the shared address;

(B) The registrant addresses the annual report to security holders, proxy statement or Notice of Internet Availability of Proxy Materials, as applicable, to the security holders as a group (for example, "ABC Fund [or Corporation] Security Holders," "Jane Doe and Household," "The Smith Family"), to each of the security holders individually (for example, "John Doe and Richard Jones") or to the security holders in a form to which each of the security holders has consented in writing;

NOTE TO PARAGRAPH (e)(1)(i)(B): Unless the registrant addresses the annual report to security holders, proxy statement or Notice of Internet Availability of Proxy Materials to the security holders as a group or to each of the security holders individually, it must obtain, from each security holder to be included in the household group, a separate affirmative written consent to the specific form of address the registrant will use.

(C) The security holders consent, in accordance with paragraph (e)(1)(ii) of this section, to delivery of one annual report to security holders or proxy statement, as applicable;

(D) With respect to delivery of the proxy statement or Notice of Internet Availability of Proxy Materials, the registrant delivers, together with or subsequent to delivery of the proxy statement, a separate proxy card for each security holder at the shared address; and

(E) The registrant includes an undertaking in the proxy statement to deliver promptly upon written or oral request a separate copy of the annual report to security holders, proxy statement or Notice of Internet Availability of Proxy Materials, as applicable, to a security holder at a shared address to which a single copy of the document was delivered.

(ii) *Consent*—(A) *Affirmative written consent.* Each security holder must affirmatively consent, in writing, to delivery of one annual report to security holders or proxy statement, as applicable. A security holder's affirmative written consent will be considered valid only if the security holder has been informed of:

(*1*) The duration of the consent;

(*2*) The specific types of documents to which the consent will apply;

(*3*) The procedures the security holder must follow to revoke consent; and

(*4*) The registrant's obligation to begin sending individual copies to a security holder within thirty days after the security holder revokes consent.

(B) *Implied consent.* The registrant need not obtain affirmative written consent from a security holder for purposes of paragraph (e)(1)(ii)(A) of this

245

§ 240.14a-3

section if all of the following conditions are met:

(*1*) The security holder has the same last name as the other security holders at the shared address or the registrant reasonably believes that the security holders are members of the same family;

(*2*) The registrant has sent the security holder a notice at least 60 days before the registrant begins to rely on this section concerning delivery of annual reports to security holders, proxy statements or Notices of Internet Availability of Proxy Materials to that security holder. The notice must:

(*i*) Be a separate written document;

(*ii*) State that only one annual report to security holders, proxy statement or Notice of Internet Availability of Proxy Materials, as applicable, will be delivered to the shared address unless the registrant receives contrary instructions;

(*iii*) Include a toll-free telephone number, or be accompanied by a reply form that is pre-addressed with postage provided, that the security holder can use to notify the registrant that the security holder wishes to receive a separate annual report to security holders, proxy statement or Notice of Internet Availability of Proxy Materials;

(*iv*) State the duration of the consent;

(*v*) Explain how a security holder can revoke consent;

(*vi*) State that the registrant will begin sending individual copies to a security holder within thirty days after the security holder revokes consent; and

(*vii*) Contain the following prominent statement, or similar clear and understandable statement, in bold-face type: "Important Notice Regarding Delivery of Security Holder Documents." This statement also must appear on the envelope in which the notice is delivered. Alternatively, if the notice is delivered separately from other communications to security holders, this statement may appear either on the notice or on the envelope in which the notice is delivered.

NOTE TO PARAGRAPH (e)(1)(ii)(B)(*2*): The notice should be written in plain English. See § 230.421(d)(2) of this chapter for a discussion of plain English principles.

17 CFR Ch. II (4-1-23 Edition)

(*3*) The registrant has not received the reply form or other notification indicating that the security holder wishes to continue to receive an individual copy of the annual report to security holders, proxy statement or Notice of Internet Availability of Proxy Materials, as applicable, within 60 days after the registrant sent the notice required by paragraph (e)(1)(ii)(B)(*2*) of this section; and

(*4*) The registrant delivers the document to a post office box or residential street address.

NOTE TO PARAGRAPH (e)(1)(ii)(B)(*4*): The registrant can assume that a street address is residential unless the registrant has information that indicates the street address is a business.

(iii) *Revocation of consent.* If a security holder, orally or in writing, revokes consent to delivery of one annual report to security holders, proxy statement or Notice of Internet Availability of Proxy Materials to a shared address, the registrant must begin sending individual copies to that security holder within 30 days after the registrant receives revocation of the security holder's consent.

(iv) *Definition of address.* Unless otherwise indicated, for purposes of this section, address means a street *address*, a post office box number, an electronic mail address, a facsimile telephone number or other similar destination to which paper or electronic documents are delivered, unless otherwise provided in this section. If the registrant has reason to believe that the address is a street address of a multi-unit building, the address must include the unit number.

NOTE TO PARAGRAPH (e)(1): A person other than the registrant making a proxy solicitation may deliver a single proxy statement to security holders of record or beneficial owners who have separate accounts and share an address if: (a) the registrant or intermediary has followed the procedures in this section; and (b) the registrant or intermediary makes available the shared address information to the person in accordance with § 240.14a-7(a)(2)(i) and (ii).

(2) Notwithstanding paragraphs (a) and (b) of this section, unless state law requires otherwise, a registrant is not

Securities and Exchange Commission § 240.14a–4

required to send an annual report to security holders, proxy statement or Notice of Internet Availability of Proxy Materials to a security holder if:

(i) An annual report to security holders and a proxy statement, or a Notice of Internet Availability of Proxy Materials, for two consecutive annual meetings; or

(ii) All, and at least two, payments (if sent by first class mail) of dividends or interest on securities, or dividend reinvestment confirmations, during a twelve month period, have been mailed to such security holder's address and have been returned as undeliverable. If any such security holder delivers or causes to be delivered to the registrant written notice setting forth his then current address for security holder communications purposes, the registrant's obligation to deliver an annual report to security holders, a proxy statement or a Notice of Internet Availability of Proxy Materials under this section is reinstated.

(f) The provisions of paragraph (a) of this section shall not apply to a communication made by means of speeches in public forums, press releases, published or broadcast opinions, statements, or advertisements appearing in a broadcast media, newspaper, magazine or other bona fide publication disseminated on a regular basis, provided that:

(1) No form of proxy, consent or authorization or means to execute the same is provided to a security holder in connection with the communication; and

(2) At the time the communication is made, a definitive proxy statement is on file with the Commission pursuant to § 240.14a–6(b).

[39 FR 40768, Nov. 20, 1974]

EDITORIAL NOTE: For FEDERAL REGISTER citations affecting § 240.14a–3, see the List of CFR Sections Affected, which appears in the Finding Aids section of the printed volume and at *www.govinfo.gov*.

§ 240.14a–4 Requirements as to proxy.

(a) The form of proxy (1) shall indicate in bold-face type whether or not the proxy is solicited on behalf of the registrant's board of directors or, if provided other than by a majority of the board of directors, shall indicate in bold-face type on whose behalf the solicitation is made;

(2) Shall provide a specifically designated blank space for dating the proxy card; and

(3) Shall identify clearly and impartially each separate matter intended to be acted upon, whether or not related to or conditioned on the approval of other matters, and whether proposed by the registrant or by security holders. No reference need be made, however, to proposals as to which discretionary authority is conferred pursuant to paragraph (c) of this section.

NOTE TO PARAGRAPH (a)(3) (ELECTRONIC FILERS): Electronic filers shall satisfy the filing requirements of Rule 14a–6(a) or (b) (§ 240.14a–6(a) or (b)) with respect to the form of proxy by filing the form of proxy as an appendix at the end of the proxy statement. Forms of proxy shall not be filed as exhibits or separate documents within an electronic submission.

(b)(1) Means shall be provided in the form of proxy whereby the person solicited is afforded an opportunity to specify by boxes a choice between approval or disapproval of, or abstention with respect to each separate matter referred to therein as intended to be acted upon, other than elections to office and votes to determine the frequency of shareholder votes on executive compensation pursuant to § 240.14a–21(b) of this chapter. A proxy may confer discretionary authority with respect to matters as to which a choice is not specified by the security holder provided that the form of proxy states in bold-face type how it is intended to vote the shares represented by the proxy in each such case.

(2) A form of proxy that provides for the election of directors shall set forth the names of persons nominated for election as directors, including any person whose nomination by a shareholder or shareholder group satisfies the requirements of an applicable state or foreign law provision, or a registrant's governing documents as they relate to the inclusion of shareholder director nominees in the registrant's proxy materials.

(3) Except as otherwise provided in § 240.14a–19, a form of proxy that provides for the election of directors may provide a means for the security holder

§ 240.14a–4

to grant authority to vote for the nominees set forth, as a group, provided that there is a similar means for the security holder to withhold authority to vote for such group of nominees (or, when applicable state law gives legal effect to votes cast against a nominee, a similar means for the security holder to vote against such group of nominees and a means for security holders to abstain from voting for such group of nominees). Any such form of proxy which is executed by the security holder in such manner as not to withhold authority to vote for the election of any nominee, or not to grant authority to vote against the election of any nominee, shall be deemed to grant authority to vote for the election of any nominee, provided that the form of proxy so states in bold-face type. Means to grant authority to vote for any nominees as a group or to withhold authority for any nominees as a group or to vote against any nominees as a group may not be provided if the form of proxy includes one or more shareholder nominees in accordance with an applicable state or foreign law provision, or a registrant's governing documents as they relate to the inclusion of shareholder director nominees in the registrant's proxy materials.

(4) When applicable state law gives legal effect to votes cast against a nominee, then in lieu of providing a means for security holders to withhold authority to vote, the form of proxy shall provide a means for security holders to vote against each nominee and a means for security holders to abstain from voting. When applicable state law does not give legal effect to votes cast against a nominee, such form of proxy shall not provide a means for security holders to vote against any nominee and such form of proxy shall clearly provide any of the following means for security holders to withhold authority to vote for each nominee:

(i) A box opposite the name of each nominee which may be marked to indicate that authority to vote for such nominee is withheld; or

(ii) An instruction in bold-face type which indicates that the security holder may withhold authority to vote for any nominee by lining through or otherwise striking out the name of any nominee; or

(iii) Designated blank spaces in which the security holder may enter the names of nominees with respect to whom the security holder chooses to withhold authority to vote; or

(iv) Any other similar means, provided that clear instructions are furnished indicating how the security holder may withhold authority to vote for any nominee.

Instruction 1 to paragraphs (b)(2), (3), and (4). Paragraphs (b)(2), (3), and (4) do not apply in the case of a merger, consolidation or other plan if the election of directors is an integral part of the plan.

(5) A form of proxy which provides for a shareholder vote on the frequency of shareholder votes to approve the compensation of executives required by section 14A(a)(2) of the Securities Exchange Act of 1934 (15 U.S.C. 78n–1(a)(2)) shall provide means whereby the person solicited is afforded an opportunity to specify by boxes a choice among 1, 2 or 3 years, or abstain.

(c) A proxy may confer discretionary authority to vote on any of the following matters:

(1) For an annual meeting of shareholders, if the registrant did not have notice of the matter at least 45 days before the date on which the registrant first sent its proxy materials for the prior year's annual meeting of shareholders (or date specified by an advance notice provision), and a specific statement to that effect is made in the proxy statement or form of proxy. If during the prior year the registrant did not hold an annual meeting, or if the date of the meeting has changed more than 30 days from the prior year, then notice must not have been received a reasonable time before the registrant sends its proxy materials for the current year.

(2) In the case in which the registrant has received timely notice in connection with an annual meeting of shareholders (as determined under paragraph (c)(1) of this section), if the registrant includes, in the proxy statement, advice on the nature of the matter and how the registrant intends to exercise its discretion to vote on each matter. However, even if the registrant

Securities and Exchange Commission § 240.14a–4

includes this information in its proxy statement, it may not exercise discretionary voting authority on a particular proposal if the proponent:

(i) Provides the registrant with a written statement, within the timeframe determined under paragraph (c)(1) of this section, that the proponent intends to deliver a proxy statement and form of proxy to holders of at least the percentage of the company's voting shares required under applicable law to carry the proposal;

(ii) Includes the same statement in its proxy materials filed under §240.14a–6; and

(iii) Immediately after soliciting the percentage of shareholders required to carry the proposal, provides the registrant with a statement from any solicitor or other person with knowledge that the necessary steps have been taken to deliver a proxy statement and form of proxy to holders of at least the percentage of the company's voting shares required under applicable law to carry the proposal.

(3) For solicitations other than for annual meetings or for solicitations by persons other than the registrant, matters which the persons making the solicitation do not know, a reasonable time before the solicitation, are to be presented at the meeting, if a specific statement to that effect is made in the proxy statement or form of proxy.

(4) Approval of the minutes of the prior meeting if such approval does not amount to ratification of the action taken at that meeting;

(5) The election of any person to any office for which a bona fide nominee is named in a proxy statement and such nominee is unable to serve or for good cause will not serve.

(6) Any proposal omitted from the proxy statement and form of proxy pursuant to §240.14a–8 or §240.14a–9 of this chapter.

(7) Matters incident to the conduct of the meeting.

(d) No proxy shall confer authority:

(1) To vote for the election of any person to any office for which a bona fide nominee is not named in the proxy statement:

(i) A person shall not be deemed to be a bona fide nominee and shall not be named as such unless the person has consented to being named in a proxy statement relating to the registrant's next annual meeting of shareholders at which directors are to be elected (or a special meeting in lieu of such meeting) and to serve if elected.

(ii) Notwithstanding paragraph (d)(1)(i) of this section, if the registrant is an investment company registered under the Investment Company Act of 1940 (15 U.S.C. 80a–1 *et seq.*) or a business development company as defined by section 2(a)(48) of the Investment Company Act of 1940 (15 U.S.C. 80a–2(a)(48)), a person shall not be deemed to be a bona fide nominee and shall not be named as such unless the person has consented to being named in the proxy statement and to serve if elected. Provided, however, that nothing in this section shall prevent any person soliciting in support of nominees who, if elected, would constitute a minority of the board of directors of an investment company registered under the Investment Company Act of 1940 or a business development company as defined by section 2(a)(48) of the Investment Company Act of 1940, from seeking authority to vote for nominees named in the registrant's proxy statement, so long as the soliciting party:

(A) Seeks authority to vote in the aggregate for the number of director positions then subject to election;

(B) Represents that it will vote for all the registrant nominees, other than those registrant nominees specified by the soliciting party;

(C) Provides the security holder an opportunity to withhold authority with respect to any other registrant nominee by writing the name of that nominee on the form of proxy; and

(D) States on the form of proxy and in the proxy statement that there is no assurance that the registrant's nominees will serve if elected with any of the soliciting party's nominees;

(2) To vote at any annual meeting other than the next annual meeting (or any adjournment thereof) to be held after the date on which the proxy statement and form of proxy are first sent or given to security holders;

(3) To vote with respect to more than one meeting (and any adjournment thereof) or more than one consent solicitation; or

§ 240.14a-5

(4) To consent to or authorize any action other than the action proposed to be taken in the proxy statement, or matters referred to in paragraph (c) of this section.

(e) The proxy statement or form of proxy shall provide, subject to reasonable specified conditions, that the shares represented by the proxy will be voted and that where the person solicited specifies by means of a ballot provided pursuant to paragraph (b) of this section a choice with respect to any matter to be acted upon, the shares will be voted in accordance with the specifications so made.

(f) No person conducting a solicitation subject to this regulation shall deliver a form of proxy, consent or authorization to any security holder unless the security holder concurrently receives, or has previously received, a definitive proxy statement that has been filed with the Commission pursuant to § 240.14a-6(b).

[17 FR 11432, Dec. 18, 1952, as amended at 31 FR 212, Jan. 7, 1966; 32 FR 20963, Dec. 29, 1967; 44 FR 68770, Nov. 29, 1979; 45 FR 76979, Nov. 21, 1980; 51 FR 42060, Nov. 20, 1986; 57 FR 48291, Oct. 22, 1992; 59 FR 67764, Dec. 30, 1994; 63 FR 29118, May 28, 1998; 63 FR 50622, Sept. 22, 1998; 64 FR 61456, Nov. 10, 1999; 72 FR 4167, Jan. 29, 2007; 76 FR 6045, Feb. 2, 2011; 75 FR 56781, Sept. 16, 2010; 86 FR 68378, Dec. 1, 2021]

§ 240.14a-5 Presentation of information in proxy statement.

(a) The information included in the proxy statement shall be clearly presented and the statements made shall be divided into groups according to subject matter and the various groups of statements shall be preceded by appropriate headings. The order of items and sub-items in the schedule need not be followed. Where practicable and appropriate, the information shall be presented in tabular form. All amounts shall be stated in figures. Information required by more than one applicable item need not be repeated. No statement need be made in response to any item or sub-item which is inapplicable.

(b) Any information required to be included in the proxy statement as to terms of securities or other subject matter which from a standpoint of practical necessity must be determined in the future may be stated in terms of present knowledge and intention. To the extent practicable, the authority to be conferred concerning each such matter shall be confined within limits reasonably related to the need for discretionary authority. Subject to the foregoing, information which is not known to the persons on whose behalf the solicitation is to be made and which it is not reasonably within the power of such persons to ascertain or procure may be omitted, if a brief statement of the circumstances rendering such information unavailable is made.

(c) Any information contained in any other proxy soliciting material which has been or will be furnished to each person solicited in connection with the same meeting or subject matter may be omitted from the proxy statement, if a clear reference is made to the particular document containing such information.

(d)(1) All printed proxy statements shall be in roman type at least as large and as legible as 10-point modern type, except that to the extent necessary for convenient presentation financial statements and other tabular data, but not the notes thereto, may be in roman type at least as large and as legible as 8-point modern type. All such type shall be leaded at least 2 points.

(2) Where a proxy statement is delivered through an electronic medium, issuers may satisfy legibility requirements applicable to printed documents, such as type size and font, by presenting all required information in a format readily communicated to investors.

(e) All proxy statements shall disclose, under an appropriate caption, the following dates:

(1) The deadline for submitting shareholder proposals for inclusion in the registrant's proxy statement and form of proxy for the registrant's next annual meeting, calculated in the manner provided in § 240.14a-8(e)(Question 5);

(2) The date after which notice of a shareholder proposal submitted outside the processes of § 240.14a-8 is considered untimely, either calculated in the manner provided by § 240.14a-4(c)(1) or as established by the registrant's advance notice provision, if any, authorized by applicable state law;

Securities and Exchange Commission § 240.14a-6

(3) The deadline for submitting nominees for inclusion in the registrant's proxy statement and form of proxy pursuant to § 240.14a–11, an applicable state or foreign law provision, or a registrant's governing documents as they relate to the inclusion of shareholder director nominees in the registrant's proxy materials for the registrant's next annual meeting of shareholders; and

(4) The deadline for providing notice of a solicitation of proxies in support of director nominees other than the registrant's nominees pursuant to § 240.14a–19 for the registrant's next annual meeting unless the registrant is an investment company registered under the Investment Company Act of 1940 (15 U.S.C. 80a–1 *et seq.*) or a business development company as defined by section 2(a)(48) of the Investment Company Act of 1940 (15 U.S.C. 80a–2(a)(48)).

(f) If the date of the next annual meeting is subsequently advanced or delayed by more than 30 calendar days from the date of the annual meeting to which the proxy statement relates, the registrant shall, in a timely manner, inform shareholders of such change, and the new dates referred to in paragraphs (e)(1) and (e)(2) of this section, by including a notice, under Item 5, in its earliest possible quarterly report on Form 10–Q (§ 249.308a of this chapter), or, in the case of investment companies, in a shareholder report under § 270.30d–1 of this chapter under the Investment Company Act of 1940, or, if impracticable, any means reasonably calculated to inform shareholders.

[17 FR 11432, Dec. 18, 1952, as amended at 36 FR 8935, May 15, 1971; 37 FR 23179, Oct. 31, 1972; 44 FR 68770, Nov. 29, 1979; 51 FR 42061, Nov. 20, 1986; 61 FR 24656, May 15, 1996; 63 FR 29118, May 28, 1998; 63 FR 46881, Sept. 3, 1998; 73 FR 977, Jan. 4, 2008; 75 FR 56782, Sept. 16, 2010; 86 FR 68379, Dec. 1, 2021]

§ 240.14a–6 Filing requirements.

(a) *Preliminary proxy statement.* Five preliminary copies of the proxy statement and form of proxy shall be filed with the Commission at least 10 calendar days prior to the date definitive copies of such material are first sent or given to security holders, or such shorter period prior to that date as the Commission may authorize upon a showing of good cause thereunder. A registrant, however, shall not file with the Commission a preliminary proxy statement, form of proxy or other soliciting material to be furnished to security holders concurrently therewith if the solicitation relates to an annual (or special meeting in lieu of the annual) meeting, or for an investment company registered under the Investment Company Act of 1940 (15 U.S.C. 80a–1 *et seq.*) or a business development company, if the solicitation relates to any meeting of security holders at which the only matters to be acted upon are:

(1) The election of directors;

(2) The election, approval or ratification of accountant(s);

(3) A security holder proposal included pursuant to Rule 14a–8 (§ 240.14a–8 of this chapter);

(4) A shareholder nominee for director included pursuant to § 240.14a–11, an applicable state or foreign law provision, or a registrant's governing documents as they relate to the inclusion of shareholder director nominees in the registrant's proxy materials.

(5) The approval or ratification of a plan as defined in paragraph (a)(6)(ii) of Item 402 of Regulation S–K (§ 229.402(a)(6)(ii) of this chapter) or amendments to such a plan;

(6) With respect to an investment company registered under the Investment Company Act of 1940 or a business development company, a proposal to continue, without change, any advisory or other contract or agreement that previously has been the subject of a proxy solicitation for which proxy material was filed with the Commission pursuant to this section;

(7) With respect to an open-end investment company registered under the Investment Company Act of 1940, a proposal to increase the number of shares authorized to be issued; and/or

(8) A vote to approve the compensation of executives as required pursuant to section 14A(a)(1) of the Securities Exchange Act of 1934 (15 U.S.C. 78n–1(a)(1)) and § 240.14a–21(a) of this chapter, or pursuant to section 111(e)(1) of the Emergency Economic Stabilization Act of 2008 (12 U.S.C. 5221(e)(1)) and

§ 240.14a-6

§ 240.14a-20 of this chapter, a vote to determine the frequency of shareholder votes to approve the compensation of executives as required pursuant to Section 14A(a)(2) of the Securities Exchange Act of 1934 (15 U.S.C. 78n-1(a)(2)) and § 240.14a-21(b) of this chapter, or any other shareholder advisory vote on executive compensation.

This exclusion from filing preliminary proxy material does not apply if the registrant comments upon or refers to a solicitation in opposition in connection with the meeting in its proxy material.

NOTE 1 TO PARAGRAPH (a): The filing of revised material does not recommence the ten day time period unless the revised material contains material revisions or material new proposal(s) that constitute a fundamental change in the proxy material.

NOTE 2 TO PARAGRAPH (a): The official responsible for the preparation of the proxy material should make every effort to verify the accuracy and completeness of the information required by the applicable rules. The preliminary material should be filed with the Commission at the earliest practicable date.

NOTE 3 TO PARAGRAPH (a): Solicitation in Opposition. For purposes of the exclusion from filing preliminary proxy material, a "solicitation in opposition" includes: [a] Any solicitation opposing a proposal supported by the registrant; {b} any solicitation supporting a proposal that the registrant does not expressly support, other than a security holder proposal included in the registrant's proxy material pursuant to § 240.14a-8; and {c} any solicitation subject to § 240.14a-19. The inclusion of a security holder proposal in the registrant's proxy material pursuant to § 240.14a-8 does not constitute a "solicitation in opposition," even if the registrant opposes the proposal and/or includes a statement in opposition to the proposal. The inclusion of a shareholder nominee in the registrant's proxy materials pursuant to an applicable state or foreign law provision, or a registrant's governing documents as they relate to the inclusion of shareholder director nominees in the registrant's proxy materials does not constitute a "solicitation in opposition" for purposes of paragraph (a) of this section, even if the registrant opposes the shareholder nominee and solicits against the shareholder nominee and in favor of a registrant nominee.

NOTE 4 TO PARAGRAPH (a): A registrant that is filing proxy material in preliminary form only because the registrant has commented on or referred to a solicitation in opposition should indicate that fact in a transmittal letter when filing the preliminary material with the Commission.

(b) *Definitive proxy statement and other soliciting material.* Eight definitive copies of the proxy statement, form of proxy and all other soliciting materials, in the same form as the materials sent to security holders, must be filed with the Commission no later than the date they are first sent or given to security holders. Three copies of these materials also must be filed with, or mailed for filing to, each national securities exchange on which the registrant has a class of securities listed and registered.

(c) *Personal solicitation materials.* If part or all of the solicitation involves personal solicitation, then eight copies of all written instructions or other materials that discuss, review or comment on the merits of any matter to be acted on, that are furnished to persons making the actual solicitation for their use directly or indirectly in connection with the solicitation, must be filed with the Commission no later than the date the materials are first sent or given to these persons.

(d) *Release dates.* All preliminary proxy statements and forms of proxy filed pursuant to paragraph (a) of this section shall be accompanied by a statement of the date on which definitive copies thereof filed pursuant to paragraph (b) of this section are intended to be released to security holders. All definitive material filed pursuant to paragraph (b) of this section shall be accompanied by a statement of the date on which copies of such material were released to security holders, or, if not released, the date on which copies thereof are intended to be released. All material filed pursuant to paragraph (c) of this section shall be accompanied by a statement of the date on which copies thereof were released to the individual who will make the actual solicitation or if not released, the date on which copies thereof are intended to be released.

(e)(1) *Public availability of information.* All copies of preliminary proxy statements and forms of proxy filed pursuant to paragraph (a) of this section shall be clearly marked "Preliminary Copies," and shall be deemed immediately available for public inspection

Securities and Exchange Commission § 240.14a–6

unless confidential treatment is obtained pursuant to paragraph (e)(2) of this section.

(2) *Confidential treatment.* If action will be taken on any matter specified in Item 14 of Schedule 14A (§ 240.14a–101), all copies of the preliminary proxy statement and form of proxy filed under paragraph (a) of this section will be for the information of the Commission only and will not be deemed available for public inspection until filed with the Commission in definitive form so long as:

(i) The proxy statement does not relate to a matter or proposal subject to § 240.13e–3 or a roll-up transaction as defined in Item 901(c) of Regulation S-K (§ 229.901(c) of this chapter);

(ii) Neither the parties to the transaction nor any persons authorized to act on their behalf have made any public communications relating to the transaction except for statements where the content is limited to the information specified in § 230.135 of this chapter; and

(iii) The materials are filed in paper and marked "Confidential, For Use of the Commission Only." In all cases, the materials may be disclosed to any department or agency of the United States Government and to the Congress, and the Commission may make any inquiries or investigation into the materials as may be necessary to conduct an adequate review by the Commission.

INSTRUCTION TO PARAGRAPH (e)(2): If communications are made publicly that go beyond the information specified in § 230.135 of this chapter, the preliminary proxy materials must be re-filed promptly with the Commission as public materials.

(f) *Communications not required to be filed.* Copies of replies to inquiries from security holders requesting further information and copies of communications which do no more than request that forms of proxy theretofore solicited be signed and returned need not be filed pursuant to this section.

(g) *Solicitations subject to § 240.14a–2(b)(1).* (1) Any person who:

(i) Engages in a solicitation pursuant to § 240.14a–2(b)(1), and

(ii) At the commencement of that solicitation owns beneficially securities of the class which is the subject of the solicitation with a market value of over $5 million,

shall furnish or mail to the Commission, not later than three days after the date the written solicitation is first sent or given to any security holder, five copies of a statement containing the information specified in the Notice of Exempt Solicitation (§ 240.14a–103) which statement shall attach as an exhibit all written soliciting materials. Five copies of an amendment to such statement shall be furnished or mailed to the Commission, in connection with dissemination of any additional communications, not later than three days after the date the additional material is first sent or given to any security holder. Three copies of the Notice of Exempt Solicitation and amendments thereto shall, at the same time the materials are furnished or mailed to the Commission, be furnished or mailed to each national securities exchange upon which any class of securities of the registrant is listed and registered.

(2) Notwithstanding paragraph (g)(1) of this section, no such submission need be made with respect to oral solicitations (other than with respect to scripts used in connection with such oral solicitations), speeches delivered in a public forum, press releases, published or broadcast opinions, statements, and advertisements appearing in a broadcast media, or a newspaper, magazine or other bona fide publication disseminated on a regular basis.

(h) *Revised material.* Where any proxy statement, form of proxy or other material filed pursuant to this section is amended or revised, two of the copies of such amended or revised material filed pursuant to this section (or in the case of investment companies registered under the Investment Company Act of 1940, three of such copies) shall be marked to indicate clearly and precisely the changes effected therein. If the amendment or revision alters the text of the material the changes in such text shall be indicated by means of underscoring or in some other appropriate manner.

(i) *Fees.* At the time of filing the proxy solicitation material, the persons upon whose behalf the solicitation

253

§ 240.14a-6

is made, other than investment companies registered under the Investment Company Act of 1940, shall pay to the Commission the following applicable fee:

(1) For preliminary proxy material involving acquisitions, mergers, spin-offs, consolidations or proposed sales or other dispositions of substantially all the assets of the company, a fee established in accordance with Rule 0-11 (§ 240.0-11 of this chapter) shall be paid. No refund shall be given.

(2) For all other proxy submissions and submissions made pursuant to § 240.14a-6(g), no fee shall be required.

(j) *Merger proxy materials.* (1) Any proxy statement, form of proxy or other soliciting material required to be filed by this section that also is either

(i) Included in a registration statement filed under the Securities Act of 1933 on Forms S-4 (§ 239.25 of this chapter), F-4 (§ 239.34 of this chapter) or N-14 (§ 239.23 of this chapter); or

(ii) Filed under § 230.424, § 230.425 or § 230.497 of this chapter is required to be filed only under the Securities Act, and is deemed filed under this section.

(2) Under paragraph (j)(1) of this section, the fee required by paragraph (i) of this section need not be paid.

(k) *Computing time periods.* In computing time periods beginning with the filing date specified in Regulation 14A (§§ 240.14a-1 to 240.14b-1 of this chapter), the filing date shall be counted as the first day of the time period and midnight of the last day shall constitute the end of the specified time period.

(l) *Roll-up transactions.* If a transaction is a roll-up transaction as defined in Item 901(c) of Regulation S-K (17 CFR 229.901(c)) and is registered (or authorized to be registered) on Form S-4 (17 CFR 229.25) or Form F-4 (17 CFR 229.34), the proxy statement of the sponsor or the general partner as defined in Item 901(d) and Item 901(a), respectively, of Regulation S-K (17 CFR 229.901) must be distributed to security holders no later than the lesser of 60 calendar days prior to the date on which the meeting of security holders is held or action is taken, or the maximum number of days permitted for giving notice under applicable state law.

17 CFR Ch. II (4-1-23 Edition)

(m) *Cover page.* Proxy materials filed with the Commission shall include a cover page in the form set forth in Schedule 14A (§ 240.14a-101 of this chapter). The cover page required by this paragraph need not be distributed to security holders.

(n) *Solicitations subject to § 240.14a-2(b)(4).* Any person who:

(1) Engages in a solicitation pursuant to § 240.14a-2(b)(4); and

(2) At the commencement of that solicitation both owns five percent (5%) or more of the outstanding securities of a class that is the subject of the proposed roll-up transaction, and engages in the business of buying and selling limited partnership interests in the secondary market, shall furnish or mail to the Commission, not later than three days after the date an oral or written solicitation by that person is first made, sent or provided to any security holder, five copies of a statement containing the information specified in the Notice of Exempt Preliminary Roll-up Communication (§ 240.14a-104). Five copies of any amendment to such statement shall be furnished or mailed to the Commission not later than three days after a communication containing revised material is first made, sent or provided to any security holder.

(o) *Solicitations before furnishing a definitive proxy statement.* Solicitations that are published, sent or given to security holders before they have been furnished a definitive proxy statement must be made in accordance with § 240.14a-12 unless there is an exemption available under § 240.14a-2.

(p) *Solicitations subject to § 240.14a-11.* Any soliciting material that is published, sent or given to shareholders in connection with § 240.14a-2(b)(7) or (b)(8) must be filed with the Commission as specified in that section.

[17 FR 11432, Dec. 18, 1952]

EDITORIAL NOTE: For FEDERAL REGISTER citations affecting § 240.14a-6, see the List of CFR Sections Affected, which appears in the Finding Aids section of the printed volume and at *www.govinfo.gov.*

Securities and Exchange Commission § 240.14a–7

§ 240.14a–7 Obligations of registrants to provide a list of, or mail soliciting material to, security holders.

(a) If the registrant has made or intends to make a proxy solicitation in connection with a security holder meeting or action by consent or authorization, upon the written request by any record or beneficial holder of securities of the class entitled to vote at the meeting or to execute a consent or authorization to provide a list of security holders or to mail the requesting security holder's materials, regardless of whether the request references this section, the registrant shall:

(1) Deliver to the requesting security holder within five business days after receipt of the request:

(i) Notification as to whether the registrant has elected to mail the security holder's soliciting materials or provide a security holder list if the election under paragraph (b) of this section is to be made by the registrant;

(ii) A statement of the approximate number of record holders and beneficial holders, separated by type of holder and class, owning securities in the same class or classes as holders which have been or are to be solicited on management's behalf, or any more limited group of such holders designated by the security holder if available or retrievable under the registrant's or its transfer agent's security holder data systems; and

(iii) The estimated cost of mailing a proxy statement, form of proxy or other communication to such holders, including to the extent known or reasonably available, the estimated costs of any bank, broker, and similar person through whom the registrant has solicited or intends to solicit beneficial owners in connection with the security holder meeting or action;

(2) Perform the acts set forth in either paragraphs (a)(2)(i) or (a)(2)(ii) of this section, at the registrant's or requesting security holder's option, as specified in paragraph (b) of this section:

(i) Send copies of any proxy statement, form of proxy, or other soliciting material, including a Notice of Internet Availability of Proxy Materials (as described in § 240.14a–16), furnished by the security holder to the record holders, including banks, brokers, and similar entities, designated by the security holder. A sufficient number of copies must be sent to the banks, brokers, and similar entities for distribution to all beneficial owners designated by the security holder. The security holder may designate only record holders and/or beneficial owners who have not requested paper and/ or e-mail copies of the proxy statement. If the registrant has received affirmative written or implied consent to deliver a single proxy statement to security holders at a shared address in accordance with the procedures in § 240.14a–3(e)(1), a single copy of the proxy statement or Notice of Internet Availability of Proxy Materials furnished by the security holder shall be sent to that address, provided that if multiple copies of the Notice of Internet Availability of Proxy Materials are furnished by the security holder for that address, the registrant shall deliver those copies in a single envelope to that address. The registrant shall send the security holder material with reasonable promptness after tender of the material to be sent, envelopes or other containers therefore, postage or payment for postage and other reasonable expenses of effecting such distribution. The registrant shall not be responsible for the content of the material; or

(ii) Deliver the following information to the requesting security holder within five business days of receipt of the request:

(A) A reasonably current list of the names, addresses and security positions of the record holders, including banks, brokers and similar entities holding securities in the same class or classes as holders which have been or are to be solicited on management's behalf, or any more limited group of such holders designated by the security holder if available or retrievable under the registrant's or its transfer agent's security holder data systems;

(B) The most recent list of names, addresses and security positions of beneficial owners as specified in § 240.14a–13(b), in the possession, or which subsequently comes into the possession, of the registrant;

(C) The names of security holders at a shared address that have consented

255

§ 240.14a–7

to delivery of a single copy of proxy materials to a shared address, if the registrant has received written or implied consent in accordance with § 240.14a–3(e)(1); and

(D) If the registrant has relied on § 240.14a–16, the names of security holders who have requested paper copies of the proxy materials for all meetings and the names of security holders who, as of the date that the registrant receives the request, have requested paper copies of the proxy materials only for the meeting to which the solicitation relates.

(iii) All security holder list information shall be in the form requested by the security holder to the extent that such form is available to the registrant without undue burden or expense. The registrant shall furnish the security holder with updated record holder information on a daily basis or, if not available on a daily basis, at the shortest reasonable intervals; provided, however, the registrant need not provide beneficial or record holder information more current than the record date for the meeting or action.

(b)(1) The requesting security holder shall have the options set forth in paragraph (a)(2) of this section, and the registrant shall have corresponding obligations, if the registrant or general partner or sponsor is soliciting or intends to solicit with respect to:

(i) A proposal that is subject to § 240.13e–3;

(ii) A roll-up transaction as defined in Item 901(c) of Regulation S-K (§ 229.901(c) of this chapter) that involves an entity with securities registered pursuant to Section 12 of the Act (15 U.S.C. 78*l*);

(iii) A roll-up transaction as defined in Item 901(c) of Regulation S-K (§ 229.901(c) of this chapter) that involves a limited partnership, unless the transaction involves only:

(A) Partnerships whose investors will receive new securities or securities in another entity that are not reported under a transaction reporting plan declared effective before December 17, 1993 by the Commission under Section 11A of the Act (15 U.S.C. 78k–1); or

(B) Partnerships whose investors' securities are reported under a transaction reporting plan declared effective before December 17, 1993 by the Commission under Section 11A of the Act (15 U.S.C. 78k–1).

(2) With respect to all other requests pursuant to this section, the registrant shall have the option to either mail the security holder's material or furnish the security holder list as set forth in this section.

(c) At the time of a list request, the security holder making the request shall:

(1) If holding the registrant's securities through a nominee, provide the registrant with a statement by the nominee or other independent third party, or a copy of a current filing made with the Commission and furnished to the registrant, confirming such holder's beneficial ownership; and

(2) Provide the registrant with an affidavit, declaration, affirmation or other similar document provided for under applicable state law identifying the proposal or other corporate action that will be the subject of the security holder's solicitation or communication and attesting that:

(i) The security holder will not use the list information for any purpose other than to solicit security holders with respect to the same meeting or action by consent or authorization for which the registrant is soliciting or intends to solicit or to communicate with security holders with respect to a solicitation commenced by the registrant; and

(ii) The security holder will not disclose such information to any person other than a beneficial owner for whom the request was made and an employee or agent to the extent necessary to effectuate the communication or solicitation.

(d) The security holder shall not use the information furnished by the registrant pursuant to paragraph (a)(2)(ii) of this section for any purpose other than to solicit security holders with respect to the same meeting or action by consent or authorization for which the registrant is soliciting or intends to solicit or to communicate with security holders with respect to a solicitation commenced by the registrant; or disclose such information to any person other than an employee, agent, or beneficial owner for whom a request was

Securities and Exchange Commission

§ 240.14a-8

made to the extent necessary to effectuate the communication or solicitation. The security holder shall return the information provided pursuant to paragraph (a)(2)(ii) of this section and shall not retain any copies thereof or of any information derived from such information after the termination of the solicitation.

(e) The security holder shall reimburse the reasonable expenses incurred by the registrant in performing the acts requested pursuant to paragraph (a) of this section.

NOTE 1 TO § 240.14A-7. Reasonably prompt methods of distribution to security holders may be used instead of mailing. If an alternative distribution method is chosen, the costs of that method should be considered where necessary rather than the costs of mailing.

NOTE 2 TO § 240.14A-7 When providing the information required by § 240.14a-7(a)(1)(ii), if the registrant has received affirmative written or implied consent to delivery of a single copy of proxy materials to a shared address in accordance with § 240.14a-3(e)(1), it shall exclude from the number of record holders those to whom it does not have to deliver a separate proxy statement.

[57 FR 48292, Oct. 22, 1992, as amended at 59 FR 63684, Dec. 8, 1994; 61 FR 24657, May 15, 1996; 65 FR 65750, Nov. 2, 2000; 72 FR 4167, Jan. 29, 2007; 72 FR 42238, Aug. 1, 2007]

§ 240.14a-8 Shareholder proposals.

This section addresses when a company must include a shareholder's proposal in its proxy statement and identify the proposal in its form of proxy when the company holds an annual or special meeting of shareholders. In summary, in order to have your shareholder proposal included on a company's proxy card, and included along with any supporting statement in its proxy statement, you must be eligible and follow certain procedures. Under a few specific circumstances, the company is permitted to exclude your proposal, but only after submitting its reasons to the Commission. We structured this section in a question-and-answer format so that it is easier to understand. The references to "you" are to a shareholder seeking to submit the proposal.

(a) *Question 1:* What is a proposal? A shareholder proposal is your recommendation or requirement that the company and/or its board of directors take action, which you intend to present at a meeting of the company's shareholders. Your proposal should state as clearly as possible the course of action that you believe the company should follow. If your proposal is placed on the company's proxy card, the company must also provide in the form of proxy means for shareholders to specify by boxes a choice between approval or disapproval, or abstention. Unless otherwise indicated, the word "proposal" as used in this section refers both to your proposal, and to your corresponding statement in support of your proposal (if any).

(b) *Question 2:* Who is eligible to submit a proposal, and how do I demonstrate to the company that I am eligible? (1) To be eligible to submit a proposal, you must satisfy the following requirements:

(i) You must have continuously held:

(A) At least $2,000 in market value of the company's securities entitled to vote on the proposal for at least three years; or

(B) At least $15,000 in market value of the company's securities entitled to vote on the proposal for at least two years; or

(C) At least $25,000 in market value of the company's securities entitled to vote on the proposal for at least one year; or

(D) The amounts specified in paragraph (b)(3) of this section. This paragraph (b)(1)(i)(D) will expire on the same date that § 240.14a-8(b)(3) expires; and

(ii) You must provide the company with a written statement that you intend to continue to hold the requisite amount of securities, determined in accordance with paragraph (b)(1)(i)(A) through (C) of this section, through the date of the shareholders' meeting for which the proposal is submitted; and

(iii) You must provide the company with a written statement that you are able to meet with the company in person or via teleconference no less than 10 calendar days, nor more than 30 calendar days, after submission of the shareholder proposal. You must include your contact information as well as business days and specific times that

257

§ 240.14a–8

you are available to discuss the proposal with the company. You must identify times that are within the regular business hours of the company's principal executive offices. If these hours are not disclosed in the company's proxy statement for the prior year's annual meeting, you must identify times that are between 9 a.m. and 5:30 p.m. in the time zone of the company's principal executive offices. If you elect to co-file a proposal, all co-filers must either:

(A) Agree to the same dates and times of availability, or

(B) Identify a single lead filer who will provide dates and times of the lead filer's availability to engage on behalf of all co-filers; and

(iv) If you use a representative to submit a shareholder proposal on your behalf, you must provide the company with written documentation that:

(A) Identifies the company to which the proposal is directed;

(B) Identifies the annual or special meeting for which the proposal is submitted;

(C) Identifies you as the proponent and identifies the person acting on your behalf as your representative;

(D) Includes your statement authorizing the designated representative to submit the proposal and otherwise act on your behalf;

(E) Identifies the specific topic of the proposal to be submitted;

(F) Includes your statement supporting the proposal; and

(G) Is signed and dated by you.

(v) The requirements of paragraph (b)(1)(iv) of this section shall not apply to shareholders that are entities so long as the representative's authority to act on the shareholder's behalf is apparent and self-evident such that a reasonable person would understand that the agent has authority to submit the proposal and otherwise act on the shareholder's behalf.

(vi) For purposes of paragraph (b)(1)(i) of this section, you may not aggregate your holdings with those of another shareholder or group of shareholders to meet the requisite amount of securities necessary to be eligible to submit a proposal.

(2) One of the following methods must be used to demonstrate your eligibility to submit a proposal:

(i) If you are the registered holder of your securities, which means that your name appears in the company's records as a shareholder, the company can verify your eligibility on its own, although you will still have to provide the company with a written statement that you intend to continue to hold the requisite amount of securities, determined in accordance with paragraph (b)(1)(i)(A) through (C) of this section, through the date of the meeting of shareholders.

(ii) If, like many shareholders, you are not a registered holder, the company likely does not know that you are a shareholder, or how many shares you own. In this case, at the time you submit your proposal, you must prove your eligibility to the company in one of two ways:

(A) The first way is to submit to the company a written statement from the "record" holder of your securities (usually a broker or bank) verifying that, at the time you submitted your proposal, you continuously held at least $2,000, $15,000, or $25,000 in market value of the company's securities entitled to vote on the proposal for at least three years, two years, or one year, respectively. You must also include your own written statement that you intend to continue to hold the requisite amount of securities, determined in accordance with paragraph (b)(1)(i)(A) through (C) of this section, through the date of the shareholders' meeting for which the proposal is submitted; or

(B) The second way to prove ownership applies only if you were required to file, and filed, a Schedule 13D (§ 240.13d–101), Schedule 13G (§ 240.13d–102), Form 3 (§ 249.103 of this chapter), Form 4 (§ 249.104 of this chapter), and/or Form 5 (§ 249.105 of this chapter), or amendments to those documents or updated forms, demonstrating that you meet at least one of the share ownership requirements under paragraph (b)(1)(i)(A) through (C) of this section. If you have filed one or more of these documents with the SEC, you may demonstrate your eligibility to submit a proposal by submitting to the company:

Securities and Exchange Commission § 240.14a-8

(1) A copy of the schedule(s) and/or form(s), and any subsequent amendments reporting a change in your ownership level;

(2) Your written statement that you continuously held at least $2,000, $15,000, or $25,000 in market value of the company's securities entitled to vote on the proposal for at least three years, two years, or one year, respectively; and

(3) Your written statement that you intend to continue to hold the requisite amount of securities, determined in accordance with paragraph (b)(1)(i)(A) through (C) of this section, through the date of the company's annual or special meeting.

(c) *Question 3:* How many proposals may I submit? Each person may submit no more than one proposal, directly or indirectly, to a company for a particular shareholders' meeting. A person may not rely on the securities holdings of another person for the purpose of meeting the eligibility requirements and submitting multiple proposals for a particular shareholders' meeting.

(d) *Question 4:* How long can my proposal be? The proposal, including any accompanying supporting statement, may not exceed 500 words.

(e) *Question 5:* What is the deadline for submitting a proposal? (1) If you are submitting your proposal for the company's annual meeting, you can in most cases find the deadline in last year's proxy statement. However, if the company did not hold an annual meeting last year, or has changed the date of its meeting for this year more than 30 days from last year's meeting, you can usually find the deadline in one of the company's quarterly reports on Form 10–Q (§ 249.308a of this chapter), or in shareholder reports of investment companies under § 270.30d–1 of this chapter of the Investment Company Act of 1940. In order to avoid controversy, shareholders should submit their proposals by means, including electronic means, that permit them to prove the date of delivery.

(2) The deadline is calculated in the following manner if the proposal is submitted for a regularly scheduled annual meeting. The proposal must be received at the company's principal executive offices not less than 120 calendar days before the date of the company's proxy statement released to shareholders in connection with the previous year's annual meeting. However, if the company did not hold an annual meeting the previous year, or if the date of this year's annual meeting has been changed by more than 30 days from the date of the previous year's meeting, then the deadline is a reasonable time before the company begins to print and send its proxy materials.

(3) If you are submitting your proposal for a meeting of shareholders other than a regularly scheduled annual meeting, the deadline is a reasonable time before the company begins to print and send its proxy materials.

(f) *Question 6:* What if I fail to follow one of the eligibility or procedural requirements explained in answers to Questions 1 through 4 of this section? (1) The company may exclude your proposal, but only after it has notified you of the problem, and you have failed adequately to correct it. Within 14 calendar days of receiving your proposal, the company must notify you in writing of any procedural or eligibility deficiencies, as well as of the time frame for your response. Your response must be postmarked, or transmitted electronically, no later than 14 days from the date you received the company's notification. A company need not provide you such notice of a deficiency if the deficiency cannot be remedied, such as if you fail to submit a proposal by the company's properly determined deadline. If the company intends to exclude the proposal, it will later have to make a submission under § 240.14a–8 and provide you with a copy under Question 10 below, § 240.14a–8(j).

(2) If you fail in your promise to hold the required number of securities through the date of the meeting of shareholders, then the company will be permitted to exclude all of your proposals from its proxy materials for any meeting held in the following two calendar years.

(g) *Question 7:* Who has the burden of persuading the Commission or its staff that my proposal can be excluded? Except as otherwise noted, the burden is on the company to demonstrate that it is entitled to exclude a proposal.

§ 240.14a–8

(h) *Question 8:* Must I appear personally at the shareholders' meeting to present the proposal? (1) Either you, or your representative who is qualified under state law to present the proposal on your behalf, must attend the meeting to present the proposal. Whether you attend the meeting yourself or send a qualified representative to the meeting in your place, you should make sure that you, or your representative, follow the proper state law procedures for attending the meeting and/or presenting your proposal.

(2) If the company holds its shareholder meeting in whole or in part via electronic media, and the company permits you or your representative to present your proposal via such media, then you may appear through electronic media rather than traveling to the meeting to appear in person.

(3) If you or your qualified representative fail to appear and present the proposal, without good cause, the company will be permitted to exclude all of your proposals from its proxy materials for any meetings held in the following two calendar years.

(i) *Question 9:* If I have complied with the procedural requirements, on what other bases may a company rely to exclude my proposal? (1) Improper under state law: If the proposal is not a proper subject for action by shareholders under the laws of the jurisdiction of the company's organization;

NOTE TO PARAGRAPH (i)(1): Depending on the subject matter, some proposals are not considered proper under state law if they would be binding on the company if approved by shareholders. In our experience, most proposals that are cast as recommendations or requests that the board of directors take specified action are proper under state law. Accordingly, we will assume that a proposal drafted as a recommendation or suggestion is proper unless the company demonstrates otherwise.

(2) *Violation of law:* If the proposal would, if implemented, cause the company to violate any state, federal, or foreign law to which it is subject;

NOTE TO PARAGRAPH (i)(2): We will not apply this basis for exclusion to permit exclusion of a proposal on grounds that it would violate foreign law if compliance with the foreign law would result in a violation of any state or federal law.

(3) *Violation of proxy rules:* If the proposal or supporting statement is contrary to any of the Commission's proxy rules, including § 240.14a-9, which prohibits materially false or misleading statements in proxy soliciting materials;

(4) *Personal grievance; special interest:* If the proposal relates to the redress of a personal claim or grievance against the company or any other person, or if it is designed to result in a benefit to you, or to further a personal interest, which is not shared by the other shareholders at large;

(5) *Relevance:* If the proposal relates to operations which account for less than 5 percent of the company's total assets at the end of its most recent fiscal year, and for less than 5 percent of its net earnings and gross sales for its most recent fiscal year, and is not otherwise significantly related to the company's business;

(6) *Absence of power/authority:* If the company would lack the power or authority to implement the proposal;

(7) *Management functions:* If the proposal deals with a matter relating to the company's ordinary business operations;

(8) *Director elections:* If the proposal:

(i) Would disqualify a nominee who is standing for election;

(ii) Would remove a director from office before his or her term expired;

(iii) Questions the competence, business judgment, or character of one or more nominees or directors;

(iv) Seeks to include a specific individual in the company's proxy materials for election to the board of directors; or

(v) Otherwise could affect the outcome of the upcoming election of directors.

(9) *Conflicts with company's proposal:* If the proposal directly conflicts with one of the company's own proposals to be submitted to shareholders at the same meeting;

NOTE TO PARAGRAPH (i)(9): A company's submission to the Commission under this section should specify the points of conflict with the company's proposal.

(10) *Substantially implemented:* If the company has already substantially implemented the proposal;

Securities and Exchange Commission § 240.14a-8

NOTE TO PARAGRAPH (i)(10): A company may exclude a shareholder proposal that would provide an advisory vote or seek future advisory votes to approve the compensation of executives as disclosed pursuant to Item 402 of Regulation S-K (§ 229.402 of this chapter) or any successor to Item 402 (a "say-on-pay vote") or that relates to the frequency of say-on-pay votes, provided that in the most recent shareholder vote required by § 240.14a-21(b) of this chapter a single year (i.e., one, two, or three years) received approval of a majority of votes cast on the matter and the company has adopted a policy on the frequency of say-on-pay votes that is consistent with the choice of the majority of votes cast in the most recent shareholder vote required by § 240.14a-21(b) of this chapter.

(11) *Duplication:* If the proposal substantially duplicates another proposal previously submitted to the company by another proponent that will be included in the company's proxy materials for the same meeting;

(12) *Resubmissions.* If the proposal addresses substantially the same subject matter as a proposal, or proposals, previously included in the company's proxy materials within the preceding five calendar years if the most recent vote occurred within the preceding three calendar years and the most recent vote was:

(i) Less than 5 percent of the votes cast if previously voted on once;
(ii) Less than 15 percent of the votes cast if previously voted on twice; or
(iii) Less than 25 percent of the votes cast if previously voted on three or more times.

(13) *Specific amount of dividends:* If the proposal relates to specific amounts of cash or stock dividends.

(j) *Question 10:* What procedures must the company follow if it intends to exclude my proposal? (1) If the company intends to exclude a proposal from its proxy materials, it must file its reasons with the Commission no later than 80 calendar days before it files its definitive proxy statement and form of proxy with the Commission. The company must simultaneously provide you with a copy of its submission. The Commission staff may permit the company to make its submission later than 80 days before the company files its definitive proxy statement and form of proxy, if the company demonstrates good cause for missing the deadline.

(2) The company must file six paper copies of the following:
(i) The proposal;
(ii) An explanation of why the company believes that it may exclude the proposal, which should, if possible, refer to the most recent applicable authority, such as prior Division letters issued under the rule; and
(iii) A supporting opinion of counsel when such reasons are based on matters of state or foreign law.

(k) *Question 11:* May I submit my own statement to the Commission responding to the company's arguments?

Yes, you may submit a response, but it is not required. You should try to submit any response to us, with a copy to the company, as soon as possible after the company makes its submission. This way, the Commission staff will have time to consider fully your submission before it issues its response. You should submit six paper copies of your response.

(l) *Question 12:* If the company includes my shareholder proposal in its proxy materials, what information about me must it include along with the proposal itself?

(1) The company's proxy statement must include your name and address, as well as the number of the company's voting securities that you hold. However, instead of providing that information, the company may instead include a statement that it will provide the information to shareholders promptly upon receiving an oral or written request.

(2) The company is not responsible for the contents of your proposal or supporting statement.

(m) *Question 13:* What can I do if the company includes in its proxy statement reasons why it believes shareholders should not vote in favor of my proposal, and I disagree with some of its statements?

(1) The company may elect to include in its proxy statement reasons why it believes shareholders should vote against your proposal. The company is allowed to make arguments reflecting its own point of view, just as you may express your own point of view in your proposal's supporting statement.

(2) However, if you believe that the company's opposition to your proposal

§ 240.14a-9

contains materially false or misleading statements that may violate our anti-fraud rule, § 240.14a-9, you should promptly send to the Commission staff and the company a letter explaining the reasons for your view, along with a copy of the company's statements opposing your proposal. To the extent possible, your letter should include specific factual information demonstrating the inaccuracy of the company's claims. Time permitting, you may wish to try to work out your differences with the company by yourself before contacting the Commission staff.

(3) We require the company to send you a copy of its statements opposing your proposal before it sends its proxy materials, so that you may bring to our attention any materially false or misleading statements, under the following timeframes:

(i) If our no-action response requires that you make revisions to your proposal or supporting statement as a condition to requiring the company to include it in its proxy materials, then the company must provide you with a copy of its opposition statements no later than 5 calendar days after the company receives a copy of your revised proposal; or

(ii) In all other cases, the company must provide you with a copy of its opposition statements no later than 30 calendar days before its files definitive copies of its proxy statement and form of proxy under § 240.14a-6.

[63 FR 29119, May 28, 1998; 63 FR 50622, 50623, Sept. 22, 1998, as amended at 72 FR 4168, Jan. 29, 2007; 72 FR 70456, Dec. 11, 2007; 73 FR 977, Jan. 4, 2008; 76 FR 6045, Feb. 2, 2011; 75 FR 56782, Sept. 16, 2010; 85 FR 70294, Nov. 4, 2020]

§ 240.14a-9 False or misleading statements.

(a) No solicitation subject to this regulation shall be made by means of any proxy statement, form of proxy, notice of meeting or other communication, written or oral, containing any statement which, at the time and in the light of the circumstances under which it is made, is false or misleading with respect to any material fact, or which omits to state any material fact necessary in order to make the statements therein not false or misleading or necessary to correct any statement in any earlier communication with respect to the solicitation of a proxy for the same meeting or subject matter which has become false or misleading.

(b) The fact that a proxy statement, form of proxy or other soliciting material has been filed with or examined by the Commission shall not be deemed a finding by the Commission that such material is accurate or complete or not false or misleading, or that the Commission has passed upon the merits of or approved any statement contained therein or any matter to be acted upon by security holders. No representation contrary to the foregoing shall be made.

(c) No nominee, nominating shareholder or nominating shareholder group, or any member thereof, shall cause to be included in a registrant's proxy materials, either pursuant to the Federal proxy rules, an applicable state or foreign law provision, or a registrant's governing documents as they relate to including shareholder nominees for director in a registrant's proxy materials, include in a notice on Schedule 14N (§ 240.14n-101), or include in any other related communication, any statement which, at the time and in the light of the circumstances under which it is made, is false or misleading with respect to any material fact, or which omits to state any material fact necessary in order to make the statements therein not false or misleading or necessary to correct any statement in any earlier communication with respect to a solicitation for the same meeting or subject matter which has become false or misleading.

NOTE: The following are some examples of what, depending upon particular facts and circumstances, may be misleading within the meaning of this section.

a. Predictions as to specific future market values.

b. Material which directly or indirectly impugns character, integrity or personal reputation, or directly or indirectly makes charges concerning improper, illegal or immoral conduct or associations, without factual foundation.

c. Failure to so identify a proxy statement, form of proxy and other soliciting material as to clearly distinguish it from the soliciting material of any other person or persons soliciting for the same meeting or subject matter.

Securities and Exchange Commission

§ 240.14a-12

d. Claims made prior to a meeting regarding the results of a solicitation.

[31 FR 212, Jan. 7, 1966, as amended at 41 FR 19933, May 14, 1976; 44 FR 38815, July 2, 1979; 44 FR 68456, Nov. 29, 1979; 75 FR 56782, Sept. 16, 2010; 85 FR 55155, Sept. 3, 2020; 87 FR 43196, July 19, 2022]

§ 240.14a-10 Prohibition of certain solicitations.

No person making a solicitation which is subject to §§ 240.14a-1 to 240.14a-10 shall solicit:

(a) Any undated or postdated proxy; or

(b) Any proxy which provides that it shall be deemed to be dated as of any date subsequent to the date on which it is signed by the security holder.

[17 FR 11434, Dec. 18, 1952]

§ 240.14a-12 Solicitation before furnishing a proxy statement.

(a) Notwithstanding the provisions of § 240.14a-3(a), a solicitation may be made before furnishing security holders with a proxy statement meeting the requirements of § 240.14a-3(a) if:

(1) Each written communication includes:

(i) The identity of the participants in the solicitation (as defined in Instruction 3 to Item 4 of Schedule 14A (§ 240.14a-101)) and a description of their direct or indirect interests, by security holdings or otherwise, or a prominent legend in clear, plain language advising security holders where they can obtain that information; and

(ii) A prominent legend in clear, plain language advising security holders to read the proxy statement when it is available because it contains important information. The legend also must explain to investors that they can get the proxy statement, and any other relevant documents, for free at the Commission's web site and describe which documents are available free from the participants; and

(2) A definitive proxy statement meeting the requirements of § 240.14a-3(a) is sent or given to security holders solicited in reliance on this section before or at the same time as the forms of proxy, consent or authorization are furnished to or requested from security holders.

(b) Any soliciting material published, sent or given to security holders in accordance with paragraph (a) of this section must be filed with the Commission no later than the date the material is first published, sent or given to security holders. Three copies of the material must at the same time be filed with, or mailed for filing to, each national securities exchange upon which any class of securities of the registrant is listed and registered. The soliciting material must include a cover page in the form set forth in Schedule 14A (§ 240.14a-101) and the appropriate box on the cover page must be marked. Soliciting material in connection with a registered offering is required to be filed only under § 230.424 or § 230.425 of this chapter, and will be deemed filed under this section.

(c) Solicitations by any person or group of persons for the purpose of opposing a solicitation subject to this regulation by any other person or group of persons with respect to the election or removal of directors at any annual or special meeting of security holders also are subject to the following provisions:

(1) *Application of this rule to annual report to security holders.* Notwithstanding the provisions of § 240.14a-3 (b) and (c), any portion of the annual report to security holders referred to in § 240.14a-3(b) that comments upon or refers to any solicitation subject to this rule, or to any participant in the solicitation, other than the solicitation by the management, must be filed with the Commission as proxy material subject to this regulation. This must be filed in electronic format unless an exemption is available under Rules 201 or 202 of Regulation S-T (§ 232.201 or § 232.202 of this chapter).

(2) *Use of reprints or reproductions.* In any solicitation subject to this § 240.14a-12(c), soliciting material that includes, in whole or part, any reprints or reproductions of any previously published material must:

(i) State the name of the author and publication, the date of prior publication, and identify any person who is quoted without being named in the previously published material.

(ii) Except in the case of a public or official document or statement, state whether or not the consent of the author and publication has been obtained to the use of the previously published material as proxy soliciting material.

(iii) If any participant using the previously published material, or anyone on his or her behalf, paid, directly or indirectly, for the preparation or prior publication of the previously published material, or has made or proposes to make any payments or give any other consideration in connection with the publication or republication of the material, state the circumstances.

INSTRUCTION 1 TO § 240.14a–12. If paper filing is permitted, file eight copies of the soliciting material with the Commission, except that only three copies of the material specified by § 240.14a–12(c)(1) need be filed.

INSTRUCTION 2 TO § 240.14a–12. Any communications made under this section after the definitive proxy statement is on file but before it is disseminated also must specify that the proxy statement is publicly available and the anticipated date of dissemination.

INSTRUCTION 3 TO § 240.14a–12. Inclusion of a nominee pursuant to § 240.14a–11, an applicable state or foreign law provision, or a registrant's governing documents as they relate to the inclusion of shareholder director nominees in the registrant's proxy materials, or solicitations by a nominating shareholder or nominating shareholder group that are made in connection with that nomination constitute solicitations in opposition subject to § 240.14a–12(c), except for purposes of § 240.14a–6(a).

[64 FR 61456, Nov. 10, 1999, as amended at 72 FR 4168, Jan. 29, 2007; 75 FR 56787, Sept. 16, 2010]

§ 240.14a–13 Obligation of registrants in communicating with beneficial owners.

(a) If the registrant knows that securities of any class entitled to vote at a meeting (or by written consents or authorizations if no meeting is held) with respect to which the registrant intends to solicit proxies, consents or authorizations are held of record by a broker, dealer, voting trustee, bank, association, or other entity that exercises fiduciary powers in nominee name or otherwise, the registrant shall:

(1) By first class mail or other equally prompt means:

(i) Inquire of each such record holder:

(A) Whether other persons are the beneficial owners of such securities and if so, the number of copies of the proxy and other soliciting material necessary to supply such material to such beneficial owners;

(B) In the case of an annual (or special meeting in lieu of the annual) meeting, or written consents in lieu of such meeting, at which directors are to be elected, the number of copies of the annual report to security holders necessary to supply such report to beneficial owners to whom such reports are to be distributed by such record holder or its nominee and not by the registrant;

(C) If the record holder has an obligation under § 240.14b–1(b)(3) or § 240.14b–2(b)(4)(ii) and (iii), whether an agent has been designated to act on its behalf in fulfilling such obligation and, if so, the name and address of such agent; and

(D) Whether it holds the registrant's securities on behalf of any respondent bank and, if so, the name and address of each such respondent bank; and

(ii) Indicate to each such record holder:

(A) Whether the registrant, pursuant to paragraph (c) of this section, intends to distribute the annual report to security holders to beneficial owners of its securities whose names, addresses and securities positions are disclosed pursuant to § 240.14b–1(b)(3) or § 240.14b–2(b)(4)(ii) and (iii);

(B) The record date; and

(C) At the option of the registrant, any employee benefit plan established by an affiliate of the registrant that holds securities of the registrant that the registrant elects to treat as exempt employee benefit plan securities;

(2) Upon receipt of a record holder's or respondent bank's response indicating, pursuant to § 240.14b–2(b)(1)(i), the names and addresses of its respondent banks, within one business day after the date such response is received, make an inquiry of and give notification to each such respondent bank in the same manner required by paragraph (a)(1) of this section; *Provided, however,* the inquiry required by paragraphs (a)(1) and (a)(2) of this section shall not cover beneficial owners of exempt employee benefit plan securities;

(3) Make the inquiry required by paragraph (a)(1) of this section at least

20 business days prior to the record date of the meeting of security holders, or

(i) If such inquiry is impracticable 20 business days prior to the record date of a special meeting, as many days before the record date of such meeting as is practicable or,

(ii) If consents or authorizations are solicited, and such inquiry is impracticable 20 business days before the earliest date on which they may be used to effect corporate action, as many days before that date as is practicable, or

(iii) At such later time as the rules of a national securities exchange on which the class of securities in question is listed may permit for good cause shown; *Provided, however,* That if a record holder or respondent bank has informed the registrant that a designated office(s) or department(s) is to receive such inquiries, the inquiry shall be made to such designated office(s) or department(s); and

(4) Supply, in a timely manner, each record holder and respondent bank of whom the inquiries required by paragraphs (a)(1) and (a)(2) of this section are made with copies of the proxy, other proxy soliciting material, and/or the annual report to security holders, in such quantities, assembled in such form and at such place(s), as the record holder or respondent bank may reasonably request in order to send such material to each beneficial owner of securities who is to be furnished with such material by the record holder or respondent bank; and

(5) Upon the request of any record holder or respondent bank that is supplied with proxy soliciting material and/or annual reports to security holders pursuant to paragraph (a)(4) of this section, pay its reasonable expenses for completing the sending of such material to beneficial owners.

NOTE 1: If the registrant's list of security holders indicates that some of its securities are registered in the name of a clearing agency registered pursuant to Section 17A of the Act (e.g., "Cede & Co.," nominee for the Depository Trust Company), the registrant shall make appropriate inquiry of the clearing agency and thereafter of the participants in such clearing agency who may hold on behalf of a beneficial owner or respondent bank, and shall comply with the above paragraph with respect to any such participant (*see* §240.14a-1(i)).

NOTE 2: The attention of registrants is called to the fact that each broker, dealer, bank, association, and other entity that exercises fiduciary powers has an obligation pursuant to §240.14b-1 and §240.14b-2 (except as provided therein with respect to exempt employee benefit plan securities held in nominee name) and, with respect to brokers and dealers, applicable self-regulatory organization requirements to obtain and forward, within the time periods prescribed therein, (a) proxies (or in lieu thereof requests for voting instructions) and proxy soliciting materials to beneficial owners on whose behalf it holds securities, and (b) annual reports to security holders to beneficial owners on whose behalf it holds securities, unless the registrant has notified the record holder or respondent bank that it has assumed responsibility to send such material to beneficial owners whose names, addresses, and securities positions are disclosed pursuant to §240.14b-1(b)(3) and §240.14b-2(b)(4)(ii) and (iii).

NOTE 3: The attention of registrants is called to the fact that registrants have an obligation, pursuant to paragraph (d) of this section, to cause proxies (or in lieu thereof requests for voting instructions), proxy soliciting material and annual reports to security holders to be furnished, in a timely manner, to beneficial owners of exempt employee benefit plan securities.

(b) Any registrant requesting pursuant to §240.14b-1(b)(3) or §240.14b-2(b)(4)(ii) and (iii) a list of names, addresses and securities positions of beneficial owners of its securities who either have consented or have not objected to disclosure of such information shall:

(1) By first class mail or other equally prompt means, inquire of each record holder and each respondent bank identified to the registrant pursuant to §240.14b-2(b)(4)(i) whether such record holder or respondent bank holds the registrant's securities on behalf of any respondent banks and, if so, the name and address of each such respondent bank;

(2) Request such list to be compiled as of a date no earlier than five business days after the date the registrant's request is received by the record holder or respondent bank; *Provided, however,* That if the record holder or respondent bank has informed the registrant that a designated office(s) or department(s) is to receive such requests, the request shall be made to

§ 240.14a-14

such designated office(s) or department(s);

(3) Make such request to the following persons that hold the registrant's securities on behalf of beneficial owners: all brokers, dealers, banks, associations and other entities that exercises fiduciary powers; *Provided however*, such request shall not cover beneficial owners of exempt employee benefit plan securities as defined in § 240.14a-1(d)(1); and, at the option of the registrant, such request may give notice of any employee benefit plan established by an affiliate of the registrant that holds securities of the registrant that the registrant elects to treat as exempt employee benefit plan securities;

(4) Use the information furnished in response to such request exclusively for purposes of corporate communications; and

(5) Upon the request of any record holder or respondent bank to whom such request is made, pay the reasonable expenses, both direct and indirect, of providing beneficial owner information.

NOTE: A registrant will be deemed to have satisfied its obligations under paragraph (b) of this section by requesting consenting and non-objecting beneficial owner lists from a designated agent acting on behalf of the record holder or respondent bank and paying to that designated agent the reasonable expenses of providing the beneficial owner information.

(c) A registrant, at its option, may send its annual report to security holders to the beneficial owners whose identifying information is provided by record holders and respondent banks, pursuant to § 240.14b-1(b)(3) or § 240.14b-2(b)(4)(ii) and (iii), provided that such registrant notifies the record holders and respondent banks, at the time it makes the inquiry required by paragraph (a) of this section, that the registrant will send the annual report to security holders to the beneficial owners so identified.

(d) If a registrant solicits proxies, consents or authorizations from record holders and respondent banks who hold securities on behalf of beneficial owners, the registrant shall cause proxies (or in lieu thereof requests or voting instructions), proxy soliciting material and annual reports to security holders to be furnished, in a timely manner, to beneficial owners of exempt employee benefit plan securities.

[51 FR 44276, Dec. 9, 1986; 52 FR 2220, Jan. 21, 1987, as amended at 52 FR 23648, June 24, 1987; 53 FR 16405, May 9, 1988; 57 FR 1099, Jan. 10, 1992; 72 FR 4168, Jan. 29, 2007]

§ 240.14a-14 Modified or superseded documents.

(a) Any statement contained in a document incorporated or deemed to be incorporated by reference shall be deemed to be modified or superseded, for purposes of the proxy statement, to the extent that a statement contained in the proxy statement or in any other subsequently filed document that also is or is deemed to be incorporated by reference modifies or replaces such statement.

(b) The modifying or superseding statement may, but need not, state it has modified or superseded a prior statement or include any other information set forth in the document that is not so modified or superseded. The making of a modifying or superseding statement shall not be deemed an admission that the modified or superseded statement, when made, constituted an untrue statement of a material fact, an omission to state a material fact necessary to make a statement not misleading, or the employment of a manipulative, deceptive, or fraudulent device, contrivance, scheme, transaction, act, practice, course of business or artifice to defraud, as those terms are used in the Securities Act of 1933, the Securities Exchange Act of 1934 ("the Act"), the Investment Company Act of 1940, or the rules and regulations thereunder.

(c) Any statement so modified shall not be deemed in its unmodified form to constitute part of the proxy statement for purposes of the Act. Any statement so superseded shall not be deemed to constitute a part of the proxy statement for purposes of the Act.

[52 FR 21936, June 10, 1987, as amended at 73 FR 17814, Apr. 1, 2008]

Securities and Exchange Commission

§ 240.14a-16

§ 240.14a-15 Differential and contingent compensation in connection with roll-up transactions.

(a) It shall be unlawful for any person to receive compensation for soliciting proxies, consents, or authorizations directly from security holders in connection with a roll-up transaction as provided in paragraph (b) of this section, if the compensation is:

(1) Based on whether the solicited proxy, consent, or authorization either approves or disapproves the proposed roll-up transaction; or

(2) Contingent on the approval, disapproval, or completion of the roll-up transaction.

(b) This section is applicable to a roll-up transaction as defined in Item 901(c) of Regulation S-K (§ 229.901(c) of this chapter), except for a transaction involving only:

(1) Finite-life entities that are not limited partnerships;

(2) Partnerships whose investors will receive new securities or securities in another entity that are not reported under a transaction reporting plan declared effective before December 17, 1993 by the Commission under section 11A of the Act (15 U.S.C. 78k-1); or

(3) Partnerships whose investors' securities are reported under a transaction reporting plan declared effective before December 17, 1993 by the Commission under section 11A of the Act (15 U.S.C. 78k-1).

[59 FR 63684, Dec. 8, 1994]

§ 240.14a-16 Internet availability of proxy materials.

(a)(1) A registrant shall furnish a proxy statement pursuant to § 240.14a-3(a), or an annual report to security holders pursuant to § 240.14a-3(b), to a security holder by sending the security holder a Notice of Internet Availability of Proxy Materials, as described in this section, 40 calendar days or more prior to the security holder meeting date, or if no meeting is to be held, 40 calendar days or more prior to the date the votes, consents or authorizations may be used to effect the corporate action, and complying with all other requirements of this section.

(2) Unless the registrant chooses to follow the full set delivery option set forth in paragraph (n) of this section, it must provide the record holder or respondent bank with all information listed in paragraph (d) of this section in sufficient time for the record holder or respondent bank to prepare, print and send a Notice of Internet Availability of Proxy Materials to beneficial owners at least 40 calendar days before the meeting date.

(b)(1) All materials identified in the Notice of Internet Availability of Proxy Materials must be publicly accessible, free of charge, at the Web site address specified in the notice on or before the time that the notice is sent to the security holder and such materials must remain available on that Web site through the conclusion of the meeting of security holders.

(2) All additional soliciting materials sent to security holders or made public after the Notice of Internet Availability of Proxy Materials has been sent must be made publicly accessible at the specified Web site address no later than the day on which such materials are first sent to security holders or made public.

(3) The Web site address relied upon for compliance under this section may not be the address of the Commission's electronic filing system.

(4) The registrant must provide security holders with a means to execute a proxy as of the time the Notice of Internet Availability of Proxy Materials is first sent to security holders.

(c) The materials must be presented on the Web site in a format, or formats, convenient for both reading online and printing on paper.

(d) The Notice of Internet Availability of Proxy Materials must contain the following:

(1) A prominent legend in bold-face type that states "Important Notice Regarding the Availability of Proxy Materials for the Shareholder Meeting To Be Held on [insert meeting date]";

(2) An indication that the communication is not a form for voting and presents only an overview of the more complete proxy materials, which contain important information and are available on the Internet or by mail, and encouraging a security holder to access and review the proxy materials before voting;

§ 240.14a–16

(3) The Internet Web site address where the proxy materials are available;

(4) Instructions regarding how a security holder may request a paper or e-mail copy of the proxy materials at no charge, including the date by which they should make the request to facilitate timely delivery, and an indication that they will not otherwise receive a paper or e-mail copy;

(5) The date, time, and location of the meeting, or if corporate action is to be taken by written consent, the earliest date on which the corporate action may be effected;

(6) A clear and impartial identification of each separate matter intended to be acted on and the soliciting person's recommendations, if any, regarding those matters, but no supporting statements;

(7) A list of the materials being made available at the specified Web site;

(8) A toll-free telephone number, an e-mail address, and an Internet Web site where the security holder can request a copy of the proxy statement, annual report to security holders, and form of proxy, relating to all of the registrant's future security holder meetings and for the particular meeting to which the proxy materials being furnished relate;

(9) Any control/identification numbers that the security holder needs to access his or her form of proxy;

(10) Instructions on how to access the form of proxy, provided that such instructions do not enable a security holder to execute a proxy without having access to the proxy statement and, if required by § 240.14a–3(b), the annual report to security holders; and

(11) Information on how to obtain directions to be able to attend the meeting and vote in person.

(e)(1) The Notice of Internet Availability of Proxy Materials may not be incorporated into, or combined with, another document, except that it may be incorporated into, or combined with, a notice of security holder meeting required under state law, unless state law prohibits such incorporation or combination.

(2) The Notice of Internet Availability of Proxy Materials may contain only the information required by paragraph (d) of this section and any additional information required to be included in a notice of security holders meeting under state law; provided that:

(i) The registrant must revise the information on the Notice of Internet Availability of Proxy Materials, including any title to the document, to reflect the fact that:

(A) The registrant is conducting a consent solicitation rather than a proxy solicitation; or

(B) The registrant is not soliciting proxy or consent authority, but is furnishing an information statement pursuant to § 240.14c–2; and

(ii) The registrant may include a statement on the Notice to educate security holders that no personal information other than the identification or control number is necessary to execute a proxy.

(f)(1) Except as provided in paragraph (h) of this section, the Notice of Internet Availability of Proxy Materials must be sent separately from other types of security holder communications and may not accompany any other document or materials, including the form of proxy.

(2) Notwithstanding paragraph (f)(1) of this section, the registrant may accompany the Notice of Internet Availability of Proxy Materials with:

(i) A pre-addressed, postage-paid reply card for requesting a copy of the proxy materials;

(ii) A copy of any notice of security holder meeting required under state law if that notice is not combined with the Notice of Internet Availability of Proxy Materials;

(iii) In the case of an investment company registered under the Investment Company Act of 1940, the company's prospectus, a summary prospectus that satisfies the requirements of § 230.498(b) or § 230.498A(b) or (c) of this chapter, a Notice under § 270.30e–3 of this chapter, or a report that is required to be transmitted to stockholders by section 30(e) of the Investment Company Act (15 U.S.C. 80a–29(e)) and its implementing regulations (e.g., §§ 270.30e–1 and 270.30e–2 of this chapter); and

(iv) An explanation of the reasons for a registrant's use of the rules detailed

Securities and Exchange Commission

§ 240.14a–16

in this section and the process of receiving and reviewing the proxy materials and voting as detailed in this section.

(g) *Plain English.* (1) To enhance the readability of the Notice of Internet Availability of Proxy Materials, the registrant must use plain English principles in the organization, language, and design of the notice.

(2) The registrant must draft the language in the Notice of Internet Availability of Proxy Materials so that, at a minimum, it substantially complies with each of the following plain English writing principles:

(i) Short sentences;

(ii) Definite, concrete, everyday words;

(iii) Active voice;

(iv) Tabular presentation or bullet lists for complex material, whenever possible;

(v) No legal jargon or highly technical business terms; and

(vi) No multiple negatives.

(3) In designing the Notice of Internet Availability of Proxy Materials, the registrant may include pictures, logos, or similar design elements so long as the design is not misleading and the required information is clear.

(h) The registrant may send a form of proxy to security holders if:

(1) At least 10 calendar days or more have passed since the date it first sent the Notice of Internet Availability of Proxy Materials to security holders and the form of proxy is accompanied by a copy of the Notice of Internet Availability of Proxy Materials; or

(2) The form of proxy is accompanied or preceded by a copy, via the same medium, of the proxy statement and any annual report to security holders that is required by § 240.14a–3(b).

(i) The registrant must file a form of the Notice of Internet Availability of Proxy Materials with the Commission pursuant to § 240.14a–6(b) no later than the date that the registrant first sends the notice to security holders.

(j) *Obligation to provide copies.* (1) The registrant must send, at no cost to the record holder or respondent bank and by U.S. first class mail or other reasonably prompt means, a paper copy of the proxy statement, information statement, annual report to security holders, and form of proxy (to the extent each of those documents is applicable) to any record holder or respondent bank requesting such a copy within three business days after receiving a request for a paper copy.

(2) The registrant must send, at no cost to the record holder or respondent bank and via e-mail, an electronic copy of the proxy statement, information statement, annual report to security holders, and form of proxy (to the extent each of those documents is applicable) to any record holder or respondent bank requesting such a copy within three business days after receiving a request for an electronic copy via e-mail.

(3) The registrant must provide copies of the proxy materials for one year after the conclusion of the meeting or corporate action to which the proxy materials relate, provided that, if the registrant receives the request after the conclusion of the meeting or corporate action to which the proxy materials relate, the registrant need not send copies via First Class mail and need not respond to such request within three business days.

(4) The registrant must maintain records of security holder requests to receive materials in paper or via e-mail for future solicitations and must continue to provide copies of the materials to a security holder who has made such a request until the security holder revokes such request.

(k) *Security holder information.* (1) A registrant or its agent shall maintain the Internet Web site on which it posts its proxy materials in a manner that does not infringe on the anonymity of a person accessing such Web site.

(2) The registrant and its agents shall not use any e-mail address obtained from a security holder solely for the purpose of requesting a copy of proxy materials pursuant to paragraph (j) of this section for any purpose other than to send a copy of those materials to that security holder. The registrant shall not disclose such information to any person other than an employee or agent to the extent necessary to send a copy of the proxy materials pursuant to paragraph (j) of this section.

(1) A person other than the registrant may solicit proxies pursuant to the

§ 240.14a–16

conditions imposed on registrants by this section, provided that:

(1) A soliciting person other than the registrant is required to provide copies of its proxy materials only to security holders to whom it has sent a Notice of Internet Availability of Proxy Materials; and

(2) A soliciting person other than the registrant must send its Notice of Internet Availability of Proxy Materials by the later of:

(i) 40 Calendar days prior to the security holder meeting date or, if no meeting is to be held, 40 calendar days prior to the date the votes, consents, or authorizations may be used to effect the corporate action; or

(ii) The date on which it files its definitive proxy statement with the Commission, provided its preliminary proxy statement is filed no later than 10 calendar days after the date that the registrant files its definitive proxy statement.

(3) *Content of the soliciting person's Notice of Internet Availability of Proxy Materials.* (i) If, at the time a soliciting person other than the registrant sends its Notice of Internet Availability of Proxy Materials, the soliciting person is not aware of all matters on the registrant's agenda for the meeting of security holders, the soliciting person's Notice on Internet Availability of Proxy Materials must provide a clear and impartial identification of each separate matter on the agenda to the extent known by the soliciting person at that time. The soliciting person's notice also must include a clear statement indicating that there may be additional agenda items of which the soliciting person is not aware and that the security holder cannot direct a vote for those items on the soliciting person's proxy card provided at that time.

(ii) If a soliciting person other than the registrant sends a form of proxy not containing all matters intended to be acted upon, the Notice of Internet Availability of Proxy Materials must clearly state whether execution of the form of proxy will invalidate a security holder's prior vote on matters not presented on the form of proxy.

(m) This section shall not apply to a proxy solicitation in connection with a business combination transaction, as defined in § 230.165 of this chapter, as well as transactions for cash consideration requiring disclosure under Item 14 of § 240.14a–101.

(n) *Full Set Delivery Option.* (1) For purposes of this paragraph (n), the term full set of proxy materials shall include all of the following documents:

(i) A copy of the proxy statement;

(ii) A copy of the annual report to security holders if required by § 240.14a–3(b); and

(iii) A form of proxy.

(2) Notwithstanding paragraphs (e) and (f)(2) of this section, a registrant or other soliciting person may:

(i) Accompany the Notice of Internet Availability of Proxy Materials with a full set of proxy materials; or

(ii) Send a full set of proxy materials without a Notice of Internet Availability of Proxy Materials if all of the information required in a Notice of Internet Availability of Proxy Materials pursuant to paragraphs (d) and (n)(4) of this section is incorporated in the proxy statement and the form of proxy.

(3) A registrant or other soliciting person that sends a full set of proxy materials to a security holder pursuant to this paragraph (n) need not comply with

(i) The timing provisions of paragraphs (a) and (l)(2) of this section; and

(ii) The obligation to provide copies pursuant to paragraph (j) of this section.

(4) A registrant or other soliciting person that sends a full set of proxy materials to a security holder pursuant to this paragraph (n) need not include in its Notice of Internet Availability of Proxy Materials, proxy statement, or form of proxy the following disclosures:

(i) Instructions regarding the nature of the communication pursuant to paragraph (d)(2) of this section;

(ii) Instructions on how to request a copy of the proxy materials; and

(iii) Instructions on how to access the form of proxy pursuant to paragraph (d)(10) of this section.

[72 FR 4168, Jan. 29, 2007, as amended at 72 FR 42238, Aug. 1, 2007; 72 FR 42238, Aug. 1, 2007; 73 FR 17814, Apr. 1, 2008; 75 FR 9081, Feb. 26, 2010; 83 FR 29204, June 22, 2018; 85 FR 26101, May 1, 2020]

§ 240.14a–17 Electronic shareholder forums.

(a) A shareholder, registrant, or third party acting on behalf of a shareholder or registrant may establish, maintain, or operate an electronic shareholder forum to facilitate interaction among the registrant's shareholders and between the registrant and its shareholders as the shareholder or registrant deems appropriate. Subject to paragraphs (b) and (c) of this section, the forum must comply with the federal securities laws, including Section 14(a) of the Act and its associated regulations, other applicable federal laws, applicable state laws, and the registrant's governing documents.

(b) No shareholder, registrant, or third party acting on behalf of a shareholder or registrant, by reason of establishing, maintaining, or operating an electronic shareholder forum, will be liable under the federal securities laws for any statement or information provided by another person to the electronic shareholder forum. Nothing in this section prevents or alters the application of the federal securities laws, including the provisions for liability for fraud, deception, or manipulation, or other applicable federal and state laws to the person or persons that provide a statement or information to an electronic shareholder forum.

(c) Reliance on the exemption in § 240.14a–2(b)(6) to participate in an electronic shareholder forum does not eliminate a person's eligibility to solicit proxies after the date that the exemption in § 240.14a–2(b)(6) is no longer available, or is no longer being relied upon, provided that any such solicitation is conducted in accordance with this regulation.

[73 FR 4458, Jan. 25, 2008]

§ 240.14a–18 Disclosure regarding nominating shareholders and nominees submitted for inclusion in a registrant's proxy materials pursuant to applicable state or foreign law, or a registrant's governing documents.

To have a nominee included in a registrant's proxy materials pursuant to a procedure set forth under applicable state or foreign law, or the registrant's governing documents addressing the inclusion of shareholder director nominees in the registrant's proxy materials, the nominating shareholder or nominating shareholder group must provide notice to the registrant of its intent to do so on a Schedule 14N (§ 240.14n–101) and file that notice, including the required disclosure, with the Commission on the date first transmitted to the registrant. This notice shall be postmarked or transmitted electronically to the registrant by the date specified by the registrant's advance notice provision or, where no such provision is in place, no later than 120 calendar days before the anniversary of the date that the registrant mailed its proxy materials for the prior year's annual meeting, except that, if the registrant did not hold an annual meeting during the prior year, or if the date of the meeting has changed by more than 30 calendar days from the prior year, then the nominating shareholder or nominating shareholder group must provide notice a reasonable time before the registrant mails its proxy materials, as specified by the registrant in a Form 8–K (§ 249.308 of this chapter) filed pursuant to Item 5.08 of Form 8–K.

INSTRUCTION TO § 240.14a–18. The registrant is not responsible for any information provided in the Schedule 14N (§ 240.14n–101) by the nominating shareholder or nominating shareholder group, which is submitted as required by this section or otherwise provided by the nominating shareholder or nominating shareholder group that is included in the registrant's proxy materials.

[75 FR 56787, Sept. 16, 2010]

§ 240.14a–19 Solicitation of proxies in support of director nominees other than the registrant's nominees.

(a) No person may solicit proxies in support of director nominees other than the registrant's nominees unless such person:

(1) Provides notice to the registrant in accordance with paragraph (b) of this section unless the information required by paragraph (b) of this section has been provided in a preliminary or definitive proxy statement previously filed by such person;

(2) Files a definitive proxy statement with the Commission in accordance with § 240.14a–6(b) by the later of:

§ 240.14a-19

(i) 25 calendar days prior to the security holder meeting date; or

(ii) Five (5) calendar days after the date that the registrant files its definitive proxy statement; and

(3) Solicits the holders of shares representing at least 67% of the voting power of shares entitled to vote on the election of directors and includes a statement to that effect in the proxy statement or form of proxy.

(b) The notice shall:

(1) Be postmarked or transmitted electronically to the registrant at its principal executive office no later than 60 calendar days prior to the anniversary of the previous year's annual meeting date, except that, if the registrant did not hold an annual meeting during the previous year, or if the date of the meeting has changed by more than 30 calendar days from the previous year, then notice must be provided by the later of 60 calendar days prior to the date of the annual meeting or the 10th calendar day following the day on which public announcement of the date of the annual meeting is first made by the registrant;

(2) Include the names of all nominees for whom such person intends to solicit proxies; and

(3) Include a statement that such person intends to solicit the holders of shares representing at least 67% of the voting power of shares entitled to vote on the election of directors in support of director nominees other than the registrant's nominees.

(c) If any change occurs with respect to such person's intent to solicit the holders of shares representing at least 67% of the voting power of shares entitled to vote on the election of directors in support of director nominees other than the registrant's nominees or with respect to the names of such person's nominees, such person shall notify the registrant promptly.

(d) A registrant shall notify the person conducting a proxy solicitation subject to this section of the names of all nominees for whom the registrant intends to solicit proxies unless the names have been provided in a preliminary or definitive proxy statement previously filed by the registrant. The notice shall be postmarked or transmitted electronically no later than 50 calendar days prior to the anniversary of the previous year's annual meeting date, except that, if the registrant did not hold an annual meeting during the previous year, or if the date of the meeting has changed by more than 30 calendar days from the previous year, then notice must be provided no later than 50 calendar days prior to the date of the annual meeting. If any change occurs with respect to the names of the registrant's nominees, the registrant shall notify the person conducting a proxy solicitation subject to this section promptly.

(e) Notwithstanding the provisions of §240.14a-4(b)(2), if any person is conducting a proxy solicitation subject to this section, the form of proxy of the registrant and the form of proxy of any person soliciting proxies pursuant to this section shall:

(1) Set forth the names of all persons nominated for election by the registrant and by any person or group of persons that has complied with this section and the name of any person whose nomination by a shareholder or shareholder group satisfies the requirements of an applicable state or foreign law provision or a registrant's governing documents as they relate to the inclusion of shareholder director nominees in the registrant's proxy materials;

(2) Provide a means for the security holder to grant authority to vote for the nominees set forth;

(3) Clearly distinguish between the nominees of the registrant, the nominees of the person or group of persons that has complied with this section and the nominees of any shareholder or shareholder group whose nominees are included in a registrant's proxy materials pursuant to the requirements of an applicable state or foreign law provision or a registrant's governing documents;

(4) Within each group of nominees referred to in paragraph (e)(3) of this section, list nominees in alphabetical order by last name;

(5) Use the same font type, style and size for all nominees;

(6) Prominently disclose the maximum number of nominees for which authority to vote can be granted; and

Securities and Exchange Commission § 240.14a-20

(7) Prominently disclose the treatment and effect of a proxy executed in a manner that grants authority to vote for the election of fewer or more nominees than the number of directors being elected and the treatment and effect of a proxy executed in a manner that does not grant authority to vote with respect to any nominees.

(f) If any person is conducting a proxy solicitation subject to this section, the form of proxy of the registrant and the form of proxy of any person soliciting proxies pursuant to this section may provide a means for the security holder to grant authority to vote for the nominees of the registrant set forth, as a group, and a means for the security holder to grant authority to vote for the nominees of any other soliciting person set forth, as a group, provided that there is a similar means for the security holder to withhold authority to vote for such groups of nominees unless the number of nominees of the registrant or of any other soliciting person is less than the number of directors being elected. Means to grant authority to vote for any nominees as a group or to withhold authority for any nominees as a group may not be provided if the form of proxy includes one or more shareholder nominees in accordance with an applicable state or foreign law provision or a registrant's governing documents as they relate to the inclusion of shareholder director nominees in the registrant's proxy materials.

(g) This section shall not apply to:

(1) A consent solicitation; or

(2) A solicitation in connection with an election of directors at an investment company registered under the Investment Company Act of 1940 (15 U.S.C. 80a-1 *et seq.*) or a business development company as defined by section 2(a)(48) of the Investment Company Act of 1940 (15 U.S.C. 80a-2(a)(48)).

INSTRUCTION 1 to paragraphs (b)(1) and (d). Where the deadline falls on a Saturday, Sunday, or holiday, the deadline will be treated as the first business day following the Saturday, Sunday, or holiday.

INSTRUCTION 2 to paragraph (f). Where applicable state law gives legal effect to votes cast against a nominee, the form of proxy may provide a means for the security holder to grant authority to vote for the nominees of the registrant set forth, as a group, and a means for the security holder to grant authority to vote for the nominees of any other soliciting person set forth, as a group, provided that, in lieu of the ability to withhold authority to vote as a group, there is a similar means for the security holder to vote against such group of nominees (as well as a means for security holders to abstain from voting for such group of nominees).

[86 FR 68380, Dec. 1, 2021]

§ 240.14a-20 Shareholder approval of executive compensation of TARP recipients.

If a solicitation is made by a registrant that is a *TARP recipient*, as defined in section 111(a)(3) of the Emergency Economic Stabilization Act of 2008 (12 U.S.C. 5221(a)(3)), during the period in which any obligation arising from financial assistance provided under the *TARP*, as defined in section 3(8) of the Emergency Economic Stabilization Act of 2008 (12 U.S.C. 5202(8)), remains outstanding and the solicitation relates to an annual (or special meeting in lieu of the annual) meeting of security holders for which proxies will be solicited for the election of directors, as required pursuant to section 111(e)(1) of the Emergency Economic Stabilization Act of 2008 (12 U.S.C. 5221(e)(1)), the registrant shall provide a separate shareholder vote to approve the compensation of executives, as disclosed pursuant to Item 402 of Regulation S-K (§ 229.402 of this chapter), including the compensation discussion and analysis, the compensation tables, and any related material.

NOTE TO § 240.14a-20: TARP recipients that are smaller reporting companies entitled to provide scaled disclosure pursuant to Item 402(l) of Regulation S-K are not required to include a compensation discussion and analysis in their proxy statements in order to comply with this section. In the case of these smaller reporting companies, the required vote must be to approve the compensation of executives as disclosed pursuant to Item 402(m) through (q) of Regulation S-K.

[75 FR 2794, Jan. 19, 2010]

§ 240.14a-21 Shareholder approval of executive compensation, frequency of votes for approval of executive compensation and shareholder approval of golden parachute compensation.

(a) If a solicitation is made by a registrant, other than an emerging growth company as defined in Rule 12b-2 (§ 240.12b-2), and the solicitation relates to an annual or other meeting of shareholders at which directors will be elected and for which the rules of the Commission require executive compensation disclosure pursuant to Item 402 of Regulation S-K (§ 229.402 of this chapter), the registrant shall, for the first annual or other meeting of shareholders on or after January 21, 2011, or for the first annual or other meeting of shareholders on or after January 21, 2013 if the registrant is a smaller reporting company, and thereafter no later than the annual or other meeting of shareholders held in the third calendar year after the immediately preceding vote under this subsection, include a separate resolution subject to shareholder advisory vote to approve the compensation of its named executive officers, as disclosed pursuant to Item 402 of Regulation S-K.

INSTRUCTION TO PARAGRAPH (a): The registrant's resolution shall indicate that the shareholder advisory vote under this subsection is to approve the compensation of the registrant's named executive officers as disclosed pursuant to Item 402 of Regulation S-K (§ 229.402 of this chapter). The following is a non-exclusive example of a resolution that would satisfy the requirements of this subsection: "RESOLVED, that the compensation paid to the company's named executive officers, as disclosed pursuant to Item 402 of Regulation S-K, including the Compensation Discussion and Analysis, compensation tables and narrative discussion is hereby APPROVED."

(b) If a solicitation is made by a registrant, other than an emerging growth company as defined in Rule 12b-2 (§ 240.12b-2), and the solicitation relates to an annual or other meeting of shareholders at which directors will be elected and for which the rules of the Commission require executive compensation disclosure pursuant to Item 402 of Regulation S-K (§ 229.402 of this chapter), the registrant shall, for the first annual or other meeting of shareholders on or after January 21, 2011, or for the first annual or other meeting of shareholders on or after January 21, 2013 if the registrant is a smaller reporting company, and thereafter no later than the annual or other meeting of shareholders held in the sixth calendar year after the immediately preceding vote under this subsection, include a separate resolution subject to shareholder advisory vote as to whether the shareholder vote required by paragraph (a) of this section should occur every 1, 2 or 3 years. Registrants required to provide a separate shareholder vote pursuant to § 240.14a-20 of this chapter shall include the separate resolution required by this section for the first annual or other meeting of shareholders after the registrant has repaid all obligations arising from financial assistance provided under the TARP, as defined in section 3(8) of the Emergency Economic Stabilization Act of 2008 (12 U.S.C. 5202(8)), and thereafter no later than the annual or other meeting of shareholders held in the sixth calendar year after the immediately preceding vote under this subsection.

(c) If a solicitation is made by a registrant, other than an emerging growth company as defined in Rule 12b-2 (§ 240.12b-2), for a meeting of shareholders at which shareholders are asked to approve an acquisition, merger, consolidation or proposed sale or other disposition of all or substantially all the assets of the registrant, the registrant shall include a separate resolution subject to shareholder advisory vote to approve any agreements or understandings and compensation disclosed pursuant to Item 402(t) of Regulation S-K (§ 229.402(t) of this chapter), unless such agreements or understandings have been subject to a shareholder advisory vote under paragraph (a) of this section. Consistent with section 14A(b) of the Exchange Act (15 U.S.C. 78n-1(b)), any agreements or understandings between an acquiring company and the named executive officers of the registrant, where the registrant is not the acquiring company, are not required to be subject to the separate shareholder advisory vote under this paragraph.

Securities and Exchange Commission § 240.14a-101

INSTRUCTIONS TO § 240.14a-21: 1. Disclosure relating to the compensation of directors required by Item 402(k) (§ 229.402(k) of this chapter) and Item 402(r) of Regulation S–K (§ 229.402(r) of this chapter) is not subject to the shareholder vote required by paragraph (a) of this section. If a registrant includes disclosure pursuant to Item 402(s) of Regulation S–K (§ 229.402(s) of this chapter) about the registrant's compensation policies and practices as they relate to risk management and risk-taking incentives, these policies and practices would not be subject to the shareholder vote required by paragraph (a) of this section. To the extent that risk considerations are a material aspect of the registrant's compensation policies or decisions for named executive officers, the registrant is required to discuss them as part of its Compensation Discussion and Analysis under § 229.402(b) of this chapter, and therefore such disclosure would be considered by shareholders when voting on executive compensation.

2. If a registrant includes disclosure of golden parachute compensation arrangements pursuant to Item 402(t) (§ 229.402(t) of this chapter) in an annual meeting proxy statement, such disclosure would be subject to the shareholder advisory vote required by paragraph (a) of this section.

3. Registrants that are smaller reporting companies entitled to provide scaled disclosure in accordance with Item 402(*l*) of Regulation S–K (§ 229.402(*l*) of this chapter) are not required to include a Compensation Discussion and Analysis in their proxy statements in order to comply with this section. For smaller reporting companies, the vote required by paragraph (a) of this section must be to approve the compensation of the named executive officers as disclosed pursuant to Item 402(m) through (q) of Regulation S–K (§ 229.402(m) through (q) of this chapter).

4. A registrant that has ceased being an emerging growth company shall include the first separate resolution described under § 240.14a–21(a) not later than the end of (i) in the case of a registrant that was an emerging growth company for less than two years after the date of first sale of common equity securities of the registrant pursuant to an effective registration statement under the Securities Act of 1933 (15 U.S.C 77a *et seq.*), the three-year period beginning on such date; and (ii) in the case of any other registrant, the one-year period beginning on the date the registrant is no longer an emerging growth company.

[76 FR 6045, Feb. 2, 2011, as amended at 82 FR 17555, Apr. 12, 2017]

§ 240.14a–101 Schedule 14A. Information required in proxy statement.

SCHEDULE 14A INFORMATION

Proxy Statement Pursuant to Section 14(a) of the Securities Exchange Act of 1934

(Amendment No.   )

Filed by the Registrant [ ]
Filed by a party other than the Registrant [ ]
Check the appropriate box:
[ ] Preliminary Proxy Statement
[ ] Confidential, for Use of the Commission Only (as permitted by Rule 14a–6(e)(2))
[ ] Definitive Proxy Statement
[ ] Definitive Additional Materials
[ ] Soliciting Material under § 240.14a–12

(Name of Registrant as Specified In Its Charter)

(Name of Person(s) Filing Proxy Statement, if other than the Registrant)
Payment of Filing Fee (Check all boxes that apply):
[ ] No fee required
[ ] Fee paid previously with preliminary materials
[ ] Fee computed on table in exhibit required by Item 25(b) per Exchange Act Rules 14a–6(i)(1) and 0–11

NOTES

Notes: A. Where any item calls for information with respect to any matter to be acted upon and such matter involves other matters with respect to which information is called for by other items of this schedule, the information called for by such other items also shall be given. For example, where a solicitation of security holders is for the purpose of approving the authorization of additional securities which are to be used to acquire another specified company, and the registrants' security holders will not have a separate opportunity to vote upon the transaction, the solicitation to authorize the securities is also a solicitation with respect to the acquisition. Under those facts, information required by Items 11, 13 and 14 shall be furnished.

B. Where any item calls for information with respect to any matter to be acted upon at the meeting, such item need be answered in the registrant's soliciting material only with respect to proposals to be made by or on behalf of the registrant.

C. Except as otherwise specifically provided, where any item calls for information for a specified period with regard to directors, executive officers, officers or other persons holding specified positions or relationships, the information shall be given with regard to any person who held any of the specified positions or relationship at any time during the period. Information, other than

§ 240.14a–101

information required by Item 404 of Regulation S-K (§ 229.404 of this chapter), need not be included for any portion of the period during which such person did not hold any such position or relationship, provided a statement to that effect is made.

D. Information may be incorporated by reference only in the manner and to the extent specifically permitted in the items of this schedule. Where incorporation by reference is used, the following shall apply:

1. Disclosure must not be incorporated by reference from a second document if that second document incorporates information pertinent to such disclosure by reference to a third document. A registrant incorporating any documents, or portions of documents, shall include a statement on the last page(s) of the proxy statement as to which documents, or portions of documents, are incorporated by reference. Information shall not be incorporated by reference in any case where such incorporation would render the statement incomplete, unclear or confusing.

2. If a document is incorporated by reference but not delivered to security holders, include an undertaking to provide, without charge, to each person to whom a proxy statement is delivered, upon written or oral request of such person and by first class mail or other equally prompt means within one business day of receipt of such request, a copy of any and all of the information that has been incorporated by reference in the proxy statement (not including exhibits to the information that is incorporated by reference unless such exhibits are specifically incorporated by reference into the information that the proxy statement incorporates), and the address (including title or department) and telephone numbers to which such a request is to be directed. This includes information contained in documents filed subsequent to the date on which definitive copies of the proxy statement are sent or given to security holders, up to the date of responding to the request.

3. If a document or portion of a document other than an annual report sent to security holders pursuant to the requirements of Rule 14a-3 (§ 240.14a-3 of this chapter) with respect to the same meeting or solicitation of consents or authorizations as that to which the proxy statement relates is incorporated by reference in the manner permitted by Item 13(b) or 14(e)(1) of this schedule, the proxy statement must be sent to security holders no later than 20 business days prior to the date on which the meeting of such security holders is held or, if no meeting is held, at least 20 business days prior to the date the votes, consents or authorizations may be used to effect the corporate action.

4. *Electronic filings.* If any of the information required by Items 13 or 14 of this Schedule is incorporated by reference from an annual or quarterly report to security holders,

17 CFR Ch. II (4–1–23 Edition)

such report, or any portion thereof incorporated by reference, shall be filed in electronic format with the proxy statement. This provision shall not apply to registered investment companies.

5. *Interactive Data File.* An Interactive Data File must be included in accordance with § 232.405 of this chapter and the EDGAR Filer Manual where applicable pursuant to § 232.405(b) of this chapter.

E. In Item 13 of this Schedule, the reference to "meets the requirement of Form S-3" or "meets the requirements of General Instruction A.2 of Form N-2" shall refer to a registrant who meets the following requirements:

(a) A registrant meets the requirements of Form S-3 if:

(1) The registrant meets the requirements of General Instruction I.A. of Form S-3 (§ 239.13 of this chapter); and

(2) One of the following is met:

(i) The registrant meets the aggregate market value requirement of General Instruction I.B.1 of Form S-3; or

(ii) Action is to be taken as described in Items 11, 12, and 14 of this schedule which concerns non-convertible debt or preferred securities issued by a registrant meeting the requirements of General Instruction I.B.2. of Form S-3 (referenced in 17 CFR 239.13); or

(iii) The registrant is a majority-owned subsidiary and one of the conditions of General Instruction I.C. of Form S-3 is met.

(b) A registrant meets the requirements of General Instruction A.2 of Form N-2 (§§ 239.14 and 274.11a 1 of this chapter) if the registrant meets the conditions included in such General Instruction, provided that General Instruction A.2.c of Form N-2 is subject to the same limitations described in paragraph (a)(2) of this Note E.

Item 1. Date, time and place information. (a) State the date, time and place of the meeting of security holders, and the complete mailing address, including ZIP Code, of the principal executive offices of the registrant, unless such information is otherwise disclosed in material furnished to security holders with or preceding the proxy statement. If action is to be taken by written consent, state the date by which consents are to be submitted if state law requires that such a date be specified or if the person soliciting intends to set a date.

(b) On the first page of the proxy statement, as delivered to security holders, state the approximate date on which the proxy statement and form of proxy are first sent or given to security holders.

(c) Furnish the information required to be in the proxy statement by Rule 14a-5(e) (§ 240.14a-5(e) of this chapter).

Item 2. Revocability of proxy. State whether or not the person giving the proxy has the power to revoke it. If the right of revocation before the proxy is exercised is limited or is

Securities and Exchange Commission

§ 240.14a-101

subject to compliance with any formal procedure, briefly describe such limitation or procedure.

Item 3. Dissenters' right of appraisal. Outline briefly the rights of appraisal or similar rights of dissenters with respect to any matter to be acted upon and indicate any statutory procedure required to be followed by dissenting security holders in order to perfect such rights. Where such rights may be exercised only within a limited time after the date of adoption of a proposal, the filing of a charter amendment or other similar act, state whether the persons solicited will be notified of such date.

Instructions. 1. Indicate whether a security holder's failure to vote against a proposal will constitute a waiver of his appraisal or similar rights and whether a vote against a proposal will be deemed to satisfy any notice requirements under State law with respect to appraisal rights. If the State law is unclear, state what position will be taken in regard to these matters.

2. Open-end investment companies registered under the Investment Company Act of 1940 are not required to respond to this item.

Item 4. Persons Making the Solicitation—(a) Solicitations not subject to Rule 14a-12(c) (§ 240.14a-12(c)). (1) If the solicitation is made by the registrant, so state. Give the name of any director of the registrant who has informed the registrant in writing that he intends to oppose any action intended to be taken by the registrant and indicate the action which he intends to oppose.

(2) If the solicitation is made otherwise than by the registrant, so state and give the names of the participants in the solicitation, as defined in paragraphs (a) (iii), (iv), (v) and (vi) of Instruction 3 to this Item.

(3) If the solicitation is to be made otherwise than by the use of the mails or pursuant to § 240.14a-16, describe the methods to be employed. If the solicitation is to be made by specially, engaged employees or paid solicitors, state (i) the material features of any contract or arrangement for such solicitation and identify the parties, and (ii) the cost or anticipated cost thereof.

(4) State the names of the persons by whom the cost of solicitation has been or will be borne, directly or indirectly.

(b) *Solicitations subject to Rule 14a-12(c) (§ 240.14a-12(c)).* (1) State by whom the solicitation is made and describe the methods employed and to be employed to solicit security holders.

(2) If regular employees of the registrant or any other participant in a solicitation have been or are to be employed to solicit security holders, describe the class or classes of employees to be so employed, and the manner and nature of their employment for such purpose.

(3) If specially engaged employees, representatives or other persons have been or are to be employed to solicit security holders, state (i) the material features of any contract or arrangement for such solicitation and the identity of the parties, (ii) the cost or anticipated cost thereof and (iii) the approximate number of such employees of employees or any other person (naming such other person) who will solicit security holders).

(4) State the total amount estimated to be spent and the total expenditures to date for, in furtherance of, or in connection with the solicitation of security holders.

(5) State by whom the cost of the solicitation will be borne. If such cost is to be borne initially by any person other than the registrant, state whether reimbursement will be sought from the registrant, and, if so, whether the question of such reimbursement will be submitted to a vote of security holders.

(6) If any such solicitation is terminated pursuant to a settlement between the registrant and any other participant in such solicitation, describe the terms of such settlement, including the cost or anticipated cost thereof to the registrant.

Instructions. 1. With respect to solicitations subject to Rule 14a-12(c) (§ 240.14a-12(c)), costs and expenditures within the meaning of this Item 4 shall include fees for attorneys, accountants, public relations or financial advisers, solicitors, advertising, printing, transportation, litigation and other costs incidental to the solicitation, except that the registrant may exclude the amount of such costs represented by the amount normally expended for a solicitation for an election of directors in the absence of a contest, and costs represented by salaries and wages of regular employees and officers, provided a statement to that effect is included in the proxy statement.

2. The information required pursuant to paragraph (b)(6) of this Item should be included in any amended or revised proxy statement or other soliciting materials relating to the same meeting or subject matter furnished to security holders by the registrant subsequent to the date of settlement.

3. For purposes of this Item 4 and Item 5 of this Schedule 14A:

(a) The terms "participant" and "participant in a solicitation" include the following:

(i) In the case of a solicitation made on behalf of the registrant, the registrant, each director of the registrant and each of the registrant's nominees for election as a director;

(ii) In the case of a solicitation made otherwise than on behalf of the registrant, each of the soliciting person's nominees for election as a director;

(iii) Any committee or group which solicits proxies, any member of such committee or group, and any person whether or not named

§ 240.14a-101

as a member who, acting alone or with one or more other persons, directly or indirectly takes the initiative, or engages, in organizing, directing, or arranging for the financing of any such committee or group;

(iv) Any person who finances or joins with another to finance the solicitation of proxies, except persons who contribute not more than $500 and who are not otherwise participants;

(v) Any person who lends money or furnishes credit or enters into any other arrangements, pursuant to any contract or understanding with a participant, for the purpose of financing or otherwise inducing the purchase, sale, holding or voting of securities of the registrant by any participant or other persons, in support of or in opposition to a participant; except that such terms do not include a bank, broker or dealer who, in the ordinary course of business, lends money or executes orders for the purchase or sale of securities and who is not otherwise a participant; and

(vi) Any person who solicits proxies.

(b) The terms "participant" and "participant in a solicitation" do not include:

(i) Any person or organization retained or employed by a participant to solicit security holders and whose activities are limited to the duties required to be performed in the course of such employment;

(ii) Any person who merely transmits proxy soliciting material or performs other ministerial or clerical duties;

(iii) Any person employed by a participant in the capacity of attorney, accountant, or advertising, public relations or financial adviser, and whose activities are limited to the duties required to be performed in the course of such employment;

(iv) Any person regularly employed as an officer or employee of the registrant or any of its subsidiaries who is not otherwise a participant; or

(v) Any officer or director of, or any person regularly employed by, any other participant, if such officer, director or employee is not otherwise a participant.

Item 5. Interest of certain Persons in Matters To Be Acted Upon (a) *Solicitations not subject to Rule 14a–12(c) (§ 240.14a–12(c)).* Describe briefly any substantial interest, direct or indirect, by security holdings or otherwise, of each of the following persons in any matter to be acted upon, other than elections to office:

(1) If the solicitation is made on behalf of the registrant, each person who has been a director or executive officer of the registrant at any time since the beginning of the last fiscal year.

(2) If the solicitation is made otherwise than on behalf of the registrant, each participant in the solicitation, as defined in paragraphs (a) (iii), (iv), (v), and (vi) of Instruction 3 to Item 4 of this Schedule 14A.

(3) Each nominee for election as a director of the registrant.

(4) Each associate of any of the foregoing persons.

(5) If the solicitation is made on behalf of the registrant, furnish the information required by Item 402(t) of Regulation S-K (§ 229.402(t) of this chapter).

INSTRUCTION TO PARAGRAPH (a). Except in the case of a solicitation subject to this regulation made in opposition to another solicitation subject to this regulation, this subitem (a) shall not apply to any interest arising from the ownership of securities of the registrant where the security holder receives no extra or special benefit not shared on a pro rata basis by all other holders of the same class.

(b) *Solicitation subject to Rule 14a–12(c) (§ 240.14a–12(c)).* With respect to any solicitation subject to Rule 14a–12(c) (§ 240.14a–12(c)):

(1) Describe briefly any substantial interest, direct or indirect, by security holdings or otherwise, of each participant as defined in paragraphs (a) (ii), (iii), (iv), (v) and (vi) of Instruction 3 to Item 4 of this Schedule 14A, in any matter to be acted upon at the meeting, and include with respect to each participant the following information, or a fair and accurate summary thereof:

(i) Name and business address of the participant.

(ii) The participant's present principal occupation or employment and the name, principal business and address of any corporation or other organization in which such employment is carried on.

(iii) State whether or not, during the past ten years, the participant has been convicted in a criminal proceeding (excluding traffic violations or similar misdemeanors) and, if so, give dates, nature of conviction, name and location of court, and penalty imposed or other disposition of the case. A negative answer need not be included in the proxy statement or other soliciting material.

(iv) State the amount of each class of securities of the registrant which the participant owns beneficially, directly or indirectly.

(v) State the amount of each class of securities of the registrant which the participant owns of record but not beneficially.

(vi) State with respect to all securities of the registrant purchased or sold within the past two years, the dates on which they were purchased or sold and the amount purchased or sold on each such date.

(vii) If any part of the purchase price or market value of any of the shares specified in paragraph (b)(1)(vi) of this Item is represented by funds borrowed or otherwise obtained for the purpose of acquiring or holding such securities, so state and indicate the amount of the indebtedness as of the latest practicable date. If such funds were borrowed or obtained otherwise than pursuant to a

Securities and Exchange Commission § 240.14a–101

margin account or bank loan in the regular course of business of a bank, broker or dealer, briefly describe the transaction, and state the names of the parties.

(viii) State whether or not the participant is, or was within the past year, a party to any contract, arrangements or understandings with any person with respect to any securities of the registrant, including, but not limited to joint ventures, loan or option arrangements, puts or calls, guarantees against loss or guarantees of profit, division of losses or profits, or the giving or withholding of proxies. If so, name the parties to such contracts, arrangements or understandings and give the details thereof.

(ix) State the amount of securities of the registrant owned beneficially, directly or indirectly, by each of the participant's associates and the name and address of each such associate.

(x) State the amount of each class of securities of any parent or subsidiary of the registrant which the participant owns beneficially, directly or indirectly.

(xi) Furnish for the participant and associates of the participant the information required by Item 404(a) of Regulation S-K (§ 229.404(a) of this chapter).

(xii) State whether or not the participant or any associates of the participant have any arrangement or understanding with any person—
(A) with respect to any future employment by the registrant or its affiliates; or
(B) with respect to any future transactions to which the registrant or any of its affiliates will or may be a party.

If so, describe such arrangement or understanding and state the names of the parties thereto.

(2) With respect to any person, other than a director or executive officer of the registrant acting solely in that capacity, who is a party to an arrangement or understanding pursuant to which a nominee for election as director is proposed to be elected, describe any substantial interest, direct or indirect, by security holdings or otherwise, that such person has in any matter to be acted upon at the meeting, and furnish the information called for by paragraphs (b)(1) (xi) and (xii) of this Item.

(3) If the solicitation is made on behalf of the registrant, furnish the information required by Item 402(t) of Regulation S-K (§ 229.402(t) of this chapter).

INSTRUCTION TO PARAGRAPH (b): For purposes of this Item 5, beneficial ownership shall be determined in accordance with Rule 13d-3 under the Act (Section 240.13d-3 of this chapter).

Item 6. Voting securities and principal holders thereof, (a) As to each class of voting securities of the registrant entitled to be voted at the meeting (or by written consents or authorizations if no meeting is held), state the number of shares outstanding and the number of votes to which each class is entitled.

(b) State the record date, if any, with respect to this solicitation. If the right to vote or give consent is not to be determined, in whole or in part, by reference to a record date, indicate the criteria for the determination of security holders entitled to vote or give consent.

(c) If action is to be taken with respect to the election of directors and if the persons solicited have cumulative voting rights: (1) Make a statement that they have such rights, (2) briefly describe such rights, (3) state briefly the conditions precedent to the exercise thereof, and (4) if discretionary authority to cumulate votes is solicited, so indicate.

(d) Furnish the information required by Item 403 of Regulation S-K (§ 229.403 of this chapter) to the extent known by the persons on whose behalf the solicitation is made.

(e) If, to the knowledge of the persons on whose behalf the solicitation is made, a change in control of the registrant has occurred since the beginning of its last fiscal year, state the name of the person(s) who acquired such control, the amount and the source of the consideration used by such person or persons; the basis of the control, the date and a description of the transaction(s) which resulted in the change of control and the percentage of voting securities of the registrant now beneficially owned directly or indirectly by the person(s) who acquired control; and the identity of the person(s) from whom control was assumed. If the source of all or any part of the consideration used is a loan made in the ordinary course of business by a bank as defined by section 3(a)(6) of the Act, the identity of such bank shall be omitted provided a request for confidentiality has been made pursuant to section 13(d)(1)(B) of the Act by the person(s) who acquired control. In lieu thereof, the material shall indicate that the identity of the bank has been so omitted and filed separately with the Commission.

Instruction. 1. State the terms of any loans or pledges obtained by the new control group for the purpose of acquiring control, and the names of the lenders or pledgees.

2. Any arrangements or understandings among members of both the former and new control groups and their associates with respect to election of directors or other matters should be described.

Item 7. Directors and executive officers. If action is to be taken with respect to the election of directors, furnish the following information in tabular form to the extent practicable. If, however, the solicitation is made on behalf of persons other than the registrant, the information required need be furnished only as to nominees of the persons making the solicitation.

§ 240.14a–101

(a) The information required by Item 103(c)(2) of Regulation S–K (§ 229.103(c)(2) of this chapter) with respect to directors and executive officers.

(b) The information required by Items 401, 404(a) and (b), 405, 407 and 408(b) of Regulation S–K (§§ 229.401, 229.404(a) and (b), 229.405, 229.407, and 229.408(b) of this chapter), other than the information required by:

(i) Paragraph (c)(3) of Item 407 of Regulation S–K (§ 229.407(c)(3) of this chapter); and

(ii) Paragraphs (e)(4) and (e)(5) of Item 407 of Regulation S–K (§§ 229.407(e)(4) and 229.407(e)(5) of this chapter) (which are required by Item 8 of this Schedule 14A).

(c) If a shareholder nominee or nominees are submitted to the registrant for inclusion in the registrant's proxy materials pursuant to § 240.14a–11 and the registrant is not permitted to exclude the nominee or nominees pursuant to the provisions of § 240.14a–11, the registrant must include in its proxy statement the disclosure required from the nominating shareholder or nominating shareholder group under Item 5 of § 240.14n–101 with regard to the nominee or nominees and the nominating shareholder or nominating shareholder group.

(d) If a registrant is required to include a shareholder nominee or nominees submitted to the registrant for inclusion in the registrant's proxy materials pursuant to a procedure set forth under applicable state or foreign law, or the registrant's governing documents providing for the inclusion of shareholder director nominees in the registrant's proxy materials, the registrant must include in its proxy statement the disclosure required from the nominating shareholder or nominating shareholder group under Item 6 of § 240.14n–101 with regard to the nominee or nominees and the nominating shareholder or nominating shareholder group.

(e) In lieu of the information required by this Item 7, investment companies registered under the Investment Company Act of 1940 (15 U.S.C. 80a) must furnish the information required by Item 22(b) of this Schedule 14A.

(f) If a person is conducting a solicitation that is subject to § 240.14a–19, the registrant must include in its proxy statement a statement directing shareholders to refer to any other soliciting person's proxy statement for information required by Item 7 of this Schedule 14A with regard to such person's nominee or nominees and a soliciting person other than the registrant must include in its proxy statement a statement directing shareholders to refer to the registrant's or other soliciting person's proxy statement for information required by Item 7 of this Schedule 14A with regard to the registrant's or other soliciting person's nominee or nominees. The statement must explain to shareholders that they can access the other soliciting person's proxy statement, and any other relevant documents, without cost on the Commission's website.

INSTRUCTION TO ITEM 7. The information disclosed pursuant to paragraphs (c) and (d) of this Item 7 will not be deemed incorporated by reference into any filing under the Securities Act of 1933 (15 U.S.C. 77a *et seq.*), the Securities Exchange Act of 1934 (15 U.S.C. 78a *et seq.*), or the Investment Company Act of 1940 (15 U.S.C. 80a–1 *et seq.*), except to the extent that the registrant specifically incorporates that information by reference.

Item 8. Compensation of directors and executive officers. Furnish the information required by Item 402 of Regulation S–K (§ 229.402 of this chapter) and paragraphs (e)(4) and (e)(5) of Item 407 of Regulation S–K (§ 229.407(e)(4) and (e)(5) of this chapter) if action is to be taken with regard to:

(a) The election of directors;

(b) Any bonus, profit sharing or other compensation plan, contract or arrangement in which any director, nominee for election as a director, or executive officer of the registrant will participate;

(c) Any pension or retirement plan in which any such person will participate; or

(d) The granting or extension to any such person of any options, warrants or rights to purchase any securities, other than warrants or rights issued to security holders as such, on a pro rata basis.

However, if the solicitation is made on behalf of persons other than the registrant, the information required need be furnished only as to nominees of the persons making the solicitation and associates of such nominees. In the case of investment companies registered under the Investment Company Act of 1940 (15 U.S.C. 80a), furnish the information required by Item 22(b)(13) of this Schedule 14A.

Instruction. If an otherwise reportable compensation plan became subject to such requirements because of an acquisition or merger and, within one year of the acquisition or merger, such plan was terminated for purposes of prospective eligibility, the registrant may furnish a description of its obligation to the designated individuals pursuant to the compensation plan. Such description may be furnished in lieu of a description of the compensation plan in the proxy statement.

Item 9. Independent public accountants. If the solicitation is made on behalf of the registrant and relates to: (1) The annual (or special meeting in lieu of annual) meeting of security holders at which directors are to be elected, or a solicitation of consents or authorizations in lieu of such meeting or (2) the election, approval or ratification of the registrant's accountant, furnish the following information describing the registrant's relationship with its independent public accountant:

(a) The name of the principal accountant selected or being recommended to security holders for election, approval or ratification for the current year. If no accountant has been selected or recommended, so state and briefly describe the reasons therefor.

(b) The name of the principal accountant for the fiscal year most recently completed if different from the accountant selected or recommended for the current year or if no accountant has yet been selected or recommended for the current year.

(c) The proxy statement shall indicate: (1) Whether or not representatives of the principal accountant for the current year and for the most recently completed fiscal year are expected to be present at the security holders' meeting, (2) whether or not they will have the opportunity to make a statement if they desire to do so, and (3) whether or not such representatives are expected to be available to respond to appropriate questions.

(d) If during the registrant's two most recent fiscal years or any subsequent interim period, (1) an independent accountant who was previously engaged as the principal accountant to audit the registrant's financial statements, or an independent accountant on whom the principal accountant expressed reliance in its report regarding a significant subsidiary, has resigned (or indicated it has declined to stand for re-election after the completion of the current audit) or was dismissed, or (2) a new independent accountant has been engaged as either the principal accountant to audit the registrant's financial statements or as an independent accountant on whom the principal accountant has expressed or is expected to express reliance in its report regarding a significant subsidiary, then, notwithstanding any previous disclosure, provide the information required by Item 304(a) of Regulation S-K (§ 229.304 of this chapter).

(e)(1) Disclose, under the caption *Audit Fees*, the aggregate fees billed for each of the last two fiscal years for professional services rendered by the principal accountant for the audit of the registrant's annual financial statements and review of financial statements included in the registrant's Form 10-Q (17 CFR 249.308a) or services that are normally provided by the accountant in connection with statutory and regulatory filings or engagements for those fiscal years.

(2) Disclose, under the caption *Audit-Related Fees*, the aggregate fees billed in each of the last two fiscal years for assurance and related services by the principal accountant that are reasonably related to the performance of the audit or review of the registrant's financial statements and are not reported under paragraph (e)(1) of this section. Registrants shall describe the nature of the services comprising the fees disclosed under this category.

(3) Disclose, under the caption *Tax Fees*, the aggregate fees billed in each of the last two fiscal years for professional services rendered by the principal accountant for tax compliance, tax advice, and tax planning. Registrants shall describe the nature of the services comprising the fees disclosed under this category.

(4) Disclose, under the caption *All Other Fees*, the aggregate fees billed in each of the last two fiscal years for products and services provided by the principal accountant, other than the services reported in paragraphs (e)(1) through (e)(3) of this section. Registrants shall describe the nature of the services comprising the fees disclosed under this category.

(5)(i) Disclose the audit committee's pre-approval policies and procedures described in 17 CFR 210.2–01(c)(7)(i).

(ii) Disclose the percentage of services described in each of paragraphs (e)(2) through (e)(4) of this section that were approved by the audit committee pursuant to 17 CFR 210.2–01(c)(7)(i)(C).

(6) If greater than 50 percent, disclose the percentage of hours expended on the principal accountant's engagement to audit the registrant's financial statements for the most recent fiscal year that were attributed to work performed by persons other than the principal accountant's full-time, permanent employees.

(7) If the registrant is an investment company, disclose the aggregate non-audit fees billed by the registrant's accountant for services rendered to the registrant, and to the registrant's investment adviser (not including any subadviser whose role is primarily portfolio management and is subcontracted with or overseen by another investment adviser), and any entity controlling, controlled by, or under common control with the adviser that provides ongoing services to the registrant for each of the last two fiscal years of the registrant.

(8) If the registrant is an investment company, disclose whether the audit committee of the board of directors has considered whether the provision of non-audit services that were rendered to the registrant's investment adviser (not including any subadviser whose role is primarily portfolio management and is subcontracted with or overseen by another investment adviser), and any entity controlling, controlled by, or under common control with the investment adviser that provides ongoing services to the registrant that were not pre-approved pursuant to 17 CFR 210.2–01(c)(7)(ii) is compatible with maintaining the principal accountant's independence.

§ 240.14a–101

Instruction to Item 9(e). For purposes of Item 9(e)(2), (3), and (4), registrants that are investment companies must disclose fees billed for services rendered to the registrant and separately, disclose fees required to be approved by the investment company registrant's audit committee pursuant to 17 CFR 210.2–01(c)(7)(ii). Registered investment companies must also disclose the fee percentages as required by item 9(e)(5)(ii) for the registrant and separately, disclose the fee percentages as required by item 9(e)(5)(ii) for the fees required to be approved by the investment company registrant's audit committee pursuant to 17 CFR 210.2–01(c)(7)(ii).

Item 10. Compensation Plans. If action is to be taken with respect to any plan pursuant to which cash or noncash compensation may be paid or distributed, furnish the following information:

(a) *Plans subject to security holder action.* (1) Describe briefly the material features of the plan being acted upon, identify each class of persons who will be eligible to participate therein, indicate the approximate number of persons in each such class, and state the basis of such participation.

(2)(i) In the tabular format specified below, disclose the benefits or amounts that will be received by or allocated to each of the following under the plan being acted upon, if such benefits or amounts are determinable:

NEW PLAN BENEFITS

Plan name		
Name and position	Dollar value ($)	Number of units
CEO. A. B. C. D. Executive Group. Non-Executive Director Group. Non-Executive Officer Employee Group.		

(ii) The table required by paragraph (a)(2)(i) of this Item shall provide information as to the following persons:

(A) Each person (stating name and position) specified in paragraph (a)(3) of Item 402 of Regulation S-K (§ 229.402(a)(3) of this chapter);

Instruction: In the case of investment companies registered under the Investment Company Act of 1940, furnish the information for Compensated Persons as defined in Item 22(b)(13) of this Schedule in lieu of the persons specified in paragraph (a)(3) of Item 402 of Regulation S-K (§ 229.402(a)(3) of this chapter).

(B) All current executive officers as a group;

(C) All current directors who are not executive officers as a group; and

(D) All employees, including all current officers who are not executive officers, as a group.

INSTRUCTION TO NEW PLAN BENEFITS TABLE

Additional columns should be added for each plan with respect to which security holder action is to be taken.

(iii) If the benefits or amounts specified in paragraph (a)(2)(i) of this item are not determinable, state the benefits or amounts which would have been received by or allocated to each of the following for the last completed fiscal year if the plan had been in effect, if such benefits or amounts may be determined, in the table specified in paragraph (a)(2)(i) of this Item:

(A) Each person (stating name and position) specified in paragraph (a)(3) of Item 402 of Regulation S-K (§ 229.402(a)(3) of this chapter);

(B) All current executive officers as a group;

(C) All current directors who are not executive officers as a group; and

(D) All employees, including all current officers who are not executive officers, as a group.

(3) If the plan to be acted upon can be amended, otherwise than by a vote of security holders, to increase the cost thereof to the registrant or to alter the allocation of the benefits as between the persons and groups specified in paragraph (a)(2) of this item, state the nature of the amendments which can be so made.

(b)(1) *Additional information regarding specified plans subject to security holder action.* With respect to any pension or retirement plan submitted for security holder action, state:

(i) The approximate total amount necessary to fund the plan with respect to past services, the period over which such amount is to be paid and the estimated annual payments necessary to pay the total amount over such period; and

(ii) The estimated annual payment to be made with respect to current services. In the case of a pension or retirement plan, information called for by paragraph (a)(2) of this Item may be furnished in the format specified by paragraph (h)(2) of Item 402 of Regulation S-K (§ 229.402(h)(2) of this chapter).

INSTRUCTION TO PARAGRAPH (b)(1)(ii). In the case of investment companies registered under the Investment Company Act of 1940 (15 U.S.C. 80a), refer to Instruction 4 in Item 22(b)(13)(i) of this Schedule in lieu of paragraph (h)(2) of Item 402 of Regulation S-K (§ 229.402(h)(2) of this chapter).

(2)(i) With respect to any specific grant of or any plan containing options, warrants or rights submitted for security holder action, state:

Securities and Exchange Commission § 240.14a-101

(A) The title and amount of securities underlying such options, warrants or rights;

(B) The prices, expiration dates and other material conditions upon which the options, warrants or rights may be exercised;

(C) The consideration received or to be received by the registrant or subsidiary for the granting or extension of the options, warrants or rights;

(D) The market value of the securities underlying the options, warrants, or rights as of the latest practicable date; and

(E) In the case of options, the federal income tax consequences of the issuance and exercise of such options to the recipient and the registrant; and

(ii) State separately the amount of such options received or to be received by the following persons if such benefits or amounts are determinable:

(A) Each person (stating name and position) specified in paragraph (a)(3) of Item 402 of Regulation S-K (§ 229.402(a)(3) of this chapter);

(B) All current executive officers as a group;

(C) All current directors who are not executive officers as a group;

(D) Each nominee for election as a director;

(E) Each associate of any of such directors, executive officers or nominees;

(F) Each other person who received or is to receive 5 percent of such options, warrants or rights; and

(G) All employees, including all current officers who are not executive officers, as a group.

(c) *Information regarding plans and other arrangements not subject to security holder action.* Furnish the information required by Item 201(d) of Regulation S-K (§ 229.201(d) of this chapter).

INSTRUCTIONS TO PARAGRAPH (c). 1. If action is to be taken as described in paragraph (a) of this Item with respect to the approval of a new compensation plan under which equity securities of the registrant are authorized for issuance, information about the plan shall be disclosed as required under paragraphs (a) and (b) of this Item and shall not be included in the disclosure required by Item 201(d) of Regulation S-K (§ 229.201(d) of this chapter). If action is to be taken as described in paragraph (a) of this Item with respect to the amendment or modification of an existing plan under which equity securities of the registrant are authorized for issuance, the registrant shall include information about securities previously authorized for issuance under the plan (including any outstanding options, warrants and rights previously granted pursuant to the plan and any securities remaining available for future issuance under the plan) in the disclosure required by Item 201(d) of Regulation S-K (§ 229.201(d) of this chapter). Any additional securities that are the subject of the amendments or modification of the existing plan shall be disclosed as required under paragraphs (a) and (b) of this Item and shall not be included in the Item 201(d) disclosure.

Instructions

1. The term *plan* as used in this Item means any plan as defined in paragraph (a)(6)(ii) of Item 402 of Regulation S-K (§ 229.402(a)(6)(ii) of this chapter).

2. If action is to be taken with respect to a material amendment or modification of an existing plan, the item shall be answered with respect to the plan as proposed to be amended or modified and shall indicate any material differences from the existing plan.

3. If the plan to be acted upon is set forth in a written document, three copies thereof shall be filed with the Commission at the time copies of the proxy statement and form of proxy are first filed pursuant to paragraph (a) or (b) of § 240.14a-6. Electronic filers shall file with the Commission a copy of such written plan document in electronic format as an appendix to the proxy statement. It need not be provided to security holders unless it is a part of the proxy statement.

4. Paragraph (b)(2)(ii) does not apply to warrants or rights to be issued to security holders as such on a pro rata basis.

5. The Commission shall be informed, as supplemental information, when the proxy statement is first filed, as to when the options, warrants or rights and the shares called for thereby will be registered under the Securities Act or, if such registration is not contemplated, the section of the Securities Act or rule of the Commission under which exemption from such registration is claimed and the facts relied upon to make the exemption available.

Item 11. Authorization or issuance of securities otherwise than for exchange. If action is to be taken with respect to the authorization or issuance of any securities otherwise than for exchange for outstanding securities of the registrant, furnish the following information:

(a) State the title and amount of securities to be authorized or issued.

(b) Furnish the information required by Item 202 of Regulation S-K (§ 229.202 of this chapter). If the terms of the securities cannot be stated or estimated with respect to any or all of the securities to be authorized, because no offering thereof is contemplated in the proximate future, and if no further authorization by security holders for the issuance thereof is to be obtained, it should be stated that the terms of the securities to be authorized, including dividend or interest rates, conversion prices, voting rights, redemption prices, maturity dates, and similar matters will be determined by the board of directors. If the securities are additional

§ 240.14a–101

shares of common stock of a class outstanding, the description may be omitted except for a statement of the preemptive rights, if any. Where the statutory provisions with respect to preemptive rights are so indefinite or complex that they cannot be stated in summarized form, it will suffice to make a statement in the form of an opinion of counsel as to the existence and extent of such rights.

(c) Describe briefly the transaction in which the securities are to be issued including a statement as to (1) the nature and approximate amount of consideration received or to be received by the registrant and (2) the approximate amount devoted to each purpose so far as determinable for which the net proceeds have been or are to be used. If it is impracticable to describe the transaction in which the securities are to be issued, state the reason, indicate the purpose of the authorization of the securities, and state whether further authorization for the issuance of the securities by a vote of security holders will be solicited prior to such issuance.

(d) If the securities are to be issued otherwise than in a public offering for cash, state the reasons for the proposed authorization or issuance and the general effect thereof upon the rights of existing security holders.

(e) Furnish the information required by Item 13(a) of this schedule.

Item 12. Modification or exchange of securities. If action is to be taken with respect to the modification of any class of securities of the registrant, or the issuance or authorization for issuance of securities of the registrant in exchange for outstanding securities of the registrant furnish the following information:

(a) If outstanding securities are to be modified, state the title and amount thereof. If securities are to be issued in exchange for outstanding securities, state the title and amount of securities to be so issued, the title and amount of outstanding securities to be exchanged therefor and the basis of the exchange.

(b) Describe any material differences between the outstanding securities and the modified or new securities in respect of any of the matters concerning which information would be required in the description of the securities in Item 202 of Regulation S-K (§ 229.202 of this chapter).

(c) State the reasons for the proposed modification or exchange and the general effect thereof upon the rights of existing security holders.

(d) Furnish a brief statement as to arrears in dividends or as to defaults in principal or interest in respect to the outstanding securities which are to be modified or exchanged and such other information as may be appropriate in the particular case to disclose adequately the nature and effect of the proposed action.

(e) Outline briefly any other material features of the proposed modification or exchange. If the plan of proposed action is set forth in a written document, file copies thereof with the Commission in accordance with § 240.14a–6.

(f) Furnish the information required by Item 13(a) of this Schedule.

Instruction. If the existing security is presently listed and registered on a national securities exchange, state whether the registrant intends to apply for listing and registration of the new or reclassified security on such exchange or any other exchange. If the registrant does not intend to make such application, state the effect of the termination of such listing and registration.

Item 13. Financial and other information. (See Notes D and E at the beginning of this Schedule.)

(a) *Information required.* If action is to be taken with respect to any matter specified in Item 11 or 12, furnish the following information:

(1) Financial statements meeting the requirements of Regulation S–X, including financial information required by Rule 3–05 and Article 11 of Regulation S–X with respect to transactions other than pursuant to which action is to be taken as described in this proxy statement (A smaller reporting company may provide the information in Rules 8–04 and 8–05 of Regulation S–X (§§ 210.8–04 and 210.8–05 of this chapter) in lieu of the financial information required by Rule 3–05 and Article 11 of Regulation S–X);

(2) Item 302 of Regulation S-K, supplementary financial information;

(3) Item 303 of Regulation S-K, management's discussion and analysis of financial condition and results of operations;

(4) Item 304 of Regulation S-K, changes in and disagreements with accountants on accounting and financial disclosure;

(5) Item 305 of Regulation S-K, quantitative and qualitative disclosures about market risk; and

(6) A statement as to whether or not representatives of the principal accountants for the current year and for the most recently completed fiscal year:

(i) Are expected to be present at the security holders' meeting;

(ii) Will have the opportunity to make a statement if they desire to do so; and

(iii) Are expected to be available to respond to appropriate questions.

(b) *Incorporation by reference.* The information required pursuant to paragraph (a) of this Item may be incorporated by reference into the proxy statement as follows:

(1) *S–3 registrants and certain N–2 registrants.* If the registrant meets the requirements of Form S–3 or General Instruction A.2 of Form

Securities and Exchange Commission

§ 240.14a–101

N–2 (see Note E to this Schedule), it may incorporate by reference to previously-filed documents any of the information required by paragraph (a) of this Item, provided that the requirements of paragraph (c) are met. Where the registrant meets the requirements of Form S–3 or General Instruction A.2 of Form N–2 and has elected to furnish the required information by incorporation by reference, the registrant may elect to update the information so incorporated by reference to information in subsequently-filed documents.

(2) *All registrants.* The registrant may incorporate by reference any of the information required by paragraph (a) of this Item, provided that the information is contained in an annual report to security holders or a previously-filed statement or report, such report or statement is delivered to security holders with the proxy statement and the requirements of paragraph (c) are met.

(c) *Certain conditions applicable to incorporation by reference.* Registrants eligible to incorporate by reference into the proxy statement the information required by paragraph (a) of this Item in the manner specified by paragraphs (b)(1) and (b)(2) may do so only if:

(1) The information is not required to be included in the proxy statement pursuant to the requirement of another Item;

(2) The proxy statement identifies on the last page(s) the information incorporated by reference; and

(3) The material incorporated by reference substantially meets the requirements of this Item or the appropriate portions of this Item.

Instructions to Item 13. 1. Notwithstanding the provisions of this Item, any or all of the information required by paragraph (a) of this Item not material for the exercise of prudent judgment in regard to the matter to be acted upon may be omitted. In the usual case the information is deemed material to the exercise of prudent judgment where the matter to be acted upon is the authorization or issuance of a material amount of senior securities, but the information is not deemed material where the matter to be acted upon is the authorization or issuance of common stock, otherwise than in an exchange, merger, consolidation, acquisition or similar transaction, the authorization of preferred stock without present intent to issue or the authorization of preferred stock for issuance for cash in an amount constituting fair value.

2. In order to facilitate compliance with Rule 2–02(a) of Regulation S–X, one copy of the definitive proxy statement filed with the Commission shall include a manually signed copy of the accountant's report. If the financial statements are incorporated by reference, a manually signed copy of the accountant's report shall be filed with the definitive proxy statement.

3. Notwithstanding the provisions of Regulation S–X, no schedules other than those prepared in accordance with Rules 12–15, 12–28 and 12–29 (or, for management investment companies, Rules 12–12 through 12–14) of that regulation need be furnished in the proxy statement.

4. Unless registered on a national securities exchange or otherwise required to furnish such information, registered investment companies need not furnish the information required by paragraph (a)(2) or (3) of this Item.

5. If the registrant submits preliminary proxy material incorporating by reference financial statements required by this Item, the registrant should furnish a draft of the financial statements if the document from which they are incorporated has not been filed with or furnished to the Commission.

6. A registered investment company need not comply with items (a)(2), (a)(3), and (a)(5) of this Item 13.

Item 14. Mergers, consolidations, acquisitions and similar matters. (See Notes A and D at the beginning of this Schedule)

Instructions to Item 14: 1. In transactions in which the consideration offered to security holders consists wholly or in part of securities registered under the Securities Act of 1933, furnish the information required by Form S–4 (§ 239.25 of this chapter), Form F–4 (§ 239.34 of this chapter), or Form N–14 (§ 239.23 of this chapter), as applicable, instead of this Item. Only a Form S–4, Form F–4, or Form N–14 must be filed in accordance with § 240.14a–6(j).

2. (a) In transactions in which the consideration offered to security holders consists wholly of cash, the information required by paragraph (c)(1) of this Item for the acquiring company need not be provided unless the information is material to an informed voting decision (e.g., the security holders of the target company are voting and financing is not assured).

(b) Additionally, if only the security holders of the target company are voting:

i. The financial information in paragraphs (b)(8)–(11) of this Item for the acquiring company and the target need not be provided; and

ii. The information in paragraph (c)(2) of this Item for the target company need not be provided.

If, however, the transaction is a going-private transaction (as defined by § 240.13e–3), then the information required by paragraph (c)(2) of this Item must be provided and to the extent that the going-private rules require the information specified in paragraph (b)(8)–(b)(11) of this Item, that information must be provided as well.

3. In transactions in which the consideration offered to security holders consists wholly of securities exempt from registration under the Securities Act of 1933 or a

§ 240.14a–101

combination of exempt securities and cash, information about the acquiring company required by paragraph (c)(1) of this Item need not be provided if only the security holders of the acquiring company are voting, unless the information is material to an informed voting decision. If only the security holders of the target company are voting, information about the target company in paragraph (c)(2) of this Item need not be provided. However, the information required by paragraph (c)(2) of this Item must be provided if the transaction is a going-private (as defined by § 240.13e–3) or roll-up (as described by Item 901 of Regulation S-K (§ 229.901 of this chapter)) transaction.

4. The information required by paragraphs (b)(8)–(11) and (c) need not be provided if the plan being voted on involves only the acquiring company and one or more of its totally held subsidiaries and does not involve a liquidation or a spin off.

5. To facilitate compliance with Rule 2–02(a) of Regulation S-X (§ 210.2–02(a) of this chapter) (technical requirements relating to accountants' reports), one copy of the definitive proxy statement filed with the Commission must include a signed copy of the accountant's report. If the financial statements are incorporated by reference, a signed copy of the accountant's report must be filed with the definitive proxy statement. Signatures may be typed if the document is filed electronically on EDGAR. See Rule 302 of Regulation S-T (§ 232.302 of this chapter).

6. Notwithstanding the provisions of Regulation S-X, no schedules other than those prepared in accordance with § 210.12–15, § 210.12–28 and § 210.12–29 of this chapter (or, for management investment companies, §§ 210.12–12 through 210.12–14 of this chapter) of that regulation need be furnished in the proxy statement.

7. If the preliminary proxy material incorporates by reference financial statements required by this Item, a draft of the financial statements must be furnished to the Commission staff upon request if the document from which they are incorporated has not been filed with or furnished to the Commission.

(a) *Applicability.* If action is to be taken with respect to any of the following transactions, provide the information required by this Item:

(1) A merger or consolidation;

(2) An acquisition of securities of another person;

(3) An acquisition of any other going business or the assets of a going business;

(4) A sale or other transfer of all or any substantial part of assets; or

(5) A liquidation or dissolution.

(b) *Transaction information.* Provide the following information for each of the parties to the transaction unless otherwise specified:

(1) *Summary term sheet.* The information required by Item 1001 of Regulation M-A (§ 229.1001 of this chapter).

(2) *Contact information.* The name, complete mailing address and telephone number of the principal executive offices.

(3) *Business conducted.* A brief description of the general nature of the business conducted.

(4) *Terms of the transaction.* The information required by Item 1004(a)(2) of Regulation M-A (§ 229.1004 of this chapter).

(5) *Regulatory approvals.* A statement as to whether any federal or state regulatory requirements must be complied with or approval must be obtained in connection with the transaction and, if so, the status of the compliance or approval.

(6) *Reports, opinions, appraisals.* If a report, opinion or appraisal materially relating to the transaction has been received from an outside party, and is referred to in the proxy statement, furnish the information required by Item 1015(b) of Regulation M-A (§ 229.1015 of this chapter).

(7) *Past contacts, transactions or negotiations.* The information required by Items 1005(b) and 1011(a)(1) of Regulation M-A (§ 229.1005 of this chapter and § 229.1011 of this chapter), for the parties to the transaction and their affiliates during the periods for which financial statements are presented or incorporated by reference under this Item.

(8)—(10) [Reserved]

(11) *Financial information.* If material, financial information required by Article 11 of Regulation S-X (§§ 210.10–01 through 229.11–03 of this chapter) with respect to this transaction.

INSTRUCTIONS TO PARAGRAPH (b)(11): 1. Present any Article 11 information required with respect to transactions other than those being voted upon (where not incorporated by reference) together with the pro forma information relating to the transaction being voted upon. In presenting this information, you must clearly distinguish between the transaction being voted upon and any other transaction.

2. If current pro forma financial information with respect to all other transactions is incorporated by reference, you need only present the pro forma effect of this transaction.

(c) *Information about the parties to the transaction*—(1) *Acquiring company.* Furnish the information required by Part B (Registrant Information) of Form S-4 (§ 239.25 of this chapter) or Form F-4 (§ 239.34 of this chapter), as applicable, for the acquiring company. However, financial statements need only be presented for the latest two fiscal years and interim periods.

(2) *Acquired company.* Furnish the information required by Part C (Information with Respect to the Company Being Acquired) of

Securities and Exchange Commission § 240.14a–101

Form S–4 (§ 239.25 of this chapter) or Form F–4 (§ 239.34 of this chapter), as applicable.

(d) *Information about parties to the transaction: registered investment companies and business development companies.* If the acquiring company or the acquired company is an investment company registered under the Investment Company Act of 1940 or a business development company as defined by Section 2(a)(48) of the Investment Company Act of 1940, provide the following information for that company instead of the information specified by paragraph (c) of this Item:

(1) Information required by Item 101 of Regulation S–K (§ 229.101 of this chapter), description of business;

(2) Information required by Item 102 of Regulation S–K (§ 229.102 of this chapter), description of property;

(3) Information required by Item 103 of Regulation S–K (§ 229.103 of this chapter), legal proceedings;

(4) Information required by Item 201(a), (b) and (c) of Regulation S–K (§ 229.201(a), (b) and (c) of this chapter), market price of and dividends on the registrant's common equity and related stockholder matters;

(5) Financial statements meeting the requirements of Regulation S–X, including financial information required by Rule 3–05 and Article 11 of Regulation S–X (§ 210.3–05 and § 210.11–01 through § 210.11–03 of this chapter) with respect to transactions other than that as to which action is to be taken as described in this proxy statement;

(6) [Reserved]

(7) Information required by Item 302 of Regulation S–K (§ 229.302 of this chapter), supplementary financial information;

(8) Information required by Item 303 of Regulation S–K (§ 229.303 of this chapter), management's discussion and analysis of financial condition and results of operations; and

(9) Information required by Item 304 of Regulation S–K (§ 229.304 of this chapter), changes in and disagreements with accountants on accounting and financial disclosure.

INSTRUCTION TO PARAGRAPH (d) OF ITEM 14: Unless registered on a national securities exchange or otherwise required to furnish such information, registered investment companies need not furnish the information required by paragraphs (d)(6), (d)(7) and (d)(8) of this Item.

(e) *Incorporation by reference.* (1) The information required by paragraph (c) of this section may be incorporated by reference into the proxy statement to the same extent as would be permitted by Form S–4 (§ 239.25 of this chapter) or Form F–4 (§ 239.34 of this chapter), as applicable.

(2) Alternatively, the registrant may incorporate by reference into the proxy statement the information required by paragraph (c) of this Item if it is contained in an annual report sent to security holders in accordance with § 240.14a–3 of this chapter with respect to the same meeting or solicitation of consents or authorizations that the proxy statement relates to and the information substantially meets the disclosure requirements of Item 14 or Item 17 of Form S–4 (§ 239.25 of this chapter) or Form F–4 (§ 239.34 of this chapter), as applicable.

Item 15. Acquisition or disposition of property. If action is to be taken with respect to the acquisition or disposition of any property, furnish the following information:

(a) Describe briefly the general character and location of the property.

(b) State the nature and amount of consideration to be paid or received by the registrant or any subsidiary. To the extent practicable, outline briefly the facts bearing upon the question of the fairness of the consideration.

(c) State the name and address of the transferer or transferee, as the case may be and the nature of any material relationship of such person to the registrant or any affiliate of the registrant.

(d) Outline briefly any other material features of the contract or transaction.

Item 16. Restatement of accounts. If action is to be taken with respect to the restatement of any asset, capital, or surplus account of the registrant furnish the following information:

(a) State the nature of the restatement and the date as of which it is to be effective.

(b) Outline briefly the reasons for the restatement and for the selection of the particular effective date.

(c) State the name and amount of each account (including any reserve accounts) affected by the restatement and the effect of the restatement thereon. Tabular presentation of the amounts shall be made when appropriate, particularly in the case of recapitalizations.

(d) To the extent practicable, state whether and the extent, if any, to which, the restatement will, as of the date thereof, alter the amount available for distribution to the holders of equity securities.

Item 17. Action with respect to reports. If action is to be taken with respect to any report of the registrant or of its directors, officers or committees or any minutes of a meeting of its security holders, furnish the following information:

(a) State whether or not such action is to constitute approval or disapproval of any of the matters referred to in such reports or minutes.

(b) Identify each of such matters which it is intended will be approved or disapproved, and furnish the information required by the appropriate item or items of this schedule with respect to each such matter.

Item 18. Matters not required to be submitted. If action is to be taken with respect to any

§ 240.14a-101

matter which is not required to be submitted to a vote of security holders, state the nature of such matter, the reasons for submitting it to a vote of security holders and what action is intended to be taken by the registrant in the event of a negative vote on the matter by the security holders.

Item 19. Amendment of character, bylaws or other documents. If action is to be taken with respect to any amendment of the registrant's charter, bylaws or other documents as to which information is not required above, state briefly the reasons for and the general effect of such amendment.

Instructions. 1. Where the matter to be acted upon is the classification of directors, state whether vacancies which occur during the year may be filled by the board of directors to serve only until the next annual meeting or may be so filled for the remainder of the full term.

2. Attention is directed to the discussion of disclosure regarding anti-takeover and similar proposals in Release No. 34-15230 (October 13, 1978).

Item 20. Other proposed action. If action is to be taken on any matter not specifically referred to in this Schedule 14A, describe briefly the substance of each such matter in substantially the same degree of detail as is required by Items 5 to 19, inclusive, of this Schedule, and, with respect to investment companies registered under the Investment Company Act of 1940, Item 22 of this Schedule. Registrants required to provide a separate shareholder vote pursuant to section 111(e)(1) of the Emergency Economic Stabilization Act of 2008 (12 U.S.C. 5221(e)(1)) and §240.14a-20 shall disclose that they are providing such a vote as required pursuant to the Emergency Economic Stabilization Act of 2008, and briefly explain the general effect of the vote, such as whether the vote is non-binding.

Item 21. Voting procedures. As to each matter which is to be submitted to a vote of security holders, furnish the following information:

(a) State the vote required for approval or election, other than for the approval of auditors.

(b) Disclose the method by which votes will be counted, including the treatment and effect under applicable state law and registrant charter and bylaw provisions of abstentions, broker non-votes, and, to the extent applicable, a security holder's withholding of authority to vote for a nominee in an election of directors.

(c) When applicable, disclose how the soliciting person intends to treat proxy authority granted in favor of any other soliciting person's nominees if such other soliciting person abandons its solicitation or fails to comply with §240.14a-19.

Item 22. Information required in investment company proxy statement. (a) *General.*

17 CFR Ch. II (4-1-23 Edition)

(1) *Definitions.* Unless the context otherwise requires, terms used in this Item that are defined in §240.14a-1 (with respect to proxy soliciting material), in §240.14c-1 (with respect to information statements), and in the Investment Company Act of 1940 shall have the same meanings provided therein and the following terms shall also apply:

(i) *Administrator.* The term "Administrator" shall mean any person who provides significant administrative or business affairs management services to a Fund.

(ii) *Affiliated broker.* The term "Affiliated Broker" shall mean any broker:

(A) That is an affiliated person of the Fund;

(B) That is an affiliated person of such person; or

(C) An affiliated person of which is an affiliated person of the Fund, its investment adviser, principal underwriter, or Administrator.

(iii) *Distribution plan.* The term "Distribution Plan" shall mean a plan adopted pursuant to Rule 12b-1 under the Investment Company Act of 1940 (§270.12b-1 of this chapter).

(iv) *Family of Investment Companies.* The term "Family of Investment Companies" shall mean any two or more registered investment companies that:

(A) Share the same investment adviser or principal underwriter; and

(B) Hold themselves out to investors as related companies for purposes of investment and investor services.

(v) *Fund.* The term "Fund" shall mean a Registrant or, where the Registrant is a series company, a separate portfolio of the Registrant.

(vi) *Fund complex.* The term "Fund Complex" shall mean two or more Funds that:

(A) Hold themselves out to investors as related companies for purposes of investment and investor services; or

(B) Have a common investment adviser or have an investment adviser that is an affiliated person of the investment adviser of any of the other Funds.

(vii) *Immediate Family Member.* The term "Immediate Family Member" shall mean a person's spouse; child residing in the person's household (including step and adoptive children); and any dependent of the person, as defined in section 152 of the Internal Revenue Code (26 U.S.C. 152).

(viii) *Officer.* The term "Officer" shall mean the president, vice-president, secretary, treasurer, controller, or any other officer who performs policy-making functions.

(ix) *Parent.* The term "Parent" shall mean the affiliated person of a specified person who controls the specified person directly or indirectly through one or more intermediaries.

(x) *Registrant.* The term "Registrant" shall mean an investment company registered under the Investment Company Act of 1940

Securities and Exchange Commission § 240.14a–101

(15 U.S.C. 80a) or a business development company as defined by section 2(a)(48) of the Investment Company Act of 1940 (15 U.S.C. 80a–2(a)(48)).

(xi) *Sponsoring Insurance Company.* The term "Sponsoring Insurance Company" of a Fund that is a separate account shall mean the insurance company that maintains the separate account and that owns the assets of the separate account.

(xii) *Subsidiary.* The term "Subsidiary" shall mean an affiliated person of a specified person who is controlled by the specified person directly, or indirectly through one or more intermediaries.

(2) [Reserved]

(3) *General disclosure.* Furnish the following information in the proxy statement of a Fund or Funds:

(i) State the name and address of the Fund's investment adviser, principal underwriter, and Administrator.

(ii) When a Fund proxy statement solicits a vote on proposals affecting more than one Fund or class of securities of a Fund (unless the proposal or proposals are the same and affect all Fund or class shareholders), present a summary of all of the proposals in tabular form on one of the first three pages of the proxy statement and indicate which Fund or class shareholders are solicited with respect to each proposal.

(iii) Unless the proxy statement is accompanied by a copy of the Fund's most recent annual report, state prominently in the proxy statement that the Fund will furnish, without charge, a copy of the annual report and the most recent semi-annual report succeeding the annual report, if any, to a shareholder upon request, providing the name, address, and toll-free telephone number of the person to whom such request shall be directed (or, if no toll-free telephone number is provided, a self-addressed postage paid card for requesting the annual report). The Fund should provide a copy of the annual report and the most recent semi-annual report succeeding the annual report, if any, to the requesting shareholder by first class mail, or other means designed to assure prompt delivery, within three business days of the request.

(iv) If the action to be taken would, directly or indirectly, establish a new fee or expense or increase any existing fee or expense to be paid by the Fund or its shareholders, provide a table showing the current and pro forma fees (with the required examples) using the format prescribed in the appropriate registration statement form under the Investment Company Act of 1940 (for open-end management investment companies, Item 3 of Form N–1A (§ 239.15A); for closed-end management investment companies, Item 3 of Form N–2 (§ 239.14); and for separate accounts that offer variable annuity contracts, Item 4 of Form N–3 (§ 239.17a)).

Instructions. 1. Where approval is sought only for a change in asset breakpoints for a pre-existing fee that would not have increased the fee for the previous year (or have the effect of increasing fees or expenses, but for any other reason would not be reflected in a pro forma fee table), describe the likely effect of the change in lieu of providing pro forma fee information.

2. An action would indirectly establish or increase a fee or expense where, for example, the approval of a new investment advisory contract would result in higher custodial or transfer agency fees.

3. The tables should be prepared in a manner designed to facilitate understanding of the impact of any change in fees or expenses.

4. A Fund that offers its shares exclusively to one or more separate accounts and thus is not required to include a fee table in its prospectus (see Item 3 of Form N–1A (§ 239.15A)) should nonetheless prepare a table showing current and pro forma expenses and disclose that the table does not reflect separate account expenses, including sales load.

(v) If action is to be taken with respect to the election of directors or the approval of an advisory contract, describe any purchases or sales of securities of the investment adviser or its Parents, or Subsidiaries of either, since the beginning of the most recently completed fiscal year by any director or any nominee for election as a director of the Fund.

Instructions. 1. Identify the parties, state the consideration, the terms of payment and describe any arrangement or understanding with respect to the composition of the board of directors of the Fund or of the investment adviser, or with respect to the selection of appointment of any person to any office with either such company.

2. Transactions involving securities in an amount not exceeding one percent of the outstanding securities of any class of the investment adviser or any of its Parents or Subsidiaries may be omitted.

(b) *Election of Directors.* If action is to be taken with respect to the election of directors of a Fund, furnish the following information in the proxy statement in addition to, in the case of business development companies, the information (and in the format) required by Item 7 and Item 8 of this Schedule 14A.

INSTRUCTIONS TO INTRODUCTORY TEXT OF PARAGRAPH (b). 1. Furnish information with respect to a prospective investment adviser to the extent applicable.

2. If the solicitation is made by or on behalf of a person other than the Fund or an investment adviser of the Fund, provide information only as to nominees of the person making the solicitation.

3. When providing information about directors and nominees for election as directors in

289

§ 240.14a–101

response to this Item 22(b), furnish information for directors or nominees who are or would be "interested persons" of the Fund within the meaning of section 2(a)(19) of the Investment Company Act of 1940 (15 U.S.C. 80a–2(a)(19)) separately from the information for directors or nominees who are not or would not be interested persons of the Fund. For example, when furnishing information in a table, you should provide separate tables (or separate sections of a single table) for directors and nominees who are or would be interested persons and for directors or nominees who are not or would not be interested persons. When furnishing information in narrative form, indicate by heading or otherwise the directors or nominees who are or would be interested persons and the directors or nominees who are not or would not be interested persons.

4. No information need be given about any director whose term of office as a director will not continue after the meeting to which the proxy statement relates.

(1) Provide the information required by the following table for each director, nominee for election as director, Officer of the Fund, person chosen to become an Officer of the Fund, and, if the Fund has an advisory board, member of the board. Explain in a footnote to the table any family relationship between the persons listed.

(1)	(2)	(3)	(4)	(5)	(6)
Name, Address, and Age.	Position(s) Held with Fund.	Term of Office and Length of Time Served.	Principal Occupation(s) During Past 5 Years.	Number of Portfolios in Fund Complex Overseen by Director or Nominee for Director.	Other Directorships Held by Director or Nominee for Director

INSTRUCTIONS TO PARAGRAPH (b)(1). 1. For purposes of this paragraph, the term "family relationship" means any relationship by blood, marriage, or adoption, not more remote than first cousin.

2. No nominee or person chosen to become a director or Officer who has not consented to act as such may be named in response to this Item. In this regard, see Rule 14a–4(d) under the Exchange Act (§ 240.14a–4(d)).

3. If fewer nominees are named than the number fixed by or pursuant to the governing instruments, state the reasons for this procedure and that the proxies cannot be voted for a greater number of persons than the number of nominees named.

4. For each director or nominee for election as director who is or would be an "interested person" of the Fund within the meaning of section 2(a)(19) of the Investment Company Act of 1940 (15 U.S.C. 80a–2(a)(19)), describe, in a footnote or otherwise, the relationship, events, or transactions by reason of which the director or nominee is or would be an interested person.

5. State the principal business of any company listed under column (4) unless the principal business is implicit in its name.

6. Include in column (5) the total number of separate portfolios that a nominee for election as director would oversee if he were elected.

7. Indicate in column (6) directorships not included in column (5) that are held by a director or nominee for election as director in any company with a class of securities registered pursuant to section 12 of the Exchange Act (15 U.S.C. 78*l*), or subject to the requirements of section 15(d) of the Exchange Act (15 U.S.C. 78o(d)), or any company registered as an investment company under the Investment Company Act of 1940, (15 U.S.C. 80a), as amended, and name the companies in which the directorships are held. Where the other directorships include directorships overseeing two or more portfolios in the same Fund Complex, identify the Fund Complex and provide the number of portfolios overseen as a director in the Fund Complex rather than listing each portfolio separately.

(2) For each individual listed in column (1) of the table required by paragraph (b)(1) of this Item, except for any director or nominee for election as director who is not or would not be an "interested person" of the Fund within the meaning of section 2(a)(19) of the Investment Company Act of 1940 (15 U.S.C. 80a–2(a)(19)), describe any positions, including as an officer, employee, director, or general partner, held with affiliated persons or principal underwriters of the Fund.

INSTRUCTION TO PARAGRAPH (b)(2). When an individual holds the same position(s) with two or more registered investment companies that are part of the same Fund Complex, identify the Fund Complex and provide the number of registered investment companies for which the position(s) are held rather than listing each registered investment company separately.

(3)(i) For each director or nominee for election as director, briefly discuss the specific experience, qualifications, attributes, or skills that led to the conclusion that the person should serve as a director for the Fund at the time that the disclosure is made in light

Securities and Exchange Commission § 240.14a-101

of the Fund's business and structure. If material, this disclosure should cover more than the past five years, including information about the person's particular areas of expertise or other relevant qualifications.

(ii) Describe briefly any arrangement or understanding between any director, nominee for election as director, Officer, or person chosen to become an Officer, and any other person(s) (naming the person(s)) pursuant to which he was or is to be selected as a director, nominee, or Officer.

INSTRUCTION TO PARAGRAPH (b)(3)(ii). Do not include arrangements or understandings with directors or Officers acting solely in their capacities as such.

(4)(i) Unless disclosed in the table required by paragraph (b)(1) of this Item, describe any positions, including as an officer, employee, director, or general partner, held by any director or nominee for election as director, who is not or would not be an "interested person" of the Fund within the meaning of section 2(a)(19) of the Investment Company Act of 1940 (15 U.S.C. 80a-2(a)(19)), or Immediate Family Member of the director or nominee, during the past five years, with:

(A) The Fund;

(B) An investment company, or a person that would be an investment company but for the exclusions provided by sections 3(c)(1) and 3(c)(7) of the Investment Company Act of 1940 (15 U.S.C. 80a-3(c)(1) and (c)(7)), having the same investment adviser, principal underwriter, or Sponsoring Insurance Company as the Fund or having an investment adviser, principal underwriter, or Sponsoring Insurance Company that directly or indirectly controls, is controlled by, or is under common control with an investment adviser, principal underwriter, or Sponsoring Insurance Company of the Fund;

(C) An investment adviser, principal underwriter, Sponsoring Insurance Company, or affiliated person of the Fund; or

(D) Any person directly or indirectly controlling, controlled by, or under common control with an investment adviser, principal underwriter, or Sponsoring Insurance Company of the Fund.

(ii) Unless disclosed in the table required by paragraph (b)(1) of this Item or in response to paragraph (b)(4)(i) of this Item, indicate any directorships held during the past five years by each director or nominee for election as director in any company with a class of securities registered pursuant to section 12 of the Exchange Act (15 U.S.C. 78*l*) or subject to the requirements of section 15(d) of the Exchange Act (15 U.S.C. 78o(d)) or any company registered as an investment company under the Investment Company Act of 1940 (15 U.S.C. 80a-1 *et seq.*), as amended, and name the companies in which the directorships were held.

INSTRUCTION TO PARAGRAPH (b)(4). When an individual holds the same position(s) with two or more portfolios that are part of the same Fund Complex, identify the Fund Complex and provide the number of portfolios for which the position(s) are held rather than listing each portfolio separately.

(5) For each director or nominee for election as director, state the dollar range of equity securities beneficially owned by the director or nominee as required by the following table:

(i) In the Fund; and

(ii) On an aggregate basis, in any registered investment companies overseen or to be overseen by the director or nominee within the same Family of Investment Companies as the Fund.

(1)	(2)	(3)
Name of Director or Nominee.	Dollar Range of Equity Securities in the Fund.	Aggregate Dollar Range of Equity Securities in All Funds Overseen or to be Overseen by Director or Nominee in Family of Investment Companies

INSTRUCTIONS TO PARAGRAPH (b)(5). 1. Information should be provided as of the most recent practicable date. Specify the valuation date by footnote or otherwise.

2. Determine "beneficial ownership" in accordance with rule 16a-1(a)(2) under the Exchange Act (§ 240.16a-1(a)(2)).

3. If action is to be taken with respect to more than one Fund, disclose in column (2) the dollar range of equity securities beneficially owned by a director or nominee in each such Fund overseen or to be overseen by the director or nominee.

4. In disclosing the dollar range of equity securities beneficially owned by a director or nominee in columns (2) and (3), use the following ranges: none, $1-$10,000, $10,001-$50,000, $50,001-$100,000, or over $100,000.

(6) For each director or nominee for election as director who is not or would not be an "interested person" of the Fund within the meaning of section 2(a)(19) of the Investment Company Act of 1940 (15 U.S.C. 80a-2(a)(19), and his Immediate Family Members, furnish the information required by the following table as to each class of securities owned beneficially or of record in:

(i) An investment adviser, principal underwriter, or Sponsoring Insurance Company of the Fund; or

(ii) A person (other than a registered investment company) directly or indirectly controlling, controlled by, or

§ 240.14a–101 17 CFR Ch. II (4–1–23 Edition)

under common control with an investment adviser, principal underwriter, or Sponsoring Insurance Company of the Fund:

(1)	(2)	(3)	(4)	(5)	(6)
Name of Director or Nominee.	Name of Owners and Relationships to Director or Nominee.	Company	Title of Class	Value of Securities	Percent of Class

INSTRUCTIONS TO PARAGRAPH (b)(6). 1. Information should be provided as of the most recent practicable date. Specify the valuation date by footnote or otherwise.

2. An individual is a "beneficial owner" of a security if he is a "beneficial owner" under either rule 13d–3 or rule 16a–1(a)(2) under the Exchange Act (§§ 240.13d–3 or 240.16a–1(a)(2)).

3. Identify the company in which the director, nominee, or Immediate Family Member of the director or nominee owns securities in column (3). When the company is a person directly or indirectly controlling, controlled by, or under common control with an investment adviser, principal underwriter, or Sponsoring Insurance Company, describe the company's relationship with the investment adviser, principal underwriter, or Sponsoring Insurance Company.

4. Provide the information required by columns (5) and (6) on an aggregate basis for each director (or nominee) and his Immediate Family Members.

(7) Unless disclosed in response to paragraph (b)(6) of this Item, describe any direct or indirect interest, the value of which exceeds $120,000, of each director or nominee for election as director who is not or would not be an "interested person" of the Fund within the meaning of section 2(a)(19) of the Investment Company Act of 1940 (15 U.S.C. 80a–2(a)(19)), or Immediate Family Member of the director or nominee, during the past five years, in:

(i) An investment adviser, principal underwriter, or Sponsoring Insurance Company of the Fund; or

(ii) A person (other than a registered investment company) directly or indirectly controlling, controlled by, or under common control with an investment adviser, principal underwriter, or Sponsoring Insurance Company of the Fund.

INSTRUCTIONS TO PARAGRAPH (b)(7). 1. A director, nominee, or Immediate Family Member has an interest in a company if he is a party to a contract, arrangement, or understanding with respect to any securities of, or interest in, the company.

2. The interest of the director (or nominee) and the interests of his Immediate Family Members should be aggregated in determining whether the value exceeds $120,000.

(8) Describe briefly any material interest, direct or indirect, of any director or nominee for election as director who is not or would not be an "interested person" of the Fund within the meaning of section 2(a)(19) of the Investment Company Act of 1940 (15 U.S.C. 80a–2(a)(19)), or Immediate Family Member of the director or nominee, in any transaction, or series of similar transactions, since the beginning of the last two completed fiscal years of the Fund, or in any currently proposed transaction, or series of similar transactions, in which the amount involved exceeds $120,000 and to which any of the following persons was or is to be a party:

(i) The Fund;

(ii) An Officer of the Fund;

(iii) An investment company, or a person that would be an investment company but for the exclusions provided by sections 3(c)(1) and 3(c)(7) of the Investment Company Act of 1940 (15 U.S.C. 80a–3(c)(1) and (c)(7)), having the same investment adviser, principal underwriter, or Sponsoring Insurance Company as the Fund or having an investment adviser, principal underwriter, or Sponsoring Insurance Company that directly or indirectly controls, is controlled by, or is under common control with an investment adviser, principal underwriter, or Sponsoring Insurance Company of the Fund;

(iv) An Officer of an investment company, or a person that would be an investment company but for the exclusions provided by sections 3(c)(1) and 3(c)(7) of the Investment Company Act of 1940 (15 U.S.C. 80a–3(c)(1) and (c)(7)), having the same investment adviser, principal underwriter, or Sponsoring Insurance Company as the Fund or

Securities and Exchange Commission § 240.14a–101

having an investment adviser, principal underwriter, or Sponsoring Insurance Company that directly or indirectly controls, is controlled by, or is under common control with an investment adviser, principal underwriter, or Sponsoring Insurance Company of the Fund;

(v) An investment adviser, principal underwriter, or Sponsoring Insurance Company of the Fund;

(vi) An Officer of an investment adviser, principal underwriter, or Sponsoring Insurance Company of the Fund;

(vii) A person directly or indirectly controlling, controlled by, or under common control with an investment adviser, principal underwriter, or Sponsoring Insurance Company of the Fund; or

(viii) An Officer of a person directly or indirectly controlling, controlled by, or under common control with an investment adviser, principal underwriter, or Sponsoring Insurance Company of the Fund.

INSTRUCTIONS TO PARAGRAPH (b)(8). 1. Include the name of each director, nominee, or Immediate Family Member whose interest in any transaction or series of similar transactions is described and the nature of the circumstances by reason of which the interest is required to be described.

2. State the nature of the interest, the approximate dollar amount involved in the transaction, and, where practicable, the approximate dollar amount of the interest.

3. In computing the amount involved in the transaction or series of similar transactions, include all periodic payments in the case of any lease or other agreement providing for periodic payments.

4. Compute the amount of the interest of any director, nominee, or Immediate Family Member of the director or nominee without regard to the amount of profit or loss involved in the transaction(s).

5. As to any transaction involving the purchase or sale of assets, state the cost of the assets to the purchaser and, if acquired by the seller within two years prior to the transaction, the cost to the seller. Describe the method used in determining the purchase or sale price and the name of the person making the determination.

6. If the proxy statement relates to multiple portfolios of a series Fund with different fiscal years, then, in determining the date that is the beginning of the last two completed fiscal years of the Fund, use the earliest date of any series covered by the proxy statement.

7. Disclose indirect, as well as direct, material interests in transactions. A person who has a position or relationship with, or interest in, a company that engages in a transaction with one of the persons listed in paragraphs (b)(8)(i) through (b)(8)(viii) of this Item may have an indirect interest in the transaction by reason of the position, relationship, or interest. The interest in the transaction, however, will not be deemed "material" within the meaning of paragraph (b)(8) of this Item where the interest of the director, nominee, or Immediate Family Member arises solely from the holding of an equity interest (including a limited partnership interest, but excluding a general partnership interest) or a creditor interest in a company that is a party to the transaction with one of the persons specified in paragraphs (b)(8)(i) through (b)(8)(viii) of this Item, and the transaction is not material to the company.

8. The materiality of any interest is to be determined on the basis of the significance of the information to investors in light of all the circumstances of the particular case. The importance of the interest to the person having the interest, the relationship of the parties to the transaction with each other, and the amount involved in the transaction are among the factors to be considered in determining the significance of the information to investors.

9. No information need be given as to any transaction where the interest of the director, nominee, or Immediate Family Member arises solely from the ownership of securities of a person specified in paragraphs (b)(8)(i) through (b)(8)(viii) of this Item and the director, nominee, or Immediate Family Member receives no extra or special benefit not shared on a pro rata basis by all holders of the class of securities.

10. Transactions include loans, lines of credit, and other indebtedness. For indebtedness, indicate the largest aggregate amount of indebtedness outstanding at any time during the period, the nature of the indebtedness and the transaction in which it was incurred, the amount outstanding as of the latest practicable date, and the rate of interest paid or charged.

11. No information need be given as to any routine, retail transaction. For example, the Fund need not disclose that a director has a credit card, bank or brokerage account, residential mortgage, or insurance policy with a person specified in paragraphs (b)(8)(i) through (b)(8)(viii) of this Item unless the director is accorded special treatment.

(9) Describe briefly any direct or indirect relationship, in which the amount involved exceeds $120,000, of any director or nominee for election as director who is not or would not be an "interested person" of the Fund within

§ 240.14a-101

the meaning of section 2(a)(19) of the Investment Company Act of 1940 (15 U.S.C. 80a–2(a)(19)), or Immediate Family Member of the director or nominee, that exists, or has existed at any time since the beginning of the last two completed fiscal years of the Fund, or is currently proposed, with any of the persons specified in paragraphs (b)(8)(i) through (b)(8)(viii) of this Item. Relationships include:

(i) Payments for property or services to or from any person specified in paragraphs (b)(8)(i) through (b)(8)(viii) of this Item;

(ii) Provision of legal services to any person specified in paragraphs (b)(8)(i) through (b)(8)(viii) of this Item;

(iii) Provision of investment banking services to any person specified in paragraphs (b)(8)(i) through (b)(8)(viii) of this Item, other than as a participating underwriter in a syndicate; and

(iv) Any consulting or other relationship that is substantially similar in nature and scope to the relationships listed in paragraphs (b)(9)(i) through (b)(9)(iii) of this Item.

INSTRUCTIONS TO PARAGRAPH (b)(9). 1. Include the name of each director, nominee, or Immediate Family Member whose relationship is described and the nature of the circumstances by reason of which the relationship is required to be described.

2. State the nature of the relationship and the amount of business conducted between the director, nominee, or Immediate Family Member and the person specified in paragraphs (b)(8)(i) through (b)(8)(viii) of this Item as a result of the relationship since the beginning of the last two completed fiscal years of the Fund or proposed to be done during the Fund's current fiscal year.

3. In computing the amount involved in a relationship, include all periodic payments in the case of any agreement providing for periodic payments.

4. If the proxy statement relates to multiple portfolios of a series Fund with different fiscal years, then, in determining the date that is the beginning of the last two completed fiscal years of the Fund, use the earliest date of any series covered by the proxy statement.

5. Disclose indirect, as well as direct, relationships. A person who has a position or relationship with, or interest in, a company that has a relationship with one of the persons listed in paragraphs (b)(8)(i) through (b)(8)(viii) of this Item may have an indirect relationship by reason of the position, relationship, or interest.

6. In determining whether the amount involved in a relationship exceeds $120,000, amounts involved in a relationship of the director (or nominee) should be aggregated with those of his Immediate Family Members.

7. In the case of an indirect interest, identify the company with which a person specified in paragraphs (b)(8)(i) through (b)(8)(viii) of this Item has a relationship; the name of the director, nominee, or Immediate Family Member affiliated with the company and the nature of the affiliation; and the amount of business conducted between the company and the person specified in paragraphs (b)(8)(i) through (b)(8)(viii) of this Item since the beginning of the last two completed fiscal years of the Fund or proposed to be done during the Fund's current fiscal year.

8. In calculating payments for property and services for purposes of paragraph (b)(9)(i) of this Item, the following may be excluded:

A. Payments where the transaction involves the rendering of services as a common contract carrier, or public utility, at rates or charges fixed in conformity with law or governmental authority; or

B. Payments that arise solely from the ownership of securities of a person specified in paragraphs (b)(8)(i) through (b)(8)(viii) of this Item and no extra or special benefit not shared on a pro rata basis by all holders of the class of securities is received.

9. No information need be given as to any routine, retail relationship. For example, the Fund need not disclose that a director has a credit card, bank or brokerage account, residential mortgage, or insurance policy with a person specified in paragraphs (b)(8)(i) through (b)(8)(viii) of this Item unless the director is accorded special treatment.

(10) If an Officer of an investment adviser, principal underwriter, or Sponsoring Insurance Company of the Fund, or an Officer of a person directly or indirectly controlling, controlled by, or under common control with an investment adviser, principal underwriter, or Sponsoring Insurance Company of the Fund, serves, or has served since the beginning of the last two completed fiscal years of the Fund, on the board of directors of a company where a director of the Fund or nominee for election as director who is not or would not be an "interested person" of the Fund within the meaning of section 2(a)(19) of the Investment Company Act of 1940 (15 U.S.C. 80a-2(a)(19)), or Immediate Family Member of the director or nominee, is, or was since the beginning

Securities and Exchange Commission § 240.14a–101

of the last two completed fiscal years of the Fund, an Officer, identify:

(i) The company;

(ii) The individual who serves or has served as a director of the company and the period of service as director;

(iii) The investment adviser, principal underwriter, or Sponsoring Insurance Company or person controlling, controlled by, or under common control with the investment adviser, principal underwriter, or Sponsoring Insurance Company where the individual named in paragraph (b)(10)(ii) of this Item holds or held office and the office held; and

(iv) The director of the Fund, nominee for election as director, or Immediate Family Member who is or was an Officer of the company; the office held; and the period of holding the office.

INSTRUCTION TO PARAGRAPH (b)(10). If the proxy statement relates to multiple portfolios of a series Fund with different fiscal years, then, in determining the date that is the beginning of the last two completed fiscal years of the Fund, use the earliest date of any series covered by the proxy statement.

(11) Provide in tabular form, to the extent practicable, the information required by Items 401(f) and (g), 404(a), 405, and 407(h) of Regulation S–K (§§ 229.401(f) and (g), 229.404(a), 229.405, and 229.407(h) of this chapter).

INSTRUCTION TO PARAGRAPH (b)(11). Information provided under paragraph (b)(8) of this Item 22 is deemed to satisfy the requirements of Item 404(a) of Regulation S–K for information about directors, nominees for election as directors, and Immediate Family Members of directors and nominees, and need not be provided under this paragraph (b)(11).

(12) Describe briefly any material pending legal proceedings, other than ordinary routine litigation incidental to the Fund's business, to which any director or nominee for director or affiliated person of such director or nominee is a party adverse to the Fund or any of its affiliated persons or has a material interest adverse to the Fund or any of its affiliated persons. Include the name of the court where the case is pending, the date instituted, the principal parties, a description of the factual basis alleged to underlie the proceeding, and the relief sought.

(13) In the case of a Fund that is an investment company registered under the Investment Company Act of 1940 (15 U.S.C. 80a), for all directors, and for each of the three highest-paid Officers that have aggregate compensation from the Fund for the most recently completed fiscal year in excess of $60,000 ("Compensated Persons"):

(i) Furnish the information required by the following table for the last fiscal year:

COMPENSATION TABLE

(1)	(2)	(3)	(4)	(5)
Name of Person, Position.	Aggregate Compensation From Fund.	Pension or Retirement Benefits Accrued as Part of Fund Expenses.	Estimated Annual Benefits Upon Retirement.	Total Compensation From Fund and Complex Paid to Directors

INSTRUCTIONS TO PARAGRAPH (b)(13)(i). 1. For column (1), indicate, if necessary, the capacity in which the remuneration is received. For Compensated Persons that are directors of the Fund, compensation is amounts received for service as a director.

2. If the Fund has not completed its first full year since its organization, furnish the information for the current fiscal year, estimating future payments that would be made pursuant to an existing agreement or understanding. Disclose in a footnote to the Compensation Table the period for which the information is furnished.

3. Include in column (2) amounts deferred at the election of the Compensated Person, whether pursuant to a plan established under Section 401(k) of the Internal Revenue Code (26 U.S.C. 401(k)) or otherwise, for the fiscal year in which earned. Disclose in a footnote to the Compensation Table the total amount of deferred compensation (including interest) payable to or accrued for any Compensated Person.

4. Include in columns (3) and (4) all pension or retirement benefits proposed to be paid under any existing plan in the event of retirement at normal retirement date, directly or indirectly, by the Fund or any of its Subsidiaries, or by other companies in the Fund Complex. Omit column (4) where retirement benefits are not determinable.

§ 240.14a–101

5. For any defined benefit or actuarial plan under which benefits are determined primarily by final compensation (or average final compensation) and years of service, provide the information required in column (4) in a separate table showing estimated annual benefits payable upon retirement (including amounts attributable to any defined benefit supplementary or excess pension award plans) in specified compensation and years of service classifications. Also provide the estimated credited years of service for each Compensated Person.

6. Include in column (5) only aggregate compensation paid to a director for service on the board and other boards of investment companies in a Fund Complex specifying the number of such other investment companies.

(ii) Describe briefly the material provisions of any pension, retirement, or other plan or any arrangement other than fee arrangements disclosed in paragraph (b)(13)(i) of this Item pursuant to which Compensated Persons are or may be compensated for any services provided, including amounts paid, if any, to the Compensated Person under any such arrangements during the most recently completed fiscal year. Specifically include the criteria used to determine amounts payable under any plan, the length of service or vesting period required by the plan, the retirement age or other event that gives rise to payments under the plan, and whether the payment of benefits is secured or funded by the Fund.

(14) State whether or not the Fund has a separately designated audit committee established in accordance with section 3(a)(58)(A) of the Act (15 U.S.C. 78c(a)(58)(A)). If the entire board of directors is acting as the Fund's audit committee as specified in section 3(a)(58)(B) of the Act (15 U.S.C. 78c(a)(58)(B)), so state. If applicable, provide the disclosure required by § 240.10A–3(d) regarding an exemption from the listing standards for audit committees. Identify the other standing committees of the Fund's board of directors, and provide the following information about each committee, including any separately designated audit committee and any nominating committee:

(i) A concise statement of the functions of the committee;

(ii) The members of the committee and, in the case of a nominating committee, whether or not the members of the committee are "interested persons" of the Fund as defined in section 2(a)(19) of the Investment Company Act of 1940 (15 U.S.C. 80a–2(a)(19)); and

(iii) The number of committee meetings held during the last fiscal year.

INSTRUCTION TO PARAGRAPH (b)(14): For purposes of Item 22(b)(14), the term "nominating committee" refers not only to nominating committees and committees performing similar functions, but also to groups of directors fulfilling the role of a nominating committee, including the entire board of directors.

(15)(i) Provide the information (and in the format) required by Items 407(b)(1), (b)(2) and (f) of Regulation S–K (§ 229.407(b)(1), (b)(2) and (f) of this chapter); and

(ii) Provide the following regarding the requirements for the director nomination process:

(A) The information (and in the format) required by Items 407(c)(1) and (c)(2) of Regulation S–K (§ 229.407(c)(1) and (c)(2) of this chapter); and

(B) If the Fund is a listed issuer (as defined in § 240.10A–3 of this chapter) whose securities are listed on a national securities exchange registered pursuant to section 6(a) of the Act (15 U.S.C. 78f(a)) or in an automated inter-dealer quotation system of a national securities association registered pursuant to section 15A of the Act (15 U.S.C. 78o–3(a)) that has independence requirements for nominating committee members, identify each director that is a member of the nominating committee that is not independent under the independence standards described in this paragraph. In determining whether the nominating committee members are independent, use the Fund's definition of independence that it uses for determining if the members of the nominating committee are independent in compliance with the independence standards applicable for the members of the nominating committee in the listing standards applicable to the Fund. If the Fund does not have independence standards for the nominating committee, use the independence standards for the nominating committee in the listing standards applicable to the Fund.

INSTRUCTION TO PARAGRAPH (b)(15)(ii)(B). If the national securities exchange or inter-

Securities and Exchange Commission § 240.14a–101

dealer quotation system on which the Fund's securities are listed has exemptions to the independence requirements for nominating committee members upon which the Fund relied, disclose the exemption relied upon and explain the basis for the Fund's conclusion that such exemption is applicable.

(16) In the case of a Fund that is a closed-end investment company:

(i) Provide the information (and in the format) required by Item 407(d)(1), (d)(2) and (d)(3) of Regulation S–K (§ 229.407(d)(1), (d)(2) and (d)(3) of this chapter); and

(ii) Identify each director that is a member of the Fund's audit committee that is not independent under the independence standards described in this paragraph. If the Fund does not have a separately designated audit committee, or committee performing similar functions, the Fund must provide the disclosure with respect to all members of its board of directors.

(A) If the Fund is a listed issuer (as defined in § 240.10A–3 of this chapter) whose securities are listed on a national securities exchange registered pursuant to section 6(a) of the Act (15 U.S.C. 78f(a)) or in an automated inter-dealer quotation system of a national securities association registered pursuant to section 15A of the Act (15 U.S.C. 78o–3(a)) that has independence requirements for audit committee members, in determining whether the audit committee members are independent, use the Fund's definition of independence that it uses for determining if the members of the audit committee are independent in compliance with the independence standards applicable for the members of the audit committee in the listing standards applicable to the Fund. If the Fund does not have independence standards for the audit committee, use the independence standards for the audit committee in the listing standards applicable to the Fund.

(B) If the Fund is not a listed issuer whose securities are listed on a national securities exchange registered pursuant to section 6(a) of the Act (15 U.S.C. 78f(a)) or in an automated inter-dealer quotation system of a national securities association registered pursuant to section 15A of the Act (15 U.S.C. 78o–3(a)), in determining whether the audit committee members are independent, use a definition of independence of a national securities exchange registered pursuant to section 6(a) of the Act (15 U.S.C. 78f(a)) or an automated inter-dealer quotation system of a national securities association registered pursuant to section 15A of the Act (15 U.S.C. 78o–3(a)) which has requirements that a majority of the board of directors be independent and that has been approved by the Commission, and state which definition is used. Whatever such definition the Fund chooses, it must use the same definition with respect to all directors and nominees for director. If the national securities exchange or national securities association whose standards are used has independence standards for the members of the audit committee, use those specific standards.

INSTRUCTION TO PARAGRAPH (b)(16)(ii). If the national securities exchange or inter-dealer quotation system on which the Fund's securities are listed has exemptions to the independence requirements for nominating committee members upon which the Fund relied, disclose the exemption relied upon and explain the basis for the Fund's conclusion that such exemption is applicable. The same disclosure should be provided if the Fund is not a listed issuer and the national securities exchange or inter-dealer quotation system selected by the Fund has exemptions that are applicable to the Fund.

(17) In the case of a Fund that is an investment company registered under the Investment Company Act of 1940 (15 U.S.C. 80a), if a director has resigned or declined to stand for re-election to the board of directors since the date of the last annual meeting of security holders because of a disagreement with the registrant on any matter relating to the registrant's operations, policies or practices, and if the director has furnished the registrant with a letter describing such disagreement and requesting that the matter be disclosed, the registrant shall state the date of resignation or declination to stand for re-election and summarize the director's description of the disagreement. If the registrant believes that the description provided by the director is incorrect or incomplete, it may include a brief statement presenting its view of the disagreement.

(18) If a shareholder nominee or nominees are submitted to the Fund

§ 240.14a–101

for inclusion in the Fund's proxy materials pursuant to § 240.14a–11 and the Fund is not permitted to exclude the nominee or nominees pursuant to the provisions of § 240.14a–11, the Fund must include in its proxy statement the disclosure required from the nominating shareholder or nominating shareholder group under Item 5 of § 240.14n–101 with regard to the nominee or nominees and the nominating shareholder or nominating shareholder group.

INSTRUCTION TO PARAGRAPH (b)(18). The information disclosed pursuant to paragraph (b)(18) of this Item will not be deemed incorporated by reference into any filing under the Securities Act of 1933 (15 U.S.C. 77a *et seq.*), the Securities Exchange Act of 1934 (15 U.S.C. 78a *et seq.*), or the Investment Company Act of 1940 (15 U.S.C. 80a–1 *et seq.*), except to the extent that the Fund specifically incorporates that information by reference.

(19) If a Fund is required to include a shareholder nominee or nominees submitted to the Fund for inclusion in the Fund's proxy materials pursuant to a procedure set forth under applicable state or foreign law or the Fund's governing documents providing for the inclusion of shareholder director nominees in the Fund's proxy materials, the Fund must include in its proxy statement the disclosure required from the nominating shareholder or nominating shareholder group under Item 6 of § 240.14n–101 with regard to the nominee or nominees and the nominating shareholder or nominating shareholder group.

INSTRUCTION TO PARAGRAPH (b)(19). The information disclosed pursuant to paragraph (b)(19) of this Item will not be deemed incorporated by reference into any filing under the Securities Act of 1933 (15 U.S.C. 77a *et seq.*), the Securities Exchange Act of 1934 (15 U.S.C. 78a *et seq.*), or the Investment Company Act of 1940 (15 U.S.C. 80a–1 *et seq.*), except to the extent that the Fund specifically incorporates that information by reference.

(20) In the case of a Fund that is an investment company registered under the Investment Company Act of 1940 (15 U.S.C. 80a) that is required to develop and implement a policy regarding the recovery of erroneously awarded compensation pursuant to § 240.10D–1(b)(1), if at any time during the last completed fiscal year the Fund was required to prepare an accounting restatement that required recovery of erroneously awarded compensation pursuant to the Fund's compensation recovery policy required by the listing standards adopted pursuant to 240.10D–1, or there was an outstanding balance as of the end of the last completed fiscal year of erroneously awarded compensation to be recovered from the application of the policy to a prior restatement, the Fund must provide the information required by Item 18 of Form N–CSR, as applicable.

(c) *Approval of investment advisory contract.* If action is to be taken with respect to an investment advisory contract, include the following information in the proxy statement.

Instruction. Furnish information with respect to a prospective investment adviser to the extent applicable (including the name and address of the prospective investment adviser).

(1) With respect to the existing investment advisory contract:

(i) State the date of the contract and the date on which it was last submitted to a vote of security holders of the Fund, including the purpose of such submission;

(ii) Briefly describe the terms of the contract, including the rate of compensation of the investment adviser;

(iii) State the aggregate amount of the investment adviser's fee and the amount and purpose of any other material payments by the Fund to the investment adviser, or any affiliated person of the investment adviser, during the last fiscal year of the Fund;

(iv) If any person is acting as an investment adviser of the Fund other than pursuant to a written contract that has been approved by the security holders of the company, identify the person and describe the nature of the services and arrangements;

(v) Describe any action taken with respect to the investment advisory contract since the beginning of the Fund's last fiscal year by the board of directors of the Fund (unless described in response to paragraph (c)(1)(vi)) of this Item 22); and

(vi) If an investment advisory contract was terminated or not renewed for any reason, state the date of such termination or non-renewal, identify

Securities and Exchange Commission §240.14a–101

the parties involved, and describe the circumstances of such termination or non-renewal.

(2) State the name, address and principal occupation of the principal executive officer and each director or general partner of the investment adviser.

Instruction. If the investment adviser is a partnership with more than ten general partners, name:

(i) The general partners with the five largest economic interests in the partnership, and, if different, those general partners comprising the management or executive committee of the partnership or exercising similar authority;

(ii) The general partners with significant management responsibilities relating to the fund.

(3) State the names and addresses of all Parents of the investment adviser and show the basis of control of the investment adviser and each Parent by its immediate Parent.

Instructions. 1. If any person named is a corporation, include the percentage of its voting securities owned by its immediate Parent.

2. If any person named is a partnership, name the general partners having the three largest partnership interests (computed by whatever method is appropriate in the particular case).

(4) If the investment adviser is a corporation and if, to the knowledge of the persons making the solicitation or the persons on whose behalf the solicitation is made, any person not named in answer to paragraph (c)(3) of this Item 22 owns, of record or beneficially, ten percent or more of the outstanding voting securities of the investment adviser, indicate that fact and state the name and address of each such person.

(5) Name each officer or director of the Fund who is an officer, employee, director, general partner or shareholder of the investment adviser. As to any officer or director who is not a director or general partner of the investment adviser and who owns securities or has any other material direct or indirect interest in the investment adviser or any other person controlling, controlled by or under common control with the investment adviser, describe the nature of such interest.

(6) Describe briefly and state the approximate amount of, where practicable, any material interest, direct or indirect, of any director of the Fund in any material transactions since the beginning of the most recently completed fiscal year, or in any material proposed transactions, to which the investment adviser of the Fund, any Parent or Subsidiary of the investment adviser (other than another Fund), or any Subsidiary of the Parent of such entities was or is to be a party.

Instructions. 1. Include the name of each person whose interest in any transaction is described and the nature of the relationship by reason of which such interest is required to be described. Where it is not practicable to state the approximate amount of the interest, indicate the approximate amount involved in the transaction.

2. As to any transaction involving the purchase or sale of assets by or to the investment adviser, state the cost of the assets to the purchaser and the cost thereof to the seller if acquired by the seller within two years prior to the transaction.

3. If the interest of any person arises from the position of the person as a partner in a partnership, the proportionate interest of such person in transactions to which the partnership is a party need not be set forth, but state the amount involved in the transaction with the partnership.

4. No information need be given in response to this paragraph (c)(6) of Item 22 with respect to any transaction that is not related to the business or operations of the Fund and to which neither the Fund nor any of its Parents or Subsidiaries is a party.

(7) Disclose any financial condition of the investment adviser that is reasonably likely to impair the financial ability of the adviser to fulfill its commitment to the fund under the proposed investment advisory contract.

(8) Describe the nature of the action to be taken on the investment advisory contract and the reasons therefor, the terms of the contract to be acted upon, and, if the action is an amendment to, or a replacement of, an investment advisory contract, the material differences between the current and proposed contract.

(9) If a change in the investment advisory fee is sought, state:

(i) The aggregate amount of the investment adviser's fee during the last year;

(ii) The amount that the adviser would have received had the proposed fee been in effect; and

(iii) The difference between the aggregate amounts stated in response to paragraphs (i) and (ii) of this item (c)(9) as a percentage of the amount stated in response to paragraph (i) of this item (c)(9).

(10) If the investment adviser acts as such with respect to any other Fund having a similar investment objective, identify and state the size of such other Fund and the rate of the investment adviser's compensation. Also indicate for any Fund identified whether the investment adviser has waived, reduced, or otherwise agreed to reduce its compensation under any applicable contract.

Instruction. Furnish the information in response to this paragraph (c)(10) of Item 22 in tabular form.

(11) Discuss in reasonable detail the material factors and the conclusions with respect thereto that form the basis for the recommendation of the board of directors that the shareholders approve an investment advisory contract. Include the following in the discussion:

(i) Factors relating to both the board's selection of the investment adviser and approval of the advisory fee and any other amounts to be paid by the Fund under the contract. This would include, but not be limited to, a discussion of the nature, extent, and quality of the services to be provided by the investment adviser; the investment performance of the Fund and the investment adviser; the costs of the services to be provided and profits to be realized by the investment adviser and its affiliates from the relationship with the Fund; the extent to which economies of scale would be realized as the Fund grows; and whether fee levels reflect these economies of scale for the benefit of Fund investors. Also indicate in the discussion whether the board relied upon comparisons of the services to be rendered and the amounts to be paid under the contract with those under other investment advisory contracts, such as contracts of the same and other investment advisers with other registered investment companies or other types of clients (e.g., pension funds and other institutional investors). If the board relied upon such comparisons, describe the comparisons that were relied on and how they assisted the board in determining to recommend that the shareholders approve the advisory contract; and

(ii) If applicable, any benefits derived or to be derived by the investment adviser from the relationship with the Fund such as soft dollar arrangements by which brokers provide research to the Fund or its investment adviser in return for allocating Fund brokerage.

Instructions. 1. Conclusory statements or a list of factors will not be considered sufficient disclosure. Relate the factors to the specific circumstances of the Fund and the investment advisory contract for which approval is sought and state how the board evaluated each factor. For example, it is not sufficient to state that the board considered the amount of the investment advisory fee without stating what the board concluded about the amount of the fee and how that affected its determination to recommend approval of the contract.

2. If any factor enumerated in paragraph (c)(11)(i) of this Item 22 is not relevant to the board's evaluation of the investment advisory contract for which approval is sought, note this and explain the reasons why that factor is not relevant.

(12) Describe any arrangement or understanding made in connection with the proposed investment advisory contract with respect to the composition of the board of directors of the Fund or the investment adviser or with respect to the selection or appointment of any person to any office with either such company.

(13) For the most recently completed fiscal year, state:

(i) The aggregate amount of commissions paid to any Affiliated Broker; and

(ii) The percentage of the Fund's aggregate brokerage commissions paid to any such Affiliated Broker.

Instruction. Identify each Affiliated Broker and the relationships that cause the broker to be an Affiliated Broker.

Securities and Exchange Commission § 240.14a–101

(14) Disclose the amount of any fees paid by the Fund to the investment adviser, its affiliated persons or any affiliated person of such person during the most recent fiscal year for services provided to the Fund (other than under the investment advisory contract or for brokerage commissions). State whether these services will continue to be provided after the investment advisory contract is approved.

(d) *Approval of distribution plan.* If action is to be taken with respect to a Distribution Plan, include the following information in the proxy statement.

Instruction. Furnish information on a prospective basis to the extent applicable.

(1) Describe the nature of the action to be taken on the Distribution Plan and the reason therefor, the terms of the Distribution Plan to be acted upon, and, if the action is an amendment to, or a replacement of, a Distribution Plan, the material differences between the current and proposed Distribution Plan.

(2) If the Fund has a Distribution Plan in effect:

(i) Provide the date that the Distribution Plan was adopted and the date of the last amendment, if any;

(ii) Disclose the persons to whom payments may be made under the Distribution Plan, the rate of the distribution fee and the purposes for which such fee may be used;

(iii) Disclose the amount of distribution fees paid by the Fund pursuant to the plan during its most recent fiscal year, both in the aggregate and as a percentage of the Fund's average net assets during the period;

(iv) Disclose the name of, and the amount of any payments made under the Distribution Plan by the Fund during its most recent fiscal year to, any person who is an affiliated person of the Fund, its investment adviser, principal underwriter, or Administrator, an affiliated person of such person, or a person that during the most recent fiscal year received 10% or more of the aggregate amount paid under the Distribution Plan by the Fund;

(v) Describe any action taken with respect to the Distribution Plan since the beginning of the Fund's most recent fiscal year by the board of directors of the Fund; and

(vi) If a Distribution Plan was or is to be terminated or not renewed for any reason, state the date or prospective date of such termination or non-renewal, identify the parties involved, and describe the circumstances of such termination or non-renewal.

(3) Describe briefly and state the approximate amount of, where practicable, any material interest, direct or indirect, of any director or nominee for election as a director of the Fund in any material transactions since the beginning of the most recently completed fiscal year, or in any material proposed transactions, to which any person identified in response to Item 22(d)(2)(iv) was or is to be a party.

Instructions. 1. Include the name of each person whose interest in any transaction is described and the nature of the relationship by reason of which such interest is required to be described. Where it is not practicable to state the approximate amount of the interest, indicate the approximate amount involved in the transaction.

2. As to any transaction involving the purchase or sale of assets, state the cost of the assets to the purchaser and the cost thereof to the seller if acquired by the seller within two years prior to the transaction.

3. If the interest of any person arises from the position of the person as a partner in a partnership, the proportionate interest of such person in transactions to which the partnership is a party need not be set forth but state the amount involved in the transaction with the partnership.

4. No information need be given in response to this paragraph (d)(3) of Item 22 with respect to any transaction that is not related to the business or operations of the Fund and to which neither the Fund nor any of its Parents or Subsidiaries is a party.

(4) Discuss in reasonable detail the material factors and the conclusions with respect thereto which form the basis for the conclusion of the board of directors that there is a reasonable likelihood that the proposed Distribution Plan (or amendment thereto) will benefit the Fund and its shareholders.

§ 240.14a-101

Instruction. Conclusory statements or a list of factors will not be considered sufficient disclosure.

Item 23. Delivery of documents to security holders sharing an address. If one annual report to security holders, proxy statement, or Notice of Internet Availability of Proxy Materials is being delivered to two or more security holders who share an address in accordance with § 240.14a-3(e)(1), furnish the following information:

(a) State that only one annual report to security holders, proxy statement, or Notice of Internet Availability of Proxy Materials, as applicable, is being delivered to multiple security holders sharing an address unless the registrant has received contrary instructions from one or more of the security holders;

(b) Undertake to deliver promptly upon written or oral request a separate copy of the annual report to security holders, proxy statement, or Notice of Internet Availability of Proxy Materials, as applicable, to a security holder at a shared address to which a single copy of the documents was delivered and provide instructions as to how a security holder can notify the registrant that the security holder wishes to receive a separate copy of an annual report to security holders, proxy statement, or Notice of Internet Availability of Proxy Materials, as applicable;

(c) Provide the phone number and mailing address to which a security holder can direct a notification to the registrant that the security holder wishes to receive a separate annual report to security holders, proxy statement, or Notice of Internet Availability of Proxy Materials, as applicable, in the future; and

(d) Provide instructions how security holders sharing an address can request delivery of a single copy of annual reports to security holders, proxy statements, or Notices of Internet Availability of Proxy Materials if they are receiving multiple copies of annual reports to security holders, proxy statements, or Notices of Internet Availability of Proxy Materials.

Item 24. Shareholder Approval of Executive Compensation. Registrants required to provide any of the separate shareholder votes pursuant to § 240.14a-21 of this chapter shall disclose that they are providing each such vote as required pursuant to section 14A of the Securities Exchange Act (15 U.S.C. 78n-1), briefly explain the general effect of each vote, such as whether each such vote is non-binding, and, when applicable, disclose the current frequency of shareholder advisory votes on executive compensation required by Rule 14a-21(a) and when the next such shareholder advisory vote will occur.

Item 25. Exhibits. Provide each of the following in an exhibit to this Schedule 14A:

(a) The legal opinion required to be filed by Item 402(u)(4)(i) of Regulation S–K (17 CFR 229.402(u)); and

(b) If a fee is required, the title of each class of securities to which the transaction applies, aggregate number of securities to which the transaction applies, per unit price or other underlying value of the transaction computed pursuant to § 240.0-11, proposed maximum aggregate value of the transaction, fee rate, amount of filing fee and, as applicable, information relating to reliance on § 240.0-11(a)(2) in the tabular form indicated.

Registered funds that must pay registration fees using Form 24F-2 (§ 274.24) are not required to respond to this Item.

CALCULATION OF FILING FEE TABLES

TABLE 1—TRANSACTION VALUATION

	Proposed maximum aggregate value of transaction	Fee rate	Amount of filing fee
Fees to Be Paid	X	X	X
Fees Previously Paid	X		X

Securities and Exchange Commission §240.14a–101

TABLE 1—TRANSACTION VALUATION—Continued

	Proposed maximum aggregate value of transaction	Fee rate	Amount of filing fee
Total Transaction Valuation	X		
Total Fees Due for Filing			X
Total Fees Previously Paid			X
Total Fee Offsets			X
Net Fee Due			X

TABLE 2—FEE OFFSET CLAIMS AND SOURCES

	Registrant or filer name	Form or filing type	File number	Initial filing date	Filing date	Fee offset claimed	Fee paid with fee offset source
Fee Offset Claims		X	X	X		X	
Fee Offset Sources	X	X	X		X		X

Instructions to the Calculation of Filing Fee Tables and Related Disclosure ("Instructions"):

1. General Requirements.

A. Applicable Table Requirements.

The "X" designation indicates the information required to be disclosed, as applicable, in tabular format. Add as many rows of each table as necessary.

B. Fee Rate.

For the current fee rate, *see* https://www.sec.gov/ofm/Article/feeamt.html.

C. Explanations.

Disclose the (i) title of each class of securities to which the transaction applies; (ii) aggregate number of securities to which the transaction apples; and (iii) per unit price or other underlying value of the transaction computed pursuant to Exchange Act Rule 0–11 (set forth the amount on which the filing fee is calculated and state how it was determined). If not otherwise explained in response to these instructions, disclose specific details relating to the fee calculation as necessary to clarify the information presented in each table, including references to the applicable provisions of Rule 0–11 (§240.0–11 of this chapter). All disclosure these Instructions require that is not specifically required to be presented in tabular format must appear in narrative format immediately after the table(s) to which it corresponds.

D. Submission Method.

If a filing fee exhibit is required to be provided pursuant to this Item 25(b), it must be submitted as required by Rule 408 of Regulation S–T (§232.408 of this chapter).

2. Table 1: Transaction Valuation Table and Related Disclosure.

A. Fees to Be Paid and Fees Previously Paid.

i. Fees to Be Paid.

Provide the information Table 1 requires for the line item "Fees to Be Paid" as follows:

c. Initial Filings.

For an initial filing on this schedule, provide the required information for the total transaction valuation.

d. Amendments with Then-Current Total Transaction Valuation Higher than Highest Total Transaction Valuation Previously Reported.

For amendments to this schedule that reflect a then-current total transaction valuation higher than the highest total transaction valuation previously reported, provide the required information for the incremental increase.

303

§ 240.14a–101

ii. Fees Previously Paid.

Provide the information Table 1 requires for the line item "Fees Previously Paid" for the prior initial filing or amendment to this schedule that reflected a then-current total transaction valuation that was the highest total transaction valuation previously reported.

B. Other Tabular Information.

Provide the following information in the table for the line items "Fees to be Paid" and "Fees Previously Paid", as applicable:

i. The proposed maximum aggregate value of the transaction computed pursuant to Exchange Act Rule 0–11;

ii. The fee rate; and

iii. The filing fee due without regard to any previous payments or offsets.

C. Totals.

i. Total Transaction Valuation.

Provide the sum of the proposed maximum aggregate values for the line items "Fees to Be Paid" and "Fees Previously Paid".

ii. Total Fees Due for Filing.

Provide the sum of the fees due without regard to any previous payments or offsets for the line items "Fees to be Paid" and "Fees Previously Paid."

iii. Total Fees Previously Paid.

Provide the aggregate of filing fees previously paid with this filing.

iv. Total Fee Offsets.

Provide the aggregate of the fee offsets that are claimed in Table 2 pursuant to Instruction 3.

v. Net Fee Due.

Provide the difference between (a) the total fees due for this schedule from the Total Fees Due for Filing row; and (b) the sum of (i) the aggregate of filing fees previously paid from the Total Fees Previously Paid row; and (ii) the aggregate fee offsets claimed from the Total Fee Offsets row.

D. Narrative Disclosure.

Explain how the transaction valuation was determined.

3. Table 2: Fee Offset Claims and Sources.

A. Terminology.

For purposes of this Instruction 3 and Table 2, the term "submission" means any (i) initial filing of, or amendment (pre-effective or post-effective), to a fee-bearing document; or (ii) fee-bearing form of prospectus filed under Rule 424 under the Securities Act (§ 230.424 of this chapter), in all cases that was accompanied by a contemporaneous fee payment. For purposes of these instructions to Table 2, a contemporaneous fee payment is the payment of a required fee that is satisfied through the actual transfer of funds, and does not include any amount of a required fee satisfied through a claimed fee offset. Instruction 3.B.ii requires a filer that claims a fee offset under Rule 0–11(a)(2) to identify previous submissions with contemporaneous fee payments that are the original source to which the fee offsets claimed on this filing can be traced. See Instruction 3.C for an example.

B. Rule 0–11(a)(2).

If relying on Rule 0–11(a)(2) to offset some or all of the filing fee due on this schedule by amounts paid in connection with earlier filings (other than this Schedule 14A) relating to the same transaction, provide the following information:

i. Fee Offset Claims.

For each earlier filed Securities Act registration statement or Exchange Act document relating to the same transaction from which a fee offset is being claimed, provide the information that Table 2 requires for the line item "Fee Offset Claims". The "Fee Offset Claimed" column requires the dollar amount of the previously paid filing fee to be offset against the currently due fee.

Note to Instruction 3.B.i.

If claiming an offset from a Securities Act registration statement, provide a detailed explanation of the basis for the claimed offset.

ii. Fee Offset Sources.

With respect to amounts claimed as an offset under Rule 0–11(a)(2), identify those submissions with contemporaneous fee payments that are the original source to which those amounts can be traced. For each submission identified, provide the information that Table 2 requires for the line item "Fee Offset Sources". The "Fee Paid with Fee Offset Source" column requires the dollar amount of the contemporaneous fee payment made with respect to each identified submission that is the source of the fee offset claimed pursuant to Rule 0–11(a)(2).

Securities and Exchange Commission

§ 240.14a-103

C. Fee Offset Source Submission Identification Example.

A filer:
- Initially files a registration statement on Form S-1 on 1/15/20X1 (assigned file number 333-123456) with a fee payment of $10,000;
- Files pre-effective amendment number 1 to the Form S-1 (333-123456) on 2/15/20X1 with a fee payment of $15,000 and the registration statement goes effective on 2/20/20X1;
- Initially files a registration statement on Form S-1 on 1/15/20X4 (assigned file number 333-123467) with a fee payment of $25,000 and relies on Rule 457(p) to claim an offset of $10,000 related to the unsold securities registered on the previously filed Form S-1 (333-123456) and apply it to the $35,000 filing fee due and the registration statement goes effective on 2/15/20X4.
- Initially files a registration statement related to a tender offer on Form S-4 (assigned file number 333-123478) on 1/15/20X7 with a fee payment of $15,000 and relies on Rule 457(p) to claim an offset of $30,000 related to the unsold securities registered on the most recently effective Form S-1 (333-123467) filed on 1/15/20X4 and apply it to the $45,000 filing fee due.
- Initially files a Schedule TO related to the same tender offer on 1/22/20X7 and relies on Rule 0-11(ε)(2) to claim an offset of $45,000 from the fee paid directly and by offset claimed on the Form S-4 (333-123478) filed 1/15/20X7 and apply it to the $45,000 filing fee due.

For the Schedule TO filed on 1/22/20X7, the filer can satisfy the submission identification requirement when it claims the $45,000 fee offset from the Form S-4 (333-123478) filed on 1/15/20X7 by referencing any combination of the Form S-4 (333-123478) filed on 1/15/20X7, the Form S-1 (333-123467) filed on 1/15/20X4, the pre-effective amendment to the Form S-1 (333-123456) filed on 2/15/20X1 or the initial filing of the Form S-1 (333-123456) on 1/15/20X1 in relation to which contemporaneous fee payments were made equal to $45,000. One example could be:
- The Form S-4 (333-123478) filed on 1/15/20X7 in relation to the payment of $15,000 made with that submission;
- the Form S-1 (333-123467) filed on 1/15/20X4 in relation to the payment of $25,000 made with that submission; and
- the pre-effective amendment to the Form S-1 (333-123456) filed on 2/15/20X1 in relation to the payment of $5,000 out of the payment of $15,000 made with that submission (it would not matter if the filer cited to this pre-effective amendment and/or the initial submission of this Form S-1 (333-123456) on 1/15/20X1 as long as singly or together they were cited as relating to a total of $5,000 in this example).

In this example, the filer could not satisfy the submission identification requirement solely by citing to the Form S-4 (333-123478) filed on 1/15/20X7 because even though the offset claimed and available from that filing was $45,000, the contemporaneous fee payment made with that filing ($15,000) was less than the offset being claimed. As a result, the filer must also identify a prior submission or submissions with an aggregate of contemporaneous fee payment(s) of $30,000 as the original source(s) to which the rest of the claimed offset can be traced.

[51 FR 42063, Nov. 20, 1986; 51 FR 45576, Dec. 19, 1986]

EDITORIAL NOTE: For FEDERAL REGISTER citations affecting § 240.14a-101, see the List of CFR Sections Affected, which appears in the Finding Aids section of the printed volume and at *www.govinfo.gov*.

§ 240.14a-102 [Reserved]

§ 240.14a-103 Notice of Exempt Solicitation. Information to be included in statements submitted by or on behalf of a person pursuant to § 240.14a-6(g).

U.S. Securities and Exchange Commission
Washington, DC 20549

Notice of Exempt Solicitation

1. Name of the Registrant:

2. Name of person relying on exemption:

3. Address of person relying on exemption:

4. Written materials. Attach written material required to be submitted pursuant to Rule 14a-6(g)(1) [§ 240.14a-6(g)(1)].

[57 FR 48294, Oct. 22, 1992]

305

§ 240.14a–104 Notice of Exempt Preliminary Roll-up Communication. Information regarding ownership interests and any potential conflicts of interest to be included in statements submitted by or on behalf of a person pursuant to § 240.14a–2(b)(4) and § 240.14a–6(n).

United States Securities and Exchange Commission Washington, D.C. 20549

Notice of Exempt Preliminary Roll-Up Communication

1. Name of registrant appearing on Securities Act of 1933 registration statement for the roll-up transaction (or, if registration statement has not been filed, name of entity into which partnerships are to be rolled up):

2. Name of partnership that is the subject of the proposed roll-up transaction:

3. Name of person relying on exemption:

4. Address of person relying on exemption:

5. Ownership interest of security holder in partnership that is the subject of the proposed roll-up transaction:

NOTE: To the extent that the holder owns securities in any other entities involved in this roll-up transaction, disclosure of these interests also should be made.

6. Describe any and all relations of the holder to the parties to the transaction or to the transaction itself:

a. The holder is engaged in the business of buying and selling limited partnership interests in the secondary market would be adversely affected if the roll-up transaction were completed.

b. The holder would suffer direct (or indirect) material financial injury if the roll-up transaction were completed since it is a service provider to an affected limited partnership.

c. The holder is engaged in another transaction that may be competitive with the pending roll-up transaction.

d. Any other relations to the parties involved in the transaction or to the transaction itself, or any benefits enjoyed by the holder not shared on a pro rata basis

by all other holders of the same class of securities of the partnership that is the subject of the proposed roll-up transaction.

[59 FR 63685, Dec. 8, 1994]

§ 240.14Ad–1 Report of proxy voting record.

(a) Subject to paragraphs (b) and (c) of this section, every institutional investment manager (as that term is defined in section 13(f)(6)(A) of the Act (15 U.S.C. 78m(f)(6)(A))) that is required to file reports under section 13(f) of the Act (15 U.S.C. 78m(f)) must file an annual report on Form N–PX (§§ 249.326 and 274.129 of this chapter) not later than August 31 of each year, for the most recent 12-month period ended June 30, containing the institutional investment manager's proxy voting record for each shareholder vote pursuant to sections 14A(a) and (b) of the Act (15 U.S.C. 78n–1(a) and (b)) with respect to each security over which the manager exercised voting power (as defined in paragraph (d) of this section).

(b) An institutional investment manager is not required to file a report on Form N–PX (§§ 249.326 and 274.129 of this chapter) for the 12-month period ending June 30 of the calendar year in which the manager's initial filing on Form 13F (§ 249.325 of this chapter) is due pursuant to § 240.13f–1. For purposes of this paragraph (b), "initial filing" on Form 13F means any quarterly filing on Form 13F if no filing on Form 13F was required for the immediately preceding calendar quarter.

(c) An institutional investment manager is not required to file a report on Form N–PX (§§ 249.326 and 274.129 of this chapter) with respect to any shareholder vote at a meeting that occurs after September 30 of the calendar year in which the manager's final filing on Form 13F (§ 249.325 of this chapter) is due pursuant to § 240.13f–1. An institutional investment manager is required to file a Form N–PX for the period July 1 through September 30 of the calendar year in which the manager's final filing on Form 13F is due pursuant to § 240.13f–1; this filing is required to be made not later than March 1 of the immediately following calendar year. For

Securities and Exchange Commission § 240.14b-1

purposes of this paragraph (c), "final filing" on Form 13F means any quarterly filing on Form 13F if no filing on Form 13F is required for the immediately subsequent calendar quarter.

(d) For purposes of this section:

(1) *Voting power* means the ability, through any contract, arrangement, understanding, or relationship, to vote a security or direct the voting of a security, including the ability to determine whether to vote a security or to recall a loaned security.

(2) *Exercise* of voting power means using voting power to influence a voting decision with respect to a security.

[87 FR 78808, Dec. 22, 2022]

EFFECTIVE DATE NOTE: 87 FR 78808, Dec. 22, 2022, § 240.14Ad–1 was added, effective July 1, 2024.

§ 240.14b-1 Obligation of registered brokers and dealers in connection with the prompt forwarding of certain communications to beneficial owners.

(a) *Definitions.* Unless the context otherwise requires, all terms used in this section shall have the same meanings as in the Act and, with respect to proxy soliciting material, as in § 240.14a-1 thereunder and, with respect to information statements, as in § 240.14c-1 thereunder. In addition, as used in this section, the term "registrant" means:

(1) The issuer of a class of securities registered pursuant to section 12 of the Act; or

(2) An investment company registered under the Investment Company Act of 1940.

(b) *Dissemination and beneficial owner information requirements.* A broker or dealer registered under Section 15 of the Act shall comply with the following requirements for disseminating certain communications to beneficial owners and providing beneficial owner information to registrants.

(1) The broker or dealer shall respond, by first class mail or other equally prompt means, directly to the registrant no later than seven business days after the date it receives an inquiry made in accordance with § 240.14a–13(a) or § 240.14c–7(a) by indicting, by means of a search card or otherwise:

(i) The approximate number of customers of the broker or dealer who are beneficial owners of the registrant's securities that are held of record by the broker, dealer, or its nominee;

(ii) The number of customers of the broker or dealer who are beneficial owners of the registrant's securities who have objected to disclosure of their names, addresses, and securities positions if the registrant has indicated, pursuant to § 240.14a–13(a)(1)(ii)(A) or § 240.14c–7(a)(1)(ii)(A), that it will distribute the annual report to security holders to beneficial owners of its securities whose names, addresses and securities positions are disclosed pursuant to paragraph (b)(3) of this section; and

(iii) The identity of the designated agent of the broker or dealer, if any, acting on its behalf in fulfilling its obligations under paragraph (b)(3) of this section; *Provided, however,* that if the broker or dealer has informed the registrant that a designated office(s) or department(s) is to receive such inquiries, receipt for purposes of paragraph (b)(1) of this section shall mean receipt by such designated office(s) or department(s).

(2) The broker or dealer shall, upon receipt of the proxy, other proxy soliciting material, information statement, and/or annual report to security holders from the registrant or other soliciting person, forward such materials to its customers who are beneficial owners of the registrant's securities no later than five business days after receipt of the proxy material, information statement or annual report to security holders.

NOTE TO PARAGRAPH (b)(2): At the request of a registrant, or on its own initiative so long as the registrant does not object, a broker or dealer may, but is not required to, deliver one annual report to security holders, proxy statement, information statement, or Notice of Internet Availability of Proxy Materials to more than one beneficial owner sharing an address if the requirements set forth in § 240.14a–3(e)(1) (with respect to annual reports to security holders, proxy statements, and Notices of Internet Availability of Proxy Materials) and § 240.14c–3(c) (with respect to annual reports to security holders, information statements, and Notices of Internet Availability of Proxy Materials) applicable to registrants, with the exception

§ 240.14b-1

of § 240.14a-3(e)(1)(i)(E), are satisfied instead by the broker or dealer.

(3) The broker or dealer shall, through its agent or directly:

(i) Provide the registrant, upon the registrant's request, with the names, addresses, and securities positions, compiled as of a date specified in the registrant's request which is no earlier than five business days after the date the registrant's request is received, of its customers who are beneficial owners of the registrant's securities and who have not objected to disclosure of such information; *Provided*, *however*, that if the broker or dealer has informed the registrant that a designated office(s) or department(s) is to receive such requests, receipt shall mean receipt by such designated office(s) or department(s); and

(ii) Transmit the data specified in paragraph (b)(3)(i) of this section to the registrant no later than five business days after the record date or other date specified by the registrant.

NOTE 1: Where a broker or dealer employs a designated agent to act on its behalf in performing the obligations imposed on the broker or dealer by paragraph (b)(3) of this section, the five business day time period for determining the date as of which the beneficial owner information is to be compiled is calculated from the date the designated agent receives the registrant's request. In complying with the registrant's request for beneficial owner information under paragraph (b)(3) of this section, a broker or dealer need only supply the registrant with the names, addresses, and securities positions of non-objecting beneficial owners.

NOTE 2: If a broker or dealer receives a registrant's request less than five business days before the requested compilation date, it must provide a list compiled as of a date that is no more than five business days after receipt and transmit the list within five business days after the compilation date.

(c) *Exceptions to dissemination and beneficial owner information requirements.* A broker or dealer registered under section 15 of the Act shall be subject to the following with respect to its dissemination and beneficial owner information requirements:

(1) With regard to beneficial owners of exempt employee benefit plan securities, the broker or dealer shall:

(i) Not include information in its response pursuant to paragraph (b)(1) of

17 CFR Ch. II (4-1-23 Edition)

this section or forward proxies (or in lieu thereof requests for voting instructions), proxy soliciting material, information statements, or annual reports to security holders pursuant to paragraph (b)(2) of this section to such beneficial owners; and

(ii) Not include in its response, pursuant to paragraph (b)(3) of this section, data concerning such beneficial owners.

(2) A broker or dealer need not satisfy:

(i) Its obligations under paragraphs (b)(2), (b)(3) and (d) of this section if the registrant or other soliciting person, as applicable, does not provide assurance of reimbursement of the broker's or dealer's reasonable expenses, both direct and indirect, incurred in connection with performing the obligations imposed by paragraphs (b)(2), (b)(3) and (d) of this section; or

(ii) Its obligation under paragraph (b)(2) of this section to forward annual reports to security holders to non-objecting beneficial owners identified by the broker or dealer, through its agent or directly, pursuant to paragraph (b)(3) of this section if the registrant notifies the broker or dealer pursuant to § 240.14a-13(c) or § 240.14c-7(c) that the registrant will send the annual report to security holders to such non-objecting beneficial owners identified by the broker or dealer and delivered in a list to the registrant pursuant to paragraph (b)(3) of this section.

(3) In its response pursuant to paragraph (b)(1) of this section, a broker or dealer shall not include information about annual reports to security holders, proxy statements or information statements that will not be delivered to security holders sharing an address because of the broker or dealer's reliance on the procedures referred to in the Note to paragraph (b)(2) of this section.

(d) Upon receipt from the soliciting person of all of the information listed in § 240.14a-16(d), the broker or dealer shall:

(1) Prepare and send a Notice of Internet Availability of Proxy Materials containing the information required in paragraph (e) of this section to beneficial owners no later than:

Securities and Exchange Commission

§ 240.14b-1

(i) With respect to a registrant, 40 calendar days prior to the security holder meeting date or, if no meeting is to be held, 40 calendar days prior to the date the votes, consents, or authorizations may be used to effect the corporate action; and

(ii) With respect to a soliciting person other than the registrant, the later of:

(A) 40 calendar days prior to the security holder meeting date or, if no meeting is to be held, 40 calendar days prior to the date the votes, consents, or authorizations may be used to effect the corporate action; or

(B) 10 calendar days after the date that the registrant first sends its proxy statement or Notice of Internet Availability of Proxy Materials to security holders.

(2) Establish a Web site at which beneficial owners are able to access the broker or dealer's request for voting instructions and, at the broker or dealer's option, establish a Web site at which beneficial owners are able to access the proxy statement and other soliciting materials, provided that such Web sites are maintained in a manner consistent with paragraphs (b), (c), and (k) of §240.14a-16;

(3) Upon receipt of a request from the registrant or other soliciting person, send to security holders specified by the registrant or other soliciting person a copy of the request for voting instructions accompanied by a copy of the intermediary's Notice of Internet Availability of Proxy Materials 10 calendar days or more after the broker or dealer sends its Notice of Internet Availability of Proxy Materials pursuant to paragraph (d)(1); and

(4) Upon receipt of a request for a copy of the materials from a beneficial owner:

(i) Request a copy of the soliciting materials from the registrant or other soliciting person, in the form requested by the beneficial owner, within three business days after receiving the beneficial owner's request;

(ii) Forward a copy of the soliciting materials to the beneficial owner, in the form requested by the beneficial owner, within three business days after receiving the materials from the registrant or other soliciting person; and

(iii) Maintain records of security holder requests to receive a paper or e-mail copy of the proxy materials in connection with future proxy solicitations and provide copies of the proxy materials to a security holder who has made such a request for all securities held in the account of that security holder until the security holder revokes such request.

(5) Notwithstanding any other provisions in this paragraph (d), if the broker or dealer receives copies of the proxy statement and annual report to security holders (if applicable) from the soliciting person with instructions to forward such materials to beneficial owners, the broker or dealer:

(i) Shall either:

(A) Prepare a Notice of Internet Availability of Proxy Materials and forward it with the proxy statement and annual report to security holders (if applicable); or

(B) Incorporate any information required in the Notice of Internet Availability of Proxy Materials that does not appear in the proxy statement into the broker or dealer's request for voting instructions to be sent with the proxy statement and annual report (if applicable);

(ii) Need not comply with the following provisions:

(A) The timing provisions of paragraph (d)(1)(ii) of this section; and

(B) Paragraph (d)(4) of this section; and

(iii) Need not include in its Notice of Internet Availability of Proxy Materials or request for voting instructions the following disclosures:

(A) Legends 1 and 3 in §240.14a-16(d)(1); and

(B) Instructions on how to request a copy of the proxy materials.

(e) *Content of Notice of Internet Availability of Proxy Materials.* The broker or dealer's Notice of Internet Availability of Proxy Materials shall:

(1) Include all information, as it relates to beneficial owners, required in a registrant's Notice of Internet Availability of Proxy Materials under §240.14a-16(d), provided that the broker or dealer shall provide its own, or its agent's, toll-free telephone number, an e-mail address, and an Internet Web

309

§ 240.14b-2

site to service requests for copies from beneficial owners;

(2) Include a brief description, if applicable, of the rules that permit the broker or dealer to vote the securities if the beneficial owner does not return his or her voting instructions; and

(3) Otherwise be prepared and sent in a manner consistent with paragraphs (e), (f), and (g) of § 240.14a–16.

[57 FR 1099, Jan. 10, 1992, as amended at 65 FR 65751, Nov. 2, 2000; 72 FR 4170, Jan. 29, 2007; 72 FR 42238, Aug. 1, 2007; 73 FR 17814, Apr. 1, 2008]

§ 240.14b-2 Obligation of banks, associations and other entities that exercise fiduciary powers in connection with the prompt forwarding of certain communications to beneficial owners.

(a) *Definitions.* Unless the context otherwise requires, all terms used in this section shall have the same meanings as in the Act and, with respect to proxy soliciting material, as in § 240.14a–1 thereunder and, with respect to information statements, as in § 240.14c–1 thereunder. In addition, as used in this section, the following terms shall apply:

(1) The term *bank* means a bank, association, or other entity that exercises fiduciary powers.

(2) The term *beneficial owner* includes any person who has or shares, pursuant to an instrument, agreement, or otherwise, the power to vote, or to direct the voting of a security.

NOTE 1: If more than one person shares voting power, the provisions of the instrument creating that voting power shall govern with respect to whether consent to disclosure of beneficial owner information has been given.

NOTE 2: If more than one person shares voting power or if the instrument creating that voting power provides that such power shall be exercised by different persons depending on the nature of the corporate action involved, all persons entitled to exercise such power shall be deemed beneficial owners; *Provided, however*, that only one such beneficial owner need be designated among the beneficial owners to receive proxies or requests for voting instructions, other proxy soliciting material, information statements, and/or annual reports to security holders, if the person so designated assumes the obligation to disseminate, in a timely manner, such materials to the other beneficial owners.

(3) The term *registrant* means:

(i) The issuer of a class of securities registered pursuant to section 12 of the Act; or

(ii) An investment company registered under the Investment Company Act of 1940.

(b) *Dissemination and beneficial owner information requirements.* A bank shall comply with the following requirements for disseminating certain communications to beneficial owners and providing beneficial owner information to registrants.

(1) The bank shall:

(i) Respond, by first class mail or other equally prompt means, directly to the registrant, no later than one business day after the date it receives an inquiry made in accordance with § 240.14a–13(a) or § 240.14c–7(a) by indicating the name and address of each of its respondent banks that holds the registrant's securities on behalf of beneficial owners, if any; and

(ii) Respond, by first class mail or other equally prompt means, directly to the registrant no later than seven business days after the date it receives an inquiry made in accordance with § 240.14a–13(a) or § 240.14c–7(a) by indicating, by means of a search card or otherwise:

(A) The approximate number of customers of the bank who are beneficial owners of the registrant's securities that are held of record by the bank or its nominee;

(B) If the registrant has indicated, pursuant to § 240.14a–13(a)(1)(ii)(A) or § 240.14c–7(a)(1)(ii)(A), that it will distribute the annual report to security holders to beneficial owners of its securities whose names, addresses, and securities positions are disclosed pursuant to paragraphs (b)(4) (ii) and (iii) of this section:

(*1*) With respect to customer accounts opened on or before December 28, 1986, the number of beneficial owners of the registrant's securities who have affirmatively consented to disclosure of their names, addresses, and securities positions; and

(*2*) With respect to customer accounts opened after December 28, 1986, the number of beneficial owners of the

Securities and Exchange Commission § 240.14b–2

registrant's securities who have not objected to disclosure of their names, addresses, and securities positions; and

(C) The identity of its designated agent, if any, acting on its behalf in fulfilling its obligations under paragraphs (b)(4) (ii) and (iii) of this section;

Provided, however, that, if the bank or respondent bank has informed the registrant that a designated office(s) or department(s) is to receive such inquiries, receipt for purposes of paragraphs (b)(1) (i) and (ii) of this section shall mean receipt by such designated office(s) or department(s).

(2) Where proxies are solicited, the bank shall, within five business days after the record date:

(i) Execute an omnibus proxy, including a power of substitution, in favor of its respondent banks and forward such proxy to the registrant; and

(ii) Furnish a notice to each respondent bank in whose favor an omnibus proxy has been executed that it has executed such a proxy, including a power of substitution, in its favor pursuant to paragraph (b)(2)(i) of this section.

(3) Upon receipt of the proxy, other proxy soliciting material, information statement, and/or annual report to security holders from the registrant or other soliciting person, the bank shall forward such materials to each beneficial owner on whose behalf it holds securities, no later than five business days after the date it receives such material and, where a proxy is solicited, the bank shall forward, with the other proxy soliciting material and/or the annual report to security holders, either:

(i) A properly executed proxy:

(A) Indicating the number of securities held for such beneficial owner;

(B) Bearing the beneficial owner's account number or other form of identification, together with instructions as to the procedures to vote the securities;

(C) Briefly stating which other proxies, if any, are required to permit securities to be voted under the terms of the instrument creating that voting power or applicable state law; and

(D) Being accompanied by an envelope addressed to the registrant or its agent, if not provided by the registrant; or

(ii) A request for voting instructions (for which registrant's form of proxy may be used and which shall be voted by the record holder bank or respondent bank in accordance with the instructions received), together with an envelope addressed to the record holder bank or respondent bank.

NOTE TO PARAGRAPH (b)(3): At the request of a registrant, or on its own initiative so long as the registrant does not object, a bank may, but is not required to, deliver one annual report to security holders, proxy statement, information statement, or Notice of Internet Availability of Proxy Materials to more than one beneficial owner sharing an address if the requirements set forth in §240.14a–3(e)(1) (with respect to annual reports to security holders, proxy statements, and Notices of Internet Availability of Proxy Materials) and §240.14c–3(c) (with respect to annual reports to security holders, information statements, and Notices of Internet Availability of Proxy Materials) applicable to registrants, with the exception of §240.14a–3(e)(1)(i)(E), are satisfied instead by the bank.

(4) The bank shall:

(i) Respond, by first class mail or other equally prompt means, directly to the registrant no later than one business day after the date it receives an inquiry made in accordance with §240.14a–13(b)(1) or §240.14c–7(b)(1) by indicating the name and address of each of its respondent banks that holds the registrant's securities on behalf of beneficial owners, if any;

(ii) Through its agent or directly, provide the registrant, upon the registrant's request, and within the time specified in paragraph (b)(4)(iii) of this section, with the names, addresses, and securities position, compiled as of a date specified in the registrant's request which is no earlier than five business days after the date the registrant's request is received, of:

(A) With respect to customer accounts opened on or before December 28, 1986, beneficial owners of the registrant's securities on whose behalf it holds securities who have consented affirmatively to disclosure of such information, subject to paragraph (b)(5) of this section; and

(B) With respect to customer accounts opened after December 28, 1986,

§ 240.14b–2

beneficial owners of the registrant's securities on whose behalf it holds securities who have not objected to disclosure of such information;

Provided, however, that if the record holder bank or respondent bank has informed the registrant that a designated office(s) or department(s) is to receive such requests, receipt for purposes of paragraphs (b)(4) (i) and (ii) of this section shall mean receipt by such designated office(s) or department(s); and

(iii) Through its agent or directly, transmit the data specified in paragraph (b)(4)(ii) of this section to the registrant no later than five business days after the date specified by the registrant.

NOTE 1: Where a record holder bank or respondent bank employs a designated agent to act on its behalf in performing the obligations imposed on it by paragraphs (b)(4) (ii) and (iii) of this section, the five business day time period for determining the date as of which the beneficial owner information is to be compiled is calculated from the date the designated agent receives the registrant's request. In complying with the registrant's request for beneficial owner information under paragraphs (b)(4) (ii) and (iii) of this section, a record holder bank or respondent bank need only supply the registrant with the names, addresses and securities positions of affirmatively consenting and non-objecting beneficial owners.

NOTE 2: If a record holder bank or respondent bank receives a registrant's request less than five business days before the requested compilation date, it must provide a list compiled as of a date that is no more than five business days after receipt and transmit the list within five business days after the compilation date.

(5) For customer accounts opened on or before December 28, 1986, unless the bank has made a good faith effort to obtain affirmative consent to disclosure of beneficial owner information pursuant to paragraph (b)(4)(ii) of this section, the bank shall provide such information as to beneficial owners who do not object to disclosure of such information. A good faith effort to obtain affirmative consent to disclosure of beneficial owner information shall include, but shall not be limited to, making an inquiry:

(i) Phrased in neutral language, explaining the purpose of the disclosure and the limitations on the registrant's use thereof;

17 CFR Ch. II (4–1–23 Edition)

(ii) Either in at least one mailing separate from other account mailings or in repeated mailings; and

(iii) In a mailing that includes a return card, postage paid enclosure.

(c) *Exceptions to dissemination and beneficial owner information requirements.* The bank shall be subject to the following respect to its dissemination and beneficial owner requirements.

(1) With regard to beneficial owners of exempt employee benefit plan securities, the bank shall not:

(i) Include information in its response pursuant to paragraph (b)(1) of this section; or forward proxies (or in lieu thereof requests for voting instructions), proxy soliciting material, information statements, or annual reports to security holders pursuant to paragraph (b)(3) of this section to such beneficial owners; or

(ii) Include in its response pursuant to paragraphs (b)(4) and (b)(5) of this section data concerning such beneficial owners.

(2) The bank need not satisfy:

(i) Its obligations under paragraphs (b)(2), (b)(3), (b)(4) and (d) of this section if the registrant or other soliciting person, as applicable, does not provide assurance of reimbursement of its reasonable expenses, both direct and indirect, incurred in connection with performing the obligations imposed by paragraphs (b)(2), (b)(3), (b)(4) and (d) of this section; or

(ii) Its obligation under paragraph (b)(3) of this section to forward annual reports to security holders to consenting and non-objecting beneficial owners identified pursuant to paragraphs (b)(4) (ii) and (iii) of this section if the registrant notifies the record holder bank or respondent bank, pursuant to § 240.14a–13(c) or § 240.14c–7(c), that the registrant will send the annual report to security holders to beneficial owners whose names addresses and securities positions are disclosed pursuant to paragraphs (b)(4) (ii) and (iii) of this section.

(3) For the purposes of determining the fees which may be charged to registrants pursuant to § 240.14a–13(b)(5), § 240.14c–7(a)(5), and paragraph (c)(2) of this section for performing obligations under paragraphs (b)(2), (b)(3), and (b)(4) of this section, an amount no

Securities and Exchange Commission § 240.14b-2

greater than that permitted to be charged by brokers or dealers for reimbursement of their reasonable expenses, both direct and indirect, incurred in connection with performing the obligations imposed by paragraphs (b)(2) and (b)(3) of § 240.14b-1, shall be deemed to be reasonable.

(4) In its response pursuant to paragraph (b)(1)(ii)(A) of this section, a bank shall not include information about annual reports to security holders, proxy statements or information statements that will not be delivered to security holders sharing an address because of the bank's reliance on the procedures referred to in the Note to paragraph (b)(3) of this section.

(d) Upon receipt from the soliciting person of all of the information listed in § 240.14a-16(d), the bank shall:

(1) Prepare and send a Notice of Internet Availability of Proxy Materials containing the information required in paragraph (e) of this section to beneficial owners no later than:

(i) With respect to a registrant, 40 calendar days prior to the security holder meeting date or, if no meeting is to be held, 40 calendar days prior to the date the votes, consents, or authorizations may be used to effect the corporate action; and

(ii) With respect to a soliciting person other than the registrant, the later of:

(A) 40 calendar days prior to the security holder meeting date or, if no meeting is to be held, 40 calendar days prior to the date the votes, consents, or authorizations may be used to effect the corporate action; or

(B) 10 calendar days after the date that the registrant first sends its proxy statement or Notice of Internet Availability of Proxy Materials to security holders.

(2) Establish a Web site at which beneficial owners are able to access the bank's request for voting instructions and, at the bank's option, establish a Web site at which beneficial owners are able to access the proxy statement and other soliciting materials, provided that such Web sites are maintained in a manner consistent with paragraphs (b), (c), and (k) of § 240.14a-16;

(3) Upon receipt of a request from the registrant or other soliciting person, send to security holders specified by the registrant or other soliciting person a copy of the request for voting instructions accompanied by a copy of the intermediary's Notice of Internet Availability of Proxy Materials 10 days or more after the bank sends its Notice of Internet Availability of Proxy Materials pursuant to paragraph (d)(1); and

(4) Upon receipt of a request for a copy of the materials from a beneficial owner:

(i) Request a copy of the soliciting materials from the registrant or other soliciting person, in the form requested by the beneficial owner, within three business days after receiving the beneficial owner's request;

(ii) Forward a copy of the soliciting materials to the beneficial owner, in the form requested by the beneficial owner, within three business days after receiving the materials from the registrant or other soliciting person; and

(iii) Maintain records of security holder requests to receive a paper or e-mail copy of the proxy materials in connection with future proxy solicitations and provide copies of the proxy materials to a security holder who has made such a request for all securities held in the account of that security holder until the security holder revokes such request.

(5) Notwithstanding any other provisions in this paragraph (d), if the bank receives copies of the proxy statement and annual report to security holders (if applicable) from the soliciting person with instructions to forward such materials to beneficial owners, the bank:

(i) Shall either:

(A) Prepare a Notice of Internet Availability of Proxy Materials and forward it with the proxy statement and annual report to security holders (if applicable); or

(B) Incorporate any information required in the Notice of Internet Availability of Proxy Materials that does not appear in the proxy statement into the bank's request for voting instructions to be sent with the proxy statement and annual report (if applicable);

(ii) Need not comply with the following provisions:

(A) The timing provisions of paragraph (d)(1)(ii) of this section; and

§ 240.14c-1

(B) Paragraph (d)(4) of this section; and

(iii) Need not include in its Notice of Internet Availability of Proxy Materials or request for voting instructions the following disclosures:

(A) Legends 1 and 3 in § 240.14a–16(d)(1); and

(B) Instructions on how to request a copy of the proxy materials.

(e) *Content of Notice of Internet Availability of Proxy Materials.* The bank's Notice of Internet Availability of Proxy Materials shall:

(1) Include all information, as it relates to beneficial owners, required in a registrant's Notice of Internet Availability of Proxy Materials under § 240.14a–16(d), provided that the bank shall provide its own, or its agent's, toll-free telephone number, e-mail address, and Internet Web site to service requests for copies from beneficial owners; and

(2) Otherwise be prepared and sent in a manner consistent with paragraphs (e), (f), and (g) of § 240.14a–16.

[57 FR 1100, Jan. 10, 1992, as amended at 65 FR 65751, Nov. 2, 2000; 72 FR 4171, Jan. 29, 2007; 72 FR 42239, Aug. 1, 2007; 73 FR 17814, Apr. 1, 2008]

REGULATION 14C: DISTRIBUTION OF INFORMATION PURSUANT TO SECTION 14(c)

ATTENTION ELECTRONIC FILERS

THIS REGULATION SHOULD BE READ IN CONJUNCTION WITH REGULATION S-T (PART 232 OF THIS CHAPTER), WHICH GOVERNS THE PREPARATION AND SUBMISSION OF DOCUMENTS IN ELECTRONIC FORMAT. MANY PROVISIONS RELATING TO THE PREPARATION AND SUBMISSION OF DOCUMENTS IN PAPER FORMAT CONTAINED IN THIS REGULATION ARE SUPERSEDED BY THE PROVISIONS OF REGULATION S-T FOR DOCUMENTS REQUIRED TO BE FILED IN ELECTRONIC FORMAT.

§ 240.14c-1 Definitions.

Unless the context otherwise requires, all terms used in this regulation have the same meanings as in the Act or elsewhere in the general rules and regulations thereunder. In addition, the following definitions apply unless the context otherwise requires:

(a) *Associate.* The term "associate," used to indicate a relationship with any person, means:

(1) Any corporation or organization (other than the registrant or a majority owned subsidiary of the registrant) of which such person is an officer or partner or is, directly or indirectly, the beneficial owner of 10 percent or more of any class of equity securities;

(2) Any trust or other estate in which such person has a substantial beneficial interest or as to which such person serves as trustee or in a similar fiduciary capacity; and

(3) Any relative or spouse of such person, or any relative of such spouse, who has the same home as such person or who is a director or officer of the registrant or any of its parents or subsidiaries.

(b) *Employee benefit plan.* For purposes of § 240.14c–7, the term "employee benefit plan" means any purchase, savings, option, bonus, appreciation, profit sharing, thrift, incentive, pension or similar plan primarily for employees, directors, trustees or officers.

(c) *Entity that exercises fiduciary powers.* The term "entity that exercises fiduciary powers" means any entity that holds securities in nominee name or otherwise on behalf of a beneficial owner but does not include a clearing agency registered pursuant to section 17A of the Act, or a broker or a dealer.

(d) *Exempt employee benefit plan securities.* For purposes of § 240.14c–7, the term "exempt employee benefit plan securities" means:

(1) Securities of the registrant held by an employee benefit plan, as defined in paragraph (b) of this section, where such plan is established by the registrant; or

(2) If notice regarding the current distribution of information statements has been given pursuant to § 240.14c–7(a)(1)(ii)(C) or if notice regarding the current request for a list of names, addresses and securities positions of beneficial owners has been given pursuant to § 240.14c–7(b)(3), securities of the registrant held by an employee benefit plan, as defined in paragraph (b) of this section, where such plan is established by an affiliate of the registrant.

(e) *Information statement.* The term "information statement" means the

Securities and Exchange Commission

§ 240.14c-2

statement required by § 240.14c-2, whether or not contained in a single document.

(f) *Last fiscal year.* The term "last fiscal year" of the registrant means the last fiscal year of the registrant ending prior to the date of the meeting with respect to which an information statement is required to be distributed, or if the information statement involves consents or authorizations in lieu of a meeting, the earliest date on which they may be used to effect corporate action.

(g) *Proxy.* The term "proxy" includes every proxy, consent or authorization within the meaning of section 14(a) of the Act. The consent or authorization may take the form of failure to object or to dissent.

(h) *Record date.* The term "record date" means the date as of which the record holders of securities entitled to vote at a meeting or by written consent or authorization shall be determined.

(i) *Record holder.* For purposes of § 240.14c-7, the term "record holder" means any broker, dealer, voting trustee, bank, association or other entity that exercises fiduciary powers which holds securities of record in nominee name or otherwise or as a participant in a clearing agency registered pursuant to section 17A of the Act.

(j) *Registrant.* The term "registrant" means:

(1) The issuer of a class of securities registered pursuant to section 12 of the Act; or

(2) An investment company registered under the Investment Company Act of 1940 that has made a public offering of its securities.

(k) *Respondent bank.* For purposes of § 240.14c-7, the term "respondent bank" means any bank, association or other entity that exercises fiduciary powers which holds securities on behalf of beneficial owners and deposits such securities for safekeeping with another bank, association or other entity that exercises fiduciary powers.

[51 FR 44279, Dec. 9, 1986, as amended at 52 FR 23649, June 24, 1987; 53 FR 16406, May 9, 1988; 57 FR 1101, Jan. 10, 1992]

§ 240.14c-2 **Distribution of information statement.**

(a)(1) In connection with every annual or other meeting of the holders of the class of securities registered pursuant to section 12 of the Act or of a class of securities issued by an investment company registered under the Investment Company Act of 1940 that has made a public offering of securities, including the taking of corporate action by the written authorization or consent of security holders, the registrant shall transmit to every security holder of the class that is entitled to vote or give an authorization or consent in regard to any matter to be acted upon and from whom proxy authorization or consent is not solicited on behalf of the registrant pursuant to section 14(a) of the Act:

(i) A written information statement containing the information specified in Schedule 14C (§ 240.14c-101);

(ii) A publicly-filed information statement, in the form and manner described in § 240.14c-3(d), containing the information specified in Schedule 14C (§ 240.14c-101); or

(iii) A written information statement included in a registration statement filed under the Securities Act of 1933 on Form S-4 or F-4 (§ 239.25 or § 239.34 of this chapter) or Form N-14 (§ 239.23 of this chapter) and containing the information specified in such Form.

(2) Notwithstanding paragraph (a)(1) of this section:

(i) In the case of a class of securities in unregistered or bearer form, such statements need to be transmitted only to those security holders whose names are known to the registrant; and

(ii) No such statements need to be transmitted to a security holder if a registrant would be excused from delivery of an annual report to security holders or a proxy statement under § 240.14a-3(e)(2) if such section were applicable.

(b) The information statement shall be sent or given at least 20 calendar days prior to the meeting date or, in the case of corporate action taken pursuant to the consents or authorizations of security holders, at least 20 calendar days prior to the earliest date on which the corporate action may be taken.

§ 240.14c-3

(c) If a transaction is a roll-up transaction as defined in Item 901(c) of Regulation S-K (17 CFR 229.901(c)) and is registered (or authorized to be registered) on Form S-4 (17 CFR 229.25) or Form F-4 (17 CFR 229.34), the information statement must be distributed to security holders no later than the lesser of 60 calendar days prior to the date on which the meeting of security holders is held or action is taken, or the maximum number of days permitted for giving notice under applicable state law.

(d) A registrant shall transmit an information statement to security holders pursuant to paragraph (a) of this section by satisfying the requirements set forth in § 240.14a–16; provided, however, that the registrant shall revise the information required in the Notice of Internet Availability of Proxy Materials, including changing the title of that notice, to reflect the fact that the registrant is not soliciting proxies for the meeting.

[51 FR 42070, Nov. 20, 1986, as amended at 56 FR 57254, Nov. 8, 1991; 57 FR 1102, Jan. 10, 1992; 57 FR 48295, Oct. 22, 1992; 72 FR 4171, Jan. 29, 2007; 72 FR 42239, Aug. 1, 2007]

§ 240.14c–3 Annual report to be furnished security holders.

(a) If the information statement relates to an annual (or special meeting in lieu of the annual) meeting, or written consent in lieu of such meeting, of security holders at which directors of the registrant, other than an investment company registered under the Investment Company Act of 1940, are to be elected, it shall be accompanied or preceded by an annual report to security holders:

(1) The annual report to security holders shall contain the information specified in paragraphs (b)(1) through (b)(11) of § 240.14a–3.

(2) [Reserved]

(b) The report sent to security holders pursuant to this rule shall be submitted in electronic format, in accordance with the EDGAR Filer Manual, to the Commission, solely for its information, not later than the date on which such report is first sent or given to security holders or the date on which preliminary copies, or definitive copies, if preliminary filing was not required, of the information statement are filed with the Commission pursuant to § 240.14c–5, whichever date is later. The report is not deemed to be "filed" with the Commission or subject to this regulation otherwise than as provided in this rule, or to the liabilities of section 18 of the Act, except to the extent that the registrant specifically requests that it be treated as a part of the information statement or incorporates it in the information statement or other filed report by reference.

(c) A registrant will be considered to have delivered a Notice of Internet Availability of Proxy Materials, annual report to security holders or information statement to security holders of record who share an address if the requirements set forth in § 240.14a–3(e)(1) are satisfied with respect to the Notice of Internet Availability of Proxy Materials, annual report to security holders or information statement, as applicable.

(d) A registrant shall furnish an annual report to security holders pursuant to paragraph (a) of this section by satisfying the requirements set forth in § 240.14a–16.

[39 FR 40770, Nov. 20, 1974, as amended at 45 FR 63647, Sept. 25, 1980; 51 FR 42071, Nov. 20, 1986; 52 FR 48984, Dec. 29, 1987; 58 FR 26519, May 4, 1993; 59 FR 52700, Oct. 19, 1994; 59 FR 67765, Dec. 30, 1994; 64 FR 62547, Nov. 16, 1999; 65 FR 65751, Nov. 2, 2000; 72 FR 4172, Jan. 29, 2007; 72 FR 42239, Aug. 1, 2007; 73 FR 977, Jan. 4, 2008; 87 FR 35413, June 10, 2022]

§ 240.14c–4 Presentation of information in information statement.

(a) The information included in the information statement shall be clearly presented and the statements made shall be divided into groups according to subject matter and the various groups of statements shall be preceded by appropriate headings. The order of items and sub-items in the schedule need not be followed. Where practicable and appropriate, the information shall be presented in tabular form. All amounts shall be stated in figures. Information required by more than one applicable item need not be repeated. No statement need be made in response to any item or sub-item which is inapplicable.

(b) Any information required to be included in the information statement

Securities and Exchange Commission

§ 240.14c-5

as to terms of securities or other subject matters which from a standpoint of practical necessity must be determined in the future may be stated in terms of present knowledge and intention. Subject to the foregoing, information which is not known to the registrant and which it is not reasonably within the power of the registrant to ascertain or procure may be omitted, if a brief statement of the circumstances rendering such information unavailable is made.

(c) All printed information statements shall be in roman type at least as large and as legible as 10-point modern type except that to the extent necessary for convenient presentation, financial statements and other tabular data, but not the notes thereto, may be in roman type at least as large and as legible as 8-point modern type. All such type shall be leaded at least 2 points.

(d) Where an information statement is delivered through an electronic medium, issuers may satisfy legibility requirements applicable to printed documents, such as type size and font, by presenting all required information in a format readily communicated to investors.

[31 FR 262, Jan. 8, 1966, as amended at 36 FR 8935, May 15, 1971; 51 FR 42071, Nov. 20, 1986; 61 FR 24657, May 15, 1996]

§ 240.14c-5 Filing requirements.

(a) *Preliminary information statement.* Five preliminary copies of the information statement shall be filed with the Commission at least 10 calendar days prior to the date definitive copies of such statement are first sent or given to security holders, or such shorter period prior to that date as the Commission may authorize upon a showing of good cause therefor. In computing the 10-day period, the filing date of the preliminary copies is to be counted as the first day and the 11th day is the date on which definitive copies of the information statement may be sent to security holders. A registrant, however, shall not file with the Commission a preliminary information statement if it relates to an annual (or special meeting in lieu of the annual) meeting, of security holders at which the only matters to be acted upon are:

(1) The election of directors;

(2) The election, approval or ratification of accountant(s);

(3) A security holder proposal identified in the registrant's information statement pursuant to Item 4 of Schedule 14C (§ 240.14c-101); and/or

(4) The approval or ratification of a plan as defined in paragraph (a)(6)(ii) of Item 402 of Regulation S-K (§ 229.402(a)(6)(ii) of this chapter) or amendments to such a plan.

This exclusion from filing a preliminary information statement does not apply if the registrant comments upon or refers to a solicitation in opposition in connection with the meeting in its information statement.

NOTE 1: The filing of revised material does not recommence the ten day time period unless the revised material contains material revisions or material new proposal(s) that constitute a fundamental change in the information statement.

NOTE 2: The officials responsible for the preparation of the information statement should make every effort to verify the accuracy and completeness of the information required by the applicable rules. The preliminary statement should be filed with the Commission at the earliest practicable date.

NOTE 3: Solicitation in Opposition—For purposes of the exclusion from filing a preliminary information statement, a "solicitation in opposition" includes: (a) Any solicitation opposing a proposal supported by the registrant; and (b) any solicitation supporting a proposal that the registrant does not expressly support, other than a security holder proposal identified in the registrant's information statement pursuant to Item 4 of Schedule 14C (§ 240.14c-101 of this chapter). The identification of a security holder proposal in the registrant's information statement does not constitute a "solicitation in opposition," even if the registrant opposes the proposal and/or includes a statement in opposition to the proposal.

NOTE 4: A registrant that is filing an information statement in preliminary form only because the registrant has commented on or referred to an opposing solicitation should indicate that fact in a transmittal letter when filing the preliminary material with the Commission.

(b) *Definitive information statement.* Eight definitive copies of the information statement, in the form in which it is furnished to security holders, must be filed with the Commission no later than the date the information statement is first sent or given to security

§ 240.14c–5

holders. Three copies of these materials also must be filed with, or mailed for filing to, each national securities exchange on which the registrant has a class of securities listed and registered.

(c) *Release dates.* All preliminary material filed pursuant to paragraph (a) of this section shall be accompanied by a statement of the date on which copies thereof filed pursuant to paragraph (b) of this section are intended to be released to security holders. All definitive material filed pursuant to paragraph (b) of this section shall be accompanied by a statement of the date on which copies of such material have been released to security holders or, if not released, the date on which copies thereof are intended to be released.

(d)(1) *Public availability of information.* All copies of material filed pursuant to paragraph (a) of this section shall be clearly marked "Preliminary Copies," and shall be deemed immediately available for public inspection unless confidential treatment is obtained pursuant to paragraph (d)(2) of this section.

(2) *Confidential treatment.* If action will be taken on any matter specified in Item 14 of Schedule 14A (§ 240.14a–101), all copies of the preliminary information statement filed under paragraph (a) of this section will be for the information of the Commission only and will not be deemed available for public inspection until filed with the Commission in definitive form so long as:

(i) The information statement does not relate to a matter or proposal subject to § 240.13e–3 or a roll-up transaction as defined in Item 901(c) of Regulation S-K (§ 229.901(c) of this chapter);

(ii) Neither the parties to the transaction nor any persons authorized to act on their behalf have made any public communications relating to the transaction except for statements where the content is limited to the information specified in § 230.135 of this chapter; and

(iii) The materials are filed in paper and marked "Confidential, For Use of the Commission Only". In all cases, the materials may be disclosed to any department or agency of the United States Government and to the Congress, and the Commission may make any inquiries or investigation into the materials as may be necessary to conduct an adequate review by the Commission.

INSTRUCTION TO PARAGRAPH (d)(2): If communications are made publicly that go beyond the information specified in § 230.135, the materials must be re-filed publicly with the Commission.

(e) *Revised information statements.* Where any information statement filed pursuant to this section is amended or revised, two of the copies of such amended or revised material filed pursuant to this section shall be marked to indicate clearly and precisely the changes effected therein. If the amendment or revision alters the text of the material, the changes in such text shall be indicated by means of underscoring or in some other appropriate manner.

(f) *Merger material.* Notwithstanding the foregoing provisions of this section, any information statement or other material included in a registration statement filed under the Securities Act of 1933 on Form N–14, S–4, or F–4 (§ 239.23, § 239.25 or § 239.34 of this chapter) shall be deemed filed both for the purposes of that Act and for the purposes of this section, but separate copies of such material need not be furnished pursuant to this section, nor shall any fee be required under paragraph (a) of this section. However, any additional material used after the effective date of the registration statement on Form N–14, S–4, or F–4 shall be filed in accordance with this section, unless separate copies of such material are required to be filed as an amendment of such registration statement.

(g) *Fees.* At the time of filing a preliminary information statement regarding an acquisition, merger, spinoff, consolidation or proposed sale or other disposition of substantially all the assets of the company, the registrant shall pay the Commission a fee, no part of which shall be refunded, established in accordance with § 240.0–11.

(h) *Cover page.* Each information statement filed with the Commission shall include a cover page in the form set forth in Schedule 14C (§ 240.14c–101).

Securities and Exchange Commission § 240.14c–7

The cover page required by this paragraph need not be distributed to security holders.

[51 FR 42071, Nov. 20, 1986, as amended at 52 FR 48984, Dec. 29, 1987; 57 FR 48295, Oct. 22, 1992; 58 FR 14684, Mar. 18, 1993; 58 FR 69226, Dec. 30, 1993; 59 FR 67765, Dec. 30, 1994; 61 FR 49960, Sept. 24, 1996; 64 FR 61459, Nov. 10, 1999; 71 FR 53263, Sept. 8, 2006; 72 FR 4172, Jan. 29, 2007]

§ 240.14c–6 False or misleading statements.

(a) No information statement shall contain any statement which, at the time and in the light of the circumstances under which it is made, is false or misleading with respect to any material fact, or which omits to state any material fact necessary in order to make the statements therein not false or misleading or necessary to correct any statement in any earlier communication with respect to the same meeting or subject matter which has become false or misleading.

(b) The fact that an information statement has been filed with or examined by the Commission shall not be deemed a finding by the Commission that such material is accurate or complete or not false or misleading, or that the Commission has passed upon the merits of or approved any statement contained therein or any matter to be acted upon by security holders. No representation contrary to the foregoing shall be made.

[31 FR 262, Jan. 8, 1966]

§ 240.14c–7 Providing copies of material for certain beneficial owners.

(a) If the registrant knows that securities of any class entitled to vote at a meeting, or by written authorizations or consents if no meeting is held, are held of record by a broker, dealer, voting trustee, or bank, association, or other entity that exercises fiduciary powers in nominee name or otherwise, the registrant shall:

(1) By first class mail or other equally prompt means:

(i) Inquire of each such record holder:

(A) Whether other persons are the beneficial owners of such securities and, if so, the number of copies of the information statement necessary to supply such material to such beneficial owners;

(B) In the case of an annual (or special meeting in lieu of the annual) meeting, or written consents in lieu of such meeting, at which directors are to be elected, the number of copies of the annual report to security holders, necessary to supply such report to such beneficial owners for whom proxy material has not been and is not to be made available and to whom such reports are to be distributed by such record holder or its nominee and not by the registrant;

(C) If the record holder or respondent bank has an obligation under § 240.14b–1(b)(3) or § 240.14b–2(b)(4) (ii) and (iii), whether an agent has been designated to act on its behalf in fulfilling such obligation, and, if so, the name and address of such agent; and

(D) Whether it holds the registrant's securities on behalf of any respondent bank and, if so, the name and address of each such respondent bank; and

(ii) Indicate to each such record holder:

(A) Whether the registrant pursuant to paragraph (c) of this section, intends to distribute the annual report to security holders to beneficial owners of its securities whose names, addresses and securities positions are disclosed pursuant to § 240.14b–1(b)(3) and § 240.14b–2(b)(4) (ii) and (iii);

(B) The record date; and

(C) At the option of the registrant, any employee benefit plan established by an affiliate of the registrant that holds securities of the registrant that the registrant elects to treat as exempt employee benefit plan securities;

(2) Upon receipt of a record holder's or respondent bank's response indicating, pursuant to § 240.14b–2(a)(1), the names and addresses of its respondent banks, within one business day after the date such response is received, make an inquiry of and give notification to each such respondent bank in the same manner required by paragraph (a)(1) of this section; *Provided, however,* the inquiry required by paragraphs (a)(1) and (a)(2) of this section shall not cover beneficial owners of exempt employee benefit plan securities;

§ 240.14c-7

(3) Make the inquiry required by paragraph (a)(1) of this section on the earlier of:

(i) At least 20 business days prior to the record date of the meeting of security holders or the record date of written consents in lieu of a meeting; or

(ii) At least 20 business days prior to the date the information statement is required to be sent or given pursuant to § 240.14c-2(b);

Provided, however, That, if a record holder or respondent bank has informed the registrant that a designated office(s) or department(s) is to receive such inquiries, the inquiry shall be made to such designated office(s) or department(s);

(4) Supply, in a timely manner, each record holder and respondent bank of whom the inquiries required by paragraphs (a)(1) and (a)(2) of this section are made with copies of the information statement and/or the annual report to security holders, in such quantities, assembled in such form and at such place(s), as the record holder or respondent bank may reasonably request in order to send such material to each beneficial owner of securities who is to be furnished with such material by the record holder or respondent bank; and

(5) Upon the request of any record holder or respondent bank that is supplied with Notices of Internet Availability of Proxy Materials, information statements and/or annual reports to security holders pursuant to paragraph (a)(3) of this section, pay its reasonable expenses for completing the sending of such material to beneficial owners.

NOTE 1: If the registrant's list of security holders indicates that some of its securities are registered in the name of a clearing agency registered pursuant to section 17A of the Act (e.g., "Cede & Co.," nominee for the Depository Trust Company), the registrant shall make appropriate inquiry of the clearing agency and thereafter of the participants in such clearing agency who may hold on behalf of a beneficial owner or respondent bank, and shall comply with the above paragraph with respect to any such participant (see § 240.14c-1 (h)).

NOTE 2: The attention of registrants is called to the fact that each broker, dealer, bank, association, and other entity that exercises fiduciary powers has an obligation pursuant to § 240.14b-1 and § 240.14b-2 (except as provided therein with respect to exempt employee benefit plan securities held in nominee name) and, with respect to brokers and dealers, applicable self-regulatory organization requirements to obtain and forward, within the time periods prescribed therein, (a) information statements to beneficial owners on whose behalf it holds securities, and (b) annual reports to security holders to beneficial owners on whose behalf it holds securities, unless the registrant has notified the record holder or respondent bank that it has assumed responsibility to send such material to beneficial owners whose names, addresses, and securities positions are disclosed pursuant to § 240.14b-1(b)(3) and § 240.14b-2(b)(4) (ii) and (iii).

NOTE 3: The attention of registrants is called to the fact that registrants have an obligation, pursuant to paragraph (d) of this section, to cause information statements and annual reports to security holders to be furnished, in accordance with § 240.14c-2, to beneficial owners of exempt employee benefit plan securities.

(b) Any registrant requesting pursuant to § 240.14b-1(b)(3) and § 240.14b-2(b)(4) (ii) and (iii) a list of names, addresses and securities positions of beneficial owners of its securities who either have consented or have not objected to disclosure of such information shall:

(1) By first class mail or other equally prompt means, inquire of each record holder and each respondent bank identified to the registrant pursuant to § 240.14b-2(e)(1) whether such record holder or respondent bank holds the registrant's securities on behalf of any respondent banks and, if so, the name and address of each such respondent bank;

(2) Request such list be compiled as of a date no earlier than five business days after the date the registant's request is received by the record holder or respondent bank; *Provided, however,* That if the record holder or respondent bank has informed the registrant that a designated office(s) or department(s) is to receive such requests, the request shall be made to such designated office(s) or department(s);

(3) Make such request to the following persons that hold the registrant's securities on behalf of beneficial owners: all brokers, dealers, banks, associations and other entities that exercise fiduciary powers; *Provided, however,* such request shall not

320

Securities and Exchange Commission

§ 240.14c-101

cover beneficial owners of exempt employee benefit plan securities as defined in § 240.14a-1(d)(1); and, at the option of the registrant, such request may give notice of any employee benefit plan established by an affiliate of the registrant that holds securities of the registrant that the registrant elects to treat as exempt employee benefit plan securities;

(4) Use the information furnished in response to such request exclusively for purposes of corporate communications; and

(5) Upon the request of any record holder or respondent bank to whom such request is made, pay the reasonable expenses, both direct and indirect, of providing beneficial owner information.

NOTE: A registrant will be deemed to have satisfied its obligations under paragraph (b) of this section by requesting consenting and non-objecting beneficial owner lists from a designated agent acting on behalf of the record holder or respondent bank and paying to that designated agent the reasonable expenses of providing the beneficial owner information.

(c) A registrant, at its option, may send by mail or other equally prompt means, its annual report to security holders to the beneficial owners whose identifying information is provided by record holders and respondent banks, pursuant to § 240.14b-1(b)(3) and § 240.14b-2(b)(4) (ii) and (iii), provided that such registrant notifies the record holders and respondent banks at the time it makes the inquiry required by paragraph (a) of this section that the registrant will send the annual report to security holders to the beneficial owners so identified.

(d) If a registrant furnishes information statements to record holders and respondent banks who hold securities on behalf of beneficial owners, the registrant shall cause information statements and annual reports to security holders to be furnished, in accordance with § 240.14c-2, to beneficial owners of exempt employee benefit plan securities.

[51 FR 44280, Dec. 9, 1986, as amended at 52 FR 23649, June 24, 1987; 53 FR 16406, May 9, 1988; 57 FR 1102, Jan. 10, 1992; 61 FR 24657, May 15, 1996; 64 FR 62547, Nov. 16, 1999; 72 FR 4172, Jan. 29, 2007]

§ 240.14c-101 Schedule 14C. Information required in information statement.

SCHEDULE 14C INFORMATION

Information Statement Pursuant to Section 14(c) of the Securities Exchange Act of 1934

(Amendment No.   )

Check the appropriate box:
[ ] Preliminary Information Statement
[ ] Confidential, for Use of the Commission Only (as permitted by Rule 14c-5(d)(2))
[ ] Definitive Information Statement

(Name of Registrant As Specified In Its Charter)

Payment of Filing Fee (Check all boxes that apply):
[ ] No fee required
[ ] Fee paid previously with preliminary materials
[ ] Fee computed on table in exhibit required by Item 25(b) of Schedule 14A (17 CFR 240.14a-101) per Item 1 of this Schedule and Exchange Act Rules 14c-5(g) and 0-11

NOTE

NOTE TO COVER PAGE: Where any item, other than Item 4, calls for information with respect to any matter to be acted upon at the meeting or, if no meeting is being held, by written authorization or consent, such item need be answered only with respect to proposals to be made by the registrant. Registrants and acquirees that meet the definition of "smaller reporting company" under Rule 12b-2 of the Exchange Act (§ 240.12b-2) shall refer to the disclosure items in Regulation S-K (§§ 229.10 through 229.1123 of this chapter) with specific attention to the scaled disclosure requirements for smaller reporting companies, if any. A smaller reporting company may provide the information in Article 8 of Regulation S-X in lieu of any financial statements required by Item 1 of § 240.14c-101.

Item 1. Information required by Items of Schedule 14A (17 CFR 240.14a-101). Furnish the information called for by all of the items of Schedule 14A of Regulation 14A (17 CFR 240.14a-101) (other than Items 1(c), 2, 4 and 5 thereof) which would be applicable to any matter to be acted upon at the meeting if proxies were to be solicited in connection with the meeting. Notes A, C, D, and E to Schedule 14A (including the requirement in Note D.5 to provide an Interactive Data File in accordance with § 232.405 of this chapter and the EDGAR Filer Manual where applicable pursuant to § 232.405(b) of this chapter) are also applicable to Schedule 14C.

Item 2. Statement that proxies are not solicited. The following statement shall be set

§ 240.14c-101

forth on the first page of the information statement in bold-face type:

WE ARE NOT ASKING YOU FOR A PROXY AND YOU ARE REQUESTED NOT TO SEND US A PROXY

Item 3. Interest of certain persons in or opposition to matters to be acted upon. (a) Describe briefly any substantial interest, direct or indirect, by security holdings or otherwise, of each of the following persons in any matter to be acted upon, other than elections to office:

(1) Each person who has been a director or officer of the registrant at any time since the beginning of the last fiscal year;

(2) Each nominee for election as a director of the registrant;

(3) Each associate of any of the foregoing persons.

(b) Give the name of any director of the registrant who has informed the registrant in writing that he intends to oppose any action to be taken by the registrant at the meeting and indicate the action which he intends to oppose.

(c) Furnish the information required by Item 402(t) of Regulation S-K (§ 229.402(t) of this chapter).

Item 4. Proposals by security holders. If any security holder entitled to vote at the meeting or by written authorization or consent has submitted to the registrant a reasonable time before the information statement is to be transmitted to security holders a proposal, other than elections to office, which is accompanied by notice of his intention to present the proposal for action at the meeting the registrant shall, if a meeting is held, make a statement to that effect, identify the proposal and indicate the disposition proposed to be made of the proposal by the registrant at the meeting.

Instructions. 1. This item need not be answered as to any proposal submitted with respect to an annual meeting if such proposal is submitted less than 60 days in advance of a day corresponding to the date of sending a proxy statement or information statement in connection with the last annual meeting of security holders.

2. If the registrant intends to rule a proposal out of order, the Commission shall be so advised 20 calendar days prior to the date the definitive copies of the information statement are filed with the Commission, together with a statement of the reasons why the proposal is not deemed to be a proper subject for action by security holders.

Item 5. Delivery of documents to security holders sharing an address. If one annual report to security holders, information statement, or Notice of Internet Availability of Proxy Materials is being delivered to two or more security holders who share an address, furnish the following information in accordance with § 240.14a-3(e)(1):

(a) State that only one annual report to security holders, information statement, or Notice of Internet Availability of Proxy Materials, as applicable, is being delivered to multiple security holders sharing an address unless the registrant has received contrary instructions from one or more of the security holders;

(b) Undertake to deliver promptly upon written or oral request a separate copy of the annual report to security holders, information statement, or Notice of Internet Availability of Proxy Materials, as applicable, to a security holder at a shared address to which a single copy of the documents was delivered and provide instructions as to how a security holder can notify the registrant that the security holder wishes to receive a separate copy of an annual report to security holders, information statement, or Notice of Internet Availability of Proxy Materials, as applicable;

(c) Provide the phone number and mailing address to which a security holder can direct a notification to the registrant that the security holder wishes to receive a separate annual report to security holders, information statement, or Notice of Internet Availability of Proxy Materials, as applicable, in the future; and

(d) Provide instructions how security holders sharing an address can request delivery of a single copy of annual reports to security holders, information statements, or Notices of Internet Availability of Proxy Materials if they are receiving multiple copies of annual reports to security holders, information statements, or Notices of Internet Availability of Proxy Materials.

[51 FR 42072, Nov. 20, 1986, as amended at 52 FR 48984, Dec. 29, 1987; 57 FR 36495, Aug. 13, 1992; 58 FR 14684, Mar. 18, 1993; 59 FR 67765, Dec. 30, 1994; 61 FR 49960, Sept. 24, 1996; 65 FR 65752, Nov. 2, 2000; 72 FR 4172, Jan. 29, 2007; 73 FR 977, Jan. 4, 2008; 76 FR 6046, Feb. 2, 2011; 86 FR 70259, Dec. 9, 2021; 87 FR 55197, Sept. 8, 2022]

REGULATION 14D

ATTENTION ELECTRONIC FILERS

THIS REGULATION SHOULD BE READ IN CONJUNCTION WITH REGULATION S-T

Securities and Exchange Commission

§ 240.14d-1

(PART 232 OF THIS CHAPTER), WHICH GOVERNS THE PREPARATION AND SUBMISSION OF DOCUMENTS IN ELECTRONIC FORMAT. MANY PROVISIONS RELATING TO THE PREPARATION AND SUBMISSION OF DOCUMENTS IN PAPER FORMAT CONTAINED IN THIS REGULATION ARE SUPERSEDED BY THE PROVISIONS OF REGULATION S-T FOR DOCUMENTS REQUIRED TO BE FILED IN ELECTRONIC FORMAT.

§ 240.14d-1 Scope of and definitions applicable to Regulations 14D and 14E.

(a) *Scope.* Regulation 14D (§§ 240.14d-1 through 240.14d-101) shall apply to any tender offer that is subject to section 14(d)(1) of the Act (15 U.S.C. 78n(d)(1)), including, but not limited to, any tender offer for securities of a class described in that section that is made by an affiliate of the issuer of such class. Regulation 14E (§§ 240.14e-1 through 240.14e-8) shall apply to any tender offer for securities (other than exempted securities) unless otherwise noted therein.

(b) The requirements imposed by sections 14(d)(1) through 14(d)(7) of the Act, Regulation 14D and Schedules TO and 14D-9 thereunder, and Rule 14e-1 of Regulation 14E under the Act, shall be deemed satisfied with respect to any tender offer, including any exchange offer, for the securities of an issuer incorporated or organized under the laws of Canada or any Canadian province or territory, if such issuer is a foreign private issuer and is not an investment company registered or required to be registered under the Investment Company Act of 1940, if less than 40 percent of the class of securities outstanding that is the subject of the tender offer is held by U.S. holders, and the tender offer is subject to, and the bidder complies with, the laws, regulations and policies of Canada and/or any of its provinces or territories governing the conduct of the offer (unless the bidder has received an exemption(s) from, and the tender offer does not comply with, requirements that otherwise would be prescribed by Regulation 14D or 14E), *provided that:*

(1) In the case of tender offers subject to section 14(d)(1) of the Act, where the consideration for a tender offer subject to this section consists solely of cash, the entire disclosure document or documents required to be furnished to holders of the class of securities to be acquired shall be filed with the Commission on Schedule 14D-1F (§ 240.14d-102) and disseminated to shareholders of the subject company residing in the United States in accordance with such Canadian laws, regulations and policies; or

(2) Where the consideration for a tender offer subject to this section includes securities of the bidder to be issued pursuant to the offer, any registration statement and/or prospectus relating thereto shall be filed with the Commission along with the Schedule 14D-1F referred to in paragraph (b)(1) of this section, and shall be disseminated, together with the home jurisdiction document(s) accompanying such Schedule, to shareholders of the subject company residing in the United States in accordance with such Canadian laws, regulations and policies.

NOTES: 1. For purposes of any tender offer, including any exchange offer, otherwise eligible to proceed in accordance with Rule 14d-1(b) under the Act, the issuer of the subject securities will be presumed to be a foreign private issuer and U.S. holders will be presumed to hold less than 40 percent of such outstanding securities, unless (a) the aggregate trading volume of that class on national securities exchanges in the United States and on NASDAQ exceeded its aggregate trading volume on securities exchanges in Canada and on the Canadian Dealing Network, Inc. ("CDN") over the 12 calendar month period prior to commencement of this offer, or if commenced in response to a prior offer, over the 12 calendar month period prior to the commencement of the initial offer (based on volume figures published by such exchanges and NASDAQ and CDN); (b) the most recent annual report or annual information form filed or submitted by the issuer with securities regulators of Ontario, Quebec, British Columbia or Alberta (or, if the issuer of the subject securities is not a reporting issuer in any of such provinces, with any other Canadian securities regulator) or with the Commission indicates that U.S. holders hold 40 percent or more of the outstanding subject class of securities; or (c) the offeror has actual knowledge that the level of U.S. ownership equals or exceeds 40 percent of such securities.

2. Notwithstanding the grant of an exemption from one or more of the applicable Canadian regulatory provisions imposing requirements that otherwise would be prescribed by Regulation 14D or 14E, the tender offer will be eligible to proceed in accordance

§ 240.14d-1

with the requirements of this section if the Commission by order determines that the applicable Canadian regulatory provisions are adequate to protect the interest of investors.

(c) *Tier I.* Any tender offer for the securities of a foreign private issuer as defined in § 240.3b-4 is exempt from the requirements of sections 14(d)(1) through 14(d)(7) of the Act (15 U.S.C. 78n(d)(1) through 78n(d)(7)), Regulation 14D (§§ 240.14d-1 through 240.14d-10) and Schedules TO (§ 240.14d-100) and 14D-9 (§ 240.14d-101) thereunder, and § 240.14e-1 and § 240.14e-2 of Regulation 14E under the Act if the following conditions are satisfied:

(1) *U.S. ownership limitation.* Except in the case of a tender offer that is commenced during the pendency of a tender offer made by a prior bidder in reliance on this paragraph or § 240.13e-4(h)(8), U.S. holders do not hold more than 10 percent of the class of securities sought in the offer (as determined under Instructions 2 or 3 to paragraphs (c) and (d) of this section).

(2) *Equal treatment.* The bidder must permit U.S. holders to participate in the offer on terms at least as favorable as those offered any other holder of the same class of securities that is the subject of the tender offer; however:

(i) *Registered exchange offers.* If the bidder offers securities registered under the Securities Act of 1933 (15 U.S.C. 77a et seq.), the bidder need not extend the offer to security holders in those states or jurisdictions that prohibit the offer or sale of the securities after the bidder has made a good faith effort to register or qualify the offer and sale of securities in that state or jurisdiction, except that the bidder must offer the same cash alternative to security holders in any such state or jurisdiction that it has offered to security holders in any other state or jurisdiction.

(ii) *Exempt exchange offers.* If the bidder offers securities exempt from registration under § 230.802 of this chapter, the bidder need not extend the offer to security holders in those states or jurisdictions that require registration or qualification, except that the bidder must offer the same cash alternative to security holders in any such state or jurisdiction that it has offered to security holders in any other state or jurisdiction.

(iii) *Cash only consideration.* The bidder may offer U.S. holders only a cash consideration for the tender of the subject securities, notwithstanding the fact that the bidder is offering security holders outside the United States a consideration that consists in whole or in part of securities of the bidder, so long as the bidder has a reasonable basis for believing that the amount of cash is substantially equivalent to the value of the consideration offered to non-U.S. holders, and either of the following conditions are satisfied:

(A) The offered security is a "margin security" within the meaning of Regulation T (12 CFR 220.2) and the issuer undertakes to provide, upon the request of any U.S. holder or the Commission staff, the closing price and daily trading volume of the security on the principal trading market for the security as of the last trading day of each of the six months preceding the announcement of the offer and each of the trading days thereafter; or

(B) If the offered security is not a "margin security" within the meaning of Regulation T (12 CFR 220.2) the issuer undertakes to provide, upon the request of any U.S. holder or the Commission staff, an opinion of an independent expert stating that the cash consideration offered to U.S. holders is substantially equivalent to the value of the consideration offered security holders outside the United States.

(iv) *Disparate tax treatment.* If the bidder offers loan notes solely to offer sellers tax advantages not available in the United States and these notes are neither listed on any organized securities market nor registered under the Securities Act of 1933 (15 U.S.C. 77a et seq.), the loan notes need not be offered to U.S. holders.

(3) *Informational documents.* (i) The bidder must disseminate any informational document to U.S. holders, including any amendments thereto, in English, on a comparable basis to that provided to security holders in the home jurisdiction.

(ii) If the bidder disseminates by publication in its home jurisdiction, the bidder must publish the information in

324

Securities and Exchange Commission § 240.14d–1

the United States in a manner reasonably calculated to inform U.S. holders of the offer.

(iii) In the case of tender offers for securities described in section 14(d)(1) of the Act (15 U.S.C. 78n(d)(1)), if the bidder publishes or otherwise disseminates an informational document to the holders of the securities in connection with the tender offer, the bidder must furnish that informational document, including any amendments thereto, in English, to the Commission on Form CB (§ 249.480 of this chapter) by the first business day after publication or dissemination. If the bidder is a foreign company, it must also file a Form F–X (§ 239.42 of this chapter) with the Commission at the same time as the submission of Form CB to appoint an agent for service in the United States.

(4) *Investment companies.* The issuer of the securities that are the subject of the tender offer is not an investment company registered or required to be registered under the Investment Company Act of 1940 (15 U.S.C. 80a–1 *et seq.*), other than a registered closed-end investment company.

(d) *Tier II.* A person conducting a tender offer (including any exchange offer) that meets the conditions in paragraph (d)(1) of this section shall be entitled to the exemptive relief specified in paragraph (d)(2) of this section, provided that such tender offer complies with all the requirements of this section other than those for which an exemption has been specifically provided in paragraph (d)(2) of this section. In addition, a person conducting a tender offer subject only to the requirements of section 14(e) of the Act (15 U.S.C. 78n(e)) and Regulation 14E thereunder (§§ 240.14e–1 through 240.14e–8) that meets the conditions in paragraph (d)(1) of the section also shall be entitled to the exemptive relief specified in paragraph (d)(2) of this section, to the extent needed under the requirements of Regulation 14E, so long as the tender offer complies with all requirements of Regulation 14E other than those for which an exemption has been specifically provided in paragraph (d)(2) of this section:

(1) *Conditions.* (i) The subject company is a foreign private issuer as defined in § 240.3b–4 and is not an investment company registered or required to be registered under the Investment Company Act of 1940 (15 U.S.C. 80a–1 *et seq.*), other than a registered closed-end investment company;

(ii) Except in the case of a tender offer that is commenced during the pendency of a tender offer made by a prior bidder in reliance on this paragraph or § 240.13e–4(i), U.S. holders do not hold more than 40 percent of the class of securities sought in the offer (as determined under Instructions 2 or 3 to paragraphs (c) and (d) of this section); and

(iii) The bidder complies with all applicable U.S. tender offer laws and regulations, other than those for which an exemption has been provided for in paragraph (d)(2) of this section.

(2) *Exemptions*—(i) *Equal treatment—loan notes.* If the bidder offers loan notes solely to offer sellers tax advantages not available in the United States and these notes are neither listed on any organized securities market nor registered under the Securities Act of 1933 (15 U.S.C. 77a *et seq.*), the loan notes need not be offered to U.S. holders, notwithstanding § 240.14d–10.

(ii) *Equal treatment—separate U.S. and foreign offers.* Notwithstanding the provisions of § 240.14d–10, a bidder conducting a tender offer meeting the conditions of paragraph (d)(1) of this section may separate the offer into multiple offers: One offer made to U.S. holders, which also may include all holders of American Depositary Shares representing interests in the subject securities, and one or more offers made to non-U.S. holders. The U.S. offer must be made on terms at least as favorable as those offered any other holder of the same class of securities that is the subject of the tender offers. U.S. holders may be included in the foreign offer(s) only where the laws of the jurisdiction governing such foreign offer(s) expressly preclude the exclusion of U.S. holders from the foreign offer(s) and where the offer materials distributed to U.S. holders fully and adequately disclose the risks of participating in the foreign offer(s).

(iii) *Notice of extensions.* Notice of extensions made in accordance with the requirements of the home jurisdiction

§ 240.14d-1

law or practice will satisfy the requirements of § 240.14e-1(d).

(iv) *Prompt payment.* Payment made in accordance with the requirements of the home jurisdiction law or practice will satisfy the requirements of § 240.14e-1(c). Where payment may not be made on a more expedited basis under home jurisdiction law or practice, payment for securities tendered during any subsequent offering period within 20 business days of the date of tender will satisfy the prompt payment requirements of § 240.14d-11(e). For purposes of this paragraph (d), a business day is determined with reference to the target's home jurisdiction.

(v) *Subsequent offering period/Withdrawal rights.* A bidder will satisfy the announcement and prompt payment requirements of § 240.14d-11(d), if the bidder announces the results of the tender offer, including the approximate number of securities deposited to date, and pays for tendered securities in accordance with the requirements of the home jurisdiction law or practice and the subsequent offering period commences immediately following such announcement. Notwithstanding section 14(d)(5) of the Act (15 U.S.C. 78n(d)(5)), the bidder need not extend withdrawal rights following the close of the offer and prior to the commencement of the subsequent offering period.

(vi) *Payment of interest on securities tendered during subsequent offering period.* Notwithstanding the requirements of § 240.14d-11(f), the bidder may pay interest on securities tendered during a subsequent offering period, if required under applicable foreign law. Paying interest on securities tendered during a subsequent offering period in accordance with this section will not be deemed to violate § 240.14d-10(a)(2).

(vii) *Suspension of withdrawal rights during counting of tendered securities.* The bidder may suspend withdrawal rights required under section 14(d)(5) of the Act (15 U.S.C. 78n(d)(5)) at the end of the offer and during the period that securities tendered into the offer are being counted, provided that:

(A) The bidder has provided an offer period including withdrawal rights for a period of at least 20 U.S. business days;

17 CFR Ch. II (4-1-23 Edition)

(B) At the time withdrawal rights are suspended, all offer conditions have been satisfied or waived, except to the extent that the bidder is in the process of determining whether a minimum acceptance condition included in the terms of the offer has been satisfied by counting tendered securities; and

(C) Withdrawal rights are suspended only during the counting process and are reinstated immediately thereafter, except to the extent that they are terminated through the acceptance of tendered securities.

(viii) *Mix and match elections and the subsequent offering period.* Notwithstanding the requirements of § 240.14d-11(b), where the bidder offers target security holders a choice between different forms of consideration, it may establish a ceiling on one or more forms of consideration offered. Notwithstanding the requirements of § 240.14d-11(f), a bidder that establishes a ceiling on one or more forms of consideration offered pursuant to this subsection may offset elections of tendering security holders against one another, subject to proration, so that elections are satisfied to the greatest extent possible and prorated to the extent that they cannot be satisfied in full. Such a bidder also may separately offset and prorate securities tendered during the initial offering period and those tendered during any subsequent offering period, notwithstanding the requirements of § 240.14d-10(c).

(ix) *Early termination of an initial offering period.* A bidder may terminate an initial offering period, including a voluntary extension of that period, if at the time the initial offering period and withdrawal rights terminate, the following conditions are met:

(A) The initial offering period has been open for at least 20 U.S. business days;

(B) The bidder has adequately discussed the possibility of and the impact of the early termination in the original offer materials;

(C) The bidder provides a subsequent offering period after the termination of the initial offering period;

(D) All offer conditions are satisfied as of the time when the initial offering period ends; and

Securities and Exchange Commission

§ 240.14d–1

(E) The bidder does not terminate the initial offering period or any extension of that period during any mandatory extension required under U.S. tender offer rules.

INSTRUCTIONS TO PARAGRAPHS (c) AND (d): 1. *Home jurisdiction* means both the jurisdiction of the subject company's incorporation, organization or chartering and the principal foreign market where the subject company's securities are listed or quoted.

2. *U.S. holder* means any security holder resident in the United States. Except as otherwise provided in Instruction 3 below, to determine the percentage of outstanding securities held by U.S. holders:

i. Calculate the U.S. ownership as of a date no more than 60 before and no more than 30 days after public announcement of the tender offer. If you are unable to calculate as of a date within these time frames, the calculation may be made as of the most recent practicable date before public announcement, but in no event earlier than 120 days before announcement;

ii. Include securities underlying American Depositary Shares convertible or exchangeable into the securities that are the subject of the tender offer when calculating the number of subject securities outstanding, as well as the number held by U.S. holders. Exclude from the calculations other types of securities that are convertible or exchangeable into the securities that are the subject of the tender offer, such as warrants, options and convertible securities. Exclude from those calculations securities held by the bidder;

iii. Use the method of calculating record ownership in Rule 12g3-2(a) under the Act (§ 240.12g3-2(a) of this chapter), except that your inquiry as to the amount of securities represented by accounts of customers resident in the United States may be limited to brokers, dealers, banks and other nominees located in the United States, the subject company's jurisdiction of incorporation or that of each participant in a business combination, and the jurisdiction that is the primary trading market for the subject securities, if different than the subject company's jurisdiction of incorporation;

iv. If, after reasonable inquiry, you are unable to obtain information about the amount of securities represented by accounts of customers resident in the United States, you may assume, for purposes of this definition, that the customers are residents of the jurisdiction in which the nominee has its principal place of business; and

v. Count securities as beneficially owned by residents of the United States as reported on reports of beneficial ownership that are provided to you or publicly filed and based on information otherwise provided to you.

3. In a tender offer by a bidder other than an affiliate of the issuer of the subject securities that is not made pursuant to an agreement with the issuer of the subject securities, the issuer of the subject securities will be presumed to be a foreign private issuer and U.S. holders will be presumed to hold less than 10 percent (40 percent in the case of paragraph (d) of this section) of such outstanding securities, unless paragraphs 3.i., ii., or iii. of the instructions to paragraphs (c) and (d) of this section indicate otherwise. In addition, where the bidder is unable to conduct the analysis of U.S. ownership set forth in Instruction 2 to paragraphs (c) and (d) of this section, the bidder may presume that the percentage of securities held by U.S. holders is less than 10 percent (40 percent in the case of paragraph (d) of this section) of the outstanding securities so long as there is a primary trading market for the subject securities outside the U.S., as defined in § 240.12h–6(f)(5) of this chapter, unless:

i. Average daily trading volume of the subject securities in the United States for a recent twelve-month period ending on a date no more than 60 days before the public announcement of the offer exceeds 10 percent (40 percent in the case of paragraph (d) of this section) of the average daily trading volume of that class of securities on a worldwide basis for the same period; or

ii. The most recent annual report or annual information filed or submitted by the issuer with securities regulators of the home jurisdiction or with the Commission or any jurisdiction in which the subject securities trade before the public announcement of the offer indicates that U.S. holders hold more than 10 percent (40 percent in the case of paragraph (d) of this section) of the outstanding subject class of securities; or

iii. The bidder knows or has reason to know, before the public announcement of the offer, that the level of U.S. ownership exceeds 10 percent (40 percent in the case of paragraph (d) of this section) of such securities. As an example, a bidder is deemed to know information about U.S. ownership of the subject class of securities that is publicly available and that appears in any filing with the Commission or any regulatory body in the issuer's jurisdiction of incorporation or (if different) the non-U.S. jurisdiction in which the primary trading market for the subject securities is located. The bidder is deemed to know information about U.S. ownership available from the issuer or obtained or readily available from any other source that is reasonably reliable, including from persons it has retained to advise it about the transaction, as well as from third-party information providers. These examples are not intended to be exclusive.

iv. The bidder knows or has reason to know that the level of U.S. ownership exceeds 10

§ 240.14d-1

percent (40 percent in the case of 14d–1(d)) of such securities.

4. *United States* means the United States of America, its territories and possessions, any State of the United States, and the District of Columbia.

5. The exemptions provided by paragraphs (c) and (d) of this section are not available for any securities transaction or series of transactions that technically complies with paragraph (c) or (d) of this section but are part of a plan or scheme to evade the provisions of Regulations 14D or 14E.

(e) Notwithstanding paragraph (a) of this section, the requirements imposed by sections 14(d)(1) through 14(d)(7) of the Act [15 U.S.C. 78n(d)(1) through 78n(d)(7)], Regulation 14D promulgated thereunder (§§ 240.14d–1 through 240.14d–10), and §§ 240.14e–1 and 240.14e–2 shall not apply by virtue of the fact that a bidder for the securities of a foreign private issuer, as defined in § 240.3b–4, the subject company of such a tender offer, their representatives, or any other person specified in § 240.14d–9(d), provides any journalist with access to its press conferences held outside of the United States, to meetings with its representatives conducted outside of the United States, or to written press-related materials released outside the United States, at or in which a present or proposed tender offer is discussed, if:

(1) Access is provided to both U.S. and foreign journalists; and

(2) With respect to any written press-related materials released by the bidder or its representatives that discuss a present or proposed tender offer for equity securities registered under Section 12 of the Act [15 U.S.C. 78*l*], the written press-related materials must state that these written press-related materials are not an extension of a tender offer in the United States for a class of equity securities of the subject company. If the bidder intends to extend the tender offer in the United States at some future time, a statement regarding this intention, and that the procedural and filing requirements of the Williams Act will be satisfied at that time, also must be included in these written press-related materials. No means to tender securities, or coupons that could be returned to indicate interest in the tender offer, may be provided as part of, or attached to, these written press-related materials.

(f) For the purpose of § 240.14d–1(e), a bidder may presume that a target company qualifies as a foreign private issuer if the target company is a foreign issuer and files registration statements or reports on the disclosure forms specifically designated for foreign private issuers, claims the exemption from registration under the Act pursuant to § 240.12g3–2(b), or is not reporting in the United States.

(g) *Definitions.* Unless the context otherwise requires, all terms used in Regulation 14D and Regulation 14E have the same meaning as in the Act and in Rule 12b–2 (§ 240.12b–2) promulgated thereunder. In addition, for purposes of sections 14(d) and 14(e) of the Act and Regulations 14D and 14E, the following definitions apply:

(1) The term *beneficial owner* shall have the same meaning as that set forth in Rule 13d–3: *Provided, however,* That, except with respect to Rule 14d–3, Rule 14d–9(d), the term shall not include a person who does not have or share investment power or who is deemed to be a beneficial owner by virtue of Rule 13d–3(d)(1) (§ 240.13d–3(d)(1));

(2) The term *bidder* means any person who makes a tender offer or on whose behalf a tender offer is made: *Provided, however,* That the term does not include an issuer which makes a tender offer for securities of any class of which it is the issuer;

(3) The term *business day* means any day, other than Saturday, Sunday or a federal holiday, and shall consist of the time period from 12:01 a.m. through 12:00 midnight Eastern time. In computing any time period under section 14(d)(5) or section 14(d)(6) of the Act or under Regulation 14D or Regulation 14E, the date of the event which begins the running of such time period shall be included *except that* if such event occurs on other than a business day such period shall begin to run on and shall include the first business day thereafter; and

(4) The term *initial offering period* means the period from the time the offer commences until all minimum time periods, including extensions, required by Regulations 14D (§§ 240.14d–1 through 240.14d–103) and 14E (§§ 240.14e–1 through 240.14e–8) have been satisfied and all conditions to the offer have

Securities and Exchange Commission § 240.14d-2

been satisfied or waived within these time periods.

(5) The term *security holders* means holders of record and beneficial owners of securities which are the subject of a tender offer;

(6) The term *security position listing* means, with respect to securities of any issuer held by a registered clearing agency in the name of the clearing agency or its nominee, a list of those participants in the clearing agency on whose behalf the clearing agency holds the issuer's securities and of the participants' respective positions in such securities as of a specified date.

(7) The term *subject company* means any issuer of securities which are sought by a bidder pursuant to a tender offer;

(8) The term *subsequent offering period* means the period immediately following the initial offering period meeting the conditions specified in § 240.14d-11.

(9) The term *tender offer material* means:

(i) The bidder's formal offer, including all the material terms and conditions of the tender offer and all amendments thereto;

(ii) The related transmittal letter (whereby securities of the subject company which are sought in the tender offer may be transmitted to the bidder or its depositary) and all amendments thereto; and

(iii) Press releases, advertisements, letters and other documents published by the bidder or sent or given by the bidder to security holders which, directly or indirectly, solicit, invite or request tenders of the securities being sought in the tender offer;

(h) *Signatures.* Where the Act or the rules, forms, reports or schedules thereunder require a document filed with or furnished to the Commission to be signed, such document shall be manually signed, or signed using either typed signatures or duplicated or facsimile versions of manual signatures. Where typed, duplicated, or facsimile signatures are used, each signatory to the filing shall manually or electronically sign a signature page or other document authenticating, acknowledging, or otherwise adopting his or her signature that appears in the filing ("authentication document"). Such authentication document shall be executed before or at the time the filing is made and shall be retained by the filer for a period of five years. The requirements set forth in § 232.302(b) must be met with regards to the use of an electronically signed authentication document pursuant to this paragraph (h). Upon request, the filer shall furnish to the Commission or its staff a copy of any or all documents retained pursuant to this section.

(h) *Signatures.* Where the Act or the rules, forms, reports or schedules thereunder require a document filed with or furnished to the Commission to be signed, such document shall be manually signed, or signed using either typed signatures or duplicated or facsimile versions of manual signatures. Where typed, duplicated, or facsimile signatures are used, each signatory to the filing shall manually or electronically sign a signature page or other document authenticating, acknowledging, or otherwise adopting his or her signature that appears in the filing ("authentication document"). Such authentication document shall be executed before or at the time the filing is made and shall be retained by the filer for a period of five years. The requirements set forth in § 232.302(b) must be met with regards to the use of an electronically signed authentication document pursuant to this paragraph (h). Upon request, the filer shall furnish to the Commission or its staff a copy of any or all documents retained pursuant to this section.

[44 FR 70340, Dec. 6, 1979, as amended at 47 FR 11470, Mar. 16, 1982; 56 FR 30071, July 1, 1991; 60 FR 26622, May 17, 1995; 61 FR 30403, June 14, 1996; 62 FR 53955, Oct. 17, 1997; 64 FR 61404, 61459, Nov. 10, 1999; 73 FR 17814, Apr. 1, 2008; 73 FR 60091, Oct. 9, 2008; 85 FR 78229, Dec. 4, 2020]

§ 240.14d-2 Commencement of a tender offer.

(a) *Date of commencement.* A bidder will have commenced its tender offer for purposes of section 14(d) of the Act (15 U.S.C. 78n) and the rules under that section at 12:01 a.m. on the date when the bidder has first published, sent or given the means to tender to security holders. For purposes of this section,

§ 240.14d-3

the means to tender includes the transmittal form or a statement regarding how the transmittal form may be obtained.

(b) *Pre-commencement communications.* A communication by the bidder will not be deemed to constitute commencement of a tender offer if:

(1) It does not include the means for security holders to tender their shares into the offer; and

(2) All written communications relating to the tender offer, from and including the first public announcement, are filed under cover of Schedule TO (§ 240.14d-100) with the Commission no later than the date of the communication. The bidder also must deliver to the subject company and any other bidder for the same class of securities the first communication relating to the transaction that is filed, or required to be filed, with the Commission.

INSTRUCTIONS TO PARAGRAPH (b)(2): 1. The box on the front of Schedule TO indicating that the filing contains pre-commencement communications must be checked.

2. Any communications made in connection with an exchange offer registered under the Securities Act of 1933 need only be filed under § 230.425 of this chapter and will be deemed filed under this section.

3. Each pre-commencement written communication must include a prominent legend in clear, plain language advising security holders to read the tender offer statement when it is available because it contains important information. The legend also must advise investors that they can get the tender offer statement and other filed documents for free at the Commission's web site and explain which documents are free from the offeror.

4. See §§ 230.135, 230.165 and 230.166 of this chapter for pre-commencement communications made in connection with registered exchange offers.

5. "Public announcement" is any oral or written communication by the bidder, or any person authorized to act on the bidder's behalf, that is reasonably designed to, or has the effect of, informing the public or security holders in general about the tender offer.

(c) *Filing and other obligations triggered by commencement.* As soon as practicable on the date of commencement, a bidder must comply with the filing requirements of § 240.14d-3(a), the dissemination requirements of § 240.14d-

4(a) or (b), and the disclosure requirements of § 240.14d-6(a).

[64 FR 61459, Nov. 10, 1999]

§ 240.14d-3 **Filing and transmission of tender offer statement.**

(a) *Filing and transmittal.* No bidder shall make a tender offer if, after consummation thereof, such bidder would be the beneficial owner of more than 5 percent of the class of the subject company's securities for which the tender offer is made, unless as soon as practicable on the date of the commencement of the tender offer such bidder:

(1) Files with the Commission a Tender Offer Statement on Schedule TO (§ 240.14d-100), including all exhibits thereto;

(2) Delivers a copy of such Schedule TO, including all exhibits thereto:

(i) To the subject company at its principal executive office; and

(ii) To any other bidder, which has filed a Schedule TO with the Commission relating to a tender offer which has not yet terminated for the same class of securities of the subject company, at such bidder's principal executive office or at the address of the person authorized to receive notices and communications (which is disclosed on the cover sheet of such other bidder's Schedule TO);

(3) Gives telephonic notice of the information required by Rule 14d-6(d)(2)(i) and (ii) (§ 240.14d-6(d)(2)(i) and (ii)) and mails by means of first class mail a copy of such Schedule TO, including all exhibits thereto:

(i) To each national securities exchange where such class of the subject company's securities is registered and listed for trading (which may be based upon information contained in the subject company's most recent Annual Report on Form 10-K (§ 249.310 of this chapter) filed with the Commission unless the bidder has reason to believe that such information is not current), which telephonic notice shall be made when practicable before the opening of each such exchange; and

(ii) To the National Association of Securities Dealers, Inc. ("NASD") if such class of the subject company's securities is authorized for quotation in the NASDAQ interdealer quotation system.

Securities and Exchange Commission § 240.14d-4

(b) *Post-commencement amendments and additional materials.* The bidder making the tender offer must file with the Commission:

(1) An amendment to Schedule TO (§ 240.14d-100) reporting promptly any material changes in the information set forth in the schedule previously filed and including copies of any additional tender offer materials as exhibits; and

(2) A final amendment to Schedule TO (§ 240.14d-100) reporting promptly the results of the tender offer.

INSTRUCTION TO PARAGRAPH (b): A copy of any additional tender offer materials or amendment filed under this section must be sent promptly to the subject company and to any exchange and/or NASD, as required by paragraph (a) of this section, but in no event later than the date the materials are first published, sent or given to security holders.

(c) *Certain announcements.* Notwithstanding the provisions of paragraph (b) of this section, if the additional tender offer material or an amendment to Schedule TO discloses only the number of shares deposited to date, and/or announces an extension of the time during which shares may be tendered, then the bidder may file such tender offer material or amendment and send a copy of such tender offer material or amendment to the subject company, any exchange and/or the NASD, as required by paragraph (a) of this section, promptly after the date such tender offer material is first published or sent or given to security holders.

[44 FR 70341, Dec. 6, 1979; 64 FR 61460, Nov. 10, 1999, as amended at 73 FR 977, Jan. 4, 2008; 73 FR 17814, Apr. 1, 2008]

§ 240.14d-4 Dissemination of tender offers to security holders.

As soon as practicable on the date of commencement of a tender offer, the bidder must publish, send or give the disclosure required by § 240.14d-6 to security holders of the class of securities that is the subject of the offer, by complying with all of the requirements of any of the following:

(a) *Cash tender offers and exempt securities offers.* For tender offers in which the consideration consists solely of cash and/or securities exempt from registration under section 3 of the Securities Act of 1933 (15 U.S.C. 77c):

(1) *Long-form publication.* The bidder makes adequate publication in a newspaper or newspapers of long-form publication of the tender offer.

(2) *Summary publication.* (i) If the tender offer is not subject to Rule 13e-3 (§ 240.13e-3), the bidder makes adequate publication in a newspaper or newspapers of a summary advertisement of the tender offer; and

(ii) Mails by first class mail or otherwise furnishes with reasonable promptness the bidder's tender offer materials to any security holder who requests such tender offer materials pursuant to the summary advertisement or otherwise.

(3) *Use of stockholder lists and security position listings.* Any bidder using stockholder lists and security position listings under § 240.14d-5 must comply with paragraph (a)(1) or (2) of this section on or before the date of the bidder's request under § 240.14d-5(a).

INSTRUCTION TO PARAGRAPH (a): Tender offers may be published or sent or given to security holders by other methods, but with respect to summary publication and the use of stockholder lists and security position listings under § 240.14d-5, paragraphs (a)(2) and (a)(3) of this section are exclusive.

(b) *Registered securities offers.* For tender offers in which the consideration consists solely or partially of securities registered under the Securities Act of 1933, a registration statement containing all of the required information, including pricing information, has been filed and a preliminary prospectus or a prospectus that meets the requirements of section 10(a) of the Securities Act (15 U.S.C. 77j(a)), including a letter of transmittal, is delivered to security holders. However, for going-private transactions (as defined by § 240.13e-3) and roll-up transactions (as described by Item 901 of Regulation S-K (§ 229.901 of this chapter)), a registration statement registering the securities to be offered must have become effective and only a prospectus that meets the requirements of section 10(a) of the Securities Act may be delivered to security holders on the date of commencement.

INSTRUCTIONS TO PARAGRAPH (b): 1. If the prospectus is being delivered by mail, mailing on the date of commencement is sufficient.

§ 240.14d-5

2. A preliminary prospectus used under this section may not omit information under §§ 230.430 or 230.430A of this chapter.

3. If a preliminary prospectus is used under this section and the bidder must disseminate material changes, the tender offer must remain open for the period specified in paragraph (d)(2) of this section.

4. If a preliminary prospectus is used under this section, tenders may be requested in accordance with § 230.162(a) of this chapter.

(c) *Adequate publication.* Depending on the facts and circumstances involved, adequate publication of a tender offer pursuant to this section may require publication in a newspaper with a national circulation or may only require publication in a newspaper with metropolitan or regional circulation or may require publication in a combination thereof: *Provided, however,* That publication in all editions of a daily newspaper with a national circulation shall be deemed to constitute adequate publication.

(d) *Publication of changes and extension of the offer.* (1) If a tender offer has been published or sent or given to security holders by one or more of the methods enumerated in this section, a material change in the information published or sent or given to security holders shall be promptly disseminated to security holders in a manner reasonably designed to inform security holders of such change; *Provided, however,* That if the bidder has elected pursuant to rule 14d-5 (f)(1) of this section to require the subject company to disseminate amendments disclosing material changes to the tender offer materials pursuant to Rule 14d-5, the bidder shall disseminate material changes in the information published or sent or given to security holders at least pursuant to Rule 14d-5.

(2) In a registered securities offer where the bidder disseminates the preliminary prospectus as permitted by paragraph (b) of this section, the offer must remain open from the date that material changes to the tender offer materials are disseminated to security holders, as follows:

(i) Five business days for a prospectus supplement containing a material change other than price or share levels;

(ii) Ten business days for a prospectus supplement containing a change in price, the amount of securities sought, the dealer's soliciting fee, or other similarly significant change;

(iii) Ten business days for a prospectus supplement included as part of a post-effective amendment; and

(iv) Twenty business days for a revised prospectus when the initial prospectus was materially deficient.

[44 FR 70341, Dec. 6, 1979, as amended at 64 FR 61460, Nov. 10, 1999; 76 FR 71876, Nov. 21, 2011]

§ 240.14d-5 Dissemination of certain tender offers by the use of stockholder lists and security position listings.

(a) *Obligations of the subject company.* Upon receipt by a subject company at its principal executive offices of a bidder's written request, meeting the requirements of paragraph (e) of this section, the subject company shall comply with the following sub-paragraphs.

(1) The subject company shall notify promptly transfer agents and any other person who will assist the subject company in complying with the requirements of this section of the receipt by the subject company of a request by a bidder pursuant to this section.

(2) The subject company shall promptly ascertain whether the most recently prepared stockholder list, written or otherwise, within the access of the subject company was prepared as of a date earlier than ten business days before the date of the bidder's request and, if so, the subject company shall promptly prepare or cause to be prepared a stockholder list as of the most recent practicable date which shall not be more than ten business days before the date of the bidder's request.

(3) The subject company shall make an election to comply and shall comply with all of the provisions of either paragraph (b) or paragraph (c) of this section. The subject company's election once made shall not be modified or revoked during the bidder's tender offer and extensions thereof.

(4) No later than the second business day after the date of the bidder's request, the subject company shall orally notify the bidder, which notification shall be confirmed in writing, of the

Securities and Exchange Commission §240.14d–5

subject company's election made pursuant to paragraph (a)(3) of this section. Such notification shall indicate (i) the approximate number of security holders of the class of securities being sought by the bidder and, (ii) if the subject company elects to comply with paragraph (b) of this section, appropriate information concerning the location for delivery of the bidder's tender offer materials and the approximate direct costs incidental to the mailing to security holders of the bidder's tender offer materials computed in accordance with paragraph (g)(2) of this section.

(b) *Mailing of tender offer materials by the subject company.* A subject company which elects pursuant to paragraph (a)(3) of this section to comply with the provisions of this paragraph shall perform the acts prescribed by the following paragraphs.

(1) The subject company shall promptly contact each participant named on the most recent security position listing of any clearing agency within the access of the subject company and make inquiry of each such participant as to the approximate number of beneficial owners of the subject company securities being sought in the tender offer held by each such participant.

(2) No later than the third business day after delivery of the bidder's tender offer materials pursuant to paragraph (g)(1) of this section, the subject company shall begin to mail or cause to be mailed by means of first class mail a copy of the bidder's tender offer materials to each person whose name appears as a record holder of the class of securities for which the offer is made on the most recent stockholder list referred to in paragraph (a)(2) of this section. The subject company shall use its best efforts to complete the mailing in a timely manner but in no event shall such mailing be completed in a substantially greater period of time than the subject company would complete a mailing to security holders of its own materials relating to the tender offer.

(3) No later than the third business day after the delivery of the bidder's tender offer materials pursuant to paragraph (g)(1) of this section, the subject company shall begin to transmit or cause to be transmitted a sufficient number of sets of the bidder's tender offer materials to the participants named on the security position listings described in paragraph (b)(1) of this section. The subject company shall use its best efforts to complete the transmittal in a timely manner but in no event shall such transmittal be completed in a substantially greater period of time than the subject company would complete a transmittal to such participants pursuant to security position listings of clearing agencies of its own material relating to the tender offer.

(4) The subject company shall promptly give oral notification to the bidder, which notification shall be confirmed in writing, of the commencement of the mailing pursuant to paragraph (b)(2) of this section and of the transmittal pursuant to paragraph (b)(3) of this section.

(5) During the tender offer and any extension thereof the subject company shall use reasonable efforts to update the stockholder list and shall mail or cause to be mailed promptly following each update a copy of the bidder's tender offer materials (to the extent sufficient sets of such materials have been furnished by the bidder) to each person who has become a record holder since the later of (i) the date of preparation of the most recent stockholder list referred to in paragraph (a)(2) of this section or (ii) the last preceding update.

(6) If the bidder has elected pursuant to paragraph (f)(1) of this section to require the subject company to disseminate amendments disclosing material changes to the tender offer materials pursuant to this section, the subject company, promptly following delivery of each such amendment, shall mail or cause to be mailed a copy of each such amendment to each record holder whose name appears on the shareholder list described in paragraphs (a)(2) and (b)(5) of this section and shall transmit or cause to be transmitted sufficient copies of such amendment to each participant named on security position listings who received sets of the bidder's tender offer materials pursuant to paragraph (b)(3) of this section.

(7) The subject company shall not include any communication other than

§ 240.14d–5

the bidder's tender offer materials or amendments thereto in the envelopes or other containers furnished by the bidder.

(8) Promptly following the termination of the tender offer, the subject company shall reimburse the bidder the excess, if any, of the amounts advanced pursuant to paragraph (f)(3)(iii) over the direct costs incidental to compliance by the subject company and its agents in performing the acts required by this section computed in accordance with paragraph (g)(2) of this section.

(c) *Delivery of stockholder lists and security position listings.* A subject company which elects pursuant to paragraph (a)(3) of this section to comply with the provisions of this paragraph shall perform the acts prescribed by the following paragraphs.

(1) No later than the third business day after the date of the bidder's request, the subject company must furnish to the bidder at the subject company's principal executive office a copy of the names and addresses of the record holders on the most recent stockholder list referred to in paragraph (a)(2) of this section; the names and addresses of participants identified on the most recent security position listing of any clearing agency that is within the access of the subject company; and the most recent list of names, addresses and security positions of beneficial owners as specified in § 240.14a–13(b), in the possession of the subject company, or that subsequently comes into its possession. All security holder list information must be in the format requested by the bidder to the extent the format is available to the subject company without undue burden or expense.

(2) If the bidder has elected pursuant to paragraph (f)(1) of this section to require the subject company to disseminate amendments disclosing material changes to the tender offer materials, the subject company shall update the stockholder list by furnishing the bidder with the name and address of each record holder named on the stockholder list, and not previously furnished to the bidder, promptly after such information becomes available to the subject company during the tender offer and any extensions thereof.

(d) *Liability of subject company and others.* Neither the subject company nor any affiliate or agent of the subject company nor any clearing agency shall be:

(1) Deemed to have made a solicitation or recommendation respecting the tender offer within the meaning of section 14(d)(4) based solely upon the compliance or noncompliance by the subject company or any affiliate or agent of the subject company with one or more requirements of this section;

(2) Liable under any provision of the Federal securities laws to the bidder or to any security holder based solely upon the inaccuracy of the current names or addresses on the stockholder list or security position listing, unless such inaccuracy results from a lack of reasonable care on the part of the subject company or any affiliate or agent of the subject company;

(3) Deemed to be an "underwriter" within the meaning of section (2)(11) of the Securities Act of 1933 for any purpose of that Act or any rule or regulation promulgated thereunder based solely upon the compliance or noncompliance by the subject company or any affiliate or agent of the subject company with one or more of the requirements of this section;

(4) Liable under any provision of the Federal securities laws for the disclosure in the bidder's tender offer materials, including any amendment thereto, based solely upon the compliance or noncompliance by the subject company or any affiliate or agent of the subject company with one or more of the requirements of this section.

(e) *Content of the bidder's request.* The bidder's written request referred to in paragraph (a) of this section shall include the following:

(1) The identity of the bidder;

(2) The title of the class of securities which is the subject of the bidder's tender offer;

(3) A statement that the bidder is making a request to the subject company pursuant to paragraph (a) of this section for the use of the stockholder list and security position listings for the purpose of disseminating a tender offer to security holders;

Securities and Exchange Commission § 240.14d-5

(4) A statement that the bidder is aware of and will comply with the provisions of paragraph (f) of this section;

(5) A statement as to whether or not it has elected pursuant to paragraph (f)(1) of this section to disseminate amendments disclosing material changes to the tender offer materials pursuant to this section; and

(6) The name, address and telephone number of the person whom the subject company shall contact pursuant to paragraph (a)(4) of this section.

(f) *Obligations of the bidder.* Any bidder who requests that a subject company comply with the provisions of paragraph (a) of this section shall comply with the following paragraphs.

(1) The bidder shall make an election whether or not to require the subject company to disseminate amendments disclosing material changes to the tender offer materials pursuant to this section, which election shall be included in the request referred to in paragraph (a) of this section and shall not be revocable by the bidder during the tender offer and extensions thereof.

(2) With respect to a tender offer subject to section 14(d)(1) of the Act in which the consideration consists solely of cash and/or securities exempt from registration under section 3 of the Securities Act of 1933, the bidder shall comply with the requirements of Rule 14d-4(a)(3).

(3) If the subject company elects to comply with paragraph (b) of this section,

(i) The bidder shall promptly deliver the tender offer materials after receipt of the notification from the subject company as provided in paragraph (a)(4) of this section;

(ii) The bidder shall promptly notify the subject company of any amendment to the bidder's tender offer materials requiring compliance by the subject company with paragraph (b)(6) of this section and shall promptly deliver such amendment to the subject company pursuant to paragraph (g)(1) of this section;

(iii) The bidder shall advance to the subject company an amount equal to the approximate cost of conducting mailings to security holders computed in accordance with paragraph (g)(2) of this section;

(iv) The bidder shall promptly reimburse the subject company for the direct costs incidental to compliance by the subject company and its agents in performing the acts required by this section computed in accordance with paragraph (g)(2) of this section which are in excess of the amount advanced pursuant to paragraph (f)(2)(iii) of this section; and

(v) The bidder shall mail by means of first class mail or otherwise furnish with reasonable promptness the tender offer materials to any security holder who requests such materials.

(4) If the subject company elects to comply with paragraph (c) of this section,

(i) The bidder shall use the stockholder list and security position listings furnished to the bidder pursuant to paragraph (c) of this section exclusively in the dissemination of tender offer materials to security holders in connection with the bidder's tender offer and extensions thereof;

(ii) The bidder shall return the stockholder lists and security position listings furnished to the bidder pursuant to paragraph (c) of this section promptly after the termination of the bidder's tender offer;

(iii) The bidder shall accept, handle and return the stockholder lists and security position listings furnished to the bidder pursuant to paragraph (c) of this section to the subject company on a confidential basis;

(iv) The bidder shall not retain any stockholder list or security position listing furnished by the subject company pursuant to paragraph (c) of this section, or any copy thereof, nor retain any information derived from any such list or listing or copy thereof after the termination of the bidder's tender offer;

(v) The bidder shall mail by means of first class mail, at its own expense, a copy of its tender offer materials to each person whose identity appears on the stockholder list as furnished and updated by the subject company pursuant to paragraphs (c)(1) and (2) of this section;

(vi) The bidder shall contact the participants named on the security position listing of any clearing agency, make inquiry of each participant as to

§ 240.14d-6

the approximate number of sets of tender offer materials required by each such participant, and furnish, at its own expense, sufficient sets of tender offer materials and any amendment thereto to each such participant for subsequent transmission to the beneficial owners of the securities being sought by the bidder;

(vii) The bidder shall mail by means of first class mail or otherwise furnish with reasonable promptness the tender offer materials to any security holder who requests such materials; and

(viii) The bidder shall promptly reimburse the subject company for direct costs incidental to compliance by the subject company and its agents in performing the acts required by this section computed in accordance with paragraph (g)(2) of this section.

(g) *Delivery of materials, computation of direct costs.* (1) Whenever the bidder is required to deliver tender offer materials or amendments to tender offer materials, the bidder shall deliver to the subject company at the location specified by the subject company in its notice given pursuant to paragraph (a)(4) of this section a number of sets of the materials or of the amendment, as the case may be, at least equal to the approximate number of security holders specified by the subject company in such notice, together with appropriate envelopes or other containers therefor: *Provided, however,* That such delivery shall be deemed not to have been made unless the bidder has complied with paragraph (f)(3)(iii) of this section at the time the materials or amendments, as the case may be, are delivered.

(2) The approximate direct cost of mailing the bidder's tender offer materials shall be computed by adding (i) the direct cost incidental to the mailing of the subject company's last annual report to shareholders (excluding employee time), less the costs of preparation and printing of the report, and postage, plus (ii) the amount of first class postage required to mail the bidder's tender offer materials. The approximate direct costs incidental to the mailing of the amendments to the bidder's tender offer materials shall be computed by adding (iii) the estimated direct costs of preparing mailing labels, of updating shareholder lists and

17 CFR Ch. II (4-1-23 Edition)

of third party handling charges plus (iv) the amount of first class postage required to mail the bidder's amendment. Direct costs incidental to the mailing of the bidder's tender offer materials and amendments thereto when finally computed may include all reasonable charges paid by the subject company to third parties for supplies or services, including costs attendant to preparing shareholder lists, mailing labels, handling the bidder's materials, contacting participants named on security position listings and for postage, but shall exclude indirect costs, such as employee time which is devoted to either contesting or supporting the tender offer on behalf of the subject company. The final billing for direct costs shall be accompanied by an appropriate accounting in reasonable detail.

NOTE TO § 240.14d-5. Reasonably prompt methods of distribution to security holders may be used instead of mailing. If alternative methods are chosen, the approximate direct costs of distribution shall be computed by adding the estimated direct costs of preparing the document for distribution through the chosen medium (including updating of shareholder lists) plus the estimated reasonable cost of distribution through that medium. Direct costs incidental to the distribution of tender offer materials and amendments thereto may include all reasonable charges paid by the subject company to third parties for supplies or services, including costs attendant to preparing shareholder lists, handling the bidder's materials, and contacting participants named on security position listings, but shall not include indirect costs, such as employee time which is devoted to either contesting or supporting the tender offer on behalf of the subject company.

[44 FR 70342, Dec. 6, 1979, as amended at 61 FR 24657, May 15, 1996; 64 FR 61460, Nov. 10, 1999]

§ 240.14d-6 Disclosure of tender offer information to security holders.

(a) *Information required on date of commencement*—(1) *Long-form publication.* If a tender offer is published, sent or given to security holders on the date of commencement by means of long-form publication under § 240.14d-4(a)(1), the long-form publication must include the information required by paragraph (d)(1) of this section.

Securities and Exchange Commission § 240.14d-6

(2) *Summary publication.* If a tender offer is published, sent or given to security holders on the date of commencement by means of summary publication under § 240.14d-4(a)(2):

(i) The summary advertisement must contain at least the information required by paragraph (d)(2) of this section; and

(ii) The tender offer materials furnished by the bidder upon request of any security holder must include the information required by paragraph (d)(1) of this section.

(3) *Use of stockholder lists and security position listings.* If a tender offer is published, sent or given to security holders on the date of commencement by the use of stockholder lists and security position listings under § 240.14d-4(a)(3):

(i) The summary advertisement must contain at least the information required by paragraph (d)(2) of this section; and

(ii) The tender offer materials transmitted to security holders pursuant to such lists and security position listings and furnished by the bidder upon the request of any security holder must include the information required by paragraph (d)(1) of this section.

(4) *Other tender offers.* If a tender offer is published or sent or given to security holders other than pursuant to § 240.14d-4(a), the tender offer materials that are published or sent or given to security holders on the date of commencement of such offer must include the information required by paragraph (d)(1) of this section.

(b) *Information required in other tender offer materials published after commencement.* Except for tender offer materials described in paragraphs (a)(2)(ii) and (a)(3)(ii) of this section, additional tender offer materials published, sent or given to security holders after commencement must include:

(1) The identities of the bidder and subject company;

(2) The amount and class of securities being sought;

(3) The type and amount of consideration being offered; and

(4) The scheduled expiration date of the tender offer, whether the tender offer may be extended and, if so, the procedures for extension of the tender offer.

INSTRUCTION TO PARAGRAPH (b): If the additional tender offer materials are summary advertisements, they also must include the information required by paragraphs (d)(2)(v) of this section.

(c) *Material changes.* A material change in the information published or sent or given to security holders must be promptly disclosed to security holders in additional tender offer materials.

(d) *Information to be included*—(1) Tender offer materials other than summary publication. The following information is required by paragraphs (a)(1), (a)(2)(ii), (a)(3)(ii) and (a)(4) of this section:

(i) The information required by Item 1 of Schedule TO (§ 240.14d-100) (Summary Term Sheet); and

(ii) The information required by the remaining items of Schedule TO (§ 240.14d-100) for third-party tender offers, except for Item 12 (exhibits) of Schedule TO (§ 240.14d-100), or a fair and adequate summary of the information.

(2) *Summary Publication.* The following information is required in a summary advertisement under paragraphs (a)(2)(i) and (a)(3)(i) of this section:

(i) The identity of the bidder and the subject company;

(ii) The information required by Item 1004(a)(1) of Regulation M-A (§ 229.1004(a)(1) of this chapter);

(iii) If the tender offer is for less than all of the outstanding securities of a class of equity securities, a statement as to whether the purpose or one of the purposes of the tender offer is to acquire or influence control of the business of the subject company;

(iv) A statement that the information required by paragraph (d)(1) of this section is incorporated by reference into the summary advertisement;

(v) Appropriate instructions as to how security holders may obtain promptly, at the bidder's expense, the bidder's tender offer materials; and

(vi) In a tender offer published or sent or given to security holders by use of stockholder lists and security position listings under § 240.14d-4(a)(3), a statement that a request is being made for such lists and listings. The summary publication also must state that

§ 240.14d-7

tender offer materials will be mailed to record holders and will be furnished to brokers, banks and similar persons whose name appears or whose nominee appears on the list of security holders or, if applicable, who are listed as participants in a clearing agency's security position listing for subsequent transmittal to beneficial owners of such securities. If the list furnished to the bidder also included beneficial owners pursuant to § 240.14d-5(c)(1) and tender offer materials will be mailed directly to beneficial holders, include a statement to that effect.

(3) *No transmittal letter.* Neither the initial summary advertisement nor any subsequent summary advertisement may include a transmittal letter (the letter furnished to security holders for transmission of securities sought in the tender offer) or any amendment to the transmittal letter.

[64 FR 61460, Nov. 10, 1999]

§ 240.14d-7 Additional withdrawal rights.

(a) *Rights.* (1) In addition to the provisions of section 14(d)(5) of the Act, any person who has deposited securities pursuant to a tender offer has the right to withdraw any such securities during the period such offer request or invitation remains open.

(2) *Exemption during subsequent offering period.* Notwithstanding the provisions of section 14(d)(5) of the Act (15 U.S.C. 78n(d)(5)) and paragraph (a) of this section, the bidder need not offer withdrawal rights during a subsequent offering period.

(b) *Notice of withdrawal.* Notice of withdrawal pursuant to this section shall be deemed to be timely upon the receipt by the bidder's depositary of a written notice of withdrawal specifying the name(s) of the tendering stockholder(s), the number or amount of the securities to be withdrawn and the name(s) in which the certificate(s) is (are) registered, if different from that of the tendering security holder(s). A bidder may impose other reasonable requirements, including certificate numbers and a signed request for withdrawal accompanied by a signature guarantee, as conditions precedent to the physical release of withdrawn securities.

[44 FR 70345, Dec. 6, 1979, as amended at 51 FR 25882, July 17, 1986; 51 FR 32630, Sept. 15, 1986; 64 FR 61461, Nov. 10, 1999; 76 FR 71876, Nov. 21, 2011]

§ 240.14d-8 Exemption from statutory pro rata requirements.

Notwithstanding the pro rata provisions of section 14(d)(6) of the Act, if any person makes a tender offer or request or invitation for tenders, for less than all of the outstanding equity securities of a class, and if a greater number of securities are deposited pursuant thereto than such person is bound or willing to take up and pay for, the securities taken up and paid for shall be taken up and paid for as nearly as may be pro rata, disregarding fractions, according to the number of securities deposited by each depositor during the period such offer, request or invitation remains open.

(Sec. 23, 48 Stat. 901; sec. 203(a), 49 Stat. 704; sec. 8, 49 Stat. 1379; sec. 10, 78 Stat. 580; sec. 3, 82 Stat. 455; secs. 3–5, 84 Stat. 1497; sec. 18, 89 Stat. 155; 15 U.S.C. 78n(e), 78w(a))

[47 FR 57680, Dec. 28, 1982]

§ 240.14d-9 Recommendation or solicitation by the subject company and others.

(a) *Pre-commencement communications.* A communication by a person described in paragraph (e) of this section with respect to a tender offer will not be deemed to constitute a recommendation or solicitation under this section if:

(1) The tender offer has not commenced under § 240.14d-2; and

(2) The communication is filed under cover of Schedule 14D-9 (§ 240.14d-101) with the Commission no later than the date of the communication.

INSTRUCTIONS TO PARAGRAPH (a)(2): 1. The box on the front of Schedule 14D-9 (§ 240.14d-101) indicating that the filing contains pre-commencement communications must be checked.

2. Any communications made in connection with an exchange offer registered under the Securities Act of 1933 need only be filed under § 230.425 of this chapter and will be deemed filed under this section.

3. Each pre-commencement written communication must include a prominent legend in clear, plain language advising security

Securities and Exchange Commission § 240.14d-9

holders to read the company's solicitation/recommendation statement when it is available because it contains important information. The legend also must advise investors that they can get the recommendation and other filed documents for free at the Commission's web site and explain which documents are free from the filer.

4. See §§ 230.135, 230.165 and 230.166 of this chapter for pre-commencement communications made in connection with registered exchange offers.

(b) *Post-commencement communications.* After commencement by a bidder under § 240.14d-2, no solicitation or recommendation to security holders may be made by any person described in paragraph (e) of this section with respect to a tender offer for such securities unless as soon as practicable on the date such solicitation or recommendation is first published or sent or given to security holders such person complies with the following:

(1) Such person shall file with the Commission a Tender Offer Solicitation/Recommendation Statement on Schedule 14D-9 (§ 240.14d-101), including all exhibits thereto; and

(2) If such person is either the subject company or an affiliate of the subject company,

(i) Such person shall hand deliver a copy of the Schedule 14D-9 to the bidder at its principal office or at the address of the person authorized to receive notices and communications (which is set forth on the cover sheet of the bidder's Schedule TO (§ 240.14d-100) filed with the Commission; and

(ii) Such person shall give telephonic notice (which notice to the extent possible shall be given prior to the opening of the market) of the information required by Items 1003(d) and 1012(a) of Regulation M—A (§ 229.1003(d) and § 229.1012(a)) and shall mail a copy of the Schedule to each national securities exchange where the class of securities is registered and listed for trading and, if the class is authorized for quotation in the NASDAQ interdealer quotation system, to the National Association of Securities Dealers, Inc. ("NASD").

(3) If such person is neither the subject company nor an affiliate of the subject company,

(i) Such person shall mail a copy of the schedule to the bidder at its principal office or at the address of the person authorized to receive notices and communications (which is set forth on the cover sheet of the bidder's Schedule TO (§ 240.14d-100) filed with the Commission); and

(ii) Such person shall mail a copy of the Schedule to the subject company at its principal office.

(c) *Amendments.* If any material change occurs in the information set forth in the Schedule 14D-9 (§ 240.14d-101) required by this section, the person who filed such Schedule 14D-9 shall:

(1) File with the Commission an amendment on Schedule 14D-9 (§ 240.14d-101) disclosing such change promptly, but not later than the date such material is first published, sent or given to security holders; and

(2) Promptly deliver copies and give notice of the amendment in the same manner as that specified in paragraph (b)(2) or (3) of this section, whichever is applicable; and

(3) Promptly disclose and disseminate such change in a manner reasonably designed to inform security holders of such change.

(d) *Information required in solicitation or recommendation.* Any solicitation or recommendation to holders of a class of securities referred to in section 14(d)(1) of the Act with respect to a tender offer for such securities shall include the name of the person making such solicitation or recommendation and the information required by Items 1 through 8 of Schedule 14D-9 (§ 240.14d-101) or a fair and adequate summary thereof: *Provided, however,* That such solicitation or recommendation may omit any of such information previously furnished to security holders of such class of securities by such person with respect to such tender offer.

(e) *Applicability.* (1) Except as is provided in paragraphs (e)(2) and (f) of this section, this section shall only apply to the following persons:

(i) The subject company, any director, officer, employee, affiliate or subsidiary of the subject company;

(ii) Any record holder or beneficial owner of any security issued by the subject company, by the bidder, or by any affiliate of either the subject company or the bidder; and

339

§ 240.14d–10

(iii) Any person who makes a solicitation or recommendation to security holders on behalf of any of the foregoing or on behalf of the bidder other than by means of a solicitation or recommendation to security holders which has been filed with the Commission pursuant to this section or Rule 14d–3 (§ 240.14d–3).

(2) Notwithstanding paragraph (e)(1) of this section, this section shall not apply to the following persons:

(i) A bidder who has filed a Schedule TO (§ 240.14d–100) pursuant to Rule 14d–3 (§ 240.14d–3);

(ii) Attorneys, banks, brokers, fiduciaries or investment advisers who are not participating in a tender offer in more than a ministerial capacity and who furnish information and/or advice regarding such tender offer to their customers or clients on the unsolicited request of such customers or clients or solely pursuant to a contract or a relationship providing for advice to the customer or client to whom the information and/or advice is given.

(iii) Any person specified in paragraph (e)(1) of this section if:

(A) The subject company is the subject of a tender offer conducted under § 240.14d–1(c);

(B) Any person specified in paragraph (e)(1) of this section furnishes to the Commission on Form CB (§ 249.480 of this chapter) the entire informational document it publishes or otherwise disseminates to holders of the class of securities in connection with the tender offer no later than the next business day after publication or dissemination;

(C) Any person specified in paragraph (e)(1) of this section disseminates any informational document to U.S. holders, including any amendments thereto, in English, on a comparable basis to that provided to security holders in the issuer's home jurisdiction; and

(D) Any person specified in paragraph (e)(1) of this section disseminates by publication in its home jurisdiction, such person must publish the information in the United States in a manner reasonably calculated to inform U.S. security holders of the offer.

(f) *Stop-look-and-listen communication.* This section shall not apply to the subject company with respect to a communication by the subject company to its security holders which only:

(1) Identifies the tender offer by the bidder;

(2) States that such tender offer is under consideration by the subject company's board of directors and/or management;

(3) States that on or before a specified date (which shall be no later than 10 business days from the date of commencement of such tender offer) the subject company will advise such security holders of (i) whether the subject company recommends acceptance or rejection of such tender offer; expresses no opinion and remains neutral toward such tender offer; or is unable to take a position with respect to such tender offer and (ii) the reason(s) for the position taken by the subject company with respect to the tender offer (including the inability to take a position); and

(4) Requests such security holders to defer making a determination whether to accept or reject such tender offer until they have been advised of the subject company's position with respect thereto pursuant to paragraph (f)(3) of this section.

(g) *Statement of management's position.* A statement by the subject company's of its position with respect to a tender offer which is required to be published or sent or given to security holders pursuant to Rule 14e–2 shall be deemed to constitute a solicitation or recommendation within the meaning of this section and section 14(d)(4) of the Act.

[44 FR 70345, Dec. 6, 1979, as amended at 64 FR 61406, 61461, Nov. 10, 1999; 73 FR 17814, Apr. 1, 2008]

§ 240.14d–10 Equal treatment of security holders.

(a) No bidder shall make a tender offer unless:

(1) The tender offer is open to all security holders of the class of securities subject to the tender offer; and

(2) The consideration paid to any security holder for securities tendered in the tender offer is the highest consideration paid to any other security holder for securities tendered in the tender offer.

Securities and Exchange Commission §240.14d–10

(b) Paragraph (a)(1) of this section shall not:

(1) Affect dissemination under Rule 14d–4 (§240.14d–4); or

(2) Prohibit a bidder from making a tender offer excluding all security holders in a state where the bidder is prohibited from making the tender offer by administrative or judicial action pursuant to a state statute after a good faith effort by the bidder to comply with such statute.

(c) Paragraph (a)(2) of this section shall not prohibit the offer of more than one type of consideration in a tender offer, *Provided*, That:

(1) Security holders are afforded equal right to elect among each of the types of consideration offered; and

(2) The highest consideration of each type paid to any security holder is paid to any other security holder receiving that type of consideration.

(d)(1) Paragraph (a)(2) of this section shall not prohibit the negotiation, execution or amendment of an employment compensation, severance or other employee benefit arrangement, or payments made or to be made or benefits granted or to be granted according to such an arrangement, with respect to any security holder of the subject company, where the amount payable under the arrangement:

(i) Is being paid or granted as compensation for past services performed, future services to be performed, or future services to be refrained from performing, by the security holder (and matters incidental thereto); and

(ii) Is not calculated based on the number of securities tendered or to be tendered in the tender offer by the security holder.

(2) The provisions of paragraph (d)(1) of this section shall be satisfied and, therefore, pursuant to this non-exclusive safe harbor, the negotiation, execution or amendment of an arrangement and any payments made or to be made or benefits granted or to be granted according to that arrangement shall not be prohibited by paragraph (a)(2) of this section, if the arrangement is approved as an employment compensation, severance or other employee benefit arrangement solely by independent directors as follows:

(i) The compensation committee or a committee of the board of directors that performs functions similar to a compensation committee of the subject company approves the arrangement, regardless of whether the subject company is a party to the arrangement, or, if the bidder is a party to the arrangement, the compensation committee or a committee of the board of directors that performs functions similar to a compensation committee of the bidder approves the arrangement; or

(ii) If the subject company's or bidder's board of directors, as applicable, does not have a compensation committee or a committee of the board of directors that performs functions similar to a compensation committee or if none of the members of the subject company's or bidder's compensation committee or committee that performs functions similar to a compensation committee is independent, a special committee of the board of directors formed to consider and approve the arrangement approves the arrangement; or

(iii) If the subject company or bidder, as applicable, is a foreign private issuer, any or all members of the board of directors or any committee of the board of directors authorized to approve employment compensation, severance or other employee benefit arrangements under the laws or regulations of the home country approves the arrangement.

INSTRUCTIONS TO PARAGRAPH (d)(2): For purposes of determining whether the members of the committee approving an arrangement in accordance with the provisions of paragraph (d)(2) of this section are independent, the following provisions shall apply:

1. If the bidder or subject company, as applicable, is a listed issuer (as defined in §240.10A–3 of this chapter) whose securities are listed either on a national securities exchange registered pursuant to section 6(a) of the Exchange Act (15 U.S.C. 78f(a)) or in an inter-dealer quotation system of a national securities association registered pursuant to section 15A(a) of the Exchange Act (15 U.S.C. 78o–3(a)) that has independence requirements for compensation committee members that have been approved by the Commission (as those requirements may be modified or supplemented), apply the bidder's or subject company's definition of independence that it uses for determining that the members of

§ 240.14d-11

the compensation committee are independent in compliance with the listing standards applicable to compensation committee members of the listed issuer.

2. If the bidder or subject company, as applicable, is not a listed issuer (as defined in § 240.10A-3 of this chapter), apply the independence requirements for compensation committee members of a national securities exchange registered pursuant to section 6(a) of the Exchange Act (15 U.S.C. 78f(a)) or an inter-dealer quotation system of a national securities association registered pursuant to section 15A(a) of the Exchange Act (15 U.S.C. 78o-3(a)) that have been approved by the Commission (as those requirements may be modified or supplemented). Whatever definition the bidder or subject company, as applicable, chooses, it must apply that definition consistently to all members of the committee approving the arrangement.

3. Notwithstanding Instructions 1 and 2 to paragraph (d)(2), if the bidder or subject company, as applicable, is a closed-end investment company registered under the Investment Company Act of 1940, a director is considered to be independent if the director is not, other than in his or her capacity as a member of the board of directors or any board committee, an "interested person" of the investment company, as defined in section 2(a)(19) of the Investment Company Act of 1940 (15 U.S.C. 80a-2(a)(19)).

4. If the bidder or the subject company, as applicable, is a foreign private issuer, apply either the independence standards set forth in Instructions 1 and 2 to paragraph (d)(2) or the independence requirements of the laws, regulations, codes or standards of the home country of the bidder or subject company, as applicable, for members of the board of directors or the committee of the board of directors approving the arrangement.

5. A determination by the bidder's or the subject company's board of directors, as applicable, that the members of the board of directors or the committee of the board of directors, as applicable, approving an arrangement in accordance with the provisions of paragraph (d)(2) are independent in accordance with the provisions of this instruction to paragraph (d)(2) shall satisfy the independence requirements of paragraph (d)(2).

INSTRUCTION TO PARAGRAPH (d): The fact that the provisions of paragraph (d) of this section extend only to employment compensation, severance and other employee benefit arrangements and not to other arrangements, such as commercial arrangements, does not raise any inference that a payment under any such other arrangement constitutes consideration paid for securities in a tender offer.

(e) If the offer and sale of securities constituting consideration offered in a tender offer is prohibited by the appropriate authority of a state after a good faith effort by the bidder to register or qualify the offer and sale of such securities in such state:

(1) The bidder may offer security holders in such state an alternative form of consideration; and

(2) Paragraph (c) of this section shall not operate to require the bidder to offer or pay the alternative form of consideration to security holders in any other state.

(f) This section shall not apply to any tender offer with respect to which the Commission, upon written request or upon its own motion, either unconditionally or on specified terms and conditions, determines that compliance with this section is not necessary or appropriate in the public interest or for the protection of investors.

[51 FR 25882, July 17, 1986, as amended at 71 FR 65408, Nov. 8, 2006]

§ 240.14d-11 Subsequent offering period.

A bidder may elect to provide a subsequent offering period of at least three business days during which tenders will be accepted if:

(a) The initial offering period of at least 20 business days has expired;

(b) The offer is for all outstanding securities of the class that is the subject of the tender offer, and if the bidder is offering security holders a choice of different forms of consideration, there is no ceiling on any form of consideration offered;

(c) The bidder immediately accepts and promptly pays for all securities tendered during the initial offering period;

(d) The bidder announces the results of the tender offer, including the approximate number and percentage of securities deposited to date, no later than 9:00 a.m. Eastern time on the next business day after the expiration date of the initial offering period and immediately begins the subsequent offering period;

(e) The bidder immediately accepts and promptly pays for all securities as they are tendered during the subsequent offering period; and

Securities and Exchange Commission

§ 240.14d–100

(f) The bidder offers the same form and amount of consideration to security holders in both the initial and the subsequent offering period.

NOTE TO § 240.14d–11: No withdrawal rights apply during the subsequent offering period in accordance with § 240.14d–7(a)(2).

[64 FR 61462, Nov. 10, 1999, as amended at 73 FR 60092, Oct. 9, 2008]

§ 240.14d–100 Schedule TO. Tender offer statement under section 14(d)(1) or 13(e)(1) of the Securities Exchange Act of 1934.

Securities and Exchange Commission,
Washington, D.C. 20549

Schedule TO

Tender Offer Statement under Section 14(d)(1) or 13(e)(1) of the Securities Exchange Act of 1934

(Amendment No. _____)*

_____

(Name of Subject Company (issuer))

_____

(Names of Filing Persons (identifying status as offeror, issuer or other person))

_____

(Title of Class of Securities)

_____

(CUSIP Number of Class of Securities)

(Name, address, and telephone numbers of person authorized to receive notices and communications on behalf of filing persons)

[ ] Check the box if the filing relates solely to preliminary communications made before the commencement of a tender offer.

Check the appropriate boxes below to designate any transactions to which the statement relates:

[ ] third-party tender offer subject to Rule 14d–1.

[ ] issuer tender offer subject to Rule 13e–4.

[ ] going-private transaction subject to Rule 13e–3.

[ ] amendment to Schedule 13D under Rule 13d–2.

Check the following box if the filing is a final amendment reporting the results of the tender offer: [ ]

If applicable, check the appropriate box(es) below to designate the appropriate rule provision(s) relied upon:

[ ] Rule 13e–4(i) (Cross-Border Issuer Tender Offer)

[ ] Rule 14d–1(d) (Cross-Border Third-Party Tender Offer)

General Instructions:

A. File eight copies of the statement, including all exhibits, with the Commission if paper filing is permitted.

B. This filing must be accompanied by a fee payable to the Commission as required by § 240.0–11.

C. If the statement is filed by a general or limited partnership, syndicate or other group, the information called for by Items 3 and 5–8 for a third-party tender offer and Items 5–8 for an issuer tender offer must be given with respect to: (i) Each partner of the general partnership; (ii) each partner who is, or functions as, a general partner of the limited partnership; (iii) each member of the syndicate or group; and (iv) each person controlling the partner or member. If the statement is filed by a corporation or if a person referred to in (i), (ii), (iii) or (iv) of this Instruction is a corporation, the information called for by the items specified above must be given with respect to: (a) Each executive officer and director of the corporation; (b) each person controlling the corporation; and (c) each executive officer and director of any corporation or other person ultimately in control of the corporation.

D. If the filing contains only preliminary communications made before the commencement of a tender offer, no signature or filing fee is required. The filer need not respond to the items in the schedule. Any pre-commencement communications that are filed under cover of this schedule need not be incorporated by reference into the schedule.

E. If an item is inapplicable or the answer is in the negative, so state. The statement published, sent or given to security holders may omit negative and not applicable responses. If the schedule includes any information that is not published, sent or given to security holders, provide that information or specifically incorporate it by reference under the appropriate item number and heading in the schedule. Do not recite the text of disclosure requirements in the schedule or any document published, sent or given to security holders. Indicate clearly the coverage of the requirements without referring to the text of the items.

F. Information contained in exhibits to the statement may be incorporated by reference in answer or partial answer to any item unless it would render the answer misleading, incomplete, unclear or confusing. A copy of any information that is incorporated by reference or a copy of the pertinent pages of a document containing the information must be submitted with this statement as an exhibit, unless it was previously filed with the Commission electronically on EDGAR. If an exhibit contains information responding to more than one item in the schedule, all information in that exhibit may be incorporated by reference once in response to the several items in the schedule for which it provides an answer. Information incorporated by reference is deemed filed with the Commission for all purposes of the Act.

§ 240.14d–100

G. A filing person may amend its previously filed Schedule 13D (§ 240.13d–101) on Schedule TO (§ 240.14d–100) if the appropriate box on the cover page is checked to indicate a combined filing and the information called for by the fourteen disclosure items on the cover page of Schedule 13D (§ 240.13d–101) is provided on the cover page of the combined filing with respect to each filing person.

H. The final amendment required by § 240.14d–3(b)(2) and § 240.13e–4(c)(4) will satisfy the reporting requirements of section 13(d) of the Act with respect to all securities acquired by the offeror in the tender offer.

I. Amendments disclosing a material change in the information set forth in this statement may omit any information previously disclosed in this statement.

J. If the tender offer disclosed on this statement involves a going-private transaction, a combined Schedule TO (§ 240.14d–100) and Schedule 13E–3 (§ 240.13e–100) may be filed with the Commission under cover of Schedule TO. The Rule 13e–3 box on the cover page of the Schedule TO must be checked to indicate a combined filing. All information called for by both schedules must be provided except that Items 1–3, 5, 8 and 9 of Schedule TO may be omitted to the extent those items call for information that duplicates the item requirements in Schedule 13E–3.

K. For purposes of this statement, the following definitions apply:

(1) The term *offeror* means any person who makes a tender offer or on whose behalf a tender offer is made;

(2) The term *issuer tender offer* has the same meaning as in Rule 13e–4(a)(2); and

(3) The term third-party tender offer means a tender offer that is not an issuer tender offer.

SPECIAL INSTRUCTIONS FOR COMPLYING WITH SCHEDULE TO

Under Sections 13(e), 14(d) and 23 of the Act and the rules and regulations of the Act, the Commission is authorized to solicit the information required to be supplied by this schedule.

Disclosure of the information specified in this schedule is mandatory. The information will be used for the primary purpose of disclosing tender offer and going-private transactions. This statement will be made a matter of public record. Therefore, any information given will be available for inspection by any member of the public.

Because of the public nature of the information, the Commission can use it for a variety of purposes, including referral to other governmental authorities or securities self-regulatory organizations for investigatory purposes or in connection with litigation involving the federal securities laws or other civil, criminal or regulatory statutes or provisions.

Failure to disclose the information required by this schedule may result in civil or criminal action against the persons involved for violation of the federal securities laws and rules.

Item 1. Summary Term Sheet

Furnish the information required by Item 1001 of Regulation M-A (§ 229.1001 of this chapter) unless information is disclosed to security holders in a prospectus that meets the requirements of § 230.421(d) of this chapter.

Item 2. Subject Company Information

Furnish the information required by Item 1002(a) through (c) of Regulation M-A (§ 229.1002 of this chapter).

Item 3. Identity and Background of Filing Person

Furnish the information required by Item 1003(a) through (c) of Regulation M-A (§ 229.1003 of this chapter) for a third-party tender offer and the information required by Item 1003(a) of Regulation M-A (§ 229.1003 of this chapter) for an issuer tender offer.

Item 4. Terms of the Transaction

Furnish the information required by Item 1004(a) of Regulation M-A (§ 229.1004 of this chapter) for a third-party tender offer and the information required by Item 1004(a) through (b) of Regulation M-A (§ 229.1004 of this chapter) for an issuer tender offer.

Item 5. Past Contacts, Transactions, Negotiations and Agreements

Furnish the information required by Item 1005(a) and (b) of Regulation M-A (§ 229.1005 of this chapter) for a third-party tender offer and the information required by Item 1005(e) of Regulation M-A (§ 229.1005) for an issuer tender offer.

Item 6. Purposes of the Transaction and Plans or Proposals

Furnish the information required by Item 1006(a) and (c)(1) through (7) of Regulation M-A (§ 229.1006 of this chapter) for a third-party tender offer and the information required by Item 1006(a) through (c) of Regulation M-A (§ 229.1006 of this chapter) for an issuer tender offer.

Item 7. Source and Amount of Funds or Other Consideration

Furnish the information required by Item 1007(a), (b) and (d) of Regulation M-A (§ 229.1007 of this chapter).

Securities and Exchange Commission § 240.14d–100

Item 8. Interest in Securities of the Subject Company

Furnish the information required by Item 1008 of Regulation M-A (§ 229.1008 of this chapter).

Item 9. Persons/Assets, Retained, Employed, Compensated or Used

Furnish the information required by Item 1009(a) of Regulation M-A (§ 229.1009 of this chapter).

Item 10. Financial Statements

If material, furnish the information required by Item 1010(a) and (b) of Regulation M-A (§ 229.1010 of this chapter) for the issuer in an issuer tender offer and for the offeror in a third-party tender offer.

Instructions to Item 10: 1. Financial statements must be provided when the offeror's financial condition is material to security holder's decision whether to sell, tender or hold the securities sought. The facts and circumstances of a tender offer, particularly the terms of the tender offer, may influence a determination as to whether financial statements are material, and thus required to be disclosed.

2. Financial statements are *not* considered material when: (a) The consideration offered consists solely of cash; (b) the offer is not subject to any financing condition; *and* either: (c) the offeror is a public reporting company under Section 13(a) or 15(d) of the Act that files reports electronically on EDGAR, or (d) the offer is for all outstanding securities of the subject class. Financial information may be required, however, in a two-tier transaction. *See* Instruction 5 below.

3. The filing person may incorporate by reference financial statements contained in any document filed with the Commission, solely for the purposes of this schedule, if: (a) The financial statements substantially meet the requirements of this item; (b) an express statement is made that the financial statements are incorporated by reference; (c) the information incorporated by reference is clearly identified by page, paragraph, caption or otherwise; and (d) if the information incorporated by reference is not filed with this schedule, an indication is made where the information may be inspected and copies obtained. Financial statements that are required to be presented in comparative form for two or more fiscal years or periods may not be incorporated by reference unless the material incorporated by reference includes the entire period for which the comparative data is required to be given. *See* General Instruction F to this schedule.

4. If the offeror in a third-party tender offer is a natural person, and such person's financial information is material, disclose the net worth of the offeror. If the offeror's net worth is derived from material amounts of assets that are not readily marketable or there are material guarantees and contingencies, disclose the nature and approximate amount of the individual's net worth that consists of illiquid assets and the magnitude of any guarantees or contingencies that may negatively affect the natural person's net worth.

5. Pro forma financial information is required in a negotiated third-party cash tender offer when securities are intended to be offered in a subsequent merger or other transaction in which remaining target securities are acquired and the acquisition of the subject company is significant to the offeror under § 210.11–01(b)(1) of this chapter. The offeror must disclose the financial information specified in Item 3(f) and Item 5 of Form S–4 (§ 239.25 of this chapter) in the schedule filed with the Commission, but may furnish only the summary financial information specified in Item 3(d), (e) and (f) of Form S–4 in the disclosure document sent to security holders. If pro forma financial information is required by this instruction, the historical financial statements specified in Item 1010 of Regulation M-A (§ 229.1010 of this chapter) are required for the bidder.

6. The disclosure materials disseminated to security holders may contain the summarized financial information specified by Item 1010(c) of Regulation M-A (§ 229.1010 of this chapter) instead of the financial information required by Item 1010(a) and (b). In that case, the financial information required by Item 1010(a) and (b) of Regulation M-A must be disclosed in the statement. If summarized financial information is disseminated to security holders, include appropriate instructions on how more complete financial information can be obtained. If the summarized financial information is prepared on the basis of a comprehensive body of accounting principles other than U.S. GAAP, the summarized financial information must be accompanied by a reconciliation as described in Instruction 8 of this Item.

7. If the offeror is not subject to the periodic reporting requirements of the Act, the financial statements required by this Item need not be audited if audited financial statements are not available or obtainable without unreasonable cost or expense. Make a statement to that effect and the reasons for their unavailability.

8. If the financial statements required by this Item are prepared on the basis of a comprehensive body of accounting principles other than U.S. GAAP, provide a reconciliation to U.S. GAAP in accordance with Item 17 of Form 20–F (§ 249.220f of this chapter), unless a reconciliation is unavailable or not obtainable without unreasonable cost or expense. At a minimum, however, when financial statements are prepared on a basis other than U.S. GAAP, a narrative description of

§ 240.14d–100

all material variations in accounting principles, practices and methods used in preparing the non-U.S. GAAP financial statements from those accepted in the U.S. must be presented.

Item 11. Additional Information.

Furnish the information required by Item 1011(a) and (c) of Regulation M–A (§ 229.1011 of this chapter).

Item 12. Exhibits

File each of the following as an exhibit to the Schedule:

(a) All documents specified in Item 1016(a), (b), (d), (g) and (h) of Regulation M–A (§ 229.1016 of this chapter); and

(b) The transaction valuation, fee rate, amount of filing fee and, as applicable, information relating to reliance on § 240.0–11(a)(2) in the tabular form indicated.

CALCULATION OF FILING FEE TABLES

TABLE 1—TRANSACTION VALUATION

	Transaction valuation	Fee rate	Amount of filing fee
Fees to Be Paid	X	X	X
Fees Previously Paid	X		X
Total Transaction Valuation	X		
Total Fees Due for Filing			X
Total Fees Previously Paid			X
Total Fee Offsets			X
Net Fee Due			X

TABLE 2—FEE OFFSET CLAIMS AND SOURCES

	Registrant or filer name	Form or filing type	File number	Initial filing date	Filing date	Fee offset claimed	Fee paid with fee offset source
Fee Offset Claims		X	X	X		X	
Fee Offset Sources	X	X	X		X		X

Instructions to the Calculation of Filing Fee Tables and Related Disclosure ("Instructions"):

1. General Requirements.

A. Applicable Table Requirements.

The "X" designation indicates the information required to be disclosed, as applicable, in tabular format. Add as many rows of each table as necessary.

B. Fee Rate.

For the current fee rate, *see* *https:// www.sec.gov/ofm/Article/feeamt.html.*

C. Explanations.

If not otherwise explained in response to these instructions, disclose specific details relating to the fee calculation as necessary to clarify the information presented in each table, including references to the applicable provisions of Rule 0–11 (§ 240.0–11 of this chapter). All disclosure these Instructions require that is not specifically required to be presented in tabular format must appear in narrative format immediately after the table(s) to which it corresponds.

D. Submission Method.

If a filing fee exhibit is required to be provided pursuant to this Item 12(b), it must be submitted as required by Rule 408 of Regulation S–T (§ 232.408 of this chapter).

2. Table 1: Transaction Valuation Table and Related Disclosure.

A. Fees to Be Paid and Fees Previously Paid.

i. Fees to Be Paid.

Provide the information Table 1 requires for the line item "Fees to Be Paid" as follows:

a. Initial Filings.

For an initial filing on this schedule, provide the required information for the total transaction valuation.

b. Amendments with Then-Current Total Transaction Valuation Higher than Highest

Securities and Exchange Commission

§ 240.14d–100

Total Transaction Valuation Previously Reported. For amendments to this schedule that reflect a then-current total transaction valuation higher than the highest total transaction valuation previously reported, provide the required information for the incremental increase.

ii. Fees Previously Paid.

Provide the information Table 1 requires for the line item "Fees Previously Paid" for the prior initial filing or amendment to this schedule that reflected a then-current total transaction valuation that was the highest total transaction valuation previously reported.

B. Other Tabular Information.

Provide the following information in the table for the line items "Fees to Be Paid" and "Fees Previously Paid", as applicable:

i. The transaction valuation computed pursuant to Exchange Act Rule 0–11;

ii. The fee rate; and

iii. The filing fee due without regard to any previous payments or offsets.

C. Totals.

i. Total Transaction Valuation.

Provide the sum of the transaction valuations for the line items "Fees to Be Paid" and "Fees Previously Paid."

ii. Total Fees Due for Filing.

Provide the sum of the fees due without regard to any previous payments or offsets for the line items "Fees to Be Paid" and "Fees Previously Paid."

iii. Total Fees Previously Paid.

Provide the aggregate of filing fees previously paid with this filing.

iv. Total Fee Offsets.

Provide the aggregate of the fee offsets that are claimed in Table 2 pursuant to Instruction 3.

v. Net Fee Due.

Provide the difference between (a) the total fees due for this schedule from the Total Fees Due for Filing row; and (b) the sum of (i) the aggregate of filing fees previously paid from the Total Fees Previously Paid row; and (ii) the aggregate fee offsets claimed from the Total Fee Offsets row.

D. Narrative Disclosure.

Explain how the transaction valuation was determined.

3. Table 2: Fee Offset Claims and Sources.

A. Terminology.

For purposes of this Instruction 3 and Table 2, the term "submission" means any (i) initial filing of, or amendment (pre-effective or post-effective), to a fee-bearing document; or (ii) fee-bearing form of prospectus filed under Rule 424 under the Securities Act (§ 230.424 of this chapter), in all cases that was accompanied by a contemporaneous fee payment. For purposes of these instructions to Table 2, a contemporaneous fee payment is the payment of a required fee that is satisfied through the actual transfer of funds, and does not include any amount of a required fee satisfied through a claimed fee offset. Instruction 3.B.ii requires a filer that claims a fee offset under Rule 0–11(a)(2) to identify previous submissions with contemporaneous fee payments that are the original source to which the fee offsets claimed on this filing can be traced. See Instruction 3.C for an example.

B. Rule 0–11(a)(2).

If relying on Rule 0–11(a)(2) to offset some or all of the filing fee due on this tender offer statement by amounts paid in connection with earlier filings (other than this Schedule TO) relating to the same transaction, provide the following information:

i. Fee Offset Claims.

For each earlier filed Securities Act registration statement or Exchange Act document relating to the same transaction from which a fee offset is being claimed, provide the information that Table 2 requires for the line item "Fee Offset Claims". The "Fee Offset Claimed" column requires the dollar amount of the previously paid filing fee to be offset against the currently due fee.

Note to Instruction 3.B.i.

If claiming an offset from a Securities Act registration statement, provide a detailed explanation of the basis for the claimed offset.

ii. Fee Offset Sources.

With respect to amounts claimed as an offset under Rule 0–11(a)(2), identify those submissions with contemporaneous fee payments that are the original source to which those amounts can be traced. For each submission identified, provide the information that Table 2 requires for the line item "Fee Offset Sources". The "Fee Paid with Fee Offset Source" column requires the dollar amount of the contemporaneous fee payment made with respect to each identified submission that is the source of the fee offset claimed pursuant to Rule 0–11(a)(2).

C. Fee Offset Source Submission Identification Example.

A filer:

• Initially files a registration statement on Form S–1 on 1/15/20X1 (assigned file number 333–123456) with a fee payment of $10,000;

• Files pre-effective amendment number 1 to the Form S–1 (333–123456) on 2/15/20X1 with a fee payment of $15,000 and the registration statement goes effective on 2/20/20X1;

• Initially files a registration statement on Form S–1 on 1/15/20X4 (assigned file number 333–123467) with a fee payment of $25,000 and relies on Rule 457(p) to claim an offset of $10,000 related to the unsold securities registered on the previously filed Form S–1 (333–123456) and apply it to the $35,000 filing fee due and the registration statement goes effective on 2/15/20X4.

• Initially files a registration statement related to a tender offer on Form S–4 (assigned file number 333–123478) on 1/15/20X7 with a fee payment of $15,000 and relies on

§ 240.14d–101

Rule 457(p) to claim an offset of $30,000 related to the unsold securities registered on the most recently effective Form S-1 (333-123467) filed on 1/15/20X4 and apply it to the $45,000 filing fee due.
• Initially files a Schedule TO related to the same tender offer on 1/22/20X7 and relies on Rule 0–11(a)(2) to claim an offset of $45,000 from the fee paid directly and by offset claimed on the Form S-4 (333-123478) filed 1/15/20X7 and apply it to the $45,000 filing fee due.

For the Schedule TO filed on 1/22/20X7, the filer can satisfy the submission identification requirement when it claims the $45,000 fee offset from the Form S-4 (333-123478) filed on 1/15/20X7 by referencing any combination of the Form S-4 (333-123478) filed on 1/15/20X7, the Form S-1 (333-123467) filed on 1/15/20X4, the pre-effective amendment to the Form S-1 (333-123456) filed on 2/15/20X1 or the initial filing of the Form S-1 (333-123456) on 1/15/20X1 in relation to which contemporaneous fee payments were made equal to $45,000.

One example could be:
• The Form S-4 (333-123478) filed on 1/15/20X7 in relation to the payment of $15,000 made with that submission;
• the Form S-1 (333-123467) filed on 1/15/20X4 in relation to the payment of $25,000 made with that submission; and
• the pre-effective amendment to the Form S-1 (333-123456) filed on 2/15/20X1 in relation to the payment of $5,000 out of the payment of $15,000 made with that submission (it would not matter if the filer cited to this pre-effective amendment and/or the initial submission of this Form S-1 (333-123456) on 1/15/20X1 as long as singly or together they were cited as relating to a total of $5,000 in this example).

In this example, the filer could not satisfy the submission identification requirement solely by citing to the Form S-4 (333-123478) filed on 1/15/20X7 because even though the offset claimed and available from that filing was $45,000, the contemporaneous fee payment made with that filing ($15,000) was less than the offset being claimed. As a result, the filer must also identify a prior submission or submissions with an aggregate of contemporaneous fee payment(s) of $30,000 as the original source(s) to which the rest of the claimed offset can be traced.

Item 13. Information Required by Schedule 13E–3

If the Schedule TO is combined with Schedule 13E–3 (§ 240.13e–100), set forth the information required by Schedule 13E–3 that is not included or covered by the items in Schedule TO.

Signature. After due inquiry and to the best of my knowledge and belief, I certify that the information set forth in this statement is true, complete and correct.

_____
(Signature)

_____
(Name and title)

_____
(Date)

Instruction to Signature: The statement must be signed by the filing person or that person's authorized representative. If the statement is signed on behalf of a person by an authorized representative (other than an executive officer of a corporation or general partner of a partnership), evidence of the representative's authority to sign on behalf of the person must be filed with the statement. The name and any title of each person who signs the statement must be typed or printed beneath the signature. See §§ 240.12b–11 and 240.14d–1(h) with respect to signature requirements.

[64 FR 61462, Nov. 10, 1999, as amended at 72 FR 45112, Aug. 10, 2007; 73 FR 17814, Apr. 1, 2008; 73 FR 60093, Oct. 9, 2008; 76 FR 6046, Feb. 2, 2011; 86 FR 70259, Dec. 9, 2021]

§ 240.14d–101 Schedule 14D–9.

Securities and Exchange Commission
Washington, D.C. 20549
Schedule 14D–9
Solicitation/Recommendation Statement under Section 14(d)(4) of the Securities Exchange Act of 1934
(Amendment No. _____)

_____
(Name of Subject Company)

_____
(Names of Persons Filing Statement)

_____
(Title of Class of Securities)

_____
(CUSIP Number of Class of Securities)

_____
(Name, address, and telephone numbers of person authorized to receive notices and communications on behalf of the persons filing statement)

[ ] Check the box if the filing relates solely to preliminary communications made before the commencement of a tender offer.

General Instructions:

A. File eight copies of the statement, including all exhibits, with the Commission if paper filing is permitted.

B. If the filing contains only preliminary communications made before the commencement of a tender offer, no signature is required. The filer need not respond to the items in the schedule. Any pre-commencement communications that are filed under cover of this schedule need not be incorporated by reference into the schedule.

C. If an item is inapplicable or the answer is in the negative, so state. The statement

Securities and Exchange Commission § 240.14d–102

published, sent or given to security holders may omit negative and not applicable responses. If the schedule includes any information that is not published, sent or given to security holders, provide that information or specifically incorporate it by reference under the appropriate item number and heading in the schedule. Do not recite the text of disclosure requirements in the schedule or any document published, sent or given to security holders. Indicate clearly the coverage of the requirements without referring to the text of the items.

D. Information contained in exhibits to the statement may be incorporated by reference in answer or partial answer to any item unless it would render the answer misleading, incomplete, unclear or confusing. A copy of any information that is incorporated by reference or a copy of the pertinent pages of a document containing the information must be submitted with this statement as an exhibit, unless it was previously filed with the Commission electronically on EDGAR. If an exhibit contains information responding to more than one item in the schedule, all information in that exhibit may be incorporated by reference once in response to the several items in the schedule for which it provides an answer. Information incorporated by reference is deemed filed with the Commission for all purposes of the Act.

E. Amendments disclosing a material change in the information set forth in this statement may omit any information previously disclosed in this statement.

Item 1. Subject Company Information

Furnish the information required by Item 1002(a) and (b) of Regulation M-A (§ 229.1002 of this chapter).

Item 2. Identity and Background of Filing Person

Furnish the information required by Item 1003(a) and (d) of Regulation M-A (§ 229.1003 of this chapter).

Item 3. Past Contacts, Transactions, Negotiations and Agreements

Furnish the information required by Item 1005(d) of Regulation M-A (§ 229.1005 of this chapter).

Item 4. The Solicitation or Recommendation

Furnish the information required by Item 1012(a) through (c) of Regulation M-A (§ 229.1012 of this chapter).

Item 5. Person/Assets, Retained, Employed, Compensated or Used

Furnish the information required by Item 1009(a) of Regulation M-A (§ 229.1009 of this chapter).

Item 6. Interest in Securities of the Subject Company

Furnish the information required by Item 1008(b) of Regulation M-A (§ 229.1008 of this chapter).

Item 7. Purposes of the Transaction and Plans or Proposals

Furnish the information required by Item 1006(d) of Regulation M-A (§ 229.1006 of this chapter).

Item 8. Additional Information

Furnish the information required by Item 1011(b) and (c) of Regulation M-A (§ 229.1011 of this chapter).

Item 9. Exhibits

File as an exhibit to the Schedule all documents specified by Item 1016(a), (e) and (g) of Regulation M-A (§ 229.1016 of this chapter).

Signature. After due inquiry and to the best of my knowledge and belief, I certify that the information set forth in this statement is true, complete and correct.

_____
(Signature)

_____
(Name and title)

_____
(Date)

Instruction to Signature: The statement must be signed by the filing person or that person's authorized representative. If the statement is signed on behalf of a person by an authorized representative (other than an executive officer of a corporation or general partner of a partnership), evidence of the representative's authority to sign on behalf of the person must be filed with the statement. The name and any title of each person who signs the statement must be typed or printed beneath the signature. See § 240.14d–1(h) with respect to signature requirements.

[64 FR 61464, Nov. 10, 1999, as amended at 73 FR 17814, Apr. 1, 2008; 76 FR 6046, Feb. 2, 2011]

§ 240.14d–102 Schedule 14D–1F. Tender offer statement pursuant to rule 14d–1(b) under the Securities Exchange Act of 1934.

Securities and Exchange Commission

Washington, DC

Schedule 14D–1F

Tender Offer Statement Pursuant to Rule 14d–1(b) Under the Securities Exchange Act of 1934

[Amendment No. _____]

_____
(Name of Subject Company [Issuer])

§ 240.14d-102

_____
(Translation of Subject Company's [Issuer's] name into English (if applicable))

_____
(Jurisdiction of Subject Company's [Issuer's] Incorporation or Organization)

_____
(Bidder)

_____
(Title of Class of Securities)

_____
(CUSIP Number of Class of Securities (if applicable))

_____
(Name, address (including zip code) and telephone number (including area code) of person(s) authorized to receive notices and communications on behalf of bidder)

_____
(Date tender offer first published, sent or given to securityholders)

General Instructions

I. ELIGIBILITY REQUIREMENTS FOR USE OF SCHEDULE 14D-1F

A. Schedule 14D-1F may be used by any person making a cash tender or exchange offer (the "bidder") for securities of any issuer incorporated or organized under the laws of Canada or any Canadian province or territory that is a foreign private issuer, where less than 40 percent of the outstanding class of such issuer's securities that is the subject of the offer is held by U.S. holders. The calculation of U.S. holders shall be made as of the end of the subject issuer's last quarter or, if such quarter terminated within 60 days of the filing date, as of the end of such issuer's preceding quarter.

Instructions

1. For purposes of this Schedule, "foreign private issuer" shall be construed in accordance with Rule 405 under the Securities Act.

2. For purposes of this Schedule, the term "U.S. holder" shall mean any person whose address appears on the records of the issuer, any voting trustee, any depositary, any share transfer agent or any person acting in a similar capacity on behalf of the issuer as being located in the United States.

3. With respect to any tender offer, including any exchange offer, otherwise eligible to proceed in accordance with Rule 14d-1(b) under the Securities Exchange Act of 1934 (the "Exchange Act"), the issuer of the subject securities will be presumed to be a foreign private issuer and U.S. holders will be presumed to hold less than 40 percent of such outstanding securities, unless (a) the aggregate trading volume of that class on national securities exchanges in the United States and on NASDAQ exceeded its aggregate trading volume on securities exchanges in Canada and on the Canadian Dealing Network, Inc. ("CDN") over the 12 calendar month period prior to commencement of this offer, or if commenced in response to a prior offer, over the 12 calendar month period prior to commencement of the initial offer (based on volume figures published by such exchanges and NASDAQ and CDN); (b) the most recent annual report or annual information form filed or submitted by the issuer with securities regulators of Ontario, Quebec, British Columbia or Alberta (or, if the issuer of the subject securities is not a reporting issuer in any of such provinces, with any other Canadian securities regulator) or with the Commission indicates that U.S. holders hold 40 percent or more of the subject class of securities; or (c) the offeror has actual knowledge that the level of U.S. ownership equals or exceeds 40 percent of such securities.

4. If this Schedule is filed during the pendency of one or more ongoing cash tender or exchange offers for securities of the class subject to this offer that was commenced or was eligible to be commenced on Schedule 13E-4F, Schedule 14D-1F and/or Form F-8 or Form F-80, the date for calculation of U.S. ownership for purposes of this Schedule shall be the same as that date used by the initial bidder or issuer.

5. For purposes of this Schedule, the class of subject securities shall not include any securities that may be converted into or are exchangeable for the subject securities.

B. Any bidder using this Schedule must extend the cash tender or exchange offer to U.S. holders of securities of the subject company upon terms and conditions not less favorable than those extended to any other holder of such securities, and must comply with the requirements of any Canadian federal, provincial and/or territorial law, regulation or policy relating to the terms and conditions of the offer.

C. This Schedule shall not be used if the subject company is an investment company registered or required to be registered under the Investment Company Act of 1940.

D. This Schedule shall not be used to comply with the reporting requirements of section 13(d) of the Exchange Act. Persons using this Schedule are reminded of their obligation to file or update a Schedule 13D where required by section 13(d)(1) of the Exchange Act and the Commission's rules and regulations thereunder.

II. FILING INSTRUCTIONS AND FEE

A.(1) The bidder must file this Schedule and any amendment to the Schedule (see Part I, Item 1.(b)), including all exhibits and other documents filed as part of the Schedule or amendment, in electronic format via the Commission's Electronic Data Gathering, Analysis, and Retrieval (EDGAR) system in accordance with the EDGAR rules set forth in Regulation S-T (17 CFR Part 232). For assistance with technical questions about EDGAR or to request an access code,

Securities and Exchange Commission § 240.14d-102

call the EDGAR Filer Support Office at (202) 551-8900. For assistance with the EDGAR rules, call the Office of EDGAR and Information Analysis at (202) 551-3610.

(2) If filing the Schedule in paper under a hardship exemption in 17 CFR 232.201 or 232.202 of Regulation S-T, or as otherwise permitted, the bidder must file with the Commission at its principal office five copies of the complete Schedule and any amendment, including exhibits and all other documents filed as a part of the Schedule or amendment. The bidder must bind, staple or otherwise compile each copy in one or more parts without stiff covers. The bidder must further bind the Schedule or amendment on the side or stitching margin in a manner that leaves the reading matter legible. The bidder must provide three additional copies of the Schedule or amendment without exhibits to the Commission.

B. An electronic filer must provide the signatures required for the Schedule or amendment in accordance with 17 CFR 232.302 of Regulation S-T. A bidder filing in paper must have the original and at least one copy of the Schedule and any amendment signed in accordance with Exchange Act Rule 12b-11(d) (17 CFR 12b-11(d)) by the persons whose signatures are required for this Schedule or amendment. The bidder must also conform the unsigned copies.

C. At the time of filing this Schedule with the Commission, the bidder shall pay to the Commission in accordance with Rule 0-11 of the Exchange Act, a fee in U.S. dollars in the amount prescribed by section 14(g)(3) of the Exchange Act. See also Rule 0-9 under the Exchange Act.

(1) Where the bidder is offering securities or other non-cash consideration for some or all of the securities to be acquired, whether or not in combination with a cash payment for the same securities, the value of the consideration shall be based on the market value of the securities to be received by the bidder as established by paragraph 3 of this section.

(2) If there is no market for the securities to be acquired by the bidder, the book value of such securities computed as of the latest practicable date prior to the date of filing the Schedule shall be used, unless the issuer of such securities is in bankruptcy or receivership or has an accumulated capital deficit, in which case one-third of the principal amount, par value or stated value of such securities shall be used.

(3) When the fee is based upon the market value of the securities, such market value shall be calculated upon the basis of either the average of the high and low prices reported in the consolidated reporting system (for exchange traded securities and last sale reported for over-the-counter securities) or the average of the bid and asked price (for other over-the-counter securities) as of a specified date within five business days prior to the date of filing the Schedule.

D. If at any time after the initial payment of the fee the aggregate consideration offered is increased, an additional filing fee based upon such increase shall be paid with the required amended filing.

E. The bidder must file the Schedule or amendment in electronic format in the English language in accordance with 17 CFR 232.306 of Regulation S-T. The bidder may file part of the Schedule or amendment, or exhibit or other attachment to the Schedule or amendment, in both French and English if the bidder included the French text to comply with the requirements of the Canadian securities administrator or other Canadian authority and, for an electronic filing, if the filing is an HTML document, as defined in 17 CFR 232.11 of Regulation S-T. For both an electronic filing and a paper filing, the bidder may provide an English translation or English summary of a foreign language document as an exhibit or other attachment to the Schedule or amendment as permitted by the rules of the applicable Canadian securities administrator.

F. A paper filer must number sequentially the signed original of the Schedule or amendment (in addition to any internal numbering that otherwise may be present) by handwritten, typed, printed or other legible form of notation from the first page through the last page of the Schedule or amendment, including any exhibits or attachments. A paper filer must disclose the total number of pages on the first page of the sequentially numbered Schedule or amendment.

III. COMPLIANCE WITH THE EXCHANGE ACT

A. Pursuant to Rule 14d-1(b) under the Exchange Act, the bidder shall be deemed to comply with the requirements of sections 14(d)(1) through 14(d)(7) of the Exchange Act, Regulation 14D under the Exchange Act and Schedule TO thereunder, and Rule 14e-1 under Regulation 14E of the Exchange Act, in connection with a cash tender or exchange offer for securities that may be made pursuant to this Schedule; *provided that*, if an exemption has been granted from requirements of Canadian federal, provincial, and/or territorial laws, regulations or policies, and the tender offer does not comply with requirements that otherwise would be prescribed by Regulation 14D or 14E, the bidder (absent an order from the Commission) shall comply with the provisions of sections 14(d)(1) through 14(d)(7) of the Exchange Act, Regulation 14D and Schedule TO thereunder, and Rule 14e-1 under Regulation 14E.

B. Any cash tender or exchange offer made pursuant to this Schedule is not exempt from the antifraud provisions of section 10(b) of the Exchange Act and Rule 10b-5 thereunder, and section 14(e) of the Exchange Act

§ 240.14d-102

and Rule 14e-3 thereunder, and this Schedule shall be deemed "filed" for purposes of section 18 of the Exchange Act.

C. The bidder's attention is directed to Regulation M (§§ 242.100 through 242.105 of this chapter) in the case of an exchange offer, and to Rule 14e-5 under the Exchange Act (§ 240.14e-5) for any exchange or cash tender offer. [See Exchange Act Release No. 29355 (June 21, 1991) containing an exemption from Rule 10b-13, the predecessor to Rule 14e-5.]

PART I—INFORMATION REQUIRED TO BE SENT TO SHAREHOLDERS

Item 1. Home Jurisdiction Documents

(a) This Schedule shall be accompanied by the entire disclosure document or documents required to be delivered to holders of securities to be acquired in the proposed transaction by the bidder pursuant to the laws, regulations or policies of Canada and/or any of its provinces or territories governing the conduct of the tender offer. It shall not include any documents incorporated by reference into such disclosure document(s) and not distributed to offerees pursuant to any such law, regulation or policy.

(b) Any amendment made by the bidder to a home jurisdiction document or documents shall be filed with the Commission under cover of this Schedule, which must indicate on the cover page the number of the amendment.

(c) In an exchange offer where securities of the bidder have been or are to be offered or cancelled in the transaction, such securities shall be registered on forms promulgated by the Commission under the Securities Act of 1933 including, where available, the Commission's Form F-8 or F-80 providing for inclusion in that registration statement of the home jurisdiction prospectus.

Item 2. Informational Legends

The following legends, to the extent applicable, shall appear on the outside front cover page of the home-jurisdiction document(s) in bold-face roman type at least as high as ten-point modern type and at least two points leaded:

"This tender offer is made for the securities of a foreign issuer and while the offer is subject to disclosure requirements of the country in which the subject company is incorporated or organized, investors should be aware that these requirements are different from those of the United States. Financial statements included herein, if any, have been prepared in accordance with foreign generally accepted accounting principles and thus may not be comparable to financial statements of United States companies.

"The enforcement by investors of civil liabilities under the federal securities laws may be affected adversely by the fact that the subject company is located in a foreign country, and that some or all of its officers and directors are residents of a foreign country.

"Investors should be aware that the bidder or its affiliates, directly or indirectly, may bid for or make purchases of the issuer's securities subject to the offer, or of the issuer's related securities, during the period of the tender offer, as permitted by applicable Canadian laws or provincial laws or regulations."

In the case of an exchange offer:

"Investors should be aware that the bidder or its affiliates, directly or indirectly, may bid for or make purchases of the issuer's securities subject to the offer or of the issuer's related securities, or of the bidder's securities to be distributed or of the bidder's related securities, during the period of the tender offer, as permitted by applicable Canadian laws or provincial laws or regulations."

NOTE TO ITEM 2. If the home-jurisdiction document(s) are delivered through an electronic medium, the issuer may satisfy the legibility requirements for the required legends relating to type size and font by presenting the legend in any manner reasonably calculated to draw security holder attention to it.

PART II—INFORMATION NOT REQUIRED TO BE SENT TO SHAREHOLDERS

The exhibits specified below shall be filed as part of the Schedule, but are not required to be sent to shareholders unless so required pursuant to the laws, regulations or policies of Canada and/or any of its provinces or territories. Exhibits shall be appropriately lettered or numbered for convenient reference.

(1) File any reports or information that, in accordance with the requirements of the home jurisdiction(s), must be made publicly available by the bidder in connection with the transaction but need not be disseminated to shareholders.

(2) File copies of any documents incorporated by reference into the home jurisdiction document(s).

(3) If any name is signed to this Schedule pursuant to power of attorney, manually signed copies of any such power of attorney shall be filed. If the name of any officer signing on behalf of the bidder is signed pursuant to a power of attorney, certified copies of the bidder's board of directors authorizing such signature also shall be filed.

(4) File the following information: The transaction valuation, fee rate, amount of filing fee and, as applicable, information relating to reliance on § 240.0-11(a)(2) in the tabular form indicated.

CALCULATION OF FILING FEE TABLES

Securities and Exchange Commission

§ 240.14d–102

TABLE 1—TRANSACTION VALUATION

	Transaction valuation	Fee rate	Amount of filing fee
Fees to Be Paid	X	X	X
Fees Previously Paid	X		X
Total Transaction Valuation	X		
Total Fees Due for Filing			X
Total Fees Previously Paid			X
Total Fee Offsets			X
Net Fee Due			X

TABLE 2—FEE OFFSET CLAIMS AND SOURCES

	Registrant or filer name	Form or filing type	File number	Initial filing date	Filing date	Fee offset claimed	Fee paid with fee offset source
Fee Offset Claims		X	X	X		X	
Fee Offset Sources	X	X	X		X		X

Instructions to the Calculation of Filing Fee Tables and Related Disclosure ("Instructions"):

1. General Requirements.

A. Applicable Table Requirements.

The "X" designation indicates the information required to be disclosed, as applicable, in tabular format. Add as many rows of each table as necessary.

B. Fee Rate.

For the current fee rate, see https://www.sec.gov/ofm/Article/feeamt.html.

C. Additional Filing Fee Provisions.

See General Instructions II.C and D for additional provisions regarding filing fees.

D. Explanations.

If not otherwise explained in response to these instructions, disclose specific details relating to the fee calculation as necessary to clarify the information presented in each table, including references to the applicable provisions of Rule 0–11 (§ 240.0–11 of this chapter). All disclosure these Instructions require that is not specifically required to be presented in tabular format must appear in narrative format immediately after the table(s) to which it corresponds.

E. Submission Method.

A filing fee exhibit required to be provided pursuant to this paragraph (4) under "Part II—Information Not Required To Be Sent To Shareholders" must be submitted as required by Rule 408 of Regulation S–T (§ 232.408 of this chapter).

2. Table 1: Transaction Valuation Table and Related Disclosure.

A. Fees to Be Paid and Fees Previously Paid.

i. Fees to Be Paid.

Provide the information Table 1 requires for the line item "Fees to Be Paid" as follows:

a. Initial Filings.

For an initial filing on this schedule, provide the required information for the total transaction valuation.

b. Amendments with Then-Current Total Transaction Valuation Higher than Highest Total Transaction Valuation Previously Reported. For amendments to this schedule that reflect a then-current total transaction valuation higher than the highest total transaction valuation previously reported, provide the required information for the incremental increase.

ii. Fees Previously Paid.

Provide the information Table 1 requires for the line item "Fees Previously Paid" for the prior initial filing or amendment to this schedule that reflected a then-current total transaction valuation that was the highest total transaction valuation previously reported.

B. Other Tabular Information.

Provide the following information in the table for the line items "Fees to be Paid" and "Fees Previously Paid":

i. The transaction valuation computed pursuant to Exchange Act Rule 0–11;

ii. The fee rate; and

353

§ 240.14d–102

iii. The filing fee due without regard to any previous payments or offsets.

C. Totals.

i. Total Transaction Valuation.

Provide the sum of the transaction valuations for the line items "Fees to be Paid" and "Fees Previously Paid."

ii. Total Fees Due for Filing.

Provide the sum of the fees due without regard to any previous payments or offsets for the line items "Fees to be Paid" and "Fees Previously Paid."

iii. Total Fees Previously Paid.

Provide the aggregate of filing fees previously paid with this filing.

iv. Total Fee Offsets.

Provide the aggregate of the fee offsets that are claimed in Table 2 pursuant to Instruction 3.

v. Net Fee Due.

Provide the difference between (a) the total fees due for this schedule from the Total Fees Due for Filing row; and (b) the sum of (i) the aggregate of filing fees previously paid from the Total Fees Previously Paid row; and (ii) the aggregate fee offsets claimed from the Total Fee Offsets row.

D. Narrative Disclosure.

Explain how the transaction valuation was determined.

3. Table 2: Fee Offset Claims and Sources.

A. Terminology.

For purposes of this Instruction 3 and Table 2, the term "submission" means any (i) initial filing of, or amendment (pre-effective or post-effective, to a fee-bearing document; or (ii) fee-bearing form of prospectus filed under Rule 424 under the Securities Act (§ 230.424 of this chapter), in all cases that was accompanied by a contemporaneous fee payment. For purposes of these instructions to Table 2, a contemporaneous fee payment is the payment of a required fee that is satisfied through the actual transfer of funds, and does not include any amount of a required fee satisfied through a claimed fee offset. Instruction 3.B.ii requires a filer that claims a fee offset under Rule 0–11(a)(2) to identify previous submissions with contemporaneous fee payments that are the original source to which the fee offsets claimed on this filing can be traced. See Instruction 3.C for an example.

B. Rule 0–11(a)(2).

If relying on Rule 0–11(a)(2) to offset some or all of the filing fee due on this tender offer statement by amounts paid in connection with earlier filings (other than this Schedule 14D–1F) relating to the same transaction, provide the following information:

i. Fee Offset Claims.

For each earlier filed Securities Act registration statement or Exchange Act document relating to the same transaction from which a fee offset is being claimed, provide the information that Table 2 requires for the line item "Fee Offset Claims". The "Fee Offset Claimed" column requires the dollar amount of the previously paid filing fee to be offset against the currently due fee.

Note to Instruction 3.B.i.

If claiming an offset from a Securities Act registration statement, provide a detailed explanation of the basis for the claimed offset.

ii. Fee Offset Sources.

With respect to amounts claimed as an offset under Rule 0–11(a)(2), identify those submissions with contemporaneous fee payments that are the original source to which those amounts can be traced. For each submission identified, provide the information that Table 2 requires for the line item "Fee Offset Sources". The "Fee Paid with Fee Offset Source" column requires the dollar amount of the contemporaneous fee payment made with respect to each identified submission that is the source of the fee offset claimed pursuant to Rule 0–11(a)(2).

C. Fee Offset Source Submission Identification Example.

A filer:

• Initially files a registration statement on Form S–1 on 1/15/20X1 (assigned file number 333–123456) with a fee payment of $10,000;

• Files pre-effective amendment number 1 to the Form S–1 (333–123456) on 2/15/20X1 with a fee payment of $15,000 and the registration statement goes effective on 2/20/20X1;

• Initially files a registration statement on Form S–1 on 1/15/20X4 (assigned file number 333–123467) with a fee payment of $25,000 and relies on Rule 457(p) to claim an offset of $10,000 related to the unsold securities registered on the previously filed Form S–1 (333–123456) and apply it to the $35,000 filing fee due and the registration statement goes effective on 2/15/20X4.

• Initially files a registration statement related to a tender offer on Form S–4 (assigned file number 333–123478) on 1/15/20X7 with a fee payment of $15,000 and relies on Rule 457(p) to claim an offset of $30,000 related to the unsold securities registered on the most recently effective Form S–1 (333–123467) filed on 1/15/20X4 and apply it to the $45,000 filing fee due.

• Initially files a Schedule TO related to the same tender offer on 1/22/20X7 and relies on Rule 0–11(a)(2) to claim an offset of $45,000 from the fee paid directly and by offset claimed on the Form S–4 (333–123478) filed 1/15/20X7 and apply it to the $45,000 filing fee due.

For the Schedule TO filed on 1/22/20X7, the filer can satisfy the submission identification requirement when it claims the $45,000 fee offset from the Form S–4 (333–123478) filed on 1/15/20X7 by referencing any combination of the Form S–4 (333–123478) filed on 1/15/20X7, the Form S–1 (333–123467) filed on 1/15/20X4, the pre-effective amendment to the Form S–1 (333–123456) filed on 2/15/20X1 or the initial filing of the Form S–1 (333–123456) on 1/15/20X1

Securities and Exchange Commission

§ 240.14d–103

in relation to which contemporaneous fee payments were made equal to $45,000.

One example could be:
- the Form S–4 (333–123478) filed on 1/15/20X7 in relation to the payment of $15,000 made with that submission;
- the Form S–1 (333–123467) filed on 1/15/20X4 in relation to the payment of $25,000 made with that submission; and
- the pre-effective amendment to the Form S–1 (333–123456) filed on 2/15/20X1 in relation to the payment of $5,000 out of the payment of $15,000 made with that submission (it would not matter if the filer cited to this pre-effective amendment and/or the initial submission of this Form S–1 (333–123456) on 1/15/20X1 as long as singly or together they were cited as relating to a total of $5,000 in this example).

In this example, the filer could not satisfy the submission identification requirement solely by citing to the Form S–4 (333–123478) filed on 1/15/20X7 because even though the offset claimed and available from that filing was $45,000, the contemporaneous fee payment made with that filing ($15,000) was less than the offset being claimed. As a result, the filer must also identify a prior submission or submissions with an aggregate of contemporaneous fee payment(s) of $30,000 as the original source(s) to which the rest of the claimed offset can be traced.

PART III—UNDERTAKINGS AND CONSENT TO SERVICE OF PROCESS

1. *Undertakings*

The Schedule shall set forth the following undertakings of the bidder:

a. The bidder undertakes to make available, in person or by telephone, representatives to respond to inquiries made by the Commission staff, and to furnish promptly, when requested to do so by the Commission staff, information relating to this Schedule or to transactions in said securities.

b. The bidder undertakes to disclose in the United States, on the same basis as it is required to make such disclosure pursuant to applicable Canadian federal and/or provincial or territorial laws, regulations or policies, or otherwise discloses, information regarding purchases of the issuer's securities in connection with the cash tender or exchange offer covered by this Schedule. Such information shall be set forth in amendments to this Schedule.

c. In the case of an exchange offer:

The bidder undertakes to disclose in the United States, on the same basis as it is required to make such disclosure pursuant to any applicable Canadian federal and/or provincial or territorial law, regulation or policy, or otherwise discloses, information regarding purchases of the issuer's or bidder's securities in connection with the offer.

2. *Consent to Service of Process*

(a) At the time of filing this Schedule, the bidder (if a non-U. S. person) shall file with the Commission a written irrevocable consent and power of attorney on Form F-X.

(b) Any change to the name or address of a registrant's agent for service shall be communicated promptly to the Commission by amendment to Form F-X referencing the file number of the registrant.

PART IV—SIGNATURES

A. The Schedule shall be signed by each person on whose behalf the Schedule is filed or its authorized representative. If the Schedule is signed on behalf of a person by his authorized representative (other than an executive officer or general partner of the bidder), evidence of the representative's authority shall be filed with the Schedule.

B. The name and any title of each person who signs the Schedule shall be typed or printed beneath his signature.

C. By signing this Schedule, the bidder consents without power of revocation that any administrative subpoena may be served, or any administrative proceeding, civil suit or civil action where the cause of action arises out of or relates to or concerns any offering made or purported to be made in connection with the filing on Schedule 14D–1F or any purchases or sales of any security in connection therewith, may be commenced against it in any administrative tribunal or in any appropriate court in any place subject to the jurisdiction of any state or of the United States by service of said subpoena or process upon the registrant's designated agent.

After due inquiry and to the best of my knowledge and belief, I certify that the information set forth in this statement is true, complete and correct.

(Signature)

(Name and Title)

(Date)

[56 FR 30071, July 1, 1991; 57 FR 10615, Mar. 27, 1992, as amended at 61 FR 24657, May 15, 1996; 62 FR 544, Jan. 3, 1997; 67 FR 36705, May 24, 2002; 73 FR 17814, Apr. 1, 2008; 86 FR 70260, Dec. 9, 2021]

§ 240.14d–103 Schedule 14D–9F. Solicitation/recommendation statement pursuant to section 14(d)(4) of the Securities Exchange Act of 1934 and rules 14d–1(b) and 14e–2(c) thereunder.

Securities and Exchange Commission Washington, DC 20549

Schedule 14D–9F

§ 240.14d–103

Solicitation/Recommendation Statement Pursuant to Section 14(d)(4) of the Securities Exchange Act of 1934 and Rules 14d–1(b) and 14e–2(c) Thereunder

[Amendment No. ____]

_____
(Name of Subject Company [Issuer])

_____
(Translation of Subject Company's [Issuer's] Name into English (if applicable))

_____
(Jurisdiction of Subject Company's [Issuer's] Incorporation or Organization)

_____
(Name(s) of Person(s) Filing Statement)

_____
(Title of Class of Securities)

_____
(CUSIP Number of Class of Securities (if applicable))

_____
(Name, address (including zip code) and telephone number (including area code) of person(s) authorized to receive notices and communications on behalf of the person(s) filing statement)

General Instructions

I. ELIGIBILITY REQUIREMENTS FOR USE OF SCHEDULE 14D–9F

A. Schedule 14D–9F is used by any issuer incorporated or organized under the laws of Canada or any Canadian province or territory that is a foreign private issuer (the "subject company"), or by any director or officer of such issuer, where the issuer is the subject of a cash tender or exchange offer for a class of its securities filed on Schedule 14D–1F. For purposes of this Schedule, "foreign private issuer" shall be construed in accordance with Rule 405 under the Securities Act.

B. Any person(s) using this Schedule must comply with the requirements of any Canadian federal, provincial and/or territorial law, regulation or policy relating to a recommendation by the subject issuer's board of directors, or any director or officer thereof, with respect to the offer.

II. FILING INSTRUCTIONS

A.(1) The subject issuer must file this Schedule and any amendment to the Schedule (see Part I, Item 1.(b)), including all exhibits and other documents filed as part of the Schedule or amendment, in electronic format via the Commission's Electronic Data Gathering, Analysis, and Retrieval (EDGAR) system in accordance with the EDGAR rules set forth in Regulation S-T (17 CFR Part 232). For assistance with technical questions about EDGAR or to request an access code, call the EDGAR Filer Support Office at (202) 551–8900. For assistance with the EDGAR rules, call the Office of EDGAR and Information Analysis at (202) 551–3610.

(2) If filing the Schedule in paper under a hardship exemption in 17 CFR 232.201 or 232.202 of Regulation S-T, or as otherwise permitted, the subject issuer must file with the Commission at its principal office five copies of the complete Schedule and any amendment, including exhibits and all other documents filed as a part of the Schedule or amendment. The subject issuer must bind, staple or otherwise compile each copy in one or more parts without stiff covers. The subject issuer must further bind the Schedule or amendment on the side or stitching margin in a manner that leaves the reading matter legible. The subject issuer must provide three additional copies of the Schedule or amendment without exhibits to the Commission.

B. An electronic filer must provide the signatures required for the Schedule or amendment in accordance with 17 CFR 232.302 of Regulation S-T. A subject issuer filing in paper must have the original and at least one copy of the Schedule and any amendment signed in accordance with Exchange Act Rule 12b–11(d) (17 CFR 12b–11(d)) by the persons whose signatures are required for this Schedule or amendment. The subject issuer must also conform the unsigned copies.

C. The subject issuer must file the Schedule or amendment in electronic format in the English language in accordance with 17 CFR 232.306 of Regulation S-T. The subject issuer may file part of the Schedule or amendment, or exhibit or other attachment to the Schedule or amendment, in both French and English if the bidder included the French text to comply with the requirements of the Canadian securities administrator or other Canadian authority and, for an electronic filing, if the filing is an HTML document, as defined in 17 CFR 232.11 of Regulation S-T. For both an electronic filing and a paper filing, the subject issuer may provide an English translation or English summary of a foreign language document as an exhibit or other attachment to the Schedule or amendment as permitted by the rules of the applicable Canadian securities administrator.

D. A paper filer must number sequentially the signed original of the Schedule or amendment (in addition to any internal numbering that otherwise may be present) by handwritten, typed, printed or other legible form of notation from the first page through the last page of the Schedule or amendment, including any exhibits or attachments. A paper filer must disclose the total number of pages on the first page of the sequentially numbered Schedule or amendment.

III. COMPLIANCE WITH THE EXCHANGE ACT

A. Pursuant to Rule 14e–2(c) under the Securities Exchange Act of 1934 (the "Exchange

Securities and Exchange Commission § 240.14d-103

Act"), this Schedule shall be filed by an issuer, a class of the securities of which is the subject of a cash tender or exchange offer filed on Schedule 14D-1F, and may be filed by any director or officer of such issuer.

B. Any recommendation with respect to a cash tender or exchange offer for a class of securities of the subject company made pursuant to this Schedule is not exempt from the antifraud provisions of section 10(b) of the Exchange Act and Rule 10b-5 thereunder and section 14(e) of the Exchange Act and Rule 14e-3 thereunder, and this Schedule shall be deemed "filed" with the Commission for purposes of section 18 of the Exchange Act.

Part I—Information Required To Be Sent to Shareholders

Item 1. Home Jurisdiction Documents

(a) This Schedule shall be accompanied by the entire disclosure document or documents required to be delivered to holders of securities to be acquired in the proposed transaction pursuant to the laws, regulations or policies of Canada and/or any of its provinces or territories governing the conduct of the offer. It shall not include any documents incorporated by reference into such disclosure document(s) and not distributed to offerees pursuant to any such law, regulation or policy.

(b) Any amendment made to a home jurisdiction document or documents shall be filed with the Commission under cover of this Schedule, which must indicate on the cover page the number of the amendment.

Item 2. Informational Legends

The following legends, to the extent applicable, shall appear on the outside front cover page of the home jurisdiction document(s) in bold-face roman type at least as high as ten-point modern type and at least two points leaded:

"This tender offer is made for the securities of a foreign issuer and while the offer is subject to disclosure requirements of the country in which the subject issuer is incorporated or organized, investors should be aware that these requirements are different from those of the United States. Financial statements included herein, if any, have been prepared in accordance with foreign generally accepted accounting principles and thus may not be comparable to financial statements of United States companies.

"The enforcement by investors of civil liabilities under the federal securities laws may be affected adversely by the fact that the issuer is located in a foreign country, and that some or all of its officers and directors are residents of a foreign country."

NOTE TO ITEM 2. If the home jurisdiction document(s) are delivered through an electronic medium, the issuer may satisfy the legibility requirements for the required legends relating to type size and font by presenting the legend in any manner reasonably calculated to draw security holder attention to it.

Part II—Information Not Required To Be Sent to Shareholders

The exhibits specified below shall be filed as part of the Schedule, but are not required to be sent to shareholders unless so required pursuant to the laws, or regulations or policies of Canada and/or any of its provinces or territories. Exhibits shall be appropriately lettered or numbered for convenient reference.

(1) File any reports or information that, in accordance with the requirements of the home jurisdiction(s), must be made publicly available by the person(s) filing this Schedule in connection with the transaction, but need not be disseminated to shareholders.

(2) File copies of any documents incorporated by reference into the home jurisdiction document(s).

(3) If any name is signed to the Schedule pursuant to power of attorney, manually signed copies of any such power of attorney shall be filed. If the name of any officer signing on behalf of the issuer is signed pursuant to a power of attorney, certified copies of a resolution of the issuer's board of directors authorizing such signature also shall be filed.

Part III—Undertaking and Consent to Service of Process

1. Undertaking

The Schedule shall set forth the following undertaking of the person filing it:

The person(s) filing this Schedule undertakes to make available, in person or by telephone, representatives to respond to inquiries made by the Commission staff, and to furnish promptly, when requested to do so by the Commission staff, information relating to this Schedule or to transactions in said securities.

2. Consent to Service of Process.

(a) At the time of filing this Schedule, the person(s) (if a non-U. S. person) so filing shall file with the Commission a written irrevocable consent and power of attorney on Form F-X.

(b) Any change to the name or address of a registrant's agent for service shall be communicated promptly to the Commission by amendment to Form F-X referencing the file number of the registrant.

Part IV—Signatures

A. The Schedule shall be signed by each person on whose behalf the Schedule is filed or its authorized representative. If the Schedule is signed on behalf of a person by

§ 240.14e-1

his authorized representative (other than an executive officer or general partner of the subject company), evidence of the representative's authority shall be filed with the Schedule.

B. The name and any title of each person who signs the Schedule shall be typed or printed beneath his signature.

C. By signing this Schedule, the persons signing consent without power of revocation that any administrative subpoena may be served, or any administrative proceeding, civil suit or civil action where the cause of action arises out of or relates to or concerns any offering made or purported to be made in connection with filing on this Schedule 14D–9F or any purchases or sales of any security in connection therewith, may be commenced against them in any administrative tribunal or in any appropriate court in any place subject to the jurisdiction of any state or of the United States by service of said subpoena or process upon the registrant's designated agent.

After due inquiry and to the best of my knowledge and belief, I certify that the information set forth in this statement is true, complete and correct.

_____
(Signature)

_____
(Name and Title)

_____
(Date)

[56 FR 30073, July 1, 1991, as amended at 61 FR 24657, May 15, 1996; 67 FR 36706, May 24, 2002; 73 FR 17814, Apr. 1, 2008]

REGULATION 14E

NOTE: For the scope of and definitions applicable to Regulation 14E, refer to § 240.14d–1.

§ 240.14e-1 Unlawful tender offer practices.

As a means reasonably designed to prevent fraudulent, deceptive or manipulative acts or practices within the meaning of section 14(e) of the Act, no person who makes a tender offer shall:

(a) Hold such tender offer open for less than twenty business days from the date such tender offer is first published or sent to security holders; provided, however, that if the tender offer involves a roll-up transaction as defined in Item 901(c) of Regulation S-K (17 CFR 229.901(c)) and the securities being offered are registered (or authorized to be registered) on Form S-4 (17 CFR 229.25) or Form F-4 (17 CFR 229.34), the offer shall not be open for less than sixty calendar days from the date the tender offer is first published or sent to security holders;

17 CFR Ch. II (4–1–23 Edition)

(b) Increase or decrease the percentage of the class of securities being sought or the consideration offered or the dealer's soliciting fee to be given in a tender offer unless such tender offer remains open for at least ten business days from the date that notice of such increase or decrease is first published or sent or given to security holders.

Provided, however, That, for purposes of this paragraph, the acceptance for payment of an additional amount of securities not to exceed two percent of the class of securities that is the subject of the tender offer shall not be deemed to be an increase. For purposes of this paragraph, the percentage of a class of securities shall be calculated in accordance with section 14(d)(3) of the Act.

(c) Fail to pay the consideration offered or return the securities deposited by or on behalf of security holders promptly after the termination or withdrawal of a tender offer. This paragraph does not prohibit a bidder electing to offer a subsequent offering period under § 240.14d–11 from paying for securities during the subsequent offering period in accordance with that section.

(d) Extend the length of a tender offer without issuing a notice of such extension by press release or other public announcement, which notice shall include disclosure of the approximate number of securities deposited to date and shall be issued no later than the earlier of: (i) 9:00 a.m. Eastern time, on the next business day after the scheduled expiration date of the offer or (ii), if the class of securities which is the subject of the tender offer is registered on one or more national securities exchanges, the first opening of any one of such exchanges on the next business day after the scheduled expiration date of the offer.

(e) The periods of time required by paragraphs (a) and (b) of this section shall be tolled for any period during which the bidder has failed to file in electronic format, absent a hardship exemption (§§ 232.201 and 232.202 of this chapter), the Schedule TO Tender Offer Statement (§ 240.14d–100), any tender offer material required to be filed by Item 12 of that Schedule pursuant to

Securities and Exchange Commission §240.14e–3

paragraph (a) of Item 1016 of Regulation M–A (§229.1016(a) of this chapter), and any amendments thereto. If such documents were filed in paper pursuant to a hardship exemption (*see* §232.201 and §232.202(d)), the minimum offering periods shall be tolled for any period during which a required confirming electronic copy of such Schedule and tender offer material is delinquent.

[44 FR 70348, Dec. 6, 1979, as amended at 51 FR 3035, Jan. 23, 1986; 51 FR 25883, July 17, 1986; 51 FR 32630, Sept. 15, 1986; 56 FR 57255, Nov. 8, 1991; 58 FR 14682, 14685, Mar. 18, 1993; 59 FR 67765, Déc. 30, 1994; 62 FR 36459, July 8, 1997; 64 FR 61465, Nov. 10, 1999; 73 FR 17814, Apr. 1, 2008]

§240.14e–2 Position of subject company with respect to a tender offer.

(a) *Position of subject company.* As a means reasonably designed to prevent fraudulent, deceptive or manipulative acts or practices withing the meaning of section 14(e) of the Act, the subject company, no later the date the tender offer is first published or sent or given, shall publish, send or give to security holders a statement disclosing that the subject company:

(1) Recommends acceptance or rejection of the bidder's tender offer;

(2) Expresses no opinion and is remaining neutral toward the bidder's tender offer; or

(3) Is unable to take a position with respect to the bidder's tender offer. Such statement shall also include the reason(s) for the position (including the inability to take a position) disclosed therein.

(b) *Material change.* If any material change occurs in the disclosure required by paragraph (a) of this section, the subject company shall promptly publish or send or give a statement disclosing such material change to security holders.

(c) Any issuer, a class of the securities of which is the subject of a tender offer filed with the Commission on Schedule 14D–1F and conducted in reliance upon and in conformity with Rule 14d–1(b) under the Act, and any director or officer of such issuer where so required by the laws, regulations and policies of Canada and/or any of its provinces or territories, in lieu of the statements called for by paragraph (a) of this section and Rule 14d–9 under the Act, shall file with the Commission on Schedule 14D–9F the entire disclosure document(s) required to be furnished to holders of securities of the subject issuer by the laws, regulations and policies of Canada and/or any of its provinces or territories governing the conduct of the tender offer, and shall disseminate such document(s) in the United States in accordance with such laws, regulations and policies.

(d) *Exemption for cross-border tender offers.* The subject company shall be exempt from this section with respect to a tender offer conducted under §240.14d–1(c).

[44 FR 70348, Dec. 6, 1979, as amended at 56 FR 30075, July 1, 1991; 64 FR 61406, Nov. 10, 1999]

§240.14e–3 Transactions in securities on the basis of material, nonpublic information in the context of tender offers.

(a) If any person has taken a substantial step or steps to commence, or has commenced, a tender offer (the "offering person"), it shall constitute a fraudulent, deceptive or manipulative act or practice within the meaning of section 14(e) of the Act for any other person who is in possession of material information relating to such tender offer which information he knows or has reason to know is nonpublic and which he knows or has reason to know has been acquired directly or indirectly from:

(1) The offering person,

(2) The issuer of the securities sought or to be sought by such tender offer, or

(3) Any officer, director, partner or employee or any other person acting on behalf of the offering person or such issuer, to purchase or sell or cause to be purchased or sold any of such securities or any securities convertible into or exchangeable for any such securities or any option or right to obtain or to dispose of any of the foregoing securities, unless within a reasonable time prior to any purchase or sale such information and its source are publicly disclosed by press release or otherwise.

(b) A person other than a natural person shall not violate paragraph (a) of this section if such person shows that:

§ 240.14e-4

(1) The individual(s) making the investment decision on behalf of such person to purchase or sell any security described in paragraph (a) of this section or to cause any such security to be purchased or sold by or on behalf of others did not know the material, nonpublic information; and

(2) Such person had implemented one or a combination of policies and procedures, reasonable under the circumstances, taking into consideration the nature of the person's business, to ensure that individual(s) making investment decision(s) would not violate paragraph (a) of this section, which policies and procedures may include, but are not limited to, (i) those which restrict any purchase, sale and causing any purchase and sale of any such security or (ii) those which prevent such individual(s) from knowing such information.

(c) Notwithstanding anything in paragraph (a) of this section to contrary, the following transactions shall not be violations of paragraph (a) of this section:

(1) Purchase(s) of any security described in paragraph (a) of this section by a broker or by another agent on behalf of an offering person; or

(2) Sale(s) by any person of any security described in paragraph (a) of this section to the offering person.

(d)(1) As a means reasonably designed to prevent fraudulent, deceptive or manipulative acts or practices within the meaning of section 14(e) of the Act, it shall be unlawful for any person described in paragraph (d)(2) of this section to communicate material, nonpublic information relating to a tender offer to any other person under circumstances in which it is reasonably foreseeable that such communication is likely to result in a violation of this section *except* that this paragraph shall not apply to a communication made in good faith,

(i) To the officers, directors, partners or employees of the offering person, to its advisors or to other persons, involved in the planning, financing, preparation or execution of such tender offer;

(ii) To the issuer whose securities are sought or to be sought by such tender offer, to its officers, directors, partners, employees or advisors or to other persons, involved in the planning, financing, preparation or execution of the activities of the issuer with respect to such tender offer; or

(iii) To any person pursuant to a requirement of any statute or rule or regulation promulgated thereunder.

(2) The persons referred to in paragraph (d)(1) of this section are:

(i) The offering person or its officers, directors, partners, employees or advisors;

(ii) The issuer of the securities sought or to be sought by such tender offer or its officers, directors, partners, employees or advisors;

(iii) Anyone acting on behalf of the persons in paragraph (d)(2)(i) of this section or the issuer or persons in paragraph (d)(2)(ii) of this section; and

(iv) Any person in possession of material information relating to a tender offer which information he knows or has reason to know is nonpublic and which he knows or has reason to know has been acquired directly or indirectly from any of the above.

[45 FR 60418, Sept. 12, 1980]

§ 240.14e-4 Prohibited transactions in connection with partial tender offers.

(a) *Definitions*. For purposes of this section:

(1) The amount of a person's "net long position" in a subject security shall equal the excess, if any, of such person's "long position" over such person's "short position." For the purposes of determining the net long position as of the end of the proration period and for tendering concurrently to two or more partial tender offers, securities that have been tendered in accordance with the rule and not withdrawn are deemed to be part of the person's long position.

(i) Such person's *long position* is the amount of subject securities that such person:

(A) Or his agent has title to or would have title to but for having lent such securities; or

(B) Has purchased, or has entered into an unconditional contract, binding on both parties thereto, to purchase but has not yet received; or

Securities and Exchange Commission § 240.14e-4

(C) Has exercised a standardized call option for; or

(D) Has converted, exchanged, or exercised an equivalent security for; or

(E) Is entitled to receive upon conversion, exchange, or exercise of an equivalent security.

(ii) Such person's *short position*, is the amount of subject securities or subject securities underlying equivalent securities that such person:

(A) Has sold, or has entered into an unconditional contract, binding on both parties thereto, to sell; or

(B) Has borrowed; or

(C) Has written a non-standardized call option, or granted any other right pursuant to which his shares may be tendered by another person; or

(D) Is obligated to deliver upon exercise of a standardized call option sold on or after the date that a tender offer is first publicly announced or otherwise made known by the bidder to holders of the security to be acquired, if the exercise price of such option is lower than the highest tender offer price or stated amount of the consideration offered for the subject security. For the purpose of this paragraph, if one or more tender offers for the same security are ongoing on such date, the announcement date shall be that of the first announced offer.

(2) The term *equivalent security* means:

(i) Any security (including any option, warrant, or other right to purchase the subject security), issued by the person whose securities are the subject of the offer, that is immediately convertible into, or exchangeable or exercisable for, a subject security, or

(ii) Any other right or option (other than a standardized call option) that entitles the holder thereof to acquire a subject security, but only if the holder thereof reasonably believes that the maker or writer of the right or option has title to and possession of the subject security and upon exercise will promptly deliver the subject security.

(3) The term *subject security* means a security that is the subject of any tender offer or request or invitation for tenders.

(4) For purposes of this rule, a person shall be deemed to "tender" a security if he:

(i) Delivers a subject security pursuant to an offer,

(ii) Causes such delivery to be made,

(iii) Guarantees delivery of a subject security pursuant to a tender offer,

(iv) Causes a guarantee of such delivery to be given by another person, or

(v) Uses any other method by which acceptance of a tender offer may be made.

(5) The term *partial tender offer* means a tender offer or request or invitation for tenders for less than all of the outstanding securities subject to the offer in which tenders are accepted either by lot or on a *pro rata* basis for a specified period, or a tender offer for all of the outstanding shares that offers a choice of consideration in which tenders for different forms of consideration may be accepted either by lot or on a *pro rata* basis for a specified period.

(6) The term *standardized call option* means any call option that is traded on an exchange, or for which quotation information is disseminated in an electronic interdealer quotation system of a registered national securities association.

(b) It shall be unlawful for any person acting alone or in concert with others, directly or indirectly, to tender any subject security in a partial tender offer:

(1) For his own account unless at the time of tender, and at the end of the proration period or period during which securities are accepted by lot (including any extensions thereof), he has a net long position equal to or greater than the amount tendered in:

(i) The subject security and will deliver or cause to be delivered such security for the purpose of tender to the person making the offer within the period specified in the offer; or

(ii) An equivalent security and, upon the acceptance of his tender will acquire the subject security by conversion, exchange, or exercise of such equivalent security to the extent required by the terms of the offer, and will deliver or cause to be delivered the subject security so acquired for the purpose of tender to the person making

§ 240.14e-5

the offer within the period specified in the offer; or

(2) For the account of another person unless the person making the tender:

(i) Possesses the subject security or an equivalent security, or

(ii) Has a reasonable belief that, upon information furnished by the person on whose behalf the tender is made, such person owns the subject security or an equivalent security and will promptly deliver the subject security or such equivalent security for the purpose of tender to the person making the tender.

(c) This rule shall not prohibit any transaction or transactions which the Commission, upon written request or upon its own motion, exempts, either unconditionally or on specified terms and conditions.

[49 FR 13870, Apr. 9, 1984, as amended at 50 FR 8102, Feb. 28, 1985. Redesignated and amended at 55 FR 50320, Dec. 6, 1990]

§ 240.14e-5 Prohibiting purchases outside of a tender offer.

(a) *Unlawful activity.* As a means reasonably designed to prevent fraudulent, deceptive or manipulative acts or practices in connection with a tender offer for equity securities, no covered person may directly or indirectly purchase or arrange to purchase any subject securities or any related securities except as part of the tender offer. This prohibition applies from the time of public announcement of the tender offer until the tender offer expires. This prohibition does not apply to any purchases or arrangements to purchase made during the time of any subsequent offering period as provided for in § 240.14d-11 if the consideration paid or to be paid for the purchases or arrangements to purchase is the same in form and amount as the consideration offered in the tender offer.

(b) *Excepted activity.* The following transactions in subject securities or related securities are not prohibited by paragraph (a) of this section:

(1) *Exercises of securities.* Transactions by covered persons to convert, exchange, or exercise related securities into subject securities, if the covered person owned the related securities before public announcement;

(2) *Purchases for plans.* Purchases or arrangements to purchase by or for a plan that are made by an agent independent of the issuer;

(3) *Purchases during odd-lot offers.* Purchases or arrangements to purchase if the tender offer is excepted under § 240.13e-4(h)(5);

(4) *Purchases as intermediary.* Purchases by or through a dealer-manager or its affiliates that are made in the ordinary course of business and made either:

(i) On an agency basis not for a covered person; or

(ii) As principal for its own account if the dealer-manager or its affiliate is not a market maker, and the purchase is made to offset a contemporaneous sale after having received an unsolicited order to buy from a customer who is not a covered person;

(5) *Basket transactions.* Purchases or arrangements to purchase a basket of securities containing a subject security or a related security if the following conditions are satisfied:

(i) The purchase or arrangement to purchase is made in the ordinary course of business and not to facilitate the tender offer;

(ii) The basket contains 20 or more securities; and

(iii) Covered securities and related securities do not comprise more than 5% of the value of the basket;

(6) *Covering transactions.* Purchases or arrangements to purchase that are made to satisfy an obligation to deliver a subject security or a related security arising from a short sale or from the exercise of an option by a non-covered person if:

(i) The short sale or option transaction was made in the ordinary course of business and not to facilitate the offer;

(ii) In the case of a short sale, the short sale was entered into before public announcement of the tender offer; and

(iii) In the case of an exercise of an option, the covered person wrote the option before public announcement of the tender offer;

(7) *Purchases pursuant to contractual obligations.* Purchases or arrangements to purchase pursuant to a contract if the following conditions are satisfied:

Securities and Exchange Commission § 240.14e–5

(i) The contract was entered into before public announcement of the tender offer;

(ii) The contract is unconditional and binding on both parties; and

(iii) The existence of the contract and all material terms including quantity, price and parties are disclosed in the offering materials;

(8) *Purchases or arrangements to purchase by an affiliate of the dealer-manager.* Purchases or arrangements to purchase by an affiliate of a dealer-manager if the following conditions are satisfied:

(i) The dealer-manager maintains and enforces written policies and procedures reasonably designed to prevent the flow of information to or from the affiliate that might result in a violation of the federal securities laws and regulations;

(ii) The dealer-manager is registered as a broker or dealer under Section 15(a) of the Act;

(iii) The affiliate has no officers (or persons performing similar functions) or employees (other than clerical, ministerial, or support personnel) in common with the dealer-manager that direct, effect, or recommend transactions in securities; and

(iv) The purchases or arrangements to purchase are not made to facilitate the tender offer;

(9) *Purchases by connected exempt market makers or connected exempt principal traders.* Purchases or arrangements to purchase if the following conditions are satisfied:

(i) The issuer of the subject security is a foreign private issuer, as defined in § 240.3b–4(c);

(ii) The tender offer is subject to the United Kingdom's City Code on Takeovers and Mergers;

(iii) The purchase or arrangement to purchase is effected by a connected exempt market maker or a connected exempt principal trader, as those terms are used in the United Kingdom's City Code on Takeovers and Mergers;

(iv) The connected exempt market maker or the connected exempt principal trader complies with the applicable provisions of the United Kingdom's City Code on Takeovers and Mergers; and

(v) The tender offer documents disclose the identity of the connected exempt market maker or the connected exempt principal trader and disclose, or describe how U.S. security holders can obtain, information regarding market making or principal purchases by such market maker or principal trader to the extent that this information is required to be made public in the United Kingdom;

(10) *Purchases during cross-border tender offers.* Purchases or arrangements to purchase if the following conditions are satisfied:

(i) The tender offer is excepted under § 240.13e–4(h)(8) or § 240.14d–1(c);

(ii) The offering documents furnished to U.S. holders prominently disclose the possibility of any purchases, or arrangements to purchase, or the intent to make such purchases;

(iii) The offering documents disclose the manner in which any information about any such purchases or arrangements to purchase will be disclosed;

(iv) The offeror discloses information in the United States about any such purchases or arrangements to purchase in a manner comparable to the disclosure made in the home jurisdiction, as defined in § 240.13e–4(i)(3); and

(v) The purchases comply with the applicable tender offer laws and regulations of the home jurisdiction; and

(11) *Purchases or arrangements to purchase pursuant to a foreign tender offer(s).* Purchases or arrangements to purchase pursuant to a foreign offer(s) where the offeror seeks to acquire subject securities through a U.S. tender offer and a concurrent or substantially concurrent foreign offer(s), if the following conditions are satisfied:

(i) The U.S. and foreign tender offer(s) meet the conditions for reliance on the Tier II cross-border exemptions set forth in § 240.14d–1(d);

(ii) The economic terms and consideration in the U.S. tender offer and foreign tender offer(s) are the same, provided that any cash consideration to be paid to U.S. security holders may be converted from the currency to be paid in the foreign tender offer(s) to U.S. dollars at an exchange rate disclosed in the U.S. offering documents;

§ 240.14e–5

(iii) The procedural terms of the U.S. tender offer are at least as favorable as the terms of the foreign tender offer(s);

(iv) The intention of the offeror to make purchases pursuant to the foreign tender offer(s) is disclosed in the U.S. offering documents; and

(v) Purchases by the offeror in the foreign tender offer(s) are made solely pursuant to the foreign tender offer(s) and not pursuant to an open market transaction(s), a private transaction(s), or other transaction(s); and

(12) *Purchases or arrangements to purchase by an affiliate of the financial advisor and an offeror and its affiliates.* (i) Purchases or arrangements to purchase by an affiliate of a financial advisor and an offeror and its affiliates that are permissible under and will be conducted in accordance with the applicable laws of the subject company's home jurisdiction, if the following conditions are satisfied:

(A) The subject company is a foreign private issuer as defined in § 240.3b–4(c);

(B) The covered person reasonably expects that the tender offer meets the conditions for reliance on the Tier II cross-border exemptions set forth in § 240.14d–1(d);

(C) No purchases or arrangements to purchase otherwise than pursuant to the tender offer are made in the United States;

(D) The United States offering materials disclose prominently the possibility of, or the intention to make, purchases or arrangements to purchase subject securities or related securities outside of the tender offer, and if there will be public disclosure of purchases of subject or related securities, the manner in which information regarding such purchases will be disseminated;

(E) There is public disclosure in the United States, to the extent that such information is made public in the subject company's home jurisdiction, of information regarding all purchases of subject securities and related securities otherwise than pursuant to the tender offer from the time of public announcement of the tender offer until the tender offer expires;

(F) Purchases or arrangements to purchase by an offeror and its affiliates must satisfy the following additional condition: the tender offer price will be increased to match any consideration paid outside of the tender offer that is greater than the tender offer price; and

(G) Purchases or arrangements to purchase by an affiliate of a financial advisor must satisfy the following additional conditions:

(*1*) The financial advisor and the affiliate maintain and enforce written policies and procedures reasonably designed to prevent the transfer of information among the financial advisor and affiliate that might result in a violation of U.S. federal securities laws and regulations through the establishment of information barriers;

(*2*) The financial advisor has an affiliate that is registered as a broker or dealer under section 15(a) of the Act (15 U.S.C. 78o(a));

(*3*) The affiliate has no officers (or persons performing similar functions) or employees (other than clerical, ministerial, or support personnel) in common with the financial advisor that direct, effect, or recommend transactions in the subject securities or related securities who also will be involved in providing the offeror or subject company with financial advisory services or dealer-manager services; and

(*4*) The purchases or arrangements to purchase are not made to facilitate the tender offer.

(ii) [Reserved]

(c) *Definitions.* For purposes of this section, the term:

(1) *Affiliate* has the same meaning as in § 240.12b–2;

(2) *Agent independent of the issuer* has the same meaning as in § 242.100(b) of this chapter;

(3) *Covered person* means:

(i) The offeror and its affiliates;

(ii) The offeror's dealer-manager and its affiliates;

(iii) Any advisor to any of the persons specified in paragraph (c)(3)(i) and (ii) of this section, whose compensation is dependent on the completion of the offer; and

(iv) Any person acting, directly or indirectly, in concert with any of the persons specified in this paragraph (c)(3) in connection with any purchase or arrangement to purchase any subject securities or any related securities;

Securities and Exchange Commission § 240.14e–7

(4) *Plan* has the same meaning as in § 242.100(b) of this chapter;

(5) *Public announcement* is any oral or written communication by the offeror or any person authorized to act on the offeror's behalf that is reasonably designed to, or has the effect of, informing the public or security holders in general about the tender offer;

(6) *Related securities* means securities that are immediately convertible into, exchangeable for, or exercisable for subject securities;

(7) *Subject securities* has the same meaning as in § 229.1000 of this chapter; and

(8) *Subject company* has the same meaning as in § 229.1000 of this chapter; and

(9) *Home jurisdiction* has the same meaning as in the Instructions to paragraphs (c) and (d) of § 240.14d–1.

(d) *Exemptive authority.* Upon written application or upon its own motion, the Commission may grant an exemption from the provisions of this section, either unconditionally or on specified terms or conditions, to any transaction or class of transactions or any security or class of security, or any person or class of persons.

[64 FR 61465, Nov. 10, 1999, as amended at 73 FR 60093, Oct. 9, 2008]

§ 240.14e–6 Repurchase offers by certain closed-end registered investment companies.

Sections 240.14e–1 and 240.14e–2 shall not apply to any offer by a closed-end management investment company to repurchase equity securities of which it is the issuer pursuant to § 270.23c–3 of this chapter.

[58 FR 19343, Apr. 14, 1993]

§ 240.14e–7 Unlawful tender offer practices in connection with roll-ups.

In order to implement section 14(h) of the Act (15 U.S.C. 78n(h)):

(a)(1) It shall be unlawful for any person to receive compensation for soliciting tenders directly from security holders in connection with a roll-up transaction as provided in paragraph (a)(2) of this section, if the compensation is:

(i) Based on whether the solicited person participates in the tender offer; or

(ii) Contingent on the success of the tender offer.

(2) Paragraph (a)(1) of this section is applicable to a roll-up transaction as defined in Item 901(c) of Regulation S-K (§ 229.901(c) of this chapter), structured as a tender offer, except for a transaction involving only:

(i) Finite-life entities that are not limited partnerships;

(ii) Partnerships whose investors will receive new securities or securities in another entity that are not reported under a transaction reporting plan declared effective before December 17, 1993 by the Commission under section 11A of the Act (15 U.S.C. 78k–1); or

(iii) Partnerships whose investors' securities are reported under a transaction reporting plan declared effective before December 17, 1993 by the Commission under section 11A of the Act (15 U.S.C. 78k–1).

(b)(1) It shall be unlawful for any finite-life entity that is the subject of a roll-up transaction as provided in paragraph (b)(2) of this section to fail to provide a security holder list or mail communications related to a tender offer that is in furtherance of the roll-up transaction, at the option of a requesting security holder, pursuant to the procedures set forth in § 240.14a–7.

(2) Paragraph (b)(1) of this section is applicable to a roll-up transaction as defined in Item 901(c) of Regulation S-K (§ 229.901(c) of this chapter), structured as a tender offer, that involves:

(i) An entity with securities registered pursuant to section 12 of the Act (15 U.S.C. 78*l*); or

(ii) A limited partnership, unless the transaction involves only:

(A) Partnerships whose investors will receive new securities or securities in another entity that are not reported under a transaction reporting plan declared effective before December 17, 1993 by the Commission under section 11A of the Act (15 U.S.C. 78k–1); or

(B) Partnerships whose investors' securities are reported under a transaction reporting plan declared effective before December 17, 1993 by the Commission under section 11A of the Act (15 U.S.C. 78k–1).

[59 FR 63685, Dec. 8, 1994]

§ 240.14e-8 Prohibited conduct in connection with pre-commencement communications.

It is a fraudulent, deceptive or manipulative act or practice within the meaning of section 14(e) of the Act (15 U.S.C. 78n) for any person to publicly announce that the person (or a party on whose behalf the person is acting) plans to make a tender offer that has not yet been commenced, if the person:

(a) Is making the announcement of a potential tender offer without the intention to commence the offer within a reasonable time and complete the offer;

(b) Intends, directly or indirectly, for the announcement to manipulate the market price of the stock of the bidder or subject company; or

(c) Does not have the reasonable belief that the person will have the means to purchase securities to complete the offer.

[64 FR 61466, Nov. 10, 1999]

§ 240.14f-1 Change in majority of directors.

If, pursuant to any arrangement or understanding with the person or persons acquiring securities in a transaction subject to section 13(d) or 14(d) of the Act, any persons are to be elected or designated as directors of the issuer, otherwise than at a meeting of security holders, and the persons so elected or designated will constitute a majority of the directors of the issuer, then, not less than 10 days prior to the date any such person take office as a director, or such shorter period prior to that date as the Commission may authorize upon a showing of good cause therefor, the issuer shall file with the Commission and transmit to all holders of record of securities of the issuer who would be entitled to vote at a meeting for election of directors, information substantially equivalent to the information which would be required by Items 6 (a), (d) and (e), 7 and 8 of Schedule 14A of Regulation 14A (§ 240.14a–101 of this chapter) to be transmitted if such person or persons were nominees for election as directors at a meeting of such security holders. Eight copies of such information shall be filed with the Commission.

[33 FR 11017, Aug. 2, 1968, as amended at 34 FR 6101, Apr. 4, 1969; 51 FR 42072, Nov. 20, 1986]

REGULATION 14N: FILINGS REQUIRED BY CERTAIN NOMINATING SHAREHOLDERS

§ 240.14n-1 Filing of Schedule 14N.

(a) A shareholder or group of shareholders that submits a nominee or nominees in accordance with § 240.14a-11 or a procedure set forth under applicable state or foreign law, or a registrant's governing documents providing for the inclusion of shareholder director nominees in the registrant's proxy materials shall file with the Commission a statement containing the information required by Schedule 14N (§ 240.14n–101) and simultaneously provide the notice on Schedule 14N to the registrant.

(b)(1) Whenever two or more persons are required to file a statement containing the information required by Schedule 14N (§ 240.14n–101), only one statement need be filed. The statement must identify all such persons, contain the required information with regard to each such person, indicate that the statement is filed on behalf of all such persons, and include, as an appendix, their agreement in writing that the statement is filed on behalf of each of them. Each person on whose behalf the statement is filed is responsible for the timely filing of that statement and any amendments thereto, and for the completeness and accuracy of the information concerning such person contained therein; such person is not responsible for the completeness or accuracy of the information concerning the other persons making the filing.

(2) If the group's members elect to make their own filings, each filing should identify all members of the group but the information provided concerning the other persons making the filing need only reflect information which the filing person knows or has reason to know.

[75 FR 56788, Sept. 16, 2010]

Securities and Exchange Commission

§ 240.14n-2 Filing of amendments to Schedule 14N.

(a) If any material change occurs with respect to the nomination, or in the disclosure or certifications set forth in the Schedule 14N (§ 240.14n-101) required by § 240.14n-1(a), the person or persons who were required to file the statement shall promptly file or cause to be filed with the Commission an amendment disclosing that change.

(b) An amendment shall be filed within 10 calendar days of the final results of the election being announced by the registrant stating the nominating shareholder's or the nominating shareholder group's intention with regard to continued ownership of their shares.

[75 FR 56788, Sept. 16, 2010]

§ 240.14n-3 Dissemination.

One copy of Schedule 14N (§ 240.14n-101) filed pursuant to §§ 240.14n-1 and 240.14n-2 shall be mailed by registered or certified mail or electronically transmitted to the registrant at its principal executive office. Three copies of the material must at the same time be filed with, or mailed for filing to, each national securities exchange upon which any class of securities of the registrant is listed and registered.

[75 FR 56788, Sept. 16, 2010]

§ 240.14n-101 Schedule 14N—Information to be included in statements filed pursuant to § 240.14n-1 and amendments thereto filed pursuant to § 240.14n-2.

Securities and Exchange Commission, Washington, DC 20549

Schedule 14N

Under the Securities Exchange Act of 1934

(Amendment No. __)*

(Name of Issuer)

_____

(Title of Class of Securities)

_____

(CUSIP Number)

_____

[ ] Solicitation pursuant to § 240.14a-2(b)(7)

[ ] Solicitation pursuant to § 240.14a-2(b)(8)

§ 240.14n-101

[ ] Notice of Submission of a Nominee or Nominees in Accordance with § 240.14a-11

[ ] Notice of Submission of a Nominee or Nominees in Accordance with Procedures Set Forth Under Applicable State or Foreign Law, or the Registrant's Governing Documents

*The remainder of this cover page shall be filled out for a reporting person's initial filing on this form, and for any subsequent amendment containing information which would alter the disclosures provided in a prior cover page.

The information required in the remainder of this cover page shall not be deemed to be "filed" for the purpose of Section 18 of the Securities Exchange Act of 1934 ("Act") or otherwise subject to the liabilities of that section of the Act but shall be subject to all other provisions of the Act.

(1) Names of reporting persons: _____

(2) Mailing address and phone number of each reporting person (or, where applicable, the authorized representative): _____

(3) Amount of securities held that are entitled to be voted on the election of directors held by each reporting person (and, where applicable, amount of securities held in the aggregate by the nominating shareholder group), but including loaned securities and net of securities sold short or borrowed for purposes other than a short sale: _____

(4) Number of votes attributable to the securities entitled to be voted on the election of directors represented by amount in Row (3) (and, where applicable, aggregate number of votes attributable to the securities entitled to be voted on the election of directors held by group): _____

Instructions for Cover Page:

(1) *Names of Reporting Persons*—Furnish the full legal name of each person for whom the report is filed—*i.e.*, each person required to sign the schedule itself—including each member of a group. Do not include the name of a person required to be identified in the report but who is not a reporting person.

(3) and (4) *Amount Held by Each Reporting Person*—Rows (3) and (4) are to

§ 240.14n-101

be completed in accordance with the provisions of Item 3 of Schedule 14N.

NOTES: Attach as many copies of parts one through three of the cover page as are needed, one reporting person per copy.

Filing persons may, in order to avoid unnecessary duplication, answer items on Schedule 14N by appropriate cross references to an item or items on the cover page(s). This approach may only be used where the cover page item or items provide all the disclosure required by the schedule item. Moreover, such a use of a cover page item will result in the item becoming a part of the schedule and accordingly being considered as "filed" for purposes of Section 18 of the Act or otherwise subject to the liabilities of that section of the Act.

SPECIAL INSTRUCTIONS FOR COMPLYING WITH SCHEDULE 14N

Under Sections 14 and 23 of the Securities Exchange Act of 1934 and the rules and regulations thereunder, the Commission is authorized to solicit the information required to be supplied by this Schedule. The information will be used for the primary purpose of determining and disclosing the holdings and interests of a nominating shareholder or nominating shareholder group. This statement will be made a matter of public record. Therefore, any information given will be available for inspection by any member of the public.

Because of the public nature of the information, the Commission can use it for a variety of purposes, including referral to other governmental authorities or securities self-regulatory organizations for investigatory purposes or in connection with litigation involving the Federal securities laws or other civil, criminal or regulatory statutes or provisions. Failure to disclose the information requested by this schedule may result in civil or criminal action against the persons involved for violation of the Federal securities laws and rules promulgated thereunder, or in some cases, exclusion of the nominee from the registrant's proxy materials.

General Instructions to Item Requirements

The item numbers and captions of the items shall be included but the text of the items is to be omitted. The answers to the items shall be prepared so as to indicate clearly the coverage of the items without referring to the text of the items. Answer every item. If an item is inapplicable or the answer is in the negative, so state.

ITEM 1(a). NAME OF REGISTRANT

ITEM 1(b). ADDRESS OF REGISTRANT'S PRINCIPAL EXECUTIVE OFFICES

ITEM 2(a). NAME OF PERSON FILING

ITEM 2(b). ADDRESS OR PRINCIPAL BUSINESS OFFICE OR, IF NONE, RESIDENCE

ITEM 2(c). TITLE OF CLASS OF SECURITIES

ITEM 2(d). CUSIP NO.

ITEM 3. OWNERSHIP

Provide the following information, in accordance with Instruction 3 to § 240.14a–11(b)(1):

(a) Amount of securities held and entitled to be voted on the election of directors (and, where applicable, amount of securities held in the aggregate by the nominating shareholder group): _____.

(b) The number of votes attributable to the securities referred to in paragraph (a) of this Item: _____.

(c) The number of votes attributable to securities that have been loaned but which the reporting person:

(i) has the right to recall; and

(ii) will recall upon being notified that any of the nominees will be included in the registrant's proxy statement and proxy card: _____.

(d) The number of votes attributable to securities that have been sold in a short sale that is not closed out, or that have been borrowed for purposes other than a short sale: _____.

(e) The sum of paragraphs (b) and (c), minus paragraph (d) of this Item, divided by the aggregate number of votes derived from all classes of securities of the registrant that are entitled to vote on the election of directors, and expressed as a percentage: _____.

Securities and Exchange Commission

§ 240.14n–101

ITEM 4. STATEMENT OF OWNERSHIP FROM A NOMINATING SHAREHOLDER OR EACH MEMBER OF A NOMINATING SHAREHOLDER GROUP SUBMITTING THIS NOTICE PURSUANT TO § 240.14A–11

(a) If the nominating shareholder, or each member of the nominating shareholder group, is the registered holder of the shares, please so state. Otherwise, attach to the Schedule 14N one or more written statements from the persons (usually brokers or banks) through which the nominating shareholder's securities are held, verifying that, within seven calendar days prior to filing the shareholder notice on Schedule 14N with the Commission and transmitting the notice to the registrant, the nominating shareholder continuously held the amount of securities being used to satisfy the ownership threshold for a period of at least three years. In the alternative, if the nominating shareholder has filed a Schedule 13D (§ 240.13d–101), Schedule 13G (§ 240.13d–102), Form 3 (§ 249.103 of this chapter), Form 4 (§ 249.104 of this chapter), and/or Form 5 (§ 249.105 of this chapter), or amendments to those documents, reflecting ownership of the securities as of or before the date on which the three-year eligibility period begins, so state and incorporate that filing or amendment by reference.

(b) Provide a written statement that the nominating shareholder, or each member of the nominating shareholder group, intends to continue to hold the amount of securities that are used for purposes of satisfying the minimum ownership requirement of § 240.14a–11(b)(1) through the date of the meeting of shareholders, as required by § 240.14a–11(b)(4). Additionally, provide a written statement from the nominating shareholder or each member of the nominating shareholder group regarding the nominating shareholder's or nominating shareholder group member's intent with respect to continued ownership after the election of directors, as required by § 240.14a–11(b)(5).

Instruction to Item 4. If the nominating shareholder or any member of the nominating shareholder group is not the registered holder of the securities and is not proving ownership for purposes of § 240.14a–11(b)(3) by providing previously filed Schedules 13D or 13G or Forms 3, 4, or 5, and the securities are held in an account with a broker or bank that is a participant in the Depository Trust Company ("DTC") or other clearing agency acting as a securities depository, a written statement or statements from that participant or participants in the following form will satisfy § 240.14a–11(b)(3):

As of [date of this statement], [name of nominating shareholder or member of the nominating shareholder group] held at least [number of securities owned continuously for at least three years] of the [registrant's] [class of securities], and has held at least this amount of such securities continuously for [at least three years]. [Name of clearing agency participant] is a participant in [name of clearing agency] whose nominee name is [nominee name].

[name of clearing agency participant]

By: [name and title of representative]

Date:

If the securities are held through a broker or bank (*e.g.* in an omnibus account) that is not a participant in a clearing agency acting as a securities depository, the nominating shareholder or member of the nominating shareholder group must (a) obtain and submit a written statement or statements (the "initial broker statement") from the broker or bank with which the nominating shareholder or member of the nominating shareholder group maintains an account that provides the information about securities ownership set forth above and (b) obtain and submit a separate written statement from the clearing agency participant through which the securities of the nominating shareholder or member of the nominating shareholder group are held, that (i) identifies the broker or bank for whom the clearing agency participant holds the securities, and (ii) states that the account of such broker or bank has held, as of the date of the separate written statement, at least the number of securities specified in the initial broker statement, and (iii) states that this account has held at least that amount of securities continuously for at least three years.

§ 240.14n-101

If the securities have been held for less than three years at the relevant entity, provide written statements covering a continuous period of three years and modify the language set forth above as appropriate.

For purposes of complying with § 240.14a-11(b)(3), loaned securities may be included in the amount of securities set forth in the written statements.

ITEM 5. DISCLOSURE REQUIRED FOR SHAREHOLDER NOMINATIONS SUBMITTED PURSUANT TO § 240.14A-11

If a nominating shareholder or nominating shareholder group is submitting this notice in connection with the inclusion of a shareholder nominee or nominees for director in the registrant's proxy materials pursuant to § 240.14a-11, provide the following information:

(a) A statement that the nominee consents to be named in the registrant's proxy statement and form of proxy and, if elected, to serve on the registrant's board of directors;

(b) Disclosure about the nominee as would be provided in response to the disclosure requirements of Items 4(b), 5(b), 7(a), (b) and (c) and, for investment companies, Item 22(b) of Schedule 14A (§ 240.14a-101), as applicable;

(c) Disclosure about the nominating shareholder or each member of a nominating shareholder group as would be required of a participant in response to the disclosure requirements of Items 4(b) and 5(b) of Schedule 14A (§ 240.14a-101), as applicable;

(d) Disclosure about whether the nominating shareholder or any member of a nominating shareholder group has been involved in any legal proceeding during the past ten years, as specified in Item 401(f) of Regulation S-K (§ 229.10 of this chapter). Disclosure pursuant to this paragraph need not be provided if provided in response to Item 5(c) of this section;

Instruction 1 to Item 5(c) and (d). Where the nominating shareholder is a general or limited partnership, syndicate or other group, the information called for in paragraphs (c) and (d) of this Item must be given with respect to:

a. Each partner of the general partnership;

b. Each partner who is, or functions as, a general partner of the limited partnership;

c. Each member of the syndicate or group; and

d. Each person controlling the partner or member.

Instruction 2 to Item 5(c) and (d). If the nominating shareholder is a corporation or if a person referred to in a., b., c. or d. of Instruction 1 to paragraphs (c) and (d) of this Item is a corporation, the information called for in paragraphs (c) and (d) of this Item must be given with respect to:

a. Each executive officer and director of the corporation;

b. Each person controlling the corporation; and

c. Each executive officer and director of any corporation or other person ultimately in control of the corporation.

(e) Disclosure about whether, to the best of the nominating shareholder's or group's knowledge, the nominee meets the director qualifications, if any, set forth in the registrant's governing documents;

(f) A statement that, to the best of the nominating shareholder's or group's knowledge, in the case of a registrant other than an investment company, the nominee meets the objective criteria for "independence" of the national securities exchange or national securities association rules applicable to the registrant, if any, or, in the case of a registrant that is an investment company, the nominee is not an "interested person" of the registrant as defined in section 2(a)(19) of the Investment Company Act of 1940 (15 U.S.C. 80a-2(a)(19)).

Instruction to Item 5(f). For this purpose, the nominee would be required to meet the definition of "independence" that is generally applicable to directors of the registrant and not any particular definition of independence applicable to members of the audit committee of the registrant's board of directors. To the extent a national securities exchange or national securities association rule imposes a standard regarding independence that requires a subjective determination by the board or a group or committee of the board (for example, requiring that the board of directors or any group or committee

370

Securities and Exchange Commission

§ 240.14n–101

of the board of directors make a determination regarding the existence of factors material to a determination of a nominee's independence), the nominee would not be required to meet the subjective determination of independence as part of the shareholder nomination process.

(g) The following information regarding the nature and extent of the relationships between the nominating shareholder or nominating shareholder group, the nominee, and/or the registrant or any affiliate of the registrant:

(1) Any direct or indirect material interest in any contract or agreement between the nominating shareholder or any member of the nominating shareholder group, the nominee, and/or the registrant or any affiliate of the registrant (including any employment agreement, collective bargaining agreement, or consulting agreement);

(2) Any material pending or threatened legal proceeding in which the nominating shareholder or any member of the nominating shareholder group and/or the nominee is a party or a material participant, and that involves the registrant, any of its executive officers or directors, or any affiliate of the registrant; and

(3) Any other material relationship between the nominating shareholder or any member of the nominating shareholder group, the nominee, and/or the registrant or any affiliate of the registrant not otherwise disclosed;

NOTE TO ITEM 5(g)(3): Any other material relationship of the nominating shareholder or any member of the nominating shareholder group or nominee with the registrant or any affiliate of the registrant may include, but is not limited to, whether the nominating shareholder or any member of the nominating shareholder group currently has, or has had in the past, an employment relationship with the registrant or any affiliate of the registrant (including consulting arrangements).

(h) The Web site address on which the nominating shareholder or nominating shareholder group may publish soliciting materials, if any; and

(i) Any statement in support of the shareholder nominee or nominees, which may not exceed 500 words for each nominee, if the nominating shareholder or nominating shareholder group elects to have such statement included in the registrant's proxy materials.

ITEM 6. DISCLOSURE REQUIRED BY § 240.14A–18

If a nominating shareholder or nominating shareholder group is submitting this notice in connection with the inclusion of a shareholder nominee or nominees for director in the registrant's proxy materials pursuant to a procedure set forth under applicable state or foreign law, or the registrant's governing documents provide the following disclosure:

(a) A statement that the nominee consents to be named in the registrant's proxy statement and form of proxy and, if elected, to serve on the registrant's board of directors;

(b) Disclosure about the nominee as would be provided in response to the disclosure requirements of Items 4(b), 5(b), 7(a), (b) and (c) and, for investment companies, Item 22(b) of Schedule 14A (§ 240.14a–101), as applicable;

(c) Disclosure about the nominating shareholder or each member of a nominating shareholder group as would be required in response to the disclosure requirements of Items 4(b) and 5(b) of Schedule 14A (§ 240.14a–101), as applicable;

(d) Disclosure about whether the nominating shareholder or any member of a nominating shareholder group has been involved in any legal proceeding during the past ten years, as specified in Item 401(f) of Regulation S–K (§ 229.10 of this chapter). Disclosure pursuant to this paragraph need not be provided if provided in response to Item 6(c) of this section;

Instruction 1 to Item 6(c) and (d). Where the nominating shareholder is a general or limited partnership, syndicate or other group, the information called for in paragraphs (c) and (d) of this Item must be given with respect to:

a. Each partner of the general partnership;

b. Each partner who is, or functions as, a general partner of the limited partnership;

c. Each member of the syndicate or group; and

§ 240.14n-101

d. Each person controlling the partner or member.

Instruction 2 to Item 6(c) and (d). If the nominating shareholder is a corporation or if a person referred to in a., b., c. or d. of Instruction 1 to paragraphs (c) and (d) of this Item is a corporation, the information called for in paragraphs (c) and (d) of this Item must be given with respect to:

a. Each executive officer and director of the corporation;

b. Each person controlling the corporation; and

c. Each executive officer and director of any corporation or other person ultimately in control of the corporation.

(e) The following information regarding the nature and extent of the relationships between the nominating shareholder or nominating shareholder group, the nominee, and/or the registrant or any affiliate of the registrant:

(1) Any direct or indirect material interest in any contract or agreement between the nominating shareholder or any member of the nominating shareholder group, the nominee, and/or the registrant or any affiliate of the registrant (including any employment agreement, collective bargaining agreement, or consulting agreement);

(2) Any material pending or threatened legal proceeding in which the nominating shareholder or any member of the nominating shareholder group and/or nominee is a party or a material participant, involving the registrant, any of its executive officers or directors, or any affiliate of the registrant; and

(3) Any other material relationship between the nominating shareholder or any member of the nominating shareholder group, the nominee, and/or the registrant or any affiliate of the registrant not otherwise disclosed; and

Instruction to Item 6(e)(3). Any other material relationship of the nominating shareholder or any member of the nominating shareholder group with the registrant or any affiliate of the registrant may include, but is not limited to, whether the nominating shareholder or any member of the nominating shareholder group currently has, or has had in the past, an employment relationship with the registrant or any affiliate of the registrant (including consulting arrangements).

(f) The Web site address on which the nominating shareholder or nominating shareholder group may publish soliciting materials, if any.

ITEM 7. NOTICE OF DISSOLUTION OF GROUP OR TERMINATION OF SHAREHOLDER NOMINATION

Notice of dissolution of a nominating shareholder group or the termination of a shareholder nomination shall state the date of the dissolution or termination.

ITEM 8. SIGNATURES

(a) The following certifications shall be provided by the filing person submitting this notice pursuant to § 240.14a–11, or in the case of a group, each filing person whose securities are being aggregated for purposes of meeting the ownership threshold set out in § 240.14a–11(b)(1) exactly as set forth below:

I, [identify the certifying individual], after reasonable inquiry and to the best of my knowledge and belief, certify that:

(1) I [or if signed by an authorized representative, the name of the nominating shareholder or each member of the nominating shareholder group, as appropriate] am [is] not holding any of the registrant's securities with the purpose, or with the effect, of changing control of the registrant or to gain a number of seats on the board of directors that exceeds the maximum number of nominees that the registrant could be required to include under § 240.14a–11(d);

(2) I [or if signed by an authorized representative, the name of the nominating shareholder or each member of the nominating shareholder group, as appropriate] otherwise satisfy [satisfies] the requirements of § 240.14a–11(b), as applicable;

(3) The nominee or nominees satisfies the requirements of § 240.14a–11(b), as applicable; and

(4) The information set forth in this notice on Schedule 14N is true, complete and correct.

(b) The following certification shall be provided by the filing person or persons submitting this notice in connection with the submission of a nominee or nominees in accordance with procedures set forth under applicable state or foreign law or the registrant's governing documents:

I, [identify the certifying individual], after reasonable inquiry and to the best of my knowledge and belief, certify that the information set forth in this notice on Schedule 14N is true, complete and correct.

Dated: _____
Signature: _____
Name/Title: _____

The original statement shall be signed by each person on whose behalf the statement is filed or his authorized representative. If the statement is signed on behalf of a person by his authorized representative other than an executive officer or general partner of the filing person, evidence of the representative's authority to sign on behalf of such person shall be filed with the statement, *provided, however,* that a power of attorney for this purpose which is already on file with the Commission may be incorporated by reference. The name and any title of each person who signs the statement shall be typed or printed beneath his signature.

Attention: Intentional misstatements or omissions of fact constitute Federal criminal violations (see 18 U.S.C. 1001).

[75 FR 56788, Sept. 16, 2010]

Exemption of Certain OTC Derivatives Dealers

§ 240.15a–1 Securities activities of OTC derivatives dealers.

PRELIMINARY NOTE: OTC derivatives dealers are a special class of broker-dealers that are exempt from certain broker-dealer requirements, including membership in a self-regulatory organization (§ 240.15b9–2), regular broker-dealer margin rules (§ 240.36a1–1), and application of the Securities Investor Protection Act of 1970 (§ 240.36a1–2). OTC derivative dealers are subject to special requirements, including limitations on the scope of their securities activities (§ 240.15a–1), specified internal risk management control systems (§ 240.15c3–4), recordkeeping obligations (§ 240.17a–3(a)(10)), and reporting responsibilities (§ 240.17a–12). They are also subject to alternative net capital treatment (§ 240.15c3–1(a)(5)). This rule 15a–1 uses a number of defined terms in setting forth the securities activities in which an OTC derivatives dealer may engage: "OTC derivatives dealer," "eligible OTC derivative instrument," "cash management securities activities," and "ancillary portfolio management securities activities." These terms are defined under Rules 3b–12 through 3b–15 (§ 240.3b–12 through § 240.3b–15).

(a) The securities activities of an OTC derivatives dealer shall:

(1) Be limited to:

(i) Engaging in dealer activities in eligible OTC derivative instruments that are securities;

(ii) Issuing and reacquiring securities that are issued by the dealer, including warrants on securities, hybrid securities, and structured notes;

(iii) Engaging in cash management securities activities;

(iv) Engaging in ancillary portfolio management securities activities; and

(v) Engaging in such other securities activities that the Commission designates by order pursuant to paragraph (b)(1) of this section; and

(2) Consist primarily of the activities described in paragraphs (a)(1)(i), (a)(1)(ii), and (a)(1)(iii) of this section; and

(3) Not consist of any other securities activities, including engaging in any transaction in any security that is not an eligible OTC derivative instrument, except as permitted under paragraphs (a)(1)(iii), (a)(1)(iv), and (a)(1)(v) of this section.

(b) The Commission, by order, entered upon its own initiative or after considering an application for exemptive relief, may clarify or expand the scope of eligible OTC derivative instruments and the scope of permissible securities activities of an OTC derivatives dealer. Such orders may:

(1) Identify other permissible securities activities;

(2) Determine that a class of fungible instruments that are standardized as to their material economic terms is within the scope of eligible OTC derivative instrument;

(3) Clarify whether certain contracts, agreements, or transactions are within the scope of eligible OTC derivative instrument; or

§ 240.15a-1

(4) Clarify whether certain securities activities are within the scope of ancillary portfolio management securities activities.

(c) To the extent an OTC derivatives dealer engages in any securities transaction pursuant to paragraphs (a)(1)(i) through (a)(1)(v) of this section, such transaction shall be effected through a registered broker or dealer (other than an OTC derivatives dealer) that, in the case of any securities transaction pursuant to paragraphs (a)(1)(i), or (a)(1)(iii) through (a)(1)(v) of this section, is an affiliate of the OTC derivatives dealer, except that this paragraph (c) shall not apply if:

(1) The counterparty to the transaction with the OTC derivatives dealer is acting as principal and is:

(i) A registered broker or dealer;

(ii) A bank acting in a dealer capacity, as permitted by U.S. law;

(iii) A foreign broker or dealer; or

(iv) An affiliate of the OTC derivatives dealer; or

(2) The OTC derivatives dealer is engaging in an ancillary portfolio management securities activity, and the transaction is in a foreign security, and a registered broker or dealer, a bank, or a foreign broker or dealer is acting as agent for the OTC derivatives dealer.

(d) To the extent an OTC derivatives dealer induces or attempts to induce any counterparty to enter into any securities transaction pursuant to paragraphs (a)(1)(i) through (a)(1)(v) of this section, any communication or contact with the counterparty concerning the transaction (other than clerical and ministerial activities conducted by an associated person of the OTC derivatives dealer) shall be conducted by one or more registered persons that, in the case of any securities transaction pursuant to paragraphs (a)(1)(i), or (a)(1)(iii) through (a)(1)(v) of this section, is associated with an affiliate of the OTC derivatives dealer, except that this paragraph (d) shall not apply if the counterparty to the transaction with the OTC derivatives dealer is:

(1) A registered broker or dealer;

(2) A bank acting in a dealer capacity, as permitted by U.S. law;

(3) A foreign broker or dealer; or

(4) An affiliate of the OTC derivatives dealer.

(e) For purposes of this section, the term *hybrid security* means a security that incorporates payment features economically similar to options, forwards, futures, swap agreements, or collars involving currencies, interest or other rates, commodities, securities, indices, quantitative measures, or other financial or economic interests or property of any kind, or any payment or delivery that is dependent on the occurrence or nonoccurrence of any event associated with a potential financial, economic, or commercial consequence (or any combination, permutation, or derivative of such contract or underlying interest).

(f) For purposes of this section, the term *affiliate* means any organization (whether incorporated or unincorporated) that directly or indirectly controls, is controlled by, or is under common control with, the OTC derivatives dealer.

(g) For purposes of this section, the term *foreign broker or dealer* means any person not resident in the United States (including any U.S. person engaged in business as a broker or dealer entirely outside the United States, except as otherwise permitted by § 240.15a-6) that is not an office or branch of, or a natural person associated with, a registered broker or dealer, whose securities activities, if conducted in the United States, would be described by the definition of "broker" in section 3(a)(4) of the Act (15 U.S.C. 78c(a)(4)) or "dealer" in section 3(a)(5) of the Act (15 U.S.C. 78c(a)(5)).

(h) For purposes of this section, the term *foreign security* means any security (including a depositary share issued by a United States bank, provided that the depositary share is initially offered and sold outside the United States in accordance with Regulation S (17 CFR 230.901 through 230.904)) issued by a person not organized or incorporated under the laws of the United States, provided the transaction that involves such security is not effected on a national securities exchange or on a market operated by a registered national securities association; or a debt security (including a convertible debt security) issued by an

Securities and Exchange Commission §240.15a-5

issuer organized or incorporated under the laws of the United States that is initially offered and sold outside the United States in accordance with Regulation S (17 CFR 230.901 through 230.904).

(i) For purposes of this section, the term *registered person* is:

(A) A natural person who is associated with a registered broker or dealer and is registered or approved under the rules of a self-regulatory organization of which such broker or dealer is a member; or

(B) If the counterparty to the transaction with the OTC derivatives dealer is a resident of a jurisdiction other than the United States, a natural person who is not resident in the United States and is associated with a broker or dealer that is registered or licensed by a foreign financial regulatory authority in the jurisdiction in which such counterparty is resident or in which such natural person is located, in accordance with applicable legal requirements, if any.

[63 FR 59396, Nov. 3, 1998]

EXEMPTION OF CERTAIN SECURITIES FROM SECTION 15(a)

§240.15a-2 Exemption of certain securities of cooperative apartment houses from section 15(a).

Shares of a corporation which represent ownership, or entitle the holders thereof to possession and occupancy, of specific apartment units in property owned by such corporations and organized and operated on a cooperative basis are hereby exempted from the operation of section 15(a) of the Securities Exchange Act of 1934, when such shares are sold by or through a real estate broker licensed under the laws of the political subdivision in which the property is located.

(Secs. 3, 48 Stat. 882, as amended, 895, as amended; 15 U.S.C. 78c, 78o)

[13 FR 8204, Dec. 22, 1948]

§240.15a-3 [Reserved]

§240.15a-4 Forty-five day exemption from registration for certain members of national securities exchanges.

(a) A natural person who is a member of a national securities exchange shall, upon termination of his association with a registered broker-dealer, be exempt, for a period of forty-five days after such termination, from the registration requirement of section 15(a) of the Act solely for the purpose of continuing to effect transactions on the floor of such exchange if (1) such person has filed with the Commission an application for registration as a broker-dealer and such person complies in all material respects with rules of the Commission applicable to registered brokers and dealers and (2) such exchange has filed with the Commission a statement that it has reviewed such application and that there do not appear to be grounds for its denial.

(b) The exemption from registration provided by this rule shall not be available to any person while there is pending before the Commission any proceeding involving any such person pursuant to section 15(b)(1)(B) of the Act.

[41 FR 18290, May 3, 1976]

§240.15a-5 Exemption of certain nonbank lenders.

A lender approved under the rules and regulations of the Small Business Administration shall be exempt from the registration requirement of section 15(a)(1) of the Act if it does not engage in the business of effecting transactions in securities or of buying and selling securities for its own account except in respect of receiving notes evidencing loans to small business concerns and selling the portion of such notes guaranteed by the Small Business Administration through or to a registered broker or dealer or to a bank, a savings institution, an insurance company, or an account over which an investment adviser registered pursuant to the Investment Advisers Act of 1940 exercises investment discretion.

[41 FR 50645, Nov. 17, 1976]

§ 240.15a-6

REGISTRATION OF BROKERS AND DEALERS

§ 240.15a-6 Exemption of certain foreign brokers or dealers.

(a) A foreign broker or dealer shall be exempt from the registration requirements of sections 15(a)(1) or 15B(a)(1) of the Act to the extent that the foreign broker or dealer:

(1) Effects transactions in securities with or for persons that have not been solicited by the foreign broker or dealer; or

(2) Furnishes research reports to major U.S. institutional investors, and effects transactions in the securities discussed in the research reports with or for those major U.S. institutional investors, provided that:

(i) The research reports do not recommend the use of the foreign broker or dealer to effect trades in any security;

(ii) The foreign broker or dealer does not initiate contact with those major U.S. institutional investors to follow up on the research reports, and does not otherwise induce or attempt to induce the purchase or sale of any security by those major U.S. institutional investors;

(iii) If the foreign broker or dealer has a relationship with a registered broker or dealer that satisfies the requirements of paragraph (a)(3) of this section, any transactions with the foreign broker or dealer in securities discussed in the research reports are effected only through that registered broker or dealer, pursuant to the provisions of paragraph (a)(3) of this section; and

(iv) The foreign broker or dealer does not provide research to U.S. persons pursuant to any express or implied understanding that those U.S. persons will direct commission income to the foreign broker or dealer; or

(3) Induces or attempts to induce the purchase or sale of any security by a U.S. institutional investor or a major U.S. institutional investor, provided that:

(i) The foreign broker or dealer:

(A) Effects any resulting transactions with or for the U.S. institutional investor or the major U.S. institutional investor through a registered broker or dealer in the manner described by paragraph (a)(3)(iii) of this section; and

(B) Provides the Commission (upon request or pursuant to agreements reached between any foreign securities authority, including any foreign government, as specified in section 3(a)(50) of the Act, and the Commission or the U.S. Government) with any information or documents within the possession, custody, or control of the foreign broker or dealer, any testimony of foreign associated persons, and any assistance in taking the evidence of other persons, wherever located, that the Commission requests and that relates to transactions under paragraph (a)(3) of this section, except that if, after the foreign broker or dealer has exercised its best efforts to provide the information, documents, testimony, or assistance, including requesting the appropriate governmental body and, if legally necessary, its customers (with respect to customer information) to permit the foreign broker or dealer to provide the information, documents, testimony, or assistance to the Commission, the foreign broker or dealer is prohibited from providing this information, documents, testimony, or assistance by applicable foreign law or regulations, then this paragraph (a)(3)(i)(B) shall not apply and the foreign broker or dealer will be subject to paragraph (c) of this section;

(ii) The foreign associated person of the foreign broker or dealer effecting transactions with the U.S. institutional investor or the major U.S. institutional investor:

(A) Conducts all securities activities from outside the U.S., except that the foreign associated persons may conduct visits to U.S. institutional investors and major U.S. institutional investors within the United States, provided that:

(*1*) The foreign associated person is accompanied on these visits by an associated person of a registered broker or dealer that accepts responsibility for the foreign associated person's communications with the U.S. institutional investor or the major U.S institutional investor; and

(*2*) Transactions in any securities discussed during the visit by the foreign

Securities and Exchange Commission § 240.15a-6

associated person are effected only through the registered broker or dealer, pursuant to paragraph (a)(3) of this section; and

(B) Is determined by the registered broker or dealer to:

(1) Not be subject to a statutory disqualification specified in section 3(a)(39) of the Act, or any substantially equivalent foreign

(i) Expulsion or suspension from membership,

(ii) Bar or suspension from association,

(iii) Denial of trading privileges,

(iv) Order denying, suspending, or revoking registration or barring or suspending association, or

(v) Finding with respect to causing any such effective foreign suspension, expulsion, or order;

(2) Not to have been convicted of any foreign offense, enjoined from any foreign act, conduct, or practice, or found to have committed any foreign act substantially equivalent to any of those listed in sections 15(b)(4) (B), (C), (D), or (E) of the Act; and

(3) Not to have been found to have made or caused to be made any false foreign statement or omission substantially equivalent to any of those listed in section 3(a)(39)(E) of the Act; and

(iii) The registered broker or dealer through which the transaction with the U.S. institutional investor or the major U.S. institutional investor is effected:

(A) Is responsible for:

(1) Effecting the transactions conducted under paragraph (a)(3) of this section, other than negotiating their terms;

(2) Issuing all required confirmations and statements to the U.S. institutional investor or the major U.S. institutional investor;

(3) As between the foreign broker or dealer and the registered broker or dealer, extending or arranging for the extension of any credit to the U.S. institutional investor or the major U.S. institutional investor in connection with the transactions;

(4) Maintaining required books and records relating to the transactions, including those required by Rules 17a-3 and 17a-4 under the Act (17 CFR 2410.17a-3 and 17a-4);

(5) Complying with Rule 15c3-1 under the Act (17 CFR 240.15c3-1) with respect to the transactions; and

(6) Receiving, delivering, and safeguarding funds and securities in connection with the transactions on behalf of the U.S. institutional investor or the major U.S. institutional investor in compliance with Rule 15c3-3 under the Act (17 CFR 240.15c3-3);

(B) Participates through an associated person in all oral communications between the foreign associated person and the U.S. institutional investor, other than a major U.S. institutional investor;

(C) Has obtained from the foreign broker or dealer, with respect to each foreign associated person, the types of information specified in Rule 17a-3(a)(12) under the Act (17 CFR 240.17a-3(a)(12)), provided that the information required by paragraph (a)(12)(d) of that Rule shall include sanctions imposed by foreign securities authorities, exchanges, or associations, including without limitation those described in paragraph (a)(3)(ii)(B) of this section;

(D) Has obtained from the foreign broker or dealer and each foreign associated person written consent to service of process for any civil action brought by or proceeding before the Commission or a self-regulatory organization (as defined in section 3(a)(26) of the Act), providing that process may be served on them by service on the registered broker or dealer in the manner set forth on the registered broker's or dealer's current Form BD; and

(E) Maintains a written record of the information and consents required by paragraphs (a)(3)(iii) (C) and (D) of this section, and all records in connection with trading activities of the U.S. institutional investor or the major U.S. institutional investor involving the foreign broker or dealer conducted under paragraph (a)(3) of this section, in an office of the registered broker or dealer located in the United States (with respect to nonresident registered brokers or dealers, pursuant to Rule 17a-7(a) under the Act (17 CFR 240.17a-7(a))), and makes these records available to the Commission upon request; or

(4) Effects transactions in securities with or for, or induces or attempts to

§ 240.15a-6

induce the purchase or sale of any security by:

(i) A registered broker or dealer, whether the registered broker or dealer is acting as principal for its own account or as agent for others, or a bank acting pursuant to an exception or exemption from the definition of "broker" or "dealer" in sections 3(a)(4)(B), 3(a)(4)(E), or 3(a)(5)(C) of the Act (15 U.S.C. 78c(a)(4)(B), 15 U.S.C. 78c(a)(4)(E), or 15 U.S.C. 78c(a)(5)(C)) or the rules thereunder;

(ii) The African Development Bank, the Asian Development Bank, the Inter-American Development Bank, the International Bank for Reconstruction and Development, the International Monetary Fund, the United Nations, and their agencies, affiliates, and pension funds;

(iii) A foreign person temporarily present in the United States, with whom the foreign broker or dealer had a bona fide, pre-existing relationship before the foreign person entered the United States;

(iv) Any agency or branch of a U.S. person permanently located outside the United States, provided that the transactions occur outside the United States; or

(v) U.S. citizens resident outside the United States, provided that the transactions occur outside the United States, and that the foreign broker or dealer does not direct its selling efforts toward identifiable groups of U.S. citizens resident abroad.

(b) When used in this rule,

(1) The term *family of investment companies* shall mean:

(i) Except for insurance company separate accounts, any two or more separately registered investment companies under the Investment Company Act of 1940 that share the same investment adviser or principal underwriter and hold themselves out to investors as related companies for purposes of investment and investor services; and

(ii) With respect to insurance company separate accounts, any two or more separately registered separate accounts under the Investment Company Act of 1940 that share the same investment adviser or principal underwriter and function under operational or accounting or control systems that are substantially similar.

(2) The term *foreign associated person* shall mean any natural person domiciled outside the United States who is an associated person, as defined in section 3(a)(18) of the Act, of the foreign broker or dealer, and who participates in the solicitation of a U.S. institutional investor or a major U.S. institutional investor under paragraph (a)(3) of this section.

(3) The term *foreign broker or dealer* shall mean any non-U.S. resident person (including any U.S. person engaged in business as a broker or dealer entirely outside the United States, except as otherwise permitted by this rule) that is not an office or branch of, or a natural person associated with, a registered broker or dealer, whose securities activities, if conducted in the United States, would be described by the definition of "broker" or "dealer" in sections 3(a)(4) or 3(a)(5) of the Act.

(4) The term *major U.S. institutional investor* shall mean a person that is:

(i) A U.S. institutional investor that has, or has under management, total assets in excess of $100 million; provided, however, that for purposes of determining the total assets of an investment company under this rule, the investment company may include the assets of any family of investment companies of which it is a part; or

(ii) An investment adviser registered with the Commission under section 203 of the Investment Advisers Act of 1940 that has total assets under management in excess of $100 million.

(5) The term *registered broker or dealer* shall mean a person that is registered with the Commission under sections 15(b), 15B(a)(2), or 15C(a)(2) of the Act.

(6) The term *United States* shall mean the United States of America, including the States and any territories and other areas subject to its jurisdiction.

(7) The term *U.S. institutional investor* shall mean a person that is:

(i) An investment company registered with the Commission under section 8 of the Investment Company Act of 1940; or

Securities and Exchange Commission

(ii) A bank, savings and loan association, insurance company, business development company, small business investment company, or employee benefit plan defined in Rule 501(a)(1) of Regulation D under the Securities Act of 1933 (17 CFR 230.501(a)(1)); a private business development company defined in Rule 501(a)(2) (17 CFR 230.501(a)(2)); an organization described in section 501(c)(3) of the Internal Revenue Code, as defined in Rule 501(a)(3) (17 CFR 230.501(a)(3)); or a trust defined in Rule 501(a)(7) (17 CFR 230.501(a)(7)).

(c) The Commission, by order after notice and opportunity for hearing, may withdraw the exemption provided in paragraph (a)(3) of this section with respect to the subsequent activities of a foreign broker or dealer or class of foreign brokers or dealers conducted from a foreign country, if the Commission finds that the laws or regulations of that foreign country have prohibited the foreign broker or dealer, or one of a class of foreign brokers or dealers, from providing, in response to a request from the Commission, information or documents within its possession, custody, or control, testimony of foreign associated persons, or assistance in taking the evidence of other persons, wherever located, related to activities exempted by paragraph (a)(3) of this section.

[54 FR 30031, July 18, 1989, as amended at 72 FR 56568, Oct. 3, 2007]

§§ 240.15a-7—240.15a-9 [Reserved]

§ 240.15a-10 Exemption of certain brokers or dealers with respect to security futures products.

(a) A broker or dealer that is registered by notice with the Commission pursuant to section 15(b)(11)(A) of the Act (15 U.S.C. 78o(b)(11)(A)) and that is not a member of either a national securities exchange registered pursuant to section 6(a) of the Act (15 U.S.C. 78f(a)) or a national securities association registered pursuant to section 15A(a) of the Act (15 U.S.C. 78o-3(a)) will be exempt from the registration requirement of section 15(a)(1) of the Act (15 U.S.C. 78o(a)(1)) solely to act as a broker or a dealer in security futures products.

(b) A broker or dealer that is registered by notice with the Commission pursuant to section 15(b)(11)(A) of the Act (15 U.S.C. 78o(b)(11)(A)) and that is a member of either a national securities exchange registered pursuant to section 6(a) of the Act (15 U.S.C. 78f(a)) or a national securities association registered pursuant to section 15A(a) of the Act (15 U.S.C. 78o-3(a)) will be exempt from the registration requirement of section 15(a)(1) of the Act (15 U.S.C. 78o(a)(1)) solely to act as a broker or a dealer in security futures products, if:

(1) The rules of any such exchange or association of which the broker or dealer is a member provides specifically for a broker or dealer that is registered by notice with the Commission pursuant to section 15(b)(11)(A) of the Act (15 U.S.C. 78o(b)(11)(A)) to become a member of such exchange or association; and

(2) The broker or dealer complies with section 11(a)–(c) of the Act (15 U.S.C. 78k(a)–(c)) with respect to any transactions in security futures products on a national securities exchange registered pursuant to section 6(a) of the Act (15 U.S.C. 78f(a)) of which it is a member, notwithstanding section 15(b)(11)(B)(ii) of the Act (15 U.S.C. 78o(b)(11)(B)(ii)).

[66 FR 45146, Aug. 27, 2001]

§ 240.15a-11 [Reserved]

§ 240.15b1-1 Application for registration of brokers or dealers.

(a) An application for registration of a broker or dealer that is filed pursuant to section 15(b) of the Act (15 U.S.C. 78o(b)) shall be filed on Form BD (§ 249.501 of this chapter) in accordance with the instructions to the form. A broker or dealer that is an OTC derivatives dealer shall indicate where appropriate on Form BD that the type of business in which it is engaged is that of acting as an OTC derivatives dealer.

(b) Every application for registration of a broker or dealer that is filed on or after January 25, 1993, shall be filed with the Central Registration Depository operated by the Financial Industry Regulatory Authority, Inc.

§ 240.15b1-2

(c) An application for registration that is filed with the Central Registration Depository pursuant to this section shall be considered a "report" filed with the Commission for purposes of Sections 15(b), 17(a), 18(a), 32(a) (15 U.S.C. 78o(b), 78q(a), 78r(a), 78ff(a)) and other applicable provisions of the Act.

[19 FR 1041, Feb. 24, 1954. Redesignated at 30 FR 11851, Sept. 16, 1965, and amended at 58 FR 14, Jan. 4, 1993; 63 FR 59397, Nov. 3, 1998; 64 FR 25147, May 10, 1999; 73 FR 4692, Jan. 28, 2008]

§ 240.15b1-2 [Reserved]

§ 240.15b1-3 Registration of successor to registered broker or dealer.

(a) In the event that a broker or dealer succeeds to and continues the business of a broker or dealer registered pursuant to section 15(b) of the Act, the registration of the predecessor shall be deemed to remain effective as the registration of the successor if the successor, within 30 days after such succession, files an application for registration on Form BD, and the predecessor files a notice of withdrawal from registration on Form BDW; *Provided, however,* That the registration of the predecessor broker or dealer will cease to be effective as the registration of the successor broker or dealer 45 days after the application for registration on Form BD is filed by such successor.

(b) Notwithstanding paragraph (a) of this section, if a broker or dealer succeeds to and continues the business of a registered predecessor broker or dealer, and the succession is based solely on a change in the predecessor's date or state of incorporation, form of organization, or composition of a partnership, the successor may, within 30 days after the succession, amend the registration of the predecessor broker or dealer on Form BD to reflect these changes. This amendment shall be deemed an application for registration filed by the predecessor and adopted by the successor.

[58 FR 10, Jan. 4, 1993]

§ 240.15b1-4 Registration of fiduciaries.

The registration of a broker or dealer shall be deemed to be the registration of any executor, administrator, guardian, conservator, assignee for the benefit of creditors, receiver, trustee in insolvency or bankruptcy, or other fiduciary, appointed or qualified by order, judgment, or decree of a court of competent jurisdiction to continue the business of such registered broker or dealer; *Provided,* That such fiduciary files with the Commission, within 30 days after entering upon the performance of his duties, a statement setting forth as to such fiduciary substantially the information required by Form BD.

(Secs. 15, 17, 48 Stat. 895, as amended, 897 as amended; 15 U.S.C. 78o, 78q)

[19 FR 1041, Feb. 24, 1954. Redesignated at 30 FR 11851, Sept. 16, 1965]

§ 240.15b1-5 Consent to service of process to be furnished by nonresident brokers or dealers and by nonresident general partners or managing agents of brokers or dealers.

(a) Each nonresident broker or dealer registered or applying for registration pursuant to section 15(b) of the Securities Exchange Act of 1934, each nonresident general partner of a broker or dealer partnership which is registered or applying for registration, and each nonresident managing agent of any other unincorporated broker or dealer which is registered or applying for registration, shall furnish to the Commission, in a form prescribed by or acceptable to it, a written irrevocable consent and power of attorney which (1) designates the Securities and Exchange Commission as an agent upon whom may be served any process, pleadings, or other papers in any civil suit or action brought in any appropriate court in any place subject to the jurisdiction of the United States, with respect to any cause of action (i) which accrues during the period beginning when such broker or dealer becomes registered pursuant to section 15 of the Securities Exchange Act of 1934 and the rules and regulations thereunder and ending either when such registration is cancelled or revoked, or when the Commission receives from such broker or dealer a notice to withdraw from such registration, whichever is earlier, (ii) which arises out of any activity, in any place subject to the jurisdiction of the United States, occurring in connection

Securities and Exchange Commission § 240.15b1-5

with the conduct of business of a broker or dealer, and (iii) which is founded directly or indirectly, upon the provisions of the Securities Act of 1933, the Securities Exchange Act of 1934, the Trust Indenture Act of 1939, the Investment Company Act of 1940, the Investment Advisers Act of 1940, or any rule or regulation under any of said Acts; and (2) stipulates and agrees that any such civil suit or action may be commended by the service of process upon the Commission and the forwarding of a copy thereof as provided in paragraph (c) of this section, and that the service as aforesaid of any such process, pleadings, or other papers upon the Commission shall be taken and held in all courts to be as valid and binding as if due personal service thereof had been made.

(b) The required consent and power of attorney shall be furnished to the Commission within the following period of time:

(1) Each nonresident broker or dealer registered at the time this section becomes effective, and each nonresident general partner or managing agent of an unincorporated broker or dealer registered at the time this section becomes effective, shall furnish such consent and power of attorney within 60 days after such date;

(2) Each broker or dealer applying for registration after the effective date of this section shall furnish, at the time of filing such application, all the consents and powers of attorney required to be furnished by such broker or dealer and by each general partner or managing agent thereof; *Provided, however,* That where an application for registration of a broker or dealer is pending at the time this section becomes effective such consents and powers of attorney shall be furnished within 30 days after this section becomes effective.

(3) Each broker or dealer registered or applying for registration who or which becomes a nonresident broker or dealer after the effective date of this section, and each general partner or managing agent, of an unincorporated broker or dealer registered or applying for registration, who becomes a nonresident after the effective date of this section, shall furnish such consent and power of attorney within 30 days thereafter.

(c) Service of any process, pleadings or other papers on the Commission under this part shall be made by delivering the requisite number of copies thereof to the Secretary of the Commission or to such other person as the Commission may authorize to act in its behalf. Whenever any process, pleadings or other papers as aforesaid are served upon the Commission, it shall promptly forward a copy thereof by registered or certified mail to the appropriate defendants at their last address of record filed with the Commission. The Commission shall be furnished a sufficient number of copies for such purpose, and one copy for its file.

(d) For purposes of this section the following definitions shall apply:

(1) The term *broker* shall have the meaning set out in section 3(a)(4) of the Securities Exchange Act of 1934.

(2) The term *dealer* shall have the meaning set out in section 3(a)(5) of the Securities Exchange Act of 1934.

(3) The term *managing agent* shall mean any person, including a trustee, who directs or manages or who participated in the directing or managing of the affairs of any unincoprorated organization or association which is not a partnership.

(4) The term *nonresident broker or dealer* shall mean (i) in the case of an individual, one who resides in or has his principal place of business in any place not subject to the jurisdiction of the United States; (ii) in the case of a corporation, one incorporated in or having its principal place of business in any place not subject to the jurisdiction of the United States; (iii) in the case of a partnership or other unincoporated organization or association, one having its principal place of business in any place not subject to the jurisdiction of the United States.

(5) A general partner or managing agent of a broker or dealer shall be deemed to be a nonresident if he resides in any place not subject to the jurisdiction of the United States.

(Sec. 319, 53 Stat. 1173, secs. 38, 211, 54 Stat. 641, 855; 15 U.S.C. 77sss, 80a-37, 80b-11)

[18 FR 2578, May 2, 1953, as amended at 23 FR 9691, Dec. 16, 1958; 29 FR 16982, Dec. 11, 1964. Redesignated at 30 FR 11851, Sept. 16, 1965]

§ 240.15b1-6 Notice to brokers and dealers of requirements regarding lost securityholders and unresponsive payees.

Brokers and dealers are hereby notified of Rule 17Ad-17 (§ 240.17Ad-17), which addresses certain requirements with respect to lost securityholders and unresponsive payees that may be applicable to them.

[78 FR 4783, Jan. 23, 2013]

§ 240.15b2-2 Inspection of newly registered brokers and dealers.

(a) *Definition.* For the purpose of this section the term *applicable financial responsibility rules* shall include:

(1) Any rule adopted by the Commission pursuant to sections 8, 15(c)(3), 17(a), or 17(e)(1)(A) of the Act;

(2) Any rule adopted by the Commission relating to hypothecation or lending of customer securities;

(3) Any other rule adopted by the Commission relating to the protection of funds or securities; and

(4) Any rule adopted by the Secretary of the Treasury pursuant to section 15C(b)(1) of the Act.

(b) Each self-regulatory organization that has responsibility for examining a broker or dealer member (including members that are government securities brokers or government securities dealers registered pursuant to section 15C(a)(1)(A) of the Act) for compliance with applicable financial responsibility rules is authorized and directed to conduct an inspection of the member, within six months of the member's registration with the Commission, to determine whether the member is operating in conformity with applicable financial responsibility rules.

(c) The examining self-regulatory organization is further authorized and directed to conduct an inspection of the member no later than twelve months from the member's registration with the Commission, to determine whether the member is operating in conformity with all other applicable provisions of the Act and rules thereunder.

(d) In each case where the examining self-regulatory organization determines that a broker or dealer member has not commenced actual operations within six months of the member's registration with the Commission, it shall delay the inspection pursuant to this section until the second six month period from the member's registration with the Commission.

(e) No inspection need be conducted as provided for in paragraphs (b) and (c) of this section if:

(1) The member was registered with the Commission prior to April 26, 1982;

(2) An inspection of the member has already been conducted by another self-regulatory organization pursuant to this section;

(3) An inspection of the member has already been conducted by the Commission pursuant to section 15(b)(2)(C) of the Act.; or

(4) The member is registered with the Commission pursuant to section 15(b)(11)(A) of the Act (15 U.S.C. 78o(b)(11)(A)).

[47 FR 11269, Mar. 16, 1982, as amended at 52 FR 16838, May 6, 1987; 53 FR 4121, Feb. 12, 1988; 66 FR 45147, Aug. 27, 2001]

§ 240.15b3-1 Amendments to application.

(a) If the information contained in any application for registration as a broker or dealer, or in any amendment thereto, is or becomes inaccurate for any reason, the broker or dealer shall promptly file with the Central Registration Depository (operated by the Financial Industry Regulatory Authority, Inc.) an amendment on Form BD correcting such information.

(b) Every amendment filed with the Central Registration Depository pursuant to this section shall constitute a "report" filed with the Commission within the meaning of Sections 15(b), 17(a), 18(a), 32(a) (15 U.S.C. 78o(b), 78q(a), 78r(a), 78ff(a)) and other applicable provisions of the Act.

[58 FR 14, Jan. 4, 1993, as amended at 64 FR 25147, May 10, 1999; 64 FR 37593, July 12, 1999; 64 FR 42595, Aug. 5, 1999; 73 FR 4692, Jan. 28, 2008]

§ 240.15b5-1 Extension of registration for purposes of the Securities Investor Protection Act of 1970 after cancellation or revocation.

Commission revocation or cancellation of the registration of a broker or dealer pursuant to section 15(b) of the Act: (i) shall be effective for all purposes, except as hereinafter provided,

Securities and Exchange Commission § 240.15b6–1

on the date of the order of revocation or cancellation or, if such order is stayed, on the date the stay is terminated; and (ii) shall be effective six months after the date of the order of revocation or cancellation (or, if such order is stayed, the date the stay is terminated) with respect to a broker's or dealer's registration status as a member within the meaning of Section 3(a)(2) of the Securities Investor Protection Act of 1970 for purposes of the application of sections 5, 6, and 7 thereof to customer claims arising prior to the date of the order of revocation or cancellation (or, if such order is stayed, the date the stay is terminated).

[39 FR 37485, Oct. 22, 1974]

§ 240.15b6–1 Withdrawal from registration.

(a) Notice of withdrawal from registration as a broker or dealer pursuant to Section 15(b) of the Act shall be filed on Form BDW (17 CFR 249.501a) in accordance with the instructions contained therein. Every notice of withdrawal from registration as a broker or dealer shall be filed with the Central Registration Depository (operated by the Financial Industry Regulatory Authority, Inc.) in accordance with applicable filing requirements. Prior to filing a notice of withdrawal from registration on Form BDW (17 CFR 249.501a), a broker or dealer shall amend Form BD (17 CFR 249.501) in accordance with § 240.15b3–1(a) to update any inaccurate information.

(b) A notice of withdrawal from registration filed by a broker or dealer pursuant to Section 15(b) of the Act (15 U.S.C. 78o(b)) shall become effective for all matters (except as provided in this paragraph (b) and in paragraph (c) of this section) on the 60th day after the filing thereof with the Commission, within such longer period of time as to which such broker or dealer consents or which the Commission by order may determine as necessary or appropriate in the public interest or for the protection of investors, or within such shorter period of time as the Commission may determine. If a notice of withdrawal from registration is filed with the Commission at any time subsequent to the date of the issuance of a Commission order instituting proceedings pursuant to Section 15(b) of the Act (15 U.S.C. 78o(b)) to censure, place limitations on the activities, functions or operations of, or suspend or revoke the registration of, such broker or dealer, or if prior to the effective date of the notice of withdrawal pursuant to this paragraph (b), the Commission institutes such a proceeding or a proceeding to impose terms or conditions upon such withdrawal, the notice of withdrawal shall not become effective pursuant to this paragraph (b) except at such time and upon such terms and conditions as the Commission deems necessary or appropriate in the public interest or for the protection of investors.

(c) With respect to a broker's or dealer's registration status as a member within the meaning of Section 3(a)(2) of the Securities Investor Protection Act of 1970 (15 U.S.C. 78ccc(a)(2)) for purposes of the application of Sections 5, 6, and 7 (15 U.S.C. 78eee, 78fff, and 78fff–1) thereof to customer claims arising prior to the effective date of withdrawal pursuant to paragraph (b) of this section, the effective date of a broker's or dealer's withdrawal from registration pursuant to this paragraph (c) shall be six months after the effective date of withdrawal pursuant to paragraph (b) of this section or such shorter period of time as the Commission may determine.

(d) Every notice of withdrawal filed with the Central Registration Depository pursuant to this section shall constitute a "report" filed with the Commission within the meaning of Sections 15(b), 17(a), 18(a), 32(a) (15 U.S.C. 78o(b), 78q(a), 78r(a), 78ff(a)) and other applicable provisions of the Act.

(e) The Commission, by order, may exempt any broker or dealer from the filing requirements provided in Form BDW (17 CFR 249.501a) under conditions that differ from the filing instructions contained in Form BDW.

[64 FR 25147, May 10, 1999, as amended at 64 FR 42595, Aug. 5, 1999; 73 FR 4692, Jan. 28, 2008]

§ 240.15b7-1 Compliance with qualification requirements of self-regulatory organizations.

No registered broker or dealer shall effect any transaction in, or induce the purchase or sale of, any security unless any natural person associated with such broker or dealer who effects or is involved in effecting such transaction is registered or approved in accordance with the standards of training, experience, competence, and other qualification standards (including but not limited to submitting and maintaining all required forms, paying all required fees, and passing any required examinations) established by the rules of any national securities exchange or national securities association of which such broker or dealer is a member or under the rules of the Municipal Securities Rulemaking Board (if it is subject to the rules of that organization).

[58 FR 27658, May 11, 1993]

§ 240.15b7-3T Operational capability in a Year 2000 environment.

(a) This section applies to every broker or dealer registered pursuant to Section 15 of the Act, (15 U.S.C. 78o) that uses computers in the conduct of its business as a broker or dealer. If you have a material Year 2000 problem, then you do not have operational capability within the meaning of Section 15(b)(7) of the Act (15 U.S.C. 78o(b)(7)).

(b)(1) You have a material Year 2000 problem under paragraph (a) of this section if, at any time on or after August 31, 1999:

(i) Any of your mission critical computer systems incorrectly identifies any date in the Year 1999 or the Year 2000; and

(ii) The error impairs or, if uncorrected, is likely to impair, any of your mission critical systems.

(2) You will be presumed to have a material Year 2000 problem if, at any time on or after August 31, 1999, you:

(i) Do not have written procedures reasonably designed to identify, assess, and remediate any Year 2000 problems in mission critical systems under your control;

(ii) Have not verified your Year 2000 remediation efforts through reasonable internal testing of mission critical systems under your control;

(iii) Have not verified your Year 2000 remediation efforts by satisfying Year 2000 testing requirements imposed by self-regulatory organizations to which you are subject; or

(iv) Have not remediated all exceptions related to your mission critical systems contained in any independent public accountant's report prepared on your behalf pursuant to § 240.17a-5(e)(5)(vi).

(c) If you have or are presumed to have a material Year 2000 problem, you must immediately notify the Commission and your designated examining authority of the problem. You must send this notice to the Commission by overnight delivery to the Division of Market Regulation, U.S. Securities and Exchange Commission, 100 F Street, NE., Washington, DC 20549-6628 Attention: Y2K Compliance.

(d)(1) If you are a broker or dealer that is not operationally capable because you have or are presumed to have a material Year 2000 problem, you may not, on or after August 31, 1999:

(i) Effect any transaction in, or induce the purchase or sale of, any security; or

(ii) Receive or hold customer funds or securities, or carry customer accounts.

(2) Notwithstanding paragraph (d)(1) of this section, you may continue to effect transactions in, or induce the purchase or sale of, a security, receive or hold customer funds or securities, or carry customer accounts:

(i) Until December 1, 1999, if you have submitted a certificate to the Commission in compliance with paragraph (e) of this section; or

(ii) Solely to the extent necessary to effect an orderly cessation or transfer of these functions.

(e)(1)(i) If you are a broker or dealer that is not operationally capable because you have or are presumed to have a material Year 2000 problem, you may, in addition to providing the Commission the notice required by paragraph (c) of this section, provide the Commission and your designated examining authority a certificate signed by your chief executive officer (or an individual with similar authority) stating:

(A) You are in the process of remediating your material Year 2000 problem;

Securities and Exchange Commission §240.15b9–1

(B) You have scheduled testing of your affected mission critical systems to verify that the material Year 2000 problem has been remediated, and specify the testing dates;

(C) The date by which you anticipate completing remediation of the material Year 2000 problem in your mission critical systems, and will therefore be operationally capable; and

(D) Based on inquiries and to the best of the chief executive officer's knowledge, you do not anticipate that the existence of the material Year 2000 problem in your mission critical systems will impair your ability, depending on the nature of your business, to ensure prompt and accurate processing of securities transactions, including order entry, execution, comparison, allocation, clearance and settlement of securities transactions, the maintenance of customer accounts, or the delivery of funds and securities; and you anticipate that the steps referred to in paragraphs (e)(1)(i)(A) through (C) of this section will result in remedying the material Year 2000 problem on or before November 15, 1999.

(ii) If the information contained in any certificate provided to the Commission pursuant to paragraph (e) of this section is or becomes misleading or inaccurate for any reason, you must promptly file an updated certificate correcting such information. In addition to the information contained in the certificate, you may provide the Commission with any other information necessary to establish that your mission critical systems will not have material Year 2000 problems on or after November 15, 1999.

(2) If you have submitted a certificate pursuant to paragraph (e)(1) of this section, you must submit a certificate to the Commission and your designated examining authority signed by your chief executive officer (or an individual with similar authority) on or before November 15, 1999, stating that, based on inquiries and to the best of the chief executive officer's knowledge, you have remediated your Year 2000 problem or that you will cease operations. This certificate must be sent to the Commission by overnight delivery to the Division of Market Regulation, U.S. Securities and Exchange Commission, 100 F Street, NE., Washington, DC 20549–6628 Attention: Y2K Compliance.

(f) Notwithstanding paragraph (d)(2) of this section, you must comply with the requirements of paragraph (d)(1) of this section if you have been so ordered by the Commission or by a court.

(g) For the purposes of this section:

(1) The term *mission critical system* means any system that is necessary, depending on the nature of your business, to ensure prompt and accurate processing of securities transactions, including order entry, execution, comparison, allocation, clearance and settlement of securities transactions, the maintenance of customer accounts, and the delivery of funds and securities; and

(2) The term *customer* includes a broker or dealer.

(h) This temporary section will expire on July 1, 2001.

[64 FR 42028, Aug. 3, 1999, as amended at 73 FR 32227, June 5, 2008]

§ 240.15b9–1 Exemption for certain exchange members.

(a) Any broker or dealer required by section 15(b)(8) of the Act to become a member of a registered national securities association shall be exempt from such requirement if it: (1) Is a member of a national securities exchange, (2) carries no customer accounts, and (3) has annual gross income derived from purchases and sales of securities otherwise than on a national securities exchange of which it is a member in an amount no greater than $1,000.

(b) The gross income limitation contained in paragraph (a) of this section, shall not apply to income derived from transactions (1) for the dealer's own account with or through another registered broker or dealer or (2) through the Intermarket Trading System.

(c) For purposes of this section, the term *Intermarket Trading System* shall mean the intermarket communications linkage operated jointly by certain self-regulatory organizations pursuant to a plan filed with, and approved by, the Commission pursuant to §242.608 of this chapter.

[48 FR 53691, Nov. 29, 1983, as amended at 70 FR 37618, June 29, 2005]

§ 240.15b9-2 Exemption from SRO membership for OTC derivatives dealers.

An OTC derivatives dealer, as defined in § 240.3b-12, shall be exempt from any requirement under section 15(b)(8) of the Act (15 U.S.C. 78o(b)(8)) to become a member of a registered national securities association.

[63 FR 59397, Nov. 3, 1998]

§ 240.15b11-1 Registration by notice of security futures product broker-dealers.

(a) A broker or dealer may register by notice pursuant to section 15(b)(11)(A) of the Act (15 U.S.C. 78o(b)(11)(A)) if it:

(1) Is registered with the Commodity Futures Trading Commission as a futures commission merchant or an introducing broker, as those terms are defined in the Commodity Exchange Act (7 U.S.C. 1, *et seq.*), respectively;

(2) Is a member of the National Futures Association or another national securities association registered under section 15A(k) of the Act (15 U.S.C. 78o-3(k)); and

(3) Is not required to register as a broker or dealer in connection with transactions in securities other than security futures products.

(b) A broker or dealer registering by notice pursuant to section 15(b)(11)(A) of the Act (15 U.S.C. 78o(b)(11)(A)) must file Form BD-N (17 CFR 249.501b) in accordance with the instructions to the form. A broker or dealer registering by notice pursuant to this section must indicate where appropriate on Form BD-N that it satisfies all of the conditions in paragraph (a) of this section.

(c) If the information contained in any notice of registration filed on Form BD-N (17 CFR 249.501b) pursuant to this section is or becomes inaccurate for any reason, the broker or dealer shall promptly file an amendment on Form BD-N correcting such information.

(d) An application for registration by notice, and any amendments thereto, that are filed on Form BD-N (17 CFR 249.501b) pursuant to this section will be considered a "report" filed with the Commission for purposes of sections 15(b), 17(a), 18(a), 32(a) (15 U.S.C. 78o(b), 78q(a), 78r(a), 78ff(a)) and other applicable provisions of the Act.

[66 FR 45146, Aug. 27, 2001]

RULES RELATING TO OVER-THE-COUNTER MARKETS

§ 240.15c1-1 Definitions.

As used in any rule adopted pursuant to section 15(c)(1) of the Act:

(a) The term *customer* shall not include a broker or dealer or a municipal securities dealer; provided, however, that the term "customer" shall include a municipal securities dealer (other than a broker or dealer) with respect to transactions in securities other than municipal securities.

(b) The term *the completion of the transaction* means:

(1) In the case of a customer who purchases a security through or from a broker, dealer or municipal securities dealer, except as provided in paragraph (b)(2) of this section, the time when such customer pays the broker, dealer or municipal securities dealer any part of the purchase price, or, if payment is effected by a bookkeeping entry, the time when such bookkeeping entry is made by the broker, dealer or municipal securities dealer for any part of the purchase price;

(2) In the case of a customer who purchases a security through or from a broker, dealer or municipal securities dealer and who makes payment therefor prior to the time when payment is requested or notification is given that payment is due, the time when such broker, dealer or municipal securities dealer delivers the security to or into the account of such customer;

(3) In the case of a customer who sells a security through or to a broker, dealer or municipal securities dealer except as provided in paragraph (b)(4) of this section, if the security is not in the custody of the broker, dealer or municipal securities dealer at the time of sale, the time when the security is delivered to the broker, dealer or municipal securities dealer, and if the security is in the custody of the broker, dealer or municipal securities dealer at the time of sale, the time when the broker, dealer or municipal securities dealer transfers the security from the account of such customer;

Securities and Exchange Commission

(4) In the case of a customer who sells a security through or to a broker, dealer or municipal securities dealer and who delivers such security to such broker, dealer or municipal securities dealer prior to the time when delivery is requested or notification is given that delivery is due, the time when such broker, dealer or municipal securities dealer makes payment to or into the account of such customer.

[41 FR 22825, June 7, 1976]

§ 240.15c1-2 Fraud and misrepresentation.

(a) The term *manipulative, deceptive, or other fraudulent device or contrivance*, as used in section 15(c)(1) of the Act (section 2, 52 Stat. 1075; 15 U.S.C. 78o(c)(1), is hereby defined to include any act, practice, or course of business which operates or would operate as a fraud or deceit upon any person.

(b) The term *manipulative, deceptive, or other fraudulent device or contrivance*, as used in section 15(c)(1) of the Act, is hereby defined to include any untrue statement of a material fact and any omission to state a material fact necessary in order to make the statements made, in the light of the circumstances under which they are made, not misleading, which statement or omission is made with knowledge or reasonable grounds to believe that it is untrue or misleading.

(c) The scope of this section shall not be limited by any specific definitions of the term "manipulative, deceptive, or other fraudulent device or contrivance" contained in other rules adopted pursuant to section 15(c)(1) of the act.

(Sec. 2, 52 Stat. 1075; 15 U.S.C. 78o)

CROSS REFERENCE: For regulation prohibiting employment of manipulative and deceptive devices as such term is used in section 15 of the Act, by any broker or dealer, see § 240.10b-3.

[13 FR 8205, Dec. 22, 1948]

§ 240.15c1-3 Misrepresentation by brokers, dealers and municipal securities dealers as to registration.

The term *manipulative, deceptive, or other fraudulent device or contrivance*, as used in section 15(c)(1) of the Act, is hereby defined to include any representation by a broker, dealer or municipal securities dealer that the registration of a broker or dealer, pursuant to section 15(b) of the Act, or the registration of a municipal securities dealer pursuant to section 15B(a) of the Act, or the failure of the Commission to deny or revoke such registration, indicates in any way that the Commission has passed upon or approved the financial standing, business, or conduct of such registered broker, dealer or municipal securities dealer or the merits of any security or any transaction or transactions therein.

[41 FR 22825, June 7, 1976]

§ 240.15c1-4 [Reserved]

§ 240.15c1-5 Disclosure of control.

The term *manipulative, deceptive, or other fraudulent device or contrivance*, as used in section 15(c)(1) of the Act, is hereby defined to include any act of any broker, dealer or municipal securities dealer controlled by, controlling, or under common control with, the issuer of any security, designed to effect with or for the account of a customer any transaction in, or to induce the purchase or sale by such customer of, such security unless such broker, dealer or municipal securities dealer, before entering into any contract with or for such customer for the purchase or sale of such security, discloses to such customer the existence of such control, and unless such disclosure, if not made in writing, is supplemented by the giving or sending of written disclosure at or before the completion of the transaction.

[41 FR 22825, June 7, 1976]

§ 240.15c1-6 Disclosure of interest in distribution.

The term *manipulative, deceptive, or other fraudulent device or contrivance*, as used in section 15(c)(1) of the Act, is hereby defined to include any act of any broker who is acting for a customer or for both such customer and some other person, or of any dealer or municipal securities dealer who receives or has promise of receiving a fee from a customer for advising such customer with respect to securities, designed to effect with or for the account of such customer any transaction in, or

§ 240.15c1-7

to induce the purchase or sale by such customer of, any security in the primary or secondary distribution of which such broker, dealer or municipal securities dealer is participating or is otherwise financially interested unless such broker, dealer or municipal securities dealer, at or before the completion of each such transaction gives or sends to such customer written notification of the existence of such participation or interest.

[41 FR 22826, June 7, 1976]

§ 240.15c1-7 Discretionary accounts.

(a) The term *manipulative, deceptive, or other fraudulent device or contrivance*, as used in section 15(c) of the Act, is hereby defined to include any act of any broker, dealer or municipal securities dealer designed to effect with or for any customer's account in respect to which such broker, dealer or municipal securities dealer or his agent or employee is vested with any discretionary power any transactions or purchase or sale which are excessive in size or frequency in view of the financial resources and character of such account.

(b) The term *manipulative, deceptive, or other fraudulent device or contrivance*, as used in section 15(c)(1) of the Act, is hereby defined to include any act of any broker, dealer or municipal securities dealer designed to effect with or for any customer's account in respect to which such broker, dealer or municipal securities dealer or his agent or employee is vested with any discretionary power any transaction of purchase or sale unless immediately after effecting such transaction such broker, dealer or municipal securities dealer makes a record of such transaction which record includes the name of such customer, the name, amount and price of the security, and the date and time when such transaction took place.

[41 FR 22826, June 7, 1976]

§ 240.15c1-8 Sales at the market.

The term *manipulative, deceptive, or other fraudulent device or contrivance*, as used in section 15(c)(1) of the Act, is hereby defined to include any representation made to a customer by a broker, dealer or municipal securities dealer who is participating or otherwise financially interested in the primary or secondary distribution of any security which is not admitted to trading on a national securities exchange that such security is being offered to such customer "at the market" or at a price related to the market price unless such broker, dealer or municipal securities dealer knows or has reasonable grounds to believe that a market for such security exists other than that made, created, or controlled by him, or by any person for whom he is acting or with whom he is associated in such distribution, or by any person controlled by, controlling or under common control with him.

[41 FR 22826, June 7, 1976]

§ 240.15c1-9 Use of pro forma balance sheets.

The term *manipulative, deceptive, or other fraudulent device or contrivance*, as used in section 15(c)(1) of the Act, is hereby defined to include the use of financial statements purporting to give effect to the receipt and application of any part of the proceeds from the sale or exchange of securities, unless the assumptions upon which each such financial statement is based are clearly set forth as part of the caption to each such statement in type at least as large as that used generally in the body of the statement.

(Sec. 2, 52 Stat. 1075; 15 U.S.C. 78o)

[13 FR 8205, Dec. 22, 1948]

§ 240.15c2-1 Hypothecation of customers' securities.

(a) *General provisions.* The term *fraudulent, deceptive, or manipulative act or practice*, as used in section 15(c) (2) of the Act, is hereby defined to include the direct or indirect hypothecation by a broker or dealer, or his arranging for or permitting, directly or indirectly, the continued hypothecation of any securities carried for the account of any customer under circumstances:

(1) That will permit the commingling of securities carried for the account of any such customer with securities carried for the account of any other customer, without first obtaining the written consent of each such customer to such hypothecation;

Securities and Exchange Commission § 240.15c2–1

(2) That will permit such securities to be commingled with securities carried for the account of any person other than a bona fide customer of such broker or dealer under a lien for a loan made to such broker or dealer; or

(3) That will permit securities carried for the account of customers to be hypothecated, or subjected to any lien or liens or claims or claims of the pledgee or pledgees, for a sum which exceeds the aggregate indebtedness of all customers in respect of securities carried for their accounts; except that this clause shall not be deemed to be violated by reason of an excess arising on any day through the reduction of the aggregate indebtedness of customers on such day, provided that funds or securities in an amount sufficient to eliminate such excess are paid or placed in transfer to pledgees for the purpose of reducing the sum of the liens or claims to which securities carried for the account of customers are subject as promptly as practicable after such reduction occurs, but before the lapse of one half hour after the commencement of banking hours on the next banking day at the place where the largest principal amount of loans of such broker or dealer are payable and, in any event, before such broker or dealer on such day has obtained or increased any bank loan collateralized by securities carried for the account of customers.

(b) *Definitions.* For the purposes of this section:

(1) The term *customer* shall not include any general or special partner or any director or officer of such broker or dealer, or any participant, as such, in any joint, group or syndicate account with such broker or dealer or with any partner, officer or director thereof. The term also shall not include a counterparty who has delivered collateral to an OTC derivatives dealer pursuant to a transaction in an eligible OTC derivative instrument, or pursuant to the OTC derivatives dealer's cash management securities activities or ancillary portfolio management securities activities, and who has received a prominent written notice from the OTC derivatives dealer that:

(i) Except as otherwise agreed in writing by the OTC derivatives dealer and the counterparty, the dealer may repledge or otherwise use the collateral in its business;

(ii) In the event of the OTC derivatives dealer's failure, the counterparty will likely be considered an unsecured creditor of the dealer as to that collateral;

(iii) The Securities Investor Protection Act of 1970 (15 U.S.C 78aaa through 78lll) does not protect the counterparty; and

(iv) The collateral will not be subject to the requirements of §240.8c–1, §240.15c2–1, §240.15c3–2, or §240.15c3–3;

(2) The term *securities carried for the account of any customer* shall be deemed to mean:

(i) Securities received by or on behalf of such broker or dealer for the account of any customer;

(ii) Securities sold and appropriated by such broker or dealer to a customer, except that if such securities were subject to a lien when appropriated to a customer they shall not be deemed to be "securities carried for the account of any customer" pending their release from such lien as promptly as practicable;

(iii) Securities sold, but not appropriated, by such broker or dealer to a customer who has made any payment therefor, to the extent that such broker or dealer owns and has received delivery of securities of like kind, except that if such securities were subject to a lien when such payment was made they shall not be deemed to be "securities carried for the account of any customer" pending their release from such lien as promptly as practicable;

(3) *Aggregate indebtedness* shall not be deemed to be reduced by reason of uncollected items. In computing aggregate indebtedness, related guaranteed and guarantor accounts shall be treated as a single account and considered on a consolidated basis, and balances in accounts carrying both long and short positions shall be adjusted by treating the market value of the securities required to cover such short positions as though such market value were a debit; and

(4) In computing the sum of the liens or claims to which securities carried for the account of customers of a

§ 240.15c2-1

broker or dealer are subject, any rehypothecation of such securities by another broker or dealer who is subject to this section or to § 240.8c–1 shall be disregarded.

(c) *Exemption for cash accounts.* The provisions of paragraph (a)(1) of this section shall not apply to any hypothecation of securities carried for the account of a customer in a special cash account within the meaning of 12 CFR 220.4(c): *Provided,* That at or before the completion of the transaction of purchase of such securities for, or of sale of such securities to, such customer, written notice is given or sent to such customer disclosing that such securities are or may be hypothecated under circumstances which will permit the commingling thereof with securities carried for the account of other customers. The term *the completion of the transaction* shall have the meaning given to such term by § 240.15c1–1(b).

(d) *Exemption for clearing house liens.* The provisions of paragraphs (a)(2), (a)(3), and (f) of this section shall not apply to any lien or claim of the clearing corporation, or similar department or association, of a national securities exchange or a registered national securities association, for a loan made and to be repaid on the same calendar day, which is incidental to the clearing of transactions in securities or loans through such corporation, department, or association: *Provided, however,* That for the purpose of paragraph (a)(3) of this section, "aggregate indebtedness of all customers in respect of securities carried for their accounts" shall not include indebtedness in respect of any securities subject to any lien or claim exempted by this paragraph.

(e) *Exemption for certain liens on securities of noncustomers.* The provisions of paragraph (a)(2) of this section shall not be deemed to prevent such broker or dealer from permitting securities not carried for the account of a customer to be subjected (1) to a lien for a loan made against securities carried for the account of customers, or (2) to a lien for a loan made and to be repaid on the same calendar day. For the purpose of this exemption, a loan shall be deemed to be "made against securities carried for the account of customers" if only securities carried for the account of customers are used to obtain or to increase such loan or as substitutes for other securities carried for the account of customers.

(f) *Notice and certification requirements.* No person subject to this section shall hypothecate any security carried for the account of a customer unless, at or prior to the time of each such hypothecation, he gives written notice to the pledgee that the security pledged is carried for the account of a customer and that such hypothecation does not contravene any provision of this section, except that in the case of an omnibus account the broker or dealer for whom such account is carried may furnish a signed statement to the person carrying such account that all securities carried therein by such broker or dealer will be securities carried for the account of his customers and that the hypothecation thereof by such broker or dealer will not contravene any provision of this section. The provisions of this paragraph shall not apply to any hypothecation of securities under any lien or claim of a pledgee securing a loan made and to be repaid on the same calendar day.

(g) The fact that securities carried for the accounts of customers and securities carried for the accounts of others are represented by one or more certificates in the custody of a clearing corporation or other subsidiary organization of either a national securities exchange or of a registered national securities association, or of a custodian bank, in accordance with a system for the central handling of securities established by a national securities exchange or a registered national securities association, pursuant to which system the hypothecation of such securities is effected by bookkeeping entries without physical delivery of such securities, shall not, in and of itself, result in a commingling of securities prohibited by paragraph (a)(1) or (a)(2) of this section, whenever a participating member, broker or dealer hypothecates securities in accordance with such system: *Provided, however,* That (1) any such custodian of any securities held by or for such system shall agree that it will not for any reason, including the assertion of any claim, right or lien of any kind, refuse or refrain from

Securities and Exchange Commission

§ 240.15c2-5

promptly delivering any such securities (other than securities then hypothecated in accordance with such system) to such clearing corporation or other subsidiary organization or as directed by it, except that nothing in such agreement shall be deemed to require the custodian to deliver any securities in contravention of any notice of levy, seizure or similar notice, or order or judgment, issued or directed by a governmental agency or court, or officer thereof, having jurisdiction over such custodian, which on its face affects such securities; (2) such systems shall have safeguards in the handling, transfer and delivery of securities and provisions for fidelity bond coverage of the employees and agents of the clearing corporation or other subsidiary organization and for periodic examinations by independent public accountants; and (3) the provisions of this paragraph (g) shall not be effective with respect to any particular system unless the agreement required by paragraph (g)(1) of this section and the safeguards and provisions required by paragraph (g)(2) of this section shall have been deemed adequate by the Commission for the protection of investors, and unless any subsequent amendments to such agreement, safeguards or provisions shall have been deemed adequate by the Commission for the protection of investors.

(Secs. 8, 15, 48 Stat. 888, 895, sec. 2, 52 Stat. 1075; 15 U.S.C. 78b. 78o)

CROSS REFERENCE: For interpretative releases applicable to § 240.15c2-1, see Nos. 2690 and 2822 in tabulation, part 241 of this chapter.

[13 FR 8205, Dec. 22, 1948, as amended at 31 FR 7741, June 1, 1966; 37 FR 73, Jan. 5, 1972; 63 FR 59397, Nov. 3, 1998]

§ 240.15c2-3 [Reserved]

§ 240.15c2-4 Transmission or maintenance of payments received in connection with underwritings.

It shall constitute a "fraudulent, deceptive, or manipulative act or practice" as used in section 15(c)(2) of the Act, for any broker, dealer or municipal securities dealer participating in any distribution of securities, other than a firm-commitment underwriting, to accept any part of the sale price of any security being distributed unless:

(a) The money or other consideration received is promptly transmitted to the persons entitled thereto; or

(b) If the distribution is being made on an "all-or-none" basis, or on any other basis which contemplates that payment is not to be made to the person on whose behalf the distribution is being made until some further event or contingency occurs, (1) the money or other consideration received is promptly deposited in a separate bank account, as agent or trustee for the persons who have the beneficial interests therein, until the appropriate event or contingency has occurred, and then the funds are promptly transmitted or returned to the persons entitled thereto, or (2) all such funds are promptly transmitted to a bank which has agreed in writing to hold all such funds in escrow for the persons who have the beneficial interests therein and to transmit or return such funds directly to the persons entitled thereto when the appropriate event or contingency has occurred.

[41 FR 22826, June 7, 1976]

§ 240.15c2-5 Disclosure and other requirements when extending or arranging credit in certain transactions.

(a) It shall constitute a "fraudulent, deceptive, or manipulative act or practice" as used in section 15(c)(2) of the Act for any broker or dealer to offer or sell any security to, or to attempt to induce the purchase of any security by, any person, in connection with which such broker or dealer directly or indirectly offers to extend any credit to or to arrange any loan for such person, or extends to or participates in arranging any loan for such person, unless such broker or dealer, before any purchase, loan or other related element of the transaction is entered into:

(1) Delivers to such person a written statement setting forth the exact nature and extent of (i) such person's obligations under the particular loan arrangement, including among other things, the specific charges which such person will incur under such loan in each period during which the loan may continue or be extended, (ii) the risks

§ 240.15c2-6

and disadvantages which such person will incur in the entire transaction, including the loan arrangement, (iii) all commissions, discounts, and other remuneration received and to be received in connection with the entire transaction including the loan arrangment, by the broker or dealer, by any person controlling, controlled by, or under common control with the broker or dealer, and by any other person participating in the transaction; *Provided, however,* That the broker or dealer shall be deemed to be in compliance with this paragraph if the customer, before any purchase, loan, or other related element of the transaction is entered into in a manner legally binding upon the customer, receives a statement from the lender, or receives a prospectus or offering circular from the broker or dealer, which statement, prospectus or offering circular contains the information required by this paragraph; and

(2) Obtains from such person information concerning his financial situation and needs, reasonably determines that the entire transaction, including the loan arrangement, is suitable for such person, and retains in his files a written statement setting forth the basis upon which the broker or dealer made such determination; *Provided, however,* That the written statement referred to in this paragraph must be made available to the customer on request.

(b) This section shall not apply to any credit extended or any loan arranged by any broker or dealer subject to the provisions of Regulation T (12 CFR part 220) if such credit is extended or such loan is arranged, in compliance with the requirements of such regulation, only for the purpose of purchasing or carrying the security offered or sold: *Provided, however,* That notwithstanding this paragraph, the provisions of paragraph (a) shall apply in full force with respect to any transaction involving the extension of or arrangement for credit by a broker or dealer (i) in a special insurance premium funding account within the meaning of section 4(k) of Regulation T (12 CFR 220.4(k)) or (ii) in compliance with the terms of § 240.3a12-5 of this chapter.

(c) This section shall not apply to any offer to extend credit or arrange

17 CFR Ch. II (4-1-23 Edition)

any loan, or to any credit extended or loan arranged, in connection with any offer or sale, or attempt to induce the purchase, of any municipal security.

(d) This section shall not apply to a transaction involving the extension of credit by an OTC derivatives dealer, as defined in § 240.3b-12, if the transaction is exempt from the provisions of Section 7(c) of the Act (15 U.S.C. 78g(c)) pursuant to § 240.36a1-1.

(Sec. 3(a)(12), 48 Stat. 882, as amended, 84 Stat. 718, 1435, 1499 (15 U.S.C. 78c(12)); sec. 7(c), 48 Stat. 886, as amended, 82 Stat. 452 (15 U.S.C. 78g(c)); sec. 11(d)(1), 48 Stat. 891 as amended, 68 Stat. 686 (15 U.S.C. 78k(d)(1)); sec. 15(c), 48 Stat. 895, as amended, 52 Stat. 1075, 84 Stat. 1653 (15 U.S.C. 78o(c)); sec. 23(a), 48 Stat. 901, as amended, 49 Stat. 704, 1379 (15 U.S.C. 78w(a))

[40 FR 6646, Feb. 13, 1975, as amended at 41 FR 22826, June 7, 1976; 63 FR 59397, Nov. 3, 1998]

§ 240.15c2-6 [Reserved]

§ 240.15c2-7 Identification of quotations.

(a) It shall constitute an attempt to induce the purchase or sale of a security by making a "fictitious quotation" within the meaning of section 15(c)(2) of the Act, for any broker or dealer to furnish or submit, directly or indirectly, any quotation for a security (other than a municipal security) to an inter-dealer quotation system unless:

(1) The inter-dealer-quotation-system is informed, if such is the case, that the quotation is furnished or submitted;

(i) By a correspondent broker or dealer for the account or in behalf of another broker or dealer, and if so, the identity of such other broker or dealer; and/or

(ii) In furtherance of one or more other arrangements (including a joint account, guarantee of profit, guarantee against loss, commission, markup, markdown, indication of interest and accommodation arrangement) between or among brokers or dealers, and if so, the identity of each broker or dealer participating in any such arrangement or arrangements: *Provided, however,* That the provisions of this subparagraph shall not apply if only one of the brokers or dealers participating in any such arrangement or arrangements furnishes or submits a quotation with respect to the security to an inter-dealer-quotation-system.

(2) The inter-dealer-quotation-system to which the quotation is furnished or submitted makes it a general practice to disclose with each published quotation, by appropriate symbol or otherwise, the category or categories (paragraph (a)(1)(i) and/or (ii) of this section) in furtherance of which the quotation is submitted, and the identities of all other brokers and dealers referred to in paragraph (a)(1) of this section where such information is supplied to the inter-dealer-quotation-system under the provisions of paragraph (a)(1) of this section.

(b) It shall constitute an attempt to induce the purchase or sale of a security by making a "fictitious quotation," within the meaning of section 15(c)(2) of the Act, for a broker or dealer to enter into any correspondent or other arrangement (including a joint account, guarantee of profit, guarantee against loss, commission, markup, markdown, indication of interest and accommodation arrangement) in furtherance of which two or more brokers or dealers furnish or submit quotations with respect to a particular security unless such broker or dealer informs all brokers or dealers furnishing or submitting such quotations of the existence of such correspondent and other arrangments, and the identity of the parties thereto.

(c) For purposes of this section:

(1) The term *inter-dealer-quotation-system* shall mean any system of general circulation to brokers and dealers which regularly disseminates quotations of identified brokers or dealers but shall not include a quotation sheet prepared and distributed by a broker or dealer in the regular course of his business and containing only quotations of such broker or dealer.

(2) The term *quotation* shall mean any bid or offer, or any indication of interest (such as OW or BW) in any bid or offer.

(3) The term *correspondent* shall mean a broker or dealer who has a direct line of communication to another broker or dealer located in a different city or geographic area.

(Sec. 15, 48 Stat. 895, as amended; 15 U.S.C. 78o)

[29 FR 11530, Aug. 12, 1964, as amended at 41 FR 22826, June 7, 1976]

§ 240.15c2-8 **Delivery of prospectus.**

(a) It shall constitute a deceptive act or practice, as those terms are used in section 15(c)(2) of the Act, for a broker or dealer to participate in a distribution of securities with respect to which a registration statement has been filed under the Securities Act of 1933 unless he complies with the requirements set forth in paragraphs (b) through (h) of this section. For the purposes of this section, a broker or dealer participating in the distribution shall mean any underwriter and any member or proposed member of the selling group.

(b) In connection with an issue of securities, the issuer of which has not previously been required to file reports pursuant to sections 13(a) or 15(d) of the Securities Exchange Act of 1934, unless such issuer has been exempted from the requirement to file reports thereunder pursuant to section 12(h) of the Act, such broker or dealer shall deliver a copy of the preliminary prospectus to any person who is expected to receive a confirmation of sale at least 48 hours prior to the sending of such confirmation. This paragraph (b) does not apply with respect to asset-backed securities (as defined in § 229.1101 of this chapter) that meet the requirements of General Instruction I.B.5 of Form S-3 (§ 239.13 of this chapter). Provided, however, this paragraph (b) shall apply to all issuances of asset-backed securities (as defined in § 229.1101(c) of this chapter) regardless of whether the issuer has previously been required to file reports pursuant to sections 13(a) or 15(d) of the Securities Exchange Act of 1934, or exempted from the requirement to file reports thereunder pursuant to section 12(h) of the Act (15 U.S.C. 78l).

(c) Such broker or dealer shall take reasonable steps to furnish to any person who makes written request for a preliminary prospectus between the filing date and a reasonable time prior to the effective date of the registration

§ 240.15c2-11

statement to which such prospectus relates, a copy of the latest preliminary prospectus on file with the Commission. Reasonable steps shall include receiving an undertaking by the managing underwriter or underwriters to send such copy to the address given in the requests.

(d) Such broker or dealer shall take reasonable steps to comply promptly with the written request of any person for a copy of the final prospectus relating to such securities during the period between the effective date of the registration statement and the later of either the termination of such distribution, or the expiration of the applicable 40- or 90-day period under section 4(3) of the Securities Act of 1933. Reasonable steps shall include receiving an undertaking by the managing underwriter or underwriters to send such copy to the address given in the requests. (The 40-day and 90-day periods referred to above shall be deemed to apply for purposes of this rule irrespective of the provisions of paragraphs (b) and (d) of § 230.174 of this chapter).

(e) Such broker or dealer shall take reasonable steps (1) to make available a copy of the preliminary prospectus relating to such securities to each of his associated persons who is expected, prior to the effective date, to solicit customers' order for such securities before the making of any such solicitation by such associated persons and (2) to make available to each such associated person a copy of any amended preliminary prospectus promptly after the filing thereof.

(f) Such broker or dealer shall take reasonable steps to make available a copy of the final prospectus relating to such securities to each of his associated persons who is expected, after the effective date, to solicit customers orders for such securities prior to the making of any such solicitation by such associated persons, unless a preliminary prospectus which is substantially the same as the final prospectus except for matters relating to the price of the stocks, has been so made available.

(g) If the broker or dealer is a managing underwriter of such distribution, he shall take reasonable steps to see to it that all other brokers or dealers participating in such distribution are promptly furnished with sufficient copies, as requested by them, of each preliminary prospectus, each amended preliminary prospectus and the final prospectus to enable them to comply with paragraphs (b), (c), (d), and (e) of this section.

(h) If the broker or dealer is a managing underwriter of such distribution, he shall take reasonable steps to see that any broker or dealer participating in the distribution or trading in the registered security is furnished reasonable quantities of the final prospectus relating to such securities, as requested by him, in order to enable him to comply with the prospectus delivery requirements of section 5(b) (1) and (2) of the Securities Act of 1933.

(i) This section shall not require the furnishing of prospectuses in any state where such furnishing would be unlawful under the laws of such state: *Provided, however,* That this provision is not to be construed to relieve a broker or dealer from complying with the requirements of section 5(b)(1) and (2) of the Securities Act of 1933.

[35 FR 18457, Dec. 4, 1970, as amended at 47 FR 11470, Mar. 16, 1982; 53 FR 11845, Apr. 11, 1988; 60 FR 26622, May 17, 1995; 70 FR 1622, Jan. 7, 2005; 79 FR 57344, Sept. 24, 2014]

§ 240.15c2-11 Publication or submission of quotations without specified information.

(a) *Unlawful activity.* As a means reasonably designed to prevent fraudulent, deceptive, or manipulative acts or practices, it shall be unlawful for:

(1) *Brokers or dealers.* A broker or dealer to publish any quotation for a security or, directly or indirectly, to submit any such quotation for publication, in any quotation medium, unless:

(i)(A) Such broker or dealer has in its records the documents and information specified in paragraph (b) of this section;

(B) Such documents and information specified in paragraph (b) of this section (excluding paragraphs (b)(5)(i)(N) through (P) of this section) are current and publicly available; and

(C) Based upon a review of the documents and information specified in paragraph (b) of this section, together

Securities and Exchange Commission § 240.15c2-11

with any other documents and information required by paragraph (c) of this section, such broker or dealer has a reasonable basis under the circumstances for believing that:

(1) The documents and information specified in paragraph (b) of this section are accurate in all material respects; and

(2) The sources of the documents and information specified in paragraph (b) of this section are reliable; or

(ii)(A) The quotation medium is a qualified interdealer quotation system that made a publicly available determination that it has performed the activities described in paragraph (a)(2)(i) through (iii) of this section; and

(B) Such quotation is published or submitted for publication within three business days after such qualified interdealer quotation system makes such publicly available determination.

(2) *Qualified interdealer quotation systems.* A qualified interdealer quotation system to make known to others the quotation of a broker or dealer that is published or submitted for publication pursuant to paragraph (a)(1)(ii) of this section, unless:

(i) Such qualified interdealer quotation system has in its records the documents and information specified in paragraph (b) of this section (excluding paragraphs (b)(5)(i)(N) through (P) of this section except where the qualified interdealer quotation system has knowledge or possession of this information);

(ii) Such documents and information specified in paragraph (b) of this section (excluding paragraphs (b)(5)(i)(N) through (P) of this section) are current and publicly available;

(iii) Based upon a review of the documents and information specified in paragraph (b) of this section (excluding paragraphs (b)(5)(i)(N) through (P) of this section, except where the qualified interdealer quotation system has knowledge or possession of this information), together with any other documents and information required by paragraph (c) of this section, such qualified interdealer quotation system has a reasonable basis under the circumstances for believing that:

(A) The documents and information specified in paragraph (b) of this section are accurate in all material respects; and

(B) The sources of the documents and information specified in paragraph (b) of this section are reliable; and

(iv) The qualified interdealer quotation system makes a publicly available determination that it has performed the activities described in paragraphs (a)(2)(i) through (iii) of this section; or

(3) *Qualified interdealer quotation systems or registered national securities Associations.* A qualified interdealer quotation system or registered national securities association to make a publicly available determination described in paragraph (f)(2)(iii)(B), (f)(3)(ii)(A), or (f)(7) of this section, unless such qualified interdealer quotation system or registered national securities association establishes, maintains, and enforces reasonably designed written policies and procedures to determine whether:

(i) The documents and information specified in paragraph (b) of this section are current and publicly available; and

(ii) The requirements of an exception under paragraph (f) of this section are met, if it makes a publicly available determination described in paragraph (f)(7) of this section.

(b) *Specified information.* (1) A copy of the prospectus specified by section 10(a) of the Securities Act of 1933 for an issuer that has filed a registration statement under the Securities Act of 1933, other than a registration statement on Form F-6, that became effective less than 90 calendar days prior to the day on which such broker or dealer publishes or submits the quotation to the quotation medium; *Provided,* That such registration statement has not thereafter been the subject of a stop order that is still in effect when the quotation is published or submitted; or

(2) A copy of the offering circular provided for under Regulation A (§§ 230.251 through 230.263 of this chapter) for an issuer that has filed an offering statement under Regulation A that was qualified less than 40 calendar days prior to the day on which such broker or dealer publishes or submits the quotation to the quotation medium; *Provided,* That the Regulation A

§ 240.15c2-11

exemption, with respect to such issuer, has not thereafter become subject to a suspension order that is still in effect when the quotation is published or submitted; or

(3) A current copy of:

(i) An annual report filed pursuant to section 13 or 15(d) of the Act, together with any periodic and current reports that have been filed thereafter under the Act by the issuer, except for current reports filed during the three business days prior to the publication or submission of the quotation; *Provided, however,* That, until such issuer has filed its first such annual report, the broker, dealer, or qualified interdealer quotation system has in its records a copy of the registration statement filed by the issuer under the Securities Act of 1933, other than a registration statement on Form F-6, that became effective within the prior 16 months, or a copy of any registration statement filed by the issuer under section 12 of the Act that became effective within the prior 16 months, together with any periodic and current reports filed thereafter under section 13 or 15(d) of the Act;

(ii) An annual report filed pursuant to Regulation A, together with any periodic and current reports filed thereafter under Regulation A by the issuer, except for current reports filed during the three business days prior to the publication or submission of the quotation; *Provided, however,* That, until such issuer has filed its first such annual report, the broker, dealer, or qualified interdealer quotation system has in its records a copy of the offering statement filed by the issuer under Regulation A, that was qualified within the prior 16 months, together with any periodic and current reports filed thereafter under Regulation A;

(iii) An annual report filed pursuant to Regulation Crowdfunding (§§ 227.100 through 227.503 of this chapter); *Provided, however,* that, until such issuer has filed its first such annual report, the broker, dealer, or qualified interdealer quotation system has in its records a copy of the Form C filed by the issuer under Regulation Crowdfunding within the prior 16 months, together with any Form C/A

and Form C/U filed thereafter under Regulation Crowdfunding;

(iv) An annual statement referred to in section 12(g)(2)(G)(i) of the Act (in the case of an issuer required to file reports pursuant to section 13 or 15(d) of the Act), together with any periodic and current reports filed thereafter under the Act by the issuer, except for current reports filed during the three business days prior to the publication or submission of the quotation; *Provided, however,* that, until such issuer has filed its first such annual statement, the broker, dealer, or qualified interdealer quotation system has in its records a copy of the registration statement filed by the issuer under the Securities Act of 1933, other than a registration statement on Form F-6, that became effective within the prior 16 months, or a copy of any registration statement filed by the issuer under section 12 of the Act, that became effective within the prior 16 months, together with any periodic and current reports filed thereafter under section 13 or 15(d) of the Act; or

(v) An annual statement referred to in section 12(g)(2)(G)(i) of the Act (in the case of an issuer of a security that falls within the provisions of section 12(g)(2)(G) of the Act); or

(4) A copy of the information that, since the first day of its most recently completed fiscal year, the issuer has published as required to establish the exemption from registration under section 12(g) of the Act pursuant to § 240.12g3-2(b) of this chapter, which the broker or dealer must make available upon the request of a person expressing an interest in a proposed transaction in the issuer's security with the broker or dealer, such as by providing the requesting person with appropriate instructions regarding how to obtain the information electronically; or

(5)(i) The following information, which must be (excluding paragraphs (b)(5)(i)(N) through (P) of this section) as of a date within 12 months prior to the publication or submission of the quotation, unless otherwise specified:

(A) The name of the issuer and any predecessors during the past five years;

Securities and Exchange Commission § 240.15c2-11

(B) The address(es) of the issuer's principal executive office and of its principal place of business;

(C) The state of incorporation or registration of the issuer and of each of its predecessors (if any) during the past five years;

(D) The title, class, and ticker symbol (if assigned) of the security;

(E) The par or stated value of the security;

(F) The number of shares or total amount of the securities outstanding as of the end of the issuer's most recent fiscal year;

(G) The name and address of the transfer agent;

(H) A description of the issuer's business;

(I) A description of products or services offered by the issuer;

(J) A description and extent of the issuer's facilities;

(K) The name and title of all company insiders;

(L) The issuer's most recent balance sheet (as of a date less than 16 months before the publication or submission of the quotation) and profit and loss and retained earnings statements (for the 12 months preceding the date of the most recent balance sheet);

(M) Similar financial information for such part of the two preceding fiscal years as the issuer or its predecessors has been in existence;

(N) Whether the broker or dealer or any associated person of the broker or dealer is affiliated, directly or indirectly, with the issuer;

(O) Whether the quotation is being published or submitted on behalf of any other broker or dealer and, if so, the name of such broker or dealer; and

(P) Whether the quotation is being submitted or published, directly or indirectly, by or on behalf of the issuer or a company insider and, if so, the name of such person and the basis for any exemption under the federal securities laws for any sales of such securities on behalf of such person.

(ii) The broker or dealer must make the documents and information specified in paragraph (b)(5)(i) of this section available upon the request of a person expressing an interest in a proposed transaction in the issuer's security with the broker or dealer, such as by providing the requesting person with appropriate instructions regarding how to obtain such publicly available documents and information electronically. If such information is made available to others upon request pursuant to this paragraph, such delivery, unless otherwise represented, shall not constitute a representation by such broker or dealer that such information is accurate but shall constitute a representation by such broker or dealer that the information is current in relation to the day the quotation is submitted, the broker or dealer has a reasonable basis under the circumstances for believing the information is accurate in all material respects, and the information was obtained from sources that the broker or dealer has a reasonable basis under the circumstances for believing are reliable. The documents and information specified in paragraph (b)(5) of this section must be reviewed where paragraphs (b)(1) through (4) of this section do not apply to such issuer. For purposes of compliance with paragraph (a)(1)(i)(B) or (a)(2)(ii) of this section, the documents and information specified in paragraph (b)(5) of this section must be reviewed for an issuer for which the documents and information specified in paragraph (b)(1), (2), (3), or (4) of this section regarding such issuer are not current.

(c) *Supplemental information.* With respect to any security the quotation of which is within the provisions of this section, the broker or dealer submitting or publishing such quotation, or any qualified interdealer quotation system that makes known to others the quotation of a broker or dealer pursuant to paragraph (a)(2) of this section, shall have in its records the following documents and information:

(1) Records related to the submission or publication of such quotation, including the identity of the person or persons for whom the quotation is being published or submitted, whether such person or persons is the issuer or a company insider, and any information regarding the transactions provided to the broker, dealer, or qualified interdealer quotation system by such person or persons;

§ 240.15c2-11

(2) A copy of any trading suspension order issued by the Commission pursuant to section 12(k) of the Act regarding any securities of the issuer or its predecessor (if any) during the 12 months preceding the date of the publication or submission of the quotation or a copy of the public release issued by the Commission announcing such trading suspension order; and

(3) A copy or a written record of any other material information (including adverse information) regarding the issuer that comes to the knowledge or possession of the broker, dealer, or qualified interdealer quotation system before the publication or submission of the quotation.

(d) *Recordkeeping.* (1)(i) The following persons shall preserve for a period of not less than three years, the first two years in an easily accessible place, the documents and information required under paragraphs (a), (b), and (c) of this section, except for the documents and information that are available on the Commission's *Electronic Data Gathering, Analysis and Retrieval System* (EDGAR):

(A) Any broker or dealer that publishes or submits a quotation pursuant to paragraph (a)(1) of this section for a security; or

(B) Any qualified interdealer quotation system that makes known to others the quotation of a broker or dealer pursuant to paragraph (a)(2) of this section for a security;

(ii) Any broker or dealer that publishes or submits a quotation pursuant to paragraph (a)(1)(ii) of this section shall preserve for a period of not less than three years, the first two years in an easily accessible place, the name of the qualified interdealer quotation system that made a publicly available determination that it has performed the activities described in paragraph (a)(2)(i) through (iii) of this section.

(2) The following persons shall preserve for a period of not less than three years, the first two years in an easily accessible place, the documents and information that demonstrate that the requirements for an exception under paragraph (f)(2), (3), (5), (6), or (7) of this section are met, except for the documents and information that are available on EDGAR:

17 CFR Ch. II (4-1-23 Edition)

(i) Any qualified interdealer quotation system or registered national securities association that makes a publicly available determination described in paragraph (f)(2)(iii)(B), (f)(3)(ii)(A), or (f)(7) of this section; and

(ii) Any broker or dealer that publishes or submits a quotation pursuant to paragraph (f) of this section; *Provided, however,* That any broker or dealer that relies on a publicly available determination described in paragraph (f)(2)(iii)(B) or (f)(3)(ii)(A) of this section shall preserve only a record of the name of the qualified interdealer quotation system or registered national securities association that determined whether the documents and information specified in paragraph (b) of this section are current and publicly available in addition to the documents and information that demonstrate that the other requirements of the exception provided in paragraph (f)(2) or (3), respectively, are met; and that any broker or dealer that relies on a publicly available determination described in paragraph (f)(7) of this section shall preserve only a record of the exception provided in paragraph (f)(1), (f)(3)(i), or (f)(4) or (5) for which the publicly available determination is made and the name of the qualified interdealer quotation system or registered national securities association that determined that the requirements of that exception are met.

(e) *Definitions.* For purposes of this section:

(1) *Company insider* shall mean any officer or director of the issuer, or person that performs a similar function, or any person who is, directly or indirectly, the beneficial owner of more than 10 percent of the outstanding units or shares of any class of any equity security of the issuer.

(2) *Current* shall mean, for the documents and information specified in:

(i) Paragraph (b)(1), (2), (4), or (5) of this section, filed, published, or are as of a date in accordance with the time frames specified in the applicable paragraph for such documents and information; or

398

Securities and Exchange Commission § 240.15c2-11

(ii) Paragraph (b)(3) of this section, the most recently required annual report or statement filed pursuant to section 13 or 15(d) of the Act and any rule(s) thereunder, Regulation A, Regulation Crowdfunding, or section 12(G)(2)(g) of the Act, together with any subsequently required periodic reports or statements, filed pursuant to section 13 or 15(d) of the Act and any rule(s) thereunder, Regulation A, Regulation Crowdfunding, or section 12(G)(2)(g) of the Act.

(3) *Interdealer quotation system* shall mean any system of general circulation to brokers or dealers that regularly disseminates quotations of identified brokers or dealers.

(4) *Issuer*, in the case of quotations for American Depositary Receipts, shall mean the issuer of the deposited shares represented by such American Depositary Receipts.

(5) *Publicly available* shall mean available on EDGAR; on the website of a state or federal agency, a qualified interdealer quotation system, a registered national securities association, an issuer, or a registered broker or dealer; or through an electronic information delivery system that is generally available to the public in the primary trading market of a foreign private issuer as defined in § 240.3b-4 of this chapter; *Provided, however,* that *publicly available* shall mean where access is not restricted by user name, password, fees, or other restraints.

(6) *Qualified interdealer quotation system* shall mean any interdealer quotation system that meets the definition of an "alternative trading system" under § 242.300(a) of this chapter and operates pursuant to the exemption from the definition of an "exchange" under § 240.3a1-1(a)(2) of this chapter.

(7) *Quotation*, except as otherwise specified in this section, shall mean any bid or offer at a specified price with respect to a security, or any indication of interest by a broker or dealer in receiving bids or offers from others for a security, or any indication by a broker or dealer that wishes to advertise its general interest in buying or selling a particular security.

(8) *Quotation medium* shall mean any "interdealer quotation system" or any publication or electronic communications network or other device that is used by brokers or dealers to make known to others their interest in transactions in any security, including offers to buy or sell at a stated price or otherwise, or invitations of offers to buy or sell.

(9) *Shell company* shall mean any issuer, other than a business combination related shell company, as defined in § 230.405 of this chapter, or an asset-backed issuer as defined in Item 1101(b) of Regulation AB (§ 229.1101(b) of this chapter), that has:

(i) No or nominal operations; and
(ii) Either:
(A) No or nominal assets;
(B) Assets consisting solely of cash and cash equivalents; or
(C) Assets consisting of any amount of cash and cash equivalents and nominal other assets.

(f) *Exceptions.* Except as provided in paragraph (d)(2) of this section, the provisions of this section shall not apply to:

(1) The publication or submission of a quotation for a security that is admitted to trading on a national securities exchange and that is traded on such an exchange on the same day as, or on the business day next preceding, the day the quotation is published or submitted.

(2)(i) The publication or submission by a broker or dealer, solely on behalf of a customer (other than a person acting as or for a dealer), of a quotation that represents the customer's unsolicited indication of interest;

(ii) Provided, however, that this paragraph (f)(2) shall not apply to a quotation:

(A) Consisting of both a bid and an offer, each of which is at a specified price, unless the quotation medium specifically identifies the quotation as representing such an unsolicited customer interest; or

(B) Published or submitted, directly or indirectly on behalf of a company insider or affiliate as defined in § 230.144(a)(1) of this chapter, unless the documents and information specified in paragraph (b) of this section are current and publicly available.

(iii) For purposes of paragraph (f)(2)(ii)(B) of this section, a broker or

399

§ 240.15c2-11

dealer that publishes or submits quotations may rely on either a:

(A) Written representation from the customer's broker that such customer is not a company insider or an affiliate if:

(1) Such representation is received prior to, and on the same day that, the quotation representing the customer's unsolicited indication of interest is published or submitted; and

(2) The broker or dealer has a reasonable basis under the circumstances for believing that the customer's broker is a reliable source; or

(B) Publicly available determination by a qualified interdealer quotation system or registered national securities association that the documents and information specified in paragraph (b) of this section are current and publicly available.

(3)(i)(A) The publication or submission, in an interdealer quotation system that specifically identifies as such unsolicited customer indications of interest of the kind described in paragraph (f)(2) of this section, of a quotation for a security that has been the subject of a bid or offer quotation (exclusive of any identified customer interests) in such a system at a specified price, with no more than four business days in succession without such a quotation;

(B) Provided, however, that this paragraph (f)(3) shall not apply to a quotation that is published or submitted by a broker or dealer for the security of an issuer that:

(1) Was the subject of a trading suspension order issued by the Commission pursuant to section 12(k) of the Act until 60 calendar days after the expiration of such order;

(2) Such broker or dealer, or any qualified interdealer quotation system or registered national securities association, has a reasonable basis under the circumstances for believing is a shell company, unless such quotation is published or submitted within the 18 months following the initial quotation for such issuer's security that is the subject of a bid or offer quotation in an interdealer quotation system at a specified price;

(C) Provided further, that this paragraph (f)(3) shall apply to the publication or submission of a quotation for a security of an issuer only if the documents and information regarding such issuer that are specified in:

(1) Paragraph (b)(3)(i), (iv), or (v) of this section are filed within 180 calendar days from the end of the issuer's most recent fiscal year or any quarterly reporting period that is covered by a report required by section 13 or 15(d) of the Act, as applicable;

(2) Paragraph (b)(3)(ii) or (iii) of this section are timely filed;

(3) Paragraph (b)(4) or (b)(5)(i) (excluding paragraphs (b)(5)(i)(N) through (P)) are current and publicly available; or

(4) Paragraph (b)(3)(i), (ii), (iii), (iv), or (v) are filed within 15 calendar days starting on the date on which a publicly available determination is made pursuant to paragraph (f)(3)(ii)(A) of this section; or

(ii) If the documents and information specified in paragraph (b) of this section (excluding paragraphs (b)(5)(i)(N) through (P)) regarding an issuer are no longer current and publicly available, timely filed, or filed within 180 calendar days, as specified in paragraph (f)(3)(i)(C) of this section, a broker or dealer may continue to publish or submit a quotation for such issuer's security in an interdealer quotation system during the time frame specified in in paragraph (f)(3)(ii)(C) if:

(A) Within the first four business days that such documents and information are no longer current and publicly available, timely filed, or filed within 180 calendar days, as applicable, a qualified interdealer quotation system or registered national securities association makes a publicly available determination that:

(1) Such documents and information are no longer current and publicly available, timely filed, or filed within 180 calendar days, as specified in paragraph (f)(3)(i)(C) of this section; and

(2) The exception provided in paragraph (f)(3)(ii) of this section is available only during the 15 calendar days starting on the date on which the publicly available determination described in paragraph (f)(3)(ii)(A)(1) of this section is made; and

(B) The broker or dealer complies with the requirements of paragraphs

Securities and Exchange Commission

§ 240.15c2-12

(d)(2) and (f)(3)(i) of this section, except for the requirement that the documents and information specified in paragraph (b) (excluding paragraphs (b)(5)(i)(N) through (P)) regarding such issuer be current and publicly available, timely filed, or filed within 180 calendar days, as applicable;

(C) Provided, however, that the provisions of this paragraph (f)(3)(ii) shall apply only during the shorter of the period beginning with the date on which a qualified interdealer quotation system or registered national securities association makes a publicly available determination identified in paragraph (f)(3)(ii)(A) and ending on:

(*1*) The date on which the documents and information specified in paragraph (b) of this section (excluding paragraphs (b)(5)(i)(N) through (P)) regarding such issuer become current and publicly available or filed; or

(*2*) The fourteenth calendar day following the date on which such publicly available determination was made.

(4) The publication or submission of a quotation for a municipal security.

(5) The publication or submission of a quotation for:

(i) A security with a worldwide average daily trading volume value of at least $100,000 reported during the 60 calendar days immediately before the publication of the quotation of such security; and

(ii) The issuer of such security has at least $50 million in total assets and $10 million in shareholders' equity as reflected in the issuer's publicly available audited balance sheet issued within six months after the end of its most recent fiscal year.

(6) The publication or submission of a quotation for a security by a broker or dealer that is named as an underwriter in a registration statement for an offering of that class of security referenced in paragraph (b)(1) of this section or in an offering statement for an offering of that class of security referenced in paragraph (b)(2) of this section; *Provided, however*, that this paragraph (f)(6) shall apply only to the publication or submission of a quotation for such security within the time frames specified in paragraph (b)(1) or (2) of this section.

(7) The publication or submission of a quotation by a broker or dealer that relies on a publicly available determination by a qualified interdealer quotation system or registered national securities association that the requirements of an exception provided in paragraph (f)(1), (f)(3)(i), or (f)(4) or (5) of this section are met; *Provided, however*, that any qualified interdealer quotation system or registered national securities association that makes a publicly available determination that the requirements of the exception provided in paragraph (f)(3)(i) of this section are met must subsequently make a publicly available determination under paragraph (f)(3)(ii)(A) of this section, as applicable.

(g) *Exemptive authority.* Upon written application or upon its own motion, the Commission may, conditionally or unconditionally, exempt by order any person, security, or transaction, or any class or classes of persons, securities, or transactions, from any provision or provisions of this section, to the extent that such exemption is necessary or appropriate in the public interest, and is consistent with the protection of investors.

[85 FR 68203, Oct. 27, 2020]

§ 240.15c2-12 Municipal securities disclosure.

PRELIMINARY NOTE: For a discussion of disclosure obligations relating to municipal securities, issuers, brokers, dealers, and municipal securities dealers should refer to Securities Act Release No. 7049, Securities Exchange Act Release No. 33741, FR-42 (March 9, 1994). For a discussion of the obligations of underwriters to have a reasonable basis for recommending municipal securities, brokers, dealers, and municipal securities dealers should refer to Securities Exchange Act Release No. 26100 (Sept. 22, 1988) and Securities Exchange Act Release No. 26985 (June 28, 1989).

(a) *General.* As a means reasonably designed to prevent fraudulent, deceptive, or manipulative acts or practices, it shall be unlawful for any broker, dealer, or municipal securities dealer (a "Participating Underwriter" when used in connection with an Offering) to act as an underwriter in a primary offering of municipal securities with an aggregate principal amount of

§ 240.15c2-12

$1,000,000 or more (an "Offering") unless the Participating Underwriter complies with the requirements of this section or is exempted from the provisions of this section.

(b) *Requirements*. (1) Prior to the time the Participating Underwriter bids for, purchases, offers, or sells municipal securities in an Offering, the Participating Underwriter shall obtain and review an official statement that an issuer of such securities deems final as of its date, except for the omission of no more than the following information: The offering price(s), interest rate(s), selling compensation, aggregate principal amount, principal amount per maturity, delivery dates, any other terms or provisions required by an issuer of such securities to be specified in a competitive bid, ratings, other terms of the securities depending on such matters, and the identity of the underwriter(s).

(2) Except in competitively bid offerings, from the time the Participating Underwriter has reached an understanding with an issuer of municipal securities that it will become a Participating Underwriter in an Offering until a final official statement is available, the Participating Underwriter shall send no later than the next business day, by first-class mail or other equally prompt means, to any potential customer, on request, a single copy of the most recent preliminary official statement, if any.

(3) The Participating Underwriter shall contract with an issuer of municipal securities or its designated agent to receive, within seven business days after any final agreement to purchase, offer, or sell the municipal securities in an Offering and in sufficient time to accompany any confirmation that requests payment from any customer, copies of a final official statement in sufficient quantity to comply with paragraph (b)(4) of this rule and the rules of the Municipal Securities Rulemaking Board.

(4) From the time the final official statement becomes available until the earlier of—

(i) Ninety days from the end of the underwriting period or

(ii) The time when the official statement is available to any person from the Municipal Securities Rulemaking Board, but in no case less than twenty-five days following the end of the underwriting period, the Participating Underwriter in an Offering shall send no later than the next business day, by first-class mail or other equally prompt means, to any potential customer, on request, a single copy of the final official statement.

(5)(i) A Participating Underwriter shall not purchase or sell municipal securities in connection with an Offering unless the Participating Underwriter has reasonably determined that an issuer of municipal securities, or an obligated person for whom financial or operating data is presented in the final official statement has undertaken, either individually or in combination with other issuers of such municipal securities or obligated persons, in a written agreement or contract for the benefit of holders of such securities, to provide the following to the Municipal Securities Rulemaking Board in an electronic format as prescribed by the Municipal Securities Rulemaking Board, either directly or indirectly through an indenture trustee or a designated agent:

(A) Annual financial information for each obligated person for whom financial information or operating data is presented in the final official statement, or, for each obligated person meeting the objective criteria specified in the undertaking and used to select the obligated persons for whom financial information or operating data is presented in the final official statement, except that, in the case of pooled obligations, the undertaking shall specify such objective criteria;

(B) If not submitted as part of the annual financial information, then when and if available, audited financial statements for each obligated person covered by paragraph (b)(5)(i)(A) of this section;

(C) In a timely manner not in excess of ten business days after the occurrence of the event, notice of any of the following events with respect to the securities being offered in the Offering:

(*1*) Principal and interest payment delinquencies;

(*2*) Non-payment related defaults, if material;

Securities and Exchange Commission § 240.15c2-12

(3) Unscheduled draws on debt service reserves reflecting financial difficulties;

(4) Unscheduled draws on credit enhancements reflecting financial difficulties;

(5) Substitution of credit or liquidity providers, or their failure to perform;

(6) Adverse tax opinions, the issuance by the Internal Revenue Service of proposed or final determinations of taxability, Notices of Proposed Issue (IRS Form 5701-TEB) or other material notices or determinations with respect to the tax status of the security, or other material events affecting the tax status of the security;

(7) Modifications to rights of security holders, if material;

(8) Bond calls, if material, and tender offers;

(9) Defeasances;

(10) Release, substitution, or sale of property securing repayment of the securities, if material;

(11) Rating changes;

(12) Bankruptcy, insolvency, receivership or similar event of the obligated person;

NOTE TO PARAGRAPH (b)(5)(i)(C)(*12*): For the purposes of the event identified in paragraph (b)(5)(i)(C)(12) of this section, the event is considered to occur when any of the following occur: The appointment of a receiver, fiscal agent or similar officer for an obligated person in a proceeding under the U.S. Bankruptcy Code or in any other proceeding under state or federal law in which a court or governmental authority has assumed jurisdiction over substantially all of the assets or business of the obligated person, or if such jurisdiction has been assumed by leaving the existing governing body and officials or officers in possession but subject to the supervision and orders of a court or governmental authority, or the entry of an order confirming a plan of reorganization, arrangement or liquidation by a court or governmental authority having supervision or jurisdiction over substantially all of the assets or business of the obligated person.

(13) The consummation of a merger, consolidation, or acquisition involving an obligated person or the sale of all or substantially all of the assets of the obligated person, other than in the ordinary course of business, the entry into a definitive agreement to undertake such an action or the termination of a definitive agreement relating to any such actions, other than pursuant to its terms, if material;

(14) Appointment of a successor or additional trustee or the change of name of a trustee, if material;

(15) Incurrence of a financial obligation of the obligated person, if material, or agreement to covenants, events of default, remedies, priority rights, or other similar terms of a financial obligation of the obligated person, any of which affect security holders, if material; and

(16) Default, event of acceleration, termination event, modification of terms, or other similar events under the terms of a financial obligation of the obligated person, any of which reflect financial difficulties; and

(D) In a timely manner, notice of a failure of any person specified in paragraph (b)(5)(i)(A) of this section to provide required annual financial information, on or before the date specified in the written agreement or contract.

(ii) The written agreement or contract for the benefit of holders of such securities also shall identify each person for whom annual financial information and notices of material events will be provided, either by name or by the objective criteria used to select such persons, and, for each such person shall:

(A) Specify, in reasonable detail, the type of financial information and operating data to be provided as part of annual financial information;

(B) Specify, in reasonable detail, the accounting principles pursuant to which financial statements will be prepared, and whether the financial statements will be audited; and

(C) Specify the date on which the annual financial information for the preceding fiscal year will be provided.

(iii) Such written agreement or contract for the benefit of holders of such securities also may provide that the continuing obligation to provide annual financial information and notices of events may be terminated with respect to any obligated person, if and when such obligated person no longer remains an obligated person with respect to such municipal securities.

(iv) Such written agreement or contract for the benefit of holders of such securities also shall provide that all

§ 240.15c2-12

documents provided to the Municipal Securities Rulemaking Board shall be accompanied by identifying information as prescribed by the Municipal Securities Rulemaking Board.

(c) *Recommendations.* As a means reasonably designed to prevent fraudulent, deceptive, or manipulative acts or practices, it shall be unlawful for any broker, dealer, or municipal securities dealer to recommend the purchase or sale of a municipal security unless such broker, dealer, or municipal securities dealer has procedures in place that provide reasonable assurance that it will receive prompt notice of any event disclosed pursuant to paragraph (b)(5)(i)(C), paragraph (b)(5)(i)(D), and paragraph (d)(2)(ii)(B) of this section with respect to that security.

(d) *Exemptions.* (1) This section shall not apply to a primary offering of municipal securities in authorized denominations of $100,000 or more, if such securities:

(i) Are sold to no more than thirty-five persons each of whom the Participating Underwriter reasonably believes:

(A) Has such knowledge and experience in financial and business matters that it is capable of evaluating the merits and risks of the prospective investment; and

(B) Is not purchasing for more than one account or with a view to distributing the securities; or

(ii) Have a maturity of nine months or less.

(2) Paragraph (b)(5) of this section shall not apply to an Offering of municipal securities if, at such time as an issuer of such municipal securities delivers the securities to the Participating Underwriters:

(i) No obligated person will be an obligated person with respect to more than $10,000,000 in aggregate amount of outstanding municipal securities, including the offered securities and excluding municipal securities that were offered in a transaction exempt from this section pursuant to paragraph (d)(1) of this section;

(ii) An issuer of municipal securities or obligated person has undertaken, either individually or in combination with other issuers of municipal securities or obligated persons, in a written agreement or contract for the benefit of holders of such municipal securities, to provide the following to the Municipal Securities Rulemaking Board in an electronic format as prescribed by the Municipal Securities Rulemaking Board:

(A) At least annually, financial information or operating data regarding each obligated person for which financial information or operating data is presented in the final official statement, as specified in the undertaking, which financial information and operating data shall include, at a minimum, that financial information and operating data which is customarily prepared by such obligated person and is publicly available; and

(B) In a timely manner not in excess of ten business days after the occurrence of the event, notice of events specified in paragraph (b)(5)(i)(C) of this section with respect to the securities that are the subject of the Offering; and

(C) Such written agreement or contract for the benefit of holders of such securities also shall provide that all documents provided to the Municipal Securities Rulemaking Board shall be accompanied by identifying information as prescribed by the Municipal Securities Rulemaking Board; and

(iii) The final official statement identifies by name, address, and telephone number the persons from which the foregoing information, data, and notices can be obtained.

(3) The provisions of paragraph (b)(5) of this section, other than paragraph (b)(5)(i)(C) of this section, shall not apply to an Offering of municipal securities, if such municipal securities have a stated maturity of 18 months or less.

(4) The provisions of paragraph (c) of this section shall not apply to municipal securities:

(i) Sold in an Offering to which paragraph (b)(5) of this section did not apply, other than Offerings exempt under paragraph (d)(2)(ii) of this section; or

(ii) Sold in an Offering exempt from this section under paragraph (d)(1) of this section.

(5) With the exception of paragraphs (b)(1) through (b)(4), this section shall

Securities and Exchange Commission § 240.15c2-12

apply to a primary offering of municipal securities in authorized denominations of $100,000 or more if such securities may, at the option of the holder thereof, be tendered to an issuer of such securities or its designated agent for redemption or purchase at par value or more at least as frequently as every nine months until maturity, earlier redemption, or purchase by an issuer or its designated agent; provided, however, that paragraphs (b)(5) and (c) of this section shall not apply to such securities outstanding on November 30, 2010, for so long as they continuously remain in authorized denominations of $100,000 or more and may, at the option of the holder thereof, be tendered to an issuer of such securities or its designated agent for redemption or purchase at par value or more at least as frequently as every nine months until maturity, earlier redemption, or purchase by an issuer or its designated agent.

(e) *Exemptive authority.* The Commission, upon written request, or upon its own motion, may exempt any broker, dealer, or municipal securities dealer, whether acting in the capacity of a Participating Underwriter or otherwise, that is a participant in a transaction or class of transactions from any requirement of this section, either unconditionally or on specified terms and conditions, if the Commission determines that such an exemption is consistent with the public interest and the protection of investors.

(f) *Definitions.* For the purposes of this rule—

(1) The term *authorized denominations of $100,000 or more* means municipal securities with a principal amount of $100,000 or more and with restrictions that prevent the sale or transfer of such securities in principal amounts of less than $100,000 other than through a primary offering; except that, for municipal securities with an original issue discount of 10 percent or more, the term means municipal securities with a minimum purchase price of $100,000 or more and with restrictions that prevent the sale or transfer of such securities, in principal amounts that are less than the original principal amount at the time of the primary offering, other than through a primary offering.

(2) The term *end of the underwriting period* means the later of such time as

(i) The issuer of municipal securities delivers the securities to the Participating Underwriters or

(ii) The Participating Underwriter does not retain, directly or as a member or an underwriting syndicate, an unsold balance of the securities for sale to the public.

(3) The term *final official statement* means a document or set of documents prepared by an issuer of municipal securities or its representatives that is complete as of the date delivered to the Participating Underwriter(s) and that sets forth information concerning the terms of the proposed issue of securities; information, including financial information or operating data, concerning such issuers of municipal securities and those other entities, enterprises, funds, accounts, and other persons material to an evaluation of the Offering; and a description of the undertakings to be provided pursuant to paragraph (b)(5)(i), paragraph (d)(2)(ii), and paragraph (d)(2)(iii) of this section, if applicable, and of any instances in the previous five years in which each person specified pursuant to paragraph (b)(5)(ii) of this section failed to comply, in all material respects, with any previous undertakings in a written contract or agreement specified in paragraph (b)(5)(i) of this section. Financial information or operating data may be set forth in the document or set of documents, or may be included by specific reference to documents available to the public on the Municipal Securities Rulemaking Board's Internet Web site or filed with the Commission.

(4) The term *issuer of municipal securities* means the governmental issuer specified in section 3(a)(29) of the Act and the issuer of any separate security, including a sepatate security as defined in rule 3b-5(a) under the Act.

(5) The term *potential customer* means (i) Any person contacted by the Participating Underwriter concerning the purchase of municipal securities that are intended to be offered or have been sold in an offering, (ii) Any person who has expressed an interest to the Participating Underwriter in possibly purchasing such municipal securities, and

405

§ 240.15c2-12

(iii) Any person who has a customer account with the Participating Underwriter.

(6) The term *preliminary official statement* means an official statement prepared by or for an issuer of municipal securities for dissemination to potential customers prior to the availability of the final official statement.

(7) The term *primary offering* means an offering of municipal securities directly or indirectly by or on behalf of an issuer of such securities, including any remarketing of municipal securities.

(i) That is accompanied by a change in the authorized denomination of such securities from $100,000 or more to less than $100,000, or

(ii) That is accompanied by a change in the period during which such securities may be tendered to an issuer of such securities or its designated agent for redemption or purchase from a period of nine months or less to a period of more than nine months.

(8) The term *underwriter* means any person who has purchased from an issuer of municipal securities with a view to, or offers or sells for an issuer of municipal securities in connection with, the offering of any municipal security, or participates or has a direct or indirect participation in any such undertaking, or participates or has a participation in the direct or indirect underwriting of any such undertaking; except, that such term shall not include a person whose interest is limited to a commission, concession, or allowance from an underwriter, broker, dealer, or municipal securities dealer not in excess of the usual and customary distributors' or sellers' commission, concession, or allowance.

(9) The term *annual financial information* means financial information or operating data, provided at least annually, of the type included in the final official statement with respect to an obligated person, or in the case where no financial information or operating data was provided in the final official statement with respect to such obligated person, of the type included in the final official statement with respect to those obligated persons that meet the objective criteria applied to select the persons for which financial information or operating data will be provided on an annual basis. Financial information or operating data may be set forth in the document or set of documents, or may be included by specific reference to documents available to the public on the Municipal Securities Rulemaking Board's Internet Web site or filed with the Commission.

(10) The term *obligated person* means any person, including an issuer of municipal securities, who is either generally or through an enterprise, fund, or account of such person committed by contract or other arrangement to support payment of all, or part of the obligations on the municipal securities to be sold in the Offering (other than providers of municipal bond insurance, letters of credit, or other liquidity facilities).

(11)(i) The term *financial obligation* means a:

(A) Debt obligation;

(B) Derivative instrument entered into in connection with, or pledged as security or a source of payment for, an existing or planned debt obligation; or

(C) Guarantee of paragraph (f)(11)(i)(A) or (B).

(ii) The term *financial obligation* shall not include municipal securities as to which a final official statement has been provided to the Municipal Securities Rulemaking Board consistent with this rule.

(g) *Transitional provision.* If on July 28, 1989, a Participating Underwriter was contractually committed to act as underwriter in an Offering of municipal securities originally issued before July 29, 1989, the requirements of paragraphs (b)(3) and (b)(4) shall not apply to the Participating Underwriter in connection with such an Offering. Paragraph (b)(5) of this section shall not apply to a Participating Underwriter that has contractually committed to act as an underwriter in an Offering of municipal securities before July 3, 1995; *except that* paragraph (b)(5)(i)(A) and paragraph (b)(5)(i)(B) shall not apply with respect to fiscal years ending prior to January 1, 1996. Paragraph (c) shall become effective on January 1, 1996. Paragraph (d)(2)(ii) and paragraph (d)(2)(iii) of this section shall not apply

Securities and Exchange Commission § 240.15c3-1

to an Offering of municipal securities commencing prior to January 1, 1996.

[54 FR 28813, July 10, 1989, as amended at 59 FR 59609, Nov. 17, 1994; 73 FR 76132, Dec. 15, 2008; 75 FR 33155, June 10, 2010; 83 FR 44742, Aug. 31, 2018]

§ 240.15c3-1 Net capital requirements for brokers or dealers.

(a) Every broker or dealer must at all times have and maintain net capital no less than the greater of the highest minimum requirement applicable to its ratio requirement under paragraph (a)(1) of this section, or to any of its activities under paragraph (a)(2) of this section, and must otherwise not be "insolvent" as that term is defined in paragraph (c)(16) of this section. In lieu of applying paragraphs (a)(1) and (a)(2) of this section, an OTC derivatives dealer shall maintain net capital pursuant to paragraph (a)(5) of this section. Each broker or dealer also shall comply with the supplemental requirements of paragraphs (a)(4) and (a)(9) of this section, to the extent either paragraph is applicable to its activities. In addition, a broker or dealer shall maintain net capital of not less than its own net capital requirement plus the sum of each broker's or dealer's subsidiary or affiliate minimum net capital requirements, which is consolidated pursuant to appendix C, § 240.15c3-1c.

RATIO REQUIREMENTS

Aggregate Indebtedness Standard

(1)(i) No broker or dealer, other than one that elects the provisions of paragraph (a)(1)(ii) of this section, shall permit its aggregate indebtedness to all other persons to exceed 1500 percent of its net capital (or 800 percent of its net capital for 12 months after commencing business as a broker or dealer).

Alternative Standard

(ii) A broker or dealer may elect not to be subject to the Aggregate Indebtedness Standard of paragraph (a)(1)(i) of this section. That broker or dealer shall not permit its net capital to be less than the greater of $250,000 or 2 percent of aggregate debit items computed in accordance with the Formula for Determination of Reserve Requirements for Brokers and Dealers (Exhibit A to Rule 15c3-3, § 240.15c3-3a). Such broker or dealer shall notify its Examining Authority, in writing, of its election to operate under this paragraph (a)(1)(ii). Once a broker or dealer has notified its Examining Authority, it shall continue to operate under this paragraph unless a change is approved upon application to the Commission. A broker or dealer that elects this standard and is not exempt from Rule 15c3-3 shall:

(A) Make the computation required by § 240.15c3-3(e) and set forth in Exhibit A, § 240.15c3-3a, on a weekly basis and, in lieu of the 1 percent reduction of certain debit items required by Note E (3) in the computation of its Exhibit A requirement, reduce aggregate debit items in such computation by 3 percent;

(B) Include in Items 7 and 8 of Exhibit A, § 240.15c3-3a, the market value of items specified therein more than 7 business days old;

(C) Exclude credit balances in accounts representing amounts payable for securities not yet received from the issuer or its agent which securities are specified in paragraphs (c)(2)(vi) (A) and (E) of this section and any related debit items from the Exhibit A requirement for 3 business days; and

(D) Deduct from net worth in computing net capital 1 percent of the contract value of all failed to deliver contracts or securities borrowed that were allocated to failed to receive contracts of the same issue and which thereby were excluded from Items 11 or 12 of Exhibit A, § 240.15c3-3a.

Futures Commission Merchants

(iii) No broker or dealer registered as a futures commission merchant shall permit its net capital to be less than the greater of its requirement under paragraph (a)(1) (i) or (ii) of this section, or 4 percent of the funds required to be segregated pursuant to the Commodity Exchange Act and the regulations thereunder (less the market value of commodity options purchased by option customers on or subject to the rules of a contract market, each such deduction not to exceed the amount of funds in the customer's account).

§ 240.15c3-1

MINIMUM REQUIREMENTS

See Appendix E (§ 240.15c3-1e) for temporary minimum requirements.

Brokers or Dealers That Carry Customer Accounts

(2)(i) A broker or dealer (other than one described in paragraphs (a)(2)(ii) or (a)(8) of this section) shall maintain net capital of not less than $250,000 if it carries customer or broker or dealer accounts and receives or holds funds or securities for those persons. A broker or dealer shall be deemed to receive funds, or to carry customer or broker or dealer accounts and to receive funds from those persons if, in connection with its activities as a broker or dealer, it receives checks, drafts, or other evidences of indebtedness made payable to itself or persons other than the requisite registered broker or dealer carrying the account of a customer, escrow agent, issuer, underwriter, sponsor, or other distributor of securities. A broker or dealer shall be deemed to hold securities for, or to carry customer or broker or dealer accounts, and hold securities of, those persons if it does not promptly forward or promptly deliver all of the securities of customers or of other brokers or dealers received by the firm in connection with its activities as a broker or dealer. A broker or dealer, without complying with this paragraph (a)(2)(i), may receive securities only if its activities conform with the provisions of paragraphs (a)(2) (iv) or (v) of this section, and may receive funds only in connection with the activities described in paragraph (a)(2)(v) of this section.

(ii) A broker or dealer that is exempt from the provisions of § 240.15c3-3 pursuant to paragraph (k)(2)(i) thereof shall maintain net capital of not less than $100,000.

Dealers

(iii) A dealer shall maintain net capital of not less than $100,000. For the purposes of this section, the term "dealer" includes:

(A) Any broker or dealer that endorses or writes options otherwise than on a registered national securities exchange or a facility of a registered national securities association; and

(B) Any broker or dealer that effects more than ten transactions in any one calendar year for its own investment account. This section shall not apply to those persons engaging in activities described in paragraphs (a)(2)(v), (a)(2)(vi) or (a)(8) of this section, or to those persons whose underwriting activities are limited solely to acting as underwriters in best efforts or all or none underwritings in conformity with paragraph (b)(2) of § 240.15c2-4, so long as those persons engage in no other dealer activities.

Brokers or Dealers That Introduce Customer Accounts And Receive Securities

(iv) A broker or dealer shall maintain net capital of not less than $50,000 if it introduces transactions and accounts of customers or other brokers or dealers to another registered broker or dealer that carries such accounts on a fully disclosed basis, and if the broker or dealer receives but does not hold customer or other broker or dealer securities. A broker or dealer operating under this paragraph (a)(2)(iv) of this section may participate in a firm commitment underwriting without being subject to the provisions of paragraph (a)(2)(iii) of this section, but may not enter into a commitment for the purchase of shares related to that underwriting.

Brokers or Dealers Engaged in the Sale of Redeemable Shares of Registered Investment Companies and Certain Other Share Accounts

(v) A broker or dealer shall maintain net capital of not less than $25,000 if it acts as a broker or dealer with respect to the purchase, sale and redemption of redeemable shares of registered investment companies or of interests or participations in an insurance company separate account directly from or to the issuer on other than a subscription way basis. A broker or dealer operating under this section may sell securities for the account of a customer to obtain funds for the immediate reinvestment in redeemable securities of registered investment companies. A broker or dealer operating under this paragraph (a)(2)(v) must promptly transmit all

Securities and Exchange Commission

§ 240.15c3-1

funds and promptly deliver all securities received in connection with its activities as a broker or dealer, and may not otherwise hold funds or securities for, or owe money or securities to, customers.

Other Brokers or Dealers

(vi) A broker or dealer that does not receive, directly or indirectly, or hold funds or securities for, or owe funds or securities to, customers and does not carry accounts of, or for, customers and does not engage in any of the activities described in paragraphs (a)(2)(i) through (v) of this section shall maintain net capital of not less than $5,000. A broker or dealer operating under this paragraph may engage in the following dealer activities without being subject to the requirements of paragraph (a)(2)(iii) of this section:

(A) In the case of a buy order, prior to executing such customer's order, it purchases as principal the same number of shares or purchases shares to accumulate the number of shares necessary to complete the order, which shall be cleared through another registered broker or dealer or

(B) In the case of a sell order, prior to executing such customer's order, it sells as principal the same number of shares or a portion thereof, which shall be cleared through another registered broker or dealer.

(3) [Reserved]

Capital Requirements for Market Makers

(4) A broker or dealer engaged in activities as a market maker as defined in paragraph (c)(8) of this section shall maintain net capital in an amount not less than $2,500 for each security in which it makes a market (unless a security in which it makes a market has a market value of $5 or less, in which event the amount of net capital shall be not less than $1,000 for each such security) based on the average number of such markets made by such broker or dealer during the 30 days immediately preceding the computation date. Under no circumstances shall it have net capital less than that required by the provisions of paragraph (a) of this section, or be required to maintain net capital of more than $1,000,000 unless required by paragraph (a) of this section.

(5)(i) In accordance with appendix F to this section (§ 240.15c3-1f), the Commission may grant an application by an OTC derivatives dealer when calculating net capital to use the market risk standards of appendix F as to some or all of its positions in lieu of the provisions of paragraph (c)(2)(vi) of this section and the credit risk standards of appendix F to its receivables (including counterparty net exposure) arising from transactions in eligible OTC derivative instruments in lieu of the requirements of paragraph (c)(2)(iv) of this section. An OTC derivatives dealer shall at all times maintain tentative net capital of not less than $100 million and net capital of not less than $20 million.

(ii) An OTC derivatives dealer that is also registered as a security-based swap dealer under section 15F of the Act (15 U.S.C. 78o-10) is subject to the capital requirements in §§ 240.18a-1, 240.18a-1a, 240.18a-1b, 240.18a-1c and 240.18a-1d instead of the capital requirements of this section and its appendices.

Market Makers, Specialists and Certain Other Dealers

(6)(i) A dealer who meets the conditions of paragraph (a)(6)(ii) of this section may elect to operate under this paragraph (a)(6) and thereby not apply, except to the extent required by this paragraph (a)(6), the provisions of paragraphs (c)(2)(vi) or appendix A (§ 240.15c3-1a) of this section to market maker and specialist transactions and, in lieu thereof, apply thereto the provisions of paragraph (a)(6)(iii) of this section.

(ii) This paragraph (a)(6) shall be available to a dealer who does not effect transactions with other than brokers or dealers, who does not carry customer accounts, who does not effect transactions in options not listed on a registered national securities exchange or facility of a registered national securities association, and whose market maker or specialist transactions are effected through and carried in a market maker or specialist account cleared by another broker or dealer as provided in paragraph (a)(6)(iv) of this section.

(iii) A dealer who elects to operate pursuant to this paragraph (a)(6) shall

§ 240.15c3-1

at all times maintain a liquidating equity in respect of securities positions in his market maker or specialist account at least equal to:

(A) An amount equal to 25 percent (5 percent in the case of exempted securities) of the market value of the long positions and 30 percent of the market value of the short positions; provided, however, in the case of long or short positions in options and long or short positions in securities other than options which relate to a bona fide hedged position as defined in paragraph (c)(2)(x)(C) of this section, such amount shall equal the deductions in respect of such positions specified by appendix A (§ 240.15c3-1a).

(B) Such lesser requirement as may be approved by the Commission under specified terms and conditions upon written application of the dealer and the carrying broker or dealer.

(C) For purposes of this paragraph (a)(6)(iii), equity in such specialist or market maker account shall be computed by (1) marking all securities positions long or short in the account to their respective current market values, (2) adding (deducting in the case of a debit balance) the credit balance carried in such specialist or market maker account, and (3) adding (deducting in the case of short positions) the market value of positions long in such account.

(iv) The dealer shall obtain from the broker or dealer carrying the market maker or specialist account a written undertaking which shall be designated "Notice Pursuant to § 240.15c3-1(a)(6) of Intention to Carry Specialist or Market Maker Account." Said undertaking shall contain the representations required by paragraph (a)(6) of this section and shall be filed with the Commission's Washington, DC, Office, the regional office of the Commission for the region in which the broker or dealer has its principal place of business and the Designated Examining Authorities of both firms prior to effecting any transactions in said account. The broker or dealer carrying such account:

(A) Shall mark the account to the market not less than daily and shall issue appropriate calls for additional equity which shall be met by noon of the following business day;

(B) Shall notify by telegraph the Commission and the Designated Examining Authorities pursuant to 17 CFR 240.17a-11, if the market maker or specialist fails to deposit any required equity within the time prescribed in paragraph (a)(6)(iv)(A) of this section; said telegraphic notice shall be received by the Commission and the Designated Examining Authorities not later than the close of business on the day said call is not met;

(C) Shall not extend further credit in the account if the equity in the account falls below that prescribed in paragraph (a)(6)(iii) of this section, and

(D) Shall take steps to liquidate promptly existing positions in the account in the event of a failure to meet a call for equity.

(v) No such carrying broker or dealer shall permit the sum of (A) the deductions required by paragraph (c)(2)(x)(A) of this section in respect of all transactions in market maker accounts guaranteed, indorsed or carried by such broker or dealer pursuant to paragraph (c)(2)(x) of this section and (B) the equity required by paragraph (iii) of this paragraph (a)(6) in respect of all transactions in the accounts of specialists of market makers in options carried by such broker or dealer pursuant to this paragraph (a)(6) to exceed 1,000 percent of such broker's or dealer's net capital as defined in paragraph (c)(2) of this section for any period exceeding five business days; *Provided,* That solely for purposes of this paragraph (a)(6)(v), deductions or equity required in a specialist or market maker account in respect of positions in fully paid securities (other than options), which do not underlie options listed on the national securities exchange or facility of a national securities association of which the specialist or market marker is a member, need not be recognized. *Provided further,* That if at any time such sum exceeds 1,000 percent of such broker's or dealer's net capital, then the broker or dealer shall immediately transmit telegraphic notice of such event to the principal office of the Commission in Washington, DC, the regional office of the Commission for the region in which the broker or dealer

Securities and Exchange Commission § 240.15c3–1

maintains its principal place of business, and such broker's or dealer's Designated Examining Authority. *Provided further,* That if at any time such sum exceeds 1,000 percent of such broker's or dealer's net capital, then such broker or dealer shall be subject to the prohibitions against withdrawal of equity capital set forth in paragraph (e) of this section, and to the prohibitions against reduction, prepayment and repayment of subordination agreements set forth in paragraph (b)(11) of § 240.15c3–1d, as if such broker or dealer's net capital were below the minimum standards specified by each of the aforementioned paragraphs.

ALTERNATIVE NET CAPITAL COMPUTATION FOR BROKER-DEALERS AUTHORIZED TO USE MODELS

(7) In accordance with appendix E to this section (§ 240.15c3–1e), the Commission may approve, in whole or in part, an application or an amendment to an application by a broker or dealer to calculate net capital using the market risk standards of appendix E to compute a deduction for market risk on some or all of its positions, instead of the provisions of paragraphs (c)(2)(vi) and (c)(2)(vii) of this section, and using the credit risk standards of appendix E to compute a deduction for credit risk on certain credit exposures arising from transactions in derivatives instruments, instead of the provisions of paragraph (c)(2)(iv) of this section, subject to any conditions or limitations on the broker or dealer the Commission may require as necessary or appropriate in the public interest or for the protection of investors. A broker or dealer that has been approved to calculate its net capital under appendix E must:

(i)(A) At all times maintain tentative net capital of not less than $5 billion and net capital of not less than the greater of $1 billion or the sum of the ratio requirement under paragraph (a)(1) of this section and:

(*1*) Two percent of the risk margin amount; or

(*2*) Four percent or less of the risk margin amount if the Commission issues an order raising the requirement to four percent or less on or after the third anniversary of this section's compliance date; or

(*3*) Eight percent or less of the risk margin amount if the Commission issues an order raising the requirement to eight percent or less on or after the fifth anniversary of this section's compliance date and the Commission had previously issued an order raising the requirement under paragraph (a)(7)(i)(B) of this section;

(B) If, after considering the capital and leverage levels of brokers or dealers subject to paragraph (a)(7) of this section, as well as the risks of their security-based swap positions, the Commission determines that it may be appropriate to change the percentage pursuant to paragraph (a)(7)(i)(A)(*2*) or (*3*) of this section, the Commission will publish a notice of the potential change and subsequently will issue an order regarding any such change.

(ii) Provide notice that same day in accordance with § 240.17a–11(g) if the broker's or dealer's tentative net capital is less than $6 billion. The Commission may, upon written application, lower the threshold at which notification is necessary under this paragraph (a)(7)(ii), either unconditionally or on specified terms and conditions, if a broker or dealer satisfies the Commission that notification at the $6 billion threshold is unnecessary because of, among other factors, the special nature of its business, its financial position, its internal risk management system, or its compliance history; and

(iii) Comply with § 240.15c3–4 as though it were an OTC derivatives dealer with respect to all of its business activities, except that paragraphs (c)(5)(xiii), (c)(5)(xiv), (d)(8), and (d)(9) of § 240.15c3–4 shall not apply.

(8) *Municipal securities brokers' brokers.* (i) A municipal securities brokers' brokers, as defined in subsection (ii) of this paragraph (a)(8), may elect not to be subject to the limitations of paragraph (c)(2)(ix) of this section provided that such brokers' broker complies with the requirements set out in paragraphs (a)(8) (iii), (iv) and (v) of this section.

(ii) The term *municipal securities brokers' broker* shall mean a municipal securities broker or dealer who acts exclusively as an undisclosed agent in the

411

§ 240.15c3-1

purchase or sale of municipal securities for a registered broker or dealer or registered municipal securities dealer, who has no "customers" as defined in this rule and who does not have or maintain any municipal securities in its proprietary or other accounts.

(iii) In order to qualify to operate under this paragraph (a)(8), a brokers' broker shall at all times have and maintain net capital of not less than $150,000.

(iv) For purposes of this paragraph (a)(8), a brokers' broker shall deduct from net worth 1% of the contract value of each municipal failed to deliver contract which is outstanding 21 business days or longer. Such deduction shall be increased by any excess of the contract price of the fail to deliver over the market value of the underlying security.

(v) For purposes of this paragraph (a)(8), a brokers' broker may exclude from its aggregate indebtedness computation indebtedness adequately collateralized by municipal securities outstanding for not more than one business day and offset by municipal securities failed to deliver of the same issue and quantity. In no event may a brokers' broker exclude any overnight bank loan attributable to the same municipal securities failed to deliver contract for more than one business day. A brokers' broker need not deduct from net worth the amount by which the market value of securities failed to receive outstanding longer than thirty (30) calendar days exceeds the contract value of those failed to receive as required by Rule 15c3-1(c)(2)(iv)(E).

Certain Additional Capital Requirements for Brokers or Dealers Engaging in Reverse Repurchase Agreements

(9) A broker or dealer shall maintain net capital in addition to the amounts required under paragraph (a) of this section in an amount equal to 10 percent of:

(i) The excess of the market value of United States Treasury Bills, Bonds and Notes subject to reverse repurchase agreements with any one party over 105 percent of the contract prices (including accrued interest) for reverse repurchase agreements with that party;

(ii) The excess of the market value of securities issued or guaranteed as to principal or interest by an agency of the United States or mortgage related securities as defined in section 3(a)(41) of the Act subject to reverse repurchase agreements with any one party over 110 percent of the contract prices (including accrued interest) for reverse repurchase agreements with that party; and

(iii) The excess of the market value of other securities subject to reverse repurchase agreements with any one party over 120 percent of the contract prices (including accrued interest) for reverse repurchase agreements with that party.

Broker-Dealers Registered as Security-Based Swap Dealers

(10) A broker or dealer registered with the Commission as a security-based swap dealer, other than a broker or dealer subject to the provisions of paragraph (a)(7) of this section, must:

(i)(A) At all times maintain net capital of not less than the greater of $20 million or the sum of the ratio requirement under paragraph (a)(1) of this section and:

(*1*) Two percent of the risk margin amount; or

(*2*) Four percent or less of the risk margin amount if the Commission issues an order raising the requirement to four percent or less on or after the third anniversary of this section's compliance date; or

(*3*) Eight percent or less of the risk margin amount if the Commission issues an order raising the requirement to eight percent or less on or after the fifth anniversary of this section's compliance date and the Commission had previously issued an order raising the requirement under paragraph (a)(10)(i)(B) of this section;

(B) If, after considering the capital and leverage levels of brokers or dealers subject to paragraph (a)(10) of this section, as well as the risks of their security-based swap positions, the Commission determines that it may be appropriate to change the percentage pursuant to paragraph (a)(10)(i)(A)(*2*) or (*3*) of this section, the Commission will publish a notice of the potential

Securities and Exchange Commission § 240.15c3–1

change and subsequently will issue an order regarding any such change; and

(ii) Comply with § 240.15c3–4 as though it were an OTC derivatives dealer with respect to all of its business activities, except that paragraphs (c)(5)(xiii) and (xiv), and (d)(8) and (9) of § 240.15c3–4 shall not apply.

(b) *Exemptions:*

(1) The provisions of this section shall not apply to any specialist:

(i) Whose securities business, except for an occasional non-specialist related securities transaction for its own account, is limited to that of acting as an options market maker on a national securities exchange;

(ii) That is a member in good standing and subject to the capital requirements of a national securities exchange;

(iii) That does not transact a business in securities with other than a broker or dealer registered with the Commission under section 15 or section 15C of the Act or a member of a national securities exchange; and

(iv) That is not a clearing member of The Options Clearing Corporation and whose securities transactions are effected through and carried in an account cleared by another broker or dealer registered with the Commission under section 15 of the Act.

(2) A member in good standing of a national securities exchange who acts as a floor broker (and whose activities do not require compliance with other provisions of this rule), may elect to comply, in lieu of the other provisions of this section, with the following financial responsibility standard: The value of the exchange membership of the member (based on the lesser of the most recent sale price or current bid price for an exchange membership) is not less than $15,000, or an amount equal to the excess of $15,000 over the value of the exchange membership is held by an independent agent in escrow: *Provided,* That the rules of such exchange require that the proceeds from the sale of the exchange membership of the member and the amount held in escrow pursuant to this paragraph shall be subject to the prior claims of the exchange and its clearing corporation and those arising directly from the closing out of contracts entered into on the floor of such exchanges.

(3) The Commission may, upon written application, exempt from the provisions of this section, either unconditionally or on specified terms and conditions, any broker or dealer who satisfies the Commission that, because of the special nature of its business, its financial position, and the safeguards it has established for the protection of customers' funds and securities, it is not necessary in the public interest or for the protection of investors to subject the particular broker or dealer to the provisions of this section.

(c) *Definitions.* For the purpose of this section:

AGGREGATE INDEBTEDNESS

(1) The term *aggregate indebtedness* shall be deemed to mean the total money liabilities of a broker or dealer arising in connection with any transaction whatsoever and includes, among other things, money borrowed, money payable against securities loaned and securities "failed to receive," the market value of securities borrowed to the extent to which no equivalent value is paid or credited (other than the market value of margin securities borrowed from customers in accordance with the provisions of 17 CFR 240.15c3–3 and margin securities borrowed from non-customers), customers' and non-customers' free credit balances, credit balances in customers' and non-customers' accounts having short positions in securities, equities in customers' and non-customers' future commodities accounts and credit balances in customers' and non-customers' commodities accounts, but excluding:

EXCLUSIONS FROM AGGREGATE INDEBTEDNESS

(i) Indebtedness adequately collateralized by securities which are carried long by the broker or dealer and which have not been sold or by securities which collateralize a secured demand note pursuant to appendix D to this section 17 CFR 240.15c3–1d; indebtedness adequately collateralized by spot commodities which are carried long by the broker or dealer and which have not been sold; or, until October 1,

1976, indebtedness adequately collateralized by municipal securities outstanding for not more than one business day and offset by municipal securities failed to deliver of the same issue and quantity, where such indebtedness is incurred by a broker or dealer effecting transactions solely in municipal securities who is either registered with the Commission or temporarily exempt from such registration pursuant to 17 CFR 240.15a–1(T) or 17 CFR 240.15Ba2–3(T);

(ii) Amounts payable against securities loaned, which securities are carried long by the broker or dealer and which have not been sold or which securities collateralize a secured demand note pursuant to Appendix (D) (17 CFR 240.15c)

(iii) Amounts payable against securities failed to receive which securities are carried long by the broker or dealer and which have not been sold or which securities collateralize a secured demand note pursuant to Appendix (D) (17 CFR 240.15c3–1d) or amounts payable against securities failed to receive for which the broker or dealer also has a receivable related to securities of the same issue and quantity thereof which are either fails to deliver or securities borrowed by the broker or dealer;

(iv) Credit balances in accounts representing amounts payable for securities or money market instruments not yet received from the issuer or its agent which securities are specified in paragraph (c)(2)(vi)(E) and which amounts are outstanding in such accounts not more than three (3) business days;

(v) Equities in customers' and non-customers' accounts segregated in accordance with the provisions of the Commodity Exchange Act and the rules and regulations thereunder;

(vi) Liability reserves established and maintained for refunds of charges required by section 27(d) of the Investment Company Act of 1940, but only to the extent of amounts on deposit in a segregated trust account in accordance with 17 CFR 270.27d–1 under the Investment Company Act of 1940;

(vii) Amounts payable to the extent funds and qualified securities are required to be on deposit and are deposited in a "Special Reserve Bank Account for the Exclusive Benefit of Customers" pursuant to 17 CFR 240.15c3–3 under the Securities Exchange Act of 1934;

(viii) Fixed liabilities adequately secured by assets acquired for use in the ordinary course of the trade or business of a broker or dealer but no other fixed liabilities secured by assets of the broker or dealer shall be so excluded unless the sole recourse of the creditor for nonpayment of such liability is to such asset;

(ix) Liabilities on open contractual commitments;

(x) Indebtedness subordinated to the claims of creditors pursuant to a satisfactory subordination agreement, as defined in Appendix (D) (17 CFR 240.15c3–1d);

(xi) Liabilities which are effectively subordinated to the claims of creditors (but which are not subject to a satisfactory subordination agreement as defined in Appendix (D) (17 CFR 240.15c3–1d)) by non-customers of the broker or dealer prior to such subordination, except such subordinations by customers as may be approved by the Examining Authority for such broker or dealer;

(xii) Credit balances in accounts of general partners;

(xiii) Deferred tax liabilities;

(xiv) Eighty-five percent of amounts payable to a registered investment company related to fail to deliver receivables of the same quantity arising out of purchases of shares of those registered investment companies; and

(xv) Eighty-five percent of amounts payable against securities loaned for which the broker or dealer has receivables related to securities of the same class and issue and quantity that are securities borrowed by the broker or dealer.

NET CAPITAL

(2) The term *net capital* shall be deemed to mean the net worth of a broker or dealer, adjusted by:

(i) *Adjustments to net worth related to unrealized profit or loss, deferred tax provisions, and certain liabilities.* (A) Adding unrealized profits (or deducting unrealized losses) in the accounts of the broker or dealer;

(B)(*1*) In determining net worth, all long and all short positions in listed

Securities and Exchange Commission § 240.15c3-1

options shall be marked to their market value and all long and all short securities and commodities positions shall be marked to their market value.

(2) In determining net worth, the value attributed to any unlisted option shall be the difference between the option's exercise value and the market value of the underlying security. In the case of an unlisted call, if the market value of the underlying security is less than the exercise value of such call it shall be given no value and in the case of an unlisted put if the market value of the underlying security is more than the exercise value of the unlisted put it shall be given no value.

(C) Adding to net worth the lesser of any deferred income tax liability related to the items in (1), (2), and (3) below, or the sum of (1), (2) and (3) below;

(1) The aggregate amount resulting from applying to the amount of the deductions computed in accordance with paragraph (c)(2)(vi) of this section and Appendices A and B, § 240.15c3-1a and 240.15c3-1b, the appropriate Federal and State tax rate(s) applicable to any unrealized gain on the asset on which the deduction was computed;

(2) Any deferred tax liability related to income accrued which is directly related to an asset otherwise deducted pursuant to this section;

(3) Any deferred tax liability related to unrealized appreciation in value of any asset(s) which has been otherwise deducted from net worth in accordance with the provisions of this section; and,

(D) Adding, in the case of future income tax benefits arising as a result of unrealized losses, the amount of such benefits not to exceed the amount of income tax liabilities accrued on the books and records of the broker or dealer, but only to the extent such benefits could have been applied to reduce accrued tax liabilities on the date of the capital computation, had the related unrealized losses been realized on that date.

(E) Adding to net worth any actual tax liability related to income accrued which is directly related to an asset otherwise deducted pursuant to this section.

(F) Subtracting from net worth any liability or expense relating to the business of the broker or dealer for which a third party has assumed the responsibility, unless the broker or dealer can demonstrate that the third party has adequate resources independent of the broker or dealer to pay the liability or expense.

(G) Subtracting from net worth any contribution of capital to the broker or dealer:

(1) Under an agreement that provides the investor with the option to withdraw the capital; or

(2) That is intended to be withdrawn within a period of one year of contribution. Any withdrawal of capital made within one year of its contribution is deemed to have been intended to be withdrawn within a period of one year, unless the withdrawal has been approved in writing by the Examining Authority for the broker or dealer.

(ii) *Subordinated liabilities.* Excluding liabilities of the broker or dealer which are subordinated to the claims of creditors pursuant to a satisfactory subordination agreement, as defined in appendix (D) (17 CFR 240.15c3-1d).

(iii) *Sole proprietors.* Deducting, in the case of a broker or dealer who is a sole proprietor, the excess of liabilities which have not been incurred in the course of business as a broker or dealer over assets not used in the business.

(iv) *Assets not readily convertible into cash.* Deducting fixed assets and assets which cannot be readily converted into cash (less any indebtedness excluded in accordance with subdivision (c)(1)(viii) of this section) including, among other things:

(A) *Fixed assets and prepaid items.* Real estate; furniture and fixtures; exchange memberships; prepaid rent, insurance and other expenses; goodwill, organization expenses;

Certain Unsecured and Partly Secured Receivables

(B) All unsecured advances and loans; deficits in customers' and non-customers' unsecured and partly secured notes; deficits in omnibus credit accounts maintained in compliance with the requirements of 12 CFR 220.7(f) of Regulation T under the Act, or similar accounts carried on behalf of another broker or dealer, after application of calls for margin, marks to the market

415

§ 240.15c3-1

or other required deposits that are outstanding 5 business days or less; deficits in customers' and non-customers' unsecured and partly secured accounts after application of calls for margin, marks to market or other required deposits that are outstanding 5 business days or less, except deficits in cash accounts as defined in 12 CFR 220.8 of Regulation T under the Act for which not more than one extension respecting a specified securities transaction has been requested and granted, and deducting for securities carried in any of such accounts the percentages specified in paragraph (c)(2)(vi) of this section or appendix A, § 240.15c3-1a; the market value of stock loaned in excess of the value of any collateral received therefor; receivables arising out of free shipments of securities (other than mutual fund redemptions) in excess of $5,000 per shipment and all free shipments (other than mutual fund redemptions) outstanding more than 7 business days, and mutual fund redemptions outstanding more than 16 business days; and any collateral deficiencies in secured demand notes as defined in appendix D, § 240.15c3-1d; a broker or dealer that participates in a loan of securities by one party to another party will be deemed a principal for the purpose of the deductions required under this section, unless the broker or dealer has fully disclosed the identity of each party to the other and each party has expressly agreed in writing that the obligations of the broker or dealer do not include a guarantee of performance by the other party and that such party's remedies in the event of a default by the other party do not include a right of setoff against obligations, if any, of the broker or dealer.

(C) Interest receivable, floor brokerage receivable, commissions receivable from other brokers or dealers (other than syndicate profits which shall be treated as required in paragraph (c)(2)(iv)(E) of this section), mutual fund concessions receivable and management fees receivable from registered investment companies, all of which receivables are outstanding longer than thirty (30) days from the date they arise; dividends receivable outstanding longer than thirty (30) days from the payable date; good faith deposits arising in connection with a non-municipal securities underwriting, outstanding longer than eleven (11) business days from the settlement of the underwriting with the issuer; receivables due from participation in municipal securities underwriting syndicates and municipal securities joint underwriting accounts which are outstanding longer than sixty (60) days from settlement of the underwriting with the issuer and good faith deposits arising in connection with an underwriting of municipal securities, outstanding longer than sixty (60) days from settlement of the underwriting with the issuer; and receivables due from participation in municipal securities secondary trading joint accounts, which are outstanding longer than sixty (60) days from the date all securities have been delivered by the account manager to the account members;

(D) *Insurance claims.* Insurance claims which, after seven (7) business days from the date the loss giving rise to the claim is discovered, are not covered by an opinion of outside counsel that the claim is valid and is covered by insurance policies presently in effect; insurance claims which after twenty (20) business days from the date the loss giving rise to the claim is discovered and which are accompanied by an opinion of outside counsel described above, have not been acknowledged in writing by the insurance carrier as due and payable; and insurance claims acknowledged in writing by the carrier as due and payable outstanding longer than twenty (20) business days from the date they are so acknowledged by the carrier; and,

(E) *Other deductions.* All other unsecured receivables; all assets doubtful of collection less any reserves established therefor; the amount by which the market value of securities failed to receive outstanding longer than thirty (30) calendar days exceeds the contract value of such fails to receive; and the funds on deposit in a "segregated trust account" in accordance with 17 CFR 270.27d-1 under the Investment Company Act of 1940, but only to the extent that the amount on deposit in such segregated trust account exceeds the

Securities and Exchange Commission § 240.15c3-1

amount of liability reserves established and maintained for refunds of charges required by sections 27(d) and 27(f) of the Investment Company Act of 1940; *Provided,* That the following need not be deducted:

(*1*) Any amounts deposited in a Customer Reserve Bank Account or PAB Reserve Bank Account pursuant to §240.15c3-3(e) or in the "special reserve account for the exclusive benefit of security-based swap customers" established pursuant to §240.15c3-3(p)(3),

(*2*) Cash and securities held in a securities account at a carrying broker or dealer (except where the account has been subordinated to the claims of creditors of the carrying broker or dealer), and

(*3*) Clearing deposits.

(F)(*1*) For purposes of this paragraph:

(*i*) The term *reverse repurchase agreement deficit* shall mean the difference between the contract price for resale of the securities under a reverse repurchase agreement and the market value of those securities (if less than the contract price).

(*ii*) The term *repurchase agreement deficit* shall mean the difference between the market value of securities subject to the repurchase agreement and the contract price for repurchase of the securities (if less than the market value of the securities).

(*iii*) As used in paragraph (c)(2)(iv)(F)(*1*) of this section, the term *contract price* shall include accrued interest.

(*iv*) Reverse repurchase agreement deficits and the repurchase agreement deficits where the counterparty is the Federal Reserve Bank of New York shall be disregarded.

(*2*)(*i*) In the case of a reverse repurchase agreement, the deduction shall be equal to the reverse repurchase agreement deficit.

(*ii*) In determining the required deductions under paragraph (c)(2)(iv)(F)(*2*)(*i*) of this section, the broker or dealer may reduce the reverse repurchase agreement deficit by:

(*A*) Any margin or other deposits held by the broker or dealer on account of the reverse repurchase agreement;

(*B*) Any excess market value of the securities over the contract price for resale of those securities under any other reverse repurchase agreement with the same party;

(*C*) The difference between the contract price for resale and the market value of securities subject to repurchase agreements with the same party (if the market value of those securities is less than the contract price); and

(*D*) Calls for margin, marks to the market, or other required deposits which are outstanding one business day or less.

(*3*) (*i*) In the case of repurchase agreements, the deduction shall be:

(*A*) The excess of the repurchase agreement deficit over 5 percent of the contract price for resale of United States Treasury Bills, Notes and Bonds, 10 percent of the contract price for the resale of securities issued or guaranteed as to principal or interest by an agency of the United States or mortgage related securities as defined in section 3(a)(41) of the Act and 20 percent of the contract price for the resale of other securities and;

(*B*) The excess of the aggregate repurchase agreement deficits with any one party over 25 percent of the broker or dealer's net capital before the application of paragraph (c)(2)(vi) of this section (less any deduction taken with respect to repurchase agreements with that party under paragraph (c)(2)(iv)(F)(*3*)(*i*)(*A*) of this section) or, if greater;

(*C*) The excess of the aggregate repurchase agreement deficits over 300 percent of the broker's or dealer's net capital before the application of paragraph (c)(2)(vi) of this section.

(*ii*) In determining the required deduction under paragraph (c)(2)(iv)(F)(*3*)(*i*) of this section, the broker or dealer may reduce a repurchase agreement deficit by:

(*A*) Any margin or other deposits held by the broker or dealer on account of a reverse repurchase agreement with the same party to the extent not otherwise used to reduce a reverse repurchase deficit;

(*B*) The difference between the contract price and the market value of securities subject to other repurchase agreements with the same party (if the market value of those securities is less than the contract price) not otherwise

§ 240.15c3-1

used to reduce a reverse repurchase agreement deficit; and

(C) Calls for margin, marks to the market, or other required deposits which are outstanding one business day or less to the extent not otherwise used to reduce a reverse repurchase agreement deficit.

(G) *Securities borrowed.* 1 percent of the market value of securities borrowed collateralized by an irrevocable letter of credit.

(H) Any receivable from an affiliate of the broker or dealer (not otherwise deducted from net worth) and the market value of any collateral given to an affiliate (not otherwise deducted from net worth) to secure a liability over the amount of the liability of the broker or dealer unless the books and records of the affiliate are made available for examination when requested by the representatives of the Commission or the Examining Authority for the broker or dealer in order to demonstrate the validity of the receivable or payable. The provisions of this subsection shall not apply where the affiliate is a registered broker or dealer, registered government securities broker or dealer or bank as defined in section 3(a)(6) of the Act or insurance company as defined in section 3(a)(19) of the Act or investment company registered under the Investment Company Act of 1940 or federally insured savings and loan association or futures commission merchant registered pursuant to the Commodity Exchange Act.

(v)(A) Deducting the market value of all short securities differences (which shall include securities positions reflected on the securities record which are not susceptible to either count or confirmation) unresolved after discovery in accordance with the following schedule:

Differences [1]	Numbers of business days after discovery
25 percent	7
50 percent	14
75 percent	21
100 percent	28

[1] Percentage of market value of short securities differences.

(B) Deducting the market value of any long securities differences, where such securities have been sold by the broker or dealer before they are adequately resolved, less any reserves established therefor;

(C) The designated examining authority for a broker or dealer may extend the periods in (v)(A) of this section for up to 10 business days if it finds that exceptional circumstances warrant an extension.

Securities Haircuts

(vi) Deducting the percentages specified in paragraphs (c)(2)(vi) (A) through (M) of this section (or the deductions prescribed for securities positions set forth in Appendix A (§ 240.15c3-1a) of the market value of all securities, money market instruments or options in the proprietary or other accounts of the broker or dealer.

(A)(*1*) In the case of a security issued or guaranteed as to principal or interest by the United States or any agency thereof, the applicable percentages of the market value of the net long or short position in each of the categories specified below are:

CATEGORY 1

(*i*) Less than 3 months to maturity—0 percent.
(*ii*) 3 months but less than 6 months to maturity—½ of 1 percent.
(*iii*) 6 months but less than 9 months to maturity—¾ of 1 percent.
(*iv*) 9 months but less than 12 months to maturity—1 percent.

CATEGORY 2

(*i*) 1 year but less than 2 years to maturity—1½ percent.
(*ii*) 2 years but less than 3 years to maturity—2 percent.

CATEGORY 3

(*i*) 3 years but less than 5 years to maturity—3%.
(*ii*) 5 years but less than 10 years to maturity—4%.

CATEGORY 4

(*i*) 10 years but less than 15 years to maturity—4½%.
(*ii*) 15 years but less than 20 years to maturity—5%.
(*iii*) 20 years but less than 25 years to maturity—5½%.
(*iv*) 25 years or more to maturity—6%.

Securities and Exchange Commission § 240.15c3-1

Brokers or dealers shall compute a deduction for each category above as follows: Compute the deductions for the net long or short positions in each subcategory above. The deduction for the category shall be the net of the aggregate deductions on the long positions and the aggregate deductions on the short positions in each category plus 50% of the lesser of the aggregate deductions on the long or short positions.

(2) A broker or dealer may elect to deduct, in lieu of the computation required under paragraph (c)(2)(vi)(A)(*1*) of this section, the applicable percentages of the market value of the net long or short positions in each of the subcategories specified in paragraph (c)(2)(vi)(A)(*1*) of this section.

(3) In computing deductions under paragraph (c)(2)(vi)(A)(*1*) of this section, a broker or dealer may elect to exclude the market value of a long or short security from one category and a security from another category, *Provided*, That:

(*i*) Such securities have maturity dates:

(*A*) Between 9 months and 15 months and within 3 months of one another.

(*B*) Between 2 years and 4 years and within 1 year of one another; or

(*C*) Between 8 years and 12 years and within 2 years of one another.

(*ii*) The net market value of the two excluded securities shall remain in the category of the security with the higher market value.

(4) In computing deductions under paragraph (c)(2)(vi)(A)(*1*) of this section, a broker or dealer may include in the categories specified in paragraph (c)(2)(vi)(A)(*1*) of this section, long or short positions in securities issued by the United States or any agency thereof that are deliverable against long or short positions in futures contracts relating to Government securities, traded on a recognized contract market approved by the Commodity Futures Trading Commission, which are held in the proprietary or other accounts of the broker or dealer. The value of the long or short positions included in the categories shall be determined by the contract value of the futures contract held in the account. The provisions of Appendix B to Rule 15c3-1 (17 CFR 240.15c3-1b) will in any event apply to the positions in futures contracts.

(5) In the case of a Government securities dealer that reports to the Federal Reserve System, that transacts business directly with the Federal Reserve System, and that maintains at all times a minimum net capital of at least $50,000,000, before application of the deductions provided for in paragraph (c)(2)(vi) of this section, the deduction for a security issued or guaranteed as to principal or interest by the United States or any agency thereof shall be 75 percent of the deduction otherwise computed under paragraph (c)(2)(vi)(A) of this section.

(B)(*1*) In the case of any municipal security which has a scheduled maturity at date of issue of 731 days or less and which is issued at par value and pays interest at maturity, or which is issued at a discount, and which is not traded flat or in default as to principal or interest, the applicable percentages of the market value on the greater of the long or short position in each of the categories specified below are:

(*i*) Less than 30 days to maturity—0%.

(*ii*) 30 days but less than 91 days to maturity—⅛ of 1%.

(*iii*) 91 days but less than 181 days to maturity—¼ of 1%.

(*iv*) 181 days but less than 271 days to maturity—⅜ of 1%.

(*v*) 271 days but less than 366 days to maturity—½ of 1%.

(*vi*) 366 days but less than 456 days to maturity—¾ of 1%.

(*vii*) 456 days but less than 732 days to maturity—1%.

(2) In the case of any municipal security, other than those specified in paragraph (c)(2)(vi)(B)(*1*), which is not traded flat or in default as to principal or interest, the applicable percentages of the market value of the greater of the long or short position in each of the categories specified below are:

(*i*) Less than 1 year to maturity—1%.

(*ii*) 1 year but less than 2 years to maturity—2%.

(*iii*) 2 years but less than 3½ years to maturity—3%.

(*iv*) 3½ years but less than 5 years to maturity—4%.

(*v*) 5 years but less than 7 years to maturity—5%.

§ 240.15c3-1

(vi) 7 years but less than 10 years to maturity—5½%.
(vii) 10 years but less than 15 years to maturity—6%.
(viii) 15 years but less than 20 years to maturity—6½%.
(ix) 20 years or more to maturity—7%.

(C) *Canadian Debt Obligations.* In the case of any security issued or unconditionally guaranteed as to principal and interest by the Government of Canada, the percentages of market value to be deducted shall be the same as in paragraph (A) of this section.

(D)(*1*) In the case of redeemable securities of an investment company registered under the Investment Company Act of 1940, which assets consist of cash or money market instruments and which is described in § 270.2a-7 of this chapter, the deduction will be 2% of the market value of the greater of the long or short position.

(*2*) In the case of redeemable securities of an investment company registered under the Investment Company Act of 1940, which assets are in the form of cash or securities or money market instruments of any maturity which are described in paragraph (c)(2)(vi) (A) through (C) or (E) of this section, the deduction shall be 7% of the market value of the greater of the long or short positions.

(*3*) In the case of redeemable securities of an investment company registered under the Investment Company Act of 1940, which assets are in the form of cash or securities or money market instruments which are described in paragraphs (c)(2)(vi) (A) through (C) or (E) and (F) of this section, the deduction shall be 9% of the market value of the long or short position.

(E) *Commercial paper, bankers' acceptances and certificates of deposit.* In the case of any short term promissory note or evidence of indebtedness which has a fixed rate of interest or is sold at a discount, which has a maturity date at date of issuance not exceeding nine months exclusive of days of grace, or any renewal thereof, the maturity of which is likewise limited and has only a minimal amount of credit risk, or in the case of any negotiable certificates of deposit or bankers' acceptance or similar type of instrument issued or guaranteed by any bank as defined in section 3(a)(6) of the Securities Exchange Act of 1934 (15 U.S.C. 78c(a)(6)), the applicable percentage of the market value of the greater of the long or short position in each of the categories specified below are:

(*1*) Less than 30 days to maturity—0 percent.
(*2*) 30 days but less than 91 days to maturity ⅛ of 1 percent.
(*3*) 91 days but less than 181 days to maturity ¼ of 1 percent.
(*4*) 181 days but less than 271 days to maturity ⅜ of 1 percent.
(*5*) 271 days but less than 1 year to maturity ½ of 1 percent; and
(*6*) With respect to any negotiable certificate of deposit or bankers acceptance or similar type of instrument issued or guaranteed by any bank, as defined above, having 1 year or more to maturity, the deduction shall be on the greater of the long or short position and shall be the same percentage as that prescribed in paragraph (c)(2)(vi)(A) of this section.

(F)(*1*) *Nonconvertible debt securities.* In the case of nonconvertible debt securities having a fixed interest rate and a fixed maturity date, which are not traded flat or in default as to principal or interest and which have only a minimal amount of credit risk, the applicable percentages of the market value of the greater of the long or short position in each of the categories specified below are:

(i) Less than 1 year to maturity—2%
(ii) 1 year but less than 2 years to maturity—3%
(iii) 2 years but less than 3 years to maturity—5%
(iv) 3 years but less than 5 years to maturity—6%
(v) 5 years but less than 10 years to maturity—7%
(vi) 10 years but less than 15 years to maturity—7½%
(vii) 15 years but less than 20 years to maturity—8%
(viii) 20 years but less than 25 years to maturity—8½%
(ix) 25 years or more to maturity—9%

(*2*) A broker or dealer may elect to exclude from the above categories long or short positions that are hedged with short or long positions in securities

Securities and Exchange Commission

§ 240.15c3-1

issued by the United States or any agency thereof or nonconvertible debt securities having a fixed interest rate and a fixed maturity date and which are not traded flat or in default as to principal or interest, and which have only a minimal amount of credit risk if such securities have maturity dates:

(*i*) Less than five years and within 6 months of each other;

(*ii*) Between 5 years and 10 years and within 9 months of each other;

(*iii*) Between 10 years and 15 years and within 2 years of each other; or

(*iv*) 15 years or more and within 10 years of each other.

The broker-dealer shall deduct the amounts specified in paragraphs (c)(2)(vi)(F) (*3*) and (*4*) of this section.

(*3*) With respect to those positions described in paragraph (c)(2)(vi)(F)(*2*) of this section that include a long or short position in securities issued by the United States or any agency thereof, the broker or dealer shall exclude the hedging short or long United States or agency securities position from the applicable haircut category under paragraph (c)(2)(vi)(A) of this section. The broker or dealer shall deduct the percentage of the market value of the hedged long or short position in nonconvertible debt securities as specified in each of the categories below:

(*i*) Less than 5 years to maturity—1½%

(*ii*) 5 years but less than 10 years to maturity—2½%

(*iii*) 10 years but less than 15 years to maturity—2¾%

(*iv*) 15 years or more to maturity—3%

(*4*) With respect to those positions described in paragraph (c)(2)(vi)(F)(*2*) of this section that include offsetting long and short positions in nonconvertible debt securities, the broker or dealer shall deduct a percentage of the market value of the hedged long or short position in nonconvertible debt securities as specified in each of the categories below:

(*i*) Less than 5 years to maturity—1¾%

(*ii*) 5 years but less than 10 years to maturity—3%

(*iii*) 10 years but less than 15 years to maturity—3¼%

(*iv*) 15 years or more to maturity—3½%

(*5*) In computing deductions under paragraph (c)(2)(vi)(F)(*3*) of this section, a broker or dealer may include in the categories specified in paragraph (c)(2)(vi)(F)(*3*) of this section, long or short positions in securities issued by the United States or any agency thereof that are deliverable against long or short positions in futures contracts relating to Government securities, traded on a recognized contract market approved by the Commodity Futures Trading Commission, which are held in the proprietary or other accounts of the broker or dealer. The value of the long or short positions included in the categories shall be determined by the contract value of the futures contract held in the account.

(*6*) The provisions of Appendix B to Rule 15c3-1 (17 CFR 240.15c3-1b) will in any event apply to the positions in futures contracts.

(G) *Convertible debt securities.* In the case of a debt security not in default which has a fixed rate of interest and a fixed maturity date and which is convertible into an equity security, the deductions shall be as follows: If the market value is 100 percent or more of the principal amount, the deduction shall be determined as specified in paragraph (c)(2)(vi)(J) of this section; if the market value is less than the principal amount, the deduction shall be determined as specified in paragraph (F) of this section; if such securities are rated as required of paragraph (F) of this section;

(H) In the case of cumulative, nonconvertible preferred stock ranking prior to all other classes of stock of the same issuer, which has only a minimal amount of credit risk and which are not in arrears as to dividends, the deduction shall be 10% of the market value of the greater of the long or short position.

(I) In order to apply a deduction under paragraphs (c)(2)(vi)(E), (c)(2)(vi)(F)(*1*), (c)(2)(vi)(F)(*2*), or (c)(2)(vi)(H) of this section, the broker or dealer must assess the creditworthiness of the security or money market instrument pursuant to policies and procedures for assessing and monitoring creditworthiness that the

§ 240.15c3-1

broker or dealer establishes, documents, maintains, and enforces. The policies and procedures must be reasonably designed for the purpose of determining whether a security or money market instrument has only a minimal amount of credit risk. Policies and procedures that are reasonably designed for this purpose should result in assessments of creditworthiness that typically are consistent with market data. A broker-dealer that opts not to make an assessment of creditworthiness under this paragraph may not apply the deductions under paragraphs (c)(2)(vi)(E), (c)(2)(vi)(F)(1), (c)(2)(vi)(F)(2), or (c)(2)(vi)(H) of this section.

NOTE TO PARAGRAPH (c)(2)(vi)(I): For a discussion of the "minimal amount of credit risk" standard, see Removal of Certain References to Credit Ratings Under the Securities Exchange Act of 1934, Exchange Act Release No. 34-71194 (Dec. 27, 2013), at http://www.sec.gov/rules/final.shtml.

All Other Securities

(J) In the case of all securities or evidences of indebtedness, except those described in appendix A, § 240.15c3-1a, which are not included in any of the percentage categories enumerated in paragraphs (c)(2)(vi) (A) through (H) of this section or paragraph (c)(2)(vi)(K)(ii) of this section, the deduction shall be 15 percent of the market value of the greater of the long or short positions and to the extent the market value of the lesser of the long or short positions exceeds 25 percent of the market value of the greater of the long or short positions, the percentage deduction on such excess shall be 15 percent of the market value of such excess. No deduction need be made in the case of:

(1) A security that is convertible into or exchangeable for another security within a period of 90 days, subject to no conditions other than the payment of money, and the other securities into which such security is convertible or for which it is exchangeable, are short in the accounts of such broker or dealer; or

(2) A security that has been called for redemption and that is redeemable within 90 days.

(K) *Securities with a limited market.* In the case of securities (other than exempted securities, nonconvertible debt securities, and cumulative nonconvertible preferred stock) which are not: (1) Traded on a national securities exchange; (2) designated as "OTC Margin Stock" pursuant to Regulation T under the Securities Exchange Act of 1934; (3) quoted on "NASDAQ"; or (4) redeemable shares of investment companies registered under the Investment Company Act of 1940, the deduction shall be as follows:

(i) In the case where there are regular quotations in an inter-dealer quotations system for the securities by three or more independent market-makers (exclusive of the computing broker or dealer) and where each such quotation represents a bona fide offer to brokers or dealers to both buy and sell in reasonable quantities at stated prices, or where a ready market as defined in paragraph (c)(11) (ii) is deemed to exist, the deduction shall be determined in accordance with paragraph (c)(2)(vi)(J) of this section;

(ii) In the case where there are regular quotations in an inter-dealer quotations system for the securities by only one or two independent market-makers (exclusive of the computing broker or dealer) and where each such quotation represents a bona fide offer to brokers or dealers both to buy and sell in reasonable quantities, at stated prices, the deduction on both the long and short position shall be 40 percent.

(L) Where a broker or dealer demonstrates that there is sufficient liquidity for any securities long or short in the proprietary or other accounts of the broker or dealer which are subject to a deduction required by paragraph (c)(2)(vi)(K) of this section, such deduction, upon a proper showing to the Examining Authority for the broker or dealer, may be appropriately decreased, but in no case shall such deduction be less than that prescribed in paragraph (c)(2)(vi)(J) of this section.

Undue Concentration

(M)(1) In the case of money market instruments, or securities of a single class or series of an issuer, including any option written, endorsed or held to purchase or sell securities of such a single class or series of an issuer (other

Securities and Exchange Commission

§ 240.15c3-1

than "exempted securities" and redeemable securities of an investment company registered pursuant to the Investment Company Act of 1940), and securities underwritten (in which case the deduction provided for herein shall be applied after 11 business days), which are long or short in the proprietary or other accounts of a broker or dealer, including securities that are collateral to secured demand notes defined in appendix D, § 240.15c3-1d, and that have a market value of more than 10 percent of the "net capital" of a broker or dealer before the application of paragraph (c)(2)(vi) of this section or appendix A, § 240.15c3-1a, there shall be an additional deduction from net worth and/or the Collateral Value for securities collateralizing a secured demand note defined in appendix D, § 240.15c3-1d, equal to 50 percent of the percentage deduction otherwise provided by this paragraph (c)(2)(vi) of this section or appendix A, § 240.15c3-1a, on that portion of the securities position in excess of 10 percent of the "net capital" of the broker or dealer before the application of paragraph (c)(2)(vi) of this section and appendix A, § 240.15c3-1a. In the case of securities described in paragraph (c)(2)(vi)(J), the additional deduction required by this paragraph (c)(2)(vi)(M) shall be 15 percent.

(2) This paragraph (c)(2)(vi)(M) shall apply notwithstanding any long or short position exemption provided for in paragraph (c)(2)(vi)(J) of this section (except for long or short position exemptions arising out of the first proviso to paragraph (c)(2)(vi)(J)) and the deduction on any such exempted position shall be 15 percent of that portion of the securities position in excess of 10 percent of the broker or dealer's net capital before the application of paragraph (c)(2)(vi) of this section and appendix A, § 240.15c3-1a.

(3) This paragraph (c)(2)(vi)(M) shall be applied to an issue of equity securities only on the market value of such securities in excess of $10,000 or the market value of 500 shares, whichever is greater, or $25,000 in the case of a debt security.

(4) This paragraph (c)(2)(vi)(M) will be applied to an issue of municipal securities having the same security provisions, date of issue, interest rate, day, month and year of maturity only if such securities have a market value in excess of $500,000 in bonds ($5,000,000 in notes) or 10 percent of tentative net capital, whichever is greater, and are held in position longer than 20 business days from the date the securities are received by the syndicate manager from the issuer.

(5) Any specialist that is subject to a deduction required by this paragraph (c)(2)(vi)(M), respecting its specialty stock, that can demonstrate to the satisfaction of the Examining Authority for such broker or dealer that there is sufficient liquidity for such specialist's specialty stock and that such deduction need not be applied in the public interest for the protection of investors, may upon a proper showing to such Examining Authority have such undue concentration deduction appropriately decreased, but in no case shall the deduction prescribed in paragraph (c)(2)(vi)(J) of this section above be reduced. Each such Examining Authority shall make and preserve for a period of not less than 3 years a record of each application granted pursuant to this paragraph (c)(2)(vi)(M)(5), which shall contain a summary of the justification for the granting of the application.

(N) Any specialist that limits its securities business to that of a specialist (except for an occasional non-specialist related securities transaction for its own account), that does not transact a business in securities with other than a broker or dealer registered with the Commission under section 15 or 15C of the Act or a member of a national securities exchange, and that is not a clearing member of The Options Clearing Corporation need not deduct from net worth in computing net capital those deductions, as to its specialty securities, set forth in paragraph (c)(2)(vi) of this section or appendix A to this section, except for paragraph (e) of this section limiting withdrawals of equity capital and appendix D to this section relating to satisfactory subordination agreements. As to a specialist that is solely an options specialist, in paragraph (e) the term "net capital" shall be deemed to mean "net capital before the application of paragraph (c)(2)(vi) of this section or appendix A

423

§ 240.15c3-1

to this section" and "excess net capital" shall be deemed to be the amount of net capital before the application of paragraph (c)(2)(vi) of this section or appendix A to this section in excess of the amount of net capital required under paragraph (a) of this section. In reports filed pursuant to §240.17a–5 and in making the record required by §240.17a–3(a)(11) each specialists shall include the deductions that would otherwise have been required by paragraph (c)(2)(vi) of this section or appendix A to this section in the absence of this paragraph (c)(2)(vi)(N).

(O) *Cleared security-based swaps.* In the case of a cleared security-based swap held in a proprietary account of the broker or dealer, deducting the amount of the applicable margin requirement of the clearing agency or, if the security-based swap references an equity security, the broker or dealer may take a deduction using the method specified in §240.15c3–1a.

(P) *Non-cleared security-based swaps*— (1) *Credit default swaps*—(i) *Short positions (selling protection).* In the case of a non-cleared security-based swap that is a short credit default swap, deducting the percentage of the notional amount based upon the current basis point spread of the credit default swap and the maturity of the credit default swap in accordance with table 1 to §240.15c3–1(c)(2)(vi)(P)(*1*)(*i*):

TABLE 1 TO § 240.15c3–1(c)(2)(vi)(P)(*1*)(*i*)

Length of time to maturity of credit default swap contract	Basis point spread					
	100 or less %	101–300 %	301–400 %	401–500 %	501–699 %	700 or more %
Less than 12 months	1.00	2.00	5.00	7.50	10.00	15.00
12 months but less than 24 months	1.50	3.50	7.50	10.00	12.50	17.50
24 months but less than 36 months	2.00	5.00	10.00	12.50	15.00	20.00
36 months but less than 48 months	3.00	6.00	12.50	15.00	17.50	22.50
48 months but less than 60 months	4.00	7.00	15.00	17.50	20.00	25.00
60 months but less than 72 months	5.50	8.50	17.50	20.00	22.50	27.50
72 months but less than 84 months	7.00	10.00	20.00	22.50	25.00	30.00
84 months but less than 120 months ...	8.50	15.00	22.50	25.00	27.50	40.00
120 months and longer	10.00	20.00	25.00	27.50	30.00	50.00

(ii) *Long positions (purchasing protection).* In the case of a non-cleared security-based swap that is a long credit default swap, deducting 50 percent of the deduction that would be required by paragraph (c)(2)(vi)(P)(*1*)(*i*) of this section if the non-cleared security-based swap was a short credit default swap, each such deduction not to exceed the current market value of the long position.

(iii) *Long and short credit default swaps.* In the case of non-cleared security-based swaps that are long and short credit default swaps referencing the same entity (in the case of non-cleared credit default swap security-based swaps referencing a corporate entity) or obligation (in the case of non-cleared credit default swap security-based swaps referencing an asset-backed security), that have the same credit events which would trigger payment by the seller of protection, that have the same basket of obligations which would determine the amount of payment by the seller of protection upon the occurrence of a credit event, that are in the same or adjacent spread category, and that are in the same or adjacent maturity category and have a maturity date within three months of the other maturity category, deducting the percentage of the notional amount specified in the higher maturity category under paragraph (c)(2)(vi)(P)(*1*)(*i*) or (*ii*) on the excess of the long or short position. In the case of non-cleared security-based swaps that are long and short credit default swaps referencing corporate entities in the same industry sector and the same spread and maturity categories prescribed in paragraph (c)(2)(vi)(P)(*1*)(*i*) of this section, deducting 50 percent of the amount required by paragraph (c)(2)(vi)(P)(*1*)(*i*) of this section on the short position plus the deduction required by paragraph (c)(2)(vi)(P)(*1*)(*ii*) of this section on the excess long position, if any. For the purposes of this section, the broker or dealer must use an industry sector

Securities and Exchange Commission

§ 240.15c3-1

classification system that is reasonable in terms of grouping types of companies with similar business activities and risk characteristics and the broker or dealer must document the industry sector classification system used pursuant to this section.

(iv) *Long security and long credit default swap.* In the case of a non-cleared security-based swap that is a long credit default swap referencing a debt security and the broker or dealer is long the same debt security, deducting 50 percent of the amount specified in paragraph (c)(2)(vi) or (vii) of this section for the debt security, provided that the broker or dealer can deliver the debt security to satisfy the obligation of the broker or dealer on the credit default swap.

(v) *Short security and short credit default swap.* In the case of a non-cleared security-based swap that is a short credit default swap referencing a debt security or a corporate entity, and the broker or dealer is short the debt security or a debt security issued by the corporate entity, deducting the amount specified in paragraph (c)(2)(vi) or (vii) of this section for the debt security. In the case of a non-cleared security-based swap that is a short credit default swap referencing an asset-backed security and the broker or dealer is short the asset-backed security, deducting the amount specified in paragraph (c)(2)(vi) or (vii) of this section for the asset-backed security.

(2) *Non-cleared security-based swaps that are not credit default swaps.* In the case of a non-cleared security-based swap that is not a credit default swap, deducting the amount calculated by multiplying the notional amount of the security-based swap and the percentage specified in paragraph (c)(2)(vi) of this section applicable to the reference security. A broker or dealer may reduce the deduction under this paragraph (c)(2)(vi)(P)(*2*) by an amount equal to any reduction recognized for a comparable long or short position in the reference security under paragraph (c)(2)(vi) of this section and, in the case of a security-based swap referencing an equity security, the method specified in §240.15c3-1a.

(vii) *Non-marketable securities.* Deducting 100 percent of the carrying value in the case of securities or evidence of indebtedness in the proprietary or other accounts of the broker or dealer, for which there is no ready market, as defined in paragraph (c)(11) of this section, and securities, in the proprietary or other accounts of the broker or dealer, which cannot be publicly offered or sold because of statutory, regulatory or contractual arrangements or other restrictions.

Open Contractual Commitments

(viii) Deducting, in the case of a broker or dealer that has open contractual commitments (other than those option positions subject to appendix A, §240.15c3-1a), the respective deductions as specified in paragraph (c)(2)(vi) of this section or appendix B, §240.15c3-1b, from the value (which shall be the market value whenever there is a market) of each net long and each net short position contemplated by any open contractual commitment in the proprietary or other accounts of the broker or dealer.

(A) The deduction for contractual commitments in those securities that are treated in paragraph (c)(2)(vi)(J) of this section shall be 30 percent unless the class and issue of the securities subject to the open contractual commitment deduction are listed for trading on a national securities exchange or are designated as NASDAQ National Market System Securities.

(B) A broker or dealer that maintains in excess of $250,000 of net capital may add back to net worth up to $150,000 of any deduction computed under this paragraph (c)(2)(viii)(B).

(C) The deduction with respect to any single commitment shall be reduced by the unrealized profit in such commitment, in an amount not greater than the deduction provided for by this paragraph (or increased by the unrealized loss), in such commitment, and in no event shall an unrealized profit on any closed transactions operate to increase net capital.

(ix) Deducting from the contract value of each failed to deliver contract that is outstanding five business days or longer (21 business days or longer in the case of municipal securities) the percentages of the market value of the

§ 240.15c3-1

underlying security that would be required by application of the deduction required by paragraph (c)(2)(vi) of this section. Such deduction, however, shall be increased by any excess of the contract price of the failed to deliver contract over the market value of the underlying security or reduced by any excess of the market value of the underlying security over the contract value of the failed to deliver contract, but not to exceed the amount of such deduction. The designated examining authority for the broker or dealer may, upon application of the broker or dealer, extend for a period up to 5 business days, any period herein specified when it is satisfied that the extension is warranted. The designated examining authority upon expiration of the extension may extend for one additional period of up to 5 business days, any period herein specified when it is satisfied that the extension is warranted.

Brokers or Dealers Carrying Accounts of Listed Options Specialists

(x)(A) With respect to any transaction of a specialist in listed options, who is either not otherwise subject to the provisions of this section or is described in paragraph (c)(2)(vi)(N) of this section, for whose specialist account a broker or dealer acts as a guarantor, endorser, or carrying broker or dealer, such broker or dealer shall adjust its net worth by deducting as of noon of each business day the amounts computed as of the prior business day pursuant to § 240.15c3-1a. The required deductions may be reduced by any liquidating equity that exists in such specialist's market-maker account as of that time and shall be increased by the extent of any liquidating deficit in such account. Noon shall be determined according to the local time where the broker or dealer is headquartered. In no event shall excess equity in the specialist's market-maker account result in an increase of the net capital of any such guarantor, endorser, or carrying broker or dealer.

(B) *Definitions.* (*1*) The term *listed option* shall mean any option traded on a registered national securities exchange or automated facility of a registered national securities association.

(*2*) For purposes of this section, the equity in an individual specialist's market-maker account shall be computed by:

(*i*) Marking all securities positions long or short in the account to their respective current market values;

(*ii*) Adding (deducting in the case of a debit balance) the credit balance carried in such specialist's market-maker account; and

(*iii*) Adding (deducting in the case of short positions) the market value of positions long in such account.

(C) No guarantor, endorser, or carrying broker or dealer shall permit the sum of the deductions required pursuant to § 240.15c3-1a in respect of all transactions in specialists' market-maker accounts guaranteed, endorsed, or carried by such broker or dealer to exceed 1,000 percent of such broker's or dealer's net capital as defined in § 240.15c3-1(c)(2) for any period exceeding three business days. If at any time such sum exceeds 1,000 percent of such broker's or dealer's net capital, then the broker or dealer shall:

(*1*) Immediately transmit telegraphic or facsimile notice of such event to the Division of Market Regulation in the headquarters office of the Commission in Washington, DC, to the regional office of the Commission for the region in which the broker or dealer maintains its principal place of business, and to its examining authority designated pursuant to section 17(d) of the Act (15 U.S.C. 78q(d)) ("Designated Examining Authority"); and

(*2*) Be subject to the prohibitions against withdrawal of equity capital set forth in § 240.15c3-1(e) and to the prohibitions against reduction, prepayment, and repayment of subordination agreements set forth in paragraph (b)(11) of § 240.15c3-1d, as if such broker or dealer's net capital were below the minimum standards specified by each of those paragraphs.

(D) If at any time there is a liquidating deficit in a specialist's market-maker account, then the broker or dealer guaranteeing, endorsing, or carrying listed options transactions in such specialist's market-maker account may not extend any further credit in that account, and shall take steps

Securities and Exchange Commission

§ 240.15c3-1

to liquidate promptly existing positions in the account. This paragraph shall not prevent the broker or dealer from, upon approval by the broker's or dealer's Designated Examining Authority, entering into hedging positions in the specialist's market-maker account. The broker or dealer also shall transmit telegraphic or facsimile notice of the deficit and its amount by the close of business of the following business day to its Designated Examining Authority and the Designated Examining Authority of the specialist, if different from its own.

(E) Upon written application to the Commission by the specialist and the broker or dealer guaranteeing, endorsing, or carrying options transactions in such specialist's market-maker account, the Commission may approve upon specified terms and conditions lesser adjustments to net worth than those specified in § 240.15c3–1a.

(xi) *Brokers or dealers carrying specialists or market makers accounts.* With respect to a broker or dealer who carries a market maker or specialist account, or with respect to any transaction in options listed on a registered national securities exchange for which a broker or dealer acts as a guarantor or endorser of options written by a specialist in a specialist account, the broker or dealer shall deduct, for each account carried or for each class or series of options guaranteed or endorsed, any deficiency in collateral required by paragraph (a)(6) of this section.

(xii)(A) *Deduction from net worth for certain undermargined accounts.* Deducting the amount of cash required in each customer's or non-customer's account to meet the maintenance margin requirements of the Examining Authority for the broker or dealer, after application of calls for margin, marks to the market or other required deposits which are outstanding 5 business days or less.

(B) Deducting the amount of cash required in the account of each security-based swap and swap customer to meet the margin requirements of a clearing agency, Examining Authority, the Commission, derivatives clearing organization, or the Commodity Futures Trading Commission, as applicable, after application of calls for margin, marks to the market, or other required deposits which are outstanding within the required time frame to collect the margin, mark to the market, or other required deposits.

(xiii) *Deduction from net worth for indebtedness collateralized by exempted securities.* Deducting, at the option of the broker or dealer, in lieu of including such amounts in aggregate indebtedness, 4 percent of the amount of any indebtedness secured by exempted securities or municipal securities if such indebtedness would otherwise be includable in aggregate indebtedness.

(xiv) *Deduction from net worth for excess deductible amounts related to fidelity bond coverage.* Deducting the amount specified by rule of the Examining Authority for the broker or dealer with respect to a requirement to maintain fidelity bond coverage.

(xv) *Deduction from net worth in lieu of collecting collateral for non-cleared security-based swap and swap transactions—* (A) *Security-based swaps.* Deducting the initial margin amount calculated pursuant to § 240.18a–3(c)(1)(i)(B) for the account of a counterparty at the broker or dealer that is subject to a margin exception set forth in § 240.18a–3(c)(1)(iii), less the margin value of collateral held in the account.

(B) *Swaps.* Deducting the initial margin amount calculated pursuant to the margin rules of the Commodity Futures Trading Commission in the account of a counterparty at the broker or dealer that is subject to a margin exception in those rules, less the margin value of collateral held in the account.

(C) *Treatment of collateral held at a third-party custodian.* For the purposes of the deductions required pursuant to paragraphs (c)(2)(xv)(A) and (B) of this section, collateral held by an independent third-party custodian as initial margin may be treated as collateral held in the account of the counterparty at the broker or dealer if:

(*1*) The independent third-party custodian is a bank as defined in section 3(a)(6) of the Act or a registered U.S. clearing organization or depository that is not affiliated with the counterparty or, if the collateral consists of foreign securities or currencies,

427

§ 240.15c3-1

a supervised foreign bank, clearing organization, or depository that is not affiliated with the counterparty and that customarily maintains custody of such foreign securities or currencies;

(2) The broker or dealer, the independent third-party custodian, and the counterparty that delivered the collateral to the custodian have executed an account control agreement governing the terms under which the custodian holds and releases collateral pledged by the counterparty as initial margin that is a legal, valid, binding, and enforceable agreement under the laws of all relevant jurisdictions, including in the event of bankruptcy, insolvency, or a similar proceeding of any of the parties to the agreement, and that provides the broker or dealer with the right to access the collateral to satisfy the counterparty's obligations to the broker or dealer arising from transactions in the account of the counterparty; and

(3) The broker or dealer maintains written documentation of its analysis that in the event of a legal challenge the relevant court or administrative authorities would find the account control agreement to be legal, valid, binding, and enforceable under the applicable law, including in the event of the receivership, conservatorship, insolvency, liquidation, or a similar proceeding of any of the parties to the agreement.

Exempted Securities

(3) The term *exempted securities* shall mean those securities deemed exempted securities by section 3(a)(12) of the Securities Exchange Act of 1934 and rules thereunder.

Contractual Commitments

(4) The term *contractual commitments* shall include underwriting, when issued, when distributed and delayed delivery contracts, the writing or endorsement of puts and calls and combinations thereof, commitments in foreign currencies, and spot (cash) commodities contracts, but shall not include uncleared regular way purchases and sales of securities and contracts in commodities futures. A series of contracts of purchase or sale of the same security conditioned, if at all, only upon issuance may be treated as an individual commitment.

Adequately Secured

(5) Indebtedness shall be deemed to be adequately secured within the meaning of this section when the excess of the market value of the collateral over the amount of the indebtedness is sufficient to make the loan acceptable as a fully secured loan to banks regularly making secured loans to brokers or dealers.

Customer

(6) The term *customer* shall mean any person from whom, or on whose behalf, a broker or dealer has received, acquired or holds funds or securities for the account of such person, but shall not include a broker or dealer or a registered municipal securities dealer, or a general, special or limited partner or director or officer of the broker or dealer, or any person to the extent that such person has a claim for property or funds which by contract, agreement, or understanding, or by operation of law, is part of the capital of the broker or dealer. *Provided, however,* That the term "customer" shall also include a broker or dealer, but only insofar as such broker or dealer maintains a special omnibus account carried with another broker or dealer in compliance with 12 CFR 220.4(b) of Regulation T under the Securities Exchange Act of 1934.

Non-Customer

(7) The term *non-customer* means a broker or dealer, registered municipal securities dealer, general partner, limited partner, officer, director and persons to the extent their claims are subordinated to the claims of creditors of the broker or dealer.

Market Maker

(8) The term *market maker* shall mean a dealer who, with respect to a particular security, (i) regularly publishes bona fide, competitive bid and offer quotations in a recognized interdealer quotation system; or (ii) furnishes bona fide competitive bid and offer quotations on request; and, (iii) is

Securities and Exchange Commission § 240.15c3-1

ready, willing and able to effect transactions in reasonable quantities at his quoted prices with other brokers or dealers.

PROMPTLY TRANSMIT AND DELIVER

(9) A broker or dealer is deemed to "promptly transmit" all funds and to "promptly deliver" all securities within the meaning of paragraphs (a)(2)(i) and (a)(2)(v) of this section where such transmission or delivery is made no later than noon of the next business day after the receipt of such funds or securities; provided, however, that such prompt transmission or delivery shall not be required to be effected prior to the settlement date for such transaction.

PROMPTLY FORWARD

(10) A broker or dealer is deemed to "promptly forward" funds or securities within the meaning of paragraph (a)(2)(i) of this section only when such forwarding occurs no later than noon of the next business day following receipt of such funds or securities.

READY MARKET

(11)(i) The term *ready market* shall include a recognized established securities market in which there exists independent bona fide offers to buy and sell so that a price reasonably related to the last sales price or current bona fide competitive bid and offer quotations can be determined for a particular security almost instantaneously and where payment will be received in settlement of a sale at such price within a relatively short time conforming to trade custom.

(ii) A *ready market* shall also be deemed to exist where securities have been accepted as collateral for a loan by a bank as defined in section 3(a)(6) of the Securities Exchange Act of 1934 and where the broker or dealer demonstrates to its Examining Authority that such securities adequately secure such loans as that term is defined in paragraph (c)(5) of this section.

EXAMINING AUTHORITY

(12) The term *Examining Authority* of a broker or dealer shall mean for the purposes of 17 CFR 240.15c3-1 and 240.15c3-1a-d the national securities exchange or national securities association of which the broker or dealer is a member or, if the broker or dealer is a member of more than one such self-regulatory organization, the organization designated by the Commission as the Examining Authority for such broker or dealer, or if the broker or dealer is not a member of any such self-regulatory organization, the Regional Office of the Commission where such broker or dealer has its principal place of business.

ENTITIES THAT HAVE A PRINCIPAL REGULATOR

(13)(i) For purposes of § 240.15c3-1e and § 240.15c3-1g, the term *entity that has a principal regulator* shall mean a person (other than a natural person) that is not a registered broker or dealer (other than a broker or dealer registered under section 15(b)(11) of the Act (15 U.S.C. 78o(b)(11)), provided that the person is:

(A) An insured depository institution as defined in section 3(c)(2) of the Federal Deposit Insurance Act (12 U.S.C. 1813(c)(2));

(B) Registered as a futures commission merchant or an introducing broker with the Commodity Futures Trading Commission;

(C) Registered with or licensed by a State insurance regulator and issues any insurance, endowment, or annuity policy or contract;

(D) A foreign bank as defined in section 1(b)(7) of the International Banking Act of 1978 (12 U.S.C. 3101(7)) that has its headquarters in a jurisdiction for which any foreign bank has been approved by the Board of Governors of the Federal Reserve System to conduct business pursuant to the standards set forth in 12 CFR 211.24(c), provided such foreign bank represents to the Commission that it is subject to the same supervisory regime as the foreign bank previously approved by the Board of Governors of the Federal Reserve System;

(E) Not primarily in the securities business, and the person is:

(*1*) A corporation organized under section 25A of the Federal Reserve Act (12 U.S.C. 611 through 633); or

§ 240.15c3-1

(2) A corporation having an agreement or undertaking with the Board of Governors of the Federal Reserve System under section 25 of the Federal Reserve Act (12 U.S.C. 601 through 604a); or

(F) A person that the Commission finds is another entity that is subject to comprehensive supervision, has in place appropriate arrangements so that information that the person provides to the Commission is sufficiently reliable for the purposes of determining compliance with § 240.15c3-1e and § 240.15c3-1g, and it is appropriate to consider the person to be an entity that has a principal regulator considering all relevant circumstances, including the person's mix of business.

(ii) For purposes of §§ 240.15c3-1e, 240.15c3-1g, 240.17h-1T, and 240.17h2T, the term *ultimate holding company that has a principal regulator* shall mean a person (other than a natural person) that:

(A) Is a financial holding company or a company that is treated as a financial holding company under the Bank Holding Company Act of 1956 (12 U.S.C. 1840 *et seq.*), or

(B) The Commission determines to be an ultimate holding company that has a principal regulator, if that person is subject to consolidated, comprehensive supervision; there are in place appropriate arrangements so that information that the person provides to the Commission is sufficiently reliable for the purposes of determining compliance with § 240.15c3-1e and § 240.15c3-1g; and it is appropriate to consider the person to be an ultimate holding company that has a principal regulator in view of all relevant circumstances, including the person's mix of business.

(14) The term *municipal securities* shall mean those securities included within the definition of "municipal securities" in section 3(a)(29) of the Securities Exchange Act of 1934.

(15) The term *tentative net capital* shall mean the net capital of a broker or dealer before deducting the securities haircuts computed pursuant to paragraph (c)(2)(vi) of this section and the charges on inventory computed pursuant to appendix B to this section (§ 240.15c3-1b). However, for purposes of paragraph (a)(5) of this section, the term *tentative net capital* means the net capital of an OTC derivatives dealer before deducting the charges for market and credit risk as computed pursuant to appendix F to this section (§ 240.15c3-1f) or paragraph (c)(2)(vi) of this section, if applicable, and increased by the balance sheet value (including counterparty net exposure) resulting from transactions in eligible OTC derivative instruments which would otherwise be deducted by virtue of paragraph (c)(2)(iv) of this section. For purposes of paragraph (a)(7) of this section, the term *tentative net capital* means the net capital of the broker or dealer before deductions for market and credit risk computed pursuant to § 240.15c3-1e or paragraph (c)(2)(vi) of this section, if applicable, and increased by the balance sheet value (including counterparty net exposure) resulting from transactions in derivative instruments which would otherwise be deducted by virtue of paragraph (c)(2)(iv) of this section. Tentative net capital shall include securities for which there is no ready market, as defined in paragraph (c)(11) of this section, if the use of mathematical models has been approved for purposes of calculating deductions from net capital for those securities pursuant to § 240.15c3-1e.

INSOLVENT

(16) For the purposes of this section, a broker or dealer is insolvent if the broker or dealer:

(i) Is the subject of any bankruptcy, equity receivership proceeding or any other proceeding to reorganize, conserve, or liquidate such broker or dealer or its property or is applying for the appointment or election of a receiver, trustee, or liquidator or similar official for such broker or dealer or its property;

(ii) Has made a general assignment for the benefit of creditors;

(iii) Is insolvent within the meaning of section 101 of title 11 of the United States Code, or is unable to meet its obligations as they mature, and has made an admission to such effect in writing or in any court or before any agency of the United States or any State; or

Securities and Exchange Commission § 240.15c3-1

(iv) Is unable to make such computations as may be necessary to establish compliance with this section or with § 240.15c3-3.

(17) The term *risk margin amount* means the sum of:

(i) The total initial margin required to be maintained by the broker or dealer at each clearing agency with respect to security-based swap transactions cleared for security-based swap customers; and

(ii) The total initial margin amount calculated by the broker or dealer with respect to non-cleared security-based swaps pursuant to § 240.18a-3(c)(1)(i)(B).

(d) *Debt-equity requirements.* No broker or dealer shall permit the total of outstanding principal amounts of its satisfactory subordination agreements (other than such agreements which qualify under this paragraph (d) as equity capital) to exceed 70 percent of its debt-equity total, as hereinafter defined, for a period in excess of 90 days or for such longer period which the Commission may, upon application of the broker or dealer, grant in the public interest or for the protection of investors. In the case of a corporation, the debt-equity total shall be the sum of its outstanding principal amounts of satisfactory subordination agreements, par or stated value of capital stock, paid in capital in excess of par, retained earnings, unrealized profit and loss or other capital accounts. In the case of a partnership, the debt-equity total shall be the sum of its outstanding principal amounts of satisfactory subordination agreements, capital accounts of partners (exclusive of such partners' securities accounts) subject to the provisions of paragraph (e) of this section, and unrealized profit and loss. In the case of a sole proprietorship, the debt-equity total shall include the sum of its outstanding principal amounts of satisfactory subordination agreements, capital accounts of the sole proprietorship and unrealized profit and loss. *Provided, however,* That a satisfactory subordination agreement entered into by a partner or stockholder which has an initial term of at least three years and has a remaining term of not less than 12 months shall be considered equity for the purposes of this paragraph (d) if:

(1) It does not have any of the provisions for accelerated maturity provided for by paragraphs (b)(9)(i), (10)(i) or (10)(ii) of Appendix (D) (17 CFR 240.15c3-1d) and is maintained as capital subject to the provisions restricting the withdrawal thereof required by paragraph (e) of this section or

(2) The partnership agreement provides that capital contributed pursuant to a satisfactory subordination agreement as defined in Appendix (D) (17 CFR 240.15c3-1d) shall in all respects be partnership capital subject to the provisions restricting the withdrawal thereof required by paragraph (e) of this section.

(e)(1) *Notice provisions relating to limitations on the withdrawal of equity capital.* No equity capital of the broker or dealer or a subsidiary or affiliate consolidated pursuant to appendix C (17 CFR 240.15c3-1c) may be withdrawn by action of a stockholder or a partner or by redemption or repurchase of shares of stock by any of the consolidated entities or through the payment of dividends or any similar distribution, nor may any unsecured advance or loan be made to a stockholder, partner, sole proprietor, employee or affiliate without written notice given in accordance with paragraph (e)(1)(iv) of this section:

(i) Two business days prior to any withdrawals, advances or loans if those withdrawals, advances or loans on a net basis exceed in the aggregate in any 30 calendar day period, 30 percent of the broker or dealer's excess net capital. A broker or dealer, in an emergency situation, may make withdrawals, advances or loans that on a net basis exceed 30 percent of the broker or dealer's excess net capital in any 30 calendar day period without giving the advance notice required by this paragraph, with the prior approval of its Examining Authority. Where a broker or dealer makes a withdrawal with the consent of its Examining Authority, it shall in any event comply with paragraph (e)(1)(ii) of this section; or

(ii) Two business days after any withdrawals, advances or loans if those withdrawals, advances or loans on a net basis exceed in the aggregate in any 30 calendar day period, 20 percent

§ 240.15c3-1

of the broker or dealer's excess net capital.

(iii) This paragraph (e)(1) does not apply to:

(A) Securities or commodities transactions in the ordinary course of business between a broker or dealer and an affiliate where the broker or dealer makes payment to or on behalf of such affiliate for such transaction and then receives payment from such affiliate for the securities or commodities transaction within two business days from the date of the transaction; or

(B) Withdrawals, advances or loans which in the aggregate in any thirty calendar day period, on a net basis, equal $500,000 or less.

(iv) Each required notice shall be effective when received by the Commission in Washington, DC, the regional office of the Commission for the region in which the broker or dealer has its principal place of business, the broker or dealer's Examining Authority and the Commodity Futures Trading Commission if such broker or dealer is registered with that Commission.

(2) *Limitations on Withdrawal of equity capital.* No equity capital of the broker or dealer or a subsidiary or affiliate consolidated pursuant to appendix C (17 CFR 240.15c3-1c) may be withdrawn by action of a stockholder or a partner or by redemption or repurchase of shares of stock by any of the consolidated entities or through the payment of dividends or any similar distribution, nor may any unsecured advance or loan be made to a stockholder, partner, sole proprietor, employee or affiliate, if after giving effect thereto and to any other such withdrawals, advances or loans and any Payments of Payment Obligations (as defined in appendix D (17 CFR 240.15c3-1d)) under satisfactory subordination agreements which are scheduled to occur within 180 days following such withdrawal, advance or loan if:

(i) The broker or dealer's net capital would be less than 120 percent of the minimum dollar amount required by paragraph (a) of this section;

(ii) The broker-dealer is registered as a futures commission merchant, its net capital would be less than 7 percent of the funds required to be segregated pursuant to the Commodity Exchange Act and the regulations thereunder (less the market value of commodity options purchased by option customers on or subject to the rules of a contract market, each such deduction not to exceed the amount of funds in the option customer's account);

(iii) The broker-dealer's net capital would be less than 25 percent of deductions from net worth in computing net capital required by paragraphs (c)(2)(vi), (f) and appendix A, of this section, unless the broker or dealer has the prior approval of the Commission to make such withdrawal;

(iv) The total outstanding principal amounts of satisfactory subordination agreements of the broker or dealer and any subsidiaries or affiliates consolidated pursuant to appendix C (17 CFR 240.15c3-1c) (other than such agreements which qualify as equity under paragraph (d) of this section) would exceed 70% of the debt-equity total as defined in paragraph (d) of this section;

(v) The broker or dealer is subject to the aggregate indebtedness limitations of paragraph (a) of this section, the aggregate indebtedness of any of the consolidated entities exceeds 1000 percent of its net capital; or

(vi) The broker or dealer is subject to the alternative net capital requirement of paragraph (f) of this section, its net capital would be less than 5 percent of aggregate debit items computed in accordance with 17 CFR 240.15c3-3a.

(3)(i) *Temporary restrictions on withdrawal of net capital.* The Commission may by order restrict, for a period of up to twenty business days, any withdrawal by the broker or dealer of equity capital or unsecured loan or advance to a stockholder, partner, sole proprietor, member, employee or affiliate under such terms and conditions as the Commission deems necessary or appropriate in the public interest or consistent with the protection of investors if the Commission, based on the information available, concludes that such withdrawal, advance or loan may be detrimental to the financial integrity of the broker or dealer, or may unduly jeopardize the broker or dealer's ability to repay its customer claims or other liabilities which may cause a significant impact on the markets or expose the customers or creditors of the

Securities and Exchange Commission

§ 240.15c3-1a

broker or dealer to loss without taking into account the application of the Securities Investor Protection Act of 1970.

(ii) An order temporarily prohibiting the withdrawal of capital shall be rescinded if the Commission determines that the restriction on capital withdrawal should not remain in effect. A hearing on an order temporarily prohibiting the withdrawal of capital will be held within two business days from the date of the request in writing by the broker or dealer.

(4)(i) *Miscellaneous provisions.* Excess net capital is that amount in excess of the amount required under paragraph (a) of this section. For the purposes of paragraphs (e)(1) and (e)(2) of this section, a broker or dealer may use the amount of excess net capital and deductions required under paragraphs (c)(2)(vi), (f) and appendix A of this section reported in its most recently required filed Form X-17A-5 for the purposes of calculating the effect of a projected withdrawal, advance or loan relative to excess net capital or deductions. The broker or dealer must assure itself that the excess net capital or the deductions reported on the most recently required filed Form X-17A-5 have not materially changed since the time such report was filed.

(ii) The term equity capital includes capital contributions by partners, par or stated value of capital stock, paid-in capital in excess of par, retained earnings or other capital accounts. The term equity capital does not include securities in the securities accounts of partners and balances in limited partners' capital accounts in excess of their stated capital contributions.

(iii) Paragraphs (e)(1) and (e)(2) of this section shall not preclude a broker or dealer from making required tax payments or preclude the payment to partners of reasonable compensation, and such payments shall not be included in the calculation of withdrawals, advances, or loans for purposes of paragraphs (e)(1) and (e)(2) of this section.

(iv) For the purpose of this paragraph (e) of this section, any transaction between a broker or dealer and a stockholder, partner, sole proprietor, employee or affiliate that results in a diminution of the broker or dealer's net capital shall be deemed to be an advance or loan of net capital.

[40 FR 29799, July 16, 1975]

EDITORIAL NOTE: For FEDERAL REGISTER citations affecting §240.15c3-1, see the List of CFR Sections Affected, which appears in the Finding Aids section of the printed volume and at *www.govinfo.gov.*

§ 240.15c3-1a Options (Appendix A to 17 CFR 240.15c3-1).

(a) *Definitions.* (1) The term *unlisted option* shall mean any option not included in the definition of listed option provided in paragraph (c)(2)(x) of §240.15c3-1.

(2) The term *option series* refers to listed option contracts of the same type (either a call or a put) and exercise style, covering the same underlying security with the same exercise price, expiration date, and number of underlying units.

(3) The term *related instrument* within an option class or product group refers to futures contracts, options on futures contracts, security-based swaps on a narrow-based security index, and swaps covering the same underlying instrument. In relation to options on foreign currencies, a related instrument within an option class also shall include forward contracts on the same underlying currency.

(4) The term *underlying instrument* refers to long and short positions, as appropriate, covering the same foreign currency, the same security, security future, or security-based swap other than a security-based swap on a narrow-based security index, or a security which is exchangeable for or convertible into the underlying security within a period of 90 days. If the exchange or conversion requires the payment of money or results in a loss upon conversion at the time when the security is deemed an underlying instrument for purposes of this section, the broker or dealer will deduct from net worth the full amount of the conversion loss. The term *underlying instrument* shall not be deemed to include securities options, futures contracts, options on futures contracts, security-based swaps on a narrow-based security index, qualified stock baskets, unlisted instruments, or swaps.

433

§ 240.15c3-1a

(5) The term *options class* refers to all options contracts covering the same underlying instrument.

(6) The term *product group* refers to two or more option classes, related instruments, underlying instruments, and qualified stock baskets in the same portfolio type (see paragraph (b)(1)(ii) of this section) for which it has been determined that a percentage of offsetting profits may be applied to losses at the same valuation point.

(b) The deduction under this Appendix A to § 240.15c3-1 shall equal the sum of the deductions specified in paragraphs (b)(1)(v)(C) or (b)(2) of this section.

THEORETICAL PRICING CHARGES

(1)(i) *Definitions.* (A) The terms *theoretical gains and losses* shall mean the gain and loss in the value of individual option series, the value of underlying instruments, related instruments, and qualified stock baskets within that option's class, at 10 equidistant intervals (valuation points) ranging from an assumed movement (both up and down) in the current market value of the underlying instrument equal to the percentage corresponding to the deductions otherwise required under § 240.15c3-1 for the underlying instrument (See paragraph (a)(1)(iii) of this section). Theoretical gains and losses shall be calculated using a theoretical options pricing model that satisfies the criteria set forth in paragraph (a)(1)(i)(B) of this section.

(B) The term *theoretical options pricing model* shall mean any mathematical model, other than a broker-dealer proprietary model, approved by a Designated Examining Authority. Such Designated Examining Authority shall submit the model to the Commission, together with a description of its methods for approving models. Any such model shall calculate theoretical gains and losses as described in paragraph (a)(1)(i)(A) of this section for all series and issues of equity, index and foreign currency options and related instruments, and shall be made available equally and on the same terms to all registered brokers or dealers. Its procedures shall include the arrangement of the vendor to supply accurate and timely data to each broker-dealer with respect to its services, and the fees for distribution of the services. The data provided to brokers or dealers shall also contain the minimum requirements set forth in paragraphs (b)(1)(v)(C) of this section and the product group offsets set forth in paragraphs (b)(1)(v)(B) of this section. At a minimum, the model shall consider the following factors in pricing the option:

(*1*) The current spot price of the underlying asset;

(*2*) The exercise price of the option;

(*3*) The remaining time until the option's expiration;

(*4*) The volatility of the underlying asset;

(*5*) Any cash flows associated with ownership of the underlying asset that can reasonably be expected to occur during the remaining life of the option; and

(*6*) The current term structure of interest rates.

(C) The term *major market foreign currency* shall mean the currency of a sovereign nation for which there is a substantial inter-bank forward currency market.

(D) The term *qualified stock basket* shall mean a set or basket of stock positions which represents no less than 50% of the capitalization for a high-capitalization or non-high-capitalization diversified market index, or, in the case of a narrow-based index, no less than 95% of the capitalization for such narrow-based index.

(ii) With respect to positions involving listed options in a single specialist's market-maker account, and, separately, with respect to positions involving listed option positions in its proprietary or other account, the broker or dealer shall group long and short positions into the following portfolio types:

(A) Equity options on the same underlying instrument and positions in that underlying instrument;

(B) Options on the same major market foreign currency, positions in that major market foreign currency, and related instruments within those options' classes;

(C) High-capitalization diversified market index options, related instruments within the option's class, and

Securities and Exchange Commission §240.15c3-1a

qualified stock baskets in the same index;

(D) Non-high-capitalization diversified index options, related instruments within the index option's class, and qualified stock baskets in the same index; and

(E) Narrow-based index options, related instruments within the index option's class, and qualified stock baskets in the same index.

(iii) Before making the computation, each broker or dealer shall obtain the theoretical gains and losses for each options series and for the related and underlying instruments within those options' class in each specialist's market-maker account guaranteed, endorsed, or carried by a broker or dealer, or in the proprietary or other accounts of that broker or dealer. For each option series, the theoretical options pricing model shall calculate theoretical prices at 10 equidistant valuation points within a range consisting of an increase or a decrease of the following percentages of the daily market price of the underlying instrument:

(A) + (−)15% for equity securities with a ready market, narrow-based indexes, and non-high-capitalization diversified indexes;

(B) + (−)6% for major market foreign currencies;

(C) + (−) 20% for all other currencies; and

(D) + (−)10% for high-capitalization diversified indexes.

(iv) As to non-clearing option specialists and market-makers, the percentages of the daily market price of the underlying instrument shall be:

(A) + (−) 4½% for major market foreign currencies; and

(B) + 6(−)8% for high-capitalization diversified indexes.

(C) + (−) 10% for a non-clearing market-maker, or specialist in non-high capitalization diversified index product group.

(v)(A) The broker or dealer shall multiply the corresponding theoretical gains and losses at each of the 10 equidistant valuation points by the number of positions held in a particular options series, the related instruments and qualified stock baskets within the option's class, and the positions in the same underlying instrument.

(B) In determining the aggregate profit or loss for each portfolio type, the broker or dealer will be allowed the following offsets in the following order, provided, that in the case of qualified stock baskets, the broker or dealer may elect to net individual stocks between qualified stock baskets and take the appropriate deduction on the remaining, if any, securities:

(1) First, a broker or dealer is allowed the following offsets within an option's class:

(i) Between options on the same underlying instrument, positions covering the same underlying instrument, and related instruments within the option's class, 100% of a position's gain shall offset another position's loss at the same valuation point;

(ii) Between index options, related instruments within the option's class, and qualified stock baskets on the same index, 95%, or such other amount as designated by the Commission, of gains shall offset losses at the same valuation point;

(2) Second, a broker-dealer is allowed the following offsets within an index product group:

(i) Among positions involving different high-capitalization diversified index option classes within the same product group, 90% of the gain in a high-capitalization diversified market index option, related instruments, and qualified stock baskets within that index option's class shall offset the loss at the same valuation point in a different high-capitalization diversified market index option, related instruments, and qualified stock baskets within that index option's class;

(ii) Among positions involving different non-high-capitalization diversified index option classes within the same product group, 75% of the gain in a non-high-capitalization diversified market index option, related instruments, and qualified stock baskets within that index option's class shall offset the loss at the same valuation point in another non-high-capitalization diversified market index option, related instruments, and qualified stock baskets within that index option's class or product group;

435

§ 240.15c3–1a

(iii) Among positions involving different narrow-based index option classes within the same product group, 90% of the gain in a narrow-based market index option, related instruments, and qualified stock baskets within that index option's class shall offset the loss at the same valuation point in another narrow-based market index option, related instruments, and qualified stock baskets within that index option's class or product group;

(iv) No qualified stock basket should offset another qualified stock basket; and

(3) Third, a broker-dealer is allowed the following offsets between product groups: Among positions involving different diversified index product groups within the same market group, 50% of the gain in a diversified market index option, a related instrument, or a qualified stock basket within that index option's product group shall offset the loss at the same valuation point in another product group;

(C) For each portfolio type, the total deduction shall be the larger of:

(1) The amount for any of the 10 equidistant valuation points representing the largest theoretical loss after applying the offsets provided in paragraph (b)(1)(v)(B) if this section; or

(2) A minimum charge equal to 25% times the multiplier for each equity and index option contract and each related instrument within the option's class or product group, or $25 for each option on a major market foreign currency with the minimum charge for futures contracts and options on futures contracts adjusted for contract size differentials, not to exceed market value in the case of long positions in options and options on futures contracts; plus

(3) In the case of portfolio types involving index options and related instruments offset by a qualified stock basket, there will be a minimum charge of 5 percent of the market value of the qualified stock basket for high-capitalization diversified and narrow-based indexes;

(4) In the case of portfolio types involving index options and related instruments offset by a qualified stock basket, there will be a minimum charge of 7 ½ percent of the market value of the qualified stock basket for

non-high-capitalization diversified indexes; and

(5) In the case of portfolio types involving security futures and equity options on the same underlying instrument and positions in that underlying instrument, there will be a minimum charge of 25 percent times the multiplier for each security future and equity option.

ALTERNATIVE STRATEGY BASED METHOD

(2) A broker or dealer may elect to apply the alternative strategy based method in accordance with the provisions of this paragraph (b)(2).

(i) *Definitions.* (A) The term *intrinsic value* or *in-the-money amount* shall mean the amount by which the exercise value, in the case of a call, is less than the current market value of the underlying instrument, and, in the case of a put, is greater than the current market value of the underlying instrument.

(B) The term *out-of-the-money amount* shall mean the amount by which the exercise value, in the case of a call, is greater than the current market value of the underlying instrument, and, in the case of a put, is less than the current market value of the underlying instrument.

(C) The term *time value* shall mean the current market value of an option contract that is in excess of its intrinsic value.

(ii) Every broker or dealer electing to calculate adjustments to net worth in accordance with the provisions of this paragraph (b)(2) must make the following adjustments to net worth:

(A) Add the time value of a short position in a listed option; and

(B) Deduct the time value of a long position in a listed option, which relates to a position in the same underlying instrument or in a related instrument within the option class or product group as recognized in the strategies enumerated in paragraph (b)(2)(iii)(D) of this section; and

(C) Add the net short market value or deduct the long market value of listed options as recognized in the strategies enumerated in paragraphs (b)(2)(iii)(E)(*1*) and (*2*) of this section.

436

Securities and Exchange Commission § 240.15c3-1a

(iii) In computing net capital after the adjustments provided for in paragraph (b)(2)(ii) of this section, every broker or dealer shall deduct the percentages specified in this paragraph (b)(2)(iii) for all listed option positions, positions covering the same underlying instrument and related instruments within the options' class or product group.

UNCOVERED CALLS

(A) Where a broker or dealer is short a call, deducting the percentage required by paragraphs (c)(2)(vi) (A) through (K) of §240.15c3-1 of the current market value of the underlying instrument for such option reduced by its out-of-the-money amount, to the extent that such reduction does not operate to increase net capital. In no event shall this deduction be less than the greater of $250 for each short call option contract for 100 shares or 50% of the aforementioned percentage.

UNCOVERED PUTS

(B) Where a broker or dealer is short a put, deducting the percentage required by paragraphs (c)(2)(vi) (A) through (K) of §240.15c3-1 of the current market value of the underlying instrument for such option reduced by its out-of-the-money amount, to the extent that such reduction does not operate to increase net capital. In no event shall the deduction provided by this paragraph be less than the greater of $250 for each short put option contract for 100 shares or 50% of the aforementioned percentage.

LONG POSITIONS

(C) Where a broker or dealer is long puts or calls, deducting 50 percent of the market value of the net long put and call positions in the same options series.

CERTAIN SECURITY POSITIONS WITH OFFSETTING OPTIONS

(D)(*1*) Where a broker or dealer is long a put for which it has an offsetting long position in the same number of units of the same underlying instrument, deducting the percentage required by paragraphs (c)(2)(vi) (A) through (K) of §240.15c3-1 of the current market value of the underlying instrument for the long offsetting position, not to exceed the out-of-the-money amount of the option. In no event shall the deduction provided by this paragraph be less than $25 for each option contract for 100 shares, provided that the minimum charge need not exceed the intrinsic value of the option.

(*2*) Where a broker or dealer is long a call for which it has an offsetting short position in the same number of units of the same underlying instrument, deducting the percentage required by paragraphs (c)(2)(vi) (A) through (K) of §240.15c3-1 of the current market value of the underlying instrument for the short offsetting position, not to exceed the out-of-the-money amount of the option. In no event shall the deduction provided by this paragraph be less than $25 for each option contract for 100 shares, provided that the minimum charge need not exceed the intrinsic value of the option.

(*3*) Where a broker or dealer is short a call for which it has an offsetting long position in the same number of units of the same underlying instrument, deducting the percentage required by paragraphs (c)(2)(vi) (A) through (K) of §240.15c3-1 of the current market value of the underlying instrument for the offsetting long position reduced by the short call's intrinsic value. In no event shall the deduction provided by this paragraph be less than $25 for each option contract for 100 shares.

CERTAIN SPREAD POSITIONS

(E)(*1*) Where a broker or dealer is short a listed call and is also long a listed call in the same class of options contracts and the long option expires on the same date as or subsequent to the short option, the deduction, after adjustments required in paragraph (b) of this section, shall be the amount by which the exercise value of the long call exceeds the exercise value of the short call. If the exercise value of the long call is less than or equal to the exercise value of the short call, no deduction is required.

(*2*) Where a broker or dealer is short a listed put and is also long a listed put in the same class of options contracts and the long option expires on the

§ 240.15c3-1a

same date as or subsequent to the short option, the deduction, after the adjustments required in paragraph (b) of this section, shall be the amount by which the exercise value of the short put exceeds the exercise value of the long put. If the exercise value of the long put is equal to or greater than the exercise value of the short put, no deduction is required.

(c) With respect to transactions involving unlisted options, every broker or dealer shall determine the value of unlisted option positions in accordance with the provision of paragraph (c)(2)(i) of § 240.15c3-1, and shall deduct the percentages of all securities positions or unlisted options in the proprietary or other accounts of the broker or dealer specified in this paragraph (c). However, where computing the deduction required for a security position as if the security position had no related unlisted option position and positions in unlisted options as if uncovered would result in a lesser deduction from net worth, the broker or dealer may compute such deductions separately.

UNCOVERED CALLS

(1) Where a broker or dealer is short a call, deducting 15 percent (or such other percentage required by paragraphs (c)(2)(vi) (A) through (K) of § 240.15c3-1) of the current market value of the security underlying such option reduced by any excess of the exercise value of the call over the current market value of the underlying security. In no event shall the deduction provided by this paragraph be less than $250 for each option contract for 100 shares.

UNCOVERED PUTS

(2) Where a broker or dealer is short a put, deducting 15 percent (or such other percentage required by paragraphs (c)(2)(vi) (A) through (K) of § 240.15c3-1) of the current market value of the security underlying the option reduced by any excess of the market value of the underlying security over the exercise value of the put. In no event shall the deduction provided by this paragraph be less than $250 for each option contract for 100 shares.

COVERED CALLS

(3) Where a broker or dealer is short a call and long equivalent units of the underlying security, deducting 15 percent (or such other percentage required by paragraphs (c)(2)(vi) (A) through (K) of § 240.15c3-1) of the current market value of the underlying security reduced by any excess of the current market value of the underlying security over the exercise value of the call. No reduction under this paragraph shall have the effect of increasing net capital.

COVERED PUTS

(4) Where a broker or dealer is short a put and short equivalent units of the underlying security, deducting 15 percent (or such other percentage required by paragraphs (c)(2)(vi) (A) through (K) of § 240.15c3-1) of the current market value of the underlying security reduced by any excess of the exercise value of the put over the market value of the underlying security. No such reduction shall have the effect of increasing net capital.

CONVERSION ACCOUNTS

(5) Where a broker or dealer is long equivalent units of the underlying security, long a put written or endorsed by a broker or dealer and short a call in its proprietary or other accounts, deducting 5 percent (or 50 percent of such other percentage required by paragraphs (c)(2)(vi) (A) through (K) of § 240.15c3-1) of the current market value of the underlying security.

(6) Where a broker or dealer is short equivalent units of the underlying security, long a call written or endorsed by a broker or dealer and short a put in his proprietary or other accounts, deducting 5 percent (or 50 percent of such other percentage required by paragraphs (c)(2)(vi) (A) through (K) of § 240.15c3-1) of the market value of the underlying security.

LONG OPTIONS

(7) Where a broker or dealer is long a put or call endorsed or written by a broker or dealer, deducting 15 percent (or such other percentage required by paragraphs (c)(2)(vi) (A) through (K) of § 240.15c3-1) of the market value of the

Securities and Exchange Commission §240.15c3–1b

underlying security, not to exceed any value attributed to such option in paragraph (c)(2)(i) of §240.15c3–1.

[62 FR 6481, Feb. 12, 1997, as amended at 78 FR 51901, Aug. 21, 2013; 79 FR 1549, Jan. 8, 2014; 84 FR 44044, Aug. 22, 2019]

§ 240.15c3–1b Adjustments to net worth and aggregate indebtedness for certain commodities transactions (appendix B to 17 CFR 240.15c3–1).

(a) Every broker or dealer in computing net capital pursuant to 17 CFR 240.15c3–1 shall comply with the following:

(1) Where a broker or dealer has an asset or liability which is treated or defined in paragraph (c) of 17 CFR 240.15c3–1, the inclusion or exclusion of all or part of such asset or liability for the computation of aggregate indebtedness and net capital shall be in accordance with paragraph (c) of 17 CFR 240.15c3–1, except as specifically provided otherwise in this appendix B. Where a commodity related asset or liability is specifically treated or defined in 17 CFR 1.17 and is not generally or specifically treated or defined in 17 CFR 240.15c3–1 or this appendix B, the inclusion or exclusion of all or part of such asset or liability for the computation of aggregate indebtedness and net capital shall be in accordance with 17 CFR 1.17.

AGGREGATE INDEBTEDNESS

(2) The term *aggregate indebtedness* as defined in paragraph (c)(1) of this section shall exclude with respect to commodity-related transactions:

(i) Indebtedness arising in connection with an advance to a non-proprietary account when such indebtedness is adequately collateralized by spot commodities eligible for delivery on a contract market and when such spot commodities are covered.

(ii) Advances received by the broker or dealer against bills of lading issued in connection with the shipment of commodities sold by the broker or dealer; and

(iii) Equity balances in the accounts of general partners.

NET CAPITAL

(3) In computing net capital as defined in paragraph (c)(2) of this section, the net worth of a broker or dealer shall be adjusted as follows with respect to commodity-related transactions:

(i) *Unrealized profit or loss for certain commodities transactions.* (A) Unrealized profits shall be added and unrealized losses shall be deducted in the commodities accounts of the broker or dealer, including unrealized profits and losses on fixed price commitments and forward contracts; and

(B) The value attributed to any commodity option which is not traded on a contract market shall be the difference between the option's strike price and the market value for the physical or futures contract which is the subject of the option. In the case of a long call commodity option, if the market value for the physical or futures contract which is the subject of the option is less than the strike price of the option, it shall be given no value. In the case of a long put commodity option, if the market value for the physical commodity or futures contract which is the subject of the option is more than the striking price of the option, it shall be given no value.

(ii) Deduct any unsecured commodity futures or option account containing a ledger balance and open trades, the combination of which liquidates to a deficit or containing a debit ledger balance only: *Provided, however,* Deficits or debit ledger balances in unsecured customers', non-customers' and proprietary accounts, which are the subject of calls for margin or other required deposits need not be deducted until the close of business on the business day following the date on which such deficit or debit ledger balance originated;

(iii) Deduct all unsecured receivables, advances and loans except for:

(A) Management fees receivable from commodity pools outstanding no longer than thirty (30) days from the date they are due;

(B) Receivables from foreign clearing organizations;

(C) Receivables from registered futures commission merchants or brokers, resulting from cleared swap transactions or, commodity futures or

§ 240.15c3–1b

option transactions, except those specifically excluded under paragraph (3)(ii) of this appendix B. In the case of an introducing broker or an applicant for registration as an introducing broker, include 50 percent of the value of a guarantee or security deposit with a futures commission merchant which carries or intends to carry accounts for the customers of the introducing broker.

(iv) Deduct all inventories (including work in process, finished goods, raw materials and inventories held for resale) except for readily marketable spot commodities; or spot commodities which adequately collateralize indebtedness under paragraph (c)(7) of 17 CFR 1.17;

(v) Guarantee deposits with commodities clearing organizations are not required to be deducted from net worth;

(vi) Stock in commodities clearing organizations to the extent of its margin value is not required to be deducted from net worth;

(vii) Deduct from net worth the amount by which any advances paid by the broker or dealer on cash commodity contracts and used in computing net capital exceeds 95 percent of the market value of the commodities covered by such contracts.

(viii) Do not include equity in the commodity accounts of partners in net worth.

(ix) In the case of all inventory, fixed price commitments and forward contracts, except for inventory and forward contracts in the inter-bank market in those foreign currencies which are purchased or sold for further delivery on or subject to the rules of a contract market and covered by an open futures contract for which there will be no charge, deduct the applicable percentage of the net position specified below:

(A) Inventory which is currently registered as deliverable on a contract market and covered by an open futures contract or by a commodity option on a physical—No charge.

(B) Inventory which is covered by an open futures contract or commodity option—5% of the market value.

(C) Inventory which is not covered—20% of the market value.

(D) Fixed price commitments (open purchases and sales) and forward contracts which are covered by an open futures contract or commodity option—10% of the market value.

(E) Fixed price commitments (open purchases and sales) and forward contracts which are not covered by an open futures contract or commodity option—20% of the market value.

(x) Deduct 4% of the market value of commodity options granted (sold) by option customers on or subject to the rules of a contract market.

(xi) [Reserved]

(xii) Deduct for undermargined customer commodity futures accounts the amount of funds required in each such account to meet maintenance margin requirements of the applicable board of trade or, if there are no such maintenance margin requirements, clearing organization margin requirements applicable to such positions, after application of calls for margin, or other required deposits which are outstanding three business days or less. If there are no such maintenance margin requirements or clearing organization margin requirements on such accounts, then deduct the amount of funds required to provide margin equal to the amount necessary after application of calls for margin, or other required deposits outstanding three days or less to restore original margin when the original margin has been depleted by 50 percent or more. *Provided*, To the extent a deficit is deducted from net worth in accordance with paragraph (a)(3)(ii) of this appendix B, such amount shall not also be deducted under this paragraph (a)(3)(xii). In the event that an owner of a customer account has deposited an asset other than cash to margin, guarantee or secure his account, the value attributable to such asset for purposes of this paragraph shall be the lesser of (A) the value attributable to such asset pursuant to the margin rules of the applicable board of trade, or (B) the market value of such asset after application of the percentage deductions specified in paragraph (a)(3)(ix) of this appendix B or, where appropriate, specified in paragraph (c)(2)(vi) or (c)(2)(vii) of § 240.15c3–1 this chapter;

Securities and Exchange Commission § 240.15c3-1b

(xiii) Deduct for undermargined non-customer and omnibus commodity futures accounts the amount of funds required in each such account to meet maintenance margin requirements of the applicable board of trade or, if there are no such maintenance margin requirements, clearing organization margin requirements applicable to such positions, after application of calls for margin, or other required deposits which are outstanding two business days or less. If there are no such maintenance margin requirements or clearing organization margin requirements, then deduct the amount of funds required to provide margin equal to the amount necessary after application of calls for margin, or other required deposits outstanding two days or less to restore original margin when the original margin has been depleted by 50 percent or more. *Provided*, To the extent a deficit is deducted from net worth in accordance with paragraph (a)(3)(ii) of this appendix B such amount shall not also be deducted under this paragraph (a)(3)(xiii). In the event that an owner of a non-customer or omnibus account has deposited an asset other than cash to margin, guarantee or secure his account, the value attributable to such asset for purposes of this paragraph shall be the lesser of (A) the value attributable to such asset pursuant to the margin rules of the applicable board of trade, or (B) the market value of such asset after application of the percentage deductions specified in paragraph (a)(3)(ix) of this appendix B or, where appropriate, specified in paragraph (c)(2)(vi) or (c)(2)(vii) of § 240.15c3-1 of this chapter;

(xiv) In the case of open futures contracts and granted (sold) commodity options held in proprietary accounts carried by the broker or dealer which are not covered by a position held by the broker or dealer or which are not the result of a "changer trade" made in accordance with the rules of a contract market, deduct:

(A) For a broker or dealer which is a clearing member of a contract market for the positions on such contract market cleared by such member, the applicable margin requirement of the applicable clearing organization;

(B) For a broker or dealer which is a member of a self-regulatory organization 150% of the applicable maintenance margin requirement of the applicable board of trade or clearing organization, whichever is greater; or

(C) For all other brokers or dealers, 200% of the applicable maintenance margin requirement of the applicable board of trade or clearing organization, whichever is greater; or

(D) For open contracts or granted (sold) commodity options for which there are no applicable maintenance margin requirements, 200% of the applicable initial margin requirement;

Provided, the equity in any such proprietary account shall reduce the deduction required by this paragraph (a)(3)(xiv) if such equity is not otherwise includable in net capital.

(xv) In the case of a broker or dealer which is a purchaser of a commodity option which is traded on a contract market the deduction shall be the same safety factor as if the broker or dealer were the grantor of such option in accordance with paragraph (a)(3)(xiv), but in no event shall the safety factor be greater than the market value attributed to such option.

(xvi) In the case of a broker or dealer which is a purchaser of a commodity option not traded on a contract market which has value and such value is used to increase net capital, the deduction is ten percent of the market value of the physical or futures contract which is the subject of such option but in no event more than the value attributed to such option.

(xvii) Deduction 5% of all unsecured receivables includable under paragraph (a)(3)(iii)(C) of this appendix B used by the broker or dealer in computing "net capital" and which are not receivable from (A) a futures commission merchant registered as such with the Commodity Futures Trading Commission, or (B) a broker or dealer which is registered as such with the Securities and Exchange Commission.

(xviii) A loan or advance or any other form of receivable shall not be considered "secured" for the purposes of paragraph (a)(3) of this appendix B unless the following conditions exist:

§ 240.15c3–1b

(A) The receivable is secured by readily marketable collateral which is otherwise unencumbered and which can be readily converted into cash: *Provided, however,* That the receivable will be considered secured only to the extent of the market value of such collateral after application of the percentage deductions specified in paragraph (a)(3)(ix) of this appendix B; and

(B)(*1*) The readily marketable collateral is in the possession or control of the broker or dealer; or

(*2*) The broker or dealer has a legally enforceable, written security agreement, signed by the debtor, and has a perfected security interest in the readily marketable collateral within the meaning of the laws of the State in which the readily marketable collateral is located.

(xix) The term *cover* for purposes of this appendix B shall mean cover as defined in 17 CFR 1.17(j).

(xx) The term *customer* for purposes of this Appendix B shall mean customer as defined in 17 CFR 1.17(b)(2). The term "non-customer" for purposes of this appendix B shall mean non-customer as defined in 17 CFR 1.17(b)(4).

(b) Every broker or dealer in computing net capital pursuant to § 240.15c3–1 must comply with the following:

(1) *Cleared swaps.* In the case of a cleared swap held in a proprietary account of the broker or dealer, deducting the amount of the applicable margin requirement of the derivatives clearing organization or, if the swap references an equity security index, the broker or dealer may take a deduction using the method specified in § 240.15c3–1a.

(2) *Non-cleared swaps*—(i) *Credit default swaps referencing broad-based security indices.* In the case of a non-cleared credit default swap for which the deductions in § 240.15c3–1e do not apply:

(A) *Short positions (selling protection).* In the case of a non-cleared swap that is a short credit default swap referencing a broad-based security index, deducting the percentage of the notional amount based upon the current basis point spread of the credit default swap and the maturity of the credit default swap in accordance table 1 to § 240.15c3–1a(b)(2)(i)(A):

TABLE 1 TO § 240.15c3–1a(b)(2)(i)(A)

Length of time to maturity of credit default swap contract	Basis point spread					
	100 or less (%)	101–300 (%)	301–400 (%)	401–500 (%)	501–699 (%)	700 or more (%)
Less than 12 months	0.67	1.33	3.33	5.00	6.67	10.00
12 months but less than 24 months	1.00	2.33	5.00	6.67	8.33	11.67
24 months but less than 36 months	1.33	3.33	6.67	8.33	10.00	13.33
36 months but less than 48 months	2.00	4.00	8.33	10.00	11.67	15.00
48 months but less than 60 months	2.67	4.67	10.00	11.67	13.33	16.67
60 months but less than 72 months	3.67	5.67	11.67	13.33	15.00	18.33
72 months but less than 84 months	4.67	6.67	13.33	15.00	16.67	20.00
84 months but less than 120 months	5.67	10.00	15.00	16.67	18.33	26.67
120 months and longer	6.67	13.33	16.67	18.33	20.00	33.33

(B) *Long positions (purchasing protection).* In the case of a non-cleared swap that is a long credit default swap referencing a broad-based security index, deducting 50 percent of the deduction that would be required by paragraph (b)(2)(i)(A) of this section if the non-cleared swap was a short credit default swap, each such deduction not to exceed the current market value of the long position.

(C) *Long and short credit default swaps.* In the case of non-cleared swaps that are long and short credit default swaps referencing the same broad-based security index, have the same credit events which would trigger payment by the seller of protection, have the same basket of obligations which would determine the amount of payment by the seller of protection upon the occurrence of a credit event, that are in the same or adjacent spread category, and that are in the same or adjacent maturity category and have a maturity date within three months of the other maturity category, deducting the percentage of the notional amount

Securities and Exchange Commission § 240.15c3–1c

specified in the higher maturity category under paragraph (b)(2)(i)(A) or (B) of this section on the excess of the long or short position.

(D) *Long basket of obligors and long credit default swap.* In the case of a non-cleared swap that is a long credit default swap referencing a broad-based security index and the broker or dealer is long a basket of debt securities comprising all of the components of the security index, deducting 50 percent of the amount specified in § 240.15c3–1(c)(2)(vi) for the component securities, provided the broker or dealer can deliver the component securities to satisfy the obligation of the broker or dealer on the credit default swap.

(E) *Short basket of obligors and short credit default swap.* In the case of a non-cleared swap that is a short credit default swap referencing a broad-based security index and the broker or dealer is short a basket of debt securities comprising all of the components of the security index, deducting the amount specified in § 240.15c3–1(c)(2)(vi) for the component securities.

(ii) *All other swaps.* (A) In the case of a non-cleared swap that is not a credit default swap for which the deductions in § 240.15c3–1e do not apply, deducting the amount calculated by multiplying the notional value of the swap by the percentage specified in:

(*1*) Section 240.15c3–1 applicable to the reference asset if § 240.15c3–1 specifies a percentage deduction for the type of asset;

(*2*) 17 CFR 1.17 applicable to the reference asset if 17 CFR 1.17 specifies a percentage deduction for the type of asset and § 240.15c3–1 does not specify a percentage deduction for the type of asset; or

(*3*) In the case of non-cleared interest rate swap, § 240.15c3–1(c)(2)(vi)(A) based on the maturity of the swap, provided that the percentage deduction must be no less than one eighth of 1 percent of the amount of a long position that is netted against a short position in the case of a non-cleared swap with a maturity of three months or more.

(B) A broker or dealer may reduce the deduction under paragraph (b)(2)(ii)(A) by an amount equal to any reduction recognized for a comparable long or short position in the reference asset or interest rate under § 240.15c3–1 or 17 CFR 1.17.

(Secs. 15(c)(3), 17(a) and 23(a), 15 U.S.C. 78o(c)(3), 78q(a), and 78w(a))

[44 FR 34886, June 15, 1979, as amended at 46 FR 37041, July 17, 1981; 49 FR 31848, Aug. 9, 1984; 84 FR 44044, Aug. 22, 2019]

§ 240.15c3–1c Consolidated computations of net capital and aggregate indebtedness for certain subsidiaries and affiliates (appendix C to 17 CFR 240.15c3–1).

(a) *Flow through capital benefits.* Every broker or dealer in computing its net capital and aggregate indebtedness pursuant to 17 CFR 240.15c3–1 shall, subject to the provisions of paragraphs (b) and (d) of this appendix, consolidate in a single computation assets and liabilities of any subsidiary or affiliate for which it guarantees, endorses or assumes directly or indirectly the obligations or liabilities. The assets and liabilities of a subsidiary or affiliate whose liabilities and obligations have not been guaranteed, endorsed, or assumed directly or indirectly by the broker or dealer may also be so consolidated if an opinion of counsel is obtained as provided for in paragraph (b) of this section.

(b) *Required counsel opinions.* (1) If the consolidation, provided for in paragraph (a) of this section, of any such subsidiary or affiliate results in the increase of the broker's or dealer's net capital and/or the decrease of the broker's or dealer's minimum net capital requirement under paragraph (a) of § 240.15c3–1 and an opinion of counsel described in paragraph (b)(2) of this section has not been obtained, such benefits shall not be recognized in the broker's or dealer's computation required by this section.

(2) Except as provided for in paragraph (b)(1) of this section, consolidation shall be permitted with respect to any subsidiaries or affiliates which are majority owned and controlled by the broker or dealer for which the broker or dealer can demonstrate to the satisfaction of the Commission, through the Examining Authority, by an opinion of counsel that the net asset values, or the portion thereof related to the parent's ownership interest in the subsidiary or affiliate may be caused by

§ 240.15c3-1d

the broker or dealer or a trustee appointed pursuant to the Securities Investor Protection Act of 1970 or otherwise, to be distributed to the broker or dealer within 30 calendar days. Such opinion shall also set forth the actions necessary to cause such a distribution to be made, identify the parties having the authority to take such actions, identify and describe the rights of other parties or classes of parties, including but not limited to customers, general creditors, subordinated lenders, minority shareholders, employees, litigants and governmental or regulatory authorities, who may delay or prevent such a distribution and such other assurances as the Commission or the Examining Authority by rule or interpretation may require. Such opinion shall be current and periodically renewed in connection with the broker's or dealer's annual audit pursuant to 17 CFR 240.17a-5 under the Securities Exchange Act of 1934 or upon any material change in circumstances.

(c) *Principles of consolidation.* In preparing a consolidated computation of net capital and/or aggregate indebtedness pursuant to this section, the following minimum and non-exclusive requirements shall be observed:

(1) Consolidated net worth shall be reduced by the estimated amount of any tax reasonably anticipated to be incurred upon distribution of the assets of the subsidiary or affiliate.

(2) Liabilities of a consolidated subsidiary or affiliate which are subordinated to the claims of present and future creditors pursuant to a satisfactory subordination agreement shall not be added to consolidated net worth unless such subordination extends also to the claims of present or future creditors of the parent broker or dealer and all consolidated subsidiaries.

(3) Subordinated liabilities of a consolidated subsidiary or affiliate which are consolidated in accordance with paragraph (c)(2) of this section may not be prepaid, repaid or accelerated if any of the entities included in such consolidation would otherwise be unable to comply with the provisions of Appendix (D), 17 CFR 240.15c3-1d.

(4) Each broker or dealer included within the consolidation shall at all times be in compliance with the net capital requirement to which it is subject.

(d) *Certain precluded acts.* No broker or dealer shall guarantee, endorse or assume directly or indirectly any obligation or liability of a subsidiary or affiliate unless the obligation or liability is reflected in the computation of net capital and/or aggregate indebtedness pursuant to 17 CFR 240.15c3-1 or this appendix (C), except as provided in paragraph (b)(1) of this section.

[40 FR 29808, July 16, 1975, as amended at 57 FR 56988, Dec. 2, 1992]

§ 240.15c3-1d Satisfactory Subordination Agreements (Appendix D to 17 CFR 240.15c3-1).

(a) *Introduction.* (1) This appendix sets forth minimum and non-exclusive requirements for satisfactory subordination agreements (hereinafter "subordination agreement"). The Examining Authority may require or the broker or dealer may include such other provisions as deemed necessary or appropriate to the extent such provisions do not cause the subordination agreement to fail to meet the minimum requirements of this Appendix (D).

(2) *Certain definitions.* For purposes of 17 CFR 240.15c3-1 and this Appendix (D):

(i) A subordination agreement may be either a subordinated loan agreement or a secured demand note agreement.

(ii) The term *subordinated loan agreement* shall mean the agreement or agreements evidencing or governing a subordinated borrowing of cash.

(iii) The term *collateral value* of any securities pledged to secure a secured demand note shall mean the market value of such securities after giving effect to the percentage deductions set forth in paragraph (c)(2)(vi) of § 240.15c3-1 except for paragraph (c)(2)(vi)(J). In lieu of the deduction under (c)(2)(vi)(J), the broker or dealer shall reduce the market value of the securities pledged to secure the secured demand note by 30 percent.

(iv) The term *payment obligation* shall mean the obligation of a broker or dealer in respect to any subordination agreement (A) to repay cash loaned to

Securities and Exchange Commission § 240.15c3-1d

the broker or dealer pursuant to a subordinated loan agreement or (B) to return a secured demand note contributed to the broker or dealer or reduce the unpaid principal amount thereof and to return cash or securities pledged as collateral to secure the secured demand note and (C) "Payment" shall mean the performance by a broker or dealer of a Payment Obligation.

(v)(A) The term *secured demand note agreement* shall mean an agreement (including the related secured demand note) evidencing or governing the contribution of a secured demand note to a broker or dealer and the pledge of securities and/or cash with the broker or dealer as collateral to secure payment of such secured demand note. The secured demand note agreement may provide that neither the lender, his heirs, executors, administrators or assigns shall be personally liable on such note and that in the event of default the broker or dealer shall look for payment of such note solely to the collateral then pledged to secure the same.

(B) The secured demand note shall be a promissory note executed by the lender and shall be payable on the demand of the broker or dealer to which it is contributed; provided, however, that the making of such demand may be conditioned upon the occurrence of any of certain events which are acceptable to the Commission and to the Examining Authority for such broker or dealer.

(C) If such note is not paid upon presentment and demand as provided for therein, the broker or dealer shall have the right to liquidate all or any part of the securities then pledged as collateral to secure payment of the same and to apply the net proceeds of such liquidation, together with any cash then included in the collateral, in payment of such note. Subject to the prior rights of the broker or dealer as pledgee, the lender, as defined herein, may retain ownership of the collateral and have the benefit of any increases and bear the risks of any decreases in the value of the collateral and may retain the right to vote securities contained within the collateral and any right to income therefrom or distributions thereon, except the broker or dealer shall have the right to receive and hold as pledgee all dividends payable in securities and all partial and complete liquidating dividends.

(D) Subject to the prior rights of the broker or dealer as pledgee, the lender may have the right to direct the sale of any securities included in the collateral, to direct the purchases of securities with any cash included therein, to withdraw excess collateral or to substitute cash or other securities as collateral, provided that the net proceeds of any such sale and the cash so substituted and the securities so purchased or substituted are held by the broker or dealer, as pledgee, and are included within the collateral to secure payment of the secured demand note, and provided further that no such transaction shall be permitted if, after giving effect thereto, the sum of the amount of any cash, plus the Collateral Value of the securities, then pledged as collateral to secure the secured demand note would be less than the unpaid principal amount of the secured demand note.

(E) Upon payment by the lender, as distinguished from a reduction by the lender which is provided for in (b)(6)(iii) or reduction by the broker or dealer as provided for in subparagraph (b)(7) of this appendix (D), of all or any part of the unpaid principal amount of the secured demand note, a broker or dealer shall issue to the lender a subordinated loan agreement in the amount of such payment (or in the case of a broker or dealer that is a partnership credit a capital account of the lender) or issue preferred or common stock of the broker or dealer in the amount of such payment, or any combination of the foregoing, as provided for in the secured demand note agreement.

(F) The term *lender* shall mean person who lends cash to a broker or dealer pursuant to a subordinated loan agreement and the person who contributes a secured demand note to a broker or dealer pursuant to a secured demand note agreement.

(b) *Minimum requirements for subordination agreements.* (1) Subject to paragraph (a) of this section, a subordination agreement shall mean a written

§ 240.15c3-1d

agreement between the broker or dealer and the lender, which (i) has a minimum term of one year, except for temporary subordination agreements provided for in paragraph (c)(5) of this appendix (D), and (ii) is a valid and binding obligation enforceable in accordance with its terms (subject as to enforcement to applicable bankruptcy, insolvency, reorganization, moratorium and other similar laws) against the broker or dealer and the lender and their respective heirs, executors, administrators, successors and assigns.

(2) *Specific amount.* All subordination agreements shall be for a specific dollar amount which shall not be reduced for the duration of the agreement except by installments as specifically provided for therein and except as otherwise provided in this appendix (D).

(3) *Effective subordination.* The subordination agreement shall effectively subordinate any right of the lender to receive any Payment with respect thereto, together with accrued interest or compensation, to the prior payment or provision for payment in full of all claims of all present and future creditors of the broker or dealer arising out of any matter occurring prior to the date on which the related Payment Obligation matures consistent with the provisions of 17 CFR 240.15c3-1 and 240.15c3-1d, except for claims which are the subject of subordination agreements which rank on the same priority as or junior to the claim of the lender under such subordination agreements.

(4) *Proceeds of subordinated loan agreements.* The subordinated loan agreement shall provide that the cash proceeds thereof shall be used and dealt with by the broker or dealer as part of its capital and shall be subject to the risks of the business.

(5) *Certain rights of the broker or dealer.* The subordination agreement shall provide that the broker or dealer shall have the right to:

(i) Deposit any cash proceeds of a subordinated loan agreement and any cash pledged as collateral to secure a secured demand note in an account or accounts in its own name in any bank or trust company;

(ii) Pledge, repledge, hypothecate and rehypothecate, any or all of the securities pledged as collateral to secure a secured demand note, without notice, separately or in common with other securities or property for the purpose of securing any indebtedness of the broker or dealer; and

(iii) Lend to itself or others any or all of the securities and cash pledged as collateral to secure a secured demand note.

(6) *Collateral for secured demand notes.* Only cash and securities which are fully paid for and which may be publicly offered or sold without registration under the Securities Act of 1933, and the offer, sale and transfer of which are not otherwise restricted, may be pledged as collateral to secure a secured demand note. The secured demand note agreement shall provide that if at any time the sum of the amount of any cash, plus the Collateral Value of any securities, then pledged as collateral to secure the secured demand note is less than the unpaid principal amount of the secured demand note, the broker or dealer must immediately transmit written notice to that effect to the lender and the Examining Authority for such broker or dealer. The secured demand note agreement shall also require that following such transmittal:

(i) The lender, prior to noon of the business day next succeeding the transmittal of such notice, may pledge as collateral additional cash or securities sufficient, after giving effect to such pledge, to bring the sum of the amount of any cash plus the Collateral Value of any securities, then pledged as collateral to secure the secured demand note, up to an amount not less than the unpaid principal amount of the secured demand note; and

(ii) Unless additional cash or securities are pledged by the lender as provided in paragraph (b)(6)(i) of this section, the broker or dealer at noon on the business day next succeeding the transmittal of notice to the lender must commence sale, for the account of the lender, of such of the securities then pledged as collateral to secure the secured demand note and apply so much of the net proceeds thereof, together with such of the cash then

Securities and Exchange Commission § 240.15c3-1d

pledged as collateral to secure the secured demand note as may be necessary to eliminate the unpaid principal amount of the secured demand note; *Provided, however,* That the unpaid principal amount of the secured demand note need not be reduced below the sum of the amount of any remaining cash, plus the Collateral Value of the remaining securities, then pledged as collateral to secure the secured demand note. The broker or dealer may not purchase for its own account any securities subject to such a sale.

(iii) The secured demand note agreement also may provide that, in lieu of the procedures specified in the provisions required by paragraph (b)(6)(ii) of this section, the lender with the prior written consent of the broker or dealer and the Examining Authority for the broker or dealer may reduce the unpaid principal amount of the secured demand note. After giving effect to such reduction, the aggregate indebtedness of the broker or dealer may not exceed 1000 percent of its net capital or, in the case of a broker or dealer operating pursuant to paragraph (a)(1)(ii) of § 240.15c3-1, net capital may not be less than 5 percent of aggregate debit items computed in accordance with § 240.15c3-3a, or, if registered as a futures commission merchant, 7 percent of the funds required to be segregated pursuant to the Commodity Exchange Act and the regulations thereunder (less the market value of commodity options purchased by option customers subject to the rules of a contract market, each such deduction not to exceed the amount of funds in the option customer's account), if greater. No single secured demand note shall be permitted to be reduced by more than 15 percent of its original principal amount and after such reduction no excess collateral may be withdrawn. No Examining Authority shall consent to a reduction of the principal amount of a secured demand note if, after giving effect to such reduction, net capital would be less than 120 percent of the minimum dollar amount required by § 240.15c3-1.

Permissive Prepayments

(7) A broker or dealer at its option but not at the option of the lender may, if the subordination agreement so provides, make a Payment of all or any portion of the Payment Obligation thereunder prior to the scheduled maturity date of such Payment Obligation (hereinafter referred to as a "Prepayment"), but in no event may any Prepayment be made before the expiration of one year from the date such subordination agreement became effective. This restriction shall not apply to temporary subordination agreements that comply with the provisions of paragraph (c)(5) of this section. No Prepayment shall be made, if, after giving effect thereto (and to all Payments of Payment Obligations under any other subordinated agreements then outstanding the maturity or accelerated maturities of which are scheduled to fall due within six months after the date such Prepayment is to occur pursuant to this provision or on or prior to the date on which the Payment Obligation in respect of such Prepayment is scheduled to mature disregarding this provision, whichever date is earlier) without reference to any projected profit or loss of the broker or dealer, either aggregate indebtedness of the broker or dealer would exceed 1000 percent of its net capital or its net capital would be less than 120 percent of the minimum dollar amount required by § 240.15c3-1 or, in the case of a broker or dealer operating pursuant to § 240.15c3-1(a)(1)(ii), its net capital would be less than 5 percent of its aggregate debit items computed in accordance with § 240.15c3-3a, or if registered as a futures commission merchant, 7 percent of the funds required to be segregated pursuant to the Commodity Exchange Act and the regulations thereunder (less the market value of commodity options purchased by option customers subject to the rules of a contract market, each such deduction not to exceed the amount of funds in the option customer's account), if greater, or its net capital would be less than 120 percent of the minimum dollar amount required by § 240.15c3-1(a)(1)(ii), or if, in the case of a broker or dealer operating pursuant to § 240.15c3-1(a)(10), its net capital would be less than 120 percent of its minimum requirement.

§ 240.15c3-1d

Suspended Repayment

(8)(i) The Payment Obligation of the broker or dealer in respect of any subordination agreement shall be suspended and shall not mature if, after giving effect to Payment of such Payment Obligation (and to all Payments of Payment Obligations of such broker or dealer under any other subordination agreement(s) then outstanding that are scheduled to mature on or before such Payment Obligation) either:

(A) The aggregate indebtedness of the broker or dealer would exceed 1200 percent of its net capital, or in the case of a broker or dealer operating pursuant to § 240.15c3-1(a)(1)(ii), its net capital would be less than 5 percent of aggregate debit items computed in accordance with § 240.15c3-3a or, if registered as a futures commission merchant, 6 percent of the funds required to be segregated pursuant to the Commodity Exchange Act and the regulations thereunder (less the market value of commodity options purchased by option customers on or subject to the rules of a contract market, each such deduction not to exceed the amount of funds in the option customer's account), if greater, or, in the case of a broker or dealer operating pursuant to § 240.15c3-1(a)(10), its net capital would be less than 120 percent of its minimum requirement; or

(B) Its net capital would be less than 120 percent of the minimum dollar amount required by § 240.15c3-1 including paragraph (a)(1)(ii), if applicable. The subordination agreement may provide that if the Payment Obligation of the broker or dealer thereunder does not mature and is suspended as a result of the requirement of this paragraph (b)(8) for a period of not less than six months, the broker or dealer shall thereupon commence the rapid and orderly liquidation of its business, but the right of the lender to receive Payment, together with accrued interest or compensation, shall remain subordinate as required by the provisions of §§ 240.15c3-1 and 240.15c3-1d.

(ii) [Reserved]

(9) *Accelerated maturity-obligation to repay to remain subordinate.* (i) Subject to the provisions of paragraph (b)(8) of this appendix, a subordination agreement may provide that the lender may, upon prior written notice to the broker or dealer and the Examining Authority given not earlier than six months after the effective date of such subordination agreement, accelerate the date on which the Payment Obligation of the broker or dealer, together with accrued interest or compensation, is scheduled to mature to a date not earlier than six months after the giving of such notice, but the right of the lender to receive Payment, together with accrued interest or compensation, shall remain subordinate as required by the provisions of 17 CFR 240.15c3-1 and 240.15c3-1d.

(ii) Notwithstanding the provisions of paragraph (b)(8) of this appendix, the Payment Obligation of the broker or dealer with respect to a subordination agreement, together with accrued interest and compensation, shall mature in the event of any receivership, insolvency, liquidation pursuant to the Securities Investor Protection Act of 1970 or otherwise, bankruptcy, assignment for the benefit of creditors, reorganization whether or not pursuant to the bankruptcy laws, or any other marshalling of the assets and liabilities of the broker or dealer but the right of the lender to receive Payment, together with accrued interest or compensation, shall remain subordinate as required by the provisions of 17 CFR 240.15c3-1 and 240.15c3-1d.

(10)(i) *Accelerated maturity of subordination agreements on event of default and event of acceleration—obligation to repay to remain subordinate.* A subordination agreement may provide that the lender may, upon prior written notice to the broker or dealer and the Examining Authority of the broker or dealer of the occurrence of any Event of Acceleration (as hereinafter defined) given no sooner than six months after the effective date of such subordination agreement, accelerate the date on which the Payment Obligation of the broker or dealer, together with accrued interest or compensation, is scheduled to mature, to the last business day of a calendar month which is not less than six months after notice of acceleration is received by the broker or dealer and the Examining Authority for the broker or dealer. Any subordination agreement containing such Events of Acceleration may also provide, that if upon such accelerated maturity date the Payment Obligation of the broker or dealer is suspended as required by paragraph (b)(8) of this appendix (D) and liquidation of the broker or dealer has not commenced on or prior to such accelerated maturity date, then notwithstanding paragraph (b)(8) of this appendix the Payment Obligation of the broker or dealer with respect to such subordination agreement shall mature on the day immediately following such accelerated maturity date and in any such event the Payment Obligations of the broker or dealer with respect to all other subordination agreements then outstanding shall also mature at the same time but the rights of the respective lenders to receive Payment, together with accrued interest or compensation, shall remain subordinate as required by the provisions of this Appendix (D). Events of Acceleration which may be included in a subordination agreement complying with this paragraph (b)(10) shall be limited to:

(A) Failure to pay interest or any installment of principal on a subordination agreement as scheduled;

(B) Failure to pay when due other money obligations of a specified material amount;

(C) Discovery that any material, specified representation or warranty of the broker or dealer which is included in the subordination agreement and on which the subordination agreement was based or continued was inaccurate in a material respect at the time made;

(D) Any specified and clearly measurable event which is included in the subordination agreement and which the lender and the broker or dealer agree (1) is a significant indication that the financial position of the broker or dealer has changed materially and adversely from agreed upon specified norms or (2) could materially and adversely affect the ability of the broker or dealer to conduct its business as conducted on the date the subordination agreement was made; or (3) is a significant change in the senior management of the broker or dealer or in the general business conducted by the broker or dealer from that which obtained on the date the subordination agreement became effective;

(E) Any continued failure to perform agreed covenants included in the subordination agreement relating to the conduct of the business of the broker or dealer or relating to the maintenance and reporting of its financial position; and

(ii) Notwithstanding the provisions of paragraph (b)(8) of this appendix, a subordination agreement may provide that, if liquidation of the business of the broker or dealer has not already commenced, the Payment Obligation of the broker or dealer shall mature, together with accrued interest or compensation, upon the occurrence of an Event of Default (as hereinafter defined). Such agreement may also provide that, if liquidation of the business of the broker or dealer has not already commenced, the rapid and orderly liquidation of the business of the broker or dealer shall then commence upon the happening of an Event of Default. Any subordination agreement which so provides for maturity of the Payment Obligation upon the occurrence of an Event of Default shall also provide that the date on which such Event of Default occurs shall, if liquidation of the broker or dealer has not already commenced, be the date on which the Payment Obligations of the broker or dealer with respect to all other subordination agreements then outstanding shall mature but the rights of the respective lenders to receive Payment, together with accrued interest or compensation, shall remain subordinate as required by the provisions of this Appendix (D). Events of Default which may be included in a subordination agreement shall be limited to:

(A) The making of an application by the Securities Investor Protection Corporation for a decree adjudicating that customers of the broker or dealer are in need of protection under the Securities Investor Protection Act of 1970 and the failure of the broker or dealer to obtain the dismissal of such application within 30 days;

(B) The aggregate indebtedness of the broker or dealer exceeding 1500 percent of its net capital or, in the case of a broker or dealer that has elected to operate under § 240.15c3–1(a)(1)(ii), its net

§ 240.15c3-1d

capital computed in accordance therewith is less than two percent of its aggregate debit items computed in accordance with § 240.15c3-3a or, if registered as a futures commission merchant, four percent of the funds required to be segregated pursuant to the Commodity Exchange Act and the regulations thereunder (less the market value of commodity options purchased by option customers on or subject to the rules of a contract market, each such deduction not to exceed the amount of funds in the option customer's account), if greater, or, in the case of a broker or dealer operating pursuant to § 240.15c3-1(a)(10), its net capital is less than its minimum requirement, throughout a period of 15 consecutive business days, commencing on the day the broker or dealer first determines and notifies the Examining Authority for the broker or dealer, or the Examining Authority or the Commission first determines and notifies the broker or dealer of such fact;

(C) The Commission shall revoke the registration of the broker or dealer;

(D) The Examining Authority shall suspend (and not reinstate within 10 days) or revoke the broker's or dealer's status as a member thereof;

(E) Any receivership, insolvency, liquidation pursuant to the Securities Investor Protection Act of 1970 or otherwise, bankruptcy, assignment for the benefit of creditors, reorganization whether or not pursuant to bankruptcy laws, or any other marshalling of the assets and liabilities of the broker or dealer.

A subordination agreement which contains any of the provisions permitted by this paragraph (b)(10) shall not contain the provision otherwise permitted by clause (i) of paragraph (b)(9).

BROKERS AND DEALERS CARRYING THE ACCOUNTS OF SPECIALISTS AND MARKET MAKERS IN LISTED OPTIONS

(11) A subordination agreement which becomes effective on or after August 1, 1977 in favor of a broker or dealer who guarantees, endorses, carries or clears specialist or market maker transactions in options listed on a national securities exchange or facility of a national securities association shall provide that reduction, prepayment or repayment of the unpaid principal amount thereof, pursuant to those terms of the agreement required or permitted by paragraphs (b)(6)(iii), (b)(7), or (b)(8)(i) of this section, shall not occur in contravention of paragraphs (a)(6)(v), (a)(7)(iv), or (c)(2)(x)(B)(*1*) of § 240.15c3-1 insofar as they apply to such broker or dealer.

(c) *Miscellaneous Provisions*—(1) *Prohibited Cancellation.* The subordination agreement shall not be subject to cancellation by either party; no Payment shall be made with respect thereto and the agreement shall not be terminated, rescinded or modified by mutual consent or otherwise if the effect thereof would be inconsistent with the requirements of 17 CFR 240.15c3-1 and 240.15c3-1d.

(2) Every broker or dealer shall immediately notify the Examining Authority for such broker or dealer if, after giving effect to all Payments of Payment Obligations under subordination agreements then outstanding that are then due or mature within the following six months without reference to any projected profit or loss of the broker or dealer either the aggregate indebtedness of the broker or dealer would exceed 1200 percent of its net capital or its net capital would be less than 120 percent of the minimum dollar amount required by § 240.15c3-1, or, in the case of a broker or dealer operating pursuant to § 240.15c3-1(a)(1)(ii), its net capital would be less than 5 percent of aggregate debit items computed in accordance with § 240.15c3-3a, or, if registered as a futures commission merchant, 6 percent of the funds required to be segregated pursuant to the Commodity Exchange Act and the regulations thereunder (less the market value of commodity options purchased by option customers on or subject to the rules of a contract market, each such deduction not to exceed the amount of funds in the option customer's account), if greater, or less than 120 percent of the minimum dollar amount required by § 240.15c3-1(a)(1)(ii), or, in the case of a broker or dealer operating pursuant to § 240.15c3-1(a)(10), its net capital would be less than 120 percent of its minimum requirement.

Securities and Exchange Commission § 240.15c3-1d

(3) *Certain legends.* If all the provisions of a satisfactory subordination agreement do not appear in a single instrument, then the debenture or other evidence of indebtedness shall bear on its face an appropriate legend stating that it is issued subject to the provisions of a satisfactory subordination agreement which shall be adequately referred to and incorporated by reference.

(4) *Legal title to securities.* All securities pledged as collateral to secure a secured demand note must be in bearer form, or registered in the name of the broker or dealer or the name of its nominee or custodian.

Temporary and Revolving Subordination Agreements

(5)(i) For the purpose of enabling a broker or dealer to participate as an underwriter of securities or other extraordinary activities in compliance with the net capital requirements of § 240.15c3-1, a broker or dealer shall be permitted, on no more than three occasions in any 12 month period, to enter into a subordination agreement on a temporary basis that has a stated term of no more than 45 days from the date such subordination agreement became effective. This temporary relief shall not apply to a broker or dealer if, within the preceding thirty calendar days, it has given notice pursuant to § 240.17a-11, or if immediately prior to entering into such subordination agreement, either:

(A) The aggregate indebtedness of the broker or dealer exceeds 1000 percent of its net capital or its net capital is less than 120 percent of the minimum dollar amount required by § 240.15c3-1, or

(B) In the case of a broker or dealer operating pursuant to § 240.15c3-1(a)(1)(ii), its net capital is less than 5 percent of aggregate debits computed in accordance with § 240.15c3-1, or, if registered as a futures commission merchant, less than 7 percent of the funds required to be segregated pursuant to the Commodity Exchange Act and the regulations thereunder (less the market value of commodity options purchased by option customers on or subject to the rules of a contract market, each such deduction not to exceed the amount of funds in the option customer's account), if greater, or less than 120 percent of the minimum dollar amount required by paragraph (a)(1)(ii) of this section, or, in the case of a broker or dealer operating pursuant to § 240.15c3-1(a)(10), its net capital would be less than 120 percent of its minimum requirement, or

(C) The amount of its then outstanding subordination agreements exceeds the limits specified in paragraph (d) of § 240.15c3-1. Such temporary subordination agreement shall be subject to all other provisions of this appendix D.

(ii) A broker or dealer shall be permitted to enter into a revolving subordinated loan agreement which provides for prepayment within less than one year of all or any portion of the Payment Obligation thereunder at the option of the broker or dealer upon the prior written approval of the Examining Authority for the broker or dealer. The Examining Authority, however, shall not approve any prepayment if:

(A) After giving effect thereto (and to all Payments of Payment Obligations under any other subordinated agreements then outstanding, the maturity or accelerated maturities of which are scheduled to fall due within six months after the date such prepayment is to occur pursuant to this provision or on or prior to the date on which the Payment Obligation in respect of such prepayment is scheduled to mature disregarding this provision, whichever date is earlier) without reference to any projected profit or loss of the broker or dealer, either aggregate indebtedness of the broker or dealer would exceed 900 percent of its net capital or its net capital would be less than 200 percent of the minimum dollar amount required by § 240.15c3-1 or, in the case of a broker or dealer operating pursuant to paragraph (a)(1)(ii) of § 240.15c3-1, its net capital would be less than 6 percent of aggregate debit items computed in accordance with § 240.15c3-3a, or, if registered as a futures commission merchant, 10 percent of the funds required to be segregated pursuant to the Commodity Exchange Act and the regulations thereunder (less the market value of commodity options purchased by option customers on or subject to the rules of a contract

§ 240.15c3–1e

market, each such deduction not to exceed the amount of funds in the option customer's account), if greater, or its net capital would be less than 200 percent of the minimum dollar amount required by paragraph (a)(1)(ii) of this section or

(B) Pre-tax losses during the latest three-month period equalled more than 15% of current excess net capital.

Any subordination agreement entered into pursuant to this paragraph (c)(5)(ii) shall be subject to all the other provisions of this Appendix D. Any such subordination agreement shall not be considered equity for purposes of subsection (d) of section 15c3–1, despite the length of the initial term of the loan.

(6)(i) *Filing.* Two copies of any proposed subordination agreement (including nonconforming subordination agreements) shall be filed at least 10 days prior to the proposed execution date of the agreement with the Commission's Regional Office for the region in which the broker or dealer maintains its principal place of business or at such other time as the Regional Office for good cause shall accept such filing. Copies of the proposed agreement shall also be filed with the Examining Authority in such quantities and at such time as the Examining Authority may require. The broker or dealer shall also file with said parties a statement setting forth the name and address of the lender, the business relationship of the lender to the broker or dealer, and whether the broker or dealer carried funds or securities for the lender at or about the time the proposed agreement was so filed. All agreements shall be examined by the Commission's Regional Office or the Examining Authority with whom such agreement is required to be filed prior to their becoming effective. No proposed agreement shall be a satisfactory subordination agreement for the purposes of this section unless and until the Examining Authority has found the agreement acceptable and such agreement has become effective in the form found acceptable.

(ii) The broker or dealer need not file with the Regional Office for the region in which the broker or dealer maintains its principal place of business (if a Regional Office is not its Examining Authority) copies of any proposed subordination agreement or the statement described above if the Examining Authority for that broker or dealer has consented to file with the Commission periodic reports (not less than monthly) summarizing for the period, on a firm-by-firm basis, the subordination agreements it has approved for that period. Such reports should include at the minimum, the amount of the loan and its duration, the name of the lender and the business relationship of the lender to the broker or dealer.

(7) *Subordination agreements in effect prior to adoption.* Any subordination agreement which has been entered into prior to December 20, 1978 and which has been deemed to be satisfactorily subordinated pursuant to 17 CFR 240.15c3–1 as in effect prior to December 20, 1978, shall continue to be deemed a satisfactory subordination agreement until the maturity of such agreement. *Provided,* That no renewal of an agreement which provides for automatic or optional renewal by the broker or dealer or lender shall be deemed to be a satisfactory subordination agreement unless such renewed agreement meets the requirements of this appendix within 6 months from December 20, 1978. *Provided, further,* That all subordination agreements must meet the requirements of this appendix within 5 years of December 20, 1978.

[40 FR 29808, July 16, 1975, as amended at 42 FR 31778, June 23, 1977; 44 FR 34887, June 15, 1979; 46 FR 35635, July 10, 1981; 47 FR 21775, May 20, 1982; 49 FR 31848, Aug. 9, 1984; 57 FR 56988, Dec. 2, 1992; 58 FR 37657, July 13, 1993; 59 FR 5945, Feb. 9, 1994; 73 FR 32228, June 5, 2008; 84 FR 44045, Aug. 22, 2019]

§ 240.15c3–1e Deductions for market and credit risk for certain brokers or dealers (Appendix E to 17 CFR 240.15c3–1).

Sections 240.15c3–1e and 240.15c3–1g set forth a program that allows a broker or dealer to use an alternative approach to computing net capital deductions, subject to the conditions described in §§ 240.15c3–1e and 240.15c3–1g, including supervision of the broker's or dealer's ultimate holding company under the program. The program is designed to reduce the likelihood that financial and operational weakness in

Securities and Exchange Commission § 240.15c3-1e

the holding company will destabilize the broker or dealer, or the broader financial system. The focus of this supervision of the ultimate holding company is its financial and operational condition and its risk management controls and methodologies.

Application

(a) A broker or dealer may apply to the Commission for authorization to compute deductions for market risk pursuant to this section in lieu of computing deductions pursuant to §§ 240.15c3-1(c)(2)(vi) and (vii) and 240.15c3-1b, and to compute deductions for credit risk pursuant to this section on credit exposures arising from transactions in derivatives instruments (if this section is used to calculate deductions for market risk on these instruments) in lieu of computing deductions pursuant to § 240.15c3-1(c)(2)(iv) and (c)(2)(xv)(A) and (B):

(1) A broker-dealer shall submit the following information to the Commission with its application:

(i) An executive summary of the information provided to the Commission with its application and an identification of the ultimate holding company of the broker or dealer;

(ii) A comprehensive description of the internal risk management control system of the broker or dealer and how that system satisfies the requirements set forth in § 240.15c3-4;

(iii) A list of the categories of positions that the broker or dealer holds in its proprietary accounts and a brief description of the methods that the broker or dealer will use to calculate deductions for market and credit risk on those categories of positions;

(iv) A description of the mathematical models to be used to price positions and to compute deductions for market risk, including those portions of the deductions attributable to specific risk, if applicable, and deductions for credit risk; a description of the creation, use, and maintenance of the mathematical models; a description of the broker's or dealer's internal risk management controls over those models, including a description of each category of persons who may input data into the models; if a mathematical model incorporates empirical correlations across risk categories, a description of the process for measuring correlations; a description of the backtesting procedures the broker or dealer will use to backtest the mathematical model used to calculate maximum potential exposure; a description of how each mathematical model satisfies the applicable qualitative and quantitative requirements set forth in paragraph (d) of this appendix E; and a statement describing the extent to which each mathematical model used to compute deductions for market and credit risk will be used as part of the risk analyses and reports presented to senior management;

(v) If the broker or dealer is applying to the Commission for approval to use scenario analysis to calculate deductions for market risk for certain positions, a list of those types of positions, a description of how those deductions will be calculated using scenario analysis, and an explanation of why each scenario analysis is appropriate to calculate deductions for market risk on those types of positions;

(vi) A description of how the broker or dealer will calculate current exposure;

(vii) A description of how the broker or dealer will determine internal credit ratings of counterparties and internal credit risk weights of counterparties, if applicable;

(viii) A written undertaking by the ultimate holding company of the broker or dealer, if it is not an ultimate holding company that has a principal regulator, in a form acceptable to the Commission, signed by a duly authorized person at the ultimate holding company, to the effect that, as a condition of Commission approval of the application of the broker or dealer to compute deductions for market and credit risk pursuant to this appendix E, the ultimate holding company agrees to:

(A) Comply with all applicable provisions of this appendix E;

(B) Comply with all applicable provisions of § 240.15c3-1g;

(C) Comply with the provisions of § 240.15c3-4 with respect to an internal risk management control system for the affiliate group as though it were an OTC derivatives dealer with respect to

§ 240.15c3-1e

all of its business activities, except that paragraphs (c)(5)(xiii), (c)(5)(xiv), (d)(8), and (d)(9) of § 240.15c3-4 shall not apply;

(D) As part of the internal risk management control system for the affiliate group, establish, document, and maintain procedures for the detection and prevention of money laundering and terrorist financing;

(E) Permit the Commission to examine the books and records of the ultimate holding company and any of its affiliates, if the affiliate is not an entity that has a principal regulator;

(F) If the disclosure to the Commission of any information required as a condition for the broker or dealer to compute deductions for market and credit risk pursuant to this appendix E could be prohibited by law or otherwise, cooperate with the Commission, to the extent permissible, including by describing any secrecy laws or other impediments that could restrict the ability of material affiliates to provide information on their operations or activities and by discussing the manner in which the ultimate holding company and the broker or dealer propose to provide the Commission with adequate information or assurances of access to information;

(G) Make available to the Commission information about the ultimate holding company or any of its material affiliates that the Commission finds is necessary to evaluate the financial and operational risk within the ultimate holding company and its material affiliates and to evaluate compliance with the conditions of eligibility of the broker or dealer to compute deductions to net capital under the alternative method of this appendix E;

(H) Make available examination reports of principal regulators for those affiliates of the ultimate holding company that are not subject to Commission examination; and

(I) Acknowledge that, if the ultimate holding company fails to comply in a material manner with any provision of its undertaking, the Commission may, in addition to any other conditions necessary or appropriate in the public interest or for the protection of investors, increase the multiplication factors the ultimate holding company

uses to calculate allowances for market and credit risk, as defined in § 240.15c3-1g(a)(2) and (a)(3) or impose any condition with respect to the broker or dealer listed in paragraph (e) of this appendix E; and

(ix) A written undertaking by the ultimate holding company of the broker or dealer, if the ultimate holding company has a principal regulator, in a form acceptable to the Commission, signed by a duly authorized person at the ultimate holding company, to the effect that, as a condition of Commission approval of the application of the broker or dealer to compute deductions for market and credit risk pursuant to this appendix E, the ultimate holding company agrees to:

(A) Comply with all applicable provisions of this appendix E;

(B) Comply with all applicable provisions of § 240.15c3-1g;

(C) Make available to the Commission information about the ultimate holding company that the Commission finds is necessary to evaluate the financial and operational risk within the ultimate holding company and to evaluate compliance with the conditions of eligibility of the broker or dealer to compute net capital under the alternative method of this appendix E; and

(D) Acknowledge that if the ultimate holding company fails to comply in a material manner with any provision of its undertaking, the Commission may, in addition to any other conditions necessary or appropriate in the public interest or for the protection of investors, impose any condition with respect to the broker or dealer listed in paragraph (e) of this appendix E;

(2) As a condition of Commission approval, the ultimate holding company of the broker or dealer, if it is not an ultimate holding company that has a principal regulator, shall include the following information with the application:

(i) A narrative description of the business and organization of the ultimate holding company;

(ii) An alphabetical list of the affiliates of the ultimate holding company (referred to as the "affiliate group," which shall include the ultimate holding company), with an identification of

Securities and Exchange Commission

§ 240.15c3-1e

the financial regulator, if any, that regulates the affiliate, and a designation of the members of the affiliate group that are material to the ultimate holding company ("material affiliates");

(iii) An organizational chart that identifies the ultimate holding company, the broker or dealer, and the material affiliates;

(iv) Consolidated and consolidating financial statements of the ultimate holding company as of the end of the quarter preceding the filing of the application;

(v) Sample computations for the ultimate holding company of allowable capital and allowances for market risk, credit risk, and operational risk, determined pursuant to § 240.15c3-1g(a)(1)-(a)(4);

(vi) A list of the categories of positions that the affiliate group holds in its proprietary accounts and a brief description of the method that the ultimate holding company proposes to use to calculate allowances for market and credit risk, pursuant to § 240.15c3-1g(a)(2) and (a)(3), on those categories of positions;

(vii) A description of the mathematical models to be used to price positions and to compute the allowance for market risk, including those portions of the allowance attributable to specific risk, if applicable, and the allowance for credit risk; a description of the creation, use, and maintenance of the mathematical models; a description of the ultimate holding company's internal risk management controls over those models, including a description of each category of persons who may input data into the models; if a mathematical model incorporates empirical correlations across risk categories, a description of the process for measuring correlations; a description of the backtesting procedures the ultimate holding company will use to backtest the mathematical model used to calculate maximum potential exposure; a description of how each mathematical model satisfies the applicable qualitative and quantitative requirements set forth in paragraph (d) of this appendix E; a statement describing the extent to which each mathematical model used to compute allowances for market and credit risk is used as part of the risk analyses and reports presented to senior management; and a description of any positions for which the ultimate holding company proposes to use a method other than VaR to compute an allowance for market risk and a description of how that allowance would be determined;

(viii) A description of how the ultimate holding company will calculate current exposure;

(ix) A description of how the ultimate holding company will determine the credit risk weights of counterparties and internal credit ratings of counterparties, if applicable;

(x) A description of how the ultimate holding company will calculate an allowance for operational risk under § 240.15c3-1g(a)(4);

(xi) For each instance in which a mathematical model used by the broker or dealer to calculate a deduction for market risk or to calculate maximum potential exposure for a particular product or counterparty differs from the mathematical model used by the ultimate holding company to calculate an allowance for market risk or to calculate maximum potential exposure for that same product or counterparty, a description of the difference(s) between the mathematical models;

(xii) A comprehensive description of the risk management control system for the affiliate group that the ultimate holding company has established to manage affiliate group-wide risk, including market, credit, liquidity and funding, legal and compliance, and operational risks, and how that system satisfies the requirements of § 240.15c3-4; and

(xiii) Sample risk reports that are provided to the persons at the ultimate holding company who are responsible for managing group-wide risk and that will be provided to the Commission pursuant to § 240.15c3-1g(b)(1)(i)(H);

(3) As a condition of Commission approval, the ultimate holding company of the broker or dealer, if the ultimate holding company has a principal regulator, shall include the following information with the broker's or dealer's application:

§ 240.15c3-1e

(i) A narrative description of the business and organization of the ultimate holding company;

(ii) An alphabetical list of the affiliates of the ultimate holding company (referred to as the "affiliate group," which shall include the ultimate holding company), with an identification of the financial regulator, if any, that regulates the affiliate, and a designation of those affiliates that are material to the ultimate holding company ("material affiliates");

(iii) An organizational chart that identifies the ultimate holding company, the broker or dealer, and the material affiliates;

(iv) Consolidated and consolidating financial statements of the ultimate holding company as of the end of the quarter preceding the filing of the application;

(v) The most recent capital measurements of the ultimate holding company, as reported to its principal regulator, calculated in accordance with the standards published by the Basel Committee on Banking Supervision, as amended from time to time;

(vi) For each instance in which a mathematical model to be used by the broker or dealer to calculate a deduction for market risk or to calculate maximum potential exposure for a particular product or counterparty differs from the mathematical model used by the ultimate holding company to calculate an allowance for market risk or to calculate maximum potential exposure for that same product or counterparty, a description of the difference(s) between the mathematical models; and

(vii) Sample risk reports that are provided to the persons at the ultimate holding company who are responsible for managing group-wide risk and that will be provided to the Commission under § 240.15c3-1g(b)(1)(i)(H);

(4) The application of the broker or dealer shall be supplemented by other information relating to the internal risk management control system, mathematical models, and financial position of the broker or dealer or the ultimate holding company of the broker or dealer that the Commission may request to complete its review of the application;

(5) The application shall be considered filed when received at the Commission's principal office in Washington, DC. A person who files an application pursuant to this section for which it seeks confidential treatment may clearly mark each page or segregable portion of each page with the words "Confidential Treatment Requested." All information submitted in connection with the application will be accorded confidential treatment, to the extent permitted by law;

(6) If any of the information filed with the Commission as part of the application of the broker or dealer is found to be or becomes inaccurate before the Commission approves the application, the broker or dealer must notify the Commission promptly and provide the Commission with a description of the circumstances in which the information was found to be or has become inaccurate along with updated, accurate information;

(7)(i) The Commission may approve the application or an amendment to the application, in whole or in part, subject to any conditions or limitations the Commission may require, if the Commission finds the approval to be necessary or appropriate in the public interest or for the protection of investors, after determining, among other things, whether the broker or dealer has met the requirements of this appendix E and is in compliance with other applicable rules promulgated under the Act and by self-regulatory organizations, and whether the ultimate holding company of the broker or dealer is in compliance with the terms of its undertakings, as provided to the Commission;

(ii) The Commission may approve the temporary use of a provisional model in whole or in part, subject to any conditions or limitations the Commission may require, if:

(A) The broker or dealer has a complete application pending under this section;

(B) The use of the provisional model has been approved by:

(1) A prudential regulator;

(2) The Commodity Futures Trading Commission or a futures association

Securities and Exchange Commission § 240.15c3–1e

registered with the Commodity Futures Trading Commission under section 17 of the Commodity Exchange Act;

(3) A foreign financial regulatory authority that administers a foreign financial regulatory system with capital requirements that the Commission has found are eligible for substituted compliance under § 240.3a71–6 if the provisional model is used for the purposes of calculating net capital;

(4) A foreign financial regulatory authority that administers a foreign financial regulatory system with margin requirements that the Commission has found are eligible for substituted compliance under § 240.3a71–6 if the provisional model is used for the purposes of calculating initial margin pursuant to § 240.18a–3; or

(5) Any other foreign supervisory authority that the Commission finds has approved and monitored the use of the provisional model through a process comparable to the process set forth in this section.

(8) A broker or dealer shall amend its application to calculate certain deductions for market and credit risk under this appendix E and submit the amendment to the Commission for approval before it may change materially a mathematical model used to calculate market or credit risk or before it may change materially its internal risk management control system;

(9) As a condition to the broker's or dealer's calculation of deductions for market and credit risk under this appendix E, an ultimate holding company that does not have a principal regulator shall submit to the Commission, as an amendment to the broker's or dealer's application, any material changes to a mathematical model or other methods used to calculate allowances for market, credit, and operational risk, and any material changes to the internal risk management control system for the affiliate group. The ultimate holding company must submit these material changes to the Commission before making them;

(10) As a condition for the broker or dealer to compute deductions for market and credit risk under this appendix E, the broker or dealer agrees that:

(i) It will notify the Commission 45 days before it ceases to compute deductions for market and credit risk under this appendix E; and

(ii) The Commission may determine by order that the notice will become effective after a shorter or longer period of time if the broker or dealer consents or if the Commission determines that a shorter or longer period of time is necessary or appropriate in the public interest or for the protection of investors; and

(11) Notwithstanding paragraph (a)(10) of this section, the Commission, by order, may revoke a broker's or dealer's exemption that allows it to use the market risk standards of this appendix E to calculate deductions for market risk, instead of the provisions of § 240.15c3–1(c)(2)(vi) and (c)(2)(vii), and the exemption to use the credit risk standards of this appendix E to calculate deductions for credit risk on certain credit exposures arising from transactions in derivatives instruments, instead of the provisions of § 240.15c3–1(c)(2)(iv), if the Commission finds that such exemption is no longer necessary or appropriate in the public interest or for the protection of investors. In making its finding, the Commission will consider the compliance history of the broker or dealer related to its use of models, the financial and operational strength of the broker or dealer and its ultimate holding company, the broker's or dealer's compliance with its internal risk management controls, and the ultimate holding company's compliance with its undertakings.

Market Risk

(b) A broker or dealer whose application, including amendments, has been approved under paragraph (a) of this appendix E shall compute a deduction for market risk in an amount equal to the sum of the following:

(1) For positions for which the Commission has approved the broker's or dealer's use of value-at risk ("VaR") models, the VaR of the positions multiplied by the appropriate multiplication

457

§ 240.15c3-1e

factor determined according to paragraph (d)(1)(iii) of this appendix E, except that the initial multiplication factor shall be three, unless the Commission determines, based on a review of the broker's or dealer's application or an amendment to the application under paragraph (a) of this appendix E, including a review of its internal risk management control system and practices and VaR models, that another multiplication factor is appropriate;

(2) For positions for which the VaR model does not incorporate specific risk, a deduction for specific risk to be determined by the Commission based on a review of the broker's or dealer's application or an amendment to the application under paragraph (a) of this appendix E and the positions involved;

(3) For positions for which the Commission has approved the broker's or dealer's application to use scenario analysis, the greatest loss resulting from a range of adverse movements in relevant risk factors, prices, or spreads designed to represent a negative movement greater than, or equal to, the worst ten-day movement over the four years preceding calculation of the greatest loss, or some multiple of the greatest loss based on the liquidity of the positions subject to scenario analysis. If historical data is insufficient, the deduction shall be the largest loss within a three standard deviation movement in those risk factors, prices, or spreads over a ten-day period, multiplied by an appropriate liquidity adjustment factor. Irrespective of the deduction otherwise indicated under scenario analysis, the resulting deduction for market risk must be at least $25 per 100 share equivalent contract for equity positions, or one-half of one percent of the face value of the contract for all other types of contracts, even if the scenario analysis indicates a lower amount. A qualifying scenario must include the following:

(i) A set of pricing equations for the positions based on, for example, arbitrage relations, statistical analysis, historic relationships, merger evaluation, or fundamental valuation of an offering of securities;

(ii) Auxiliary relationships mapping risk factors to prices; and

(iii) Data demonstrating the effectiveness of the scenario in capturing market risk, including specific risk; and

(4) For all remaining positions, the deductions specified in §§ 240.15c3-1(c)(2)(vi), (c)(2)(vii), and applicable appendices to § 240.15c3-1.

Credit Risk

(c) A broker or dealer whose application, including amendments, has been approved under paragraph (a) of this appendix E shall compute a deduction for credit risk on transactions in derivative instruments (if this appendix E is used to calculate a deduction for market risk on those instruments) in an amount equal to the sum of the following:

(1) A counterparty exposure charge in an amount equal to the sum of the following:

(i) The net replacement value in the account of each counterparty that is insolvent, or in bankruptcy, or that has senior unsecured long-term debt in default; and

(ii) For a counterparty not otherwise described in paragraph (c)(1)(i) of this appendix E, the credit equivalent amount of the broker's or dealer's exposure to the counterparty, as defined in paragraph (c)(4)(i) of this appendix E, multiplied by the credit risk weight of the counterparty, as defined in paragraph (c)(4)(vi) of this appendix E, multiplied by 8%;

(2) A concentration charge by counterparty in an amount equal to the sum of the following:

(i) For each counterparty with a credit risk weight of 20% or less, 5% of the amount of the current exposure to the counterparty in excess of 5% of the tentative net capital of the broker or dealer;

(ii) For each counterparty with a credit risk weight of greater than 20% but less than 50%, 20% of the amount of the current exposure to the counterparty in excess of 5% of the tentative net capital of the broker or dealer; and

(iii) For each counterparty with a credit risk weight of greater than 50%, 50% of the amount of the current exposure to the counterparty in excess of

Securities and Exchange Commission

§ 240.15c3-1e

5% of the tentative net capital of the broker or dealer; and

(3) A portfolio concentration charge of 100 percent of the amount of the broker's or dealer's aggregate current exposure for all counterparties in excess of 10 percent of the tentative net capital of the broker or dealer;

(4) *Terms.* (i) The *credit equivalent amount* of the broker's or dealer's exposure to a counterparty is the sum of the broker's or dealer's maximum potential exposure to the counterparty, as defined in paragraph (c)(4)(ii) of this appendix E, multiplied by the appropriate multiplication factor, and the broker's or dealer's current exposure to the counterparty, as defined in paragraph (c)(4)(iii) of this appendix E. The broker or dealer must use the multiplication factor determined according to paragraph (d)(1)(v) of this appendix E, except that the initial multiplication factor shall be one, unless the Commission determines, based on a review of the broker's or dealer's application or an amendment to the application approved under paragraph (a) of this appendix E, including a review of its internal risk management control system and practices and VaR models, that another multiplication factor is appropriate;

(ii) The *maximum potential exposure* is the VaR of the counterparty's positions with the broker or dealer, after applying netting agreements with the counterparty meeting the requirements of paragraph (c)(4)(iv) of this appendix E, taking into account the value of collateral from the counterparty held by the broker or dealer in accordance with paragraph (c)(4)(v) of this appendix E, and taking into account the current replacement value of the counterparty's positions with the broker or dealer;

(iii) The *current exposure* of the broker or dealer to a counterparty is the current replacement value of the counterparty's positions with the broker or dealer, after applying netting agreements with the counterparty meeting the requirements of paragraph (c)(4)(iv) of this appendix E and taking into account the value of collateral from the counterparty held by the broker or dealer in accordance with paragraph (c)(4)(v) of this appendix E;

(iv) *Netting agreements.* A broker or dealer may include the effect of a netting agreement that allows the broker or dealer to net gross receivables from and gross payables to a counterparty upon default of the counterparty if:

(A) The netting agreement is legally enforceable in each relevant jurisdiction, including in insolvency proceedings;

(B) The gross receivables and gross payables that are subject to the netting agreement with a counterparty can be determined at any time; and

(C) For internal risk management purposes, the broker-dealer monitors and controls its exposure to the counterparty on a net basis;

(v) *Collateral.* When calculating maximum potential exposure and current exposure to a counterparty, the fair market value of collateral pledged and held may be taken into account provided:

(A) The collateral is marked to market each day and is subject to a daily margin maintenance requirement;

(B) The collateral is subject to the broker's or dealer's physical possession or control;

(*1*) The collateral is subject to the broker's or dealer's physical possession or control and may be liquidated promptly by the firm without intervention by any other party; or

(*2*) The collateral is held by an independent third-party custodian that is a bank as defined in section 3(a)(6) of the Act or a registered U.S. clearing organization or depository that is not affiliated with the counterparty or, if the collateral consists of foreign securities or currencies, a supervised foreign bank, clearing organization, or depository that is not affiliated with the counterparty and that customarily maintains custody of such foreign securities or currencies;

(C) The collateral is liquid and transferable;

(D) The collateral agreement is legally enforceable by the broker or dealer against the counterparty and any other parties to the agreement;

(E) The collateral does not consist of securities issued by the counterparty or a party related to the broker or dealer or to the counterparty;

§ 240.15c3-1e

(F) The Commission has approved the broker's or dealer's use of a VaR model to calculate deductions for market risk for the type of collateral in accordance with this appendix E; and

(G) The collateral is not used in determining the credit rating of the counterparty;

(vi) *Credit risk weights of counterparties.* A broker or dealer that computes its deductions for credit risk pursuant to this Appendix E shall apply a credit risk weight for transactions with a counterparty of either 20%, 50%, or 150% based on an internal credit rating the broker or dealer determines for the counterparty.

(A) As part of its initial application or in an amendment, the broker or dealer may request Commission approval to apply a credit risk weight of either 20%, 50%, or 150% based on internal calculations of credit ratings, including internal estimates of the maturity adjustment. Based on the strength of the broker's or dealer's internal credit risk management system, the Commission may approve the application. The broker or dealer must make and keep current a record of the basis for the credit rating of each counterparty;

(B) For the portion of a current exposure covered by a written guarantee where that guarantee is an unconditional and irrevocable guarantee of the due and punctual payment and performance of the obligation and the broker or dealer can demand immediate payment from the guarantor after any payment is missed without having to make collection efforts, the broker or dealer may substitute the credit risk weight of the guarantor for the credit risk weight of the counterparty; and

(C) As part of its initial application or in an amendment, the broker or dealer may request Commission approval to reduce deductions for credit risk through the use of credit derivatives.

VaR Models

(d) To be approved, each VaR model must meet the following minimum qualitative and quantitative requirements:

(1) *Qualitative requirements.* (i) The VaR model used to calculate market or credit risk for a position must be integrated into the daily internal risk management system of the broker or dealer;

(ii) The VaR model must be reviewed both periodically and annually. The periodic review may be conducted by the broker's or dealer's internal audit staff, but the annual review must be conducted by a registered public accounting firm, as that term is defined in section 2(a)(12) of the Sarbanes-Oxley Act of 2002 (15 U.S.C. 7201 *et seq.*); and

(iii) For purposes of computing market risk, the broker or dealer must determine the appropriate multiplication factor as follows:

(A) Beginning three months after the broker or dealer begins using the VaR model to calculate market risk, the broker or dealer must conduct backtesting of the model by comparing its actual daily net trading profit or loss with the corresponding VaR measure generated by the VaR model, using a 99 percent, one-tailed confidence level with price changes equivalent to a one business-day movement in rates and prices, for each of the past 250 business days, or other period as may be appropriate for the first year of its use;

(B) On the last business day of each quarter, the broker or dealer must identify the number of backtesting exceptions of the VaR model, that is, the number of business days in the past 250 business days, or other period as may be appropriate for the first year of its use, for which the actual net trading loss, if any, exceeds the corresponding VaR measure; and

(C) The broker or dealer must use the multiplication factor indicated in Table 1 of this appendix E in determining its market risk until it obtains the next quarter's backtesting results;

TABLE 1—MULTIPLICATION FACTOR BASED ON THE NUMBER OF BACKTESTING EXCEPTIONS OF THE VaR MODEL

Number of exceptions	Multiplication factor
4 or fewer	3.00
5	3.40
6	3.50
7	3.65
8	3.75

Securities and Exchange Commission § 240.15c3-1e

TABLE 1—MULTIPLICATION FACTOR BASED ON THE NUMBER OF BACKTESTING EXCEPTIONS OF THE VaR MODEL—Continued

Number of exceptions	Multiplication factor
9	3.85
10 or more	4.00

(iv) For purposes of incorporating specific risk into a VaR model, a broker or dealer must demonstrate that it has methodologies in place to capture liquidity, event, and default risk adequately for each position. Furthermore, the models used to calculate deductions for specific risk must:

(A) Explain the historical price variation in the portfolio;

(B) Capture concentration (magnitude and changes in composition);

(C) Be robust to an adverse environment; and

(D) Be validated through backtesting; and

(v) For purposes of computing the credit equivalent amount of the broker's or dealer's exposures to a counterparty, the broker or dealer must determine the appropriate multiplication factor as follows:

(A) Beginning three months after it begins using the VaR model to calculate maximum potential exposure, the broker or dealer must conduct backtesting of the model by comparing, for at least 80 counterparties with widely varying types and sizes of positions with the firm, the ten-business day change in its current exposure to the counterparty based on its positions held at the beginning of the ten-business day period with the corresponding ten-business day maximum potential exposure for the counterparty generated by the VaR model;

(B) As of the last business day of each quarter, the broker or dealer must identify the number of backtesting exceptions of the VaR model, that is, the number of ten-business day periods in the past 250 business days, or other period as may be appropriate for the first year of its use, for which the change in current exposure to a counterparty exceeds the corresponding maximum potential exposure; and

(C) The broker or dealer will propose, as part of its application, a schedule of multiplication factors, which must be approved by the Commission based on the number of backtesting exceptions of the VaR model. The broker or dealer must use the multiplication factor indicated in the approved schedule in determining the credit equivalent amount of its exposures to a counterparty until it obtains the next quarter's backtesting results, unless the Commission determines, based on, among other relevant factors, a review of the broker's or dealer's internal risk management control system, including a review of the VaR model, that a different adjustment or other action is appropriate;

(2) *Quantitative requirements.* (i) For purposes of determining market risk, the VaR model must use a 99 percent, one-tailed confidence level with price changes equivalent to a ten business-day movement in rates and prices;

(ii) For purposes of determining maximum potential exposure, the VaR model must use a 99 percent, one-tailed confidence level with price changes equivalent to a one-year movement in rates and prices; or based on a review of the broker's or dealer's procedures for managing collateral and if the collateral is marked to market daily and the broker or dealer has the ability to call for additional collateral daily, the Commission may approve a time horizon of not less than ten business days;

(iii) The VaR model must use an effective historical observation period of at least one year. The broker or dealer must consider the effects of market stress in its construction of the model. Historical data sets must be updated at least monthly and reassessed whenever market prices or volatilities change significantly; and

(iv) The VaR model must take into account and incorporate all significant, identifiable market risk factors applicable to positions in the accounts of the broker or dealer, including:

(A) Risks arising from the non-linear price characteristics of derivatives and the sensitivity of the market value of those positions to changes in the volatility of the derivatives' underlying rates and prices;

(B) Empirical correlations with and across risk factors or, alternatively, risk factors sufficient to cover all the

§ 240.15c3-1f

market risk inherent in the positions in the proprietary or other trading accounts of the broker or dealer, including interest rate risk, equity price risk, foreign exchange risk, and commodity price risk;

(C) Spread risk, where applicable, and segments of the yield curve sufficient to capture differences in volatility and imperfect correlation of rates along the yield curve for securities and derivatives that are sensitive to different interest rates; and

(D) Specific risk for individual positions.

Additional Conditions

(e) As a condition for the broker or dealer to use this appendix E to calculate certain of its capital charges, the Commission may impose additional conditions on the broker or dealer, which may include, but are not limited to restricting the broker's or dealer's business on a product-specific, category-specific, or general basis; submitting to the Commission a plan to increase the broker's or dealer's net capital or tentative net capital; filing more frequent reports with the Commission; modifying the broker's or dealer's internal risk management control procedures; or computing the broker's or dealer's deductions for market and credit risk in accordance with § 240.15c3–1(c)(2)(iv), (vi), and (vii), (c)(2)(xv)(A) and (B), as appropriate, and § 240.15c–1b, as appropriate. If it is not an ultimate holding company that has a principal regulator, the Commission also may require, as a condition of continuation of the exemption, the ultimate holding company of the broker or dealer to file more frequent reports or to modify its group-wide internal risk management control procedures. If the Commission finds it is necessary or appropriate in the public interest or for the protection of investors, the Commission may impose additional conditions on either the broker-dealer, or the ultimate holding company, if it is an ultimate holding company that does not have a principal regulator, if:

(1) The broker or dealer is required by § 240.15c3–1(a)(7)(ii) to provide notice to the Commission that the broker's or dealer's tentative net capital is less than $6 billion;

(2) The broker or dealer or the ultimate holding company of the broker or dealer fails to meet the reporting requirements set forth in § 240.17a–5 or 240.15c3–1g(b), as applicable;

(3) Any event specified in § 240.17a–11 occurs;

(4) There is a material deficiency in the internal risk management control system or in the mathematical models used to price securities or to calculate deductions for market and credit risk or allowances for market and credit risk, as applicable, of the broker or dealer or the ultimate holding company of the broker or dealer;

(5) The ultimate holding company of the broker or dealer fails to comply with its undertakings that the broker or dealer has filed with its application pursuant to paragraph (a)(1)(viii) or (a)(1)(ix) of this appendix E;

(6) The broker or dealer fails to comply with this appendix E; or

(7) The Commission finds that imposition of other conditions is necessary or appropriate in the public interest or for the protection of investors.

[69 FR 34462, June 21, 2004, as amended at 79 FR 1549, Jan. 8, 2014; 79 FR 38451, July 8, 2014; 84 FR 44046, Aug. 22, 2019]

§ 240.15c3–1f Optional market and credit risk requirements for OTC derivatives dealers (Appendix F to 17 CFR 240.15c3–1).

Application Requirements

(a) An OTC derivatives dealer may apply to the Commission for authorization to compute capital charges for market and credit risk pursuant to this Appendix F in lieu of computing securities haircuts pursuant to § 240.15c3–1(c)(2)(vi).

(1) An OTC derivatives dealer's application shall contain the following information:

(i) *Executive summary.* An OTC derivatives dealer shall include in its application an Executive Summary of information provided to the Commission.

(ii) *Description of methods for computing market risk charges.* An OTC derivatives dealer shall provide a description of all statistical models used for pricing OTC derivative instruments and for computing value-at-risk

Securities and Exchange Commission

§ 240.15c3-1f

("VAR"), a description of the applicant's controls over those models, and a statement regarding whether the firm has developed its own internal VAR models. If the OTC derivatives dealer's VAR model incorporates empirical correlations across risk categories, the dealer shall describe its process for measuring correlations and describe the qualitative and quantitative aspects of the model which at a minimum must adhere to the criteria set forth in paragraph (e) of this appendix F. The application shall further state whether the OTC derivatives dealer intends to use an alternative method for computing its market risk charge for equity instruments and, if applicable, a description of how its own theoretical pricing model contains the minimum pricing factors set forth in appendix A (§ 240.15c3-1a). The application shall also describe any category of securities having no ready market or any category of debt securities which are below investment grade for which the OTC derivatives dealer wishes to use its VAR model to calculate its market risk charge or for which it wishes to use an alternative method for computing this charge and a description of how those charges would be determined.

(iii) *Internal risk management control systems.* An OTC derivatives dealer shall provide a comprehensive description of its internal risk management control systems and how those systems adhere to the requirements set forth in § 240.15c3-4(a) through (d).

(2) The Commission may approve the application after reviewing the application to determine whether the OTC derivatives dealer:

(i) Has adopted internal risk management control systems that meet the requirements set forth in § 240.15c3-4; and

(ii) Has adopted a VAR model that meets the requirements set forth in paragraphs (e)(1) and (e)(2) of this appendix F.

(3) If the OTC derivatives dealer materially amends its VAR model or internal risk management control systems as described in its application, including any material change in the categories of non-marketable securities that it wishes to include in its VAR model, the dealer shall file an application describing the changes which must be approved by the Commission before the changes may be implemented. After reviewing the application for changes to the dealer's VAR model or internal risk management control systems to determine whether, with the changes, the OTC derivatives dealer's VAR model and internal risk management control systems would meet the requirements set forth in this appendix F and § 240.15c3-4, the Commission may approve the application.

(4) The applications provided for in this paragraph (a) shall be considered filed when received at the Commission's principal office in Washington, DC. All applications filed pursuant to this paragraph (a) shall be deemed to be confidential.

Compliance With § 240.15c3-4

(b) An OTC derivatives dealer must be in compliance in all material respects with § 240.15c3-4 regarding its internal risk management control systems in order to be in compliance with § 240.15c3-1.

Market Risk

(c) An OTC derivatives dealer electing to apply this appendix F shall compute a capital charge for market risk which shall be the aggregate of the charges computed below:

(1) *Value-at-Risk.* An OTC derivatives dealer shall deduct from net worth an amount for market risk for eligible OTC derivative instruments and other positions in its proprietary or other accounts equal to the VAR of these positions obtained from its proprietary VAR model, multiplied by the appropriate multiplication factor in paragraph (e)(1)(iv)(C) of this appendix F. The OTC derivatives dealer may not elect to calculate its capital charges under this paragraph (c)(1) until its application to use the VAR model has been approved by the Commission.

(2) *Alternative method for equities.* An OTC derivatives dealer may elect to use this alternative method to calculate its market risk for equity instruments, including OTC options, upon approval by the Commission on application by the dealer. Under this alternative method, the deduction for

§ 240.15c3-1f

market risk must be the amount computed pursuant to appendix A to Rule 15c3-1 (§ 240.15c3-1a). In this computation, the OTC derivatives dealer may use its own theoretical pricing model provided that it contains the minimum pricing factors set forth in appendix A.

(3) *Non-marketable securities.* An OTC derivatives dealer may not use a VAR model to determine a capital charge for any category of securities having no ready market or any category of debt securities which are below investment grade or any derivative instrument based on the value of these categories of securities, unless the Commission has granted, pursuant to paragraph (a)(1) of this appendix F, its application to use its VAR model for any such category of securities. The dealer in any event may apply, pursuant to paragraph (a)(1) of this appendix F, for an alternative treatment for any such category of securities, rather than calculate the market risk capital charge for such category of securities under § 240.15c3-1(c)(2)(vi) and (vii).

(4) *Residual positions.* To the extent that a position has not been included in the calculation of the market risk charge in paragraphs (c)(1) through (c)(3) of this section, the market risk charge for the position shall be computed under § 240.15c3-1(c)(2)(vi).

Credit Risk

(d) The capital charge for credit risk arising from an OTC derivatives dealer's transactions in eligible OTC derivative instruments shall be:

(1) The net replacement value in the account of a counterparty (including the effect of legally enforceable netting agreements and the application of liquid collateral) that is insolvent, or in bankruptcy, or that has senior unsecured long-term debt in default;

(2) As to a counterparty not otherwise described in paragraph (d)(1) of this section, the net replacement value in the account of the counterparty (including the effect of legally enforceable netting agreements and the application of liquid collateral) multiplied by 8%, and further multiplied by a counterparty factor of 20%, 50%, or 100% based on an internal credit rating the OTC derivatives dealer determines for the counterparty; and

(3) A concentration charge where the net replacement value in the account of any one counterparty (other than a counterparty described in paragraph (d)(1) of this section) exceeds 25% of the OTC derivatives dealer's tentative net capital, calculated as follows:

(i) For counterparties for which an OTC derivatives dealer assigns an internal rating for senior unsecured long-term debt or commercial paper that would apply a 20% counterparty factor under paragraph (d)(2) of this section, 5% of the amount of the net replacement value in excess of 25% of the OTC derivatives dealer's tentative net capital;

(ii) For counterparties for which an OTC derivatives dealer assigns an internal rating for senior unsecured long-term debt that would apply a 50% counterparty factor under paragraph (d)(2) of this section, 20% of the amount of the net replacement value in excess of 25% of the OTC derivatives dealer's tentative net capital;

(iii) For counterparties for which an OTC derivatives dealer assigns an internal rating for senior unsecured long-term debt that would apply a 100% counterparty factor under paragraph (d)(2) of this section, 50% of the amount of the net replacement value in excess of 25% of the OTC derivatives dealer's tentative net capital.

(4) Counterparties may be rated by the OTC derivatives dealer, or by an affiliated bank or affiliated broker-dealer of the OTC derivatives dealer, upon approval by the Commission on application by the OTC derivatives dealer. Based on the strength of the OTC derivatives dealer's internal credit risk management system, the Commission may approve the application. The OTC derivatives dealer must make and keep current a record of the basis for the credit rating for each counterparty.

VAR Models

(e) An OTC derivatives dealer's VAR model must meet the following qualitative and quantitative requirements:

(1) *Qualitative requirements.* An OTC derivatives dealer applying this appendix F must have a VAR model that

Securities and Exchange Commission

§ 240.15c3–1f

meets the following minimum qualitative requirements:

(i) The OTC derivatives dealer's VAR model must be integrated into the firm's daily risk management process;

(ii) The OTC derivatives dealer must conduct appropriate stress tests of the VAR model, and develop appropriate procedures to follow in response to the results of such tests;

(iii) The OTC derivatives dealer must conduct periodic reviews (which may be performed by internal audit staff) of its VAR model. The OTC derivatives dealer's VAR model also must be subject to annual reviews conducted by independent public accountants; and

(iv) The OTC derivatives dealer must conduct backtesting of the VAR model pursuant to the following procedures:

(A) Beginning one year after the OTC derivatives dealer begins using its VAR model to calculate its net capital, the OTC derivatives dealer must conduct backtesting by comparing each of its most recent 250 business days' actual net trading profit or loss with the corresponding daily VAR measures generated for determining market risk capital charges and calibrated to a one-day holding period and a 99 percent, one-tailed confidence level;

(B) Once each quarter, the OTC derivatives dealer must identify the number of exceptions, that is, the number of business days for which the actual daily net trading loss, if any, exceeded the corresponding daily VAR measure; and

(C) An OTC derivatives dealer must use the multiplication factor indicated in Table 1 of this appendix F in determining its capital charge for market risk until it obtains the next quarter's backtesting results, unless the Commission determines that a different adjustment or other action is appropriate.

TABLE 5—MULTIPLICATION FACTOR BASED ON RESULTS OF BACKTESTING

Number of exceptions	Multiplication factor
4 or fewer	3.00
5	3.40
6	3.50
7	3.65
8	3.75
9	3.85

TABLE 5—MULTIPLICATION FACTOR BASED ON RESULTS OF BACKTESTING—Continued

Number of exceptions	Multiplication factor
10 or more	4.00

(2) *Quantitative requirements.* An OTC derivatives dealer applying this appendix F must have a VAR model that meets the following minimum quantitative requirements:

(i) The VAR measures must be calculated on a daily basis using a 99 percent, one-tailed confidence level with a price change equivalent to a ten-business day movement in rates and prices;

(ii) The effective historical observation period for VAR measures must be at least one year, and the weighted average time lag of the individual observations cannot be less than six months. Historical data sets must be updated at least every three months and reassessed whenever market prices or volatilities are subject to large changes;

(iii) The VAR measures must include the risks arising from the non-linear price characteristics of options positions and the sensitivity of the market value of the positions to changes in the volatility of the underlying rates or prices. An OTC derivatives dealer must measure the volatility of options positions by different maturities;

(iv) The VAR measures may incorporate empirical correlations within and across risk categories, provided that the OTC derivatives dealer has described its process for measuring correlations in its application to apply this appendix F and the Commission has approved its application. In the event that the VAR measures do not incorporate empirical correlations across risk categories, the OTC derivatives dealer must add the separate VAR measures for the four major risk categories in paragraph (e)(2)(v) of this appendix F to determine its aggregate VAR measure; and

(v) The OTC derivatives dealer's VAR model must use risk factors sufficient to measure the market risk inherent in all covered positions. The risk factors must address, at a minimum, the following major risk categories: interest

§ 240.15c3-1g

rate risk, equity price risk, foreign exchange rate risk, and commodity price risk. For material exposures in the major currencies and markets, modeling techniques must capture, at a minimum, spread risk and must incorporate enough segments of the yield curve to capture differences in volatility and less-than-perfect correlation of rates along the yield curve. An OTC derivatives dealer must provide the Commission with evidence that the OTC derivatives dealer's VAR model takes account of specific risk in positions, including specific equity risk, if the OTC derivatives dealer intends to utilize its VAR model to compute capital charges for equity price risk.

[63 FR 59398, Nov. 3, 1998, as amended at 79 FR 1549, Jan. 8, 2014]

§ 240.15c3-1g Conditions for ultimate holding companies of certain brokers or dealers (Appendix G to 17 CFR 240.15c3-1).

As a condition for a broker or dealer to compute certain of its deductions to capital in accordance with § 240.15c3-1e, pursuant to its undertaking, the ultimate holding company of the broker or dealer shall:

CONDITIONS REGARDING COMPUTATION OF ALLOWABLE CAPITAL AND RISK ALLOWANCES

(a) If it is not an ultimate holding company that has a principal regulator, as that term is defined in § 240.15c3-1(c)(13), calculate allowable capital and allowances for market, credit, and operational risk on a consolidated basis as follows:

(1) *Allowable capital.* The ultimate holding company must compute allowable capital as the sum of:

(i) Common shareholders' equity on the consolidated balance sheet of the holding company less:

(A) Goodwill;

(B) Deferred tax assets, except those permitted for inclusion in Tier 1 capital by the Board of Governors of the Federal Reserve System ("Federal Reserve") (12 CFR 225, appendix A);

(C) Other intangible assets; and

(D) Other deductions from common stockholders' equity as required by the Federal Reserve in calculating Tier 1 capital (as defined in 12 CFR 225, appendix A);

(ii) Cumulative and non-cumulative preferred stock, except that the amount of cumulative preferred stock may not exceed 33% of the items included in allowable capital pursuant to paragraph (a)(1)(i) of this appendix G, excluding cumulative preferred stock, provided that:

(A) The stock does not have a maturity date;

(B) The stock cannot be redeemed at the option of the holder of the instrument;

(C) The stock has no other provisions that will require future redemption of the issue; and

(D) The issuer of the stock can defer or eliminate dividends;

(iii) The sum of the following items on the consolidated balance sheet, to the extent that the sum does not exceed the sum of the items included in allowable capital pursuant to paragraphs (a)(1)(i) and (ii) of this Appendix G:

(A) Cumulative preferred stock in excess of the 33% limit specified in paragraph (a)(1)(ii) of this appendix G and subject to the conditions of paragraphs (a)(1)(ii)(A) through (D) of this appendix G;

(B) Subordinated debt if the original weighted average maturity of the subordinated debt is at least five years; each subordinated debt instrument states clearly on its face that repayment of the debt is not protected by any Federal agency or the Securities Investor Protection Corporation; the subordinated debt is unsecured and subordinated in right of payment to all senior indebtedness of the ultimate holding company; and the subordinated debt instrument permits acceleration only in the event of bankruptcy or reorganization of the ultimate holding company under Chapters 7 (liquidation) and 11 (reorganization) of the U.S. Bankruptcy Code; and

(C) As part of the broker's or dealer's application to calculate deductions for market and credit risk under § 240.15c3-1e, an ultimate holding company may request to include, for a period of three years after adoption of this appendix G, long-term debt that has an original weighted average maturity of at least

Securities and Exchange Commission § 240.15c3-1g

five years and that cannot be accelerated, except upon the occurrence of certain events as the Commission may approve. As part of a subsequent amendment to the broker's or dealer's application, the broker or dealer may request permission for the ultimate holding company to include long-term debt that meets these criteria in allowable capital for up to an additional two years; and

(iv) Hybrid capital instruments that are permitted for inclusion in Tier 2 capital by the Federal Reserve (as defined in 12 CFR 225, appendix A);

(2) *Allowance for market risk.* The ultimate holding company shall compute an allowance for market risk for all proprietary positions, including debt instruments, equity instruments, commodity instruments, foreign exchange contracts, and derivative contracts, as the aggregate of the following:

(i) *Value at risk.* The VaR of its positions, multiplied by the appropriate multiplication factor as set forth in §240.15c3-1e(d). The VaR of the positions must be obtained using approved VaR models meeting the applicable qualitative and quantitative requirements of §240.15c3-1e(d); and

(ii) *Alternative method.* For positions for which there does not exist adequate historical data to support a VaR model, the ultimate holding company must propose a model that produces a suitable allowance for market risk for those positions;

(3) *Allowance for credit risk.* The ultimate holding company shall compute an allowance for credit risk for certain assets on the consolidated balance sheet and certain off-balance sheet items, including loans and loan commitments, exposures due to derivatives contracts, structured financial products, and other extensions of credit, and credit substitutes as follows:

(i) By multiplying the credit equivalent amount of the ultimate holding company's exposure to the counterparty, as defined in paragraphs (a)(3)(i)(A), (B) and (C) of this appendix G, by the appropriate credit risk weight, as defined in paragraph (a)(3)(i)(F) of this appendix G, of the asset, off-balance sheet item, or counterparty, then multiplying that product by 8%, in accordance with the following:

(A) For certain loans and loan commitments, the credit equivalent amount is determined by multiplying the nominal amount of the contract by the following credit conversion factors:

(*1*) 0% credit conversion factor for loan commitments that:

(*i*) May be unconditionally cancelled by the lender; or

(*ii*) May be cancelled by the lender due to credit deterioration of the borrower;

(*2*) 20% credit conversion factor for:

(*i*) Loan commitments of less than one year; or

(*ii*) Short-term self-liquidating trade related contingencies, including letters of credit;

(*3*) 50% credit conversion factor for loan commitments with an original maturity of greater than one year that contain transaction contingencies, including performance bonds, revolving underwriting facilities, note issuance facilities and bid bonds; and

(*4*) 100% credit conversion factor for bankers' acceptances, stand-by letters of credit, and forward purchases of assets, and similar direct credit substitutes;

(B) For derivatives contracts and for repurchase agreements, reverse repurchase agreements, stock lending and borrowing, and similar collateralized transactions, the credit equivalent amount is the sum of the ultimate holding company's maximum potential exposure to the counterparty, as defined in paragraph (a)(3)(i)(E) of this appendix G, multiplied by the appropriate multiplication factor, and the ultimate holding company's current exposure to the counterparty, as defined in paragraph (a)(3)(i)(D) of this appendix G. The ultimate holding company must use the multiplication factor determined according to §240.15c3-1e(d)(1)(v), except that the initial multiplication factor shall be one, unless the Commission determines, based on a review of the group-wide internal risk management control system and practices, including a review of the VaR models, that another multiplication factor is appropriate;

(C) The credit equivalent amount for other assets shall be the asset's book

§ 240.15c3–1g

value on the ultimate holding company's consolidated balance sheet or other amount as determined according to the standards published by the Basel Committee on Banking Supervision, as amended from time to time;

(D) The *current exposure* is the current replacement value of a counterparty's positions, after applying netting agreements with that counterparty meeting the requirements of § 240.15c3–1e(c)(4)(iv) and taking into account the value of collateral from the counterparty in accordance with § 240.15c3–1e(c)(4)(v);

(E) The *maximum potential exposure* is the VaR of the counterparty's positions with the member of the affiliate group, after applying netting agreements with the counterparty meeting the requirements of paragraph (c)(4)(iv) of § 240.15c3–1e, taking into account the value of collateral from the counterparty held by the member of the affiliate in accordance with paragraph (c)(4)(v) of § 240.15c3–1e, and taking into account the current replacement value of the counterparty's positions with the member of the affiliate group, except that for repurchase agreements, reverse repurchase agreements, stock lending and borrowing, and similar collateralized transactions, maximum potential exposure must be calculated using a time horizon of not less than five days;

(F) Credit ratings and credit risk weights shall be determined according to the provisions of paragraphs (c)(4)(vi)(A) and (c)(4)(vi)(B) of § 240.15c3–1e, respectively;

(G) As part of the broker's or dealer's initial application or in an amendment, the ultimate holding company may request Commission approval to reduce allowances for credit risk through the use of credit derivatives;

(H) For the portion of a current exposure covered by a written guarantee, where that guarantee is an unconditional and irrevocable guarantee of the due and punctual payment and performance of the obligation and the ultimate holding company or member of the affiliate group can demand payment after any payment is missed without having to make collection efforts, the ultimate holding company or member of the affiliate group may substitute the credit risk weight of the guarantor for the credit risk weight of the counterparty; or

(ii) As part of the broker's or dealer's initial application or in an amendment to the application, the ultimate holding company may request Commission approval to use a method of calculating credit risk that is consistent with standards published by the Basel Committee on Banking Supervision in International Convergence of Capital Measurement and Capital Standards (July 1988), as amended from time to time; and

(4) *Allowance for operational risk.* The ultimate holding company shall compute an allowance for operational risk in accordance with the standards published by the Basel Committee on Banking Supervision, as amended from time to time.

CONDITIONS REGARDING REPORTING REQUIREMENTS

(b) File reports with the Commission in accordance with the following:

(1) If it is not an ultimate holding company that has a principal regulator, as that term is defined in § 240.15c3–1(c)(13), the ultimate holding company shall file with the Commission:

(i) A report as of the end of each month, filed not later than 30 calendar days after the end of the month. A monthly report need not be filed for a month-end that coincides with a fiscal quarter-end. The monthly report shall include:

(A) A consolidated balance sheet and income statement (including notes to the financial statements) for the ultimate holding company and statements of allowable capital and allowances for market, credit, and operational risk computed pursuant to paragraph (a) of this appendix G, *except* that the consolidated balance sheet and income statement for the first month of the fiscal year may be filed at a later time to which the Commission agrees (when reviewing the affiliated broker's or dealer's application under § 240.15c3–1e(a)). A statement of comprehensive

Securities and Exchange Commission § 240.15c3-1g

income (as defined in § 210.1-02 of Regulation S-X of this chapter) shall be included in place of an income statement, if required by the applicable generally accepted accounting principles.

(B) A graph reflecting, for each business line, the daily intra-month VaR;

(C) Consolidated credit risk information, including aggregate current exposure and current exposures (including commitments) listed by counterparty for the 15 largest exposures;

(D) The 10 largest commitments listed by counterparty;

(E) Maximum potential exposure listed by counterparty for the 15 largest exposures;

(F) The aggregate maximum potential exposure;

(G) A summary report reflecting the geographic distribution of the ultimate holding company's exposures on a consolidated basis for each of the top ten countries to which it is exposed (by residence of the main operating group of the counterparty); and

(H) Certain regular risk reports provided to the persons responsible for managing group-wide risk as the Commission may request from time to time;

(ii) A quarterly report as of the end of each fiscal quarter, filed not later than 35 calendar days after the end of the quarter. The quarterly report shall include, in addition to the information contained in the monthly report as required by paragraph (b)(1)(i) of this appendix G, the following:

(A) Consolidating balance sheets and income statements for the ultimate holding company. The consolidating balance sheet must provide information regarding each material affiliate of the ultimate holding company in a separate column, but may aggregate information regarding members of the affiliate group that are not material affiliates into one column. Statements of comprehensive income (as defined in § 210.1-02 of Regulation S-X) shall be included in place of an income statement, if required by the applicable generally accepted accounting principles;

(B) The results of backtesting of all internal models used to compute allowable capital and allowances for market and credit risk indicating, for each model, the number of backtesting exceptions;

(C) A description of all material pending legal or arbitration proceedings, involving either the ultimate holding company or any of its affiliates, that are required to be disclosed by the ultimate holding company under generally accepted accounting principles;

(D) The aggregate amount of unsecured borrowings and lines of credit, segregated into categories, scheduled to mature within twelve months from the most recent fiscal quarter as to each material affiliate; and

(E) For a quarter-end that coincides with the ultimate holding company's fiscal year-end, the ultimate holding company need not include consolidated and consolidating balance sheets and income statements (or statements of comprehensive income, as applicable) in its quarterly reports. The consolidating balance sheet and income statement (or statement of comprehensive income, as applicable) for the quarter-end that coincides with the fiscal year-end may be filed at a later time to which the Commission agrees (when reviewing the affiliated broker's or dealer's application under § 240.15c3-1e(a));

(iii) An annual audited report as of the end of the ultimate holding company's fiscal year, filed not later than 65 calendar days after the end of the fiscal year. The annual report shall include:

(A) Consolidated financial statements for the ultimate holding company audited by a registered public accounting firm, as that term is defined in section 2(a)(12) of the Sarbanes-Oxley Act of 2002 (15 U.S.C. 7201 *et seq.*). The audit shall be made in accordance with the rules promulgated by the Public Company Accounting Oversight Board. The audited financial statements must include a supporting schedule containing statements of allowable capital and allowances for market, credit, and operational risk computed pursuant to paragraph (a) of this appendix G; and

(B) A supplemental report entitled "Accountant's Report on Internal Risk Management Control System" prepared by a registered public accounting firm, as that term is defined in section

§ 240.15c3–1g

2(a)(12) of the Sarbanes-Oxley Act of 2002 (15 U.S.C. 7201 *et seq.*), indicating the results of the registered public accounting firm's review of the ultimate holding company's compliance with § 240.15c3–4. The procedures are to be performed and the report is to be prepared in accordance with procedures agreed upon by the ultimate holding company and the registered public accounting firm conducting the review. The agreed-upon procedures are to be performed and the report is to be prepared in accordance with rules promulgated by the Public Company Accounting Oversight Board. The ultimate holding company must file, before commencement of the initial review, the procedures agreed upon by the ultimate holding company and the registered public accounting firm with the Division of Market Regulation, Office of Financial Responsibility, at Commission's principal office in Washington, DC. Before commencement of each subsequent review, the ultimate holding company must notify the Commission of any changes in the procedures;

(iv) An organizational chart, as of the ultimate holding company's fiscal year-end, concurrently with its quarterly report for the quarter-end that coincides with its fiscal year-end. The ultimate holding company must provide quarterly updates of the organizational chart if a material change in the information provided to the Commission has occurred;

(2) If the ultimate holding company is an entity that has a principal regulator, as that term is defined in § 240.15c3–1(c)(13), the ultimate holding company must file with the Commission:

(i) A quarterly report as of the end of each fiscal quarter, filed not later than 35 calendar days after the end of the quarter, or a later time to which the Commission may agree upon application. The quarterly report shall include:

(A) Consolidated (including notes to the financial statements) and consolidating balance sheets and income statements for the ultimate holding company. Statements of comprehensive income (as defined in § 210.1–02 of Regulation S-X) shall be included in place of income statements, if required by the applicable generally accepted accounting principles;

(B) Its most recent capital measurements computed in accordance with the standards published by the Basel Committee on Banking Supervision, as amended from time to time, as reported to its principal regulator;

(C) Certain regular risk reports provided to the persons responsible for managing group-wide risk as the Commission may request from time to time; and

(D) For a quarter-end that coincides with the ultimate holding company's fiscal year-end, the ultimate holding company need not include consolidated and consolidating balance sheets and income statements (or statements of comprehensive income, as applicable) in its quarterly reports. The consolidating balance sheet and income statement (or statement of comprehensive income, as applicable) for the quarter-end that coincides with the fiscal year-end may be filed at a later time to which the Commission agrees (when reviewing the affiliated broker's or dealer's application under § 240.15c3–1e(a)).

(ii) An annual audited report as of the end of the ultimate holding company's fiscal year, filed with the Commission when required to be filed by any regulator;

(3) The reports that the ultimate holding company must file in accordance with paragraph (b) of this appendix G will be considered filed when two copies are received at the Commission's principal office in Washington, DC. A person who files reports pursuant to this section for which he or she seeks confidential treatment may clearly mark each page or segregable portion of each page with the words "Confidential Treatment Requested." The copies shall be addressed to the Division of Market Regulation, Risk Assessment Group; and

(4) The reports that the ultimate holding company must file with the Commission in accordance with paragraph (b) of this Appendix G will be accorded confidential treatment to the extent permitted by law.

Securities and Exchange Commission

§ 240.15c3-1g

CONDITIONS REGARDING RECORDS TO BE MADE

(c) If it is not an ultimate holding company that has a principal regulator, make and keep current the following records:

(1) A record of the results of funding and liquidity stress tests that the ultimate holding company has conducted in response to the following events at least once each quarter and a record of the contingency plan to respond to each of these events:

(i) A credit rating downgrade of the ultimate holding company;

(ii) An inability of the ultimate holding company to access capital markets for unsecured short-term funding;

(iii) An inability of the ultimate holding company to access liquid assets in regulated entities across international borders when the events described in paragraphs (c)(1)(i) or (ii) of this appendix G occur; and

(iv) An inability of the ultimate holding company to access credit or assets held at a particular institution when the events described in paragraphs (c)(1)(i) or (ii) of this appendix G occur;

(2) A record of the basis for the determination of credit risk weights for each counterparty;

(3) A record of the basis for the determination of internal credit ratings for each counterparty; and

(4) A record of the calculations of allowable capital and allowances for market, credit and operational risk computed currently at least once per month on a consolidated basis.

CONDITIONS REGARDING PRESERVATION OF RECORDS

(d)(1) Must preserve the following information, documents, and reports for a period of not less than three years in an easily accessible place using any media acceptable under § 240.17a-4(f):

(i) The documents created in accordance with paragraph (c) of this Appendix G;

(ii) Any application or documents filed with the Commission pursuant to § 240.15c3-1e and this appendix G and any written responses received from the Commission;

(iii) All reports and notices filed with the Commission pursuant to § 240.15c3-1e and this appendix G; and

(iv) If the ultimate holding company does not have a principal regulator, all written policies and procedures concerning the group-wide internal risk management control system established pursuant to § 240.15c3-1e(a)(1)(viii)(C); and

(2) The ultimate holding company may maintain the records referred to in paragraph (d)(1) of this appendix G either at the ultimate holding company, at an affiliate, or at a records storage facility, provided that the records are located within the United States. If the records are maintained by an entity other than the ultimate holding company, the ultimate holding company shall obtain and file with the Commission a written undertaking by the entity maintaining the records, in a form acceptable to the Commission, signed by a duly authorized person at the entity maintaining the records, to the effect that the records will be treated as if the ultimate holding company were maintaining the records pursuant to this section and that the entity maintaining the records will permit examination of such records at any time or from time to time during business hours by representatives or designees of the Commission and will promptly furnish the Commission or its designee a true, legible, complete, and current paper copy of any or all or any part of such records. The election to operate pursuant to the provisions of this paragraph shall not relieve the ultimate holding company that is required to maintain and preserve such records from any of its reporting or recordkeeping responsibilities under this section.

CONDITIONS REGARDING NOTIFICATION

(e) The ultimate holding company of a broker or dealer that computes certain of its capital charges in accordance with § 240.15c3-1e shall:

(1) Send notice promptly (but within 24 hours) after the occurrence of the following events:

(i) The early warning indications of low capital as the Commission may agree;

§ 240.15c3-2

(ii) The ultimate holding company files a Form 8-K (17 CFR 249.308) with the Commission; and

(iii) A material affiliate declares bankruptcy or otherwise becomes insolvent; and

(2) If it is not an ultimate holding company that has a principal regulator, as defined in § 240.15c3-1(c)(13), send notice promptly (but within 24 hours) after the occurrence of the following events:

(i) The ultimate holding company becomes aware that an NRSRO has determined to reduce materially its assessment of the creditworthiness of a material affiliate or the credit rating(s) assigned to one or more outstanding short or long-term obligations of a material affiliate;

(ii) The ultimate holding company becomes aware that any financial regulatory agency or self-regulatory organization has taken significant enforcement or regulatory action against a material affiliate; and

(iii) The occurrence of any backtesting exception under § 240.15c3-1e(d)(1)(iii) or (iv) that would require that the ultimate holding company use a higher multiplication factor in the calculation of its allowances for market or credit risk;

(3) Every notice given or transmitted by paragraph (e) of this appendix G will be given or transmitted to the Division of Market Regulation, Office of Financial Responsibility, at the principal office of the Commission in Washington, DC. A person who files notification pursuant to this section for which he or she seeks confidential treatment may clearly mark each page or segregable portion of each page with the words "Confidential Treatment Request." For the purposes of this appendix G, "notice" shall be given or transmitted by telegraphic notice or facsimile transmission. The notice described by paragraph (e)(2) of this appendix G may be transmitted by overnight delivery. Notices filed pursuant to this paragraph will be accorded confidential treatment to the extent permitted by law; and

(4) Upon the written request of the ultimate holding company, or upon its own motion, the Commission may grant an extension of time or an exemption from any of the requirements of this paragraph (e) either unconditionally or on specified terms and conditions as are necessary or appropriate in the public interest or for the protection of investors.

[69 FR 34467, June 21, 2004, as amended at 79 FR 1550, Jan. 8, 2014; 83 FR 50222, Oct. 4, 2018]

§ 240.15c3-2 [Reserved]

§ 240.15c3-3 Customer protection—reserves and custody of securities.

Except where otherwise noted, § 240.15c3-3 applies to a broker or dealer registered under section 15(b) of the Act (15 U.S.C. 78o(b)), including a broker or dealer also registered as a security-based swap dealer or major security-based swap participant under section 15F(b) of the Act (15 U.S.C. 78o-10(b)). A security-based swap dealer or major security-based swap participant registered under section 15F(b) of the Act that is not also registered as a broker or dealer under section 15(b) of the Act is subject to the requirements under § 240.18a-4.

(a) *Definitions.* For the purpose of this section:

(1) The term *customer* shall mean any person from whom or on whose behalf a broker or dealer has received or acquired or holds funds or securities for the account of that person. The term shall not include a broker or dealer, a municipal securities dealer, or a government securities broker or government securities dealer. The term shall, however, include another broker or dealer to the extent that broker or dealer maintains an omnibus account for the account of customers with the broker or dealer in compliance with Regulation T (12 CFR 220.1 through 220.12). The term shall not include a general partner or director or principal officer of the broker or dealer or any other person to the extent that person has a claim for property or funds which by contract, agreement or understanding, or by operation of law, is part of the capital of the broker or dealer or is subordinated to the claims of creditors of the broker or dealer. In addition, the term shall not include a person to the extent that the person has a claim for security futures products held in a futures account, or any

Securities and Exchange Commission

§ 240.15c3-3

security futures product and any futures product held in a "proprietary account" as defined by the Commodity Futures Trading Commission in § 1.3(y) of this chapter. The term also shall not include a counterparty who has delivered collateral to an OTC derivatives dealer pursuant to a transaction in an eligible OTC derivative instrument, or pursuant to the OTC derivatives dealer's cash management securities activities or ancillary portfolio management securities activities, and who has received a prominent written notice from the OTC derivatives dealer that:

(i) Except as otherwise agreed in writing by the OTC derivatives dealer and the counterparty, the dealer may repledge or otherwise use the collateral in its business;

(ii) In the event of the OTC derivatives dealer's failure, the counterparty will likely be considered an unsecured creditor of the dealer as to that collateral;

(iii) The Securities Investor Protection Act of 1970 (SIPA) does not protect the counterparty; and

(iv) The collateral will not be subject to the requirements of § 240.8c-1, § 240.15c2-1, § 240.15c3-2, or § 240.15c3-3.

(2) The term *securities carried for the account of a customer* (hereinafter also "customer securities") shall mean:

(i) Securities received by or on behalf of a broker or dealer for the account of any customer and securities carried long by a broker or dealer for the account of any customer; and

(ii) Securities sold to, or bought for, a customer by a broker or dealer.

(3) The term *fully paid securities* means all securities carried for the account of a customer in a cash account as defined in Regulation T (12 CFR 220.1 *et seq.*), as well as securities carried for the account of a customer in a margin account or any special account under Regulation T that have no loan value for margin purposes, and all margin equity securities in such accounts if they are fully paid: *Provided, however*, that the term *fully paid securities* does not apply to any securities purchased in transactions for which the customer has not made full payment.

(4) The term *margin securities* means those securities carried for the account of a customer in a margin account as defined in section 4 of Regulation T (12 CFR 220.4), as well as securities carried in any other account (such accounts hereinafter referred to as "margin accounts") other than the securities referred to in paragraph (a)(3) of this section.

(5) The term *excess margin securities* shall mean those securities referred to in paragraph (a)(4) of this section carried for the account of a customer having a market value in excess of 140 percent of the total of the debit balances in the customer's account or accounts encompassed by paragraph (a)(4) of this section which the broker or dealer identifies as not constituting margin securities.

(6) The term *qualified security* shall mean a security issued by the United States or a security in respect of which the principal and interest are guaranteed by the United States.

(7) The term *bank* means a bank as defined in section 3(a)(6) of the Act and will also mean any building and loan, savings and loan or similar banking institution subject to supervision by a Federal banking authority. With respect to a broker or dealer that maintains its principal place of business in Canada, the term "bank" also means a Canadian bank subject to supervision by a Canadian authority.

(8) The term *free credit balances* means liabilities of a broker or dealer to customers which are subject to immediate cash payment to customers on demand, whether resulting from sales of securities, dividends, interest, deposits or otherwise, excluding, however, funds in commodity accounts which are segregated in accordance with the Commodity Exchange Act or in a similar manner, or which are funds carried in a proprietary account as that term is defined in regulations under the Commodity Exchange Act. The term "free credit balances" also includes, if subject to immediate cash payment to customers on demand, funds carried in a securities account pursuant to a self-regulatory organization portfolio margining rule approved by the Commission under section 19(b) of the Act (15 U.S.C. 78s(b)) ("SRO portfolio margining rule"), including variation margin or initial margin, marks to market, and proceeds resulting from margin

§ 240.15c3-3

paid or released in connection with closing out, settling or exercising futures contracts and options thereon.

(9) The term *other credit balances* means cash liabilities of a broker or dealer to customers other than free credit balances and funds in commodity accounts which are segregated in accordance with the Commodity Exchange Act or in a similar manner, or funds carried in a proprietary account as that term is defined in regulations under the Commodity Exchange Act. The term "other credit balances" also includes funds that are cash liabilities of a broker or dealer to customers other than free credit balances and are carried in a securities account pursuant to an SRO portfolio margining rule, including variation margin or initial margin, marks to market, and proceeds resulting from margin paid or released in connection with closing out, settling or exercising futures contracts and options thereon.

(10) The term *funds carried for the account of any customer* (hereinafter also "customer funds") shall mean all free credit and other credit balances carried for the account of the customer.

(11) The term *principal officer* shall mean the president, executive vice president, treasurer, secretary or any other person performing a similar function with the broker or dealer.

(12) The term *household members and other persons related to principals* includes husbands or wives, children, sons-in-law or daughters-in-law and any household relative to whose support a principal contributes directly or indirectly. For purposes of this paragraph (a)(12), a principal shall be deemed to be a director, general partner, or principal officer of the broker or dealer.

(13) The term *affiliated person* includes any person who directly or indirectly controls a broker or dealer or any person who is directly or indirectly controlled by or under common control with the broker or dealer. Ownership of 10% or more of the common stock of the relevant entity will be deemed prima facie control of that entity for purposes of this paragraph.

(14) The term *securities account* shall mean an account that is maintained in accordance with the requirements of section 15(c)(3) of the Act (15 U.S.C. 78o(c)(3)) and § 240.15c3-3.

(15) The term *futures account* (also referred to as "commodity account") shall mean an account that is maintained in accordance with the segregation requirements of section 4d of the Commodity Exchange Act (7 U.S.C. 6d) and the rules thereunder.

(16) The term *PAB account* means a proprietary securities account of a broker or dealer (which includes a foreign broker or dealer, or a foreign bank acting as a broker or dealer) other than a delivery-versus-payment account or a receipt-versus-payment account. The term does not include an account that has been subordinated to the claims of creditors of the carrying broker or dealer.

(17) The term *Sweep Program* means a service provided by a broker or dealer where it offers to its customer the option to automatically transfer free credit balances in the securities account of the customer to either a money market mutual fund product as described in § 270.2a-7 of this chapter or an account at a bank whose deposits are insured by the Federal Deposit Insurance Corporation.

(b) *Physical possession or control of securities.* (1) A broker or dealer shall promptly obtain and shall thereafter maintain the physical possession or control of all fully-paid securities and excess margin securities carried by a broker or dealer for the account of customers.

(2) A broker or dealer shall not be deemed to be in violation of the provisions of paragraph (b)(1) of this section regarding physical possession or control of customers' securities if, solely as the result of normal business operations, temporary lags occur between the time when a security is required to be in the possession or control of the broker or dealer and the time that it is placed in the broker's or dealer's physical possession or under its control, provided that the broker or dealer takes timely steps in good faith to establish prompt physical possession or control. The burden of proof shall be on the broker or dealer to establish that the failure to obtain physical possession or control of securities carried for the account of customers as required

Securities and Exchange Commission § 240.15c3-3

by paragraph (b)(1) of this section is merely temporary and solely the result of normal business operations including same day receipt and redelivery (turnaround), and to establish that it has taken timely steps in good faith to place them in its physical possession or control.

(3) A broker or dealer shall not be deemed to be in violation of the provisions of paragraph (b)(1) of this section regarding physical possession or control of fully-paid or excess margin securities borrowed from any person, provided that the broker or dealer and the lender, at or before the time of the loan, enter into a written agreement that, at a minimum;

(i) Sets forth in a separate schedule or schedules the basis of compensation for any loan and generally the rights and liabilities of the parties as to the borrowed securities;

(ii) Provides that the lender will be given a schedule of the securities actually borrowed at the time of the borrowing of the securities;

(iii) Specifies that the broker or dealer:

(A) Must provide to the lender, upon the execution of the agreement or by the close of the business day of the loan if the loan occurs subsequent to the execution of the agreement, collateral, which fully secures the loan of securities, consisting exclusively of cash or United States Treasury bills and Treasury notes or an irrevocable letter of credit issued by a bank as defined in section 3(a)(6)(A)–(C) of the Act (15 U.S.C. 78c(a)(6)(A)–(C)) or such other collateral as the Commission designates as permissible by order as necessary or appropriate in the public interest and consistent with the protection of investors after giving consideration to the collateral's liquidity, volatility, market depth and location, and the issuer's creditworthiness; and

(B) Must mark the loan to the market not less than daily and, in the event that the market value of all the outstanding securities loaned at the close of trading at the end of the business day exceeds 100 percent of the collateral then held by the lender, the borrowing broker or dealer must provide additional collateral of the type described in paragraph (b)(3)(iii)(A) of this section to the lender by the close of the next business day as necessary to equal, together with the collateral then held by the lender, not less than 100 percent of the market value of the securities loaned; and

(iv) Contains a prominent notice that the provisions of the SIPA may not protect the lender with respect to the securities loan transaction and that, therefore, the collateral delivered to the lender may constitute the only source of satisfaction of the broker's or dealer's obligation in the event the broker or dealer fails to return the securities.

(4)(i) Notwithstanding paragraph (k)(2)(i) of this section, a broker or dealer that retains custody of securities that are the subject of a repurchase agreement between the broker or dealer and a counterparty shall:

(A) Obtain the repurchase agreement in writing;

(B) Confirm in writing the specific securities that are the subject of a repurchase transaction pursuant to such agreement at the end of the trading day on which the transaction is initiated and at the end of any other day during which other securities are substituted if the substitution results in a change to issuer, maturity date, par amount or coupon rate as specified in the previous confirmation;

(C) Advise the counterparty in the repurchase agreement that the Securities Investor Protection Corporation has taken the position that the provisions of the SIPA do not protect the counterparty with respect to the repurchase agreement; and

(D) Maintain possession or control of securities that are the subject of the agreement.

(ii) For purpose of this paragraph (b)(4), securities are in the broker's or dealer's control only if they are in the control of the broker or dealer within the meaning of § 240.15c3–3 (c)(1), (c)(3), (c)(5) or (c)(6) of this title.

(iii) A broker or dealer shall not be in violation of the requirement to maintain possession or control pursuant to paragraph (b)(4)(i)(D) during the trading day if:

(A) In the written repurchase agreement, the counterparty grants the broker or dealer the right to substitute

475

§ 240.15c3–3

other securities for those subject to the agreement; and

(B) The provision in the written repurchase agreement governing the right, if any, to substitute is immediately preceded by the following disclosure statement, which must be prominently displayed:

REQUIRED DISCLOSURE

The [seller] is not permitted to substitute other securities for those subject to this agreement and therefore must keep the [buyer's] securities segregated at all times, unless in this agreement the [buyer] grants the [seller] the right to substitute other securities. If the [buyer] grants the right to substitute, this means that the [buyer's] securities will likely be commingled with the [seller's] own securities during the trading day. The [buyer] is advised that, during any trading day that the [buyer's] securities are commingled with the [seller's] securities, they will be subject to liens granted by the [seller] to its clearing bank and may be used by the [seller] for deliveries on other securities transactions. Whenever the securities are commingled, the [seller's] ability to resegregate substitute securities for the [buyer] will be subject to the [seller's] ability to satisfy the clearing lien or to obtain substitute securities.

(iv) A confirmation issued in accordance with paragraph (b)(4)(i)(B) of this section shall specify the issuer, maturity date, coupon rate, par amount and market value of the security and shall further identify a CUSIP or mortgage-backed security pool number, as appropriate, except that a CUSIP or a pool number is not required on the confirmation if it is identified in internal records of the broker or dealer that designate the specific security of the counterparty. For purposes of this paragraph (b)(4)(iv), the market value of any security that is the subject of the repurchase transaction shall be the most recently available bid price plus accrued interest, obtained by any reasonable and consistent methodology.

(v) This paragraph (b)(4) shall not apply to a repurchase agreement between the broker or dealer and another broker or dealer (including a government securities broker or dealer), a registered municipal securities dealer, or a general partner or director or principal officer of the broker or dealer or any person to the extent that the person's claim is explicitly subordinated to the claims of creditors of the broker or dealer.

(5) A broker or dealer is required to obtain and thereafter maintain the physical possession or control of securities carried for a PAB account, unless the broker or dealer has provided written notice to the account holder that the securities may be used in the ordinary course of its securities business, and has provided an opportunity for the account holder to object.

(c) *Control of securities.* Securities under the control of a broker or dealer shall be deemed to be securities which:

(1) Are represented by one or more certificates in the custody or control of a clearing corporation or other subsidiary organization of either national securities exchanges or of a registered national securities association, or of a custodian bank in accordance with a system for the central handling of securities complying with the provisions of §§ 240.8c–1(g) and 240.15c2–1(g) the delivery of which certificates to the broker or dealer does not require the payment of money or value, and if the books or records of the broker or dealer identify the customers entitled to receive specified quantities or units of the securities so held for such customers collectively; or

(2) Are carried for the account of any customer by a broker or dealer and are carried in an omnibus credit account in the name of such broker or dealer with another broker or dealer in compliance with the requirements of section 7(f) of Regulation T (12 CFR 220.7(f)), such securities being deemed to be under the control of such broker or dealer to the extent that it has instructed such carrying broker or dealer to maintain physical possession or control of them free of any charge, lien, or claim of any kind in favor of such carrying broker or dealer or any persons claiming through such carrying broker or dealer; or

(3) Are the subject of bona fide items of transfer; provided that securities shall be deemed not to be the subject of bona fide items of transfer if, within 40 calendar days after they have been transmitted for transfer by the broker or dealer to the issuer or its transfer agent, new certificates conforming to the instructions of the broker or dealer

Securities and Exchange Commission

§ 240.15c3-3

have not been received by the broker or deal, the broker or dealer has not received a written statement by the issuer or its transfer agent acknowledging the transfer instructions and the possession of the securities or the broker or dealer has not obtained a revalidation of a window ticket from a transfer agent with respect to the certificate delivered for transfer; or

(4) Are in the custody of a foreign depository, foreign clearing agency or foreign custodian bank which the Commission upon application from a broker or dealer, a registered national securities exchange or a registered national securities association, or upon its own motion shall designate as a satisfactory control location for securities; or

(5) Are in the custody or control of a bank as defined in section 3(a)(6) of the Act, the delivery of which securities to the broker or dealer does not require the payment of money or value and the bank having acknowledged in writing that the securities in its custody or control are not subject to any right, charge, security interest, lien or claim of any kind in favor of a bank or any person claiming through the bank; or

(6)(i) Are held in or are in transit between offices of the broker or dealer; or (ii) are held by a corporate subsidiary if the broker or dealer owns and exercises a majority of the voting rights of all of the voting securities of such subsidiary, assumes or guarantees all of the subsidiary's obligations and liabilities, operates the subsidiary as a branch office of the broker or dealer, and assumes full responsibility for compliance by the subsidiary and all of its associated persons with the provisions of the Federal securities laws as well as for all of the other acts of the subsidiary and such associated persons; or

(7) Are held in such other locations as the Commission shall upon application from a broker or dealer find and designate to be adequate for the protection of customer securities.

(d) *Requirement to reduce securities to possession or control.* Not later than the next business day, a broker or dealer, as of the close of the preceding business day, shall determine from its books or records the quantity of fully paid securities and excess margin securities in its possession or control and the quantity of fully paid securities and excess margin securities not in its possession or control. In making this daily determination inactive margin accounts (accounts having no activity by reason of purchase or sale of securities, receipt or delivery of cash or securities or similar type events) may be computed not less than once weekly. If such books or records indicate, as of such close of the business day, that such broker or dealer has not obtained physical possession or control of all fully paid and excess margin securities as required by this section and there are securities of the same issue and class in any of the following noncontrol locations:

(1) Securities subject to a lien securing moneys borrowed by the broker or dealer or securities loaned to another broker or dealer or a clearing corporation, then the broker or dealer shall, not later than the business day following the day on which such determination is made, issue instructions for the release of such securities from the lien or return of such loaned securities and shall obtain physical possession or control of such securities within two business days following the date of issuance of the instructions in the case of securities subject to lien securing borrowed moneys and within five business days following the date of issuance of instructions in the case of securities loaned; or

(2) Securities included on the broker's or dealer's books or records as failed to receive more than 30 calendar days, then the broker or dealer shall, not later than the business day following the day on which such determination is made, take prompt steps to obtain physical possession or control of securities so failed to receive through a buy-in procedure or otherwise; or

(3) Securities receivable by the broker or dealer as a security dividend receivable, stock split or similar distribution for more than 45 calendar days, then the broker or dealer shall, not later than the business day following the day on which such determination is made, take prompt steps to obtain physical possession or control of securities so receivable through a buy-in procedure or otherwise; or

§ 240.15c3-3

(4) Securities included on the broker's or dealer's books or records that allocate to a short position of the broker or dealer or a short position for another person, excluding positions covered by paragraph (m) of this section, for more than 30 calendar days, then the broker or dealer must, not later than the business day following the day on which the determination is made, take prompt steps to obtain physical possession or control of such securities. For the purposes of this paragraph (d)(4), the 30 day time period will not begin to run with respect to a syndicate short position established in connection with an offering of securities until the completion of the underwriter's participation in the distribution as determined pursuant to § 242.100(b) of Regulation M of this chapter (17 CFR 242.100 through 242.105); or

(5) A broker or dealer which is subject to the requirements of § 240.15c3-3 with respect to physical possession or control of fully paid and excess margin securities shall prepare and maintain a current and detailed description of the procedures which it utilizes to comply with the possession or control requirements set forth in this section. The records required herein shall be made available upon request to the Commission and to the designated examining authority for such broker or dealer.

(e) *Special reserve bank accounts for the exclusive benefit of customers and PAB accounts.* (1) Every broker or dealer must maintain with a bank or banks at all times when deposits are required or hereinafter specified a "Special Reserve Bank Account for the Exclusive Benefit of Customers" (hereinafter referred to as the *Customer Reserve Bank Account*) and a "Special Reserve Bank Account for Brokers and Dealers" (hereinafter referred to as the *PAB Reserve Bank Account*), each of which will be separate from the other and from any other bank account of the broker or dealer. Such broker or dealer must at all times maintain in the Customer Reserve Bank Account and the PAB Reserve Bank Account, through deposits made therein, cash and/or qualified securities in amounts computed in accordance with the formula attached as Exhibit A (17 CFR 240.15c3-3a), as applied to customer and PAB accounts respectively.

(2) With respect to each computation required pursuant to paragraph (e)(1) of this section, a broker or dealer must not accept or use any of the amounts under items comprising Total Credits under the formula referred to in paragraph (e)(1) of this section except for the specified purposes indicated under items comprising Total Debits under the formula, and, to the extent Total Credits exceed Total Debits, at least the net amount thereof must be maintained in the Customer Reserve Bank Account and PAB Reserve Bank Account pursuant to paragraph (e)(1) of this section.

(3) *Reserve Bank Account computations.* (i) Computations necessary to determine the amount required to be deposited in the Customer Reserve Bank Account and PAB Reserve Bank Account as specified in paragraph (e)(1) of this section must be made weekly, as of the close of the last business day of the week, and the deposit so computed must be made no later than one hour after the opening of banking business on the second following business day; *provided, however,* a broker or dealer which has aggregate indebtedness not exceeding 800 percent of net capital (as defined in § 240.15c3-1) and which carries aggregate customer funds (as defined in paragraph (a)(10) of this section), as computed at the last required computation pursuant to this section, not exceeding $1,000,000, may in the alternative make the Customer Reserve Bank Account computation monthly, as of the close of the last business day of the month, and, in such event, must deposit not less than 105 percent of the amount so computed no later than one hour after the opening of banking business on the second following business day.

(ii) If a broker or dealer, computing on a monthly basis, has, at the time of any required computation, aggregate indebtedness in excess of 800 percent of net capital, such broker or dealer must thereafter compute weekly as aforesaid until four successive weekly Customer Reserve Bank Account computations are made, none of which were made at a time when its aggregate indebtedness exceeded 800 percent of its net capital.

Securities and Exchange Commission § 240.15c3-3

(iii) A broker or dealer that does not carry the accounts of a "customer" as defined by this section or conduct a proprietary trading business may make the computation to be performed with respect to PAB accounts under paragraph (e)(1) of this section monthly rather than weekly. If a broker or dealer performing the computation with respect to PAB accounts under paragraph (e)(1) of this section on a monthly basis is, at the time of any required computation, required to deposit additional cash or qualified securities in the PAB Reserve Bank Account, the broker or dealer must thereafter perform the computation required with respect to PAB accounts under paragraph (e)(1) of this section weekly until four successive weekly computations are made, none of which is made at a time when the broker or dealer was required to deposit additional cash or qualified securities in the PAB Reserve Bank Account.

(iv) Computations in addition to the computations required in this paragraph (e)(3), may be made as of the close of any business day, and the deposits so computed must be made no later than one hour after the opening of banking business on the second following business day.

(v) The broker or dealer must make and maintain a record of each such computation made pursuant to this paragraph (e)(3) or otherwise and preserve each such record in accordance with § 240.17a-4.

(4) If the computation performed under paragraph (e)(3) of this section with respect to PAB accounts results in a deposit requirement, the requirement may be satisfied to the extent of any excess debit in the computation performed under paragraph (e)(3) of this section with respect to customer accounts of the same date. However, a deposit requirement resulting from the computation performed under paragraph (e)(3) of this section with respect to customer accounts cannot be satisfied with excess debits from the computation performed under paragraph (e)(3) of this section with respect to PAB accounts.

(5) In determining whether a broker or dealer maintains the minimum deposits required under this section, the broker or dealer must exclude the total amount of any cash deposited with an affiliated bank. The broker or dealer also must exclude cash deposited with a non-affiliated bank to the extent that the amount of the deposit exceeds 15% of the bank's equity capital as reported by the bank in its most recent Call Report or any successor form the bank is required to file by its appropriate Federal banking agency (as defined by section 3 of the Federal Deposit Insurance Act (12 U.S.C. 1813)).

(f) *Notification of banks.* A broker or dealer required to maintain a Customer Reserve Bank Account and PAB Reserve Bank Account prescribed by paragraph (e)(1) of this section or who maintains a Special Account referred to in paragraph (k) of this section must obtain and preserve in accordance with § 240.17a-4 a written notification from each bank with which it maintains a Customer Reserve Bank Account, a PAB Reserve Bank Account, or a Special Account that the bank was informed that all cash and/or qualified securities deposited therein are being held by the bank for the exclusive benefit of the customers and account holders of the broker or dealer in accordance with the regulations of the Commission, and are being kept separate from any other accounts maintained by the broker or dealer with the bank, and the broker or dealer must have a written contract with the bank which provides that the cash and/or qualified securities will at no time be used directly or indirectly as security for a loan to the broker or dealer by the bank and will not be subject to any right, charge, security interest, lien, or claim of any kind in favor of the bank or any person claiming through the bank.

(g) *Withdrawals from the reserve bank account.* A broker or dealer may make withdrawals from a Customer Reserve Bank Account and a PAB Reserve Bank Account if and to the extent that at the time of the withdrawal the amount remaining in the Customer Reserve Bank Account and PAB Reserve Bank Account is not less than the amount then required by paragraph (e) of this section. A bank may presume that any request for withdrawal from a reserve bank account is in conformity and compliance with this paragraph

§ 240.15c3-3

(g) On any business day on which a withdrawal is made, the broker or dealer shall make a record of the computation on the basis of which he makes such withdrawal, and he shall preserve such computation in accordance with § 240.17a-4.

(h) *Buy-in of short security differences.* A broker or dealer shall within 45 calendar days after the date of the examination, count, verification and comparison of securities pursuant to § 240.17a-13 or otherwise or to the annual report of financial condition in accordance with § 240.17a-5 or 240.17a-12, buy-in all short security differences which are not resolved during the 45-day period.

(i) *Notification in the event of failure to make a required deposit.* If a broker or dealer shall fail to make in its Customer Reserve Bank Account, PAB Reserve Bank Account or special account a deposit, as required by this section, the broker or dealer shall by telegram immediately notify the Commission and the regulatory authority for the broker or dealer, which examines such broker or dealer as to financial responsibility and shall promptly thereafter confirm such notification in writing.

(j) *Treatment of free credit balances.* (1) A broker or dealer must not accept or use any free credit balance carried for the account of any customer of the broker or dealer unless such broker or dealer has established adequate procedures pursuant to which each customer for whom a free credit balance is carried will be given or sent, together with or as part of the customer's statement of account, whenever sent but not less frequently than once every three months, a written statement informing the customer of the amount due to the customer by the broker or dealer on the date of the statement, and that the funds are payable on demand of the customer.

(2) A broker or dealer must not convert, invest, or transfer to another account or institution, credit balances held in a customer's account except as provided in paragraphs (j)(2)(i) and (ii) of this section.

(i) A broker or dealer is permitted to invest or transfer to another account or institution, free credit balances in a customer's account only upon a specific order, authorization, or draft from the customer, and only in the manner, and under the terms and conditions, specified in the order, authorization, or draft.

(ii) A broker or dealer is permitted to transfer free credit balances held in a customer's securities account to a product in its Sweep Program or to transfer a customer's interest in one product in a Sweep Program to another product in a Sweep Program, *provided:*

(A) For an account opened on or after the effective date of this paragraph (j)(2)(ii), the customer gives prior written affirmative consent to having free credit balances in the customer's securities account included in the Sweep Program after being notified:

(*1*) Of the general terms and conditions of the products available through the Sweep Program; and

(*2*) That the broker or dealer may change the products available under the Sweep Program.

(B) For any account:

(*1*) The broker or dealer provides the customer with the disclosures and notices regarding the Sweep Program required by each self-regulatory organization of which the broker or dealer is a member;

(*2*) The broker or dealer provides notice to the customer, as part of the customer's quarterly statement of account, that the balance in the bank deposit account or shares of the money market mutual fund in which the customer has a beneficial interest can be liquidated on the customer's order and the proceeds returned to the securities account or remitted to the customer; and

(*3*)(*i*) The broker or dealer provides the customer with written notice at least 30 calendar days before:

(*A*) Making changes to the terms and conditions of the Sweep Program;

(*B*) Making changes to the terms and conditions of a product currently available through the Sweep Program;

(*C*) Changing, adding or deleting products available through the Sweep Program; or

(*D*) Changing the customer's investment through the Sweep Program from one product to another.

Securities and Exchange Commission § 240.15c3-3

(*ii*) The notice must describe the new terms and conditions of the Sweep Program or product or the new product, and the options available to the customer if the customer does not accept the new terms and conditions or product.

(k) *Exemptions.* (1) The provisions of this section shall not be applicable to a broker or dealer meeting all of the following conditions:

(i) The broker's or dealer's transactions as dealer (as principal for its own account) are limited to the purchase, sale, and redemption of redeemable securities of registered investment companies or of interests or participations in an insurance company separate account, whether or not registered as an investment company; except that a broker or dealer transacting business as a sole proprietor may also effect occasional transactions in other securities for its own account with or through another registered broker or dealer;

(ii) The broker's or dealer's transactions as broker (agent) are limited to:

(*a*) The sale and redemption of redeemable securities of registered investment companies or of interests or participations in an insurance company separate account, whether or not registered as an investment company;

(*b*) the solicitation of share accounts for savings and loan associations insured by an instrumentality of the United States; and

(*c*) the sale of securities for the account of a customer to obtain funds for immediate reinvestment in redeemable securities of registered investment companies; and

(iii) The broker or dealer promptly transmits all funds and delivers all securities received in connection with its activities as a broker or dealer, and does not otherwise hold funds or securities for, or owe money or securities to, customers.

(iv) Notwithstanding the foregoing, this section shall not apply to any insurance company which is a registered broker-dealer, and which otherwise meets all of the conditions in paragraphs (k)(1) (i), (ii), and (iii) of this section, solely by reason of its participation in transactions that are a part of the business of insurance, including the purchasing, selling, or holding of securities for or on behalf of such company's general and separate accounts.

(2) The provisions of this section shall not be applicable to a broker or dealer:

(i) Who carries no margin accounts, promptly transmits all customer funds and delivers all securities received in connection with its activities as a broker or dealer, does not otherwise hold funds or securities for, or owe money or securities to, customers and effectuates all financial transactions between the broker or dealer and its customers through one or more bank accounts, each to be designated as "Special Account for the Exclusive Benefit of Customers of (name of the broker or dealer)"; or

(ii) Who, as an introducing broker or dealer, clears all transactions with and for customers on a fully disclosed basis with a clearing broker or dealer, and who promptly transmits all customer funds and securities to the clearing broker or dealer which carries all of the accounts of such customers and maintains and preserves such books and records pertaining thereto pursuant to the requirements of §§ 240.17a-3 and 240.17a-4 of this chapter, as are customarily made and kept by a clearing broker or dealer.

(3) Upon written application by a broker or dealer, the Commission may exempt such broker or dealer from the provisions of this section, either unconditionally or on specified terms and conditions, if the Commission finds that the broker or dealer has established safeguards for the protection of funds and securities of customers comparable with those provided for by this section and that it is not necessary in the public interest or for the protection of investors to subject the particular broker or dealer to the provisions of this section.

(l) *Delivery of securities.* Nothing stated in this section shall be construed as affecting the absolute right of a customer of a broker or dealer to receive in the course of normal business operations following demand made on the broker or dealer, the physical delivery of certificates for:

§ 240.15c3-3

(1) Fully-paid securities to which he is entitled, and,

(2) Margin securities upon full payment by such customer to the broker or dealer of the customer's indebtedness to the broker or dealer; and, subject to the right of the broker or dealer under Regulation T (12 CFR 220) to retain collateral for its own protection beyond the requirements of Regulation T, excess margin securities not reasonably required to collateralize such customer's indebtedness to the broker or dealer.

(m) *Completion of sell orders on behalf of customers.* If a broker or dealer executes a sell order of a customer (other than an order to execute a sale of securities which the seller does not own) and if for any reason whatever the broker or dealer has not obtained possession of the securities from the customer within 10 business days after the settlement date, the broker or dealer shall immediately thereafter close the transaction with the customer by purchasing securities of like kind and quantity: *Provided, however,* The term *customer* for the purpose of this paragraph (m) shall not include a broker or dealer who maintains an omnibus credit account with another broker or dealer in compliance with section 7(f) of Regulation T (12 CFR 220.7(f)).

NOTE TO PARAGRAPH (m): See 38 FR 12103, May 9, 1973 for an order suspending indefinitely the operation of paragraph (m) as to sell orders for exempted securities (e.g., U.S. Government and municipal obligations).

(n) *Extensions of time.* If a registered national securities exchange or a registered national securities association is satisfied that a broker or dealer is acting in good faith in making the application and that exceptional circumstances warrant such action, such exchange or association, on application of the broker or dealer, may extend any period specified in paragraphs (d)(2) through (4), (h) and (m) of this section, relating to the requirement that such broker or dealer take action within a designated period of time to buy-in a security, for one or more limited periods commensurate with the circumstances. Each such exchange or association shall make and preserve for a period of not less than 3 years a record of each extension granted pursuant to paragraph (n) of this section which shall contain a summary of the justification for the granting of the extension.

(o) *Security futures products*—(1) *Where security futures products shall be held.* A broker or dealer registered with the Commission pursuant to section 15(b)(1) of the Act (15 U.S.C. 78o(b)(1)) that is also a futures commission merchant registered with the Commodity Futures Trading Commission pursuant to section 4f(a)(1) of the Commodity Exchange Act (7 U.S.C. 6f(a)(1)):

(i) Shall hold a customer's security futures products in either a securities account or a futures account; and

(ii) Shall establish written policies or procedures for determining whether customer security futures products will be placed in a securities account or a futures account and, if applicable, the process by which a customer may elect the type or types of account in which security futures products will be held (including the procedure to be followed if a customer fails to make an election of account type).

(2) *Disclosure and record requirements.* (i) Except as provided in paragraph (o)(2)(ii), before a broker or dealer registered with the Commission pursuant to section 15(b)(1) of the Act (15 U.S.C. 78o(b)(1)) accepts the first order for a security futures product from or on behalf of a customer, the broker or dealer shall furnish the customer with a disclosure document containing the following information:

(A) A description of the protections provided by the requirements set forth under this section and SIPA applicable to a securities account;

(B) A description of the protections provided by the requirements set forth under section 4d of the Commodity Exchange Act (7 U.S.C. 6d) applicable to a futures account;

(C) A statement indicating whether the customer's security futures products will be held in a securities account or a futures account, or whether the firm permits customers to make or change an election of account type; and

(D) A statement that, with respect to holding the customer's security futures products in a securities account or a futures account, the alternative regulatory scheme is not available to the

482

Securities and Exchange Commission

§ 240.15c3-3

customer with relation to that account.

(ii) Where a customer account containing an open security futures product position is transferred to a broker or dealer registered with the Commission pursuant to section 15(b)(1) of the Act (15 U.S.C. 78o(b)(1)), that broker or dealer may instead provide the statements described in paragraphs (o)(2)(i)(C) and (o)(2)(i)(D) of this section no later than ten business days after the date the account is received.

(3) *Changes in account type.* A broker or dealer registered with the Commission pursuant to section 15(b)(1) of the Act (15 U.S.C. 78o(b)(1)) that is also a futures commission merchant registered pursuant to section 4f(a)(1) of the Commodity Exchange Act (7 U.S.C. 6f(a)(1)) may change the type of account in which a customer's security futures products will be held; *provided* that:

(i) The broker or dealer creates a record of each change in account type, including the name of the customer, the account number, the date the broker or dealer received the customer's request to change the account type, if applicable, and the date the change in account type became effective; and

(ii) The broker or dealer, at least ten days before the customer's account type is changed:

(A) Notifies the customer in writing of the date that the change will become effective; and

(B) Provides the customer with the disclosures described in paragraph (o)(2)(i) of this section.

(p) *Segregation requirements for security-based swaps.* The following requirements apply to the security-based swap activities of a broker or dealer.

(1) *Definitions.* For the purposes of this paragraph:

(i) The term *cleared security-based swap* means a security-based swap that is, directly or indirectly, submitted to and cleared by a clearing agency registered with the Commission pursuant to section 17A of the Act (15 U.S.C. 78q-1);

(ii) The term *excess securities collateral* means securities and money market instruments carried for the account of a security-based swap customer that have a market value in excess of the current exposure of the broker or dealer (after reducing the current exposure by the amount of cash in the account) to the security-based swap customer, excluding:

(A) Securities and money market instruments held in a qualified clearing agency account but only to the extent the securities and money market instruments are being used to meet a margin requirement of the clearing agency resulting from a security-based swap transaction of the security-based swap customer; and

(B) Securities and money market instruments held in a qualified registered security-based swap dealer account or in a third-party custodial account but only to the extent the securities and money market instruments are being used to meet a regulatory margin requirement of a security-based swap dealer resulting from the broker or dealer entering into a non-cleared security-based swap transaction with the security-based swap dealer to offset the risk of a non-cleared security-based swap transaction between the broker or dealer and the security-based swap customer;

(iii) The term *qualified clearing agency account* means an account of a broker or dealer at a clearing agency registered with the Commission pursuant to section 17A of the Act (15 U.S.C. 78q-1) that holds funds and other property in order to margin, guarantee, or secure cleared security-based swap transactions for the security-based swap customers of the broker or dealer that meets the following conditions:

(A) The account is designated "Special Clearing Account for the Exclusive Benefit of the Cleared Security-Based Swap Customers of [name of broker or dealer]";

(B) The clearing agency has acknowledged in a written notice provided to and retained by the broker or dealer that the funds and other property in the account are being held by the clearing agency for the exclusive benefit of the security-based swap customers of the broker or dealer in accordance with the regulations of the

483

§ 240.15c3–3

Commission and are being kept separate from any other accounts maintained by the broker or dealer with the clearing agency; and

(C) The account is subject to a written contract between the broker or dealer and the clearing agency which provides that the funds and other property in the account shall be subject to no right, charge, security interest, lien, or claim of any kind in favor of the clearing agency or any person claiming through the clearing agency, except a right, charge, security interest, lien, or claim resulting from a cleared security-based swap transaction effected in the account.

(iv) The term *qualified registered security-based swap dealer account* means an account at a security-based swap dealer that is registered with the Commission pursuant to section 15F of the Act that meets the following conditions:

(A) The account is designated "Special Reserve Account for the Exclusive Benefit of the Security-Based Swap Customers of [name of broker or dealer]";

(B) The security-based swap dealer has acknowledged in a written notice provided to and retained by the broker or dealer that the funds and other property held in the account are being held by the security-based swap dealer for the exclusive benefit of the security-based swap customers of the broker or dealer in accordance with the regulations of the Commission and are being kept separate from any other accounts maintained by the broker or dealer with the security-based swap dealer;

(C) The account is subject to a written contract between the broker or dealer and the security-based swap dealer which provides that the funds and other property in the account shall be subject to no right, charge, security interest, lien, or claim of any kind in favor of the security-based swap dealer or any person claiming through the security-based swap dealer, except a right, charge, security interest, lien, or claim resulting from a non-cleared security-based swap transaction effected in the account; and

(D) The account and the assets in the account are not subject to any type of subordination agreement between the broker or dealer and the security-based swap dealer.

(v) The term *qualified security* means:

(A) Obligations of the United States;

(B) Obligations fully guaranteed as to principal and interest by the United States; and

(C) General obligations of any State or a political subdivision of a State that:

(*1*) Are not traded flat and are not in default;

(*2*) Were part of an initial offering of $500 million or greater; and

(*3*) Were issued by an issuer that has published audited financial statements within 120 days of its most recent fiscal year end.

(vi) The term *security-based swap customer* means any person from whom or on whose behalf the broker or dealer has received or acquired or holds funds or other property for the account of the person with respect to a cleared or non-cleared security-based swap transaction. The term does not include a person to the extent that person has a claim for funds or other property which by contract, agreement or understanding, or by operation of law, is part of the capital of the broker or dealer or, in the case of an affiliate of the broker or dealer, is subordinated to all claims of customers (including PAB customers) and security-based swap customers of the broker or dealer.

(vii) The term *special reserve account for the exclusive benefit of security-based swap customers* means an account at a bank that meets the following conditions:

(A) The account is designated "Special Reserve Account for the Exclusive Benefit of the Security-Based Swap Customers of [name of broker or dealer]";

(B) The account is subject to a written acknowledgement by the bank provided to and retained by the broker or dealer that the funds and other property held in the account are being held by the bank for the exclusive benefit of the security-based swap customers of the broker or dealer in accordance with the regulations of the Commission and are being kept separate from any other accounts maintained by the broker or dealer with the bank; and

Securities and Exchange Commission § 240.15c3-3

(C) The account is subject to a written contract between the broker or dealer and the bank which provides that the funds and other property in the account shall at no time be used directly or indirectly as security for a loan or other extension of credit to the broker or dealer by the bank and, shall be subject to no right, charge, security interest, lien, or claim of any kind in favor of the bank or any person claiming through the bank.

(viii) The term *third-party custodial account* means an account carried by an independent third-party custodian that meets the following conditions:

(A) The account is established for the purposes of meeting regulatory margin requirements of another security-based swap dealer;

(B) The account is carried by a bank as defined in section 3(a)(6) of the Act or a registered U.S. clearing organization or depository or, if the collateral to be held in the account consists of foreign securities or currencies, a supervised foreign bank, clearing organization, or depository that customarily maintains custody of such foreign securities or currencies;

(C) The account is designated for and on behalf of the broker or dealer for the benefit of its security-based swap customers and the account is subject to a written acknowledgement by the bank, clearing organization, or depository provided to and retained by the broker or dealer that the funds and other property held in the account are being held by the bank, clearing organization, or depository for the exclusive benefit of the security-based swap customers of the broker or dealer and are being kept separate from any other accounts maintained by the broker or dealer with the bank, clearing organization, or depository; and

(D) The account is subject to a written contract between the broker or dealer and the bank, clearing organization, or depository which provides that the funds and other property in the account shall at no time be used directly or indirectly as security for a loan or other extension of credit to the security-based swap dealer by the bank, clearing organization, or depository and, shall be subject to no right, charge, security interest, lien, or claim of any kind in favor of the bank, clearing organization, or depository or any person claiming through the bank, clearing organization, or depository.

(2) *Physical possession or control of excess securities collateral.* (i) A broker or dealer must promptly obtain and thereafter maintain physical possession or control of all excess securities collateral carried for the security-based swap accounts of security-based swap customers.

(ii) A broker or dealer has *control* of excess securities collateral only if the securities and money market instruments:

(A) Are represented by one or more certificates in the custody or control of a clearing corporation or other subsidiary organization of either national securities exchanges, or of a custodian bank in accordance with a system for the central handling of securities complying with the provisions of §§ 240.8c–1(g) and 240.15c2–1(g) the delivery of which certificates to the broker or dealer does not require the payment of money or value, and if the books or records of the broker or dealer identify the security-based swap customers entitled to receive specified quantities or units of the securities so held for such security-based swap customers collectively;

(B) Are the subject of bona fide items of transfer; provided that securities and money market instruments shall be deemed not to be the subject of bona fide items of transfer if, within 40 calendar days after they have been transmitted for transfer by the broker or dealer to the issuer or its transfer agent, new certificates conforming to the instructions of the broker or dealer have not been received by the broker or dealer, the broker or dealer has not received a written statement by the issuer or its transfer agent acknowledging the transfer instructions and the possession of the securities or money market instruments, or the broker or dealer has not obtained a revalidation of a window ticket from a transfer agent with respect to the certificate delivered for transfer;

(C) Are in the custody or control of a bank as defined in section 3(a)(6) of the Act, the delivery of which securities or money market instruments to the

§ 240.15c3–3

broker or dealer does not require the payment of money or value and the bank having acknowledged in writing that the securities and money market instruments in its custody or control are not subject to any right, charge, security interest, lien or claim of any kind in favor of a bank or any person claiming through the bank;

(D)(*1*) Are held in or are in transit between offices of the broker or dealer; or

(*2*) Are held by a corporate subsidiary if the broker or dealer owns and exercises a majority of the voting rights of all of the voting securities of such subsidiary, assumes or guarantees all of the subsidiary's obligations and liabilities, operates the subsidiary as a branch office of the broker or dealer, and assumes full responsibility for compliance by the subsidiary and all of its associated persons with the provisions of the Federal securities laws as well as for all of the other acts of the subsidiary and such associated persons; or

(E) Are held in such other locations as the Commission shall upon application from a broker or dealer find and designate to be adequate for the protection of security-based swap customer securities.

(iii) Each business day the broker or dealer must determine from its books and records the quantity of excess securities collateral in its possession or control as of the close of the previous business day and the quantity of excess securities collateral not in its possession or control as of the previous business day. If the broker or dealer did not obtain possession or control of all excess securities collateral on the previous business day as required by this section and there are securities or money market instruments of the same issue and class in any of the following non-control locations:

(A) Securities or money market instruments subject to a lien securing an obligation of the broker or dealer, then the broker or dealer, not later than the next business day on which the determination is made, must issue instructions for the release of the securities or money market instruments from the lien and must obtain physical possession or control of the securities or money market instruments within two business days following the date of the instructions;

(B) Securities or money market instruments held in a qualified clearing agency account, then the broker or dealer, not later than the next business day on which the determination is made, must issue instructions for the release of the securities or money market instruments by the clearing agency and must obtain physical possession or control of the securities or money market instruments within two business days following the date of the instructions;

(C) Securities or money market instruments held in a qualified registered security-based swap dealer account maintained by another security-based swap dealer or in a third-party custodial account, then the broker or dealer, not later than the next business day on which the determination is made, must issue instructions for the release of the securities or money market instruments by the security-based swap dealer or the third-party custodian and must obtain physical possession or control of the securities or money market instruments within two business days following the date of the instructions;

(D) Securities or money market instruments loaned by the broker or dealer, then the broker or dealer, not later than the next business day on which the determination is made, must issue instructions for the return of the loaned securities or money market instruments and must obtain physical possession or control of the securities or money market instruments within five business days following the date of the instructions;

(E) Securities or money market instruments failed to receive more than 30 calendar days, then the broker or dealer, not later than the next business day on which the determination is made, must take prompt steps to obtain physical possession or control of the securities or money market instruments through a buy-in procedure or otherwise;

(F) Securities or money market instruments receivable by the broker or dealer as a security dividend, stock split or similar distribution for more than 45 calendar days, then the broker

Securities and Exchange Commission

§ 240.15c3-3

or dealer, not later than the next business day on which the determination is made, must take prompt steps to obtain physical possession or control of the securities or money market instruments through a buy-in procedure or otherwise; or

(G) Securities or money market instruments included on the broker's or dealer's books or records that allocate to a short position of the broker or dealer or a short position for another person, for more than 30 calendar days, then the broker or dealer must, not later than the business day following the day on which the determination is made, take prompt steps to obtain physical possession or control of such securities or money market instruments.

(3) *Deposit requirement for special reserve account for the exclusive benefit of security-based swap customers.* (i) A broker or dealer must maintain a special reserve account for the exclusive benefit of security-based swap customers that is separate from any other bank account of the broker or dealer. The broker or dealer must at all times maintain in the special reserve account for the exclusive benefit of security-based swap customers, through deposits into the account, cash and/or qualified securities in amounts computed in accordance with the formula set forth in § 240.15c3-3b. In determining the amount maintained in a special reserve account for the exclusive benefit of security-based swap customers, the broker or dealer must deduct:

(A) The percentage of the value of a general obligation of a State or a political subdivision of a State specified in § 240.15c3-1(c)(2)(vi);

(B) The aggregate value of general obligations of a State or a political subdivision of a State to the extent the amount of the obligations of a single issuer (after applying the deduction in paragraph (p)(3)(i)(A) of this section) exceeds two percent of the amount required to be maintained in the special reserve account for the exclusive benefit of security-based swap customers;

(C) The aggregate value of all general obligations of States or political subdivisions of States to the extent the amount of the obligations (after applying the deduction in paragraph (p)(3)(i)(A) of this section) exceeds 10 percent of the amount required to be maintained in the special reserve account for the exclusive benefit of security-based swap customers;

(D) The amount of cash deposited with a single non-affiliated bank to the extent the amount exceeds 15 percent of the equity capital of the bank as reported by the bank in its most recent Call Report or any successor form the bank is required to file by its appropriate federal banking agency (as defined by section 3 of the Federal Deposit Insurance Act (12 U.S.C. 1813)); and

(E) The total amount of cash deposited with an affiliated bank.

(ii) A broker or dealer must not accept or use credits identified in the items of the formula set forth in § 240.15c3-3b except for the specified purposes indicated under items comprising Total Debits under the formula, and, to the extent Total Credits exceed Total Debits, at least the net amount thereof must be maintained in the Special Reserve Account pursuant to paragraph (p)(3)(i) of this section.

(iii)(A) The computations necessary to determine the amount required to be maintained in the special reserve account for the exclusive benefit of security-based swap customers must be made weekly as of the close of the last business day of the week and any deposit required to be made into the account must be made no later than one hour after the opening of banking business on the second following business day. The broker or dealer may make a withdrawal from the special reserve account for the exclusive benefit of security-based swap customers only if the amount remaining in the account after the withdrawal is equal to or exceeds the amount required to be maintained in the account pursuant to paragraph (p)(3) of this section.

(ii)(B) Computations in addition to the computations required pursuant to paragraph (p)(3)(iii)(A) of this section may be made as of the close of any business day, and deposits so computed must be made no later than one hour after the open of banking business on the second following business day.

487

§ 240.15c3–3a

(iv) A broker or dealer must promptly deposit into a special reserve account for the exclusive benefit of security-based swap customers cash and/or qualified securities of the broker or dealer if the amount of cash and/or qualified securities in one or more special reserve accounts for the exclusive benefit of security-based swap customers falls below the amount required to be maintained pursuant to this section.

(4) *Requirements for non-cleared security-based swaps*—(i) *Notice.* A broker or dealer registered under section 15F(b) of the Act (15 U.S.C. 78o–10(b)) as a security-based swap dealer or major security-based swap participant must provide the notice required pursuant to section 3E(f)(1)(A) of the Act (15 U.S.C. 78c–5(f)) in writing to a duly authorized individual prior to the execution of the first non-cleared security-based swap transaction with the counterparty occurring after the compliance date of this section.

(ii) *Subordination*—(A) *Counterparty that elects to have individual segregation at an independent third-party custodian.* A broker or dealer must obtain an agreement from a counterparty whose funds or other property to meet a margin requirement of the broker or dealer are held at a third-party custodian in which the counterparty agrees to subordinate its claims against the broker or dealer for the funds or other property held at the third-party custodian to the claims of customers (including PAB customers) and security-based swap customers of the broker or dealer but only to the extent that funds or other property provided by the counterparty to the independent third-party custodian are not treated as *customer property* as that term is defined in 11 U.S.C. 741 or *customer* property as defined in 15 U.S.C. 78*lll*(4) in a liquidation of the broker or dealer.

(B) *Counterparty that elects to have no segregation.* A broker or dealer registered under section 15F(b) of the Act as a security-based swap dealer must obtain an agreement from a counterparty that is an affiliate of the broker or dealer that affirmatively chooses not to require segregation of funds or other property pursuant to section 3E(f) of the Act (15 U.S.C. 78c–5(f)) in which the counterparty agrees to subordinate all of its claims against the broker or dealer to the claims of customers (including PAB customers) and security-based swap customers of the broker or dealer.

[37 FR 25226, Nov. 29, 1972; 38 FR 6277, Mar. 8, 1973, as amended at 42 FR 23790, May 10, 1977; 44 FR 1975, Jan. 9, 1979; 45 FR 37688, June 4, 1980; 47 FR 21775, May 20, 1982; 47 FR 23920, June 2, 1982; 50 FR 41340, Oct. 10, 1985; 52 FR 30333, Aug. 14, 1987; 63 FR 59400, Nov. 3, 1998; 67 FR 58299, Sept. 13, 2002; 68 FR 12783, Mar. 17, 2003; 78 FR 51902, Aug. 21, 2013; 84 FR 44047, Aug. 22, 2019]

§ 240.15c3–3a Exhibit A—Formula for determination of customer and PAB account reserve requirements of brokers and dealers under § 240.15c3–3.

	Credits	Debits
1. Free credit balances and other credit balances in customers' security accounts. (See Note A)	XXX	
2. Monies borrowed collateralized by securities carried for the accounts of customers (See Note B)	XXX	
3. Monies payable against customers' securities loaned (See Note C)	XXX	
4. Customers' securities failed to receive (See Note D)	XXX	
5. Credit balances in firm accounts which are attributable to principal sales to customers.	XXX	
6. Market value of stock dividends, stock splits and similar distributions receivable outstanding over 30 calendar days	XXX	
7. Market value of short security count differences over 30 calendar days old	XXX	
8. Market value of short securities and credits (not to be offset by longs or by debits) in all suspense accounts over 30 calendar days	XXX	
9. Market value of securities which are in transfer in excess of 40 calendar days and have not been confirmed to be in transfer by the transfer agent or the issuer during the 40 days	XXX	
10. Debit balances in customers' cash and margin accounts excluding unsecured accounts and accounts doubtful of collection. (See Note E)		XXX
11. Securities borrowed to effectuate short sales by customers and securities borrowed to make delivery on customers' securities failed to deliver		XXX
12. Failed to deliver of customers' securities not older than 30 calendar days		XXX
13. Margin required and on deposit with the Options Clearing Corporation for all option contracts written or purchased in customer accounts. (See Note F)		XXX

Securities and Exchange Commission § 240.15c3-3a

	Credits	Debits
14. Margin required and on deposit with a clearing agency registered with the Commission under section 17A of the Act (15 U.S.C. 78q–1) or a derivatives clearing organization registered with the Commodity Futures Trading Commission under section 5b of the Commodity Exchange Act (7 U.S.C. 7a–1) related to the following types of positions written, purchased or sold in customer accounts: (1) security futures products and (2) futures contracts (and options thereon) carried in a securities account pursuant to an SRO portfolio margining rule (See Note G) .... Total credits .... Total debits	....	XXX
15. Excess of total credits (sum of items 1–9) over total debits (sum of items 10–14) required to be on deposit in the "Reserve Bank Account" (§ 240.15c3–3(e)). If the computation is made monthly as permitted by this section, the deposit must be not less than 105% of the excess of total credits over total debits.	....	XXX

NOTES REGARDING THE CUSTOMER RESERVE BANK ACCOUNT COMPUTATION

NOTE A. Item 1 must include all outstanding drafts payable to customers which have been applied against free credit balances or other credit balances and must also include checks drawn in excess of bank balances per the records of the broker or dealer.

NOTE B. Item 2 must include the amount of options-related or security futures product-related Letters of Credit obtained by a member of a registered clearing agency or a derivatives clearing organization which are collateralized by customers' securities, to the extent of the member's margin requirement at the registered clearing agency or derivatives clearing organization. Item 2 must also include the amount of Letters of Credit which are collateralized by customers' securities and related to other futures contracts (and options thereon) carried in a securities account pursuant to an SRO portfolio margining rule.

NOTE C. Item 3 must include in addition to monies payable against customers' securities loaned the amount by which the market value of securities loaned exceeds the collateral value received from the lending of such securities.

NOTE D. Item 4 must include in addition to customers' securities failed to receive the amount by which the market value of securities failed to receive and outstanding more than thirty (30) calendar days exceeds their contract value.

NOTE E. (1) Debit balances in margin accounts must be reduced by the amount by which a specific security (other than an exempted security) which is collateral for margin accounts exceeds in aggregate value 15 percent of the aggregate value of all securities which collateralize all margin accounts receivable; provided, however, the required reduction must not be in excess of the amounts of the debit balance required to be excluded because of this concentration rule. A specified security is deemed to be collateral for a margin account only to the extent it represents in value not more than 140 percent of the customer debit balance in a margin account.

(2) Debit balances in special omnibus accounts, maintained in compliance with the requirements of Section 7(f) of Regulation T (12 CFR 220.7(f)) or similar accounts carried on behalf of another broker or dealer, must be reduced by any deficits in such accounts (or if a credit, such credit must be increased) less any calls for margin, mark to the market, or other required deposits which are outstanding 5 business days or less.

(3) Debit balances in customers' cash and margin accounts included in the formula under Item 10 must be reduced by an amount equal to 1 percent of their aggregate value.

(4) Debit balances in cash and margin accounts of household members and other persons related to principals of a broker or dealer and debit balances in cash and margin accounts of affiliated persons of a broker or dealer must be excluded from the Reserve Formula, unless the broker or dealer can demonstrate that such debit balances are directly related to credit items in the formula.

(5) Debit balances in margin accounts (other than omnibus accounts) must be reduced by the amount by which any

single customer's debit balance exceeds 25% (to the extent such amount is greater than $50,000) of the broker-dealer's tentative net capital (*i.e.*, net capital prior to securities haircuts) unless the broker or dealer can demonstrate that the debit balance is directly related to credit items in the Reserve Formula. Related accounts (*e.g.*, the separate accounts of an individual, accounts under common control or subject to cross guarantees) will be deemed to be a single customer's accounts for purposes of this provision.

If the registered national securities exchange or the registered national securities association having responsibility for examining the broker or dealer ("designated examining authority") is satisfied, after taking into account the circumstances of the concentrated account including the quality, diversity, and marketability of the collateral securing the debit balances or margin accounts subject to this provision, that the concentration of debit balances is appropriate, then such designated examining authority may grant a partial or plenary exception from this provision. The debit balance may be included in the reserve formula computation for five business days from the day the request is made.

(6) Debit balances in joint accounts, custodian accounts, participation in hedge funds or limited partnerships or similar type accounts or arrangements that include both assets of a person or persons who would be excluded from the definition of customer ("noncustomer") and assets of a person or persons who would be included in the definition of customer must be included in the Reserve Formula in the following manner: If the percentage ownership of the non-customer is less than 5 percent then the entire debit balance shall be included in the formula; if such percentage ownership is between 5 percent and 50 percent then the portion of the debit balance attributable to the non-customer must be excluded from the formula unless the broker or dealer can demonstrate that the debit balance is directly related to credit items in the formula; or if such percentage ownership is greater than 50 percent, then the entire debit balance must be excluded from the formula unless the broker or dealer can demonstrate that the debit balance is directly related to credit items in the formula.

NOTE F. Item 13 must include the amount of margin required and on deposit with the Options Clearing Corporation to the extent such margin is represented by cash, proprietary qualified securities and letters of credit collateralized by customers' securities.

NOTE G. (a) Item 14 must include the amount of margin required and on deposit with a clearing agency registered with the Commission under section 17A of the Act (15 U.S.C. 78q–1) or a derivatives clearing organization registered with the Commodity Futures Trading Commission under section 5b of the Commodity Exchange Act (7 U.S.C. 7a–1) for customer accounts to the extent that the margin is represented by cash, proprietary qualified securities, and letters of credit collateralized by customers' securities.

(b) Item 14 will apply only if the broker or dealer has the margin related to security futures products, or futures (and options thereon) carried in a securities account pursuant to an approved SRO portfolio margining program on deposit with:

(1) A registered clearing agency or derivatives clearing organization that:

(i) Maintains security deposits from clearing members in connection with regulated options or futures transactions and assessment power over member firms that equal a combined total of at least $2 billion, at least $500 million of which must be in the form of security deposits. For the purposes of this Note G, the term "security deposits" refers to a general fund, other than margin deposits or their equivalent, that consists of cash or securities held by a registered clearing agency or derivative clearing organization; or

(ii) Maintains at least $3 billion in margin deposits; or

(iii) Does not meet the requirements of paragraphs (b)(1)(i) through (b)(1)(iii) of this Note G, if the Commission has determined, upon a written request for exemption by or for the benefit of the broker or dealer, that the broker or dealer may utilize such a registered clearing agency or derivatives clearing organization. The Commission may, in its sole discretion, grant such an exemption subject to such conditions as are appropriate under the circumstances, if the Commission determines that such conditional or unconditional exemption is necessary or appropriate in the public interest, and is consistent with the protection of investors; and

(2) A registered clearing agency or derivatives clearing organization that, if it holds funds or securities deposited as margin for security futures products or futures in a portfolio margin account in a bank, as defined in section 3(a)(6) of the Act (15 U.S.C. 78c(a)(6)), obtains and preserves written notification from the bank at which it holds such funds and securities or at which such funds and securities are held on its behalf. The written notification will state that all funds and/or securities deposited with the bank as margin (including customer security futures products and futures in a portfolio margin account), or held by the bank and pledged to such registered clearing agency or derivatives clearing agency as margin, are being held by the bank for the exclusive benefit of clearing members of the registered clearing agency or derivatives clearing organization (subject to the interest of such registered clearing agency or derivatives clearing organization therein), and are being kept separate from any other accounts maintained by the registered clearing agency or derivatives clearing organization with the bank. The written notification also will provide that such funds and/or securities will at no time be used directly or indirectly as security for a loan to the registered clearing agency or derivatives clearing organization by the bank, and will be subject to no right, charge, security interest, lien, or claim of any kind in favor of the bank or any person claiming through the bank. This provision, however, will not prohibit a registered clearing agency or derivatives clearing organization from pledging customer funds or securities as collateral to a bank for any purpose that the rules of the Commission or the registered clearing agency or derivatives clearing organization otherwise permit; and

(3) A registered clearing agency or derivatives clearing organization establishes, documents, and maintains:

(i) Safeguards in the handling, transfer, and delivery of cash and securities;

(ii) Fidelity bond coverage for its employees and agents who handle customer funds or securities. In the case of agents of a registered clearing agency or derivatives clearing organization, the agent may provide the fidelity bond coverage; and

(iii) Provisions for periodic examination by independent public accountants; and

(iv) A derivatives clearing organization that, if it is not otherwise registered with the Commission, has provided the Commission with a written undertaking, in a form acceptable to the Commission, executed by a duly authorized person at the derivatives clearing organization, to the effect that, with respect to the clearance and settlement of the customer security futures products and futures in a portfolio margin account of the broker or dealer, the derivatives clearing organization will permit the Commission to examine the books and records of the derivatives clearing organization for compliance with the requirements set forth in §240.15c3–3a, Note G (b)(1) through (3).

(c) Item 14 will apply only if a broker or dealer determines, at least annually, that the registered clearing agency or derivatives clearing organization with which the broker or dealer has on deposit margin related to securities future products or futures in a portfolio margin account meets the conditions of this Note G.

NOTES REGARDING THE PAB RESERVE BANK ACCOUNT COMPUTATION

NOTE 1. Broker-dealers should use the formula in Exhibit A for the purposes of computing the PAB reserve requirement, except that references to "accounts," "customer accounts, or "customers" will be treated as references to PAB accounts.

NOTE 2. Any credit (including a credit applied to reduce a debit) that is included in the computation required by §240.15c3–3 with respect to customer accounts (the "customer reserve computation") may not be included as a

§ 240.15c3-3b

credit in the computation required by § 240.15c3-3 with respect to PAB accounts (the "PAB reserve computation").

NOTE 3. Note E(1) to § 240.15c3-3a does not apply to the PAB reserve computation.

NOTE 4. Note E(3) to § 240.15c3-3a which reduces debit balances by 1% does not apply to the PAB reserve computation.

NOTE 5. Interest receivable, floor brokerage, and commissions receivable of another broker or dealer from the broker or dealer (excluding clearing deposits) that are otherwise allowable assets under § 240.15c3-1 need not be included in the PAB reserve computation, provided the amounts have been clearly identified as payables on the books of the broker or dealer. Commissions receivable and other receivables of another broker or dealer from the broker or dealer that are otherwise non-allowable assets under § 240.15c3-1 and clearing deposits of another broker or dealer may be included as "credit balances" for purposes of the PAB reserve computation, provided the commissions receivable and other receivables are subject to immediate cash payment to the other broker or dealer and the clearing deposit is subject to payment within 30 days.

NOTE 6. Credits included in the PAB reserve computation that result from the use of securities held for a PAB account ("PAB securities") that are pledged to meet intra-day margin calls in a cross-margin account established between the Options Clearing Corporation and any regulated derivatives clearing organization may be reduced to the extent that the excess margin held by the other clearing corporation in the cross-margin relationship is used the following business day to replace the PAB securities that were previously pledged. In addition, balances resulting from a portfolio margin account that are segregated pursuant to Commodity Futures Trading Commission regulations need not be included in the PAB Reserve Bank Account computation.

NOTE 7. Deposits received prior to a transaction pending settlement which are $5 million or greater for any single transaction or $10 million in aggregate may be excluded as credits from the PAB reserve computation if such balances are placed and maintained in a separate PAB Reserve Bank Account by 12 p.m. Eastern Time on the following business day. Thereafter, the money representing any such deposits may be withdrawn to complete the related transactions without performing a new PAB reserve computation.

NOTE 8. A credit balance resulting from a PAB reserve computation may be reduced by the amount that items representing such credits are swept into money market funds or mutual funds of an investment company registered under the Investment Company Act of 1940 on or prior to 10 a.m. Eastern Time on the deposit date provided that the credits swept into any such fund are not subject to any right, charge, security interest, lien, or claim of any kind in favor of the investment company or the broker or dealer. Any credits that have been swept into money market funds or mutual funds must be maintained in the name of a particular broker or for the benefit of another broker.

NOTE 9. Clearing deposits required to be maintained at registered clearing agencies may be included as debits in the PAB reserve computation to the extent the percentage of the deposit, which is based upon the clearing agency's aggregate deposit requirements (*e.g.*, dollar trading volume), that relates to the proprietary business of other brokers and dealers can be identified.

NOTE 10. A broker or dealer that clears PAB accounts through an affiliate or third party clearing broker must include these PAB account balances and the omnibus PAB account balance in its PAB reserve computation.

[78 FR 51904, Aug. 21, 2013, as amended at 79 FR 1550, Jan. 8, 2014]

§ 240.15c3-3b **Exhibit B—Formula for determination of security-based swap customer reserve requirements of brokers and dealers under § 240.15c3-3.**

Securities and Exchange Commission § 240.15c3-3b

	Credits	Debits
1. Free credit balances and other credit balances in the accounts carried for security-based swap customers (See Note A)	$____	
2. Monies borrowed collateralized by securities in accounts carried for security-based swap customers (See Note B)	$____	
3. Monies payable against security-based swap customers' securities loaned (See Note C)	$____	
4. Security-based swap customers' securities failed to receive (See Note D)	$____	
5. Credit balances in firm accounts which are attributable to principal sales to security-based swap customers	$____	
6. Market value of stock dividends, stock splits and similar distributions receivable outstanding over 30 calendar days	$____	
7. Market value of short security count differences over 30 calendar days old	$____	
8. Market value of short securities and credits (not to be offset by longs or by debits) in all suspense accounts over 30 calendar days	$____	
9. Market value of securities which are in transfer in excess of 40 calendar days and have not been confirmed to be in transfer by the transfer agent or the issuer during the 40 days	$____	
10. Debit balances in accounts carried for security-based swap customers, excluding unsecured accounts and accounts doubtful of collection (See Note E)	....	$____
11. Securities borrowed to effectuate short sales by security-based swap customers and securities borrowed to make delivery on security-based swap customers' securities failed to deliver	....	$____
12. Failed to deliver of security-based swap customers' securities not older than 30 calendar days	....	$____
13. Margin required and on deposit with the Options Clearing Corporation for all option contracts written or purchased in accounts carried for security-based swap customers (See Note F)	....	$____
14. Margin related to security futures products written, purchased or sold in accounts carried for security-based swap customers required and on deposit in a qualified clearing agency account at a clearing agency registered with the Commission under section 17A of the Act (15 U.S.C. 78q–1) or a derivatives clearing organization registered with the Commodity Futures Trading Commission under section 5b of the Commodity Exchange Act (7 U.S.C. 7a–1) (See Note G)	....	$____
15. Margin related to cleared security-based swap transactions in accounts carried for security-based swap customers required and on deposit in a qualified clearing agency account at a clearing agency registered with the Commission pursuant to section 17A of the Act (15 U.S.C. 78q–1)	....	$____
16. Margin related to non-cleared security-based swap transactions in accounts carried for security-based swap customers required and held in a qualified registered security-based swap dealer account at a security-based swap dealer or at a third-party custodial account	....	$____
Total Credits	$____	
Total Debits	....	$____
Excess of Credits over Debits	$____	

Note A. Item 1 must include all outstanding drafts payable to security-based swap customers which have been applied against free credit balances or other credit balances and must also include checks drawn in excess of bank balances per the records of the broker or dealer.

Note B. Item 2 must include the amount of options-related or security futures product-related Letters of Credit obtained by a member of a registered clearing agency or a derivatives clearing organization which are collateralized by security-based swap customers' securities, to the extent of the member's margin requirement at the registered clearing agency or derivatives clearing organization.

Note C. Item 3 must include in addition to monies payable against security-based swap customers' securities loaned the amount by which the market value of securities loaned exceeds the collateral value received from the lending of such securities.

Note D. Item 4 must include in addition to security-based swap customers' securities failed to receive the amount by which the market value of securities failed to receive and outstanding more than thirty (30) calendar days exceeds their contract value.

Note E. (1) Debit balances in accounts carried for security-based swap customers must be reduced by the amount by which a specific security (other than an exempted security) which is collateral for margin requirements exceeds in aggregate value 15 percent of the aggregate value of all securities which collateralize all accounts receivable; provided, however, the required reduction must not be in excess of the amount of the debit balance required to be excluded because of this concentration rule. A specified security is deemed to be collateral for an account only to the extent it is not an excess margin security.

(2) Debit balances in special omnibus accounts, maintained in compliance with the requirements of section 4(b) of Regulation T under the Act (12 CFR 220.4(b)) or similar accounts carried on behalf of a security-based swap dealer, must be reduced by any deficits in such accounts (or if a credit, such credit must be increased) less any calls for margin, marks to the market, or other required deposits which are outstanding 5 business days or less.

(3) Debit balances in security-based swap customers' accounts included in the formula under item 10 must be reduced by an amount equal to 1 percent of their aggregate value.

(4) Debit balances in accounts of household members and other persons related to principals of a broker or dealer and debit balances in accounts of affiliated persons of a broker or dealer must be excluded from the reserve formula, unless the broker or dealer can demonstrate that such debit balances are directly related to credit items in the formula.

(5) Debit balances in accounts (other than omnibus accounts) must be reduced by the amount by which any single security-based swap customer's debit balance exceeds 25 percent (to the extent such amount is greater than $50,000) of the broker's or dealer's tentative net capital (*i.e.*, net capital prior to securities haircuts) unless the broker or dealer can demonstrate that the debit balance is directly related to credit items in the Reserve Formula. Related accounts (e.g., ≤ the separate accounts of an individual, accounts under common control or subject to cross guarantees) will be deemed to be a single security-based swap customer's account for purposes of this provision.

If the registered national securities exchange or the registered national securities association having responsibility for examining the broker or dealer ("designated examining authority") is satisfied, after taking into account the circumstances of the concentrated account including the quality, diversity, and marketability of the collateral securing the debit balances in accounts subject to this provision, that the concentration of debit balances is appropriate, then such designated examining authority may, by order, grant a partial or plenary exception from this provision. The debit balance may be included in the reserve formula computation for five business days from the day the request is made.

§ 240.15c3-4

(6) Debit balances of joint accounts, custodian accounts, participations in hedge funds or limited partnerships or similar type accounts or arrangements that include both assets of a person who would be excluded from the definition of security-based swap customer ("non-security-based swap customer") and assets of a person or persons includible in the definition of security-based swap customer must be included in the Reserve Formula in the following manner: if the percentage ownership of the non-security-based swap customer is less than 5 percent then the entire debit balance shall be included in the formula; if such percentage ownership is between 5 percent and 50 percent then the portion of the debit balance attributable to the non-security-based swap customer must be excluded from the formula unless the broker or dealer can demonstrate that the debit balance is directly related to credit items in the formula; if such percentage ownership is greater than 50 percent, then the entire debit balance must be excluded from the formula unless the broker or dealer can demonstrate that the debit balance is directly related to credit items in the formula.

Note F. Item 13 must include the amount of margin required and on deposit with Options Clearing Corporation to the extent such margin is represented by cash, proprietary qualified securities, and letters of credit collateralized by security-based swap customers' securities.

Note G. (a) Item 14 must include the amount of margin required and on deposit with a clearing agency registered with the Commission under section 17A of the Act (15 U.S.C. 78q–1) or a derivatives clearing organization registered with the Commodity Futures Trading Commission under section 5b of the Commodity Exchange Act (7 U.S.C. 7a–1) for security-based swap customer accounts to the extent that the margin is represented by cash, proprietary qualified securities, and letters of credit collateralized by security-based swap customers' securities.

(b) Item 14 will apply only if the broker or dealer has the margin related to security futures products on deposit with:

(1) A registered clearing agency or derivatives clearing organization that:

(i) Maintains security deposits from clearing members in connection with regulated options or futures transactions and assessment power over member firms that equal a combined total of at least $2 billion, at least $500 million of which must be in the form of security deposits. For purposes of this Note G, the term "security deposits" refers to a general fund, other than margin deposits or their equivalent, that consists of cash or securities held by a registered clearing agency or derivative clearing organization;

(ii) Maintains at least $3 billion in margin deposits; or

(iii) Does not meet the requirements of paragraphs (b)(1)(i) through (b)(1)(ii) of this Note G, if the Commission has determined, upon a written request for exemption by or for the benefit of the broker or dealer, that the broker or dealer may utilize such a registered clearing agency or derivatives clearing organization. The Commission may, in its sole discretion, grant such an exemption subject to such conditions as are appropriate under the circumstances, if the Commission determines that such conditional or unconditional exemption is necessary or appropriate in the public interest, and is consistent with the protection of investors; and

(2) A registered clearing agency or derivatives clearing organization that, if it holds funds or securities deposited as margin for security futures products in a bank, as defined in section 3(a)(6) of the Act (15 U.S.C. 78c(a)(6)), obtains and preserves written notification from the bank at which it holds such funds and securities or at which such funds and securities are held on its behalf. The written notification will state that all funds and/or securities deposited with the bank as margin (including security-based swap customer security futures products margin), or held by the bank and pledged to such registered clearing agency or derivatives clearing agency as margin, are being held by the bank for the exclusive benefit of clearing members of the registered clearing agency or derivatives clearing organization (subject to the interest of such registered clearing agency or derivatives clearing organization therein), and are being kept separate from any other accounts maintained by the registered clearing agency or derivatives clearing organization with the bank. The written notification also will provide that such funds and/or securities will at no time be used directly or indirectly as security for a loan to the registered clearing agency or derivatives clearing organization by the bank, and will be subject to no right, charge, security interest, lien, or claim of any kind in favor of the bank or any person claiming through the bank. This provision, however, will not prohibit a registered clearing agency or derivatives clearing organization from pledging security-based swap customer funds or securities as collateral to a bank for any purpose that the rules of the Commission or the registered clearing agency or derivatives clearing organization otherwise permit; and

(3) A registered clearing agency or derivatives clearing organization that establishes, documents, and maintains:

(i) Safeguards in the handling, transfer, and delivery of cash and securities;

(ii) Fidelity bond coverage for its employees and agents who handle security-based swap customer funds or securities. In the case of agents of a registered clearing agency or derivatives clearing organization, the agent may provide the fidelity bond coverage; and

(iii) Provisions for periodic examination by independent public accountants; and

(4) A derivatives clearing organization that, if it is not otherwise registered with the Commission, has provided the Commission with a written undertaking, in a form acceptable to the Commission, executed by a duly authorized person at the derivatives clearing organization, to the effect that, with respect to the clearance and settlement of the security-based swap customer security futures products of the broker or dealer, the derivatives clearing organization will permit the Commission to examine the books and records of the derivatives clearing organization for compliance with the requirements set forth in § 240.15c3–3a, Note G. (b)(1) through (3).

(c) Item 14 will apply only if a broker or dealer determines, at least annually, that the registered clearing agency or derivatives clearing organization with which the broker or dealer has on deposit margin related to security futures products meets the conditions of this Note G.

[84 FR 44050, Aug. 22, 2019]

§ 240.15c3-4 Internal risk management control systems for OTC derivatives dealers.

(a) An OTC derivatives dealer shall establish, document, and maintain a system of internal risk management controls to assist it in managing the risks associated with its business activities, including market, credit, leverage, liquidity, legal, and operational risks.

(b) An OTC derivatives dealer shall consider the following when adopting its internal control system guidelines, policies, and procedures:

(1) The ownership and governance structure of the OTC derivatives dealer;

(2) The composition of the governing body of the OTC derivatives dealer;

(3) The management philosophy of the OTC derivatives dealer;

(4) The scope and nature of established risk management guidelines;

(5) The scope and nature of the permissible OTC derivatives activities;

(6) The sophistication and experience of relevant trading, risk management, and internal audit personnel;

Securities and Exchange Commission

§ 240.15c3-4

(7) The sophistication and functionality of information and reporting systems; and

(8) The scope and frequency of monitoring, reporting, and auditing activities.

(c) An OTC derivatives dealer's internal risk management control system shall include the following elements:

(1) A risk control unit that reports directly to senior management and is independent from business trading units;

(2) Separation of duties between personnel responsible for entering into a transaction and those responsible for recording the transaction in the books and records of the OTC derivatives dealer;

(3) Periodic reviews (which may be performed by internal audit staff) and annual reviews (which must be conducted by independent certified public accountants) of the OTC derivatives dealer's risk management systems;

(4) Definitions of risk, risk monitoring, and risk management; and

(5) Written guidelines, approved by the OTC derivatives dealer's governing body, that include and discuss the following:

(i) The OTC derivatives dealer's consideration of the elements in paragraph (b) of this section;

(ii) The scope, and the procedures for determining the scope, of authorized activities or any nonquantitative limitation on the scope of authorized activities;

(iii) Quantitative guidelines for managing the OTC derivatives dealer's overall risk exposure;

(iv) The type, scope, and frequency of reporting by management on risk exposures;

(v) The procedures for and the timing of the governing body's periodic review of the risk monitoring and risk management written guidelines, systems, and processes;

(vi) The process for monitoring risk independent of the business or trading units whose activities create the risks being monitored;

(vii) The performance of the risk management function by persons independent from or senior to the business or trading units whose activities create the risks;

(viii) The authority and resources of the groups or persons performing the risk monitoring and risk management functions;

(ix) The appropriate response by management when internal risk management guidelines have been exceeded;

(x) The procedures to monitor and address the risk that an OTC derivatives transaction contract will be unenforceable;

(xi) The procedures requiring the documentation of the principal terms of OTC derivatives transactions and other relevant information regarding such transactions;

(xii) The procedures authorizing specified employees to commit the OTC derivatives dealer to particular types of transactions;

(xiii) The procedures to prevent the OTC derivatives dealer from engaging in any securities transaction that is not permitted under § 240.15a-1; and

(xiv) The procedures to prevent the OTC derivatives dealer from improperly relying on the exceptions to § 240.15a-1(c) and § 240.15a-1(d), including the procedures to determine whether a counterparty is acting in the capacity of principal or agent.

(d) Management must periodically review, in accordance with written procedures, the OTC derivatives dealer's business activities for consistency with risk management guidelines including that:

(1) Risks arising from the OTC derivatives dealer's OTC derivatives activities are consistent with prescribed guidelines;

(2) Risk exposure guidelines for each business unit are appropriate for the business unit;

(3) The data necessary to conduct the risk monitoring and risk management function as well as the valuation process over the OTC derivatives dealer's portfolio of products is accessible on a timely basis and information systems are available to capture, monitor, analyze, and report relevant data;

(4) Procedures are in place to enable management to take action when internal risk management guidelines have been exceeded;

(5) Procedures are in place to monitor and address the risk that an OTC

495

§ 240.15c3-5

derivatives transaction contract will be unenforceable;

(6) Procedures are in place to identify and address any deficiencies in the operating systems and to contain the extent of losses arising from unidentified deficiencies;

(7) Procedures are in place to authorize specified employees to commit the OTC derivatives dealer to particular types of transactions, to specify any quantitative limits on such authority, and to provide for the oversight of their exercise of such authority;

(8) Procedures are in place to prevent the OTC derivatives dealer from engaging in any securities transaction that is not permitted under § 240.15a-1;

(9) Procedures are in place to prevent the OTC derivatives dealer from improperly relying on the exceptions to § 240.15a-1(c) and § 240.15a-1(d), including procedures to determine whether a counterparty is acting in the capacity of principal or agent;

(10) Procedures are in place to provide for adequate documentation of the principal terms of OTC derivatives transactions and other relevant information regarding such transactions;

(11) Personnel resources with appropriate expertise are committed to implementing the risk monitoring and risk management systems and processes; and

(12) Procedures are in place for the periodic internal and external review of the risk monitoring and risk management functions.

[63 FR 59400, Nov. 3, 1998]

§ 240.15c3-5 Risk management controls for brokers or dealers with market access.

(a) For the purpose of this section:

(1) The term *market access* shall mean:

(i) Access to trading in securities on an exchange or alternative trading system as a result of being a member or subscriber of the exchange or alternative trading system, respectively; or

(ii) Access to trading in securities on an alternative trading system provided by a broker-dealer operator of an alternative trading system to a non-broker-dealer.

(2) The term *regulatory requirements* shall mean all federal securities laws, rules and regulations, and rules of self-regulatory organizations, that are applicable in connection with market access.

(b) A broker or dealer with market access, or that provides a customer or any other person with access to an exchange or alternative trading system through use of its market participant identifier or otherwise, shall establish, document, and maintain a system of risk management controls and supervisory procedures reasonably designed to manage the financial, regulatory, and other risks of this business activity. Such broker or dealer shall preserve a copy of its supervisory procedures and a written description of its risk management controls as part of its books and records in a manner consistent with § 240.17a-4(e)(7). A broker-dealer that routes orders on behalf of an exchange or alternative trading system for the purpose of accessing other trading centers with protected quotations in compliance with Rule 611 of Regulation NMS (§ 242.611) for NMS stocks, or in compliance with a national market system plan for listed options, shall not be required to comply with this rule with regard to such routing services, except with regard to paragraph (c)(1)(ii) of this section.

(c) The risk management controls and supervisory procedures required by paragraph (b) of this section shall include the following elements:

(1) *Financial risk management controls and supervisory procedures.* The risk management controls and supervisory procedures shall be reasonably designed to systematically limit the financial exposure of the broker or dealer that could arise as a result of market access, including being reasonably designed to:

(i) Prevent the entry of orders that exceed appropriate pre-set credit or capital thresholds in the aggregate for each customer and the broker or dealer and, where appropriate, more finely-tuned by sector, security, or otherwise by rejecting orders if such orders would exceed the applicable credit or capital thresholds; and

(ii) Prevent the entry of erroneous orders, by rejecting orders that exceed appropriate price or size parameters, on an order-by-order basis or over a

Securities and Exchange Commission § 240.15c6-1

short period of time, or that indicate duplicative orders.

(2) *Regulatory risk management controls and supervisory procedures.* The risk management controls and supervisory procedures shall be reasonably designed to ensure compliance with all regulatory requirements, including being reasonably designed to:

(i) Prevent the entry of orders unless there has been compliance with all regulatory requirements that must be satisfied on a pre-order entry basis;

(ii) Prevent the entry of orders for securities for a broker or dealer, customer, or other person if such person is restricted from trading those securities;

(iii) Restrict access to trading systems and technology that provide market access to persons and accounts pre-approved and authorized by the broker or dealer; and

(iv) Assure that appropriate surveillance personnel receive immediate post-trade execution reports that result from market access.

(d) The financial and regulatory risk management controls and supervisory procedures described in paragraph (c) of this section shall be under the direct and exclusive control of the broker or dealer that is subject to paragraph (b) of this section.

(1) Notwithstanding the foregoing, a broker or dealer that is subject to paragraph (b) of this section may reasonably allocate, by written contract, after a thorough due diligence review, control over specific regulatory risk management controls and supervisory procedures described in paragraph (c)(2) of this section to a customer that is a registered broker or dealer, provided that such broker or dealer subject to paragraph (b) of this section has a reasonable basis for determining that such customer, based on its position in the transaction and relationship with an ultimate customer, has better access than the broker or dealer to that ultimate customer and its trading information such that it can more effectively implement the specified controls or procedures.

(2) Any allocation of control pursuant to paragraph (d)(1) of this section shall not relieve a broker or dealer that is subject to paragraph (b) of this section from any obligation under this section, including the overall responsibility to establish, document, and maintain a system of risk management controls and supervisory procedures reasonably designed to manage the financial, regulatory, and other risks of market access.

(e) A broker or dealer that is subject to paragraph (b) of this section shall establish, document, and maintain a system for regularly reviewing the effectiveness of the risk management controls and supervisory procedures required by paragraphs (b) and (c) of this section and for promptly addressing any issues.

(1) Among other things, the broker or dealer shall review, no less frequently than annually, the business activity of the broker or dealer in connection with market access to assure the overall effectiveness of such risk management controls and supervisory procedures. Such review shall be conducted in accordance with written procedures and shall be documented. The broker or dealer shall preserve a copy of such written procedures, and documentation of each such review, as part of its books and records in a manner consistent with § 240.17a–4(e)(7) and § 240.17a–4(b), respectively.

(2) The Chief Executive Officer (or equivalent officer) of the broker or dealer shall, on an annual basis, certify that such risk management controls and supervisory procedures comply with paragraphs (b) and (c) of this section, and that the broker or dealer conducted such review, and such certifications shall be preserved by the broker or dealer as part of its books and records in a manner consistent with § 240.17a–4(b).

(f) The Commission, by order, may exempt from the provisions of this section, either unconditionally or on specified terms and conditions, any broker or dealer, if the Commission determines that such exemption is necessary or appropriate in the public interest consistent with the protection of investors.

[75 FR 69825, Nov. 15, 2010]

§ 240.15c6-1 Settlement cycle.

(a) Except as provided in paragraphs (b), (c), and (d) of this section, a broker

§ 240.15c6–1

or dealer shall not effect or enter into a contract for the purchase or sale of a security (other than an exempted security, government security, municipal security, commercial paper, bankers' acceptances, or commercial bills) that provides for payment of funds and delivery of securities later than the second business day after the date of the contract unless otherwise expressly agreed to by the parties at the time of the transaction.

(b) Paragraphs (a) and (c) of this section shall not apply to contracts:

(1) For the purchase or sale of limited partnership interests that are not listed on an exchange or for which quotations are not disseminated through an automated quotation system of a registered securities association;

(2) For the purchase or sale of securities that the Commission may from time to time, taking into account then existing market practices, exempt by order from the requirements of paragraph (a) of this section, either unconditionally or on specified terms and conditions, if the Commission determines that such exemption is consistent with the public interest and the protection of investors.

(c) Paragraph (a) of this section shall not apply to contracts for the sale for cash of securities that are priced after 4:30 p.m. Eastern time on the date such securities are priced and that are sold by an issuer to an underwriter pursuant to a firm commitment underwritten offering registered under the Securities Act of 1933 or sold to an initial purchaser by a broker-dealer participating in such offering provided that a broker or dealer shall not effect or enter into a contract for the purchase or sale of such securities that provides for payment of funds and delivery of securities later than the fourth business day after the date of the contract unless otherwise expressly agreed to by the parties at the time of the transaction.

(d) For purposes of paragraphs (a) and (c) of this section, the parties to a contract shall be deemed to have expressly agreed to an alternate date for payment of funds and delivery of securities at the time of the transaction for a contract for the sale for cash of securities pursuant to a firm commitment offering if the managing underwriter and the issuer have agreed to such date for all securities sold pursuant to such offering and the parties to the contract have not expressly agreed to another date for payment of funds and delivery of securities at the time of the transaction.

[58 FR 52903, Oct. 13, 1993, as amended at 60 FR 26622, May 17, 1995; 82 FR 15601, Mar. 29, 2017]

EFFECTIVE DATE NOTE: 88 FR 13952, Mar. 6, 2023, § 240.15c6–1 was revised, effective May 5, 2023. For the convenience of the user, the revised text is set forth as follows:

§ 240.15c6–1 Settlement cycle.

(a) Except as provided in paragraphs (b), (c), and (d) of this section, a broker or dealer shall not effect or enter into a contract for the purchase or sale of a security (other than an exempted security, a government security, a municipal security, commercial paper, bankers' acceptances, or commercial bills) that provides for payment of funds and delivery of securities later than the first business day after the date of the contract unless otherwise expressly agreed to by the parties at the time of the transaction.

(b) Paragraph (a) of this section shall not apply to:

(1) Contracts for the purchase or sale of limited partnership interests that are not listed on an exchange or for which quotations are not disseminated through an automated quotation system of a registered securities association;

(2) Security-based swaps; or

(3) Contracts for the purchase or sale of securities that the Commission may from time to time, taking into account then existing market practices, exempt by order from the requirements of paragraph (a) of this section, either unconditionally or on specified terms and conditions, if the Commission determines that such exemption is consistent with the public interest and the protection of investors.

(c) Paragraph (a) of this section shall not apply to contracts for the sale for cash of securities that are priced after 4:30 p.m. Eastern Time (ET) on the date such securities are priced and that are sold by an issuer to an underwriter pursuant to a firm commitment underwritten offering registered under the Securities Act of 1933 or sold to an initial purchaser by a broker-dealer participating in such offering provided that a broker or dealer shall not effect or enter into a contract for the purchase or sale of such securities that provides for payment of funds and delivery of securities later than the second business day after the date of the contract unless

Securities and Exchange Commission § 240.15d-1

otherwise expressly agreed to by the parties at the time of the transaction.

(d) For purposes of paragraphs (a) and (c) of this section, the parties to a contract shall be deemed to have expressly agreed to an alternate date for payment of funds and delivery of securities at the time of the transaction for a contract for the sale for cash of securities pursuant to a firm commitment offering if the managing underwriter and the issuer have agreed to such date for all securities sold pursuant to such offering and the parties to the contract have not expressly agreed to another date for payment of funds and delivery of securities at the time of the transaction.

§ 240.15c6-2 Same-day allocation, confirmation, and affirmation.

(a) Any broker or dealer engaging in the allocation, confirmation, or affirmation process with another party or parties to achieve settlement of a securities transaction that is subject to the requirements of § 240.15c6-1(a) shall:

(1) Enter into a written agreement with the relevant parties to ensure completion of the allocation, confirmation, affirmation, or any combination thereof, for the transaction as soon as technologically practicable and no later than the end of the day on trade date in such form as necessary to achieve settlement of the transaction; or

(2) Establish, maintain, and enforce written policies and procedures reasonably designed to ensure completion of the allocation, confirmation, affirmation, or any combination thereof, for the transaction as soon as technologically practicable and no later than the end of the day on trade date in such form as necessary to achieve settlement of the transaction.

(b) To ensure completion of the allocation, confirmation, affirmation, or any combination thereof for the transaction as soon as technologically practicable and no later than the end of the day on trade date, the reasonably designed written policies and procedures required by paragraph (a)(2) of this section shall:

(1) Identify and describe any technology systems, operations, and processes that the broker or dealer uses to coordinate with other relevant parties, including investment advisers and custodians, to ensure completion of the allocation, confirmation, or affirmation process for the transaction;

(2) Set target time frames on trade date for completing the allocation, confirmation, and affirmation for the transaction;

(3) Describe the procedures that the broker or dealer will follow to ensure the prompt communication of trade information, investigate any discrepancies in trade information, and adjust trade information to help ensure that the allocation, confirmation, and affirmation can be completed by the target time frames on trade date;

(4) Describe how the broker or dealer plans to identify and address delays if another party, including an investment adviser or a custodian, is not promptly completing the allocation or affirmation for the transaction, or if the broker or dealer experiences delays in promptly completing the confirmation; and

(5) Measure, monitor, and document the rates of allocations, confirmations, and affirmations completed as soon as technologically practicable and no later than the end of the day on trade date.

[88 FR 13953, Mar. 6, 2023]

EFFECTIVE DATE NOTE: At 88 FR 13953, Mar. 6, 2023, § 240.15c6-2 was added, effective May 5, 2023.

REGULATION 15D: REPORTS OF REGISTRANTS UNDER THE SECURITIES ACT OF 1933

ANNUAL REPORTS

§ 240.15d-1 Requirement of annual reports.

Every registrant under the Securities Act of 1933 shall file an annual report, on the appropriate form authorized or prescribed therefor, for the fiscal year in which the registration statement under the Securities Act of 1933 became effective and for each fiscal year thereafter, unless the registrant is exempt from such filing by section 15(d) of the Act or rules thereunder. Annual reports shall be filed within the period specified in the appropriate report form.

[47 FR 17052, Apr. 21, 1982, as amended at 61 FR 49960, Sept. 24, 1996]

§ 240.15d-2 Special financial report.

(a) If the registration statement under the Securities Act of 1933 did not contain certified financial statements for the registrant's last full fiscal year (or for the life of the registrant if less than a full fiscal year) preceding the fiscal year in which the registration statement became effective, the registrant shall, within 90 days after the effective date of the registration statement, file a special report furnishing certified financial statements for such last full fiscal year or other period, as the case may be, meeting the requirements of the form appropriate for annual reports of the registrant. If the registrant is a foreign private issuer as defined in § 230.405 of this chapter, then the special financial report shall be filed on the appropriate form for annual reports of the registrant and shall be filed by the later of 90 days after the date on which the registration statement became effective, or four months following the end of the registrant's latest full fiscal year.

(b) The report shall be filed under cover of the facing sheet of the form appropriate for annual reports of the registrant, shall indicate on the facing sheet that it contains only financial statements for the fiscal year in question, and shall be signed in accordance with the requirements of the annual report form.

[13 FR 9326, Dec. 31, 1948, as amended at 36 FR 1891, Feb. 3, 1971; 58 FR 60306, Nov. 15, 1993; 73 FR 58324, Oct. 6, 2008; 83 FR 50222, Oct. 4, 2018]

§ 240.15d-3 Reports for depositary shares registered on Form F-6.

Annual and other reports are not required with respect to Depositary Shares registered on Form F-6 (§ 230.36 of this chapter). The exemption in this section does not apply to any deposited securities registered on any other form under the Securities Act of 1933.

[62 FR 39768, July 24, 1997]

§ 240.15d-4 Reporting by Form 40-F registrants.

A registrant that is eligible to use Forms 40-F and 6-K and files reports in accordance therewith shall be deemed to satisfy the requirements of Regulation 15D (§§ 240.15d-1 through 240.15d-21 of this chapter).

[56 FR 30075, July 1, 1991]

§ 240.15d-5 Reporting by successor issuers.

(a) Where in connection with a succession by merger, consolidation, exchange of securities, acquisition of assets or otherwise, securities of any issuer that is not required to file reports pursuant to section 15(d) (15 U.S.C. 78o(d)) of the Act are issued to the holders of any class of securities of another issuer that is required to file such reports, the duty to file reports pursuant to such section shall be deemed to have been assumed by the issuer of the class of securities so issued. The successor issuer shall, after the consummation of the succession, file reports in accordance with section 15(d) of the Act (15 U.S.C. 78o(d)) and the rules and regulations thereunder, unless that issuer is exempt from filing such reports or the duty to file such reports is suspended under section 15(d) of the Act (15 U.S.C. 78o(d)).

(b) An issuer that is deemed to be a successor issuer according to paragraph (a) of this section shall file reports on the same forms as the predecessor issuer except as follows:

(1) An issuer that is not a foreign issuer shall not be eligible to file on Form 20-F (§ 240.220f of this chapter).

(2) A foreign private issuer shall be eligible to file on Form 20-F.

(c) The provisions of paragraph (a) of this section shall not apply to an issuer of securities in connection with a succession that was registered on Form F-8 (§ 239.38 of this chapter), Form F-10 (§ 239.40 of this chapter) or Form F-80 (§ 239.41 of this chapter).

[36 FR 3805, Feb. 27, 1971, as amended at 48 FR 46740, Oct. 14, 1983; 56 FR 30075, July 1, 1991; 62 FR 39768, July 24, 1997]

§ 240.15d-6 Suspension of duty to file reports.

If the duty of an issuer to file reports pursuant to section 15(d) of the Act as to any fiscal year is suspended as provided in section 15(d) of the Act, such issuer shall, within 30 days after the beginning of the first fiscal year, file a notice on Form 15 informing the Commission of such suspension unless

Securities and Exchange Commission

§ 240.15d-10

Form 15 has already been filed pursuant to Rule 12h-3. If the suspension resulted from the issuer's merger into, or consolidation with, another issuer or issuers, the notice shall be filed by the successor issuer.

(Secs. 12(g)(4), 12(h), 13(a), 15(d), 23(a), 48 Stat. 892, 894, 895, 901; sec. 203(a), 49 Stat. 704; secs. 3, 8, 49 Stat. 1377, 1379; secs. 3, 4, 6, 78 Stat. 565–568, 569, 570–574; sec. 18, 89 Stat. 155; sec. 204, 91 Stat. 1500; 15 U.S.C. 78l(g)(4), 78l(h), 78m(a), 78o(d), 78w(a))

[49 FR 12690, Mar. 30, 1984]

OTHER REPORTS

§ 240.15d-10 Transition reports.

(a) Every issuer that changes its fiscal closing date shall file a report covering the resulting transition period between the closing date of its most recent fiscal year and the opening date of its new fiscal year; *Provided, however,* that an issuer shall file an annual report for any fiscal year that ended before the date on which the issuer determined to change its fiscal year end. In no event shall the transition report cover a period of 12 or more months.

(b) The report pursuant to this section shall be filed for the transition period not more than the number of days specified in paragraph (j) of this section after either the close of the transition period or the date of the determination to change the fiscal closing date, whichever is later. The report shall be filed on the form appropriate for annual reports of the issuer, shall cover the period from the close of the last fiscal year end and shall indicate clearly the period covered. The financial statements for the transition period filed therewith shall be audited. Financial statements, which may be unaudited, shall be filed for the comparable period of the prior year, or a footnote, which may be unaudited, shall state for the comparable period of the prior year, revenues, gross profits, income taxes, income or loss from continuing operations and net income or loss. The effects of any discontinued operations as classified under the provisions of generally accepted accounting principles also shall be shown, if applicable. Per share data based upon such income or loss and net income or loss shall be presented in conformity with applicable accounting standards. Where called for by the time span to be covered, the comparable period financial statements or footnote shall be included in subsequent filings.

(c) If the transition period covers a period of less than six months, in lieu of the report required by paragraph (b) of this section, a report may be filed for the transition period on Form 10-Q (§ 249.308 of this chapter) not more than the number of days specified in paragraph (j) of this section after either the close of the transition period or the date of the determination to change the fiscal closing date, whichever is later. The report on Form 10-Q shall cover the period from the close of the last fiscal year end and shall indicate clearly the period covered. The financial statements filed therewith need not be audited but, if they are not audited, the issuer shall file with the first annual report for the newly adopted fiscal year separate audited statements of income and cash flows covering the transition period. The notes to financial statements for the transition period included in such first annual report may be integrated with the notes to financial statements for the full fiscal period. A separate audited balance sheet as of the end of the transition period shall be filed in the annual report only if the audited balance sheet as of the end of the fiscal year before the transition period is not filed. Schedules need not be filed in transition reports on Form 10-Q.

(d) Notwithstanding the foregoing in paragraphs (a), (b), and (c) of this section, if the transition period covers a period of one month or less, the issuer need not file a separate transition report if either:

(1) The first report required to be filed by the issuer for the newly adopted fiscal year after the date of the determination to change the fiscal year end is an annual report, and that report covers the transition period as well as the fiscal year; or

(2)(i) The issuer files with the first annual report for the newly adopted fiscal year separate audited statements of income and cash flows covering the transition period; and

§ 240.15d-10

(ii) The first report required to be filed by the issuer for the newly adopted fiscal year after the date of the determination to change the fiscal year end is a quarterly report on Form 10–Q; and

(iii) Information on the transition period is included in the issuer's quarterly report on Form 10–Q for the first quarterly period (except the fourth quarter) of the newly adopted fiscal year that ends after the date of the determination to change the fiscal year. The information covering the transition period required by Part II and Item 2 of Part I may be combined with the information regarding the quarter. However, the financial statements required by Part I, which may be unaudited, shall be furnished separately for the transition period.

(e) Every issuer required to file quarterly reports on Form 10–Q pursuant to § 240.15d–13 that changes its fiscal year end shall:

(1) File a quarterly report on Form 10–Q within the time period specified in General Instruction A.1. to that form for any quarterly period (except the fourth quarter) of the old fiscal year that ends before the date on which the issuer determined to change its fiscal year end, except that the issuer need not file such quarterly report if the date on which the quarterly period ends also is the date on which the transition period ends;

(2) File a quarterly report on Form 10–Q within the time specified in General Instruction A.1 to that form for each quarterly period of the old fiscal year within the transition period. In lieu of a quarterly report for any quarter of the old fiscal year within the transition period, the issuer may file a quarterly report on Form 10–Q for any period of three months within the transition period that coincides with a quarter of the newly adopted fiscal year if the quarterly report is filed within the number of days specified in paragraph (j) of this section after the end of such three month period, provided the issuer thereafter continues filing quarterly reports on the basis of the quarters of the newly adopted fiscal year;

(3) Commence filing quarterly reports for the quarters of the new fiscal year no later than the quarterly report for the first quarter of the new fiscal year that ends after the date on which the issuer determined to change the fiscal year end; and

(4) Unless such information is or will be included in the transition report, or the first annual report on Form 10–K for the newly adopted fiscal year, include in the initial quarterly report on Form 10–Q for the newly adopted fiscal year information on any period beginning on the first day after the period covered by the issuer's final quarterly report on Form 10–Q or annual report on Form 10–K for the old fiscal year. The information covering such period required by Part II and Item 2 of Part I may be combined with the information regarding the quarter. However, the financial statements required by Part I, which may be unaudited, shall be furnished separately for such period.

NOTE TO PARAGRAPHS (c) AND (e): If it is not practicable or cannot be cost-justified to furnish in a transition report on Form 10–Q or a quarterly report for the newly adopted fiscal year financial statements for corresponding periods of the prior year where required, financial statements may be furnished for the quarters of the preceding fiscal year that most nearly are comparable if the issuer furnishes an adequate discussion of seasonal and other factors that could affect the comparability of information or trends reflected, an assessment of the comparability of the data, and a representation as to the reason recasting has not been undertaken.

(f) Every successor issuer that has a different fiscal year from that of its predecessor(s) shall file a transition report pursuant to this section, containing the required information about each predecessor, for the transition period, if any, between the close of the fiscal year covered by the last annual report of each predecessor and the date of succession. The report shall be filed for the transition period on the form appropriate for annual reports of the issuer not more than the number of days specified in paragraph (j) of this section after the date of the succession, with financial statements in conformity with the requirements set forth in paragraph (b) of this section. If the transition period covers a period of less than six months, in lieu of a transition report on the form appropriate

Securities and Exchange Commission § 240.15d-10

for the issuer's annual reports, the report may be filed for the transition period on Form 10-Q not more than the number of days specified in paragraph (j) of this section after the date of the succession, with financial statements in conformity with the requirements set forth in paragraph (c) of this section. Notwithstanding the foregoing, if the transition period covers a period of one month or less, the successor issuer need not file a separate transition report if the information is reported by the successor issuer in conformity with the requirements set forth in paragraph (d) of this section.

(g)(1) Paragraphs (a) through (f) of this section shall not apply to foreign private issuers.

(2) Every foreign private issuer that changes its fiscal closing date shall file a report covering the resulting transition period between the closing date of its most recent year and the opening date of its new fiscal year. In no event shall a transition report cover a period longer than 12 months.

(3) The report for the transition period shall be filed on Form 20-F (§ 249.220f of this chapter) responding to all items to which such issuer is required to respond when Form 20-F is used as an annual report. The financial statements for the transition period filed therewith shall be audited. The report shall be filed within four months after either the close of the transition period or the date on which the issuer made the determination to change the fiscal closing date, whichever is later.

(4) If the transition period covers a period of six or fewer months, in lieu of the report required by paragraph (g)(3) of this section, a report for the transition period may be filed on Form 20-F responding to Items 5, 8.A.7., 13, 14, and 17 or 18 within three months after either the close of the transition period or the date on which the issuer made the determination to change the fiscal closing date, whichever is later. The financial statements required by either Item 17 or Item 18 shall be furnished for the transition period. Such financial statements may be unaudited and condensed as permitted in Article 10 of Regulation S-X (§ 210.10-01 of this chapter), but if the financial statements are unaudited and condensed, the issuer shall file with the first annual report for the newly adopted fiscal year separate audited statements of income and cash flows covering the transition period.

(5) Notwithstanding the foregoing in paragraphs (g)(2), (g)(3), and (g)(4) of this section, if the transition period covers a period of one month or less, a foreign private issuer need not file a separate transition report if the first annual report for the newly adopted fiscal year covers the transition period as well as the fiscal year.

(h) The provisions of this rule shall not apply to investment companies required to file reports pursuant to Rule 30a-1 (§ 270.30a-1 of this chapter) under the Investment Company Act of 1940 (15 U.S.C. 80a-1 et seq.).

(i) No filing fee shall be required for a transition report filed pursuant to this section.

(j)(1) For transition reports to be filed on the form appropriate for annual reports of the issuer, the number of days shall be:

(i) 60 days (75 days for fiscal years ending before December 15, 2006) for large accelerated filers (as defined in § 240.12b-2);

(ii) 75 days for accelerated filers (as defined in § 240.12b-2); and

(iii) 90 days for all other issuers; and

(2) For transition reports to be filed on Form 10-Q (§ 249.308 of this chapter), the number of days shall be:

(i) 40 days for large accelerated filers and accelerated filers (as defined in § 240.12b-2); and

(ii) 45 days for all other issuers.

(k)(1) Paragraphs (a) through (g) of this section shall not apply to asset-backed issuers.

(2) Every asset-backed issuer that changes its fiscal closing date shall file a report covering the resulting transition period between the closing date of its most recent fiscal year and the opening date of its new fiscal year. In no event shall a transition report cover a period longer than 12 months.

(3) The report for the transition period shall be filed on Form 10-K (§ 249.310 of this chapter) responding to all items to which such asset-backed issuer is required to respond pursuant to General Instruction J. of Form 10-K. Such report shall be filed within 90

§ 240.15d-11

days after the later of either the close of the transition period or the date on which the issuer made the determination to change the fiscal closing date.

(4) Notwithstanding the foregoing in paragraphs (k)(2) and (k)(3) of this section, if the transition period covers a period of one month or less, an asset-backed issuer need not file a separate transition report if the first annual report for the newly adopted fiscal year covers the transition period as well as the fiscal year.

(5) Any obligation of the asset-backed issuer to file distribution reports pursuant to § 240.15d-17 will continue to apply regardless of a change in the asset-backed issuer's fiscal closing date.

NOTE 1: In addition to the report or reports required to be filed pursuant to this section, every issuer, except a foreign private issuer or an investment company required to file reports pursuant to § 270.30b1-1 of this chapter, that changes its fiscal closing date is required to file a Form 8-K (§ 249.308 of this chapter) report that includes the information required by Item 5.03 of Form 8-K within the period specified in General Instruction B.1. to that form.

NOTE 2: The report or reports to be filed pursuant to this section must include the certification required by § 240.15d-14.

[54 FR 10318, Mar. 13, 1989, as amended at 56 FR 30075, July 1, 1991; 64 FR 53912, Oct. 5, 1999; 67 FR 57289, Sept. 9, 2002; 67 FR 58505, Sept. 16, 2002; 69 FR 15618, Mar. 25, 2004; 69 FR 68236, Nov. 23, 2004; 70 FR 1622, Jan. 7, 2005; 70 FR 76642, Dec. 27, 2005; 73 FR 978, Jan. 4, 2008; 73 FR 58324, Oct. 6, 2008; 81 FR 82020, Nov. 18, 2016; 83 FR 50222, Oct. 4, 2018]

§ 240.15d-11 Current reports on Form 8-K (§ 249.308 of this chapter).

(a) Except as provided in paragraph (b) of this section, every registrant subject to § 240.15d-1 shall file a current report on Form 8-K within the period specified in that form unless substantially the same information as that required by Form 8-K has been previously reported by the registrant.

(b) This section shall not apply to foreign governments, foreign private issuers required to make reports on Form 6-K (17 CFR 249.306) pursuant to § 240.15d-16, issuers of American Depositary Receipts for securities of any foreign issuer, or investment companies required to file reports pursuant to § 270.30a-1 of this chapter under the Investment Company Act of 1940, except where such an investment company is required to file:

(1) Notice of a blackout period pursuant to § 245.104 of this chapter;

(2) Disclosure pursuant to Instruction 2 to § 240.14a-11(b)(1) of information concerning outstanding shares and voting; or

(3) Disclosure pursuant to Instruction 2 to § 240.14a-11(b)(10) of the date by which a nominating shareholder or nominating shareholder group must submit the notice required pursuant to § 240.14a-11(b)(10).

(c) No failure to file a report on Form 8-K that is required solely pursuant to Item 1.01, 1.02, 2.03, 2.04, 2.05, 2.06, 4.02(a), 5.02(e) or 6.03 of Form 8-K shall be deemed to be a violation of 15 U.S.C. 78j(b) and § 240.10b-5.

[42 FR 4429, Jan. 25, 1977, as amended at 50 FR 27939, July 9, 1985; 68 FR 4355, Jan. 28, 2002; 69 FR 15618, Mar. 25, 2004; 70 FR 1622, Jan. 7, 2005; 71 FR 53263, Sept. 8, 2006; 75 FR 56792, Sept. 16, 2010; 81 FR 82020, Nov. 18, 2016]

§ 240.15d-13 Quarterly reports on Form 10-Q (§ 249.308 of this chapter).

(a) Except as provided in paragraphs (b) and (c) of this section, every issuer that has securities registered pursuant to the Securities Act and is required to file annual reports pursuant to section 15(d) of the Act on Form 10-K (§ 249.310 of this chapter) shall file a quarterly report on Form 10-Q (§ 249.308 of this chapter) within the period specified in General Instruction A.1 to that form for each of the first three quarters of each fiscal year of the issuer, commencing with the first fiscal quarter following the most recent fiscal year for which full financial statements were included in the registration statement, or, if the registration statement included financial statements for an interim period after the most recent fiscal year end meeting the requirements of Article 10 of Regulation S-X, or Rule 8-03 of Regulation S-X for smaller reporting companies, for the first fiscal quarter after the quarter reported upon in the registration statement. The first quarterly report of the issuer shall be filed either within 45 days after the effective date of the registration statement or on or before the

Securities and Exchange Commission § 240.15d-14

date on which such report would have been required to be filed if the issuer had been required to file reports on Form 10-Q as of its last fiscal quarter, whichever is later.

(b) The provisions of this rule shall not apply to the following issuers:

(1) Investment companies required to file reports pursuant to § 270.30a-1;

(2) Foreign private issuers required to file reports pursuant to § 240.15d-16; and

(3) Asset-backed issuers required to file reports pursuant to § 240.15d-17.

(c) Part I of the quarterly reports on Form 10-Q need not be filed by:

(1) Mutual life insurance companies; or

(2) Mining companies not in the production stage but engaged primarily in the exploration for the development of mineral deposits other than oil, gas or coal, if all of the following conditions are met:

(i) The registrant has not been in production during the current fiscal year or the two years immediately prior thereto; except that being in production for an aggregate period of not more than eight months over the three-year period shall not be a violation of this condition.

(ii) Receipts from the sale of mineral products or from the operations of mineral producing properties by the registrant and its subsidiaries combined have not exceeded $500,000 in any of the most recent six years and have not aggregated more than $1,500,000 in the most recent six fiscal years.

(d) Notwithstanding the foregoing provisions of this section, the financial information required by Part I of Form 10-Q shall not be deemed to be "filed" for the purpose of section 18 of the Act or otherwise subject to the liabilities of that section of the Act, but shall be subject to all other provisions of the Act.

(e) Notwithstanding the foregoing provisions of this section, the financial information required by Part I of Form 10-Q, or financial information submitted in lieu thereof pursuant to paragraph (d) of this section, shall not be deemed to be "filed" for the purpose of section 18 of the Act or otherwise subject to the liabilities of that section of the Act, but shall be subject to all other provisions of the Act.

[42 FR 24065, May 12, 1977, as amended at 46 FR 63255, Dec. 31, 1981; 50 FR 27939, July 9, 1985; 54 FR 10319, Mar. 13, 1989, 61 FR 30403, June 14, 1996; 70 FR 1622, Jan. 7, 2005; 73 FR 978, Jan. 4, 2008; 81 FR 82020, Nov. 18, 2016]

§ 240.15d-14 Certification of disclosure in annual and quarterly reports.

(a) Each report, including transition reports, filed on Form 10-Q, Form 10-K, Form 20-F or Form 40-F (§ 249.308a, § 249.310, § 249.220f or § 249.240f of this chapter) under section 15(d) of the Act (15 U.S.C. 78o(d)), other than a report filed by an Asset-Backed Issuer (as defined in § 229.1101 of this chapter) or a report on Form 20-F filed under § 240.15d-19, must include certifications in the form specified in the applicable exhibit filing requirements of such report, and such certifications must be filed as an exhibit to such report. Each principal executive and principal financial officer of the issuer, or persons performing similar functions, at the time of filing of the report must sign a certification. The principal executive and principal financial officers of an issuer may omit the portion of the introductory language in paragraph 4 as well as language in paragraph 4(b) of the certification that refers to the certifying officers' responsibility for designing, establishing and maintaining internal control over financial reporting for the issuer until the issuer becomes subject to the internal control over financial reporting requirements in § 240.13a-15 or § 240.15d-15.

(b) Each periodic report containing financial statements filed by an issuer pursuant to section 15(d) of the Act (15 U.S.C. 78o(d)) must be accompanied by the certifications required by Section 1350 of Chapter 63 of Title 18 of the United States Code (18 U.S.C. 1350) and such certifications must be furnished as an exhibit to such report as specified in the applicable exhibit requirements for such report. Each principal executive and principal financial officer of the issuer (or equivalent thereof) must sign a certification. This requirement may be satisfied by a single certification signed by an issuer's principal executive and principal financial officers.

505

§ 240.15d–15

(c) A person required to provide a certification specified in paragraph (a), (b) or (d) of this section may not have the certification signed on his or her behalf pursuant to a power of attorney or other form of confirming authority.

(d) Each annual report and transition report filed on Form 10–K (§ 249.310 of this chapter) by an asset-backed issuer under section 15(d) of the Act (15 U.S.C. 78o(d)) must include a certification in the form specified in the applicable exhibit filing requirements of such report and such certification must be filed as an exhibit to such report. Terms used in paragraphs (d) and (e) of this section have the same meaning as in Item 1101 of Regulation AB (§ 229.1101 of this chapter).

(e) With respect to asset-backed issuers, the certification required by paragraph (d) of this section must be signed by either:

(1) The senior officer in charge of securitization of the depositor if the depositor is signing the report; or

(2) The senior officer in charge of the servicing function of the servicer if the servicer is signing the report on behalf of the issuing entity. If multiple servicers are involved in servicing the pool assets, the senior officer in charge of the servicing function of the master servicer (or entity performing the equivalent function) must sign if a representative of the servicer is to sign the report on behalf of the issuing entity.

(f) The certification requirements of this section do not apply to an Interactive Data File, as defined in § 232.11 of this chapter (Rule 11 of Regulation S–T).

[67 FR 57289, Sept. 9, 2002, as amended at 68 FR 36666, June 18, 2003; 70 FR 1622, Jan. 7, 2005; 70 FR 6572, Feb. 8, 2005; 70 FR 42247, July 21, 2005; 71 FR 76596, Dec. 21, 2006; 73 FR 979, Jan. 4, 2008; 74 FR 6819, Feb. 10, 2009; 83 FR 40878, Aug. 16, 2018]

§ 240.15d–15 Controls and procedures.

(a) Every issuer that files reports under section 15(d) of the Act (15 U.S.C. 78o(d)), other than an Asset Backed Issuer (as defined in § 229.1101 of this chapter), a small business investment company registered on Form N–5 (§§ 239.24 and 274.5 of this chapter), or a unit investment trust as defined in section 4(2) of the Investment Company Act of 1940 (15 U.S.C. 80a–4(2)), must maintain disclosure controls and procedures (as defined in paragraph (e) of this section) and, if the issuer either had been required to file an annual report pursuant to section 13(a) or 15(d) of the Act (15 U.S.C. 78m(a) or 78o(d)) for the prior fiscal year or had filed an annual report with the Commission for the prior fiscal year, internal control over financial reporting (as defined in paragraph (f) of this section).

(b) Each such issuer's management must evaluate, with the participation of the issuer's principal executive and principal financial officers, or persons performing similar functions, the effectiveness of the issuer's disclosure controls and procedures, as of the end of each fiscal quarter, except that management must perform this evaluation:

(1) In the case of a foreign private issuer (as defined in § 240.3b–4) as of the end of each fiscal year; and

(2) In the case of an investment company registered under section 8 of the Investment Company Act of 1940 (15 U.S.C. 80a–8), within the 90-day period prior to the filing date of each report requiring certification under § 270.30a–2 of this chapter.

(c) The management of each such issuer, that either had been required to file an annual report pursuant to section 13(a) or 15(d) of the Act (15 U.S.C. 78m(a) or 78o(d)) for the prior fiscal year or previously had filed an annual report with the Commission for the prior fiscal year, other than an investment company registered under section 8 of the Investment Company Act of 1940, must evaluate, with the participation of the issuer's principal executive and principal financial officers, or persons performing similar functions, the effectiveness, as of the end of each fiscal year, of the issuer's internal control over financial reporting. The framework on which management's evaluation of the issuer's internal control over financial reporting is based must be a suitable, recognized control framework that is established by a body or group that has followed due-process procedures, including the broad distribution of the framework for public comment. Although there are many

Securities and Exchange Commission §240.15d-16

different ways to conduct an evaluation of the effectiveness of internal control over financial reporting to meet the requirements of this paragraph, an evaluation that is conducted in accordance with the interpretive guidance issued by the Commission in Release No. 34-55929 will satisfy the evaluation required by this paragraph.

(d) The management of each such issuer that previously either had been required to file an annual report pursuant to section 13(a) or 15(d) of the Act (15 U.S.C. 78m(a) or 78o(d)) for the prior fiscal year or previously had filed an annual report with the Commission for the prior fiscal year, other than an investment company registered under section 8 of the Investment Company Act of 1940 (15 U.S.C. 80a-8), must evaluate, with the participation of the issuer's principal executive and principal financial officers, or persons performing similar functions, any change in the issuer's internal control over financial reporting, that occurred during each of the issuer's fiscal quarters, or fiscal year in the case of a foreign private issuer, that has materially affected, or is reasonably likely to materially affect, the issuer's internal control over financial reporting.

(e) For purposes of this section, the term disclosure controls and procedures means controls and other procedures of an issuer that are designed to ensure that information required to be disclosed by the issuer in the reports that it files or submits under the Act (15 U.S.C. 78a et seq.) is recorded, processed, summarized and reported, within the time periods specified in the Commission's rules and forms. Disclosure controls and procedures include, without limitation, controls and procedures designed to ensure that information required to be disclosed by an issuer in the reports that it files or submits under the Act is accumulated and communicated to the issuer's management, including its principal executive and principal financial officers, or persons performing similar functions, as appropriate to allow timely decisions regarding required disclosure.

(f) The term *internal control over financial reporting* is defined as a process designed by, or under the supervision of, the issuer's principal executive and principal financial officers, or persons performing similar functions, and effected by the issuer's board of directors, management and other personnel, to provide reasonable assurance regarding the reliability of financial reporting and the preparation of financial statements for external purposes in accordance with generally accepted accounting principles and includes those policies and procedures that:

(1) Pertain to the maintenance of records that in reasonable detail accurately and fairly reflect the transactions and dispositions of the assets of the issuer;

(2) Provide reasonable assurance that transactions are recorded as necessary to permit preparation of financial statements in accordance with generally accepted accounting principles, and that receipts and expenditures of the issuer are being made only in accordance with authorizations of management and directors of the issuer; and

(3) Provide reasonable assurance regarding prevention or timely detection of unauthorized acquisition, use or disposition of the issuer's assets that could have a material effect on the financial statements.

[68 FR 36667, June 18, 2003, as amended at 70 FR 1622, Jan. 7, 2005; 71 FR 76596, Dec. 21, 2006; 72 FR 35322, June 27, 2007]

§240.15d-16 Reports of foreign private issuers on Form 6-K [17 CFR 249.306].

(a) Every foreign private issuer which is subject to Rule 15d-1 [17 CFR 240.15d-1] shall make reports on Form 6-K, except that this rule shall not apply to:

(1) Investment companies required to file reports pursuant to §270.30a-1 of this chapter;

(2) Issuers of American depositary receipts for securities of any foreign issuer; and

(3) Asset-backed issuers, as defined in §229.1101 of this chapter.

(b) Such reports shall be transmitted promptly after the information required by Form 6-K is made public by the issuer, by the country of its domicile or under the laws of which it was incorporated or organized or by a foreign securities exchange with which the issuer has filed the information.

§ 240.15d–17

(c) Reports furnished pursuant to this rule shall not be deemed to be "filed" for the purpose of section 18 of the Act or otherwise subject to the liabilities of that section.

[32 FR 7849, May 30, 1967, as amended at 44 FR 70137, Dec. 6, 1979; 47 FR 54781, Dec. 6, 1982; 50 FR 27939, July 9, 1985; 56 FR 30075, July 1, 1991; 70 FR 1622, Jan. 7, 2005; 81 FR 82020, Nov. 18, 2016]

§ 240.15d–17 Reports of asset-backed issuers on Form 10–D (§ 249.312 of this chapter).

Every asset-backed issuer subject to § 240.15d–1 shall make reports on Form 10–D (§ 249.312 of this chapter). Such reports shall be filed within the period specified in Form 10–D.

[70 FR 1622, Jan. 7, 2005]

§ 240.15d–18 Compliance with servicing criteria for asset-backed securities.

(a) This section applies to every class of asset-backed securities subject to the reporting requirements of section 15(d) of the Act (15 U.S.C. 78o(d)). Terms used in this section have the same meaning as in Item 1101 of Regulation AB (§ 229.1101 of this chapter).

(b) *Reports on assessments of compliance with servicing criteria for asset-backed securities required.* With regard to a class of asset-backed securities subject to the reporting requirements of section 15(d) of the Act, the annual report on Form 10–K (§ 249.308 of this chapter) for such class must include from each party participating in the servicing function a report regarding its assessment of compliance with the servicing criteria specified in paragraph (d) of Item 1122 of Regulation AB (§ 229.1122(d) of this chapter), as of and for the period ending the end of each fiscal year, with respect to asset-backed securities transactions taken as a whole involving the party participating in the servicing function and that are backed by the same asset type backing the class of asset-backed securities (including the asset-backed securities transaction that is to be the subject of the report on Form 10–K for that fiscal year).

(c) *Attestation reports on assessments of compliance with servicing criteria for asset-backed securities required.* With respect to each report included pursuant to paragraph (b) of this section, the annual report on Form 10–K must also include a report by a registered public accounting firm that attests to, and reports on, the assessment made by the asserting party. The attestation report on assessment of compliance with servicing criteria for asset-backed securities must be made in accordance with standards for attestation engagements issued or adopted by the Public Company Accounting Oversight Board.

NOTE TO § 240.15d–18: If multiple parties are participating in the servicing function, a separate assessment report and attestation report must be included for each party participating in the servicing function. A party participating in the servicing function means any entity (e.g., master servicer, primary servicers, trustees) that is performing activities that address the criteria in paragraph (d) of Item 1122 of Regulation AB (§ 229.1122(d) of this chapter), unless such entity's activities relate only to 5% or less of the pool assets.

[70 FR 1622, Jan. 7, 2005]

§ 240.15d–19 Reports by shell companies on Form 20–F.

Every foreign private issuer that was a shell company, other than a business combination related shell company, immediately before a transaction that causes it to cease to be a shell company shall, within four business days of completion of that transaction, file a report on Form 20–F (§ 249.220f of this chapter) containing the information that would be required if the issuer were filing a form for registration of securities on Form 20–F to register under the Act all classes of the issuer's securities subject to the reporting requirements of section 13 (15 U.S.C. 78m) or section 15(d) (15 U.S.C. 78o(d)) of the Act upon consummation of the transaction, with such information reflecting the registrant and its securities upon consummation of the transaction.

[70 FR 42247, July 21, 2005]

§ 240.15d–20 Plain English presentation of specified information.

(a) Any information included or incorporated by reference in a report filed under section 15(d) of the Act (15 U.S.C. 78o(d)) that is required to be disclosed pursuant to Item 402, 403, 404 or

Securities and Exchange Commission

§ 240.15d-22

407 of Regulation S-K (§ 229.402, § 229.403, § 229.404 or § 229.407 of this chapter) must be presented in a clear, concise and understandable manner. You must prepare the disclosure using the following standards:

(1) Present information in clear, concise sections, paragraphs and sentences;

(2) Use short sentences;

(3) Use definite, concrete, everyday words;

(4) Use the active voice;

(5) Avoid multiple negatives;

(6) Use descriptive headings and subheadings;

(7) Use a tabular presentation or bullet lists for complex material, wherever possible;

(8) Avoid legal jargon and highly technical business and other terminology;

(9) Avoid frequent reliance on glossaries or defined terms as the primary means of explaining information. Define terms in a glossary or other section of the document only if the meaning is unclear from the context. Use a glossary only if it facilitates understanding of the disclosure; and

(10) In designing the presentation of the information you may include pictures, logos, charts, graphs and other design elements so long as the design is not misleading and the required information is clear. You are encouraged to use tables, schedules, charts and graphic illustrations that present relevant data in an understandable manner, so long as such presentations are consistent with applicable disclosure requirements and consistent with other information in the document. You must draw graphs and charts to scale. Any information you provide must not be misleading.

(b) [Reserved]

NOTE TO § 240.15d-20: In drafting the disclosure to comply with this section, you should avoid the following:

1. Legalistic or overly complex presentations that make the substance of the disclosure difficult to understand;

2. Vague "boilerplate" explanations that are imprecise and readily subject to different interpretations;

3. Complex information copied directly from legal documents without any clear and concise explanation of the provision(s); and

4. Disclosure repeated in different sections of the document that increases the size of the document but does not enhance the quality of the information.

[71 FR 53263, Sept. 8, 2006, as amended at 73 FR 979, Jan. 4, 2008]

EXEMPTION OF CERTAIN ISSUERS FROM SECTION 15(d) OF THE ACT

§ 240.15d-21 Reports for employee stock purchase, savings and similar plans.

(a) Separate annual and other reports need not be filed pursuant to section 15(d) of the Act with respect to any employee stock purchase, savings or similar plan: *Provided,*

(1) The issuer of the stock or other securities offered to employees through their participation in the plan files annual reports on Form 10-K (§ 249.310 of this chapter); and

(2) Such issuer furnishes, as a part of its annual report on such form or as an amendment thereto, the financial statements required by Form 11-K (§ 249.311 of this chapter) with respect to the plan.

(b) If the procedure permitted by this Rule is followed, the financial statements required by Form 11-K with respect to the plan shall be filed within 120 days after the end of the fiscal year of the plan, either as a part of or as an amendment to the annual report of the issuer for its last fiscal year, *provided that* if the fiscal year of the plan ends within 62 days prior to the end of the fiscal year of the issuer, such information, financial statements and exhibits may be furnished as a part of the issuer's next annual report. If a plan subject to the Employee Retirement Income Security Act of 1974 uses the procedure permitted by this Rule, the financial statements required by Form 11-K shall be filed within 180 days after the plan's fiscal year end.

[27 FR 7871, Aug. 9, 1962, as amended at 55 FR 23929, June 13, 1990; 73 FR 979, Jan. 4, 2008]

§ 240.15d-22 Reporting regarding asset-backed securities under section 15(d) of the Act.

(a) With respect to an offering of asset-backed securities registered pursuant to § 230.415(a)(1)(vii) or § 230.415(a)(1)(xii) of this chapter:

§ 240.15d–23

(1) Annual and other reports need not be filed pursuant to section 15(d) of the Act (15 U.S.C. 78o(d)) regarding any class of securities to which such registration statement relates until the first bona fide sale in a takedown of securities under the registration statement; and

(2) The starting and suspension dates for any reporting obligation under section 15(d) of the Act (15 U.S.C. 78o(d)) with respect to a takedown of any class of asset-backed securities are determined separately for each takedown of securities under the registration statement.

(b) The duty to file annual and other reports pursuant to section 15(d) of the Act (15 U.S.C. 78o(d)) regarding any class of asset-backed securities is suspended:

(1) As to any semi-annual fiscal period, if, at the beginning of the semi-annual fiscal period, other than a period in the fiscal year within which the registration statement became effective, or, for offerings conducted pursuant to § 230.415(a)(1)(vii) or § 230.415(a)(1)(xii), the takedown for the offering occurred, there are no asset-backed securities of such class that were sold in a registered transaction held by non-affiliates of the depositor and a certification on Form 15 (17 CFR 249.323) has been filed; or

(2) When there are no asset-backed securities of such class that were sold in a registered transaction still outstanding, immediately upon filing with the Commission a certification on Form 15 (17 CFR 249.323) if the issuer of such class has filed all reports required by Section 13(a), without regard to Rule 12b-25 (17 CFR 249.322), for the shorter of its most recent three fiscal years and the portion of the current year preceding the date of filing Form 15, or the period since the issuer became subject to such reporting obligation. If the certification on Form 15 is subsequently withdrawn or denied, the issuer shall, within 60 days, file with the Commission all reports which would have been required if such certification had not been filed.

NOTE 1 TO PARAGRAPH (b): Securities held of record by a broker, dealer, bank or nominee for any of them for the accounts of customers shall be considered as held by the separate accounts for which the securities are held.

NOTE 2 TO PARAGRAPH (b): An issuer may not suspend reporting if the issuer and its affiliates acquire and resell securities as part of a plan or scheme to evade the reporting obligations of Section 15(d).

(c) This section does not affect any other reporting obligation applicable with respect to any classes of securities from additional takedowns under the same or different registration statements or any reporting obligation that may be applicable pursuant to section 12 of the Act (15 U.S.C. 78*l*).

[76 FR 52555, Aug. 23, 2011, as amended at 79 FR 57344, Sept. 24, 2014]

§ 240.15d–23 Reporting regarding certain securities underlying asset-backed securities under section 15(d) of the Act.

(a) Regarding a class of asset-backed securities, if the asset pool for the asset-backed securities includes a pool asset representing an interest in or the right to the payments or cash flows of another asset pool, then no separate annual and other reports need be filed pursuant to section 15(d) of the Act (15 U.S.C. 78o(d)) because of the separate registration of the distribution of the pool asset under the Securities Act (15 U.S.C. 77a *et seq.*), if the following conditions are met:

(1) Both the issuing entity for the asset-backed securities and the entity that issued the pool asset were established under the direction of the same sponsor and depositor;

(2) The pool asset was created solely to satisfy legal requirements or otherwise facilitate the structuring of the asset-backed securities transaction;

(3) The pool asset is not part of a scheme to avoid the registration or reporting requirements of the Act;

(4) The pool asset is held by the issuing entity and is a part of the asset pool for the asset-backed securities; and

(5) The offering of the asset-backed securities and the offering of the pool asset were both registered under the Securities Act (15 U.S.C. 77a *et seq.*).

(b) Paragraph (a) of this section does not affect any reporting obligation applicable with respect to the asset-

Securities and Exchange Commission § 240.15g–2

backed securities or any other reporting obligation that may be applicable with respect to the pool asset or any other securities by the issuer of that pool asset pursuant to section 12 or 15(d) of the Act (15 U.S.C. 78*l* or 78o(d)).

(c) This section does not affect any obligation to provide information regarding the pool asset or the asset pool underlying the pool asset in a filing with respect to the asset-backed securities. See Item 1100(d) of Regulation AB (§ 229.1100(d) of this chapter).

(d) Terms used in this section have the same meaning as in Item 1101 of Regulation AB (§ 229.1101 of this chapter).

[70 FR 1623, Jan. 7, 2005]

§ 240.15g–1 Exemptions for certain transactions.

The following transactions shall be exempt from 17 CFR 240.15g–2, 17 CFR 240.15g–3, 17 CFR 240.15g–4, 17 CFR 240.15g–5, and 17 CFR 240.15g–6:

(a) Transactions by a broker or dealer:

(1) Whose commissions, commission equivalents, mark-ups, and markdowns from transactions in penny stocks during each of the immediately preceding three months and during eleven or more of the preceding twelve months, or during the immediately preceding six months, did not exceed five percent of its total commissions, commission equivalents, mark-ups, and mark-downs from transactions in securities during those months; and

(2) Who has not been a market maker in the penny stock that is the subject of the transaction in the immediately preceding twelve months.

NOTE: Prior to April 28, 1993, commissions, commission equivalents, mark-ups, and mark-downs from transactions in designated securities, as defined in 17 CFR 240.15c2–6(d)(2) as of April 15, 1992, may be considered to be commissions, commission equivalents, mark-ups, and mark-downs from transactions in penny stocks for purposes of paragraph (a)(1) of this section.

(b) Transactions in which the customer is an institutional accredited investor, as defined in 17 CFR 230.501(a)(1), (2), (3), (7), (8), (9), (12), or (13).

NOTE 1 TO PARAGRAPH (b): Though the definition of "family client" from rule 501(a)(13) includes both natural persons and institutions, only family clients that are institutions may be considered institutional accredited investors.

(c) Transactions that meet the requirements of Regulation D (17 CFR 230.500 *et seq.*), or transactions with an issuer not involving any public offering pursuant to section 4(a)(2) of the Securities Act of 1933.

(d) Transactions in which the customer is the issuer, or a director, officer, general partner, or direct or indirect beneficial owner of more than five percent of any class of equity security of the issuer, of the penny stock that is the subject of the transaction.

(e) Transactions that are not recommended by the broker or dealer.

(f) Any other transaction or class of transactions or persons or class of persons that, upon prior written request or upon its own motion, the Commission conditionally or unconditionally exempts by order as consistent with the public interest and the protection of investors.

[57 FR 18032, Apr. 28, 1992, as amended at 77 FR 18685, Mar. 28, 2012; 85 FR 64278, Oct. 9, 2020]

§ 240.15g–2 Penny stock disclosure document relating to the penny stock market.

(a) It shall be unlawful for a broker or dealer to effect a transaction in any penny stock for or with the account of a customer unless, prior to effecting such transaction, the broker or dealer has furnished to the customer a document containing the information set forth in Schedule 15G, § 240.15g–100, and has obtained from the customer a signed and dated acknowledgment of receipt of the document.

(b) Regardless of the form of acknowledgment used to satisfy the requirements of paragraph (a) of this section, it shall be unlawful for a broker or dealer to effect a transaction in any penny stock for or with the account of a customer less than two business days after the broker or dealer sends such document.

(c) The broker or dealer shall preserve, as part of its records, a copy of the written acknowledgment required

§ 240.15g-3

by paragraph (a) of this section for the period specified in 17 CFR 240.17a-4(b) of this chapter.

(d) Upon request of the customer, the broker or dealer shall furnish the customer with a copy of the information set forth on the Commission's Web site at *http://www.sec.gov/investor/pubs/ microcapstock.htm*.

[58 FR 37417, July 12, 1993, as amended at 70 FR 40632, July 13, 2005]

§ 240.15g-3 Broker or dealer disclosure of quotations and other information relating to the penny stock market.

(a) *Requirement.* It shall be unlawful for a broker or dealer to effect a transaction in any penny stock with or for the account of a customer unless such broker or dealer discloses to such customer, within the time periods and in the manner required by paragraph (b) of this section, the following information:

(1) The inside bid quotation and the inside offer quotation for the penny stock.

(2) If paragraph (a)(1) of this section does not apply because of the absence of an inside bid quotation and an inside offer quotation:

(i) With respect to a transaction effected with or for a customer on a principal basis (other than as provided in paragraph (a)(2)(ii) of this section):

(A) The dealer shall disclose its offer price for the security:

(*1*) If during the previous five days the dealer has effected no fewer than three *bona fide* sales to other dealers consistently at its offer price for the security current at the time of those sales, and

(*2*) If the dealer reasonably believes in good faith at the time of the transaction with the customer that its offer price accurately reflects the price at which it is willing to sell one or more round lots to another dealer. For purposes of paragraph (a)(2)(i)(A) of this section, "consistently" shall constitute, at a minimum, seventy-five percent of the dealer's *bona fide* inter-dealer sales during the previous five-day period, and, if the dealer has effected only three *bona fide* inter-dealer sales during such period, all three of such sales.

(B) The dealer shall disclose its bid price for the security:

(*1*) If during the previous five days the dealer has effected no fewer than three *bona fide* purchases from other dealers consistently at its bid price for the security current at the time of those purchases, and

(*2*) If the dealer reasonably believes in good faith at the time of the transaction with the customer that its bid price accurately reflects the price at which it is willing to buy one or more round lots from another dealer. For purposes of paragraph (a)(2)(i)(B) of this section, "consistently" shall constitute, at a minimum, seventy-five percent of the dealer's *bona fide* inter-dealer purchases during the previous five-day period, and, if the dealer has effected only three *bona fide* inter-dealer purchases during such period, all three of such purchases.

(C) If the dealer's bid or offer prices to the customer do not satisfy the criteria of paragraphs (a)(2)(i)(A) or (a)(2)(i)(B) of this section, the dealer shall disclose to the customer:

(*1*) That it has not effected inter-dealer purchases or sales of the penny stock consistently at its bid or offer price, and

(*2*) The price at which it last purchased the penny stock from, or sold the penny stock to, respectively, another dealer in a *bona fide* transaction.

(ii) With respect to transactions effected by a broker or dealer with or for the account of the customer:

(A) On an agency basis or

(B) On a basis other than as a market maker in the security, where, after having received an order from the customer to purchase a penny stock, the dealer effects the purchase from another person to offset a contemporaneous sale of the penny stock to such customer, or, after having received an order from the customer to sell the penny stock, the dealer effects the sale to another person to offset a contemporaneous purchase from such customer, the broker or dealer shall disclose the best independent interdealer bid and offer prices for the penny stock that the broker or dealer obtains through reasonable diligence. A broker-dealer shall be deemed to have

Securities and Exchange Commission § 240.15g-4

exercised reasonable diligence if it obtains quotations from three market makers in the security (or all known market makers if there are fewer than three).

(3) With respect to bid or offer prices and transaction prices disclosed pursuant to paragraph (a) of this section, the broker or dealer shall disclose the number of shares to which the bid and offer prices apply.

(b) *Timing.* (1) The information described in paragraph (a) of this section:

(i) Shall be provided to the customer orally or in writing prior to effecting any transaction with or for the customer for the purchase or sale of such penny stock; and

(ii) Shall be given or sent to the customer in writing, at or prior to the time that any written confirmation of the transaction is given or sent to the customer pursuant to 17 CFR 240.10b-10 of this chapter.

(2) A broker or dealer, at the time of making the disclosure pursuant to paragraph (b)(1)(i) of this section, shall make and preserve as part of its records, a record of such disclosure for the period specified in 17 CFR 240.17a-4(b).

(c) *Definitions.* For purposes of this section:

(1) The term *bid price* shall mean the price most recently communicated by the dealer to another broker or dealer at which the dealer is willing to purchase one or more round lots of the penny stock, and shall not include indications of interest.

(2) The term *offer price* shall mean the price most recently communicated by the dealer to another broker or dealer at which the dealer is willing to sell one or more round lots of the penny stock, and shall not include indications of interest.

(3) The term *inside bid quotation* for a security shall mean the highest bid quotation for the security displayed by a market maker in the security on a Qualifying Electronic Quotation System, at any time in which at least two market makers are contemporaneously displaying on such system bid and offer quotations for the security at specified prices.

(4) The term *inside offer quotation* for a security shall mean the lowest offer quotation for the security displayed by a market maker in the security on a Qualifying Electronic Quotation System, at any time in which at least two market makers are contemporaneously displaying on such system bid and offer quotations for the security at specified prices.

(5) The term *Qualifying Electronic Quotation System* shall mean an automated interdealer quotation system that has the characteristics set forth in section 17B(b)(2) of the Act, or such other automated interdealer quotation system designated by the Commission for purposes of this section.

[57 FR 18033, Apr. 28, 1992]

§ 240.15g-4 Disclosure of compensation to brokers or dealers.

PRELIMINARY NOTE: Brokers and dealers may wish to refer to Securities Exchange Act Release No. 30608 (April 20, 1992) for a discussion of the procedures for computing compensation in active and competitive markets, inactive and competitive markets, and dominated and controlled markets.

(a) *Disclosure requirement.* It shall be unlawful for any broker or dealer to effect a transaction in any penny stock for or with the account of a customer unless such broker or dealer discloses to such customer, within the time periods and in the manner required by paragraph (b) of this section, the aggregate amount of any compensation received by such broker or dealer in connection with such transaction.

(b) *Timing.* (1) The information described in paragraph (a) of this section:

(i) Shall be provided to the customer orally or in writing prior to effecting any transaction with or for the customer for the purchase or sale of such penny stock; and

(ii) Shall be given or sent to the customer in writing, at or prior to the time that any written confirmation of the transaction is given or sent to the customer pursuant to 17 CFR 240.10b-10.

(2) A broker or dealer, at the time of making the disclosure pursuant to paragraph (b)(1)(i) of this section, shall make and preserve as part of its records, a record of such disclosure for the period specified in 17 CFR 240.17a-4(b).

§ 240.15g-5

(c) *Definition of compensation.* For purposes of this section, *compensation* means, with respect to a transaction in a penny stock:

(1) If a broker is acting as agent for a customer, the amount of any remuneration received or to be received by it from such customer in connection with such transaction;

(2) If, after having received a buy order from a customer, a dealer other than a market maker purchased the penny stock as principal from another person to offset a contemporaneous sale to such customer or, after having received a sell order from a customer, sold the penny stock as principal to another person to offset a contemporaneous purchase from such customer, the difference between the price to the customer and such contemporaneous purchase or sale price; or

(3) If the dealer otherwise is acting as principal for its own account, the difference between the price to the customer and the prevailing market price.

(d) *Active and competitive* market. For purposes of this section only, a market may be deemed to be "active and competitive" in determining the prevailing market price with respect to a transaction by a market maker in a penny stock if the aggregate number of transactions effected by such market maker in the penny stock in the five business days preceding such transaction is less than twenty percent of the aggregate number of all transactions in the penny stock reported on a Qualifying Electronic Quotation System (as defined in 17 CFR 240.15g–3(c)(5)) during such five-day period. No presumption shall arise that a market is not "active and competitive" solely by reason of a market maker not meeting the conditions specified in this paragraph.

[57 FR 18034, Apr. 28, 1992]

§ 240.15g-5 **Disclosure of compensation of associated persons in connection with penny stock transactions.**

(a) *General.* It shall be unlawful for a broker or dealer to effect a transaction in any penny stock for or with the account of a customer unless the broker or dealer discloses to such customer, within the time periods and in the manner required by paragraph (b) of this section, the aggregate amount of cash compensation that any associated person of the broker or dealer who is a natural person and has communicated with the customer concerning the transaction at or prior to receipt of the customer's transaction order, other than any person whose function is solely clerical or ministerial, has received or will receive from any source in connection with the transaction and that is determined at or prior to the time of the transaction, including separate disclosure, if applicable, of the source and amount of such compensation that is not paid by the broker or dealer.

(b) *Timing.* (1) The information described in paragraph (a) of this section:

(i) Shall be provided to the customer orally or in writing prior to effecting any transaction with or for the customer for the purchase or sale of such penny stock; and

(ii) Shall be given or sent to the customer in writing, at or prior to the time that any written confirmation of the transaction is given or sent to the customer pursuant to 17 CFR 240.10b–10.

(2) A broker or dealer, at the time of making the disclosure pursuant to paragraph (b)(1)(i) of this section, shall make and preserve as part of its records, a record of such disclosure for the period specified in 17 CFR 240.17a–4(b).

(c) *Contingent compensation arrangements.* Where a portion or all of the cash or other compensation that the associated person may receive in connection with the transaction may be determined and paid following the transaction based on aggregate sales volume levels or other contingencies, the written disclosure required by paragraph (b)(1)(ii) of this section shall state that fact and describe the basis upon which such compensation is determined.

[57 FR 18034, Apr. 28, 1992]

§ 240.15g-6 **Account statements for penny stock customers.**

(a) *Requirement.* It shall be unlawful for any broker or dealer that has effected the sale to any customer, other than in a transaction that is exempt pursuant to 17 CFR 240.15g-1, of any security that is a penny stock on the last trading day of any calendar month, or

Securities and Exchange Commission § 240.15g-6

any successor of such broker or dealer, to fail to give or send to such customer a written statement containing the information described in paragraphs (c) and (d) of this section with respect to each such month in which such security is held for the customer's account with the broker or dealer, within ten days following the end of such month.

(b) *Exemptions.* A broker or dealer shall be exempted from the requirement of paragraph (a) of this section under either of the following circumstances:

(1) If the broker or dealer does not effect any transactions in penny stocks for or with the account of the customer during a period of six consecutive calendar months, then the broker or dealer shall not be required to provide monthly statements for each quarterly period that is immediately subsequent to such six-month period and in which the broker or dealer does not effect any transaction in penny stocks for or with the account of the customer, *provided* that the broker or dealer gives or sends to the customer written statements containing the information described in paragraphs (d) and (e) of this section on a quarterly basis, within ten days following the end of each such quarterly period.

(2) If, on all but five or fewer trading days of any quarterly period, a security has a price of five dollars or more, the broker or dealer shall not be required to provide a monthly statement covering the security for subsequent quarterly periods, until the end of any such subsequent quarterly period on the last trading day of which the price of the security is less than five dollars.

(c) *Price determinations.* For purposes of paragraphs (a) and (b) of this section, the price of a security on any trading day shall be determined at the close of business in accordance with the provisions of 17 CFR 240.3a51-1(d)(1).

(d) *Market and price information.* The statement required by paragraph (a) of this section shall contain at least the following information with respect to each penny stock covered by paragraph (a) of this section, as of the last trading day of the period to which the statement relates:

(1) The identity and number of shares or units of each such security held for the customer's account; and

(2) The estimated market value of the security, to the extent that such estimated market value can be determined in accordance with the following provisions:

(i) The highest inside bid quotation for the security on the last trading day of the period to which the statement relates, multiplied by the number of shares or units of the security held for the customer's account; or

(ii) If paragraph (d)(2)(i) of this section is not applicable because of the absence of an inside bid quotation, and if the broker or dealer furnishing the statement has effected at least ten separate Qualifying Purchases in the security during the last five trading days of the period to which the statement relates, the weighted average price per share paid by the broker or dealer in all Qualifying Purchases effected during such five-day period, multiplied by the number of shares or units of the security held for the customer's account; or

(iii) If neither of paragraphs (d)(2)(i) nor (d)(2)(ii) of this section is applicable, a statement that there is "no estimated market value" with respect to the security.

(e) *Legend.* In addition to the information required by paragraph (d) of this section, the written statement required by paragraph (a) of this section shall include a conspicuous legend that is identified with the penny stocks described in the statement and that contains the following language:

If this statement contains an estimated value, you should be aware that this value may be based on a limited number of trades or quotes. Therefore, you may not be able to sell these securities at a price equal or near to the value shown. However, the broker-dealer furnishing this statement may not refuse to accept your order to sell these securities. Also, the amount you receive from a sale generally will be reduced by the amount of any commissions or similar charges. If an estimated value is not shown for a security, a value could not be determined because of a lack of information.

(f) *Preservation of records.* Any broker or dealer subject to this section shall preserve, as part of its records, copies of the written statements required by

515

§ 240.15g-8

paragraph (a) of this section and keep such records for the periods specified in 17 CFR 240.17a-4(b).

(g) *Definitions.* For purposes of this section:

(1) The term *Quarterly period* shall mean any period of three consecutive full calendar months.

(2) The *inside bid quotation* for a security shall mean the highest bid quotation for the security displayed by a market maker in the security on a Qualifying Electronic Quotation System, at any time in which at least two market makers are contemporaneously displaying on such system bid and offer quotations for the security at specified prices.

(3) The term *Qualifying Electronic Quotation System* shall mean an automated interdealer quotation system that has the characteristics set forth in section 17B(b)(2) of the Act, or such other automated interdealer quotation system designated by the Commission for purposes of this section.

(4) The term *Qualifying Purchases* shall mean *bona fide* purchases by a broker or dealer of a penny stock for its own account, each of which involves at least 100 shares, but excluding any block purchase involving more than one percent of the outstanding shares or units of the security.

[57 FR 18034, Apr. 28, 1992]

§ 240.15g-8 Sales of escrowed securities of blank check companies.

As a means reasonably designed to prevent fraudulent, deceptive, or manipulative acts or practices, it shall be unlawful for any person to sell or offer to sell any security that is deposited and held in an escrow or trust account pursuant to Rule 419 under the Securities Act of 1933 (17 CFR 230.419), or any interest in or related to such security, other than pursuant to a qualified domestic relations order as defined by the Internal Revenue Code of 1986, as amended (26 U.S.C. 1 *et seq.*), or Title I of the Employee Retirement Income Security Act (29 U.S.C. 1001 *et seq.*), or the rules thereunder.

[57 FR 18045, Apr. 28, 1992]

§ 240.15g-9 Sales practice requirements for certain low-priced securities.

(a) As a means reasonably designed to prevent fraudulent, deceptive, or manipulative acts or practices, it shall be unlawful for a broker or dealer to sell a penny stock to, or to effect the purchase of a penny stock by, any person unless:

(1) The transaction is exempt under paragraph (c) of this section; or

(2) Prior to the transaction:

(i) The broker or dealer has approved the person's account for transactions in penny stocks in accordance with the procedures set forth in paragraph (b) of this section; and

(ii)(A) The broker or dealer has received from the person an agreement to the transaction setting forth the identity and quantity of the penny stock to be purchased; and

(B) Regardless of the form of agreement used to satisfy the requirements of paragraph (a)(2)(ii)(A) of this section, it shall be unlawful for such broker or dealer to sell a penny stock to, or to effect the purchase of a penny stock by, for or with the account of a customer less than two business days after the broker or dealer sends such agreement.

(b) In order to approve a person's account for transactions in penny stocks, the broker or dealer must:

(1) Obtain from the person information concerning the person's financial situation, investment experience, and investment objectives;

(2) Reasonably determine, based on the information required by paragraph (b)(1) of this section and any other information known by the broker-dealer, that transactions in penny stocks are suitable for the person, and that the person (or the person's independent adviser in these transactions) has sufficient knowledge and experience in financial matters that the person (or the person's independent adviser in these transactions) reasonably may be expected to be capable of evaluating the risks of transactions in penny stocks;

(3) Deliver to the person a written statement:

Securities and Exchange Commission § 240.15g–100

(i) Setting forth the basis on which the broker or dealer made the determination required by paragraph (b)(2) of this section;

(ii) Stating in a highlighted format that it is unlawful for the broker or dealer to effect a transaction in a penny stock subject to the provisions of paragraph (a)(2) of this section unless the broker or dealer has received, prior to the transaction, a written agreement to the transaction from the person; and

(iii) Stating in a highlighted format immediately preceding the customer signature line that:

(A) The broker or dealer is required by this section to provide the person with the written statement; and

(B) The person should not sign and return the written statement to the broker or dealer if it does not accurately reflect the person's financial situation, investment experience, and investment objectives; and

(4)(i) Obtain from the person a signed and dated copy of the statement required by paragraph (b)(3) of this section; and

(ii) Regardless of the form of statement used to satisfy the requirements of paragraph (b)(4)(i) of this section, it shall be unlawful for such broker or dealer to sell a penny stock to, or to effect the purchase of a penny stock by, for or with the account of a customer less than two business days after the broker or dealer sends such statement.

(c) For purposes of this section, the following transactions shall be exempt:

(1) Transactions that are exempt under 17 CFR 240.15g–1 (a), (b), (d), (e), and (f).

(2) Transactions that meet the requirements of 17 CFR 230.506 (including, where applicable, the requirements of 17 CFR 230.501 through 230.503, and 17 CFR 230.507 through 230.508), or transactions with an issuer not involving any public offering pursuant to section 4(a)(2) of the Securities Act of 1933.

(3) Transactions in which the purchaser is an established customer of the broker or dealer.

(d) For purposes of this section:

(1) The term *penny stock* shall have the same meaning as in 17 CFR 240.3a51–1.

(2) The term *established customer* shall mean any person for whom the broker or dealer, or a clearing broker on behalf of such broker or dealer, carries an account, and who in such account:

(i) Has effected a securities transaction, or made a deposit of funds or securities, more than one year previously; or

(ii) Has made three purchases of penny stocks that occurred on separate days and involved different issuers.

[54 FR 35481, Aug. 28, 1989. Redesignated and amended at 58 FR 37417, July 12, 1993; 70 FR 40632, July 13, 2005; 81 FR 83553, Nov. 21, 2016]

§ 240.15g–100 Schedule 15G—Information to be included in the document distributed pursuant to 17 CFR 240.15g–2.

SECURITIES AND EXCHANGE COMMISSION

Washington, DC 20549

SCHEDULE 15G

Under the Securities Exchange Act of 1934

Instructions to Schedule 15G

A. Schedule 15G (Schedule) may be provided to customers in its entirety either on paper or electronically. It may also be provided to customers electronically through a link to the SEC's Web site.

1. *If the Schedule is sent in paper form*, the format and typeface of the Schedule must be reproduced exactly as presented. For example, words that are capitalized must remain capitalized, and words that are underlined or bold must remain underlined or bold. The typeface must be clear and easy to read. The Schedule may be reproduced either by photocopy or by printing.

2. *If the Schedule is sent electronically*, the e-mail containing the Schedule must have as a subject line "Important Information on Penny Stocks." The Schedule reproduced in the text of the e-mail must be clear, easy-to-read type presented in a manner reasonably calculated to draw the customer's attention to the language in the document, especially words that are capitalized, underlined or in bold.

§ 240.15g-100

3. If the Schedule is sent electronically using a hyperlink to the SEC Web site, the e-mail containing the hyperlink must have as a subject line: "Important Information on Penny Stocks." Immediately before the hyperlink, the text of the e-mail must reproduce the following statement in clear, easy-to-read type presented in a manner reasonably calculated to draw the customer's attention to the words: "We are required by the U.S. Securities and Exchange Commission to give you the following disclosure statement: *http://www.sec.gov/investor/schedule15g.htm*. It explains some of the risks of investing in penny stocks. Please read it carefully before you agree to purchase or sell a penny stock."

B. Regardless of how the Schedule is provided to the customer, the communication must also provide the name, address, telephone number and e-mail address of the broker. E-mail messages may also include any privacy or confidentiality information that the broker routinely includes in e-mail messages sent to customers. No other information may be included in these communications, other than instructions on how to provide a signed and dated acknowledgement of receipt of the Schedule.

C. The document entitled "Important Information on Penny Stocks" must be distributed as Schedule 15G and must be no more than two pages in length if provided in paper form.

D. The disclosures made through the Schedule are in addition to any other disclosures that are required under the Federal securities laws.

E. Recipients of the document must not be charged any fee for the document.

F. The content of the Schedule is as follows:

[next page]

Important Information on Penny Stocks

The U.S. Securities and Exchange Commission (SEC) requires your broker to give this statement to you, and to obtain your signature to show that you have received it, before your first trade in a penny stock. This statement contains important information—and you should read it carefully before you sign it, and before you decide to purchase or sell a penny stock.

In addition to obtaining your signature, the SEC requires your broker to wait at least two business days after sending you this statement before executing your first trade to give you time to carefully consider your trade.

Penny Stocks Can Be Very Risky

Penny stocks are low-priced shares of small companies. Penny stocks may trade infrequently—which means that it may be difficult to sell penny stock shares once you have them. Because it may also be difficult to find quotations for penny stocks, they may be impossible to accurately price. Investors in penny stock should be prepared for the possibility that they may lose their whole investment.

While penny stocks generally trade over-the-counter, they may also trade on U.S. securities exchanges, facilities of U.S. exchanges, or foreign exchanges. You should learn about the market in which the penny stock trades to determine how much demand there is for this stock and how difficult it will be to sell. Be especially careful if your broker is offering to sell you newly issued penny stock that has no established trading market.

The securities you are considering have not been approved or disapproved by the SEC. Moreover, the SEC has not passed upon the fairness or the merits of this transaction nor upon the accuracy or adequacy of the information contained in any prospectus or any other information provided by an issuer or a broker or dealer.

Information You Should Get

In addition to this statement, your broker is required to give you a statement of your financial situation and investment goals explaining why his or her firm has determined that penny stocks are a suitable investment for you. In addition, your broker is required to obtain your agreement to the proposed penny stock transaction.

Before you buy penny stock, Federal law requires your salesperson to tell you the "*offer*" and the "*bid*" on the stock, and the "*compensation*" the salesperson and the firm receive for the

Securities and Exchange Commission

§ 240.15l-1

trade. The firm also must send a confirmation of these prices to you after the trade. You will need this price information to determine what profit or loss, if any, you will have when you sell your stock.

The offer price is the wholesale price at which the dealer is willing to sell stock to other dealers. The bid price is the wholesale price at which the dealer is willing to buy the stock from other dealers. In its trade with you, the dealer may add a retail charge to these wholesale prices as compensation (called a "markup" or "markdown").

The difference between the bid and the offer price is the dealer's *"spread."* A spread that is large compared with the purchase price can make a resale of a stock very costly. To be profitable when you sell, the bid price of your stock must rise above the amount of this spread and the compensation charged by both your selling and purchasing dealers. *Remember that if the dealer has no bid price, you may not be able to sell the stock after you buy it, and may lose your whole investment.*

After you buy penny stock, your brokerage firm must send you a monthly account statement that gives an estimate of the value of each penny stock in your account, if there is enough information to make an estimate. If the firm has not bought or sold any penny stocks for your account for six months, it can provide these statements every three months.

Additional information about low-priced securities—including penny stocks—is available on the SEC's Web site at *http://www.sec.gov/investor/pubs/microcapstock.htm*. In addition, your broker will send you a copy of this information upon request. The SEC encourages you to learn all you can before making this investment.

Brokers' Duties and Customers' Rights and Remedies

Remember that your salesperson is not an impartial advisor—he or she is being paid to sell you stock. Do not rely only on the salesperson, but seek outside advice before you buy any stock. You can get the disciplinary history of a salesperson or firm from NASD at 1-800-289-9999 or contact NASD via the Internet at *http://www.nasd.com*. You can also get additional information from your state securities official. The North American Securities Administrators Association, Inc. can give you contact information for your state. You can reach NASAA at (202) 737-0900 or via the Internet at *http://www.nasaa.org*.

If you have problems with a salesperson, contact the firm's compliance officer. You can also contact the securities regulators listed above. Finally, if you are a victim of fraud, you may have rights and remedies under state and Federal law. In addition to the regulators listed above, you also may contact the SEC with complaints at (800) SEC-0330 or via the Internet at *help@sec.gov*.

[70 FR 40632, July 13, 2005]

§ 240.15l-1 Regulation best interest.

(a) *Best interest obligation.* (1) A broker, dealer, or a natural person who is an associated person of a broker or dealer, when making a recommendation of any securities transaction or investment strategy involving securities (including account recommendations) to a retail customer, shall act in the best interest of the retail customer at the time the recommendation is made, without placing the financial or other interest of the broker, dealer, or natural person who is an associated person of a broker or dealer making the recommendation ahead of the interest of the retail customer.

(2) The best interest obligation in paragraph (a)(1) of this section shall be satisfied if:

(i) *Disclosure obligation.* The broker, dealer, or natural person who is an associated person of a broker or dealer, prior to or at the time of the recommendation, provides the retail customer, in writing, full and fair disclosure of:

(A) All material facts relating to the scope and terms of the relationship with the retail customer, including:

(*1*) That the broker, dealer, or such natural person is acting as a broker, dealer, or an associated person of a broker or dealer with respect to the recommendation;

(*2*) The material fees and costs that apply to the retail customer's transactions, holdings, and accounts; and

§ 240.15l–1

(3) The type and scope of services provided to the retail customer, including any material limitations on the securities or investment strategies involving securities that may be recommended to the retail customer; and

(B) All material facts relating to conflicts of interest that are associated with the recommendation.

(ii) *Care obligation.* The broker, dealer, or natural person who is an associated person of a broker or dealer, in making the recommendation, exercises reasonable diligence, care, and skill to:

(A) Understand the potential risks, rewards, and costs associated with the recommendation, and have a reasonable basis to believe that the recommendation could be in the best interest of at least some retail customers;

(B) Have a reasonable basis to believe that the recommendation is in the best interest of a particular retail customer based on that retail customer's investment profile and the potential risks, rewards, and costs associated with the recommendation and does not place the financial or other interest of the broker, dealer, or such natural person ahead of the interest of the retail customer;

(C) Have a reasonable basis to believe that a series of recommended transactions, even if in the retail customer's best interest when viewed in isolation, is not excessive and is in the retail customer's best interest when taken together in light of the retail customer's investment profile and does not place the financial or other interest of the broker, dealer, or such natural person making the series of recommendations ahead of the interest of the retail customer.

(iii) *Conflict of interest obligation.* The broker or dealer establishes, maintains, and enforces written policies and procedures reasonably designed to:

(A) Identify and at a minimum disclose, in accordance with paragraph (a)(2)(i) of this section, or eliminate, all conflicts of interest associated with such recommendations;

(B) Identify and mitigate any conflicts of interest associated with such recommendations that create an incentive for a natural person who is an associated person of a broker or dealer to place the interest of the broker, dealer, or such natural person ahead of the interest of the retail customer;

(C)(*1*) Identify and disclose any material limitations placed on the securities or investment strategies involving securities that may be recommended to a retail customer and any conflicts of interest associated with such limitations, in accordance with subparagraph (a)(2)(i), and

(*2*) Prevent such limitations and associated conflicts of interest from causing the broker, dealer, or a natural person who is an associated person of the broker or dealer to make recommendations that place the interest of the broker, dealer, or such natural person ahead of the interest of the retail customer; and

(D) Identify and eliminate any sales contests, sales quotas, bonuses, and non-cash compensation that are based on the sales of specific securities or specific types of securities within a limited period of time.

(iv) *Compliance obligation.* In addition to the policies and procedures required by paragraph (a)(2)(iii) of this section, the broker or dealer establishes, maintains, and enforces written policies and procedures reasonably designed to achieve compliance with Regulation Best Interest.

(b) *Definitions.* Unless otherwise provided, all terms used in this rule shall have the same meaning as in the Securities Exchange Act of 1934. In addition, the following definitions shall apply for purposes of this section:

(1) *Retail customer* means a natural person, or the legal representative of such natural person, who:

(i) Receives a recommendation of any securities transaction or investment strategy involving securities from a broker, dealer, or a natural person who is an associated person of a broker or dealer; and

(ii) Uses the recommendation primarily for personal, family, or household purposes.

(2) *Retail customer investment profile* includes, but is not limited to, the retail customer's age, other investments, financial situation and needs, tax status, investment objectives, investment experience, investment time horizon, liquidity needs, risk tolerance, and any

Securities and Exchange Commission § 240.15Aj–1

other information the retail customer may disclose to the broker, dealer, or a natural person who is an associated person of a broker or dealer in connection with a recommendation.

(3) *Conflict of interest* means an interest that might incline a broker, dealer, or a natural person who is an associated person of a broker or dealer —consciously or unconsciously—to make a recommendation that is not disinterested.

[84 FR 33491, July 12, 2019]

NATIONAL AND AFFILIATED SECURITIES ASSOCIATIONS

§ 240.15Aa–1 Registration of a national or an affiliated securities association.

Any application for registration of an association as a national, or as an affiliated, securities association shall be made in triplicate on Form X–15AA–1 accompanied by three copies of the exhibits prescribed by the Commission to be filed in connection therewith.

(Sec. 15A, 52 Stat. 1070; 15 U.S.C. 78*o*–3)

[13 FR 8209, Dec. 22, 1948. Redesignated at 30 FR 11851, Sept. 16, 1965]

§ 240.15Aj–1 Amendments and supplements to registration statements of securities associations.

Every association applying for registration or registered as a national securities association or as an affiliated securities association shall keep its registration statement up-to-date in the manner prescribed below:

(a) *Amendments.* Promptly after the discovery of any inaccuracy in the registration statement or in any amendment or supplement thereto the association shall file with the Commission an amendment correcting such inaccuracy.

(b) *Current supplements.* Promptly after any change which renders no longer accurate any information contained or incorporated in the registration statement or in any amendment or supplement thereto the association shall file with the Commission a current supplement setting forth such change, except that:

(1) Supplements setting forth changes in the information called for in Exhibit C need not be filed until 10 days after the calendar month in which the changes occur.

(2) No current supplements need be filed with respect to changes in the information called for in Exhibit B.

(3) If changes in the information called for in items (1) and (2) of Exhibit C are reported in any record which is published at least once a month by the association and promptly filed in triplicate with the Commission, no current supplement need be filed with respect thereto.

(c) *Annual supplements.* (1) Promptly after March 1 of each year, the association shall file with the Commission an annual consolidated supplement as of such date on Form X–15AJ–2 (§ 249.803) except that:

(i) If the securities association publishes or cooperates in the publication of the information required in Items 6(a) and 6(b) of Form X–15AJ–2 on an annual or more frequent basis, in lieu of filing such an item the securities association may:

(A) Identify the publication in which such information is available, the name, address, and telephone number of the person from whom such publication may be obtained, and the price thereof; and

(B) Certify to the accuracy of such information as of its date.

(ii) Promptly after March 1, 1995, and every three years thereafter each association shall file complete Exhibit A to Form X–15AJ–2. The information contained in this exhibit shall be up to date as of the latest practicable date within 3 months of the date on which these exhibits are filed. If the association publishes or cooperates in the publication of the information required in this exhibit on an annual or more frequent basis, in lieu of filing such exhibit the association may:

(A) Identify the publication in which such information is available, the name, address, and telephone number of the person from whom such publication may be obtained, and the price thereof; and

(B) Certify to the accuracy of such information as of its date. If a securities association keeps the information required in this exhibit up to date and makes it available to the Commission and the public upon request, in lieu of

§ 240.15AI2-1

filing such an exhibit a securities association may certify that the information is kept up to date and is available to the Commission and the public upon request.

(2) Promptly after the close of each fiscal year of the association, it shall file with the Commission a supplement setting forth its balance sheet as of the close of such year and its income and expense statement for such year.

(d) *Filing, dating, etc.* Each amendment or supplement shall be filed in triplicate, at least one of which must be signed and attested, in the same manner as required in the case of the original registration statement, and must conform to the requirements of Form X–15Aj–1, except that the annual consolidated supplement shall be filed on Form X–15Aj–2. All amendments and supplements shall be dated and numbered in order of filing. One amendment or supplement may include any number of changes. In addition to the formal filing of amendments and supplements above described, each association shall send to the Commission three copies of any notices, reports, circulars, loose-leaf insertions, riders, new additions, lists or other records of changes covered by amendments or supplements when, as and if such records are made available to members of the association.

(Sec. 15A, 52 Stat. 1070; 15 U.S.C. 78*o*–3)

[13 FR 8209, Dec. 22, 1948, as amended at 18 FR 6259, Oct. 1, 1953. Redesignated at 30 FR 11851, Sept. 16, 1965; 59 FR 66700, Dec. 28, 1994]

§ 240.15Al2–1 [Reserved]

§ 240.15Ba1–1 **Definitions.**

As used in the rules and regulations prescribed by the Commission pursuant to section 15B of the Act (15 U.S.C. 78*o*–4) in §§ 240.15Ba1–1 through 240.15Ba1–8 and 240.15Bc4–1:

(a) *Guaranteed investment contract* has the same meaning as in section 15B(e)(2) of the Act (15 U.S.C. 78*o*–4(e)(2)); *provided, however,* that the contract relates to investments of proceeds of municipal securities or municipal escrow investments.

(b) *Investment strategies* has the same meaning as in section 15B(e)(3) of the Act (15 U.S.C. 78*o*–4(e)(3)), and includes plans or programs for the investment of proceeds of municipal securities that are not municipal derivatives or guaranteed investment contracts, and the recommendation of and brokerage of municipal escrow investments.

(c) *Managing agent* means any person, including a trustee, who directs or manages, or who participates in directing or managing, the affairs of any unincorporated organization or association other than a partnership.

(d)(1) *Municipal advisor.*

(i) *In general.* Except as otherwise provided in paragraphs (d)(2) and (d)(3) of this section, the term *municipal advisor* has the same meaning as in section 15B(e)(4) of the Act (15 U.S.C. 78*o*–4(e)(4)). Under section 15B(e)(4)(A) of the Act (15 U.S.C. 78*o*-4(e)(4)(A)), the term *municipal advisor* means a person (who is not a municipal entity or an employee of a municipal entity) that provides advice to or on behalf of a municipal entity or obligated person with respect to municipal financial products or the issuance of municipal securities, including advice with respect to the structure, timing, terms, and other similar matters concerning such financial products or issues; or undertakes a solicitation of a municipal entity or an obligated person. Under section 15B(e)(4)(C) of the Act (15 U.S.C. 78*o*-4(e)(4)(C)) and paragraph (d)(2) of this section, a *municipal advisor* does not include a person that engages in specified excluded activities.

(ii) *Advice standard.* For purposes of the municipal advisor definition under paragraph (d)(1)(i) of this section, advice excludes, among other things, the provision of general information that does not involve a recommendation regarding municipal financial products or the issuance of municipal securities (including with respect to the structure, timing, terms and other similar matters concerning such financial products or issues).

(iii) *Certain types of municipal advisors.* Under section 15B(e)(4)(B) of the Act (15 U.S.C. 78*o*-4(e)(4)(B)), *municipal advisors* include, without limitation, financial advisors, guaranteed investment contract brokers, third-party marketers, placement agents, solicitors, finders, and swap advisors, to the extent that such persons otherwise

Securities and Exchange Commission § 240.15Ba1-1

meet the requirements of the municipal advisor definition in this paragraph (d)(1).

(2) *Exclusions from municipal advisor definition.* Pursuant to section 15B(e)(4)(C) of the Act (15 U.S.C. 78o-4(e)(4)(C)), the term *municipal advisor* excludes the following persons with respect to the specified excluded activities:

(i) *Serving as an underwriter.* A broker, dealer, or municipal securities dealer serving as an underwriter of a particular issuance of municipal securities to the extent that the broker, dealer, or municipal securities dealer engages in activities that are within the scope of an underwriting of such issuance of municipal securities.

(ii) *Registered investment advisers—In general.* Any investment adviser registered under the Investment Advisers Act of 1940 (15 U.S.C. 80b-1 *et seq.*) or any person associated with such registered investment adviser to the extent that such registered investment adviser or such person is providing investment advice in such capacity. Solely for purposes of this paragraph (d)(2)(ii), investment advice does not include advice concerning whether and how to issue municipal securities, advice concerning the structure, timing, and terms of an issuance of municipal securities and other similar matters, advice concerning municipal derivatives, or a solicitation of a municipal entity or obligated person.

(iii) *Registered commodity trading advisors.* Any commodity trading advisor registered under the Commodity Exchange Act (7 U.S.C. 1 *et seq.*), or person associated with a registered commodity trading advisor, to the extent that such registered commodity trading advisor or such person is providing advice that is related to swaps (as defined in Section 1a(47) of the Commodity Exchange Act (7 U.S.C. 1a(47)) and section 3(a)(69) of the Act (15 U.S.C. 78c(a)(69)), and any rules and regulations thereunder).

(iv) *Attorneys.* Any attorney to the extent that the attorney is offering legal advice or providing services that are of a traditional legal nature with respect to the issuance of municipal securities or municipal financial products to a client of such attorney that is a municipal entity, obligated person, or other participant in the transaction. To the extent an attorney represents himself or herself as a financial advisor or financial expert regarding the issuance of municipal securities or municipal financial products, however, the attorney is not excluded with respect to such financial activities under this paragraph (d)(2)(iv).

(v) *Engineers.* Any engineer to the extent that the engineer is providing engineering advice.

(3) *Exemptions from municipal advisor definition.* The Commission exempts the following persons from the definition of municipal advisor to the extent they are engaging in the specified activities:

(i) *Accountants.* Any accountant to the extent that the accountant is providing audit or other attest services, preparing financial statements, or issuing letters for underwriters for, or on behalf of, a municipal entity or obligated person.

(ii) *Public officials and employees.* (A) Any person serving as a member of a governing body, an advisory board, or a committee of, or acting in a similar official capacity with respect to, or as an official of, a municipal entity or obligated person to the extent that such person is acting within the scope of such person's official capacity.

(B) Any employee of a municipal entity or obligated person to the extent that such person is acting within the scope of such person's employment.

(iii) *Banks.* Any bank, as defined in section 3(a)(6) of the Act (15 U.S.C. 78c(a)(6)), to the extent the bank provides advice with respect to the following:

(A) Any investments that are held in a deposit account, savings account, certificate of deposit, or other deposit instrument issued by a bank;

(B) Any extension of credit by a bank to a municipal entity or obligated person, including the issuance of a letter of credit, the making of a direct loan, or the purchase of a municipal security by the bank for its own account;

(C) Any funds held in a sweep account that meets the requirements of section 3(a)(4)(B)(v) of the Act (15 U.S.C. 78c(a)(4)(B)(v)); or

§ 240.15Ba1-1

(D) Any investment made by a bank acting in the capacity of an indenture trustee or similar capacity.

(iv) *Responses to requests for proposals or qualifications.* Any person providing a response in writing or orally to a request for proposals or qualifications from a municipal entity or obligated person for services in connection with a municipal financial product or the issuance of municipal securities; *provided, however,* that such person does not receive separate direct or indirect compensation for advice provided as part of such response.

(v) *Swap dealers.* (A) A swap dealer (as defined in Section 1a(49) of the Commodity Exchange Act (7 U.S.C. 1a(49)) and the rules and regulations thereunder) registered under the Commodity Exchange Act or associated person of the swap dealer recommending a municipal derivative or a trading strategy that involves a municipal derivative, so long as the registered swap dealer or associated person is not *acting as an advisor* to the municipal entity or obligated person with respect to the municipal derivative or trading strategy pursuant to Section 4s(h)(4) of the Commodity Exchange Act and the rules and regulations thereunder.

(B) For purposes of determining whether a swap dealer is *acting as an advisor* in this paragraph (d)(3)(v), the municipal entity or obligated person involved in the transaction will be treated as a *special entity* under Section 4s(h)(2) of the Commodity Exchange Act and the rules and regulations thereunder (even if such municipal entity or obligated person does not satisfy the definition of *special entity* under those provisions).

(vi) *Participation by an independent registered municipal advisor.* Any person engaging in municipal advisory activities in a circumstance in which a municipal entity or obligated person is otherwise represented by an independent registered municipal advisor with respect to the same aspects of a municipal financial product or an issuance of municipal securities, provided that the following requirements are met:

(A) *Independent registered municipal advisor.* An independent registered municipal advisor is providing advice with respect to the same aspects of the municipal financial product or issuance of municipal securities. For purposes of this paragraph (d)(3)(vi), the term *independent registered municipal advisor* means a municipal advisor registered pursuant to section 15B of the Act (15 U.S.C. 78*o*-4) and the rules and regulations thereunder and that is not, and within at least the past two years was not, associated (as defined in section 15B(e)(7) (15 U.S.C. 78*o*-4(e)(7)) of the Act) with the person seeking to rely on this paragraph (d)(3)(vi).

(B) *Required representation.* A person seeking to rely on this paragraph (d)(3)(vi) receives from the municipal entity or obligated person a representation in writing that it is represented by, and will rely on the advice of, an independent registered municipal advisor, provided that the person receiving such representation has a reasonable basis for relying on the representation.

(C) *Required disclosures.* (*1*) With respect to a municipal entity, such person discloses in writing to the municipal entity that, by obtaining such representation from the municipal entity, such person is not a municipal advisor and is not subject to the fiduciary duty set forth in section 15B(c)(1) of the Act (15 U.S.C. 78*o*-4(c)(1)) with respect to the municipal financial product or issuance of municipal securities, and provides a copy of such disclosure to the independent registered municipal advisor.

(*2*) With respect to an obligated person, such person discloses in writing to the obligated person that, by obtaining such representation from the obligated person, such person is not a municipal advisor with respect to the municipal financial product or issuance of municipal securities, and provides a copy of such disclosure to the independent registered municipal advisor.

(*3*) Each such disclosure must be made at a time and in a manner reasonably designed to allow the municipal entity or obligated person to assess the material incentives and conflicts of interest that such person may have in connection with the municipal advisory activities.

(vii) *Persons that provide advice on certain investment strategies.* A person that

Securities and Exchange Commission § 240.15Ba1–1

provides advice with respect to investment strategies that are not plans or programs for the investment of the proceeds of municipal securities or the recommendation of and brokerage of municipal escrow investments.

(viii) *Certain solicitations.* A person that undertakes a solicitation of a municipal entity or obligated person for the purpose of obtaining or retaining an engagement by a municipal entity or by an obligated person of a broker, dealer, municipal securities dealer, or municipal advisor for or in connection with municipal financial products that are investment strategies to the extent that those investment strategies are not plans or programs for the investment of the proceeds of municipal securities or the recommendation of and brokerage of municipal escrow investments.

(4) *Special rule for separately identifiable departments or divisions of banks for municipal advisory purposes.* If a bank engages in municipal advisory activities through a separately identifiable department or division that meets the requirements of this paragraph (d)(4), the determination of whether those municipal advisory activities cause any person to be a municipal advisor may be made separately for such department or division. In such event, that department or division, rather than the bank itself, shall be deemed to be the municipal advisor.

(i) *Separately identifiable department or division.* For purposes of this paragraph (d)(4), a *separately identifiable department or division* of a bank is that unit of the bank which conducts all of the municipal advisory activities of the bank, provided that the following requirements are met:

(A) *Supervision.* Such unit is under the direct supervision of an officer or officers designated by the board of directors of the bank as responsible for the day-to-day conduct of the bank's municipal advisory activities, including the supervision of all bank employees engaged in the performance of such activities.

(B) *Separate records.* All of the records relating to the bank's municipal advisory activities are separately maintained in, or extractable from, such unit's own facilities or the facilities of the bank, and such records are so maintained or otherwise accessible as to permit independent examination thereof and enforcement of applicable provisions of the Act, the rules and regulations thereunder, and the rules of the Municipal Securities Rulemaking Board relating to municipal advisors.

(ii) [Reserved]

(e) *Municipal advisory activities* means the following activities specified in section 15B(e)(4)(A) of the Act (15 U.S.C. 78o–4(e)(4)(A)) and paragraph (d)(1) of this section that, absent the availability of an exclusion under paragraph (d)(2) of this section or an exemption under paragraph (d)(3) of this section, would cause a person to be a municipal advisor:

(1) Providing advice to or on behalf of a municipal entity or obligated person with respect to municipal financial products or the issuance of municipal securities, including advice with respect to the structure, timing, terms, and other similar matters concerning such financial products or issues; or

(2) Solicitation of a municipal entity or an obligated person.

(f) *Municipal derivatives* means any swap (as defined in Section 1a(47) of the Commodity Exchange Act (7 U.S.C. 1a(47)) and section 3(a)(69) of the Act (15 U.S.C. 78c(a)(69)), including any rules and regulations thereunder) or security-based swap (as defined in section 3(a)(68) of the Act (15 U.S.C. 78c(a)(68)), including any rules and regulations thereunder) to which:

(1) A municipal entity is a counterparty; or

(2) An obligated person, acting in such capacity, is a counterparty.

(g) *Municipal entity* means any State, political subdivision of a State, or municipal corporate instrumentality of a State or of a political subdivision of a State, including:

(1) Any agency, authority, or instrumentality of the State, political subdivision, or municipal corporate instrumentality;

(2) Any plan, program, or pool of assets sponsored or established by the State, political subdivision, or municipal corporate instrumentality or any agency, authority, or instrumentality thereof; and

§ 240.15Ba1-1

(3) Any other issuer of municipal securities.

(h) *Municipal escrow investments.* (1) *In general.* Except as otherwise provided in paragraph (h)(2) of this section, *municipal escrow investments* means proceeds of municipal securities and any other funds of a municipal entity that are deposited in an escrow account to pay the principal of, premium, if any, and interest on one or more issues of municipal securities.

(2) *Reasonable reliance on representations.* In determining whether or not funds to be invested or reinvested constitute municipal escrow investments for purposes of this section, a person may rely on representations in writing made by a knowledgeable official of the municipal entity or obligated person whose funds are to be invested or reinvested regarding the nature of such investments, provided that the person seeking to rely on such representations has a reasonable basis for such reliance.

(i) *Municipal financial product* has the same meaning as in section 15B(e)(5) of the Act (15 U.S.C. 78o–4(e)(5)).

(j) *Non-resident* means:

(1) In the case of an individual, one who resides in or has his principal office and place of business in any place not subject to the jurisdiction of the United States;

(2) In the case of a corporation, one incorporated in or having its principal office and place of business in any place not subject to the jurisdiction of the United States; or

(3) In the case of a partnership or other unincorporated organization or association, one having its principal office and place of business in any place not subject to the jurisdiction of the United States.

(k) *Obligated person* has the same meaning as in section 15B(e)(10) of the Act (15 U.S.C. 78o–4(e)(10)); *provided, however,* that the term *obligated person* shall not include:

(1) A person who provides municipal bond insurance, letters of credit, or other liquidity facilities;

(2) A person whose financial information or operating data is not material to a municipal securities offering, without reference to any municipal bond insurance, letter of credit, liquidity facility, or other credit enhancement; or

(3) The federal government.

(l) *Principal office and place of business* means the executive office of the municipal advisor from which the officers, partners, or managers of the municipal advisor direct, control, and coordinate the activities of the municipal advisor.

(m)(1) *Proceeds of municipal securities—In general.* Except as otherwise provided in paragraphs (m)(2) and (m)(3) of this section, *proceeds of municipal securities* means monies derived by a municipal entity from the sale of municipal securities, investment income derived from the investment or reinvestment of such monies, and any monies of a municipal entity or obligated person held in funds under legal documents for the municipal securities that are reasonably expected to be used as security or a source of payment for the payment of the debt service on the municipal securities, including reserves, sinking funds, and pledged funds created for such purpose, and the investment income derived from the investment or reinvestment of monies in such funds. When such monies are spent to carry out the authorized purposes of municipal securities, they cease to be proceeds of municipal securities.

(2) *Exception for Section 529 college savings plans.* Solely for purposes of this paragraph (m), monies derived from a municipal security issued by an education trust established by a State under Section 529(b) of the Internal Revenue Code (26 U.S.C. 529(b)) are not proceeds of municipal securities.

(3) *Reasonable reliance on representations.* In determining whether or not funds to be invested constitute proceeds of municipal securities for purposes of this section, a person may rely on representations in writing made by a knowledgeable official of the municipal entity or obligated person whose funds are to be invested regarding the nature of such funds, provided that the person seeking to rely on such representations has a reasonable basis for such reliance.

(n) *Solicitation of a municipal entity or obligated person* has the same meaning as in section 15B(e)(9) of the Act (15

U.S.C. 78o–4(e)(9)); *provided, however,* that a solicitation does not include:

(1) Advertising by a broker, dealer, municipal securities dealer, municipal advisor, or investment adviser; or

(2) Solicitation of an obligated person, if such obligated person is not acting in the capacity of an obligated person or the solicitation of the obligated person is not in connection with the issuance of municipal securities or with respect to municipal financial products.

[78 FR 67633, Nov. 12, 2013]

§ 240.15Ba1–2 Registration of municipal advisors and information regarding certain natural persons.

(a) *Form MA.* A person applying for registration with the Commission as a municipal advisor pursuant to section 15B of the Act (15 U.S.C. 78o–4) must complete Form MA (17 CFR 249.1300) in accordance with the instructions in the Form and file the Form electronically with the Commission.

(b) *Form MA–I.* (1) A person applying for registration or registered with the Commission as a municipal advisor pursuant to section 15B of the Act (15 U.S.C. 78o–4) must complete Form MA–I (17 CFR 249.1310) with respect to each natural person who is a person associated with the municipal advisor (as defined in section 15B(e)(7) of the Act (15 U.S.C. 78o–4(e)(7))) and engaged in municipal advisory activities on its behalf in accordance with the instructions in the Form and file the Form electronically with the Commission.

(2) A natural person applying for registration with the Commission as a municipal advisor pursuant to section 15B of the Act (15 U.S.C. 78o–4), in addition to completing and filing Form MA pursuant to paragraph (a) of this section, must complete Form MA–I (17 CFR 249.1310) in accordance with the instructions in the Form and file the Form electronically with the Commission.

(c) *When filed.* Each Form MA (17 CFR 249.1300) shall be considered filed with the Commission upon submission of a completed Form MA, together with all additional required documents, including all required filings of Form MA–I (17 CFR 249.1310), to the Commission's Electronic Data Gathering, Analysis, and Retrieval system.

(d) *Form MA and Form MA–I are reports.* Each Form MA (17 CFR 249.1300) and Form MA–I (17 CFR 249.1310) required to be filed under this section shall constitute a report within the meaning of sections 15B(c), 17(a), 18(a), 32(a) of the Act (15 U.S.C. 78o–4(c), 78q(a), 78r(a), 78ff(a)) and other applicable provisions of the Act.

[78 FR 67633, Nov. 12, 2013]

§ 240.15Ba1–3 Exemption of certain natural persons from registration under section 15B(a)(1)(B) of the Act.

A natural person municipal advisor shall be exempt from section 15B(a)(1)(B) of the Act (15 U.S.C. 78o–4(a)(1)(B)) if he or she:

(a) Is an associated person of an advisor that is registered with the Commission pursuant to section 15B(a)(2) of the Act (15 U.S.C. 78o–4(a)(2)) and the rules and regulations thereunder; and

(b) Engages in municipal advisory activities solely on behalf of a registered municipal advisor.

[78 FR 67633, Nov. 12, 2013]

§ 240.15Ba1–4 Withdrawal from municipal advisor registration.

(a) *Form MA–W.* Notice of withdrawal from registration as a municipal advisor shall be filed on Form MA–W (17 CFR 249.1320) in accordance with the instructions to the Form.

(b) *Electronic filing.* Any notice of withdrawal on Form MA–W (17 CFR 249.1320) must be filed electronically.

(c) *Effective date.* A notice of withdrawal from registration shall become effective for all matters on the 60th day after the filing thereof, within such longer period of time as to which the municipal advisor consents or which the Commission by order may determine as necessary or appropriate in the public interest or for the protection of investors, or within such shorter period of time as the Commission may determine. If a notice of withdrawal from registration is filed at any time subsequent to the date of the issuance of a Commission order instituting proceedings pursuant to section 15B(c) of the Act (15 U.S.C. 78o–4(c)) to censure, place limitations on the activities, functions or operations of, or suspend or revoke the registration of, the municipal advisor, or if prior to the effective date of the notice of withdrawal pursuant to this paragraph (c), the Commission institutes such a proceeding or a proceeding to impose terms or conditions upon such withdrawal, the notice of withdrawal shall not become effective pursuant to this paragraph (c) except at such time and upon such terms and conditions as the Commission deems necessary or appropriate in the public interest or for the protection of investors.

(d) *Form MA–W is a report.* Each Form MA–W (17 CFR 249.1320) required to be filed under this section shall constitute a report within the meaning of sections 15B(c), 17(a), 18(a), 32(a) of the Act (15 U.S.C. 78o–4(c), 78q(a), 78r(a), 78ff(a)) and other applicable provisions of the Act.

[78 FR 67633, Nov. 12, 2013]

§ 240.15Ba1-5 Amendments to Form MA and Form MA–I.

(a) *When amendment is required—Form MA.* A registered municipal advisor shall promptly amend the information contained in its Form MA (17 CFR 249.1300):

(1) At least annually, within 90 days of the end of a municipal advisor's fiscal year, or of the end of the calendar year for a sole proprietor; and

(2) More frequently, if required by the General Instructions (17 CFR 249.1300), as applicable.

(b) *When amendment is required—Form MA–I.* A registered municipal advisor shall promptly amend the information contained in Form MA–I (17 CFR 249.1310) by filing an amended Form MA–I whenever the information contained in the Form MA–I becomes inaccurate for any reason.

(c) *Electronic filing of amendments.* A registered municipal advisor shall file all amendments to Form MA (17 CFR 249.1300) and Form MA–I (17 CFR 249.1310) electronically.

(d) *Amendments to Form MA and Form MA–I are reports.* Each amendment required to be filed under this section shall constitute a report within the meaning of sections 15B(c), 17(a), 18(a), 32(a) of the Act (15 U.S.C. 78o–4(c), 78q(a), 78r(a), 78ff(a)) and other applicable provisions of the Act.

[78 FR 67633, Nov. 12, 2013]

§ 240.15Ba1-6 Consent to service of process to be filed by non-resident municipal advisors; legal opinion to be provided by non-resident municipal advisors.

(a)(1) Each non-resident municipal advisor applying for registration pursuant to section 15B(a) of the Act (15 U.S.C. 78o–4(a)) shall, at the time of filing of the municipal advisor's application on Form MA (17 CFR 249.1300), file with the Commission a written irrevocable consent and power of attorney on Form MA–NR (17 CFR 249.1330) to appoint an agent in the United States, other than a Commission member, official, or employee, upon whom may be served any process, pleadings, or other papers in any action brought against the non-resident municipal advisor to enforce this chapter.

(2) Each municipal advisor applying for registration pursuant to or registered under section 15B of the Act (15 U.S.C. 78o–4) shall, at the time of filing the relevant Form MA (17 CFR 249.1300) or Form MA–I (17 CFR 249.1310), file with the Commission a written irrevocable consent and power of attorney on Form MA–NR (17 CFR 249.1330) to appoint an agent in the United States, other than a Commission member, official, or employee, upon whom may be served any process, pleadings, or other papers in any action brought against the municipal advisor's non-resident general partner or non-resident managing agent, or non-resident natural persons who are persons associated with the municipal advisor (as defined in section 15B(e)(7) of the Act (15 U.S.C. 78o–4(e)(7))) and engaged in municipal advisory activities on its behalf, to enforce this chapter.

(b) The registered municipal advisor shall communicate promptly to the Commission by filing a new Form MA–NR (17 CFR 249.1330) any change to the name or address of the agent for service of process of each such non-resident municipal advisor, general partner, managing agent, or natural persons who are persons associated with the municipal advisor (as defined in section 15B(e)(7) of the Act (15 U.S.C. 78o–

Securities and Exchange Commission § 240.15Ba1-8

4(e)(7))) and engaged in municipal advisory activities on its behalf.

(c)(1) Each registered non-resident municipal advisor must promptly appoint a successor agent for service of process and file a new Form MA–NR (17 CFR 249.1330) if the non-resident municipal advisor discharges its identified agent for service of process or if its agent for service of process is unwilling or unable to accept service on behalf of the non-resident municipal advisor.

(2) Each registered municipal advisor must require each of its non-resident general partners or non-resident managing agents, or non-resident natural persons who are persons associated with the municipal advisor (as defined in section 15B(e)(7) of the Act (15 U.S.C. 78o–4(e)(7))) and engaged in municipal advisory activities on its behalf, to promptly appoint a successor agent for service of process and the registered municipal advisor must file a new Form MA–NR (17 CFR 249.1330) if such non-resident general partner, managing agent, or associated person discharges the identified agent for service of process or if the agent for service of process is unwilling or unable to accept service on behalf such person.

(d) Each non-resident municipal advisor applying for registration pursuant to section 15B(a) of the Act (15 U.S.C. 78o–4(a)) shall provide an opinion of counsel on Form MA (17 CFR 249.1300) that the municipal advisor can, as a matter of law, provide the Commission with access to the books and records of the municipal advisor as required by law and that the municipal advisor can, as a matter of law, submit to inspection and examination by the Commission.

(e) Form MA–NR (17 CFR 249.1330) must be filed electronically.

[78 FR 67633, Nov. 12, 2013]

§ 240.15Ba1-7 Registration of successor to municipal advisor.

(a) In the event that a municipal advisor succeeds to and continues the business of a municipal advisor registered pursuant to section 15B(a) of the Act (15 U.S.C. 78o–4(a)), the registration of the predecessor shall be deemed to remain effective as the registration of the successor if the successor, within 30 days after the succession, files an application for registration on Form MA (17 CFR 249.1300), and the predecessor files a notice of withdrawal from registration on Form MA–W (17 CFR 249.1320); *provided, however,* that the registration of the predecessor municipal advisor will cease to be effective as the registration of the successor municipal advisor 45 days after the application for registration on Form MA is filed by the successor.

(b) Notwithstanding paragraph (a) of this section, if a municipal advisor succeeds to and continues the business of a registered predecessor municipal advisor, and the succession is based solely on a change in the predecessor's date or state of incorporation, form of organization, or composition of a partnership, the successor may, within 30 days after the succession, amend the registration of the predecessor municipal advisor on Form MA (17 CFR 249.1300) to reflect these changes. This amendment shall be deemed an application for registration filed by the predecessor and adopted by the successor.

[78 FR 67633, Nov. 12, 2013]

§ 240.15Ba1-8 Books and records to be made and maintained by municipal advisors.

(a) Every person registered or required to be registered under section 15B of the Act (15 U.S.C. 78o-4) and the rules and regulations thereunder shall make and keep true, accurate, and current the following books and records relating to its municipal advisory activities:

(1) Originals or copies of all written communications received, and originals or copies of all written communications sent, by such municipal advisor (including inter-office memoranda and communications) relating to municipal advisory activities, regardless of the format of such communications;

(2) All check books, bank statements, general ledgers, cancelled checks and cash reconciliations of the municipal advisor;

(3) A copy of each version of the municipal advisor's policies and procedures, if any, that:

(i) Are in effect; or

(ii) At any time within the last five years were in effect, not including those in effect prior to July 1, 2014;

529

§ 240.15Ba1–8

(4) A copy of any document created by the municipal advisor that was material to making a recommendation to a municipal entity or obligated person or that memorializes the basis for that recommendation;

(5) All written agreements (or copies thereof) entered into by the municipal advisor with any municipal entity, employee of a municipal entity, or an obligated person or otherwise relating to the business of such municipal advisor as such;

(6) A record of the names of persons who are currently, or within the past five years were, associated with the municipal advisor, not including persons associated with the municipal advisor prior to July 1, 2014;

(7) Books and records containing a list or other record of:

(i) The names, titles, and business and residence addresses of all persons associated with the municipal advisor;

(ii) All municipal entities or obligated persons with which the municipal advisor is engaging or has engaged in municipal advisory activities in the past five years, not including those prior to July 1, 2014;

(iii) The name and business address of each person to whom the municipal advisor provides or agrees to provide, directly or indirectly, payment to solicit a municipal entity, an employee of a municipal entity, or an obligated person on its behalf; and

(iv) The name and business address of each person that provides or agrees to provide, directly or indirectly, payment to the municipal advisor to solicit a municipal entity, an employee of a municipal entity, or an obligated person on its behalf; and

(8) Written consents to service of process from each natural person who is a person associated with the municipal advisor and engages in municipal advisory activities solely on behalf of such municipal advisor.

(b)(1) All books and records required to be made under this section shall be maintained and preserved for a period of not less than five years, the first two years in an easily accessible place.

(2) Partnership articles and any amendments thereto, articles of incorporation, charters, minute books, and stock certificate books of the municipal advisor and of any predecessor, excluding those that were only in effect prior to July 1, 2014, shall be maintained in the principal office of the municipal advisor and preserved until at least three years after termination of the business or withdrawal from registration as a municipal advisor.

(c) A municipal advisor subject to paragraph (a) of this section, before ceasing to conduct or discontinuing business as a municipal advisor, shall arrange for and be responsible for the preservation of the books and records required to be maintained and preserved under this section for the remainder of the period specified in this section, and shall notify the Commission in writing, at its principal office in Washington, DC, of the exact address where such books and records will be maintained during such period.

(d) *Electronic storage permitted.* (1) *General.* The records required to be maintained and preserved pursuant to this part may be maintained and preserved for the required time on:

(i) Electronic storage media, including any digital storage medium or system that meets the terms of this section; or

(ii) Paper documents.

(2) *General requirements.* The municipal advisor must:

(i) Arrange and index the records in a way that permits easy location, access, and retrieval of any particular record;

(ii) Provide promptly any of the following that the Commission (by its staff or other representatives) may request:

(A) A legible, true, and complete copy of the record in the medium and format in which it is stored;

(B) A legible, true, and complete printout of the record; and

(C) Means to access, view, and print the records; and

(iii) Separately store, for the time required for preservation of the record, a duplicate copy of the record on any medium allowed by this section.

(3) *Special requirements for electronic storage media.* In the case of records on electronic storage media, the municipal advisor must establish and maintain procedures:

(i) To maintain and preserve the records, so as to reasonably safeguard

Securities and Exchange Commission § 240.15Ba1-8

them from loss, alteration, or destruction;

(ii) To limit access to the records to properly authorized personnel and the Commission (including its staff and other representatives); and

(iii) To reasonably ensure that any reproduction of a non-electronic record on electronic storage media is complete, true, and legible when retrieved.

(e)(1) Any book or other record made, kept, maintained, and preserved in compliance with §§ 240.17a–3 and 240.17a–4, rules of the Municipal Securities Rulemaking Board, or § 275.204–2 under the Investment Advisers Act of 1940 (15 U.S.C. 80b–1 *et seq.*), which is substantially the same as a book or other record required to be made, kept, maintained, and preserved under this section, shall satisfy the requirements of this section.

(2) A record made and kept pursuant to any provision of paragraph (a) of this section that contains all the information required under any other provision of paragraph (a) of this section, need not be maintained in duplicate in order to meet the requirements of the other provisions of paragraph (a) of this section.

(f)(1) Except as provided in paragraph (f)(3) of this section, each non-resident municipal advisor registered or applying for registration pursuant to section 15B of the Act (15 U.S.C. 78*o*-4) and the rules and regulations thereunder shall keep, maintain, and preserve, at a place within the United States designated in a notice from such municipal advisor as provided in paragraph (f)(2) of this section, true, correct, complete, and current copies of books and records that such municipal advisor is required to make, keep current, maintain or preserve pursuant to any provisions of any rule or regulation of the Commission adopted under the Act.

(2) Except as provided in paragraph (f)(3) of this section, each non-resident municipal advisor subject to paragraph (f)(1) of this section shall furnish to the Commission a written notice specifying the address of the place within the United States where the copies of the books and records required to be kept, maintained, and preserved by such municipal advisor pursuant to paragraph (f)(1) of this section are located. Each non-resident municipal advisor registered or applying for registration when this paragraph becomes effective shall file such notice within 30 calendar days after this paragraph becomes effective. Each non-resident municipal advisor that files an application for registration after this paragraph becomes effective shall file such notice with such application for registration.

(3) Notwithstanding the provisions of paragraphs (f)(1) and (2) of this section, a non-resident municipal advisor need not keep, maintain, or preserve within the United States copies of the books and records referred to in paragraphs (f)(1) and (2) of this section, if:

(i) Such non-resident municipal advisor files with the Commission, at the time or within the period provided by paragraph (f)(2) of this section, a written undertaking, in a form acceptable to the Commission and signed by a duly authorized person, to furnish to the Commission, upon demand, at the Commission's principal office in Washington, DC, or at any Regional Office of the Commission designated in such demand, true, correct, complete, and current copies of any or all of the books and records which such municipal advisor is required to make, keep current, maintain, or preserve pursuant to any provision of any rule or regulation of the Commission adopted under the Act, or any part of such books and records that may be specified in such demand. Such undertaking shall be in substantially the following form:

The undersigned hereby undertakes to furnish at its own expense to the Securities and Exchange Commission at the Commission's principal office in Washington, DC or at any Regional Office of the Commission specified in a demand for copies of books and records made by or on behalf of the Commission, true, correct, complete, and current copies of any or all, or any part, of the books and records that the undersigned is required to make, keep current, maintain, or preserve pursuant to any provision of any rule or regulation of the Securities and Exchange Commission under the Securities Exchange Act of 1934. This undertaking shall be suspended during any period when the undersigned is making, keeping current, maintaining, and preserving copies of all of said books and records at a place within the United States in compliance with 17 CFR 240.15Ba1–7(f)(1) and (2). This undertaking shall be binding

§ 240.15Ba2-1

upon the undersigned and the heirs, successors and assigns of the undersigned, and the written irrevocable consents and powers of attorney of the undersigned, its general partners, and managing agents filed with the Securities and Exchange Commission shall extend to and cover any action to enforce the same.

and

(ii) Such non-resident municipal advisor furnishes to the Commission, at such municipal advisor's own expense 14 calendar days after written demand therefor forwarded to such municipal advisor by registered mail at such municipal advisor's last address of record filed with the Commission and signed by the Secretary of the Commission or such person as the Commission may authorize to act in its behalf, true, correct, complete, and current copies of any or all books and records which such municipal advisor is required to make, keep current, maintain, or preserve pursuant to any provision of any rule or regulation of the Commission adopted under the Act, or any part of such books and records that may be specified in said written demand. Such copies shall be furnished to the Commission at the Commission's principal office in Washington, DC, or at any Regional Office of the Commission which may be specified in said written demand.

[78 FR 67633, Nov. 12, 2013, as amended at 79 FR 2779, Jan. 16, 2014]

§ 240.15Ba2-1 Application for registration of municipal securities dealers which are banks or separately identifiable departments or divisions of banks.

(a) An application for registration, pursuant to Section 15B(a) of the Act, of a municipal securities dealer which is a bank (as defined in section 3(a)(6) of the Act) or a separately identifiable department or division of a bank (as defined by the Municipal Securities Rulemaking Board), shall be filed with the Commission on Form MSD (§ 249.950 of this chapter), in accordance with the instructions contained therein.

(b) If the information contained in any application for registration pursuant to paragraph (a) of this section, or in any amendment to such application, is or becomes inaccurate for any reason, applicant shall promptly file an amendment on Form MSD (§ 249.950 of this chapter) correcting such information.

(c) Every amendment filed pursuant to this rule shall constitute a "report" within the meaning of sections 17 and 32(a) of the Act (15 U.S.C. 78q and 78ff(a)).

[40 FR 49776, Oct. 24, 1975]

§ 240.15Ba2-2 Application for registration of non-bank municipal securities dealers whose business is exclusively intrastate.

(a) An application for registration, pursuant to section 15B(a) of the Act, of a municipal securities dealer who is not subject to the requirements of § 240.15Ba2-1, that is filed on or after January 25, 1993, shall be filed with the Central Registration Depository (operated by the Financial Industry Regulatory Authority, Inc.) on Form BD in accordance with the instructions contained therein.

(b) Every applicant shall file with its application for registration a statement that such applicant is filing for registration as an intrastate dealer in accordance with the requirements of this section. Such statement shall be deemed a part of the application for registration.

(c) If the information contained in any application for registration filed pursuant to paragraph (a) of this section, or in any amendment to such application, is or becomes inaccurate for any reason, the dealer shall promptly file with the Central Registration Depository an amendment on Form BD correcting such information.

(d) Every application or amendment filed with the Central Registration Depository pursuant to this section shall constitute a "report" filed with the Commission within the meaning of Sections 15(b), 15B(c), 17(a), 18(a), 32(a) (15 U.S.C. 78o(b), 78o-4(c), 78q(a), 78r(a), 78ff(a)) and other applicable provisions of the Act.

[58 FR 14, Jan. 4, 1993, as amended at 64 FR 25148, May 10, 1999; 64 FR 37594, July 12, 1999; 64 FR 42596, Aug. 5, 1999; 73 FR 4692, Jan. 28, 2008]

§ 240.15Ba2-4 Registration of successor to registered municipal securities dealer.

(a) In the event that a municipal securities dealer succeeds to and continues the business of a registered municipal securities dealer, the registration of the predecessor shall be deemed to remain effective as the registration of the successor if the successor, within 30 days after such succession, files an application for registration on Form MSD, in the case of a municipal securities dealer that is a bank or a separately identifiable department or division of a bank, or Form BD, in the case of any other municipal securities dealer, and the predecessor files a notice of withdrawal from registration on Form MSDW or Form BDW, as the case may be; *Provided, however,* That the registration of the predecessor dealer will cease to be effective as the registration of the successor dealer 45 days after the application for registration on Form MSD or Form BD is filed by such successor.

(b) Notwithstanding paragraph (a) of this section, if a municipal securities dealer succeeds to and continues the business of a registered predecessor municipal securities dealer, and the succession is based solely on a change in the predecessor's date or state of incorporation, form of organization, or composition of a partnership, the successor may, within 30 days after the succession, amend the registration of the predecessor dealer on Form MSD, in the case of a predecessor municipal securities dealer that is a bank or a separately identifiable department or division of a bank, or on Form BD, in the case of any other municipal securities dealer, to reflect these changes. This amendment shall be deemed an application for registration filed by the predecessor and adopted by the successor.

[58 FR 10, Jan. 4, 1993]

§ 240.15Ba2-5 Registration of fiduciaries.

The registration of a municipal securities dealer shall be deemed to be the registration of any executor, administrator, guardian, conservator, assignee for the benefit of creditors, receiver, trustee in insolvency or bankruptcy, or other fiduciary, appointed or qualified by order, judgment, or decree of a court of competent jurisdiction to continue the business of such registered municipal securities dealer, provided that such fiduciary files with the Commission, within 30 days after entering upon the performance of his duties, a statement setting forth as to such fiduciary substantially the information required by Form MSD, if the municipal securities dealer is a bank or a separately identifiable department of a bank, or Form BD, if the municipal securities dealer is other than a bank or a separately identifiable department or division of a bank.

[41 FR 28948, July 14, 1976]

§ 240.15Ba2-6 [Reserved]

§ 240.15Bc3-1 Withdrawal from registration of municipal securities dealers.

(a) Notice of withdrawal from registration as a municipal securities dealer pursuant to Section 15B(c) (15 U.S.C. 78o–4(c)) shall be filed on Form MSDW (17 CFR 249.1110), in the case of a municipal securities dealer which is a bank or a separately identifiable department or division of a bank, or Form BDW (17 CFR 249.501a), in the case of any other municipal securities dealer, in accordance with the instructions contained therein. Prior to filing a notice of withdrawal from registration on Form MSDW (17 CFR 249.1110) or Form BDW (17 CFR 249.501a), a municipal securities dealer shall amend Form MSD (17 CFR 249.1100) in accordance with § 240.15Ba2-1(b) or amend Form BD (17 CFR 249.501) in accordance with § 240.15Ba2-2(c) to update any inaccurate information.

(b) Every notice of withdrawal from registration as a municipal securities dealer that is filed on Form BDW (17 CFR 249.501a) shall be filed with the Central Registration Depository (operated by the Financial Industry Regulatory Authority, Inc.) in accordance with applicable filing requirements. Every notice of withdrawal of Form MSDW (17 CFR 249.1110) shall be filed with the Commission.

(c) A notice of withdrawal from registration filed by a municipal securities dealer pursuant to Section 15B(c)

§ 240.15Bc4–1

(15 U.S.C. 78o–4(c)) shall become effective for all matters on the 60th day after the filing thereof with the Commission, within such longer period of time as to which such municipal securities dealer consents or which the Commission by order may determine as necessary or appropriate in the public interest or for the protection of investors, or within such shorter period of time as the Commission may determine. If a notice of withdrawal from registration is filed with the Commission at any time subsequent to the date of the issuance of a Commission order instituting proceedings pursuant to Section 15B(c) (15 U.S.C. 78o–4(c)) to censure, place limitations on the activities, functions or operations of, or suspend or revoke the registration of, such municipal securities dealer, or if prior to the effective date of the notice of withdrawal pursuant to this paragraph (c), the Commission institutes such a proceeding or a proceeding to impose terms or conditions upon such withdrawal, the notice of withdrawal shall not become effective pursuant to this paragraph (c) except at such time and upon such terms and conditions as the Commission deems necessary or appropriate in the public interest or for the protection of investors.

(d) Every notice of withdrawal filed with the Central Registration Depository pursuant to this section shall constitute a ''report'' filed with the Commission within the meaning of Sections 15B(c), 17(a), 18(a), 32(a) (15 U.S.C. 78o–4(c), 78q(a), 78r(a), 78ff(a)) and other applicable provisions of the Act.

(e) The Commission, by order, may exempt any broker or dealer from the filing requirements provided in Form BDW (17 CFR 249.501a) under conditions that differ from the filing instructions contained in Form BDW.

[64 FR 25148, May 10, 1999, as amended at 64 FR 42596, Aug. 5, 1999; 73 FR 4692, Jan. 28, 2008]

§ 240.15Bc4–1 Persons associated with municipal advisors.

A person associated, seeking to become associated, or, at the time of the alleged misconduct, associated or seeking to become associated with a municipal advisor, shall be subject to a Commission order that censures or places limitations on the activities or functions of such person, or suspends for a period not exceeding twelve months or bars such person from being associated with a broker, dealer, investment adviser, municipal securities dealer, municipal advisor, transfer agent, or nationally recognized statistical rating organization, if the Commission finds, on the record after notice and opportunity for hearing, that such censure, placing of limitations, suspension, or bar is in the public interest and that such person has committed any act, or is subject to an order or finding, enumerated in subparagraph (A), (D), (E), (H), or (G) of paragraph (4) of section 15(b) of the Act (15 U.S.C. 78o(b)(4)(A), 78o(b)(4)(D), 78o(b)(4)(E), 78o(b)(4)(H), 78o(b)(4)(G)), has been convicted of any offense specified in subparagraph (B) of such paragraph (4) (15 U.S.C. 78o(b)(4)(B)) within 10 years of the commencement of the proceedings under section 15B(c)(4) (15 U.S.C. 78o–4(c)(4)), or is enjoined from any action, conduct, or practice specified in subparagraph (C) of such paragraph (4) (15 U.S.C. 78o(b)(4)(C)). It shall be unlawful for any person as to whom an order entered pursuant to section 15B(c)(4) of the Act (15 U.S.C. 78o–4(c)(4)) or section 15B(c)(5) of the Act (15 U.S.C. 78o–4(c)(5)) suspending or barring him from being associated with a municipal advisor is in effect willfully to become, or to be, associated with a municipal advisor without the consent of the Commission, and it shall be unlawful for any municipal advisor to permit such a person to become, or remain, a person associated with it without the consent of the Commission, if such municipal advisor knew, or, in the exercise of reasonable care should have known, of such order.

[78 FR 67638, Nov. 12, 2013]

§ 240.15Bc7–1 Availability of examination reports.

(a) Upon written request, copies of any report of an examination of a municipal securities dealer made by the Commission or furnished to it by an appropriate regulatory agency pursuant to section 17(c)(3) of the Act or by a registered securities association pursuant to section 15B(c)(7)(B) of the Act

Securities and Exchange Commission § 240.15Bc7-1

shall be made available to the Municipal Securities Rulemaking Board (the "Board") by the Commission subject to the following limitations:

(1) The Board shall establish by rule and shall maintain adequate procedures for ensuring the confidentiality of any information made available to it by the Commission pursuant to section 15B(c)(7)(B) of the Act;

(2) Information made available to the Board shall not identify any municipal securities broker, municipal securities dealer, or associated person that is the subject of a non-public examination report.

(b) If information to be made available to the Board is furnished to the Commission on a separate form prepared by an appropriate regulatory agency other than the Commission or by a registered securities association, that form, rather than a copy of any report of an examination, will be made available to the Board, provided that the conditions set forth in this paragraph are satisfied. Within sixty days of every six month period ending May 31 and November 30, each appropriate regulatory agency or registered securities association making available information on a separate form shall furnish to the Commission two copies of a form containing the information set forth in paragraphs (b)(1) through (b)(8) of this section. The Commission shall make one copy of the form promptly available to the Board. Copies of any forms furnished pursuant to this paragraph shall not identify any municipal securities broker, municipal securities dealer, or associated person that is the subject of an examination from which information was derived for the form; however, the Commission may obtain for its own use, upon request, the identity of any such examinee or the full examination reports. Furnished forms shall include the following information:

(1) The report period.

(2)(i) With respect to a registered securities association, the number of examinations that formed the basis of the report and, of these examinations, the number that were routine, special, and financial/operational.

(ii) With respect to an appropriate regulatory agency that is a bank agency, the number of examinations that formed the basis of the report and, of these examinations, the number that were routine, special, and financial/operational. The number of examinations that formed the basis of the report of bank dealers and the number of examinations of separately identifiable departments or divisions of banks effecting municipal securities transactions.

(3) Indications of the violations of each Board rule found in examinations that formed the basis for the report.

(4) Copies of public notices issued during the report period of any formal actions and non-public information regarding any actions taken on violations of Board rules.

(5) Any comments concerning any questionable practices relating to municipal securities activities, whether or not covered by provisions of the Act and the rules and regulations thereunder, including the rules of the Board.

(6) Descriptions of any significant or recurring customer complaints relating to municipal securities activities received by the appropriate regulatory agency or registered securities association during the report period or by municipal securities dealers during the 12 month period preceding the examination.

(7) Description of any novel issues or interpretations arising under the Board's rules.

(8) Description of any changes to existing Board rules or additional rules that would improve the regulatory scheme for municipal securities professionals or assist in the enforcement of the Board's rules.

(c) Copies of any report of an examination of a municipal securities broker or municipal securities dealer made by the Commission or furnished to it pursuant to section 15B(c)(7)(B) or 17(c)(3) of the Act, or separate forms made available to the Commission pursuant to paragraph (b) of this section, will be maintained in a non-public file.

[50 FR 48556, Nov. 26, 1985]

§ 240.15Ca1-1

REGISTRATION OF GOVERNMENT SECURITIES BROKERS AND GOVERNMENT SECURITIES DEALERS

SOURCE: Sections 240.15.Ca1–1 through 240.15Cc1–1 appear at 52 FR 16839, May 6, 1987, unless otherwise noted.

§ 240.15Ca1-1 Notice of government securities broker-dealer activities.

(a) Every government securities broker or government securities dealer that is a broker or dealer registered pursuant to section 15 or 15B of the Act (other than a financial institution as defined in section 3(a)(46) of the Act) shall file with the Commission written notice on Form BD (§ 249.501 of this chapter) in accordance with the instructions contained therein that it is a government securities broker or government securities dealer. After July 25, 1987, every broker or dealer subject to this paragraph shall file notice that it is a government securities broker or government securities dealer prior to or on the date it begins acting as a government securities broker or government securities dealer.

(b) Every government securities broker or government securities dealer required to file notice under paragraph (a) of this section shall file with the Commission written notice on Form BD in accordance with the instructions contained therein when it ceases to be a government securities broker or government securities dealer. Notice shall be filed within 30 days after the date the broker or dealer has ceased acting as a government securities broker or a government securities dealer.

(c) Any notice required pursuant to this section shall be considered filed with the Commission if it is filed with the Central Registration Depository (operated by the Financial Industry Regulatory Authority, Inc.) in accordance with applicable filing requirements.

[52 FR 16839, May 6, 1987, as amended at 58 FR 14, Jan. 4, 1993; 64 FR 25148, May 10, 1999; 73 FR 4693, Jan. 28, 2008]

§ 240.15Ca2-1 Application for registration as a government securities broker or government securities dealer.

(a) An application for registration pursuant to Section 15C(a)(1)(A) of the Act, of a government securities broker or government securities dealer that is filed on or after January 25, 1993, shall be filed with the Central Registration Depository (operated by the Financial Industry Regulatory Authority, Inc.) on Form BD in accordance with the instructions contained therein.

(b) Every application or amendment filed pursuant to this section shall constitute a "report" filed with the Commission within the meaning of Sections 15, 15C, 17(a), 18, 32(a), and other applicable provisions of the Act.

[58 FR 15, Jan. 4, 1993, as amended at 64 FR 37594, July 12, 1999; 64 FR 42596, Aug. 5, 1999; 73 FR 4693, Jan. 28, 2008]

§ 240.15Ca2-2 [Reserved]

§ 240.15Ca2-3 Registration of successor to registered government securities broker or government securities dealer.

(a) In the event that a government securities broker or government securities dealer succeeds to and continues the business of a government securities broker or government securities dealer registered pursuant to section 15C(a)(1)(A) of the Act, the registration of the predecessor shall be deemed to remain effective as the registration of the successor if the successor, within 30 days after such succession, files an application for registration on Form BD, and the predecessor files a notice of withdrawal from registration on Form BDW; *Provided, however,* That the registration of the predecessor government securities broker or government securities dealer will cease to be effective as the registration of the successor government securities broker or government securities dealer 45 days after the application for registration on Form BD is filed by such successor.

(b) Notwithstanding paragraph (a) of this section, if a government securities broker or government securities dealer succeeds to and continues the business of a predecessor government securities broker or government securities dealer that is registered pursuant to section 15C(a)(1)(A) of the Act, and the succession is based solely on a change in the predecessor's date or state of incorporation, form of organization, or composition of a partnership, the successor may, within 30 days after the succession, amend the registration of the predecessor broker or dealer on Form BD to reflect these changes. This amendment shall be deemed an application for registration filed by the predecessor and adopted by the successor.

[58 FR 11, Jan. 4, 1993]

§ 240.15Ca2-4 Registration of fiduciaries.

The registration of a government securities broker or government securities dealer pursuant to section 15C of the Act shall be deemed to be the registration of any executor, administrator, guardian, conservator, assignee for the benefit of creditors, receiver, trustee in insolvency or bankruptcy, or other fiduciary, appointed or qualified by order, judgment, or decree of a court of competent jurisdiction to continue the business of such registered government securities broker or government securities dealer, provided that such fiduciary files with the Commission, no more than 30 days after entering upon the performance of its duties, a statement setting forth as to such fiduciary substantially the information required by Form BD.

§ 240.15Ca2-5 Consent to service of process to be furnished by non-resident government securities brokers or government securities dealers and by non-resident general partners or managing agents of government securities brokers or government securities dealers.

(a) Each non-resident government securities broker or government securities dealer applying for registration pursuant to section 15C(a)(1)(A) of the Act, each non-resident general partner of a government securities broker or government securities dealer partnership that is applying for such registration, and each non-resident managing agent of any other unincorporated government securities broker or government securities dealer that is applying for registration, shall furnish to the Commission, in a form acceptable to the Commission, a written irrevocable consent and power of attorney that—

(1) Designates the Securities and Exchange Commission as an agent of such government securities broker or government securities dealer upon whom may be served any process, pleadings, or other papers in any civil suit or action brought in any appropriate court in any place subject to the jurisdiction of the United States, with respect to any cause of action,

(i) That accrues during the period beginning when such government securities broker or government securities dealer becomes registered pursuant to section 15C(a)(1)(A) of the Act and ending either when such registration is cancelled or revoked, or when a notice filed by such government securities broker or government securities dealer to withdraw from such registration becomes effective, whichever is earlier,

(ii) That arises out of any activity, in any place subject to the jurisdiction of the United States, occurring in connection with the conduct of the business of such government securities broker or government securities dealer, and

(iii) That is founded, directly or indirectly, upon the Securities Act of 1933, the Securities Exchange Act of 1934, the Trust Indenture Act of 1939, the Investment Company Act of 1940, the Investment Advisers Act of 1940, or any rule or regulation under any of those Acts, and

(2) Stipulates and agrees that any such civil suit or action may be commenced against such government securities broker or government securities dealer by the service of process upon the Commission and the forwarding of a copy thereof as provided in paragraph (c) of this section and that the service as aforesaid of any such process, pleadings, or other papers upon the Commission shall be taken and held in all courts to be as valid and binding as if due process service thereof had been made.

(b) Each government securities broker or government securities dealer registered pursuant to section 15C(a)(1)(A) of the Act that becomes a non-resident government securities

§ 240.15Cc1-1   17 CFR Ch. II (4-1-23 Edition)

broker or government securities dealer, and each general partner or managing agent of an unincorporated government securities broker or government securities dealer registered or applying for registration pursuant to section 15C(a)(1)(A) of the Act who becomes a non-resident after such registration or filing of an application for such registration, shall furnish such consent and power of attorney no more than 30 days thereafter.

(c) Service of any process, pleadings, or other papers on the Commission under this rule shall be made by delivering the requisite number of copies thereof to the Secretary of the Commission or to such other person as the Commission may authorize to act in its behalf. Whenever any process, pleadings, or other papers as aforesaid are served upon the Commission, it shall promptly forward a copy thereof by registered or certified mail to the appropriate defendants at their last address of record filed with the Commission; but any failure by the Commission to forward such a copy shall have no effect on the validity of the service made upon the Commission. The Commission shall be furnished a sufficient number of copies for such purpose, and one copy for its file.

(d) For purposes of this rule the following definitions shall apply:

(1) The term *managing agent* shall mean any person, including a trustee, who directs or manages or who participates in the directing or managing of the affairs of any unincorporated organization or association that is not a partnership.

(2) The term *non-resident government securities broker or government securities dealer* shall mean (i) in the case of an individual, one who is domiciled in or has his principal place of business in any place not subject to the jurisdiction of the United States, (ii) in the case of a corporation, one incorporated in or having its principal place of business in any place not subject to the jurisdiction of the United States; (iii) in the case of a partnership or other unincorporated organization or association, one having its principal place of business in any place not subject to the jurisdiction of the United States.

(3) A general partner or managing agent of a government securities broker or government securities dealer shall be deemed to be a non-resident if he is domiciled in any place not subject to the jurisdiction of the United States.

§ 240.15Cc1-1 Withdrawal from registration of government securities brokers or government securities dealers.

(a) Notice of withdrawal from registration as a government securities broker or government securities dealer pursuant to Section 15C(a)(1)(A) of the Act (15 U.S.C. 78o-5(a)(1)(A)) shall be filed on Form BDW (17 CFR 249.501a) in accordance with the instructions contained therein. Every notice of withdrawal from registration as a government securities broker or dealer shall be filed with the Central Registration Depository (operated by the Financial Industry Regulatory Authority, Inc.) in accordance with applicable filing requirements. Prior to filing a notice of withdrawal from registration on Form BDW (17 CFR 249.501a), a government securities broker or government securities dealer shall amend Form BD (17 CFR 249.501) in accordance with 17 CFR 400.5(a) to update any inaccurate information.

(b) A notice of withdrawal from registration filed by a government securities broker or government securities dealer shall become effective for all matters on the 60th day after the filing thereof with the Commission, within such longer period of time as to which such government securities broker or government securities dealer consents or the Commission by order may determine as necessary or appropriate in the public interest or for the protection of investors, or within such shorter period of time as the Commission may determine. If a notice of withdrawal from registration is filed with the Commission at any time subsequent to the date of the issuance of a Commission order instituting proceedings pursuant to Section 15C(c) (15 U.S.C. 78o-5(c)) to censure, place limitations on the activities, functions or operations of, or suspend or revoke the registration of such government securities broker or government securities dealer, or if

Securities and Exchange Commission § 240.15Fb1-1.

prior to the effective date of the notice of withdrawal pursuant to this paragraph (b), the Commission institutes such a proceeding or a proceeding to impose terms or conditions upon such withdrawal, the notice of withdrawal shall not become effective pursuant to this paragraph (b) except at such time and upon such terms and conditions as the Commission deems necessary or appropriate in the public interest or for the protection of investors.

(c) Every notice of withdrawal filed with the Central Registration Depository pursuant to this section shall constitute a "report" filed with the Commission within the meaning of Sections 15(b), 15C(c), 17(a), 18(a), 32(a) (15 U.S.C. 78o(b), 78o-5(c), 78q(a), 78r(a), 78ff(a)) and other applicable provisions of the Act.

(d) The Commission, by order, may exempt any broker or dealer from the filing requirements provided in Form BDW (17 CFR 249.501a) under conditions that differ from the filing instructions contained in Form BDW.

[64 FR 25148, May 10, 1999, as amended at 64 FR 42596, Aug. 5, 1999; 73 FR 4693, Jan. 28, 2008]

REGISTRATION AND REGULATION OF SECURITY-BASED SWAP DEALERS AND MAJOR SECURITY-BASED SWAP PARTICIPANTS

SOURCE: Sections 240.15Fb1-1 through 240.15Fb6-2 appear at 80 FR 49013, Aug. 14, 2015, unless otherwise noted.

§ 240.15Fb1-1. Signatures.

(a) Required signatures to, or within, any electronic submission (including, without limitation, signatories within the forms and certifications required by §§ 240.15Fb2-1, 240.15Fb2-4, and 240.15Fb6-2) must be in typed form rather than manual format. Signatures in an HTML, XML or XBRL document that are not required may, but are not required to, be presented in a graphic or image file within the electronic filing. When used in connection with an electronic filing, the term "signature" means an electronic entry in the form of a magnetic impulse or other form of computer data compilation of any letters or series of letters or characters comprising a name, executed, adopted or authorized as a signature.

(b) Each signatory to an electronic filing (including, without limitation, each signatory to the forms and certifications required by §§ 240.15Fb2-1, 240.15Fb2-4, and 240.15Fb6-2) shall manually or electronically sign a signature page or other document authenticating, acknowledging, or otherwise adopting his or her signature that appears in typed form within the electronic filing ("authentication document"). Such authentication document shall be executed before or at the time the electronic filing is made. The requirements set forth in § 232.302(b) must be met with regards to the use of an electronically signed authentication document pursuant to this paragraph (b). Upon request, the security-based swap dealer or major security-based swap participant shall furnish to the Commission or its staff a copy of any or all documents retained pursuant to this paragraph (b).

(c) A person required to provide a signature on an electronic submission (including, without limitation, each signatory to the forms and certifications required by §§ 240.15Fb2-1, 240.15Fb2-4, and 240.15Fb6-2) may not have the form or certification signed on his or her behalf pursuant to a power of attorney or other form of confirming authority.

(d) Each manually or electronically signed signature page or other document authenticating, acknowledging, or otherwise adopting his or her signature that appears in typed form within the electronic filing ("authentication document")—

(1) On Schedule F to Form SBSE (§ 249.1600 of this chapter), SBSE-A (§ 249.1600a of this chapter), or SBSE-BD (§ 249.1600b of this chapter), as appropriate, shall be retained by the filer until at least three years after the form or certification has been replaced or is no longer effective;

(2) On Form SBSE-C (§ 249.1600c of this chapter) shall be retained by the filer until at least three years after the Form was filed with the Commission.

[80 FR 49013, Aug. 14, 2015, as amended at 85 FR 78229, Dec. 4, 2020]

§ 240.15Fb2–1 Registration of security-based swap dealers and major security-based swap participants.

(a) *Application.* An application for registration of a security-based swap dealer or a major security-based swap participant that is filed pursuant to Section 15F(b) of the Securities Exchange Act of 1934 (15 U.S.C. 78o–10(b)) shall be filed on Form SBSE (§ 249.1600 of this chapter) or Form SBSE–A (§ 249.1600a of this chapter) or Form SBSE–BD (§ 249.1600b of this chapter), as appropriate, in accordance with paragraph (c) and the instructions to the forms. Applicants shall also file as part of their application the required certifications on Form SBSE–C (§ 249.1600c of this chapter).

(b) *Senior Officer Certification.* A senior officer shall certify on Form SBSE–C (§ 249.1600c of this chapter) that;

(1) After due inquiry, he or she has reasonably determined that the security-based swap dealer or major security-based swap participant has developed and implemented written policies and procedures reasonably designed to prevent violation of federal securities laws and the rules thereunder, and

(2) He or she has documented the process by which he or she reached such determination.

(c) *Filing*—(1) *Electronic filing.* Every application for registration of a security-based swap dealer or major security-based swap participant and any additional registration documents shall be filed electronically with the Commission through the Commission's EDGAR system.

(2) *Filing date.* An application of a security-based swap dealer or a major security-based swap participant submitted pursuant to paragraph (a) of this section shall be considered filed when an applicant has submitted a complete Form SBSE–C (§ 249.1600c of this chapter) and a complete Form SBSE (§ 249.1600 of this chapter), Form SBSE–A (§ 249.1600a of this chapter), or Form SBSE–BD (§ 249.1600b of this chapter), as appropriate, and all required additional documents electronically with the Commission.

(d) *Conditional registration.* (1) An applicant that has submitted a complete Form SBSE–C (§ 249.1600c of this chapter) and a complete Form SBSE (§ 249.1600 of this chapter) or Form SBSE–A (§ 249.1600a of this chapter) or Form SBSE–BD (§ 249.1600b of this chapter), as applicable, in accordance with paragraph (c) within the time periods set forth in § 240.3a67–8 (if the person is a major security-based swap participant) or § 240.3a71–2(b) (if the person is a security-based swap dealer), and has not withdrawn its registration shall be conditionally registered.

(2) Notwithstanding paragraph (d)(1) of this section, an applicant that is a nonresident security-based swap dealer or nonresident major security-based swap participant (each as defined in § 240.15Fb2–4(a)) that is unable to provide the certification and opinion of counsel required by § 240.15Fb2–4(c)(1) shall instead provide a conditional certification and opinion of counsel as discussed in paragraph (d)(3) of this section, and upon the provision of such conditional certification and opinion of counsel, shall be conditionally registered, if the nonresident applicant submits a Form SBSE–C (§ 249.1600c of this chapter) and a Form SBSE (§ 249.1600 of this chapter), SBSE–A (§ 249.1600a of this chapter) or SBSE–BD (§ 249.1600b of this chapter), as applicable, in accordance with paragraph (c) of this section within the time periods set forth in § 240.3a67–8 (if the person is a major security-based swap participant) or § 240.3a71–2(b) (if the person is a security-based swap dealer), that is complete in all respects but for the failure to provide the certification and the opinion of counsel required by § 240.15Fb2–4(c)(1), and has not withdrawn from registration.

(3) For purposes of this section, a conditional certification and opinion of counsel means a certification as required by § 240.15Fb2–4(c)(1)(i) and an opinion of counsel as required by § 240.15Fb2–4(c)(1)(ii) that identify, and are conditioned upon, the occurrence of a future action that would provide the Commission with adequate assurances of prompt access to the books and records of the nonresident security-based swap dealer or nonresident major security-based swap participant, and the ability of the nonresident security-based swap dealer or nonresident major

Securities and Exchange Commission

§ 240.15Fb2–3

security-based swap participant to submit to onsite inspection and examination by the Commission. Such future action could include:

(i) Entry by the Commission and the foreign financial regulatory authority of the jurisdiction(s) in which the nonresident security-based swap dealer or nonresident major security-based swap participant maintains the books and records that are addressed by the certification and opinion of counsel required by § 240.15Fb2–4(c)(1) into a memorandum of understanding, agreement, protocol, or other regulatory arrangement providing the Commission with adequate assurances of:

(A) Prompt access to the books and records of the nonresident security-based swap dealer or nonresident major security-based swap participant; and

(B) The ability of the nonresident security-based swap dealer or nonresident major security-based swap participant to submit to onsite inspection or examination by the Commission; or

(ii) Issuance by the Commission of an order granting substituted compliance in accordance with § 240.3a71–6 to the jurisdiction(s) in which the nonresident security-based swap dealer or nonresident major security-based swap participant maintains the books and records that are addressed by the certification and opinion of counsel required by § 240.15Fb2–4(c)(1); or

(iii) Any other action that would provide the Commission with the assurances required by § 240.15Fb2–4(c)(1)(i) and by § 240.15Fb2–4(c)(1)(ii).

(e) *Commission Decision.* (1) The Commission may deny or grant ongoing registration to a security-based swap dealer or major security-based swap participant based on a security-based swap dealer's or major security-based swap participant's application, filed pursuant to paragraph (a) of this section. The Commission will grant ongoing registration if it finds that the requirements of section 15F(b) of the Securities Exchange Act of 1934 (15 U.S.C. 78o–10(b)) are satisfied. The Commission may institute proceedings to determine whether ongoing registration should be denied if it does not or cannot make such finding or if the applicant is subject to a statutory disqualification (as described in sections 3(a)(39)(A) through (F) of the Securities Exchange Act of 1934 (15 U.S.C. 78c(a)(39)(A)–(F)), or the Commission is aware of inaccurate statements in the application. Such proceedings shall include notice of the grounds for denial under consideration and opportunity for hearing. At the conclusion of such proceedings, the Commission shall grant or deny such registration.

(2) If an applicant that is a nonresident security-based swap dealer or nonresident major security-based swap participant has become conditionally registered in reliance on paragraph (d)(2) of this section, the applicant will remain conditionally registered until the Commission acts to grant or deny ongoing registration in accordance with (e)(1) of this section. If none of the future actions in paragraph (d)(3) that are included in an applicant's conditional certification and opinion of counsel occurs within 24 months of the compliance date for § 240.15Fb2–1, and there is not otherwise a basis that would provide the Commission with the assurances required by § 240.15Fb2–4(c)(1)(i) and by § 240.15Fb2–4(c)(1)(ii), the Commission may institute proceedings thereafter to determine whether ongoing registration should be denied, in accordance with paragraph (e)(1) of this section.

[80 FR 49013, Aug. 14, 2015, as amended at 85 FR 6352, Feb. 4, 2020]

§ 240.15Fb2–3 Amendments to Form SBSE, Form SBSE–A, and Form SBSE–BD.

If a security-based swap dealer or a major security-based swap participant finds that the information contained in its Form SBSE (§ 249.1600 of this chapter), Form SBSE–A (§ 249.1600a of this chapter), or Form SBSE–BD (§ 249.1600b of this chapter), as appropriate, or in any amendment thereto, is or has become inaccurate for any reason, the security-based swap dealer or a major security-based swap participant shall promptly file an amendment electronically with the Commission through the Commission's EDGAR system on the appropriate Form to correct such information.

§ 240.15Fb2–4

§ 240.15Fb2–4 Nonresident security-based swap dealers and major security-based swap participants.

(a) *Definition.* For purposes of this section, the terms *nonresident security-based swap dealer* and *nonresident major security-based swap participant* shall mean:

(1) In the case of an individual, one who resides, or has his or her principal place of business, in any place not in the United States;

(2) In the case of a corporation, one incorporated in or having its principal place of business in any place not in the United States; or

(3) In the case of a partnership or other unincorporated organization or association, one having its principal place of business in any place not in the United States.

(b) *Power of attorney.* (1) Each nonresident security-based swap dealer and nonresident major security-based swap participant registered or applying for registration pursuant to Section 15F(b) of the Securities Exchange Act of 1934 (15 U.S.C. 78o–10(b)) shall obtain a written irrevocable consent and power of attorney appointing an agent in the United States, other than the Commission or a Commission member, official or employee, upon whom may be served any process, pleadings, or other papers in any action brought against the nonresident security-based swap dealer or nonresident major security-based swap participant to enforce the Securities Exchange Act of 1934 (15 U.S.C. 78a *et seq.*). This consent and power of attorney must be signed by the nonresident security-based swap dealer or nonresident major security-based swap participant and the named agent(s) for service of process.

(2) Each nonresident security-based swap dealer and nonresident major security-based swap participant registered or applying for registration pursuant to section 15F(b) of the Securities Act of 1934 (15 U.S.C. 78o–10(b)) shall, at the time of filing its application on Form SBSE (§ 249.1600 of this chapter), Form SBSE–A (§ 249.1600a of this chapter), or Form SBSE–BD (§ 249.1600b of this chapter), as appropriate, furnish to the Commission the name and address of its United States agent for service of process on Schedule F to the appropriate form.

(3) Any change of a nonresident security-based swap dealer's and nonresident major security-based swap participant's agent for service of process and any change of name or address of a nonresident security-based swap dealer's and nonresident major security-based swap participant's existing agent for service of process shall be communicated promptly to the Commission through amendment of the Schedule F of Form SBSE (§ 249.1600 of this chapter), Form SBSE–A (§ 249.1600a of this chapter), or Form SBSE–BD (§ 249.1600b of this chapter), as appropriate.

(4) Each nonresident security-based swap dealer and nonresident major security-based swap participant must promptly appoint a successor agent for service of process, consistent with the process described in paragraph (b)(1), if the nonresident security-based swap dealer and nonresident major security-based swap participant discharges its identified agent for service of process or if its agent for service of process is unwilling or unable to accept service on behalf of the nonresident security-based swap dealer or nonresident major security-based swap participant.

(5) Each nonresident security-based swap dealer and nonresident major security-based swap participant must maintain, as part of its books and records, the agreement identified in paragraphs (b)(1) and (b)(4) of this section for at least three years after the agreement is terminated.

(c) *Access to books and records*—(1) *Certification and opinion of counsel.* Each nonresident security-based swap dealer and nonresident major security-based swap participant applying for registration pursuant to Section 15F(b) of the Securities Exchange Act of 1934 (15 U.S.C. 78o–10(b)) shall:

(i) Certify on Schedule F of Form SBSE (§ 249.1600 of this chapter), Form SBSE–A (§ 249.1600a of this chapter), or Form SBSE–BD (§ 249.1600b of this chapter), as appropriate, that the nonresident security-based swap dealer and nonresident major security-based swap participant can, as a matter of law, and will provide the Commission with prompt access to the books and records

Securities and Exchange Commission
§ 240.15Fb2-6

of such nonresident security-based swap dealer and nonresident major security-based swap participant, and can, as a matter of law, and will submit to onsite inspection and examination by the Commission; and

(ii) Provide an opinion of counsel that the nonresident security-based swap dealer and nonresident major security-based swap participant can, as a matter of law, provide the Commission with prompt access to the books and records of such nonresident security-based swap dealer and nonresident major security-based swap participant, and can, as a matter of law, submit to onsite inspection and examination by the Commission.

(2) *Amendments.* Each nonresident security-based swap dealer and nonresident major security-based swap participant shall re-certify, on Schedule F to Form SBSE (§ 249.1600 of this chapter), Form SBSE-A (§ 249.1600a of this chapter), or Form SBSE-BD (§ 249.1600b of this chapter), as applicable, within 90 days after any changes in the legal or regulatory framework that would impact the nonresident security-based swap dealer's or nonresident major security-based swap participant's ability to provide, or the manner in which it provides the Commission with prompt access to its books and records, or would impact the Commission's ability to inspect and examine the nonresident security-based swap dealer or nonresident major security-based swap participant. The re-certification shall be accompanied by a revised opinion of counsel describing how, as a matter of law, the nonresident security-based swap dealer or nonresident major security-based swap participant will continue to meet its obligations to provide the Commission with prompt access to its books and records and to be subject to Commission inspection and examination under the new regulatory regime.

§ 240.15Fb2-5 **Registration of successor to registered security-based swap dealer or a major security-based swap participant.**

(a) In the event that a security-based swap dealer or major security-based swap participant succeeds to and continues the business of a security-based swap dealer or major security-based swap participant registered pursuant to Section 15F(b) of the Securities Exchange Act of 1934 (15 U.S.C. 78o-10(b)), the registration of the predecessor shall be deemed to remain effective as the registration of the successor if the successor, within 30 days after such succession, files an application for registration in accordance with § 240.15Fb2-1, and the predecessor files a notice of withdrawal from registration on Form SBSE-W (§ 249.1601 of this chapter).

(b) Notwithstanding paragraph (a) of this section, if a security-based swap dealer or major security-based swap participant succeeds to and continues the business of a registered predecessor security-based swap dealer or major security-based swap participant, and the succession is based solely on a change in the predecessor's date or state of incorporation, form of organization, or composition of a partnership, the successor may, within 30 days after the succession, amend the registration of the predecessor security-based swap dealer or major security-based swap participant on Form SBSE (§ 249.1600 of this chapter), Form SBSE-A (§ 249.1600a of this chapter), or Form SBSE-BD (§ 249.1600b of this chapter), as appropriate, to reflect these changes. This amendment shall be deemed an application for registration filed by the predecessor and adopted by the successor.

§ 240.15Fb2-6 **Registration of fiduciaries.**

The registration of a security-based swap dealer or a major security-based swap participant shall be deemed to be the registration of any executor, administrator, guardian, conservator, assignee for the benefit of creditors, receiver, trustee in insolvency or bankruptcy, or other fiduciary, appointed or qualified by order, judgment, or decree of a court of competent jurisdiction to continue the business of such registered security-based swap dealer or a major security-based swap participant; *Provided,* that such fiduciary files with the Commission, within 30 days after entering upon the performance of his or her duties, an amended Form SBSE (§ 249.1600 of this chapter), Form SBSE-

§ 240.15Fb3-1

A (§ 249.1600a of this chapter), or Form SBSE-BD (§ 249.1600b of this chapter), as appropriate, indicating the fiduciary's position with respect to management of the firm and, as an additional document, a copy of the order, judgment, decree, or other document appointing the fiduciary.

§ 240.15Fb3-1 Duration of registration.

(a) *General.* A person registered as a security-based swap dealer or major security-based swap participant in accordance with § 240.15Fb2-1 will continue to be so registered until the effective date of any cancellation, revocation or withdrawal of such registration.

(b) *Conditional registration.* Notwithstanding paragraph (a) of this section, conditional registration shall expire on the date the registrant withdraws from registration or the Commission grants or denies the person's ongoing registration in accordance with § 240.15Fb2-1(e).

§ 240.15Fb3-2 Withdrawal from registration.

(a) Notice of withdrawal from registration as a security-based swap dealer or major security-based swap participant pursuant to Section 15F(b) of the Securities Exchange Act of 1934 (15 U.S.C. 78o-10(b)) shall be filed on Form SBSE-W (§ 249.1601 of this chapter) in accordance with the instructions contained therein. Every notice of withdrawal from registration as a security-based swap dealer or major security-based swap participant shall be filed electronically with the Commission through the Commission's EDGAR system. Prior to filing a notice of withdrawal from registration on Form SBSE-W, a security-based swap dealer or major security-based swap participant shall amend its Form SBSE (§ 249.1600 of this chapter), Form SBSE-A (§ 249.1600a of this chapter) or Form SBSE-BD (§ 249.1600b of this chapter), as appropriate, in accordance with § 240.15Fb2-3(a) to update any inaccurate information.

(b) A notice of withdrawal from registration filed by a security-based swap dealer or major security-based swap participant pursuant to Section 15F(b) of the Securities Exchange Act of 1934 (15 U.S.C. 78o-10(b)) shall become effective for all matters (except as provided in this paragraph (b)) on the 60th day after the filing thereof with the Commission or its designee, within such longer period of time as to which such security-based swap dealer or major security-based swap participant consents or which the Commission by order may determine as necessary or appropriate in the public interest or for the protection of investors, or within such shorter period of time as the Commission may determine. If a notice of withdrawal from registration is filed with the Commission at any time subsequent to the date of the issuance of a Commission order instituting proceedings to censure, place limitations on the activities, functions or operations of, or suspend or revoke the registration of, such security-based swap dealer or major security-based swap participant, or if prior to the effective date of the notice of withdrawal pursuant to this paragraph (b), the Commission institutes such a proceeding or a proceeding to impose terms or conditions upon such withdrawal, the notice of withdrawal shall not become effective pursuant to this paragraph (b) except at such time and upon such terms and conditions as the Commission deems necessary or appropriate in the public interest or for the protection of investors.

§ 240.15Fb3-3 Cancellation and revocation of registration.

(a) *Cancellation.* If the Commission finds that any person registered pursuant to § 240.15Fb2-1 is no longer in existence or has ceased to do business as a security-based swap dealer or major security-based swap participant, the Commission shall by order cancel the registration of such person.

(b) *Revocation.* The Commission, by order, shall censure, place limitations on the activities, functions, or operations of, or revoke the registration of any security-based swap dealer or major security-based swap participant that has registered with the Commission if it makes a finding as specified in Section 15F(l)(2) of the Securities Exchange Act of 1934 (15 U.S.C. 78o-10(l)(2)).

Securities and Exchange Commission § 240.15Fh-2

§ 240.15Fb6-1 [Reserved]

§ 240.15Fb6-2 Associated person certification.

(a) *Certification.* No registered security-based swap dealer or major security-based swap participant shall act as a security-based swap dealer or major security-based swap participant unless it has certified electronically on Form SBSE-C (Section 249.1600c of this chapter) that it neither knows, nor in the exercise of reasonable care should have known, that any person associated with such security-based swap dealer or major security-based swap participant who effects or is involved in effecting security-based swaps on behalf of the security-based swap dealer or major security-based swap participant is subject to a statutory disqualification, as described in Sections 3(a)(39)(A) through (F) of the Securities Exchange Act of 1934 (15 U.S.C. 78c(a)(39)(A)-(F)), unless otherwise specifically provided by rule, regulation or order of the Commission.

(b) To support the certification required by paragraph (a) of this section, the security-based swap dealer's or major security-based swap participant's Chief Compliance Officer, or his or her designee, shall review and sign the questionnaire or application for employment, which the security-based swap dealer or major security-based swap participant is required to obtain pursuant to the relevant recordkeeping rule applicable to such security-based swap dealer or major security-based swap participant, executed by each associated person who is a natural person and who effects or is involved in effecting security based swaps on the security-based swap dealer's or major security-based swap participant's behalf. The questionnaire or application shall serve as a basis for a background check of the associated person to verify that the person is not subject to statutory disqualification.

§ 240.15Fh-1 Scope and reliance on representations.

(a) *Scope.* Sections 240.15Fh-1 through 240.15Fh-6, and 240.15Fk-1 are not intended to limit, or restrict, the applicability of other provisions of the federal securities laws, including but not limited to section 17(a) of the Securities Act of 1933 and sections 9 and 10(b) of the Act, and rules and regulations thereunder, or other applicable laws and rules and regulations. Sections 240.15Fh-1 through 240.15Fh-6, and 240.15Fk-1 apply, as relevant, in connection with entering into security-based swaps and continue to apply, as appropriate, over the term of executed security-based swaps. Sections 240.15Fh-3(a) through 240.15Fh-3(f), 240.15Fh-4(b) and 240.15Fh-5 are not applicable to security-based swaps that security-based swap dealers or major security-based swap participants enter into with their majority-owned affiliates. For these purposes the counterparties to a security-based swap are majority-owned affiliates if one counterparty directly or indirectly owns a majority interest in the other, or if a third party directly or indirectly owns a majority interest in both counterparties to the security-based swap, where "majority interest" is the right to vote or direct the vote of a majority of a class of voting securities of an entity, the power to sell or direct the sale of a majority of a class of voting securities of an entity, or the right to receive upon dissolution or the contribution of a majority of the capital of a partnership.

(b) *Reliance on representations.* A security-based swap dealer or major security-based swap participant may rely on written representations from the counterparty or its representative to satisfy its due diligence requirements under § 240.15Fh, unless it has information that would cause a reasonable person to question the accuracy of the representation.

[81 FR 30144, May 13, 2016]

§ 240.15Fh-2 Definitions.

As used in §§ 240.15Fh-1 through 240.15Fh-6:

(a) *Act as an advisor to a special entity.* A security-based swap dealer *acts as an advisor to a special entity* when it recommends a security-based swap or a trading strategy that involves the use of a security-based swap to the special entity, unless:

(1) With respect to a special entity as defined in § 240.15Fh-2(d)(3):

§ 240.15Fh-3

(i) The special entity represents in writing that it has a fiduciary as defined in section 3 of the Employee Retirement Income Security Act of 1974 (29 U.S.C. 1002) that is responsible for representing the special entity in connection with the security-based swap;

(ii) The fiduciary represents in writing that it acknowledges that the security-based swap dealer is not acting as an advisor; and

(iii) The special entity represents in writing:

(A) That it will comply in good faith with written policies and procedures reasonably designed to ensure that any recommendation the special entity receives from the security-based swap dealer involving a security-based swap transaction is evaluated by a fiduciary before the transaction is entered into; or

(B) That any recommendation the special entity receives from the security-based swap dealer involving a security-based swap transaction will be evaluated by a fiduciary before the transaction is entered into.

(2) With respect to any special entity:

(i) The special entity represents in writing that:

(A) It acknowledges that the security-based swap dealer is not acting as an advisor; and

(B) The special entity will rely on advice from a qualified independent representative as defined in § 240.15Fh-5(a); and

(ii) The security-based swap dealer discloses to the special entity that it is not undertaking to act in the best interest of the special entity, as otherwise required by section 15F(h)(4) of the Act.

(b) *Eligible contract participant* means any person as defined in section 3(a)(65) of the Act and the rules and regulations thereunder and in section 1a of the Commodity Exchange Act (7 U.S.C. 1a) and the rules and regulations thereunder.

(c) *Security-based swap dealer or major security-based swap participant* includes, where relevant, an associated person of the security-based swap dealer or major security-based swap participant.

(d) *Special entity* means:

(1) A Federal agency;

(2) A State, State agency, city, county, municipality, other political subdivision of a State, or any instrumentality, department, or a corporation of or established by a State or political subdivision of a State;

(3) Any employee benefit plan, subject to Title I of the Employee Retirement Income Security Act of 1974 (29 U.S.C. 1002);

(4) Any employee benefit plan defined in section 3 of the Employee Retirement Income Security Act of 1974 (29 U.S.C. 1002) and not otherwise defined as a special entity, unless such employee benefit plan elects not to be a special entity by notifying a security-based swap dealer or major security-based swap participant of its election prior to entering into a security-based swap with the particular security-based swap dealer or major security-based swap participant;

(5) Any governmental plan, as defined in section 3(32) of the Employee Retirement Income Security Act of 1974 (29 U.S.C. 1002(32)); or

(6) Any endowment, including an endowment that is an organization described in section 501(c)(3) of the Internal Revenue Code of 1986.

(e) A person is *subject to a statutory disqualification* for purposes of § 240.15Fh-5 if that person would be subject to a statutory disqualification, as described in section 3(a)(39)(A)–(F) of the Act.

[81 FR 30144, May 13, 2016]

§ 240.15Fh-3 Business conduct requirements.

(a) *Counterparty status*—(1) *Eligible contract participant.* A security-based swap dealer or a major security-based swap participant shall verify that a counterparty meets the eligibility standards for an eligible contract participant before entering into a security-based swap with that counterparty, provided that the requirements of this paragraph (a)(1) shall not apply to a transaction executed on a registered national securities exchange.

(2) *Special entity.* A security-based swap dealer or a major security-based swap participant shall verify whether a counterparty is a special entity before entering into a security-based swap

Securities and Exchange Commission § 240.15Fh-3

with that counterparty, unless the transaction is executed on a registered or exempt security-based swap execution facility or registered national securities exchange, and the security-based swap dealer or major security-based swap participant does not know the identity of the counterparty at a reasonably sufficient time prior to execution of the transaction to permit the security-based swap dealer or major security-based swap participant to comply with the obligations of paragraph (a) of this section.

(3) *Special entity election.* In verifying the special entity status of a counterparty pursuant to § 240.15Fh-3(a)(2), a security-based swap dealer or major security-based swap participant shall verify whether a counterparty is eligible to elect not to be a special entity under § 240.15Fh-2(d)(4) and, if so, notify such counterparty of its right to make such an election.

(b) *Disclosure.* At a reasonably sufficient time prior to entering into a security-based swap, a security-based swap dealer or major security-based swap participant shall disclose to a counterparty, other than a security-based swap dealer, major security-based swap participant, swap dealer or major swap participant, material information concerning the security-based swap in a manner reasonably designed to allow the counterparty to assess the material risks and characteristics and material incentives or conflicts of interest, as described below, so long as the identity of the counterparty is known to the security-based swap dealer or major security-based swap participant at a reasonably sufficient time prior to execution of the transaction to permit the security-based swap dealer or major security-based swap participant to comply with the obligations of paragraph (b) of this section.

(1) *Material risks and characteristics* means the material risks and characteristics of the particular security-based swap, which may include:

(i) Market, credit, liquidity, foreign currency, legal, operational, and any other applicable risks; and

(ii) The material economic terms of the security-based swap, the terms relating to the operation of the security-based swap, and the rights and obligations of the parties during the term of the security-based swap.

(2) *Material incentives or conflicts of interest* means any material incentives or conflicts of interest that the security-based swap dealer or major security-based swap participant may have in connection with the security-based swap, including any compensation or other incentives from any source other than the counterparty in connection with the security-based swap to be entered into with the counterparty.

(3) *Record.* The security-based swap dealer or major security-based swap participant shall make a written record of the non-written disclosures made pursuant to this paragraph (b), and provide a written version of these disclosures to its counterparties in a timely manner, but in any case no later than the delivery of the trade acknowledgment of the particular transaction pursuant to § 240.15Fi-1.

(c) *Daily mark.* A security-based swap dealer or major security-based swap participant shall disclose the daily mark to the counterparty, other than a security-based swap dealer, major security-based swap participant, swap dealer or major swap participant, which shall be:

(1) For a cleared security-based swap, upon request of the counterparty, the daily mark that the security-based swap dealer or major security-based swap participant receives from the appropriate clearing agency;

(2) For an uncleared security-based swap, the midpoint between the bid and offer, or the calculated equivalent thereof, as of the close of business, unless the parties agree in writing otherwise to a different time, on each business day during the term of the security-based swap. The daily mark may be based on market quotations for comparable security-based swaps, mathematical models or a combination thereof. The security-based swap dealer or major security-based swap participant shall also disclose its data sources and a description of the methodology and assumptions used to prepare the daily mark, and promptly disclose any material changes to such data sources, methodology and assumptions during the term of the security-based swap; and

§ 240.15Fh–3

(3) The security-based swap dealer or major security-based swap participant shall provide the daily mark without charge to the counterparty and without restrictions on the internal use of the daily mark by the counterparty.

(d) *Disclosure regarding clearing rights.* A security-based swap dealer or major security-based swap participant shall disclose the following information to a counterparty, other than a security-based swap dealer, major security-based swap participant, swap dealer or major swap participant, so long as the identity of the counterparty is known to the security-based swap dealer or major security-based swap participant at a reasonably sufficient time prior to execution of the transaction to permit the security-based swap dealer or major security-based swap participant to comply with the obligations of paragraph (d) of this section:

(1) *For security-based swaps subject to clearing requirement.* Before entering into a security-based swap subject to the clearing requirement under section 3C(a) of the Act, a security-based swap dealer or major security-based swap participant shall:

(i) Disclose to the counterparty the names of the clearing agencies that accept the security-based swap for clearing, and through which of those clearing agencies the security-based swap dealer or major security-based swap participant is authorized or permitted, directly or through a designated clearing member, to clear the security-based swap; and

(ii) Notify the counterparty that it shall have the sole right to select which of the clearing agencies described in paragraph (d)(1)(i) of this section shall be used to clear the security-based swap subject to section 3C(g)(5) of the Act.

(2) *For security-based swaps not subject to clearing requirement.* Before entering into a security-based swap not subject to the clearing requirement under section 3C(a) of the Act, a security-based swap dealer or major security-based swap participant shall:

(i) Determine whether the security-based swap is accepted for clearing by one or more clearing agencies;

(ii) Disclose to the counterparty the names of the clearing agencies that accept the security-based swap for clearing, and whether the security-based swap dealer or major security-based swap participant is authorized or permitted, directly or through a designated clearing member, to clear the security-based swap through such clearing agencies; and

(iii) Notify the counterparty that it may elect to require clearing of the security-based swap and shall have the sole right to select the clearing agency at which the security-based swap will be cleared, provided it is a clearing agency at which the security-based swap dealer or major security-based swap participant is authorized or permitted, directly or through a designated clearing member, to clear the security-based swap.

(3) *Record.* The security-based swap dealer or major security-based swap participant shall make a written record of the non-written disclosures made pursuant to this paragraph (d), and provide a written version of these disclosures to its counterparties in a timely manner, but in any case no later than the delivery of the trade acknowledgement of the particular transaction pursuant to § 240.15Fi–1.

(c) *Know your counterparty.* Each security-based swap dealer shall establish, maintain and enforce written policies and procedures reasonably designed to obtain and retain a record of the essential facts concerning each counterparty whose identity is known to the security-based swap dealer that are necessary for conducting business with such counterparty. For purposes of paragraph (e) of this section, the *essential facts concerning a counterparty* are:

(1) Facts required to comply with applicable laws, regulations and rules;

(2) Facts required to implement the security-based swap dealer's credit and operational risk management policies in connection with transactions entered into with such counterparty; and

(3) Information regarding the authority of any person acting for such counterparty.

(f) *Recommendations of security-based swaps or trading strategies.* (1) A security-based swap dealer that recommends a security-based swap or trading strategy involving a security-

Securities and Exchange Commission § 240.15Fh-3

based swap to a counterparty, other than a security-based swap dealer, major security-based swap participant, swap dealer, or major swap participant, must:

(i) Undertake reasonable diligence to understand the potential risks and rewards associated with the recommended security-based swap or trading strategy involving a security-based swap; and

(ii) Have a reasonable basis to believe that a recommended security-based swap or trading strategy involving a security-based swap is suitable for the counterparty. To establish a reasonable basis for a recommendation, a security-based swap dealer must have or obtain relevant information regarding the counterparty, including the counterparty's investment profile, trading objectives, and its ability to absorb potential losses associated with the recommended security-based swap or trading strategy involving a security-based swap.

(2) A security-based swap dealer may also fulfill its obligations under paragraph (f)(1)(ii) of this section with respect to an institutional counterparty, if:

(i) The security-based swap dealer reasonably determines that the counterparty, or an agent to which the counterparty has delegated decision-making authority, is capable of independently evaluating investment risks with regard to the relevant security-based swap or trading strategy involving a security-based swap;

(ii) The counterparty or its agent affirmatively represents in writing that it is exercising independent judgment in evaluating the recommendations of the security-based swap dealer with regard to the relevant security-based swap or trading strategy involving a security-based swap; and

(iii) The security-based swap dealer discloses that it is acting in its capacity as a counterparty, and is not undertaking to assess the suitability of the security-based swap or trading strategy for the counterparty.

(3) A security-based swap dealer will be deemed to have satisfied its obligations under paragraph (f)(2)(i) of this section if it receives written representations, as provided in § 240.15Fh-1(b), that:

(i) In the case of a counterparty that is not a special entity, the counterparty has complied in good faith with written policies and procedures that are reasonably designed to ensure that the persons responsible for evaluating the recommendation and making trading decisions on behalf of the counterparty are capable of doing so; or

(ii) In the case of a counterparty that is a special entity, satisfy the terms of the safe harbor in § 240.15Fh-5(b).

(4) For purposes of paragraph (f)(2) of this section, an institutional counterparty is a counterparty that is an eligible contract participant as defined in clauses (A)(i), (ii), (iii), (iv), (viii), (ix) or (x), or clause (B)(ii) (other than a person described in clause (A)(v)) of section 1a(18) of the Commodity Exchange Act (7 U.S.C. 1(a)(18)) and the rules and regulations thereunder, or any person (whether a natural person, corporation, partnership, trust or otherwise) with total assets of at least $50 million.

(g) *Fair and balanced communications.* A security-based swap dealer or major security-based swap participant shall communicate with counterparties in a fair and balanced manner based on principles of fair dealing and good faith. In particular:

(1) Communications must provide a sound basis for evaluating the facts with regard to any particular security-based swap or trading strategy involving a security-based swap;

(2) Communications may not imply that past performance will recur or make any exaggerated or unwarranted claim, opinion or forecast; and

(3) Any statement referring to the potential opportunities or advantages presented by a security-based swap shall be balanced by an equally detailed statement of the corresponding risks.

(h) *Supervision*—(1) *In general.* A security-based swap dealer or major security-based swap participant shall establish and maintain a system to supervise, and shall diligently supervise, its business and the activities of its associated persons. Such a system shall be

§ 240.15Fh–3

reasonably designed to prevent violations of the provisions of applicable federal securities laws and the rules and regulations thereunder relating to its business as a security-based swap dealer or major security-based swap participant, respectively.

(2) *Minimum requirements.* The system required by paragraph (h)(1) of this section shall, at a minimum, provide for:

(i) The designation of at least one person with authority to carry out the supervisory responsibilities of the security-based swap dealer or major security-based swap participant for each type of business in which it engages for which registration as a security-based swap dealer or major security-based swap participant is required;

(ii) The use of reasonable efforts to determine that all supervisors are qualified, either by virtue of experience or training, to carry out their assigned responsibilities; and

(iii) Establishment, maintenance and enforcement of written policies and procedures addressing the supervision of the types of security-based swap business in which the security-based swap dealer or major security-based swap participant is engaged and the activities of its associated persons that are reasonably designed to prevent violations of applicable federal securities laws and the rules and regulations thereunder, and that include, at a minimum:

(A) Procedures for the review by a supervisor of transactions for which registration as a security-based swap dealer or major security-based swap participant is required;

(B) Procedures for the review by a supervisor of incoming and outgoing written (including electronic) correspondence with counterparties or potential counterparties and internal written communications relating to the security-based swap dealer's or major security-based swap participant's business involving security-based swaps;

(C) Procedures for a periodic review, at least annually, of the security-based swap business in which the security-based swap dealer or major security-based swap participant engages that is reasonably designed to assist in detecting and preventing violations of applicable federal securities laws and the rules and regulations thereunder;

(D) Procedures to conduct a reasonable investigation regarding the good character, business repute, qualifications, and experience of any person prior to that person's association with the security-based swap dealer or major security-based swap participant;

(E) Procedures to consider whether to permit an associated person to establish or maintain a securities or commodities account or a trading relationship in the name of, or for the benefit of such associated person, at another security-based swap dealer, broker, dealer, investment adviser, or other financial institution; and if permitted, procedures to supervise the trading at the other security-based swap dealer, broker, dealer, investment adviser, or financial institution;

(F) A description of the supervisory system, including the titles, qualifications and locations of supervisory persons and the responsibilities of each supervisory person with respect to the types of business in which the security-based swap dealer or major security-based swap participant is engaged;

(G) Procedures prohibiting an associated person who performs a supervisory function from supervising his or her own activities or reporting to, or having his or her compensation or continued employment determined by, a person or persons he or she is supervising; provided, however, that if the security-based swap dealer or major security-based swap participant determines, with respect to any of its supervisory personnel, that compliance with this requirement is not possible because of the firm's size or a supervisory person's position within the firm, the security-based swap dealer or major security-based swap participant must document the factors used to reach such determination and how the supervisory arrangement with respect to such supervisory personnel otherwise complies with paragraph (h)(1) of this section, and include a summary of such determination in the annual compliance report prepared by the security-based swap dealer's or major security-based swap participant's chief compliance officer pursuant to § 240.15Fk–1(c);

Securities and Exchange Commission § 240.15Fh–4

(H) Procedures reasonably designed to prevent the supervisory system required by paragraph (h)(1) of this section from being compromised due to the conflicts of interest that may be present with respect to the associated person being supervised, including the position of such person, the revenue such person generates for the security-based swap dealer or major security-based swap participant, or any compensation that the associated person conducting the supervision may derive from the associated person being supervised; and

(I) Procedures reasonably designed, taking into consideration the nature of such security-based swap dealer's or major security-based swap participant's business, to comply with the duties set forth in section 15F(j) of the Act.

(3) *Failure to supervise.* A security-based swap dealer or major security-based swap participant or an associated person of a security-based swap dealer or major security-based swap participant shall not be deemed to have failed to diligently supervise any other person, if such other person is not subject to his or her supervision, or if:

(i) The security-based swap dealer or major security-based swap participant has established and maintained written policies and procedures as required in § 240.15Fh–3(h)(2)(iii), and a documented system for applying those policies and procedures, that would reasonably be expected to prevent and detect, insofar as practicable, any violation of the federal securities laws and the rules and regulations thereunder relating to security-based swaps; and

(ii) The security-based swap dealer or major security-based swap participant, or associated person of the security-based swap dealer or major security-based swap participant, has reasonably discharged the duties and obligations required by such written policies and procedures and documented system and did not have a reasonable basis to believe that such written policies and procedures and documented system were not being followed.

(4) *Maintenance of written supervisory procedures.* A security-based swap dealer or major security-based swap participant shall:

(i) Promptly amend its written supervisory procedures as appropriate when material changes occur in applicable securities laws or rules or regulations thereunder, and when material changes occur in its business or supervisory system; and

(ii) Promptly communicate any material amendments to its supervisory procedures to all associated persons to whom such amendments are relevant based on their activities and responsibilities.

[81 FR 30144, May 13, 2016]

§ 240.15Fh–4 **Antifraud provisions for security-based swap dealers and major security-based swap participants; special requirements for security-based swap dealers acting as advisors to special entities.**

(a) *Antifraud provisions.* It shall be unlawful for a security-based swap dealer or major security-based swap participant:

(1) To employ any device, scheme, or artifice to defraud any special entity or prospective customer who is a special entity;

(2) To engage in any transaction, practice, or course of business that operates as a fraud or deceit on any special entity or prospective customer who is a special entity; or

(3) To engage in any act, practice, or course of business that is fraudulent, deceptive, or manipulative.

(b) *Special requirements for security-based swap dealers acting as advisors to special entities.* A security-based swap dealer that acts as an advisor to a special entity regarding a security-based swap shall comply with the following requirements:

(1) *Duty.* The security-based swap dealer shall have a duty to make a reasonable determination that any security-based swap or trading strategy involving a security-based swap recommended by the security-based swap dealer is in the best interests of the special entity.

(2) *Reasonable efforts.* The security-based swap dealer shall make reasonable efforts to obtain such information that the security-based swap dealer considers necessary to make a reasonable determination that a security-

§ 240.15Fh-5

based swap or trading strategy involving a security-based swap is in the best interests of the special entity. This information shall include, but not be limited to:

(i) The authority of the special entity to enter into a security-based swap;

(ii) The financial status of the special entity, as well as future funding needs;

(iii) The tax status of the special entity;

(iv) The hedging, investment, financing or other objectives of the special entity;

(v) The experience of the special entity with respect to entering into security-based swaps, generally, and security-based swaps of the type and complexity being recommended;

(vi) Whether the special entity has the financial capability to withstand changes in market conditions during the term of the security-based swap; and

(vii) Such other information as is relevant to the particular facts and circumstances of the special entity, market conditions and the type of security-based swap or trading strategy involving a security-based swap being recommended.

(3) *Exception.* The requirements of this paragraph (b) shall not apply with respect to a security-based swap if:

(i) The transaction is executed on a registered or exempt security-based swap execution facility or registered national securities exchange; and

(ii) The security-based swap dealer does not know the identity of the counterparty at a reasonably sufficient time prior to execution of the transaction to permit the security-based swap dealer to comply with the obligations of paragraph (b) of this section.

[81 FR 30144, May 13, 2016]

§ 240.15Fh-5 Special requirements for security-based swap dealers and major security-based swap participants acting as counterparties to special entities.

(a)(1) A security-based swap dealer or major security-based swap participant that offers to enter into or enters into a security-based swap with a special entity, other than a special entity defined in § 240.15Fh-2(d)(3), must have a reasonable basis to believe that the special entity has a qualified independent representative. For these purposes, a qualified independent representative is a representative that:

(i) Has sufficient knowledge to evaluate the transaction and risks;

(ii) Is not subject to a statutory disqualification;

(iii) Undertakes a duty to act in the best interests of the special entity;

(iv) Makes appropriate and timely disclosures to the special entity of material information concerning the security-based swap;

(v) Evaluates, consistent with any guidelines provided by the special entity, the fair pricing and the appropriateness of the security-based swap;

(vi) In the case of a special entity defined in §§ 240.15Fh-2(d)(2) or (5), is a person that is subject to rules of the Commission, the Commodity Futures Trading Commission or a self-regulatory organization subject to the jurisdiction of the Commission or the Commodity Futures Trading Commission prohibiting it from engaging in specified activities if certain political contributions have been made, *provided that* this paragraph (a)(1)(vi) shall not apply if the independent representative is an employee of the special entity; and

(vii) Is independent of the security-based swap dealer or major security-based swap participant.

(A) A representative of a special entity is independent of a security-based swap dealer or major security-based swap participant if the representative does not have a relationship with the security-based swap dealer or major security-based swap participant, whether compensatory or otherwise, that reasonably could affect the independent judgment or decision-making of the representative.

(B) A representative of a special entity will be deemed to be independent of a security-based swap dealer or major security-based swap participant if:

(*1*) The representative is not and, within one year of representing the special entity in connection with the security-based swap, was not an associated person of the security-based swap dealer or major security-based swap participant;

Securities and Exchange Commission § 240.15Fh–5

(2) The representative provides timely disclosures to the special entity of all material conflicts of interest that could reasonably affect the judgment or decision making of the representative with respect to its obligations to the special entity and complies with policies and procedures reasonably designed to manage and mitigate such material conflicts of interest; and

(3) The security-based swap dealer or major security-based swap participant did not refer, recommend, or introduce the representative to the special entity within one year of the representative's representation of the special entity in connection with the security-based swap.

(2) A security-based swap dealer or major security-based swap participant that offers to enter into or enters into a security-based swap with a special entity as defined in § 240.15Fh–2(d)(3) must have a reasonable basis to believe that the special entity has a representative that is a fiduciary as defined in section 3 of the Employee Retirement Income Security Act of 1974 (29 U.S.C. 1002).

(b) *Safe harbor.* (1) A security-based swap dealer or major security-based swap participant shall be deemed to have a reasonable basis to believe that the special entity, other than a special entity defined in § 240.15Fh–2(d)(3), has a representative that satisfies the applicable requirements of paragraph (a)(1) of this section, provided that:

(i) The special entity represents in writing to the security-based swap dealer or major security-based swap participant that it has complied in good faith with written policies and procedures reasonably designed to ensure that it has selected a representative that satisfies the applicable requirements of paragraph (a)(1) of this section, and that such policies and procedures provide for ongoing monitoring of the performance of such representative consistent with the requirements of paragraph (a)(1) of this section; and

(ii) The representative represents in writing to the special entity and security-based swap dealer or major security-based swap participant that the representative:

(A) Has policies and procedures reasonably designed to ensure that it satisfies the applicable requirements of paragraph (a)(1) of this section;

(B) Meets the independence test in paragraph (a)(1)(vii) of this section; has the knowledge required under paragraph (a)(1)(i) of this section; is not subject to a statutory disqualification under paragraph (a)(1)(ii) of this section; undertakes a duty to act in the best interests of the special entity as required under paragraph (a)(1)(iii) of this section; and is subject to the requirements regarding political contributions, as applicable, under paragraph (a)(1)(vi) of this section; and

(C) Is legally obligated to comply with the applicable requirements of paragraph (a)(1) of this section by agreement, condition of employment, law, rule, regulation, or other enforceable duty.

(2) A security-based swap dealer or major security-based swap participant shall be deemed to have a reasonable basis to believe that a special entity defined in § 240.15Fh–2(d)(3) of this section has a representative that satisfies the applicable requirements in paragraph (a)(2) of this section, provided that the special entity provides in writing to the security-based swap dealer or major security-based swap participant the representative's name and contact information, and represents in writing that the representative is a fiduciary as defined in section 3 of the Employee Retirement Income Security Act of 1974 (29 U.S.C. 1002).

(c) Before initiation of a security-based swap with a special entity, a security-based swap dealer shall disclose to the special entity in writing the capacity in which the security-based swap dealer is acting in connection with the security-based swap and, if the security-based swap dealer engages in business with the counterparty in more than one capacity, the security-based swap dealer shall disclose the material differences between such capacities and any other financial transaction or service involving the counterparty.

(d) The requirements of this section shall not apply with respect to a security-based swap if:

(1) The transaction is executed on a registered or exempt security-based

553

§ 240.15Fh-6

swap execution facility or registered national securities exchange; and

(2) The security-based swap dealer or major security-based swap participant does not know the identity of the counterparty at a reasonably sufficient time prior to execution of the transaction to permit the security-based swap dealer or major security-based swap participant to comply with the obligations of paragraphs (a) through (c) of this section.

[81 FR 30144, May 13, 2016]

§ 240.15Fh-6 Political contributions by certain security-based swap dealers.

(a) *Definitions.* For the purposes of this section:

(1) The term *contribution* means any gift, subscription, loan, advance, or deposit of money or anything of value made:

(i) For the purpose of influencing any election for federal, state or local office;

(ii) For payment of debt incurred in connection with any such election; or

(iii) For transition or inaugural expenses incurred by the successful candidate for state or local office.

(2) The term *covered associate* means:

(i) Any general partner, managing member or executive officer, or other person with a similar status or function;

(ii) Any employee who solicits a municipal entity to enter into a security-based swap with the security-based swap dealer and any person who supervises, directly or indirectly, such employee; and

(iii) A political action committee controlled by the security-based swap dealer or by a person described in paragraphs (a)(2)(i) and (ii) of this section.

(3) The term *executive officer of a security-based swap dealer* means:

(i) The president;

(ii) Any vice president in charge of a principal business unit, division or function (such as sales, administration or finance);

(iii) Any other officer of the security-based swap dealer who performs a policy-making function; or

(iv) Any other person who performs similar policy-making functions for the security-based swap dealer.

17 CFR Ch. II (4-1-23 Edition)

(4) The term *municipal entity* is defined in section 15B(e)(8) of the Act.

(5) The term *official of a municipal entity* means any person (including any election committee for such person) who was, at the time of the contribution, an incumbent, candidate or successful candidate for elective office of a municipal entity, if the office:

(i) Is directly or indirectly responsible for, or can influence the outcome of, the selection of a security-based swap dealer by a municipal entity; or

(ii) Has authority to appoint any person who is directly or indirectly responsible for, or can influence the outcome of, the selection of a security-based swap dealer by a municipal entity.

(6) The term *payment* means any gift, subscription, loan, advance, or deposit of money or anything of value.

(7) The term *regulated person* means:

(i) A person that is subject to rules of the Commission, the Commodity Futures Trading Commission or a self-regulatory organization subject to the jurisdiction of the Commission or the Commodity Futures Trading Commission prohibiting it from engaging in specified activities if certain political contributions have been made, or its officers or employees;

(ii) A general partner, managing member or executive officer of such person, or other individual with a similar status or function; or

(iii) An employee of such person who solicits a municipal entity for the security-based swap dealer and any person who supervises, directly or indirectly, such employee.

(8) The term *solicit* means a direct or indirect communication by any person with a municipal entity for the purpose of obtaining or retaining an engagement related to a security-based swap.

(b) *Prohibitions and exceptions.* (1) It shall be unlawful for a security-based swap dealer to offer to enter into, or enter into, a security-based swap, or a trading strategy involving a security-based swap, with a municipal entity within two years after any contribution to an official of such municipal entity was made by the security-based swap dealer, or by any covered associate of the security-based swap dealer.

Securities and Exchange Commission § 240.15Fh–6

(2) The prohibition in paragraph (b)(1) of this section does not apply:

(i) If the only contributions made by the security-based swap dealer to an official of such municipal entity were made by a covered associate, if a natural person:

(A) To officials for whom the covered associate was entitled to vote at the time of the contributions, *if* the contributions in the aggregate do not exceed $350 to any one official per election; or

(B) To officials for whom the covered associate was not entitled to vote at the time of the contributions, *if* the contributions in the aggregate do not exceed $150 to any one official, per election;

(ii) To a security-based swap dealer as a result of a contribution made by a natural person more than six months prior to becoming a covered associate of the security-based swap dealer, *however*, this exclusion shall not apply if the natural person, after becoming a covered associate, solicits the municipal entity on behalf of the security-based swap dealer to offer to enter into, or to enter into, security-based swap, or a trading strategy involving a security-based swap; or

(iii) With respect to a security-based swap that is executed on a registered national securities exchange or registered or exempt security-based swap execution facility where the security-based swap dealer does not know the identity of the counterparty to the transaction at a reasonably sufficient time prior to execution of the transaction to permit the security-based swap dealer to comply with the obligations of paragraph (b)(1) of this section.

(3) No security-based swap dealer or any covered associate of the security-based swap dealer shall:

(i) Provide or agree to provide, directly or indirectly, payment to any person to solicit a municipal entity to offer to enter into, or to enter into, a security-based swap or any trading strategy involving a security-based swap with that security-based swap dealer unless such person is a regulated person; or

(ii) Coordinate, or solicit any person or political action committee to make, any:

(A) Contribution to an official of a municipal entity with which the security-based swap dealer is offering to enter into, or has entered into, a security-based swap or a trading strategy involving a security-based swap; or

(B) Payment to a political party of a state or locality with which the security-based swap dealer is offering to enter into, or has entered into, a security-based swap or a trading strategy involving a security-based swap.

(c) *Circumvention of rule.* No security-based swap dealer shall, directly or indirectly, through or by any other person or means, do any act that would result in a violation of paragraph (a) or (b) of this section.

(d) *Requests for exemption.* The Commission, upon application, may conditionally or unconditionally exempt a security-based swap dealer from the prohibition under paragraph (b)(1) of this section. In determining whether to grant an exemption, the Commission will consider, among other factors:

(1) Whether the exemption is necessary or appropriate in the public interest and consistent with the protection of investors and the purposes of the Act;

(2) Whether the security-based swap dealer:

(i) Before the contribution resulting in the prohibition was made, adopted and implemented policies and procedures reasonably designed to prevent violations of this section;

(ii) Prior to or at the time the contribution which resulted in such prohibition was made, had no actual knowledge of the contribution; and

(iii) After learning of the contribution:

(A) Has taken all available steps to cause the contributor involved in making the contribution which resulted in such prohibition to obtain a return of the contribution; and

(B) Has taken such other remedial or preventive measures as may be appropriate under the circumstances;

(3) Whether, at the time of the contribution, the contributor was a covered associate or otherwise an employee of the security-based swap dealer, or was seeking such employment;

§ 240.15Fi-1

(4) The timing and amount of the contribution which resulted in the prohibition;

(5) The nature of the election (*e.g.*, federal, state or local); and

(6) The contributor's apparent intent or motive in making the contribution that resulted in the prohibition, as evidenced by the facts and circumstances surrounding the contribution.

(e) *Prohibitions inapplicable.* (1) The prohibitions under paragraph (b) of this section shall not apply to a contribution made by a covered associate of the security-based swap dealer if:

(i) The security-based swap dealer discovered the contribution within 120 calendar days of the date of such contribution;

(ii) The contribution did not exceed $350; and

(iii) The covered associate obtained a return of the contribution within 60 calendar days of the date of discovery of the contribution by the security-based swap dealer.

(2) A security-based swap dealer that has more than 50 covered associates may not rely on paragraph (e)(1) of this section more than three times in any 12-month period, while a security-based swap dealer that has 50 or fewer covered associates may not rely on paragraph (e)(1) of this section more than twice in any 12-month period.

(3) A security-based swap dealer may not rely on paragraph (e)(1) of this section more than once for any covered associate, regardless of the time between contributions.

[81 FR 30144, May 13, 2016]

§ 240.15Fi-1 Definitions.

For the purposes of §§ 240.15Fi-1 through 240.15Fi-5:

(a) The term *bilateral portfolio compression exercise* means an exercise by which two security-based swap counterparties wholly terminate or change the notional value of some or all of the security-based swaps submitted by the counterparties for inclusion in the portfolio compression exercise and, depending on the methodology employed, replace the terminated security-based swaps with other security-based swaps whose combined notional value (or some other measure of risk) is less than the combined notional value (or some other measure of risk) of the terminated security-based swaps in the exercise.

(b) The term *business day* means any day other than a Saturday, Sunday, or legal holiday.

(c) Solely for purposes of § 240.15Fi-2, the term *clearing agency* means a clearing agency as defined in section 3(a)(23) of the Securities Exchange Act of 1934 (15 U.S.C. 78c(a)(23)) that is registered pursuant to section 17A of the Securities Exchange Act of 1934 (15 U.S.C. 78q-1) and provides central counterparty services for security-based swap transactions.

(d) The term *clearing transaction* means a security-based swap that has a clearing agency as a direct counterparty.

(e) The term *day of execution* means the calendar day of the counterparty to the security-based swap transaction that ends the latest, provided that if a security-based swap transaction is:

(1) Entered into after 4:00 p.m. in the place of a counterparty; or

(2) Entered into on a day that is not a business day in the place of a counterparty, then such security-based swap transaction shall be deemed to have been entered into by that counterparty on the immediately succeeding business day of that counterparty, and the day of execution shall be determined with reference to such business day.

(f) The term *execution* means the point at which the counterparties become irrevocably bound to a transaction under applicable law.

(g) The term *financial counterparty* means a counterparty that is not a security-based swap dealer or a major security-based swap participant and that is one of the following:

(1) A swap dealer;

(2) A major swap participant;

(3) A commodity pool as defined in section 1a(10) of the Commodity Exchange Act (7 U.S.C. 1a(10));

(4) A private fund as defined in section 202(a)(29) of the Investment Advisers Act of 1940 (15 U.S.C. 80b-2(a));

(5) An employee benefit plan as defined in paragraphs (3) and (32) of section 3 of the Employee Retirement Income Security Act of 1974 (29 U.S.C. 1002); and

Securities and Exchange Commission § 240.15Fi-2

(6) A person predominantly engaged in activities that are in the business of banking, or in activities that are financial in nature, as defined in section 4(k) of the Bank Holding Company Act of 1956 (12 U.S.C. 1843k).

(h) The term *fully offsetting security-based swaps* means security-based swaps of equivalent terms where no net cash flow would be owed to either counterparty after the offset of payment obligations thereunder.

(i) The term *material terms* means each term that is required to be reported to a registered security-based swap data repository or the Commission pursuant to § 242.901 of this chapter; provided, however, that such definition does not include any term that is not relevant to the ongoing rights and obligations of the parties and the valuation of the security-based swap.

(j) The term *multilateral portfolio compression exercise* means an exercise by which multiple security-based swap counterparties wholly terminate or change the notional value of some or all of the security-based swaps submitted by the counterparties for inclusion in the portfolio compression exercise and, depending on the methodology employed, replace the terminated security-based swaps with other security-based swaps whose combined notional value (or some other measure of risk) is less than the combined notional value (or some other measure of risk) of the terminated security-based swaps in the exercise.

(k) The term *national securities exchange* means an exchange as defined in section 3(a)(1) of the Securities Exchange Act of 1934 (15 U.S.C. 78c(a)(1)) that is registered pursuant to section 6 of the Securities Exchange Act of 1934 (15 U.S.C. 78f).

(l) The term *portfolio reconciliation* means any process by which the counterparties to one or more security-based swaps:

(1) Exchange the material terms of all security-based swaps in the security-based swap portfolio between the counterparties;

(2) Exchange each counterparty's valuation of each security-based swap in the security-based swap portfolio between the counterparties as of the close of business on the immediately preceding business day; and

(3) Resolve any discrepancy in valuations or material terms.

(m) The term *prudential regulator* has the meaning given to the term in section 3(a)(74) of the Act (15 U.S.C. 78c(a)(74)) and includes the Board of Governors of the Federal Reserve System, the Office of the Comptroller of the Currency, the Federal Deposit Insurance Corporation, the Farm Credit Association, and the Federal Housing Finance Agency, as applicable to the security-based swap dealer or major security-based swap participant.

(n) The term *security-based swap execution facility* means a security-based swap execution facility as defined in section 3(a)(77) of the Securities Exchange Act of 1934 (15 U.S.C. 78c(a)(77)) that is registered pursuant to section 3D of the Securities Exchange Act of 1934 (15 U.S.C. 78c-4).

(o) The term *security-based swap portfolio* means all security-based swaps currently in effect between a particular security-based swap dealer or major security-based swap participant and a particular counterparty.

(p) The term *trade acknowledgment* means a written or electronic record of a security-based swap transaction sent by one counterparty of the security-based swap transaction to the other.

(q) The term *valuation* means the current market value or net present value of a security-based swap.

(r) The term *verification* means the process by which a trade acknowledgment has been manually, electronically, or by some other legally equivalent means, signed by the receiving counterparty.

[85 FR 6412, Feb. 4, 2020]

§ 240.15Fi-2 **Acknowledgment and verification of security-based swap transactions.**

(a) *Trade acknowledgment requirement.* In any transaction in which a security-based swap dealer or major security-based swap participant purchases from or sells to any counterparty a security-based swap, a trade acknowledgment must be provided by:

(1) The security-based swap dealer, if the transaction is between a security-

§ 240.15Fi-2

based swap dealer and a major security-based swap participant;

(2) The security-based swap dealer or major security-based swap participant, if only one counterparty in the transaction is a security-based swap dealer or major security-based swap participant; or

(3) The counterparty that the counterparties have agreed will provide the trade acknowledgment in any transaction other than one described by paragraph (a)(1) or (a)(2) of this section.

(b) *Prescribed time.* Any trade acknowledgment required by paragraph (a) of this section must be provided promptly, but in any event by the end of the first business day following the day of execution.

(c) *Form and content of trade acknowledgment.* Any trade acknowledgment required by paragraph (a) of this section must be provided through electronic means that provide reasonable assurance of delivery and a record of transmittal, and must disclose all the terms of the security-based swap transaction.

(d) *Trade verification.* (1) A security-based swap dealer or major security-based swap participant must establish, maintain, and enforce written policies and procedures that are reasonably designed to obtain prompt verification of the terms of a trade acknowledgment provided pursuant to paragraph (a) of this section.

(2) A security-based swap dealer or major security-based swap participant must promptly verify the accuracy of, or dispute with its counterparty, the terms of a trade acknowledgment it receives pursuant to paragraph (a) of this section.

(e) *Exception for clearing transactions.* A security-based swap dealer or major security-based swap participant is excepted from the requirements of this section with respect to any clearing transaction.

(f) Exception for transactions executed on a security-based swap execution facility or national securities exchange or accepted for clearing by a clearing agency.

(1) A security-based swap dealer or major security-based swap participant is excepted from the requirements of

17 CFR Ch. II (4–1–23 Edition)

this subsection with respect to any security-based swap transaction executed on a security-based swap execution facility or national securities exchange, provided that the rules, procedures or processes of the security-based swap execution facility or national securities exchange provide for the acknowledgment and verification of all terms of the security-based swap transaction no later than the time required by paragraphs (b) and (d)(2) of this section.

(2) A security-based swap dealer or major security-based swap participant is excepted from the requirements of this subsection with respect to any security-based swap transaction that is submitted for clearing to a clearing agency, provided that:

(i) The security-based swap transaction is submitted for clearing as soon as technologically practicable, but in any event no later than the time established for providing a trade acknowledgment under paragraph (b) of this section; and

(ii) The rules, procedures or processes of the clearing agency provide for the acknowledgment and verification of all terms of the security-based swap transaction prior to or at the same time that the security-based swap transaction is accepted for clearing.

(3) If a security-based swap dealer or major security-based swap participant receives notice that a security-based swap transaction has not been acknowledged and verified pursuant to the rules, procedures or processes of a security-based swap execution facility or a national securities exchange, or accepted for clearing by a clearing agency, the security-based swap dealer or major security-based swap participant shall comply with the requirements of this section with respect to such security-based swap transaction as if such security-based swap transaction were executed at the time the security-based swap dealer or major security-based swap participant receives such notice.

(g) *Exemption from § 240.10b–10.* A security-based swap dealer or major security-based swap participant that is also a broker or dealer, is purchasing from or selling to any counterparty, and that complies with paragraph (a) or

558

Securities and Exchange Commission § 240.15Fi-3

(d)(2) of this section with respect to the security-based swap transaction, is exempt from the requirements of § 240.10b-10 with respect to the security-based swap transaction.

[81 FR 39844, June 17, 2016]

§ 240.15Fi-3 Security-based swap portfolio reconciliation.

(a) *Security-based swaps with security-based swap dealers or major security-based swap participants.* Each security-based swap dealer and major security-based swap participant shall engage in portfolio reconciliation as follows for all security-based swaps in which its counterparty is also a security-based swap dealer or major security-based swap participant.

(1) Each security-based swap dealer or major security-based swap participant shall agree in writing with each of its counterparties on the terms of the portfolio reconciliation including, if applicable, agreement on the selection of any third party service provider who may be performing the portfolio reconciliation.

(2) The portfolio reconciliation may be performed on a bilateral basis by the counterparties or by a third party selected by the counterparties in accordance with paragraph (a)(1) of this section.

(3) The portfolio reconciliation shall be performed no less frequently than:

(i) Once each business day for each security-based swap portfolio that includes 500 or more security-based swaps;

(ii) Once each week for each security-based swap portfolio that includes more than 50 but fewer than 500 security-based swaps on any business day during the week; and

(iii) Once each calendar quarter for each security-based swap portfolio that includes no more than 50 security-based swaps at any time during the calendar quarter.

(4) Each security-based swap dealer and major security-based swap participant shall resolve immediately any discrepancy in a material term of a security-based swap identified as part of a portfolio reconciliation or otherwise.

(5) Each security-based swap dealer and major security-based swap participant shall establish, maintain, and follow written policies and procedures reasonably designed to resolve any discrepancy in a valuation identified as part of a portfolio reconciliation or otherwise as soon as possible, but in any event within five business days after the date on which the discrepancy is first identified, provided that the security-based swap dealer and major security-based swap participant establishes, maintains, and follows written policies and procedures reasonably designed to identify how the security-based swap dealer or major security-based swap participant will comply with any variation margin requirements under section 15F(e) of the Act (15 U.S.C. 78o-10(e)) and § 240.18a-3 (and any subsequent regulations promulgated pursuant to section 15F(e) of the Act (15 U.S.C. 78o-10(e))) pending resolution of the discrepancy in valuation. For purposes of this paragraph (a)(5), a difference between the lower valuation and the higher valuation of less than 10 percent of the higher valuation need not be deemed a discrepancy.

(b) *Security-based swaps with entities other than security-based swap dealers or major security-based swap participants.* Each security-based swap dealer and major security-based swap participant shall establish, maintain, and follow written policies and procedures reasonably designed to ensure that it engages in portfolio reconciliation for all security-based swaps in which its counterparty is neither a security-based swap dealer nor a major security-based swap participant as follows.

(1) Each security-based swap dealer or major security-based swap participant shall agree in writing with each of its counterparties on the terms of the portfolio reconciliation including, if applicable, agreement on the selection of any third party service provider who may be performing the reconciliation.

(2) The portfolio reconciliation may be performed on a bilateral basis by the counterparties or by one or more third parties selected by the counterparties in accordance with paragraph (b)(1) of this section.

(3) The portfolio reconciliation will be required to be performed no less frequently than:

(i) Once each calendar quarter for each security-based swap portfolio that includes more than 100 security-based swaps at any time during the calendar quarter; and

(ii) Once annually for each security-based swap portfolio that includes no more than 100 security-based swaps at any time during the calendar year.

(4) Each security-based swap dealer or major security-based swap participant shall establish, maintain, and follow written procedures reasonably designed to resolve any discrepancies in the valuation or material terms of each security-based swap identified as part of a portfolio reconciliation or otherwise with a counterparty that is neither a security-based swap dealer nor major security-based swap participant in a timely fashion. For purposes of this paragraph (b)(4), a difference between the lower valuation and the higher valuation of less than 10 percent of the higher valuation need not be deemed a discrepancy.

(c) *Reporting of security-based swap valuation disputes*—(1) *Notice requirement.* Each security-based swap dealer and major security-based swap participant shall promptly notify the Commission, in a form and manner acceptable to the Commission, and any applicable prudential regulator of any security-based swap valuation dispute in excess of $20,000,000 (or its equivalent in any other currency), at either the transaction or portfolio level, if not resolved within:

(i) Three business days, if the dispute is with a counterparty that is a security-based swap dealer or major security-based swap participant; or

(ii) Five business days, if the dispute is with a counterparty that is not a security-based swap dealer or major security-based swap participant.

(2) *Amendments.* Each security-based swap dealer and major security-based swap participant shall notify the Commission, in a form and manner acceptable to the Commission, and any applicable prudential regulator, if the amount of any security-based swap valuation dispute that was the subject of a previous notice made pursuant to paragraph (c)(1) of this section increases or decreases by more than $20,000,000 (or its equivalent in any other currency), at either the transaction or portfolio level. Such amended notice shall be provided to the Commission and any applicable prudential regulator no later than the last business day of the calendar month in which the applicable security-based swap valuation dispute increases or decreases by the applicable dispute amount.

(d) *Reconciliation of cleared security-based swaps.* Nothing in this section shall apply to any security-based swap that is, directly or indirectly, submitted to and cleared by a clearing agency registered pursuant to section 17A of the Act (15 U.S.C. 78q–1) or by a clearing agency that the Commission has exempted from registration by rule or order pursuant to section 17A of the Act (15 U.S.C. 78q–1).

[85 FR 6413, Feb. 4, 2020]

§ 240.15Fi–4 Security-based swap portfolio compression.

(a) *Portfolio compression with security-based swap dealers and major security-based swap participants*—(1) *Bilateral offset.* Each security-based swap dealer and major security-based swap participant shall establish, maintain, and follow written policies and procedures for terminating each fully offsetting security-based swap between a security-based swap dealer or major security-based swap participant and another security-based swap dealer or major security-based swap participant in a timely fashion, when appropriate.

(2) *Bilateral compression.* Each security-based swap dealer and major security-based swap participant shall establish, maintain, and follow written policies and procedures for periodically engaging in bilateral portfolio compression exercises, when appropriate, with each counterparty that is also a security-based swap dealer or major security-based swap participant. Such policies and procedures shall address, among other things, the evaluation of bilateral portfolio compression exercises that are initiated, offered, or sponsored by any third party.

(3) *Multilateral compression.* Each security-based swap dealer and major security-based swap participant shall establish, maintain, and follow written policies and procedures for periodically engaging in multilateral portfolio compression exercises, when appropriate,

Securities and Exchange Commission § 240.15Fi–5

with each counterparty that is also a security-based swap dealer or major security-based swap participant. Such policies and procedures shall address, among other things, the evaluation of multilateral portfolio compression exercises that are initiated, offered, or sponsored by any third party.

(b) *Portfolio compression with counterparties other than security-based swap dealers and major security-based swap participants.* Each security-based swap dealer and major security-based swap participant shall establish, maintain, and follow written policies and procedures for periodically terminating fully offsetting security-based swaps and for engaging in bilateral or multilateral portfolio compression exercises with respect to security-based swaps in which its counterparty is an entity other than a security-based swap dealer or major security-based swap participant, when appropriate and to the extent requested by any such counterparty.

(c) *Portfolio compression of cleared security-based swaps.* Nothing in this section shall apply to any security-based swap that is, directly or indirectly, submitted to and cleared by a clearing agency registered pursuant to section 17A of the Act (15 U.S.C. 78q–1) or by a clearing agency that the Commission has exempted from registration by rule or order pursuant to section 17A of the Act (15 U.S.C. 78q–1).

[85 FR 6414, Feb. 4, 2020]

§ 240.15Fi–5 Security-based swap trading relationship documentation.

(a) *Scope*—(1) *Applicability.* The requirements of this section shall not apply to:

(i) Security-based swaps executed prior to the date on which a security-based swap dealer or major security-based swap participant is required to be in compliance with this section;

(ii) Any security-based swap that is, directly or indirectly, submitted to and cleared by a clearing agency registered pursuant to section 17A of the Act (15 U.S.C. 78q–1) or by a clearing agency that the Commission has exempted from registration by rule or order pursuant to section 17A of the Act (15 U.S.C. 78q–1); and

(iii) Security-based swaps executed anonymously on a national securities exchange or a security-based swap execution facility, *Provided that:*

(A) Such security-based swaps are intended to be cleared and are actually submitted for clearing to a clearing agency;

(B) All terms of such security-based swaps conform to the rules of the clearing agency; and

(C) Upon acceptance of such security-based swap by the clearing agency:

(*1*) The original security-based swap is extinguished;

(*2*) The original security-based swap is replaced by equal and opposite security-based swaps with the clearing agency; and

(*3*) All terms of the security-based swap shall conform to the product specifications of the cleared security-based swap established under the clearing agency's rules; and *Provided further,* That if a security-based swap dealer or major security-based swap participant receives notice that a security-based swap transaction has not been accepted for clearing by a clearing agency, the security-based swap dealer or major security-based swap participant shall be required to comply with the requirements of this section in all respects promptly after receipt of such notice.

(2) *Policies and procedures.* Each security-based swap dealer and major security-based swap participant shall establish, maintain, and follow written policies and procedures reasonably designed to ensure that the security-based swap dealer or major security-based swap participant executes written security-based swap trading relationship documentation with its counterparty that complies with the requirements of this section. The policies and procedures shall be approved in writing by a senior officer of the security-based swap dealer or major security-based swap participant, and a record of the approval shall be retained. Other than trade acknowledgements and verifications of security-based swap transactions under § 240.15Fi–2, the security-based swap trading relationship documentation shall be executed prior to, or contemporaneously with, executing a security-based swap with any counterparty.

561

§ 240.15Fi-5

(b) *Security-based swap trading relationship documentation.* (1) The security-based swap trading relationship documentation shall be in writing and shall include all terms governing the trading relationship between the security-based swap dealer or major security-based swap participant and its counterparty, including, without limitation, terms addressing payment obligations, netting of payments, events of default or other termination events, calculation and netting of obligations upon termination, transfer of rights and obligations, governing law, valuation, and dispute resolution.

(2) The security-based swap trading relationship documentation shall include all trade acknowledgements and verifications of security-based swap transactions under § 240.15Fi-2.

(3) The security-based swap trading relationship documentation shall include credit support arrangements, which shall contain, in accordance with applicable requirements under Commission regulations or regulations adopted by prudential regulators and without limitation, the following:

(i) Initial and variation margin requirements, if any;

(ii) Types of assets that may be used as margin and asset valuation haircuts, if any;

(iii) Investment and rehypothecation terms for assets used as margin for uncleared security-based swaps, if any; and

(iv) Custodial arrangements for margin assets, including whether margin assets are to be segregated with an independent third party, in accordance with the notice requirement in section 3E(f)(1)(A) of the Act (15 U.S.C. 78c–5(f)(1)(A)) (and either § 240.15c3–3(p)(4)(i) or § 240.18a–4(d)(1) thereunder, as applicable), if any.

(4)(i) The security-based swap trading relationship documentation between security-based swap dealers, between major security-based swap participants, between a security-based swap dealer and major security-based swap participant, between a security-based swap dealer or major security-based swap participant and a financial counterparty, and, if requested by any other counterparty, between a security-based swap dealer or major security-based swap participant and such counterparty, shall include written documentation in which the parties agree on the process, which may include any agreed upon methods, procedures, rules, and inputs, for determining the value of each security-based swap at any time from execution to the termination, maturity, or expiration of such security-based swap for the purposes of complying with the margin requirements under section 15F(e) of the Act (15 U.S.C. 78o–10(e)) and § 240.18a–3 (and any subsequent regulations promulgated pursuant to section 15F(e) of the Act (15 U.S.C. 78o–10(e))), and the risk management requirements under section 15F(j) of the Act (15 U.S.C. 78o–10(j)) of the Act and § 240.15Fh–3(h)(2)(iii)(I) (and any subsequent regulations promulgated pursuant to section 15F(j) of the Act (15 U.S.C. 78o–10(j))). To the maximum extent practicable, the valuation of each security-based swap shall be based on recently executed transactions, valuations provided by independent third parties, or other objective criteria.

(ii) Such documentation shall include either:

(A) Alternative methods for determining the value of the security-based swap for the purposes of complying with this paragraph (b)(4) in the event of the unavailability or other failure of any input required to value the security-based swap for such purposes; or

(B) A valuation dispute resolution process by which the value of the security-based swap shall be determined for the purposes of complying with this paragraph (b)(4).

(iii) A security-based swap dealer or major security-based swap participant is not required to disclose to the counterparty confidential, proprietary information about any model it may use to value a security-based swap.

(iv) The parties may agree on changes or procedures for modifying or amending the documentation at any time.

(5) The security-based swap trading relationship documentation of a security-based swap dealer or major security-based swap participant shall include the following:

(i) A statement of whether the security-based swap dealer or major security-based swap participant is an insured depository institution (as defined in 12 U.S.C. 1813) or a financial company (as defined in section 201(a)(11) of the Dodd-Frank Act, 12 U.S.C. 5381(a)(11));

(ii) A statement of whether the counterparty is an insured depository institution or financial company;

(iii) A statement that in the event either the security-based swap dealer or major security-based swap participant or its counterparty becomes a covered financial company (as defined in section 201(a)(8) of the Dodd-Frank Wall Street Reform and Consumer Protection Act, 12 U.S.C. 5381(a)(8)) or is an insured depository institution for which the Federal Deposit Insurance Corporation (FDIC) has been appointed as a receiver (the "covered party"), certain limitations under Title II of the Dodd-Frank Act or the Federal Deposit Insurance Act may apply to the right of the non-covered party to terminate, liquidate, or net any security-based swap by reason of the appointment of the FDIC as receiver, notwithstanding the agreement of the parties in the security-based swap trading relationship documentation, and that the FDIC may have certain rights to transfer security-based swaps of the covered party under section 210(c)(9)(A) of the Dodd-Frank Wall Street Reform and Consumer Protection Act, 12 U.S.C. 5390(c)(9)(A), or 12 U.S.C. 1821(e)(9)(A); and

(iv) An agreement between the security-based swap dealer or major security-based swap participant and its counterparty to provide notice if either it or its counterparty becomes or ceases to be an insured depository institution or a financial company.

(6) The security-based swap trading relationship documentation of each security-based swap dealer and major security-based swap participant shall contain a notice that, upon acceptance of a security-based swap by a clearing agency:

(i) The original security-based swap is extinguished;

(ii) The original security-based swap is replaced by equal and opposite security-based swaps with the clearing agency; and

(iii) All terms of the security-based swap shall conform to the product specifications of the cleared security-based swap established under the clearing agency's rules.

(c) *Audit of security-based swap trading relationship documentation.* Each security-based swap dealer and major security-based swap participant shall have an independent auditor conduct periodic audits sufficient to identify any material weakness in its documentation policies and procedures required by this section. A record of the results of each audit shall be retained.

[85 FR 6414, Feb. 4, 2020]

§ 240.15Fk–1 **Designation of chief compliance officer for security-based swap dealers and major security-based swap participants.**

(a) *In general.* A security-based swap dealer and major security-based swap participant shall designate an individual to serve as a chief compliance officer on its registration form.

(b) *Duties.* The chief compliance officer shall:

(1) Report directly to the board of directors or to the senior officer of the security-based swap dealer or major security-based swap participant; and

(2) Take reasonable steps to ensure that the registrant establishes, maintains and reviews written policies and procedures reasonably designed to achieve compliance with the Act and the rules and regulations thereunder relating to its business as a security-based swap dealer or major security-based swap participant by:

(i) Reviewing the compliance of the security-based swap dealer or major security-based swap participant with respect to the security-based swap dealer and major security-based swap participant requirements described in section 15F of the Act, and the rules and regulations thereunder, where the review shall involve preparing the registrant's annual assessment of its written policies and procedures reasonably designed to achieve compliance with section 15F of the Act, and the rules and regulations thereunder, by the security-based swap dealer or major security-based swap participant;

§ 240.15Fk-1

(ii) Taking reasonable steps to ensure that the registrant establishes, maintains and reviews policies and procedures reasonably designed to remediate non-compliance issues identified by the chief compliance officer through any means, including any:

(A) Compliance office review;

(B) Look-back;

(C) Internal or external audit finding;

(D) Self-reporting to the Commission and other appropriate authorities; or

(E) Complaint that can be validated; and

(iii) Taking reasonable steps to ensure that the registrant establishes and follows procedures reasonably designed for the handling, management response, remediation, retesting, and resolution of non-compliance issues;

(3) In consultation with the board of directors or the senior officer of the security-based swap dealer or major security-based swap participant, take reasonable steps to resolve any material conflicts of interest that may arise; and

(4) Administer each policy and procedure that is required to be established pursuant to section 15F of the Act and the rules and regulations thereunder.

(c) *Annual reports*—(1) *In general.* The chief compliance officer shall annually prepare and sign a compliance report that contains a description of the written policies and procedures of the security-based swap dealer or major security-based swap participant described in paragraph (b) of this section (including the code of ethics and conflict of interest policies).

(2) *Requirements.* (i) Each compliance report shall also contain, at a minimum, a description of:

(A) The security-based swap dealer or major security-based swap participant's assessment of the effectiveness of its policies and procedures relating to its business as a security-based swap dealer or major security-based participant;

(B) Any material changes to the registrant's policies and procedures since the date of the preceding compliance report;

(C) Any areas for improvement, and recommended potential or prospective changes or improvements to its compliance program and resources devoted to compliance;

(D) Any material non-compliance matters identified; and

(E) The financial, managerial, operational, and staffing resources set aside for compliance with the Act and the rules and regulations thereunder relating to its business as a security-based swap dealer or major security-based swap participant, including any material deficiencies in such resources.

(ii) A compliance report under paragraph (c)(1) of this section also shall:

(A) Be submitted to the Commission within 30 days following the deadline for filing the security-based swap dealer's or major security-based swap participant's annual financial report with the Commission pursuant to section 15F of the Act and rules and regulations thereunder;

(B) Be submitted to the board of directors and audit committee (or equivalent bodies) and the senior officer of the security-based swap dealer or major security-based swap participant prior to submission to the Commission;

(C) Be discussed in one or more meetings conducted by the senior officer with the chief compliance officer(s) in the preceding 12 months, the subject of which addresses the obligations in this section; and

(D) Include a certification by the chief compliance officer or senior officer that, to the best of his or her knowledge and reasonable belief and under penalty of law, the information contained in the compliance report is accurate and complete in all material respects.

(iii) *Extensions of time.* A security-based swap dealer or major security-based swap participant may request from the Commission an extension of time to submit its compliance report, provided the registrant's failure to timely submit the report could not be eliminated by the registrant without unreasonable effort or expense. Extensions of the deadline will be granted at the discretion of the Commission.

Securities and Exchange Commission § 240.15Ga–1

(iv) *Incorporation by reference.* A security-based swap dealer or major security-based swap participant may incorporate by reference sections of a compliance report that have been submitted within the current or immediately preceding reporting period to the Commission.

(v) *Amendments.* A security-based swap dealer or major security-based swap participant shall promptly submit an amended compliance report if material errors or omissions in the report are identified. An amendment must contain the certification required under paragraph (c)(2)(ii)(D) of this section.

(d) *Compensation and removal.* The compensation and removal of the chief compliance officer shall require the approval of a majority of the board of directors of the security-based swap dealer or major security-based swap participant.

(e) *Definitions.* For purposes of this section, references to:

(1) The *board* or *board of directors* shall include a body performing a function similar to the board of directors.

(2) The *senior officer* shall include the chief executive officer or other equivalent officer.

(3) *Complaint that can be validated* shall include any written complaint by a counterparty involving the security-based swap dealer or major security-based swap participant or associated person of a security-based swap dealer or major security-based swap participant that can be supported upon reasonable investigation.

(4) A *material non-compliance matter* means any non-compliance matter about which the board of directors of the security-based swap dealer or major security-based swap participant would reasonably need to know to oversee the compliance of the security-based swap dealer or major security-based swap participant, and that involves, without limitation:

(i) A violation of the federal securities laws relating to its business as a security-based swap dealer or major security-based swap participant by the firm or its officers, directors, employees or agents;

(ii) A violation of the policies and procedures relating to its business as a security-based swap dealer or major security-based swap participant by the firm or its officers, directors, employees or agents; or

(iii) A weakness in the design or implementation of the policies and procedures relating to its business as a security-based swap dealer or major security-based swap participant.

[81 FR 30144, May 13, 2016]

§ 240.15Ga–1 **Repurchases and replacements relating to asset-backed securities.**

(a) *General.* With respect to any asset-backed security (as that term is defined in Section 3(a)(79) of the Securities Exchange Act of 1934 (15 U.S.C. 78c(a)(79)) for which the underlying transaction agreements contain a covenant to repurchase or replace an underlying asset for breach of a representation or warranty, a securitizer (as that term is defined in Section 15G(a) of the Securities Exchange Act of 1934) shall disclose fulfilled and unfulfilled repurchase requests across all trusts by providing the information required in paragraph (a)(1) of this section concerning all assets securitized by the securitizer that were the subject of a demand to repurchase or replace for breach of the representations and warranties concerning the pool assets for all asset-backed securities held by non-affiliates of the securitizer during the reporting period.

§ 240.15Ga–1　　　　　　　　　　　　　　　　　　　17 CFR Ch. II (4–1–23 Edition)

Name of Issuing Entity	Check if Registered	Name of Originator	Total Assets in ABS by Originator		Assets That Were Subject of Demand		Assets That Were Repurchased or Replaced		Assets Pending Repurchase or Replacement (within cure period)		Demand in Dispute		Demand Withdrawn		Demand Rejected	
			(#)	($)	(% of princ ipal balan ce)	(#)	($)	(% of princ ipal balan ce)	(#)	($)	(% of princ ipal balan ce)	(#)	($)	(% of princ ipal balan ce)	(#)	($)	(% of princ ipal balan ce)	(#)	($)	(% of princ ipal balan ce)	(#)	($)	(% of princ ipal balan ce)
(a)	(b)	(c)	(d)	(e)	(f)	(g)	(h)	(i)	(j)	(k)	(l)	(m)	(n)	(o)	(p)	(q)	(r)	(s)	(t)	(u)	(v)	(w)	(x)
Asset Class X																							
Issuing Entity A CIK #	X	Originator 1	#	$		#	$		#	$		#	$		#	$		#	$		#	$	
		Originator 2	#	$		#	$		#	$		#	$		#	$		#	$		#	$	
Total			#	$		#	$		#	$		#	$		#	$		#	$		#	$	
Asset Class Y																							
Issuing Entity B		Originator 3	#	$		#	$		#	$		#	$		#	$		#	$		#	$	
Total			#	$		#	$		#	$		#	$		#	$		#	$		#	$	
Total			#	$		#	$		#	$		#	$		#	$		#	$		#	$	

(1) The table shall:

(i) Disclose the asset class and group the issuing entities by asset class (column (a)).

(ii) Disclose the name of the issuing entity (as that term is defined in Item 1101(f) of Regulation AB (17 CFR

Securities and Exchange Commission § 240.15Ga–1

229.1101(f)) of the asset-backed securities. List the issuing entities in order of the date of formation (column (a)).

INSTRUCTION TO PARAGRAPH (a)(1)(ii): Include all issuing entities with outstanding asset-backed securities during the reporting period.

(iii) For each named issuing entity, indicate by check mark whether the transaction was registered under the Securities Act of 1933 (column (b)) and disclose the CIK number of the issuing entity (column (a)).

(iv) Disclose the name of the originator of the underlying assets (column (c)).

INSTRUCTION TO PARAGRAPH (a)(1)(iv): Include all originators that originated assets in the asset pool for each issuing entity.

(v) Disclose the number, outstanding principal balance and percentage by principal balance of assets at the time of securitization (columns (d) through (f)).

(vi) Disclose the number, outstanding principal balance and percentage by principal balance of assets that were subject of a demand to repurchase or replace for breach of representations and warranties (columns (g) through (i)).

(vii) Disclose the number, outstanding principal balance and percentage by principal balance of assets that were repurchased or replaced for breach of representations and warranties (columns (j) through (l)).

(viii) Disclose the number, outstanding principal balance and percentage by principal balance of assets that are pending repurchase or replacement for breach of representations and warranties due to the expiration of a cure period (columns (m) through (o)).

(ix) Disclose the number, outstanding principal balance and percentage by principal balance of assets that are pending repurchase or replacement for breach of representations and warranties because the demand is currently in dispute (columns (p) through (r)).

(x) Disclose the number, outstanding principal balance and percentage by principal balance of assets that were not repurchased or replaced because the demand was withdrawn (columns (s) through (u)).

(xi) Disclose the number, outstanding principal balance and percentage by principal balance of assets that were not repurchased or replaced because the demand was rejected (columns (v) through (x)).

INSTRUCTION TO PARAGRAPHS (a)(1)(vi) THROUGH (xi): For purposes of these (a)(1)(vi) through (xi) the outstanding principal balance shall be the principal balance as of the reporting period end date and the percentage by principal balance shall be the outstanding principal balance of an asset divided by the outstanding principal balance of the asset pool as of the reporting period end date.

(xii) Provide totals by asset class, issuing entity and for all issuing entities for columns that require number of assets and principal amounts (columns (d), (e), (g), (h), (j), (k), (m), (n) (p), (q), (s), (t), (v) and (w)).

INSTRUCTION 1 TO PARAGRAPH (a)(1): The table should include any activity during the reporting period, including activity related to assets subject to demands made prior to the beginning of the reporting period.

INSTRUCTION 2 TO PARAGRAPH (a)(1): Indicate by footnote and provide narrative disclosure in order to further explain the information presented in the table, as appropriate.

(2) If any of the information required by this paragraph (a) is unknown and not available to the securitizer without unreasonable effort or expense, such information may be omitted, provided the securitizer provides the information it possesses or can acquire without unreasonable effort or expense, and the securitizer includes a statement showing that unreasonable effort or expense would be involved in obtaining the omitted information. Further, if a securitizer requested and was unable to obtain all information with respect to investor demands upon a trustee that occurred prior to July 22, 2010, so state by footnote. In this case, also state that the disclosures do not contain investor demands upon a trustee made prior to July 22, 2010.

(b) In the case of multiple affiliated securitizers for a single asset-backed securities transaction, if one securitizer has filed all the disclosures required in order to meet the obligations under paragraph (a) of this section, other affiliated securitizers shall not be required to separately provide

§ 240.15Ga-2

and file the same disclosures related to the same asset-backed security.

(c) The disclosures in paragraph (a) of this section shall be provided by a securitizer:

(1) For the three year period ended December 31, 2011, by any securitizer that issued an asset-backed security during the period, or organized and initiated an asset-backed securities transaction during the period, by securitizing an asset, either directly or indirectly, including through an affiliate, in each case, if the underlying transaction agreements provide a covenant to repurchase or replace an underlying asset for breach of a representation or warranty and the securitizer has asset-backed securities, containing such a covenant, outstanding and held by non-affiliates as of the end of the three year period. If a securitizer has no activity to report, it shall indicate by checking the appropriate box on Form ABS-15G (17 CFR 249.1400). The requirement of this paragraph (c)(1) applies to all issuances of asset-backed securities whether or not publicly registered under the provisions of the Securities Act of 1933. The disclosures required by this paragraph (c)(1) shall be filed no later than February 14, 2012.

INSTRUCTION TO PARAGRAPH (c)(1): For demands made prior to January 1, 2009, the disclosure should include any related activity subsequent to January 1, 2009 associated with such demand.

(2) For each calendar quarter, by any securitizer that issued an asset-backed security during the period, or organized and initiated an asset-backed securities transaction by securitizing an asset, either directly or indirectly, including through an affiliate, or had outstanding asset-backed securities held by non-affiliates during the period, in each case, if the underlying transaction agreements provide a covenant to repurchase or replace an underlying asset for breach of a representation or warranty. The disclosures required by this paragraph (c)(2) shall be filed no later than 45 calendar days after the end of such calendar quarter:

(i) Except that, a securitizer may suspend its duty to provide periodic quarterly disclosures if no activity occurred during the initial filing period in paragraph (c)(1) of this section or during a calendar quarter that is required to be reported under paragraph (a) of this section. A securitizer shall indicate that it has no activity to report by checking the appropriate box on Form ABS-15G (17 CFR 249.1400). Thereafter, a periodic quarterly report required by this paragraph (c)(2) will only be required if a change in the demand, repurchase or replacement activity occurs that is required to be reported under paragraph (a) of this section during a calendar quarter; and

(ii) Except that, annually, any securitizer that has suspended its duty to provide quarterly disclosures pursuant to paragraph (c)(2)(i) of this section must confirm that no activity occurred during the previous calendar year by checking the appropriate box on Form ABS-15G (17 CFR 249.1400). The confirmation required by this paragraph (c)(2)(ii) shall be filed no later than 45 days after each calendar year.

(3) Except that, if a securitizer has no asset-backed securities outstanding held by non-affiliates, the duty under paragraph (c)(2) of this section to file periodically the disclosures required by paragraph (a) of this section shall be terminated immediately upon filing a notice on Form ABS-15G (17 CFR 249.1400).

[76 FR 4511, Jan. 26, 2011, as amended at 76 FR 54375, Sept. 1, 2011; 79 FR 57344, Sept. 24, 2014]

§ 240.15Ga-2 Findings and conclusions of third-party due diligence reports.

(a) The issuer or underwriter of an offering of any asset-backed security (as that term is defined in Section 3(a)(79) of the Act (15 U.S.C. 78c(a)(79))) that is to be rated by a nationally recognized statistical rating organization must furnish Form ABS-15G (§ 249.1400 of this chapter) to the Commission containing the findings and conclusions of any third-party due diligence report obtained by the issuer or underwriter at least five business days prior to the first sale in the offering.

Instruction to paragraph (a): Disclosure of the findings and conclusions includes, but is not limited to, disclosure of the criteria against which the loans were evaluated, and how the evaluated loans compared to those criteria along with the basis for including any loans

Securities and Exchange Commission § 240.16a-1

not meeting those criteria. This disclosure is only required for an initial rating and does not need to be furnished in connection with any subsequent rating actions. For purposes of this rule, the date of first sale is the date on which the first investor is irrevocably contractually committed to invest, which, depending on the terms and conditions of the contract, could be the date on which the issuer receives the investor's subscription agreement or check.

(b) In the case where the issuer and one or more underwriters have obtained the same third-party due diligence report related to a particular asset-backed securities transaction, if any one such party has furnished all the disclosures required in order to meet the obligations under paragraph (a) of this section, the other party or parties are not required to separately furnish the same disclosures related to such third-party due diligence report.

(c) If the disclosure required by this rule has been made in the prospectus (including an attribution to the third-party that provided the third-party due diligence report), the issuer or underwriter may refer to that section of the prospectus in Form ABS-15G rather than providing the findings and conclusions itself directly in Form ABS-15G.

(d) For purposes of paragraphs (a) and (b) of this section, *issuer* is defined in Rule 17g-10(d)(2) (§ 240.17g-10(d)(2) of this chapter) and *third-party due diligence report* means any report containing findings and conclusions of any *due diligence services* as defined in Rule 17g-10(d)(1) (§ 240.17g-10(d)(1) of this chapter) performed by a third party.

(e) The requirements of this rule would not apply to an offering of an asset-backed security if certain conditions are met, including:

(1) The offering is not required to be, and is not, registered under the Securities Act of 1933;

(2) The issuer of the rated security is not a U.S. person (as defined in § 230.902(k)); and

(3) All offers and sales of the security by any issuer, sponsor, or underwriter linked to the security will occur outside the United States (as that phrase is used in §§ 230.901 through 230.905 (Regulation S)).

(f) The requirements of this rule would not apply to an offering of an asset-backed security if certain conditions are met, including:

(1) The issuer of the rated security is a municipal issuer; and

(2) The offering is not required to be, and is not, registered under the Securities Act of 1933.

(g) For purposes of paragraph (f) of this section, a municipal issuer is an *issuer* (as that term is defined in Rule 17g-10(d)(2) (§ 240.17g-10(d)(2) of this chapter)) that is any State or Territory of the United States, the District of Columbia, any political subdivision of any State, Territory or the District of Columbia, or any public instrumentality of one or more States, Territories or the District of Columbia.

(h) An offering of an asset-backed security that is exempted from the requirements of this rule pursuant to paragraph (f) of this section remains subject to the requirements of Section 15E(s)(4)(A) of the Act (15 U.S.C. 78o-7(s)(4)(A)), which requires that the issuer or underwriter of any asset-backed security shall make publicly available the findings and conclusions of any third-party due diligence report obtained by the issuer or underwriter.

[79 FR 55261, Sept. 15, 2014; 79 FR 61576, Oct. 14, 2014, as amended at 84 84 FR 40258, Sept. 13, 2019]

§ 240.16a-1 Definition of terms.

Terms defined in this rule shall apply solely to section 16 of the Act and the rules thereunder. These terms shall not be limited to section 16(a) of the Act but also shall apply to all other subsections under section 16 of the Act.

(a) The term *beneficial owner* shall have the following applications:

(1) Solely for purposes of determining whether a person is a beneficial owner of more than ten percent of any class of equity securities registered pursuant to section 12 of the Act, the term "beneficial owner" shall mean any person who is deemed a beneficial owner pursuant to section 13(d) of the Act and the rules thereunder; *provided, however,* that the following institutions or persons shall not be deemed the beneficial owner of securities of such class held for the benefit of third parties or in customer or fiduciary accounts in the

§ 240.16a-1

ordinary course of business (or in the case of an employee benefit plan specified in paragraph (a)(1)(vi) of this section, of securities of such class allocated to plan participants where participants have voting power) as long as such shares are acquired by such institutions or persons without the purpose or effect of changing or influencing control of the issuer or engaging in any arrangement subject to Rule 13d-3(b) (§ 240.13d-3(b)):

(i) A broker or dealer registered under section 15 of the Act (15 U.S.C. 78o);

(ii) A bank as defined in section 3(a)(6) of the Act (15 U.S.C. 78c);

(iii) An insurance company as defined in section 3(a)(19) of the Act (15 U.S.C. 78c);

(iv) An investment company registered under section 8 of the Investment Company Act of 1940 (15 U.S.C. 80a-8);

(v) Any person registered as an investment adviser under Section 203 of the Investment Advisers Act of 1940 (15 U.S.C. 80b-3) or under the laws of any state;

(vi) An employee benefit plan as defined in Section 3(3) of the Employee Retirement Income Security Act of 1974, as amended, 29 U.S.C. 1001 et seq. ("ERISA") that is subject to the provisions of ERISA, or any such plan that is not subject to ERISA that is maintained primarily for the benefit of the employees of a state or local government or instrumentality, or an endowment fund;

(vii) A parent holding company or control person, provided the aggregate amount held directly by the parent or control person, and directly and indirectly by their subsidiaries or affiliates that are not persons specified in § 240.16a-1 (a)(1)(i) through (x), does not exceed one percent of the securities of the subject class;

(viii) A savings association as defined in Section 3(b) of the Federal Deposit Insurance Act (12 U.S.C. 1813);

(ix) A church plan that is excluded from the definition of an investment company under section 3(c)(14) of the Investment Company Act of 1940 (15 U.S.C. 80a-30);

(x) A non-U.S. institution that is the functional equivalent of any of the institutions listed in paragraphs (a)(1)(i) through (ix) of this section, so long as the non-U.S. institution is subject to a regulatory scheme that is substantially comparable to the regulatory scheme applicable to the equivalent U.S. institution and the non-U.S. institution is eligible to file a Schedule 13G pursuant to § 240.13d-1(b)(1)(ii)(J); and

(xi) A group, provided that all the members are persons specified in § 240.16a-1 (a)(1)(i) through (x).

NOTE TO PARAGRAPH (a): Pursuant to this section, a person deemed a beneficial owner of more than ten percent of any class of equity securities registered under section 12 of the Act would file a Form 3 (§ 249.103), but the securities holdings disclosed on Form 3, and changes in beneficial ownership reported on subsequent Forms 4 (§ 249.104) or 5 (§ 249.105), would be determined by the definition of "beneficial owner" in paragraph (a)(2) of this section.

(2) Other than for purposes of determining whether a person is a beneficial owner of more than ten percent of any class of equity securities registered under Section 12 of the Act, the term *beneficial owner* shall mean any person who, directly or indirectly, through any contract, arrangement, understanding, relationship or otherwise, has or shares a direct or indirect pecuniary interest in the equity securities, subject to the following:

(i) The term *pecuniary interest* in any class of equity securities shall mean the opportunity, directly or indirectly, to profit or share in any profit derived from a transaction in the subject securities.

(ii) The term *indirect pecuniary interest* in any class of equity securities shall include, but not be limited to:

(A) Securities held by members of a person's immediate family sharing the same household; provided, however, that the presumption of such beneficial ownership may be rebutted; see also § 240.16a-1(a)(4);

(B) A general partner's proportionate interest in the portfolio securities held by a general or limited partnership. The general partner's proportionate interest, as evidenced by the partnership agreement in effect at the time of the transaction and the partnership's most recent financial statements, shall be the greater of:

Securities and Exchange Commission

§ 240.16a-1

(1) The general partner's share of the partnership's profits, including profits attributed to any limited partnership interests held by the general partner and any other interests in profits that arise from the purchase and sale of the partnership's portfolio securities; or

(2) The general partner's share of the partnership capital account, including the share attributable to any limited partnership interest held by the general partner.

(C) A performance-related fee, other than an asset-based fee, received by any broker, dealer, bank, insurance company, investment company, investment adviser, investment manager, trustee or person or entity performing a similar function; *provided, however,* that no pecuniary interest shall be present where:

(1) The performance-related fee, regardless of when payable, is calculated based upon net capital gains and/or net capital appreciation generated from the portfolio or from the fiduciary's overall performance over a period of one year or more; and

(2) Equity securities of the issuer do not account for more than ten percent of the market value of the portfolio. A right to a nonperformance-related fee alone shall not represent a pecuniary interest in the securities;

(D) A person's right to dividends that is separated or separable from the underlying securities. Otherwise, a right to dividends alone shall not represent a pecuniary interest in the securities;

(E) A person's interest in securities held by a trust, as specified in § 240.16a-8(b); and

(F) A person's right to acquire equity securities through the exercise or conversion of any derivative security, whether or not presently exercisable.

(iii) A shareholder shall not be deemed to have a pecuniary interest in the portfolio securities held by a corporation or similar entity in which the person owns securities if the shareholder is not a controlling shareholder of the entity and does not have or share investment control over the entity's portfolio.

(3) Where more than one person subject to section 16 of the Act is deemed to be a beneficial owner of the same equity securities, all such persons must report as beneficial owners of the securities, either separately or jointly, as provided in § 240.16a-3(j). In such cases, the amount of short-swing profit recoverable shall not be increased above the amount recoverable if there were only one beneficial owner.

(4) Any person filing a statement pursuant to section 16(a) of the Act may state that the filing shall not be deemed an admission that such person is, for purposes of section 16 of the Act or otherwise, the beneficial owner of any equity securities covered by the statement.

(5) The following interests are deemed not to confer beneficial ownership for purposes of section 16 of the Act:

(i) Interests in portfolio securities held by any investment company registered under the Investment Company Act of 1940 (15 U.S.C. 80a-1 *et seq.*); and

(ii) Interests in securities comprising part of a broad-based, publicly traded market basket or index of stocks, approved for trading by the appropriate federal governmental authority.

(b) The term *call equivalent position* shall mean a derivative security position that increases in value as the value of the underlying equity increases, including, but not limited to, a long convertible security, a long call option, and a short put option position.

(c) The term *derivative securities* shall mean any option, warrant, convertible security, stock appreciation right, or similar right with an exercise or conversion privilege at a price related to an equity security, or similar securities with a value derived from the value of an equity security, but shall not include:

(1) Rights of a pledgee of securities to sell the pledged securities;

(2) Rights of all holders of a class of securities of an issuer to receive securities pro rata, or obligations to dispose of securities, as a result of a merger, exchange offer, or consolidation involving the issuer of the securities;

(3) Rights or obligations to surrender a security, or have a security withheld, upon the receipt or exercise of a derivative security or the receipt or vesting of equity securities, in order to satisfy

§ 240.16a-2

the exercise price or the tax withholding consequences of receipt, exercise or vesting;

(4) Interests in broad-based index options, broad-based index futures, and broad-based publicly traded market baskets of stocks approved for trading by the appropriate federal governmental authority;

(5) Interests or rights to participate in employee benefit plans of the issuer;

(6) Rights with an exercise or conversion privilege at a price that is not fixed; or

(7) Options granted to an underwriter in a registered public offering for the purpose of satisfying over-allotments in such offering.

(d) The term *equity security of such issuer* shall mean any equity security or derivative security relating to an issuer, whether or not issued by that issuer.

(e) The term *immediate family* shall mean any child, stepchild, grandchild, parent, stepparent, grandparent, spouse, sibling, mother-in-law, father-in-law, son-in-law, daughter-in-law, brother-in-law, or sister-in-law, and shall include adoptive relationships.

(f) The term "officer" shall mean an issuer's president, principal financial officer, principal accounting officer (or, if there is no such accounting officer, the controller), any vice-president of the issuer in charge of a principal business unit, division or function (such as sales, administration or finance), any other officer who performs a policy-making function, or any other person who performs similar policy-making functions for the issuer. Officers of the issuer's parent(s) or subsidiaries shall be deemed officers of the issuer if they perform such policy-making functions for the issuer. In addition, when the issuer is a limited partnership, officers or employees of the general partner(s) who perform policy-making functions for the limited partnership are deemed officers of the limited partnership. When the issuer is a trust, officers or employees of the trustee(s) who perform policy-making functions for the trust are deemed officers of the trust.

NOTE: "Policy-making function" is not intended to include policy-making functions that are not significant. If pursuant to Item 401(b) of Regulation S-K (§ 229.401(b)) the issuer identifies a person as an "executive officer," it is presumed that the Board of Directors has made that judgment and that the persons so identified are the officers for purposes of Section 16 of the Act, as are such other persons enumerated in this paragraph (f) but not in Item 401(b).

(g) The term *portfolio securities* shall mean all securities owned by an entity, other than securities issued by the entity.

(h) The term *put equivalent position* shall mean a derivative security position that increases in value as the value of the underlying equity decreases, including, but not limited to, a long put option and a short call option position.

[56 FR 7265, Feb. 21, 1991, as amended at 56 FR 19927, May 1, 1991; 61 FR 30391, June 14, 1996; 63 FR 2868, Jan. 16, 1998; 73 FR 60093, Oct. 9, 2008; 76 FR 71876, Nov. 21, 2011]

§ 240.16a-2 Persons and transactions subject to section 16.

Any person who is the beneficial owner, directly or indirectly, of more than ten percent of any class of equity securities ("ten percent beneficial owner") registered pursuant to section 12 of the Act (15 U.S.C. 78*l*), any director or officer of the issuer of such securities, and any person specified in section 30(h) of the Investment Company Act of 1940 (15 U.S.C. 80a-29(h)), including any person specified in § 240.16a-8, shall be subject to the provisions of section 16 of the Act (15 U.S.C. 78p). The rules under section 16 of the Act apply to any class of equity securities of an issuer whether or not registered under section 12 of the Act. The rules under section 16 of the Act also apply to non-equity securities as provided by the Investment Company Act of 1940. With respect to transactions by persons subject to section 16 of the Act:

(a) A transaction(s) carried out by a director or officer in the six months prior to the director or officer becoming subject to section 16 of the Act shall be subject to section 16 of the Act and reported on the first required Form 4 only if the transaction(s) occurred within six months of the transaction giving rise to the Form 4 filing obligation and the director or officer became subject to section 16 of the Act solely as a result of the issuer registering a

Securities and Exchange Commission § 240.16a–3

class of equity securities pursuant to section 12 of the Act.

(b) A transaction(s) following the cessation of director or officer status shall be subject to section 16 of the Act only if:

(1) Executed within a period of less than six months of an opposite transaction subject to section 16(b) of the Act that occurred while that person was a director or officer; and

(2) Not otherwise exempted from section 16(b) of the Act pursuant to the provisions of this chapter.

NOTE TO PARAGRAPH (b): For purposes of this paragraph, an acquisition and a disposition each shall be an opposite transaction with respect to the other.

(c) The transaction that results in a person becoming a ten percent beneficial owner is not subject to section 16 of the Act unless the person otherwise is subject to section 16 of the Act. A ten percent beneficial owner not otherwise subject to section 16 of the Act must report only those transactions conducted while the beneficial owner of more than ten percent of a class of equity securities of the issuer registered pursuant to section 12 of the Act.

(d)(1) Transactions by a person or entity shall be exempt from the provisions of section 16 of the Act for the 12 months following appointment and qualification, to the extent such person or entity is acting as:

(i) Executor or administrator of the estate of a decedent;

(ii) Guardian or member of a committee for an incompetent;

(iii) Receiver, trustee in bankruptcy, assignee for the benefit of creditors, conservator, liquidating agent, or other similar person duly authorized by law to administer the estate or assets of another person; or

(iv) Fiduciary in a similar capacity.

(2) Transactions by such person or entity acting in a capacity specified in paragraph (d)(1) of this section after the period specified in that paragraph shall be subject to section 16 of the Act only where the estate, trust or other entity is a beneficial owner of more than ten percent of any class of equity security registered pursuant to section 12 of the Act.

[56 FR 7265, Feb. 21, 1991, as amended at 61 FR 30392, June 14, 1996; 67 FR 43535, June 28, 2002; 76 FR 71877, Nov. 21, 2011]

§ 240.16a–3 Reporting transactions and holdings.

(a) Initial statements of beneficial ownership of equity securities required by section 16(a) of the Act shall be filed on Form 3. Statements of changes in beneficial ownership required by that section shall be filed on Form 4. Annual statements shall be filed on Form 5. At the election of the reporting person, any transaction required to be reported on Form 5 may be reported on an earlier filed Form 4. All such statements shall be prepared and filed in accordance with the requirements of the applicable form.

(b) A person filing statements pursuant to section 16(a) of the Act with respect to any class of equity securities registered pursuant to section 12 of the Act need not file an additional statement on Form 3:

(1) When an additional class of equity securities of the same issuer becomes registered pursuant to section 12 of the Act; or

(2) When such person assumes a different or an additional relationship to the same issuer (for example, when an officer becomes a director).

(c) Any issuer that has equity securities listed on more than one national securities exchange may designate one exchange as the only exchange with which reports pursuant to section 16(a) of the Act need be filed. Such designation shall be made in writing and shall be filed with the Commission and with each national securities exchange on which any equity security of the issuer is listed at the time of such election. The reporting person's obligation to file reports with each national securities exchange on which any equity security of the issuer is listed shall be satisfied by filing with the exchange so designated.

(d) Any person required to file a statement with respect to securities of a single issuer under both section 16(a) of the Act (15 U.S.C. 78p(a)) and section 30(h) of the Investment Company Act of 1940 (15 U.S.C. 80a–29(h)) may file a

§ 240.16a-3

single statement containing the required information, which will be deemed to be filed under both Acts.

(e) [Reserved]

(f)(1) A Form 5 shall be filed by every person who at any time during the issuer's fiscal year was subject to section 16 of the Act with respect to such issuer, except as provided in paragraph (f)(2) of this section. The Form shall be filed within 45 days after the issuer's fiscal year end, and shall disclose the following holdings and transactions not reported previously on Forms 3, 4 or 5:

(i) All transactions during the most recent fiscal year that were exempt from section 16(b) of the Act, except:

(A) Exercises and conversions of derivative securities exempt under either § 240.16b-3 or § 240.16b-6(b), dispositions by bona fide gifts exempt under § 240.16b-5, and any transaction exempt under § 240.16b-3(d), § 240.16b-3(e), or § 240.16b-3(f), (these are required to be reported on Form 4);

(B) Transactions exempt from section 16(b) of the Act pursuant to § 240.16b-3(c), which shall be exempt from section 16(a) of the Act; and

(C) Transactions exempt from section 16(a) of the Act pursuant to another rule;

(ii) Transactions that constituted small acquisitions pursuant to § 240.16a-6(a);

(iii) All holdings and transactions that should have been reported during the most recent fiscal year, but were not; and

(iv) With respect to the first Form 5 requirement for a reporting person, all holdings and transactions that should have been reported in each of the issuer's last two fiscal years but were not, based on the reporting person's reasonable belief in good faith in the completeness and accuracy of the information.

(2) Notwithstanding the above, no Form 5 shall be required where all transactions otherwise required to be reported on the Form 5 have been reported before the due date of the Form 5.

Persons no longer subject to section 16 of the Act, but who were subject to the Section at any time during the issuer's fiscal year, must file a Form 5 unless paragraph (f)(2) is satisfied. *See also* § 240.16a-2(b) regarding the reporting obligations of persons ceasing to be officers or directors.

(g)(1) A Form 4 must be filed to report: All transactions not exempt from section 16(b) of the Act; all transactions exempt from section 16(b) of the Act pursuant to § 240.16b-3(d), § 240.16b-3(e), or § 240.16b-3(f); and dispositions by bona fide gifts and all exercises and conversions of derivative securities, regardless of whether exempt from section 16(b) of the Act. Form 4 must be filed before the end of the second business day following the day on which the subject transaction has been executed.

(2) Solely for purposes of section 16(a)(2)(C) of the Act and paragraph (g)(1) of this section, the date on which the executing broker, dealer or plan administrator notifies the reporting person of the execution of the transaction is deemed the date of execution for a transaction where the following conditions are satisfied:

(i) the transaction is pursuant to a contract, instruction or written plan for the purchase or sale of equity securities of the issuer (as defined in § 16a-1(d)) that satisfies the affirmative defense conditions of § 240.10b5-1(c) of this chapter; and

(ii) the reporting person does not select the date of execution.

(3) Solely for purposes of section 16(a)(2)(C) of the Act and paragraph (g)(1) of this section, the date on which the plan administrator notifies the reporting person that the transaction has been executed is deemed the date of execution for a discretionary transaction (as defined in § 16b-3(b)(1)) for which the reporting person does not select the date of execution.

(4) In the case of the transactions described in paragraphs (g)(2) and (g)(3) of this section, if the notification date is later than the third business day following the trade date of the transaction, the date of execution is deemed to be the third business day following the trade date of the transaction.

(5) At the option of the reporting person, transactions that are reportable on Form 5 may be reported on Form 4, so long as the Form 4 is filed no later than the due date of the Form 5 on

Securities and Exchange Commission §240.16a-4

which the transaction is otherwise required to be reported.

(h) The date of filing with the Commission shall be the date of receipt by the Commission.

(i) *Signatures.* Where Section 16 of the Act, or the rules or forms thereunder, require a document filed with or furnished to the Commission to be signed, such document shall be manually signed, or signed using either typed signatures or duplicated or facsimile versions of manual signatures. Where typed, duplicated, or facsimile signatures are used, each signatory to the filing shall manually or electronically sign a signature page or other document authenticating, acknowledging, or otherwise adopting his or her signature that appears in the filing ("authentication document"). Such authentication document shall be executed before or at the time the filing is made and shall be retained by the filer for a period of five years. The requirements set forth in §232.302(b) must be met with regards to the use of an electronically signed authentication document pursuant to this paragraph (i). Upon request, the filer shall furnish to the Commission or its staff a copy of any or all documents retained pursuant to this section.

(j) Where more than one person subject to section 16 of the Act is deemed to be a beneficial owner of the same equity securities, all such persons must report as beneficial owners of the securities, either separately or jointly. Where persons in a group are deemed to be beneficial owners of equity securities pursuant to §240.16a-1(a)(1) due to the aggregation of holdings, a single Form 3, 4 or 5 may be filed on behalf of all persons in the group. Joint and group filings must include all required information for each beneficial owner, and such filings must be signed by each beneficial owner, or on behalf of such owner by an authorized person.

(k) Any issuer that maintains a corporate Web site shall post on that Web site by the end of the business day after filing any Form 3, 4 or 5 filed under section 16(a) of the Act as to the equity securities of that issuer. Each such form shall remain accessible on such issuer's Web site for at least a 12-month period. In the case of an issuer that is an investment company and that does not maintain its own Web site, if any of the issuer's investment adviser, sponsor, depositor, trustee, administrator, principal underwriter, or any affiliated person of the investment company maintains a Web site that includes the name of the issuer, the issuer shall comply with the posting requirements by posting the forms on one such Web site.

[56 FR 7265, Feb. 21, 1991, as amended at 60 FR 26622, May 17, 1995; 61 FR 30392, 30404, June 14, 1996; 67 FR 43535, June 28, 2002; 67 FR 56467, Sept. 3, 2002; 68 FR 25799, May 13, 2003; 76 FR 71877, Nov. 21, 2011; 84 FR 12728, Apr. 2, 2019; 85 FR 78230, Dec. 4, 2020; 87 FR 80430, Dec. 29, 2022]

§240.16a-4 Derivative securities.

(a) For purposes of section 16 of the Act, both derivative securities and the underlying securities to which they relate shall be deemed to be the same class of equity securities, *except that* the acquisition or disposition of any derivative security shall be separately reported.

(b) The exercise or conversion of a call equivalent position shall be reported on Form 4 and treated for reporting purposes as:

(1) A purchase of the underlying security; and

(2) A closing of the derivative security position.

(c) The exercise or conversion of a put equivalent position shall be reported on Form 4 and treated for reporting purposes as:

(1) A sale of the underlying security; and

(2) A closing of the derivative security position.

(d) The disposition or closing of a long derivative security position, as a result of cancellation or expiration, shall be exempt from section 16(a) of the Act if exempt from section 16(b) of the Act pursuant to §240.16b-6(d).

NOTE TO §240.16a-4: A purchase or sale resulting from an exercise or conversion of a derivative security may be exempt from section 16(b) of the Act pursuant to §240.16b-3 or §240.16b-6(b).

[56 FR 7265, Feb. 21, 1991, as amended at 56 FR 19927, May 1, 1991; 61 FR 30392, June 14, 1996]

§ 240.16a–5 Odd-lot dealers.

Transactions by an odd-lot dealer (a) in odd-lots as reasonably necessary to carry on odd-lot transactions, or (b) in round lots to offset odd-lot transactions previously or simultaneously executed or reasonably anticipated in the usual course of business, shall be exempt from the provisions of section 16(a) of the Act with respect to participation by such odd-lot dealer in such transaction.

§ 240.16a–6 Small acquisitions.

(a) Any acquisition of an equity security or the right to acquire such securities, other than an acquisition from the issuer (including an employee benefit plan sponsored by the issuer), not exceeding $10,000 in market value shall be reported on Form 5, subject to the following conditions:

(1) Such acquisition, when aggregated with other acquisitions of securities of the same class (including securities underlying derivative securities, but excluding acquisitions exempted by rule from section 16(b) or previously reported on Form 4 or Form 5) within the prior six months, does not exceed a total of $10,000 in market value; and

(2) The person making the acquisition does not within six months thereafter make any disposition, other than by a transaction exempt from section 16(b) of the Act.

(b) If an acquisition no longer qualifies for the reporting deferral in paragraph (a) of this section, all such acquisitions that have not yet been reported must be reported on Form 4 before the end of the second business day following the day on which the conditions of paragraph (a) of this section are no longer met.

[56 FR 7265, Feb. 21, 1991, as amended at 61 FR 30392, June 14, 1996; 67 FR 56467, Sept. 3, 2002]

§ 240.16a–7 Transactions effected in connection with a distribution.

(a) Any purchase and sale, or sale and purchase, of a security that is made in connection with the distribution of a substantial block of securities shall be exempt from the provisions of section 16(a) of the Act, to the extent specified in this rule, subject to the following conditions:

(1) The person effecting the transaction is engaged in the business of distributing securities and is participating in good faith, in the ordinary course of such business, in the distribution of such block of securities; and

(2) The security involved in the transaction is:

(i) Part of such block of securities and is acquired by the person effecting the transaction, with a view to distribution thereof, from the issuer or other person on whose behalf such securities are being distributed or from a person who is participating in good faith in the distribution of such block of securities; or

(ii) A security purchased in good faith by or for the account of the person effecting the transaction for the purpose of stabilizing the market price of securities of the class being distributed or to cover an over-allotment or other short position created in connection with such distribution.

(b) Each person participating in the transaction must qualify on an individual basis for an exemption pursuant to this section.

§ 240.16a–8 Trusts.

(a) *Persons subject to section 16*—(1) *Trusts.* A trust shall be subject to section 16 of the Act with respect to securities of the issuer if the trust is a beneficial owner, pursuant to § 240.16a–1(a)(1), of more than ten percent of any class of equity securities of the issuer registered pursuant to section 12 of the Act ("ten percent beneficial owner").

(2) *Trustees, beneficiaries, and settlors.* In determining whether a trustee, beneficiary, or settlor is a ten percent beneficial owner with respect to the issuer:

(i) Such persons shall be deemed the beneficial owner of the issuer's securities held by the trust, to the extent specified by § 240.16a–1(a)(1); and

(ii) Settlors shall be deemed the beneficial owner of the issuer's securities held by the trust where they have the power to revoke the trust without the consent of another person.

(b) *Trust Holdings and Transactions.* Holdings and transactions in the issuer's securities held by a trust shall be reported by the trustee on behalf of

Securities and Exchange Commission

§ 240.16a-9

the trust, if the trust is subject to section 16 of the Act, except as provided below. Holdings and transactions in the issuer's securities held by a trust (whether or not subject to section 16 of the Act) may be reportable by other parties as follows:

(1) *Trusts.* The trust need not report holdings and transactions in the issuer's securities held by the trust in an employee benefit plan subject to the Employee Retirement Income Security Act over which no trustee exercises investment control.

(2) *Trustees.* If, as provided by §240.16a–1(a)(2), a trustee subject to section 16 of the Act has a pecuniary interest in any holding or transaction in the issuer's securities held by the trust, such holding or transaction shall be attributed to the trustee and shall be reported by the trustee in the trustee's individual capacity, as well as on behalf of the trust. With respect to performance fees and holdings of the trustee's immediate family, trustees shall be deemed to have a pecuniary interest in the trust holdings and transactions in the following circumstances:

(i) A performance fee is received that does not meet the proviso of §240.16a–1(a)(2)(ii)(C); or

(ii) At least one beneficiary of the trust is a member of the trustee's immediate family. The pecuniary interest of the immediate family member(s) shall be attributed to and reported by the trustee.

(3) *Beneficiaries.* A beneficiary subject to section 16 of the Act shall have or share reporting obligations with respect to transactions in the issuer's securities held by the trust, if the beneficiary is a beneficial owner of the securities pursuant to §240.16a–1(a)(2), as follows:

(i) If a beneficiary shares investment control with the trustee with respect to a trust transaction, the transaction shall be attributed to and reported by both the beneficiary and the trust;

(ii) If a beneficiary has investment control with respect to a trust transaction without consultation with the trustee, the transaction shall be attributed to and reported by the beneficiary only; and

(iii) In making a determination as to whether a beneficiary is the beneficial owner of the securities pursuant to §240.16a–1(a)(2), beneficiaries shall be deemed to have a pecuniary interest in the issuer's securities held by the trust to the extent of their pro rata interest in the trust where the trustee does not exercise exclusive investment control.

NOTE TO PARAGRAPH (b)(3): Transactions and holdings attributed to a trust beneficiary may be reported by the trustee on behalf of the beneficiary, provided that the report is signed by the beneficiary or other authorized person. Where the transactions and holdings are attributed both to the trustee and trust beneficiary, a joint report may be filed in accordance with §240.16a–3(j).

(4) *Settlors.* If a settlor subject to section 16 of the Act reserves the right to revoke the trust without the consent of another person, the trust holdings and transactions shall be attributed to and reported by the settlor instead of the trust; *Provided, however,* That if the settlor does not exercise or share investment control over the issuer's securities held by the trust, the trust holdings and transactions shall be attributed to and reported by the trust instead of the settlor.

(c) *Remainder interests.* Remainder interests in a trust are deemed not to confer beneficial ownership for purposes of section 16 of the Act, provided that the persons with the remainder interests have no power, directly or indirectly, to exercise or share investment control over the trust.

(d) A trust, trustee, beneficiary or settlor becoming subject to section 16(a) of the Act pursuant to this rule also shall be subject to sections 16(b) and 16(c) of the Act.

[56 FR 7265, Feb. 21, 1991, as amended at 56 FR 19927, May 1, 1991; 61 FR 30392, June 14, 1996; 67 FR 56467, Sept. 3, 2002]

§ 240.16a-9 Stock splits, stock dividends, and pro rata rights.

The following shall be exempt from section 16 of the Act:

(a) The increase or decrease in the number of securities held as a result of a stock split or stock dividend applying equally to all securities of a class, including a stock dividend in which equity securities of a different issuer are distributed; and

§ 240.16a–10

(b) The acquisition of rights, such as shareholder or pre-emptive rights, pursuant to a pro rata grant to all holders of the same class of equity securities registered under section 12 of the Act.

NOTE: The exercise or sale of a pro rata right shall be reported pursuant to § 240.16a–4 and the exercise shall be eligible for exemption from section 16(b) of the Act pursuant to § 240.16b–6(b).

[56 FR 7265, Feb. 21, 1991, as amended at 61 FR 30393, June 14, 1996]

§ 240.16a–10 Exemptions under section 16(a).

Except as provided in § 240.16a–6, any transaction exempted from the requirements of section 16(a) of the Act, insofar as it is otherwise subject to the provisions of section 16(b), shall be likewise exempt from section 16(b) of the Act.

§ 240.16a–11 Dividend or interest reinvestment plans.

Any acquisition of securities resulting from the reinvestment of dividends or interest on securities of the same issuer shall be exempt from section 16 of the Act if the acquisition is made pursuant to a plan providing for the regular reinvestment of dividends or interest and the plan provides for broad-based participation, does not discriminate in favor of employees of the issuer, and operates on substantially the same terms for all plan participants.

[61 FR 30393, June 14, 1996]

§ 240.16a–12 Domestic relations orders.

The acquisition or disposition of equity securities pursuant to a domestic relations order, as defined in the Internal Revenue Code or Title I of the Employee Retirement Income Security Act, or the rules thereunder, shall be exempt from section 16 of the Act.

[61 FR 30393, June 14, 1996]

§ 240.16a–13 Change in form of beneficial ownership.

A transaction, other than the exercise or conversion of a derivative security or deposit into or withdrawal from a voting trust, that effects only a change in the form of beneficial ownership without changing a person's pecuniary interest in the subject equity securities shall be exempt from section 16 of the Act.

[61 FR 30393, June 14, 1996]

EXEMPTION OF CERTAIN TRANSACTIONS FROM SECTION 16(b)

SOURCE: Sections 240.16b–1 through 240.16b–8 appear at 56 FR 7270, Feb. 21, 1991, unless otherwise noted.

§ 240.16b–1 Transactions approved by a regulatory authority.

Any purchase and sale, or sale and purchase, of a security shall be exempt from section 16(b) of the Act, if the transaction is effected by an investment company registered under the Investment Company Act of 1940 (15 U.S.C. 80a–1 *et seq.*) and both the purchase and sale of such security have been exempted from the provisions of section 17(a) (15 U.S.C. 80a–17(a)) of the Investment Company Act of 1940, by rule or order of the Commission.

[56 FR 7270, Feb. 21, 1991, as amended at 61 FR 30404, June 14, 1996; 76 FR 71877, Nov. 21, 2011]

§ 240.16b–2 [Reserved]

§ 240.16b–3 Transactions between an issuer and its officers or directors.

(a) *General.* A transaction between the issuer (including an employee benefit plan sponsored by the issuer) and an officer or director of the issuer that involves issuer equity securities shall be exempt from section 16(b) of the Act if the transaction satisfies the applicable conditions set forth in this section.

(b) *Definitions*—(1) A *Discretionary Transaction* shall mean a transaction pursuant to an employee benefit plan that:

(i) Is at the volition of a plan participant;

(ii) Is not made in connection with the participant's death, disability, retirement or termination of employment;

(iii) Is not required to be made available to a plan participant pursuant to a provision of the Internal Revenue Code; and

(iv) Results in either an intra-plan transfer involving an issuer equity securities fund, or a cash distribution

Securities and Exchange Commission § 240.16b–3

funded by a volitional disposition of an issuer equity security.

(2) An *Excess Benefit Plan* shall mean an employee benefit plan that is operated in conjunction with a Qualified Plan, and provides only the benefits or contributions that would be provided under a Qualified Plan but for any benefit or contribution limitations set forth in the Internal Revenue Code of 1986, or any successor provisions thereof.

(3)(i) A *Non-Employee Director* shall mean a director who:

(A) Is not currently an officer (as defined in § 240.16a-1(f)) of the issuer or a parent or subsidiary of the issuer, or otherwise currently employed by the issuer or a parent or subsidiary of the issuer;

(B) Does not receive compensation, either directly or indirectly, from the issuer or a parent or subsidiary of the issuer, for services rendered as a consultant or in any capacity other than as a director, except for an amount that does not exceed the dollar amount for which disclosure would be required pursuant to § 229.404(a) of this chapter; and

(C) Does not possess an interest in any other transaction for which disclosure would be required pursuant to § 229.404(a) of this chapter.

(ii) Notwithstanding paragraph (b)(3)(i) of this section, a *Non-Employee Director* of a closed-end investment company shall mean a director who is not an "interested person" of the issuer, as that term is defined in Section 2(a)(19) of the Investment Company Act of 1940.

(4) A *Qualified Plan* shall mean an employee benefit plan that satisfies the coverage and participation requirements of sections 410 and 401(a)(26) of the Internal Revenue Code of 1986, or any successor provisions thereof.

(5) A *Stock Purchase Plan* shall mean an employee benefit plan that satisfies the coverage and participation requirements of sections 423(b)(3) and 423(b)(5), or section 410, of the Internal Revenue Code of 1986, or any successor provisions thereof.

(c) *Tax-conditioned plans.* Any transaction (other than a Discretionary Transaction) pursuant to a Qualified Plan, an Excess Benefit Plan, or a Stock Purchase Plan shall be exempt without condition.

(d) *Acquisitions from the issuer.* Any transaction, other than a Discretionary Transaction, involving an acquisition from the issuer (including without limitation a grant or award), whether or not intended for a compensatory or other particular purpose, shall be exempt if:

(1) The transaction is approved by the board of directors of the issuer, or a committee of the board of directors that is composed solely of two or more Non-Employee Directors;

(2) The transaction is approved or ratified, in compliance with section 14 of the Act, by either: the affirmative votes of the holders of a majority of the securities of the issuer present, or represented, and entitled to vote at a meeting duly held in accordance with the applicable laws of the state or other jurisdiction in which the issuer is incorporated; or the written consent of the holders of a majority of the securities of the issuer entitled to vote; *provided that* such ratification occurs no later than the date of the next annual meeting of shareholders; or

(3) The issuer equity securities so acquired are held by the officer or director for a period of six months following the date of such acquisition, *provided that* this condition shall be satisfied with respect to a derivative security if at least six months elapse from the date of acquisition of the derivative security to the date of disposition of the derivative security (other than upon exercise or conversion) or its underlying equity security.

(e) *Dispositions to the issuer.* Any transaction, other than a Discretionary Transaction, involving the disposition to the issuer of issuer equity securities, whether or not intended for a compensatory or other particular purpose, shall be exempt, provided that the terms of such disposition are approved in advance in the manner prescribed by either paragraph (d)(1) or paragraph (d)(2) of this section.

(f) *Discretionary Transactions.* A Discretionary Transaction shall be exempt only if effected pursuant to an election made at least six months following the date of the most recent election, with respect to any plan of the issuer, that

§ 240.16b-4

effected a Discretionary Transaction that was:

(1) An acquisition, if the transaction to be exempted would be a disposition; or

(2) A disposition, if the transaction to be exempted would be an acquisition.

NOTES TO § 240.16b-3

NOTE (1): The exercise or conversion of a derivative security that does not satisfy the conditions of this section is eligible for exemption from section 16(b) of the Act to the extent that the conditions of § 240.16b-6(b) are satisfied.

NOTE (2): Section 16(a) reporting requirements applicable to transactions exempt pursuant to this section are set forth in § 240.16a-3(f) and (g) and § 240.16a-4.

NOTE (3): The approval conditions of paragraphs (d)(1), (d)(2) and (e) of this section require the approval of each specific transaction, and are not satisfied by approval of a plan in its entirety except for the approval of a plan pursuant to which the terms and conditions of each transaction are fixed in advance, such as a formula plan. Where the terms of a subsequent transaction (such as the exercise price of an option, or the provision of an exercise or tax withholding right) are provided for in a transaction as initially approved pursuant to paragraphs (d)(1), (d)(2) or (e), such subsequent transaction shall not require further specific approval.

NOTE (4): For purposes of determining a director's status under those portions of paragraph (b)(3)(i) that reference §229.404(a) of this chapter, an issuer may rely on the disclosure provided under § 229.404(a) of this chapter for the issuer's most recent fiscal year contained in the most recent filing in which disclosure required under § 229.404(a) is presented. Where a transaction disclosed in that filing was terminated before the director's proposed service as a Non-Employee Director, that transaction will not bar such service. The issuer must believe in good faith that any current or contemplated transaction in which the director participates will not be required to be disclosed under §229.404(a) of this chapter, based on information readily available to the issuer and the director at the time such director proposes to act as a Non-Employee Director. At such time as the issuer believes in good faith, based on readily available information, that a current or contemplated transaction with a director will be required to be disclosed under § 229.404(a) in a future filing, the director no longer is eligible to serve as a Non-Employee Director; *provided, however,* that this determination does not result in retroactive loss of a Rule 16b-3 exemption for a transaction previously approved by the director while serving as a Non-Employee Di-

17 CFR Ch. II (4-1-23 Edition)

rector consistent with this note. In making the determinations specified in this Note, the issuer may rely on information it obtains from the director, for example, pursuant to a response to an inquiry.

[61 FR 30393, June 14, 1996, as amended at 70 FR 46089, Aug. 9, 2005; 71 FR 53263, Sept. 8, 2006]

§ 240.16b-4 [Reserved]

§ 240.16b-5 Bona fide gifts and inheritance.

Both the acquisition and the disposition of equity securities shall be exempt from the operation of section 16(b) of the Act if they are: (a) Bona fide gifts; or (b) transfers of securities by will or the laws of descent and distribution.

§ 240.16b-6 Derivative securities.

(a) The establishment of or increase in a call equivalent position or liquidation of or decrease in a put equivalent position shall be deemed a purchase of the underlying security for purposes of section 16(b) of the Act, and the establishment of or increase in a put equivalent position or liquidation of or decrease in a call equivalent position shall be deemed a sale of the underlying securities for purposes of section 16(b) of the Act: *Provided, however,* That if the increase or decrease occurs as a result of the fixing of the exercise price of a right initially issued without a fixed price, where the date the price is fixed is not known in advance and is outside the control of the recipient, the increase or decrease shall be exempt from section 16(b) of the Act with respect to any offsetting transaction within the six months prior to the date the price is fixed.

(b) The closing of a derivative security position as a result of its exercise or conversion shall be exempt from the operation of section 16(b) of the Act, and the acquisition of underlying securities at a fixed exercise price due to the exercise or conversion of a call equivalent position or the disposition of underlying securities at a fixed exercise price due to the exercise of a put equivalent position shall be exempt from the operation of section 16(b) of the Act: *Provided, however,* That the acquisition of underlying securities from

Securities and Exchange Commission § 240.16b-7

the exercise of an out-of-the-money option, warrant, or right shall not be exempt unless the exercise is necessary to comport with the sequential exercise provisions of the Internal Revenue Code (26 U.S.C. 422A).

NOTE TO PARAGRAPH (b): The exercise or conversion of a derivative security that does not satisfy the conditions of this section is eligible for exemption from section 16(b) of the Act to the extent that the conditions of § 240.16b-3 are satisfied.

(c) In determining the short-swing profit recoverable pursuant to section 16(b) of the Act from transactions involving the purchase and sale or sale and purchase of derivative and other securities, the following rules apply:

(1) Short-swing profits in transactions involving the purchase and sale or sale and purchase of derivative securities that have identical characteristics (e.g., purchases and sales of call options of the same strike price and expiration date, or purchases and sales of the same series of convertible debentures) shall be measured by the actual prices paid or received in the short-swing transactions.

(2) Short-swing profits in transactions involving the purchase and sale or sale and purchase of derivative securities having different characteristics but related to the same underlying security (e.g., the purchase of a call option and the sale of a convertible debenture) or derivative securities and underlying securities shall not exceed the difference in price of the underlying security on the date of purchase or sale and the date of sale or purchase. Such profits may be measured by calculating the short-swing profits that would have been realized had the subject transactions involved purchases and sales solely of the derivative security that was purchased or solely of the derivative security that was sold, valued as of the time of the matching purchase or sale, and calculated for the lesser of the number of underlying securities actually purchased or sold.

(d) Upon cancellation or expiration of an option within six months of the writing of the option, any profit derived from writing the option shall be recoverable under section 16(b) of the Act. The profit shall not exceed the premium received for writing the option. The disposition or closing of a long derivative security position, as a result of cancellation or expiration, shall be exempt from section 16(b) of the Act where no value is received from the cancellation or expiration.

[56 FR 7270, Feb. 21, 1991, as amended at 61 FR 30394, June 14, 1996]

§ 240.16b-7 Mergers, reclassifications, and consolidations.

(a) The following transactions shall be exempt from the provisions of section 16(b) of the Act:

(1) The acquisition of a security of a company, pursuant to a merger, reclassification or consolidation, in exchange for a security of a company that before the merger, reclassification or consolidation, owned 85 percent or more of either:

(i) The equity securities of all other companies involved in the merger, reclassification or consolidation, or in the case of a consolidation, the resulting company; or

(ii) The combined assets of all the companies involved in the merger, reclassification or consolidation, computed according to their book values before the merger, reclassification or consolidation as determined by reference to their most recent available financial statements for a 12 month period before the merger, reclassification or consolidation, or such shorter time as the company has been in existence.

(2) The disposition of a security, pursuant to a merger, reclassification or consolidation, of a company that before the merger, reclassification or consolidation, owned 85 percent or more of either:

(i) The equity securities of all other companies involved in the merger, reclassification or, in the case of a consolidation, the resulting company; or

(ii) The combined assets of all the companies undergoing merger, reclassification or consolidation, computed according to their book values before the merger, reclassification or consolidation as determined by reference to their most recent available financial statements for a 12 month period before the merger, reclassification or consolidation.

§ 240.16b-8

(b) A merger within the meaning of this section shall include the sale or purchase of substantially all the assets of one company by another in exchange for equity securities which are then distributed to the security holders of the company that sold its assets.

(c) The exemption provided by this section applies to any securities transaction that satisfies the conditions specified in this section and is not conditioned on the transaction satisfying any other conditions.

(d) Notwithstanding the foregoing, if a person subject to section 16 of the Act makes any non-exempt purchase of a security in any company involved in the merger, reclassification or consolidation and any non-exempt sale of a security in any company involved in the merger, reclassification or consolidation within any period of less than six months during which the merger, reclassification or consolidation took place, the exemption provided by this section shall be unavailable to the extent of such purchase and sale.

[70 FR 46089, Aug. 9, 2005]

§ 240.16b-8 Voting trusts.

Any acquisition or disposition of an equity security or certificate representing equity securities involved in the deposit or withdrawal from a voting trust or deposit agreement shall be exempt from section 16(b) of the Act if substantially all of the assets held under the voting trust or deposit agreement immediately after the deposit or immediately prior to the withdrawal consisted of equity securities of the same class as the security deposited or withdrawn: *Provided, however,* That this exemption shall not apply if there is a non-exempt purchase or sale of an equity security of the class deposited within six months (including the date of withdrawal or deposit) of a non-exempt sale or purchase, respectively, of any certificate representing such equity security (other than the actual deposit or withdrawal).

EXEMPTION OF CERTAIN TRANSACTIONS FROM SECTION 16(c)

SOURCE: Sections 240.16c-1 through 240.16c-4 appear at 56 FR 7273, Feb. 21, 1991, unless otherwise noted.

§ 240.16c-1 Brokers.

Any transaction shall be exempt from section 16(c) of the Act to the extent necessary to render lawful the execution by a broker of an order for an account in which the broker has no direct or indirect interest.

§ 240.16c-2 Transactions effected in connection with a distribution.

Any transaction shall be exempt from section 16(c) of the Act to the extent necessary to render lawful any sale made by or on behalf of a dealer in connection with a distribution of a substantial block of securities, where the sale is represented by an over-allotment in which the dealer is participating as a member of an underwriting group, or the dealer or a person acting on the dealer's behalf intends in good faith to offset such sale with a security to be acquired by or on behalf of the dealer as a participant in an underwriting, selling, or soliciting-dealer group of which the dealer is a member at the time of the sale, whether or not the security to be acquired is subject to a prior offering to existing security holders or some other class of persons.

§ 240.16c-3 Exemption of sales of securities to be acquired.

(a) Whenever any person is entitled, incident to ownership of an issued security and without the payment of consideration, to receive another security "when issued" or "when distributed," the sale of the security to be acquired shall be exempt from the operation of section 16(c) of the Act: *Provided,* That:

(1) The sale is made subject to the same conditions as those attaching to the right of acquisition;

(2) Such person exercises reasonable diligence to deliver such security to the purchaser promptly after the right of acquisition matures; and

(3) Such person reports the sale on the appropriate form for reporting transactions by persons subject to section 16(a) of the Act.

(b) This section shall not exempt transactions involving both a sale of the issued security and a sale of a security "when issued" or "when distributed" if the combined transactions result in a sale of more securities than the aggregate of issued securities

Securities and Exchange Commission

§ 240.17a-2

owned by the seller plus those to be received for the other security "when issued" or "when distributed."

§ 240.16c-4 Derivative securities.

Establishing or increasing a put equivalent position shall be exempt from section 16(c) of the Act, so long as the amount of securities underlying the put equivalent position does not exceed the amount of underlying securities otherwise owned.

ARBITRAGE TRANSACTIONS

§ 240.16e-1 Arbitrage transactions under section 16.

It shall be unlawful for any director or officer of an issuer of an equity security which is registered pursuant to section 12 of the Act to effect any foreign or domestic arbitrage transaction in any equity security of such issuer, whether registered or not, unless he shall include such transaction in the statements required by section 16(a) and shall account to such issuer for the profits arising from such transaction, as provided in section 16(b). The provision of section 16(c) shall not apply to such arbitrage transactions. The provisions of section 16 shall not apply to any bona fide foreign or domestic arbitrage transaction insofar as it is effected by any person other than such director or officer of the issuer of such security.

(Secs. 4, 12, 13, 15, 16, 19, 24, 48 Stat. 77, 892, 894, 895, 896, 85, as amended, 901; 15 U.S.C. 77d, 78*l*, 78m, 78o, 78p, 77s, 78x)

[30 FR 2025, Feb. 13, 1965]

PRESERVATION OF RECORDS AND REPORTS OF CERTAIN STABILIZING ACTIVITIES

§ 240.17a-1 Recordkeeping rule for national securities exchanges, national securities associations, registered clearing agencies and the Municipal Securities Rulemaking Board.

(a) Every national securities exchange, national securities association, registered clearing agency and the Municipal Securities Rulemaking Board shall keep and preserve at least one copy of all documents, including all correspondence, memoranda, papers, books, notices, accounts, and other such records as shall be made or received by it in the course of its business as such and in the conduct of its self-regulatory activity.

(b) Every national securities exchange, national securities association, registered clearing agency and the Municipal Securities Rulemaking Board shall keep all such documents for a period of not less than five years, the first two years in an easily accessible place, subject to the destruction and disposition provisions of Rule 17a-6.

(c) Every national securities exchange, registered securities association, registered clearing agency and the Municipal Securities Rulemaking Board shall, upon request of any representative of the Commission, promptly furnish to the possession of such representative copies of any documents required to be kept and preserved by it pursuant to paragraphs (a) and (b) of this section.

[45 FR 79426, Dec. 1, 1980]

§ 240.17a-2 Recordkeeping requirements relating to stabilizing activities.

(a) *Scope of section.* This section shall apply to any person who effects any purchase of a security subject to § 242.104 of this chapter for the purpose of, or who participates in a syndicate or group that engages in, "stabilizing," as defined in § 242.100 of this chapter, the price of any security; or effects a purchase that is a "syndicate covering transaction," as defined in § 242.100 of this chapter; or imposes a "penalty bid," as defined in § 242.100 of this chapter:

(1) With respect to which a registration statement has been, or is to be, filed pursuant to the Securities Act of 1933 (15 U.S.C. 77a *et seq.*); or

(2) Which is being, or is to be, offered pursuant to an exemption from registration under Regulation A (§§ 230.251 through 230.263 of this chapter) adopted under the Securities Act of 1933 (15 U.S.C. 77a *et seq.*); or

(3) Which is being, or is to be, otherwise offered, if the aggregate offering price of the securities being offered exceeds $5,000,000.

(b) *Definitions.* For purposes of this section, the following definitions shall apply:

(1) The term *manager* shall mean the person stabilizing or effecting syndicate covering transactions or imposing a penalty bid for its sole account or for the account of a syndicate or group in which it is a participant, and who, by contract or otherwise, deals with the issuer, organizes the selling effort, receives some benefit from the underwriting that is not shared by other underwriters, or represents any other underwriters in such matters as maintaining the records of the distribution and arranging for allotments of the securities offered.

(2) The term *exempted security* means an exempted security as defined in section 3(a)(12) of the Act, including securities issued, or guaranteed both as to principal and interest, by the International Bank for Reconstruction and Development.

(c) *Records relating to stabilizing, syndicate covering transactions, and penalty bids required to be maintained by manager.* Any person subject to this section who acts as a manager and stabilizes or effects syndicate covering transactions or imposes a penalty bid shall:

(1) Promptly record and maintain the following separately retrievable information, for a period of not less than three years, the first two years in an easily accessible place; *Provided, however,* That if the information is in a record required to be made pursuant to § 240.17a–3 or § 240.17a–4, or otherwise preserved, such information need not be maintained in a separate file if the person can sort promptly and retrieve the information as if it had been kept in a separate file as a record made pursuant to, and preserves the information in accordance with the time periods specified in, this paragraph (c)(1):

(i) The name and class of any security stabilized or any security in which syndicate covering transactions have been effected or a penalty bid has been imposed;

(ii) The price, date, and time at which each stabilizing purchase or syndicate covering transaction was effected by the manager or by any participant in the syndicate or group, and whether any penalties were assessed;

(iii) The names and the addresses of the members of the syndicate or group;

(iv) Their respective commitments, or, in the case of a standby or contingent underwriting, the percentage participation of each member of the syndicate or group therein; and

(v) The dates when any penalty bid was in effect.

(2) Promptly furnish to each of the members of the syndicate or group the name and class of any security being stabilized, and the date and time at which the first stabilizing purchase was effected by the manager or by any participant in the syndicate or group; and

(3) Promptly notify each of the members of such syndicate or group of the date and time when stabilizing was terminated.

(d) *Notification to manager.* Any person who has a participation in a syndicate account but who is not a manager of such account, and who effects one or more stabilizing purchases or syndicate covering transactions for its sole account or for the account of a syndicate or group, shall within three business days following such purchase notify the manager of the price, date, and time at which such stabilizing purchase or syndicate covering transaction was effected, and shall in addition notify the manager of the date and time when such stabilizing purchase or syndicate covering transaction was terminated. The manager shall maintain such notifications in a separate file, together with the information required by paragraph (c)(1) of this section, for a period of not less than three years, the first two years in an easily accessible place.

(Secs. 9(a)(6), 10(b), 17(a) and 23(a) of the Act, 15 U.S.C. 78i(a)(6), 78j(b), 78q(a) and 78w(a))

[48 FR 41378, Sept. 15, 1983, as amended at 62 FR 544, Jan. 3, 1997]

§ 240.17a–3 **Records to be made by certain exchange members, brokers and dealers.**

This section applies to the following types of entities: A member of a national securities exchange who transacts a business in securities directly with others than members of a national securities exchange; a broker or

Securities and Exchange Commission

§ 240.17a–3

dealer who transacts a business in securities through the medium of a member of a national securities exchange; a broker or dealer, including an *OTC derivatives dealer* as that term is defined in § 240.3b–12, registered pursuant to section 15 of the Act (15 U.S.C. 78o); a security-based swap dealer registered pursuant to section 15F of the Act (15 U.S.C. 78o–10) that is also a broker or dealer, including an OTC derivatives dealer, registered pursuant to section 15 of the Act; and a major security-based swap participant registered pursuant to section 15F of the Act that is also a broker or dealer, including an OTC derivatives dealer, registered pursuant to section 15 of the Act. Section 240.18a–5 (rather than this section) applies to the following types of entities: A security-based swap dealer registered pursuant to section 15F of the Act that is not also a broker or dealer, including an OTC derivatives dealer, registered pursuant to section 15 of the Act; and a major security-based swap participant registered pursuant to section 15F of the Act that is not also a broker or dealer, including an OTC derivatives dealer, registered pursuant to section 15 of the Act.

(a) Every member of a national securities exchange who transacts a business in securities directly with others than members of a national securities exchange, every broker or dealer who transacts a business in securities through the medium of any such member, and every broker or dealer registered pursuant to section 15 of the Act (15 U.S.C. 78o) must make and keep current the following books and records relating to its business:

(1) Blotters (or other records of original entry) containing an itemized daily record of all purchases and sales of securities (including security-based swaps), all receipts and deliveries of securities (including certificate numbers), all receipts and disbursements of cash and all other debits and credits. Such records must show the account for which each such purchase or sale was effected, the name and amount of securities, the unit and aggregate purchase or sale price, if any (including the financial terms for security-based swaps), the trade date, and the name or other designation of the person from whom such securities were purchased or received or to whom sold or delivered. For security-based swaps, such records must also show, for each transaction, the type of security-based swap, the reference security, index, or obligor, the date and time of execution, the effective date, the scheduled termination date, the notional amount(s) and the currenc(ies) in which the notional amount(s) is expressed, the unique transaction identifier, and the counterparty's unique identification code.

(2) Ledgers (or other records) reflecting all assets and liabilities, income and expense and capital accounts.

(3) Ledger accounts (or other records) itemizing separately as to each cash, margin, or security-based swap account of every customer and of such member, broker or dealer and partners thereof, all purchases, sales, receipts and deliveries of securities (including security-based swaps) and commodities for such account, and all other debits and credits to such account; and, in addition, for a security-based swap, the type of security-based swap, the reference security, index, or obligor, the date and time of execution, the effective date, the scheduled termination date, the notional amount(s) and the currenc(ies) in which the notional amount(s) is expressed, the unique transaction identifier, and the counterparty's unique identification code.

(4) Ledgers (or other records) reflecting the following:

(i) Securities in transfer;

(ii) Dividends and interest received;

(iii) Securities borrowed and securities loaned;

(iv) Moneys borrowed and moneys loaned (together with a record of the collateral therefor and any substitutions in such collateral);

(v) Securities failed to receive and failed to deliver;

(vi) All long and all short securities record differences arising from the examination, count, verification, and comparison pursuant to §§ 240.17a–5, 240.17a–12, 240.17a–13, and 240.18a–7, as applicable (by date of examination, count, verification, and comparison showing for each security the number of long or short count differences); and

585

§ 240.17a-3

(vii) Repurchase and reverse repurchase agreements.

(5) A securities record or ledger reflecting separately for each:

(i) Security, other than a security-based swap, as of the clearance dates all "long" or "short" positions (including securities in safekeeping and securities that are the subjects of repurchase or reverse repurchase agreements) carried by such member, broker or dealer for its account or for the account of its customers or partners, or others, and showing the location of all securities long and the offsetting position to all securities short, including long security count differences and short security count differences classified by the date of the physical count and verification in which they were discovered, and in all cases the name or designation of the account in which each position is carried.

(ii) Security-based swap, the reference security, index, or obligor, the unique transaction identifier, the counterparty's unique identification code, whether it is a "bought" or "sold" position in the security-based swap, whether the security-based swap is cleared or not cleared, and if cleared, identification of the clearing agency where the security-based swap is cleared.

(6)(i) A memorandum of each brokerage order, and of any other instruction, given or received for the purchase or sale of a security, except for the purchase or sale of a security-based swap, whether executed or unexecuted.

(A) The memorandum must show the terms and conditions of the order or instructions and of any modification or cancellation thereof, the account for which entered, the time the order was received, the time of entry, the price at which executed, the identity of each associated person, if any, responsible for the account, the identity of any other person who entered or accepted the order on behalf of the customer, or, if a customer entered the order on an electronic system, a notation of that entry; and, to the extent feasible, the time of execution or cancellation. The memorandum need not show the identity of any person, other than the associated person responsible for the account, who may have entered or accepted the order if the order is entered into an electronic system that generates the memorandum and if that system is not capable of receiving an entry of the identity of any person other than the responsible associated person; in that circumstance, the member, broker or dealer must produce upon request by a representative of a securities regulatory authority a separate record which identifies each other person. An order entered pursuant to the exercise of discretionary authority by the member, broker or dealer, or associated person thereof, must be so designated. The term *instruction* must include instructions between partners and employees of a member, broker or dealer. The term *time of entry* means the time when the member, broker or dealer transmits the order or instruction for execution.

(B) The memorandum need not be made as to a purchase, sale or redemption of a security on a subscription way basis directly from or to the issuer, if the member, broker or dealer maintains a copy of the customer's or non-customer's subscription agreement regarding a purchase, or a copy of any other document required by the issuer regarding a sale or redemption.

(ii) A memorandum of each brokerage order, and of any other instruction, given or received for the purchase or sale of a security-based swap, whether executed or unexecuted. The memorandum must show the terms and conditions of the order or instructions and of any modification or cancellation thereof; the account for which entered; the time the order was received; the time of entry; the price at which executed; the identity of each associated person, if any, responsible for the account; the identity of any other person who entered or accepted the order on behalf of the customer, or, if a customer entered the order on an electronic system, a notation of that entry; and, to the extent feasible, the time of cancellation, if applicable. The memorandum also must include the type of the security-based swap, the reference security, index, or obligor, the date and time of execution, the effective date, the scheduled termination, the notional amount(s) and the currenc(ies) in which the notional

Securities and Exchange Commission § 240.17a–3

amount(s) is expressed, the unique transaction identifier, and the counterparty's unique identification code. An order entered pursuant to the exercise of discretionary authority must be so designated.

(7)(i) A memorandum of each purchase or sale of a security, other than for the purchase or sale of a security-based swap, for the account of the member, broker or dealer showing the price and, to the extent feasible, the time of execution; and, in addition, where the purchase or sale is with a customer other than a broker or dealer, a memorandum of each order received, showing the time of receipt; the terms and conditions of the order and of any modification thereof; the account for which it was entered; the identity of each associated person, if any, responsible for the account; the identity of any other person who entered or accepted the order on behalf of the customer, or, if a customer entered the order on an electronic system, a notation of that entry. The memorandum need not show the identity of any person other than the associated person responsible for the account who may have entered the order if the order is entered into an electronic system that generates the memorandum and if that system is not capable of receiving an entry of the identity of any person other than the responsible associated person. In the circumstance in the preceding sentence, the member, broker or dealer must produce upon request by a representative of a securities regulatory authority a separate record that identifies each other person. An order with a customer other than a member, broker or dealer entered pursuant to the exercise of discretionary authority by the member, broker or dealer, or associated person thereof, must be so designated.

(ii) A memorandum of each purchase or sale of a security-based swap for the account of the member, broker or dealer showing the price; and, in addition, where the purchase or sale is with a customer other than a broker or dealer, a memorandum of each order received, showing the time of receipt; the terms and conditions of the order and of any modification thereof; the account for which it was entered; the identity of any other person who entered or accepted the order on behalf of the customer, or, if a customer entered the order on an electronic system, a notation of that entry. The memorandum must also include the type of security-based swap, the reference security, index, or obligor, the date and time of execution, the effective date, the scheduled termination date, the notional amount(s) and the currenc(ies) in which the notional amount(s) is expressed, the unique transaction identifier, and the counterparty's unique identification code. An order entered pursuant to the exercise of discretionary authority must be so designated.

(8)(i) With respect to a security other than a security-based swap, copies of confirmations of all purchases and sales of securities, including all repurchase and reverse repurchase agreements, and copies of notices of all other debits and credits for securities, cash and other items for the account of customers and partners of such member, broker or dealer.

(ii) With respect to a security-based swap, copies of the security-based swap trade acknowledgment and verification made in compliance with § 240.15Fi–2.

(9) A record with respect to each cash, margin, and security-based swap account with such member, broker or dealer indicating, as applicable:

(i) The name and address of the beneficial owner of such account;

(ii) Except with respect to exempt employee benefit plan securities as defined in § 240.14a–1(d), but only to the extent such securities are held by employee benefit plans established by the issuer of the securities, whether or not the beneficial owner of securities registered in the name of such members, brokers or dealers, or a registered clearing agency or its nominee objects to disclosure of his or her identity, address, and securities positions to issuers;

(iii) In the case of a margin account, the signature of such owner; provided that, in the case of a joint account or an account of a corporation, such records are required only in respect of the person or persons authorized to transact business for such account; and

587

§ 240.17a-3

(iv) For each security-based swap account, a record of the unique identification code of such counterparty, the name and address of such counterparty, and a record of the authorization of each person the counterparty has granted authority to transact business in the security-based swap account.

(10) A record of all puts, calls, spreads, straddles, and other options in which such member, broker or dealer has any direct or indirect interest or which such member, broker or dealer, has granted or guaranteed, containing, at least, an identification of the security, and the number of units involved. An OTC derivatives dealer must also keep a record of all eligible OTC derivative instruments as defined in § 240.3b–13 in which the OTC derivatives dealer has any direct or indirect interest or which it has written or guaranteed, containing, at a minimum, an identification of the security or other instrument, the number of units involved, and the identity of the counterparty.

(11) A record of the proof of money balances of all ledger accounts in the form of trial balances and a record of the computation of aggregate indebtedness and net capital, as of the trial balance date, pursuant to § 240.15c3–1 or § 240.18a–1, as applicable. The computation need not be made by any member, broker or dealer unconditionally exempt from § 240.15c3–1 pursuant to § 240.15c3–1(b)(1) or (3). Such trial balances and computations must be prepared currently at least once a month.

(12)(i) A questionnaire or application for employment executed by each *associated person* as that term is defined in paragraph (g)(4) of this section of the member, broker or dealer, which questionnaire or application must be approved in writing by an authorized representative of the member, broker or dealer and must contain at least the following information with respect to the associated person:

(A) The associated person's name, address, social security number, and the starting date of the associated person's employment or other association with the member, broker or dealer;

(B) The associated person's date of birth;

(C) A complete, consecutive statement of all the associated person's business connections for at least the preceding ten years, including whether the employment was part-time or full-time;

(D) A record of any denial of membership or registration, and of any disciplinary action taken, or sanction imposed, upon the associated person by any federal or state agency, or by any national securities exchange or national securities association, including any finding that the associated person was a cause of any disciplinary action or had violated any law;

(E) A record of any denial, suspension, expulsion, or revocation of membership or registration of any member, broker or dealer with which the associated person was associated in any capacity when such action was taken;

(F) A record of any permanent or temporary injunction entered against the associated person, or any member, broker, dealer, security-based swap dealer or major security-based swap participant with which the associated person was associated in any capacity at the time such injunction was entered;

(G) A record of any arrest or indictment for any felony, or any misdemeanor pertaining to securities, commodities, banking, insurance or real estate (including, but not limited to, acting or being associated with a broker or dealer, investment company, investment adviser, futures sponsor, bank, or savings and loan association), fraud, false statements or omissions, wrongful taking of property or bribery, forgery, counterfeiting, or extortion, and the disposition of the foregoing; and

(H) A record of any other name or names by which the associated person has been known or which the associated person has used.

(I) Provided, however, that if such associated person has been registered as a registered representative of such member, broker or dealer with, or the associated person's employment has been approved by a registered national securities association or a registered national securities exchange, then retention of a full, correct, and complete copy of any and all applications for

Securities and Exchange Commission § 240.17a–3

such registration or approval will be deemed to satisfy the requirements of this paragraph (a)(12)(i).

(ii) A record listing every associated person of the member, broker or dealer which shows, for each associated person, every office of the member, broker or dealer, where the associated person regularly conducts the business of handling funds or securities or effecting any transactions in, or inducing or attempting to induce the purchase or sale of any security for the member, broker or dealer and the Central Registration Depository number, if any, and every internal identification number or code assigned to that person by the member, broker or dealer.

(13) Records required to be maintained pursuant to paragraph (d) of §240.17f–2.

(14) Copies of all Forms X–17F–1A filed pursuant to §240.17f–1, all agreements between reporting institutions regarding registration or other aspects of §240.17f–1, and all confirmations or other information received from the Commission or its designee as a result of inquiry.

(15) Records required to be maintained pursuant to paragraph (e) of §240.17f–2.

(16)(i) The following records regarding any internal broker-dealer system of which such a broker or dealer is the sponsor:

(A) A record of the broker's or dealer's customers that have access to an internal broker-dealer system sponsored by such broker or dealer (identifying any affiliations between such customers and the broker or dealer);

(B) Daily summaries of trading in the internal broker-dealer system, including:

(*1*) Securities for which transactions have been executed through use of such system; and

(*2*) Transaction volume (separately stated for trading occurring during hours when consolidated trade reporting facilities are and are not in operation):

(*i*) With respect to equity securities, stated in number of trades, number of shares, and total U.S. dollar value;

(*ii*) With respect to debt securities, stated in total settlement value in U.S. dollars; and

(*iii*) With respect to other securities, stated in number of trades, number of units of securities, and in dollar value, or other appropriate commonly used measure of value of such securities; and

(C) Time-sequenced records of each transaction effected through the internal broker-dealer system, including date and time executed, price, size, security traded, counterparty identification information, and method of execution (if internal broker-dealer system allows alternative means or locations for execution, such as routing to another market, matching with limit orders, or executing against the quotations of the broker or dealer sponsoring the system).

(ii) For purposes of paragraph (a) of this section, the term:

(A) *Internal broker-dealer system* means any facility, other than a national securities exchange, an exchange exempt from registration based on limited volume, or an alternative trading system as defined in Regulation ATS, §§242.300 through 242.303 of this chapter, that provides a mechanism, automated in full or in part, for collecting, receiving, disseminating, or displaying system orders and facilitating agreement to the basic terms of a purchase or sale of a security between a customer and the sponsor, or between two customers of the sponsor, through use of the internal broker-dealer system or through the broker or dealer sponsor of such system;

(B) *Sponsor* means any broker or dealer that organizes, operates, administers, or otherwise directly controls an internal broker-dealer trading system or, if the operator of the internal broker-dealer system is not a registered broker or dealer, any broker or dealer that, pursuant to contract, affiliation, or other agreement with the system operator, is involved on a regular basis with executing transactions in connection with use of the internal broker-dealer system, other than solely for its own account or as a customer with access to the internal broker-dealer system; and

(C) *System order* means any order or other communication or indication submitted by any customer with access to the internal broker-dealer system

§ 240.17a-3

for entry into a trading system announcing an interest in purchasing or selling a security. The term "system order" does not include inquiries or indications of interest that are not entered into the internal broker-dealer system.

(17) For each account with a natural person as a customer or owner:

(i)(A) An account record including the customer's or owner's name, tax identification number, address, telephone number, date of birth, employment status (including occupation and whether the customer is an associated person of a member, broker or dealer), annual income, net worth (excluding value of primary residence), and the account's investment objectives. In the case of a joint account, the account record must include personal information for each joint owner who is a natural person; however, financial information for the individual joint owners may be combined. The account record must indicate whether it has been signed by the associated person responsible for the account, if any, and approved or accepted by a principal of the member, broker or dealer. For accounts in existence on the effective date of this section, the member, broker or dealer must obtain this information within three years of the effective date of the section.

(B) A record indicating that:

(1) The member, broker or dealer has furnished to each customer or owner within three years of the effective date of this section, and to each customer or owner who opened an account after the effective date of this section within thirty days of the opening of the account, and thereafter at intervals no greater than thirty-six months, a copy of the account record or an alternate document with all information required by paragraph (a)(17)(i)(A) of this section. The member, broker or dealer may elect to send this notification with the next statement mailed to the customer or owner after the opening of the account. The member, broker or dealer may choose to exclude any tax identification number and date of birth from the account record or alternative document furnished to the customer or owner. The member, broker or dealer must include with the account record or alternative document provided to each customer or owner an explanation of any terms regarding investment objectives. The account record or alternate document furnished to the customer or owner must include or be accompanied by prominent statements that the customer or owner should mark any corrections and return the account record or alternate document to the member, broker or dealer, and that the customer or owner should notify the member, broker or dealer of any future changes to information contained in the account record.

(2) For each account record updated to reflect a change in the name or address of the customer or owner, the member, broker or dealer furnished a notification of that change to the customer's old address, or to each joint owner, and the associated person, if any, responsible for that account, on or before the 30th day after the date the member, broker or dealer received notice of the change.

(3) For each change in the account's investment objectives the member, broker or dealer has furnished to each customer or owner, and the associated person, if any, responsible for that account a copy of the updated customer account record or alternative document with all information required to be furnished by paragraph (a)(17)(i)(B)(1) of this section, on or before the 30th day after the date the member, broker or dealer received notice of any change, or, if the account was updated for some reason other than the firm receiving notice of a change, after the date the account record was updated. The member, broker or dealer may elect to send this notification with the next statement scheduled to be mailed to the customer or owner.

(C) For purposes of this paragraph (a)(17), the neglect, refusal, or inability of a customer or owner to provide or update any account record information required under paragraph (a)(17)(i)(A) of this section will excuse the member, broker or dealer from obtaining that required information.

(D) The account record requirements in paragraph (a)(17)(i)(A) of this section will only apply to accounts for which the member, broker or dealer is, or has

Securities and Exchange Commission § 240.17a–3

within the past 36 months been, required to make a suitability determination under the federal securities laws or under the requirements of a self-regulatory organization of which it is a member. Additionally, the furnishing requirement in paragraph (a)(17)(i)(B)(*1*) of this section will not be applicable to an account for which, within the last 36 months, the member, broker or dealer has not been required to make a suitability determination under the federal securities laws or under the requirements of a self-regulatory organization of which it is a member. This paragraph (a)(17)(i)(D) does not relieve a member, broker or dealer from any obligation arising from the rules of a self-regulatory organization of which it is a member regarding the collection of information from a customer or owner.

(ii) If an account is a discretionary account, a record containing the dated signature of each customer or owner granting the authority and the dated signature of each natural person to whom discretionary authority was granted.

(iii) A record for each account indicating that each customer or owner was furnished with a copy of each written agreement entered into on or after the effective date of this paragraph pertaining to that account and that, if requested by the customer or owner, the customer or owner was furnished with a fully executed copy of each agreement.

(18) A record:

(i) As to each associated person of each written customer complaint received by the member, broker or dealer concerning that associated person. The record must include the complainant's name, address, and account number; the date the complaint was received; the name of any other associated person identified in the complaint; a description of the nature of the complaint; and the disposition of the complaint. Instead of the record, a member, broker or dealer may maintain a copy of each original complaint in a separate file by the associated person named in the complaint along with a record of the disposition of the complaint.

(ii) Indicating that each customer of the member, broker or dealer has been provided with a notice containing the address and telephone number of the department of the member, broker or dealer to which any complaints as to the account may be directed.

(19) A record:

(i) As to each associated person listing each purchase and sale of a security attributable, for compensation purposes, to that associated person. The record must include the amount of compensation if monetary and a description of the compensation if nonmonetary. In lieu of making this record, a member, broker or dealer may elect to produce the required information promptly upon request of a representative of a securities regulatory authority.

(ii) Of all agreements pertaining to the relationship between each associated person and the member, broker or dealer including a summary of each associated person's compensation arrangement or plan with the member, broker or dealer, including commission and concession schedules and, to the extent that compensation is based on factors other than remuneration per trade, the method by which the compensation is determined.

(20) A record, which need not be separate from the advertisements, sales literature, or communications, documenting that the member, broker or dealer has complied with, or adopted policies and procedures reasonably designed to establish compliance with, applicable federal requirements and rules of a self-regulatory organization of which the member, broker or dealer is a member which require that advertisements, sales literature, or any other communications with the public by a member, broker or dealer or its associated persons be approved by a principal.

(21) A record for each office listing, by name or title, each person at that office who, without delay, can explain the types of records the firm maintains at that office and the information contained in those records.

(22) A record listing each principal of a member, broker or dealer responsible for establishing policies and procedures that are reasonably designed to ensure

§ 240.17a–3

compliance with any applicable federal requirements or rules of a self-regulatory organization of which the member, broker or dealer is a member that require acceptance or approval of a record by a principal.

(23) A record documenting the credit, market, and liquidity risk management controls established and maintained by the broker or dealer to assist it in analyzing and managing the risks associated with its business activities, *Provided*, that the records required by this paragraph (a)(23) need only be made if the broker or dealer has more than:

(i) $1,000,000 in aggregate credit items as computed under § 240.15c3–3a; or

(ii) $20,000,000 in capital, which includes debt subordinated in accordance with § 240.15c3–1d.

(24) A record of the date that each Form CRS was provided to each retail investor, including any Form CRS provided before such retail investor opens an account.

(25) A record of the daily calculation of the current exposure and, if applicable, the initial margin amount for each account of a counterparty required under § 240.18a–3(c).

(26) A record of compliance with possession or control requirements under § 240.15c3–3(p)(2).

(27) A record of the reserve computation required under § 240.15c3–3(p)(3).

(28) A record of each security-based swap transaction that is not verified under § 240.15Fi–2 within five business days of execution that includes, at a minimum, the unique transaction identifier and the counterparty's unique identification code.

(29) A record documenting that the broker or dealer has complied with the business conduct standards as required under § 240.15Fh–6.

(30) A record documenting that the broker or dealer has complied with the business conduct standards as required under §§ 240.15Fh–1 through 240.15Fh–5 and 240.15Fk–1.

(31)(i) A record of each security-based swap portfolio reconciliation, whether conducted pursuant to § 240.15Fi–3 or otherwise, including the dates of the security-based swap portfolio reconciliation, the number of portfolio reconciliation discrepancies, the number of security-based swap valuation disputes (including the time-to-resolution of each valuation dispute and the age of outstanding valuation disputes, categorized by transaction and counterparty), and the name of the third-party entity performing the security-based swap portfolio reconciliation, if any.

(ii) A copy of each notification required to be provided to the Commission pursuant to § 240.15Fi–3(c).

(iii) A record of each bilateral offset and each bilateral portfolio compression exercise or multilateral portfolio compression exercise in which it participates, whether conducted pursuant to § 240.15Fi–4 or otherwise, including the dates of the offset or compression, the security-based swaps included in the offset or compression, the identity of the counterparties participating in the offset or compression, the results of the compression, and the name of the third-party entity performing the offset or compression, if any.

(32)–(34) [Reserved]

(35) For each retail customer to whom a recommendation of any securities transaction or investment strategy involving securities is or will be provided:

(i) A record of all information collected from and provided to the retail customer pursuant to § 240.15*l*–1, as well as the identity of each natural person who is an associated person, if any, responsible for the account.

(ii) For purposes of this paragraph (a)(35), the neglect, refusal, or inability of the retail customer to provide or update any information described in paragraph (a)(35)(i) of this section shall excuse the broker, dealer, or associated person from obtaining that required information.

(b) A broker or dealer may comply with the recordkeeping requirements of the Commodity Exchange Act and chapter I of this title applicable to swap dealers and major swap participants in lieu of complying with paragraphs (a)(1), (3), and (5) of this section solely with respect to required information regarding security-based swap transactions and positions if:

(1) The broker or dealer is registered as a security-based swap dealer or major security-based swap participant

Securities and Exchange Commission § 240.17a-3

pursuant to section 15F of the Act (15 U.S.C. 78*o*–10);

(2) The broker or dealer is registered as a swap dealer or major swap participant pursuant to section 4s of the Commodity Exchange Act and chapter I of this title;

(3) The broker or dealer is subject to 17 CFR 23.201, 23.202, 23.402, and 23.501 with respect to its swap-related books and records;

(4) The broker or dealer preserves all of the data elements necessary to create the records required by paragraphs (a)(1), (3), and (5) of this section as they pertain to security-based swap and swap transactions and positions;

(5) The broker or dealer upon request furnishes promptly to representatives of the Commission the records required by paragraphs (a)(1), (3), and (5) of this section as well as the records required by 17 CFR 23.201, 23.202, 23.402, and 23.501 as they pertain to security-based swap and swap transactions and positions in the format applicable to that category of record as set forth in this section; and

(6) The broker or dealer provides notice of its intent to utilize this paragraph (b) by notifying in writing the Commission, both at the principal office of the Commission in Washington, DC, and at the regional office of the Commission for the region in which the registrant has its principal place of business, as well as by notifying in writing the registrant's designated examining authority.

(c) A member of a national securities exchange, or a broker or dealer registered pursuant to section 15 of the Act (15 U.S.C. 78*o*), that introduces accounts on a fully-disclosed basis, is not required to make or keep such records of transactions cleared for such member, broker or dealer as are made and kept by a clearing broker or dealer pursuant to the requirements of this section and §240.17a–4. Nothing in this paragraph (c) will be deemed to relieve such member, broker or dealer from the responsibility that such books and records be accurately maintained and preserved as specified in this section and §240.17a–4.

(d) For purposes of transactions in municipal securities by municipal securities brokers and municipal securities dealers, compliance with Rule G–8 of the Municipal Securities Rulemaking Board or any successor rule will be deemed to be in compliance with this section.

(e) The provisions of this section will not apply to security futures product transactions and positions in a *futures account* (as that term is defined in §240.15c3–3(a)(15)); provided, that the Commodity Futures Trading Commission's recordkeeping rules apply to those transactions and positions.

(f) Every member, broker or dealer must make and keep current, as to each office, the books and records described in paragraphs (a)(1), (6), (7), (12), and (17), (a)(18)(i), and (a)(19) through (22) of this section.

(g) When used in this section:

(1) The term *office* means any location where one or more associated persons regularly conduct the business of handling funds or securities or effecting any transactions in, or inducing or attempting to induce the purchase or sale of, any security.

(2) The term *principal* means any individual registered with a registered national securities association as a principal or branch manager of a member, broker or dealer or any other person who has been delegated supervisory responsibility over associated persons by the member, broker or dealer.

(3) The term *securities regulatory authority* means the Commission, any self-regulatory organization, or any securities commission (or any agency or office performing like functions) of the States.

(4) The term *associated person* means a "person associated with a broker or dealer" or "person associated with a security-based swap dealer or major security-based swap participant" as defined in sections 3(a)(18) and (70) of the Act (15 U.S.C. 78c(a)(18) and (70)) respectively, but does not include persons whose functions are solely clerical or ministerial.

CROSS REFERENCE: For interpretative release applicable to §240.17a–3, see No. 3040 in tabulation, part 241 of this chapter.

[13 FR 8212, Dec. 22, 1948]

EDITORIAL NOTE: For FEDERAL REGISTER citations affecting §240.17a–3, see the List of CFR Sections Affected, which appears in the

§ 240.17a-4

Finding Aids section of the printed volume and at *www.govinfo.gov.*

§ 240.17a-4 Records to be preserved by certain exchange members, brokers and dealers.

This section applies to the following types of entities: A member of a national securities exchange who transacts a business in securities directly with others than members of a national securities exchange; a broker or dealer who transacts a business in securities through the medium of a member of a national securities exchange; a broker or dealer, including an *OTC derivatives dealer* as that term is defined in § 240.3b-12, registered pursuant to section 15 of the Act (15 U.S.C. 78o); a security-based swap dealer registered pursuant to section 15F of the Act (15 U.S.C. 78o-10) that is also a broker or dealer, including an OTC derivatives dealer, registered pursuant to section 15 of the Act; and a major security-based swap participant registered pursuant to section 15F of the Act that is also a broker or dealer, including an OTC derivatives dealer, registered pursuant to section 15 of the Act. Section 240.18a-6 (rather than this section) applies to the following types of entities: A security-based swap dealer registered pursuant to section 15F of the Act that is not also a broker or dealer, including an OTC derivatives dealer, registered pursuant to section 15 of the Act; and a major security-based swap participant registered pursuant to section 15F of the Act that is not also a broker or dealer, including an OTC derivatives dealer, registered pursuant to section 15 of the Act.

(a) Every member, broker or dealer subject to § 240.17a-3 must preserve for a period of not less than 6 years, the first two years in an easily accessible place, all records required to be made pursuant to § 240.17a-3(a)(1) through (3), (5), and (21) and (22), and analogous records created pursuant to § 240.17a-3(e).

(b) Every member, broker or dealer subject to § 240.17a-3 must preserve for a period of not less than three years, the first two years in an easily accessible place:

(1) All records required to be made pursuant to § 240.17a-3(a)(4), (6) through (11), (16), (18) through (20), and (25) through (31), and analogous records created pursuant to § 240.17a-3(e).

(2) All check books, bank statements, cancelled checks and cash reconciliations.

(3) All bills receivable or payable (or copies thereof), paid or unpaid, relating to the member, broker or dealer's business as such.

(4) Originals of all communications received and copies of all communications sent (and any approvals thereof) by the member, broker or dealer (including inter-office memoranda and communications) relating to its business as such, including all communications which are subject to rules of a self-regulatory organization of which the member, broker or dealer is a member regarding communications with the public. As used in this paragraph (b)(4), the term *communications* includes sales scripts and recordings of telephone calls required to be maintained pursuant to section 15F(g)(1) of the Act (15 U.S.C. 78o-10(g)(1)).

(5) All trial balances, computations of aggregate indebtedness and net capital (and working papers in connection therewith), financial statements, branch office reconciliations, and internal audit working papers, relating to the member, broker or dealer's business as such.

(6) All guarantees of accounts and all powers of attorney and other evidence of the granting of any discretionary authority given in respect of any account, and copies of resolutions empowering an agent to act on behalf of a corporation.

(7) All written agreements (or copies thereof) entered into by such member, broker or dealer relating to its business as such, including agreements with respect to any account. Written agreements with respect to a security-based swap customer or non-customer, including governing documents or any document establishing the terms and conditions of the customer's or non-customer's security-based swaps must be maintained with the customer's or non-customer's account records.

(8) Records which contain the following information in support of amounts included in the report prepared as of the fiscal year end on Part II or IIA of Form X-17A-5 (§ 249.617 of

Securities and Exchange Commission § 240.17a–4

this chapter), as applicable, and in the annual financial statements filed with the Commission required by § 240.17a–5(d), § 240.17a–12(b), or § 240.18a–7(c), as applicable:

(i) Money balance and position, long or short, including description, quantity, price, and valuation of each security including contractual commitments in customers' accounts, in cash and fully secured accounts, partly secured accounts, unsecured accounts, and in securities accounts payable to customers;

(ii) Money balance and position, long or short, including description, quantity, price and valuation of each security including contractual commitments in non-customers' accounts, in cash and fully secured accounts, partly secured and unsecured accounts, and in securities accounts payable to non-customers;

(iii) Position, long or short, including description, quantity, price and valuation of each security including contractual commitments included in the Computation of Net Capital as commitments, securities owned, securities owned not readily marketable, and other investments owned not readily marketable;

(iv) Amount of secured demand note, description of collateral securing such secured demand note including quantity, price and valuation of each security and cash balance securing such secured demand note;

(v) Description of futures commodity contracts or swaps, contract value on trade date, market value, gain or loss, and liquidating equity or deficit in customers' and non-customers' accounts;

(vi) Description of futures commodity contracts or swaps, contract value on trade date, market value, gain or loss, and liquidating equity or deficit in trading and investment accounts;

(vii) Description, money balance, quantity, price, and valuation of each spot commodity, and swap position or commitments in customers' and non-customers' accounts;

(viii) Description, money balance, quantity, price, and valuation of each spot commodity, and swap position or commitments in trading and investment accounts;

(ix) Number of shares, description of security, exercise price, cost and market value of put and call options including short out of the money options having no market or exercise value, showing listed and unlisted put and call options separately;

(x) Quantity, price, and valuation of each security underlying the haircut for undue concentration made in the Computation for Net Capital;

(xi) Description, quantity, price and valuation of each security and commodity position or contractual commitment, long or short, in each joint account in which the broker or dealer has an interest, including each participant's interest and margin deposit;

(xii) Description, settlement date, contract amount, quantity, market price, and valuation for each aged failed to deliver requiring a charge in the Computation of Net Capital pursuant to § 240.15c3–1 or § 240.18a–1, as applicable;

(xiii) Detail relating to information for possession or control requirements under § 240.15c3–3 or § 240.18a–4, as applicable and reported in Part II or IIA of Form X–17A–5 (§ 249.617 of this chapter), as applicable;

(xiv) Detail relating to information for security-based swap possession or control requirements under § 240.15c3–3 or § 240.18a–4, as applicable, and reported in Part II or IIA of Form X–17A–5 (§ 249.617 of this chapter);

(xv) Detail of all items, not otherwise substantiated, which are charged or credited in the Computation of Net Capital pursuant to § 240.15c3–1 or § 240.18a–1, as applicable, such as cash margin deficiencies, deductions related to securities values and undue concentration, aged securities differences, and insurance claims receivable;

(xvi) Detail relating to the calculation of the risk margin amount pursuant to § 240.15c3–1(c)(17) or § 240.18a–1(c)(6), as applicable; and

(xvii) Other schedules which are specifically prescribed by the Commission as necessary to support information reported as required by §§ 240.17a–5, 240.17a–12, and 240.18a–7, as applicable.

(9) The records required to be made pursuant to § 240.15c3–3(d)(5) and (o) or § 240.18a–4, as applicable.

§ 240.17a–4

(10) The records required to be made pursuant to § 240.15c3–4 and the results of the periodic reviews conducted pursuant to § 240.15c3–4(d).

(11) All notices relating to an internal broker-dealer system provided to the customers of the broker or dealer that sponsors such internal broker-dealer system, as defined in paragraph (a)(16)(ii)(A) of § 240.17a–3. Notices, whether written or communicated through the internal broker-dealer trading system or other automated means, must be preserved under this paragraph (b)(11) if they are provided to all customers with access to an internal broker-dealer system, or to one or more classes of customers. Examples of notices to be preserved under this paragraph (b)(11) include, but are not limited to, notices addressing hours of system operations, system malfunctions, changes to system procedures, maintenance of hardware and software, and instructions pertaining to access to the internal broker-dealer system.

(12) The records required to be made pursuant to § 240.15c3–1e(c)(4)(vi) or § 240.18a–1(e)(2)(iii)(F)(2), as applicable.

(13) The written policies and procedures the broker-dealer establishes, documents, maintains, and enforces to assess creditworthiness for the purpose of § 240.15c3–1(c)(2)(vi)(E), (c)(2)(vi)(F)(1) and (2), and (c)(2)(vi)(H) or § 240.18a–1(c)(1)(vi)(2), as applicable.

(14) A copy of information required to be reported under §§ 242.901 through 242.909 of this chapter (Regulation SBSR).

(15) Copies of documents, communications, disclosures, and notices related to business conduct standards as required under §§ 240.15Fh–1 through 240.15Fh–6 and 240.15Fk–1.

(16) Copies of documents used to make a reasonable determination with respect to special entities, including information relating to the financial status, the tax status, the investment or financing objectives of the special entity as required under section 15F(h)(4)(C) and (5)(A) of the Act (15 U.S.C. 78o–10(h)(4)(C) and (5)(A)).

(c) Every member, broker or dealer subject to § 240.17a–3 must preserve for a period of not less than six years after the closing of any customer's account any account cards or records which relate to the terms and conditions with respect to the opening and maintenance of the account.

(d) Every member, broker or dealer subject to § 240.17a–3 must preserve during the life of the enterprise and of any successor enterprise all partnership articles or, in the case of a corporation, all articles of incorporation or charter, minute books, and stock certificate books (or, in the case of any other form of legal entity, all records such as articles of organization or formation, and minute books used for a purpose similar to those records required for corporations or partnerships), all Forms BD (§ 249.501 of this chapter), all Forms BDW (§ 249.501a of this chapter), all Forms SBSE–BD (§ 249.1600b of this chapter), all Forms SBSE–C (§ 249.1600c of this chapter), all Forms SBSE–W (§ 249.1601 of this chapter), all amendments to these forms, and all licenses or other documentation showing the registration of the member, broker or dealer with any securities regulatory authority or the Commodity Futures Trading Commission.

(e) Every member, broker or dealer subject to § 240.17a–3 must maintain and preserve in an easily accessible place:

(1) All records required under § 240.17a–3(a)(12) until at least three years after the associated person's employment and any other connection with the member, broker or dealer has terminated.

(2) All records required under § 240.17a–3(a)(13) until at least three years after the termination of employment or association of those persons required by § 240.17f–2 to be fingerprinted.

(3) All records required pursuant to § 240.17a–3(a)(15) during the life of the enterprise.

(4) All records required pursuant to § 240.17a–3(a)(14) for three years.

(5) All account record information required pursuant to § 240.17a–3(a)(17) and all records required pursuant to § 240.17a–3(a)(35), in each case until at least six years after the earlier of the date the account was closed or the date on which the information was collected, provided, replaced, or updated.

Securities and Exchange Commission § 240.17a-4

(6) Each report which a securities regulatory authority or the Commodity Futures Trading Commission has requested or required the member, broker or dealer to make and furnish to it pursuant to an order or settlement, and each securities regulatory authority, Commodity Futures Trading Commission, or prudential regulator examination report until three years after the date of the report.

(7) Each compliance, supervisory, and procedures manual, including any updates, modifications, and revisions to the manual, describing the policies and practices of the member, broker or dealer with respect to compliance with applicable laws and rules, and supervision of the activities of each natural person associated with the member, broker or dealer until three years after the termination of the use of the manual.

(8) All reports produced to review for unusual activity in customer accounts until eighteen months after the date the report was generated. In lieu of maintaining the reports, a member, broker or dealer may produce promptly the reports upon request by a representative of a securities regulatory authority. If a report was generated in a computer system that has been changed in the most recent eighteen month period in a manner such that the report cannot be reproduced using historical data in the same format as it was originally generated, the report may be produced by using the historical data in the current system, but must be accompanied by a record explaining each system change which affected the reports. If a report is generated in a computer system that has been changed in the most recent eighteen month period in a manner such that the report cannot be reproduced in any format using historical data, the member, broker or dealer must promptly produce upon request a record of the parameters that were used to generate the report at the time specified by a representative of a securities regulatory authority, including a record of the frequency with which the reports were generated.

(9) All records required pursuant to § 240.17a-3(a)(23) until three years after the termination of the use of the risk management controls documented therein.

(10) All records required pursuant to § 240.17a-3(a)(24), as well as a copy of each Form CRS, until at least six years after such record or Form CRS is created.

(11) The written policies and procedures required pursuant to §§ 240.15Fi-3, 240.15Fi-4, and 240.15Fi-5 until three years after termination of the use of the policies and procedures.

(12)(i) Each written agreement with counterparties on the terms of portfolio reconciliation with those counterparties as required to be created under § 240.15Fi-3(a)(1) and (b)(1) until three years after the termination of the agreement and all transactions governed thereby.

(ii) Security-based swap trading relationship documentation with counterparties required to be created under § 240.15Fi-5 until three years after the termination of such documentation and all transactions governed thereby.

(iii) A record of the results of each audit required to be performed pursuant to § 240.15Fi-5(c) until three years after the conclusion of the audit.

(f) Subject to the conditions set forth in this paragraph (f), the records required to be maintained and preserved pursuant to § 240.17a-3 and this section may be immediately produced or reproduced by means of an electronic recordkeeping system or by means of micrographic media and be maintained and preserved for the required time in that form.

(1) For purposes of this paragraph (f):

(i) The term *micrographic media* means microfilm or microfiche, or any similar medium;

(ii) The term *electronic recordkeeping system* means a system that preserves records in a digital format in a manner that permits the records to be viewed and downloaded;

(iii) The term *designated executive officer* means a member of senior management of the member, broker, or dealer who has access to and the ability to provide records maintained and preserved on the electronic recordkeeping system either directly or through a *designated specialist* who reports directly or indirectly to the designated executive officer;

§ 240.17a-4

(iv) The term *designated officer* means an employee of the member, broker, or dealer who reports directly or indirectly to the designated executive officer and who has access to and the ability to provide records maintained and preserved on the electronic recordkeeping system either directly or through a *designated specialist* who reports directly or indirectly to the designated officer;

(v) The term *designated specialist* means an employee of the member, broker, or dealer who has access to, and the ability to provide records maintained and preserved on, the electronic recordkeeping system; and

(vi) The term *designated third party* means a person that is not affiliated with the member, broker, or dealer who has access to and the ability to provide records maintained and preserved on the electronic recordkeeping system.

(2) An electronic recordkeeping system must:

(i)(A) Preserve a record for the duration of its applicable retention period in a manner that maintains a complete time-stamped audit trail that includes:

(*1*) All modifications to and deletions of the record or any part thereof;

(*2*) The date and time of actions that create, modify, or delete the record;

(*3*) If applicable, the identity of the individual creating, modifying, or deleting the record; and

(*4*) Any other information needed to maintain an audit trail of the record in a way that maintains security, signatures, and data to ensure the authenticity and reliability of the record and will permit re-creation of the original record if it is modified or deleted; or

(B) Preserve the records exclusively in a non-rewriteable, non-erasable format;

(ii) Verify automatically the completeness and accuracy of the processes for storing and retaining records electronically;

(iii) If applicable, serialize the original and duplicate units of the storage media, and time-date the required period of retention for the information placed on such electronic storage media;

(iv) Have the capacity to readily download and transfer copies of a record and its audit trail (if applicable) in both a human readable format and in a reasonably usable electronic format and to readily download and transfer the information needed to locate the electronic record, as required by the staffs of the Commission, the self-regulatory organizations of which the member, broker, or dealer is a member, or any State securities regulator having jurisdiction over the member, broker, or dealer; and

(v)(A) Include a backup electronic recordkeeping system that meets the other requirements of this paragraph (f) and that retains the records required to be maintained and preserved pursuant to § 240.17a-3 and in accordance with this section in a manner that will serve as a redundant set of records if the original electronic recordkeeping system is temporarily or permanently inaccessible; or

(B) Have other redundancy capabilities that are designed to ensure access to the records required to be maintained and preserved pursuant to § 240.17a-3 and this section.

(3) A member, broker, or dealer using an electronic recordkeeping system must:

(i) At all times have available, for examination by the staffs of the Commission, the self-regulatory organizations of which the member, broker, or dealer is a member, or any State securities regulator having jurisdiction over the member, broker, or dealer, facilities for immediately producing the records preserved by means of the electronic recordkeeping system and for producing copies of those records.

(ii) Be ready at all times to provide, and immediately provide, any record stored by means of the electronic recordkeeping system that the staffs of the Commission, the self-regulatory organizations of which the member, broker, or dealer is a member, or any State securities regulator having jurisdiction over the member, broker, or dealer may request.

(iii) For a broker-dealer operating pursuant to paragraph (f)(2)(i)(B) of this section, the member, broker, or dealer must have in place an audit system providing for accountability regarding inputting of records required

Securities and Exchange Commission § 240.17a-4

to be maintained and preserved pursuant to § 240.17a-3 and this section to the electronic recordkeeping system and inputting of any changes made to every original and duplicate record maintained and preserved thereby.

(A) At all times, a member, broker, or dealer must be able to have the results of such audit system available for examination by the staffs of the Commission and the self-regulatory organization of which the broker or dealer is a member.

(B) The audit results must be preserved for the time required for the audited records.

(iv) Organize, maintain, keep current, and provide promptly upon request by the staffs of the Commission, the self-regulatory organizations of which the member, broker, or dealer is a member, or any State securities regulator having jurisdiction over the member, broker, or dealer all information necessary to access and locate records preserved by means of the electronic recordkeeping system.

(v)(A) Have at all times filed with the designated examining authority for the member, broker, or dealer the following undertakings with respect to such records signed by either a designated executive officer or designated third party (hereinafter, the "undersigned"):

The undersigned hereby undertakes to furnish promptly to the U.S. Securities and Exchange Commission ("Commission"), its designees or representatives, any self- regulatory organization of which [Name of the Member, Broker, or Dealer] is a member, or any State securities regulator having jurisdiction over [Name of the Member, Broker, or Dealer], upon reasonable request, such information as is deemed necessary by the staff of the Commission, any self-regulatory organization of which [Name of the Member, Broker, or Dealer] is a member, or any State securities regulator having jurisdiction over [Name of the Member, Broker, or Dealer], and to download copies of a record and its audit trail (if applicable) preserved by means of an electronic recordkeeping system of [Name of the Member, Broker, or Dealer] into both a human readable format and a reasonably usable electronic format in the event of a failure on the part of [Name of the Member, Broker, or Dealer] to download a requested record or its audit trail (if applicable).

Furthermore, the undersigned hereby undertakes to take reasonable steps to provide access to the information preserved by means of an electronic recordkeeping system of [Name of the Member, Broker, or Dealer], including, as appropriate, downloading any record required to be maintained and preserved by [Name of the Member, Broker, or Dealer] pursuant to §§ 240.17a-3 and 240.17a-4 in a format acceptable to the staff of the Commission, any self-regulatory organization of which [Name of the Member, Broker, or Dealer] is a member, or any State securities regulator having jurisdiction over [Name of the Member, Broker, or Dealer]. Specifically, the undersigned will take reasonable steps to, in the event of a failure on the part of [Name of the Member, Broker, or Dealer] to download the record into a human readable format or a reasonably usable electronic format and after reasonable notice to [Name of the Member, Broker, or Dealer], download the record into a human readable format or a reasonably usable electronic format at the request of the staffs of the Commission, any self-regulatory organization of which [Name of the Member, Broker, or Dealer] is a member, or any State securities regulator having jurisdiction over [Name of the Member, Broker, or Dealer].

(B) A designated executive officer who signs the undertaking required pursuant to paragraph (f)(3)(v)(A) of this section may:

(1) Appoint in writing up to two designated officers who will take the steps necessary to fulfill the obligations of the designated executive officer set forth in the undertakings in the event the designated executive officer is unable to fulfill those obligations; and

(2) Appoint in writing up to three designated specialists.

(C) The appointment of, or reliance on, a designated officer or designated specialist does not relieve the designated executive officer of the obligations set forth in the undertaking.

(4) A broker-dealer using a micrographic media system must:

(i) At all times have available, for examination by the staffs of the Commission, self-regulatory organizations of which it is a member, and any State securities regulator having jurisdiction over the member, broker, or dealer, facilities for immediate, easily readable projection or production of micrographic media and for producing easily readable images;

(ii) Be ready at all times to provide, and immediately provide, any facsimile enlargement which the staffs of the

599

§ 240.17a-4

Commission, any self-regulatory organization of which it is a member, or any State securities regulator having jurisdiction over the member, broker, or dealer may request;

(iii) Store, separately from the original, a duplicate copy of the record stored on any medium acceptable under this section for the time required; and

(iv) Organize and index accurately all information maintained on both original and duplicate storage media.

(A) At all times, a member, broker, or dealer must be able to have such indexes available for examination by the staffs of the Commission, the self-regulatory organizations of which the broker or dealer is a member, and any State securities regulator having jurisdiction over the member, broker or, dealer.

(B) Each index must be duplicated and the duplicate copies must be stored separately from the original copy of each index.

(C) Original and duplicate indexes must be preserved for the time required for the indexed records.

(g) If a person who has been subject to § 240.17a-3 ceases to transact a business in securities directly with others than members of a national securities exchange, or ceases to transact a business in securities through the medium of a member of a national securities exchange, or ceases to be registered pursuant to section 15 of the Act (15 U.S.C. 78*o*) such person must, for the remainder of the periods of time specified in this section, continue to preserve the records which it theretofore preserved pursuant to this section.

(h) For purposes of transactions in municipal securities by municipal securities brokers and municipal securities dealers, compliance with Rule G-9 of the Municipal Securities Rulemaking Board or any successor rule will be deemed to be in compliance with this section.

(i)(1)(i) If the records required to be maintained and preserved pursuant to the provisions of § 240.17a-3 and this section are prepared or maintained by an outside service bureau, depository, bank, or other recordkeeping service, including a recordkeeping service that owns and operates the servers or other storage devices on which the records are preserved or maintained, (none of which operate pursuant to § 240.17a-3(c)) on behalf of the member, broker, or dealer required to maintain and preserve such records, such outside entity must file with the Commission a written undertaking in a form acceptable to the Commission, signed by a duly authorized person, to the effect that such records are the property of the member, broker, or dealer required to maintain and preserve such records and will be surrendered promptly on request of the member, broker, or dealer and including the following provision:

With respect to any books and records maintained or preserved on behalf of [Name of the Member, Broker, or Dealer], the undersigned hereby undertakes to permit examination of such books and records at any time or from time to time during business hours by representatives or designees of the Securities and Exchange Commission and to promptly furnish to said Commission or its designee true, correct, complete and current hard copies of any or all or any part of such books and records.

(ii)(A) If the records required to be maintained and preserved pursuant to the provisions of § 240.17a-3 and this section are maintained and preserved by means of an electronic recordkeeping system as defined in paragraph (f) of this section utilizing servers or other storage devices that are owned or operated by an outside entity (including an affiliate) and the broker, dealer, or member has *independent access* to the records as defined in paragraph (i)(1)(ii)(B) of this section, the outside entity may file with the Commission the following undertaking signed by a duly authorized person in lieu of the undertaking required under paragraph (i)(1)(i) of this section:

The undersigned hereby acknowledges that the records of [name of member, broker, or dealer] are the property of [name of member, broker, or dealer] and [name of member, broker, or dealer] has represented: one, that it is subject to rules of the Securities and Exchange Commission governing the maintenance and preservation of certain records, two, that it has independent access to the records maintained by [name of outside entity], and, three, that it consents to [name of outside entity] fulfilling the obligations set forth in this undertaking. The undersigned undertakes that [name of outside entity] will facilitate within its ability, and not impede

Securities and Exchange Commission

§ 240.17a–4

or prevent, the examination, access, download, or transfer of the records by a representative or designee of the Securities and Exchange Commission as permitted under the law. Further, the undersigned undertakes to facilitate within its ability, and not impede or prevent, a trustee appointed under the Securities Investor Protection Act of 1970 to liquidate [name of member, broker, or dealer] in accessing, downloading, or transferring the records as permitted under the law.

(B) A broker, dealer, or member utilizing servers or other storage devices that are owned or operated by an outside entity has independent access to records with respect to such outside entity if it can regularly access the records without the need of any intervention of the outside entity and through such access:

(*1*) Permit examination of the records at any time or from time to time during business hours by representatives or designees of the Commission; and

(*2*) Promptly furnish to the Commission or its designee a true, correct, complete and current hard copy of any or all or any part of such records.

(2) An agreement with an outside entity will not relieve such member, broker, or dealer from the responsibility to prepare and maintain records as specified in this section or in § 240.17a–3.

(j) Every member, broker and dealer subject to this section must furnish promptly to a representative of the Commission legible, true, complete, and current copies of those records of the member, broker, or dealer that are required to be preserved under this section, or any other records of the member, broker, or dealer subject to examination under section 17(b) of the Act (15 U.S.C. 78*q*(b)) that are requested by the representative of the Commission. The member, broker, or dealer must furnish a record and its audit trail (if applicable) preserved on an electronic recordkeeping system pursuant to paragraph (f) of this section in a reasonably usable electronic format, if requested by a representative of the Commission.

(k)(1) Except as provided in paragraph (k)(2) of this section, upon request of any designee or representative of the Commission or of any self-regulatory organization of which it is a member, every member, broker or dealer subject to this section must request and obtain from its customers documentation regarding an exchange of security futures products for physical securities, including documentation of underlying cash transactions and exchanges. Upon receipt of such documentation, the member, broker or dealer must promptly provide that documentation to the requesting designee or representative.

(2) This paragraph (k) does not apply to an underlying cash transaction(s) or exchange(s) that was effected through a member, broker or dealer registered with the Commission and is of a type required to be recorded pursuant to § 240.17a–3.

(l) Records for the most recent two year period required to be made pursuant to § 240.17a–3(f) and paragraphs (b)(4) and (e)(7) of this section which relate to an office shall be maintained at the office to which they relate. If an office is a private residence where only one associated person (or multiple associated persons who reside at that location and are members of the same immediate family) regularly conducts business, and it is not held out to the public as an office nor are funds or securities of any customer of the member, broker or dealer handled there, the member, broker or dealer need not maintain records at that office, but the records must be maintained at another location within the same State as the member, broker or dealer may select. Rather than maintain the records at each office, the member, broker or dealer may choose to produce the records promptly at the request of a representative of a securities regulatory authority at the office to which they relate or at another location agreed to by the representative.

(m) When used in this section:

(1) The term *office* has the meaning set forth in § 240.17a–3(g)(1).

(2) The term *principal* has the meaning set forth in § 240.17a–3(g)(2).

(3) The term *securities regulatory authority* has the meaning set forth in § 240.17a–3(g)(3).

(4) The term *associated person* has the meaning set forth in § 240.17a–3(g)(4).

(5) The term *business as such* includes security-based swap activity.

§ 240.17a–5

CROSS REFERENCE: For interpretative releases applicable to § 240.17a–4, see No. 3040 and No. 8024 in tabulation, part 241 of this chapter.

[13 FR 8212, Dec. 22, 1948]

EDITORIAL NOTE: For FEDERAL REGISTER citations affecting § 240.17a–4, see the List of CFR Sections Affected, which appears in the Finding Aids section of the printed volume and at *www.govinfo.gov*.

§ 240.17a–5 Reports to be made by certain brokers and dealers.

This section applies to the following types of entities: Except as provided in this introductory text, a broker or dealer, including an *OTC derivatives dealer* as that term is defined in § 240.3b–12 registered pursuant to section 15 of the Act (15 U.S.C. 78*o*); a broker or dealer, other than an OTC derivatives dealer, registered pursuant to section 15 of the Act that is also a security-based swap dealer registered pursuant to section 15F of the Act (15 U.S.C. 78*o*–10); and a broker or dealer, including an OTC derivatives dealer, registered pursuant to section 15 of the Act that is also a major-security-based swap participant registered pursuant to section 15F of the Act. Section 240.18a–7 (rather than this section) applies to the following types of entities: A security-based swap dealer registered pursuant to section 15F of the Act that is not also a broker or dealer, other than an OTC derivatives dealer, registered pursuant to section 15 of the Act; a security-based swap dealer registered pursuant to section 15F of the Act that is also an OTC derivatives dealer; and a major security-based swap participant registered pursuant to section 15F of the Act that is not also a broker or dealer, including an OTC derivatives dealer, registered pursuant to section 15 of the Act.

(a) *Monthly and quarterly reports.* (1)(i) Every broker or dealer subject to this paragraph (a) who clears transactions or carries customer accounts must file with the Commission Part I of Form X–17A–5 (§ 249.617 of this chapter) within 10 business days after the end of each month.

(ii) Every broker or dealer subject to this paragraph (a) who clears transactions or carries customer accounts and every broker or dealer that is registered as a security-based swap dealer or major security-based swap participant under section 15F of the Act (15 U.S.C. 78*o*–10) must file with the Commission an executed Part II of Form X–17A–5 (§ 249.617 of this chapter) within 17 business days after the end of the calendar quarter and within 17 business days after the end of the fiscal year of the broker or dealer where that date is not the end of a calendar quarter. Certain of such brokers or dealers must file with the Commission an executed Part IIA in lieu thereof if the nature of their business is limited as described in the instructions to Part II of Form X–17A–5 (§ 249.617 of this chapter).

(iii) Every broker or dealer that neither clears transactions nor carries customer accounts and that is not registered as a security-based swap dealer or major security-based swap participant under section 15F of the Act (15 U.S.C. 78*o*–10) must file with the Commission an executed Part IIA of Form X–17A–5 (§ 249.617 of this chapter) within 17 business days after the end of each calendar quarter and within 17 business days after the end of the fiscal year of the broker or dealer where that date is not the end of a calendar quarter.

(iv) Upon receiving written notice from the Commission or the examining authority designated pursuant to section 17(d) of the Act (15 U.S.C. 78q(d)) ("designated examining authority"), a broker or dealer who receives such notice must file with the Commission on a monthly basis, or at such times as will be specified, an executed Part II or Part IIA of Form X–17A–5 (§ 249.617 of this chapter), and such other financial or operational information as will be required by the Commission or the designated examining authority.

(2) The reports provided for in this paragraph (a) that must be filed with the Commission will be considered filed when received at the Commission's principal office in Washington, DC, and the regional office of the Commission for the region in which the broker or dealer has its principal place of business. All reports filed pursuant to this paragraph (a) will be deemed to be confidential.

602

Securities and Exchange Commission § 240.17a–5

(3) The provisions of paragraph (a)(1) of this section will not apply to a member of a national securities exchange or a registered national securities association if said exchange or association maintains records containing the information required by Part I, Part II, or Part IIA of Form X–17A–5 (§ 249.617 of this chapter), as to such member, and transmits to the Commission a copy of the applicable parts of Form X–17A–5 (§ 249.617 of this chapter) as to such member, pursuant to a plan, the procedures and provisions of which have been submitted to and declared effective by the Commission. Any such plan filed by a national securities exchange or a registered national securities association may provide that when a member is also a member of one or more national securities exchanges, or of one or more national securities exchanges and a registered national securities association, the information required to be submitted with respect to any such member may be submitted by only one specified national securities exchange or registered national securities association. For the purposes of this section, a plan filed with the Commission by a national securities exchange or a registered national securities association will not become effective unless the Commission, having due regard for the fulfillment of the Commission's duties and responsibilities under the provisions of the Act, declares the plan to be effective. Further, the Commission, in declaring any such plan effective, may impose such terms and conditions relating to the provisions of the plan and the period of its effectiveness as may be deemed necessary or appropriate in the public interest, for the protection of investors, or to carry out the Commission's duties and responsibilities under the Act.

(4) Every broker or dealer subject to this paragraph (a) must file Form Custody (§ 249.639 of this chapter) with its designated examining authority within 17 business days after the end of each calendar quarter and within 17 business days after the end of the fiscal year of the broker or dealer where that date is not the end of a calendar quarter. The designated examining authority must maintain the information obtained through the filing of Form Custody and must promptly transmit that information to the Commission at such time as it transmits the applicable part of Form X–17A–5 (§ 249.617 of this chapter) as required in paragraph (a)(2) of this section.

(5) Broker-dealers that have been authorized by the Commission to compute net capital pursuant to § 240.15c3–1e must file the following additional reports with the Commission:

(i) For each product for which the broker or dealer calculates a deduction for market risk other than in accordance with § 240.15c3–1e(b)(1) or (3), the product category and the amount of the deduction for market risk within 17 business days after the end of the month;

(ii) A graph reflecting, for each business line, the daily intra-month value at risk within 17 business days after the end of the month;

(iii) The aggregate value at risk for the broker or dealer within 17 business days after the end of the month;

(iv) For each product for which the broker or dealer uses scenario analysis, the product category and the deduction for market risk within 17 business days after the end of the month;

(v) Credit risk information on derivatives exposures within 17 business days after the end of the month, including:

(A) Overall current exposure;

(B) Current exposure (including commitments) listed by counterparty for the 15 largest exposures;

(C) The ten largest commitments listed by counterparty;

(D) The broker's or dealer's maximum potential exposure listed by counterparty for the 15 largest exposures;

(E) The broker's or dealer's aggregate maximum potential exposure;

(F) A summary report reflecting the broker's or dealer's current and maximum potential exposures by credit rating category; and

(G) A summary report reflecting the broker's or dealer's current exposure for each of the top ten countries to which the broker or dealer is exposed (by residence of the main operating group of the counterparty);

§ 240.17a–5

(vi) Regular risk reports supplied to the broker's or dealer's senior management in the format described in the application, within 17 business days after the end of the month;

(vii) [Reserved]

(viii) A report identifying the number of business days for which the actual daily net trading loss exceeded the corresponding daily VaR within 17 business days after the end of each calendar quarter; and

(ix) The results of backtesting of all internal models used to compute allowable capital, including VaR and credit risk models, indicating the number of backtesting exceptions within 17 business days after the end of the calendar quarter.

(6) Upon written application by a broker or dealer to its designated examining authority, the designated examining authority may extend the time for filing the information required by this paragraph (a). The designated examining authority for the broker or dealer will maintain, in the manner prescribed in § 240.17a–1, a record of each extension granted.

(b) *Report filed upon termination of membership interest.* (1) If a broker or dealer holding any membership interest in a national securities exchange or registered national securities association ceases to be a member in good standing of such exchange or association, such broker or dealer must, within two business days after such event, file with the Commission Part II or Part IIA of Form X–17A–5 (§ 249.617 of this chapter) as determined by the standards set forth in paragraphs (a)(1)(ii) through (iv) of this section as of the date of such event. The report must be filed at the Commission's principal office in Washington, DC, and with the regional office of the Commission for the region in which the broker or dealer has its principal place of business; *provided, however,* that such report need not be made or filed if the Commission, upon written request or upon its own motion, exempts such broker or dealer, either unconditionally or on specified terms and conditions, from such requirement; *provided, further,* that the Commission may, upon request of the broker or dealer, grant extensions of time for filing the report specified herein for good cause shown.

(2) The broker or dealer must attach to the report required by paragraph (b)(1) of this section an oath or affirmation that to the best knowledge and belief of the person making the oath or affirmation the information contained in the report is true and correct. The oath or affirmation must be made before a person duly authorized to administer such oaths or affirmations. If the broker or dealer is a sole proprietorship, the oath or affirmation must be made by the proprietor; if a partnership, by a general partner; if a corporation, by a duly authorized officer; or if a limited liability company or limited liability partnership, by the chief executive officer, chief financial officer, manager, managing member, or those members vested with management authority for the limited liability company or limited liability partnership.

(3) For the purposes of this paragraph (b) "membership interest" will include the following: full membership, allied membership, associated membership, floor privileges, and any other interest that entitles a broker or dealer to the exercise of any privilege on an exchange or with an association.

(4) For the purposes of this paragraph (b), any broker or dealer will be deemed to have ceased to be a member in good standing of such exchange or association when the broker or dealer has resigned, withdrawn, or been suspended or expelled from a membership interest in such exchange or association, or has directly or through any associated person sold or entered into an agreement for the sale of a membership interest which would on consummation thereof result in the termination of the broker's or dealer's membership interest in such exchange or association.

(5) Whenever any national securities exchange or registered national securities association takes any action which causes any broker or dealer which is a member of such exchange or association to cease to be a member in good standing of such exchange or association or when such exchange or association learns of any action by such member of any other person which causes such broker or dealer to cease to be a

Securities and Exchange Commission

§ 240.17a–5

member in good standing of such exchange or association, such exchange or association will report such action promptly to the Commission, furnishing information as to the circumstances surrounding the event, and will send a copy of such notification to the broker or dealer and notify such broker or dealer of its responsibilities under this paragraph (b).

(c) *Customer Statements*—(1) *Who must furnish the statements.* Every broker or dealer must file with the Commission at its principal office in Washington, DC, with the regional office of the Commission for the region in which the broker or dealer has its principal place of business, and with each national securities exchange and registered national securities association of which it is a member, and must send to its customers the statements prescribed by paragraphs (c) (2) and (3) of this section, except as provided in paragraph (c)(5) of this section or if the activities of such broker or dealer are limited to any one or combination of the following and are conducted in the manner prescribed herein:

(i) As introducing broker or dealer, the forwarding of all the transactions of customers of the introducing broker or dealer to a clearing broker or dealer on a fully disclosed basis: *Provided,* That such clearing broker or dealer reflects such transactions on its books and records in accounts it carries in the names of such customers and that the introducing broker or dealer does not hold funds or securities for, or owe funds or securities to, customers other than funds and securities promptly forwarded to the clearing broker or dealer or to customers;

(ii) The prompt forwarding of subscriptions for securities to the issuer, underwriter or other distributor of such securities and of receiving checks, drafts, notes, or other evidences of indebtedness payable solely to the issuer, underwriter or other distributor who delivers the security directly to the subscriber or to a custodian bank, if the broker or dealer does not otherwise hold funds or securities for, or owe money or securities to, customers;

(iii) The sale and redemption of redeemable shares of registered investment companies or the solicitation of share accounts of savings and loan associations and otherwise qualified to maintain net capital of no less than what is required under § 240.15c3–1(a)(2)(iv) or the offering to extend any credit to or participate in arranging a loan for a customer to purchase insurance in connection with the sale of redeemable shares of registered investment companies; or

(iv) Conduct which would exempt the broker or dealer from the provisions of § 240.17a–13 by reason of the provisions of paragraph (a) of that section.

(2) *Audited statements to be furnished.* Audited statements must be furnished within 105 days after the end of the fiscal year of the broker or dealer. The statements may be furnished 30 days after that time limit has expired if the broker or dealer sends them with the next mailing of the broker's or dealer's quarterly customer statements of account. In that case, the broker or dealer must include a statement in that mailing of the amount of the broker's or dealer's net capital and its required net capital in accordance with § 240.15c3–1, as of a fiscal month end that is within the 75-day period immediately preceding the date the statements are sent to customers. The audited statements must include the following:

(i) A Statement of Financial Condition with appropriate notes prepared in accordance with U.S. generally accepted accounting principles which must be audited if the financial statements furnished in accordance with paragraph (d) of this section are required to be certified;

(ii) A footnote containing a statement of the amount of the broker's or dealer's net capital and its required net capital, computed in accordance with § 240.15c3–1. Such statement must include summary financial statements of subsidiaries consolidated pursuant to Appendix C of § 240.15c3–1, where material, and the effect thereof on the net capital and required net capital of the broker or dealer;

(iii) A statement indicating that the Statement of Financial Condition of the most recent financial report of the broker or dealer under paragraph (d)(1)(i)(A) of this section is available for examination at the principal office

605

§ 240.17a–5

of the broker or dealer and at the regional office of the Commission for the region in which the broker or dealer has its principal place of business; and

(iv) If, in connection with the most recent annual reports required under paragraph (d) of this section, the report of the independent public accountant required under paragraph (d)(1)(i)(C) of this section covering the report of the broker or dealer required under paragraph (d)(1)(i)(B)(*1*) of this section identifies one or more *material weaknesses*, a statement by the broker or dealer that one or more *material weaknesses* have been identified and that a copy of the report of the independent public accountant required under paragraph (d)(1)(i)(C) of this section is currently available for the customer's inspection at the principal office of the Commission in Washington, DC, and the regional office of the Commission for the region in which the broker or dealer has its principal place of business.

(3) *Unaudited statements to be furnished.* Unaudited statements dated 6 months after the date of the audited statements required to be furnished by paragraphs (c)(1) and (2) of this section must be furnished within 65 days after the date of the unaudited statements. The unaudited statements may be furnished 70 days after that time limit has expired if the broker or dealer sends them with the next mailing of the broker's or dealer's quarterly customer statements of account. In that case, the broker or dealer must include a statement in that mailing of the amount of the broker's or dealer's net capital and its required net capital in accordance with § 240.15c3–1, as of a fiscal month end that is within the 75-day period immediately preceding the date the statements are sent to customers. The unaudited statements must contain the information specified in paragraphs (c)(2)(i) and (ii) of this section.

(4) *Definition of "customer."* For purposes of this paragraph (c), the term *customer* includes any person other than:

(i) Another broker or dealer who is exempted by paragraph (c)(1) of this section;

(ii) A general, special or limited partner or director or officer of a broker or dealer; or

17 CFR Ch. II (4–1–23 Edition)

(iii) Any person to the extent that such person has a claim for property or funds which by contract, agreement or understanding, or by operation of law, is part of the capital of the broker or dealer or is subordinated to the claims of creditors of the broker or dealer, for or with whom a broker or dealer has effected a securities transaction in a particular month, which month must be either the month preceding the balance sheet date or the month following the balance sheet date in which the statement is sent.

(iv) The term "customer" also includes any person for whom the broker or dealer holds securities for safekeeping or as collateral or for whom the broker or dealer carries a free credit balance in the month in which customers are determined for purposes of this paragraph (c).

(5) *Exemption from sending certain financial information to customers.* A broker or dealer is not required to send to its customers the statements prescribed by paragraphs (c)(2) and (c)(3) of this section if the following conditions are met:

(i) The broker or dealer semi-annually sends its customers, at the times it otherwise is required to send its customers the statements prescribed by paragraphs (c)(2) and (c)(3) of this section, a financial disclosure statement that includes:

(A) The amount of the broker's or dealer's net capital and its required net capital in accordance with § 240.15c3–1, as of the date of the statements prescribed by paragraphs (c)(2) and (c)(3) of this section;

(B) To the extent required under paragraph (c)(2)(ii) of this section, a description of the effect on the broker's or dealer's net capital and required net capital of the consolidation of the assets and liabilities of subsidiaries or affiliates consolidated pursuant to Appendix C of § 240.15c3–1; and

(C) Any statements otherwise required by paragraphs (c)(2)(iii) and (iv) of this section.

(ii) The financial disclosure statement is given prominence in the materials delivered to customers of the broker or dealer and includes an appropriate caption stating that customers may obtain the statements prescribed

Securities and Exchange Commission §240.17a–5

by paragraphs (c)(2) and (c)(3) of this section, at no cost, by:

(A) Accessing the broker's or dealer's Website at the specified Internet Uniform Resource Locator (URL); or

(B) Calling the broker's or dealer's specified toll-free telephone number.

(iii) Not later than 90 days after the date of the audited statements prescribed by paragraph (c)(2) of this section and not later than 75 days after the date of the unaudited statements prescribed by paragraph (c)(3) of this section, the broker or dealer publishes the statements on its Website, accessible by hyperlinks in either textual or button format, which are separate, prominent links, are clearly visible, and are placed in each of the following locations:

(A) On the broker's or dealer's Website home page; and

(B) On each page at which a customer can enter or log on to the broker's or dealer's Website; and

(C) If the Websites for two or more brokers or dealers can be accessed from the same home page, on the home page of the Website of each broker or dealer.

(iv) The broker or dealer maintains a toll-free telephone number that customers can call to request a copy of the statements prescribed by paragraphs (c)(2) and (c)(3) of this section.

(v) If a customer requests a copy of the statements prescribed by paragraphs (c)(2) and (c)(3) of this section, the broker or dealer sends it promptly at no cost to the customer.

(d) *Annual reports.* (1)(i) Except as provided in paragraphs (d)(1)(iii) and (iv) of this section, every broker or dealer registered under section 15 of the Act (15 U.S.C. 78*o*) must file annually:

(A) A financial report as described in paragraph (d)(2) of this section; and

(B)(*1*) If the broker or dealer did not claim it was exempt from §240.15c3–3 throughout the most recent fiscal year or the broker or dealer is subject to §240.15c3–3(p), a compliance report as described in paragraph (d)(3) of this section executed by the person who makes the oath or affirmation under paragraph (e)(2) of this section; or

(*2*) If the broker or dealer did claim it was exempt from §240.15c3–3 throughout the most recent fiscal year and the broker or dealer is not subject to §240.15c3–3(p), an exemption report as described in paragraph (d)(4) of this section executed by the person who makes the oath or affirmation under paragraph (e)(2) of this section;

(C) Except as provided in paragraph (e)(1)(i) of this section, a report prepared by an independent public accountant, under the engagement provisions in paragraph (g) of this section, covering each report required to be filed under paragraphs (d)(1)(i)(A) and (B) of this section.

(ii) The reports required to be filed under this paragraph (d) must be as of the same fiscal year end each year, unless a change is approved in writing by the designated examining authority for the broker or dealer under paragraph (n) of this section. A copy of the written approval must be sent to the Commission's principal office in Washington, DC, and the regional office of the Commission for the region in which the broker or dealer has its principal place of business.

(iii) A broker or dealer succeeding to and continuing the business of another broker or dealer need not file the reports under this paragraph (d) as of a date in the fiscal year in which the succession occurs if the predecessor broker or dealer has filed reports in compliance with this paragraph (d) as of a date in such fiscal year.

(iv) A broker or dealer that is a member of a national securities exchange, has transacted a business in securities solely with or for other members of a national securities exchange, and has not carried any margin account, credit balance, or security for any person who is defined as a *customer* in paragraph (c)(4) of this section, is not required to file reports under this paragraph (d).

(2) *Financial report.* The financial report must contain:

(i) A Statement of Financial Condition, a Statement of Income, a Statement of Cash Flows, a Statement of Changes in Stockholders' or Partners' or Sole Proprietor's Equity, and a Statement of Changes in Liabilities Subordinated to Claims of General Creditors. The statements must be prepared in accordance with U.S. generally accepted accounting principles

§ 240.17a-5

and must be in a format that is consistent with the statements contained in Part II or Part IIA of Form X-17A-5 (§ 249.617 of this chapter), as applicable. If the Statement of Financial Condition filed in accordance with instructions to Part II or Part IIA of Form X-17A-5 (§ 249.617 of this chapter), as applicable, is not consolidated, a summary of financial data, including the assets, liabilities, and net worth or stockholders' equity, for subsidiaries not consolidated in the applicable Part II or Part IIA as filed by the broker or dealer must be included in the notes to the financial statements reported on by the independent public accountant.

(ii) Supporting schedules that include, from Part II or Part IIA of Form X-17A-5 (§ 249.617 of this chapter), a Computation of Net Capital under § 240.15c3-1, a Computation for Determination of Customer Reserve Requirements under § 240.15c3-3a (Exhibit A of § 240.15c3-3), a Computation for Determination of PAB Requirements under Exhibit A of § 240.15c3-3, a Computation for Determination of Security-Based Swap Customer Reserve Requirements under § 240.15c3-3b (Exhibit B of § 240.15c3-3), Information Relating to the Possession or Control Requirements for Customers under § 240.15c3-3, and Information Relating to the Possession or Control Requirements for Security-Based Swap Customers under § 240.15c3-3, as applicable.

(iii) If any of the Computation of Net Capital under § 240.15c3-1, the Computation for Determination of Customer Reserve Requirements Under Exhibit A of § 240.15c3-3, or the Computation for Determination of Security-Based Swap Customer Reserve Requirements under Exhibit B of § 240.15c3-3, as applicable, in the financial report is materially different from the corresponding computation in the most recent Part II or Part IIA of Form X-17A-5 (§ 249.617 of this chapter), as applicable, filed by the broker or dealer pursuant to paragraph (a) of this section, a reconciliation, including appropriate explanations, between the computation in the financial report and the computation in the most recent Part II or Part IIA of Form X-17A-5, as applicable, filed by the broker or dealer. If no material differences exist, a statement so indicating must be included in the financial report.

(3) *Compliance report.* (i) The compliance report must contain:

(A) Statements as to whether:

(*1*) The broker or dealer has established and maintained *Internal Control Over Compliance* as that term is defined in paragraph (d)(3)(ii) of this section;

(*2*) The Internal Control Over Compliance of the broker or dealer was effective during the most recent fiscal year;

(*3*) The Internal Control Over Compliance of the broker or dealer was effective as of the end of the most recent fiscal year;

(*4*) The broker or dealer was in compliance with §§ 240.15c3-1, 240.15c3-3(e) and, if applicable, 240.15c3-3(p)(3) as of the end of the most recent fiscal year; and

(*5*) The information the broker or dealer used to state whether it was in compliance with §§ 240.15c3-1, 240.15c3-3(e) and, if applicable, 240.15c3-3(p)(3) was derived from the books and records of the broker or dealer.

(B) If applicable, a description of each identified material weakness in the Internal Control Over Compliance of the broker or dealer during the most recent fiscal year.

(C) If applicable, a description of an instance of non-compliance with § 240.15c3-1, § 240.15c3-3(e), or, if applicable, § 240.15c3-3(p)(3) as of the end of the most recent fiscal year.

(ii) The term *Internal Control Over Compliance* means internal controls that have the objective of providing the broker or dealer with reasonable assurance that non-compliance with § 240.15c3-1, § 240.15c3-3, § 240.17a-13, or any rule of the designated examining authority of the broker or dealer that requires account statements to be sent to the customers of the broker or dealer (an "Account Statement Rule") will be prevented or detected on a timely basis.

(iii) The broker or dealer is not permitted to conclude that its Internal Control Over Compliance was effective during the most recent fiscal year if there were one or more material weaknesses in its Internal Control Over Compliance during the most recent fiscal year. The broker or dealer is not permitted to conclude that its Internal

Securities and Exchange Commission §240.17a–5

Control Over Compliance was effective as of the end of the most recent fiscal year if there were one or more material weaknesses in its internal control as of the end of the most recent fiscal year. A *material weakness* is a deficiency, or a combination of deficiencies, in Internal Control Over Compliance such that there is a reasonable possibility that non-compliance with §240.15c3–1, §240.15c3–3(e), or §240.15c3–3(p)(3) will not be prevented or detected on a timely basis or that non-compliance to a material extent with §240.15c3–3, except for paragraph (e), §240.15c3–3(p), except for paragraph (p)(3), §240.17a–13, or any Account Statement Rule will not be prevented or detected on a timely basis. A deficiency in Internal Control Over Compliance exists when the design or operation of a control does not allow the management or employees of the broker or dealer, in the normal course of performing their assigned functions, to prevent or detect on a timely basis non-compliance with §240.15c3–1, §240.15c3–3, or §240.17a–13, or any Account Statement Rule.

(4) *Exemption report.* The exemption report must contain the following statements made to the best knowledge and belief of the broker or dealer:

(i) A statement that identifies the provisions in §240.15c3–3(k) under which the broker or dealer claimed an exemption from §240.15c3–3;

(ii) A statement that the broker or dealer met the identified exemption provisions in §240.15c3–3(k) throughout the most recent fiscal year without exception or that it met the identified exemption provisions in §240.15c3–3(k) throughout the most recent fiscal year except as described under paragraph (d)(4)(iii) of this section; and

(iii) If applicable, a statement that identifies each exception during the most recent fiscal year in meeting the identified exemption provisions in §240.15c3–3(k) and that briefly describes the nature of each exception and the approximate date(s) on which the exception existed.

(5) The annual reports must be filed not more than sixty (60) calendar days after the end of the fiscal year of the broker or dealer.

(6) *Filing of annual reports.* The annual reports must be filed with the Commission at the regional office of the Commission for the region in which the broker or dealer has its principal place of business and to the Commission's principal office in Washington, DC, or the annual reports may be filed with the Commission electronically in accordance with directions provided on the Commission's website. The annual reports must also be filed at the principal office of the designated examining authority for the broker or dealer and with the Securities Investor Protection Corporation ("SIPC") if the broker or dealer is a member of SIPC. Copies of the reports must be provided to all self-regulatory organizations of which the broker or dealer is a member, unless the self-regulatory organization by rule waives the requirement in this paragraph (d)(6).

(e) *Nature and form of reports.* The annual reports filed pursuant to paragraph (d) of this section must be prepared and filed in accordance with the following requirements:

(1)(i) The broker or dealer is not required to engage an independent public accountant to provide the reports required under paragraph (d)(1)(i)(C) of this section if, since the date of the registration of the broker or dealer under section 15 of the Act (15 U.S.C. 78o) or of the previous annual reports filed under paragraph (d) of this section:

(A) The securities business of the broker or dealer has been limited to acting as broker (agent) for a single issuer in soliciting subscriptions for securities of that issuer, the broker has promptly transmitted to the issuer all funds and promptly delivered to the subscriber all securities received in connection with the transaction, and the broker has not otherwise held funds or securities for or owed money or securities to customers; or

(B) The securities business of the broker or dealer has been limited to buying and selling evidences of indebtedness secured by mortgage, deed of trust, or other lien upon real estate or leasehold interests, and the broker or dealer has not carried any margin account, credit balance, or security for any securities customer.

(ii) A broker or dealer that files an annual report under paragraph (d) of

§ 240.17a-5

this section that is not covered by a report prepared by an independent public accountant must include in the oath or affirmation required by paragraph (e)(2) of this section a statement of the facts and circumstances relied upon as a basis for exemption from the requirement that the annual report filed under paragraph (d) of this section be covered by reports prepared by an independent public accountant.

(2) The broker or dealer must attach to the financial report an oath or affirmation that, to the best knowledge and belief of the person making the oath or affirmation:

(i) The financial report is true and correct; and

(ii) Neither the broker or dealer, nor any partner, officer, director, or equivalent person, as the case may be, has any proprietary interest in any account classified solely as that of a customer. The oath or affirmation must be made before a person duly authorized to administer such oaths or affirmations. If the broker or dealer is a sole proprietorship, the oath or affirmation must be made by the proprietor; if a partnership, by a general partner; if a corporation, by a duly authorized officer; or if a limited liability company or limited liability partnership, by the chief executive officer, chief financial officer, manager, managing member, or those members vested with management authority for the limited liability company or limited liability partnership.

(3) The annual reports filed under paragraph (d) of this section are not confidential, except that, if the Statement of Financial Condition in a format that is consistent with Part II or Part IIA of Form X-17A-5 (§ 249.617 of this chapter) is bound separately from the balance of the annual reports filed under paragraph (d) of this section, and each page of the balance of the annual reports is stamped "confidential," then the balance of the annual reports will be deemed confidential to the extent permitted by law. However, the annual reports, including the confidential portions, will be available for official use by any official or employee of the U.S. or any State, by national securities exchanges and registered national securities associations of which the broker or dealer filing such a report is a member, by the Public Company Accounting Oversight Board, and by any other person if the Commission authorizes disclosure of the annual reports to that person as being in the public interest. Nothing contained in this paragraph (e)(3) may be construed to be in derogation of the rules of any registered national securities association or national securities exchange that give to customers of a broker or dealer the right, upon request to the broker or dealer, to obtain information relative to its financial condition.

(4) The broker or dealer must file with SIPC a report on the SIPC annual general assessment reconciliation or exclusion from membership forms that contains such information and is in such format as determined by SIPC by rule and approved by the Commission.

(f)(1) *Qualifications of independent public accountant.* The independent public accountant must be qualified and independent in accordance with § 210.2-01 of this chapter and the independent public accountant must be registered with the Public Company Accounting Oversight Board if required by the Sarbanes-Oxley Act of 2002.

(2) *Statement regarding independent public accountant.* (i) Every broker or dealer that is required to file annual reports under paragraph (d) of this section must file no later than December 10 of each year (or 30 calendar days after the effective date of its registration as a broker or dealer, if earlier) a statement as prescribed in paragraph (f)(2)(ii) of this section with the Commission's principal office in Washington, DC, the regional office of the Commission for the region in which its principal place of business is located, and the principal office of the designated examining authority for the broker or dealer. The statement must be dated no later than December 1 (or 20 calendar days after the effective date of its registration as a broker or dealer, if earlier). If the engagement of an independent public accountant is of a continuing nature, providing for successive engagements, no further filing is required. If the engagement is for a single year, or if the most recent engagement has been terminated or

Securities and Exchange Commission

§ 240.17a–5

amended, a new statement must be filed by the required date.

(ii) The statement must be headed "Statement regarding independent public accountant under Rule 17a–5(f)(2)" and must contain the following information and representations:

(A) Name, address, telephone number, and registration number of the broker or dealer.

(B) Name, address, and telephone number of the independent public accountant.

(C) The date of the fiscal year of the annual reports of the broker or dealer covered by the engagement.

(D) Whether the engagement is for a single year or is of a continuing nature.

(E) A representation that the independent public accountant has undertaken the items enumerated in paragraphs (g)(1) and (2) of this section.

(F) Except as provided in paragraph (f)(2)(iii) of this section, a representation that the broker or dealer agrees to allow representatives of the Commission or its designated examining authority, if requested in writing for purposes of an examination of the broker or dealer, to review the audit documentation associated with the reports of the independent public accountant filed under paragraph (d)(1)(i)(C) of this section. For purposes of this paragraph, "audit documentation" has the meaning provided in standards of the Public Company Accounting Oversight Board. The Commission anticipates that, if requested, it will accord confidential treatment to all documents it may obtain from an independent public accountant under this paragraph to the extent permitted by law.

(G) Except as provided in paragraph (f)(2)(iii) of this section, a representation that the broker or dealer agrees to allow the independent public accountant to discuss with representatives of the Commission and its designated examining authority, if requested in writing for purposes of an examination of the broker or dealer, the findings associated with the reports of the independent public accountant filed under paragraph (d)(1)(i)(C) of this section.

(iii) If a broker or dealer neither clears transactions nor carries customer accounts, the broker or dealer is not required to include the representations in paragraphs (f)(2)(ii)(F) and (G) of this section.

(iv) Any broker or dealer that is not required to file reports prepared by an independent public accountant under paragraph (d)(1)(i)(C) of this section must file a statement required under paragraph (f)(2)(i) of this section indicating the date as of which the unaudited reports will be prepared.

(3) *Replacement of accountant.* A broker or dealer must file a notice that must be received by the Commission's principal office in Washington, DC, the regional office of the Commission for the region in which its principal place of business is located, and the principal office of the designated examining authority for the broker or dealer not more than 15 business days after:

(i) The broker or dealer has notified the independent public accountant that provided the reports the broker or dealer filed under paragraph (d)(1)(i)(C) of this section for the most recent fiscal year that the independent public accountant's services will not be used in future engagements; or

(ii) The broker or dealer has notified an independent public accountant that was engaged to provide the reports required under paragraph (d)(1)(i)(C) of this section that the engagement has been terminated; or

(iii) An independent public accountant has notified the broker or dealer that the independent public accountant would not continue under an engagement to provide the reports required under paragraph (d)(1)(i)(C) of this section; or

(iv) A new independent public accountant has been engaged to provide the reports required under paragraph (d)(1)(i)(C) of this section without any notice of termination having been given to or by the previously engaged independent public accountant.

(v) The notice must include:

(A) The date of notification of the termination of the engagement or of the engagement of the new independent public accountant, as applicable; and

(B) The details of any issues arising during the 24 months (or the period of the engagement, if less than 24 months)

§ 240.17a–5

preceding the termination or new engagement relating to any matter of accounting principles or practices, financial statement disclosure, auditing scope or procedure, or compliance with applicable rules of the Commission, which issues, if not resolved to the satisfaction of the former independent public accountant, would have caused the independent public accountant to make reference to them in the report of the independent public accountant. The issues required to be reported include both those resolved to the former independent public accountant's satisfaction and those not resolved to the former accountant's satisfaction. Issues contemplated by this section are those that occur at the decision-making level—that is, between principal financial officers of the broker or dealer and personnel of the accounting firm responsible for rendering its report. The notice must also state whether the accountant's report filed under paragraph (d)(1)(i)(C) of this section for any of the past two fiscal years contained an adverse opinion or a disclaimer of opinion or was qualified as to uncertainties, audit scope, or accounting principles, and must describe the nature of each such adverse opinion, disclaimer of opinion, or qualification. The broker or dealer must also request the former independent public accountant to furnish the broker or dealer with a letter addressed to the Commission stating whether the independent public accountant agrees with the statements contained in the notice of the broker or dealer and, if not, stating the respects in which the independent public accountant does not agree. The broker or dealer must file three copies of the notice and the accountant's letter, one copy of which must be manually signed by the sole proprietor, a general partner, or a duly authorized corporate, limited liability company, or limited liability partnership officer or member, as appropriate, and by the independent public accountant, respectively.

(g) *Engagement of independent public accountant.* The independent public accountant engaged by the broker or dealer to provide the reports required under paragraph (d)(1)(i)(C) of this section must, as part of the engagement, undertake the following, as applicable:

(1) To prepare an independent public accountant's report based on an examination of the financial report required to be filed by the broker or dealer under paragraph (d)(1)(i)(A) of this section in accordance with standards of the Public Company Accounting Oversight Board; and

(2)(i) To prepare an independent public accountant's report based on an examination of the statements required under paragraphs (d)(3)(i)(A)(*2*) through (*5*) of this section in the compliance report required to be filed by the broker or dealer under paragraph (d)(1)(i)(B)(*1*) of this section in accordance with standards of the Public Company Accounting Oversight Board; or

(ii) To prepare an independent public accountant's report based on a review of the statements required under paragraphs (d)(4)(i) through (iii) of this section in the exemption report required to be filed by the broker or dealer under paragraph (d)(1)(i)(B)(*2*) of this section in accordance with standards of the Public Company Accounting Oversight Board.

(h) *Notification of non-compliance or material weakness.* If, during the course of preparing the independent public accountant's reports required under paragraph (d)(1)(i)(C) of this section, the independent public accountant determines that the broker or dealer is not in compliance with § 240.15c3–1, § 240.15c3–3, or § 240.17a–13 or any rule of the designated examining authority of the broker or dealer that requires account statements to be sent to the customers of the broker or dealer, as applicable, or the independent public accountant determines that any material weaknesses (as defined in paragraph (d)(3)(iii) of this section) exist, the independent public accountant must immediately notify the chief financial officer of the broker or dealer of the nature of the non-compliance or material weakness. If the notice from the accountant concerns an instance of non-compliance that would require a broker or dealer to provide a notification under § 240.15c3–1, § 240.15c3–3, or § 240.17a–11, or if the notice concerns a

Securities and Exchange Commission § 240.17a–5

material weakness, the broker or dealer must provide a notification in accordance with § 240.15c3–1, § 240.15c3–3, or § 240.17a–11, as applicable, and provide a copy of the notification to the independent public accountant. If the independent public accountant does not receive the notification within one business day, or if the independent public accountant does not agree with the statements in the notification, then the independent public accountant must notify the Commission and the designated examining authority within one business day. The report from the accountant must, if the broker or dealer failed to file a notification, describe any instances of non-compliance that required a notification under § 240.15c3–1, § 240.15c3–3, or § 240.17a–11, or any material weaknesses. If the broker or dealer filed a notification, the report from the accountant must detail the aspects of the notification of the broker or dealer with which the accountant does not agree.

NOTE 1 TO PARAGRAPH (h): The attention of the broker or dealer and the independent public accountant is called to the fact that under § 240.17a–11(a)(1), among other things, a broker or dealer whose net capital declines below the minimum required pursuant to § 240.15c3–1 must give notice of such deficiency that same day in accordance with § 240.17a–11(h) and the notice must specify the broker or dealer's net capital requirement and its current amount of net capital. The attention of the broker or dealer and accountant also is called to the fact that under § 240.15c3–3(i), if a broker or dealer fails to make a reserve bank account or special reserve account deposit, as required by § 240.15c3–3, the broker or dealer must immediately notify the Commission and the regulatory authority for the broker or dealer, which examines such broker or dealer as to financial responsibility and must promptly thereafter confirm such notification in writing.

(i) *Reports of the independent public accountant required under paragraph (d)(1)(i)(C) of this section*—(1) *Technical requirements.* The independent public accountant's reports must:

(i) Be dated;
(ii) Be signed manually;
(iii) Indicate the city and state where issued; and
(iv) Identify without detailed enumeration the items covered by the reports.

(2) *Representations.* The independent public accountant's reports must:

(i) State whether the examinations or review, as applicable, were made in accordance with standards of the Public Company Accounting Oversight Board;

(ii) Identify any examination and, if applicable, review procedures deemed necessary by the independent public accountant under the circumstances of the particular case that have been omitted and the reason for their omission.

(iii) Nothing in this section may be construed to imply authority for the omission of any procedure that independent public accountants would ordinarily employ in the course of an examination or review made for the purpose of expressing the opinions or conclusions required under this section.

(3) *Opinion or conclusion to be expressed.* The independent public accountant's reports must state clearly:

(i) The opinion of the independent public accountant with respect to the financial report required under paragraph (d)(1)(i)(A) of this section and the accounting principles and practices reflected in that report;

(ii) The opinion of the independent public accountant with respect to the financial report required under paragraph (d)(1)(i)(A) of this section, as to the consistency of the application of the accounting principles, or as to any changes in those principles, that have a material effect on the financial statements; and

(iii)(A) The opinion of the independent public accountant with respect to the statements required under paragraphs (d)(3)(i)(A)(*2*) through (*5*) of this section in the compliance report required under paragraph (d)(1)(i)(B)(*1*) of this section; or

(B) The conclusion of the independent public accountant with respect to the statements required under paragraphs (d)(4)(i) through (iii) of this section in the exemption report required under paragraph (d)(1)(i)(B)(*2*) of this section.

(4) *Exceptions.* Any matters to which the independent public accountant

§ 240.17a–5

takes exception must be clearly identified, the exceptions must be specifically and clearly stated, and, to the extent practicable, the effect of each such exception on any related items contained in the annual reports required under paragraph (d) of this section must be given.

(j) [Reserved]

(k) *Supplemental reports.* Each broker or dealer that computes certain of its capital charges in accordance with § 240.15c3–1e must file concurrently with the annual audit report a supplemental report on management controls, which must be prepared by a registered public accounting firm (as that term is defined in section 2(a)(12) of the Sarbanes-Oxley Act of 2002 (15 U.S.C. 7201 *et seq.*)). The supplemental report must indicate the results of the accountant's review of the internal risk management control system established and documented by the broker or dealer in accordance with § 240.15c3–4. This review must be conducted in accordance with procedures agreed upon by the broker or dealer and the registered public accounting firm conducting the review. The agreed upon procedures are to be performed and the report is to be prepared in accordance with the rules promulgated by the Public Company Accounting Oversight Board. The purpose of the review is to confirm that the broker or dealer has established, documented, and is in compliance with the internal risk management controls established in accordance with § 240.15c3–4. Before commencement of the review and no later than December 10 of each year, the broker or dealer must file a statement with the Division of Trading and Markets, Office of Financial Responsibility, at the Commission's principal office in Washington, DC that includes:

(1) A description of the agreed-upon procedures agreed to by the broker or dealer and the registered public accounting firm; and

(2) A notice describing changes in those agreed-upon procedures, if any. If there are no changes, the broker or dealer should so indicate.

(l) *Use of certain statements filed with the Securities and Exchange Commission.* At the request of any broker or dealer who is an investment company registered under the Investment Company Act of 1940, or a sponsor or depositor of such a registered investment company who effects transactions in securities only with, or on behalf of, such registered investment company, the Commission will accept the financial statements filed pursuant to section 13 or 15(d) of the Act or section 30 of the Investment Company Act of 1940 and the rules and regulations promulgated thereunder as a filing pursuant to paragraph (d) of this section. Such a filing must be deemed to satisfy the requirements of this section for any calendar year in which such financial statements are filed, provided that the statements so filed meet the requirements of the other rules under which they are filed with respect to time of filing and content.

(m) *Extentions and exemptions.* (1) A broker's or dealer's designated examining authority may extend the period under paragraph (d) of this section for filing annual reports. The designated examining authority for the broker or dealer must maintain, in the manner prescribed in § 240.17a–1, a record of each extension granted.

(2) Any "bank" as defined in section 3(a)(6) of the Act (15 U.S.C. 78c) and any "insurance company" as defined in section 3(a)(19) of the Act (15 U.S.C. 78c) registered as a broker or dealer to sell variable contracts but exempt from § 240.15c3–1 shall be exempt from the provisions of this section.

(3) On written request of any national securities exchange, registered national securities association, broker or dealer, or on its own motion, the Commission may grant an extension of time or an exemption from any of the requirements of this section either unconditionally or on specified terms and conditions.

(4) The provisions of § 240.17a–5 will not apply to a broker or dealer registered pursuant to section 15(b)(11)(A) of the Act (15 U.S.C. 78*o*(b)(11)(A)) that is not a member of either a national securities exchange pursuant to section 6(a) of the Act (15 U.S.C. 78f(a)) or a national securities association registered pursuant to section 15A(a) of the Act (15 U.S.C. 78*o*–3(a)).

(n) *Notification of change of fiscal year.*
(1) In the event any broker or dealer

Securities and Exchange Commission §240.17a-7

finds it necessary to change its fiscal year, it must file, with the Commission's principal office in Washington, DC, the regional office of the Commission for the region in which the broker or dealer has its principal place of business and the principal office of the designated examining authority for such broker or dealer, a notice of such change.

(2) Such notice must contain a detailed explanation of the reasons for the change. Any change in the filing period for the annual report must be approved in writing by the designated examining authority of the broker or dealer

(o) *Filing requirements.* For purposes of filing requirements as described in this section, filing will be deemed to have been accomplished upon receipt at the Commission's principal office in Washington, DC, with duplicate originals simultaneously filed at the locations prescribed in the particular paragraph of this section which is applicable.

(p) *Compliance with § 240.17a-12.* An OTC derivatives dealer may comply with § 240.17a-5 by complying with the provisions of § 240.17a-12.

CROSS REFERENCE: For interpretative release applicable to § 240.17a-5, see No. 51 in tabulation, part 211 of this chapter.

[40 FR 59713, Dec. 30, 1975]

EDITORIAL NOTE: For FEDERAL REGISTER citations affecting § 240.17a-5, see the List of CFR Sections Affected, which appears in the Finding Aids section of the printed volume and at *www.govinfo.gov.*

§ 240.17a-6 Right of national securities exchange, national securities association, registered clearing agency or the Municipal Securities Rulemaking Board to destroy or dispose of documents.

(a) Any document kept by or on file with a national securities exchange, national securities association, registered clearing agency or the Municipal Securities Rulemaking Board pursuant to the Act or any rule or regulation thereunder may be destroyed or otherwise disposed of by such exchange, association, clearing agency or the Municipal Securities Rulemaking Board at the end of five years or at such earlier date as is specified in a plan for the destruction or disposition of any such documents if such plan has been filed with the Commission by such exchange, association, clearing agency or the Municipal Securities Rulemaking Board and has been declared effective by the Commission.

(b) Such plan may provide that any such document may be transferred to microfilm or other recording medium after such time as specified in the plan and thereafter be maintained and preserved in that form. If a national securities exchange, association, clearing agency or the Municipal Securities Rulemaking Board uses microfilm or other recording medium it shall:

(1) Be ready at all times to provide, and immediately provide, easily readable projection of the microfilm or other recording medium and easily readable hard copy thereof;

(2) Provide indexes permitting the immediate location of any such document on the microfilm or other recording medium; and

(3) In the case of microfilm, store a duplicate copy of the microfilm separately from the original microfilm for the time required.

(c) For the purposes of this rule a plan filed with the Commission by a national securities exchange, association, clearing agency or the Municipal Securities Rulemaking Board shall not become effective unless the Commission, having due regard for the public interest and for the protection of investors, declares the plan to be effective. The Commission in its declaration may limit the applications, reports, and documents as to which it shall apply, and may impose any other terms and conditions to the plan and to the period of its effectiveness which it deems necessary or appropriate in the public interest or for the protection of investors.

[45 FR 79426, Dec. 1, 1980]

§ 240.17a-7 Records of non-resident brokers and dealers.

(a)(1) Except as provided in paragraphs (b) and (c) of this section, each non-resident broker or dealer registered or applying for registration pursuant to section 15 of the Securities Exchange Act of 1934, as amended, shall keep, maintain, and preserve, at a

§ 240.17a-7

place within the United States designated in a notice from him as provided in paragraph (a)(2) of this section, true, correct, complete and current copies of the books and records which he is required to make, keep current, maintain or preserve pursuant to any provision of any rule or regulation of the Commission adopted under the act.

(2) Except as provided in paragraph (b) of this section, each non-resident broker or dealer subject to this section shall furnish to the Commission a written notice specifying the address of the place within the United States where the copies of the books and records required to be kept and preserved by him pursuant to paragraph (a)(1) of this section are located. Each non-resident broker or dealer registered or applying for registration when this section becomes effective shall file such notice within 30 days after such rule becomes effective. Each non-resident broker or dealer who files an application for registration after this section becomes effective shall file such notice with such application for registration.

(b) Notwithstanding the provisions of paragraph (a) of this section, a non-resident broker or dealer subject to this section need not keep or preserve within the United States copies of the books and records referred to in said paragraph (a) of this section, if:

(1) Such broker or dealer files with the Commission, at the time or within the period provided by paragraph (a)(2) of this section, a written undertaking in form acceptable to the Commission and signed by a person thereunto duly authorized, to furnish to the Commission, upon demand, at its principal office in Washington, DC, or at any Regional Office of the Commission designated in such demand, true, correct, complete and current copies of any or all of the books and records which he is required to make, keep current, maintain, or preserve pursuant to any provision of any rule or regulation of the Commission adopted under the act, or any part of such books and records which may be specified in such demand. Such undertaking shall be in substantially the following form:

The undersigned hereby undertakes to furnish at his own expense to the Securities and Exchange Commission at its principal office in Washington, DC, or at any Regional Office of said Commission specified in a demand for copies of books and records made by or on behalf of said Commission, true, correct, complete, and current copies of any or all, or any part, of the books and records which the undersigned is required to make, keep current or preserve pursuant to any provision of any rule or regulation of the Securities and Exchange Commission under the Securities Exchange Act of 1934. This undertaking shall be suspended during any period when the undersigned is making, keeping current, and preserving copies of all of said books and records at a place within the United States in compliance with § 240.17a-7 (Rule X-17A-7) under the Securities Exchange Act of 1934. This undertaking shall be binding upon the undersigned and the heirs, successors and assigns of the undersigned, and the written irrevocable consents and powers of attorney of the undersigned, its general partners and managing agents filed with the Securities and Exchange Commission shall extend to and cover any action to enforce same.

and

(2) Such broker or dealer furnishes to the Commission at his own expense within 14 days after written demand therefor forwarded to him by registered mail at his last address of record filed with the Commission and signed by the Secretary of the Commission or such other person as the Commission may authorize to act in its behalf, true, correct, complete and current copies of any or all books and records which such broker or dealer is required to make, keep current or preserve pursuant to any provision of any rule or regulation of the Commission adopted under the act, or any part of such books and records which may be specified in said written demand. Such copies shall be furnished to the Commission at its principal office in Washington, DC, or at any Regional Office of the Commission which may be specified in said written demand.

(c) The provisions of this section shall not apply to a broker or dealer registered pursuant to section 15(b)(11)(A) of the Act (15 U.S.C. 78*o*(b)(11)(A)) that is not a member of either a national securities exchange pursuant to section 6(a) of the Act (15 U.S.C. 78f(a)) or a national securities association registered pursuant to section 15A(a) of the Act (15 U.S.C. 78*o*-3(a)).

Securities and Exchange Commission § 240.17a–10

(d) For purposes of this section the following definitions shall apply:

(1) The term *broker* shall have the meaning set out in section 3(a)(4) of the Securities Exchange Act of 1934;

(2) The term *dealer* shall have the meaning set out in section 3(a)(5) of the Securities Exchange Act of 1934;

(3) The term *non-resident broker or dealer* shall mean (i) in the case of an individual, one who resides in or has his principal place of business in any place not subject to the jurisdiction of the United States; (ii) in the case of a corporation, one incorporated in or having its principal place of business in any place not subject to the jurisdiction of the United States; (iii) in the case of a partnership of other unincorporated organization or association, one having its principal place of business in any place not subject to the jurisdiction of the United States.

[21 FR 5524, July 24, 1956, as amended at 59 FR 5945, Feb. 9, 1994; 67 FR 58300, Sept. 13, 2002; 73 FR 32228, June 5, 2008]

§ 240.17a–8 Financial recordkeeping and reporting of currency and foreign transactions.

Every registered broker or dealer who is subject to the requirements of the Currency and Foreign Transactions Reporting Act of 1970 shall comply with the reporting, recordkeeping and record retention requirements of chapter X of title 31 of the Code of Federal Regulations. Where chapter X of title 31 of the Code of Federal Regulations and § 240.17a–4 of this chapter require the same records or reports to be preserved for different periods of time, such records or reports shall be preserved for the longer period of time.

[46 FR 61455, Dec. 17, 1981, as amended at 76 FR 11328, Mar. 2, 2011]

§ 240.17a–9T Records to be made and retained by certain exchange members, brokers and dealers.

This section applies to every member, broker or dealer registered pursuant to Section 15 of the Act, (15 U.S.C. 78*o*), that is required to maintain, as of December 29, December 30 and December 31, 1999, minimum net capital of $250,000 pursuant to § 240.15c3–1(a)(2)(i).

(a) You must make before January 1, 2000, for each of December 29, December 30 and December 31, 1999, separate copies of the blotters pursuant to § 240.17a–3(a)(1).

(b) You must make before January 1, 2000, as of the close of business for each of December 29, December 30 and December 31, 1999, a separate copy of the securities record or ledger pursuant to § 240.17a–3(a)(5).

(c) You must preserve these records for a period of not less than one year.

(d) The provisions of § 240.17a–4(i) shall apply as if part of this § 240.17a–9T.

(e) You may preserve these records in any format that is acceptable and in compliance with the conditions described in § 240.17a–4(f).

(f) You must furnish promptly to a representative of the Commission such legible, true and complete copies of those records, as may be requested.

(g) This temporary section will expire on July 1, 2001.

[64 FR 42029, Aug. 3, 1999]

§ 240.17a–10 Report on revenue and expenses.

(a)(1) Every broker or dealer exempted from the filing requirements of paragraph (a) of § 240.17a–5 shall, not later than 17 business days after the close of each calendar year, file the Facing Page, a Statement of Income (Loss) and balance sheet from Part IIA of Form X–17A–5 (§ 249.617 of this chapter) and Schedule I of Form X–17A–5 (§ 249.617 of this chapter) for such calendar year.

(2) Every broker or dealer subject to the filing requirements of paragraph (a) of § 240.17a–5 shall submit Schedule I of Form X–17A–5 (§ 249.617 of this chapter) with its Form X–17A–5 (§ 249.617 of this chapter) for the calendar quarter ending December 31 of each year.

(b) The provisions of paragraph (a) of this section shall not apply to a member of a national securities exchange or a registered national securities association which maintains records containing the information required by Form X–17A–5 (§ 249.617 of this chapter) as to each of its members, and which transmits to the Commission a copy of the record as to each such member, pursuant to a plan the procedures and provisions of which have been submitted to and declared effective by the

§ 240.17a-11

Commission. Any such plan filed by a national securities exchange or a registered national securities association may provide that when a member is also a member of one or more national securities exchanges, or of one or more national securities exchanges and a registered national securities association, the information required to be submitted with respect to any such member may be transmitted by only one specified national securities exchange or registered national securities association. For the purpose of this section, a plan filed with the Commission by a national securities exchange or a registered national securities association shall not become effective unless the Commission, having due regard for the public interest, for the protection of investors, and for the fulfillment of the Commission's functions under the provisions of the Act, declares the plan to be effective. Further, the Commission, in declaring any such plan effective, may impose such terms and conditions relating to the provisions of the plan and the period of its effectiveness as may be deemed necessary or appropriate in the public interest, for the protection of investors, or to carry out the Commission's duties under the Act.

(c) Individual reports filed by, or on behalf of, brokers, dealers, or members of national securities exchanges pursuant to this section are to be considered nonpublic information, except in cases where the Commission determines that it is in the public interest to direct otherwise.

(d) In the event any broker or dealer finds that it cannot file the annual report required by paragraph (a) of this section within the time specified without undue hardship, it may file with the Commission's principal office in Washington, DC, prior to the date upon which the report is due, an application for an extension of time to a specified date which shall not be later than 60 days after the close of the calendar year for which the report is to be made. The application shall state the reasons for the requested extension and shall contain an agreement to file the report on or before the specified date.

(Sec. 17, 48 Stat. 897; 15 U.S.C. 78q)

[33 FR 10390, July 20, 1968, as amended at 35 FR 3804, Feb. 27, 1970; 35 FR 7644, May 16, 1970; 37 FR 13615, July 12, 1972; 40 FR 59717, Dec. 30, 1975; 42 FR 23789, May 10, 1977; 46 FR 60193, Dec. 9, 1981]

§ 240.17a-11 Notification provisions for brokers and dealers.

This section applies to the following types of entities: Except as provided in this introductory text, a broker or dealer, including an *OTC derivatives dealer* as that term is defined in § 240.3b-12, registered pursuant to section 15 of the Act (15 U.S.C. 78*o*); a broker or dealer, other than an OTC derivatives dealer, registered pursuant to section 15 of the Act that is also a security-based swap dealer registered pursuant to section 15F of the Act (15 U.S.C. 78*o*-10); and a broker or dealer, including an OTC derivatives dealer, registered pursuant to section 15 of the Act that is also a major-security-based swap participant registered pursuant to section 15F of the Act. Section 240.18a-8 (rather than this section) applies to the following types of entities: A security-based swap dealer registered pursuant to section 15F of the Act that is not also a broker or dealer, other than an OTC derivatives dealer, registered pursuant to section 15 of the Act; a security-based swap dealer registered pursuant to section 15F of the Act that is also an OTC derivatives dealer; and a major security-based swap participant registered pursuant to section 15F of the Act that is not also a broker or dealer, including an OTC derivatives dealer, registered pursuant to section 15 of the Act.

(a)(1) Every broker or dealer whose net capital declines below the minimum amount required pursuant to § 240.15c3-1, or is insolvent as that term is defined in § 240.15c3-1(c)(16), must give notice of such deficiency that same day in accordance with paragraph (h) of this section. The notice must specify the broker or dealer's net capital requirement and its current amount of net capital. If a broker or dealer is informed by its designated examining authority or the Commission that it is, or has been, in violation of

Securities and Exchange Commission § 240.17a–11

§ 240.15c3–1 and the broker or dealer has not given notice of the capital deficiency under this section, the broker or dealer, even if it does not agree that it is, or has been, in violation of § 240.15c3–1, must give notice of the claimed deficiency, which notice may specify the broker's or dealer's reasons for its disagreement.

(2) In addition to the requirements of paragraph (b)(1) of this section, an OTC derivatives dealer or broker or dealer permitted to compute net capital pursuant to the alternative method of § 240.15c3–1e must also provide notice if its tentative net capital falls below the minimum amount required pursuant to § 240.15c3–1. The notice must specify the tentative net capital requirements, and current amount of net capital and tentative net capital, of the OTC derivatives dealer or the broker or dealer permitted to compute net capital pursuant to the alternative method of § 240.15c3–1e.

(b) Every broker or dealer must send notice promptly (but within 24 hours) after the occurrence of the events specified in paragraphs (b)(1) through (5) of this section in accordance with paragraph (h) of this section:

(1) If a computation made by a broker or dealer subject to the aggregate indebtedness standard of § 240.15c3–1 shows that its aggregate indebtedness is in excess of 1,200 percent of its net capital; or

(2) If a computation made by a broker or dealer, which has elected the alternative standard of § 240.15c3–1, shows that its net capital is less than 5 percent of aggregate debit items computed in accordance with § 240.15c3–3a Exhibit A: Formula for Determination Reserve Requirement of Brokers and Dealers under § 240.15c3–3; or

(3) If a computation made by a broker or dealer pursuant to § 240.15c3–1 shows that its total net capital is less than 120 percent of the broker's or dealer's required minimum net capital, or if a computation made by an OTC derivatives dealer pursuant to § 240.15c3–1 shows that its total tentative net capital is less than 120 percent of the dealer's required minimum tentative net capital.

(4) The occurrence of the fourth and each subsequent backtesting exception under § 240.15c3–1f(e)(1)(iv) during any 250 business day measurement period.

(5) If a computation made by a broker or dealer pursuant to § 240.15c3–1 shows that the total amount of money payable against all securities loaned or subject to a repurchase agreement or the total contract value of all securities borrowed or subject to a reverse repurchase agreement is in excess of 2500 percent of its tentative net capital; *provided*, however, that for purposes of this leverage test transactions involving government securities, as defined in section 3(a)(42) of the Act (15 U.S.C. 78c(a)(42)), must be excluded from the calculation; *provided* further, however, that a broker or dealer will not be required to send the notice required by this paragraph (c)(5) if it reports monthly its securities lending and borrowing and repurchase and reverse repurchase activity (including the total amount of money payable against securities loaned or subject to a repurchase agreement and the total contract value of securities borrowed or subject to a reverse repurchase agreement) to its designated examining authority in a form acceptable to its designated examining authority.

(c) Every broker or dealer that fails to make and keep current the books and records required by § 240.17a–3, must give notice of this fact that same day in accordance with paragraph (h) of this section, specifying the books and records which have not been made or which are not current. The broker or dealer must also transmit a report in accordance with paragraph (h) of this section within 48 hours of the notice stating what the broker or dealer has done or is doing to correct the situation.

(d) Whenever any broker or dealer discovers, or is notified by an independent public accountant under § 240.17a–12(i)(2), of the existence of any material inadequacy as defined in § 240.17a–12(h)(2), or whenever any broker or dealer discovers, or is notified by an independent public accountant under § 240.17a–5(h), of the existence of any material weakness as defined in § 240.17a–5(d)(3)(iii), the broker or dealer must:

(1) Give notice, in accordance with paragraph (h) of this section, of the

619

§ 240.17a–12

material inadequacy or material weakness within 24 hours of the discovery or notification of the material inadequacy or material weakness; and

(2) Transmit a report in accordance with paragraph (h) of this section, within 48 hours of the notice stating what the broker or dealer has done or is doing to correct the situation.

(e) [Reserved]

(f) If a broker-dealer fails to make in its special reserve account for the exclusive benefit of security-based swap customers a deposit, as required by § 240.15c3–3(p), the broker-dealer must give immediate notice in writing in accordance with paragraph (h) of this section.

(g) Every national securities exchange or national securities association that learns that a broker or dealer has failed to send notice or transmit a report as required by this section, even after being advised by the securities exchange or the national securities association to send notice or transmit a report, must immediately give notice of such failure in accordance with paragraph (h) of this section.

(h) Every notice or report required to be given or transmitted by this section must be given or transmitted to the principal office of the Commission in Washington DC and the regional office of the Commission for the region in which the broker or dealer has its principal place of business, or to an email address provided on the Commission's website, and to the designated examining authority of which such broker or dealer is a member, and to the Commodity Futures Trading Commission (CFTC) if the broker or dealer is registered as a futures commission merchant with the CFTC. The report required by paragraph (c) or (d)(2) of this section may be transmitted by overnight delivery.

(i) Other notice provisions relating to the Commission's financial responsibility or reporting rules are contained in §§ 240.15c3–1, 240.15c3–1d, 240.15c3–3, 240.17a–5, and 240.17a–12.

(j) The provisions of this section will not apply to a broker or dealer registered pursuant to section 15(b)(11)(A) of the Act (15 U.S.C. 78o(b)(11)(A)) that is not a member of either a national securities exchange pursuant to section 6(a) of the Act (15 U.S.C. 78f(a)) or a national securities association registered pursuant to section 15A(a) of the Act (15 U.S.C. 78o–3(a)).

[58 FR 37657, July 13, 1993, as amended at 59 FR 5945, Feb. 9, 1994; 63 FR 59401, Nov. 3, 1998; 67 FR 58300, Sept. 13, 2002; 69 FR 34472, June 21, 2004; 73 FR 32228, June 5, 2008; 78 FR 51907, Aug. 21, 2013; 78 FR 51933, Aug. 21, 2013; 84 FR 68655, Dec. 16, 2019]

§ 240.17a–12 Reports to be made by certain OTC derivatives dealers.

(a) *Filing of quarterly reports.* (1) This paragraph (a) shall apply to every OTC derivatives dealer registered pursuant to Section 15 of the Act (15 U.S.C. 78o).

(i) Every OTC derivatives dealer shall file Part II of Form X–17A–5 (§ 249.617 of this chapter) within 17 business days after the end of each calendar quarter and within 17 business days after the date selected for the annual audit of financial statements where said date is other than the end of the calendar quarter.

(ii) Upon receiving from the Commission written notice that additional reporting is required, an OTC derivatives dealer shall file monthly, or at such times as shall be specified, Part II of Form X–17A–5 (§ 249.617 of this chapter) and such other financial or operational information as shall be required by the Commission.

(2) The reports provided for in this paragraph (a) shall be considered filed when received at the Commission's principal office in Washington, DC. All reports filed pursuant to this paragraph (a) shall be deemed to be confidential.

(3) Upon written application by an OTC derivatives dealer to the Commission, the Commission may extend the time for filing the information required by this paragraph (a). The written application shall be filed with the Commission at its principal office in Washington DC.

(b) *Annual filing of audited financial statements.* (1)(i) Every OTC derivatives dealer registered pursuant to Section 15 of the Act (15 U.S.C. 78o) shall file annually, on a calendar or fiscal year basis, a report which shall be audited by a certified public accountant. Reports filed pursuant to this paragraph

Securities and Exchange Commission § 240.17a-12

(b) shall be as of the same fixed or determinable date each year, unless a change is approved in writing by the Commission.

(ii) An OTC derivatives dealer succeeding to and continuing the business of another OTC derivatives dealer need not file a report under this paragraph (b) as of a date in the fiscal or calendar year in which the succession occurs if the predecessor OTC derivatives dealer has filed a report in compliance with this paragraph (b) as of a date in such fiscal or calendar year.

(2) The annual audit report shall contain a Statement of Financial Condition (in a format and on a basis which is consistent with the total reported on the Statement of Financial Condition contained in Form X–17A–5 (§ 249.617 of this chapter), Part II, a Statement of Income, a Statement of Cash Flows, a Statement of Changes in Stockholders' or Partners' or Sole Proprietor's Equity, and a Statement of Changes in Liabilities Subordinated to Claims of General Creditors. Such statements shall be in a format which is consistent with such statements as contained in Form X–17A–5 (§ 249.617 of this chapter), Part II. If the Statement of Financial Condition filed in accordance with instructions to Form X–17A–5 (§ 249.617 of this chapter), Part II, is not consolidated, a summary of financial data for subsidiaries not consolidated in the Part II Statement of Financial Condition as filed by the OTC derivatives dealer shall be included in the notes to the consolidated statement of financial condition reported on by the certified public accountant. The summary financial data shall include the assets, liabilities, and net worth or stockholders' equity of the unconsolidated subsidiaries.

NOTE 1 TO PARAGRAPH (b)(2). If there is other comprehensive income in the period(s) presented, the financial report must contain a Statement of Comprehensive Income (as defined in § 210.1–02 of Regulation S–X of this chapter) in place of a Statement of Income.

(3) Supporting schedules shall include, from Part II of Form X–17A–5 (§ 249.617 of this chapter), a Computation of Net Capital under § 240.15c3–1.

(4) A reconciliation, including appropriate explanations, of the Computation of Net Capital under § 240.15c3–1 contained in the audit report with the broker's or dealer's corresponding unaudited most recent Part II filing shall be filed with the report when material differences exist. If no material differences exist, a statement so indicating shall be filed.

(5) The annual audit report shall be filed not more than sixty days after the date of the financial statements.

(6) Two copies of the annual audit report shall be filed at the Commission's principal office in Washington, DC.

(c) *Nature and form of reports.* The financial statements filed pursuant to paragraph (b) of this section shall be prepared and filed in accordance with the following requirements:

(1) An audit shall be conducted by a certified public accountant who shall be in fact independent as defined in paragraph (f) of this section, and it shall give an opinion covering the statements filed pursuant to paragraph (b) of this section.

(2) Attached to the report shall be an oath or affirmation that, to the best knowledge and belief of the person making such oath or affirmation, the financial statements and schedules are true and correct and neither the OTC derivatives dealer, nor any partner, officer, or director, as the case may be, has any significant interest in any counterparty or in any account classified solely as that of a counterparty. The oath or affirmation shall be made before a person duly authorized to administer such oaths or affirmations. If the OTC derivatives dealer is a sole proprietorship, the oath or affirmation shall be made by the proprietor; if a partnership, by a general partner; or if a corporation, by a duly authorized officer.

(3) All of the statements filed pursuant to paragraph (b) of this section shall be confidential except that they shall be available for use by any official or employee of the United States or by any other person to whom the Commission authorizes disclosure of such information as being in the public interest.

(d) *Qualification of accountants.* The Commission will not recognize any person as a certified public accountant who is not duly registered and in good

§ 240.17a–12

standing as such under the laws of the State of his principal office.

(e) *Designation of accountant.* (1) Every OTC derivatives dealer shall file no later than December 10 of each year with the Commission's principal office in Washington, DC a statement indicating the existence of an agreement, dated no later than December 1 of that year, with a certified public accountant covering a contractual commitment to conduct the OTC derivatives dealer's annual audit during the following calendar year.

(2) If the agreement is of a continuing nature, providing for successive yearly audits, no further filing is required. If the agreement is for a single audit, or if the continuing agreement previously filed has been terminated or amended, a new statement must be filed by the required date.

(3) The statement shall be headed "Notice pursuant to § 240.17a–12(e)" and shall contain the following information:

(i) Name, address, telephone number, and registration number of the OTC derivatives dealer;

(ii) Name, address, and telephone number of the certified public accounting firm; and

(iii) The audit date of the OTC derivatives dealer for the year covered by the agreement.

(4) Notwithstanding the date of filing specified in paragraph (e)(1) of this section, every OTC derivatives dealer shall file the notice provided for in paragraph (e) of this section within 30 days following the effective date of registration as an OTC derivatives dealer.

(f) *Independence of accountant.* A certified public accountant shall be independent in accordance with the provisions of § 210.2–01(b) and (c) of this chapter.

(g) *Replacement of accountant.* (1) An OTC derivatives dealer shall file a notice that must be received by the Commission's principal office in Washington, DC not more than 15 business days after:

(i) The OTC derivatives dealer has notified the certified public accountant whose opinion covered the most recent financial statements filed under paragraph (b) of this section that the certified public accountant's services will not be utilized in future engagements; or

(ii) The OTC derivatives dealer has notified a certified public accountant who was engaged to give an opinion covering the financial statements to be filed under paragraph (b) of this section that the engagement has been terminated; or

(iii) A certified public accountant has notified the OTC derivatives dealer that it will not continue under an engagement or give an opinion covering the financial statements to be filed under paragraph (b) of this section; or

(iv) A new certified public accountant has been engaged to give an opinion covering the financial statements to be filed under paragraph (b) of this section without any notice of termination having been given to or by the previously engaged certified public accountant.

(2) Such notice shall state the date of notification of the termination of the engagement of the former certified public accountant or the engagement of the new certified public accountant, as applicable, and the details of any disagreements existing during the 24 months (or the period of the engagement, if less) preceding such termination or new engagement relating to any matter of accounting principles or practices, financial statement disclosure, auditing scope or procedure, or compliance with applicable rules of the Commission, which disagreements, if not resolved to the satisfaction of the former certified public accountant, would have caused the former certified public accountant to make reference to them in connection with the report on the subject matter of the disagreements. The disagreements required to be reported in response to the preceding sentence include both those resolved to the former certified public accountant's satisfaction and those not resolved to the former certified public accountant's satisfaction. Disagreements contemplated by this section are those that occur at the decision-making level (i.e., between principal financial officers of the OTC derivatives dealer and personnel of the certified public accounting firm responsible for rendering its report). The notice shall also state whether the certified public

Securities and Exchange Commission § 240.17a–12

accountant's report on the financial statements for any of the past two years contained an adverse opinion or a disclaimer of opinion or was qualified as to uncertainties, audit scope, or accounting principles, and describe the nature of each such adverse opinion, disclaimer of opinion, or qualification. The OTC derivatives dealer shall also request the former certified public accountant to furnish the OTC derivatives dealer with a letter addressed to the Commission stating whether the former certified public accountant agrees with the statements contained in the notice of the OTC derivatives dealer and, if not, stating the respects in which the former certified public accountant does not agree. The OTC derivatives dealer shall file three copies of the notice and the certified public accountant's letter, one copy of which shall be manually signed by the sole proprietor, or a general partner or a duly authorized corporate officer, as appropriate, and by the certified public accountant.

(h) *Audit objectives.* (1) The audit shall be made in accordance with U.S. Generally Accepted Auditing Standards and shall include a review of the accounting system, the internal accounting controls, and procedures for safeguarding securities including appropriate tests thereof for the period since the date of the prior audited financial statements. The audit shall include all procedures necessary under the circumstances to enable the certified public accountant to express an opinion on the statement of financial condition, results of operations, cash flows, and the Computation of Net Capital under § 240.15c3–1. The scope of the audit and review of the accounting system, the internal accounting controls, and procedures for safeguarding securities shall be sufficient to provide reasonable assurance that any material inadequacies existing at the date of the examination in the following are disclosed:

(i) The accounting system;

(ii) The internal accounting controls; and

(iii) The procedures for safeguarding securities.

(2) A material inadequacy in the accounting system, internal accounting controls, procedures for safeguarding securities, and practices and procedures referred to in paragraph (h) (1) of this section that must be reported under these audit objectives includes any condition which has contributed substantially to or, if appropriate corrective action is not taken, could reasonably be expected to:

(i) Inhibit an OTC derivatives dealer from promptly completing securities transactions or promptly discharging its responsibilities to counterparties, other brokers and dealers, or creditors;

(ii) Result in material financial loss;

(iii) Result in material misstatements of the OTC derivatives dealer's financial statements; or

(iv) Result in violations of the Commission's recordkeeping or financial responsibility rules to an extent that could reasonably be expected to result in the conditions described in paragraphs (h)(2)(i), (ii), or (iii) of this section.

(i) *Extent and timing of audit procedures.* (1) The extent and timing of audit procedures are matters for the certified public accountant to determine on the basis of its review and evaluation of existing internal controls and other audit procedures performed in accordance with U.S. Generally Accepted Auditing Standards and the audit objectives set forth in paragraph (h) of this section.

(2) If, during the course of the audit or interim work, the certified public accountant determines that any material inadequacies exist in the accounting system, internal accounting controls, procedures for safeguarding securities, or as otherwise defined in paragraph (h)(2) of this section, then the certified public accountant shall call it to the attention of the chief financial officer of the OTC derivatives dealer, who shall inform the Commission by telegraphic or facsimile notice within 24 hours thereafter as set forth in § 240.17a–11. The OTC derivatives dealer shall also furnish the certified public accountant with a copy of said notice to the Commission by telegram or facsimile within the same 24 hour period. If the certified public accountant fails

§ 240.17a-12

to receive such notice from the OTC derivatives dealer within that 24 hour period, or if the certified public accountant disagrees with the statements contained in the notice of the OTC derivatives dealer, the certified public accountant shall inform the Commission by report of material inadequacy within 24 hours thereafter as set forth in § 240.17a-11. Such report from the certified public accountant shall, if the OTC derivatives dealer failed to file a notice, describe any material inadequacies found to exist. If the OTC derivatives dealer filed a notice, the certified public accountant shall file a report detailing the aspects, if any, of the OTC derivatives dealer's notice with which the certified public accountant does not agree.

(j) *Accountant's report, general provisions*—(1) *Technical requirements.* The certified public accountant's report shall be dated; be signed manually; indicate the city and state where issued; and identify without detailed enumeration the financial statements and schedules covered by the report.

(2) *Representations as to the audit.* The certified public accountant's report shall state that the audit was made in accordance with U.S. Generally Accepted Auditing Standards; state whether the certified public accountant reviewed the procedures followed for safeguarding securities; and designate any auditing procedures deemed necessary by the certified public accountant under the circumstances of the particular case that have been omitted, and the reason for their omission. Nothing in this section shall be construed to imply authority for the omission of any procedure which certified public accountants would ordinarily employ in the course of an audit made for the purpose of expressing the opinions required under this section.

(3) *Opinion to be expressed.* The certified public accountant's report shall state clearly the opinion of the certified public accountant:

(i) In respect of the financial statements and schedules covered by the report and the accounting principles and practices reflected therein; and

(ii) As to the consistency of the application of the accounting principles, or as to any changes in such principles which have a material effect on the financial statements.

(4) *Exceptions.* Any matters to which the certified public accountant takes exception shall be clearly identified, explained, and, to the extent practicable, the effect of each such exception on the related financial statements shall be provided.

(5) *Definitions.* For the purpose of this section, the terms *audit* (or *examination*), *accountant's report,* and *certified* shall have the meanings given in § 210.1-02 of this chapter.

(k) *Accountant's report on material inadequacies and reportable conditions.* The OTC derivatives dealer shall file concurrently with the annual audit report a supplemental report by the certified public accountant describing any material inadequacies or any matter that would be deemed to be a reportable condition under U.S. Generally Accepted Auditing Standards that are unresolved as of the date of the certified public accountant's report. The report shall also describe any material inadequacies found to have existed since the date of the previous audit. The supplemental report shall indicate any corrective action taken or proposed by the OTC derivatives dealer with regard to any identified material inadequacies or reportable conditions. If the audit did not disclose any material inadequacies or reportable conditions, the supplemental report shall so state.

(l) *Accountant's report on management controls.* (1) The OTC derivatives dealer shall file concurrently with the annual audit report a supplemental report by the certified public accountant indicating the results of the certified public accountant's review of the OTC derivatives dealer's internal risk management control system with respect to the requirements of § 240.15c3-4. This review shall be conducted in accordance with procedures agreed to by the OTC derivatives dealer and the certified public accountant conducting the review. The purpose of the review is to confirm that the OTC derivatives dealer has established, documented, and maintained an internal risk management control system in accordance with § 240.15c3-4, and is in compliance with that internal risk management control system.

Securities and Exchange Commission § 240.17a-13

(2) The agreed-upon procedures are to be performed, and the report is to be prepared, in accordance with U.S. Generally Accepted Attestation Standards.

(3) Prior to the commencement of the initial review, every OTC derivatives dealer shall file the procedures to be performed pursuant to paragraph (1)(1) of this section with the Commission's principal office in Washington, DC. Prior to the commencement of any subsequent review, every OTC derivatives dealer shall file with the Commission's principal office in Washington, DC a notice of changes to the agreed-upon procedures.

(m) *Accountant's report on inventory pricing and modeling.* (1) The OTC derivatives dealer shall file concurrently with the annual audit report a supplemental report by the certified public accountant indicating the results of the certified public accountant's review of the broker's or dealer's inventory pricing and modeling procedures. This review shall be conducted in accordance with procedures agreed to by the OTC derivatives dealer and by the certified public accountant conducting the review. The purpose of the review is to confirm that the pricing and modeling procedures relied upon by the OTC derivatives dealer conform to the procedures submitted to the Commission as part of its OTC derivatives dealer application, and that the procedures comply with the qualitative and quantitative standards set forth in § 240.15c3-1f.

(2) The agreed-upon procedures are to be performed and the report is to be prepared in accordance with U.S. Generally Accepted Attestation Standards.

(3) Every OTC derivatives dealer shall file prior to the commencement of the initial review, the procedures to be performed pursuant to paragraph (m)(1) of this section with the Commission's principal office in Washington, DC. Prior to the commencement of each subsequent review, every OTC derivatives dealer shall file with the Commission's principal office in Washington, DC notice of changes in the agreed-upon procedures.

(n) *Extensions and exemptions.* Upon the written request of the OTC derivatives dealer, or on its own motion, the Commission may grant an extension of time or an exemption from any of the requirements of this section either unconditionally or on specified terms and conditions.

(o) *Notification of change of fiscal year.* (1) In the event any OTC derivatives dealer finds it necessary to change its fiscal year, it must file a notice of such change with the Commission's principal office in Washington, DC.

(2) Such notice shall contain a detailed explanation of the reasons for the change. Any change in the filing period for the audit report must be approved by the Commission.

(p) *Filing requirements.* For purposes of filing requirements as described in § 240.17a-12, these filings shall be deemed to have been accomplished upon receipt at the Commission's principal office in Washington, DC.

[63 FR 59401, Nov. 3, 1998, as amended at 69 FR 34494, June 21, 2004; 83 FR 50223, Oct. 4, 2018; 84 FR 68656, Dec. 16, 2019; 86 FR 31116, June 11, 2021]

§ 240.17a-13 Quarterly security counts to be made by certain exchange members, brokers, and dealers.

(a) This section shall apply to every member of a national securities exchange who transacts a business in securities directly with or for others than members of a national securities exchange, every broker or dealer (other than a member) who transacts a business in securities through the medium of any member of a national securities exchange, and every broker or dealer registered pursuant to section 15 of the Act; except that a broker or dealer meeting all of the following conditions shall be exempt from the provisions of this section:

(1) His dealer transactions (as principal for his own account) are limited to the purchase, sale, and redemption of redeemable shares of registered investment companies or of interests or participations in an insurance company separate account, whether or not registered as an investment company; except that a broker or dealer transacting business as a sole proprietor may also effect occasional transactions in other securities for his own account with or through another registered broker-dealer;

625

§ 240.17a-13

(2) His transactions as broker (agent) are limited to:

(i) The sale and redemption of redeemable securities of registered investment companies or of interests or participations in an insurance company separate account, whether or not registered as an investment company;

(ii) The solicitation of share accounts for savings and loan associations insured by an instrumentality of the United States; and

(iii) The sale of securities for the account of a customer to obtain funds for immediate reinvestment in redeemable securities of registered investment companies; and

(3) He promptly transmits all funds and delivers all securities received in connection with his activities as a broker or dealer, and does not otherwise hold funds or securities for, or owe money or securities to, customers.

Notwithstanding the foregoing, this rule shall not apply to any insurance company which is a registered broker-dealer, and which otherwise meets all of the conditions in paragraphs (a)(1), (2), and (3) of this section, solely by reason of its participation in transactions that are a part of the business of insurance, including the purchasing, selling, or holding of securities for or on behalf of such company's general and separate accounts.

(b) Any member, broker, or dealer who is subject to the provisions of this rule shall at least once in each calendar quarter-year:

(1) Physically examine and count all securities held including securities that are the subjects of repurchase or reverse repurchase agreements;

(2) Account for all securities in transfer, in transit, pledged, loaned, borrowed, deposited, failed to receive, failed to deliver, subject to repurchase or reverse repurchase agreements or otherwise subject to his control or direction but not in his physical possession by examination and comparison of the supporting detail records with the appropriate ledger control accounts;

(3) Verify all securities in transfer, in transit, pledge, loaned, borrowed, deposited, failed to receive, failed to deliver, subject to repurchase or reverse repurchase agreements or otherwise subject to his control or direction but not in his physical possession, where such securities have been in said status for longer than thirty days;

(4) Compare the results of the count and verification with his records; and

(5) Record on the books and records of the member, broker, or dealer all unresolved differences setting forth the security involved and date of comparison in a security count difference account no later than 7 business days after the date of each required quarterly security examination, count, and verification in accordance with the requirements provided in paragraph (c) of this section. *Provided, however,* That no examination, count, verification, and comparison for the purpose of this section shall be within 2 months of or more than 4 months following a prior examination, count, verification, and comparison made hereunder.

(c) The examination, count, verification, and comparison may be made either as of a date certain or on a cyclical basis covering the entire list of securities. In either case the recordation shall be effected within 7 business days subsequent to the examination, count, verification, and comparison of a particular security. In the event that an examination, count, verification, and comparison is made on a cyclical basis, it shall not extend over more than 1 calendar quarter-year, and no security shall be examined, counted, verified, or compared for the purpose of this rule less than 2 months or more than 4 months after a prior examination, count, verification, and comparison.

(d) The examination, count, verification, and comparison shall be made or supervised by persons whose regular duties do not require them to have direct responsibility for the proper care and protection of the securities or the making or preservation of the subject records.

(e) The provisions of this section shall not apply to a broker or dealer registered pursuant to section 15(b)(11)(A) of the Act (15 U.S.C. 78o(b)(11)(A)) that is not a member of either a national securities exchange pursuant to section 6(a) of the Act (15 U.S.C. 78f(a)) or a national securities

Securities and Exchange Commission § 240.17a–14

association registered pursuant to section 15A(a) of the Act (15 U.S.C. 78*o*–3(a)).

(f) The Commission may, upon written request, exempt from the provisions of this section, either unconditionally or on specified terms and conditions, any member, broker, or dealer who satisfies the Commission that it is not necessary in the public interest and for the protection of investors to subject the particular member, broker, or dealer to certain or all of the provisions of this section, because of the special nature of his business, the safeguards he has established for the protection of customers' funds and securities, or such other reason as the Commission deems appropriate.

[36 FR 21179, Nov. 4, 1971, as amended at 42 FR 23790, May 10, 1977; 52 FR 22299, June 11, 1987; 67 FR 58300, Sept. 13, 2002]

§ 240.17a–14 Form CRS, for preparation, filing and delivery of Form CRS.

(a) *Scope of section.* This section shall apply to every broker or dealer registered with the Commission pursuant to section 15 of the Act that offers services to a retail investor.

(b) *Form CRS.* You must:

(1) Prepare Form CRS 17 CFR 249.640, by following the instructions in the form.

(2) File your current Form CRS electronically with the Commission through the Central Registration Depository ("Web CRD®") operated by the Financial Industry Regulatory Authority, Inc., and thereafter, file an amended Form CRS in accordance with the instructions in Form CRS.

(3) Amend your Form CRS as required by the instructions in the form.

(c) *Delivery of Form CRS.* You must:

(1) Deliver to each retail investor your current Form CRS before or at the earliest of:

(i) A recommendation of an account type, a securities transaction; or an investment strategy involving securities;

(ii) Placing an order for the retail investor; or

(iii) The opening of a brokerage account for the retail investor.

(2) Deliver to each retail investor who is an existing customer your current Form CRS before or at the time you:

(i) Open a new account that is different from the retail investor's existing account(s);

(ii) Recommend that the retail investor roll over assets from a retirement account into a new or existing account or investment; or

(iii) Recommend or provide a new brokerage service or investment that does not necessarily involve the opening of a new account and would not be held in an existing account.

(3) Post the current Form CRS prominently on your public website, if you have one, in a location and format that is easily accessible for retail investors.

(4) Communicate any changes made to Form CRS to each retail investor who is an existing customer within 60 days after the amendments are required to be made and without charge. The communication can be made by delivering the amended Form CRS or by communicating the information through another disclosure that is delivered to the retail investor.

(5) Deliver a current Form CRS to each retail investor within 30 days upon request.

(d) *Other disclosure obligations.* Delivering a Form CRS in compliance with this section does not relieve you of any other disclosure obligations arising under the federal securities laws and regulations or other laws or regulations (including the rules of a self-regulatory organization).

(e) *Definitions.* For purposes of this section:

(1) *Current Form CRS* means the most recent version of the Form CRS.

(2) *Retail investor* means a natural person, or the legal representative of such natural person, who seeks to receive or receives services primarily for personal, family or household purposes.

(f) *Transition rule.* (1) If you are registered with the Commission prior to June 30, 2020, pursuant to Section 15 of the Act, you must file your initial Form CRS with the Commission in accordance with section (b)(2) of this section, beginning on May 1, 2020, and by no later than June 30, 2020.

(2) On or after June 30, 2020, if you file an application for registration with

§ 240.17a-18

the Commission or have an application for registration pending with the Commission as a broker or dealer pursuant to Section 15 of the Act, you must begin to comply with this section by the date on which your registration application becomes effective pursuant to Section 15 of the Act, including by filing your Form CRS in accordance with paragraph (b)(2) of this section.

(3) Within 30 days after the date by which you are first required by paragraph (f) of this section to electronically file your initial Form CRS with the Commission, you must deliver to each of your existing customers who is a retail investor your current Form CRS.

(4) As of the date by which you are first required to electronically file your Form CRS with the Commission pursuant to this section, you must begin using your Form CRS as required to comply with paragraph (c) of this rule.

[84 FR 33629, July 12, 2019]

§ 240.17a-18 [Reserved]

§ 240.17a-19 Form X-17A-19 Report by national securities exchanges and registered national securities associations of changes in the membership status of any of their members.

Every national securities exchange and every registered national securities association shall file with the Commission at its principal office in Washington, DC, and with the Securities Investor Protection Corporation such information as is required by § 249.635 of this chapter on Form X-17A-19 within 5 business days of the occurrence of the initiation of the membership of any person or the suspension or termination of the membership of any member. Nothing in this section shall be deemed to relieve a national securities exchange or a registered national securities association of its responsibilities under § 240.17a-5(b)(5) except that, to the extent a national securities exchange or a registered national securities association promptly files a report on Form X-17A-19 including therewith, inter alia, information sufficient to satisfy the requirements of § 240.17a-5(b)(5), it shall not be required to file a report pursuant to § 240.17a-5(b). Upon the occurrence of the events described in this paragraph, every national securities exchange and every registered national securities association shall notify in writing such member of its responsibilities under § 240.17a-5(b).

[45 FR 39841, June 12, 1980]

§ 240.17a-21 Reports of the Municipal Securities Rulemaking Board.

(a) *Annual Report of the Municipal Securities Rulemaking Board.* The Municipal Securities Rulemaking Board shall file annual reports with the Commission as follows:

(1) Prior to October 1, 1976, the Municipal Securities Rulemaking Board shall file with the Commission an annual report for the period from its formation until June 30, 1976 and shall include whatever information, data and recommendations it considers advisable with regard to matters within its jurisdiction.

(2) Prior to December 1, 1977, the Municipal Securities Rulemaking Board shall file with the Commission an annual report for the period from July 1, 1976 until September 30, 1977 and shall include whatever information, data and recommendations it considers advisable with regard to matters within its jurisdiction.

(3) Prior to December 1 of each year beginning in 1978, the Municipal Securities Rulemaking Board shall file with the Commission an annual report for the twelve months immediately preceding October 1 of that year and shall include whatever information, data and recommendations it considers advisable with regard to matters within its jurisdiction.

(4) The Municipal Securities Rulemaking Board shall include in its annual report a statement and an analysis of its expenses and operations including:

(i) A balance sheet as of the end of the period covered by the report and a statement of revenues and expenses for the Board for that period;

(ii) The rules of the Board including any written interpretations of the rules or staff interpretive letters, except that this information may be included in the annual report once every three years and shall be up to date as

Securities and Exchange Commission § 240.17a–22

of the latest practicable date within 3 months of the date on which this information is filed. If the Board publishes or cooperates in the publication of this information on an annual or more frequent basis, in lieu of including such information in the annual report the Board may:

(A) Identify the publication in which such information is available, the name, address, and telephone number of the person from whom such publication may be obtained, and the price thereof; and

(B) Certify to the accuracy of such information as of its date. If the Board keeps this information up to date and makes it available to the Commission and the public upon request, in lieu of filing such information the Board may certify that the information is kept up to date and is available to the Commission and the public upon request;

(iii) The following information concerning members of the Board:

(A) Name;

(B) Dates of commencement and termination of present term of office;

(C) Length of time each member has held such office;

(D) Name of principal organization with which connected;

(E) Title; and

(F) City wherein the principal office of such organization is located;

(iv) Address of the Board, the name and address of each person authorized to receive notices on behalf of the Board from the Commission, and the name and address of counsel to the Board, if any; and

(v) A list, including addresses, as of the latest practicable date, alphabetically arranged, of all municipal securities brokers and municipal securities dealers which have paid to the Board fees and charges to defray the costs and expenses of operating the Board.

(5) Within 10 days after the discovery of any material inaccuracy in its annual report or in any amendment thereto the Municipal Securities Rulemaking Board shall file with the Commission an amendment correcting such inaccuracy.

(b) *Supplemental reports of the Municipal Securities Rulemaking Board.* The Municipal Securities Rulemaking Board shall file supplemental reports to the Commission as follows:

(1) Within 10 days after issuing or making generally available to municipal securities brokers and municipal securities dealers any materials (including notices, circulars, bulletins, lists, periodicals, etc.), the Municipal Securities Rulemaking Board shall file with the Commission three copies of such material (unless such material is filed with the Commission pursuant to Rule 19b–4).

(2) Within 10 days after any action is taken which renders no longer accurate any of the information required by paragraphs (a)(3) (iii), (iv), (v), and (vi) of this section to be contained in the annual report of the Municipal Securities Rulemaking Board (except action reported to the Commission pursuant to Rule 19b–4), the Board shall file with the Commission written notification in triplicate setting forth the nature of such action and the effective date thereof. Such notice may be filed either in the form of a letter or in the form of a notice made generally available to municipal securities brokers and municipal securities dealers.

[41 FR 36200, Aug. 27, 1976, as amended at 59 FR 66701, Dec. 28, 1994]

§ 240.17a–22 **Supplemental material of registered clearing agencies.**

Within ten days after issuing, or making generally available, to its participants or to other entities with whom it has a significant relationship, such as pledgees, transfer agents, or self-regulatory organizations, any material (including, for example, manuals, notices, circulars, bulletins, lists, or periodicals), a registered clearing agency shall file three copies of such material with the Commission. A registered clearing agency for which the Commission is not the appropriate regulatory agency shall at the same time file one copy of such material with its appropriate regulatory agency.

[45 FR 73914, Nov. 7, 1980]

§ 240.17a-25

§ 240.17a-25 Electronic submission of securities transaction information by exchange members, brokers, and dealers.

(a) Every member, broker, or dealer subject to § 240.17a-3 shall, upon request, electronically submit to the Commission the securities transaction information as required in this section:

(1) If the transaction was a proprietary transaction effected or caused to be effected by the member, broker, or dealer for any account in which such member, broker, or dealer, or person associated with the member, broker, or dealer, is directly or indirectly interested, such member, broker or dealer shall submit the following information:

(i) Clearing house number, or alpha symbol of the member, broker, or dealer submitting the information;

(ii) Clearing house number(s), or alpha symbol(s) of the member(s), broker(s) or dealer(s) on the opposite side of the transaction;

(iii) Identifying symbol assigned to the security;

(iv) Date transaction was executed;

(v) Number of shares, or quantity of bonds or options contracts, for each specific transaction; whether each transaction was a purchase, sale, or short sale; and, if an options contract, whether open long or short or close long or short;

(vi) Transaction price;

(vii) Account number; and

(viii) The identity of the exchange or other market where the transaction was executed.

(2) If the transaction was effected or caused to be effected by the member, broker, or dealer for any customer account, such member, broker, or dealer shall submit the following information:

(i) Information contained in paragraphs (a)(1)(i) through (a)(1)(viii) of this section;

(ii) Customer name, address(es), branch office number, registered representative number, whether the order was solicited or unsolicited, date account opened, and the customer's tax identification number(s); and

(iii) If the transaction was effected for a customer of another member, broker, or dealer, whether the other member, broker, or dealer was acting as principal or agent on the transaction.

(b) In addition to the information in paragraph (a) of this section, a member, broker, or dealer shall, upon request, electronically submit to the Commission the following securities transaction information for transactions involving entities that trade using multiple accounts:

(1)(i) If part or all of an account's transactions at the reporting member, broker, or dealer have been transferred or otherwise forwarded to one or more accounts at another member, broker, or dealer, an identifier for this type of transaction; and

(ii) If part or all of an account's transactions at the reporting member, broker, or dealer have been transferred or otherwise received from one or more other members, brokers, or dealers, an identifier for this type of transaction.

(2)(i) If part or all of an account's transactions at the reporting member, broker, or dealer have been transferred or otherwise received from another account at the reporting member, broker, or dealer, an identifier for this type of transaction; and

(ii) If part or all of an account's transactions at the reporting member, broker, or dealer have been transferred or otherwise forwarded to one or more other accounts at the reporting member, broker, or dealer, an identifier for this type of transaction.

(3) If an account's transaction was processed by a depository institution, the identifier assigned to the account by the depository institution.

(c) Every member, broker, or dealer shall, upon request, submit to the Commission and, keep current, information containing the full name, title, address, telephone number(s), facsimile number(s), and electronic-mail address(es) for each person designated by the member, broker, or dealer as responsible for processing securities transaction information requests from the Commission.

(d) The member, broker, or dealer should comply with the format for the electronic submission of the securities transaction information described in paragraphs (a) and (b) of this section as specified by the member, broker, or

Securities and Exchange Commission §240.17d–2

dealer's designated self-regulatory organization under §240.17d–1, unless otherwise specified by Commission rule.

[66 FR 35843, July 9, 2001]

§240.17d–1 Examination for compliance with applicable financial responsibility rules.

(a) Where a member of SIPC is a member of more than one self-regulatory organization, the Commission shall designate by written notice to one of such organizations responsibility for examining such member for compliance with applicable financial responsibility rules. In making such designations the Commission shall take into consideration the regulatory capabilities and procedures of the self-regulatory organizations, availability of staff, convenience of location, unnecessary regulatory duplication, and such other factors as the Commission may consider germane to the protection of investors, the cooperation and coordination among self-regulatory organizations, and the development of a national market system and a national system for the clearance and settlement of securities transactions.

(b) Upon designation of responsibility pursuant to paragraph (a) of this section, all other self-regulatory organizations of which such person is a member shall be relieved of such responsibility to the extent specified.

(c) After the Commission has acted pursuant to paragraphs (a) and (b) of this section, any self-regulatory organization relieved of responsibility with respect to a member may notify customers of, and persons doing business with, such member of the limited nature of its responsibility for such member's compliance with applicable financial responsibility rules.

[41 FR 18809, May 7, 1976]

§240.17d–2 Program for allocation of regulatory responsibility.

(a) Any two or more self-regulatory organizations may file with the Commission within ninety (90) days of the effective date of this rule, and thereafter as changes in designation are necessary or appropriate, a plan for allocating among the self-regulatory organizations the responsibility to receive regulatory reports from persons who are members or participants of more than one of such self-regulatory organizations to examine such persons for compliance, or to enforce compliance by such persons, with specified provisions of the Securities Exchange Act of 1934, the rules and regulations thereunder, and the rules of such self-regulatory organizations, or to carry out other specified regulatory functions with respect to such persons.

(b) Any plan filed hereunder may contain provisions for the allocation among the parties of expenses reasonably incurred by the self-regulatory organization having regulatory responsibilities under the plan.

(c) After appropriate notice and opportunity for comment, the Commission may, by written notice, declare such a plan, or any part of the plan, effective if it finds the plan, or any part thereof, necessary or appropriate in the public interest and for the protection of investors, to foster cooperation and coordination among self-regulatory organizations, or to remove impediments to and foster the development of the national market system and a national system for the clearance and settlement of securities transactions and in conformity with the factors set forth in section 17(d) of the Securities Exchange Act of 1934.

(d) Upon the effectiveness of such a plan or part thereof, any self-regulatory organization which is a party to the plan shall be relieved of responsibility as to any person for whom such responsibility is allocated under the plan to another self-regulatory organization to the extent of such allocation.

(e) Nothing herein shall preclude any self-regulatory organization from entering into more than one plan filed hereunder.

(f) After the Commission has declared a plan or part thereof effective pursuant to paragraph (c) of this section or acted pursuant to paragraph (g) of this section, a self-regulatory organization relieved of responsibility may notify customers of, and persons doing business with, such member or participant of the limited nature of its responsibility for such member's or participant's acts, practices, and course of business.

§ 240.17f-1

(g) In the event that plans declared effective pursuant to paragraph (c) of this section do not provide for all members or participants or do not allocate all regulatory responsibilities, the Commission may, after due consideration of the factors enumerated in section 17(d)(1) and notice and opportunity for comment, designate one or more of the self-regulatory organizations responsible for specified regulatory responsibilities with respect to such members or participants.

[41 FR 49093, Nov. 8, 1976]

§ 240.17f-1 Requirements for reporting and inquiry with respect to missing, lost, counterfeit or stolen securities.

(a) *Definitions.* For purposes of this section:

(1) The term *reporting institution* shall include every national securities exchange, member thereof, registered securities association, broker, dealer, municipal securities dealer, government securities broker, government securities dealer, registered transfer agent, registered clearing agency, participant therein, member of the Federal Reserve System and bank whose deposits are insured by the Federal Deposit Insurance Corporation;

(2) The term *uncertificated security* shall mean a security not represented by an instrument and the transfer of which is registered upon books maintained for that purpose by or on behalf of the issuer;

(3) The term *global certificate securities issue* shall mean a securities issue for which a single master certificate representing the entire issue is registered in the nominee name of a registered clearing agency and for which beneficial owners cannot receive negotiable securities certificates;

(4) The term *customer* shall mean any person with whom the reporting institution has entered into at least one prior securities-related transaction; and

(5) The term *securities-related transaction* shall mean a purpose, sale or pledge of investment securities, or a custodial arrangement for investment securities.

(6) The term *securities certificate* means any physical instrument that represents or purports to represent ownership in a security that was printed by or on behalf of the issuer thereof and shall include any such instrument that is or was:

(i) Printed but not issued;

(ii) Issued and outstanding, including treasury securities;

(iii) Cancelled, which for this purpose means either or both of the procedures set forth in § 240.17Ad-19(a)(1); or

(iv) Counterfeit or reasonably believed to be counterfeit.

(7) The term *issuer* shall include an issuer's:

(i) Transfer agent(s), paying agent(s), tender agent(s), and person(s) providing similar services; and

(ii) Corporate predecessor(s) and successor(s).

(8) The term *missing* shall include any securities certificate that:

(i) Cannot be located or accounted for, but is not believed to be lost or stolen; or

(ii) A transfer agent claims or believes was destroyed in any manner other than by the transfer agent's own certificate destruction procedures as provided in § 240.17Ad-19.

(b) Every reporting institution shall register with the Commission or its designee in accordance with instructions issued by the Commission except:

(1) A member of a national securities exchange who effects securities transactions through the trading facilities of the exchange and has not received or held customer securities within the last six months;

(2) A reporting institution that, within the last six months, limited its securities activities exclusively to uncertificated securities, global securities issues or any securities issue for which neither record nor beneficial owners can obtain a negotiable securities certificate; or

(3) A reporting institution whose business activities, within the last six months, did not involve the handling of securities certificates.

(c) *Reporting requirements*—(1) *Stolen securities.* (i) Every reporting institution shall report to the Commission or its designee, and to a registered transfer agent for the issue, the discovery of the theft or loss of any securities certificates where there is substantial

Securities and Exchange Commission § 240.17f–1

basis for believing that criminal activity was involved. Such report shall be made within one business day of the discovery and, if the certificate numbers of the securities cannot be ascertained at that time, they shall be reported as soon thereafter as possible.

(ii) Every reporting institution shall promptly report to the Federal Bureau of Investigation upon the discovery of the theft or loss of any securities certificate where there is substantial basis for believing that criminal activity was involved.

(2) *Missing or lost securities.* Every reporting institution shall report to the Commission or its designee, and to a registered transfer agent for the issue, the discovery of the loss of any securities certificate where criminal actions are not suspected when the securities certificate has been missing or lost for a period of two business days. Such report shall be made within one business day of the end of such period except that:

(i) Securities certificates lost, missing, or stolen while in transit to customers, transfer agents, banks, brokers or dealers shall be reported by the delivering institution by the later of two business days after notice of non-receipt or as soon after such notice as the certificate numbers of the securities can be ascertained.

(ii) Where a shipment of retired securities certificates is in transit between any transfer agents, banks, brokers, dealers, or other reporting institutions, with no affiliation existing between such entities, and the delivering institution fails to receive notice of receipt or non-receipt of the certificates, the delivering institution shall act to determine the facts. In the event of non-delivery where the certificates are not recovered by the delivering institution, the delivering institution shall report the certificates as lost, stolen, or missing to the Commission or its designee within a reasonable time under the circumstances but in any event within twenty business days from the date of shipment.

(iii) Securities certificates considered lost or missing as a result of securities counts or verifications required by rule, regulation or otherwise (e.g., dividend record date verification made as a result of firm policy or internal audit function report) shall be reported by the later of ten business days after completion of such securities count or verification or as soon after such count or verification as the certificate numbers of the securities can be ascertained.

(iv) Securities certificates not received during the completion of delivery, deposit or withdrawal shall be reported in the following manner:

(A) Where delivery of the securities certificates is through a clearing agency, the delivering institution shall supply to the receiving institution the certificate number of the security within two business days from the date of request from the receiving institution. The receiving institution shall report within one business day of notification of the certificate number;

(B) Where the delivery of securities certificates is in person and where the delivering institution has a receipt, the delivering institution shall supply the receiving institution the certificate numbers of the securities within two business days from the date of request from the receiving institution. The receiving institution shall report within one business day of notification of the certificate number;

(C) Where the delivery of securities certificates is in person and where the delivering institution has no receipt, the delivering institution shall report within two business days of notification of non-receipt by the receiving institution; or

(D) Where delivery of securities certificates is made by mail or via draft, if payment is not received within ten business days, the delivering institution shall confirm with the receiving institution the failure to receive such delivery; if confirmation shows non-receipt, the delivering institution shall report within two business days of such confirmation.

(3) *Counterfeit securities.* Every reporting institution shall report the discovery of any counterfeit securities certificate to the Commission or its designee, to a registered transfer agent for the issue, and to the Federal Bureau of Investigation within one business day of such discovery.

§ 240.17f-1

(4) *Transfer agent reporting obligations.* Every transfer agent shall make the reports required above only if it receives notification of the loss, theft or counterfeiting from a non-reporting institution or if it receives notification other than on a Form X–17F–1A or if the certificate was in its possession at the time of the loss.

(5) *Recovery.* Every reporting institution that originally reported a lost, missing or stolen securities certificate pursuant to this Section shall report recovery of that securities certificate to the Commission or its designee and to a registered transfer agent for the issue within one business day of such recovery or finding. Every reporting institution that originally made a report in which criminality was indicated also shall notify the Federal Bureau of Investigation that the securities certificate has been recovered.

(6) *Information to be reported.* All reports made pursuant to this Section shall include, if applicable or available, the following information with respect to each securities certificate:

(i) Issuer;
(ii) Type of security and series;
(iii) Date of issue;
(iv) Maturity date;
(v) Denomination;
(vi) Interest rate;
(vii) Certificate number, including alphabetical prefix or suffix;
(viii) Name in which registered;
(ix) Distinguishing characteristics, if counterfeit;
(x) Date of discovery of loss or recovery;
(xi) CUSIP number;
(xii) Financial Industry Numbering System ("FINS") Number; and
(xiii) Type of loss.

(7) *Forms.* Reporting institutions shall make all reports to the Commission or its designee and to a registered transfer agent for the issue pursuant to this section on Form X–17F–1A. Reporting institutions shall make reports to the Federal Bureau of Investigation pursuant to this Section on Form X–17F–1A, unless the reporting institution is a member of the Federal Reserve System or a bank whose deposits are insured by the Federal Deposit Insurance Corporation, in which case reports may be made on the form required by the institution's appropriate regulatory agency for reports to the Federal Bureau of Investigation.

(d) *Required inquiries.* (1) Every reporting institution (except a reporting institution that, acting in its capacity as transfer agent, paying agent, exchange agent or tender agent for an equity issue, or registrar for a bond or other debt issue, compares all transactions against a shareholder or bondholder list and a current list of stop transfers) shall inquire of the Commission or its designee with respect to every securities certificate which comes into its possession or keeping, whether by pledge, transfer or otherwise, to ascertain whether such securities certificate has been reported as missing, lost, counterfeit or stolen, unless:

(i) The securities certificate is received directly from the issuer or issuing agent at issuance;

(ii) The securities certificate is received from another reporting institution or from a Federal Reserve Bank or Branch;

(iii) The securities certificate is received from a customer of the reporting institution; and

(A) Is registered in the name of such customer or its nominee; or

(B) Was previously sold to such customer, as verified by the internal records of the reporting institution;

(iv) The securities certificate is received as part of a transaction which has an aggregate face value of $10,000 or less in the case of bonds, or market value of $10,000 or less in the case of stocks; or

(v) The securities certificate is received directly from a drop which is affiliated with a reporting institution for the purposes of receiving or delivering certificates on behalf of the reporting institution.

(2) *Form of inquiry.* Inquiries shall be made in such manner as prescribed by the Commission or its designee.

(3) A reporting institution shall make required inquiries by the end of the fifth business day after a securities certificate comes into its possession or keeping, provided that such inquiries shall be made before the certificate is sold, used as collateral, or sent to another reporting institution.

Securities and Exchange Commission § 240.17f-2

(e) *Permissive reports and inquiries.* Every reporting insitution may report to or inquire of the Commission or its designee with respect to any securities certificate not otherwise required by this section to be the subject of a report or inquiry. The Commission on written request or upon its own motion may permit reports to and inquiries of the system by any other person or entity upon such terms and conditions as it deems appropriate and necessary in the public interest and for the protection of investors.

(f) *Exemptions.* The following types of securities are not subject to paragraphs (c) and (d) of this section:

(1) Security issues not assigned CUSIP numbers;

(2) Bond coupons;

(3) Uncertificated securities;

(4) Global securities issues; and

(5) Any securities issue for which neither record nor beneficial owners can obtain a negotiable securities certificates.

(g) *Recordkeeping.* Every reporting institution shall maintain and preserve in an easily accessible place for three years copies of all Forms X–17F–1A filed pursuant to this section, all agreements between reporting institutions regarding registration or other aspects of this section, and all confirmations or other information received from the Commission or its designee as a result of inquiry.

(Secs. 2, 17, and 23, 15 U.S.C. 78b, 78q, 78w)

[44 FR 31503, May 31, 1979; 45 FR 14022, Mar. 3, 1980, as amended at 53 FR 37289, Sept. 26, 1988; 53 FR 40721, Oct. 18, 1988; 68 FR 74400, Dec. 23, 2003]

§ 240.17f-2 Fingerprinting of securities industry personnel.

(a) *Exemptions for the fingerprinting requirement.* Except as otherwise provided in paragraph (a)(1) or (2) of this section, every member of a national securities exchange, broker, dealer, registered transfer agent and registered clearing agency shall require that each of its partners, directors, officers and employees be fingerprinted and shall submit, or cause to be submitted, the fingerprints of such persons to the Attorney General of the United States or its designee for identification and appropriate processing.

(1) *Permissive exemptions.* Every member of a national securities exchange, broker, dealer, registered transfer agent and registered clearing agency may claim one or more of the exemptions in paragraph (a)(1) (i), (ii), (iii) or (iv) of this section; *Provided,* That all the requirements of paragraph (e) of this section are also satisfied.

(i) *Member of a national securities exchange, broker, dealer or registered clearing agency.* Every person who is a partner, director, officer or employee of a member of a national securities exchange, broker, dealer, or registered clearing agency shall be exempt if that person:

(A) Is not engaged in the sale of securities;

(B) Does not regularly have access to the keeping, handling or processing of (*1*) securities, (*2*) monies, or (*3*) the original books and records relating to the securities or the monies; and

(C) Does not have direct supervisory responsibility over persons engaged in the activities referred to in paragraphs (a)(1)(i) (A) and (B) of this section.

(ii) *Registered transfer agents.* Every person who is a partner, director, officer or employee of a registered transfer agent shall be exempt if that person:

(A) Is not engaged in transfer agent functions (as defined in section 3(a)(25) of the Securities Exchange Act of 1934) or activities incidental thereto; or

(B) Meets the conditions in paragraphs (a)(1)(i) (B) and (C) of this section.

(iii) *Registered broker-dealers engaged in sales of certain securities.* Every partner, director, officer and employee of a registered broker or dealer who satisfies paragraph (a)(1)(i)(B) of this section shall be exempt if that broker or dealer:

(A) Is engaged exclusively in the sale of shares of registered open-end management investment companies, variable contracts, or interests in limited partnerships, unit investment trusts or real estate investment trusts; *Provided,* That those securities ordinarily are not evidenced by certificates;

(B) Is current in its continuing obligation under §§ 240.15b1–1 and 15b3–1(b) to update Item 10 of Form BD to disclose the existence of any statutory disqualification set forth in sections

635

§ 240.17f-2

3(a)(39), 15(b)(4) and 15(b)(6) of the Securities Exchange Act of 1934;

(C) Has insurance or bonding indemnifying it for losses to customers caused by the fraudulent or criminal acts of any of its partners, directors, officers or employees for whom an exemption is being claimed under paragraph (a)(1)(iii) of this section; and

(D) Is subject to the jurisdiction of a state insurance department with respect to its sale of variable contracts.

(iv) *Illegible fingerprint cards.* Every person who is a partner, director, officer or employee shall be exempt if that member of a national securities exchange, broker, dealer, registered transfer agent or registered clearing agency, on at least three occasions:

(A) Attempts in good faith to obtain from such person a complete set of fingerprints acceptable to the Attorney General or its designee for identification and appropriate processing by requiring that person to be fingerprinted, by having that person's fingerprints rolled by a person competent to do so and by submitting the fingerprint cards for that person to the Attorney General of the United States or its designee in accordance with proper procedures;

(B) Has that person's fingerprint cards returned to it by the Attorney General of the United States or its designee without that person's fingerprints having been identified because the fingerprints were illegible; and

(C) Retains the returned fingerprint cards and any other required records in accordance with paragraph (d) of this section and §§ 240.17a-3(a)(13), 17a-4(e)(2) and 240.17Ad-7(e)(1) under the Securities Exchange Act of 1934.

(2) *Other exemptions by application to the Commission.* The Commission, upon specified terms, conditions and periods, may grant exemptions to any class of partners, directors, officers or employees of any member of a national securities exchange, broker, dealer, registered transfer agent or registered clearing agency, if the Commission finds that such action is not inconsistent with the public interest or the protection of investors.

(b) *Fingerprinting pursuant to other law.* Every member of a national securities exchange, broker, dealer, registered transfer agent and registered clearing agency may satisfy the fingerprinting requirement of section 17(f)(2) of the Securities Exchange Act of 1934 as to any partner, director, officer or employee, if:

(1) The person, in connection with his or her present employment with such organization, has been fingerprinted pursuant to any other law, statute, rule or regulation of any state or federal government or agency thereof;

(2) The fingerprint cards for that person are submitted, or are caused to be submitted, to the Attorney General of the United States or its designee for identification and appropriate processing, and the Attorney General or its designee has processed those fingerprint cards; and

(3) The processed fingerprint cards or any substitute records, together with any information received from the Attorney General or its designee, are maintained in accordance with paragraph (d) of this section.

(c) *Fingerprinting plans of self-regulatory organizations.* The fingerprinting requirement of section 17(f)(2) of the Securities Exchange Act of 1934 may be satisfied by submitting appropriate and complete fingerprint cards to a registered national securities exchange or to a registered national securities association which, pursuant to a plan filed with, and declared effective by, the Commission, forwards such fingerprint cards to the Attorney General of the United States or its designee for identification and appropriate processing. Any plan filed by a registered national securities exchange or a registered national securities association shall not become effective, unless declared effective by the Commission as not inconsistent with the public interest or the protection of investors; and, in declaring any such plan effective, the Commission may impose any terms and conditions relating to the provisions of the plan and the period of its effectiveness as it may deem necessary or appropriate in the public interest, for the protection of investors, or otherwise in furtherance of the purposes of the Securities Exchange Act of 1934.

(d) *Record maintenance*—(1) *Maintenance of processed fingerprint cards and other related information.* Every member

Securities and Exchange Commission § 240.17f–2

of a national securities exchange, broker, dealer, registered transfer agent and registered clearing agency shall maintain the processed fingerprint card or any substitute record when such card is not returned after processing, together with any information received from the Attorney General or its designee, for every person required to be fingerprinted under section 17(f)(2) of the Securities Exchange Act of 1934 and for persons who have complied with this section pursuant to paragraph (b) or (c) of this section. Every substitute record shall state the name of the person whose fingerprint card was submitted to the Attorney General of the United States, the name of the member of a national securities exchange, broker, dealer, registered transfer agent or registered clearing agency that submitted the fingerprint card, the name of the person or organization that rolled the fingerprints, the date on which the fingerprints were rolled, and the date the fingerprint card was submitted to the Attorney General of the United States. The processed fingerprint card and every other substitute record containing the information required by this paragraph, together with any information received from the Attorney General of the United States, shall be kept in an easily accessible place at the organization's principal office and shall be made available upon request to the Commission, the appropriate regulatory agency (if not the Commission) or other designated examining authority. The organization's principal office must provide to the regional, branch or satellite office actually employing the person written evidence that the person's fingerprints have been processed by the FBI, and must provide to that office a copy of any criminal history record information received from the FBI. All fingerprint cards, records and information required to be maintained under this paragraph shall be retained for a period of not less than three years after termination of that person's employment or relationship with the organization.

(2) *Record maintenance by designated examining authorities.* The records required to be maintained and preserved by a member of a national securities exchange, broker, or dealer pursuant to the requirements of paragraph (d)(1) of this section may be maintained and preserved on behalf of that member, broker, or dealer by a self-regulatory organization that is also the designated examining authority for that member, broker or dealer, *Provided* That the self-regulatory organization has filed in accordance with § 240.17f–2(c) a fingerprinting plan or amendments to an existing plan concerning the storage and maintenance of records and that plan, as amended, has been declared effective by the Commission, and *Provided Further* That:

(i) Such records are subject at any time, or from time to time, to reasonable periodic, special or other examinations by representatives of the Commission; and

(ii) The self-regulatory organization furnishes to the Commission, upon demand, at either the principal office or at the regional office complete, correct and current hard copies of any and all such records.

(3) *Reproduction of records on microfilm.* The records required to be maintained pursuant to paragraph (d)(1) of this section may be produced or reproduced on microfilm and preserved in that form. If such microfilm substitution for hard copy is made by a member of a national securities exchange, broker, dealer, registered transfer agent or registered clearing agency, or by a self-regulatory organization maintaining and storing records pursuant to paragraph (d)(2) of this section, it shall at all times:

(i) Have available for examination by the Commission, the appropriate regulatory agency (if not the Commission) or other designated examining authority, facilities for the immediate, easily readable projection of the microfilm and for the production of easily readable and legible facsimile enlargements;

(ii) File and index the films in such a manner as to permit the immediate location and retrieval of any particular record;

(iii) Be ready to provide, and immediately provide, any facsimile enlargement which the Commission, the appropriate regulatory agency (if not the

§ 240.17g-1

Commission) or other designated examining authority by their examiners or other representatives may request; and

(iv) For the period for which the microfilm records are required to be maintained, store separately from the original microfilm records a copy of the microfilm records.

(e) *Notice requirement.* Every member of a national securities exchange, broker, dealer, registered transfer agent and registered clearing agency that claims one or more of the exemptions in paragraph (a)(1) of this section shall make and keep current a statement entitled "Notice Pursuant to Rule 17f–2" containing the information specified in paragraph (e)(1) of this section.

(1) *Contents of statement.* The Notice required by paragraph (e) of this section shall:

(i) State the name of the organization and state whether it is a member of a national securities exchange, broker, dealer, registered transfer agent, or registered clearing agency;

(ii) Identify by division, department, class, or name and position within the organization all persons who are claimed to have satisfied the fingerprinting requirement of section 17(f)(2) of the Securities Exchange Act of 1934 pursuant to paragraph (b) of this section;

(iii) Identify by division, department, class, title or position within the organization all persons claimed to be exempt under paragraphs (a)(1)(i) through (iii) of this section, and identify by name all persons claimed to be exempt under paragraph (a)(1)(iv). Persons identified under this paragraph (e)(1)(iii) shall be exempt from the requirement of section 17(f)(2) of the Securities Exchange Act of 1934 unless notified to the contrary by the Commission;

(iv) Describe, in generic terms, the nature of the duties of the person or classes of persons, and the nature of the functions and operations of the divisions and departments, identified as exempt in paragraph (e)(1)(iii) of this section; and

(v) Describe the security measures utilized to ensure that only those persons who have been fingerprinted in accordance with the fingerprinting requirement of section 17(f)(2) of the Securities Exchange Act of 1934 or who are exempt under paragraph (a)(1)(iv) of this section have access to the keeping, handling or processing of securities or monies or the original books and records relating thereto.

(2) *Record maintenance.* A copy of the Notice required to be made and kept current under paragraph (e) of this section shall be kept in an easily accessible place at the organization's principal office and at the office employing the persons for whom exemptions are claimed and shall be made available upon request for inspection by the Commission, appropriate regulatory agency (if not the Commission) or other designated examining authority.

(3) *Exemption from the notice requirement.* A registered transfer agent that performs transfer agent functions only on behalf of itself as an issuer and that receives fewer than 500 items for transfer and fewer than 500 items for processing during any six consecutive months shall be exempt from the notice requirement of paragraph (c) of this section.

[47 FR 54060, Dec. 1, 1982]

NATIONALLY RECOGNIZED STATISTICAL RATING ORGANIZATIONS

SOURCE: 72 FR 33620, June 18, 2007, unless otherwise noted.

§ 240.17g-1 Application for registration as a nationally recognized statistical rating organization.

(a) *Initial application.* A credit rating agency applying to the Commission to be registered under section 15E of the Act (15 U.S.C. 78o–7) as a nationally recognized statistical rating organization must file with the Commission two paper copies of an initial application on Form NRSRO (§ 249b.300 of this chapter) that follows all applicable instructions for the Form.

(b) *Application to register for an additional class of credit ratings.* A nationally recognized statistical rating organization applying to register for an additional class of the credit ratings described in section 3(a)(62)(B) of the Act (15 U.S.C. 78c(a)(62)(B)) must file with the Commission two paper copies of an

Securities and Exchange Commission

§ 240.17g–1

application to add a class of credit ratings on Form NRSRO that follows all applicable instructions for the Form. The application will be subject to the requirements of section 15E(a)(2) of the Act (15 U.S.C. 78o–7(a)(2)).

(c) *Supplementing an application prior to final action by the Commission.* An applicant must promptly file with the Commission two paper copies of a written notice if information submitted to the Commission in an initial application to be registered as a nationally recognized statistical rating organization or in an application to register for an additional class of credit ratings is found to be or becomes materially inaccurate prior to the date of a Commission order granting or denying the application. The notice must identify the information that was found to be materially inaccurate. The applicant also must promptly file with the Commission two paper copies of an application supplement on Form NRSRO that follows all applicable instructions for the Form.

(d) *Withdrawing an application.* An applicant may withdraw an initial application to be registered as a nationally recognized statistical rating organization or an application to register for an additional class of credit ratings prior to the date of a Commission order granting or denying the application. To withdraw the application, the applicant must furnish the Commission with two paper copies of a written notice of withdrawal executed by a duly authorized person.

(e) *Update of registration.* A nationally recognized statistical rating organization amending materially inaccurate information in its application for registration pursuant to section 15E(b)(1) of the Act (15 U.S.C. 78o–7(b)(1)) must promptly file with the Commission an update of its registration on Form NRSRO that follows all applicable instructions for the Form. A Form NRSRO and the information and documents in Exhibits 2 through 9 to Form NRSRO, as applicable, filed under this paragraph must be filed electronically with the Commission on EDGAR as a PDF document in the format required by the EDGAR Filer Manual, as defined in Rule 11 of Regulation S–T (§ 232.11 of this chapter).

(f) *Annual certification.* A nationally recognized statistical rating organization amending its application for registration pursuant to section 15E(b)(2) of the Act (15 U.S.C. 78o–7(b)(2)) must file with the Commission an annual certification on Form NRSRO that follows all applicable instructions for the Form not later than 90 days after the end of each calendar year. A Form NRSRO and the information and documents in Exhibits 1 through 9 to Form NRSRO filed under this paragraph must be filed electronically with the Commission on EDGAR as a PDF document in the format required by the EDGAR Filer Manual, as defined in Rule 11 of Regulation S–T.

(g) *Withdrawal from registration.* A nationally recognized statistical rating organization withdrawing from registration pursuant to section 15E(e)(1) of the Act (15 U.S.C. 78o–7(e)(1)) must furnish the Commission with a notice of withdrawal from registration on Form NRSRO that follows all applicable instructions for the Form. The withdrawal from registration will become effective 45 calendar days after the notice is furnished to the Commission upon such terms and conditions as the Commission may establish as necessary in the public interest or for the protection of investors. A Form NRSRO furnished under this paragraph must be furnished electronically with the Commission on EDGAR as a PDF document in the format required by the EDGAR Filer Manual, as defined in Rule 11 of Regulation S–T.

(h) *Filing or furnishing Form NRSRO.* A Form NRSRO filed or furnished, as applicable, under any paragraph of this section will be considered filed with or furnished to the Commission on the date the Commission receives a complete and properly executed Form NRSRO that follows all applicable instructions for the Form. Information filed or furnished, as applicable, on a confidential basis and for which confidential treatment has been requested pursuant to applicable Commission rules will be accorded confidential treatment to the extent permitted by law.

(i) *Public availability of Form NRSRO.* A nationally recognized statistical rating organization must make its current

§ 240.17g-2

Form NRSRO and information and documents in Exhibits 1 through 9 to Form NRSRO publicly and freely available on an easily accessible portion of its corporate Internet Web site within 10 business days after the date of the Commission order granting an initial application for registration as a nationally recognized statistical rating organization or an application to register for an additional class of credit ratings and within 10 business days after filing with or furnishing to, as applicable, the Commission a Form NRSRO under paragraph (e), (f), or (g) of this section. In addition, a nationally recognized statistical rating organization must make its most recently filed Exhibit 1 to Form NRSRO freely available in writing to any individual who requests a copy of the Exhibit.

[13 FR 8178, Dec. 22, 1948, as amended at 79 FR 55262, Sept. 15, 2014]

§ 240.17g-2 Records to be made and retained by nationally recognized statistical rating organizations.

(a) *Records required to be made and retained.* A nationally recognized statistical rating organization must make and retain the following books and records, which must be complete and current:

(1) Records of original entry into the accounting system of the nationally recognized statistical rating organization and records reflecting entries to and balances in all general ledger accounts of the nationally recognized statistical rating organization for each fiscal year.

(2) Records with respect to each current credit rating of the nationally recognized statistical rating organization indicating (as applicable):

(i) The identity of any credit analyst(s) that participated in determining the credit rating;

(ii) The identity of the person(s) that approved the credit rating before it was issued;

(iii) If a quantitative model was a substantial component in the process of determining the credit rating of a security or money market instrument issued by an asset pool or as part of any asset-backed securities transaction, a record of the rationale for any material difference between the credit rating implied by the model and the final credit rating issued; and

(iv) Whether the credit rating was solicited or unsolicited.

(3) An account record for each person (for example, an obligor, issuer, underwriter, or other user) that has paid the nationally recognized statistical rating organization for the issuance or maintenance of a credit rating indicating:

(i) The identity and address of the person; and

(ii) The credit rating(s) determined or maintained for the person.

(4) An account record for each subscriber to the credit ratings and/or credit analysis reports of the nationally recognized statistical rating organization indicating the identity and address of the subscriber.

(5) A record listing the general types of services and products offered by the nationally recognized statistical rating organization.

(6) A record documenting the established procedures and methodologies used by the nationally recognized statistical rating organization to determine credit ratings.

(7) A record that lists each security and money market instrument and its corresponding credit rating issued by an asset pool or as part of any asset-backed securities transaction where the nationally recognized statistical rating organization, in determining the credit rating for the security or money market instrument, treats assets within such pool or as a part of such transaction that are not subject to a credit rating of the nationally recognized statistical rating organization by any or a combination of the following methods:

(i) Determining credit ratings for the unrated assets;

(ii) Performing credit assessments or determining private credit ratings for the unrated assets;

(iii) Determining credit ratings or private credit ratings, or performing credit assessments for the unrated assets by taking into consideration the internal credit analysis of another person; or

(iv) Determining credit ratings or private credit ratings, or performing credit assessments for the unrated assets by taking into consideration (but not necessarily adopting) the credit

Securities and Exchange Commission § 240.17g–2

ratings of another nationally recognized statistical rating organization.

(8) For each outstanding credit rating, a record showing all rating actions and the date of such actions from the initial credit rating to the current credit rating identified by the name of the rated security or obligor and, if applicable, the CUSIP of the rated security or the Central Index Key (CIK) number of the rated obligor.

(9) A record documenting the policies and procedures the nationally recognized statistical rating organization is required to establish, maintain, and enforce pursuant to section 15E(h)(4)(A) of the Act (15 U.S.C. 78o–7(h)(4)(A)) and § 240.17g–8(c).

(b) *Records required to be retained.* A nationally recognized statistical rating organization must retain the following books and records (excluding drafts of documents) that relate to its business as a credit rating agency:

(1) Significant records (for example, bank statements, invoices, and trial balances) underlying the information included in the annual financial reports the nationally recognized statistical rating organization filed with or furnished to, as applicable, the Commission pursuant to § 240.17g–3.

(2) Internal records, including nonpublic information and work papers, used to form the basis of a credit rating issued by the nationally recognized statistical rating organization.

(3) Credit analysis reports, credit assessment reports, and private credit rating reports of the nationally recognized statistical rating organization and internal records, including nonpublic information and work papers, used to form the basis for the opinions expressed in these reports.

(4) Compliance reports and compliance exception reports.

(5) Internal audit plans, internal audit reports, documents relating to internal audit follow-up measures, and all records identified by the internal auditors of the nationally recognized statistical rating organization as necessary to perform the audit of an activity that relates to its business as a credit rating agency.

(6) Marketing materials of the nationally recognized statistical rating organization that are published or otherwise made available to persons that are not associated with the nationally recognized statistical rating organization.

(7) External and internal communications, including electronic communications, received and sent by the nationally recognized statistical rating organization and its employees that relate to initiating, determining, maintaining, monitoring, changing,, or withdrawing a credit rating.

(8) Any written communications received from persons not associated with the nationally recognized statistical rating organization that contain complaints about the performance of a credit analyst in initiating, determining, maintaining, monitoring, changing, or withdrawing a credit rating.

(9) Internal documents that contain information, analysis, or statistics that were used to develop a procedure or methodology to treat the credit ratings of another nationally recognized statistical rating organization for the purpose of determining a credit rating for a security or money market instrument issued by an asset pool or part of any asset-backed securities transaction.

(10) For each security or money market instrument identified in the record required to be made and retained under paragraph (a)(7) of this section, any document that contains a description of how assets within such pool or as a part of such transaction not rated by the nationally recognized statistical rating organization but rated by another nationally recognized statistical rating organization were treated for the purpose of determining the credit rating of the security or money market instrument.

(11) Forms NRSRO (including Exhibits and accompanying information and documents) the nationally recognized statistical rating organization filed with or furnished to, as applicable, the Commission.

(12) The internal control structure the nationally recognized statistical rating organization is required to establish, maintain, enforce, and document pursuant to section 15E(c)(3)(A) of the Act (15 U.S.C. 78o–7(c)(3)(A)).

§ 240.17g-3

(13) The policies and procedures the nationally recognized statistical rating organization is required to establish, maintain, enforce, and document pursuant to § 240.17g-8(a).

(14) The policies and procedures the nationally recognized statistical rating organization is required to establish, maintain, enforce, and document pursuant to § 240.17g-8(b).

(15) The standards of training, experience, and competence for credit analysts the nationally recognized statistical rating organization is required to establish, maintain, enforce, and document pursuant to § 240.17g-9.

(c) *Record retention periods.* The records required to be retained pursuant to paragraphs (a) and (b) of this section must be retained for three years after the date the record is made or received, except that a record identified in paragraph (a)(9), (b)(12), (b)(13), (b)(14), or (b)(15) of this section must be retained until three years after the date the record is replaced with an updated record.

(d) *Manner of retention.* An original, or a true and complete copy of the original, of each record required to be retained pursuant to paragraphs (a) and (b) of this section must be maintained in a manner that, for the applicable retention period specified in paragraph (c) of this section, makes the original record or copy easily accessible to the principal office of the nationally recognized statistical rating organization and to any other office that conducted activities causing the record to be made or received.

(e) *Third-party record custodian.* The records required to be retained pursuant to paragraphs (a) and (b) of this section may be made or retained by a third-party record custodian, provided the nationally recognized statistical rating organization furnishes the Commission at its principal office in Washington, DC with a written undertaking of the custodian executed by a duly authorized person. The undertaking must be in substantially the following form:

The undersigned acknowledges that books and records it has made or is retaining for [the nationally recognized statistical rating organization] are the exclusive property of [the nationally recognized statistical rating organization]. The undersigned undertakes that upon the request of [the nationally recognized statistical rating organization] it will promptly provide the books and records to [the nationally recognized statistical rating organization] or the U.S. Securities and Exchange Commission ("Commission") or its representatives and that upon the request of the Commission it will promptly permit examination by the Commission or its representatives of the records at any time or from time to time during business hours and promptly furnish to the Commission or its representatives a true and complete copy of any or all or any part of such books and records.

A nationally recognized statistical rating organization that engages a third-party record custodian remains responsible for complying with every provision of this section.

(f) A nationally recognized statistical rating organization must promptly furnish the Commission or its representatives with legible, complete, and current copies, and, if specifically requested, English translations of those records of the nationally recognized statistical rating organization required to be retained pursuant to paragraphs (a) and (b) this section, or any other records of the nationally recognized statistical rating organization subject to examination under section 17(b) of the Act (15 U.S.C. 78q(b)) that are requested by the Commission or its representatives.

[72 FR 33620, June 18, 2007, as amended at 74 FR 6482, Feb. 9, 2009; 74 FR 63863, Dec. 4, 2009; 79 FR 55263, Nov. 14, 2014]

§ 240.17g-3 Annual financial and other reports to be filed or furnished by nationally recognized statistical rating organizations.

(a) A nationally recognized statistical rating organization must annually, not more than 90 calendar days after the end of its fiscal year (as indicated on its current Form NRSRO):

(1) File with the Commission a financial report, as of the end of the fiscal year, containing audited financial statements of the nationally recognized statistical rating organization or audited consolidated financial statements of its parent if the nationally recognized statistical rating organization is a separately identifiable division or department of the parent. The audited financial statements must:

Securities and Exchange Commission

§ 240.17g-3

(i) Include a balance sheet, an income statement (or a statement of comprehensive income, as defined in § 210.1-02 of Regulation S-X of this chapter, if required by the applicable generally accepted accounting principles noted in paragraph (a)(1)(ii) of this section) and statement of cash flows, and a statement of changes in ownership equity;

(ii) Be prepared in accordance with generally accepted accounting principles in the jurisdiction in which the nationally recognized statistical rating organization or its parent is incorporated, organized, or has its principal office; and

(iii) Be certified by an accountant who is qualified and independent in accordance with paragraphs (a), (b), and (c)(1), (2), (3), (4), (5) and (8) of § 210.2-01 of this chapter. The accountant must give an opinion on the financial statements in accordance with paragraphs (a) through (d) of § 210.2-02 of this chapter.

(2) File with the Commission a financial report, as of the end of the fiscal year, containing, if applicable, unaudited consolidating financial statements of the parent of the nationally recognized statistical rating organization that include the nationally recognized statistical rating organization.

NOTE TO PARAGRAPH (a)(2): This financial report must be filed only if the audited financial statements provided pursuant to paragraph (a)(1) of this section are consolidated financial statements of the parent of the nationally recognized statistical rating organization.

(3) File with the Commission an unaudited financial report, as of the end of the fiscal year, providing information concerning the revenue of the nationally recognized statistical rating organization in each of the following categories (as applicable) for the fiscal year:

(i) Revenue from determining and maintaining credit ratings;

(ii) Revenue from subscribers;

(iii) Revenue from granting licenses or rights to publish credit ratings; and

(iv) Revenue from all other services and products (include descriptions of any major sources of revenue).

(4) File with the Commission an unaudited financial report, as of the end of the fiscal year, providing the total aggregate and median annual compensation of the credit analysts of the nationally recognized statistical rating organization for the fiscal year.

NOTE TO PARAGRAPH (a)(4): In calculating total and median annual compensation, the nationally recognized statistical rating organization may exclude deferred compensation, provided such exclusion is noted in the report.

(5) File with the Commission an unaudited financial report, as of the end of the fiscal year, listing the 20 largest issuers and subscribers that used credit rating services provided by the nationally recognized statistical rating organization by amount of net revenue attributable to the issuer or subscriber during the fiscal year. Additionally, include on the list any obligor or underwriter that used the credit rating services provided by the nationally recognized statistical rating organization if the net revenue attributable to the obligor or underwriter during the fiscal year equaled or exceeded the net revenue attributable to the 20th largest issuer or subscriber. Include the net revenue amount for each person on the list.

NOTE TO PARAGRAPH (a)(5): A person is deemed to have "used the credit rating services" of the nationally recognized statistical rating organization if the person is any of the following: an obligor that is rated by the nationally recognized statistical rating organization (regardless of whether the obligor paid for the credit rating); an issuer that has securities or money market instruments subject to a credit rating of the nationally recognized statistical rating organization (regardless of whether the issuer paid for the credit rating); any other person that has paid the nationally recognized statistical rating organization to determine a credit rating with respect to a specific obligor, security, or money market instrument; or a subscriber to the credit ratings, credit ratings data, or credit analysis of the nationally recognized statistical rating organization. In calculating net revenue attributable to a person, the nationally recognized statistical rating organization should include all revenue earned by the nationally recognized statistical rating organization for any type of service or product, regardless of whether related to credit rating services, and net of any rebates and allowances paid or owed to the person by the nationally recognized statistical rating organization.

(6) Furnish the Commission with an unaudited report, as of the end of the fiscal year, of the number of credit ratings actions (upgrades, downgrades, placements on credit watch, and withdrawals) taken during the fiscal year in each class of credit ratings identified in section 3(a)(62)(B) of the Act (15 U.S.C. 78c(a)(62)(B)) for which the nationally recognized statistical rating organization is registered with the Commission.

NOTE TO PARAGRAPH (a)(6): A nationally recognized statistical rating organization registered in the class of credit ratings described in section 3(a)(62)(B)(iv) of the Act (15 U.S.C. 78c(a)(62)(B)(iv)) must include credit ratings actions taken on credit ratings of any security or money market instrument issued by an asset pool or as part of any asset-backed securities transaction for purposes of reporting the number of credit ratings actions in this class.

(7)(i) File with the Commission an unaudited report containing an assessment by management of the effectiveness during the fiscal year of the internal control structure governing the implementation of and adherence to policies, procedures, and methodologies for determining credit ratings the nationally recognized statistical rating organization is required to establish, maintain, enforce, and document pursuant to section 15E(c)(3)(A) of the Act (15 U.S.C. 78o–7(c)(3)(A)) that includes:

(A) A description of the responsibility of management in establishing and maintaining an effective internal control structure;

(B) A description of each material weakness in the internal control structure identified during the fiscal year, if any, and a description, if applicable, of how each identified material weakness was addressed; and

(C) A statement as to whether the internal control structure was effective as of the end of the fiscal year.

(ii) Management is not permitted to conclude that the internal control structure of the nationally recognized statistical rating organization was effective as of the end of the fiscal year if there were one or more material weaknesses in the internal control structure as of the end of the fiscal year.

(iii) For purposes of this paragraph (a)(7), a deficiency in the internal control structure exists when the design or operation of a control does not allow management or employees, in the normal course of performing their assigned functions, to prevent or detect a failure of the nationally recognized statistical rating organization to:

(A) Implement a policy, procedure, or methodology for determining credit ratings in accordance with the policies and procedures of the nationally recognized statistical rating organization; or

(B) Adhere to an implemented policy, procedure, or methodology for determining credit ratings.

(iv) For purposes of this paragraph (a)(7), a material weakness exists if a deficiency, or a combination of deficiencies, in the design or operation of the internal control structure creates a reasonable possibility that a failure identified in paragraph (a)(7)(iii) of this section that is material will not be prevented or detected on a timely basis.

(8) File with the Commission an unaudited annual report on the compliance of the nationally recognized statistical rating organization with the securities laws and the policies and procedures of the nationally recognized statistical rating organization pursuant to section 15E(j)(5)(B) of the Act (15 U.S.C. 78o–7(j)(5)(B)).

(b)(1) The nationally recognized statistical rating organization must attach to the reports filed or furnished, as applicable, pursuant to paragraphs (a)(1) through (6) of this section a signed statement by a duly authorized person associated with the nationally recognized statistical rating organization stating that the person has responsibility for the reports and, to the best knowledge of the person, the reports fairly present, in all material respects, the financial condition, results of operations, cash flows, revenues, analyst compensation, and credit rating actions of the nationally recognized statistical rating organization for the period presented; and

(2) The nationally recognized statistical rating organization must attach to the report filed pursuant to paragraph (a)(7) of this section a signed

Securities and Exchange Commission §240.17g–5

statement by the chief executive officer of the nationally recognized statistical rating organization or, if the nationally recognized statistical rating organization does not have a chief executive officer, an individual performing similar functions, stating that the chief executive officer or equivalent individual has responsibility for the report and, to the best knowledge of the chief executive officer or equivalent individual, the report fairly presents, in all material respects: an assessment by management of the effectiveness of the internal control structure during the fiscal year that includes a description of the responsibility of management in establishing and maintaining an effective internal control structure; a description of each material weakness in the internal control structure identified during the fiscal year, if any, and a description, if applicable, of how each identified material weakness was addressed; and an assessment by management of the effectiveness of the internal control structure as of the end of the fiscal year.

(c) The Commission may grant an extension of time or an exemption with respect to any requirements in this section either unconditionally or on specified terms and conditions on the written request of a nationally recognized statistical rating organization if the Commission finds that such extension or exemption is necessary or appropriate in the public interest and consistent with the protection of investors.

(d) *Electronic filing.* The reports must be filed with or furnished to, as applicable, the Commission electronically on EDGAR as PDF documents in the format required by the EDGAR Filer Manual, as defined in Rule 11 of Regulation S–T.

(e) *Confidential treatment.* Information in a report filed or furnished, as applicable, on a confidential basis and for which confidential treatment has been requested pursuant to applicable Commission rules will be accorded confidential treatment to the extent permitted by law. Confidential treatment may be requested by marking each page "Confidential Treatment Requested" and by complying with Commission rules governing confidential treatment.

[72 FR 33620, June 18, 2007, as amended at 74 FR 6482, Feb. 9, 2009; 79 FR 55263, Sept. 15, 2014; 79 FR 61576, Nov. 14, 2014; 83 FR 50223, Oct. 4, 2018]

§ 240.17g–4 **Prevention of misuse of material nonpublic information.**

(a) The written policies and procedures a nationally recognized statistical rating organization establishes, maintains, and enforces to prevent the misuse of material, nonpublic information pursuant to section 15E(g)(1) of the Act (15 U.S.C. 78o–7(g)(1)) must include policies and procedures reasonably designed to prevent:

(1) The inappropriate dissemination within and outside the nationally recognized statistical rating organization of material nonpublic information obtained in connection with the performance of credit rating services;

(2) A person within the nationally recognized statistical rating organization from purchasing, selling, or otherwise benefiting from any transaction in securities or money market instruments when the person is aware of material nonpublic information obtained in connection with the performance of credit rating services that affects the securities or money market instruments; and

(3) The inappropriate dissemination within and outside the nationally recognized statistical rating organization of a pending credit rating action before issuing the credit rating on the Internet or through another readily accessible means.

(b) For the purposes of this section, the term *person within a nationally recognized statistical rating organization* means a nationally recognized statistical rating organization, its credit rating affiliates identified on Form NRSRO, and any partner, officer, director, branch manager, and employee of the nationally recognized statistical rating organization or its credit rating affiliates (or any person occupying a similar status or performing similar functions).

§ 240.17g–5 **Conflicts of interest.**

(a) A person within a nationally recognized statistical rating organization

§ 240.17g–5

is prohibited from having a conflict of interest relating to the issuance or maintenance of a credit rating identified in paragraph (b) of this section, unless:

(1) The nationally recognized statistical rating organization has disclosed the type of conflict of interest in Exhibit 6 to Form NRSRO in accordance with section 15E(a)(1)(B)(vi) of the Act (15 U.S.C. 78o–7(a)(1)(B)(vi)) and § 240.17g–1;

(2) The nationally recognized statistical rating organization has established and is maintaining and enforcing written policies and procedures to address and manage conflicts of interest in accordance with section 15E(h) of the Act (15 U.S.C. 78o–7(h)); and

(3) In the case of the conflict of interest identified in paragraph (b)(9) of this section relating to issuing or maintaining a credit rating for a security or money market instrument issued by an asset pool or as part of any asset-backed securities transaction, the nationally recognized statistical rating organization:

(i) Maintains on a password-protected Internet Web site a list of each such security or money market instrument for which it is currently in the process of determining an initial credit rating in chronological order and identifying the type of security or money market instrument, the name of the issuer, the date the rating process was initiated, and the Internet Web site address where the issuer, sponsor, or underwriter of the security or money market instrument represents that the information described in paragraphs (a)(3)(iii)(C) through (E) of this section can be accessed;

(ii) Provides free and unlimited access to such password-protected Internet Web site during the applicable calendar year to any nationally recognized statistical rating organization that provides it with a copy of the certification described in paragraph (e) of this section that covers that calendar year, provided that such certification indicates that the nationally recognized statistical rating organization providing the certification either:

(A) Determined and maintained credit ratings for at least 10% of the issued securities and money market instruments for which it accessed information pursuant to 17 CFR 240.17g–5(a)(3)(iii) in the calendar year prior to the year covered by the certification, if it accessed such information for 10 or more issued securities or money market instruments; or

(B) Has not accessed information pursuant to 17 CFR 240.17g–5(a)(3) 10 or more times during the most recently ended calendar year; and

(iii) Obtains from the issuer, sponsor, or underwriter of each such security or money market instrument a written representation that can reasonably be relied upon that the issuer, sponsor, or underwriter will:

(A) Maintain the information described in paragraphs (a)(3)(iii)(C) through (E) of this section available at an identified password-protected Internet Web site that presents the information in a manner indicating which information currently should be relied on to determine or monitor the credit rating;

(B) Provide access to such password-protected Internet Web site during the applicable calendar year to any nationally recognized statistical rating organization that provides it with a copy of the certification described in paragraph (e) of this section that covers that calendar year, provided that such certification indicates that the nationally recognized statistical rating organization providing the certification either:

(*1*) Determined and maintained credit ratings for at least 10% of the issued securities and money market instruments for which it accessed information pursuant to 17 CFR 240.17g–5(a)(3)(iii) in the calendar year prior to the year covered by the certification, if it accessed such information for 10 or more issued securities or money market instruments; or

(*2*) Has not accessed information pursuant to 17 CFR 240.17g–5(a)(3) 10 or more times during the most recently ended calendar year.

(C) Post on such password-protected Internet Web site all information the issuer, sponsor, or underwriter provides to the nationally recognized statistical rating organization, or contracts with

Securities and Exchange Commission § 240.17g–5

a third party to provide to the nationally recognized statistical rating organization, for the purpose of determining the initial credit rating for the security or money market instrument, including information about the characteristics of the assets underlying or referenced by the security or money market instrument, and the legal structure of the security or money market instrument, at the same time such information is provided to the nationally recognized statistical rating organization; and

(D) Post on such password-protected Internet Web site all information the issuer, sponsor, or underwriter provides to the nationally recognized statistical rating organization, or contracts with a third party to provide to the nationally recognized statistical rating organization, for the purpose of undertaking credit rating surveillance on the security or money market instrument, including information about the characteristics and performance of the assets underlying or referenced by the security or money market instrument at the same time such information is provided to the nationally recognized statistical rating organization.

(E) Post on such password-protected Internet Web site, promptly after receipt, any executed Form ABS Due Diligence–15E (§ 249b.500 of this chapter) containing information about the security or money market instrument delivered by a person employed to provide third-party due diligence services with respect to the security or money market instrument.

(iv) The provisions of paragraphs (a)(3)(i) through (iii) of this section will not apply to a nationally recognized statistical rating organization when issuing or maintaining a credit rating for a security or money market instrument issued by an asset pool or as part of any asset-backed securities transaction, if:

(A) The issuer of the security or money market instrument is not a U.S. person (as defined in § 230.902(k) of this chapter); and

(B) The nationally recognized statistical rating organization has a reasonable basis to conclude that all offers and sales of the security or money market instrument by any issuer, sponsor, or underwriter linked to the security or money market instrument will occur outside the United States (as that phrase is used in §§ 230.901 through 230.905 (Regulation S) of this chapter).

(b) *Conflicts of interest.* For purposes of this section, each of the following is a conflict of interest:

(1) Being paid by issuers or underwriters to determine credit ratings with respect to securities or money market instruments they issue or underwrite.

(2) Being paid by obligors to determine credit ratings with respect to the obligors.

(3) Being paid for services in addition to determining credit ratings by issuers, underwriters, or obligors that have paid the nationally recognized statistical rating organization to determine a credit rating.

(4) Being paid by persons for subscriptions to receive or access the credit ratings of the nationally recognized statistical rating organization and/or for other services offered by the nationally recognized statistical rating organization where such persons may use the credit ratings of the nationally recognized statistical rating organization to comply with, and obtain benefits or relief under, statutes and regulations using the term *nationally recognized statistical rating organization.*

(5) Being paid by persons for subscriptions to receive or access the credit ratings of the nationally recognized statistical rating organization and/or for other services offered by the nationally recognized statistical rating organization where such persons also may own investments or have entered into transactions that could be favorably or adversely impacted by a credit rating issued by the nationally recognized statistical rating organization.

(6) Allowing persons within the nationally recognized statistical rating organization to directly own securities or money market instruments of, or having other direct ownership interests in, issuers or obligors subject to a credit rating determined by the nationally recognized statistical rating organization.

(7) Allowing persons within the nationally recognized statistical rating

§ 240.17g–5

organization to have a business relationship that is more than an arms length ordinary course of business relationship with issuers or obligors subject to a credit rating determined by the nationally recognized statistical rating organization.

(8) Having a person associated with the nationally recognized statistical rating organization that is a broker or dealer engaged in the business of underwriting securities or money market instruments.

(9) Issuing or maintaining a credit rating for a security or money market instrument issued by an asset pool or as part of any asset-backed securities transaction that was paid for by the issuer, sponsor, or underwriter of the security or money market instrument;

(10) Any other type of conflict of interest relating to the issuance of credit ratings by the nationally recognized statistical rating organization that is material to the nationally recognized statistical rating organization and that is identified by the nationally recognized statistical rating organization in Exhibit 6 to Form NRSRO in accordance with section 15E(a)(1)(B)(vi) of the Act (15 U.S.C. 78o–7(a)(1)(B)(vi)) and § 240.17g–1.

(c) *Prohibited conflicts.* A nationally recognized statistical rating organization is prohibited from having the following conflicts of interest relating to the issuance or maintenance of a credit rating as a credit rating agency:

(1) The nationally recognized statistical rating organization issues or maintains a credit rating solicited by a person that, in the most recently ended fiscal year, provided the nationally recognized statistical rating organization with net revenue (as reported under § 240.17g–3) equaling or exceeding 10% of the total net revenue of the nationally recognized statistical rating organization for the fiscal year;

(2) The nationally recognized statistical rating organization issues or maintains a credit rating with respect to a person (excluding a sovereign nation or an agency of a sovereign nation) where the nationally recognized statistical rating organization, a credit analyst that participated in determining the credit rating, or a person responsible for approving the credit rating, directly owns securities of, or has any other direct ownership interest in, the person that is subject to the credit rating;

(3) The nationally recognized statistical rating organization issues or maintains a credit rating with respect to a person associated with the nationally recognized statistical rating organization;

(4) The nationally recognized statistical rating organization issues or maintains a credit rating where a credit analyst who participated in determining the credit rating, or a person responsible for approving the credit rating, is an officer or director of the person that is subject to the credit rating;

(5) The nationally recognized statistical rating organization issues or maintains a credit rating with respect to an obligor or security where the nationally recognized statistical rating organization or a person associated with the nationally recognized statistical rating organization made recommendations to the obligor or the issuer, underwriter, or sponsor of the security about the corporate or legal structure, assets, liabilities, or activities of the obligor or issuer of the security;

(6) The nationally recognized statistical rating organization issues or maintains a credit rating where the fee paid for the rating was negotiated, discussed, or arranged by a person within the nationally recognized statistical rating organization who has responsibility for participating in determining credit ratings or for developing or approving procedures or methodologies used for determining credit ratings, including qualitative and quantitative models;

(7) The nationally recognized statistical rating organization issues or maintains a credit rating where a credit analyst who participated in determining or monitoring the credit rating, or a person responsible for approving the credit rating received gifts, including entertainment, from the obligor being rated, or from the issuer, underwriter, or sponsor of the securities being rated, other than items provided

Securities and Exchange Commission § 240.17g–5

in the context of normal business activities such as meetings that have an aggregate value of no more than $25; or

(8) The nationally recognized statistical rating organization issues or maintains a credit rating where a person within the nationally recognized statistical rating organization who participates in determining or monitoring the credit rating, or developing or approving procedures or methodologies used for determining the credit rating, including qualitative and quantitative models, also:

(i) Participates in sales or marketing of a product or service of the nationally recognized statistical rating organization or a product or service of an affiliate of the nationally recognized statistical rating organization; or

(ii) Is influenced by sales or marketing considerations.

(d) For the purposes of this section, the term *person within a nationally recognized statistical rating organization* means a nationally recognized statistical rating organization, its credit rating affiliates identified on Form NRSRO, and any partner, officer, director, branch manager, and employee of the nationally recognized statistical rating organization or its credit rating affiliates (or any person occupying a similar status or performing similar functions).

(e) *Certification.* In order to access a password-protected Internet Web site described in paragraph (a)(3) of this section, a nationally recognized statistical rating organization must furnish to the Commission, for each calendar year for which it is requesting a password, the following certification, signed by a person duly authorized by the certifying entity:

The undersigned hereby certifies that it will access the Internet Web sites described in 17 CFR 240.17g–5(a)(3) solely for the purpose of determining or monitoring credit ratings. Further, the undersigned certifies that it will keep the information it accesses pursuant to 17 CFR 240.17g–5(a)(3) confidential and treat it as material nonpublic information subject to its written policies and procedures established, maintained, and enforced pursuant to section 15E(g)(1) of the Act (15 U.S.C. 78o–7(g)(1)) and 17 CFR 240.17g–4. Further, the undersigned certifies that it will determine and maintain credit ratings for at least 10% of the issued securities and money market instruments for which it accesses information pursuant to 17 CFR 240.17g–5(a)(3)(iii), if it accesses such information for 10 or more issued securities or money market instruments in the calendar year covered by the certification. Further, the undersigned certifies one of the following as applicable: (1) In the most recent calendar year during which it accessed information pursuant to 17 CFR 240.17g–5(a)(3), the undersigned accessed information for [Insert Number] issued securities and money market instruments through Internet Web sites described in 17 CFR 240.17g–5(a)(3) and determined and maintained credit ratings for [Insert Number] of such securities and money market instruments; or (2) The undersigned previously has not accessed information pursuant to 17 CFR 240.17g–5(a)(3) 10 or more times during the most recently ended calendar year.

(f) Upon written application by a nationally recognized statistical rating organization, the Commission may exempt, either unconditionally or on specified terms and conditions, such nationally recognized statistical rating organization from the provisions of paragraph (c)(8) of this section if the Commission finds that due to the small size of the nationally recognized statistical rating organization it is not appropriate to require the separation within the nationally recognized statistical rating organization of the production of credit ratings from sales and marketing activities and such exemption is in the public interest.

(g) In a proceeding pursuant to section 15E(d)(1) of the Act (15 U.S.C. 78o–7(d)(1)), the Commission shall suspend or revoke the registration of a nationally recognized statistical rating organization if the Commission finds, in lieu of a finding specified under sections 15E(d)(1)(A), (B), (C), (D), (E), or (F) of the Act (15 U.S.C. 78o–7(d)(1)(A) through (F)), that the nationally recognized statistical rating organization has violated a rule issued under section 15E(h) of the Act (15 U.S.C. 78o–7(h)) and that the violation affected a credit rating.

[72 FR 33620, June 18, 2007, as amended at 74 FR 6482, Feb. 9, 2009; 74 FR 63864, Dec. 4, 2009; 79 FR 55264, Sept. 15, 2014; 79 FR 61576, Oct. 14, 2014; 84 FR 40258, Sept. 13, 2019]

§ 240.17g-6 Prohibited acts and practices.

(a) *Prohibitions.* A nationally recognized statistical rating organization is prohibited from engaging in any of the following unfair, coercive, or abusive practices:

(1) Conditioning or threatening to condition the issuance of a credit rating on the purchase by an obligor or issuer, or an affiliate of the obligor or issuer, of any other services or products, including pre-credit rating assessment products, of the nationally recognized statistical rating organization or any person associated with the nationally recognized statistical rating organization.

(2) Issuing, or offering or threatening to issue, a credit rating that is not determined in accordance with the nationally recognized statistical rating organization's established procedures and methodologies for determining credit ratings, based on whether the rated person, or an affiliate of the rated person, purchases or will purchase the credit rating or any other service or product of the nationally recognized statistical rating organization or any person associated with the nationally recognized statistical rating organization.

(3) Modifying, or offering or threatening to modify, a credit rating in a manner that is contrary to the nationally recognized statistical rating organization's established procedures and methodologies for modifying credit ratings based on whether the rated person, or an affiliate of the rated person, purchases or will purchase the credit rating or any other service or product of the nationally recognized statistical rating organization or any person associated with the nationally recognized statistical rating organization.

(4) Issuing or threatening to issue a lower credit rating, lowering or threatening to lower an existing credit rating, refusing to issue a credit rating, or withdrawing or threatening to withdraw a credit rating, with respect to securities or money market instruments issued by an asset pool or as part of any asset-backed securities transaction, unless all or a portion of the assets within such pool or part of such transaction also are rated by the nationally recognized statistical rating organization, where such practice is engaged in by the nationally recognized statistical rating organization for an anticompetitive purpose.

[13 FR 8178, Dec. 22, 1948, as amended at 79 FR 55264, Sept. 15, 2014]

§ 240.17g-7 Disclosure requirements.

(a) *Disclosures to be made when taking a rating action.* Except as provided in paragraph (a)(3) of this section, a nationally recognized statistical rating organization must publish the items described in paragraphs (a)(1) and (2) of this section, as applicable, when taking a rating action with respect to a credit rating assigned to an obligor, security, or money market instrument in a class of credit ratings for which the nationally recognized statistical rating organization is registered. For purposes of this section, the term *rating action* means any of the following: the publication of an expected or preliminary credit rating assigned to an obligor, security, or money market instrument before the publication of an initial credit rating; an initial credit rating; an upgrade or downgrade of an existing credit rating (including a downgrade to, or assignment of, default); and an affirmation or withdrawal of an existing credit rating if the affirmation or withdrawal is the result of a review of the credit rating assigned to the obligor, security, or money market instrument by the nationally recognized statistical rating organization using applicable procedures and methodologies for determining credit ratings. The items described in paragraphs (a)(1) and (2) of this section must be published in the same manner as the credit rating that is the result or subject of the rating action and made available to the same persons who can receive or access the credit rating that is the result or subject of the rating action.

(1) *Information disclosure form.* A form generated by the nationally recognized statistical rating organization that meets the requirements of paragraphs (a)(1)(i) through (iii) of this section.

(i) *Format.* The form generated by the nationally recognized statistical rating organization must be in a format that:

(A) Organizes the information into numbered items that are identified by

Securities and Exchange Commission

§ 240.17g-7

the type of information being disclosed and a reference to the paragraph in this section that specifies the disclosure of the information, and are in the order that the paragraphs specifying the information to be disclosed are codified in this section;

Note to paragraph (a)(1)(i)(A): A given item in the form should be identified by a title that identifies the type of information and references paragraph (a)(1)(ii)(A), (B), (C), (D), (E), (F), (G), (H), (I), (J), (K), (L), (M), (N), or (a)(2) of this section based on the information being disclosed in the item. For example, the information specified in paragraph (a)(1)(ii)(C) of this section should be identified with the caption "Main Assumptions and Principles Used to Construct the Rating Methodology used to Determine the Credit Rating as required by Paragraph (a)(1)(ii)(C) of Rule 17g-7"). The form must organize the items of information in the following order: items 1 through 14 must contain the information specified in paragraphs (a)(1)(ii)(A) through (N) of this section, respectively, and item 15 must contain the certifications specified in paragraph (a)(2) of this section (the information specified in each paragraph comprising a separate item). For example, item 3 must contain the information specified in paragraph (a)(1)(ii)(C) of this section.

(B) Is easy to use and helpful for users of credit ratings to understand the information contained in the form; and

(C) Provides the content described in paragraphs (a)(1)(ii)(K) through (M) of this section in a manner that is directly comparable across types of obligors, securities, and money market instruments.

(ii) *Content.* The form generated by the nationally recognized statistical rating organization must contain the following information about the credit rating:

(A) The symbol, number, or score in the rating scale used by the nationally recognized statistical rating organization to denote credit rating categories and notches within categories assigned to the obligor, security, or money market instrument that is the subject of the credit rating and, as applicable, the identity of the obligor or the identity and a description of the security or money market instrument;

(B) The version of the procedure or methodology used to determine the credit rating;

(C) The main assumptions and principles used in constructing the procedures and methodologies used to determine the credit rating, including qualitative methodologies and quantitative inputs, and, if the credit rating is for a structured finance product, assumptions about the correlation of defaults across the underlying assets;

(D) The potential limitations of the credit rating, including the types of risks excluded from the credit rating that the nationally recognized statistical rating organization does not comment on, including, as applicable, liquidity, market, and other risks;

(E) Information on the uncertainty of the credit rating including:

(*1*) Information on the reliability, accuracy, and quality of the data relied on in determining the credit rating; and

(*2*) A statement relating to the extent to which data essential to the determination of the credit rating were reliable or limited, including:

(*i*) Any limits on the scope of historical data; and

(*ii*) Any limits on accessibility to certain documents or other types of information that would have better informed the credit rating;

(F) Whether and to what extent the nationally recognized statistical rating organization used due diligence services of a third party in taking the rating action, and, if the nationally recognized statistical rating organization used such services, either:

(*1*) A description of the information that the third party reviewed in conducting the due diligence services and a summary of the findings and conclusions of the third party; or

(*2*) A cross-reference to a Form ABS Due Diligence-15E executed by the third party that is published with the form, provided the cross-referenced Form ABS Due Diligence-15E (§ 249b.500 of this chapter) contains a description of the information that the third party reviewed in conducting the due diligence services and a summary of the

§ 240.17g–7

findings and conclusions of the third party;

(G) If applicable, how servicer or remittance reports were used, and with what frequency, to conduct surveillance of the credit rating;

(H) A description of the types of data about any obligor, issuer, security, or money market instrument that were relied upon for the purpose of determining the credit rating;

(I) A statement containing an overall assessment of the quality of information available and considered in determining the credit rating for the obligor, security, or money market instrument, in relation to the quality of information available to the nationally recognized statistical rating organization in rating similar obligors, securities, or money market instruments;

(J) Information relating to conflicts of interest of the nationally recognized statistical rating organization, which must include:

(*1*) As applicable, a statement that the nationally recognized statistical rating organization was:

(*i*) Paid to determine the credit rating by the obligor being rated or the issuer, underwriter, depositor, or sponsor of the security or money market instrument being rated;

(*ii*) Paid to determine the credit rating by a person other than the obligor being rated or the issuer, underwriter, depositor, or sponsor of the security or money market instrument being rated; or

(*iii*) Not paid to determine the credit rating;

(*2*) If applicable, in a statement required under paragraph (a)(1)(ii)(J)(*1*)(*i*) or (*ii*) of this section, a statement that the nationally recognized statistical rating organization also was paid for services other than determining credit ratings during the most recently ended fiscal year by the person that paid the nationally recognized statistical rating organization to determine the credit rating; and

(*3*) If the rating action results from a review conducted pursuant to section 15E(h)(4)(A) of the Act (15 U.S.C. 78o–7(h)(4)(A)) and § 240.17g–8(c), the following information (as applicable):

(*i*) If the rating action is a revision of a credit rating pursuant to § 240.17g–8(c)(2)(i)(A), an explanation that the reason for the action is the discovery that a credit rating assigned to the obligor, security, or money market instrument in one or more prior rating actions was influenced by a conflict of interest, including a description of the nature of the conflict, the date and associated credit rating of each prior rating action that the nationally recognized statistical rating organization has determined was influenced by the conflict, and a description of the impact the conflict had on the prior rating action or actions; or

(*ii*) If the rating action is an affirmation of a credit rating pursuant to § 240.17g–8(c)(2)(i)(B), an explanation that the reason for the action is the discovery that a credit rating assigned to the obligor, security, or money market instrument in one or more prior rating actions was influenced by a conflict of interest, including a description of the nature of the conflict, an explanation of why no rating action was taken to revise the credit rating notwithstanding the presence of the conflict, the date and associated credit rating of each prior rating action the nationally recognized statistical rating organization has determined was influenced by the conflict, and a description of the impact the conflict had on the prior rating action or actions.

(K) An explanation or measure of the potential volatility of the credit rating, including:

(*1*) Any factors that are reasonably likely to lead to a change in the credit rating; and

(*2*) The magnitude of the change that could occur under different market conditions determined by the nationally recognized statistical rating organization to be relevant to the rating;

(L) Information on the content of the credit rating, including:

(*1*) If applicable, the historical performance of the credit rating; and

(*2*) The expected probability of default and the expected loss in the event of default;

(M) Information on the sensitivity of the credit rating to assumptions made by the nationally recognized statistical rating organization, including:

(*1*) Five assumptions made in the ratings process that, without accounting

Securities and Exchange Commission § 240.17g-7

for any other factor, would have the greatest impact on the credit rating if the assumptions were proven false or inaccurate; provided that, if the nationally recognized statistical rating organization has made fewer than five such assumptions, it need only disclose information on the assumptions that would have an impact on the credit rating; and

(2) An analysis, using specific examples, of how each of the assumptions identified in paragraph (a)(1)(ii)(M)(*1*) of this section impacts the credit rating;

(N)(*1*) If the credit rating is assigned to an asset-backed security as defined in section 3(a)(79) of the Act (15 U.S.C. 78c(a)(79)), information on:

(*i*) The representations, warranties, and enforcement mechanisms available to investors which were disclosed in the prospectus, private placement memorandum or other offering documents for the asset-backed security and that relate to the asset pool underlying the asset-backed security; and

(*ii*) How they differ from the representations, warranties, and enforcement mechanisms in issuances of similar securities;

(2) A nationally recognized statistical rating organization must include the information required under paragraph (a)(1)(ii)(N)(*1*) of this section only if the rating action is a preliminary credit rating, an initial credit rating, or, in the case of a rating action other than a preliminary credit rating or initial credit rating, the rating action is the first rating action taken after a material change in the representations, warranties, or enforcement mechanisms described in paragraph (a)(1)(ii)(N)(*1*) of this section and the rating action involves an asset-backed security that was initially rated by the nationally recognized statistical rating organization on or after September 26, 2011.

(iii) *Attestation.* The nationally recognized statistical rating organization must attach to the form a signed statement by a person within the nationally recognized statistical rating organization stating that the person has responsibility for the rating action and, to the best knowledge of the person:

(A) No part of the credit rating was influenced by any other business activities;

(B) The credit rating was based solely upon the merits of the obligor, security, or money market instrument being rated; and

(C) The credit rating was an independent evaluation of the credit risk of the obligor, security, or money market instrument.

(2) *Third-party due diligence certification.* Any executed Form ABS Due Diligence-15E (§ 249b.500 of this chapter) containing information about the security or money market instrument subject to the rating action that is received by the nationally recognized statistical rating organization or obtained by the nationally recognized statistical rating organization through an Internet Web site maintained by the issuer, sponsor, or underwriter of the security or money market instrument pursuant to § 240.17g-5(a)(3).

(3) *Exemption.* The provisions of paragraphs (a)(1) and (2) of this section do not apply to a rating action if:

(i) The rated obligor or issuer of the rated security or money market instrument is not a U.S. person (as defined in § 230.902(k) of this chapter); and

(ii) The nationally recognized statistical rating organization has a reasonable basis to conclude that:

(A) With respect to any security or money market instrument issued by a rated obligor, all offers and sales by any issuer, sponsor, or underwriter linked to the security or money market instrument will occur outside the United States (as that phrase is used in §§ 230.901 through 230.905 (Regulation S) of this chapter); or

(B) With respect to a rated security or money market instrument, all offers and sales by any issuer, sponsor, or underwriter linked to the security or money market instrument will occur outside the United States (as that phrase is used in §§ 230.901 through 230.905 (Regulation S) of this chapter).

(b) *Disclosure of credit rating histories*—(1) *Credit ratings subject to the disclosure requirement.* A nationally recognized statistical rating organization must publicly disclose for free on an easily accessible portion of its corporate Internet Web site:

§ 240.17g-7

(i) For a class of credit rating in which the nationally recognized statistical rating organization is registered with the Commission as of the effective date of paragraph (b) of this section, the credit rating assigned to each obligor, security, and money market instrument in the class that was outstanding as of, or initially determined on or after, the date three years prior to the effective date of this rule, and any subsequent upgrade or downgrade of the credit rating (including a downgrade to, or assignment of, default), and a withdrawal of the credit rating; and

(ii) For a class of credit rating in which the nationally recognized statistical rating organization is registered with the Commission after the effective date of paragraph (b) of this section, the credit rating assigned to each obligor, security, and money market instrument in the class that was outstanding as of, or initially determined on or after, the date three years prior to the date the nationally recognized statistical rating organization is registered in the class, and any subsequent upgrade or downgrade of the credit rating (including a downgrade to, or assignment of, default), and a withdrawal of the credit rating.

(2) *Information.* A nationally recognized statistical rating organization must include, at a minimum, the following information with each credit rating disclosed pursuant to paragraph (b)(1) of this section:

(i) The identity of the nationally recognized statistical rating organization disclosing the rating action;

(ii) The date of the rating action;

(iii) If the rating action is taken with respect to a credit rating of an obligor as an entity, the following identifying information about the obligor, as applicable:

(A) The Legal Entity Identifier issued by a utility endorsed or otherwise governed by the Global LEI Regulatory Oversight Committee or the Global LEI Foundation (LEI) of the obligor, if available, or, if an LEI is not available, the Central Index Key (CIK) number of the obligor, if available; and

(B) The name of the obligor.

(iv) If the rating action is taken with respect to a credit rating of a security or money market instrument, as applicable:

(A) The LEI of the issuer of the security or money market instrument, if available, or, if an LEI is not available, the CIK number of the issuer of the security or money market instrument, if available;

(B) The name of the issuer of the security or money market instrument; and

(C) The CUSIP of the security or money market instrument;

(v) A classification of the rating action as either:

(A) An addition to the rating history disclosure because the credit rating was outstanding as of the date three years prior to the effective date of the requirements in paragraph (b) of this section or because the credit rating was outstanding as of the date three years prior to the nationally recognized statistical rating organization becoming registered in the class of credit ratings;

(B) An initial credit rating;

(C) An upgrade of an existing credit rating;

(D) A downgrade of an existing credit rating, which would include classifying the obligor, security, or money market instrument as in default, if applicable; or

(E) A withdrawal of an existing credit rating and, if the classification is withdrawal, the nationally recognized statistical rating organization also must classify the reason for the withdrawal as either:

(*1*) The obligor defaulted, or the security or money market instrument went into default;

(*2*) The obligation subject to the credit rating was extinguished by payment in full of all outstanding principal and interest due on the obligation according to the terms of the obligation; or

(*3*) The credit rating was withdrawn for reasons other than those set forth in paragraph (b)(2)(v)(E)(*1*) or (*2*) of this section; and

(vi) The classification of the class or subclass that applies to the credit rating as either:

(A) Financial institutions, brokers, or dealers;

(B) Insurance companies;

(C) Corporate issuers; or

Securities and Exchange Commission § 240.17g–8

(D) Issuers of structured finance products in one of the following subclasses:

(*1*) Residential mortgage backed securities ("RMBS") (for purposes of this subclass, RMBS means a securitization primarily of residential mortgages);

(*2*) Commercial mortgage backed securities ("CMBS") (for purposes of this subclass, CMBS means a securitization primarily of commercial mortgages);

(*3*) Collateralized loan obligations ("CLOs") (for purposes of this subclass, a CLO means a securitization primarily of commercial loans);

(*4*) Collateralized debt obligations ("CDOs") (for purposes of this subclass, a CDO means a securitization primarily of other debt instruments such as RMBS, CMBS, CLOs, CDOs, other asset backed securities, and corporate bonds);

(*5*) Asset-backed commercial paper conduits ("ABCP") (for purposes of this subclass, ABCP means short term notes issued by a structure that securitizes a variety of financial assets, such as trade receivables or credit card receivables, which secure the notes);

(*6*) Other asset-backed securities ("other ABS") (for purposes of this subclass, other ABS means a securitization primarily of auto loans, auto leases, floor plans, credit card receivables, student loans, consumer loans, or equipment leases); or

(*7*) Other structured finance products ("other SFPs") (for purposes of this subclass, other SFPs means any structured finance product not identified in paragraphs (b)(2)(iv)(D)(*1*) through (*6*)) of this section; or

(E) Issuers of government securities, municipal securities, or securities issued by a foreign government in one of the following subclasses:

(*1*) Sovereign issuers;

(*2*) U.S. public finance; or

(*3*) International public finance; and

(vii) The credit rating symbol, number, or score in the applicable rating scale of the nationally recognized statistical rating organization assigned to the obligor, security, or money market instrument as a result of the rating action or, if the credit rating remained unchanged as a result of the action, the credit rating symbol, number, or score in the applicable rating scale of the nationally recognized statistical rating organization assigned to the obligor, security, or money market instrument as of the date of the rating action (in either case, include a credit rating in a default category, if applicable).

(3) *Format and frequency of updating.* The information identified in paragraph (b)(2) of this section must be disclosed in an interactive data file that uses an XBRL (eXtensible Business Reporting Language) format and the List of XBRL Tags for nationally recognized statistical rating organizations as published on the Internet Web site of the Commission, and must be updated no less frequently than monthly.

(4) *Timing.* The nationally recognized statistical rating organization must disclose the information required in paragraph (b)(2) of this section:

(i) Within twelve months from the date the rating action is taken, if the credit rating subject to the action was paid for by the obligor being rated or by the issuer, underwriter, depositor, or sponsor of the security being rated; or

(ii) Within twenty-four months from the date the rating action is taken, if the credit rating subject to the action is not a credit rating described in paragraph (b)(4)(i) of this section.

(5) *Removal of a credit rating history.* The nationally recognized statistical rating organization may cease disclosing a rating history of an obligor, security, or money market instrument if at least 15 years have elapsed since a rating action classified as a withdrawal of a credit rating pursuant to paragraph (b)(2)(v)(E) of this section was disclosed in the rating history of the obligor, security, or money market instrument.

[79 FR 55264, Sept. 15, 2014, as amended at 84 FR 40258, Sept. 13, 2019]

§ 240.17g–8 Policies, procedures, and internal controls.

(a) *Policies and procedures with respect to the procedures and methodologies used to determine credit ratings.* A nationally recognized statistical rating organization must establish, maintain, enforce, and document policies and procedures reasonably designed to ensure:

(1) That the procedures and methodologies, including qualitative and

§ 240.17g-8

quantitative data and models, the nationally recognized statistical rating organization uses to determine credit ratings are approved by its board of directors or a body performing a function similar to that of a board of directors.

(2) That the procedures and methodologies, including qualitative and quantitative data and models, the nationally recognized statistical rating organization uses to determine credit ratings are developed and modified in accordance with the policies and procedures of the nationally recognized statistical rating organization.

(3) That material changes to the procedures and methodologies, including changes to qualitative and quantitative data and models, the nationally recognized statistical rating organization uses to determine credit ratings are:

(i) Applied consistently to all current and future credit ratings to which the changed procedures or methodologies apply; and

(ii) To the extent that the changes are to surveillance or monitoring procedures and methodologies, applied to current credit ratings to which the changed procedures or methodologies apply within a reasonable period of time, taking into consideration the number of credit ratings impacted, the complexity of the procedures and methodologies used to determine the credit ratings, and the type of obligor, security, or money market instrument being rated.

(4) That the nationally recognized statistical rating organization promptly publishes on an easily accessible portion of its corporate Internet Web site:

(i) Material changes to the procedures and methodologies, including to qualitative models or quantitative inputs, the nationally recognized statistical rating organization uses to determine credit ratings, the reason for the changes, and the likelihood the changes will result in changes to any current credit ratings; and

(ii) Notice of the existence of a significant error identified in a procedure or methodology, including a qualitative or quantitative model, the nationally recognized statistical rating organization uses to determine credit ratings that may result in a change to current credit ratings.

(5) That the nationally recognized statistical rating organization discloses the version of a credit rating procedure or methodology, including the qualitative methodology or quantitative inputs, used with respect to a particular credit rating.

(b) *Policies and procedures with respect to credit rating symbols, numbers, or scores.* A nationally recognized statistical rating organization must establish, maintain, enforce, and document policies and procedures that are reasonably designed to:

(1) Assess the probability that an issuer of a security or money market instrument will default, fail to make timely payments, or otherwise not make payments to investors in accordance with the terms of the security or money market instrument.

(2) Clearly define each symbol, number, or score in the rating scale used by the nationally recognized statistical rating organization to denote a credit rating category and notches within a category for each class of credit ratings for which the nationally recognized statistical rating organization is registered (including subclasses within each class) and to include such definitions in Exhibit 1 to Form NRSRO (§ 249b.300 of this chapter).

(3) Apply any symbol, number, or score defined pursuant to paragraph (b)(2) of this section in a manner that is consistent for all types of obligors, securities, and money market instruments for which the symbol, number, or score is used.

(c) *Policies and procedures with respect to look-back reviews.* The policies and procedures a nationally recognized statistical rating organization is required to establish, maintain, and enforce pursuant to section 15E(h)(4)(A) of the Act (15 U.S.C. 78o–7(h)(4)(A)) must address instances in which a review conducted pursuant to those policies and procedures determines that a conflict of interest influenced a credit rating assigned to an obligor, security, or money market instrument by including, at a minimum, procedures that are reasonably designed to ensure that the nationally recognized statistical rating organization will:

Securities and Exchange Commission

§ 240.17g–8

(1) Promptly determine whether the current credit rating assigned to the obligor, security, or money market instrument must be revised so that it no longer is influenced by a conflict of interest and is solely a product of the documented procedures and methodologies the nationally recognized statistical rating organization uses to determine credit ratings; and

(2)(i) Promptly publish, based on the determination of whether a current credit rating referred to in paragraph (c)(1) of this section must be revised (as applicable):

(A) A revised credit rating, if appropriate, and include with the publication of the revised credit rating the information required by § 240.17g–7(a)(1)(ii)(J)(*3*)(*i*); or

(B) An affirmation of the credit rating, if appropriate, and include with the publication of the affirmation the information required by § 240.17g–7(a)(1)(ii)(J)(*3*)(*ii*).

(ii) If the credit rating is not revised or affirmed pursuant to paragraph (c)(2)(i) of this section within fifteen calendar days of the date of the discovery that the credit rating was influenced by a conflict of interest, publish a rating action placing the credit rating on watch or review and include with the publication an explanation that the reason for the action is the discovery that the credit rating was influenced by a conflict of interest.

(d) *Internal control structures.* A nationally recognized statistical rating organization must take into consideration the factors identified in paragraphs (d)(1) through (4) of this section when establishing, maintaining, enforcing, and documenting an effective internal control structure governing the implementation of and adherence to policies, procedures, and methodologies for determining credit ratings pursuant to section 15E(c)(3)(A) of the Act.

(1) With respect to establishing the internal control structure, the nationally recognized statistical rating organization must take into consideration:

(i) Controls reasonably designed to ensure that a newly developed methodology or proposed update to an in-use methodology for determining credit ratings is subject to an appropriate review process (for example, by persons who are independent from the persons that developed the methodology or methodology update) and to management approval prior to the new or updated methodology being employed by the nationally recognized statistical rating organization to determine credit ratings;

(ii) Controls reasonably designed to ensure that a newly developed methodology or update to an in-use methodology for determining credit ratings is disclosed to the public for consultation prior to the new or updated methodology being employed by the nationally recognized statistical rating organization to determine credit ratings, that the nationally recognized statistical rating organization makes comments received as part of the consultation publicly available, and that the nationally recognized statistical rating organization considers the comments before implementing the methodology;

(iii) Controls reasonably designed to ensure that in-use methodologies for determining credit ratings are periodically reviewed (for example, by persons who are independent from the persons who developed and/or use the methodology) in order to analyze whether the methodology should be updated;

(iv) Controls reasonably designed to ensure that market participants have an opportunity to provide comment on whether in-use methodologies for determining credit ratings should be updated, that the nationally recognized statistical rating organization makes any such comments received publicly available, and that the nationally recognized statistical rating organization considers the comments;

(v) Controls reasonably designed to ensure that newly developed or updated quantitative models proposed to be incorporated into a credit rating methodology are evaluated and validated prior to being put into use;

(vi) Controls reasonably designed to ensure that quantitative models incorporated into in-use credit rating methodologies are periodically reviewed and back-tested;

(vii) Controls reasonably designed to ensure that a nationally recognized statistical rating organization engages in analysis before commencing the rating of a class of obligors, securities, or

§ 240.17g–8

money market instruments the nationally recognized statistical rating organization has not previously rated to determine whether the nationally recognized statistical rating organization has sufficient competency, access to necessary information, and resources to rate the type of obligor, security, or money market instrument;

(viii) Controls reasonably designed to ensure that a nationally recognized statistical rating organization engages in analysis before commencing the rating of an "exotic" or "bespoke" type of obligor, security, or money market instrument to review the feasibility of determining a credit rating;

(ix) Controls reasonably designed to ensure that measures (for example, statistics) are used to evaluate the performance of credit ratings as part of the review of in-use methodologies for determining credit ratings to analyze whether the methodologies should be updated or the work of the analysts employing the methodologies should be reviewed;

(x) Controls reasonably designed to ensure that, with respect to determining credit ratings, the work and conclusions of the lead credit analyst developing an initial credit rating or conducting surveillance on an existing credit rating is reviewed by other analysts, supervisors, or senior managers before a rating action is formally taken (for example, having the work reviewed through a rating committee process);

(xi) Controls reasonably designed to ensure that a credit analyst documents the steps taken in developing an initial credit rating or conducting surveillance on an existing credit rating with sufficient detail to permit an after-the-fact review or internal audit of the rating file to analyze whether the analyst adhered to the nationally recognized statistical rating organization's procedures and methodologies for determining credit ratings;

(xii) Controls reasonably designed to ensure that the nationally recognized statistical rating organization conducts periodic reviews or internal audits of rating files to analyze whether analysts adhere to the nationally recognized statistical rating organization's procedures and methodologies for determining credit ratings; and

(xiii) Any other controls necessary to establish an effective internal control structure taking into consideration the nature of the business of the nationally recognized statistical rating organization, including its size, activities, organizational structure, and business model.

(2) With respect to maintaining the internal control structure, the nationally recognized statistical rating organization must take into consideration:

(i) Controls reasonably designed to ensure that the nationally recognized statistical rating organization conducts periodic reviews of whether it has devoted sufficient resources to implement and operate the documented internal control structure as designed;

(ii) Controls reasonably designed to ensure that the nationally recognized statistical rating organization conducts periodic reviews or ongoing monitoring to evaluate the effectiveness of the internal control structure and whether it should be updated;

(iii) Controls reasonably designed to ensure that any identified deficiencies in the internal control structure are assessed and addressed on a timely basis;

(iv) Any other controls necessary to maintain an effective internal control structure taking into consideration the nature of the business of the nationally recognized statistical rating organization, including its size, activities, organizational structure, and business model.

(3) With respect to enforcing the internal control structure, the nationally recognized statistical rating organization must take into consideration:

(i) Controls designed to ensure that additional training is provided or discipline taken with respect to employees who fail to adhere to requirements imposed by the internal control structure;

(ii) Controls designed to ensure that a process is in place for employees to report failures to adhere to the internal control structure; and

(iii) Any other controls necessary to enforce an effective internal control structure taking into consideration the nature of the business of the nationally

Securities and Exchange Commission § 240.17g-10

recognized statistical rating organization, including its size, activities, organizational structure, and business model.

(4) With respect to documenting the internal control structure, the nationally recognized statistical rating organization must take into consideration any controls necessary to document an effective internal control structure taking into consideration the nature of the business of the nationally recognized statistical rating organization, including its size, activities, organizational structure, and business model.

[79 FR 55267, Sept. 15, 2014]

§ 240.17g-9 Standards of training, experience, and competence for credit analysts.

(a) A nationally recognized statistical rating organization must establish, maintain, enforce, and document standards of training, experience, and competence for the individuals it employs to participate in the determination of credit ratings that are reasonably designed to achieve the objective that the nationally recognized statistical rating organization produces accurate credit ratings in the classes of credit ratings for which the nationally recognized statistical rating organization is registered.

(b) The nationally recognized statistical rating organization must consider the following when establishing the standards required under paragraph (a) of this section:

(1) If the credit rating procedures and methodologies used by the individual involve qualitative analysis, the knowledge necessary to effectively evaluate and process the data relevant to the creditworthiness of the obligor being rated or the issuer of the securities or money market instruments being rated;

(2) If the credit rating procedures and methodologies used by the individual involve quantitative analysis, the technical expertise necessary to understand any models and model inputs that are a part of the procedures and methodologies;

(3) The classes and subclasses of credit ratings for which the individual participates in determining credit ratings and the factors relevant to such classes and subclasses, including the geographic location, sector, industry, regulatory and legal framework, and underlying assets, applicable to the obligors or issuers in the classes and subclasses; and

(4) The complexity of the obligors, securities, or money market instruments for which the individual participates in determining credit ratings.

(c) The nationally recognized statistical rating organization must include the following in the standards required under paragraph (a) of this section:

(1) A requirement for periodic testing of the individuals employed by the nationally recognized statistical rating organization to participate in the determination of credit ratings on their knowledge of the procedures and methodologies used by the nationally recognized statistical rating organization to determine credit ratings in the classes and subclasses of credit ratings for which the individual participates in determining credit ratings; and

(2) A requirement that at least one individual with an appropriate level of experience in performing credit analysis, but not less than three years, participates in the determination of a credit rating.

[79 FR 55269, Sept. 15, 2014]

§ 240.17g-10 Certification of providers of third-party due diligence services in connection with asset-backed securities.

(a) The written certification that a person employed to provide third-party due diligence services is required to provide to a nationally recognized statistical rating organization pursuant to section 15E(s)(4)(B) of the Act (15 U.S.C. 78o-7(s)(4)(B)) must be on Form ABS Due Diligence-15E (§ 249b.500 of this chapter).

(b) The written certification must be signed by an individual who is duly authorized by the person providing the third-party due diligence services to make such a certification.

(c) A person employed to provide third-party due diligence services will be deemed to have satisfied its obligations under section 15E(s)(4)(B) of the Act (15 U.S.C. 78o-7(s)(4)(B)) if the person promptly delivers an executed Form ABS Due Diligence-15E (§ 249b.500

§ 240.17h–1T

of this chapter) after completion of the due diligence services to:

(1) A nationally recognized statistical rating organization that provided a written request for the Form prior to the completion of the due diligence services stating that the services relate to a credit rating the nationally recognized statistical rating organization is producing;

(2) A nationally recognized statistical rating organization that provides a written request for the Form after the completion of the due diligence services stating that the services relate to a credit rating the nationally recognized statistical rating organization is producing; and

(3) The issuer or underwriter of the asset-backed security for which the due diligence services relate that maintains the Internet Web site with respect to the asset-backed security pursuant to § 240.17g–5(a)(3).

(d) For purposes of section 15E(s)(4)(B) of the Act (15 U.S.C. 78o–7(s)(4)(B)) and this section:

(1) The term *due diligence services* means a review of the assets underlying an asset-backed security, as defined in section 3(a)(79) of the Act (15 U.S.C. 78c(a)(79)) for the purpose of making findings with respect to:

(i) The accuracy of the information or data about the assets provided, directly or indirectly, by the securitizer or originator of the assets;

(ii) Whether the origination of the assets conformed to, or deviated from, stated underwriting or credit extension guidelines, standards, criteria, or other requirements;

(iii) The value of collateral securing the assets;

(iv) Whether the originator of the assets complied with federal, state, or local laws or regulations; or

(v) Any other factor or characteristic of the assets that would be material to the likelihood that the issuer of the asset-backed security will pay interest and principal in accordance with applicable terms and conditions.

(2) The term *issuer* includes a sponsor, as defined in § 229.1101 of this chapter, or depositor, as defined in § 229.1101 of this chapter, that participates in the issuance of an asset-backed security, as defined in section 3(a)(79) of the Act (15 U.S.C. 78c(a)(79)).

(3) The term *originator* has the same meaning as in section 15G(a)(4) of the Act (15 U.S.C. 78o–9(a)(4)).

(4) The term *securitizer* has the same meaning as in section 15G(a)(3) of the Act (15 U.S.C. 78o–9(a)(3)).

[79 FR 55270, Sept. 15, 2014]

§ 240.17h–1T Risk assessment recordkeeping requirements for associated persons of brokers and dealers.

(a) *Requirement to maintain and preserve information.* (1) Every broker or dealer registered with the Commission pursuant to section 15 of the Act, and every municipal securities dealer registered pursuant to Section 15B of the Act for which the Commission is the appropriate regulatory agency, unless exempt pursuant to paragraph (d) of this section, shall maintain and preserve the following information:

(i) An organizational chart which includes the broker or dealer and all its associated persons. Included in the organizational chart shall be a designation of which associated persons are Material Associated Persons as that term is used in paragraph (a)(2) of this section;

(ii) Written policies, procedures, or systems concerning the broker or dealer's:

(A) Method(s) for monitoring and controlling financial and operational risks to it resulting from the activities of any of its associated persons, other than a natural person;

(B) Financing and capital adequacy, including information regarding sources of funding, together with a narrative discussion by management of the liquidity of the material assets, the structure of debt capital, and sources of alternative funding; and

(C) Trading positions and risks, such as records regarding reporting responsibilities for trading activities, policies relating to restrictions or limitations on trading securities and financial instruments or products, and a description of the types of reviews conducted to monitor existing positions, and limitations or restrictions on trading activities.

Securities and Exchange Commission § 240.17h-1T

(iii) A description of all material pending legal or arbitration proceedings involving a Material Associated Person or the broker or dealer that are required to be disclosed by the ultimate holding company under generally accepted accounting principles on a consolidated basis;

(iv) Consolidated and consolidating balance sheets, prepared in accordance with generally accepted accounting principles, which may be unaudited and which shall include the notes to the financial statements, as of quarter end for the broker or dealer and its ultimate holding company;

(v) Quarterly consolidated and consolidating income statements and consolidated cash flow statements, prepared in accordance with generally accepted accounting principles, which may be unaudited and which shall include the notes to the financial statements, for the broker or dealer and its ultimate holding company;

NOTE 1 TO PARAGRAPH (a)(1)(v). Statements of comprehensive income (as defined in §210.1–02 of Regulation S–X of this chapter) must be included in place of income statements, if required by the applicable generally accepted accounting principles.

(vi) The amount as of quarter end, and at month end if greater than quarter end, of the aggregate long and short securities and commodities positions held by each Material Associated Person, including a separate listing of each single unhedged securities or commodities position, other than U.S. government or agency securities, that exceeds the Materiality Threshold at any month end;

(vii) The notional or contractual amounts, and in the case of options, the value of the underlying instruments, as of quarter end, of financial instruments with off-balance sheet risk and financial instruments with concentrations of credit risk where the Material Associated Person operates a trading book, with a separate entry of each commitment where the credit risk (defined as the possibility that a loss may occur from the failure of another party to perform according to the terms of a contract) with respect to a counterparty exceeds the Materiality Threshold at quarter end;

(viii) The aggregate amount as of quarter end, and the amount at month end if greater than quarter end, of all bridge loans and those other material unsecured extensions of credit (not including intra-group receivables) with an initial or remaining maturity of less than one year by each Material Associated Person, together with the allowance for losses for such transactions, including a specific description of any extensions of credit to a single borrower exceeding the Materiality Threshold at any month end;

(ix) The aggregate amount as of quarter end, and the amount at month end if greater than quarter end, of commercial paper, secured and other unsecured borrowing, bank loans, lines of credit, or any other borrowings, and the principal installments of long-term or medium-term debt, scheduled to mature within twelve months from the most recent fiscal quarter for the broker or dealer and each Material Associated Person; and

(x) Data relating to real estate activities, including mortgage loans and investments in real estate, but not including trading positions in whole loans, conducted by each Material Associated Person, including:

(A) Real estate loans and investments by type of property, such as construction and development, residential, commercial and industrial or farmland;

(B) The geographic distribution, as of quarter end, by type of loan or investment where the amount exceeds the Materiality Threshold at quarter end;

(C) The aggregate carrying value of loans which each Material Associated Person deems to be not current as to interest or principal, together with the Material Associated Person's criteria for the determination of which loans are not current, or which are in the process of foreclosure or that have been restructured;

(D) The allowance for losses on loans and on investment real estate by type of loan or investment, and the activity in the allowance for losses account; and

(E) Information about risk concentration in the real estate investment and loan portfolio, including information about risk concentration to

§ 240.17h–1T

a single borrower or location of property if the risk concentration exceeds the Materiality Threshold at quarter end.

(2) The determination of whether an associated person of a broker or dealer is a Material Associated Person shall involve consideration of all aspects of the activities of, and the relationship between, both entities, including without limitation, the following factors:

(i) The legal relationship between the broker or dealer and the associated person;

(ii) The overall financing requirements of the broker or dealer and the associated person, and the degree, if any, to which the broker or dealer and the associated person are financially dependent on each other;

(iii) The degree, if any, to which the broker or dealer or its customers rely on the associated person for operational support or services in connection with the broker's or dealer's business;

(iv) The level of risk present in the activities of the broker's or dealer's associated persons; and

(v) The extent to which the associated person has the authority or the ability to cause a withdrawal of capital from the broker or dealer.

(3) The information, reports and records required by the provisions of this section shall be maintained and preserved in accordance with the provisions of § 240.17a–4 and shall be kept for a period of not less than three years in an easily accessible place.

(4) For the purposes of this section and § 240.17h–2T, the term "Materiality Threshold" shall mean the greater of:

(i) $100 million; or

(ii) 10 percent of the broker or dealer's tentative net capital based on the most recently filed Form X–17A–5 or 10 percent of the Material Associated Person's tangible net worth, whichever is greater.

(b) *Special provisions with respect to material associated persons subject to the supervision of certain domestic regulators.* A broker or dealer shall be deemed to be in compliance with the recordkeeping requirements of paragraph (a) of this section with respect to a Material Associated Person if:

(1) Such Material Associated Person is subject to examination by, or the reporting requirements of, a Federal banking agency and the broker or dealer maintains in accordance with the provisions of this section copies of all reports submitted by such Material Associated Person with the Federal banking agency pursuant to section 5211 of the Revised Statutes, section 9 of the Federal Reserve Act, section 7(a) of the Federal Deposit Insurance Act, section 10(b) of the Home Owners' Loan Act, or section 5 of the Bank Holding Company Act of 1956 other than the Form FR 2068; or

(2) If such Material Associated Person is subject to the supervision of an insurance commissioner or other similar official or agency of a state, and the broker or dealer maintains in accordance with the provisions of this section copies of the Annual and Quarterly Statements with Schedules and Exhibits prepared by the insurance company on forms prescribed by the National Association of Insurance Commissioners; or

(3) In the event an insurance company is not required to prepare Quarterly Statements on forms prescribed by the National Association of Insurance Commissioners, the broker or dealer must maintain and preserve the records required by paragraph (a) of this section on a quarterly basis; or

(4) In the case of a Material Associated Person that is subject to the supervision of the Commodity Futures Trading Commission, the broker or dealer maintains in accordance with the provisions of this section copies of the reports filed on Forms 1 FR-FCM or 1 FR-IB by such Material Associated Person with the Commodity Futures Trading Commission.

(c) *Special provisions with respect to material associated persons subject to the supervision of a foreign financial regulatory authority.* A broker or dealer shall be deemed to be in compliance with the recordkeeping requirements of paragraph (a) of this section with respect to a Material Associated Person if such broker or dealer maintains in accordance with the provisions of this section copies of the reports filed by such Material Associated Persons with

Securities and Exchange Commission

§ 240.17h–1T

a Foreign Financial Regulatory Authority. The broker or dealer shall maintain a copy of the original report and a copy translated into the English language. For the purposes of this section, the term Foreign Financial Regulatory Authority shall have the meaning set forth in section 3(a)(51) of the Act.

(d) *Exemptions.* (1) The provisions of this section shall not apply to any broker or dealer which is exempt from the provisions of § 240.15c3–3:

(i) Pursuant to paragraph (k)(1) of § 240.15c3–3; or

(ii) Pursuant to paragraph (k)(2) of § 240.15c3–3; or

(iii) If the broker or dealer does not qualify for an exemption from the provisions of § 240.15c3–3 and such broker or dealer does not hold funds or securities for, or owe money or securities to, customers and does not carry the accounts of or for customers; unless

(iv) In the case of paragraphs (d)(1)(ii) or (d)(1)(iii) of this section, the broker or dealer maintains capital including debt subordinated in accordance with appendix D of § 240.15c3–1 equal to or greater than $20,000,000.

(2) The provisions of this section shall not apply to any broker or dealer which maintains capital including debt subordinated in accordance with appendix D of section 240.15c3–1 of less than $250,000, even if the broker or dealer hold funds or securities for, or owes money or securities to, customers or carries the accounts of or for customers.

(3) In calculating capital for the purposes of this paragraph, a broker or dealer shall include the equity capital and subordinated debt of any other registered brokers or dealers that are associated with the broker or dealer and are not otherwise exempt from the provisions pursuant to paragraph (d)(1)(i) of this section.

(4) The provisions of this section shall not apply to a broker or dealer that computes certain of its capital charges in accordance with § 240.15c3–1e if that broker or dealer is affiliated with an ultimate holding company that is not an ultimate holding company that has a principal regulator, as defined in § 240.15c3–1(c)(13).

(5) The Commission may, upon written application by a Reporting Broker or Dealer, exempt from the provisions of this section, either unconditionally or on specified terms and conditions, any brokers or dealers associated with such Reporting Broker or Dealer. The term "Reporting Broker or Dealer" shall mean, in the case of a broker or dealer that is associated with other registered brokers or dealers, the broker or dealer which maintains the greatest amount of net capital as reported on its most recently fixed Form X–17A–5. In granting exemptions under this section, the Commission shall consider, among other factors, whether the records and other information required to be maintained pursuant to this section concerning the Material Associated Persons of the broker or dealer associated with the Reporting Broker or Dealer will be available to the Commission pursuant to § 240.17h–2T.

(e) *Location of records.* A broker or dealer required to maintain records concerning a Material Associated Person pursuant to this section may maintain those records either at the Material Associated Person or at a records storage facility provided that the records are located within the boundaries of the United States and the records are kept in an easily accessible place, as that term is used in § 240.17a–4. In order to operate pursuant to the provisions of this paragraph, the Material Associated Person or other entity maintaining the records shall file with the Commission a written undertaking in form acceptable to the Commission, signed by a duly authorized person, to the effect that the records will be treated as if the broker or dealer was maintaining the records pursuant to this section and that the entity maintaining the records undertakes to permit examination of such records at any time or from time to time during business hours by representatives or designees of the Commission and to promptly furnish the Commission or its designee true, correct, complete and current hard copy of any or all or any part of such records. The election to operate pursuant to the provisions of this paragraph shall not relieve the broker or dealer required to maintain and preserve such records from any of

§ 240.17h–2T

its responsibilities under this section or section 240.17h–2T.

(f) *Confidentiality.* All information obtained by the Commission pursuant to the provisions of this section from a broker or dealer concerning a Material Associated Person shall be deemed confidential information for the purposes of section 24(b) of the Act.

(g) *Temporary implementation schedule.* Every broker or dealer subject to the requirements of this section shall maintain and preserve the information required by paragraphs (a)(1)(i), (ii), and (iii) of this section commencing September 30, 1992. Commencing December 31, 1992, the provisions of this section shall apply in their entirety.

[57 FR 32168, July 21, 1992, as amended at 58 FR 25774, Apr. 28, 1993; 69 FR 34472, June 21, 2004; 69 FR 34494, June 21, 2004; 76 FR 50122, Aug. 12, 2011; 78 FR 42865, July 18, 2013; 83 FR 50223, Oct. 4, 2018]

§ 240.17h–2T **Risk assessment reporting requirements for brokers and dealers.**

(a) *Reporting requirements of risk assessment information required to be maintained by section 240.17h–1T.* (1) Every broker or dealer registered with the Commission pursuant to section 15 of the Act, and every municipal securities dealer registered pursuant to section 15B of the Act for which the Commission is the appropriate regulatory agency, unless exempt pursuant to paragraph (b) of this section, shall file a Form 17–H within 60 calendar days after the end of each fiscal quarter. The Form 17–H for the fourth fiscal quarter shall be filed within 60 calendar days of the end of the fiscal year. The cumulative year-end financial statements required by section 240.17h–1T may be filed separately within 105 calendar days of the end of the fiscal year.

(2) The reports required to be filed pursuant to paragraph (a)(1) of this section shall be considered filed when received at the Commission's principal office in Washington, DC.

(3) For the purposes of this section, the term Material Associated Person shall have the meaning used in § 240.17h–1T.

(b) *Exemptions.* (1) The provisions of this section shall not apply to any broker or dealer which is exempt from the provisions of section 240.15c3–3:

(i) Pursuant to paragraph (k)(1) of § 240.15c3–3; or

(ii) Pursuant to paragraph (k)(2) of § 240.15c3–3; or

(iii) If the broker or dealer does not qualify for an exemption from the provisions of § 240.15c3–3 and such broker or dealer does not hold funds or securities for, or owe money or securities to, customers and does not carry the accounts of or for customers; unless

(iv) In the case of paragraphs (b)(1)(ii) or (b)(1)(iii) of this section, the broker or dealer maintains capital including debt subordinated in accordance with appendix D of § 240.15c3–1 equal to or greater than $20,000,000.

(2) The provisions of this section shall not apply to any broker or dealer which maintains capital including debt subordinated in accordance with appendix D of § 240.15c3–1 of less than $250,000, even if the broker or dealer hold funds or securities for, or owes money or securities to, customers'or carries the accounts of or for customers.

(3) In calculating capital and subordinated debt for the purposes of this section, a broker or dealer shall include the equity capital and subordinated debt of any other registered brokers or dealers that are associated with the broker or dealer and are not otherwise exempt from the provisions pursuant to paragraph (b)(1)(i) of this section.

(4) The provisions of this section shall not apply to a broker or dealer that computes certain of its capital charges in accordance with § 240.15c3–1e if that broker or dealer is affiliated with an ultimate holding company that is not an ultimate holding company that has a principal regulator, as defined in § 240.15c3–1(c)(13).

(5) The Commission may, upon written application by a Reporting Broker or Dealer, exempt from the provisions of this section, either unconditionally or on specified terms and conditions, any brokers or dealers associated with the Reporting Broker or Dealer. The term "Reporting Broker or Dealer" shall mean, in the case of a broker or dealer that is associated with other registered brokers or dealers, the broker or dealer which maintains the

Securities and Exchange Commission § 240.17h-2T

greatest amount of net capital as reported on its most recently filed Form X-17A-5. In granting exemptions under this section, the Commission shall consider, among other factors, whether the records and other information required to be maintained pursuant to § 240.17h-1T concerning the Material Associated Persons of the broker or dealer associated with the Reporting Broker or Dealer will be available to the Commission pursuant to the provisions of this section.

(c) *Special provisions with respect to material associated persons subject to the supervision of certain domestic regulators.* A broker or dealer shall be deemed to be in compliance with the reporting requirements of paragraph (a) of this section with respect to a Material Associated Person if:

(1) Such Material Associated Person is subject to examination by or the reporting requirements of a Federal banking agency and the broker or dealer or such Material Associated Person furnishes in accordance with paragraph (a) of this section copies of reports filed on Form FR Y-9C, Form FR Y-6, Form FR Y-7, and Form FR 2068 by the Material Associated Person with the Federal banking agency pursuant to section 5211 of the Revised Statutes, section 9 of the Federal Reserve Act, section 7(a) of the Federal Deposit Insurance Act, section 10(b) of the Home Owners' Loan Act, or section 5 of the Bank Holding Company Act of 1956; or

(2) If the Material Associated Person is subject to the supervision of an insurance commissioner or other similar official agency of a state; and

(i) In the case of a Material Associated Person organized as a public stock company, the broker or dealer furnishes in accordance with the provisions of this section copies of the filings made by the insurance company pursuant to sections 13 or 15 of the Act and the Investment Company Act of 1940; or

(ii) In the case of Material Associated Person organized as a mutual insurance company or a non-public stock company, the broker or dealer furnishes in accordance with the provisions of this section copies of the Annual and Quarterly Statements prepared by the insurance company on forms prescribed by the National Association of Insurance Commissioners. The Annual Statement furnished to the Commission pursuant to this section shall include: The classification (distribution by state) section from the schedule of real estate; distribution by state, the interest overdue (more than three months), in process of foreclosure, and foreclosed properties transferred to real estate during the year sections from the schedule of mortgages; and the quality and maturity distribution of all bonds at statement values and by major types of issues section from the schedule of bonds and stocks. All other Schedules and Exhibits to such Annual and Quarterly Statements shall be maintained at the broker-dealer pursuant to the provisions of § 240.17h-1T but not furnished to the Commission.

(iii) In the event an insurance company organized as a stock or mutual company is not required to prepare Quarterly Statements, the broker or dealer must file with the Commission a Form 17-H in accordance with the provisions of this section on a quarterly basis.

(3) In the case of a Material Associated Person that is subject to the supervision of the Commodity Futures Trading Commission, the broker or dealer furnishes in accordance with the provisions of this section copies of the reports filed by the Material Associated Person with the Commodity Futures Trading Commission on Forms 1 FR-FCM or 1 FR-IB.

(4) No broker or dealer shall be required to furnish to the Commission any examination report of any Federal banking agency or any supervisory recommendations or analyses contained therein with respect to a Material Associated Person that is subject to the regulation of a Federal banking agency. All information received by the Commission pursuant to this section concerning a Material Associated Person that is subject to examination by or the reporting requirements of a Federal banking agency shall be deemed confidential for the purposes of section 24(b) of the Act.

(5) The furnishing of any information or documents by a broker or dealer

§ 240.17Ab2–1

pursuant to this section shall not constitute an admission for any purpose that a Material Associated Person is otherwise subject to the Act. Any documents or information furnished to the Commission by a broker or dealer pursuant to this rule shall not be deemed to be "filed" for the purposes of the liabilities set forth in section 18 of the Act.

(d) *Special provisions with respect to material associated persons subject to the supervision of a foreign financial regulatory authority.* A broker or dealer shall be deemed to be in compliance with the reporting requirements of this section with respect to a Material Associated Person if such broker or dealer furnishes in accordance with the provisions of this section copies of the reports filed by such Material Associated Person with a Foreign Financial Regulatory Authority. The broker or dealer shall file a copy of the original report and a copy translated into the English language. For the purposes of this section, the term Foreign Financial Regulatory Authority shall have the meaning set forth in section 3(a)(51) of the Act.

(e) *Confidentiality.* All information obtained by the Commission pursuant to the provisions of this section from a broker or dealer concerning a Material Associated Person shall be deemed confidential information for the purposes of section 24(b) of the Act.

(f) *Temporary implementation schedule.* Every broker or dealer subject to the requirements of this section shall file the information required by Items 1, 2 and 3 of Form 17–H by October 31, 1992. Commencing December 31, 1992, the provisions of this section shall apply in their entirety.

[57 FR 32170, July 21, 1992, as amended at 69 FR 34472, June 21, 2004; 69 FR 34494, June 21, 2004; 78 FR 42865, July 18, 2013]

§ 240.17Ab2–1 **Registration of clearing agencies.**

(a) An application for registration or for exemption from registration as a clearing agency, as defined in section 3(a)(23) of the Act, or an amendment to any such application shall be filed with the Commission on Form CA–1, in accordance with the instructions thereto.

(b) Any applicant for registration or for exemption from registration as a clearing agency whose application is filed with the Commission on or before November 24, 1975, on and in accordance with the instructions to Form CA–1, with respect to the clearing agency activities described in the application shall, during the period from December 1, 1975 until the Commission grants registration, denies registration or grants an exemption from registration, be exempt from the registration provisions of section 17A(b) of the Act and the rules and regulations thereunder and, unless the Commission shall otherwise provide by rule or by order, the provisions of the Act and the rules and regulations thereunder which would be applicable to clearing agencies as a result of registration under the Act.

(c)(1) The Commission, upon the request of a clearing agency, may grant registration of the clearing agency in accordance with sections 17A(b) and 19(a)(1) of the Act but exempt the registrant from one or more of the requirements as to which the Commission is directed to make a determination pursuant to paragraphs (A) through (I) of section 17A(b)(3) of the Act, provided that any such registration shall be effective only for eighteen months from the date the registration is made effective (or such longer period as the Commission may provide by order).

(2) In the case of any clearing agency registered in accordance with paragraph (c)(1) of this section, not later than nine months from the date such registration is made effective the Commission either will grant registration in accordance with sections 17A(b) and 19(a)(1) of the Act, without exempting the registrant from one or more of the requirements as to which the Commission is directed to make a determination pursuant to subparagraphs (A) through (I) of section 17A(b)(3) of the Act, or will institute proceedings in accordance with section 19(a)(1)(B) of the Act to determine whether registration should be denied at the expiration of the registration granted in accordance with paragraph (c)(1) of this section.

(d) The filing of an amendment to an application for registration or for exemption from registration as a clearing agency, which registration or exemption has not been granted, or the filing of additional information or documents prior to the granting of registration or an exemption from registration shall extend to ninety days from the date such filing is made (or to such longer period as to which the applicant consents) the period within which the Commission shall grant registration, institute proceedings to determine whether such registration shall be denied, or conditionally or unconditionally exempt registrant from the registration and other provisions of section 17A of the Act or the rules or regulations thereunder.

(e) If any information reported at items 1–3 of Form CA-1 is or becomes inaccurate, misleading or incomplete for any reason, whether before or after registration or an exemption from registration has been granted, the registrant shall file promptly an amendment on Form CA-1 correcting the inaccurate, misleading or incomplete information.

(f) Every application for registration or for exemption from registration as a clearing agency or amendment to, or additional information or document filed in connection with, any such application shall constitute a "report" or "application" within the meaning of sections 17, 17A, 19 and 32(a) of the Act.

[40 FR 52358, Nov. 10, 1975]

§ 240.17Ab2-2 **Determinations affecting covered clearing agencies.**

(a) The Commission may, if it deems appropriate, upon application by any clearing agency or member of a clearing agency, or on its own initiative, determine whether a covered clearing agency is systemically important in multiple jurisdictions. In determining whether a covered clearing agency is systemically important in multiple jurisdictions, the Commission may consider:

(1) Whether the covered clearing agency is a designated clearing agency; and

(2) Whether the clearing agency has been determined to be systemically important by one or more jurisdictions other than the United States through a process that includes consideration of whether the foreseeable effects of a failure or disruption of the designated clearing agency could threaten the stability of each relevant jurisdiction's financial system.

(b) The Commission may, if it deems appropriate, determine whether any of the activities of a clearing agency providing central counterparty services, in addition to clearing agencies registered with the Commission for the purpose of clearing security-based swaps, have a more complex risk profile. In determining whether a clearing agency's activity has a more complex risk profile, the Commission may consider whether the clearing agency clears financial instruments that are characterized by discrete jump-to-default price changes or that are highly correlated with potential participant defaults.

(c) The Commission may, if it deems appropriate, upon application by any clearing agency or member of a clearing agency, or on its own initiative, determine whether to rescind any determination made pursuant to paragraph (a) or (b) of this section. In determining whether to rescind any such determination, the Commission may consider a change in circumstances such that the covered clearing agency no longer meets the criteria supporting the determination in effect.

(d) The Commission shall publish notice of its intention to consider making a determination under paragraph (a), (b), or (c) of this section, together with a brief statement of the grounds under consideration therefor, and provide at least a 30-day public comment period prior to any such determination, giving all interested persons an opportunity to submit written data, views, and arguments concerning such proposed determination. The Commission may provide the clearing agency subject to the proposed determination opportunity for hearing regarding the proposed determination.

(e) Notice of determinations under paragraph (a), (b), or (c) of this section shall be given by prompt publication thereof, together with a statement of written reasons therefor.

§ 240.17Ac2-1

(f) For purposes of this rule, the terms *covered clearing agency*, *designated clearing agency*, and *systemically important in multiple jurisdictions* shall have the meanings set forth in § 240.17Ad-22(a).

[81 FR 70901, Oct. 13, 2016]

§ 240.17Ac2-1 Application for registration of transfer agents.

(a) An application for registration, pursuant to section 17A(c) of the Act, of a transfer agent for which the Commission is the appropriate regulatory agency, as defined in section 3(a)(34)(B) of the Act, shall be filed with the Commission on Form TA-1, in accordance with the instructions contained therein and shall become effective on the thirtieth day following the date on which the application is filed, unless the Commission takes affirmative action to accelerate, deny or postpone such registration in accord- ance with the provisions of section 17A(c) of the Act.

(b) The filing of any amendment to an application for registration as a transfer agent pursuant to paragraph (a) of this section, which registration has not become effective, shall postpone the effective date of the registration until the thirtieth day following the date on which the amendment is filed, unless the Commission takes affirmative action to accelerate, deny or postpone the registration in accordance with the provisions of section 17A(c) of the Act.

(c) If any of the information reported on Form TA-1 (§ 249b.100 of this chapter) becomes inaccurate, misleading, or incomplete, the registrant shall correct the information by filing an amendment within sixty days following the date on which the information becomes inaccurate, misleading, or incomplete.

(d) Every registration and amendment filed pursuant to this section shall be filed with the Commission electronically in the Commission's EDGAR system. Transfer agents should refer to Form TA-1 and the instructions to the form (§ 249b.100 of this chapter) and to the EDGAR Filer Manual (§ 232.301 of this chapter) for the technical requirements and instructions for electronic filing. Transfer agents that have previously filed a Form TA-1 with the Commission must refile the information on their Form TA-1, as amended, in electronic format in EDGAR as an amended Form TA-1.

(e) Every registration and amendment filed pursuant to this section shall constitute a "report" or "application" within the meaning of sections 17, 17A(c), and 32(a) of the Act.

[40 FR 51184, Nov. 4, 1975, as amended at 51 FR 12127, Apr. 9, 1986; 71 FR 74708, Dec. 12, 2006]

§ 240.17Ac2-2 Annual reporting requirement for registered transfer agents.

(a) Every transfer agent registered on December 31 must file a report covering the reporting period on Form TA-2 (§ 249b.102 of this chapter) by March 31 following the end of the reporting period. Form TA-2 must be completed in accordance with the instructions contained in the Form. A transfer agent may file an amendment to Form TA-2 pursuant to the instructions on the form to correct information that has become inaccurate, incomplete, or misleading. A transfer agent may file an amendment at any time; however, in order to be timely filed, all required portions of the form must be completed and filed in accordance with this section and the instructions to the form by the date the form is required to be filed with the Commission.

(1) A registered transfer agent that received fewer than 1,000 items for transfer in the reporting period and that did not maintain master securityholder files for more than 1,000 individual securityholder accounts as of December 31 of the reporting period must complete Questions 1 through 5, 11, and the signature section of Form TA-2.

(2) A named transfer agent that engaged a service company to perform all of its transfer agent functions during the reporting period must complete Questions 1 through 3 and the signature section of Form TA-2.

(3) A named transfer agent that engaged a service company to perform some but not all of its transfer agent functions during the reporting period must complete all of Form TA-2 but should enter zero (0) for those questions that relate to transfer agent

Securities and Exchange Commission § 240.17Ad–1

functions performed by the service company on behalf of the named transfer agent.

(b) For purposes of this section, the term *reporting period* shall mean the calendar year ending December 31 for which Form TA–2 is being filed. The term *named transfer agent* shall have the same meaning as defined in § 240.17Ad–9(j). The term *service company* shall have the same meaning as defined in § 240.17Ad–9(k).

(c) Every annual report and amendment filed pursuant to this section shall be filed with the Commission electronically in the Commission's EDGAR system. Transfer agents should refer to Form TA–2 and the instructions to the form (§ 249b.102 of this chapter) and the EDGAR Filer Manual (§ 232.301 of this chapter) for further information regarding electronic filing. Every registered transfer agent must file an electronic Form TA–1 with the Commission, or an electronic amendment to its Form TA–1 if the transfer agent previously filed a paper Form TA–1 with the Commission, before it may file an electronic Form TA–2 or Form TA–W with the Commission.

[65 FR 36610, June 9, 2000, as amended at 71 FR 74708, Dec. 12, 2006]

§ 240.17Ac3–1 Withdrawal from registration with the Commission.

(a) Notice of withdrawal from registration as a transfer agent with the Commission pursuant to section 17A(c)(4) of the Act shall be filed on Form TA–W in accordance with the instructions contained thereon.

(b) Except as hereinafter provided, a notice to withdraw from registration filed by a transfer agent pursuant to section 17A(c)(4) of the Act shall become effective on the sixtieth day after the filing thereof with the Commission or within such shorter period of time as the Commission may determine. If a notice to withdraw from registration is filed with the Commission at any time subsequent to the date of issuance of a Commission order instituting proceedings pursuant to section 17A(c)(3) of the Act, or if prior to the effective date of the notice of withdrawal the Commission institutes such a proceeding or a proceeding to impose terms and conditions upon such withdrawal, the notice of withdrawal shall not become effective except at such time and upon such terms and conditions as the Commission deems necessary or appropriate in the public interest, for the protection of investors, or in furtherance of the purposes of section 17A.

(c) Every withdrawal from registration filed pursuant to this section shall be filed with the Commission electronically in the Commission's EDGAR system. Transfer agents should refer to Form TA–W and the instructions to the form (§ 249b.101 of this chapter) and the EDGAR Filer Manual (§ 232.301 of this chapter) for further information regarding electronic filing.

(d) Every notice of withdrawal filed pursuant to this rule shall constitute a "report" within the meaning of sections 17 and 32(a) of the Act.

[42 FR 44984, Sept. 8, 1977, as amended at 71 FR 74709, Dec. 12, 2006]

§ 240.17Ad–1 Definitions.

As used in this section and §§ 240.17Ad–2, 240.17Ad–3, 240.17Ad–4, 240.17Ad–5, 240.17Ad–6, and 240.17Ad–7:

(a)(1) The term *item* means:

(i) A certificate or certificates of the same issue of securities covered by one ticket (or, if there is no ticket, presented by one presentor) presented for transfer, or an instruction to a transfer agent which holds securities registered in the name of the presentor to transfer or to make available all or a portion of those securities;

(ii) Each line on a "deposit shipment control list" or a "withdrawal shipment control list" submitted by a registered clearing agency; or

(iii) In the case of an outside registrar, each certificate to be countersigned.

(2) If a "deposit shipment control list" or "withdrawal shipment control list" contains both routine and non-routine transfer instructions, a registered transfer agent shall at its option:

(i) Retain all transfer instructions listed on the shipment control list and treat each line on the shipment control list as a routine item; or

(ii) Return promptly to the registered clearing agency a shipment control list line containing non-routine

§ 240.17Ad-1

transfer instructions (together with a copy of the shipment control list, an explanation for the return instructions and all routine transfer instructions reflected on the same line) and treat each line on the shipment control list that reflects retained transfer instructions as a routine item.

(3) A *deposit shipment control list* means a list of transfer instructions that accompanies certificates to be cancelled and reissued in the nominee name of a registered clearing agency.

(4) A *withdrawal shipment control list* means a list of instructions (either in paper or electronic medium) that:

(i) Directs issuance of certificates in the names of persons or entities other than the registered clearing agency; and

(ii) Accompanies certificates to be cancelled which are registered in the nominee name of a registered clearing agency, or directs the transfer agent to reduce certificate or position balances maintained by the transfer agent on behalf of a registered clearing agency under that clearing agency's transfer agent custody program

(b) The term *outside registrar* with respect to a transfer item means a transfer agent which performs only the registrar function for the certificate or certificates presented for transfer and includes the persons performing similar functions with respect to debt issues.

(c) An item is *made available* when

(1) In the case of an item for which the services of an outside registrar are not required, or which has been received from an outside registrar after processing, the transfer agent dispatches or mails the item to, or the item is awaiting pick-up by, the presentor or a person designated by the presentor, or

(2) In the case of an item for which the services of an outside registrar are required, the transfer agent dispatches or mails the item to, or the item is awaiting pick-up by, the outside registrar, or

(3) In the case of an item for which an outside registrar has completed processing, the outside registrar dispatches or mails the item to, or the item is awaiting pick-up by, the presenting transfer agent.

(d) The *transfer* of an item is accomplished when, in accordance with the presenter's instructions, all acts necessary to cancel the certificate or certificates presented for transfer and to issue a new certificate or certificates, including the performance of the registrar function, are completed and the item is made available to the presenter by the transfer agent, or when, in accordance with the presenter's instructions, a transfer agent which holds securities registered in the name of the presenter completes all acts necessary to issue a new certificate or certificates representing all or a portion of those securities and makes available the new certificate or certificates to the presenter or a person designated by the presenter or, with respect to those transfers of record ownership to be accomplished without the physical issuance of certificates, completes registration of change in ownership of all or a portion of those securities.

(e) The *turnaround* of an item is completed when transfer is accomplished or, when an outside registrar is involved, the transfer agent in accordance with the presenter's instructions completes all acts necessary to cancel the certificate or certificates presented for transfer and to issue a new certificate or certificates, and the item is made available to an outside registrar.

(f) The term *process* means the accomplishing by an outside registrar of all acts necessary to perform the registrar function and to make available to the presenting transfer agent the completed certificate or certificates or to advise the presenting transfer agent, orally or in writing, why performance of the registrar function is delayed or may not be completed.

(g) The *receipt* of an item or a written inquiry or request occurs when the item or written inquiry or request arrives at the premises at which the transfer agent performs transfer agent functions, as defined in section 3(a)(25) of the Act.

(h) A *business day* is any day during which the transfer agent is normally open for business and excludes Saturdays, Sundays, and legal holidays, or other holidays normally observed by the transfer agent.

Securities and Exchange Commission § 240.17Ad-2

(i) An item is *routine* if it does not (1) require requisitioning certificates of an issue for which the transfer agent, under the terms of its agency, does not maintain a supply of certificates; (2) include a certificate as to which the transfer agent has received notice of a stop order, adverse claim, or any other restriction on transfer; (3) require any additional certificates, documentation, instructions, assignments, guarantees, endorsements, explanations, or opinions of counsel before transfer may be effected; (4) require review of supporting documentation other than assignments, endorsements or stock powers, certified corporate resolutions, signature, or other common and ordinary guarantees, or appropriate tax, or tax waivers; (5) involve a transfer in connection with a reorganization, tender offer, exchange, redemption, or liquidation; (6) include a warrant, right, or convertible security presented for transfer of record ownership within five business days before any day upon which exercise or conversion privileges lapse or change; (7) include a warrant, right, or convertible security presented for exercise or conversion; or (8) include a security of an issue which within the previous 15 business days was offered to the public, pursuant to a registration statement effective under the Securities Act of 1933, in an offering not of a continuing nature.

(j) The term *depository-eligible securities issue* means an issue of securities that is eligible for deposit at any securities depository that is registered with the Commission under the Securities Exchange Act of 1934 as a clearing agency.

(Secs. 2, 17, 17A and 23(a) (15 U.S.C. 78b, 78q, 78q-1 and 78w(a)); secs. 3, 17A and 23(a), 15 U.S.C. 78c, 78q-1 and 78w(a))

[42 FR 32411, June 24, 1977, as amended at 49 FR 40575, Oct. 17, 1984; 51 FR 36351, Oct. 14, 1986]

§ 240.17Ad-2 Turnaround, processing, and forwarding of items.

(a) Every registered transfer agent (except when acting as an outside registrar) shall turnaround within three business days of receipt at least 90 percent of all routine items received for transfer during a month. For the purposes of this paragraph, items received at or before noon on a business day shall be deemed to have been received at noon on that day, and items received after noon on a business day or received on a day not a business day shall be deemed to have been received at noon on the next business day.

(b) Every registered transfer agent acting as an outside registrar shall process at least 90 percent of all items received during a month (1) by the opening of business on the next business day, in the case of items received at or before noon on a business day, and (2) by noon of the next business day, in the case of items received after noon on a business day. For the purposes of paragraphs (b) and (d) of this section, "items received" shall not include any item enumerated in § 240.17Ad-1(i) (5), (6), (7), or (8) or any item which is not accompanied by a debit or cancelled certificate. For the purposes of this paragraph, items received on a day not a business day shall be deemed to have been received before noon on the next business day.

(c) Any registered transfer agent which fails to comply with paragraph (a) of this section with respect to any month shall, within ten business days following the end of such month, file with the Commission and the transfer agent's appropriate regulatory agency, if it is not the Commission, a written notice in accordance with paragraph (h) of this section. Such notice shall state the number of routine items and the number of non-routine items received for transfer during the month, the number of routine items which the registered transfer agent failed to turnaround in accordance with the requirements of paragraph (a) of this section, the percentage that such routine items represent of all routine items received during the month, the reasons for such failure, the steps which have been taken, are being taken or will be taken to prevent a future failure and the number of routine items, aged in increments of one business day, which as of the close of business on the last business day of the month have been in its possession for more than four business days and have not been turned around.

(d) Any registered transfer agent which fails to comply with paragraph (b) of this section with respect to any

671

§ 240.17Ad-3

month shall, within ten business days following the end of such month, file with the Commission and the transfer agent's appropriate regulatory agency, if it is not the Commission, a written notice in accordance with paragraph (h) of this section. Such notice shall state the number of items received for processing during the month, the number of items which the registered transfer agent failed to process in accordance with the requirements of paragraph (b) of this section, the percentage that such items represent of all items received during the month, the reasons for such failure and the steps which have been taken, are being taken or will be taken to prevent a future failure and the number of items which as of the close of business on the last business day of the month have been in the transfer agent's possession for more than the time allowed for processing and have not been processed.

(e)(1) Except as provided in paragraph (e)(2) of this section, all routine items not turned around within three business days of receipt as required by paragraph (a) of this section and all items not processed within the periods required by paragraph (b) of this section shall be turned around promptly, and all nonroutine items shall receive diligent and continuous attention and shall be turned around as soon as possible.

(2) A transfer agent that is exempt under § 240.17Ad-4(b) and that has received 30 days notice of depository-eligibility of an issue for which it performs transfer agent functions shall turnaround ninety percent of all routine items received during a month within five business days of receipt. Such transfer agent shall devote diligent and continuous attention to the remaining ten percent of routine items and shall turnaround these items as soon as possible.

(f) A registered transfer agent which receives items at locations other than the premises at which it performs transfer agent functions shall have appropriate procedures to assure, and shall assure, that items are forwarded to such premises promptly.

(g) A registered transfer agent which receives processed items from an outside registrar shall have appropriate procedures to assure, and shall assure, that such items are made available promptly to the presenter.

(h) Any notice required by this section or § 240.17Ad-4 shall be filed as follows:

(1) Any notice required to be filed with the Commission shall be filed in triplicate with the principal office of the Commission in Washington, DC 20549 and, in the case of a registered transfer agent for which the Commission is the appropriate regulatory agency, an additional copy shall be filed with the regional office of the Commission for the region in which the registered transfer agent has its principal office for transfer agent activities.

(2) Any notice required to be filed with the Comptroller of the Currency shall be filed with the Office of the Comptroller of the Currency, Administrator of National Banks, Washington, DC 20219.

(3) Any notice required to be filed with the Board of Governors of the Federal Reserve System shall be filed with the Board of Governors of the Federal Reserve System, Washington, DC 20251 and with the Federal Reserve Bank of the district in which the registered transfer agent's principal banking operations are conducted.

(4) Any notice required to be filed with the Federal Deposit Insurance Corporation shall be filed with the Federal Deposit Insurance Corporation, Washington, DC 20429.

[42 FR 32412, June 24, 1977, as amended at 49 FR 40575, Oct. 17, 1984; 59 FR 5946, Feb. 9, 1994; 73 FR 32228, June 5, 2008]

§ 240.17Ad-3 Limitations on expansion.

(a) Any registered transfer agent which is required to file any notice pursuant to § 240.17Ad-2 (c) or (d) for each of three consecutive months shall not from the fifth business day after the end of the third such month until the end of the next following period of three successive months during which no such notices have been required:

(1) Initiate the performance of any transfer agent function or activity for an issue for which the transfer agent

Securities and Exchange Commission

§ 240.17Ad-4

does not perform, or is not under agreement to perform, transfer agent functions prior to such fifth business day; and

(2) With respect to an issue for which transfer agent functions are being performed on such fifth business day, initiate for that issue the performance of an additional transfer agent function or activity which the transfer agent does not perform, or is not under agreement to perform, prior to such fifth business day.

(b) Any registered transfer agent which for each of two consecutive months fails to turn around at least 75% of all routine items in accordance with the requirements of § 240.17Ad-2(a) or to process at least 75% of all items in accordance with the requirements of § 240.17Ad-2(b) shall be subject to the limitations imposed by paragraph (a) of this section and further shall, within twenty business days after the close of the second such month, send to the chief executive officer of each issuer for which such registered transfer agent acts a copy of the written notice filed pursuant to § 240.17Ad-2 (c) or (d) with respect to the second such month.

(Secs. 2, 17, 17A and 23(a) (15 U.S.C. 78b, 78q, 78q-1 and 78w(a)))

[42 FR 32412, June 24, 1977]

§ 240.17Ad-4 Applicability of §§ 240.17Ad-2, 240.17Ad-3 and 240.17Ad-6(a) (1) through (7) and (11).

(a) Sections 240.17Ad-2, 240.17Ad-3 and 240.17Ad-6(a) (1) through (7) and (11) shall not apply to interests in limited partnerships, to redeemable securities of investment companies registered under section 8 of the Investment Company Act of 1940, or to interests in dividend reinvestment programs.

(b)(1) For purposes of this section, *exempt transfer agent* means a transfer agent that during any six consecutive months shall have received fewer than 500 items for transfer and fewer than 500 items for processing.

(2) Except as provided in paragraph (c) of this section, an exempt transfer agent that satisfies the requirements of paragraph (b)(3) shall be exempt from the provisions of §§ 240.17Ad-2 (a), (b), (c), (d) and (h), 240.17Ad-3 and 240.17Ad-6(a) (2) through (7) and (11).

(3) Within ten business days following the close of the sixth consecutive month described in paragraph (b)(1) of this section, an exempt transfer agent shall:

(i) If its appropriate regulatory agency is either the Commission or the Office of the Comptroller of the Currency, prepare and maintain in its possession a document certifying that the transfer agent qualifies as exempt under paragraph (b)(1) of this section; or

(ii) If its appropriate regulatory agency is either the Board of Governors of the Federal Reserve System or the Federal Deposit Insurance Corporation, file with the appropriate regulatory agency a notice certifying that it qualifies as exempt under paragraph (b)(1) of this section.

(c) Within five business days following the close of each month, every exempt transfer agent shall calculate the number of items which it received during the preceding six months. Whenever any exempt transfer agent no longer qualifies as such under paragraph (b)(1), within ten business days after the end of such month: (1) It shall prepare and maintain in its possession a document so stating, if subject to paragraph (b)(3)(i) of this section; or (2) it shall file with its appropriate regulatory agency a notice to that effect, if subject to paragraph (b)(3)(ii) of this section. Thereafter, beginning with the first month following the month in which such document is required to be prepared or such notice is required to be filed, the registered transfer agent no longer shall be exempt under paragraph (b) of this section. Any registered transfer agent which has ceased to be an exempt transfer agent under this paragraph shall not qualify again for exemption until it has conducted its transfer agent operations pursuant to the foregoing sections for six consecutive months following the month in which it was required to prepare the document or prepare and file the notice specified in this paragraph.

(Secs. 2, 17, 17A and 23(a) (15 U.S.C. 78b, 78q, 78q-1 and 78w(a)))

[42 FR 32413, June 24, 1977, as amended at 48 FR 28246, June 21, 1983]

§ 240.17Ad-5 Written inquiries and requests.

(a) When any person makes a written inquiry to a registered transfer agent concerning the status of an item presented for transfer during the preceding six months by such person or anyone acting on his behalf, which inquiry identifies the issue, the number of shares (or principal amount of debt securities or number of units if relating to any other kind of security) presented, the approximate date of presentment and the name in which it is registered, the registered transfer agent shall, within five business days following receipt of the inquiry, respond, stating whether the item has been received; if received, whether it has been transferred; if received and not transferred, the reason for the delay and what additional matter, if any, is necessary before transfer may be effected; and, if received and transferred, the date and manner in which the completed item was made available, the addressee and address to which it was made available and the number of any new certificate which was registered and the name in which it was registered. If a new certificate is dispatched or mailed to the presentor within five business days following receipt of an inquiry pertaining to that certificate, no further response to the inquiry shall be required pursuant to this paragraph.

(b) When any broker-dealer requests in writing that a registered transfer agent acknowledge the transfer instructions and the possession of a security presented for transfer by such broker-dealer or revalidate a window ticket with respect to such security and the request identifies the issue, the number of shares (or principal amount of debt securities or number of units if relating to any other kind of security), the approximate date of presentment, the certificate number and the name in which it is registered, every registered transfer agent shall, within five business days following receipt of the request, in writing, confirm or deny possession of the security, and, if the registered transfer agent has possession, (1) acknowledge the transfer instructions or (2) revalidate the window ticket. If a new certificate is dispatched or mailed to the presentor within five business days following receipt of a request pertaining to that certificate, no further response to the inquiry shall be required pursuant to this paragraph.

(c) When any person, or anyone acting under his authority, requests in writing that a transfer agent confirm possession as of a given date of a certificate presented by such person during the 30 days before the date the inquiry is received and the request identifies the issue, the number of shares (or principal amount of debt securities or number of units if relating to any other kind of security), the approximate date of presentment, the certificate number and the name in which the certificate was registered, every registered transfer agent shall, within ten business days following receipt of the request and upon assurance of payment of a reasonable fee if required by such transfer agent, make available a written response to such person, or anyone acting under his authority, confirming or denying possession of such security as of such given date.

(d) When any person requests in writing a transcript of such person's account with respect to a particular issue, either as the account appears currently or as it appeared on a specific date not more than six months prior to the date the registered transfer agent receives the request, every registered transfer agent shall, within twenty business days following receipt of the request and upon assurance of payment of a reasonable fee if required by such transfer agent, make available to such person a transcript, ledger or statement of account in sufficient detail to permit reconstruction of such account as of the date for which the transcript was requested.

(e)(1) *Response to written inquiries concerning dividend and interest payments.* A registered transfer agent shall respond, within ten business days of receipt, to current claims that contain sufficient detail. A registered transfer agent shall respond, within twenty business days of receipt, to aged claims that contain sufficient detail. The response shall indicate in writing that the inquiry has been received, whether the claim requires further research and, if so, a reasonable estimate of how

Securities and Exchange Commission § 240.17Ad–5

long that research may take. If no further research is required, the response shall indicate whether that claim is being or will be paid and, if not, the reason for not paying the claim. A registered transfer agent shall devote diligent attention to unresolved inquiries and shall resolve all inquiries as soon as possible.

(2) *Misdirected written inquiries concerning dividend and interest payments.* In the event that a transfer agent is not the dividend disbursing or interest paying agent for an issue that is the subject of a claim under this section, but performed those or any transfer agent services for that issue within the preceding three years, the transfer agent shall provide in writing to the inquirer, within ten business days of receipt of the inquiry, the name and address of the current dividend disbursing or interest paying agent. If the transfer agent did not perform those or other transfer agent services for the issue within the preceding three years, the transfer agent must respond to the inquiry and may respond by returning the inquiry with a statement that the transfer agent is not the current dividend disbursing or interest paying agent and that it does not know the name and address of the current dividend disbursing or interest paying agent.

(3) As used in this paragraph:

(i) A *current claim* means a written inquiry concerning non-payment or incorrect payment of dividends or interest, the payment date for which occurred within the preceding six months.

(ii) An *aged claim* means a written inquiry concerning non-payment or incorrect payment of dividends or interest, the payment date for which occurred more than six months before the inquiry.

(iii) *Sufficient detail* means a written inquiry or request that identifies: The issue; the name(s) in which the securities are registered; the number of shares (or principal amount of debt securities or number of units for any other kind of security) involved; the approximate record date(s) or payment date(s) relating to the claim; and, with respect to registered broker-dealers, registered clearing agencies, or banks, certificate numbers.

(f) *Telephone response.* (1) A transfer agent may satisfy the written response requirements of this section by a telephone response to the inquirer if:

(i) The telephone response resolves that inquiry; and

(ii) The inquirer does not request a written response.

(2) When any person makes a written inquiry or request that would qualify under paragraph (e) of this section except that it fails to provide sufficient detail as specified in paragraph (e)(3)(iii) of this section, a registered transfer agent may telephone the inquirer to obtain the necessary additional detail within the time periods specified in paragraph (e)(1) of this section. If the transfer agent does not receive the additional detail within ten business days, the transfer agent immediately shall make a written request for the additional information.

(g)(1) When any person makes a written inquiry or request which would qualify under paragraph (a), (b), (c), or (d) of this section except that it fails to provide all of the information specified in those paragraphs, or requests information which refers to a time earlier than the time periods specified in those paragraphs, a registered transfer agent shall confirm promptly receipt of the inquiry or request and respond to it as soon as possible.

(2) When any person makes a written inquiry or request which would qualify under paragraph (e) of this section except that it fails to provide sufficient detail as specified in paragraph (e)(3)(iii) of this section, a registered transfer agent must respond to the inquiry within the time periods specified in paragraph (e)(1) of this section. A registered transfer agent may respond to such an inquiry in accordance with paragraph (e)(1) of this section as though sufficient detail had been provided, or may return it to the inquirer, requesting the additional necessary details.

(Secs. 2, 17, 17A and 23(a) (15 U.S.C. 78b, 78q, 78q–1 and 78w(a)))

[42 FR 32413, June 24, 1977, as amended at 51 FR 5707, Feb. 18, 1986]

§ 240.17Ad-6 Recordkeeping.

(a) Every registered transfer agent shall make and keep current the following:

(1) A receipt, ticket, schedule, log or other record showing the business day each routine item and each non-routine item is (i) received from the presenter and, if applicable, from the outside registrar and (ii) made available to the presenter and, if applicable, to the outside registrar;

(2) A log, tally, journal, schedule or other record showing for each month:

(i) The number of routine items received;

(ii) The number of routine items received during the month that were turned around within three business days of receipt;

(iii) The number of routine items received during the month that were not turned around within three business days of receipt;

(iv) The number of non-routine items received during the month;

(v) The number of non-routine items received during the month that were turned around;

(vi) The number of routine items that, as of the close of business on the last business day of each month, have been in such registered transfer agent's possession for more than four business days, aged in increments of one business day (beginning on the fifth business day); and

(vii) The number of non-routine items in such registered transfer agent's possession as of the close of business on the last business day of each month;

(3) With respect to items for which the registered transfer agent acts as an outside registrar:

(i) A receipt, ticket, schedule, log or other record showing the date and time:

(A) Each item is (1) received from the presenting transfer agent and (2) made available to the presenting transfer agent;

(B) Each written or oral notice of refusal to perform the registrar function is made available to the presenting transfer agent (and the substance of the notice); and

(ii) A log, tally, journal, schedule or other record showing for each month:

(A) The number of items received;

(B) The number of items processed within the time required by § 240.17Ad-2(b); and

(C) The number of items not processed within the time required by § 240.17Ad-2(b);

(4) A record of calculations demonstrating the registered transfer agent's monitoring of its performance under § 240.17Ad-2 (a) and (b);

(5) A copy of any written notice filed pursuant to § 240.17Ad-2;

(6) Any written inquiry or request, including those not subject to the requirements of § 240.17Ad-5, concerning an item, showing the date received; a copy of any written response to an inquiry or request, showing the date dispatched or mailed to the presenter; if no response to an inquiry or request was made, the date the certificate involved was made available to the presenter; or, in the case of an inquiry or request under § 240.17Ad-5(a) responded to by telephone, a telephone log or memorandum showing the date and substance of any telephone response to the inquiry;

(7) A log, journal, schedule or other record showing the number of inquiries subject to § 240.17Ad-5 (a), (b), (c) and (d) received during each month but not responded to within the required time frames and the number of such inquiries pending as of the close of business on the last business day of each month;

(8) Any document, resolution, contract, appointment or other writing, any supporting document, concerning the appointment and the termination of such appointment of such registered transfer agent to act in any capacity for any issue on behalf of the issuer, on behalf of itself as the issuer or on behalf of any person who was engaged by the issuer to act on behalf of the issuer;

(9) Any record of an active (i.e., unreleased) stop order, notice of adverse claim or any other restriction on transfer;

(10) A copy of any transfer journal and registrar journal prepared by such registered transfer agent; and

(11) Any document upon which the transfer agent bases its determination that an item received for transfer was

Securities and Exchange Commission § 240.17Ad-7

received in connection with a reorganization, tender offer, exchange, redemption, liquidation, conversion or the sale of securities registered pursuant to the Securities Act of 1933 and, accordingly, was not routine under § 240.17Ad–1(i) (5) or (8).

(b) Every registered transfer agent which, under the terms of its agency, maintains securityholder records for an issue or which acts as a registrar for an issue shall, with respect to such issue, obtain from the issuer or its transfer agent and retain documentation setting forth the total number of shares or principal amount of debt securities or total number of units if relating to any other kind of security authorized and the total issued and outstanding pursuant to issuer authorization.

(c) Every registered transfer agent which, under the terms of its agency, maintains securityholder records for an issue shall, with respect to such issue, retain each cancelled registered bond, debenture, share, warrant or right, other registered evidence of indebtedness, or other certificate of ownership and all accompanying documentation, except legal papers returned to the presentor.

(Secs. 2, 17, 17A and 23(a) (15 U.S.C. 78b, 78q, 78q–1 and 78w(a)))

[42 FR 32413, June 24, 1977]

§ 240.17Ad–7 Record retention.

(a) The records required by § 240.17Ad–6(a)(1), (3)(i), (6) or (11) shall be maintained for a period of not less than two years, the first six months in an easily accessible place.

(b) The records required by § 240.17Ad–6(a) (2), (3)(ii), (4), (5) or (7) shall be maintained for a period of not less than two years, the first year in an easily accessible place.

(c) The records required by § 240.17Ad–6(a) (8), (9) and (10) and (b) shall be maintained in an easily accessible place during the continuance of the transfer agency and shall be maintained for one year after termination of the transfer agency.

(d) The records required by § 240.17Ad–6(c) shall be maintained for a period of not less than six years, the first six months in an easily accessible place.

(e) Every registered transfer agent shall maintain in an easily accessible place:

(1) All records required under § 240.17f–2(d) until at least three years after the termination of employment of those persons required by § 240.17f–2 to be fingerprinted; and

(2) All records required pursuant to § 240.17f–2(e).

(f) Subject to the conditions set forth in this section, the records required to be maintained pursuant to § 240.17Ad–6 may be retained using electronic or micrographic media and may be preserved in those formats for the time required by § 240.17Ad–7. Records stored electronically or micrographically in accordance with this paragraph may serve as a substitute for the hard copy records required to be maintained pursuant to § 240.17Ad–6.

(1) For purposes of this section:

(i) The term *micrographic media* means microfilm or microfiche or any similar medium.

(ii) The term *electronic storage media* means any digital storage medium or system.

(iii) The term *ARA* means your appropriate regulatory agency as that term is defined in 15 U.S.C. 78c(a)(34).

(2) If you as a registered transfer agent use electronic storage media or micrographic media to store your records, you must:

(i) Have available at all times for examination by the staffs of the Commission and of your ARA facilities to project or produce immediately easily readable images of such records;

(ii) Be ready at all times to provide such records that the staffs of the Commission and your ARA or their representatives may request;

(iii) Create an accurate index of such records, store the index with those records, and have the index available at all times for examination by the staffs of the Commission and your ARA;

(iv) Have quality assurance procedures to verify the quality and accuracy of the electronic or micrographic recording process; and

(v) Maintain separately from the originals duplicates of the records and

§ 240.17Ad-7

the index that you store on electronic storage media or micrographic media. You may store the duplicates of the indexed records on any medium permitted by this section. You must preserve the duplicate records and index for the same time that is required by this section for the indexed records, and you must have them available at all times for examination by the staffs of the Commission and your ARA.

(3) Any electronic storage media that you use to store your records must:

(i) Ensure the security and integrity of the records by means of manual and automated controls that assure the authenticity and quality of the electronic facsimile, detect attempts to alter or remove the records, and provide means to recover altered, damaged, or lost records resulting from any cause;

(ii) Externally label all removable units of storage media using a unique identifier that allows the manual association of that removable storage unit with its place and order in the recordkeeping system; and

(iii) Uniquely identify files and internally label each file with its unique name, the date and time of file creation, the date and time of last modification or extension, and a file sequence number when the file spans more than one volume.

(4) If you use electronic storage media or micrographic media to store your records, you must establish an audit system that accounts for the inputting of and any changes to every record that is stored on electronic storage media or micrographic media. The results of such audit system must:

(i) Be available at all times for examination by the staffs of the Commission and your ARA; and

(ii) Be preserved for the same time that is required by this section for the underlying records.

(5) If you use electronic storage media or micrographic media to store your records, you must:

(i) Maintain, keep current, and provide promptly upon request by the staffs of the Commission and your ARA all information necessary to access the records and indexes stored on electronic storage media or micrographic media; and

(ii) Place, or have a third party place on your behalf, in escrow with an independent third party and keep current a copy of the physical and logical format of the electronic storage or micrographic media, the field format of all different information types written on the electronic storage media and source code, and the appropriate documentation and information necessary to access records and indexes. The independent escrow agent must file an undertaking signed by a duly authorized person with the Commission and your ARA stating that:

"[Name of Third Party] hereby undertakes to furnish promptly upon request to the U.S. Securities and Exchange Commission, its designees, or representatives, upon reasonable request, a current copy of the physical and logical format of the electronic storage or micrographic media, the field format of all different information types written on the electronic storage media and source code, and the appropriate documentation and information necessary to access the records and indexes of [Name of Transfer Agent]'s electronic records management system."

(6) (i) If you use a third party to maintain or preserve some or all of the required records using electronic storage media or micrographic media, such third party shall file a written undertaking signed by a duly authorized person with the Commission and your ARA stating that:

"With respect to any books and records maintained or preserved on behalf of [Name of Transfer Agent], [Name of Third Party] hereby undertakes to permit examination of such books and records at any time or from time to time during business hours by representatives or designees of the U.S. Securities and Exchange Commission, and to promptly furnish to said Commission or its designee true, correct, complete, and current hard copies of any or all or any part of such books and records."

(ii) Agreement with a third party to maintain your records shall not relieve you from the responsibility to prepare and maintain records as specified in this section or in § 240.17Ad-6.

(g) If the records required to be maintained and preserved by a registered transfer agent pursuant to the requirements of §§ 240.17Ad-6 and 240.17Ad-7 are maintained and preserved on behalf of the registered transfer agent by an

Securities and Exchange Commission § 240.17Ad–9

outside service bureau, other recordkeeping service or the issuer, the registered transfer agent shall obtain, from such outside service bureau, other recordkeeping service or the issuer, an agreement, in writing, to the effect that:

(1) Such records are subject at any time, or from time to time, to reasonable periodic, special, or other examinations by representatives of the Commission and the appropriate regulatory agency for such registered transfer agent if it is not the Commission; and

(2) The outside service bureau, recordkeeping service, or issuer will furnish to the Commission and the appropriate regulatory agency, upon demand, at either the principal office or at any regional office, complete, correct and current hard copies of any and all such records.

(h) When a registered transfer agent ceases to perform transfer agent functions for an issue, the responsibility of such transfer agent under § 240.17Ad–7 to retain the records required to be made and kept current under § 240.17Ad–6(a) (1), (6), (9), (10) and (11), (b) and (c) shall end upon the delivery of such records to the successor transfer agent.

(i) The records required by §§ 240.17Ad–17(d) and 240.17Ad–19(c) shall be maintained for a period of not less than three years, the first year in an easily accessible place.

[42 FR 32414, June 24, 1977, as amended at 47 FR 54063, Dec. 1, 1982; 62 FR 52237, Oct. 7, 1997; 66 FR 21659, May 1, 2001; 68 FR 74401, Dec. 23, 2003; 68 FR 75054, Dec. 29, 2003; 78 FR 4874, Jan. 23, 2013]

§ 240.17Ad–8 Securities position listings.

(a) For purposes of this section, the term *securities position listing* means, with respect to the securities of any issuer held by a registered clearing agency in the name of the clearing agency or its nominee, a list of those participants in the clearing agency on whose behalf the clearing agency holds the issuer's securities and of the participants' respective positions in such securities as of a specified date.

(b) Upon request, a registered clearing agency shall furnish a securities position listing promptly to each issuer whose securities are held in the name of the clearing agency or its nominee. A registered clearing agency may charge issuers requesting securities position listings a fee designed to recover the reasonable costs of providing the securities position listing to the issuer.

(Secs. 2, 17A, and 23(a) (15 U.S.C. 78b, 78q–1, and 78w(a)))

[44 FR 76777, Dec. 28, 1979]

§ 240.17Ad–9 Definitions.

As used in this section and §§ 240.17Ad–10, 240.17Ad–11, 240.17Ad–12 and 240.17Ad–13:

(a) *Certificate detail*, with respect to certificated securities, includes, at a minimum, all of the following, and with respect to uncertificated securities, includes items (2) through (8):

(1) The certificate number.

(2) The number of shares for equity securities or the principal dollar amount for debt securities;

(3) The securityholder's registration;

(4) The address of the registered securityholder;

(5) The issue date of the security;

(6) The cancellation date of the security;

(7) In the case of redeemable securities of investment companies, an appropriate description of each debit and credit (i.e., designation indicating purchase, redemption, or transfer); and

(8) Any other identifying information about securities and securityholders the transfer agent reasonably deems essential to its recordkeeping system for the efficient and effective research of record differences.

(b) *Master securityholder file* is the official list of individual securityholder accounts. With respect to uncertificated securities of companies registered under the Investment Company Act of 1940, the master securityholder file may consist of multiple, but linked, automated files.

(c) A *subsidiary file* is any list or record of accounts, securityholders, or certificates that evidences debits or credits that have not been posted to the master securityholder file.

(d) A *control book* is the record or other document that shows the total number of shares (in the case of equity securities) or the principal dollar

§ 240.17Ad-10

amount (in the case of debt securities) authorized and issued by the issuer.

(e) A *credit* is an addition of appropriate certificate detail to the master securityholder file.

(f) A *debit* is a cancellation of appropriate certificate detail from the master securityholder file.

(g) A *record difference* occurs when either:

(1) The total number of shares or total principal dollar amount of securities in the master securityholder file does not equal the number of shares or principal dollar amount in the control book; or

(2) The security transferred or redeemed contains certificate detail different from the certificate detail currently on the master securityholder file, which difference cannot be immediately resolved.

(h) A *recordkeeping transfer agent* is the registered transfer agent that maintains and updates the master securityholder file.

(i) A *co-transfer agent* is the registered transfer agent that transfers securities but does not maintain and update the master securityholder file.

(j) A *named transfer agent* is the registered transfer agent that is engaged by an issuer to perform transfer agent functions for an issue of securities but has engaged a service company to perform some or all of those functions.

(k) A *service company* is the registered transfer agent engaged by a named transfer agent to perform transfer agent functions for that named transfer agent.

(l) A *file* includes automated and manual records.

(Secs. 2, 17(a), 17A(d) and 23(a) thereof, 15 U.S.C. 78b, 78q(a), 78q-1(d) and 78w(a))

[48 FR 28246, June 21, 1983]

§ 240.17Ad-10 Prompt posting of certificate detail to master securityholder files, maintenance of accurate securityholder files, communications between co-transfer agents and recordkeeping transfer agents, maintenance of current control book, retention of certificate detail and "buy-in" of physical overissuance.

(a)(1) Every recordkeeping transfer agent shall promptly and accurately post to the master securityholder file debits and credits containing minimum and appropriate certificate detail representing every security transferred, purchased, redeemed or issued; *Provided, however*, That if a security transferred or redeemed contains certificate detail different from that currently posted to the master securityholder file, the credit shall be posted to the master securityholder file and the debit and related certificate detail shall be maintained in a subsidiary file until resolved. The recordkeeping transfer agent shall exercise diligent and continuous attention to resolve the resulting record difference and, once resolved, shall post to the master securityholder file the debit maintained in the subsidiary file. Postings of certificate detail shall remain on the master securityholder file until a debit to a securityholder account is appropriate.

(2) As used in this paragraph, the term *promptly* means the following number of days after issuance, purchase, transfer, or redemption of a security:

(i) With respect to recordkeeping transfer agents (other than transfer agents that perform transfer agent functions with respect to redeemable securities issued by investment companies registered under section 8 of the Investment Company Act of 1940) that are exempt transfer agents under § 240.17Ad-4(b), 30 calendar days;

(ii) With respect to recordkeeping transfer agents (other than transfer agents that perform transfer agent functions with respect to redeemable securities issued by investment companies registered under section 8 of the Investment Company Act of 1940) that:

(A) Perform transfer agent functions solely for their own or their affiliated companies' securities issues, and

(B) Employ batch posting systems, ten business days; and

(iii) With respect to all other recordkeeping transfer agents, five business days; *Provided, however*, That all securities transferred, purchased, redeemed or issued prior to record date, but posted subsequent thereto, shall be posted as of the record date.

(3) With respect to posting certificate detail from transfer journals received by the recordkeeping transfer agent

from a co-transfer agent, the time frames set forth in paragraph (a)(2) shall commence upon receipt of those journals by the recordkeeping transfer agent.

(b) Every recordkeeping transfer agent shall maintain and keep current an accurate master securityholder file and subsidiary files. If such transfer agent has any record difference, its master securityholder file and subsidiary files must accurately represent all relevant debits and credits until the record difference is resolve. The recordkeeping transfer agent shall exercise diligent and continuous attention to resolve all record differences.

(c)(1) Every co-transfer agent shall dispatch or mail promptly to the recordkeeping transfer agent a record of debits and credits for every security transferred or issued. For the purposes of this paragraph, "promptly" means within two business days following transfer of each security, and, with respect to transfers occurring within five business days of record date, daily.

(2) Within three business days following the end of each month, every co-transfer agent shall mail to the recordkeeping transfer agent for each issue of securities for which it acts as a co-transfer agent, a report setting forth:

(i) The principal dollar amount of debt securities or the number of shares and related market value of equity securities comprising any buy-in executed by the co-transfer agent during the preceding month pursuant to paragraph (g) of this section; and

(ii) The reason for the buy-in.

(d) Every co-transfer agent shall respond promptly to all inquiries from the recordkeeping transfer agent regarding records required to be dispatched or mailed by the co-transfer agent pursuant to §240.17Ad–10(c). For the purposes of this paragraph, "promptly" means within five business days of receipt of an inquiry from a recordkeeping transfer agent.

(e) Every recordkeeping transfer agent shall maintain and keep current an accurate control book for each issue of securities. A change in the control book shall not be made except upon written authorization from a duly authorized agent of the issuer.

(f) Every recordkeeping transfer agent shall retain a record of all certificate detail deleted from the master securityholder file for a period of six years from the date of deletion. In lieu of maintaining a hard copy, a recordkeeping transfer agent may comply with this paragraph by complying with §240.17Ad–7(f) or §240.17Ad–7(g).

(g)(1) A registered transfer agent, in the event of any actual physical overissuance that such transfer agent caused and of which it has knowledge, shall, within 60 days of the discovery of such overissuance, buy in securities equal to the number of shares in the case of equity securities or the principal dollar amount in the case of debt securities. During the sixty-day period, the registered transfer agent shall devote diligent attention to resolving the overissuance and recovering the certificates. This paragraph requires a buy-in only by the transfer agent that erroneously issued the certificate(s) giving rise to the physical overissuance, and applies only to those physical overissuances created by transfers or issuances subsequent to September 30, 1983.

(2) If a transfer agent obtains a letter from the party holding the overissued certificates that confirms that the overissued certificate(s) will be returned to the transfer agent not later than thirty days after the expiration of the sixty-day period, the transfer agent need not buy in securities by the sixtieth day. If, however, the certificate(s) are not returned to the transfer agent within the additional thirty-day period, the transfer agent immediately must execute the buy-in in accordance with paragraph (g)(1) of this section.

(3) If the certificates involved are covered by a surety bond indemnifying the transfer agent for all expenses incurred as a result of actual overissuance, the transfer agent need not buy in the securities. The transfer agent, however, shall devote diligent attention to resolving the overissuance and recovering the certificates.

(4) For purposes of this paragraph, *discovery of the overissuance* occurs when the transfer agent identifies the erroneously issued certificate(s) and the registered securityholder(s).

§ 240.17Ad-11

(h) Subsequent to the effective date of this section, registered transfer agents that:

(1) Assume the maintenance and updating of master securityholder files from predecessor transfer agents,

(2) Establish a new master securityholder file for a particular issue, or

(3) Convert from manual to automated systems,

must carry over any existing certificate detail required by this section on the master securityholder file.

A recordkeeping transfer agent shall not be required to add certificate detail to the master securityholder file respecting certificates issued prior to the effective date of this section.

(Secs. 2, 17(a), 17A(d) and 23(a) thereof, 15 U.S.C. 78b, 78q(a), 78q-1(d) and 78w(a))

[48 FR 28246, June 21, 1983, as amended at 51 FR 5708, Feb. 18, 1986]

§ 240.17Ad-11 Reports regarding aged record differences, buy-ins and failure to post certificate detail to master securityholder and subsidiary files.

(a) *Definitions.* (1) *Issuer capitalization* means the market value of the issuer's authorized and outstanding equity securities or, with respect to a municipal securities issuer, the market value of all debt issues for which the transfer agent performs recordkeeping functions on behalf of that issuer, determined by reference to the control book and current market prices.

(2) An *aged record difference* is a record difference that has existed for more than thirty calendar days.

(b) *Reports to Issuers.* (1) Within ten business days following the end of each month, every recordkeeping transfer agent shall report the information specified in paragraph (d)(1) of this section to the persons specified in paragraph (b)(3) of this section, when the aggregate market value of aged record differences in all equity securities issues or debt securities issues maintained on behalf of a particular issuer exceeds the thresholds set forth in the table below.

Issuer capitalization	Aggregate market value of aged record differences exceeds	
	For equity securities	For debt securities
(1) $5 million or less	$50,000	$100,000
(2) Greater than $5 million but less than $50 million	250,000	500,000
(3) Greater than $50 million but less than $150 million	500,000	1,000,000
(4) Greater than $150 million	1,000,000	2,000,000

(2) Within ten business days following the end of each month (or within ten days thereafter in the case of a named transfer agent that receives a report from a service company pursuant to paragraph (b)(3)(i)(C)), every recordkeeping transfer agent shall report the information specified in paragraph (d)(2) of this section to the persons specified in paragraph (b)(3) of this section, with respect to each issue of securities for which it acts as recordkeeping transfer agent, concerning any securities bought-in pursuant to § 240.17Ad-10(g) or reported as bought-in pursuant to § 240.17Ad-10(c) during the preceding month.

(3) The report shall be sent:

(i) By every recordkeeping transfer agent (other than a recordkeeping transfer agent that performs transfer agent functions solely for its own securities):

(A) To the official performing corporate secretary functions for the issuer of the securities for which the aged record difference exists or for which the buy-in occurred;

(B) With respect to an issue of municipal securities, to the chief financial officer of the issuer of the securities for which the aged record difference exists or for which the buy-in occurred; or

(C) If it acts as a service company, to the named transfer agent; and

(ii) By every named transfer agent that is engaged by an issuer to maintain and update the master securityholder file:

(A) To the official performing corporate secretary functions for the issuer of the securities for which the aged record difference exists or for which the buy-in occurred; or

(B) With respect to an issue of municipal securities, to the chief financial officer of the issuer of the securities for which the aged record difference exists or for which the buy-in occurred.

Securities and Exchange Commission §240.17Ad–12

(c) *Reports to appropriate regulatory agencies* (1) Within ten business days following the end of each calendar quarter, every recordkeeping transfer agent shall report the information specified in paragraph (d)(1) of this section to its appropriate regulatory agency in accordance with §240.17Ad–2(h), when the aggregate market value of aged record differences for all issues for which it performs recordkeeping functions exceeds the thresholds specified below:

(i) $300,000 if it is a recordkeeping transfer agent for 5 or fewer issues;
(ii) $500,000 for 6–24 issues;
(iii) $800,000 for 25–49 issues;
(iv) $1 million for 50–74 issues;
(v) $1.2 million for 75–99 issues;
(vi) $1.4 million for 100–499 issues;
(vii) $1.6 million for 500–999 issues;
(viii) $2.6 million for 1,000–1,999 issues; and
(ix) An additional $1 million for each additional 1,000 issues.

(2) Within ten business days following the end of each calendar quarter, every recordkeeping transfer agent shall report the information specified in paragraph (d)(2) of this section to its appropriate regulatory agency in accordance with §240.17Ad–2(h), concerning buy-ins of all issues for which it acts as recordkeeping transfer agent, when the aggregate market value of all buy-ins executed pursuant to §240.17Ad–10(g) during that calendar quarter exceeds $100,000.

(3) When the recordkeeping transfer agent has any debits or credits for securities transferred, purchased, redeemed or issued that are unposted to the master securityholder and/or subsidiary files for more than five business days after debits and credits are required to be posted to the master securityholder file or subsidiary files pursuant to §240.17Ad–10, it shall immediately report such fact to its appropriate regulatory agency in accordance with §240.17Ad–2(h) and shall state in that report what steps have been, and are being, taken to correct the situation.

(d) *Content of reports.* (1) Each report pursuant to paragraphs (b)(1) and (c)(1) of this section shall set forth with respect to each issue of securities:

(i) The principal dollar amount and related market value of debt securities or the number of shares and related market value of equity securities comprising the aged record difference (including information concerning aged record differences existing as of the effective date of this section);
(ii) The reasons for the aged record difference; and
(iii) The steps being taken or to be taken to resolve the aged record difference.

(2) Each report pursuant to paragraphs (b)(2) and (c)(2) of this section shall set forth with respect to each issue of securities:

(i) The principal dollar amount of debt securities and related market value or the number of shares and related market value of equity securities comprising any buy-in executed pursuant to §240.17Ad–10(g);
(ii) The party that executed the buy-in; and
(iii) The reason for the buy-in.

(e) For purposes of this section, the market value of an issue shall be determined as of the last business day on which market value information is available during the reporting period.

(f) A copy of any report required under this section shall be retained by the reporting transfer agent for a period of not less than three years, the first year in an easily accessible place.

(Secs. 2, 17(a), 17A(d) and 23(a) thereof, 15 U.S.C. 78b, 78q(a), 78q–1(d) and 78w(a))

[48 FR 28247, June 21, 1983]

§240.17Ad–12 Safeguarding of funds and securities.

(a) Any registered transfer agent that has custody or possession of any funds or securities related to its transfer agent activities shall assure that:

(1) All such securities are held in safekeeping and are handled, in light of all facts and circumstances, in a manner reasonably free from risk of theft, loss or destruction (other than by a transfer agent's certificate destruction procedures pursuant to §240.17Ad–19); and

(2) All such funds are protected, in light of all facts and circumstances, against misuse. In evaluating which particular safeguards and procedures

§ 240.17Ad-13

must be employed, the cost of the various safeguards and procedures as well as the nature and degree of potential financial exposure are two relevant factors.

(b) For purposes of this section, the term *securities* shall have the same meaning as the term *securities certificate* as defined in § 240.17f–1(a)(6).

(Secs. 2, 17(a), 17A(d) and 23(a) thereof, 15 U.S.C. 78b, 78q(a), 78q–1(d) and 78w(a))

[48 FR 28248, June 21, 1983, as amended at 68 FR 74401, Dec. 23, 2003]

§ 240.17Ad–13 Annual study and evaluation of internal accounting control.

(a) *Accountant's report.* Every registered transfer agent, except as provided in paragraph (d) of this section, shall file annually with the Commission and the transfer agent's appropriate regulatory agency in accordance with § 240.17Ad–2(h), a report specified in paragraph (a)(1) of this section prepared by an independent accountant concerning the transfer agent's system of internal accounting control and related procedures for the transfer of record ownership and the safeguarding of related securities and funds. That report shall be filed within 90 calendar days of the date of the study and evaluation set forth in paragraph (a)(1).

(1) The accountant's report shall:

(i) State whether the study and evaluation was made in accordance with generally accepted auditing standards using the criteria set forth in paragraph (a)(3) of this section;

(ii) Describe any material inadequacies found to exist as of the date of the study and evaluation and any corrective action taken, or if no material inadequacy existed, the report shall so state;

(iii) Comment on the current status of any material inadequacy described in the immediately preceding report; and

(iv) Indicate the date of the study and evaluation.

(2) The study and evaluation of the transfer agent's system of internal accounting control for the transfer of record ownership and the safeguarding of related securities and funds shall cover the following:

(i) Transferring securities related to changes of ownership (i.e., cancellation of certificates or other instruments evidencing prior ownership and issuance of certificates or instruments evidencing current ownership);

(ii) Registering changes of ownership on the books and records of the issuer;

(iii) Transferring record ownership as a result of corporate actions (e.g., issuance, retirement, redemption, liquidation, conversion, exchange, tender offer or other types of reorganization);

(iv) Dividend disbursement or interest paying-agent activities;

(v) Administering dividend reinvestment programs; and

(vi) Distributing statements respecting initial offerings of securities.

(3) For purposes of this report, the objectives of a transfer agent's system of internal accounting control for the transfer of record ownership and the safeguarding of related securities and funds should be to provide reasonable, but not absolute, assurance that securities and funds are safeguarded against loss from unauthorized use or disposition and that transfer agent activities are performed promptly and accurately. For purposes of this report, a material inadequacy is a condition for which the independent accountant believes that the prescribed procedures or the degree of compliance with them do not reduce to a relatively low level the risk that errors or irregularities, in amounts that would have a significant adverse effect on the transfer agent's ability promptly and accurately to transfer record ownership and safeguard related securities and funds, would occur or not be detected within a timely period by employees in the normal course of performing their assigned functions. Occurrence of errors or irregularities more frequently than in isolated instances may be evidence that the system has a material inadequacy. A significant adverse effect on a transfer agent's ability promptly and accurately to transfer record ownership and safeguard related securities and funds could result from any condition or conditions that individually, or taken as a whole, would reasonably be expected to:

(i) Inhibit the transfer agent from promptly and accurately discharging

Securities and Exchange Commission § 240.17Ad-14

its responsibilities under its contractual agreement with the issuer;

(ii) Result in material financial loss to the transfer agent; or

(iii) Result in a violation of § 240.17Ad-2, 17Ad-10 or 17Ad-12(a).

(b) *Notice of corrective action.* If the accountant's report describes any material inadequacy, the transfer agent shall, within sixty calendar days after receipt of the report, notify the Commission and its appropriate regulatory agency in writing regarding the corrective action taken or proposed to be taken.

(c) *Record retention.* The accountant's report and any documents required by paragraph (b) of this section shall be maintained by the transfer agent for at least three years, the first year in an easily accessible place.

(d) *Exemptions.* The requirements of § 240.17Ad-13 shall not apply to registered transfer agents that qualify for exemptions pursuant to this paragraph, 17Ad-13(d).

(1) A registered transfer agent shall be exempt if it performs transfer agent functions solely for:

(i) Its own securities;

(ii) Securities issued by a subsidiary in which it owns 51% or more of the subsidiary's capital stock; and

(iii) Securities issued by another corporation that owns 51% or more of the capital stock of the registered transfer agent.

(2) A registered transfer agent shall be exempt if it:

(i) Is an exempt transfer agent pursuant to § 240.17AD-4(b); and

(ii) In the case of a transfer agent that performs transfer agent functions for redeemable securities issued by companies registered under section 8 of the Investment Company Act of 1940, maintains master securityholder files consisting of fewer than 1000 shareholder accounts, in the aggregate, for each of such issues for which it performs transfer agent functions.

(3) A registered transfer agent shall be exempt if it is a bank or financial institution subject to regulation by the Board of Governors of the Federal Reserve System, the Office of the Comptroller of the Currency or the Federal Deposit Insurance Corporation, provided that it is not notified to the contrary by its appropriate regulatory agency and provided that a report similar in scope to the requirements of § 240.17Ad-13(a) is prepared for either the bank's board of directors or an audit committee of the board of directors.

(Secs. 2, 17(a), 17A(d) and 23(a) thereof, 15 U.S.C. 78b, 78q(a), 78q-1(d) and 78w(a))

[48 FR 28248, June 21, 1983]

§ 240.17Ad-14 Tender agents.

(a) *Establishing book-entry depository accounts.* When securities of a subject company have been declared eligible by one or more qualified registered securities depositories for the services of those depositories at the time a tender or exchange offer is commenced, no registered transfer agent shall act on behalf of the bidder as a depositary, in the case of a tender offer, or an exchange agent, in the case of an exchange offer, in connection with a tender or exchange offer, unless that transfer agent has established, within two business days after commencement of the offer, specially designated accounts. These accounts shall be maintained throughout the duration of the offer, including protection periods, with all qualified registered securities depositories holding the subject company's securities, for purposes of receiving from depository participants securities being tendered to the bidder by book-entry delivery pursuant to transmittal letters and other documentation and for purposes of allowing tender agents to return to depository participants by book-entry movement securities withdrawn from the offer.

(b) *Exclusions.* The rule shall not apply to tender or exchange offers (1) that are made for a class of securities of a subject company that has fewer than (i) 500 security holders of record for that class, or (ii) 500,000 shares of that class outstanding; or (2) that are made exclusively to security holders of fewer than 100 shares of a class of securities.

(c) *Definitions.* For purposes of this rule, (1) the terms *subject company, business day, security holders,* and *transmittal letter* shall be given the meanings provided in § 240.14d-1(b); (2) unless the context otherwise requires, a tender or

§ 240.17Ad-15

exchange offer shall be deemed to have commenced as specified in § 240.14d-2; (3) the term *bidder* shall mean any person who makes a tender or exchange offer or on whose behalf a tender or exchange offer is made; (4) a *qualified registered securities depository* shall mean a registered clearing agency having rules and procedures approved by the Commission pursuant to section 19 of the Securities Exchange Act of 1934 to enable book-entry delivery of the securities of the subject company to, and return of those securities from, the transfer agent through the facilities of that securities depository; and (5) the term *depositary* refers to that agent of the bidder receiving securities from tendering depository participants and paying those participants for shares tendered. The term *exchange agent* refers to the agent performing like functions in connection with an exchange offer.

(d) *Exemptions.* The Commission may exempt from the provisions of this rule, either unconditionally or on specified terms and conditions, any registered transfer agent, tender or exchange offer, or class of tender or exchange offers, if the Commission determines that an exemption is consistent with the public interest, the protection of investors, the prompt and accurate clearance and settlement of securities transactions, the maintenance of fair and orderly markets, or the removal of impediments to a national clearance and settlement system.

(Secs. 2, 11A(a)(1)(B), 14(d)(4), 15(c)(3), 15(c)(6), 17A(a), 17A(d)(1), and 23(a) of the Securities Exchange Act of 1934 (15 U.S.C. 78b, 78k–1(a)(1)(B), 78n(d)(4), 78o(c)(3), 78o(c)(6), 78q–1(a), 78q–1(d)(1) and 78w(a)))

[49 FR 3071, Jan. 25, 1984]

§ 240.17Ad-15 Signature guarantees.

(a) *Definitions.* For purposes of this section, the following terms shall mean:

(1) *Act* means the Securities Exchange Act of 1934;

(2) *Eligible Guarantor Institution* means:

(i) Banks (as that term is defined in section 3(a) of the Federal Deposit Insurance Act [12 U.S.C. 1813(a)]);

(ii) Brokers, dealers municipal securities dealers, municipal securities brokers, government securities dealers, and government securities brokers, as those terms are defined under the Act;

(iii) Credit unions (as that term is defined in Section 19 (b)(1)(A) of the Federal Reserve Act [12 U.S.C. 461(b)]);

(iv) National securities exchanges, registered securities associations, clearing agencies, as those terms are used under the Act; and

(v) Savings associations (as that term is defined in section 3(b) of the Federal Deposit Insurance Act [12 U.S.C. 1813(b)]).

(3) *Guarantee* means a guarantee of the signature of the person endorsing a certificated security, or originating an instruction to transfer ownership of a security or instructions concerning transfer of securities.

(b) *Acceptance of signature guarantees.* A registered transfer agent shall not, directly or indirectly, engage in any activity in connection with a guarantee, including the acceptance or rejection of such guarantee, that results in the inequitable treatment of any eligible guarantor institution or a class of institutions.

(c) *Transfer agent's standards and procedures.* Every registered transfer agent shall establish:

(1) Written standards for the acceptance of guarantees of securities transfers from eligible guarantor institutions; and

(2) Procedures, including written guidelines where appropriate, to ensure that those standards are used in determining whether to accept or reject guarantees from eligible guarantor institutions. Such standards and procedures shall not establish terms and conditions (including those pertaining to financial condition) that, as written or applied, treat different classes of eligible guarantor institutions inequitably, or result in the rejection of a guarantee from an eligible guarantor institution solely because the guarantor institution is of a particular type specified in paragraphs (a)(2)(i)–(a)(2)(v) of this section.

(d) *Rejection of items presented for transfer.* (1) No registered transfer agent shall reject a request for transfer of a certificated or uncertificated security because the certificate, instruction, or documents accompanying the

Securities and Exchange Commission § 240.17Ad–15

certificate or instruction includes an unacceptable guarantee, unless the transfer agent determines that the guarantor, if it is an eligible guarantor institution, does not satisfy the transfer agent's written standards or procedures.

(2) A registered transfer agent shall notify the guarantor and the presenter of the rejection and the reasons for the rejection within two business days after rejecting a transfer request because of a determination that the guarantor does not satisfy the transfer agent's written standards or procedures. Notification to the presenter may be accomplished by making the rejected item available to the presenter. Notification to the guarantor may be accomplished by telephone, facsimile, or ordinary mail.

(e) *Record retention.* (1) Every registered transfer agent shall maintain a copy of the standards and procedures specified in paragraph (c) of this section in an easily accessible place.

(2) Every registered transfer agent shall make available a copy of the standards and procedures specified in paragraph (c) of this section to any person requesting a copy of such standards and procedures. The registered transfer agent shall respond within three days of a request for such standards and procedures by sending the requesting party a copy of the requested transfer agent's standards and procedures.

(3) Every registered transfer agent shall maintain, for a period of three years following the date of the rejection, a record of transfers rejected, including the reason for the rejection, who the guarantor was and whether the guarantor failed to meet the transfer agent's guarantee standards.

(f) *Exclusions.* Nothing in this section shall prohibit a transfer agent from rejecting a request for transfer of a certificated or uncertificated security:

(1) For reasons unrelated to acceptance of the guarantor institution;

(2) Because the person acting on behalf of the guarantor institution is not authorized by that institution to act on its behalf, provided that the transfer agent maintains a list of people authorized to act on behalf of that guarantor institution; or

(3) Because the eligible guarantor institution of a type specified in paragraph (a)(2)(ii) of this section is neither a member of a clearing corporation nor maintains net capital of at least $100,000.

(g) *Signature guarantee program.* (1) A registered transfer agent shall be deemed to comply with paragraph (c) of this section if its standards and procedures include:

(i) Rejecting a request for transfer because the guarantor is neither a member of nor a participant in a signature guarantee program; or

(ii) Accepting a guarantee from an eligible guarantor institution who, at the time of issuing the guarantee, is a member of or participant in a signature guarantee program.

(2) Within the first six months after revising its standards and procedures to include a signature guarantee program, the transfer agent shall not reject a request for transfer because the guarantor is neither a member of nor participant in a signature guarantee program, unless the transfer agent has given that guarantor ninety days written notice of the transfer agent's intent to reject transfers with guarantees from non-participating or non-member guarantors.

(3) For purposes of paragraph (g) of this section, the term "signature guarantee program," means a program, the terms and conditions of which the transfer agent reasonably determines:

(i) To facilitate the equitable treatment of eligible guarantor institutions; and

(ii) To promote the prompt, accurate and safe transfer of securities by providing:

(A) Adequate protection to the transfer agent against risk of financial loss in the event persons have no recourse against the eligible guarantor institution; and

(B) Adequate protection to the transfer agent against the issuance of unauthorized guarantees.

[57 FR 1095, Jan. 10, 1992]

§ 240.17Ad-16 Notice of assumption or termination of transfer agent services.

(a) A registered transfer agent that ceases to perform transfer agent services on behalf of an issuer of securities, including a registered transfer agent that ceases to perform transfer agent services on behalf of an issuer of securities because of a merger or acquisition by another transfer agent, shall send written notice of such termination to the appropriate qualified registered securities depository on or before the later of ten calendar days prior to the effective date of such termination or the day the transfer agent is notified of the effective date of such termination. Such notice shall include the full name, address, telephone number, and Financial Industry Number Standard ("FINS") number of the transfer agent ceasing to perform the transfer agent services for the issuer; the issuer's name; the issue or issues handled and their CUSIP number(s); and if known, the name, address, and telephone number of the transfer agent that thereafter will provide transfer services for the issuer. If no successor transfer agent is known, the notice shall include the name and address of a contact person at the issuer.

(b) A registered transfer agent that changes its name or address or that assumes transfer agent services on behalf of an issuer of securities, including a transfer agent that assumes transfer agent services on behalf of an issuer of securities because of a merger or acquisition of another transfer agent, shall send written notice of such to the appropriate qualified registered securities depository on or before the later of ten calendar days prior to the effective date of such change in status or the day the transfer agent is notified of the effective date of such change in status. A notice regarding a change of name or address shall include the full name, address, telephone number, and FINS number of the transfer agent and the location where certificates are received for transfer. A notice regarding the assumption of transfer agent services on behalf of an issuer of securities, including assumption of transfer agent services resulting from the merger or acquisition of another transfer agent, shall include the full name, address, telephone number, and FINS number of the transfer agent assuming the transfer agent services for the issuer; the issuer's name; and the issue or issues handled and their CUSIP number(s).

(c) The notice described in paragraphs (a) and (b) of this section shall be delivered by means of secure communication. For purposes of this section, secure communication shall include telegraph, overnight mail, facsimile, or any other form of secure communication.

(d)(1) The appropriate qualified registered securities depository that receives notices pursuant to paragraphs (a) and (b) of this section shall deliver within 24 hours a copy of such notices to each qualified registered securities depository. A qualified registered securities depository that receives notice pursuant to this section shall deliver a copy of such notices to its own participants within 24 hours.

(2) A qualified registered securities depository may comply with its notice requirements under paragraph (d)(1) of this section by making available the notice of all material information from the notice within 24 hours in a manner set forth in the rules of the qualified registered securities depository.

(3) A qualified registered securities depository shall maintain such notices for a period of not less than two years, the first six months in an easily accessible place. Such notice shall be made available to the Commission or other persons as the Commission may designate by order.

(4) A registered transfer agent that provides notice pursuant to paragraphs (a) and (b) of this section shall maintain such notice for a period of not less than two years, the first six months in an easily accessible place.

(e) For purposes of this section, a *qualified registered securities depository* shall mean a clearing agency registered under section 17A of the Act (15 U.S.C. 78q-1) that performs clearing agency functions as described in section 3(a)(23)(A)(i) of the Act (15 U.S.C. 78c(a)(23)(A)(i)) and that has rules and procedures concerning its responsibility for maintaining, updating, and

Securities and Exchange Commission

§ 240.17Ad-17

providing appropriate access to the information it receives pursuant to this section.

(f) For purposes of this section, an *appropriate qualified registered securities depository* shall mean the qualified registered securities depository that the Commission so designates by order or, in the absence of such designation, the qualified registered securities depository that is the largest holder of record of all qualified registered securities depositories as of the most recent record date.

[59 FR 63661, Dec. 8, 1994]

§ 240.17Ad-17 Lost securityholders and unresponsive payees.

(a)(1) Every recordkeeping transfer agent whose master securityholder file includes accounts of lost securityholders and every broker or dealer that has customer security accounts that include accounts of lost securityholders shall exercise reasonable care to ascertain the correct addresses of such securityholders. In exercising reasonable care to ascertain such lost securityholders' correct addresses, each such recordkeeping transfer agent and each such broker or dealer shall conduct two database searches using at least one information database service. The transfer agent, broker, or dealer shall search by taxpayer identification number or by name if a search based on taxpayer identification number is not reasonably likely to locate the securityholder. Such database searches must be conducted without charge to a lost securityholder and with the following frequency:

(i) Between three and twelve months of such securityholder becoming a lost securityholder; and

(ii) Between six and twelve months after the first search for such lost securityholder by the transfer agent, broker, or dealer.

(2) A transfer agent, broker, or dealer may not use a search method or service to establish contact with lost securityholders that results in a charge to a lost securityholder prior to completing the searches set forth in paragraph (a)(1) of this section.

(3) A transfer agent, broker, or dealer need not conduct the searches set forth in paragraph (a)(1) of this section for a lost securityholder if:

(i) It has received documentation that such securityholder is deceased; or

(ii) The aggregate value of assets listed in the lost securityholder's account, including all dividend, interest, and other payments due to the lost securityholder and all securities owned by the lost securityholder as recorded in the master securityholder files of the transfer agent or in the customer security account records of the broker or dealer, is less than $25; or

(iii) The securityholder is not a natural person.

(b) For purposes of this section:

(1) *Information data base service* means either:

(i) Any automated data base service that contains addresses from the entire United States geographic area, contains the names of at least 50% of the United States adult population, is indexed by taxpayer identification number or name, and is updated at least four times a year; or

(ii) Any service or combination of services which produces results comparable to those of the service described in paragraph (b)(1)(i) of this section in locating lost securityholders.

(2) *Lost securityholder* means a securityholder:

(i) To whom an item of correspondence that was sent to the securityholder at the address contained in the transfer agent's master securityholder file or customer security account records of the broker or dealer has been returned as undeliverable; provided, however, that if such item is re-sent within one month to the lost securityholder, the transfer agent, broker, or dealer may deem the securityholder to be a lost securityholder as of the day the resent item is returned as undeliverable; and

(ii) For whom the transfer agent, broker, or dealer has not received information regarding the securityholder's new address.

(c)(1) The paying agent, as defined in paragraph (c)(2) of this section, shall provide not less than one written notification to each unresponsive payee, as defined in paragraph (c)(3) of this section, stating that such unresponsive

§ 240.17Ad-18

payee has been sent a check that has not yet been negotiated. Such notification may be sent with a check or other mailing subsequently sent to the unresponsive payee but must be provided no later than seven (7) months (or 210 days) after the sending of the not yet negotiated check. The paying agent shall not be required to send a written notice to an unresponsive payee if such unresponsive payee would be considered a lost securityholder by a transfer agent, broker, or dealer.

(2) The term *paying agent* shall include any issuer, transfer agent, broker, dealer, investment adviser, indenture trustee, custodian, or any other person that accepts payments from the issuer of a security and distributes the payments to the holders of the security.

(3) A securityholder shall be considered an *unresponsive payee* if a check is sent to the securityholder by the paying agent and the check is not negotiated before the earlier of the paying agent's sending the next regularly scheduled check or the elapsing of six (6) months (or 180 days) after the sending of the not yet negotiated check. A securityholder shall no longer be considered an *unresponsive payee* when the securityholder negotiates the check or checks that caused the securityholder to be considered an *unresponsive payee*.

(4) A paying agent shall be excluded from the requirements of paragraph (c)(1) of this section where the value of the not yet negotiated check is less than $25.

(5) The requirements of paragraph (c)(1) of this section shall have no effect on state escheatment laws.

(d) Every recordkeeping transfer agent, every broker or dealer that has customer security accounts, and every paying agent shall maintain records to demonstrate compliance with the requirements set forth in this section, which records shall include written procedures that describe the transfer agent's, broker's, dealer's, or paying agent's methodology for complying with this section, and shall retain such records in accordance with Rule 17Ad–7(i) (§ 240.17Ad–7(i)).

[62 FR 52237, Oct. 7, 1997; 63 FR 1884, Jan. 12, 1998, as amended at 68 FR 14316, Mar. 25, 2003; 78 FR 4784, Jan. 23, 2013]

§ 240.17Ad-18 Year 2000 Reports to be made by certain transfer agents.

(a) Each registered non-bank transfer agent must file Part I of Form TA-Y2K (§ 249.619 of this chapter) with the Commission describing the transfer agent's preparation for Year 2000 Problems. Part I of Form TA-Y2K shall be filed no later than August 31, 1998, and April 30, 1999. Part I of Form TA-Y2K shall reflect the transfer agent's preparation for the Year 2000 as of July 15, 1998, and March 15, 1999, respectively.

(b) Each registered non-bank transfer agent, except for those transfer agents that qualify for the exemption in paragraph (d) of § 240.17Ad–13, must file with the Commission Part II of Form TA-Y2K (§ 249.619 of this chapter) in addition to Part I of Form TA-Y2K. Part II of Form TA-Y2K report shall address the following topics:

(1) Whether the board of directors (or similar body) of the transfer agent has approved and funded plans for preparing and testing its computer systems for Year 2000 Problems;

(2) Whether the plans of the transfer agent exist in writing and address all mission critical computer systems of the transfer agent wherever located throughout the world;

(3) Whether the transfer agent has assigned existing employees, has hired new employees, or has engaged third parties to provide assistance in addressing Year 2000 Problems; and if so, a description of the work that these groups of individuals have performed as of the date of each report;

(4) The current progress on each stage of preparation for potential problems caused by Year 2000 Problems. These stages are:

(i) Awareness of potential Year 2000 Problems;

(ii) Assessment of what steps the transfer agent must take to address Year 2000 Problems;

(iii) Implementation of the steps needed to address Year 2000 Problems;

(iv) Internal testing of software designed to address Year 2000 Problems, including the number and description of the material exceptions resulting from such testing that are unresolved as of the reporting date;

(v) Point-to point or industry-wide testing of software designed to address

Securities and Exchange Commission § 240.17Ad-19

Year 2000 Problems (including testing with other transfer agents, other financial institutions, and customers), including the number and description of the material exceptions resulting from such testing that are unresolved as of the reporting date; and

(vi) Implementation of tested software that will address Year 2000 Problems;

(5) Whether the transfer agent has written contingency plans in the event that, after December 31, 1999, it has computer problems caused by Year 2000 Problems; and

(6) What levels of the transfer agent's management are responsible for addressing potential problems caused by Year 2000 Problems, including a description of the responsibilities for each level of management regarding the Year 2000 Problems;

(7) Any additional material information in both reports concerning its management of Year 2000 Problems that could help the Commission assess the transfer agent's readiness for the Year 2000.

(8) Part II of Form TA-Y2K (§ 249.619 of this chapter) shall be filed no later than August 31, 1998, and April 30, 1999. Part II of Form TA-Y2K shall reflect the transfer agent's preparation for the Year 2000 as of July 15, 1998, and March 15, 1999, respectively.

(c) Any non-bank transfer agent that registers between the adoption of the final rule and December 31, 1999, must file with the Commission Part I of Form TA-Y2K (§ 249.619 of this chapter) no later than 30 days after their registration becomes effective. New transfer agents whose registration with the Commission becomes effective between January 1, 1999, and April 30, 1999, would be required to file the second report due on April 30, 1999.

(d) For purposes of this section, the term Year 2000 Problem shall include problems arising from:

(1) Computer software incorrectly reading the date "01/01/00" as being the year 1900 or another incorrect year;

(2) Computer software incorrectly identifying a date in the Year 1999 or any year thereafter;

(3) Computer software failing to detect that the Year 2000 is a leap year; or

(4) Any other computer software error that is directly or indirectly caused by paragraph (d)(1), (2), or (3) of this section.

(e) For purposes of this section, the term non-bank transfer agent means a transfer agent whose:

(1) Appropriate regulatory agency, as that term is defined by 15 U.S.C. 78(c)(34)(B), is the Securities and Exchange Commission; and

(2) Is not a savings association, as defined by Section 3 of the Federal Deposit Insurance Act, 12 U.S.C. 1813, which is regulated by the Office of Thrift Supervision.

(f) *Nature and form of reports.* No later than April 30, 1999, every non-bank transfer agent required to file Part II of Form TA-Y2K (§ 249.619 of this chapter) pursuant to paragraph (b)(8) of this section shall file with its Form TA-Y2K an original and two copies of a report prepared by an independent public accountant regarding the non-bank transfer agent's process, as of March 15, 1999, for addressing Year 2000 Problems with the Commission's principal office in Washington, DC. The independent public accountant's report shall be prepared in accordance with standards that have been reviewed by the Commission and that have been issued by a national organization that is responsible for promulgating authoritative accounting and auditing standards.

[63 FR 37693, July 13, 1998, as amended at 63 FR 58635, Nov. 2, 1998]

§ 240.17Ad-19 Requirements for cancellation, processing, storage, transportation, and destruction or other disposition of securities certificates.

(a) *Definitions.* For purposes of this section:

(1) The terms *cancelled* or *cancellation* means the process in which a securities certificate:

(i) Is physically marked to clearly indicate that it no longer represents a claim against the issuer; and

(ii) Is voided on the records of the transfer agent.

(2) The term *cancelled certificate facility* means any location where securities certificates are cancelled and thereafter processed, stored, transported, destroyed or otherwise disposed of.

§ 240.17Ad-19

(3) The term *certificate number* means a unique identification or serial number that is assigned and affixed by an issuer or transfer agent to each securities certificate.

(4) The term *controlled access* means the practice of permitting the entry of only authorized personnel to areas where securities certificates are cancelled and thereafter processed, stored, transported, destroyed or otherwise disposed of.

(5) The term *CUSIP number* means the unique identification number that is assigned to each securities issue.

(6) The term *destruction* means the physical ruination of a securities certificate by a transfer agent as part of the certificate destruction procedures that make the reconstruction of the certificate impossible.

(7) The term *otherwise disposed of* means any disposition other than by destruction.

(8) The term *securities certificate* has the same meaning that it has in § 240.17f-1(a)(6).

(b) *Required procedures for the cancellation, storage, transportation, destruction, or other disposition of securities certificates.* Every transfer agent involved in the handling, processing, or storage of securities certificates shall establish and implement written procedures for the cancellation, storage, transportation, destruction, or other disposition of securities certificates. This requirement applies to any agent that the transfer agent uses to perform any of these activities.

(c) *Written procedures.* The written procedures required by paragraph (b) of this section at a minimum shall provide that:

(1) There is controlled access to any cancelled certificate facility;

(2) Each cancelled certificate be marked with the word "CANCELLED" by stamp or perforation on the face of the certificate unless the transfer agent has procedures adopted pursuant to this rule for the destruction of cancelled certificates within three business days of their cancellation;

(3) A record that is indexed and retrievable by CUSIP and certificate number that contains the CUSIP number, certificate number with any prefix or suffix, denomination, registration, issue date, and cancellation date of each cancelled certificate;

(4) A record that is indexed and retrievable by CUSIP and certificate number of each destroyed securities certificate or securities certificate otherwise disposed of, the records must contain for each destroyed or otherwise disposed of certificate the CUSIP number, certificate number with any prefix or suffix, denomination, registration, issue date, and cancellation date, and additionally for any certificate otherwise disposed of a record of how it was disposed of, the name and address of the party to whom it was disposed, and the date of disposition;

(5) The physical transportation of cancelled certificates be made in a secure manner and that the transfer agent maintain separately a record of the CUSIP number and certificate number of each certificate in transit;

(6) Authorized personnel of the transfer agent or its designee supervise and witness the intentional destruction of any cancelled certificate and retain copies of all records relating to certificates which were destroyed; and

(7) Reports to the Lost and Stolen Securities Program be effected in a timely and complete manner, as provided in § 240.17f-1 of any cancelled certificate that is lost, stolen, missing, or counterfeit.

(d) *Recordkeeping.* Every transfer agent subject to this section shall maintain records that demonstrate compliance with the requirements set forth in this section and that describe the transfer agent's methodology for complying with this section for three years, the first year in an easily accessible place.

(e) *Exemptive authority.* Upon written application or upon its own motion, the Commission may grant an exemption from any of the provisions of this section, either unconditionally or on specific terms and conditions, to any transfer agent or any class of transfer agents and to any securities certificate or any class of securities certificates.

[68 FR 74401, Dec. 23, 2003]

Securities and Exchange Commission §240.17Ad–21T

§ 240.17Ad–20 Issuer restrictions or prohibitions on ownership by securities intermediaries.

(a) Except as provided in paragraph (c) of this section, no registered transfer agent shall transfer any equity security registered pursuant to section 12 or any equity security that subjects an issuer to reporting under section 15(d) of the Act (15 U.S.C. 78*l* or 15 U.S.C. 78o(d)) if such security is subject to any restriction or prohibition on transfer to or from a securities intermediary in its capacity as such.

(b) The term *securities intermediary* means a clearing agency registered under section 17A of the Act (15 U.S.C. 78q–1) or a person, including a bank, broker, or dealer, that in the ordinary course of its business maintains securities accounts for others in its capacity as such.

(c) The provisions of this section shall not apply to any equity security issued by a partnership as defined in rule 901(b) of Regulation S–K (§ 229.901(b) of this chapter).

[70 FR 70862, Dec. 7, 2004]

§ 240.17Ad–21T Operational capability in a Year 2000 environment.

(a) This section applies to every registered non-bank transfer agent that uses computers in the conduct of its business as a transfer agent.

(b)(1) You have a material Year 2000 problem if, at any time on or after August 31, 1999:

(i) Any of your mission critical computer systems incorrectly identifies any date in the Year 1999 or the Year 2000, and

(ii) The error impairs or, if uncorrected, is likely to impair, any of your mission critical systems under your control.

(2) You will be presumed to have a material Year 2000 problem if, at any time on or after August 31, 1999, you:

(i) Do not have written procedures reasonably designed to identify, assess, and remediate any material Year 2000 problems in your mission critical systems under your control;

(ii) Have not verified your Year 2000 remediation efforts through reasonable internal testing of your mission critical systems under your control and reasonable testing of your external links under your control; or

(iii) Have not remediated all exceptions related to your mission critical systems contained in any independent public accountant's report prepared on your behalf pursuant to § 240.17Ad–18(f).

(c) If you have or are presumed to have a material Year 2000 problem, you must immediately notify the Commission and your issuers of the problem. You must send this notice to the Commission by overnight delivery to the Division of Market Regulation, U.S. Securities and Exchange Commission, 100 F Street, NE., Washington, DC 20549–6628 Attention: Y2K Compliance.

(d)(1) If you are a registered non-bank transfer agent that has or is presumed to have a material Year 2000 problem, you may not, on or after August 31, 1999, engage in any transfer agent function, including:

(i) Countersigning such securities upon issuance;

(ii) Monitoring the issuance of such securities with a view to preventing unauthorized issuance;

(iii) Registering the transfer of such securities;

(iv) Exchanging or converting such securities; or

(v) Transferring record ownership of securities by bookkeeping entry without physical issuance of securities certificates.

(2) Notwithstanding paragraph (d)(1) of this section, you may continue to engage in transfer agent functions:

(i) Until December 1, 1999, if you have submitted a certificate to the Commission in compliance with paragraph (e) of this section; or

(ii) Solely to the extent necessary to effect an orderly cessation or transfer of these functions.

(e)(1)(i) If you are a registered non-bank transfer agent that has or is presumed to have a material Year 2000 problem, you may, in addition to providing the Commission the notice required by paragraph (c) of this section, provide the Commission and your issuers a certificate signed by your chief executive officer (or an individual with similar authority) stating:

(A) You are in the process of remediating your material Year 2000 problem;

§ 240.17Ad-21T

(B) You have scheduled testing of your affected mission critical systems to verify that the material Year 2000 problem has been remediated, and specify the testing dates;

(C) The date by which you anticipate completing remediation of the material Year 2000 problem in your mission critical systems; and

(D) Based on inquiries and to the best of the chief executive officer's knowledge, you do not anticipate that the existence of the material Year 2000 problem in your mission critical systems will impair your ability, depending on the nature of your business, to assure the prompt and accurate transfer and processing of securities, the maintenance of master securityholder files, or the production and retention of required records; and you anticipate that the steps referred to in paragraphs (e)(1)(i)(A) through (C) of this section will result in remedying the material Year 2000 problem on or before November 15, 1999.

(ii) If the information contained in any certificate provided to the Commission pursuant to paragraph (e) of this section is or becomes misleading or inaccurate for any reason, you must promptly file an updated certificate correcting such information. In addition to the information contained in the certificate, you may provide the Commission with any other information necessary to establish that your mission critical systems will not have material Year 2000 problems on or after November 15, 1999.

(2) If you have submitted a certificate pursuant to paragraph (e)(1) of this section, you must submit a certificate to the Commission and your issuers signed by your chief executive officer (or an individual with similar authority) on or before November 15, 1999, stating that, based on inquiries and to the best of the chief executive officer's knowledge, you have remediated your Year 2000 problem or that you will cease operations. This certificate must be sent to the Commission by overnight delivery to the Division of Market Regulation, U.S. Securities and Exchange Commission, 100 F Street, NE., Washington, DC 20549-6628 Attention: Y2K Compliance.

(f) Notwithstanding paragraph (d)(2) of this section, you must comply with the requirements of paragraph (d)(1) of this section if you have been so ordered by the Commission or by a court.

(g) Beginning August 31, 1999, and ending March 31, 2000, you must make backup records for all master securityholder files at the close of each business day and must preserve these backup records for a rolling five business day period in a manner that will allow for the transfer and conversion of the records to a successor transfer agent. If you have a material Year 2000 problem, you must preserve for at least one year the five day backup records immediately preceding the day the problem was discovered. In addition, you must make at the close of business on December 27 through 31, 1999, a backup copy for all master securityholder files and preserve these records for at least one year. Such backup records must permit the timely restoration of such systems to their condition existing prior to experiencing the material Year 2000 problem. Copies of the backup records must be kept in an easily accessible place but must not be located with or held in the same computer system as the primary records, and you must be able to immediately produce or reproduce them. You must furnish promptly to a representative of the Commission such legible, true, and complete copies of those records, as may be requested.

(h) For the purposes of this section:

(1) The term *mission critical system* means any system that is necessary, depending on the nature of your business, to assure the prompt and accurate transfer and processing of securities, the maintenance of master securityholder files, and the production and retention of required records as described in paragraph (d) of this section;

(2) The term *customer* includes an issuer, transfer agent, or other person for which you provide transfer agent services;

(3) The term *registered non-bank transfer agent* means a transfer agent, whose appropriate regulatory agency is the Commission and not the Office of the Comptroller of the Currency, the Board of Governors of the Federal Reserve

Securities and Exchange Commission § 240.17Ad-22

System, or the Federal Deposit Insurance Corporation; and

(4) The term *master securityholder file* has the same definition as defined in § 240.17Ad-9(b).

(i) This temporary section will expire on July 1, 2001.

[64 FR 42029, Aug. 3, 1999, as amended at 73 FR 32228, June 5, 2008]

§ 240.17Ad-22 Standards for clearing agencies.

(a) *Definitions*. For purposes of this section:

(1) *Backtesting* means an ex-post comparison of actual outcomes with expected outcomes derived from the use of margin models.

(2) *Central counterparty* means a clearing agency that interposes itself between the counterparties to securities transactions, acting functionally as the buyer to every seller and the seller to every buyer.

(3) *Central securities depository* means a clearing agency that is a securities depository as described in Section 3(a)(23)(A) of the Act (15 U.S.C. 78c(a)(23)(A)).

(4) *Clearing agency involved in activities with a more complex risk profile* means a clearing agency registered with the Commission under Section 17A of the Act (15 U.S.C. 78q-1) that:

(i) Provides central counterparty services for security-based swaps;

(ii) Has been determined by the Commission to be involved in activities with a more complex risk profile at the time of its initial registration; or

(iii) Is subsequently determined by the Commission to be involved in activities with a more complex risk profile pursuant to § 240.17Ab2-2(b).

(5) *Covered clearing agency* means a registered clearing agency that provides the services of a central counterparty or central securities depository.

(6) *Designated clearing agency* means a clearing agency registered with the Commission under Section 17A of the Exchange Act (15 U.S.C. 78q-1) that is designated systemically important by the Financial Stability Oversight Council pursuant to the Payment, Clearing, and Settlement Supervision Act of 2010 (12 U.S.C. 5461 *et seq.*) and for which the Commission is the supervisory agency as defined in Section 803(8) of the Payment, Clearing, and Settlement Supervision Act of 2010 (12 U.S.C. 5461 *et seq.*).

(7) *Financial market utility* has the same meaning as defined in Section 803(6) of the Payment, Clearing, and Settlement Supervision Act of 2010 (12 U.S.C. 5462(6)).

(8) *Link* means, for purposes of paragraph (e)(20) of this section, a set of contractual and operational arrangements between two or more clearing agencies, financial market utilities, or trading markets that connect them directly or indirectly for the purposes of participating in settlement, cross margining, expanding their services to additional instruments or participants, or for any other purposes material to their business.

(9) *Model validation* means an evaluation of the performance of each material risk management model used by a covered clearing agency (and the related parameters and assumptions associated with such models), including initial margin models, liquidity risk models, and models used to generate clearing or guaranty fund requirements, performed by a qualified person who is free from influence from the persons responsible for the development or operation of the models or policies being validated.

(10) *Net capital* as used in paragraph (b)(7) of this section means net capital as defined in § 240.15c3-1 for broker-dealers or any similar risk adjusted capital calculation for all other prospective clearing members.

(11) *Normal market conditions* as used in paragraphs (b)(1) and (2) of this section means conditions in which the expected movement of the price of cleared securities would produce changes in a clearing agency's exposures to its participants that would be expected to breach margin requirements or other risk control mechanisms only one percent of the time.

(12) *Participant family* means that if a participant directly, or indirectly through one or more intermediaries, controls, is controlled by, or is under common control with, another participant then the affiliated participants shall be collectively deemed to be a single participant family for purposes

§ 240.17Ad–22

of paragraphs (b)(3), (d)(14), (e)(4), and (e)(7) of this section.

(13) *Potential future exposure* means the maximum exposure estimated to occur at a future point in time with an established single-tailed confidence level of at least 99 percent with respect to the estimated distribution of future exposure.

(14) *Qualifying liquid resources* means, for any covered clearing agency, the following, in each relevant currency:

(i) Cash held either at the central bank of issue or at creditworthy commercial banks;

(ii) Assets that are readily available and convertible into cash through prearranged funding arrangements, such as:

(A) Committed arrangements without material adverse change provisions, including:

(*1*) Lines of credit;

(*2*) Foreign exchange swaps; and

(*3*) Repurchase agreements; or

(B) Other prearranged funding arrangements determined to be highly reliable even in extreme but plausible market conditions by the board of directors of the covered clearing agency following a review conducted for this purpose not less than annually; and

(iii) Other assets that are readily available and eligible for pledging to (or conducting other appropriate forms of transactions with) a relevant central bank, if the covered clearing agency has access to routine credit at such central bank in a jurisdiction that permits said pledges or other transactions by the covered clearing agency.

(15) *Security-based swap* means a security-based swap as defined in Section 3(a)(68) of the Act (15 U.S.C. 78c(a)(68)).

(16) *Sensitivity analysis* means an analysis that involves analyzing the sensitivity of a model to its assumptions, parameters, and inputs that:

(i) Considers the impact on the model of both moderate and extreme changes in a wide range of inputs, parameters, and assumptions, including correlations of price movements or returns if relevant, which reflect a variety of historical and hypothetical market conditions;

(ii) Uses actual portfolios and, where applicable, hypothetical portfolios that reflect the characteristics of proprietary positions and customer positions;

(iii) Considers the most volatile relevant periods, where practical, that have been experienced by the markets served by the clearing agency; and

(iv) Tests the sensitivity of the model to stressed market conditions, including the market conditions that may ensue after the default of a member and other extreme but plausible conditions as defined in a covered clearing agency's risk policies.

(17) *Stress testing* means the estimation of credit or liquidity exposures that would result from the realization of potential stress scenarios, such as extreme price changes, multiple defaults, or changes in other valuation inputs and assumptions.

(18) *Systemically important in multiple jurisdictions* means, with respect to a covered clearing agency, a covered clearing agency that has been determined by the Commission to be systemically important in more than one jurisdiction pursuant to § 240.17Ab2–2.

(19) *Transparent* means, for the purposes of paragraphs (e)(1), (2), and (10) of this section, to the extent consistent with other statutory and Commission requirements on confidentiality and disclosure, that documentation required under paragraphs (e)(1), (2), and (10) is disclosed to the Commission and, as appropriate, to other relevant authorities, to clearing members and to customers of clearing members, to the owners of the covered clearing agency, and to the public.

(b) A registered clearing agency that performs central counterparty services shall establish, implement, maintain and enforce written policies and procedures reasonably designed to:

(1) Measure its credit exposures to its participants at least once a day and limit its exposures to potential losses from defaults by its participants under normal market conditions so that the operations of the clearing agency would not be disrupted and non-defaulting participants would not be exposed to losses that they cannot anticipate or control.

(2) Use margin requirements to limit its credit exposures to participants under normal market conditions and use risk-based models and parameters

Securities and Exchange Commission § 240.17Ad–22

to set margin requirements and review such margin requirements and the related risk-based models and parameters at least monthly.

(3) Maintain sufficient financial resources to withstand, at a minimum, a default by the participant family to which it has the largest exposure in extreme but plausible market conditions; provided that a registered clearing agency acting as a central counterparty for security-based swaps shall maintain additional financial resources sufficient to withstand, at a minimum, a default by the two participant families to which it has the largest exposures in extreme but plausible market conditions, in its capacity as a central counterparty for security-based swaps. Such policies and procedures may provide that the additional financial resources may be maintained by the security-based swap clearing agency generally or in separately maintained funds.

(4) Provide for an annual model validation consisting of evaluating the performance of the clearing agency's margin models and the related parameters and assumptions associated with such models by a qualified person who is free from influence from the persons responsible for the development or operation of the models being validated.

(5) Provide the opportunity for a person that does not perform any dealer or security-based swap dealer services to obtain membership on fair and reasonable terms at the clearing agency to clear securities for itself or on behalf of other persons.

(6) Have membership standards that do not require that participants maintain a portfolio of any minimum size or that participants maintain a minimum transaction volume.

(7) Provide a person that maintains net capital equal to or greater than $50 million with the ability to obtain membership at the clearing agency, provided that such persons are able to comply with other reasonable membership standards, with any net capital requirements being scalable so that they are proportional to the risks posed by the participant's activities to the clearing agency; provided, however, that the clearing agency may provide for a higher net capital requirement as a condition for membership at the clearing agency if the clearing agency demonstrates to the Commission that such a requirement is necessary to mitigate risks that could not otherwise be effectively managed by other measures and the Commission approves the higher net capital requirement as part of a rule filing or clearing agency registration application.

(c) *Record of financial resources and annual audited financial statements.* (1) Each fiscal quarter (based on calculations made as of the last business day of the clearing agency's fiscal quarter), or at any time upon Commission request, a registered clearing agency that performs central counterparty services shall calculate and maintain a record, in accordance with § 240.17a–1 of this chapter, of the financial and qualifying liquid resources necessary to meet the requirements, as applicable, of paragraphs (b)(3), (e)(4), and (e)(7) of this section, and sufficient documentation to explain the methodology it uses to compute such financial resources or qualifying liquid resources requirement.

(2) Within 60 days after the end of its fiscal year, each registered clearing agency shall post on its Web site its annual audited financial statements. Such financial statements shall:

(i) Include, for the clearing agency and its subsidiaries, consolidated balance sheets as of the end of the two most recent fiscal years and statements of income, changes in stockholders' equity and other comprehensive income and cash flows for each of the two most recent fiscal years;

(ii) Be prepared in accordance with U.S. generally accepted accounting principles, except that for a clearing agency that is a corporation or other organization incorporated or organized under the laws of any foreign country the consolidated financial statements may be prepared in accordance with U.S. generally accepted accounting principles or International Financial Reporting Standards as issued by the International Accounting Standards Board;

(iii) Be audited in accordance with standards of the Public Company Accounting Oversight Board by a registered public accounting firm that is

§ 240.17Ad-22

qualified and independent in accordance with 17 CFR 210.2–01; and

(iv) Include a report of the registered public accounting firm that complies with paragraphs (a) through (d) of 17 CFR 210.2–02.

(d) Each registered clearing agency that is not a covered clearing agency shall establish, implement, maintain and enforce written policies and procedures reasonably designed to, as applicable:

(1) Provide for a well-founded, transparent, and enforceable legal framework for each aspect of its activities in all relevant jurisdictions.

(2) Require participants to have sufficient financial resources and robust operational capacity to meet obligations arising from participation in the clearing agency; have procedures in place to monitor that participation requirements are met on an ongoing basis; and have participation requirements that are objective and publicly disclosed, and permit fair and open access.

(3) Hold assets in a manner that minimizes risk of loss or of delay in its access to them; and invest assets in instruments with minimal credit, market and liquidity risks.

(4) Identify sources of operational risk and minimize them through the development of appropriate systems, controls, and procedures; implement systems that are reliable, resilient and secure, and have adequate, scalable capacity; and have business continuity plans that allow for timely recovery of operations and fulfillment of a clearing agency's obligations.

(5) Employ money settlement arrangements that eliminate or strictly limit the clearing agency's settlement bank risks, that is, its credit and liquidity risks from the use of banks to effect money settlements with its participants; and require funds transfers to the clearing agency to be final when effected.

(6) Be cost-effective in meeting the requirements of participants while maintaining safe and secure operations.

(7) Evaluate the potential sources of risks that can arise when the clearing agency establishes links either cross-border or domestically to clear or settle trades, and ensure that the risks are managed prudently on an ongoing basis.

(8) Have governance arrangements that are clear and transparent to fulfill the public interest requirements in Section 17A of the Act (15 U.S.C. 78q–1) applicable to clearing agencies, to support the objectives of owners and participants, and to promote the effectiveness of the clearing agency's risk management procedures.

(9) Provide market participants with sufficient information for them to identify and evaluate the risks and costs associated with using its services.

(10) Immobilize or dematerialize securities certificates and transfer them by book entry to the greatest extent possible when the clearing agency provides central securities depository services.

(11) Make key aspects of the clearing agency's default procedures publicly available and establish default procedures that ensure that the clearing agency can take timely action to contain losses and liquidity pressures and to continue meeting its obligations in the event of a participant default.

(12) Ensure that final settlement occurs no later than the end of the settlement day; and require that intraday or real-time finality be provided where necessary to reduce risks.

(13) Eliminate principal risk by linking securities transfers to funds transfers in a way that achieves delivery versus payment.

(14) Institute risk controls, including collateral requirements and limits to cover the clearing agency's credit exposure to each participant family exposure fully, that ensure timely settlement in the event that the participant with the largest payment obligation is unable to settle when the clearing agency provides central securities depository services and extends intraday credit to participants.

(15) State to its participants the clearing agency's obligations with respect to physical deliveries and identify and manage the risks from these obligations.

(e) Each covered clearing agency shall establish, implement, maintain

Securities and Exchange Commission § 240.17Ad–22

and enforce written policies and procedures reasonably designed to, as applicable:

(1) Provide for a well-founded, clear, transparent, and enforceable legal basis for each aspect of its activities in all relevant jurisdictions.

(2) Provide for governance arrangements that:

(i) Are clear and transparent;

(ii) Clearly prioritize the safety and efficiency of the covered clearing agency;

(iii) Support the public interest requirements in Section 17A of the Act (15 U.S.C. 78q–1) applicable to clearing agencies, and the objectives of owners and participants;

(iv) Establish that the board of directors and senior management have appropriate experience and skills to discharge their duties and responsibilities;

(v) Specify clear and direct lines of responsibility; and

(vi) Consider the interests of participants' customers, securities issuers and holders, and other relevant stakeholders of the covered clearing agency.

(3) Maintain a sound risk management framework for comprehensively managing legal, credit, liquidity, operational, general business, investment, custody, and other risks that arise in or are borne by the covered clearing agency, which:

(i) Includes risk management policies, procedures, and systems designed to identify, measure, monitor, and manage the range of risks that arise in or are borne by the covered clearing agency, that are subject to review on a specified periodic basis and approved by the board of directors annually;

(ii) Includes plans for the recovery and orderly wind-down of the covered clearing agency necessitated by credit losses, liquidity shortfalls, losses from general business risk, or any other losses;

(iii) Provides risk management and internal audit personnel with sufficient authority, resources, independence from management, and access to the board of directors;

(iv) Provides risk management and internal audit personnel with a direct reporting line to, and oversight by, a risk management committee and an independent audit committee of the board of directors, respectively; and

(v) Provides for an independent audit committee.

(4) Effectively identify, measure, monitor, and manage its credit exposures to participants and those arising from its payment, clearing, and settlement processes, including by:

(i) Maintaining sufficient financial resources to cover its credit exposure to each participant fully with a high degree of confidence;

(ii) To the extent not already maintained pursuant to paragraph (e)(4)(i) of this section, for a covered clearing agency providing central counterparty services that is either systemically important in multiple jurisdictions or a clearing agency involved in activities with a more complex risk profile, maintaining additional financial resources at the minimum to enable it to cover a wide range of foreseeable stress scenarios that include, but are not limited to, the default of the two participant families that would potentially cause the largest aggregate credit exposure for the covered clearing agency in extreme but plausible market conditions;

(iii) To the extent not already maintained pursuant to paragraph (e)(4)(i) of this section, for a covered clearing agency not subject to paragraph (e)(4)(ii) of this section, maintaining additional financial resources at the minimum to enable it to cover a wide range of foreseeable stress scenarios that include, but are not limited to, the default of the participant family that would potentially cause the largest aggregate credit exposure for the covered clearing agency in extreme but plausible market conditions;

(iv) Including prefunded financial resources, exclusive of assessments for additional guaranty fund contributions or other resources that are not prefunded, when calculating the financial resources available to meet the standards under paragraphs (e)(4)(i) through (iii) of this section, as applicable;

(v) Maintaining the financial resources required under paragraphs (e)(4)(ii) and (iii) of this section, as applicable, in combined or separately maintained clearing or guaranty funds;

§ 240.17Ad-22

(vi) Testing the sufficiency of its total financial resources available to meet the minimum financial resource requirements under paragraphs (e)(4)(i) through (iii) of this section, as applicable, by:

(A) Conducting stress testing of its total financial resources once each day using standard predetermined parameters and assumptions;

(B) Conducting a comprehensive analysis on at least a monthly basis of the existing stress testing scenarios, models, and underlying parameters and assumptions, and considering modifications to ensure they are appropriate for determining the covered clearing agency's required level of default protection in light of current and evolving market conditions;

(C) Conducting a comprehensive analysis of stress testing scenarios, models, and underlying parameters and assumptions more frequently than monthly when the products cleared or markets served display high volatility or become less liquid, or when the size or concentration of positions held by the covered clearing agency's participants increases significantly; and

(D) Reporting the results of its analyses under paragraphs (e)(4)(vi)(B) and (C) of this section to appropriate decision makers at the covered clearing agency, including but not limited to, its risk management committee or board of directors, and using these results to evaluate the adequacy of and adjust its margin methodology, model parameters, models used to generate clearing or guaranty fund requirements, and any other relevant aspects of its credit risk management framework, in supporting compliance with the minimum financial resources requirements set forth in paragraphs (e)(4)(i) through (iii) of this section;

(vii) Performing a model validation for its credit risk models not less than annually or more frequently as may be contemplated by the covered clearing agency's risk management framework established pursuant to paragraph (e)(3) of this section;

(viii) Addressing allocation of credit losses the covered clearing agency may face if its collateral and other resources are insufficient to fully cover its credit exposures, including the repayment of any funds the covered clearing agency may borrow from liquidity providers; and

(ix) Describing the covered clearing agency's process to replenish any financial resources it may use following a default or other event in which use of such resources is contemplated.

(5) Limit the assets it accepts as collateral to those with low credit, liquidity, and market risks, and set and enforce appropriately conservative haircuts and concentration limits if the covered clearing agency requires collateral to manage its or its participants' credit exposure; and require a review of the sufficiency of its collateral haircuts and concentration limits to be performed not less than annually.

(6) Cover, if the covered clearing agency provides central counterparty services, its credit exposures to its participants by establishing a risk-based margin system that, at a minimum:

(i) Considers, and produces margin levels commensurate with, the risks and particular attributes of each relevant product, portfolio, and market;

(ii) Marks participant positions to market and collects margin, including variation margin or equivalent charges if relevant, at least daily and includes the authority and operational capacity to make intraday margin calls in defined circumstances;

(iii) Calculates margin sufficient to cover its potential future exposure to participants in the interval between the last margin collection and the close out of positions following a participant default;

(iv) Uses reliable sources of timely price data and uses procedures and sound valuation models for addressing circumstances in which pricing data are not readily available or reliable;

(v) Uses an appropriate method for measuring credit exposure that accounts for relevant product risk factors and portfolio effects across products;

(vi) Is monitored by management on an ongoing basis and is regularly reviewed, tested, and verified by:

(A) Conducting backtests of its margin model at least once each day using standard predetermined parameters and assumptions;

(B) Conducting a sensitivity analysis of its margin model and a review of its parameters and assumptions for backtesting on at least a monthly basis, and considering modifications to ensure the backtesting practices are appropriate for determining the adequacy of the covered clearing agency's margin resources;

(C) Conducting a sensitivity analysis of its margin model and a review of its parameters and assumptions for backtesting more frequently than monthly during periods of time when the products cleared or markets served display high volatility or become less liquid, or when the size or concentration of positions held by the covered clearing agency's participants increases or decreases significantly; and

(D) Reporting the results of its analyses under paragraphs (e)(6)(vi)(B) and (C) of this section to appropriate decision makers at the covered clearing agency, including but not limited to, its risk management committee or board of directors, and using these results to evaluate the adequacy of and adjust its margin methodology, model parameters, and any other relevant aspects of its credit risk management framework; and

(vii) Requires a model validation for the covered clearing agency's margin system and related models to be performed not less than annually, or more frequently as may be contemplated by the covered clearing agency's risk management framework established pursuant to paragraph (e)(3) of this section.

(7) Effectively measure, monitor, and manage the liquidity risk that arises in or is borne by the covered clearing agency, including measuring, monitoring, and managing its settlement and funding flows on an ongoing and timely basis, and its use of intraday liquidity by, at a minimum, doing the following:

(i) Maintaining sufficient liquid resources at the minimum in all relevant currencies to effect same-day and, where appropriate, intraday and multiday settlement of payment obligations with a high degree of confidence under a wide range of foreseeable stress scenarios that includes, but is not limited to, the default of the participant family that would generate the largest aggregate payment obligation for the covered clearing agency in extreme but plausible market conditions;

(ii) Holding qualifying liquid resources sufficient to meet the minimum liquidity resource requirement under paragraph (e)(7)(i) of this section in each relevant currency for which the covered clearing agency has payment obligations owed to clearing members;

(iii) Using the access to accounts and services at a Federal Reserve Bank, pursuant to Section 806(a) of the Payment, Clearing, and Settlement Supervision Act of 2010 (12 U.S.C. 5465(a)), or other relevant central bank, when available and where determined to be practical by the board of directors of the covered clearing agency, to enhance its management of liquidity risk;

(iv) Undertaking due diligence to confirm that it has a reasonable basis to believe each of its liquidity providers, whether or not such liquidity provider is a clearing member, has:

(A) Sufficient information to understand and manage the liquidity provider's liquidity risks; and

(B) The capacity to perform as required under its commitments to provide liquidity to the covered clearing agency;

(v) Maintaining and testing with each liquidity provider, to the extent practicable, the covered clearing agency's procedures and operational capacity for accessing each type of relevant liquidity resource under paragraph (e)(7)(i) of this section at least annually;

(vi) Determining the amount and regularly testing the sufficiency of the liquid resources held for purposes of meeting the minimum liquid resource requirement under paragraph (e)(7)(i) of this section by, at a minimum:

(A) Conducting stress testing of its liquidity resources at least once each day using standard and predetermined parameters and assumptions;

(B) Conducting a comprehensive analysis on at least a monthly basis of the existing stress testing scenarios, models, and underlying parameters and assumptions used in evaluating liquidity needs and resources, and considering modifications to ensure they are

§ 240.17Ad-22

appropriate for determining the clearing agency's identified liquidity needs and resources in light of current and evolving market conditions;

(C) Conducting a comprehensive analysis of the scenarios, models, and underlying parameters and assumptions used in evaluating liquidity needs and resources more frequently than monthly when the products cleared or markets served display high volatility or become less liquid, when the size or concentration of positions held by the clearing agency's participants increases significantly, or in other appropriate circumstances described in such policies and procedures; and

(D) Reporting the results of its analyses under paragraphs (e)(7)(vi)(B) and (C) of this section to appropriate decision makers at the covered clearing agency, including but not limited to, its risk management committee or board of directors, and using these results to evaluate the adequacy of and adjust its liquidity risk management methodology, model parameters, and any other relevant aspects of its liquidity risk management framework;

(vii) Performing a model validation of its liquidity risk models not less than annually or more frequently as may be contemplated by the covered clearing agency's risk management framework established pursuant to paragraph (e)(3) of this section;

(viii) Addressing foreseeable liquidity shortfalls that would not be covered by the covered clearing agency's liquid resources and seek to avoid unwinding, revoking, or delaying the same-day settlement of payment obligations;

(ix) Describing the covered clearing agency's process to replenish any liquid resources that the clearing agency may employ during a stress event; and

(x) Undertaking an analysis at least once a year that evaluates the feasibility of maintaining sufficient liquid resources at a minimum in all relevant currencies to effect same-day and, where appropriate, intraday and multiday settlement of payment obligations with a high degree of confidence under a wide range of foreseeable stress scenarios that includes, but is not limited to, the default of the two participant families that would potentially cause the largest aggregate payment obligation for the covered clearing agency in extreme but plausible market conditions if the covered clearing agency provides central counterparty services and is either systemically important in multiple jurisdictions or a clearing agency involved in activities with a more complex risk profile.

(8) Define the point at which settlement is final to be no later than the end of the day on which the payment or obligation is due and, where necessary or appropriate, intraday or in real time.

(9) Conduct its money settlements in central bank money, where available and determined to be practical by the board of directors of the covered clearing agency, and minimize and manage credit and liquidity risk arising from conducting its money settlements in commercial bank money if central bank money is not used by the covered clearing agency.

(10) Establish and maintain transparent written standards that state its obligations with respect to the delivery of physical instruments, and establish and maintain operational practices that identify, monitor, and manage the risks associated with such physical deliveries.

(11) When the covered clearing agency provides central securities depository services:

(i) Maintain securities in an immobilized or dematerialized form for their transfer by book entry, ensure the integrity of securities issues, and minimize and manage the risks associated with the safekeeping and transfer of securities;

(ii) Implement internal auditing and other controls to safeguard the rights of securities issuers and holders and prevent the unauthorized creation or deletion of securities, and conduct periodic and at least daily reconciliation of securities issues it maintains; and

(iii) Protect assets against custody risk through appropriate rules and procedures consistent with relevant laws, rules, and regulations in jurisdictions where it operates.

(12) Eliminate principal risk by conditioning the final settlement of one obligation upon the final settlement of

Securities and Exchange Commission § 240.17Ad-22

the other, regardless of whether the covered clearing agency settles on a gross or net basis and when finality occurs if the covered clearing agency settles transactions that involve the settlement of two linked obligations.

(13) Ensure the covered clearing agency has the authority and operational capacity to take timely action to contain losses and liquidity demands and continue to meet its obligations by, at a minimum, requiring the covered clearing agency's participants and, when practicable, other stakeholders to participate in the testing and review of its default procedures, including any close-out procedures, at least annually and following material changes thereto.

(14) Enable, when the covered clearing agency provides central counterparty services for security-based swaps or engages in activities that the Commission has determined to have a more complex risk profile, the segregation and portability of positions of a participant's customers and the collateral provided to the covered clearing agency with respect to those positions and effectively protect such positions and related collateral from the default or insolvency of that participant.

(15) Identify, monitor, and manage the covered clearing agency's general business risk and hold sufficient liquid net assets funded by equity to cover potential general business losses so that the covered clearing agency can continue operations and services as a going concern if those losses materialize, including by:

(i) Determining the amount of liquid net assets funded by equity based upon its general business risk profile and the length of time required to achieve a recovery or orderly wind-down, as appropriate, of its critical operations and services if such action is taken;

(ii) Holding liquid net assets funded by equity equal to the greater of either (x) six months of the covered clearing agency's current operating expenses, or (y) the amount determined by the board of directors to be sufficient to ensure a recovery or orderly wind-down of critical operations and services of the covered clearing agency, as contemplated by the plans established under paragraph (e)(3)(ii) of this section, and which:

(A) Shall be in addition to resources held to cover participant defaults or other risks covered under the credit risk standard in paragraph (b)(3) or paragraphs (e)(4)(i) through (iii) of this section, as applicable, and the liquidity risk standard in paragraphs (e)(7)(i) and (ii) of this section; and

(B) Shall be of high quality and sufficiently liquid to allow the covered clearing agency to meet its current and projected operating expenses under a range of scenarios, including in adverse market conditions; and

(iii) Maintaining a viable plan, approved by the board of directors and updated at least annually, for raising additional equity should its equity fall close to or below the amount required under paragraph (e)(15)(ii) of this section.

(16) Safeguard the covered clearing agency's own and its participants' assets, minimize the risk of loss and delay in access to these assets, and invest such assets in instruments with minimal credit, market, and liquidity risks.

(17) Manage the covered clearing agency's operational risks by:

(i) Identifying the plausible sources of operational risk, both internal and external, and mitigating their impact through the use of appropriate systems, policies, procedures, and controls;

(ii) Ensuring that systems have a high degree of security, resiliency, operational reliability, and adequate, scalable capacity; and

(iii) Establishing and maintaining a business continuity plan that addresses events posing a significant risk of disrupting operations.

(18) Establish objective, risk-based, and publicly disclosed criteria for participation, which permit fair and open access by direct and, where relevant, indirect participants and other financial market utilities, require participants to have sufficient financial resources and robust operational capacity to meet obligations arising from participation in the clearing agency, and monitor compliance with such participation requirements on an ongoing basis.

§ 240.17Ad-22

(19) Identify, monitor, and manage the material risks to the covered clearing agency arising from arrangements in which firms that are indirect participants in the covered clearing agency rely on the services provided by direct participants to access the covered clearing agency's payment, clearing, or settlement facilities.

(20) Identify, monitor, and manage risks related to any link the covered clearing agency establishes with one or more other clearing agencies, financial market utilities, or trading markets.

(21) Be efficient and effective in meeting the requirements of its participants and the markets it serves, and have the covered clearing agency's management regularly review the efficiency and effectiveness of its:

(i) Clearing and settlement arrangements;

(ii) Operating structure, including risk management policies, procedures, and systems;

(iii) Scope of products cleared or settled; and

(iv) Use of technology and communication procedures.

(22) Use, or at a minimum accommodate, relevant internationally accepted communication procedures and standards in order to facilitate efficient payment, clearing, and settlement.

(23) Provide for the following:

(i) Publicly disclosing all relevant rules and material procedures, including key aspects of its default rules and procedures;

(ii) Providing sufficient information to enable participants to identify and evaluate the risks, fees, and other material costs they incur by participating in the covered clearing agency;

(iii) Publicly disclosing relevant basic data on transaction volume and values;

(iv) A comprehensive public disclosure that describes its material rules, policies, and procedures regarding its legal, governance, risk management, and operating framework, accurate in all material respects at the time of publication, that includes:

(A) *Executive summary.* An executive summary of the key points from paragraphs (e)(23)(iv)(B), (C), and (D) of this section;

(B) *Summary of material changes since the last update of the disclosure.* A summary of the material changes since the last update of paragraph (e)(23)(iv)(C) or (D) of this section;

(C) *General background on the covered clearing agency.* A description of:

(*1*) The covered clearing agency's function and the markets it serves;

(*2*) Basic data and performance statistics on the covered clearing agency's services and operations, such as basic volume and value statistics by product type, average aggregate intraday exposures to its participants, and statistics on the covered clearing agency's operational reliability; and

(*3*) The covered clearing agency's general organization, legal and regulatory framework, and system design and operations; and

(D) *Standard-by-standard summary narrative.* A comprehensive narrative disclosure for each applicable standard set forth in paragraphs (e)(1) through (23) of this section with sufficient detail and context to enable a reader to understand the covered clearing agency's approach to controlling the risks and addressing the requirements in each standard; and

(v) Updating the public disclosure under paragraph (e)(23)(iv) of this section every two years, or more frequently following changes to its system or the environment in which it operates to the extent necessary to ensure statements previously provided under paragraph (e)(23)(iv) of this section remain accurate in all material respects.

(f) For purposes of enforcing the Payment, Clearing, and Settlement Supervision Act of 2010 (12 U.S.C. 5461 *et seq.*), a designated clearing agency for which the Commission acts as supervisory agency shall be subject to, and the Commission shall have the authority under, the provisions of paragraphs (b) through (n) of Section 8 of the Federal Deposit Insurance Act (12 U.S.C. 1818) in the same manner and to the same extent as if such designated clearing agency were an insured depository institution and the Commission were the appropriate Federal banking agency for such insured depository institution.

[77 FR 66285, Nov. 2, 2012, as amended at 81 FR 70901, Oct. 13, 2016; 85 FR 28867, May 14, 2020]

§ 240.17Ad–24 Exemption from clearing agency definition for certain registered security-based swap dealers, registered security-based swap execution facilities, and entities engaging in dealing activity in security-based swaps that are eligible for an exception under § 240.3a71–2(a) (or subject to the period set forth in § 240.3a71–2(b)).

A registered security-based swap dealer, a registered security-based swap execution facility, or an entity engaging in dealing activity in security-based swaps that is eligible for an exception under § 240.3a71–2(a) (or subject to the period set forth in § 240.3a71–2(b)) shall be exempt from inclusion in the term "clearing agency," as defined in section 3(a)(23)(A) of the Act, where such registered security-based swap dealer, registered security-based swap execution facility, or entity engaging in dealing activity in security-based swaps that is eligible for an exception under § 240.3a71–2(a) (or subject to the period set forth in § 240.3a71–2(b)) would be deemed to be a clearing agency solely by reason of:

(a) Functions performed by such institution as part of customary dealing activities or providing facilities for comparison of data respecting the terms of settlement of securities transactions effected on such registered security-based swap execution facility, respectively; or

(b) Acting on behalf of a clearing agency or participant therein in connection with the furnishing by the clearing agency of services to its participants or the use of services of the clearing agency by its participants.

[86 FR 7643, Feb. 1, 2021]

§ 240.17Ad–27 Straight-through processing by clearing agencies that provide a central matching service.

(a) A clearing agency that provides a central matching service must establish, implement, maintain, and enforce written policies and procedures reasonably designed to facilitate straight-through processing of securities transactions at the clearing agency.

(b) A clearing agency that provides a central matching service must submit to the Commission every twelve months a report that includes the following:

(1) A summary of the clearing agency's policies and procedures required under paragraph (a) of this section, current as of the last day of the twelve-month period covered by the report required under paragraph (b) of this section;

(2) A qualitative description of the clearing agency's progress in facilitating straight-through processing during the twelve-month period covered by the report required under paragraph (b) of this section;

(3) A quantitative presentation of data that includes:

(i) The total number of trades submitted to the clearing agency for processing;

(ii) The total number of allocations submitted to the clearing agency;

(iii) The total number of confirmations submitted to the clearing agency, as well as the total number of confirmations cancelled by a user;

(iv) The percentage of confirmations submitted to the clearing agency that are affirmed on trade date, specifying to the extent practicable the relevant timeframe in which the affirmation is processed on trade date;

(v) The percentage of allocations and confirmations submitted to the clearing agency that are matched and automatically confirmed through the clearing agency's services; and

(vi) Metrics concerning the use of manual and automated processes by the clearing agency's users with respect to its services that may be used to assess progress in facilitating straight-through processing.

(4) Each of the data sets required under paragraph (b)(3) of this section shall be:

(i) Organized on a month-by-month basis, beginning with January of each year, for the twelve months covered by the report required under paragraph (b) of this section;

(ii) Separated, where applicable, between the use of central matching and

§ 240.18a–1

electronic trade confirmation services offered by the clearing agency;

(iii) Separated, as appropriate, by asset class;

(iv) Separated by type of user; and

(v) Presented on an anonymized and aggregated basis.

(5) A qualitative description of the actions the clearing agency intends to take to further facilitate straight-through processing of securities transactions at the clearing agency during the twelve-month period that follows the period covered by the report required under paragraph (b) of this section.

(c) Each report required under paragraph (b) of this section must be filed within 60 days of the end of the twelve-month period covered by the report required under paragraph (b) of this section, and the twelve-month period covered by each report shall commence on January 1 of the calendar year.

(d) The report required under paragraph (b) of this section must be filed electronically on EDGAR and must be provided in an Interactive Data File in accordance with § 232.405 of this chapter (Rule 405 of Regulation S–T) and the EDGAR Filer Manual.

[88 FR 13953, Mar. 6, 2023]

EFFECTIVE DATE NOTE: At 88 FR 13953, Mar. 6, 2023, § 240.17Ad–27 was added, effective May 5, 2023.

CAPITAL, MARGIN AND SEGREGATION REQUIREMENTS FOR SECURITY-BASED SWAP DEALERS AND MAJOR SECURITY-BASED SWAP PARTICIPANTS

§ 240.18a–1 Net capital requirements for security-based swap dealers for which there is not a prudential regulator.

Sections 240.18a–1, 240.18a–1a, 240.18a–1b, 240.18a–1c, and 240.18a–1d apply to a security-based swap dealer registered under section 15F of the Act (15 U.S.C. 78*o*–10), including a security-based swap dealer that is an *OTC derivatives dealer* as that term is defined in § 240.3b–12. A security-based swap dealer registered under section 15F of the Act (15 U.S.C. 78*o*–10) that is also a broker or dealer registered under section 15 of the Act (15 U.S.C. 78*o*), other than an OTC derivatives dealer, is subject to the net capital requirements in § 240.15c3–1 and its appendices. A security-based swap dealer registered under section 15F of the Act that has a prudential regulator is not subject to § 240.18a–1, 240.18a–1a, 240.18a–1b, 240.18a–1c, and 240.18a–1d.

(a) *Minimum requirements.* Every registered security-based swap dealer must at all times have and maintain net capital no less than the greater of the highest minimum requirements applicable to its business under paragraph (a)(1) or (2) of this section, and tentative net capital no less than the minimum requirement under paragraph (a)(2) of this section.

(1)(i) A security-based swap dealer must at all times maintain net capital of not less than the greater of $20 million or:

(A) Two percent of the risk margin amount; or

(B) Four percent or less of the risk margin amount if the Commission issues an order raising the requirement to four percent or less on or after the third anniversary of this section's compliance date; or

(C) Eight percent or less of the risk margin amount if the Commission issues an order raising the requirement to eight percent or less on or after the fifth anniversary of this section's compliance date and the Commission had previously issued an order raising the requirement under paragraph (a)(1)(ii) of this section;

(ii) If, after considering the capital and leverage levels of security-based swap dealers subject to this paragraph (a)(1), as well as the risks of their security-based swap positions, the Commission determines that it may be appropriate to change the percentage pursuant to paragraph (a)(1)(i)(B) or (C) of this section, the Commission will publish a notice of the potential change and subsequently will issue an order regarding any such change.

(2) In accordance with paragraph (d) of this section, the Commission may approve, in whole or in part, an application or an amendment to an application by a security-based swap dealer to calculate net capital using the market risk standards of paragraph (d) to compute a deduction for market risk on some or all of its positions, instead of the provisions of paragraphs (c)(1)(iv), (vi), and (vii) of this section, and

Securities and Exchange Commission

§ 240.18a-1

§ 240.18a–1b, and using the credit risk standards of paragraph (d) to compute a deduction for credit risk on certain credit exposures arising from transactions in derivatives instruments, instead of the provisions of paragraphs (c)(1)(iii) and (c)(1)(ix)(A) and (B) of this section, subject to any conditions or limitations on the security-based swap dealer the Commission may require as necessary or appropriate in the public interest or for the protection of investors. A security-based swap dealer that has been approved to calculate its net capital under paragraph (d) of this section must at all times maintain tentative net capital of not less than $100 million and net capital of not less than the greater of $20 million or:

(i)(A) Two percent of the risk margin amount;

(B) Four percent or less of the risk margin amount if the Commission issues an order raising the requirement to four percent or less on or after the third anniversary of this section's compliance date; or

(C) Eight percent or less of the risk margin amount if the Commission issues an order raising the requirement to eight percent or less on or after the fifth anniversary of this section's compliance date and the Commission had previously issued an order raising the requirement under paragraph (a)(2)(ii) of this section;

(ii) If, after considering the capital and leverage levels of security-based swap dealers subject to this paragraph (a)(2), as well as the risks of their security-based swap positions, the Commission determines that it may be appropriate to change the percentage pursuant to paragraph (a)(2)(i)(B) or (C) of this section, the Commission will publish a notice of the potential change and subsequently will issue an order regarding any such change; and

(b) A security-based swap dealer must at all times maintain net capital in addition to the amounts required under paragraph (a)(1) or (2) of this section, as applicable, in an amount equal to 10 percent of:

(1) The excess of the market value of United States Treasury Bills, Bonds and Notes subject to reverse repurchase agreements with any one party over 105 percent of the contract prices (including accrued interest) for reverse repurchase agreements with that party;

(2) The excess of the market value of securities issued or guaranteed as to principal or interest by an agency of the United States or mortgage related securities as defined in section 3(a)(41) of the Act subject to reverse repurchase agreements with any one party over 110 percent of the contract prices (including accrued interest) for reverse repurchase agreements with that party; and

(3) The excess of the market value of other securities subject to reverse repurchase agreements with any one party over 120 percent of the contract prices (including accrued interest) for reverse repurchase agreements with that party.

(c) *Definitions.* For purpose of this section:

(1) *Net capital.* The term *net capital* shall be deemed to mean the net worth of a security-based swap dealer, adjusted by:

(i) *Adjustments to net worth related to unrealized profit or loss and deferred tax provisions.*

(A) Adding unrealized profits (or deducting unrealized losses) in the accounts of the security-based swap dealer;

(B)(*1*) In determining net worth, all long and all short positions in listed options shall be marked to their market value and all long and all short securities and commodities positions shall be marked to their market value.

(*2*) In determining net worth, the value attributed to any unlisted option shall be the difference between the option's exercise value and the market value of the underlying security. In the case of an unlisted call, if the market value of the underlying security is less than the exercise value of such call it shall be given no value and in the case of an unlisted put if the market value of the underlying security is more than the exercise value of the unlisted put it shall be given no value.

(C) Adding to net worth the lesser of any deferred income tax liability related to the items in paragraphs

707

§ 240.18a–1

(c)(1)(i)(C)(*1*) through (*3*) of this section, or the sum of paragraphs (c)(1)(i)(C)(*1*), (*2*), and (*3*) of this section;

(*1*) The aggregate amount resulting from applying to the amount of the deductions computed in accordance with paragraphs (c)(1)(vi) and (vii) of this section and Appendices A and B, §§ 240.18a–1a and 240.18a–1b, the appropriate Federal and State tax rate(s) applicable to any unrealized gain on the asset on which the deduction was computed;

(*2*) Any deferred tax liability related to income accrued which is directly related to an asset otherwise deducted pursuant to this section;

(*3*) Any deferred tax liability related to unrealized appreciation in value of any asset(s) which has been otherwise deducted from net worth in accordance with the provisions of this section; and

(D) Adding, in the case of future income tax benefits arising as a result of unrealized losses, the amount of such benefits not to exceed the amount of income tax liabilities accrued on the books and records of the security-based swap dealer, but only to the extent such benefits could have been applied to reduce accrued tax liabilities on the date of the capital computation, had the related unrealized losses been realized on that date.

(E) Adding to net worth any actual tax liability related to income accrued which is directly related to an asset otherwise deducted pursuant to this section.

(ii) *Subordinated liabilities.* Excluding liabilities of the security-based swap dealer that are subordinated to the claims of creditors pursuant to a satisfactory subordinated loan agreement, as defined in § 240.18a–1d.

(iii) *Assets not readily convertible into cash.* Deducting fixed assets and assets which cannot be readily converted into cash, including, among other things:

(A) *Fixed assets and prepaid items.* Real estate; furniture and fixtures; exchange memberships; prepaid rent, insurance and other expenses; goodwill; organization expenses;

(B) *Certain unsecured and partly secured receivables.* All unsecured advances and loans; deficits in customers' and non-customers' unsecured and partly secured notes; deficits in customers' and non-customers' unsecured and partly secured accounts after application of calls for margin, marks to the market or other required deposits that are outstanding for more than the required time frame to collect the margin, marks to the market, or other required deposits; and the market value of stock loaned in excess of the value of any collateral received therefore.

(C) *Insurance claims.* Insurance claims that, after seven (7) business days from the date the loss giving rise to the claim is discovered, are not covered by an opinion of outside counsel that the claim is valid and is covered by insurance policies presently in effect; insurance claims that after twenty (20) business days from the date the loss giving rise to the claim is discovered and that are accompanied by an opinion of outside counsel described above, have not been acknowledged in writing by the insurance carrier as due and payable; and insurance claims acknowledged in writing by the carrier as due and payable outstanding longer than twenty (20) business days from the date they are so acknowledged by the carrier; and

(D) *Other deductions.* All other unsecured receivables; all assets doubtful of collection less any reserves established therefore; the amount by which the market value of securities failed to receive outstanding longer than thirty (30) calendar days exceeds the contract value of such fails to receive, and the funds on deposit in a ''segregated trust account'' in accordance with 17 CFR 270.27d–1 under the Investment Company Act of 1940, but only to the extent that the amount on deposit in such segregated trust account exceeds the amount of liability reserves established and maintained for refunds of charges required by sections 27(d) and 27(f) of the Investment Company Act of 1940; *Provided,* That any amount deposited in the ''special reserve account for the exclusive benefit of the security-based swap customers'' established pursuant to § 240.18a–4 and clearing deposits shall not be so deducted.

(E) *Repurchase agreements.* (*1*) For purposes of this paragraph:

(i) The term *reverse repurchase agreement deficit* shall mean the difference between the contract price for resale of

Securities and Exchange Commission § 240.18a-1

the securities under a reverse repurchase agreement and the market value of those securities (if less than the contract price).

(*ii*) The term *repurchase agreement deficit* shall mean the difference between the market value of securities subject to the repurchase agreement and the contract price for repurchase of the securities (if less than the market value of the securities).

(*iii*) As used in this paragraph (c)(1)(iii)(E)(*1*), the term *contract price* shall include accrued interest.

(*iv*) Reverse repurchase agreement deficits and the repurchase agreement deficits where the counterparty is the Federal Reserve Bank of New York shall be disregarded.

(*2*)(*i*) In the case of a reverse repurchase agreement, the deduction shall be equal to the reverse repurchase agreement deficit.

(*ii*) In determining the required deductions under paragraph (c)(1)(iii)(E)(*2*)(*i*) of this section, the security-based swap dealer may reduce the reverse repurchase agreement deficit by: Any margin or other deposits held by the security-based swap dealer on account of the reverse repurchase agreement; any excess market value of the securities over the contract price for resale of those securities under any other reverse repurchase agreement with the same party; the difference between the contract price for resale and the market value of securities subject to repurchase agreements with the same party (if the market value of those securities is less than the contract price); and calls for margin, marks to the market, or other required deposits that are outstanding one business day or less.

(*3*) In the case of repurchase agreements, the deduction shall be:

(*i*) The excess of the repurchase agreement deficit over 5 percent of the contract price for resale of United States Treasury Bills, Notes and Bonds, 10 percent of the contract price for the resale of securities issued or guaranteed as to principal or interest by an agency of the United States or mortgage related securities as defined in section 3(a)(41) of the Act and 20 percent of the contract price for the resale of other securities; and

(*ii*) The excess of the aggregate repurchase agreement deficits with any one party over 25 percent of the security-based swap dealer's net capital before the application of paragraphs (c)(1)(vi) and (vii) of this section (less any deduction taken with respect to repurchase agreements with that party under paragraph (c)(1)(iii)(E)(*3*)(*i*) of this section) or, if greater; the excess of the aggregate repurchase agreement deficits over 300 percent of the security-based swap dealer's net capital before the application of paragraphs (c)(1)(vi) and (vii) of this section.

(*iii*) In determining the required deduction under paragraphs (c)(1)(iii)(E)(*3*)(*i*) and (*ii*) of this section, the security-based swap dealer may reduce a repurchase agreement by any margin or other deposits held by the security-based swap dealer on account of a reverse repurchase agreement with the same party to the extent not otherwise used to reduce a reverse repurchase agreement deficit; the difference between the contract price and the market value of securities subject to other repurchase agreements with the same party (if the market value of those securities is less than the contract price) not otherwise used to reduce a reverse repurchase agreement deficit; and calls for margin, marks to the market, or other required deposits that are outstanding one business day or less to the extent not otherwise used to reduce a reverse repurchase agreement deficit.

(F) *Securities borrowed.* One percent of the market value of securities borrowed collateralized by an irrevocable letter of credit.

(G) *Affiliate receivables and collateral.* Any receivable from an affiliate of the security-based swap dealer (not otherwise deducted from net worth) and the market value of any collateral given to an affiliate (not otherwise deducted from net worth) to secure a liability over the amount of the liability of the security-based swap dealer unless the books and records of the affiliate are made available for examination when requested by the representatives of the Commission in order to demonstrate the validity of the receivable or payable. The provisions of this subsection shall not apply where the affiliate is a registered security-based swap dealer, registered broker or dealer, registered government securities broker or dealer, bank as defined in section 3(a)(6) of the Act, insurance company as defined in section 3(a)(19) of the Act, investment company registered under the Investment Company Act of 1940, federally insured savings and loan association, or futures commission merchant or swap dealer registered pursuant to the Commodity Exchange Act.

(iv) *Non-marketable securities.* Deducting 100 percent of the carrying value in the case of securities or evidence of indebtedness in the proprietary or other accounts of the security-based swap dealer, for which there is no ready market, as defined in paragraph (c)(4) of this section, and securities, in the proprietary or other accounts of the security-based swap dealer, that cannot be publicly offered or sold because of statutory, regulatory or contractual arrangements or other restrictions.

(v) Deducting from the contract value of each failed to deliver contract that is outstanding five business days or longer (21 business days or longer in the case of municipal securities) the percentages of the market value of the underlying security that would be required by application of the deduction required by paragraph (c)(1)(vii) of this section. Such deduction, however, shall be increased by any excess of the contract price of the failed to deliver contract over the market value of the underlying security or reduced by any excess of the market value of the underlying security over the contract value of the failed to deliver contract, but not to exceed the amount of such deduction. The Commission may, upon application of the security-based swap dealer, extend for a period up to 5 business days, any period herein specified when it is satisfied that the extension is warranted. The Commission upon expiration of the extension may extend for one additional period of up to 5 business days, any period herein specified when it is satisfied that the extension is warranted.

(vi)(A) *Cleared security-based swaps.* In the case of a cleared security-based swap held in a proprietary account of the security-based swap dealer, deducting the amount of the applicable margin requirement of the clearing agency or, if the security-based swap references an equity security, the security-based swap dealer may take a deduction using the method specified in §240.18a–1a.

(B) *Non-cleared security-based swaps—* (*1*) *Credit default swaps—*(i) *Short positions (selling protection).* In the case of a non-cleared security-based swap that is a short credit default swap, deducting the percentage of the notional amount based upon the current basis point spread of the credit default swap and the maturity of the credit default swap in accordance with table 1 to §240.18a–1(c)(1)(vi)(B)(*1*)(*i*):

TABLE 1 TO §240.18A–1(C)(1)(VI)(B)(*1*)(*I*)

Length of time to maturity of credit default swap contract	Basis point spread					
	100 or less (%)	101–300 (%)	301–400 (%)	401–500 (%)	501–699 (%)	700 or more (%)
Less than 12 months	1.00	2.00	5.00	7.50	10.00	15.00
12 months but less than 24 months	1.50	3.50	7.50	10.00	12.50	17.50
24 months but less than 36 months	2.00	5.00	10.00	12.50	15.00	20.00
36 months but less than 48 months	3.00	6.00	12.50	15.00	17.50	22.50
48 months but less than 60 months	4.00	7.00	15.00	17.50	20.00	25.00
60 months but less than 72 months	5.50	8.50	17.50	20.00	22.50	27.50
72 months but less than 84 months	7.00	10.00	20.00	22.50	25.00	30.00
84 months but less than 120 months	8.50	15.00	22.50	25.00	27.50	40.00
120 months and longer	10.00	20.00	25.00	27.50	30.00	50.00

Securities and Exchange Commission § 240.18a–1

(ii) *Long positions (purchasing protection).* In the case of a non-cleared security-based swap that is a long credit default swap, deducting 50 percent of the deduction that would be required by paragraph (c)(1)(vi)(B)(*1*)(*i*) of this section if the non-cleared security-based swap was a short credit default swap, each such deduction not to exceed the current market value of the long position.

(iii) *Long and short credit default swaps.* In the case of non-cleared security-based swaps that are long and short credit default swaps referencing the same entity (in the case of non-cleared credit default swap security-based swaps referencing a corporate entity) or obligation (in the case of non-cleared credit default swap security-based swaps referencing an asset-backed security), that have the same credit events which would trigger payment by the seller of protection, that have the same basket of obligations which would determine the amount of payment by the seller of protection upon the occurrence of a credit event, that are in the same or adjacent spread category, and that are in the same or adjacent maturity category and have a maturity date within three months of the other maturity category, deducting the percentage of the notional amount specified in the higher maturity category under paragraph (c)(1)(vi)(B)(*1*)(*i*) or (*ii*) on the excess of the long or short position. In the case of non-cleared security-based swaps that are long and short credit default swaps referencing corporate entities in the same industry sector and the same spread and maturity categories prescribed in paragraph (c)(1)(vi)(B)(*1*)(*i*) of this section, deducting 50 percent of the amount required by paragraph (c)(1)(vi)(B)(*1*)(*i*) of this section on the short position plus the deduction required by paragraph (c)(1)(vi)(B)(*1*)(*ii*) of this section on the excess long position, if any. For the purposes of this section, the security-based swap dealer must use an industry sector classification system that is reasonable in terms of grouping types of companies with similar business activities and risk characteristics and the security-based swap dealer must document the industry sector classification system used pursuant to this section.

(iv) *Long security and long credit default swap.* In the case of a non-cleared security-based swap that is a long credit default swap referencing a debt security and the security-based swap dealer is long the same debt security, deducting 50 percent of the amount specified in § 240.15c3–1(c)(2)(vi) or (vii) for the debt security, provided that the security-based swap dealer can deliver the debt security to satisfy the obligation of the security-based swap dealer on the credit default swap.

(v) *Short security and short credit default swap.* In the case of a non-cleared security-based swap that is a short credit default swap referencing a debt security or a corporate entity, and the security-based swap dealer is short the debt security or a debt security issued by the corporate entity, deducting the amount specified in § 240.15c3–1(c)(2)(vi) or (vii) for the debt security. In the case of a non-cleared security-based swap that is a short credit default swap referencing an asset-backed security and the security-based swap dealer is short the asset-backed security, deducting the amount specified in § 240.15c3–1(c)(2)(vi) or (vii) for the asset-backed security.

(2) *All other security-based swaps.* In the case of a non-cleared security-based swap that is not a credit default swap, deducting the amount calculated by multiplying the notional amount of the security-based swap and the percentage specified in § 240.15c3–1(c)(2)(vi) applicable to the reference security. A security-based swap dealer may reduce the deduction under this paragraph (c)(1)(vi)(B)(*2*) by an amount equal to any reduction recognized for a comparable long or short position in the reference security under § 240.15c3–1(c)(2)(vi) and, in the case of a security-based swap referencing an equity security, the method specified in § 240.18a–1a.

(vii) *All other securities, money market instruments or options.* Deducting the percentages specified in § 240.15c3–1(c)(2)(vi) of the market value of all securities, money market instruments, and options in the proprietary accounts of the security-based swap dealer.

(viii) *Deduction from net worth for certain undermargined accounts.* Deducting the amount of cash required in the account of each security-based swap and swap customer to meet the margin requirements of a clearing agency, the Commission, derivatives clearing organization, or the Commodity Futures Trading Commission, as applicable, after application of calls for margin, marks to the market, or other required deposits which are outstanding within the required time frame to collect the margin, mark to the market, or other required deposits.

(ix) *Deduction from net worth in lieu of collecting collateral for non-cleared security-based swap and swap transactions—*
(A) *Security-based swaps.* Deducting the initial margin amount calculated pursuant to §240.18a–3(c)(1)(i)(B) for the account of a counterparty at the security-based swap dealer that is subject to a margin exception set forth in §240.18a–3(c)(1)(iii), less the margin value of collateral held in the account.

(B) *Swaps.* Deducting the initial margin amount calculated pursuant to the margin rules of the Commodity Futures Trading Commission in the account of a counterparty at the security-based swap dealer that is subject to a margin exception in those rules, less the margin value of collateral held in the account.

(C) *Treatment of collateral held at a third-party custodian.* For the purposes of the deductions required pursuant to paragraphs (c)(1)(ix)(A) and (B) of this section, collateral held by an independent third-party custodian as initial margin may be treated as collateral held in the account of the counterparty at the security-based swap dealer if:

(*1*) The independent third-party custodian is a bank as defined in section 3(a)(6) of the Act or a registered U.S. clearing organization or depository that is not affiliated with the counterparty or, if the collateral consists of foreign securities or currencies, a supervised foreign bank, clearing organization, or depository that is not affiliated with the counterparty and that customarily maintains custody of such foreign securities or currencies;

(*2*) The security-based swap dealer, the independent third-party custodian, and the counterparty that delivered the collateral to the custodian have executed an account control agreement governing the terms under which the custodian holds and releases collateral pledged by the counterparty as initial margin that is a legal, valid, binding, and enforceable agreement under the laws of all relevant jurisdictions, including in the event of bankruptcy, insolvency, or a similar proceeding of any of the parties to the agreement, and that provides the security-based swap dealer with the right to access the collateral to satisfy the counterparty's obligations to the security-based swap dealer arising from transactions in the account of the counterparty; and

(*3*) The security-based swap dealer maintains written documentation of its analysis that in the event of a legal challenge the relevant court or administrative authorities would find the account control agreement to be legal, valid, binding, and enforceable under the applicable law, including in the event of the receivership, conservatorship, insolvency, liquidation, or a similar proceeding of any of the parties to the agreement.

(x)(A) Deducting the market value of all short securities differences (which shall include securities positions reflected on the securities record which are not susceptible to either count or confirmation) unresolved after discovery in accordance with the schedule in table 2 to §240.18a–1(c)(1)(x)(A):

TABLE 2 TO §240.18A–1(c)(1)(x)(A)

Differences [1]	Number of business days after discovery
25 percent	7
50 percent	14
75 percent	21
100 percent	28

[1] Percentage of market value of short securities differences.

(B) Deducting the market value of any long securities differences, where such securities have been sold by the security-based swap dealer before they are adequately resolved, less any reserves established therefor;

(C) The Commission may extend the periods in paragraph (c)(1)(x)(A) of this section for up to 10 business days if it finds that exceptional circumstances warrant an extension.

Securities and Exchange Commission § 240.18a–1

(2) The term *exempted securities* shall mean those securities deemed exempted securities by section 3(a)(12) of the Act (15 U.S.C. 78c(a)(12)) and the rules thereunder.

(3) *Customer.* The term *customer* shall mean any person from whom, or on whose behalf, a security-based swap dealer has received, acquired or holds funds or securities for the account of such person, but shall not include a security-based swap dealer, a broker or dealer, a registered municipal securities dealer, or a general, special or limited partner or director or officer of the security-based swap dealer, or any person to the extent that such person has a claim for property or funds which by contract, agreement, or understanding, or by operation of law, is part of the capital of the security-based swap dealer.

(4) *Ready market.* The term *ready market* shall include a recognized established securities market in which there exist independent bona fide offers to buy and sell so that a price reasonably related to the last sales price or current bona fide competitive bid and offer quotations can be determined for a particular security almost instantaneously and where payment will be received in settlement of a sale at such price within a relatively short time conforming to trade custom.

(5) The term *tentative net capital* means the net capital of the security-based swap dealer before deducting the haircuts computed pursuant to paragraphs (c)(1)(vi) and (vii) of this section and the charges on inventory computed pursuant to § 240.18a–1b. However, for purposes of paragraph (a)(2) of this section, the term *tentative net capital* means the net capital of the security-based swap dealer before deductions for market and credit risk computed pursuant to paragraph (d) of this section or paragraphs (c)(1)(vi) and (vii) of this section, if applicable, and increased by the balance sheet value (including counterparty net exposure) resulting from transactions in derivative instruments which would otherwise be deducted pursuant to paragraph (c)(1)(iii) of this section. Tentative net capital shall include securities for which there is no ready market, as defined in paragraph (c)(4) of this section, if the use of mathematical models has been approved for purposes of calculating deductions from net capital for those securities pursuant to paragraph (d) of this section.

(6) The term *risk margin amount* means the sum of:

(i) The total initial margin required to be maintained by the security-based swap dealer at each clearing agency with respect to security-based swap transactions cleared for security-based swap customers; and

(ii) The total initial margin amount calculated by the security-based swap dealer with respect to non-cleared security-based swaps pursuant to § 240.18a–3(c)(1)(i)(B).

(d) *Application to use models to compute deductions for market and credit risk.* (1) A security-based swap dealer may apply to the Commission for authorization to compute deductions for market risk under this paragraph (d) in lieu of computing deductions pursuant to paragraphs (c)(1)(iv), (vi), and (vii) of this section, and § 240.18a–1b, and to compute deductions for credit risk pursuant to this paragraph (d) on credit exposures arising from transactions in derivatives instruments (if this paragraph (d) is used to calculate deductions for market risk on these instruments) in lieu of computing deductions pursuant to paragraphs (c)(1)(iii) and (c)(1)(ix)(A) and (B) of this section:

(i) A security-based swap dealer shall submit the following information to the Commission with its application:

(A) An executive summary of the information provided to the Commission with its application and an identification of the ultimate holding company of the security-based swap dealer;

(B) A comprehensive description of the internal risk management control system of the security-based swap dealer and how that system satisfies the requirements set forth in § 240.15c3–4;

(C) A list of the categories of positions that the security-based swap dealer holds in its proprietary accounts and a brief description of the methods that the security-based swap dealer will use to calculate deductions for market and credit risk on those categories of positions;

713

§ 240.18a–1

(D) A description of the mathematical models to be used to price positions and to compute deductions for market risk, including those portions of the deductions attributable to specific risk, if applicable, and deductions for credit risk; a description of the creation, use, and maintenance of the mathematical models; a description of the security-based swap dealer's internal risk management controls over those models, including a description of each category of persons who may input data into the models; if a mathematical model incorporates empirical correlations across risk categories, a description of the process for measuring correlations; a description of the backtesting procedures the security-based swap dealer will use to backtest the mathematical models used to calculate maximum potential exposure; a description of how each mathematical model satisfies the applicable qualitative and quantitative requirements set forth in this paragraph (d); and a statement describing the extent to which each mathematical model used to compute deductions for market risk and credit risk will be used as part of the risk analyses and reports presented to senior management;

(E) If the security-based swap dealer is applying to the Commission for approval to use scenario analysis to calculate deductions for market risk for certain positions, a list of those types of positions, a description of how those deductions will be calculated using scenario analysis, and an explanation of why each scenario analysis is appropriate to calculate deductions for market risk on those types of positions;

(F) A description of how the security-based swap dealer will calculate current exposure;

(G) A description of how the security-based swap dealer will determine internal credit ratings of counterparties and internal credit risk weights of counterparties, if applicable;

(H) For each instance in which a mathematical model to be used by the security-based swap dealer to calculate a deduction for market risk or to calculate maximum potential exposure for a particular product or counterparty differs from the mathematical model used by the ultimate holding company to calculate an allowance for market risk or to calculate maximum potential exposure for that same product or counterparty, a description of the difference(s) between the mathematical models; and

(I) Sample risk reports that are provided to management at the security-based swap dealer who are responsible for managing the security-based swap dealer's risk.

(ii) [Reserved].

(2) The application of the security-based swap dealer shall be supplemented by other information relating to the internal risk management control system, mathematical models, and financial position of the security-based swap dealer that the Commission may request to complete its review of the application;

(3) The application shall be considered filed when received at the Commission's principal office in Washington, DC. A person who files an application pursuant to this section for which it seeks confidential treatment may clearly mark each page or segregable portion of each page with the words "Confidential Treatment Requested." All information submitted in connection with the application will be accorded confidential treatment, to the extent permitted by law;

(4) If any of the information filed with the Commission as part of the application of the security-based swap dealer is found to be or becomes inaccurate before the Commission approves the application, the security-based swap dealer must notify the Commission promptly and provide the Commission with a description of the circumstances in which the information was found to be or has become inaccurate along with updated, accurate information;

(5)(i) The Commission may approve the application or an amendment to the application, in whole or in part, subject to any conditions or limitations the Commission may require if the Commission finds the approval to be necessary or appropriate in the public interest or for the protection of investors, after determining, among other things, whether the security-based swap dealer has met the requirements of this paragraph (d) and is in

Securities and Exchange Commission § 240.18a-1

compliance with other applicable rules promulgated under the Act;

(ii) The Commission may approve the temporary use of a provisional model in whole or in part, subject to any conditions or limitations the Commission may require, if:

(A) The security-based swap dealer has a complete application pending under this section;

(B) The use of the provisional model has been approved by:

(*1*) A prudential regulator;

(*2*) The Commodity Futures Trading Commission or a futures association registered with the Commodity Futures Trading Commission under section 17 of the Commodity Exchange Act;

(*3*) A foreign financial regulatory authority that administers a foreign financial regulatory system with capital requirements that the Commission has found are eligible for substituted compliance under § 240.3a71-6 if the provisional model is used for the purposes of calculating net capital;

(*4*) A foreign financial regulatory authority that administers a foreign financial regulatory system with margin requirements that the Commission has found are eligible for substituted compliance under § 240.3a71-6 if the provisional model is used for the purposes of calculating initial margin pursuant to § 240.18a-3; or

(*5*) Any other foreign supervisory authority that the Commission finds has approved and monitored the use of the provisional model through a process comparable to the process set forth in this section.

(6) A security-based swap dealer shall amend its application to calculate certain deductions for market and credit risk under this paragraph (d) and submit the amendment to the Commission for approval before it may change materially a mathematical model used to calculate market or credit risk or before it may change materially its internal risk management control system;

(7) As a condition for the security-based swap dealer to compute deductions for market and credit risk under this paragraph (d), the security-based swap dealer agrees that:

(i) It will notify the Commission 45 days before it ceases to compute deductions for market and credit risk under this paragraph (d); and

(ii) The Commission may determine by order that the notice will become effective after a shorter or longer period of time if the security-based swap dealer consents or if the Commission determines that a shorter or longer period of time is necessary or appropriate in the public interest or for the protection of investors; and

(8) Notwithstanding paragraph (d)(7) of this section, the Commission, by order, may revoke a security-based swap dealer's exemption that allows it to use the market risk standards of this paragraph (d) to calculate deductions for market risk, and the exemption to use the credit risk standards of this paragraph (d) to calculate deductions for credit risk on certain credit exposures arising from transactions in derivatives instruments if the Commission finds that such exemption is no longer necessary or appropriate in the public interest or for the protection of investors. In making its finding, the Commission will consider the compliance history of the security-based swap dealer related to its use of models, the financial and operational strength of the security-based swap dealer and its ultimate holding company, and the security-based swap dealer's compliance with its internal risk management controls.

(9) To be approved, each value-at-risk ("VaR") model must meet the following minimum qualitative and quantitative requirements:

(i) *Qualitative requirements.* (A) The VaR model used to calculate market or credit risk for a position must be integrated into the daily internal risk management system of the security-based swap dealer;

(B) The VaR model must be reviewed both periodically and annually. The periodic review may be conducted by the security-based swap dealer's internal audit staff, but the annual review must be conducted by a registered public accounting firm, as that term is defined in section 2(a)(12) of the Sarbanes-Oxley Act of 2002 (15 U.S.C. 7201 *et seq.*); and

§ 240.18a-1

(C) For purposes of computing market risk, the security-based swap dealer must determine the appropriate multiplication factor as follows:

(1) Beginning three months after the security-based swap dealer begins using the VaR model to calculate market risk, the security-based swap dealer must conduct backtesting of the model by comparing its actual daily net trading profit or loss with the corresponding VaR measure generated by the VaR model, using a 99 percent, one-tailed confidence level with price changes equivalent to a one business-day movement in rates and prices, for each of the past 250 business days, or other period as may be appropriate for the first year of its use;

(2) On the last business day of each quarter, the security-based swap dealer must identify the number of backtesting exceptions of the VaR model, that is, the number of business days in the past 250 business days, or other period as may be appropriate for the first year of its use, for which the actual net trading loss, if any, exceeds the corresponding VaR measure; and

(3) The security-based swap dealer must use the multiplication factor indicated in table 3 to § 240.18a-1(d)(9)(i)(C)(3) in determining its market risk until it obtains the next quarter's backtesting results;

TABLE 3 TO § 240.18a-1(d)(9)(i)(C)(3)—MULTIPLICATION FACTOR BASED ON THE NUMBER OF BACKTESTING EXCEPTIONS OF THE VaR MODEL

Number of exceptions	Multiplication factor
4 or fewer	3.00
5	3.40
6	3.50
7	3.65
8	3.75
9	3.85
10 or more	4.00

(4) For purposes of incorporating specific risk into a VaR model, a security-based swap dealer must demonstrate that it has methodologies in place to capture liquidity, event, and default risk adequately for each position. Furthermore, the models used to calculate deductions for specific risk must:

(i) Explain the historical price variation in the portfolio;

17 CFR Ch. II (4-1-23 Edition)

(ii) Capture concentration (magnitude and changes in composition);

(iii) Be robust to an adverse environment;

(iv) Capture name-related basis risk;

(v) Capture event risk; and

(vi) Be validated through backtesting.

(5) For purposes of computing the credit equivalent amount of the security-based swap dealer's exposures to a counterparty, the security-based swap dealer must determine the appropriate multiplication factor as follows:

(i) Beginning three months after it begins using the VaR model to calculate maximum potential exposure, the security-based swap dealer must conduct backtesting of the model by comparing, for at least 80 counterparties with widely varying types and sizes of positions with the firm, the ten-business day change in its current exposure to the counterparty based on its positions held at the beginning of the ten-business day period with the corresponding ten-business day maximum potential exposure for the counterparty generated by the VaR model;

(ii) As of the last business day of each quarter, the security-based swap dealer must identify the number of backtesting exceptions of the VaR model, that is, the number of ten-business day periods in the past 250 business days, or other period as may be appropriate for the first year of its use, for which the change in current exposure to a counterparty exceeds the corresponding maximum potential exposure; and

(iii) The security-based swap dealer will propose, as part of its application, a schedule of multiplication factors, which must be approved by the Commission based on the number of backtesting exceptions of the VaR model. The security-based swap dealer must use the multiplication factor indicated in the approved schedule in determining the credit equivalent amount of its exposures to a counterparty until it obtains the next quarter's backtesting results, unless the Commission determines, based on, among other relevant factors, a review

Securities and Exchange Commission § 240.18a-1

of the security-based swap dealer's internal risk management control system, including a review of the VaR model, that a different adjustment or other action is appropriate.

(ii) *Quantitative requirements.* (A) For purposes of determining market risk, the VaR model must use a 99 percent, one-tailed confidence level with price changes equivalent to a ten business-day movement in rates and prices;

(B) For purposes of determining maximum potential exposure, the VaR model must use a 99 percent, one-tailed confidence level with price changes equivalent to a one-year movement in rates and prices; or based on a review of the security-based swap dealer's procedures for managing collateral and if the collateral is marked to market daily and the security-based swap dealer has the ability to call for additional collateral daily, the Commission may approve a time horizon of not less than ten business days;

(C) The VaR model must use an effective historical observation period of at least one year. The security-based swap dealer must consider the effects of market stress in its construction of the model. Historical data sets must be updated at least monthly and reassessed whenever market prices or volatilities change significantly; and

(D) The VaR model must take into account and incorporate all significant, identifiable market risk factors applicable to positions in the accounts of the security-based swap dealer, including:

(*1*) Risks arising from the non-linear price characteristics of derivatives and the sensitivity of the market value of those positions to changes in the volatility of the derivatives' underlying rates and prices;

(*2*) Empirical correlations with and across risk factors or, alternatively, risk factors sufficient to cover all the market risk inherent in the positions in the proprietary or other trading accounts of the security-based swap dealer, including interest rate risk, equity price risk, foreign exchange risk, and commodity price risk;

(*3*) Spread risk, where applicable, and segments of the yield curve sufficient to capture differences in volatility and imperfect correlation of rates along the yield curve for securities and derivatives that are sensitive to different interest rates; and

(*4*) Specific risk for individual positions:

(iii) *Additional conditions.* As a condition for the security-based swap dealer to use this paragraph (d) to calculate certain of its capital charges, the Commission may impose additional conditions on the security-based swap dealer, which may include, but are not limited to restricting the security-based swap dealer's business on a product-specific, category-specific, or general basis; submitting to the Commission a plan to increase the security-based swap dealer's net capital or tentative net capital; filing more frequent reports with the Commission; modifying the security-based swap dealer's internal risk management control procedures; or computing the security-based swap dealer's deductions for market and credit risk in accordance with paragraphs (c)(1)(iii), (iv), (vi), (vii), and (c)(1)(ix)(A) and (B), as appropriate, and §240.18a-1b, as appropriate. If the Commission finds it is necessary or appropriate in the public interest or for the protection of investors, the Commission may impose additional conditions on the security-based swap dealer, if:

(A) The security-based swap dealer fails to meet the reporting requirements set forth in §240.18a-7;

(B) Any event specified in §240.18a-8 occurs;

(C) There is a material deficiency in the internal risk management control system or in the mathematical models used to price securities or to calculate deductions for market and credit risk or allowances for market and credit risk, as applicable, of the security-based swap dealer;

(D) The security-based swap dealer fails to comply with this paragraph (d); or

(E) The Commission finds that imposition of other conditions is necessary or appropriate in the public interest or for the protection of investors.

(e) *Models to compute deductions for market risk and credit risk*—(1) *Market risk.* A security-based swap dealer

§ 240.18a–1

whose application, including amendments, has been approved under paragraph (d) of this section, shall compute a deduction for market risk in an amount equal to the sum of the following:

(i) For positions for which the Commission has approved the security-based swap dealer's use of VaR models, the VaR of the positions multiplied by the appropriate multiplication factor determined according to paragraph (d) of this section, except that the initial multiplication factor shall be three, unless the Commission determines, based on a review of the security-based swap dealer's application or an amendment to the application under paragraph (d) of this section, including a review of its internal risk management control system and practices and VaR models, that another multiplication factor is appropriate;

(ii) For positions for which the VaR model does not incorporate specific risk, a deduction for specific risk to be determined by the Commission based on a review of the security-based swap dealer's application or an amendment to the application under paragraph (d) of this section and the positions involved;

(iii) For positions for which the Commission has approved the security-based swap dealer's application to use scenario analysis, the greatest loss resulting from a range of adverse movements in relevant risk factors, prices, or spreads designed to represent a negative movement greater than, or equal to, the worst ten-day movement of the four years preceding calculation of the greatest loss, or some multiple of the greatest loss based on the liquidity of the positions subject to scenario analysis. If historical data is insufficient, the deduction shall be the largest loss within a three standard deviation movement in those risk factors, prices, or spreads over a ten-day period, multiplied by an appropriate liquidity adjustment factor. Irrespective of the deduction otherwise indicated under scenario analysis, the resulting deduction for market risk must be at least $25 per 100 share equivalent contract for equity positions, or one-half of one percent of the face value of the contract for all other types of contracts, even if the scenario analysis indicates a lower amount. A qualifying scenario must include the following:

(A) A set of pricing equations for the positions based on, for example, arbitrage relations, statistical analysis, historic relationships, merger evaluations, or fundamental valuation of an offering of securities;

(B) Auxiliary relationships mapping risk factors to prices; and

(C) Data demonstrating the effectiveness of the scenario in capturing market risk, including specific risk; and

(iv) For all remaining positions, the deductions specified in § 240.15c3–1(c)(2)(vi), § 240.15c3–1(c)(2)(vii), and applicable appendices to § 240.15c3–1.

(2) *Credit risk.* A security-based swap dealer whose application, including amendments, has been approved under paragraph (d) of this section may compute a deduction for credit risk on transactions in derivatives instruments (if this paragraph (e) is used to calculate a deduction for market risk on those positions) in an amount equal to the sum of the following:

(i) *Counterparty exposure charge.* A counterparty exposure charge in an amount equal to the sum of the following:

(A) The net replacement value in the account of each counterparty that is insolvent, or in bankruptcy, or that has senior unsecured long-term debt in default; and

(B) For a counterparty not otherwise described in paragraph (e)(2)(i)(A) of this section, the *credit equivalent amount* of the security-based swap dealer's exposure to the counterparty, as defined in paragraph (e)(2)(iii)(A) of this section, multiplied by the credit risk weight of the counterparty, as determined in accordance with paragraph (e)(2)(iii)(F) of this section, multiplied by eight percent; and

(ii) *Counterparty concentration charge.* A concentration charge by counterparty in an amount equal to the sum of the following:

(A) For each counterparty with a credit risk weight of 20 percent or less, 5 percent of the amount of the current exposure to the counterparty in excess of 5 percent of the tentative net capital of the security-based swap dealer;

Securities and Exchange Commission §240.18a-1

(B) For each counterparty with a credit risk weight of greater than 20 percent but less than 50 percent, 20 percent of the amount of the current exposure to the counterparty in excess of 5 percent of the tentative net capital of the security-based swap dealer; and

(C) For each counterparty with a credit risk weight of greater than 50 percent, 50 percent of the amount of the current exposure to the counterparty in excess of 5 percent of the tentative net capital of the security-based swap dealer;

(iii) *Terms.* (A) The *credit equivalent amount* of the security-based swap dealer's exposure to a counterparty is the sum of the security-based swap dealer's *maximum potential exposure* to the counterparty, as defined in paragraph (e)(2)(iii)(B) of this section, multiplied by the appropriate multiplication factor, and the security-based swap dealer's *current exposure* to the counterparty, as defined in paragraph (e)(2)(iii)(C) of this section. The security-based swap dealer must use the multiplication factor determined according to paragraph (d)(9)(i)(C)(*5*) of this section, except that the initial multiplication factor shall be one, unless the Commission determines, based on a review of the security-based swap dealer's application or an amendment to the application approved under paragraph (d) of this section, including a review of its internal risk management control system and practices and VaR models, that another multiplication factor is appropriate;

(B) The *maximum potential exposure* is the VaR of the counterparty's positions with the security-based swap dealer, after applying netting agreements with the counterparty meeting the requirements of paragraph (e)(2)(iii)(D) of this section, taking into account the value of collateral from the counterparty held by the security-based swap dealer in accordance with paragraph (e)(2)(iii)(E) of this section, and taking into account the current replacement value of the counterparty's positions with the security-based swap dealer;

(C) The *current exposure* of the security-based swap dealer to a counterparty is the current replacement value of the counterparty's positions with the security-based swap dealer, after applying netting agreements with the counterparty meeting the requirements of paragraph (e)(2)(iii)(D) of this section and taking into account the value of collateral from the counterparty held by the security-based swap dealer in accordance with paragraph (e)(2)(iii)(E) of this section;

(D) *Netting agreements.* A security-based swap dealer may include the effect of a netting agreement that allows the security-based swap dealer to net gross receivables from and gross payables to a counterparty upon default of the counterparty if:

(*1*) The netting agreement is legally enforceable in each relevant jurisdiction, including in insolvency proceedings;

(*2*) The gross receivables and gross payables that are subject to the netting agreement with a counterparty can be determined at any time; and

(*3*) For internal risk management purposes, the security-based swap dealer monitors and controls its exposure to the counterparty on a net basis;

(E) *Collateral.* When calculating maximum potential exposure and current exposure to a counterparty, the fair market value of collateral pledged and held may be taken into account provided:

(*1*) The collateral is marked to market each day and is subject to a daily margin maintenance requirement;

(*2*)(*i*) The collateral is subject to the security-based swap dealer's physical possession or control and may be liquidated promptly by the firm without intervention by any other party; or

(*ii*) The collateral is held by an independent third-party custodian that is a bank as defined in section 3(a)(6) of the Act or a registered U.S. clearing organization or depository that is not affiliated with the counterparty or, if the collateral consists of foreign securities or currencies, a supervised foreign bank, clearing organization, or depository that is not affiliated with the counterparty and that customarily maintains custody of such foreign securities or currencies;

(*3*) The collateral is liquid and transferable;

§ 240.18a–1

(4) The collateral agreement is legally enforceable by the security-based swap dealer against the counterparty and any other parties to the agreement;

(5) The collateral does not consist of securities issued by the counterparty or a party related to the security-based swap dealer or to the counterparty;

(6) The Commission has approved the security-based swap dealer's use of a VaR model to calculate deductions for market risk for the type of collateral in accordance with paragraph (d) of this section; and

(7) The collateral is not used in determining the credit rating of the counterparty;

(F) *Credit risk weights of counterparties.* A security-based swap dealer that computes its deductions for credit risk pursuant to this paragraph (e)(2) shall apply a credit risk weight for transactions with a counterparty of either 20 percent, 50 percent, or 150 percent based on an internal credit rating the security-based swap dealer determines for the counterparty.

(*1*) As part of its initial application or in an amendment, the security-based swap dealer may request Commission approval to apply a credit risk weight of either 20 percent, 50 percent, or 150 percent based on internal calculations of credit ratings, including internal estimates of the maturity adjustment. Based on the strength of the security-based swap dealer's internal credit risk management system, the Commission may approve the application. The security-based swap dealer must make and keep current a record of the basis for the credit risk weight of each counterparty;

(*2*) As part of its initial application or in an amendment, the security-based swap dealer may request Commission approval to determine credit risk weights based on internal calculations, including internal estimates of the maturity adjustment. Based on the strength of the security-based swap dealer's internal credit risk management system, the Commission may approve the application. The security-based swap dealer must make and keep current a record of the basis for the credit risk weight of each counterparty; and

17 CFR Ch. II (4–1–23 Edition)

(*3*) As part of its initial application or in an amendment, the security-based swap dealer may request Commission approval to reduce deductions for credit risk through the use of credit derivatives.

(f) *Internal risk management control systems.* A security-based swap dealer must comply with § 240.15c3–4 as if it were an OTC derivatives dealer with respect to all of its business activities, except that § 240.15c3–4(c)(5)(xiii) and (xiv) and (d)(8) and (9) shall not apply.

(g) *Debt-equity requirements.* No security-based swap dealer shall permit the total of outstanding principal amounts of its satisfactory subordination agreements (other than such agreements which qualify under this paragraph (g) as equity capital) to exceed 70 percent of its debt-equity total, as hereinafter defined, for a period in excess of 90 days or for such longer period which the Commission may, upon application of the security-based swap dealer, grant in the public interest or for the protection of investors. In the case of a corporation, the debt-equity total shall be the sum of its outstanding principal amounts of satisfactory subordination agreements, par or stated value of capital stock, paid in capital in excess of par, retained earnings, unrealized profit and loss or other capital accounts. In the case of a partnership, the debt-equity total shall be the sum of its outstanding principal amounts of satisfactory subordination agreements, capital accounts of partners (exclusive of such partners' securities accounts) subject to the provisions of paragraph (h) of this section, and unrealized profit and loss. *Provided, however,* that a satisfactory subordinated loan agreement entered into by a partner or stockholder which has an initial term of at least three years and has a remaining term of not less than 12 months shall be considered equity for the purposes of this paragraph (g) if:

(1) It does not have any of the provisions for accelerated maturity provided for by paragraph (b)(8)(i) or (b)(9)(i) or (ii) of § 240.18a–1d and is maintained as capital subject to the provisions restricting the withdrawal thereof required by paragraph (h) of this section; or

Securities and Exchange Commission § 240.18a–1

(2) The partnership agreement provides that capital contributed pursuant to a satisfactory subordination agreement as defined in § 240.18a–1d shall in all respects be partnership capital subject to the provisions restricting the withdrawal thereof required by paragraph (h) of this section.

(h) *Provisions relating to the withdrawal of equity capital*—(1) *Notice provisions relating to limitations on the withdrawal of equity capital.* No equity capital of the security-based swap dealer or a subsidiary or affiliate consolidated pursuant to § 240.18a–1c may be withdrawn by action of a stockholder or a partner or by redemption or repurchase of shares of stock by any of the consolidated entities or through the payment of dividends or any similar distribution, nor may any unsecured advance or loan be made to a stockholder, partner, employee or affiliate without written notice given in accordance with paragraph (h)(1)(iv) of this section:

(i) Two business days prior to any withdrawals, advances or loans if those withdrawals, advances or loans on a net basis exceed in the aggregate in any 30 calendar day period, 30 percent of the security-based swap dealer's excess net capital. A security-based swap dealer, in an emergency situation, may make withdrawals, advances or loans that on a net basis exceed 30 percent of the security-based swap dealer's excess net capital in any 30 calendar day period without giving the advance notice required by this paragraph, with the prior approval of the Commission. Where a security-based swap dealer makes a withdrawal with the consent of the Commission, it shall in any event comply with paragraph (h)(1)(ii) of this section; or

(ii) Two business days after any withdrawals, advances or loans if those withdrawals, advances or loans on a net basis exceed in the aggregate in any 30 calendar day period, 20 percent of the security-based swap dealer's excess net capital.

(iii) This paragraph (h)(1) does not apply to:

(A) Securities or commodities transactions in the ordinary course of business between a security-based swap dealer and an affiliate where the security-based swap dealer makes payment to or on behalf of such affiliate for such transaction and then receives payment from such affiliate for the securities or commodities transaction within two business days from the date of the transaction; or

(B) Withdrawals, advances or loans which in the aggregate in any thirty calendar day period, on a net basis, equal $500,000 or less.

(iv) Each required notice shall be effective when received by the Commission in Washington, DC, the regional office of the Commission for the region in which the security-based swap dealer has its principal place of business, and the Commodity Futures Trading Commission if such security-based swap dealer is registered with that Commission.

(2) *Limitations on withdrawal of equity capital.* No equity capital of the security-based swap dealer or a subsidiary or affiliate consolidated pursuant to § 240.18a–1c may be withdrawn by action of a stockholder or a partner or by redemption or repurchase of shares of stock by any of the consolidated entities or through the payment of dividends or any similar distribution, nor may any unsecured advance or loan be made to a stockholder, partner, employee or affiliate, if after giving effect thereto and to any other such withdrawals, advances or loans and any Payments of Payments Obligations (as defined in § 240.18a–1d) under satisfactory subordinated loan agreements which are scheduled to occur within 180 days following such withdrawal, advance or loan if:

(i) The security-based swap dealer's net capital would be less than 120 percent of the minimum dollar amount required by paragraph (a) of this section; or

(ii) The total outstanding principal amounts of satisfactory subordinated loan agreements of the security-based swap dealer and any subsidiaries or affiliates consolidated pursuant to § 240.18a–1c (other than such agreements which qualify as equity under paragraph (g) of this section) would exceed 70 percent of the debt-equity total as defined in paragraph (g) of this section.

§ 240.18a–1a

(3) *Temporary restrictions on withdrawal of net capital.* (i) The Commission may by order restrict, for a period up to twenty business days, any withdrawal by the security-based swap dealer of equity capital or unsecured loan or advance to a stockholder, partner, member, employee or affiliate under such terms and conditions as the Commission deems necessary or appropriate in the public interest or consistent with the protection of investors if the Commission, based on the information available, concludes that such withdrawal, advance or loan may be detrimental to the financial integrity of the security-based swap dealer, or may unduly jeopardize the security-based swap dealer's ability to repay its customer claims or other liabilities which may cause a significant impact on the markets or expose the customers or creditors of the security-based swap dealer to loss.

(ii) An order temporarily prohibiting the withdrawal of capital shall be rescinded if the Commission determines that the restriction on capital withdrawal should not remain in effect. A hearing on an order temporarily prohibiting withdrawal of capital will be held within two business days from the date of the request in writing by the security-based swap dealer.

(4) *Miscellaneous provisions.* (i) Excess net capital is that amount in excess of the amount required under paragraph (a) of this section. For the purposes of paragraphs (h)(1) and (2) of this section, a security-based swap dealer may use the amount of excess net capital and deductions required under paragraphs (c)(1)(vi) and (vii) and § 240.18a–1a reported in its most recently required filed Part II of Form X–17A–5 for the purposes of calculating the effect of a projected withdrawal, advance or loan relative to excess net capital or deductions. The security-based swap dealer must assure itself that the excess net capital or the deductions reported on the most recently required filed Part II of Form X–17A–5 have not materially changed since the time such report was filed.

(ii) The term equity capital includes capital contributions by partners, par or stated value of capital stock, paid-in capital in excess of par, retained earnings or other capital accounts. The term equity capital does not include securities in the securities accounts of partners and balances in limited partners' capital accounts in excess of their stated capital contributions.

(iii) Paragraphs (h)(1) and (2) of this section shall not preclude a security-based swap dealer from making required tax payments or preclude the payment to partners of reasonable compensation, and such payments shall not be included in the calculation of withdrawals, advances, or loans for purposes of paragraphs (h)(1) and (2) of this section.

(iv) For the purpose of this paragraph (h), any transactions between a security-based swap dealer and a stockholder, partner, employee or affiliate that results in a diminution of the security-based swap dealer's net capital shall be deemed to be an advance or loan of net capital.

[84 FR 44052, Aug. 22, 2019, as amended at 85 FR 68656, Dec. 16, 2019]

§ 240.18a–1a Options.

(a)(1) *Definitions.* The term *unlisted option* means any option not included in the definition of listed option provided in § 240.15c3–1(c)(2)(x).

(2) The term *option series* refers to listed option contracts of the same type (either a call or a put) and exercise style, covering the same underlying security with the same exercise price, expiration date, and number of underlying units.

(3) The term *related instrument* within an option class or product group refers to futures contracts, options on futures contracts, security-based swaps on a narrow-based security index, and swaps covering the same underlying instrument. In relation to options on foreign currencies, a related instrument within an option class also shall include forward contracts on the same underlying currency.

(4) The term *underlying instrument* refers to long and short positions, as appropriate, covering the same foreign currency, the same security, security future, or security-based swap other than a security-based swap on a narrow-based security index, or a security

Securities and Exchange Commission § 240.18a–1a

which is exchangeable for or convertible into the underlying security within a period of 90 days. If the exchange or conversion requires the payment of money or results in a loss upon conversion at the time when the security is deemed an underlying instrument for purposes of this Appendix A, the broker or dealer will deduct from net worth the full amount of the conversion loss. The term *underlying instrument* shall not be deemed to include securities options, futures contracts, options on futures contracts, security-based swaps on a narrow-based security index, qualified stock baskets, unlisted instruments, or swaps.

(5) The term *options class* refers to all options contracts covering the same underlying instrument.

(6) The term *product group* refers to two or more option classes, related instruments, underlying instruments, and qualified stock baskets in the same portfolio type (see paragraph (b)(1)(ii) of this section) for which it has been determined that a percentage of offsetting profits may be applied to losses at the same valuation point.

(b) The deduction under this Appendix A must equal the sum of the deductions specified in paragraph (b)(1)(iv)(C) of this section.

(1)(i) *Definitions.* (A) The terms *theoretical gains and losses* mean the gain and loss in the value of individual option series, the value of underlying instruments, related instruments, and qualified stock baskets within that option's class, at 10 equidistant intervals (valuation points) ranging from an assumed movement (both up and down) in the current market value of the underlying instrument equal to the percentage corresponding to the deductions otherwise required under §240.15c3–1 for the underlying instrument (see paragraph (b)(1)(iii) of this section). Theoretical gains and losses shall be calculated using a theoretical options pricing model that satisfies the criteria set forth in paragraph (b)(1)(i)(B) of this section.

(B) The term *theoretical options pricing model* means any mathematical model, other than a security-based swap dealer's proprietary model, the use of which has been approved by the Commission. Any such model shall calculate theoretical gains and losses as described in paragraph (b)(1)(i)(A) of this section for all series and issues of equity, index and foreign currency options and related instruments, and shall be made available equally and on the same terms to all security-based swap dealers. Its procedures shall include the arrangement of the vendor to supply accurate and timely data to each security-based swap dealer with respect to its services, and the fees for distribution of the services. The data provided to security-based swap dealers shall also contain the minimum requirements set forth in paragraphs (b)(1)(iv)(C) of this section and the product group offsets set forth in paragraphs (b)(1)(iv)(B) of this section. At a minimum, the model shall consider the following factors in pricing the option:

(*1*) The current spot price of the underlying asset;

(*2*) The exercise price of the option;

(*3*) The remaining time until the option's expiration;

(*4*) The volatility of the underlying asset;

(*5*) Any cash flows associated with ownership of the underlying asset that can reasonably be expected to occur during the remaining life of the option; and

(*6*) The current term structure of interest rates.

(C) The term *major market foreign currency* means the currency of a sovereign nation for which there is a substantial inter-bank forward currency market.

(D) The term *qualified stock basket* means a set or basket of stock positions which represents no less than 50 percent of the capitalization for a high-capitalization or non-high-capitalization diversified market index, or, in the case of a narrow-based index, no less than 95 percent of the capitalization for such narrow-based index.

(ii) With respect to positions involving listed options in its proprietary or other account, the security-based swap dealer shall group long and short positions into the following portfolio types:

(A) Equity options on the same underlying instrument and positions in that underlying instrument;

(B) Options on the same major market foreign currency, positions in that

§ 240.18a–1a

major market foreign currency, and related instruments within those options' classes;

(C) High-capitalization diversified market index options, related instruments within the option's class, and qualified stock baskets in the same index;

(D) Non-high-capitalization diversified index options, related instruments within the index option's class, and qualified stock baskets in the same index; and

(E) Narrow-based index options, related instruments within the index option's class, and qualified stock baskets in the same index.

(iii) Before making the computation, each security-based swap dealer shall obtain the theoretical gains and losses for each option series and for the related and underlying instruments within those options' class in the proprietary or other accounts of that security-based swap dealer. For each option series, the theoretical options pricing model shall calculate theoretical prices at 10 equidistant valuation points within a range consisting of an increase or a decrease of the following percentages of the daily market price of the underlying instrument:

(A) +(−) 15 percent for equity securities with a ready market, narrow-based indexes, and non-high-capitalization diversified indexes;

(B) +(−) 6 percent for major market foreign currencies;

(C) +(−) 20 percent for all other currencies; and

(D) +(−)10 percent for high-capitalization diversified indexes.

(iv)(A) The security-based swap dealer shall multiply the corresponding theoretical gains and losses at each of the 10 equidistant valuation points by the number of positions held in a particular option series, the related instruments and qualified stock baskets within the option's class, and the positions in the same underlying instrument.

(B) In determining the aggregate profit or loss for each portfolio type, the security-based swap dealer will be allowed the following offsets in the following order, provided, that in the case of qualified stock baskets, the security-based swap dealer may elect to net individual stocks between qualified stock baskets and take the appropriate deduction on the remaining, if any, securities:

(*1*) First, a security-based swap dealer is allowed the following offsets within an option's class:

(*i*) Between options on the same underlying instrument, positions covering the same underlying instrument, and related instruments within the option's class, 100 percent of a position's gain shall offset another position's loss at the same valuation point;

(*ii*) Between index options, related instruments within the option's class, and qualified stock baskets on the same index, 95 percent, or such other amount as designated by the Commission, of gains shall offset losses at the same valuation point;

(*2*) Second, a security-based swap dealer is allowed the following offsets within an index product group:

(*i*) Among positions involving different high-capitalization diversified index option classes within the same product group, 90 percent of the gain in a high-capitalization diversified market index option, related instruments, and qualified stock baskets within that index option's class shall offset the loss at the same valuation point in a different high-capitalization diversified market index option, related instruments, and qualified stock baskets within that index option's class;

(*ii*) Among positions involving different non-high-capitalization diversified index option classes within the same product group, 75 percent of the gain in a non-high-capitalization diversified market index option, related instruments, and qualified stock baskets within that index option's class shall offset the loss at the same valuation point in another non-high-capitalization diversified market index option, related instruments, and qualified stock baskets within that index option's class or product group;

(*iii*) Among positions involving different narrow-based index option classes within the same product group, 90 percent of the gain in a narrow-based market index option, related instruments, and qualified stock baskets within that index option's class shall offset the loss at the same valuation

Securities and Exchange Commission § 240.18a–1b

point in another narrow-based market index option, related instruments, and qualified stock baskets within that index option's class or product group;

(*iv*) No qualified stock basket should offset another qualified stock basket; and

(3) Third, a security-based swap dealer is allowed the following offsets between product groups: Among positions involving different diversified index product groups within the same market group, 50 percent of the gain in a diversified market index option, a related instrument, or a qualified stock basket within that index option's product group shall offset the loss at the same valuation point in another product group;

(C) For each portfolio type, the total deduction shall be the larger of:

(*1*) The amount for any of the 10 equidistant valuation points representing the largest theoretical loss after applying the offsets provided in paragraph (b)(1)(iv)(B) if this section; or

(*2*) A minimum charge equal to 25 percent times the multiplier for each equity and index option contract and each related instrument within the option's class or product group, or $25 for each option on a major market foreign currency with the minimum charge for futures contracts and options on futures contracts adjusted for contract size differentials, not to exceed market value in the case of long positions in options and options on futures contracts; plus

(3) In the case of portfolio types involving index options and related instruments offset by a qualified stock basket, there will be a minimum charge of 5 percent of the market value of the qualified stock basket for high-capitalization diversified and narrow-based indexes;

(4) In the case of portfolio types involving index options and related instruments offset by a qualified stock basket, there will be a minimum charge of 7½ percent of the market value of the qualified stock basket for non-high-capitalization diversified indexes; and

(5) In the case of portfolio types involving security futures and equity options on the same underlying instrument and positions in that underlying instrument, there will be a minimum charge of 25 percent times the multiplier for each security-future and equity option.

[84 FR 44061, Aug. 22, 2019]

§ 240.18a–1b **Adjustments to net worth for certain commodities transactions.**

(a) Every registered security-based swap dealer in computing net capital pursuant to § 240.18a–1 shall comply with the following:

(1) Where a security-based swap dealer has an asset or liability which is treated or defined in paragraph (c) of § 240.18a–1, the inclusion or exclusion of all or part of such asset or liability for net capital shall be in accordance with § 240.18a–1, except as specifically provided otherwise in this section. Where a commodity related asset or liability, including a swap-related asset or liability, is specifically treated or defined in 17 CFR 1.17 and is not generally or specifically treated or defined in § 240.18a–1 or this section, the inclusion or exclusion of all or part of such asset or liability for net capital shall be in accordance with 17 CFR 1.17.

(2) In computing net capital as defined in § 240.18a–1(c)(1), the net worth of a security-based swap dealer shall be adjusted as follows with respect to commodity-related transactions:

(i)(A) Unrealized profits shall be added and unrealized losses shall be deducted in the commodities accounts of the security-based swap dealer, including unrealized profits and losses on fixed price commitments and forward contracts; and

(B) The value attributed to any commodity option which is not traded on a contract market shall be the difference between the option's strike price and the market value for the physical or futures contract which is the subject of the option. In the case of a long call commodity option, if the market value for the physical or futures contract which is the subject of the option is less than the strike price of the option, it shall be given no value. In the case of a long put commodity option, if the market value for the physical commodity or futures contract which is the subject of the option is more than the

725

§ 240.18a–1b

striking price of the option, it shall be given no value.

(ii) Deduct any unsecured commodity futures or option account containing a ledger balance and open trades, the combination of which liquidates to a deficit or containing a debit ledger balance only: *Provided, however,* Deficits or debit ledger balances in unsecured customers', non-customers' and proprietary accounts, which are the subject of calls for margin or other required deposits need not be deducted until the close of business on the business day following the date on which such deficit or debit ledger balance originated;

(iii) Deduct all unsecured receivables, advances and loans except for:

(A) Management fees receivable from commodity pools outstanding no longer than thirty (30) days from the date they are due;

(B) Receivables from foreign clearing organizations;

(C) Receivables from registered futures commission merchants or brokers, resulting from cleared swap transactions or, commodity futures or option transactions, except those specifically excluded under paragraph (a)(2)(ii) of this section.

(iv) Deduct all inventories (including work in process, finished goods, raw materials and inventories held for resale) except for readily marketable spot commodities; or spot commodities which adequately collateralize indebtedness under 17 CFR 1.17(c)(7);

(v) Guarantee deposits with commodities clearing organizations are not required to be deducted from net worth;

(vi) Stock in commodities clearing organizations to the extent of its margin value is not required to be deducted from net worth;

(vii) Deduct from net worth the amount by which any advances paid by the security-based swap dealer on cash commodity contracts and used in computing net capital exceeds 95 percent of the market value of the commodities covered by such contracts.

(viii) Do not include equity in the commodity accounts of partners in net worth.

(ix) In the case of all inventory, fixed price commitments and forward contracts, except for inventory and forward contracts in the inter-bank market in those foreign currencies which are purchased or sold for further delivery on or subject to the rules of a contract market and covered by an open futures contract for which there will be no charge, deduct the applicable percentage of the net position specified below:

(A) Inventory which is currently registered as deliverable on a contract market and covered by an open futures contract or by a commodity option on a physical—No charge.

(B) Inventory which is covered by an open futures contract or commodity option—5 percent of the market value.

(C) Inventory which is not covered—20 percent of the market value.

(D) Fixed price commitments (open purchases and sales) and forward contracts which are covered by an open futures contract or commodity option—10 percent of the market value.

(E) Fixed price commitments (open purchases and sales) and forward contracts which are not covered by an open futures contract or commodity option—20 percent of the market value.

(x) Deduct for undermargined customer commodity futures accounts the amount of funds required in each such account to meet maintenance margin requirements of the applicable board of trade or, if there are no such maintenance margin requirements, clearing organization margin requirements applicable to such positions, after application of calls for margin, or other required deposits which are outstanding three business days or less. If there are no such maintenance margin requirements or clearing organization margin requirements on such accounts, then deduct the amount of funds required to provide margin equal to the amount necessary after application of calls for margin, or other required deposits outstanding three days or less to restore original margin when the original margin has been depleted by 50 percent or more. *Provided,* To the extent a deficit is deducted from net worth in accordance with paragraph (a)(2)(ii) of this section, such amount shall not also be deducted under this paragraph (a)(2)(x). In the event that an owner of a customer account has deposited an asset other than cash to margin, guarantee

Securities and Exchange Commission § 240.18a-1b

or secure his account, the value attributable to such asset for purposes of this paragraph shall be the lesser of the value attributable to such asset pursuant to the margin rules of the applicable board of trade, or the market value of such asset after application of the percentage deductions specified in paragraph (a)(2)(ix) of this section or, where appropriate, specified in § 240.18a-1(c)(1)(iv), (vi), or (vii) of this part;

(xi) Deduct for undermargined noncustomer and omnibus commodity futures accounts the amount of funds required in each such account to meet maintenance margin requirements of the applicable board of trade or, if there are no such maintenance margin requirements, clearing organization margin requirements applicable to such positions, after application of calls for margin, or other required deposits which are outstanding two business days or less. If there are no such maintenance margin requirements or clearing organization margin requirements, then deduct the amount of funds required to provide margin equal to the amount necessary after application of calls for margin, or other required deposits outstanding two days or less to restore original margin when the original margin has been depleted by 50 percent or more. *Provided,* To the extent a deficit is deducted from net worth in accordance with paragraph (a)(2)(ii) of this section such amount shall not also be deducted under this paragraph (a)(2)(xi). In the event that an owner of a non-customer or omnibus account has deposited an asset other than cash to margin, guarantee or secure the account, the value attributable to such asset for purposes of this paragraph shall be the lesser of the value attributable to such asset pursuant to the margin rules of the applicable board of trade, or the market value of such asset after application of the percentage deductions specified in paragraph (a)(2)(ix) of this section or, where appropriate, specified in § 240.18a-1(c)(1)(iv), (vi), or (vii) of this part;

(xii) In the case of open futures contracts and granted (sold) commodity options held in proprietary accounts carried by the security-based swap dealer which are not covered by a position held by the security-based swap dealer or which are not the result of a "changer trade" made in accordance with the rules of a contract market, deduct:

(A) For a security-based swap dealer which is a clearing member of a contract market for the positions on such contract market cleared by such member, the applicable margin requirement of the applicable clearing organization;

(B) For a security-based swap dealer which is a member of a self-regulatory organization, 150 percent of the applicable maintenance margin requirement of the applicable board of trade or clearing organization, whichever is greater; or

(C) For all other security-based swap dealers, 200 percent of the applicable maintenance margin requirement of the applicable board of trade or clearing organization, whichever is greater; or

(D) For open contracts or granted (sold) commodity options for which there are no applicable maintenance margin requirements, 200 percent of the applicable initial margin requirement; *Provided,* the equity in any such proprietary account shall reduce the deduction required by this paragraph (a)(2)(xii) if such equity is not otherwise includable in net capital.

(xiii) In the case of a security-based swap dealer which is a purchaser of a commodity option which is traded on a contract market, the deduction shall be the same safety factor as if the security-based swap dealer were the grantor of such option in accordance with paragraph (a)(2)(xii) of this section, but in no event shall the safety factor be greater than the market value attributed to such option.

(xiv) In the case of a security-based swap dealer which is a purchaser of a commodity option not traded on a contract market which has value and such value is used to increase net capital, the deduction is ten percent of the market value of the physical or futures contract which is the subject of such option but in no event more than the value attributed to such option.

(xv) A loan or advance or any other form of receivable shall not be considered "secured" for the purposes of

727

§ 240.18a–1b

paragraph (a)(2) of this section unless the following conditions exist:

(A) The receivable is secured by readily marketable collateral which is otherwise unencumbered and which can be readily converted into cash: *Provided, however,* That the receivable will be considered secured only to the extent of the market value of such collateral after application of the percentage deductions specified in paragraph (a)(2)(ix) of this section; and

(B)(*1*) The readily marketable collateral is in the possession or control of the security-based swap dealer; or

(*2*) The security-based swap dealer has a legally enforceable, written security agreement, signed by the debtor, and has a perfected security interest in the readily marketable collateral within the meaning of the laws of the State in which the readily marketable collateral is located.

(xvi) The term *cover* for purposes of this section shall mean cover as defined in 17 CFR 1.17(j).

(xvii) The term *customer* for purposes of this section shall mean customer as defined in 17 CFR 1.17(b)(2). The term *non-customer* for purposes of this section shall mean non-customer as defined in 17 CFR 1.17(b)(4).

(b) Every registered security-based swap dealer in computing net capital pursuant to § 240.18a–1 shall comply with the following:

(1) *Cleared swaps.* In the case of a cleared swap held in a proprietary account of the security-based swap dealer, deducting the amount of the applicable margin requirement of the derivatives clearing organization or, if the swap references an equity security index, the security-based swap dealer may take a deduction using the method specified in § 240.18a–1a.

(2) *Non-cleared swaps*—(i) *Credit default swaps referencing broad-based security indices.* In the case of a non-cleared credit default swap for which the deductions in § 240.18a–1(e) do not apply:

(A) *Short positions (selling protection).* In the case of a non-cleared swap that is a short credit default swap referencing a broad-based security index, deducting the percentage of the notional amount based upon the current basis point spread of the credit default swap and the maturity of the credit default swap in accordance with table 1 to § 240.18a–1b(b)(2)(i)(A):

TABLE 1 TO § 240.18a–1b(b)(2)(i)(A)

Length of time to maturity of credit default swap contract	Basis point spread					
	100 or less (%)	101–300 (%)	301–400 (%)	401–500 (%)	501–699 (%)	700 or more (%)
Less than 12 months	0.67	1.33	3.33	5.00	6.67	10.00
12 months but less than 24 months	1.00	2.33	5.00	6.67	8.33	11.67
24 months but less than 36 months	1.33	3.33	6.67	8.33	10.00	13.33
36 months but less than 48 months	2.00	4.00	8.33	10.00	11.67	15.00
48 months but less than 60 months	2.67	4.67	10.00	11.67	13.33	16.67
60 months but less than 72 months	3.67	5.67	11.67	13.33	15.00	18.33
72 months but less than 84 months	4.67	6.67	13.33	15.00	16.67	20.00
84 months but less than 120 months	5.67	10.00	15.00	16.67	18.33	26.67
120 months and longer	6.67	13.33	16.67	18.33	20.00	33.33

(B) *Long positions (purchasing protection).* In the case of a non-cleared swap that is a long credit default swap referencing a broad-based security index, deducting 50 percent of the deduction that would be required by paragraph (b)(2)(i)(A) of this section if the non-cleared swap was a short credit default swap, each such deduction not to exceed the current market value of the long position.

(C) *Long and short credit default swaps.* In the case of non-cleared swaps that are long and short credit default

Securities and Exchange Commission

§ 240.18a–1d

swaps referencing the same broad-based security index, have the same credit events which would trigger payment by the seller of protection, have the same basket of obligations which would determine the amount of payment by the seller of protection upon the occurrence of a credit event, that are in the same or adjacent spread category, and that are in the same or adjacent maturity category and have a maturity date within three months of the other maturity category, deducting the percentage of the notional amount specified in the higher maturity category under paragraph (b)(2)(i)(A) or (B) of this section on the excess of the long or short position.

(D) *Long basket of obligors and long credit default swap.* In the case of a non-cleared swap that is a long credit default swap referencing a broad-based security index and the security-based swap dealer is long a basket of debt securities comprising all of the components of the security index, deducting 50 percent of the amount specified in § 240.15c3–1(c)(2)(vi) for the component securities, provided the security-based swap dealer can deliver the component securities to satisfy the obligation of the security-based swap dealer on the credit default swap.

(E) *Short basket of obligors and short credit default swap.* In the case of a non-cleared swap that is a short credit default swap referencing a broad-based security index and the security-based swap dealer is short a basket of debt securities comprising all of the components of the security index, deducting the amount specified in § 240.15c3–1(c)(2)(vi) for the component securities.

(ii) *All other swaps.* (A) In the case of any non-cleared swap that is not a credit default swap for which the deductions in § 240.18a–1(e) do not apply, deducting the amount calculated by multiplying the notional value of the swap by the percentage specified in:

(*1*) Section 240.15c3–1 applicable to the reference asset if § 240.15c3–1 specifies a percentage deduction for the type of asset;

(*2*) 17 CFR 1.17 applicable to the reference asset if 17 CFR 1.17 specifies a percentage deduction for the type of asset and § 240.15c3–1 does not specify a percentage deduction for the type of asset; or

(*3*) In the case of a non-cleared interest rate swap, § 240.15c3–1(c)(2)(vi)(A) based on the maturity of the swap, provided that the percentage deduction must be no less than one eighth of 1 percent of the amount of a long position that is netted against a short position in the case of a non-cleared swap with a maturity of three months or more.

(B) A security-based swap dealer may reduce the deduction under paragraph (b)(2)(ii) of this section by an amount equal to any reduction recognized for a comparable long or short position in the reference asset or interest rate under 17 CFR 1.17 or § 240.15c3–1.

[84 FR 44063, Aug. 22, 2019]

§ 240.18a–1c Consolidated Computations of Net Capital for Certain Subsidiaries and Affiliates of Security-Based Swap Dealers.

Every security-based swap dealer in computing its net capital pursuant to § 240.18a–1 shall include in its computation all liabilities or obligations of a subsidiary or affiliate that the security-based swap dealer guarantees, endorses, or assumes either directly or indirectly.

[84 FR 44065, Aug. 22, 2019]

§ 240.18a–1d Satisfactory Subordinated Loan Agreements.

(a) *Introduction*—(1) *Minimum requirements.* This section sets forth minimum and non-exclusive requirements for satisfactory subordinated loan agreements. The Commission may require or the security-based swap dealer may include such other provisions as deemed necessary or appropriate to the extent such provisions do not cause the subordinated loan agreement to fail to meet the minimum requirements of this section.

(2) *Certain definitions.* For purposes of § 240.18a–1 and this section:

(i) The term *"subordinated loan agreement"* shall mean the agreement or agreements evidencing or governing a subordinated borrowing of cash.

(ii) The term *"Payment Obligation"* shall mean the obligation of a security-based swap dealer to repay cash loaned

729

§ 240.18a–1d

to the security-based swap dealer pursuant to a subordinated loan agreement and "Payment" shall mean the performance by a security-based swap dealer of a Payment Obligation.

(iii) The term *"lender"* shall mean the person who lends cash to a security-based swap dealer pursuant to a subordinated loan agreement.

(b) *Minimum requirements for subordinated loan agreements*—(1) *Subordinated loan agreement.* Subject to paragraph (a) of this section, a subordinated loan agreement shall mean a written agreement between the security-based swap dealer and the lender, which has a minimum term of one year, and is a valid and binding obligation enforceable in accordance with its terms (subject as to enforcement to applicable bankruptcy, insolvency, reorganization, moratorium and other similar laws) against the security-based swap dealer and the lender and their respective heirs, executors, administrators, successors and assigns.

(2) *Specific amount.* All subordinated loan agreements shall be for a specific dollar amount which shall not be reduced for the duration of the agreement except by installments as specifically provided for therein and except as otherwise provided in this section.

(3) *Effective subordination.* The subordinated loan agreement shall effectively subordinate any right of the lender to receive any Payment with respect thereto, together with accrued interest or compensation, to the prior payment or provision for payment in full of all claims of all present and future creditors of the security-based swap dealer arising out of any matter occurring prior to the date on which the related Payment Obligation matures consistent with the provisions of §§ 240.18a–1 and 240.18a–1d, except for claims which are the subject of subordinated loan agreements that rank on the same priority as or junior to the claim of the lender under such subordinated loan agreements.

(4) *Proceeds of subordinated loan agreements.* The subordinated loan agreement shall provide that the cash proceeds thereof shall be used and dealt with by the security-based swap dealer as part of its capital and shall be subject to the risks of the business.

17 CFR Ch. II (4–1–23 Edition)

(5) *Certain rights of the security-based swap dealer.* The subordinated loan agreement shall provide that the security-based swap dealer shall have the right to deposit any cash proceeds of a subordinated loan agreement in an account or accounts in its own name in any bank or trust company.

(6) *Permissive prepayments.* A security-based swap dealer at its option but not at the option of the lender may, if the subordinated loan agreement so provides, make a Payment of all or any portion of the Payment Obligation thereunder prior to the scheduled maturity date of such Payment Obligation (hereinafter referred to as a "Prepayment"), but in no event may any Prepayment be made before the expiration of one year from the date such subordinated loan agreement became effective. No Prepayment shall be made, if, after giving effect thereto (and to all Payments of Payment Obligations under any other subordinated loan agreements then outstanding the maturity or accelerated maturities of which are scheduled to fall due within six months after the date such Prepayment is to occur pursuant to this provision or on or prior to the date on which the Payment Obligation in respect of such Prepayment is scheduled to mature disregarding this provision, whichever date is earlier) without reference to any projected profit or loss of the security-based swap dealer, either its net capital would fall below 120 percent of its minimum requirement under § 240.18a–1, or, if the security-based swap dealer is approved to calculate net capital under § 240.18a–1(d), its tentative net capital would fall to an amount below 120 percent of the minimum requirement. Notwithstanding the above, no Prepayment shall occur without the prior written approval of the Commission.

(7) *Suspended repayment.* The Payment Obligation of the security-based swap dealer in respect of any subordinated loan agreement shall be suspended and shall not mature if, after giving effect to Payment of such Payment Obligation (and to all Payments of Payment Obligations of such security-based swap dealer under any other subordinated loan agreement(s) then

730

Securities and Exchange Commission § 240.18a–1d

outstanding that are scheduled to mature on or before such Payment Obligation) either its net capital would fall below 120 percent of its minimum requirement under § 240.18a–1, or, if the security-based swap dealer is approved to calculate net capital under § 240.18a–1(d), its tentative net capital would fall to an amount below 120 percent of the minimum requirement. The subordinated loan agreement may provide that if the Payment Obligation of the security-based swap dealer thereunder does not mature and is suspended as a result of the requirement of this paragraph (b)(7) for a period of not less than six months, the security-based swap dealer shall thereupon commence the rapid and orderly liquidation of its business, but the right of the lender to receive Payment, together with accrued interest or compensation, shall remain subordinate as required by the provisions of §§ 240.18a–1 and 240.18a–1d.

(8) *Accelerated maturity—obligation to repay to remain subordinate.* (i) Subject to the provisions of paragraph (b)(7) of this section, a subordinated loan agreement may provide that the lender may, upon prior written notice to the security-based swap dealer and the Commission given not earlier than six months after the effective date of such subordinated loan agreement, accelerate the date on which the Payment Obligation of the security-based swap dealer, together with accrued interest or compensation, is scheduled to mature to a date not earlier than six months after the giving of such notice, but the right of the lender to receive Payment, together with accrued interest or compensation, shall remain subordinate as required by the provisions of §§ 240.18a–1 and 240.18a–1d.

(ii) Notwithstanding the provisions of paragraph (b)(7) of this section, the Payment Obligation of the security-based swap dealer with respect to a subordinated loan agreement, together with accrued interest and compensation, shall mature in the event of any receivership, insolvency, liquidation, bankruptcy, assignment for the benefit of creditors, reorganization whether or not pursuant to the bankruptcy laws, or any other marshalling of the assets and liabilities of the security-based swap dealer but the right of the lender to receive Payment, together with accrued interest or compensation, shall remain subordinate as required by the provisions of §§ 240.18a–1 and 240.18a–1d.

(9) *Accelerated maturity of subordinated loan agreements on event of default and event of acceleration—obligation to repay to remain subordinate.* (i) A subordinated loan agreement may provide that the lender may, upon prior written notice to the security-based swap dealer and the Commission of the occurrence of any Event of Acceleration (as hereinafter defined) given no sooner than six months after the effective date of such subordinated loan agreement, accelerate the date on which the Payment Obligation of the security-based swap dealer, together with accrued interest or compensation, is scheduled to mature, to the last business day of a calendar month which is not less than six months after notice of acceleration is received by the security-based swap dealer and the Commission. Any subordinated loan agreement containing such Events of Acceleration may also provide, that if upon such accelerated maturity date the Payment Obligation of the security-based swap dealer is suspended as required by paragraph (b)(7) of this section and liquidation of the security-based swap dealer has not commenced on or prior to such accelerated maturity date, then notwithstanding paragraph (b)(7) the Payment Obligation of the security-based swap dealer with respect to such subordinated loan agreement shall mature on the day immediately following such accelerated maturity date and in any such event the Payment Obligations of the security-based swap dealer with respect to all other subordinated loan agreements then outstanding shall also mature at the same time but the rights of the respective lenders to receive Payment, together with accrued interest or compensation, shall remain subordinate as required by the provisions of this section. Events of Acceleration which may be included in a subordinated loan agreement complying with this paragraph (b)(9) shall be limited to:

(A) Failure to pay interest or any installment of principal on a subordinated loan agreement as scheduled;

§ 240.18a–1d

(B) Failure to pay when due other money obligations of a specified material amount;

(C) Discovery that any material, specified representation or warranty of the security-based swap dealer which is included in the subordinated loan agreement and on which the subordinated loan agreement was based or continued was inaccurate in a material respect at the time made;

(D) Any specified and clearly measurable event which is included in the subordinated loan agreement and which the lender and the security-based swap dealer agree:

(1) Is a significant indication that the financial position of the security-based swap dealer has changed materially and adversely from agreed upon specified norms; or

(2) Could materially and adversely affect the ability of the security-based swap dealer to conduct its business as conducted on the date the subordinated loan agreement was made; or

(3) Is a significant change in the senior management of the security-based swap dealer or in the general business conducted by the security-based swap dealer from that which obtained on the date the subordinated loan agreement became effective;

(E) Any continued failure to perform agreed covenants included in the subordinated loan agreement relating to the conduct of the business of the security-based swap dealer or relating to the maintenance and reporting of its financial position; and

(ii) Notwithstanding the provisions of paragraph (b)(7) of this section, a subordinated loan agreement may provide that, if liquidation of the business of the security-based swap dealer has not already commenced, the Payment Obligation of the security-based swap dealer shall mature, together with accrued interest or compensation, upon the occurrence of an Event of Default (as hereinafter defined). Such agreement may also provide that, if liquidation of the business of the security-based swap dealer has not already commenced, the rapid and orderly liquidation of the business of the security-based swap dealer shall then commence upon the happening of an Event of Default. Any subordinated loan agreement which so provides for maturity of the Payment Obligation upon the occurrence of an Event of Default shall also provide that the date on which such Event of Default occurs shall, if liquidation of the security-based swap dealer has not already commenced, be the date on which the Payment Obligations of the security-based swap dealer with respect to all other subordinated loan agreements then outstanding shall mature but the rights of the respective lenders to receive Payment, together with accrued interest or compensation, shall remain subordinate as required by the provisions of this section. Events of Default which may be included in a subordinated loan agreement shall be limited to:

(A) The net capital of the security-based swap dealer falling to an amount below its minimum requirement under § 240.18a–1, or, if the security-based swap dealer is approved to calculate net capital under § 240.18a–1(d), its tentative net capital falling below the minimum requirement, throughout a period of 15 consecutive business days, commencing on the day the security-based swap dealer first determines and notifies the Commission, or the Commission first determines and notifies the security-based swap dealer of such fact;

(B) The Commission revoking the registration of the security-based swap dealer;

(C) The Commission suspending (and not reinstating within 10 days) the registration of the security-based swap dealer;

(D) Any receivership, insolvency, liquidation, bankruptcy, assignment for the benefit of creditors, reorganization whether or not pursuant to bankruptcy laws, or any other marshalling of the assets and liabilities of the security-based swap dealer. A subordinated loan agreement that contains any of the provisions permitted by this paragraph (b)(9) shall not contain the provision otherwise permitted by paragraph (b)(8)(i) of this section.

(c) *Miscellaneous provisions*—(1) *Prohibited cancellation.* The subordinated loan agreement shall not be subject to cancellation by either party; no Payment shall be made with respect thereto and the agreement shall not be terminated, rescinded or modified by mutual consent or otherwise if the effect thereof would be inconsistent with the requirements of §§ 240.18a–1 and 240.18a–1d.

(2) *Notification.* Every security-based swap dealer shall immediately notify the Commission if, after giving effect to all Payments of Payment Obligations under subordinated loan agreements then outstanding that are then due or mature within the following six months without reference to any projected profit or loss of the security-based swap dealer, either its net capital would fall below 120 percent of its minimum requirement under § 240.18a–1, or, if the security-based swap dealer is approved to calculate net capital under § 240.18a–1(d), its tentative net capital would fall to an amount below 120 percent of the minimum requirement.

(3) *Certain legends.* If all the provisions of a satisfactory subordinated loan agreement do not appear in a single instrument, then the debenture or other evidence of indebtedness shall bear on its face an appropriate legend stating that it is issued subject to the provisions of a satisfactory subordinated loan agreement which shall be adequately referred to and incorporated by reference.

(4) *Revolving subordinated loan agreements.* A security-based swap dealer shall be permitted to enter into a revolving subordinated loan agreement that provides for prepayment within less than one year of all or any portion of the Payment Obligation thereunder at the option of the security-based swap dealer upon the prior written approval of the Commission. The Commission, however, shall not approve any prepayment if:

(i) After giving effect thereto (and to all Payments of Payment Obligations under any other subordinated loan agreements then outstanding, the maturity or accelerated maturities of which are scheduled to fall due within six months after the date such prepayment is to occur pursuant to this provision or on or prior to the date on which the Payment Obligation in respect of such prepayment is scheduled to mature disregarding this provision, whichever date is earlier) without reference to any projected profit or loss of the security-based swap dealer, either its net capital would fall below 120 percent of its minimum requirement under § 240.18a–1, or, if the security-based swap dealer is approved to calculate net capital under § 240.18a–1(d), its tentative net capital would fall to an amount below 120 percent of the minimum requirement; or

(ii) Pre-tax losses during the latest three-month period equaled more than 15 percent of current excess net capital. Any subordinated loan agreement entered into pursuant to this paragraph (c)(4) shall be subject to all the other provisions of this section. Any such subordinated loan agreement shall not be considered equity for purposes of § 240.18a–1(g), despite the length of the initial term of the loan.

(5) *Filing.* Two copies of any proposed subordinated loan agreement (including nonconforming subordinated loan agreements) shall be filed at least 30 days prior to the proposed execution date of the agreement with the Commission. The security-based swap dealer shall also file with the Commission a statement setting forth the name and address of the lender, the business relationship of the lender to the security-based swap dealer, and whether the security-based swap dealer carried an account for the lender for effecting transactions in security-based swaps at or about the time the proposed agreement was so filed. All agreements shall be examined by the Commission prior to their becoming effective. No proposed agreement shall be a satisfactory subordinated loan agreement for the purposes of this section unless and until the Commission has found the agreement acceptable and such agreement has become effective in the form found acceptable.

[84 FR 44065, Aug. 22, 2019]

§ 240.18a–2 **Capital requirements for major security-based swap participants for which there is not a prudential regulator.**

(a) Every major security-based swap participant for which there is not a

§ 240.18a-3

prudential regulator and is not registered as a broker or dealer pursuant to section 15(b) of the Act (15 U.S.C. 78o(b)) must at all times have and maintain positive tangible net worth.

(b) The term *tangible net worth* means the net worth of the major security-based swap participant as determined in accordance with generally accepted accounting principles in the United States, excluding goodwill and other intangible assets. In determining net worth, all long and short positions in security-based swaps, swaps, and related positions must be marked to their market value. A major security-based swap participant must include in its computation of tangible net worth all liabilities or obligations of a subsidiary or affiliate that the participant guarantees, endorses, or assumes either directly or indirectly.

(c) Every major security-based swap participant must comply with § 240.15c3-4 as though it were an OTC derivatives dealer with respect to its security-based swap and swap activities, except that § 240.15c3-4(c)(5)(xiii) and (xiv) and (d)(8) and (9) shall not apply.

[84 FR 44068, Aug. 22, 2019]

§ 240.18a-3 Non-cleared security-based swap margin requirements for security-based swap dealers and major security-based swap participants for which there is not a prudential regulator.

(a) Every security-based swap dealer and major security-based swap participant for which there is not a prudential regulator must comply with this section.

(b) *Definitions.* For the purposes of this section:

(1) The term *account* means an account carried by a security-based swap dealer or major security-based swap participant that holds one or more non-cleared security-based swaps for a counterparty.

(2) The term *commercial end user* means a counterparty that qualifies for an exception from clearing under section 3C(g)(1) of the Act (15 U.S.C. 78o-3(g)(1)) and implementing regulations or satisfies the criteria in section 3C(g)(4) of the Act (15 U.S.C. 78o-3(g)(4)) and implementing regulations.

(3) The term *counterparty* means a person with whom the security-based swap dealer or major security-based swap participant has entered into a non-cleared security-based swap transaction.

(4) The term *initial margin amount* means the amount calculated pursuant to paragraph (d) of this section.

(5) The term *non-cleared security-based swap* means a security-based swap that is not, directly or indirectly, submitted to and cleared by a clearing agency registered pursuant to section 17A of the Act (15 U.S.C. 78q-1) or by a clearing agency that the Commission has exempted from registration by rule or order pursuant to section 17A of the Act (15 U.S.C. 78q-1).

(6) The term *security-based swap legacy account* means an account that holds no security-based swaps entered into after the compliance date of this section and that only is used to hold one or more security-based swaps entered into prior to the compliance date of this section and collateral for those security-based swaps.

(c) *Margin requirements*—(1) *Security-based swap dealers*—(i) *Calculation required.* A security-based swap dealer must calculate with respect to each account of a counterparty as of the close of each business day:

(A) The amount of the current exposure in the account of the counterparty; and

(B) The initial margin amount for the account of the counterparty.

(ii) *Account equity requirements.* Except as provided in paragraph (c)(1)(iii) of this section, a security-based swap dealer must take an action required in paragraph (c)(1)(ii)(A) or (B) of this section by no later than the close of business of the first business day following the day of the calculation required under paragraph (c)(1)(i) of this section or, if the counterparty is located in another country and more than four time zones away, the second business day following the day of the calculation required under paragraph (c)(1)(i) of this section:

(A)(*1*) Collect from the counterparty collateral in an amount equal to the current exposure that the security-based swap dealer has to the counterparty; or

Securities and Exchange Commission § 240.18a–3

(2) Deliver to the counterparty collateral in an amount equal to the current exposure that the counterparty has to the security-based swap dealer, provided that such amount does not include the initial margin amount collected from the counterparty under paragraph (c)(1)(ii)(B) of this section; and

(B) Collect from the counterparty collateral in an amount equal to the initial margin amount.

(iii) *Exceptions*—(A) *Commercial end users.* The requirements of paragraph (c)(1)(ii) of this section do not apply to an account of a counterparty that is a commercial end user.

(B) *Counterparties that are financial market intermediaries.* The requirements of paragraph (c)(1)(ii)(B) of this section do not apply to an account of a counterparty that is a security-based swap dealer, swap dealer, broker or dealer, futures commission merchant, bank, foreign bank, or foreign broker or dealer.

(C) *Counterparties that use third-party custodians.* The requirements of paragraph (c)(1)(ii)(B) of this section do not apply to an account of a counterparty that delivers the collateral to meet the initial margin amount to an independent third-party custodian.

(D) *Security-based swap legacy accounts.* The requirements of paragraph (c)(1)(ii) of this section do not apply to a security-based swap legacy account.

(E) *Bank for International Settlements, European Stability Mechanism, and Multilateral development banks.* The requirements of paragraph (c)(1)(ii) of this section do not apply to an account of a counterparty that is the Bank for International Settlements or the European Stability Mechanism, or is the International Bank for Reconstruction and Development, the Multilateral Investment Guarantee Agency, the International Finance Corporation, the Inter-American Development Bank, the Asian Development Bank, the African Development Bank, the European Bank for Reconstruction and Development, the European Investment Bank, the European Investment Fund, the Nordic Investment Bank, the Caribbean Development Bank, the Islamic Development Bank, the Council of Europe Development Bank, or any other multilateral development bank that provides financing for national or regional development in which the U.S. government is a shareholder or contributing member.

(F) *Sovereign entities.* The requirements of paragraph (c)(1)(ii)(B) of this section do not apply to an account of a counterparty that is a central government (including the U.S. government) or an agency, department, ministry, or central bank of a central government if the security-based swap dealer has determined that the counterparty has only a minimal amount of credit risk pursuant to policies and procedures or credit risk models established pursuant to § 240.15c3–1 or § 240.18a–1 (as applicable).

(G) *Affiliates.* The requirements of paragraph (c)(1)(ii)(B) of this section do not apply to an account of a counterparty that is an affiliate of the security-based swap dealer.

(H) *Threshold amount.* (1) A security-based swap dealer may elect not to collect the initial margin amount required under paragraph (c)(1)(ii)(B) of this section to the extent that the sum of that amount plus all other credit exposures resulting from non-cleared swaps and non-cleared security-based swaps of the security-based swap dealer and its affiliates with the counterparty and its affiliates does not exceed $50 million. For purposes of this calculation, a security-based swap dealer need not include any exposures arising from non-cleared security based swap transactions with a counterparty that is a commercial end user, and non-cleared swap transactions with a counterparty that qualifies for an exception from margin requirements pursuant to section 4s(e)(4) of the Commodity Exchange Act (7 U.S.C. 6s(e)(4)).

(2) *One-time deferral.* Notwithstanding paragraph (c)(1)(iii)(H)(*1*) of this section, a security-based swap dealer may defer collecting the initial margin amount required under paragraph (c)(1)(ii)(B) of this section for up to two months following the month in which a counterparty no longer qualifies for this threshold exception for the first time.

(I) *Minimum transfer amount.* Notwithstanding any other provision of this rule, a security-based swap dealer is

§ 240.18a–3

not required to collect or deliver collateral pursuant to this section with respect to a particular counterparty unless and until the total amount of collateral that is required to be collected or delivered, and has not yet been collected or delivered, with respect to the counterparty is greater than $500,000.

(2) *Major security-based swap participants*—(i) *Calculation required.* A major security-based swap participant must with respect to each account of a counterparty calculate as of the close of each business day the amount of the current exposure in the account of the counterparty.

(ii) *Account equity requirements.* Except as provided in paragraph (c)(2)(iii) of this section, a major security-based swap participant must take an action required in paragraph (c)(2)(ii)(A) or (B) of this section by no later than the close of business of the first business day following the day of the calculation required under paragraph (c)(2)(i) or, if the counterparty is located in another country and more than four time zones away, the second business day following the day of the calculation required under paragraph (c)(2)(i) of this section:

(A) Collect from the counterparty collateral in an amount equal to the current exposure that the major security-based swap participant has to the counterparty; or

(B) Deliver to the counterparty collateral in an amount equal to the current exposure that the counterparty has to the major security-based swap participant.

(iii) *Exceptions*—(A) *Commercial end users.* The requirements of paragraph (c)(2)(ii)(A) of this section do not apply to an account of a counterparty that is a commercial end user.

(B) *Security-based swap legacy accounts.* The requirements of paragraph (c)(2)(ii) of this section do not apply to a security-based swap legacy account.

(C) *Bank for International Settlements, European Stability Mechanism, and Multilateral development banks.* The requirements of paragraph (c)(2)(ii)(A) of this section do not apply to an account of a counterparty that is the Bank for International Settlements or the European Stability Mechanism, or is the International Bank for Reconstruction and Development, the Multilateral Investment Guarantee Agency, the International Finance Corporation, the Inter-American Development Bank, the Asian Development Bank, the African Development Bank, the European Bank for Reconstruction and Development, the European Investment Bank, the European Investment Fund, the Nordic Investment Bank, the Caribbean Development Bank, the Islamic Development Bank, the Council of Europe Development Bank, or any other multilateral development bank that provides financing for national or regional development in which the U.S. government is a shareholder or contributing member.

(D) *Minimum transfer amount.* Notwithstanding any other provision of this rule, a major security-based swap participant is not required to collect or deliver collateral pursuant to this section with respect to a particular counterparty unless and until the total amount of collateral that is required to be collected or delivered, and has not yet been collected or delivered, with respect to the counterparty is greater than $500,000.

(3) *Deductions for collateral.* (i) The fair market value of collateral delivered by a counterparty or the security-based swap dealer must be reduced by the amount of the standardized deductions the security-based swap dealer would apply to the collateral pursuant to § 240.15c3–1 or § 240.18a–1, as applicable, for the purpose of paragraph (c)(1)(ii) of this section.

(ii) Notwithstanding paragraph (c)(3)(i) of this section, the fair market value of assets delivered as collateral by a counterparty or the security-based swap dealer may be reduced by the amount of the standardized deductions prescribed in 17 CFR 23.156 if the security-based swap dealer applies these standardized deductions consistently with respect to the particular counterparty.

(4) *Collateral requirements.* A security-based swap dealer or a major security-based swap participant when calculating the amounts under paragraphs (c)(1) and (2) of this section may take into account the fair market value of

Securities and Exchange Commission § 240.18a-3

collateral delivered by a counterparty provided:

(i) The collateral:

(A) Has a ready market;

(B) Is readily transferable;

(C) Consists of cash, securities, money market instruments, a major foreign currency, the settlement currency of the non-cleared security-based swap, or gold;

(D) Does not consist of securities and/or money market instruments issued by the counterparty or a party related to the security-based swap dealer, the major security-based swap participant, or the counterparty; and

(E) Is subject to an agreement between the security-based swap dealer or the major security-based swap participant and the counterparty that is legally enforceable by the security-based swap dealer or the major security-based swap participant against the counterparty and any other parties to the agreement; and

(ii) The collateral is either:

(A) Subject to the physical possession or control of the security-based swap dealer or the major security-based swap participant and may be liquidated promptly by the security-based swap dealer or the major security-based swap participant without intervention by any other party; or

(B) The collateral is carried by an independent third-party custodian that is a bank as defined in section 3(a)(6) of the Act or a registered U.S. clearing organization or depository that is not affiliated with the counterparty or, if the collateral consists of foreign securities or currencies, a supervised foreign bank, clearing organization, or depository that is not affiliated with the counterparty and that customarily maintains custody of such foreign securities or currencies.

(5) *Qualified netting agreements.* A security-based swap dealer or major security-based swap participant may include the effect of a netting agreement that allows the security-based swap dealer or major security-based swap participant to net gross receivables from and gross payables to a counterparty upon the default of the counterparty, for the purposes of the calculations required pursuant to paragraphs (c)(1)(i) and (c)(2)(i) of this section, if:

(i) The netting agreement is legally enforceable in each relevant jurisdiction, including in insolvency proceedings;

(ii) The gross receivables and gross payables that are subject to the netting agreement with a counterparty can be determined at any time; and

(iii) For internal risk management purposes, the security-based swap dealer or major security-based swap participant monitors and controls its exposure to the counterparty on a net basis.

(6) *Frequency of calculations increased.* The calculations required pursuant to paragraphs (c)(1)(i) and (c)(2)(i) of this section must be made more frequently than the close of each business day during periods of extreme volatility and for accounts with concentrated positions.

(7) *Liquidation.* A security-based swap dealer or major security-based swap participant must take prompt steps to liquidate positions in an account that does not meet the margin requirements of this section to the extent necessary to eliminate the margin deficiency.

(d) *Calculating initial margin amount.* A security-based swap dealer must calculate the initial margin amount required by paragraph (c)(1)(i)(B) of this section for non-cleared security-based swaps as follows:

(1) *Standardized approach*—(i) *Credit default swaps.* For credit default swaps, the security-based swap dealer must use the method specified in § 240.18a–1(c)(1)(vi)(B)(*1*) or, if the security-based swap dealer is registered with the Commission as a broker or dealer, the method specified in § 240.15c3–1(c)(2)(vi)(P)(*1*).

(ii) *All other security-based swaps.* For security-based swaps other than credit default swaps, the security-based swap dealer must use the method specified in § 240.18a–1(c)(1)(vi)(B)(*2*) or, if the security-based swap dealer is registered with the Commission as a broker or dealer, the method specified in § 240.15c3–1(c)(2)(vi)(P)(*2*).

(2) *Model approach.* (i) For security-based swaps other than equity security-based swaps, a security-based swap dealer may apply to the Commission

737

§ 240.18a–3

for authorization to use and be responsible for a model to calculate the initial margin amount required by paragraph (c)(1)(i)(B) of this section subject to the application process in § 240.15c3–1e or § 240.18a–1(d), as applicable. The model must use a 99 percent, one-tailed confidence level with price changes equivalent to a ten business-day movement in rates and prices, and must use risk factors sufficient to cover all the material price risks inherent in the positions for which the initial margin amount is being calculated, including foreign exchange or interest rate risk, credit risk, equity risk, and commodity risk, as appropriate. Empirical correlations may be recognized by the model within each broad risk category, but not across broad risk categories.

(ii) Notwithstanding paragraph (d)(2)(i) of this section, a security-based swap dealer that is not registered as a broker or dealer pursuant to Section 15(b) of the Act (15 U.S.C. 78o(b)), other than as an OTC derivatives dealer, may apply to the Commission for authorization to use a model to calculate the initial margin amount required by paragraph (c)(1)(i)(B) of this section for equity security-based swaps, subject to the application process and model requirements of paragraph (d)(2)(i) of this section; provided, however, the account of the counterparty subject to the requirements of this paragraph may not hold equity security positions other than equity security-based swaps and equity swaps.

(e) *Risk monitoring and procedures.* A security-based swap dealer must monitor the risk of each account and establish, maintain, and document procedures and guidelines for monitoring the risk of accounts as part of the risk management control system required by § 240.15c3–4. The security-based swap dealer must review, in accordance with written procedures, at reasonable periodic intervals, its non-cleared security-based swap activities for consistency with the risk monitoring procedures and guidelines required by this section. The security-based swap dealer also must determine whether information and data necessary to apply the risk monitoring procedures and guidelines required by this section are accessible

17 CFR Ch. II (4–1–23 Edition)

on a timely basis and whether information systems are available to adequately capture, monitor, analyze, and report relevant data and information. The risk monitoring procedures and guidelines must include, at a minimum, procedures and guidelines for:

(1) Obtaining and reviewing account documentation and financial information necessary for assessing the amount of current and potential future exposure to a given counterparty permitted by the security-based swap dealer;

(2) Determining, approving, and periodically reviewing credit limits for each counterparty, and across all counterparties;

(3) Monitoring credit risk exposure to the security-based swap dealer from non-cleared security-based swaps, including the type, scope, and frequency of reporting to senior management;

(4) Using stress tests to monitor potential future exposure to a single counterparty and across all counterparties over a specified range of possible market movements over a specified time period;

(5) Managing the impact of credit exposure related to non-cleared security-based swaps on the security-based swap dealer's overall risk exposure;

(6) Determining the need to collect collateral from a particular counterparty, including whether that determination was based upon the creditworthiness of the counterparty and/or the risk of the specific non-cleared security-based swap contracts with the counterparty;

(7) Monitoring the credit exposure resulting from concentrated positions with a single counterparty and across all counterparties, and during periods of extreme volatility; and

(8) Maintaining sufficient equity in the account of each counterparty to protect against the largest individual potential future exposure of a non-cleared security-based swap carried in the account of the counterparty as measured by computing the largest maximum possible loss that could result from the exposure.

[85 FR 44068, Aug. 22, 2020]

§ 240.18a-4 Segregation requirements for security-based swap dealers and major security-based swap participants.

Section 240.18a-4 applies to a security-based swap dealer or major security-based swap participant registered under section 15F(b) of the Act (15 U.S.C. 78o-10(b)), including a security-based swap dealer that is an *OTC derivatives dealer* as that term is defined in § 240.3b-12. A security-based swap dealer registered under section 15F of the Act (15 U.S.C. 78o-10) that is also a broker or dealer registered under section 15 of the Act (15 U.S.C. 78o), other than an *OTC derivatives dealer*, is subject to the customer protection requirements under § 240.15c3-3, including paragraph (p) of that rule with respect to its security-based swap activity.

(a) *Definitions.* For the purposes of this section:

(1) The term *cleared security-based swap* means a security-based swap that is, directly or indirectly, submitted to and cleared by a clearing agency registered with the Commission pursuant to section 17A of the Act (15 U.S.C. 78q-1);

(2) The term *excess securities collateral* means securities and money market instruments carried for the account of a security-based swap customer that have a market value in excess of the current exposure of the security-based swap dealer (after reducing the current exposure by the amount of cash in the account) to the security-based swap customer, excluding:

(i) Securities and money market instruments held in a qualified clearing agency account but only to the extent the securities and money market instruments are being used to meet a margin requirement of the clearing agency resulting from a security-based swap transaction of the security-based swap customer; and

(ii) Securities and money market instruments held in a qualified registered security-based swap dealer account or in a third-party custodial account but only to the extent the securities and money market instruments are being used to meet a regulatory margin requirement of another security-based swap dealer resulting from the security-based swap dealer entering into a non-cleared security-based swap transaction with the other security-based swap dealer to offset the risk of a non-cleared security-based swap transaction between the security-based swap dealer and the security-based swap customer.

(3) The term *foreign major security-based swap participant* has the meaning set forth in § 240.3a67-10(a)(6).

(4) The term *foreign security-based swap dealer* has the meaning set forth in § 240.3a71-3(a)(7).

(5) The term *qualified clearing agency account* means an account of a security-based swap dealer at a clearing agency registered with the Commission pursuant to section 17A of the Act (15 U.S.C. 78q-1) that holds funds and other property in order to margin, guarantee, or secure cleared security-based swap transactions for the security-based swap customers of the security-based swap dealer that meets the following conditions:

(i) The account is designated "Special Clearing Account for the Exclusive Benefit of the Cleared Security-Based Swap Customers of [name of security-based swap dealer]";

(ii) The clearing agency has acknowledged in a written notice provided to and retained by the security-based swap dealer that the funds and other property in the account are being held by the clearing agency for the exclusive benefit of the security-based swap customers of the security-based swap dealer in accordance with the regulations of the Commission and are being kept separate from any other accounts maintained by the security-based swap dealer with the clearing agency; and

(iii) The account is subject to a written contract between the security-based swap dealer and the clearing agency which provides that the funds and other property in the account shall be subject to no right, charge, security interest, lien, or claim of any kind in favor of the clearing agency or any person claiming through the clearing agency, except a right, charge, security interest, lien, or claim resulting from a cleared security-based swap transaction effected in the account.

(6) The term *qualified registered security-based swap dealer account* means an account at another security-based swap

§ 240.18a–4

dealer registered with the Commission pursuant to section 15F of the Act that meets the following conditions:

(i) The account is designated "Special Reserve Account for the Exclusive Benefit of the Security-Based Swap Customers of [name of security-based swap dealer]";

(ii) The other security-based swap dealer has acknowledged in a written notice provided to and retained by the security-based swap dealer that the funds and other property held in the account are being held by the other security-based swap dealer for the exclusive benefit of the security-based swap customers of the security-based swap dealer in accordance with the regulations of the Commission and are being kept separate from any other accounts maintained by the security-based swap dealer with the other security-based swap dealer;

(iii) The account is subject to a written contract between the security-based swap dealer and the other security-based swap dealer which provides that the funds and other property in the account shall be subject to no right, charge, security interest, lien, or claim of any kind in favor of the other security-based swap dealer or any person claiming through the other security-based swap dealer, except a right, charge, security interest, lien, or claim resulting from a non-cleared security-based swap transaction effected in the account; and

(iv) The account and the assets in the account are not subject to any type of subordination agreement between the security-based swap dealer and the other security-based swap dealer.

(7) The term *qualified security* means:

(i) Obligations of the United States;

(ii) Obligations fully guaranteed as to principal and interest by the United States; and

(iii) General obligations of any State or a political subdivision of a State that:

(A) Are not traded flat and are not in default;

(B) Were part of an initial offering of $500 million or greater; and

(C) Were issued by an issuer that has published audited financial statements within 120 days of its most recent fiscal year end.

(8) The term *security-based swap customer* means any person from whom or on whose behalf the security-based swap dealer has received or acquired or holds funds or other property for the account of the person with respect to a cleared or non-cleared security-based swap transaction. The term does not include a person to the extent that person has a claim for funds or other property which by contract, agreement or understanding, or by operation of law, is part of the capital of the security-based swap dealer or is subordinated to all claims of security-based swap customers of the security-based swap dealer.

(9) The term *special reserve account for the exclusive benefit of security-based swap customers* means an account at a bank that meets the following conditions:

(i) The account is designated "Special Reserve Account for the Exclusive Benefit of the Security-Based Swap Customers of [name of security-based swap dealer]";

(ii) The account is subject to a written acknowledgement by the bank provided to and retained by the security-based swap dealer that the funds and other property held in the account are being held by the bank for the exclusive benefit of the security-based swap customers of the security-based swap dealer in accordance with the regulations of the Commission and are being kept separate from any other accounts maintained by the security-based swap dealer with the bank; and

(iii) The account is subject to a written contract between the security-based swap dealer and the bank which provides that the funds and other property in the account shall at no time be used directly or indirectly as security for a loan or other extension of credit to the security-based swap dealer by the bank and, shall be subject to no right, charge, security interest, lien, or claim of any kind in favor of the bank or any person claiming through the bank.

(10) The term *third-party custodial account* means an account carried by an independent third-party custodian that meets the following conditions:

(i) The account is established for the purposes of meeting regulatory margin

Securities and Exchange Commission § 240.18a-4

requirements of another security-based swap dealer;

(ii) The account is carried by a bank as defined in section 3(a)(6) of the Act or a registered U.S. clearing organization or depository or, if the collateral to be held in the account consists of foreign securities or currencies, a supervised foreign bank, clearing organization, or depository that customarily maintains custody of such foreign securities or currencies;

(iii) The account is designated for and on behalf of the security-based swap dealer for the benefit of its security-based swap customers and the account is subject to a written acknowledgement by the bank, clearing organization, or depository provided to and retained by the security-based swap dealer that the funds and other property held in the account are being held by the bank, clearing organization, or depository for the exclusive benefit of the security-based swap customers of the security-based swap dealer and are being kept separate from any other accounts maintained by the security-based swap dealer with the bank, clearing organization, or depository; and

(iv) The account is subject to a written contract between the security-based swap dealer and the bank, clearing organization, or depository which provides that the funds and other property in the account shall at no time be used directly or indirectly as security for a loan or other extension of credit to the security-based swap dealer by the bank, clearing organization, or depository and, shall be subject to no right, charge, security interest, lien, or claim of any kind in favor of the bank, clearing organization, or depository or any person claiming through the bank, clearing organization, or depository.

(11) The term *U.S. person* has the meaning set forth in § 240.3a71-3(a)(4).

(b) *Physical possession or control of excess securities collateral.* (1) A security-based swap dealer must promptly obtain and thereafter maintain physical possession or control of all excess securities collateral carried for the security-based swap accounts of security-based swap customers.

(2) A security-based swap dealer has control of excess securities collateral only if the securities and money market instruments:

(i) Are represented by one or more certificates in the custody or control of a clearing corporation or other subsidiary organization of either national securities exchanges, or of a custodian bank in accordance with a system for the central handling of securities complying with the provisions of §§ 240.8c-1(g) and 240.15c2-1(g) the delivery of which certificates to the security-based swap dealer does not require the payment of money or value, and if the books or records of the security-based swap dealer identify the security-based swap customers entitled to receive specified quantities or units of the securities so held for such security-based swap customers collectively;

(ii) Are the subject of bona fide items of transfer; provided that securities and money market instruments shall be deemed not to be the subject of bona fide items of transfer if, within 40 calendar days after they have been transmitted for transfer by the security-based swap dealer to the issuer or its transfer agent, new certificates conforming to the instructions of the security-based swap dealer have not been received by the security-based swap dealer, the security-based swap dealer has not received a written statement by the issuer or its transfer agent acknowledging the transfer instructions and the possession of the securities or money market instruments, or the security-based swap dealer has not obtained a revalidation of a window ticket from a transfer agent with respect to the certificate delivered for transfer;

(iii) Are in the custody or control of a bank as defined in section 3(a)(6) of the Act, the delivery of which securities or money market instruments to the security-based swap dealer does not require the payment of money or value and the bank having acknowledged in writing that the securities and money market instruments in its custody or control are not subject to any right, charge, security interest, lien or claim of any kind in favor of a bank or any person claiming through the bank;

(iv)(A) Are held in or are in transit between offices of the security-based swap dealer; or (B) Are held by a corporate subsidiary if the security-based

741

§ 240.18a–4

swap dealer owns and exercises a majority of the voting rights of all of the voting securities of such subsidiary, assumes or guarantees all of the subsidiary's obligations and liabilities, operates the subsidiary as a branch office of the security-based swap dealer, and assumes full responsibility for compliance by the subsidiary and all of its associated persons with the provisions of the Federal securities laws as well as for all of the other acts of the subsidiary and such associated persons; or

(v) Are held in such other locations as the Commission shall upon application from a security-based swap dealer find and designate to be adequate for the protection of security-based swap customer securities.

(3) Each business day the security-based swap dealer must determine from its books and records the quantity of excess securities collateral in its possession or control as of the close of the previous business day and the quantity of excess securities collateral not in its possession or control as of the previous business day. If the security-based swap dealer did not obtain possession or control of all excess securities collateral on the previous business day as required by this section and there are securities or money market instruments of the same issue and class in any of the following non-control locations:

(i) Securities or money market instruments subject to a lien securing an obligation of the security-based swap dealer, then the security-based swap dealer, not later than the next business day on which the determination is made, must issue instructions for the release of the securities or money market instruments from the lien and must obtain physical possession or control of the securities or money market instruments within two business days following the date of the instructions;

(ii) Securities or money market instruments held in a qualified clearing agency account, then the security-based swap dealer, not later than the next business day on which the determination is made, must issue instructions for the release of the securities or money market instruments by the clearing agency and must obtain physical possession or control of the securities or money market instruments within two business days following the date of the instructions;

(iii) Securities or money market instruments held in a qualified registered security-based swap dealer account maintained by another security-based swap dealer or in a third-party custodial account, then the security-based swap dealer, not later than the next business day on which the determination is made, must issue instructions for the release of the securities or money market instruments by the other security-based swap dealer or by the third-party custodian and must obtain physical possession or control of the securities or money market instruments within two business days following the date of the instructions;

(iv) Securities or money market instruments loaned by the security-based swap dealer, then the security-based swap dealer, not later than the next business day on which the determination is made, must issue instructions for the return of the loaned securities or money market instruments and must obtain physical possession or control of the securities or money market instruments within five business days following the date of the instructions;

(v) Securities or money market instruments failed to receive for more than 30 calendar days, then the security-based swap dealer, not later than the next business day on which the determination is made, must take prompt steps to obtain physical possession or control of the securities or money market instruments through a buy-in procedure or otherwise;

(vi) Securities or money market instruments receivable by the security-based swap dealer as a security dividend, stock split or similar distribution for more than 45 calendar days, then the security-based swap dealer, not later than the next business day on which the determination is made, must take prompt steps to obtain physical possession or control of the securities or money market instruments through a buy-in procedure or otherwise; or

(vii) Securities or money market instruments included on the security-based swap dealer's books or records that allocate to a short position of the security-based swap dealer or a short

Securities and Exchange Commission § 240.18a–4

position for another person, for more than 30 calendar days, then the security-based swap dealer must, not later than the business day following the day on which the determination is made, take prompt steps to obtain physical possession or control of such securities or money market instruments.

(c) *Deposit requirement for special reserve account for the exclusive benefit of security-based swap customers.* (1) A security-based swap dealer must maintain a special reserve account for the exclusive benefit of security-based swap customers that is separate from any other bank account of the security-based swap dealer. The security-based swap dealer must at all times maintain in the special reserve account for the exclusive benefit of security-based swap customers, through deposits into the account, cash and/or qualified securities in amounts computed in accordance with the formula set forth in § 240.18a–4a.

(i) In determining the amount maintained in a special reserve account for the exclusive benefit of security-based swap customers, the security-based swap dealer must deduct:

(A) The percentage of the value of a general obligation of a State or a political subdivision of a State specified in § 240.15c3–1(c)(2)(vi);

(B) The aggregate value of general obligations of a State or a political subdivision of a State to the extent the amount of the obligations of a single issuer (after applying the deduction in paragraph (c)(1)(i)(A) of this section) exceeds two percent of the amount required to be maintained in the special reserve account for the exclusive benefit of security-based swap customers;

(C) The aggregate value of all general obligations of States or political subdivisions of States to the extent the amount of the obligations (after applying the deduction in paragraph (c)(1)(i)(A) of this section) exceeds 10 percent of the amount required to be maintained in the special reserve account for the exclusive benefit of security-based swap customers;

(D) The amount of cash deposited with a single non-affiliated bank to the extent the amount exceeds 15 percent of the equity capital of the bank as reported by the bank in its most recent Call Report or any successor form the bank is required to file by its appropriate federal banking agency (as defined by section 3 of the Federal Deposit Insurance Act (12 U.S.C. 1813)); and

(E) The total amount of cash deposited with an affiliated bank.

(ii) *Exception.* A security-based swap dealer for which there is a prudential regulator need not take the deduction specified in paragraph (c)(1)(i)(D) of this section if it maintains the special reserve account for the exclusive benefit of security-based swap customers itself rather than at an affiliated or non-affiliated bank.

(2) A security-based swap dealer must not accept or use credits identified in the items of the formula set forth in § 240.18a–4a except for the specified purposes indicated under items comprising Total Debits under the formula, and, to the extent Total Credits exceed Total Debits, at least the net amount thereof must be maintained in the Special Reserve Account pursuant to paragraph (c)(1) of this section.

(3)(i) The computations necessary to determine the amount required to be maintained in the special reserve account for the exclusive benefit of security-based swap customers must be made weekly as of the close of the last business day of the week and any deposit required to be made into the account must be made no later than one hour after the opening of banking business on the second following business day. The security-based swap dealer may make a withdrawal from the special reserve account for the exclusive benefit of security-based swap customers only if the amount remaining in the account after the withdrawal is equal to or exceeds the amount required to be maintained in the account pursuant to paragraph (c)(1) of this section.

(ii) Computations in addition to the computations required pursuant to paragraph (c)(3)(i) of this section may be made as of the close of any business day, and deposits so computed must be made no later than one hour after the open of banking business on the second following business day.

§ 240.18a–4

(4) A security-based swap dealer must promptly deposit into a special reserve account for the exclusive benefit of security-based swap customers cash and/or qualified securities of the security-based swap dealer if the amount of cash and/or qualified securities in one or more special reserve accounts for the exclusive benefit of security-based swap customers falls below the amount required to be maintained pursuant to this section.

(d) *Requirements for non-cleared security-based swaps*—(1) *Notice.* A security-based swap dealer and a major security-based swap participant must provide the notice required pursuant to section 3E(f)(1)(A) of the Act (15 U.S.C. 78c–5(f)) in writing to a duly authorized individual prior to the execution of the first non-cleared security-based swap transaction with the counterparty occurring after the compliance date of this section.

(2) *Subordination*—(i) *Counterparty that elects to have individual segregation at an independent third-party custodian.* A security-based swap dealer must obtain an agreement from a counterparty whose funds or other property to meet a margin requirement of the security-based swap dealer are held at a third-party custodian in which the counterparty agrees to subordinate its claims against the security-based swap dealer for the funds or other property held at the third-party custodian to the claims of security-based swap customers of the security-based swap dealer but only to the extent that funds or other property provided by the counterparty to the third-party custodian are not treated as *customer property* as that term is defined in 11 U.S.C. 741 in a liquidation of the security-based swap dealer.

(ii) *Counterparty that elects to have no segregation.* A security-based swap dealer must obtain an agreement from a counterparty that affirmatively chooses not to require segregation of funds or other property pursuant to section 3E(f) of the Act (15 U.S.C. 78c–5(f)) in which the counterparty agrees to subordinate all of its claims against the security-based swap dealer to the claims of security-based swap customers of the security-based swap dealer.

(e) *Segregation and disclosure requirements for foreign security-based swap dealers and foreign major security-based swap participants*—(1) *Segregation requirements for foreign security-based swap dealers*—(i) *Foreign bank.* Section 3E of the Act (15 U.S.C. 78c–5) and this section thereunder apply to a foreign security-based swap dealer registered under section 15F of the Act (15 U.S.C. 78o–10) that is a foreign bank, foreign savings bank, foreign cooperative bank, foreign savings and loan association, foreign building and loan association, or foreign credit union:

(A) With respect to a security-based swap customer that is a U.S. person, and

(B) With respect to a security-based swap customer that is not a U.S. person if the foreign security-based swap dealer holds funds or other property arising out of a transaction had by such person with a branch or agency (as defined in section 1(b) of the International Banking Act of 1978) in the United States of such foreign security-based swap dealer.

(ii) *Not a foreign bank.* Section 3E of the Act (15 U.S.C. 78c–5) and this section thereunder apply to a foreign security-based swap dealer registered under section 15F of the Act (15 U.S.C. 78o–10) that is not a foreign bank, foreign savings bank, foreign cooperative bank, foreign savings and loan association, foreign building and loan association, or foreign credit union:

(A) *Cleared security-based swaps.* With respect to all cleared security-based swap transactions, if such foreign security-based swap dealer has received or acquired or holds funds or other property for at least one security-based swap customer that is a U.S. person with respect to a cleared security-based swap transaction with such U.S. person, and

(B) *Non-cleared security-based swaps.* With respect to funds or other property such foreign security-based swap dealer has received or acquired or holds for a security-based swap customer that is a U.S. person with respect to a non-cleared security-based swap transaction with such U.S. person.

(2) *Segregation requirements for foreign major security-based swap participants.* Section 3E of the Act (15 U.S.C. 78c–5)

and this section thereunder apply to a foreign major security-based swap participant registered under section 15F of the Act (15 U.S.C. 78o–10), with respect to a counterparty that is a U.S. person.

(3) *Disclosure requirements for foreign security-based swap dealers.* A foreign security-based swap dealer registered under section 15F of the Act (15 U.S.C. 78o–10) must disclose in writing to a security-based swap customer that is a U.S. person, prior to receiving, acquiring, or holding funds or other property for such security-based swap customer with respect to a security-based swap transaction, the potential treatment of the funds or other property segregated by such foreign security-based swap dealer pursuant to section 3E of the Act (15 U.S.C. 78c–5), and the rules and regulations thereunder, in insolvency proceedings under U.S. bankruptcy law and any applicable foreign insolvency laws. Such disclosure must include whether the foreign security-based swap dealer is subject to the segregation requirement set forth in section 3E of the Act (15 U.S.C. 78c–5), and the rules and regulations thereunder, with respect to the funds or other property received, acquired, or held for the security-based swap customer that will receive the disclosure, whether the foreign security-based swap dealer could be subject to the stockbroker liquidation provisions in the U.S. Bankruptcy Code, whether the segregated funds or other property could be afforded customer property treatment under U.S. bankruptcy law, and any other relevant considerations that may affect the treatment of the funds or other property segregated under section 3E of the Act (15 U.S.C. 78c–5), and the rules and regulations thereunder, in insolvency proceedings of the foreign security-based swap dealer.

(f) *Exemption.* The requirements of this section do not apply if the following conditions are met:

(1) The security-based swap dealer does not:

(i) Effect transactions in cleared security-based swaps for or on behalf of another person;

(ii) Have any open transactions in cleared security-based swaps executed for or on behalf of another person; and

(iii) Hold or control any money, securities, or other property to margin, guarantee, or secure a cleared security-based swap transaction executed for or on behalf of another person (including money, securities, or other property accruing to another person as a result of a cleared security-based swap transaction);

(2) The security-based swap dealer provides the notice required pursuant to section 3E(f)(1)(A) of the Act (15 U.S.C. 78c–5(f)(1)(A)) in writing to a duly authorized individual prior to the execution of the first non-cleared security-based swap transaction with the counterparty occurring after the compliance date of this section; and

(3) The security-based swap dealer discloses in writing to a counterparty before engaging in the first non-cleared security-based swap transaction with the counterparty that any margin collateral received and held by the security-based swap dealer will not be subject to a segregation requirement and how a claim of a counterparty for the collateral would be treated in a bankruptcy or other formal liquidation proceeding of the security-based swap dealer.

[84 FR 44071, Aug. 22, 2019]

§ 240.18a–4a Exhibit A—Formula for determination of security-based swap customer reserve requirements under § 240.18a–4.

	Credits	Debits
1. Free credit balances and other credit balances in the accounts carried for security-based swap customers (See Note A)	$____	
2. Monies borrowed collateralized by securities in accounts carried for security-based swap customers (See Note B)	$____	
3. Security-based swap customers' securities failed to receive (See Note C)	$____	
4. Credit balances in firm accounts which are attributable to principal sales to security-based swap customers	$____	
5. Market value of stock dividends, stock splits and similar distributions receivable outstanding over 30 calendar days	$____	
6. Market value of short security count differences over 30 calendar days old	$____	

§ 240.18a–4a   17 CFR Ch. II (4–1–23 Edition)

	Credits	Debits
7. Market value of short securities and credits (not to be offset by longs or by debits) in all suspense accounts over 30 calendar days	$_____	
8. Market value of securities which are in transfer in excess of 40 calendar days and have not been confirmed to be in transfer by the transfer agent or the issuer during the 40 days		$_____
9. Securities borrowed to effectuate short sales by security-based swap customers and securities borrowed to make delivery on security-based swap customers' securities failed to deliver		$_____
10. Failed to deliver of security-based swap customers' securities not older than 30 calendar days		$_____
11. Margin required and on deposit with the Options Clearing Corporation for all option contracts written or purchased in accounts carried for security-based swap customers (See Note D)		$_____
12. Margin related to security futures products written, purchased or sold in accounts carried for security-based swap customers required and on deposit in a qualified clearing agency account at a clearing agency registered with the Commission under section 17A of the Act (15 U.S.C. 78q–1) or a derivatives clearing organization registered with the Commodity Futures Trading Commission under section 5b of the Commodity Exchange Act (7 U.S.C. 7a–1) (See Note E)		$_____
13. Margin related to cleared security-based swap transactions in accounts carried for security-based swap customers required and on deposit in a qualified clearing agency account at a clearing agency registered with the Commission pursuant to section 17A of the Act (15 U.S.C. 78q–1)		$_____
14. Margin related to non-cleared security-based swap transactions in accounts carried for security-based swap customers required and held in a qualified registered security-based swap dealer account at another security-based swap dealer or at a third-party custodial account		$_____
Total Credits	$_____	
Total Debits		$_____
Excess of Credits over Debits	$_____	

Note A. Item 1 must include all outstanding drafts payable to security-based swap customers which have been applied against free credit balances or other credit balances and must also include checks drawn in excess of bank balances per the records of the security-based swap dealer.

Note B. Item 2 shall include the amount of options-related or security futures product-related Letters of Credit obtained by a member of a registered clearing agency or a derivatives clearing organization which are collateralized by security-based swap customers' securities, to the extent of the member's margin requirement at the registered clearing agency or derivatives clearing organization.

Note C. Item 3 must include in addition to security-based swap customers' securities failed to receive the amount by which the market value of securities failed to receive and outstanding more than thirty (30) calendar days exceeds their contract value.

Note D. Item 11 must include the amount of margin required and on deposit with Options Clearing Corporation to the extent such margin is represented by cash, proprietary qualified securities, and letters of credit collateralized by security-based swap customers' securities.

Note E. (a) Item 12 must include the amount of margin required and on deposit with a clearing agency registered with the Commission under section 17A of the Act (15 U.S.C. 78q–1) or a derivatives clearing organization registered with the Commodity Futures Trading Commission under section 5b of the Commodity Exchange Act (7 U.S.C. 7a–1) for security-based swap customer accounts to the extent that the margin is represented by cash, proprietary qualified securities, and letters of credit collateralized by security-based swap customers' securities.

(b) Item 12 will apply only if the security-based swap dealer has the margin related to security futures products on deposit with:

(1) A registered clearing agency or derivatives clearing organization that:

(i) Maintains security deposits from clearing members in connection with regulated options or futures transactions and assessment power over member firms that equal a combined total of at least $2 billion, at least $500 million of which must be in the form of security deposits. For purposes of this Note E the term "security deposits" refers to a general fund, other than margin deposits or their equivalent, that consists of cash or securities held by a registered clearing agency or derivative clearing organization;

(ii) Maintains at least $3 billion in margin deposits; or

(iii) Does not meet the requirements of paragraphs (b)(1)(i) through (b)(1)(ii) of this Note E, if the Commission has determined, upon a written request for exemption by or for the benefit of the security-based swap dealer, that the security-based swap dealer may utilize such a registered clearing agency or derivatives clearing organization. The Commission may, in its sole discretion, grant such an exemption subject to such conditions as are appropriate under the circumstances, if the Commission determines that such conditional or unconditional exemption is necessary or appropriate in the public interest, and is consistent with the protection of investors; and

(2) A registered clearing agency or derivatives clearing organization that, if it holds funds or securities deposited as margin for security futures products in a bank, as defined in section 3(a)(6) of the Act (15 U.S.C. 78c(a)(6)), obtains and preserves written notification from the bank at which it holds such funds and securities or at which such funds and securities are held on its behalf. The written notification will state that all funds and/or securities deposited with the bank as margin (including security-based swap customer security futures products margin), or held by the bank and pledged to such registered clearing agency or derivatives clearing agency as margin, are being held by the bank for the exclusive benefit of clearing members of the registered clearing agency or derivatives clearing organization (subject to the interest of such registered clearing agency or derivatives clearing organization therein), and are being kept separate from any other accounts maintained by the registered clearing agency or derivatives clearing organization with the bank. The written notification also will provide that such funds and/or securities will at no time be used directly or indirectly as security for a loan to the registered clearing agency or derivatives clearing organization by the bank, and will be subject to no right, charge, security interest, lien, or claim of any kind in favor of the bank or any person claiming through the bank. This provision, however, will not prohibit a registered clearing agency or derivatives clearing organization from pledging security-based swap customer funds or securities as collateral to a bank for any purpose that the rules of the Commission or the registered clearing agency or derivatives clearing organization otherwise permit; and

(3) A registered clearing agency or derivatives clearing organization that establishes, documents, and maintains:

(i) Safeguards in the handling, transfer, and delivery of cash and securities;

Securities and Exchange Commission § 240.18a–5

(ii) Fidelity bond coverage for its employees and agents who handle security-based swap customer funds or securities. In the case of agents of a registered clearing agency or derivatives clearing organization, the agent may provide the fidelity bond coverage; and

(iii) Provisions for periodic examination by independent public accountants; and

(4) A derivatives clearing organization that, if it is not otherwise registered with the Commission, has provided the Commission with a written undertaking, in a form acceptable to the Commission, executed by a duly authorized person at the derivatives clearing organization, to the effect that, with respect to the clearance and settlement of the security-based swap customer security futures products of the security-based swap dealer, the derivatives clearing organization will permit the Commission to examine the books and records of the derivatives clearing organization for compliance with the requirements set forth in § 240.15c3–3a, Note E. (b)(1) through (3).

(c) Item 12 will apply only if a security-based swap dealer determines, at least annually, that the registered clearing agency or derivatives clearing organization with which the security-based swap dealer has on deposit margin related to security futures products meets the conditions of this Note E.

[84 FR 44075, Aug. 22, 2019]

§ 240.18a–5 Records to be made by certain security-based swap dealers and major security-based swap participants.

This section applies to the following types of entities: A security-based swap dealer registered pursuant to section 15F of the Act (15 U.S.C. 78o–10) that is not also a broker or dealer, including an *OTC derivatives dealer* as that term is defined in § 240.3b–12, registered pursuant to section 15 of the Act (15 U.S.C. 78o); and a major security-based swap participant registered pursuant to section 15F of the Act that is not also a broker or dealer, including an OTC derivatives dealer, registered pursuant to section 15 of the Act. Section 240.17a–3 (rather than this section) applies to the following types of entities: A member of a national securities exchange who transacts a business in securities directly with others than members of a national securities exchange; a broker or dealer who transacts a business in securities through the medium of a member of a national securities exchange; a broker or dealer, including an OTC derivatives dealer, registered pursuant to section 15 of the Act; a security-based swap dealer registered pursuant to section 15F of the Act that is also a broker or dealer, including an OTC derivatives dealer, registered pursuant to section 15 of the Act; and a major security-based swap participant registered pursuant to section 15F of the Act that is also a broker or dealer, including an OTC derivatives dealer, registered pursuant to section 15 of the Act.

(a) This paragraph (a) applies only to security-based swap dealers and major security-based swap participants registered under section 15F of the Act for which there is no prudential regulator. Each security-based swap dealer and major security-based swap participant subject to this paragraph (a) must make and keep current the following books and records:

(1) Blotters (or other records of original entry) containing an itemized daily record of all purchases and sales of securities (including security-based swaps), all receipts and deliveries of securities (including certificate numbers), all receipts and disbursements of cash and all other debits and credits. Such records must show the account for which each such purchase or sale was effected, the name and amount of securities, the unit and aggregate purchase or sale price, if any (including the financial terms for security-based swaps), the trade date, and the name or other designation of the person from whom such securities were purchased or received or to whom sold or delivered. For security-based swaps, such records must also show, for each transaction, the type of security-based swap, the reference security, index, or obligor, the date and time of execution, the effective date, the scheduled termination date, the notional amount(s) and the currenc(ies) in which the notional amount(s) is expressed, the unique transaction identifier, and the counterparty's unique identification code.

(2) Ledgers (or other records) reflecting all assets and liabilities, income and expense and capital accounts.

(3) Ledger accounts (or other records) itemizing separately as to each account for every customer or non-customer of such security-based swap dealer or major security-based swap participant, all purchases and sales, receipts and deliveries of securities (including security-based swaps) and commodities for such account and all other debits and credits to such account; and in addition, for a security-based swap,

747

§ 240.18a–5

the type of security-based swap, the reference security, index, or obligor, the date and time of execution, the effective date, the scheduled termination date, the notional amount(s) and the currenc(ies) in which the notional amount(s) is expressed, the unique transaction identifier, and the counterparty's unique identification code.

(4) A securities record or ledger reflecting separately for each:

(i) Security, other than a security-based swap, as of the clearance dates all "long" or "short" positions (including securities in safekeeping and securities that are the subjects of repurchase or reverse repurchase agreements) carried by such security-based swap dealer or major security-based swap participant for its account or for the account of its customers and showing the location of all securities long and the offsetting position to all securities short, including long security count differences and short security count differences classified by the date of the physical count and verification in which they were discovered, and, in all cases the name or designation of the account in which each position is carried.

(ii) Security-based swap, the reference security, index, or obligor, the unique transaction identifier, the counterparty's unique identification code, whether it is a "bought" or "sold" position in the security-based swap, whether the security-based swap is cleared or not cleared, and if cleared, identification of the clearing agency where the security-based swap is cleared.

(5) A memorandum of each purchase or sale of a security-based swap for the account of the security-based swap dealer or major security-based swap participant showing the price. The memorandum must also include the type of security-based swap, the reference security, index, or obligor, the date and time of execution, the effective date, the scheduled termination date, the notional amount(s) and the currenc(ies) in which the notional amount(s) is expressed, the unique transaction identifier, and the counterparty's unique identification code. An order entered pursuant to the exercise of discretionary authority must be so designated.

(6) With respect to a security other than a security-based swap, copies of confirmations of all purchases and sales of securities. With respect to a security-based swap, copies of the security-based swap trade acknowledgment and verification made in compliance with § 240.15Fi–2.

(7) For each security-based swap account, a record of the unique identification code of such counterparty, the name and address of such counterparty, and a record of the authorization of each person the counterparty has granted authority to transact business in the security-based swap account.

(8) A record of all puts, calls, spreads, straddles and other options in which such security-based swap dealer or major security-based swap participant has any direct or indirect interest or which such security-based swap dealer or major security-based swap participant has granted or guaranteed, containing, at least, an identification of the security, and the number of units involved.

(9) A record of the proof of money balances of all ledger accounts in the form of trial balances, and a record of the computation of net capital or tangible net worth, as applicable, as of the trial balance date, pursuant to § 240.18a–1 or § 240.18a–2, respectively. Such trial balances and computations must be prepared currently at least once per month.

(10)(i) A questionnaire or application for employment executed by each "associated person" (as defined in paragraph (d) of this section) of the security-based swap dealer or major security-based swap participant who effects or is involved in effecting security-based swaps on the security-based swap dealer's or major security-based swap participant's behalf, which questionnaire or application must be approved in writing by an authorized representative of the security-based swap dealer or major security-based swap participant and must contain at least the following information with respect to the associated person:

(A) The associated person's name, address, social security number, and the

Securities and Exchange Commission § 240.18a–5

starting date of the associated person's employment or other association with the security-based swap dealer or major security-based swap participant;

(B) The associated person's date of birth;

(C) A complete, consecutive statement of all the associated person's business connections for at least the preceding ten years, including whether the employment was part-time or full-time;

(D) A record of any denial of membership or registration, and of any disciplinary action taken, or sanction imposed, upon the associated person by any Federal or state agency, or by any national securities exchange or national securities association, including any finding that the associated person was a cause of any disciplinary action or had violated any law;

(E) A record of any denial, suspension, expulsion or revocation of membership or registration of any broker, dealer, security-based swap dealer or major security-based swap participant with which the associated person was associated in any capacity at the time such action was taken;

(F) A record of any permanent or temporary injunction entered against the associated person, or any broker, dealer, security-based swap dealer or major security-based swap participant with which the associated person was associated in any capacity at the time such injunction was entered;

(G) A record of any arrest or indictment for any felony, or any misdemeanor pertaining to securities, commodities, banking, insurance or real estate (including, but not limited to, acting or being associated with a broker or dealer, security-based swap dealer, major security-based swap participant, investment company, investment adviser, futures sponsor, bank, or savings and loan association), fraud, false statements or omissions, wrongful taking of property or bribery, forgery, counterfeiting or extortion, and the disposition of the foregoing; and

(H) A record of any other name or names by which the associated person has been known or which the associated person has used.

(ii) A record listing every associated person of the security-based swap dealer or major security-based swap participant which shows, for each associated person, every office of the security-based swap dealer or major security-based swap participant where the associated person regularly conducts the business of handling funds or securities or effecting any transactions in, or inducing or attempting to induce the purchase or sale of any security, for the security-based swap dealer or major security-based swap participant and the Central Registration Depository number, if any, and every internal identification number or code assigned to that person by the security-based swap dealer or major security-based swap participant.

(iii) Notwithstanding paragraph (a)(10)(i) of this section:

(A) A security-based swap dealer or major security-based swap participant is not required to make and keep current a questionnaire or application for employment executed by an associated person if the security-based swap dealer or major security-based swap participant is excluded from the prohibition in section 15F(b)(6) of the Exchange Act (15 U.S.C. 78o–10(b)(6)) with respect to such associated person; and

(B) A questionnaire or application for employment executed by an associated person who is not a U.S. person (as that term is defined in §240.3a71–3(a)(4)(i)(A)) need not include the information described in paragraphs (a)(10)(i)(A) through (H) of this section, unless the security-based swap dealer or major security-based swap participant is required to obtain such information under applicable law in the jurisdiction in which the associated person is employed or located or obtains such information in conducting a background check that is customary for such firms in that jurisdiction and the creation or maintenance of records reflecting that information, would not result in a violation of applicable law in the jurisdiction in which the associated person is employed or located; *provided, however,* the security-based swap dealer or major security-based swap participant must comply with section 15F(b)(6) of the Exchange Act (15 U.S.C. 78o–10(b)(6)).

(11) [Reserved]

§ 240.18a-5

(12) A record of the daily calculation of the current exposure and, if applicable, the initial margin amount for each account of a counterparty required under § 240.18a-3(c).

(13) A record of compliance with possession or control requirements under § 240.18a-4(b).

(14) A record of the reserve computation required under § 240.18a-4(c).

(15) A record of each security-based swap transaction that is not verified under § 240.15Fi-2 within five business days of execution that includes, at a minimum, the unique transaction identifier and the counterparty's unique identification code.

(16) A record documenting that the security-based swap dealer has complied with the business conduct standards as required under § 240.15Fh-6.

(17) A record documenting that the security-based swap dealer or major security-based swap participant has complied with the business conduct standards as required under §§ 240.15Fh-1 through 240.15Fh-5 and 240.15Fk-1.

(18)(i) A record of each security-based swap portfolio reconciliation, whether conducted pursuant to § 240.15Fi-3 or otherwise, including the dates of the security-based swap portfolio reconciliation, the number of portfolio reconciliation discrepancies, the number of security-based swap valuation disputes (including the time-to-resolution of each valuation dispute and the age of outstanding valuation disputes, categorized by transaction and counterparty), and the name of the third-party entity performing the security-based swap portfolio reconciliation, if any.

(ii) A copy of each notification required to be provided to the Commission pursuant to § 240.15Fi-3(c).

(iii) A record of each bilateral offset and each bilateral portfolio compression exercise or multilateral portfolio compression exercise in which it participates, whether conducted pursuant to § 240.15Fi-4 or otherwise, including the dates of the offset or compression, the security-based swaps included in the offset or compression, the identity of the counterparties participating in the offset or compression, the results of the compression, and the name of the third-party entity performing the offset or compression, if any.

(b) This paragraph (b) applies only to security-based swap dealers and major security-based swap participants registered under section 15F of the Act for which there is a prudential regulator. Each security-based swap dealer and major security-based swap participant subject to this paragraph (b) must make and keep current the following books and records:

(1) For security-based swaps and any other positions related to the firm's business as such, blotters (or other records of original entry) containing an itemized daily record of all purchases and sales of securities (including security-based swaps), all receipts and deliveries of securities (including certificate numbers), all receipts and disbursements of cash and all other debits and credits. Such records must show, the account for which each such purchase and sale was effected, the name and amount of securities, the unit and aggregate purchase or sale price (if any, including the financial terms for security-based swaps), the trade date, and the name or other designation of the person from whom such securities were purchased or received or to whom sold or delivered. For security-based swaps, such records must also show, for each transaction, the type of security-based swap, the reference security, index, or obligor, the date and time of execution, the effective date, the scheduled termination date, the notional amount(s) and the currenc(ies) in which the notional amount(s) is expressed, the unique transaction identifier, and the counterparty's unique identification code.

(2) Ledger accounts (or other records) itemizing separately as to each account for every security-based swap customer or non-customer of such security-based swap dealer or major security-based swap participant, all purchases, sales, receipts and deliveries of securities (including security-based swaps) and commodities for such account and all other debits and credits to such account; and in addition, for a security-based swap, the type of security-based swap, the reference security, index, or obligor, the date and time of execution, the effective date, the

Securities and Exchange Commission § 240.18a–5

scheduled termination date, the notional amount(s) and the currenc(ies) in which the notional amount(s) is expressed, the unique transaction identifier, and the counterparty's unique identification code.

(3) For security-based swaps and any securities positions related to the firm's business as a security-based swap dealer or a major security-based swap participant, a securities record or ledger reflecting separately for each:

(i) Security, other than a security-based swap, as of the clearance dates all "long" or "short" positions (including securities in safekeeping and securities that are the subjects of repurchase or reverse repurchase agreements) carried by such security-based swap dealer or major security-based swap participant for its account or for the account of its customers and showing the location of all securities long and the offsetting position to all securities short, including long security count differences and short security count differences classified by the date of the physical count and verification in which they were discovered, and in all cases the name or designation of the account in which each position is carried.

(ii) Security-based swap, the reference security, index, or obligor, the unique transaction identifier, the counterparty's unique identification code, whether it is a "bought" or "sold" position in the security-based swap, whether the security-based swap is cleared or not cleared, and if cleared, identification of the clearing agency where the security-based swap is cleared.

(4) A memorandum of each brokerage order, and of any other instruction, given or received for the purchase or sale of a security-based swap, whether executed or unexecuted. The memorandum must show the terms and conditions of the order or instructions and of any modification or cancellation thereof; the account for which entered; the time the order was received; the time of entry; the price at which executed; the identity of each associated person, if any, responsible for the account; the identity of any other person who entered or accepted the order on behalf of the customer, or, if a customer entered the order on an electronic system, a notation of that entry; and, to the extent feasible, the time of execution or cancellation. The memorandum also must include the type of the security-based swap, the reference security, index, or obligor, the date and time of execution, the effective date, the scheduled termination date, the notional amount(s) and the currenc(ies) in which the notional amount(s) is expressed, the unique transaction identifier, and the counterparty's unique identification code. An order entered pursuant to the exercise of discretionary authority by the security-based swap dealer or major security-based swap participant, or associated person thereof, must be so designated. The term *instruction* must include instructions between partners and employees of a security-based swap dealer or major security-based swap participant. The term *time of entry* means the time when the security-based swap dealer or major security-based swap participant transmits the order or instruction for execution.

(5) A memorandum of each purchase or sale of a security-based swap for the account of the security-based swap dealer or major security-based swap participant showing the price. The memorandum must also include the type of security-based swap, the reference security, index, or obligor, the date and time of execution, the effective date, the scheduled termination date, the notional amount(s) and the currenc(ies) in which the notional amount(s) is expressed, the unique transaction identifier, and the counterparty's unique identification code. An order entered pursuant to the exercise of discretionary authority must be so designated.

(6) With respect to a security other than a security-based swap, copies of confirmations of all purchases and sales of securities related to the business of a security-based swap dealer or major security-based swap participant. With respect to a security-based swap, copies of the security-based swap trade acknowledgment and verification made in compliance with § 240.15Fi–2.

(7) For each security-based swap account, a record of the counterparty's unique identification code, the name

751

§ 240.18a–5

and address of such counterparty, and a record of the authorization of each person the counterparty has granted authority to transact business in the security-based swap account.

(8)(i) A questionnaire or application for employment executed by each "associated person" (as defined in paragraph (c) of this section) of the security-based swap dealer or major security-based swap participant who effects or is involved in effecting security-based swaps on the security-based swap dealer's or major security-based swap participant's behalf, which questionnaire or application must be approved in writing by an authorized representative of the security-based swap dealer or major security-based swap participant and must contain at least the following information with respect to the associated person:

(A) The associated person's name, address, social security number, and the starting date of the associated person's employment or other association with the security-based swap dealer or major security-based swap participant;

(B) The associated person's date of birth;

(C) A complete, consecutive statement of all the associated person's business connections for at least the preceding ten years, including whether the employment was part-time or full-time;

(D) A record of any denial of membership or registration, and of any disciplinary action taken, or sanction imposed, upon the associated person by any Federal or state agency, or by any national securities exchange or national securities association, including any finding that the associated person was a cause of any disciplinary action or had violated any law;

(E) A record of any denial, suspension, expulsion or revocation of membership or registration of any broker, dealer, security-based swap dealer or major security-based swap participant with which the associated person was associated in any capacity at the time such action was taken;

(F) A record of any permanent or temporary injunction entered against the associated person, or any broker, dealer, security-based swap dealer or major security-based swap participant with which the associated person was associated in any capacity at the time such injunction was entered;

(G) A record of any arrest or indictment for any felony, or any misdemeanor pertaining to securities, commodities, banking, insurance or real estate (including, but not limited to, acting or being associated with a broker or dealer, security-based swap dealer, major security-based swap participant, investment company, investment adviser, futures sponsor, bank, or savings and loan association), fraud, false statements or omissions, wrongful taking of property or bribery, forgery, counterfeiting or extortion, and the disposition of the foregoing; and

(H) A record of any other name or names by which the associated person has been known or which the associated person has used.

(ii) A record listing every associated person of the security-based swap dealer or major security-based swap participant which shows, for each associated person, every office of the security-based swap dealer or major security-based swap participant where the associated person regularly conducts the business of handling funds or securities or effecting any transactions in, or inducing or attempting to induce the purchase or sale of any security, for the security-based swap dealer or major security-based swap participant and every internal identification number or code assigned to that person by the security-based swap dealer or major security-based swap participant.

(iii) Notwithstanding paragraph (b)(8)(i) of this section;

(A) A security-based swap dealer or major security-based swap participant is not required to make and keep current a questionnaire or application for employment executed by an associated person if the security-based swap dealer or major security-based swap participant is excluded from the prohibition in section 15F(b)(6) of the Exchange Act (15 U.S.C. 78o–10(b)(6)) with respect to such associated person; and

(B) A questionnaire or application for employment executed by an associated person who is not a U.S. person (as that term is defined in § 240.3a71–3(a)(4)(i)(A)) need not include the information described in paragraphs

Securities and Exchange Commission § 240.18a–5

(b)(8)(i)(A) through (H) of this section, unless the security-based swap dealer or major security-based swap participant is required to obtain such information under applicable law in the jurisdiction in which the associated person is employed or located or obtains such information in conducting a background check that is customary for such firms in that jurisdiction and the creation or maintenance of records reflecting that information would not result in a violation of applicable law in the jurisdiction in which the associated person is employed or located; *provided, however,* the security-based swap dealer or major security-based swap participant must comply with Section 15F(b)(6) of the Exchange Act (15 U.S.C. 78o–10(b)(6)).

(9) A record of compliance with possession or control requirements under § 240.18a–4(b).

(10) A record of the reserve computation required under § 240.18a–4(c).

(11) A record of each security-based swap transaction that is not verified under § 240.15Fi–2 within five business days of execution that includes, at a minimum, the unique transaction identifier and the counterparty's unique identification code.

(12) A record documenting that the security-based swap dealer has complied with the business conduct standards as required under § 240.15Fh–6.

(13) A record documenting that the security-based swap dealer or major security-based swap participant has complied with the business conduct standards as required under § 240.15Fh–1 through § 240.15Fh–5 and § 240.15Fk–1.

(14)(i) A record of each security-based swap portfolio reconciliation, whether conducted pursuant to § 240.15Fi–3 or otherwise, including the dates of the security-based swap portfolio reconciliation, the number of portfolio reconciliation discrepancies, the number of security-based swap valuation disputes (including the time-to-resolution of each valuation dispute and the age of outstanding valuation disputes, categorized by transaction and counterparty), and the name of the third-party entity performing the security-based swap portfolio reconciliation, if any.

(ii) A copy of each notification required to be provided to the Commission pursuant to § 240.15Fi–3(c).

(iii) A record of each bilateral offset and each bilateral portfolio compression exercise or multilateral portfolio compression exercise in which it participates, whether conducted pursuant to § 240.15Fi–4 or otherwise, including the dates of the offset or compression, the security-based swaps included in the offset or compression, the identity of the counterparties participating in the offset or compression, the results of the compression, and the name of the third-party entity performing the offset or compression, if any.

(c) A security-based swap dealer or major security-based swap participant may comply with the recordkeeping requirements of the Commodity Exchange Act and chapter I of this title applicable to swap dealers and major swap participants in lieu of complying with paragraphs (a)(1), (3), and (4) or paragraphs (b)(1) through (3) of this section, as applicable, solely with respect to required information regarding security-based swap transactions and positions if:

(1) The security-based swap dealer or major security-based swap participant is registered as a security-based swap dealer or major security-based swap participant pursuant to section 15F of the Act;

(2) The security-based swap dealer or major security-based swap participant is registered as a swap dealer or major swap participant pursuant to section 4s of the Commodity Exchange Act and chapter I of this title;

(3) The security-based swap dealer or major security-based swap participant is subject to 17 CFR 23.201, 23.202, 23.402, and 23.501 with respect to its swap-related books and records;

(4) The security-based swap dealer or major security-based swap participant preserves all of the data elements necessary to create the records required by paragraphs (a)(1), (3), and (4) or paragraphs (b)(1) through (3) of this section, as applicable, as they pertain to security-based swap and swap transactions and positions;

(5) The security-based swap dealer or major security-based swap participant upon request furnishes promptly to

753

§ 240.18a-6

representatives of the Commission the records required by paragraphs (a)(1), (3), and (4) or paragraphs (b)(1) through (3) of this section, as applicable, as well as the records required by 17 CFR 23.201, 23.202, 23.402, and 23.501 as they pertain to security-based swap and swap transactions and positions in the format applicable to that category of record as set forth in this section; and

(6) The security-based swap dealer or major security-based swap participant provides notice of its intent to utilize this paragraph (c) by notifying in writing the Commission, both at the principal office of the Commission in Washington, DC and at the regional office of the Commission for the region in which the registrant has its principal place of business.

(d)(1) The term *associated person* means for purposes of this section a *person associated with a security-based swap dealer or major security-based swap participant* as that term is defined in section 3(a)(70) of the Act (15 U.S.C. 78c(a)(70)).

(2) The term *associated person*, as to an entity supervised by a prudential regulator, includes only those persons whose activities relate to its business as a security-based swap dealer or major security-based swap participant.

[84 FR 68656, Dec. 16, 2019, as amended at 85 FR 6353, 6416, Feb. 4, 2020]

§ 240.18a-6 Records to be preserved by certain security-based swap dealers and major security-based swap participants.

This section applies to the following types of entities: A security-based swap dealer registered pursuant to section 15F of the Act (15 U.S.C. 78o-10) that is not also a broker or dealer, including an *OTC derivatives dealer* as that term is defined in § 240.3b-12, registered pursuant to section 15 of the Act (15 U.S.C. 78o); and a major security-based swap participant registered pursuant to section 15F of the Act that is not also a broker or dealer, including an OTC derivatives dealer, registered pursuant to section 15 of the Act. Section 240.17a-4 (rather than this section) applies to the following types of entities: A member of a national securities exchange who transacts a business in securities directly with others than members of a national securities exchange; a broker or dealer who transacts a business in securities through the medium of a member of a national securities exchange; a broker or dealer, including an OTC derivatives dealer, registered pursuant to section 15 of the Act; a security-based swap dealer registered pursuant to section 15F of the Act that is also a broker or dealer, including an OTC derivatives dealer, registered pursuant to section 15 of the Act; and a major security-based swap participant registered pursuant to section 15F of the Act that is also a broker or dealer, including an OTC derivatives dealer, registered pursuant to section 15 of the Act.

(a)(1) Every security-based swap dealer and major security-based swap participant for which there is no prudential regulator must preserve for a period not less than six years, the first two years in an easily accessible place, all records required to be made pursuant to § 240.18a-5(a)(1) through (4).

(2) Every security-based swap dealer and major security-based swap participant for which there is a prudential regulator must preserve for a period not less than six years, the first two years in an easily accessible place, all records required to be made pursuant to § 240.18a-5(b)(1) through (3).

(b)(1) Every security-based swap dealer and major security-based swap participant for which there is no prudential regulator must preserve for a period of not less than three years, the first two years in an easily accessible place:

(i) All records required to be made pursuant to § 240.18a-5(a)(5) through (9) and (12) through (18).

(ii) All check books, bank statements, cancelled checks, and cash reconciliations.

(iii) All bills receivable or payable (or copies thereof), paid or unpaid, relating to the business of such security-based swap dealer or major security-based swap participant, as such.

(iv) Originals of all communications received and copies of all communications sent (and any approvals thereof) by the security-based swap dealer or major security-based swap participant (including inter-office memoranda and

Securities and Exchange Commission

§ 240.18a–6

communications) relating to its business as such. As used in this paragraph (b)(1)(iv), the term "communications" includes sales scripts and recordings of telephone calls required to be maintained pursuant to section 15F(g)(1) of the Act (15 U.S.C. 78*o*–10(g)(1)).

(v) All trial balances and computations of net capital or tangible net worth requirements (and working papers in connection therewith), as applicable, financial statements, branch office reconciliations, and internal audit working papers, relating to the business of such security-based swap dealer or major security-based swap participant as such.

(vi) All guarantees of security-based swap accounts and all powers of attorney and other evidence of the granting of any discretionary authority given in respect of any security-based swap account, and copies of resolutions empowering an agent to act on behalf of a corporation.

(vii) All written agreements (or copies thereof) entered into by such security-based swap dealer or major security-based swap participant relating to its business as such, including agreements with respect to any account. Written agreements with respect to a security-based swap customer or non-customer, including governing documents or any document establishing the terms and conditions of the customer's or non-customer's security-based swaps must be maintained with the customer's or non-customer's account records.

(viii) Records which contain the following information in support of amounts included in the report prepared as of the audit date on Part II of Form X–17A–5 (§ 249.617 of this chapter) and in annual financial statements required by § 240.18a–7(d):

(A) Money balance and position, long or short, including description, quantity, price, and valuation of each security, including contractual commitments, in security-based swap customers' accounts, in fully secured accounts, partly secured accounts, unsecured accounts, and in securities accounts payable to security-based swap customers;

(B) Money balance and position, long or short, including description, quantity, price, and valuation of each security, including contractual commitments, in security-based swap non-customers' accounts, in fully secured accounts, partly secured accounts, unsecured accounts, and in security-based swap accounts payable to non-security-based swap customers;

(C) Position, long or short, including description, quantity, price, and valuation of each security, including contractual commitments, included in the Computation of Net Capital as commitments, securities owned, securities owned not readily marketable, and other investments owned not readily marketable;

(D) Description of futures commodity contracts or swaps, contract value on trade date, market value, gain or loss, and liquidating equity or deficit in customers' and non-customers' accounts;

(E) Description of futures commodity contracts or swaps, contract value on trade date, market value, gain or loss and liquidating equity or deficit in trading and investment accounts;

(F) Description, money balance, quantity, price, and valuation of each spot commodity and swap position or commitments in customers' and non-customers' accounts;

(G) Description, money balance, quantity, price, and valuation of each spot commodity and swap position or commitments in trading and investment accounts;

(H) Number of shares, description of security, exercise price, cost, and market value of put and call options, including short out of the money options having no market or exercise value, showing listed and unlisted put and call options separately;

(I) Quantity, price, and valuation of each security underlying the haircut for undue concentration made in the Computation of Net Capital pursuant to § 240.18a–1;

(J) Description, quantity, price, and valuation of each security and commodity position or contractual commitment, long or short, in each joint account in which the security-based swap dealer or major security-based swap participant has an interest, including each participant's interest and margin deposit;

§ 240.18a–6

(K) Description, settlement date, contract amount, quantity, market price, and valuation for each aged failed to deliver requiring a charge in the Computation of Net Capital pursuant to § 240.18a–1;

(L) Detail relating to information for possession or control requirements under § 240.18a–4 and reported on Part II of Form X–17A–5 (§ 249.617 of this chapter);

(M) Detail of all items, not otherwise substantiated, which are charged or credited in the Computation of Net Capital pursuant to §§ 240.18a–1 and 240.18a–2, such as cash margin deficiencies, deductions related to securities values and undue concentration, aged securities differences, and insurance claims receivable;

(N) Detail relating to the calculation of the risk margin amount pursuant to § 240.18a–1(c)(6); and

(O) Other schedules which are specifically prescribed by the Commission as necessary to support information reported as required by § 240.18a–7.

(ix) The records required to be made pursuant to § 240.15c3–4 and the results of the periodic reviews conducted pursuant to § 240.15c3–4(d).

(x) The records required to be made pursuant to § 240.18a–1(e)(2)(iii)(F)(*1*) and (*2*).

(xi) A copy of information required to be reported under §§ 242.901 through 242.909 of this chapter (Regulation SBSR).

(xii) Copies of documents, communications, disclosures, and notices related to business conduct standards as required under §§ 240.15Fh–1 through 240.15Fh–6 and 240.15Fk–1.

(xiii) Copies of documents used to make a reasonable determination with respect to special entities, including information relating to the financial status, the tax status, and the investment or financing objectives of the special entity as required under sections 15F(h)(4)(C) and (5)(A) of the Act (15 U.S.C. 78*o*–10(h)(4)(C) and (5)(A)).

(2) Every security-based swap dealer and major security-based swap participant for which there is a prudential regulator must preserve for a period of not less than three years, the first two years in an easily accessible place:

17 CFR Ch. II (4–1–23 Edition)

(i) All records required to be made pursuant to § 240.18a–5(b)(4) through (7) and (9) through (14).

(ii) Originals of all communications received and copies of all communications sent (and any approvals thereof) by the security-based swap dealer or major security-based swap participant (including inter-office memoranda and communications) relating to its business as a security-based swap dealer or major security-based swap participant. As used in this paragraph (b)(2)(ii), the term "communications" includes sales scripts and recordings of telephone calls required to be maintained pursuant to section 15F(g)(1) of the Act (15 U.S.C. 78*o*–10(g)(1)).

(iii) All guarantees of security-based swap accounts and all powers of attorney and other evidence of the granting of any discretionary authority given in respect of any security-based swap account, and copies of resolutions empowering an agent to act on behalf of a corporation.

(iv) All written agreements (or copies thereof) entered into by such security-based swap dealer or major security-based swap participant relating to its business as a security-based swap dealer or major security-based swap participant, including agreements with respect to any account. Written agreements with respect to a security-based swap customer or non-customer, including governing documents or any document establishing the terms and conditions of the customer's or non-customer's security-based swaps, must be maintained with the customer's or non-customer's account records.

(v) Detail relating to information for possession or control requirements under § 240.18a–4 and reported on Part IIC of Form X–17A–5 (§ 249.617 of this chapter) that is in support of amounts included in the report prepared as of the audit date on Part IIC of Form X–17A–5 (§ 249.617 of this chapter) and in the registrant's annual reports required by § 240.18a–7(c).

(vi) A copy of information required to be reported under Regulation SBSR (§§ 242.901 through 242.909 of this chapter).

(vii) Copies of documents, communications, disclosures, and notices related to business conduct standards as

Securities and Exchange Commission

§ 240.18a–6

required under §§ 240.15Fh–1 through 240.15Fh–6 and 240.15Fk–1.

(viii) Copies of documents used to make a reasonable determination with respect to special entities, including information relating to the financial status, the tax status, and the investment or financing objectives of the special entity as required under sections 15F(h)(4)(C) and (5)(A) of the Act.

(c) Every security-based swap dealer and major security-based swap participant subject to this section must preserve during the life of the enterprise and of any successor enterprise all partnership articles or, in the case of a corporation, all articles of incorporation or charter, minute books, and stock certificate books (or, in the case of any other form of legal entity, all records such as articles of organization or formation and minute books used for a purpose similar to those records required for corporations or partnerships), all Forms SBSE (§ 249.1600 of this chapter), all Forms SBSE–A (§ 249.1600a of this chapter), all Forms SBSE–C (§ 249.1600c of this chapter), all Forms SBSE–W (§ 249.1601 of this chapter), all amendments to these forms, and all licenses or other documentation showing the registration of the security-based swap dealer or major security-based swap participant with any securities regulatory authority or the Commodity Futures Trading Commission.

(d) Every security-based swap dealer and major security-based swap participant subject to this section must maintain and preserve in an easily accessible place:

(1) All records required under § 240.18a–5(a)(10) or (b)(8) until at least three years after the associated person's employment and any other connection with the security-based swap dealer or major security-based swap participant has terminated.

(2)(i) For security-based swap dealers and major security-based swap participants for which there is not a prudential regulator, each report which a securities regulatory authority or the Commodity Futures Trading Commission has requested or required the security-based swap dealer or major security-based swap participant to make and furnish to it pursuant to an order or settlement, and each securities regulatory authority or Commodity Futures Trading Commission examination report until three years after the date of the report.

(ii) For security-based swap dealers and major security-based swap participants for which there is a prudential regulator, each report related to security-based swap activities which a securities regulatory authority, the Commodity Futures Trading Commission, or a prudential regulator has requested or required the security-based swap dealer or major security-based swap participant to make and furnish to it pursuant to an order or settlement, and each securities regulatory authority, Commodity Futures Trading Commission, or prudential regulator examination report until three years after the date of the report.

(3)(i) For security-based swap dealers and major security-based swap participants for which there is not a prudential regulator, each compliance, supervisory, and procedures manual, including any updates, modifications, and revisions to the manual, describing the policies and practices of the security-based swap dealer or major security-based swap participant with respect to compliance with applicable laws and rules, and supervision of the activities of each natural person associated with the security-based swap dealer or major security-based swap participant until three years after the termination of the use of the manual.

(ii) For security-based swap dealers and major security-based swap participants for which there is a prudential regulator, each compliance, supervisory, and procedures manual, including any updates, modifications, and revisions to the manual, describing the policies and practices of the security-based swap dealer or major security-based swap participant with respect to compliance with applicable laws and rules relating to security-based swap activities, and supervision of the activities of each natural person associated with the security-based swap dealer or major security-based swap participant until three years after the termination of the use of the manual.

(4) The written policies and procedures required pursuant to §§ 240.15Fi–3,

§ 240.18a–6

240.15Fi–4, and 240.15Fi–5 until three years after termination of the use of the policies and procedures.

(5)(i) Each written agreement with counterparties on the terms of portfolio reconciliation with those counterparties as required to be created under § 240.15Fi–3(a)(1) and (b)(1) until three years after the termination of the agreement and all transactions governed thereby.

(ii) Security-based swap trading relationship documentation with counterparties required to be created under § 240.15Fi–5 until three years after the termination of such documentation and all transactions governed thereby.

(iii) A record of the results of each audit required to be performed pursuant to § 240.15Fi–5(c) until three years after the conclusion of the audit.

(e) Subject to the conditions set forth in this paragraph (e), the records required to be maintained and preserved pursuant to § 240.18a–5 and this section may be immediately produced or reproduced by means of an electronic recordkeeping system and be maintained and preserved for the required time in that form.

(1) For purposes of this paragraph (e):

(i) The term *electronic recordkeeping system* means a system that preserves records in a digital format in a manner that permits the records to be viewed and downloaded;

(ii) The term *designated executive officer* means a member of senior management of the security-based swap dealer or major security-based swap participant who has access to and the ability to provide records maintained and preserved on the electronic recordkeeping system either directly or through a *designated specialist* who reports directly or indirectly to the designated executive officer;

(iii) The term *designated officer* means an employee of the security-based swap dealer or major security-based swap participant who reports directly or indirectly to the designated executive officer and who has access to and the ability to provide records maintained and preserved on the electronic recordkeeping system either directly or through a *designated specialist* who reports directly or indirectly to the designated officer;

17 CFR Ch. II (4–1–23 Edition)

(iv) The term *designated specialist* means an employee of the security-based swap dealer or major security-based swap participant who has access to, and the ability to provide records maintained and preserved on, the electronic recordkeeping system; and

(v) The term *designated third party* means a person that is not affiliated with the security-based swap dealer or major security-based swap participant who has access to and the ability to provide records maintained and preserved on the electronic recordkeeping system.

(2) An electronic recordkeeping system of a security-based swap dealer or major security-based swap participant without a prudential regulator must:

(i)(A) Preserve a record for the duration of its applicable retention period in a manner that maintains a complete time-stamped audit trail that includes:

(*1*) All modifications to and deletions of the record or any part thereof;

(*2*) The date and time of actions that create, modify, or delete the record;

(*3*) If applicable, the identity of the individual creating, modifying, or deleting the record; and

(*4*) Any other information needed to maintain an audit trail of the record in a way that maintains security, signatures, and data to ensure the authenticity and reliability of the record and will permit re-creation of the original record if it is modified or deleted; or

(B) Preserve the records exclusively in a non-rewriteable, non-erasable format;

(ii) Verify automatically the completeness and accuracy of the processes for storing and retaining records electronically;

(iii) If applicable, serialize the original and duplicate units of the storage media, and time-date the required period of retention for the information placed on such electronic storage media;

(iv) Have the capacity to readily download and transfer copies of a record and its audit trail (if applicable) in both a human readable format and in a reasonably usable electronic format and to readily download and transfer the information needed to locate the electronic record, as required by the staffs of the Commission, or any

Securities and Exchange Commission

§ 240.18a-6

State regulator having jurisdiction over the security-based swap dealer or major security-based swap participant; and

(v)(A) Include a backup electronic recordkeeping system that meets the other requirements of this paragraph (e) and that retains the records required to be maintained and preserved pursuant to § 240.18a-5 and in accordance with this section in a manner that will serve as a redundant set of records if the original electronic recordkeeping system is temporarily or permanently inaccessible; or

(B) Have other redundancy capabilities that are designed to ensure access to the records required to be maintained and preserved pursuant to § 240.18a-5 and this section.

(3) A security-based swap dealer or major security-based swap participant using an electronic recordkeeping system must:

(i) At all times have available, for examination by the staffs of the Commission or any State regulator having jurisdiction over the security-based swap dealer or major security-based swap participant, facilities for immediately producing the records preserved by means of the electronic recordkeeping system and for producing copies of those records.

(ii) Be ready at all times to provide, and immediately provide, any record stored by means of the electronic recordkeeping system that the staffs of the Commission or any State regulator having jurisdiction over the security-based swap dealer or major security-based swap participant may request.

(iii) For a security-based swap dealer or major security-based swap participant operating pursuant to paragraph (e)(2)(i)(B) of this section, the security-based swap dealer or major security-based swap participant must have in place an audit system providing for accountability regarding inputting of records required to be maintained and preserved pursuant to § 240.18a-5 and this section to the electronic recordkeeping system and inputting of any changes made to every original and duplicate record maintained and preserved thereby.

(A) At all times a security-based swap dealer and major security-based swap participant must be able to have the results of such audit system available for examination by the staff of the Commission.

(B) The audit results must be preserved for the time required for the audited records.

(iv) Organize, maintain, keep current, and provide promptly upon request by the staffs of the Commission or any State regulator having jurisdiction over the security-based swap dealer or major security-based swap participant all information necessary to access and locate records preserved by means of the electronic recordkeeping system.

(v)(A) Have at all times filed with the Commission the following undertakings with respect to such records signed by either a designated executive officer or designated third party (hereinafter, the "undersigned"):

The undersigned hereby undertakes to furnish promptly to the U.S. Securities and Exchange Commission ("Commission") and its designees or representatives, or any State securities regulator having jurisdiction over [Name of the Security-Based Swap Dealer or Major Security-Based Swap Participant], upon reasonable request, such information as is deemed necessary by the staff of the Commission or any State regulator having jurisdiction over [Name of the Security-Based Swap Dealer or Major Security-Based Swap Participant], to download copies of a record and its audit trail (if applicable) preserved by means of an electronic recordkeeping system of [Name of the Security-Based Swap Dealer or Major Security-Based Swap Participant] into both a human readable format and a reasonably usable electronic format in the event of a failure on the part of [Name of the Security-Based Swap Dealer or Major Security-Based Swap Participant] to download a requested record or its audit trail (if applicable).

Furthermore, the undersigned hereby undertakes to take reasonable steps to provide access to the information preserved by means of an electronic recordkeeping system of [Name of the Security-Based Swap Dealer or Major Security-Based Swap Participant], including, as appropriate, downloading any record required to be maintained and preserved by [Name of the Security-Based Swap Dealer or Major Security-Based Swap Participant] pursuant to §§ 240.18a-5 and 240.18a-6 in a format acceptable to the staff of the Commission or any State regulator having jurisdiction over [Name of the Security-Based Swap Dealer or Major Security-Based Swap Participant]. Specifically, the undersigned

§ 240.18a-6

will take reasonable steps to, in the event of a failure on the part of [Name of the Security-Based Swap Dealer or Major Security-Based Swap Participant] to download the record into a human readable format or a reasonably usable electronic format and after reasonable notice to [Name of the Security-Based Swap Dealer or Major Security-Based Swap Participant], download the record into a human readable format or a reasonably usable electronic format at the request of the staff of the Commission or any State regulator having jurisdiction [Name of the Security-Based Swap Dealer or Major Security-Based Swap Participant].

(B) A designated executive officer who signs the undertaking required pursuant to paragraph (e)(3)(v)(A) of this section may:

(1) Appoint in writing up to two designated officers who will take the steps necessary to fulfill the obligations of the designated executive officer set forth in the undertakings in the event the designated executive officer is unable to fulfill those obligations; and

(2) Appoint in writing up to three designated specialists.

(C) The appointment of, or reliance on, a designated officer or designated specialist does not relieve the designated executive officer of the obligations set forth in the undertaking.

(f)(1)(i) If the records required to be maintained and preserved pursuant to the provisions of §240.18a-5 and this section are prepared or maintained by a third party, including by a third party that owns and operates the servers or other storage devices on which the records are preserved or maintained, on behalf of the security-based swap dealer or major security-based swap participant, the third party must file with the Commission a written undertaking in a form acceptable to the Commission, signed by a duly authorized person, to the effect that such records are the property of the security-based swap dealer or major security-based swap participant and will be surrendered promptly on request of the security-based swap dealer or major security-based swap participant and including the following provision:

With respect to any books and records maintained or preserved on behalf of [SBSD or MSBSP], the undersigned hereby undertakes to permit examination of such books and records at any time or from time to time during business hours by representatives or designees of the Securities and Exchange Commission, and to promptly furnish to said Commission or its designee true, correct, complete, and current hard copies of any or all or any part of such books and records.

(ii)(A) If the records required to be maintained and preserved pursuant to the provisions of §240.18a-5 and this section are maintained and preserved by means of an electronic recordkeeping system as defined in paragraph (e) of this section utilizing servers or other storage devices that are owned or operated by a third party (including an affiliate) and the security-based swap dealer or major security-based swap participant has *independent access* to the records as defined in paragraph (f)(1)(ii)(B) of this section, the third party may file with the Commission the following undertaking signed by a duly authorized person in lieu of the undertaking required under paragraph (f)(1)(i) of this section:

The undersigned hereby acknowledges that the records of [SBSD or MSBSP] are the property of [SBSD or MSBSP] and [SBSD or MSBSP] has represented: one, that it is subject to rules of the Securities and Exchange Commission governing the maintenance and preservation of certain records, two, that it has independent access to the records maintained by [name of third party], and, three, that it consents to [name of third party] fulfilling the obligations set forth in this undertaking. The undersigned undertakes that [name of third party] will facilitate within its ability, and not impede or prevent, the examination, access, download, or transfer of the records by a representative or designee of the Securities and Exchange Commission as permitted under the law.

(B) A security-based swap dealer or major security-based swap participant utilizing servers or other storage devices that are owned or operated by a third party has independent access to records with respect to such third party if it can regularly access the records without the need of any intervention of the third party and through such access:

(1) Permit examination of the records at any time or from time to time during business hours by representatives or designees of the Commission; and

(2) Promptly furnish to the Commission or its designee a true, correct, complete and current hard copy of any or all or any part of such records.

Securities and Exchange Commission § 240.18a-7

(2) Agreement with a third party will not relieve such security-based swap dealer or major security-based swap participant from the responsibility to prepare and maintain records as specified in this section or in § 240.18a-5.

(g) Every security-based swap dealer and major security-based swap participant subject to this section must furnish promptly to a representative of the Commission legible, true, complete, and current copies of those records of the security-based swap dealer or major security-based swap participant that are required to be preserved under this section, or any other records of the security-based swap dealer or major security-based swap participant subject to examination or required to be made or maintained pursuant to section 15F of the Act that are requested by a representative of the Commission. The security-based swap dealer and major security-based swap participant must furnish a record and its audit trail (if applicable) preserved on an electronic recordkeeping system pursuant to paragraph (e) of this section in a reasonably usable electronic format, if requested by a representative of the Commission.

(h) When used in this section:

(1) The term *securities regulatory authority* means the Commission, any self-regulatory organization, or any securities commission (or any agency or office performing like functions) of the States.

(2) The term *associated person* has the meaning set forth in § 240.18a-5(d).

[84 FR 68659, Dec. 16, 2019, as amended at 85 FR 6416, Feb. 4, 2020; 85 FR 33021, June 1, 2020; 87 FR 66450, Nov. 3, 2022]

§ 240.18a-7 **Reports to be made by certain security-based swap dealers and major security-based swap participants.**

This section applies to the following types of entities: A security-based swap dealer registered pursuant to section 15F of the Act (15 U.S.C. 78o-10) that is not also a broker or dealer, other than an *OTC derivatives dealer* as that term is defined in § 240.3b-12, registered pursuant to section 15 of the Act (15 U.S.C. 78o); a security-based swap dealer registered pursuant to section 15F of the Act that is also an OTC derivatives dealer registered pursuant to section 15 of the Act; and a major security-based swap participant registered pursuant to section 15F of the Act that is not also a broker or dealer, including an OTC derivatives dealer, registered pursuant to section 15 of the Act. Section 240.17a-5 (rather than this section) applies to the following types of entities: Except as provided above, a broker or dealer, including an OTC derivatives dealer, registered pursuant to section 15 of the Act; a broker or dealer, other than an OTC derivatives dealer, registered pursuant to section 15 of the Act that is also a security-based swap dealer registered pursuant to section 15F of the Act; and a broker or dealer, including an OTC derivatives dealer, registered pursuant to section 15 of the Act that is also a major-security-based swap participant registered pursuant to section 15F of the Act.

(a) *Filing of reports.* (1) Every security-based swap dealer or major security-based swap participant for which there is no prudential regulator must file with the Commission or its designee Part II of Form X-17A-5 (§ 249.617 of this chapter) within 17 business days after the end of each month.

(2) Every security-based swap dealer or major security-based swap participant for which there is a prudential regulator must file with the Commission or its designee Part IIC of Form X-17A-5 (§ 249.617 of this chapter) within 30 calendar days after the end of each calendar quarter.

(3) Security-based swap dealers that have been authorized by the Commission to compute net capital pursuant to § 240.18a-1(d), must file the following additional reports with the Commission:

(i) For each product for which the security-based swap dealer calculates a deduction for market risk other than in accordance with § 240.18a-1(e)(1)(i) and (iii), the product category and the amount of the deduction for market risk within 17 business days after the end of the month;

(ii) A graph reflecting, for each business line, the daily intra-month value at risk within 17 business days after the end of the month;

(iii) The aggregate value at risk for the security-based swap dealer within

§ 240.18a–7

17 business days after end of the month;

(iv) For each product for which the security-based swap dealer uses scenario analysis, the product category and the deduction for market risk within 17 business days after the end of the month;

(v) Credit risk information on security-based swap, mixed swap and swap exposures, within 17 business days after the end of the month, including:

(A) Overall current exposure;

(B) Current exposure (including commitments) listed by counterparty for the 15 largest exposures;

(C) The ten largest commitments listed by counterparty;

(D) The broker's or dealer's maximum potential exposure listed by counterparty for the 15 largest exposures;

(E) The broker's or dealer's aggregate maximum potential exposure;

(F) A summary report reflecting the broker's or dealer's current and maximum potential exposures by credit rating category; and

(G) A summary report reflecting the broker's or dealer's current exposure for each of the top ten countries to which the broker or dealer is exposed (by residence of the main operating group of the counterparty);

(vi) Regular risk reports supplied to the security-based swap dealer's senior management in the format described in the application, within 17 business days after the end of the month;

(vii) [Reserved]

(viii) A report identifying the number of business days for which the actual daily net trading loss exceeded the corresponding daily VaR within 17 business days after the end of each calendar quarter; and

(ix) The results of backtesting of all internal models used to compute allowable capital, including VaR and credit risk models, indicating the number of backtesting exceptions within 17 business days after the end of each calendar quarter.

(b) *Customer disclosures.* (1) Every security-based swap dealer or major security-based swap participant for which there is no prudential regulator must make publicly available on its website within 10 business days after the date the firm is required to file with the Commission the annual reports pursuant to paragraph (c) of this section:

(i) A Statement of Financial Condition with appropriate notes prepared in accordance with U.S. generally accepted accounting principles which must be audited;

(ii) A statement of the amount of the security-based swap dealer's net capital and its required net capital, computed in accordance with § 240.18a–1. Such statement must include summary financial statements of subsidiaries consolidated pursuant to § 240.18a–1c (appendix C to § 240.18a–1 (Rule 18a–1)), where material, and the effect thereof on the net capital and required net capital of the security-based swap dealer; and

(iii) If, in connection with the most recent annual reports required under paragraph (c) of this section, the report of the independent public accountant required under paragraph (c)(1)(i)(C) of this section covering the report of the security-based swap dealer required under paragraph (c)(1)(i)(B)(*1*) of this section identifies one or more material weaknesses, a copy of the report.

(2) Every security-based swap dealer or major security-based swap participant for which there is no prudential regulator must make publicly available on its website unaudited statements as of the date that is 6 months after the date of the most recent audited statements filed with the Commission under paragraph (c)(1) of this section. These reports must be made publicly available within 30 calendar days of the date of the statements.

(3) The information that is made publicly available pursuant to paragraphs (b)(1) and (2) of this section must also be made available in writing, upon request, to any person that has a security-based swap account. The security-based swap dealer or major security-based swap participant must maintain a toll-free telephone number to receive such requests.

(c) *Annual reports*—(1) *Reports required to be filed.* (i) Except as provided in paragraph (c)(1)(iii) of this section, every security-based swap dealer or major security-based swap participant registered pursuant to section 15F of

Securities and Exchange Commission § 240.18a-7

the Act for which there is no prudential regulator must file annually, as applicable:

(A) A financial report as described in paragraph (c)(2) of this section;

(B)(*1*) If the security-based swap dealer did not claim it was exempt from § 240.18a-4 throughout the most recent fiscal year, a compliance report as described in paragraph (c)(3) of this section executed by the person who makes the oath or affirmation under paragraph (d)(1) of this section; or

(*2*) If the security-based swap dealer did claim it was exempt from § 240.18a-4 throughout the most recent fiscal year, an exemption report as described in paragraph (c)(4) of this section executed by the person who makes the oath or affirmation under paragraph (d)(1) of this section; and

(C) A report prepared by an independent public accountant, under the engagement provisions in paragraph (e) of this section, covering each report required to be filed under paragraphs (c)(1)(i)(A) and (B) of this section, as applicable.

(ii) The reports required to be filed under this paragraph (c) must be as of the same fiscal year end each year, unless a change is approved in writing by the Commission. The original request for a change must be filed at the Commission's principal office in Washington, DC. A copy of the written approval must be sent to the regional office of the Commission for the region in which the security-based swap dealer or major security-based swap participant has its principal place of business.

(iii) A security-based swap dealer or major security-based swap participant succeeding to and continuing the business of another security-based swap dealer or major security-based swap participant need not file reports under this paragraph (c) as of a date in the fiscal year in which the succession occurs if the predecessor security-based swap dealer or major security-based swap participant has filed the reports in compliance with this paragraph (c) as of a date in such fiscal year.

(2) *Financial report.* The financial report must contain:

(i)(A) A Statement of Financial Condition, a Statement of Income, a Statement of Cash Flows, a Statement of Changes in Stockholders' or Partners' or Sole Proprietor's Equity, and Statement of Changes in Liabilities Subordinated to Claims of General Creditors. The statements must be prepared in accordance with U.S. generally accepted accounting principles and must be in a format that is consistent with the statements contained in Part II of Form X-17A-5 (§ 249.617 of this chapter).

(B) If there is other comprehensive income in the period(s) presented, the financial report must contain a Statement of Comprehensive Income (as defined in § 210.1-02 of this chapter) in place of a Statement of Income.

(ii) Supporting schedules that include, from Part II of Form X-17A-5 (§ 249.617 of this chapter), a Computation of Net Capital under § 240.18a-1, a Computation of Tangible Net Worth under § 240.18a-2, a Computation for Determination of Security-Based Swap Customer Reserve Requirements under § 240.18a-4a (Exhibit A of § 240.18a-4), and Information Relating to the Possession or Control Requirements for Security-Based Swap Customers under § 240.18a-4, as applicable.

(iii) If any of the Computation of Net Capital under § 240.18a-1, the Computation of Tangible Net Worth under § 240.18a-2, or the Computation for Determination of Security-Based Swap Customer Reserve Requirements under Exhibit A of § 240.18a-4 in the financial report is materially different from the corresponding computation in the most recent Part II of Form X-17A-5 (§ 249.617 of this chapter) filed by the registrant pursuant to paragraph (a) of this section, a reconciliation, including appropriate explanations, between the computation in the financial report and the computation in the most recent Part II of Form X-17A-5 filed by the registrant. If no material differences exist, a statement so indicating must be included in the financial report.

(3) *Compliance report.* (i) The compliance report must contain:

(A) Statements as to whether:

(*1*) The security-based swap dealer has established and maintained Internal Control Over Compliance as that term is defined in paragraph (c)(3)(ii) of this section;

§ 240.18a–7

(2) The Internal Control Over Compliance of the security-based swap dealer was effective during the most recent fiscal year;

(3) The Internal Control Over Compliance of the security-based swap dealer was effective as of the end of the most recent fiscal year;

(4) The security-based swap dealer was in compliance with §§ 240.18a–1 and 240.18a–4(c) as of the end of the most recent fiscal year; and

(5) The information the security-based swap dealer used to state whether it was in compliance with §§ 240.18a–1 and 240.18a–4(c) was derived from the books and records of the security-based swap dealer.

(B) If applicable, a description of each identified material weakness in the Internal Control Over Compliance of the security-based swap dealer during the most recent fiscal year.

(C) If applicable, a description of an instance of non-compliance with § 240.18a–1 or § 240.18a–4(c) as of the end of the most recent fiscal year.

(ii) The term *Internal Control Over Compliance* means internal controls that have the objective of providing the security-based swap dealer with reasonable assurance that non-compliance with § 240.18a–1, § 240.18a–4(c), § 240.18a–9, or § 240.17a–13, as applicable, will be prevented or detected on a timely basis.

(iii) The security-based swap dealer is not permitted to conclude that its Internal Control Over Compliance was effective during the most recent fiscal year if there were one or more material weaknesses in its Internal Control Over Compliance during the most recent fiscal year. The security-based swap dealer is not permitted to conclude that its Internal Control Over Compliance was effective as of the end of the most recent fiscal year if there were one or more material weaknesses in its internal control as of the end of the most recent fiscal year. A *material weakness* is a deficiency, or a combination of deficiencies, in Internal Control Over Compliance such that there is a reasonable possibility that non-compliance with § 240.18a–1 or § 240.18a–4(c) will not be prevented, or detected on a timely basis or that non-compliance to a material extent with § 240.18a–4, except for paragraph (c), or § 240.18a–9 or § 240.17a–13, as applicable, will not be prevented or detected on a timely basis. A deficiency in Internal Control Over Compliance exists when the design or operation of a control does not allow the management or employees of the security-based swap dealer in the normal course of performing their assigned functions, to prevent or detect on a timely basis non-compliance with § 240.18a–1, § 240.18a–4, § 240.18a–9, or § 240.17a–13, as applicable.

(4) *Exemption report.* The exemption report must contain the following statements made to the best knowledge and belief of the security-based swap dealer:

(i) A statement that the security-based swap dealer met the exemption provisions in § 240.18a–4(f) throughout the most recent fiscal year without exception or that it met the exemption provisions in § 240.18a–4(f) throughout the most recent fiscal year except as described under paragraph (c)(4)(ii) of this section; and

(ii) If applicable, a statement that identifies each exception during the most recent fiscal year in meeting the exemption provisions in § 240.18a–4(f) and that briefly describes the nature of each exception and the approximate date(s) on which the exception existed.

(5) *Timing of filing.* The annual reports must be filed not more than sixty (60) calendar days after the end of the fiscal year of the security-based swap dealer or major security-based swap participant.

(6) *Location of filing.* The annual reports must be filed with the Commission at the regional office of the Commission for the region in which the security-based swap dealer or major security-based swap participant has its principal place of business and the Commission's principal office in Washington, DC, or the annual reports may be filed with the Commission electronically in accordance with directions provided on the Commission's website.

(d) *Nature and form of reports.* The annual reports filed pursuant to paragraph (c) of this section must be prepared and filed in accordance with the following requirements:

Securities and Exchange Commission §240.18a-7

(1)(i) The security-based swap dealer or major security-based swap participant must attach to each of the confidential and non-confidential portions of the annual reports separately bound under paragraph (d)(2) of this section a complete and executed Part III of Form X-17A-5 (§249.617 of this chapter). The security-based swap dealer or major security-based swap participant must attach to the financial report an oath or affirmation that, to the best knowledge and belief of the person making the oath or affirmation:

(A) The financial report is true and correct; and

(B) Neither the registrant, nor any partner, officer, director, or equivalent person, as the case may be, has any proprietary interest in any account classified solely as that of a customer.

(ii) The oath or affirmation must be made before a person duly authorized to administer such oaths or affirmations. If the security-based swap dealer or major security-based swap participant is a sole proprietorship, the oath or affirmation must be made by the proprietor; if a partnership, by a general partner; if a corporation, by a duly authorized officer; or if a limited liability company or limited liability partnership, by the chief executive officer, chief financial officer, manager, managing member, or those members vested with management authority for the limited liability company or limited liability partnership.

(2) The annual reports filed under paragraph (c) of this section are not confidential, except that, if the Statement of Financial Condition is in a format that is consistent with Part II of Form X-17A-5 (§249.617 of this chapter), and is bound separately from the balance of the annual reports filed under paragraph (c) of this section, and each page of the balance of the annual report is stamped "confidential," then the balance of the annual reports will be deemed confidential to the extent permitted by law. However, the annual reports, including the confidential portions, will be available for official use by any official or employee of the U.S. or any State, and by any other person if the Commission authorizes disclosure of the annual reports to that person as being in the public interest. Nothing contained in this paragraph (d)(2) may be construed to be in derogation of the right of customers of a security-based swap dealer or major security-based swap participant, upon request to the security-based swap dealer or major security-based swap participant, to obtain information relative to its financial condition.

(e) *Independent public accountant*—(1) *Qualifications of independent public accountant.* The independent public accountant must be qualified and independent in accordance with §210.2-01 of this chapter.

(2) *Statement regarding independent public accountant.* (i) Every security-based swap dealer or major security-based swap participant that is required to file annual reports under paragraph (c) of this section must file no later than December 10 of each year (or 30 days after effective date of its registration as a security-based swap dealer or major security-based swap participant if earlier) a statement as prescribed in paragraph (e)(2)(ii) of this section with the Commission's principal office in Washington, DC and the regional office of the Commission for the region in which its principal place of business is located. The statement must be dated no later than December 1 (or 20 calendar days after the effective date of its registration as a security-based swap dealer or major security-based swap participant, if earlier). If the engagement of an independent public accountant is of a continuing nature, providing for successive engagements, no further filing is required. If the engagement is for a single year, or if the most recent engagement has been terminated or amended, a new statement must be filed by the required date.

(ii) The statement must be headed "Statement regarding independent public accountant under Rule 18a-7(e)(2)" and must contain the following information and representations:

(A) Name, address, telephone number and registration number of the security-based swap dealer or major security-based swap participant.

(B) Name, address, and telephone number of the independent public accountant.

(C) The date of the fiscal year of the annual reports of the security-based

765

§ 240.18a-7

swap dealer or major security-based swap participant covered by the engagement.

(D) Whether the engagement is for a single year or is of a continuing nature.

(E) A representation that the independent public accountant has undertaken the items enumerated in paragraphs (f)(1) and (2) of this section.

(3) *Replacement of accountant.* A security-based swap dealer or major security-based swap participant must file a notice that must be received by the Commission's principal office in Washington, DC and the regional office of the Commission for the region in which its principal place of business is located not more than 15 business days after:

(i) The security-based swap dealer or major security-based swap participant has notified the independent public accountant that provided the reports the security-based swap dealer or major security-based swap participant filed under paragraph (c)(1)(i)(C) of this section for the most recent fiscal year that the independent public accountant's services will not be used in future engagements; or

(ii) The security-based swap dealer or major security-based swap participant has notified an independent public accountant that was engaged to provide the reports required under paragraph (c)(1)(i)(C) of this section that the engagement has been terminated; or

(iii) An independent public accountant has notified the security-based swap dealer or major security-based swap participant that the independent public accountant would not continue under an engagement to provide the reports required under paragraph (c)(1)(i)(C) of this section; or

(iv) A new independent public accountant has been engaged to provide the reports required under paragraph (c)(1)(i)(C) of this section without any notice of termination having been given to or by the previously engaged independent public accountant.

(v) The notice must include:

(A) The date of notification of the termination of the engagement or of the engagement of the new independent public accountant, as applicable; and

(B) The details of any issues arising during the 24 months (or the period of the engagement, if less than 24 months) preceding the termination or new engagement relating to any matter of accounting principles or practices, financial statement disclosure, auditing scope or procedure, or compliance with applicable rules of the Commission, which issues, if not resolved to the satisfaction of the former independent public accountant, would have caused the independent public accountant to make reference to them in the report of the independent public accountant. The issues required to be reported include both those resolved to the former independent public accountant's satisfaction and those not resolved to the former accountant's satisfaction. Issues contemplated by this section are those which occur at the decision-making level—that is, between principal financial officers of the security-based swap dealer or major security-based swap participant and personnel of the accounting firm responsible for rendering its report. The notice must also state whether the accountant's report filed under paragraph (c)(1)(i)(C) of this section for any of the past two fiscal years contained an adverse opinion or a disclaimer of opinion or was qualified as to uncertainties, audit scope, or accounting principles, and must describe the nature of each such adverse opinion, disclaimer of opinion, or qualification. The security-based swap dealer or major security-based swap participant must also request the former independent public accountant to furnish the security-based swap dealer or major security-based swap participant with a letter addressed to the Commission stating whether the independent public accountant agrees with the statements contained in the notice of the security-based swap dealer or major security-based swap participant and, if not, stating the respects in which the independent public accountant does not agree. The security-based swap dealer or major security-based swap participant must file three copies of the notice and the accountant's letter, one copy of which must be manually signed by the sole proprietor, or a general partner or a duly authorized corporate, limited liability company,

Securities and Exchange Commission § 240.18a-7

or limited liability partnership officer or member, as appropriate, and by the independent public accountant, respectively.

(f) *Engagement of the independent public accountant.* The independent public accountant engaged by the security-based swap dealer or major security-based swap participant to provide the reports required under paragraph (c)(1)(i)(C) of this section must, as part of the engagement, undertake the following, as applicable:

(1) To prepare an independent public accountant's report based on an examination of the financial report required to be filed by the security-based swap dealer or major security-based swap participant under paragraph (c)(1)(i)(A) of this section in accordance with generally accepted auditing standards in the United States or the standards of the Public Company Accounting Oversight Board; and

(2)(i) To prepare an independent public accountant's report based on an examination of the statements required under paragraphs (c)(3)(i)(A)(*2*) through (*5*) of this section in the compliance report required to be filed by the security-based swap dealer under paragraph (c)(1)(i)(B)(*1*) of this section in accordance with generally accepted auditing standards in the United States or the standards of the Public Company Accounting Oversight Board; or

(ii) To prepare an independent public accountant's report based on a review of the statements required under paragraphs (c)(4)(i) through (ii) of this section in the exemption report required to be filed by the security-based swap dealer under paragraph (c)(1)(i)(B)(*2*) of this section in accordance with generally accepted auditing standards in the United States or the standards of the Public Company Accounting Oversight Board.

(g) *Notification of non-compliance or material weakness.* If, during the course of preparing the independent public accountant's reports required under paragraph (c)(1)(i)(C) of this section, the independent public accountant determines that:

(1) A security-based swap dealer is not in compliance with § 240.18a-1, § 240.18a-4, § 240.18a-9, or § 240.17a-13, as applicable, or the independent public accountant determines that any material weaknesses (as defined in paragraph (c)(3)(iii) of this section) exist, the independent public accountant must immediately notify the chief financial officer of the security-based swap dealer of the nature of the non-compliance or material weakness. If the notice from the accountant concerns an instance of non-compliance that would require a security-based swap dealer to provide a notification under § 240.18a-8, or if the notice concerns a material weakness, the security-based swap dealer must provide a notification in accordance with § 240.18a-8, as applicable, and provide a copy of the notification to the independent public accountant. If the independent public accountant does not receive the notification within one business day, or if the independent public accountant does not agree with the statements in the notification, then the independent public accountant must notify the Commission within one business day. The report from the accountant must, if the security-based swap dealer failed to file a notification, describe any instances of non-compliance that required a notification under § 240.18a-8 or any material weakness. If the security-based swap dealer filed a notification, the report from the accountant must detail the aspects of the notification of the security-based swap dealer with which the accountant does not agree; or

(2) A major security-based swap participant is not in compliance with § 240.18a-2, the independent public accountant must immediately notify the chief financial officer of the major security-based swap participant of the nature of the non-compliance. If the notice from the accountant concerns an instance of non-compliance that would require a major security-based swap participant to provide a notification under § 240.18a-8, the major security-based swap participant must provide a notification in accordance with § 240.18a-8 and provide a copy of the notification to the independent public accountant. If the independent public accountant does not receive the notification within one business day, or if the independent public accountant does not agree with the statements in the

§ 240.18a-7

notification, then the independent public accountant must notify the Commission within one business day. The report from the accountant must, if the major security-based swap participant failed to file a notification, describe any instances of non-compliance that required a notification under § 240.18a-8. If the major security-based swap participant filed a notification, the report from the accountant must detail the aspects of the notification of the major security-based swap participant with which the accountant does not agree.

NOTE 1 TO PARAGRAPH (g): The attention of the security-based swap dealer, major security-based swap participant, and the independent public accountant is called to the fact that under § 240.18a-8(a), among other things, a security-based swap dealer or major security-based swap participant whose net capital or tangible net worth, as applicable, declines below the minimum required pursuant to § 240.18a-1 or § 240.18a-2, as applicable, must give notice of such deficiency that same day in accordance with § 240.18a-8(h) and the notice must specify the security-based swap dealer's net capital requirement and its current amount of net capital, or the extent of the major security-based swap participant's failure to maintain positive tangible net worth, as applicable.

(h) *Reports of the independent public accountant required under paragraph (c)(1)(i)(C) of this section*—(1) *Technical requirements.* The independent public accountant's reports must:

(i) Be dated;

(ii) Be signed manually;

(iii) Indicate the city and state where issued; and

(iv) Identify without detailed enumeration the items covered by the reports.

(2) *Representations.* The independent public accountant's reports must:

(i) State whether the examinations were made in accordance with generally accepted auditing standards in the United States or the standards of the Public Company Accounting Oversight Board; and

(ii) Identify any examination procedures deemed necessary by the independent public accountant under the circumstances of the particular case which have been omitted and the reason for their omission.

(iii) Nothing in this section may be construed to imply authority for the omission of any procedure that independent public accountants would ordinarily employ in the course of an examination for the purpose of expressing the opinions required under this section.

(3) *Opinion to be expressed.* The independent public accountant's reports must state clearly:

(i) The opinion of the independent public accountant with respect to the financial report required under paragraph (c)(1)(i)(C) of this section and the accounting principles and practices reflected in that report;

(ii) The opinion of the independent public accountant with respect to the financial report required under paragraph (c)(1)(i)(C) of this section, as to the consistency of the application of the accounting principles, or as to any changes in those principles which have a material effect on the financial statements; and

(iii)(A) The opinion of the independent public accountant with respect to the statements required under paragraphs (c)(3)(i)(A)(*2*) through (*5*) of this section in the compliance report required under paragraph (c)(1)(i)(B)(*1*) of this section; or

(B) The conclusion of the independent public accountant with respect to the statements required under paragraphs (c)(4)(i) and (ii) of this section in the exemption report required under paragraph (c)(1)(i)(B)(*2*) of this section.

(4) *Exceptions.* Any matters to which the independent public accountant takes exception must be clearly identified, the exceptions must be specifically and clearly stated, and, to the extent practicable, the effect of each such exception on any related items contained in the annual reports required under paragraph (c) of this section must be given.

(i) *Notification of change of fiscal year.* (1) In the event any security-based swap dealer or major security-based swap participant for which there is no prudential regulator finds it necessary to change its fiscal year, it must file, with the Commission's principal office in Washington, DC and the regional office of the Commission for the region

Securities and Exchange Commission § 240.18a-8

in which the security-based swap dealer or major security-based swap participant has its principal place of business, a notice of such change.

(2) Such notice must contain a detailed explanation of the reasons for the change. Any change in the filing period for the annual reports must be approved by the Commission.

(j) *Filing requirements.* For purposes of filing requirements as described in this section, filing will be deemed to have been accomplished upon receipt at the Commission's principal office in Washington, DC, with duplicate originals simultaneously filed at the locations prescribed in the particular paragraph of this section which is applicable.

[84 FR 68662, Dec. 16, 2019]

§ 240.18a-8 **Notification provisions for security-based swap dealers and major security-based swap participants.**

This section applies to the following types of entities: A security-based swap dealer registered pursuant to section 15F of the Act (15 U.S.C. 78*o*-10) that is not also a broker or dealer, other than an *OTC derivatives dealer* as that term is defined in § 240.3b-12, registered pursuant to section 15 of the Act (15 U.S.C. 78*o*); a security-based swap dealer registered pursuant to section 15F of the Act that is also an OTC derivatives dealer; and a major security-based swap participant registered pursuant to section 15F of the Act that is not also a broker or dealer, including an OTC derivatives dealer, registered pursuant to section 15 of the Act. Section 240.17a-11 (rather than this section) applies to the following types of entities: Except as provided above, a broker or dealer, including an OTC derivatives dealer, registered pursuant to section 15 of the Act; a broker or dealer, other than an OTC derivatives dealer, registered pursuant to section 15 of the Act that is also a security-based swap dealer registered pursuant to section 15F of the Act; and a broker or dealer, including an OTC derivatives dealer, registered pursuant to section 15 of the Act that is also a major-security-based swap participant registered pursuant to section 15F of the Act.

(a)(1)(i) Every security-based swap dealer for which there is no prudential regulator whose net capital declines below the minimum amount required pursuant to § 240.18a-1 must give notice of such deficiency that same day in accordance with paragraph (h) of this section. The notice must specify the security-based swap dealer's net capital requirement and its current amount of net capital. If a security-based swap dealer is informed by the Commission that it is, or has been, in violation of § 240.18a-1 and the security-based swap dealer has not given notice of the capital deficiency under this section, the security-based swap dealer, even if it does not agree that it is, or has been, in violation of § 240.18a-1, must give notice of the claimed deficiency, which notice may specify the security-based swap dealer's reasons for its disagreement.

(ii) Every security-based swap dealer for which there is no prudential regulator whose tentative net capital declines below the minimum amount required pursuant to § 240.18a-1 must give notice of such deficiency that same day in accordance with paragraph (h) of this section. The notice must specify the security-based swap dealer's tentative net capital requirement and its current amount of tentative net capital. If a security-based swap is informed by the Commission that it is, or has been, in violation of § 240.18a-1 and the security-based swap dealer has not given notice of the capital deficiency under this section, the security-based swap dealer, even if it does not agree that it is, or has been, in violation of § 240.18a-1, must give notice of the claimed deficiency, which notice may specify the security-based swap dealer's reasons for its disagreement.

(2) Every major security-based swap participant for which there is no prudential regulator who fails to maintain a positive tangible net worth pursuant to § 240.18a-2 must give notice of such deficiency that same day in accordance with paragraph (h) of this section. The notice must specify the extent to which the firm has failed to maintain positive tangible net worth. If a major security-based swap participant is informed by the Commission that it is, or has been, in violation of § 240.18a-2 and the major security-based swap participant has not given notice of the capital

§ 240.18a-8

deficiency under this section, the major security-based swap participant, even if it does not agree that it is, or has been, in violation of § 240.18a-2, must give notice of the claimed deficiency, which notice may specify the major security-based swap participant's reasons for its disagreement.

(b) Every security-based swap dealer or major security-based swap participant for which there is no prudential regulator must send notice promptly (but within 24 hours) after the occurrence of the events specified in paragraphs (b)(1) through (3) or paragraph (b)(4) of this section, as applicable, in accordance with paragraph (h) of this section:

(1) If a computation made by a security-based swap dealer pursuant to § 240.18a-1 shows that its total net capital is less than 120 percent of the security-based swap dealer's required minimum net capital;

(2) If a computation made by a security-based swap dealer authorized by the Commission to compute net capital pursuant to § 240.18a-1(d) shows that its total tentative net capital is less than 120 percent of the security-based swap dealer's required minimum tentative net capital;

(3) If the level of tangible net worth of a major security-based swap participant falls below $20 million; and

(4) The occurrence of the fourth and each subsequent backtesting exception under § 240.18a-1(d)(9) during any 250 business day measurement period.

(c) Every security-based swap dealer that files a notice of adjustment of its reported capital category with the Federal Reserve Board, the Office of the Comptroller of the Currency or the Federal Deposit Insurance Corporation must give notice of this fact that same day by transmitting a copy notice of the adjustment of reported capital category in accordance with paragraph (h) of this section.

(d) Every security-based swap dealer or major security-based swap participant that fails to make and keep current the books and records required by § 240.18a-5 or § 240.17a-3, as applicable, must give notice of this fact that same day in accordance with paragraph (h) of this section, specifying the books and records which have not been made or which are not current. The security-based swap dealer or major security-based swap participant must also transmit a report in accordance with paragraph (h) of this section within 48 hours of the notice stating what the security-based swap dealer or major security-based swap participant has done or is doing to correct the situation.

(e) Whenever any security-based swap dealer for which there is no prudential regulator discovers, or is notified by an independent public accountant under § 240.18a-7(g), of the existence of any material weakness, as defined in § 240.18a-7(c)(3)(iii), the security-based swap dealer must:

(1) Give notice, in accordance with paragraph (h) of this section, of the material weakness within 24 hours of the discovery or notification of the material weakness; and

(2) Transmit a report in accordance with paragraph (h) of this section, within 48 hours of the notice stating what the security-based swap dealer has done or is doing to correct the situation.

(f) [Reserved]

(g) If a security-based swap dealer fails to make in its special reserve account for the exclusive benefit of security-based swap customers a deposit, as required by § 240.18a-4(c), the security-based swap dealer must give immediate notice in writing in accordance with paragraph (h) of this section.

(h) Every notice or report required to be given or transmitted by this section must be given or transmitted to the principal office of the Commission in Washington, DC and the regional office of the Commission for the region in which the security-based swap dealer or major security-based swap participant has its principal place of business, or to an email address provided on the Commission's website, and to the Commodity Futures Trading Commission (CFTC) if the security-based swap dealer or major security-based swap participant is registered as a futures commission merchant with the CFTC. The report required by paragraph (d) or (e)(2) of this section may be transmitted by overnight delivery.

[84 FR 68667, Dec. 16, 2019]

Securities and Exchange Commission § 240.18a-9

§ 240.18a-9 Quarterly security counts to be made by certain security-based swap dealers.

This section applies to a security-based swap dealer registered pursuant to section 15F of the Act (15 U.S.C. 78*o*-10) that does not have a prudential regulator and that is not also a broker or dealer, including an *OTC derivatives dealer* as that term is defined in § 240.3b-12, registered pursuant to section 15 of the Act (15 U.S.C. 78*o*). Section 240.17a-13 (rather than this section) applies to the following entities (if not exempt under the provisions of § 240.17a-13): A member of a national securities exchange who transacts a business in securities directly with others than members of a national securities exchange; a broker or dealer who transacts a business in securities through the medium of a member of a national securities exchange; a broker or dealer, including an OTC derivatives dealer, registered pursuant to section 15 of the Act; a security-based swap dealer registered pursuant to section 15F of the Act that is also a broker or dealer, including an OTC derivatives dealer, registered pursuant to section 15 of the Act; and a major security-based swap participant that is also a broker or dealer, including an OTC derivatives dealer, registered pursuant to section 15 of the Act.

(a) Any security-based swap dealer that is subject to the provisions of this section must at least once in each calendar quarter-year:

(1) Physically examine and count all securities held including securities that are the subjects of repurchase or reverse repurchase agreements;

(2) Account for all securities in transfer, in transit, pledged, loaned, borrowed, deposited, failed to receive, failed to deliver, subject to repurchase or reverse repurchase agreements or otherwise subject to its control or direction but not in its physical possession by examination and comparison of the supporting detailed records with the appropriate ledger control accounts;

(3) Verify all securities in transfer, in transit, pledged, loaned, borrowed, deposited, failed to receive, failed to deliver, subject to repurchase or reverse repurchase agreements or otherwise subject to its control or direction but not in its physical possession, where such securities have been in said status for longer than thirty days;

(4) Compare the results of the count and verification with its records; and

(5) Record on the books and records of the security-based swap dealer all unresolved differences setting forth the security involved and date of comparison in a security count difference account no later than 7 business days after the date of each required quarterly security examination, count, and verification in accordance with the requirements provided in paragraph (b) of this section. *Provided, however,* that no examination, count, verification, and comparison for the purpose of this section is within 2 months of or more than 4 months following a prior examination, count, verification, and comparison made under this paragraph (a)(5).

(b) The examination, count, verification, and comparison may be made either as of a date certain or on a cyclical basis covering the entire list of securities. In either case the recordation must be effected within 7 business days subsequent to the examination, count, verification, and comparison of a particular security. In the event that an examination, count, verification, and comparison is made on a cyclical basis, it may not extend over more than 1 calendar quarter-year, and no security may be examined, counted, verified, or compared for the purpose of this section within 2 months of or more than 4 months after a prior examination, count, verification, and comparison.

(c) The examination, count, verification, and comparison must be made or supervised by persons whose regular duties do not require them to have direct responsibility for the proper care and protection of the securities or the making or preservation of the subject records.

[84 FR 68668, Dec. 16, 2019]

§ 240.18a-10 Alternative compliance mechanism for security-based swap dealers that are registered as swap dealers and have limited security-based swap activities.

(a) A security-based swap dealer may comply with capital, margin, segregation, recordkeeping, and reporting requirements of the Commodity Exchange Act and chapter I of this title applicable to swap dealers in lieu of complying with §§ 240.18a-1 and 240.18a-3 through 240.18a-9 if:

(1) The security-based swap dealer is registered as such pursuant to section 15F(b) of the Act and the rules thereunder;

(2) The security-based swap dealer is registered as a swap dealer pursuant to section 4s of the Commodity Exchange Act and the rules thereunder;

(3) The security-based swap dealer is not registered as a broker or dealer pursuant to section 15 of the Act or the rules thereunder;

(4) The security-based swap dealer meets the conditions to be exempt from § 240.18a-4 specified in paragraph (f) of that section; and

(5) As of the most recently ended quarter of the fiscal year of the security-based swap dealer, the aggregate gross notional amount of the outstanding security-based swap positions of the security-based swap dealer did not exceed the lesser of the maximum fixed-dollar amount specified in paragraph (f) of this section or 10 percent of the combined aggregate gross notional amount of the security-based swap and swap positions of the security-based swap dealer.

(b) A security-based swap dealer operating under this section must:

(1) Comply with capital, margin, segregation, recordkeeping, and reporting requirements of the Commodity Exchange Act and chapter I of this title applicable to swap dealers and treat security-based swaps or collateral related to security-based swaps as swaps or collateral related to swaps, as applicable, pursuant to those requirements to the extent the requirements do not specifically address security-based swaps or collateral related to security-based swaps;

(2) Disclose in writing to each counterparty to a security-based swap before entering into the first transaction with the counterparty after the date the security-based swap dealer begins operating under this section that the security-based swap dealer is operating under this section and is therefore complying with the applicable capital, margin, segregation, recordkeeping, and reporting requirements of the Commodity Exchange Act and the rules promulgated by the Commodity Futures Trading Commission thereunder in lieu of complying with the capital, margin, segregation, recordkeeping, and reporting requirements promulgated by the Commission in §§ 240.18a-1 and 240.18a-3 through 240.18a-9;

(3) Immediately notify the Commission and the Commodity Futures Trading Commission in writing if the security-based swap dealer fails to meet a condition specified in paragraph (a) of this section;

(4) Simultaneously notify the Commission if the security-based swap dealer is required to send a notice concerning its capital, books and records, liquidity, margin operations, or segregation operations to the Commodity Futures Trading Commission by transmitting to the Commission a copy of the notice being sent to the Commodity Futures Trading Commission; and

(5) Furnish promptly to a representative of the Commission legible, true, complete, and current copies of those records of the security-based swap dealer that are required to be preserved under the Commodity Exchange Act and chapter I of this title applicable to swap dealers, or any other records of the security-based swap dealer subject to examination pursuant to section 15F of the Act (15 U.S.C. 78o-10) that are requested by a representative of the Commission.

(c) A security-based swap dealer that fails to meet one or more of the conditions specified in paragraph (a) of this section must begin complying with §§ 240.18a-1 and 240.18a-3 through 240.18a-9 no later than:

(1) Two months after the end of the month in which the security-based swap dealer fails to meet a condition in paragraph (a) of this section; or

Securities and Exchange Commission § 240.19b–4

(2) A longer period of time as granted by the Commission by order subject to any conditions imposed by the Commission.

(d)(1) A person applying to register as a security-based swap dealer that intends to operate under this section beginning on the date of its registration must provide prior written notice to the Commission and the Commodity Futures Trading Commission of its intent to operate under the conditions of this section.

(2) A security-based swap dealer that elects to operate under this section beginning on a date after the date of its registration as a security-based swap dealer must:

(i) Provide prior written notice to the Commission and the Commodity Futures Trading Commission of its intent to operate under the conditions of this section; and

(ii) Continue to comply with §§ 240.18a–1 and 240.18a–3 through 240.18a–9 for at least:

(A) Two months after the end of the month in which the security-based swap dealer provides the notice; or

(B) A shorter period of time as granted by the Commission by order subject to any conditions imposed by the Commission.

(e) The notices required by this section must be sent by facsimile transmission to the principal office of the Commission and the regional office of the Commission for the region in which the security-based swap dealer has its principal place of business or to an email address provided on the Commission's website, and to the principal office of the Commodity Futures Trading Commission in a manner consistent with the notification requirements of the Commodity Futures Trading Commission. The notice must include a brief summary of the reason for the notice and the contact information of an individual who can provide further information about the matter that is the subject of the notice.

(f)(1) The maximum fixed-dollar amount is $250 billion until the three-year anniversary of the compliance date of this section at which time the maximum fixed-dollar amount is $50 billion unless the Commission issues an order to:

(i) Maintain the maximum fixed-dollar amount at $250 billion for an additional period of time or indefinitely; or

(ii) Lower the maximum fixed-dollar amount to an amount that is less than $250 billion but greater than $50 billion.

(2) If, after considering the levels of security-based swap activity of security-based swap dealers operating under this section, the Commission determines that it may be appropriate to change the maximum fixed-dollar amount pursuant paragraph (f)(1)(i) or (ii) of this section, the Commission will publish a notice of the potential change and subsequently will issue an order regarding any such change.

[84 FR 44076, Aug. 22, 2019, as amended at 84 FR 68668, Dec. 16, 2019]

SUSPENSION AND EXPULSION OF EXCHANGE MEMBERS

§ 240.19a3–1 [Reserved]

§ 240.19b–3 [Reserved]

§ 240.19b–4 **Filings with respect to proposed rule changes by self-regulatory organizations.**

(a) *Definitions.* As used in this section:

(1) The term *advance notice* means a notice required to be made by a designated clearing agency pursuant to Section 806(e) of the Payment, Clearing and Settlement Supervision Act (12 U.S.C. 5465(e));

(2) The term *designated clearing agency* means a clearing agency that is registered with the Commission, and for which the Commission is the Supervisory Agency (as determined in accordance with section 803(8) of the Payment, Clearing and Settlement Supervision Act (12 U.S.C. 5462(8)), that has been designated by the Financial Stability Oversight Council pursuant to section 804 of the Payment, Clearing and Settlement Supervision Act (12 U.S.C. 5463) as systemically important or likely to become systemically important;

(3) The term *Payment, Clearing and Settlement Supervision Act* means Title VIII of the Dodd-Frank Wall Street Reform and Consumer Protection Act (124 Stat. 1802, 1803, 1807, 1809, 1811, 1814, 1816, 1818, 1820, 1821; 12 U.S.C. 5461 *et seq.*);

§ 240.19b-4

(4) The term *proposed rule change* has the meaning set forth in Section 19(b)(1) of the Act (15 U.S.C. 78s(b)(1));

(5) The term *security-based swap submission* means a submission of identifying information required to be made by a clearing agency pursuant to section 3C(b)(2) of the Act (15 U.S.C. 78c-3(b)(2)) for each security-based swap, or any group, category, type or class of security-based swaps, that such clearing agency plans to accept for clearing;

(6) The term *stated policy, practice, or interpretation* means:

(i) Any material aspect of the operation of the facilities of the self-regulatory organization; or

(ii) Any statement made generally available to the membership of, to all participants in, or to persons having or seeking access (including, in the case of national securities exchanges or registered securities associations, through a member) to facilities of, the self-regulatory organization ("specified persons"), or to a group or category of specified persons, that establishes or changes any standard, limit, or guideline with respect to:

(A) The rights, obligations, or privileges of specified persons or, in the case of national securities exchanges or registered securities associations, persons associated with specified persons; or

(B) The meaning, administration, or enforcement of an existing rule.

(b)(1) Filings with respect to proposed rule changes by a self-regulatory organization, except filings with respect to proposed rules changes by self-regulatory organizations submitted pursuant to section 19(b)(7) of the Act (15 U.S.C. 78s(b)(7)), shall be made electronically on Form 19b-4 (17 CFR 249.819).

(2) For purposes of Section 19(b) of the Act and this rule, a "business day" is any day other than a Saturday, Sunday, Federal holiday, a day that the Office of Personnel Management has announced that Federal agencies in the Washington, DC area are closed to the public, a day on which the Commission is subject to a Federal government shutdown or a day on which the Commission's Washington, DC office is otherwise not open for regular business.

(c) A stated policy, practice, or interpretation of the self-regulatory organization shall be deemed to be a proposed rule change unless (1) it is reasonably and fairly implied by an existing rule of the self-regulatory organization or (2) it is concerned solely with the administration of the self-regulatory organization and is not a stated policy, practice, or interpretation with respect to the meaning, administration, or enforcement of an existing rule of the self-regulatory organization.

(d) Regardless of whether it is made generally available, an interpretation of an existing rule of the self-regulatory organization shall be deemed to be a proposed rule change if (1) it is approved or ratified by the governing body of the self-regulatory organization and (2) it is not reasonably and fairly implied by that rule.

(e) For the purposes of this paragraph, *new derivative securities product* means any type of option, warrant, hybrid securities product or any other security, other than a single equity option or a security futures product, whose value is based, in whole or in part, upon the performance of, or interest in, an underlying instrument.

(1) The listing and trading of a new derivative securities product by a self-regulatory organization shall not be deemed a proposed rule change, pursuant to paragraph (c)(1) of this section, if the Commission has approved, pursuant to section 19(b) of the Act (15 U.S.C. 78s(b)), the self-regulatory organization's trading rules, procedures and listing standards for the product class that would include the new derivative securities product and the self-regulatory organization has a surveillance program for the product class.

(2) Recordkeeping and reporting:

(i) Self-regulatory organizations shall retain at their principal place of business a file, available to Commission staff for inspection, of all relevant records and information pertaining to each new derivative securities product traded pursuant to this paragraph (e) for a period of not less than five years, the first two years in an easily accessible place, as prescribed in § 240.17a-1.

(ii) When relying on this paragraph (e), a self-regulatory organization shall submit Form 19b-4(e) (17 CFR 249.820) to the Commission within five business

Securities and Exchange Commission

§ 240.19b–4

days after commencement of trading a new derivative securities product.

(f) A proposed rule change may take effect upon filing with the Commission pursuant to Section 19(b)(3)(A) of the Act, 15 U.S.C. 78s(b)(3)(A), if properly designated by the self-regulatory organization as:

(1) Constituting a stated policy, practice, or interpretation with respect to the meaning, administration, or enforcement of an existing rule;

(2) Establishing or changing a due, fee, or other charge applicable only to a member;

(3) Concerned solely with the administration of the self-regulatory organization;

(4) Effecting a change in an existing service of a registered clearing agency that either:

(i)(A) Does not adversely affect the safeguarding of securities or funds in the custody or control of the clearing agency or for which it is responsible; and

(B) Does not significantly affect the respective rights or obligations of the clearing agency or persons using the service; or

(ii)(A) Primarily affects the clearing operations of the clearing agency with respect to products that are not securities, including futures that are not security futures, swaps that are not security-based swaps or mixed swaps, and forwards that are not security forwards; and

(B) Either

(*1*) Does not significantly affect any securities clearing operations of the clearing agency or any rights or obligations of the clearing agency with respect to securities clearing or persons using such securities-clearing service, or

(*2*) Does significantly affect any securities clearing operations of the clearing agency or the rights or obligations of the clearing agency with respect to securities clearing or persons using such securities-clearing service, but is necessary to maintain fair and orderly markets for products that are not securities, including futures that are not security futures, swaps that are not security-based swaps or mixed swaps, and forwards that are not security forwards. Proposed rule changes filed pursuant to this subparagraph II must also be filed in accordance with the procedures of Section 19(b)(1) for approval pursuant to Section 19(b)(2) and the regulations thereunder within fifteen days of being filed under Section 19(b)(3)(A).

(5) Effecting a change in an existing order-entry or trading system of a self-regulatory organization that:

(i) Does not significantly affect the protection of investors or the public interest;

(ii) Does not impose any significant burden on competition; and

(iii) Does not have the effect of limiting the access to or availability of the system; or

(6) Effecting a change that:

(i) Does not significantly affect the protection of investors or the public interest;

(ii) Does not impose any significant burden on competition; and

(iii) By its terms, does not become operative for 30 days after the date of the filing, or such shorter time as the Commission may designate if consistent with the protection of investors and the public interest; provided that the self-regulatory organization has given the Commission written notice of its intent to file the proposed rule change, along with a brief description and text of the proposed rule change, at least five business days prior to the date of filing of the proposed rule change, or such shorter time as designated by the Commission.

(g) Proceedings to determine whether a proposed rule change should be disapproved will be conducted pursuant to 17 CFR 201.700 and 201.701 (Initiation of Proceedings for SRO Proposed Rule Changes and for Proposed NMS Plans and Plan Amendments).

(h) Notice of orders issued pursuant to section 19(b) of the Act will be given by prompt publication thereof, together with a statement of written reasons therefor.

(i) Self-regulatory organizations shall retain at their principal place of business a file, available to interested persons for public inspection and copying, of all filings, notices and submissions made pursuant to this section

§ 240.19b-4

and all correspondence and other communications reduced to writing (including comment letters) to and from such self-regulatory organization concerning any such filing, notice or submission, whether such correspondence and communications are received or prepared before or after the filing, notice or submission of the proposed rule change, advance notice or security-based swap submission, as applicable.

(j) Filings by a self-regulatory organization submitted on Form 19b-4 (17 CFR 249.819) electronically shall contain an electronic signature. For the purposes of this section, the term *electronic signature* means an electronic entry in the form of a magnetic impulse or other form of computer data compilation of any letter or series of letters or characters comprising a name, executed, adopted or authorized as a signature. The signatory to an electronically submitted rule filing shall manually sign a signature page or other document, in the manner prescribed by Form 19b-4, authenticating, acknowledging or otherwise adopting his or her signature that appears in typed form within the electronic filing. Such document shall be executed before or at the time the rule filing is electronically submitted and shall be retained by the filer in accordance with § 240.17a-1.

(k) If the conditions of this section and Form 19b-4 (17 CFR 249.819) are otherwise satisfied, all filings submitted electronically on or before 5:30 p.m. Eastern Standard Time or Eastern Daylight Saving Time, whichever is currently in effect, on a business day, shall be deemed filed on that business day, and all filings submitted after 5:30 p.m. Eastern Standard Time or Eastern Daylight Saving Time, whichever is currently in effect, shall be deemed filed on the next business day.

(l) The self-regulatory organization shall post each proposed rule change, and any amendments thereto, on its Web site within two business days after the filing of the proposed rule change, and any amendments thereto, with the Commission. If a self-regulatory organization does not post a proposed rule change on its Web site on the same day that it filed the proposal with the Commission, then the self-regulatory organization shall inform the Commission of the date on which it posted such proposal on its Web site. Such proposed rule change and amendments shall be maintained on the self-regulatory organization's Web site until:

(1) In the case of a proposed rule change filed under section 19(b)(2) of the Act (15 U.S.C. 78s(b)(2)), the Commission approves or disapproves the proposed rule change or the self-regulatory organization withdraws the proposed rule change, or any amendments, or is notified that the proposed rule change is not properly filed; or

(2) In the case of a proposed rule change filed under section 19(b)(3)(A) of the Act (15 U.S.C. 78s(b)(3)(A)), or any amendment thereto, 60 days after the date of filing, unless the self-regulatory organization withdraws the proposed rule change or is notified that the proposed rule change is not properly filed; and

(3) In the case of proposed rule changes approved by the Commission pursuant to section 19(b)(2) of the Act (15 U.S.C. 78s(b)(2)) or noticed by the Commission pursuant to section 19(b)(3)(A) of the Act (15 U.S.C. 78s(b)(3)(A)), the self-regulatory organization updates its rule text as required by paragraph (m) of this section; and

(4) In the case of a proposed rule change, or any amendment thereto, that has been disapproved, withdrawn or not properly filed, the self-regulatory organization shall remove the proposed rule change, or any amendment, from its Web site within two business days of notification of disapproval, improper filing, or withdrawal by the SRO of the proposed rule change.

(m)(1) Each self-regulatory organization shall post and maintain a current and complete version of its rules on its Web site.

(2) A self-regulatory organization, other than a self-regulatory organization that is registered with the Commission under section 6(g) of the Act (15 U.S.C. 78f(g)) or pursuant to section 15A(k) of the Act (15 U.S.C. 78o-1(k)), shall update its Web site to reflect rule changes filed pursuant to section 19(b)(2) of the Act (15 U.S.C. 78s(b)(2)) within two business days after it has

Securities and Exchange Commission § 240.19b–4

been notified of the Commission's approval of a proposed rule change, and to reflect rule changes filed pursuant to section 19(b)(3)(A) of the Act (15 U.S.C. 78s(b)(3)(A)) within two business days of the Commission's notice of such proposed rule change.

(3) A self-regulatory organization that is registered with the Commission under section 6(g) of the Act (15 U.S.C. 78f(g)) or pursuant to section 15A(k) of the Act (15 U.S.C. 78o–1(k)), shall update its Web site to reflect rule changes filed pursuant to section 19(b)(2) of the Act by two business days after the later of:

(A) Notification that the Commission has approved a proposed rule change; and

(B)(i) The filing of a written certification with the Commodity Futures Trading Commission under section 5c(c) of the Commodity Exchange Act (7 U.S.C. 7a–2(c));

(ii) Receipt of notice from the Commodity Futures Trading Commission that it has determined that review of the proposed rule change is not necessary; or

(iii) Receipt of notice from the Commodity Futures Trading Commission that it has approved the proposed rule change.

(4) If a rule change is not effective for a certain period, the self-regulatory organization shall clearly indicate the effective date in the relevant rule text.

(n)(1)(i) A designated clearing agency shall provide an advance notice to the Commission of any proposed change to its rules, procedures, or operations that could materially affect the nature or level of risks presented by such designated clearing agency. Except as provided in paragraph (n)(1)(ii) of this section, such advance notice shall be submitted to the Commission electronically on Form 19b–4 (referenced in 17 CFR 249.819). The Commission shall, upon the filing of any advance notice, provide for prompt publication thereof.

(ii) Any designated clearing agency that files an advance notice with the Commission prior to December 10, 2013, shall file such advance notice in electronic format to a dedicated email address to be established by the Commission. The contents of an advance notice filed pursuant to this paragraph (n)(1)(ii) shall contain the information required to be included for advance notices in the General Instructions for Form 19b–4 (referenced in 17 CFR 249.819).

(2)(i) For purposes of this paragraph (n), the phrase *materially affect the nature or level of risks presented*, when used to qualify determinations on a change to rules, procedures, or operations at the designated clearing agency, means matters as to which there is a reasonable possibility that the change could affect the performance of essential clearing and settlement functions or the overall nature or level of risk presented by the designated clearing agency.

(ii) Changes to rules, procedures, or operations that could materially affect the nature or level of risks presented by a designated clearing agency may include, but are not limited to, changes that materially affect participant and product eligibility, risk management, daily or intraday settlement procedures, default procedures, system safeguards, governance or financial resources of the designated clearing agency.

(iii) Changes to rules, procedures, or operations that may not materially affect the nature or level of risks presented by a designated clearing agency include, but are not limited to:

(A) Changes to an existing procedure, control, or service that do not modify the rights or obligations of the designated clearing agency or persons using its payment, clearing, or settlement services and that do not adversely affect the safeguarding of securities, collateral, or funds in the custody or control of the designated clearing agency or for which it is responsible; or

(B) Changes concerned solely with the administration of the designated clearing agency or related to the routine, daily administration, direction, and control of employees;

(3) The designated clearing agency shall post the advance notice, and any amendments thereto, on its Web site within two business days after the filing of the advance notice, and any amendments thereto, with the Commission. Such advance notice and amendments shall be maintained on

§ 240.19b-4

the designated clearing agency's Web site until the earlier of:

(i) The date the designated clearing agency withdraws the advance notice or is notified that the advance notice is not properly filed; or

(ii) The date the designated clearing agency posts a notice of effectiveness as required by paragraph (n)(4)(ii) of this section.

(4)(i) The designated clearing agency shall post a notice on its Web site within two business days of the date that any change to its rules, procedures, or operations referred to in an advance notice has been permitted to take effect as such date is determined in accordance with Section 806(e) of the Payment, Clearing and Settlement Supervision Act (12 U.S.C. 5465).

(ii) The designated clearing agency shall post a notice on its Web site within two business days of the effectiveness of any change to its rules, procedures, or operations referred to in an advance notice.

(5) A designated clearing agency shall provide copies of all materials submitted to the Commission relating to an advance notice with the Board of Governors of the Federal Reserve System contemporaneously with such submission to the Commission.

(6) The publication and Web site posting requirements contained in paragraphs (n)(1), (n)(3), and (n)(4) of this section do not apply to any information contained in an advance notice for which a designated clearing agency has requested confidential treatment following the procedures set forth in § 240.24b-2.

(o)(1) Every clearing agency that is registered with the Commission that plans to accept a security-based swap, or any group, category, type, or class of security-based swaps for clearing shall submit to the Commission a security-based swap submission and provide notice to its members of such security-based swap submission.

(2)(i) Except as provided in paragraph (o)(2)(ii) of this section, a clearing agency shall submit each security-based swap submission to the Commission electronically on Form 19b-4 (referenced in 17 CFR 249.819) with the information required to be submitted for a security-based swap submission, as

17 CFR Ch. II (4-1-23 Edition)

provided in § 240.19b-4 and Form 19b-4. Any information submitted to the Commission electronically on Form 19b-4 that is not complete or otherwise in compliance with this section and Form 19b-4 shall not be considered a security-based swap submission and the Commission shall so inform the clearing agency within twenty-one business days of the submission on Form 19b-4 (referenced in 17 CFR 249.819).

(ii) Any clearing agency that files a security-based swap submission with the Commission prior to December 10, 2013, shall file such security-based swap submission in electronic format to a dedicated email address to be established by the Commission. The contents of a security-based swap submission filed pursuant to this paragraph (o)(2)(ii) shall contain the information required to be included for security-based swap submissions in the General Instructions for Form 19b-4.

(3) A security-based swap submission submitted by a clearing agency to the Commission shall include a statement that includes, but is not limited to:

(i) How the security-based swap submission is consistent with Section 17A of the Act (15 U.S.C. 78q-1);

(ii) Information that will assist the Commission in the quantitative and qualitative assessment of the factors specified in Section 3C of the Act (15 U.S.C. 78c-3), including, but not limited to:

(A) The existence of significant outstanding notional exposures, trading liquidity, and adequate pricing data;

(B) The availability of a rule framework, capacity, operational expertise and resources, and credit support infrastructure to clear the contract on terms that are consistent with the material terms and trading conventions on which the contract is then traded;

(C) The effect on the mitigation of systemic risk, taking into account the size of the market for such contract and the resources of the clearing agency available to clear the contract;

(D) The effect on competition, including appropriate fees and charges applied to clearing; and

(E) The existence of reasonable legal certainty in the event of the insolvency of the relevant clearing agency

778

Securities and Exchange Commission § 240.19b–5

or one or more of its clearing members with regard to the treatment of customer and security-based swap counterparty positions, funds, and property;

(iii) A description of how the rules of the clearing agency prescribe that all security-based swaps submitted to the clearing agency with the same terms and conditions are economically equivalent within the clearing agency and may be offset with each other within the clearing agency, as applicable to the security-based swaps described in the security-based swap submission; and

(iv) A description of how the rules of the clearing agency provide for non-discriminatory clearing of a security-based swap executed bilaterally or on or through the rules of an unaffiliated national securities exchange or security-based swap execution facility, as applicable to the security-based swaps described in the security-based swap submission.

(4) A clearing agency shall submit security-based swaps to the Commission for review by group, category, type or class of security-based swaps, to the extent reasonable and practicable to do so.

(5) A clearing agency shall post each security-based swap submission, and any amendments thereto, on its Web site within two business days after the submission of the security-based swap submission, and any amendments thereto, with the Commission. Such security-based swap submission and amendments shall be maintained on the clearing agency's Web site until the Commission makes a determination regarding the security-based swap submission or the clearing agency withdraws the security-based swap submission, or is notified that the security-based swap submission is not properly filed.

(6) In connection with any security-based swap submission that is submitted by a clearing agency to the Commission, the clearing agency shall provide any additional information requested by the Commission as necessary to assess any of the factors it determines to be appropriate in order to make the determination of whether the clearing requirement applies.

(7) Notices of orders issued pursuant to Section 3C of the Act (15 U.S.C. 78c–3), regarding security-based swap submissions will be given by prompt publication thereof, together with a statement of written reasons therefor.

[45 FR 73914, Nov. 7, 1980, as amended at 59 FR 66701, Dec. 28, 1994; 63 FR 70967, Dec. 22, 1998; 66 FR 43742, Aug. 20, 2001; 69 FR 60300, Oct. 8, 2004; 73 FR 16189, Mar. 27, 2008; 76 FR 4072, Jan. 24, 2011; 76 FR 20509, Apr. 13, 2011; 76 FR 41092, July 13, 2011; 77 FR 41648, July 13, 2012; 77 FR 73305, Dec. 10, 2012; 78 FR 21057, Apr. 9, 2013; 85 FR 65497, Oct. 15, 2020]

§ 240.19b–5 Temporary exemption from the filing requirements of Section 19(b) of the Act.

PRELIMINARY NOTES

1. The following section provides for a temporary exemption from the rule filing requirement for self-regulatory organizations that file proposed rule changes concerning the operation of a pilot trading system pursuant to section 19(b) of the Act (15 U.S.C. 78s(b), as amended). All other requirements under the Act that are applicable to self-regulatory organizations continue to apply.

2. The disclosures made pursuant to the provisions of this section are in addition to any other applicable disclosure requirements under the federal securities laws.

(a) For purposes of this section, the term *specialist* means any member subject to a requirement of a self-regulatory organization that such member regularly maintain a market in a particular security.

(b) For purposes of this section, the term *trading system* means the rules of a self-regulatory organization that:

(1) Determine how the orders of multiple buyers and sellers are brought together; and

(2) Establish non-discretionary methods under which such orders interact with each other and under which the buyers and sellers entering such orders agree to the terms of trade.

(c) For purposes of this section, the term *pilot trading system* shall mean a trading system operated by a self-regulatory organization that is not substantially similar to any trading system or pilot trading system operated by such self-regulatory organization at

§ 240.19b-5

any time during the preceding year, and that:

(1)(i) Has been in operation for less than two years;

(ii) Is independent of any other trading system operated by such self-regulatory organization that has been approved by the Commission pursuant to section 19(b) of the Act, (15 U.S.C. 78s(b));

(iii) With respect to each security traded on such pilot trading system, during at least two of the last four consecutive calendar months, has traded no more than 5 percent of the average daily trading volume of such security in the United States; and

(iv) With respect to all securities traded on such pilot trading system, during at least two of the last four consecutive calendar months, has traded no more than 20 percent of the average daily trading volume of all trading systems operated by such self-regulatory organization; or

(2)(i) Has been in operation for less than two years;

(ii) With respect to each security traded on such pilot trading system, during at least two of the last four consecutive calendar months, has traded no more than 1 percent of the average daily trading volume of such security in the United States; and

(iii) With respect to all securities traded on such pilot trading system, during at least two of the last four consecutive calendar months, has traded no more than 20 percent of the average daily trading volume of all trading systems operated by such self-regulatory organization; or

(3)(i) Has been in operation for less than two years; and

(ii)(A) Satisfied the definition of *pilot trading system* under paragraph (c)(1) of this section no more than 60 days ago, and continues to be independent of any other trading system operated by such self-regulatory organization that has been approved by the Commission pursuant to section 19(b) of the Act, (15 U.S.C. 78s(b)); or

(B) Satisfied the definition of *pilot trading system* under paragraph (c)(2) of this section no more than 60 days ago.

(d) A pilot trading system shall be deemed *independent* of any other trading system operated by a self-regulatory organization if:

(1) Such pilot trading system trades securities other than the issues of securities that trade on any other trading system operated by such self-regulatory organization that has been approved by the Commission pursuant to section 19(b) of the Act, (15 U.S.C. 78s(b));

(2) Such pilot trading system does not operate during the same trading hours as any other trading system operated by such self-regulatory organization that has been approved by the Commission pursuant to section 19(b) of the Act, (15 U.S.C. 78s(b)); or

(3) No specialist or market maker on any other trading system operated by such self-regulatory organization that has been approved by the Commission pursuant to section 19(b) of the Act, (15 U.S.C. 78s(b)), is permitted to effect transactions on the pilot trading system in securities in which they are a specialist or market maker.

(e) A self-regulatory organization shall be exempt temporarily from the requirement under section 19(b) of the Act, (15 U.S.C. 78s(b)), to submit on Form 19b-4, 17 CFR 249.819, proposed rule changes for establishing a pilot trading system, if the self-regulatory organization complies with the following requirements:

(1) *Form PILOT.* The self-regulatory organization:

(i) Files Part I of Form PILOT, 17 CFR 249.821, in accordance with the instructions therein, at least 20 days prior to commencing operation of the pilot trading system;

(ii) Files an amendment on Part I of Form PILOT at least 20 days prior to implementing a material change to the operation of the pilot trading system; and

(iii) Files a quarterly report on Part II of Form PILOT within 30 calendar days after the end of each calendar quarter in which the market has operated after the effective date of this section.

(2) *Fair access.* (i) The self-regulatory organization has in place written rules to ensure that all members of the self-regulatory organization have fair access to the pilot trading system, and that information regarding orders on

Securities and Exchange Commission § 240.19b–5

the pilot trading system is equally available to all members of the self-regulatory organization with access to such pilot trading system.

(ii) Notwithstanding the requirement in paragraph (e)(2)(i) of this section, a specialist on the pilot trading system may have preferred access to information regarding orders that it represents in its capacity as specialist.

(iii) The rules established by a self-regulatory organization pursuant to paragraph (e)(2)(i) of this section will be considered rules governing the pilot trading system for purposes of the temporary exemption under this section.

(3) *Trading rules and procedures and listing standards.* (i) The self-regulatory organization has in place written trading rules and procedures and listing standards necessary to operate the pilot trading system.

(ii) The rules established by a self-regulatory organization pursuant to paragraph (e)(3)(i) of this section will be considered rules governing the pilot trading system for purposes of the temporary exemption under this section.

(4) *Surveillance.* The self-regulatory organization establishes internal procedures for the effective surveillance of trading activity on the self-regulatory organization's pilot trading system.

(5) *Clearance and settlement.* The self-regulatory organization establishes reasonable clearance and settlement procedures for transactions effected on the self-regulatory organizations pilot trading system.

(6) *Types of securities.* The self-regulatory organization permits to trade on the pilot trading system only securities registered under section 12 of the Act, (15 U.S.C. 78*l*).

(7) *Activities of specialists.* (i) The self-regulatory organization does not permit any member to be a specialist in a security on the pilot trading system and a specialist in a security on a trading system operated by such self-regulatory organization that has been approved by the Commission pursuant to section 19(b) of the Act, (15 U.S.C. 78s(b)), or on another pilot trading system operated by such self-regulatory organization, if such securities are related securities, except that a member may be a specialist in related securities that the Commission, upon application by the self-regulatory organization, later determines is necessary or appropriate in the public interest and consistent with the protection of investors;

(ii) Notwithstanding paragraph (e)(7)(i) of this section, a self-regulatory organization may permit a member to be a specialist in any security on a pilot trading system, if the pilot trading system is operated during trading hours different from the trading hours of the trading system in which such member is a specialist.

(iii) For purposes of paragraph (e)(7) of this section, the term *related securities* means any two securities in which:

(A) The value of one security is determined, in whole or significant part, by the performance of the other security; or

(B) The value of both securities is determined, in whole or significant part, by the performance of a third security, combination of securities, index, indicator, interest rate or other common factor.

(8) *Examinations, inspections, and investigations.* The self-regulatory organization cooperates with the examination, inspection, or investigation by the Commission of transactions effected on the pilot trading system.

(9) *Recordkeeping.* The self-regulatory organization shall retain at its principal place of business and make available to Commission staff for inspection, all the rules and procedures relating to each pilot trading system operating pursuant to this section for a period of not less than five years, the first two years in an easily accessible place, as prescribed in §240.17a–1.

(10) *Public availability of pilot trading system rules.* The self-regulatory organization makes publicly available all trading rules and procedures, including those established under paragraphs (e)(2) and (e)(3) of this section.

(11) Every notice or amendment filed pursuant to this paragraph (e) shall constitute a "report" within the meaning of sections 11A, 17(a), 18(a), and 32(a), (15 U.S.C. 78k–1, 78q(a), 78r(a), and 78ff(a)), and any other applicable provisions of the Act. All notices or reports filed pursuant to this paragraph (e) shall be deemed to be confidential until

§ 240.19b-7

the pilot trading system commences operation.

(f)(1) A self-regulatory organization shall request Commission approval, pursuant to section 19(b)(2) of the Act, (15 U.S.C. 78s(b)(2)), for any rule change relating to the operation of a pilot trading system by submitting Form 19b-4, 17 CFR 249.819, no later than two years after the commencement of operation of such pilot trading system, or shall cease operation of the pilot trading system.

(2) Simultaneous with a request for Commission approval pursuant to section 19(b)(2) of the Act, (15 U.S.C. 78s(b)(2)), a self-regulatory organization may request Commission approval pursuant to section 19(b)(3)(A) of the Act, (15 U.S.C. 78s(b)(3)(A)), for any rule change relating to the operation of a pilot trading system by submitting Form 19b-4, 17 CFR 249.819, effective immediate upon filing, to continue operations of such trading system for a period not to exceed six months.

(g) Notwithstanding paragraph (e) of this section, rule changes with respect to pilot trading systems operated by a self-regulatory organization shall not be exempt from the rule filing requirements of section 19(b)(2) of the Act, (15 U.S.C. 78s(b)(2)), if the Commission determines, after notice to the SRO and opportunity for the SRO to respond, that exemption of such rule changes is not necessary or appropriate in the public interest or consistent with the protection of investors.

[63 FR 70920, Dec. 22, 1998]

§ 240.19b-7 Filings with respect to proposed rule changes submitted pursuant to Section 19(b)(7) of the Act.

PRELIMINARY NOTE: A self-regulatory organization also must refer to Form 19b-7 (17 CFR 249.822) for further requirements with respect to the filing of proposed rule changes.

(a) Filings with respect to proposed rule changes by a self-regulatory organization submitted pursuant to section 19(b)(7) of the Act (15 U.S.C. 78s(b)(7)) shall be made electronically on Form 19b-7 (17 CFR 249.822).

(b) A proposed rule change will not be deemed filed on the date it is received by the Commission unless:

(1) A completed Form 19b-7 (17 CFR 249.822) is submitted electronically; and

(2) In order to elicit meaningful comment, it is accompanied by:

(i) A clear and accurate statement of the basis and purpose of such rule change, including the impact on competition or efficiency, if any; and

(ii) A summary of any written comments (including e-mail) received by the self-regulatory organization on the proposed rule change.

(c) Self-regulatory organizations shall retain at their principle place of business a file, available to interested persons for public inspection and copying, of all filings made pursuant to this section and all correspondence and other communications reduced to writing (including comment letters) to and from such self-regulatory organization concerning such filing, whether such correspondence and communications are received or prepared before or after the filing of the proposed rule change.

(d) Filings with respect to proposed rule changes by a self-regulatory organization submitted on Form 19b-7 (17 CFR 249.822) electronically shall contain an electronic signature. For the purposes of this section, the term electronic signature means an electronic entry in the form of a magnetic impulse or other form of computer data compilation of any letter or series of letters or characters comprising a name, executed, adopted or authorized as a signature. The signatory to an electronically submitted rule filing shall manually sign a signature page or other document, in the manner prescribed by Form 19b-7, authenticating, acknowledging or otherwise adopting his or her signature that appears in typed form within the electronic filing. Such document shall be executed before or at the time the rule filing is electronically submitted and shall be retained by the filer in accordance with 17 CFR 240.17a-1.

(e) If the conditions of this section and Form 19b-7 (17 CFR 249.822) are otherwise satisfied, all filings submitted electronically on or before 5:30 p.m. Eastern Standard Time or Eastern Daylight Saving Time, whichever is currently in effect, on a business day, shall be deemed filed on that business day, and all filings submitted after 5:30

Securities and Exchange Commission §240.19c–3

p.m. Eastern Standard Time or Eastern Daylight Saving Time, whichever is currently in effect, shall be deemed filed on the next business day.

(f) The self-regulatory organization shall post the proposed rule change, and any amendments thereto, submitted on Form 19b–7 (17 CFR 249.822), on its Web site within two business days after the filing of the proposed rule change, and any amendments thereto, with the Commission. Unless the self-regulatory organization withdraws the proposed rule change or is notified that the proposed rule change is not properly filed, such proposed rule change and amendments shall be maintained on the self-regulatory organization's Web site until 60 days after:

(1) The filing of a written certification with the Commodity Futures Trading Commission under section 5c(c) of the Commodity Exchange Act (7 U.S.C. 7a–2(c));

(2) The Commodity Futures Trading Commission determines that review of the proposed rule change is not necessary; or

(3) The Commodity Futures Trading Commission approves the proposed rule change; and

(4) In the case of a proposed rule change, or any amendment thereto, that has been withdrawn or not properly filed, the self-regulatory organization shall remove the proposed rule change, or any amendment, from its Web site within two business days of notification of improper filing or withdrawal by the self-regulatory organization of the proposed rule change.

(g)(1) Each self-regulatory organization shall post and maintain a current and complete version of its rules on its Web site.

(2) The self-regulatory organization shall update its Web site to reflect rule changes filed pursuant to section 19(b)(7) of the Act (15 U.S.C. 78s(b)(7)), by two business days after the later of:

(A) The Commission's notice of such proposed rule change; and

(B)(i) The filing of a written certification with the Commodity Futures Trading Commission under section 5c(c) of the Commodity Exchange Act (7 U.S.C. 7a–2(c));

(ii) Receipt of notice from the Commodity Futures Trading Commission that it has determined that review of the proposed rule change is not necessary; or

(iii) Receipt of notice from the Commodity Futures Trading Commission that it has approved the proposed rule change.

(3) If a rule change is not effective for a certain period, the self-regulatory organization shall clearly indicate the effective date in the relevant rule text.

[66 FR 43743, Aug. 20, 2001, as amended at 73 FR 16189, Mar. 27, 2008]

§240.19c–1 Governing certain off-board agency transactions by members of national securities exchanges.

The rules of each national securities exchange shall provide as follows:

No rule, stated policy, or practice of this exchange shall prohibit or condition, or be construed to prohibit or condition or otherwise limit, directly or indirectly, the ability of any member acting as agent to effect any transaction otherwise than on this exchange with another person (except when such member also is acting as agent for such other person in such transaction), in any equity security listed on this exchange or to which unlisted trading privileges on this exchange have been extended.

(Secs. 2, 3, 6, 11, 17, 19, 23, Pub. L. 78–291, 48 Stat. 881, 882, 885, 891, 897, 898, 901, as amended by secs. 2, 3, 6, 14, 16, 18, Pub. L. 94–29, 89 Stat. 97, 104, 110, 137, 146, 155 (15 U.S.C. 78b, 78c, 78f, 78k, 78q, 78s, 78w, as amended by Pub. L. 94–29 (June 4, 1975)); sec. 7 Pub. L. 94–29, 89 Stat. 111 (15 U.S.C. 78k–1))

[43 FR 1328, Jan. 9, 1978]

§240.19c–3 Governing off-board trading by members of national securities exchanges.

The rules of each national securities exchange shall provide as follows:

(a) No rule, stated policy or practice of this exchange shall prohibit or condition, or be construed to prohibit, condition or otherwise limit, directly or indirectly, the ability of any member to effect any transaction otherwise than on this exchange in any reported security listed and registered on this exchange or as to which unlisted trading privileges on this exchange have been extended (other than a put option

783

§ 240.19c–4

or call option issued by the Options Clearing Corporation) which is not a covered security.

(b) For purposes of this rule,

(1) The term *Act* shall mean the Securities Exchange Act of 1934, as amended.

(2) The term *exchange* shall mean a national securities exchange registered as such with the Securities and Exchange Commission pursuant to section 6 of the Act.

(3) The term *covered security* shall mean (i) Any equity security or class of equity securities which

(A) Was listed and registered on an exchange on April 26, 1979, and

(B) Remains listed and registered on at least one exchange continuously thereafter;

(ii) Any equity security or class of equity securities which

(A) Was traded on one or more exchanges on April 26, 1979, pursuant to unlisted trading privileges permitted by section 12(f)(1)(A) of the Act, and

(B) Remains traded on any such exchange pursuant to such unlisted trading privileges continuously thereafter; and

(iii) Any equity security or class of equity securities which

(A) Is issued in connection with a statutory merger, consolidation or similar plan or reorganization (including a reincorporation or change of domicile) in exchange for an equity security or class of equity securities described in paragraph (b)(3)(i) or (ii) of this rule,

(B) Is listed and registered on an exchange after April 26, 1979, and

(C) Remains listed and registered on at least one exchange continuously thereafter.

(4) The term *reported security* shall mean any security or class of securities for which transaction reports are collected, processed and made available pursuant to an effective transaction reporting plan.

(5) The term *transaction report* shall mean a report containing the price and volume associated with a completed transaction involving the purchase or sale of a security.

(6) The term *effective transaction reporting plan* shall mean any plan approved by the Commission pursuant to

17 CFR Ch. II (4–1–23 Edition)

§ 242.601 of this chapter for collecting, processing, and making available transaction reports with respect to transactions in an equity security or class of equity securities.

[45 FR 41134, June 18, 1980, as amended at 70 FR 37618, June 29, 2005]

§ 240.19c–4 Governing certain listing or authorization determinations by national securities exchanges and associations.

(a) The rules of each exchange shall provide as follows: No rule, stated policy, practice, or interpretation of this exchange shall permit the listing, or the continuance of the listing, of any common stock or other equity security of a domestic issuer, if the issuer of such security issues any class of security, or takes other corporate action, with the effect of nullifying, restricting or disparately reducing the per share voting rights of holders of an outstanding class or classes of common stock of such issuer registered pursuant to section 12 of the Act.

(b) The rules of each association shall provide as follows: No rule, stated policy, practice, or interpretation of this association shall permit the authorization for quotation and/or transaction reporting through an automated interdealer quotation system ("authorization"), or the continuance of authorization, of any common stock or other equity security of a domestic issuer, if the issuer of such security issues any class of security, or takes other corporate action, with the effect of nullifying, restricting, or disparately reducing the per share voting rights of holders of an outstanding class or classes of common stock of such issuer registered pursuant to section 12 of the Act.

(c) For the purposes of paragraphs (a) and (b) of this section, the following shall be presumed to have the effect of nullifying, restricting, or disparately reducing the per share voting rights of an outstanding class or classes of common stock:

(1) Corporate action to impose any restriction on the voting power of shares of the common stock of the issuer held by a beneficial or record holder based on the number of shares

Securities and Exchange Commission § 240.19c-4

held by such beneficial or record holder;

(2) Corporate action to impose any restriction on the voting power of shares of the common stock of the issuer held by a beneficial or record holder based on the length of time such shares have been held by such beneficial or record holder;

(3) Any issuance of securities through an exchange offer by the issuer for shares of an outstanding class of the common stock of the issuer, in which the securities issued have voting rights greater than or less than the per share voting rights of any outstanding class of the common stock of the issuer.

(4) Any issuance of securities pursuant to a stock dividend, or any other type of distribution of stock, in which the securities issued have voting rights greater than the per share voting rights of any outstanding class of the common stock of the issuer.

(d) For the purpose of paragraphs (a) and (b) of this section, the following, standing alone, shall be presumed not to have the effect of nullifying, restricting, or disparately reducing the per share voting rights of holders of an outstanding class or classes of common stock:

(1) The issuance of securities pursuant to an initial registered public offering;

(2) The issuance of any class of securities, through a registered public offering, with voting rights not greater than the per share voting rights of any outstanding class of the common stock of the issuer;

(3) The issuance of any class of securities to effect a bona fide merger or acquisition, with voting rights not greater than the per share voting rights of any outstanding class of the common stock of the issuer.

(4) Corporate action taken pursuant to state law requiring a state's domestic corporation to condition the voting rights of a beneficial or record holder of a specified threshold percentage of the corporation's voting stock on the approval of the corporation's independent shareholders.

(e) *Definitions.* The following terms shall have the following meanings for purposes of this section, and the rules of each exchange and association shall include such definitions for the purposes of the prohibition in paragraphs (a) and (b), respectively, of this section:

(1) The term *Act* shall mean the Securities Exchange Act of 1934, as amended.

(2) The term *common stock* shall include any security of an issuer designated as common stock and any security of an issuer, however designated, which, by statute or by its terms, is a common stock (e.g., a security which entitles the holders thereof to vote generally on matters submitted to the issuer's security holders for a vote).

(3) The term *equity security* shall include any equity security defined as such pursuant to Rule 3a11-1 under the Act (17 CFR 240.3a11-1).

(4) The term *domestic issuer* shall mean an issuer that is not a "foreign private issuer" as defined in Rule 3b-4 under the Act (17 CFR 240.3b-4).

(5) The term *security* shall include any security defined as such pursuant to section 3(a)(10) of the Act, but shall exclude any class of security having a preference or priority over the issuer's common stock as to dividends, interest payments, redemption or payments in liquidation, if the voting rights of such securities only become effective as a result of specified events, not relating to an acquisition of the common stock of the issuer, which reasonably can be expected to jeopardize the issuer's financial ability to meet its payment obligations to the holders of that class of securities.

(6) The term *exchange* shall mean a national securities exchange, registered as such with the Securities and Exchange Commission pursuant to section 6 of the Act (15 U.S.C. 78f), which makes transaction reports available pursuant to § 242.601 of this chapter; and

(7) The term *association* shall mean a national securities association registered as such with the Securities and Exchange Commission pursuant to section 15A of the Act.

(f) An exchange or association may adopt a rule, stated policy, practice, or interpretation, subject to the procedures specified by section 19(b) of the Act, specifying what types of securities issuances and other corporate actions are covered by, or excluded from, the

§ 240.19c-5

prohibition in paragraphs (a) and (b) of this section, respectively, if such rule, stated policy, practice, or interpretation is consistent with the protection of investors and the public interest, and otherwise in furtherance of the purposes of the Act and this section.

[53 FR 26394, July 12, 1988, as amended at 70 FR 37618, June 29, 2005]

§ 240.19c-5 Governing the multiple listing of options on national securities exchanges.

(a) The rules of each national securities exchange that provides a trading market in standardized put or call options shall provide as follows:

(1) On and after January 22, 1990, but not before, no rule, stated policy, practice, or interpretation of this exchange shall prohibit or condition, or be construed to prohibit or condition or otherwise limit, directly or indirectly, the ability of this exchange to list any stock options class first listed on an exchange on or after January 22, 1990, because that options class is listed on another options exchange.

(2) During the period from January 22, 1990, to January 21, 1991, but not before, no rule, stated policy, practice, or interpretation of this exchange shall prohibit or condition, or be construed to prohibit or condition or otherwise limit, directly or indirectly, the ability of this exchange to list up to ten classes of standardized stock options overlying exchange-listed stocks that were listed on another options exchange before January 22, 1990. These ten classes shall be in addition to any option on an exchange-listed stock trading on this exchange that was traded on more than one options exchange before January 22, 1990.

(3) On and after January 21, 1991, but not before, no rule, stated policy, practice, or interpretation of this exchange shall prohibit or condition, or be construed to prohibit or condition or otherwise limit, directly or indirectly, the ability of this exchange to list any stock options class because that options class is listed on another options exchange.

(b) For purposes of paragraph (a)(2) of this Rule, if any options class is delisted from an options exchange as a result of a merger of the equity security underlying the option or a failure of the underlying security to satisfy that exchange's options listing standards, then the exchange is permitted to select a replacement option from among those standardized options overlying exchange-listed stocks that were listed on another options exchange before January 22, 1990.

(c) For purposes of this Rule, the term *exchange* shall mean a national securities exchange, registered as such with the Commission pursuant to Section 6 of the Securities Exchange Act of 1934, as amended.

(d) For purposes of this Rule, the term *standardized option* shall have the same meaning as that term is defined in Rule 9b-1 under the Securities Exchange Act of 1934, as amended, 17 CFR 240.9b-1.

(e) For purposes of this Rule, the term *options class* shall have the same meaning as that term is defined in Rule 9b-1 under the Securities Exchange Act of 1934, as amended, 17 CFR 240.9b-1.

[54 FR 23976, June 5, 1989]

§ 240.19d-1 Notices by self-regulatory organizations of final disciplinary actions, denials, bars, or limitations respecting membership, association, participation, or access to services, and summary suspensions.

(a) *General.* If any self-regulatory organization for which the Commission is the appropriate regulatory agency takes any action described in this rule to which the person affected thereby has consented and such action:

(1) Conditions or limits membership or participation in, association with a member of, or access to services offered by, such organization or a member thereof and

(2) Is based upon a statutory disqualification defined in section 3(a)(39) of the Act, notice thereof shall be filed under Rule 19h-1 and not under this rule.

(b) The notice requirement of section 19(d)(1) of the Act, concerning an action subject to such section taken by a self-regulatory organization for which the Commission is the appropriate regulatory agency, shall be satisfied by any notice with respect to such action (including a notice filed pursuant to

Securities and Exchange Commission

§ 240.19d-1

this rule) which contains the information required in the statement supporting the organization's determination required by section 6(d) (1) or (2), section 15A(h) (1) or (2), or section 17A(b)(5) (A) or (B) of the Act, as appropriate.

(c)(1) Any self-regulatory organization for which the Commission is the appropriate regulatory agency that takes any final disciplinary action with respect to any person shall promptly file a notice thereof with the Commission in accordance with paragraph (d) of this section. For the purposes of this rule, a "final disciplinary action" shall mean the imposition of any final disciplinary sanction pursuant to section 6(b)(6), 15A(b)(7), or 17A(b)(3)(G) of the Act or other action of a self-regulatory organization which, after notice and opportunity for hearing, results in any final disposition of charges of:

(i) One or more violations of—
(A) The rules of such organization;
(B) The provisions of the Act or rules thereunder; or
(C) In the case of a municipal securities broker or dealer, the rules of the Municipal Securities Rulemaking Board;

(ii) Acts or practices constituting a statutory disqualification of a type defined in subparagraph (D) or (E) (except prior convictions) of section 3(a)(39) of the Act; or

(iii) In the case of a proceeding by a national securities exhange or registered securities association based on section 6(c)(3)(A)(ii), 6(c)(3)(B)(ii), 15A(g)(3)(A)(ii), or 15A(g)(3)(B)(ii) of the Act, acts or practices inconsistent with just and equitable principles of trade.

Provided, however, That in the case of a disciplinary action in which a national securities exchange imposes a fine not exceeding $1000 or suspends floor privileges of a clerical employee for not more than five days for violation of any of its regulations concerning personal decorum on a trading floor, the disposition shall not be considered "final" for purposes of this paragraph if the sanctioned person has not sought an adjudication, including a hearing, or otherwise exhausted his administrative remedies at the exchange with respect to the matter. *Provided further,* That this exemption from the notice requirement of this paragraph shall not be available where a decorum sanction is imposed at, or results from, a hearing on the matter.

(2) Any disciplinary action, other than a decorum sanction not deemed "final" under paragraph (c)(1) of this section, taken by a self-regulatory organization for which the Commission is the appropriate regulatory agency against any person for violation of a rule of the self-regulatory organization which has been designated as a minor rule violation pursuant to a plan or any amendment thereto filed with and declared effective by the Commission under this paragraph, shall not be considered "final" for purposes of paragraph (c)(1) of this section if the sanction imposed consists of a fine not exceeding $2500 and the sanctioned person has not sought an adjudication, including a hearing, or otherwise exhausted his administrative remedies at the self-regulatory organization with resepect to the matter. After appropriate notice of the terms of substance of the filing or a description of the subjects and issues involved and opportunity for interested persons to submit written comment, the Commission may, by order, declare such plan or amendment effective if it finds that such plan or amendment is consistent with the public interest, the protection of investors, or otherwise in furtherance of the purposes of the Act. The Commission in its order may restrict the categories of violations to be designated as minor rule violations and may impose any other terms or conditions to the plan (including abbreviated reporting of selected minor rule violations) and to the period of its effectiveness which it deems necessary or appropriate in the public interest, for the protection of investors or otherwise in furtherance of the purposes of the Act.

(d) *Contents of notice required by paragraph (c)(1).* Any notice filed pursuant to paragraph (c)(1) of this section, shall consist of the following, as appropriate:

(1) The name of the respondent concerned together with his last known place of residence or business as reflected on the records of the self-regulatory organization and the name of

§ 240.19d-1

the person, committee, or other organizational unit which brought the charges involved; except that, as to any respondent who has been found not to have violated a provision covered by a charge, identifying information with respect to such person may be deleted insofar as the notice reports the disposition of that charge, unless, prior to the filing of the notice, the respondent requests otherwise;

(2) A statement describing the investigative or other origin of the action;

(3) As charged in the proceeding, the specific provisions of the Act, the rules or regulations thereunder, the rules of the organization, and, in the case of a registered securities association, the rules of the Municipal Securities Rulemaking Board, and, in the event a violation of other statutes or rules constitutes a violation of any rule of the organization, such other statutes or rules; and a statement describing the answer of the respondent to the charges;

(4) A statement setting forth findings of fact with respect to any act or practice which such respondent was charged with having engaged in or omitted; the conclusion of the organization as to whether such respondent is deemed to have violated any provision covered by the charges; and a statement of the organization in support of the resolution of the principal issues raised in the proceedings;

(5) A statement describing any sanction imposed, the reasons therefor, and the date upon which such sanction has or will become effective, together with a finding if appropriate, as to whether such respondent was a cause of any sanction imposed upon any other person; and

(6) Such other matters as the organization may deem relevant.

(e) *Notice of final denial, bar, prohibition, termination or limitation based on qualification or administrative rules.* Any final action of a self-regulatory organization for which the Commission is the appropriate regulatory agency that is taken with respect to any person constituting a denial, bar, prohibition, or limitation of membership, participation or association with a member, or of access to services offered by a self-regulatory organization or a member

17 CFR Ch. II (4-1-23 Edition)

thereof, and which is based on an alleged failure of any person to:

(1) Pass any test or examination required by the rules of the Commission or such organization;

(2) Comply with other qualification standards established by rules of the Commission or such organization; or

(3) Comply with any administrative requirements of such organization (including failure to pay entry or other dues or fees or to file prescribed forms or reports) not involving charges of violations which may lead to a disciplinary sanction shall not be considered a "disciplinary action" for purposes of paragraph (c) of this rule; but notice thereof shall be promptly filed with the Commission in accordance with paragraph (f) of this section, *Provided, however,* That no disposition of a matter shall be considered "final" pursuant to this paragraph which results merely from a notice of such failure to the person affected, if such person has not sought an adjudication, including a hearing, or otherwise exhausted his administrative remedies within such organization with respect to such a matter.

(f) *Contents of notice required by paragraph (e).* Any notice filed pursuant to paragraph (e) of this section shall consist of the following, as appropriate:

(1) The name of each person concerned together with his last known place of residence or business as reflected on the records of the organization;

(2) The specific provisions of the Act, the rules or regulations thereunder, the rules of the organization, and, in the case of a registered securities association, the rules of the Municipal Securities Rulemaking Board, upon which the action of the organization was based, and a statement describing the answer of the person concerned;

(3) A statement setting forth findings of fact and conclusions as to each alleged failure of the person to pass any required examination, comply with other qualification standards, or comply with administrative obligations, and a statement of the organization in support of the resolution of the principal issues raised in the proceeding;

(4) The date upon which such action has or will become effective; and

Securities and Exchange Commission § 240.19d-1

(5) Such other matters as the organization may deem relevant.

(g) *Notice of final action based upon prior adjudicated statutory disqualifications.* Any self-regulatory organization for which the Commission is the appropriate regulatory agency that takes any final action with respect to any person which:

(1) Denies or conditions membership or participation in, or association with a member of, such organization or prohibits or limits access to services offered by such organization or a member thereof; and

(2) Is based upon a statutory disqualification of a type defined in subparagraph (A), (B), or (C) of section 3(a)(39) of the Act or consisting of a prior conviction, as described in subparagraph (E) of said section 3(a)(39), shall promptly file a notice of such action with the Commission in accordance with paragraph (h) of this section, *provided, however,* That no disposition of a matter shall be considered "final" pursuant to this paragraph where such person has not sought an adjudication, including a hearing, or otherwise exhausted his administrative remedies within such organization with respect to such a matter.

(h) *Contents of notice required by paragraph (g).* Any notice filed pursuant to paragraph (g) of this section shall consist of the following, as appropriate:

(1) The name of the person concerned together with his last known place of residence or business as reflected on the record of the organization;

(2) A statement setting forth the principal issues raised, the answer of any person concerned, and a statement of the organization in support of the resolution of the principal issues raised in the proceeding;

(3) Any description furnished by or on behalf of the person concerned of the activities engaged in by the person since the adjudication upon which the disqualification is based;

(4) Any description furnished by or on behalf of the person concerned of the prospective business or employment in which the person plans to engage and the manner and extent of supervision to be exercised over and by such person;

(5) A copy of the order or decision of the court, the Commission or the self-regulatory organization which adjudicated the matter giving rise to such statutory disqualification;

(6) The nature of the action taken and the date upon which such action is to be made effective; and

(7) Such other matters as the organization deems relevant.

(i) *Notice of summary suspension of membership, participation, or association, or summary limitation or prohibition of access to services.* If any self-regulatory organization for which the Commission is the appropriate regulatory agency summarily suspends a member, participant, or person associated with a member, or summarily limits or prohibits any person with respect to access to or services offered by the organization or (in the case of a national securities exchange or a registered securities association) a member thereof pursuant to the provisions of section 6(d)(3), 15A(h)(3) or 17A(b)(5) (C) of the Act, such organization shall, within 24 hours of the effectiveness of such summary suspension, limitation or prohibition notify the Commission of such action, which notice shall contain at least the following information:

(1) The name of the person concerned together with his last known place of residence or business as reflected on the records of the organization;

(2) The date upon which such summary action has or will become effective;

(3) If such summary action is based upon the provisions of section 6(d)(3)(A), 15A(h)(3)(A), or 17A(b)(5)(C)(i) of the Act, a copy of the relevant order or decision of the self-regulatory organization;

(4) If such summary action is based upon the provisions of section 6(d)(3) (B) or (C), 15A(h)(3) (B) or (C), or 17A(b)(5)(C) (ii) or (iii) of the Act, a statement describing, as appropriate:

(i) The financial or operating difficulty of the member or participant upon which such organization determined the member or particpant could not be permitted to continue to do business with safety to investors, creditors, other members or participants, or the organization;

§ 240.19d-2

(ii) The pertinent failure to meet qualification requirements or other prerequisites for access and the basis upon which such organization determined that the person concerned could not be permitted to have access with safety to investors, creditors, other members, or the organization; or

(iii) The default of any delivery of funds or securities to a clearing agency by a participant.

(5) The nature and effective date of the suspension, limitation or prohibition; and

(6) Such other matters as the organization deems relevant.

(j) Notice of limitation or prohibition of access to services by delisting of security. Any national securities exchange for which the Commission is the appropriate regulatory agency that delists a security pursuant to section 12(d) of the Act (15 U.S.C. 78l(d)), and Sec. 240.12d2-2 must file a notice with the Commission in accordance with paragraph (k) of this section.

(k) Contents of notice required by paragraph (j) of this section. The national securities exchange shall file notice pursuant to paragraph (j) of this section on Form 25 (§ 249.25 of this chapter). Form 25 shall serve as notification to the Commission of such limitation or prohibition of access to services. The national securities exchange must attach a copy of its delisting determination to Form 25 and file Form 25 with the attachment on EDGAR.

[42 FR 36415, July 14, 1977, as amended at 49 FR 23831, June 8, 1984; 71 FR 42469, July 22, 2005]

§ 240.19d-2 Applications for stays of disciplinary sanctions or summary suspensions by a self-regulatory organization.

If any self-regulatory organization imposes any final disciplinary sanction as to which a notice is required to be filed with the Commission pursuant to Section 19(d)(1) of the Exchange Act, 15 U.S.C. 78s(d)(1), pursuant to Section 6(b)(6), 15A(b)(7) or 17A(b)(3)(G) of the Act (15 U.S.C. 78f(b)(6), 78o-3(b)(7) or 78q-1(b)(3)(G)), or summarily suspends or limits or prohibits access pursuant to Section 6(d)(3), 15A(h)(3) or 17A(b)(5)(C) of the Act (15 U.S.C. 78f(d)(3), 78o-3(h)(3) or 78q-1(b)(5)(C)), any person aggrieved thereby for which the Commission is the appropriate regulatory agency may file with the Commission a written motion for a stay of imposition of such action pursuant to Rule 401 of the Commission's Rules of Practice, § 201.401 of this chapter.

[60 FR 32825, June 23, 1995]

§ 240.19d-3 Applications for review of final disciplinary sanctions, denials of membership, participation or association, or prohibitions or limitations of access to services imposed by self-regulatory organizations.

Applications to the Commission for review of any final disciplinary sanction, denial or conditioning of membership, participation, bar from association, or prohibition or limitation with respect to access to services offered by a self-regulatory organization or a member thereof by any such organization shall be made pursuant to Rule 420 of the Commission's Rules of Practice, § 201.420 of this chapter.

[60 FR 32825, June 23, 1995]

§ 240.19d-4 Notice by the Public Company Accounting Oversight Board of disapproval of registration or of disciplinary action.

(a) *Definitions*—(1) *Board* means the Public Company Accounting Oversight Board.

(2) *Public accounting firm* shall have the meaning set forth in 15 U.S.C. 7201(a)(11).

(3) *Registered public accounting firm* shall have the meaning set forth in 15 U.S.C. 7201(a)(12).

(4) *Associated person* shall mean a person associated with a registered public accounting firm as defined in 15 U.S.C. 7201(a)(9).

(b)(1) *Notice of disapproval of registration.* If the Board disapproves a completed application for registration by a public accounting firm, the Board shall file a notice of its disapproval with the Commission within 30 days and serve a copy on the public accounting firm.

(2) *Contents of the notice.* The notice required by paragraph (b)(1) of this section shall provide the following information:

(i) The name of the public accounting firm and the public accounting firm's last known address as reflected in the Board's records;

(ii) The basis for the Board's disapproval, and a copy of the Board's written notice of disapproval; and

(iii) Such other information as the Board may deem relevant.

(c)(1) *Notice of disciplinary action.* If the Board imposes any final disciplinary sanction on any registered public accounting firm or any associated person of a registered public accounting firm under 15 U.S.C. 7215(b)(3) or 7215(c), the Board shall file a notice of the disciplinary sanction with the Commission within 30 days and serve a copy on the person sanctioned.

(2) *Contents of the notice.* The notice required by paragraph (c)(1) of this section shall provide the following information:

(i) The name of the registered public accounting firm or the associated person, together with the firm's or the person's last known address as reflected in the Board's records;

(ii) A description of the acts or practices, or omissions to act, upon which the sanction is based;

(iii) A statement of the sanction imposed, the reasons therefor, or a copy of the Board's statement justifying the sanction, and the effective date of such sanction; and

(iv) Such other information as the Board may deem relevant.

[69 FR 13182, Mar. 19, 2004]

§ 240.19g2-1 **Enforcement of compliance by national securities exchanges and registered securities associations with the Act and rules and regulations thereunder.**

(a) In enforcing compliance, within the meaning of section 19(g) of the Act, with the Act and the rules and regulations thereunder by its members and persons associated with its members, a national securities exchange or registered securities association is not required:

(1) To enforce compliance with sections 12 (other than sections 12(j) and 12(k)), 13, 14 (other than section 14(b)), 15(d) and 16 and the rules thereunder except to the extent of any action normally taken with respect to any person which is not a member or a person associated with a member;

(2) To enforce compliance with respect to persons associated with a member, other than securities persons or persons who control a member; and

(3) To conduct examinations as to qualifications of, require filing of periodic reports by, or conduct regular inspections (including examinations of books and records) of, persons associated with a member, other than securities persons whose functions are not solely clerical or ministerial.

(b) For the purpose of this rule:

(1) A *securities person* is a person who is a general partner or officer (or person occupying a similar status or performing similar functions) or employee of a member; *Provided, however,* That a registered broker or dealer which controls, is controlled by, or is under common control with, the member and the general partners and officers (and persons occupying similar status or performing similar functions) and employees of such a registered broker or dealer shall be securities persons if they effect, directly or indirectly, transactions in securities through the member by use of facilities maintained or supervised by such exchange or association; and

(2) *Control* means the power to direct or cause the direction of the management or policies of a company whether through ownership of securities, by contract or otherwise; *Provided, however,* That:

(i) Any person who, directly or indirectly, (A) has the right to vote 25 percent or more of the voting securities, (B) is entitled to receive 25 percent or more of the net profits, or (C) is a director (or person occupying a similar status or performing similar functions) of a company shall be presumed to be a person who controls such company;

(ii) Any person not covered by paragraph (b)(2)(i) of this section shall be presumed not to be a person who controls such company; and

(iii) Any presumption may be rebutted on an appropriate showing.

(Secs. 3, 6, 19, 23, 48 Stat. 882, 885, 898, as amended (15 U.S.C. 78c, 78f, 78s, 78w); sec. 15A, 52 Stat. 1070, as amended (15 U.S.C. 78*o*-3))

[41 FR 51808, Nov. 24, 1976]

§ 240.19h-1 Notice by a self-regulatory organization of proposed admission to or continuance in membership or participation or association with a member of any person subject to a statutory disqualification, and applications to the Commission for relief therefrom.

(a) *Notice of admission or continuance notwithstanding a statutory disqualification.* (1) Any self-regulatory organization proposing, conditionally or unconditionally, to admit to, or continue any person in, membership or participation or (in the case of a national securities exchange or registered securities association) association with a member, notwithstanding a statutory disqualification, as defined in section 3(a)(39) of the Act, with respect to such person, shall file a notice with the Commission of such proposed admission or continuance. If such disqualified person has not consented to the terms of such proposal, notice of the organization's action shall be filed pursuant to rule 19d-1 under the Act and not this rule.

(2) With respect to a person associated with a member of a national securities exchange or registered securities association, notices need be filed with the Commission pursuant to this rule only if such person:

(i) Controls such member, is a general partner or officer (or person occupying a similar status or performing similar functions) of such member, is an employee who, on behalf of such member, is engaged in securities advertising, public relations, research, sales, trading, or training or supervision of other employees who engage or propose to engage in such activities, except clerical and ministerial persons engaged in such activities, or is an employee with access to funds, securities or books and records, or

(ii) Is a broker or dealer not registered with the Commission, or controls such (unregistered) broker or dealer or is a general partner or officer (or person occupying a similar status or performing similar functions) of such broker or dealer.

(3) A notice need not be filed with the Commission pursuant to this rule if:

(i) The person subject to the statutory disqualification is already a participant in, a member of, or a person associated with a member of, a self-regulatory organization, and the terms and conditions of the proposed admission by another self-regulatory organization are the same in all material respects as those imposed or not disapproved in connection with such person's prior admission or continuance pursuant to an order of the Commission under paragraph (d) of this section or other substantially equivalent written communication.

(ii) The self-regulatory organization finds, after reasonable inquiry, that except for the identity of the employer concerned, the terms and conditions of the proposed admission or continuance are the same in all material respects as those imposed or not disapproved in connection with a prior admission or continuance of the person subject to the statutory disqualification pursuant to an order of the Commission under paragraph (d) of this section or other substantially equivalent written communication and that there is no intervening conduct or other circumstance that would cause the employment to be inconsistent with the public interest or the protection of investors;

(iii) The disqualification consists of (A) an injunction from engaging in any action, conduct, or practice specified in section 15(b)(4)(C) of the Act, which injunction was entered 10 or more years prior to the proposed admission or continuance—*Provided, however,* That in the case of a final or permanent injunction which was preceded by a preliminary injunction against the same person in the same court proceeding, such ten-year period shall begin to run from the date of such preliminary injunction—and/or (B) a finding by the Commission or a self-regulatory organization of a willful violation of the Act, the Securities Act of 1933, the Investment Advisers Act of 1940, the Investment Company Act of 1940, or a rule or regulation under one or more of such Acts and the sanction for such violation is no longer in effect;

(iv) The disqualification previously (A) was a basis for the institution of an administrative proceeding pursuant to a provision of the federal securities laws, and (B) was considered by the Commission in determining a sanction against such person in the proceeding; and the Commission concluded in such

Securities and Exchange Commission § 240.19h-1

proceeding that it would not restrict or limit the future securities activities of such person in the capacity now proposed or, if it imposed any such restrictions or limitations for a specified time period, such time period has elapsed;

(v) The disqualification consists of a court order or judgment of injunction or conviction, and such order or judgment (A) expressly includes a provision that, on the basis of such order or judgment, the Commission will not institute a proceeding against such person pursuant to section 15(b) or 15B of the Act or that the future securities activities of such persons in the capacity now proposed will not be restricted or limited or (B) includes such restrictions or limitations for a specified time period and such time period has elapsed; or

(vi) In the case of a person seeking to become associated with a broker or dealer or municipal securities dealer, the Commission has previously consented to such proposed association pursuant to section 15(b)(6) or 15B(c)(4) of the Act.

In the case of an admission to membership, participation, or association, if an exception provided for in this paragraph (a)(3) is applicable, the self-regulatory organization shall, pursuant to its rules, determine when the admission to membership, participation, or association shall become effective.

(4) If a self-regulatory organization determines to admit to, or continue any person in, membership, participation, or association with a member pursuant to an exception from the notice requirements provided in paragraph (a)(3)(ii), (iv) or (v) of this section, such organization shall, within 14 calendar days of its making of such determination, furnish to the Commission, by letter, a notification setting forth, as appropriate:

(i) The name of the person subject to the statutory disqualification;

(ii) The name of the person's prospective and immediately preceding employers who are (were) brokers or dealers or municipal securities dealers;

(iii) The name of the person's prospective supervisor(s);

(iv) The respective places of such employments as reflected on the records of the self-regulatory organization;

(v) If applicable, the findings of the self-regulatory organization referred to in paragraph (a)(3)(ii) of this section and the nature (including relevant dates) of the previous Commission or court determination referred to in paragraph (a)(3)(iv) or (v) of this section; and

(vi) An identification of any other self-regulatory organization which has indicated its agreement with the terms and conditions of the proposed admission or continuance;

(5) If a notice or notification has been previously filed or furnished pursuant to this rule by a self-regulatory organization, any other such organization need not file or furnish a separate notice or notification pursuant to this rule with respect to the same matter if such other organization agrees with the terms and conditions of the membership, participation or association reflected in the notice or notification so filed or furnished, and such agreement is set forth in the notice or notification.

(6) The notice requirements of sections 6(c)(2), 15A(g)(2), and 17A(b)(4)(A) of the Act concerning an action of a self-regulatory organization subject to one (or more) of such sections and this paragraph (a) shall be satisfied by a notice with respect to such action filed in accordance with paragraph (c) of this section.

(7) The Commission, by written notice to a self-regulatory organization on or before the thirtieth day after receipt of a notice under this Rule, may direct that such organization not admit to membership, participation, or association with a member any person who is subject to a statutory disqualification for a period not to exceed an additional 60 days beyond the initial 30 day notice period in order that the Commission may extend its consideration of the proposal; *Provided, however,* That during such extended period of consideration, the Commission will not direct the self-regulatory organization to bar the proposed admission to membership, participation or association with a member pursuant to section 6(c)(2), 15A(g)(2), or 17A(b)(4)(A) of the Act, and the Commission will not institute proceedings pursuant to section 15(b) or 15B of the Act on the basis

§ 240.19h-1

of such disqualification if the self-regulatory organization has permitted the admission to membership, participation or association with a member, on a temporary basis, pending a final Commission determination.

(b) *Preliminary notifications.* Promptly after receiving an application for admission to, or continuance in, participation or membership in, or association with a member of, a self-regulatory organization which would be required to file with the Commission a notice thereof pursuant to paragraph (a) of this section if such admission or continuance is ultimately proposed by such organization, the organization shall file with the Commission a notification of such receipt. Such notification shall include, as appropriate:

(1) The date of such receipt;

(2) The names of the person subject to the statutory disqualification and the prospective employer concerned together with their respective last known places of residence or business as reflected on the records of the organization;

(3) The basis for any such disqualification including (if based on a prior adjudication) a copy of the order or decision of the court, the Commission, or the self-regulatory organization which adjudicated the matter giving rise to the disqualification; and

(4) The capacity in which the person concerned is proposed to be employed.

(c) *Contents of notice of admission or continuance.* A notice filed with the Commission pursuant to paragraph (a) of this section shall contain the following, as appropriate:

(1) The name of the person concerned together with his last known place of residence or business as reflected on the records of the self-regulatory organization;

(2) The basis for any such disqualification from membership, participation or association including (if based on a prior adjudication) a copy of the order or decision of the court, the Commission or the self-regulatory organization which adjudicated the matter giving rise to such disqualification;

(3) In the case of an admission, the date upon which it is proposed by the organization that such membership, participation or association shall become effective, which shall be not less than 30 days from the date upon which the Commission receives the notice;

(4) A description by or on behalf of the person concerned of the activities engaged in by the person since the disqualification arose, the prospective business or employment in which the person plans to engage and the manner and extent of supervision to be exercised over and by such person. This description shall be accompanied by a written statement submitted to the self-regulatory organization by the proposed employer setting forth the terms and conditions of such employment and supervision. The description also shall include (i) the qualifications, experience and disciplinary records of the proposed supervisors of the person and their family relationship (if any) to that person; (ii) the findings and results of all examinations conducted, during the two years preceding the filing of the notice, by self-regulatory organizations of the main office of the proposed employer and of the branch office(s) in which the employment will occur or be subject to supervisory controls; (iii) a copy of a completed Form U-4 with respect to the proposed association of such person and a certification by the self-regulatory organization that such person is fully qualified under all applicable requirements to engage in the proposed activities; and (iv) the name and place of employment of any other associated person of the proposed employer who is subject to a statutory disqualification (other than a disqualification specified in paragraph (a)(3)(iii) of this section);

(5) If a hearing on the matter has been held by the organization, a certified record of the hearing together with copies of any exhibits introduced therein;

(6) All written submissions not included in a certified oral hearing record which were considered by the organization in its disposition of the matter;

(7) An identification of any other self-regulatory organization which has indicated its agreement with the terms and conditions of the proposed admission or continuance;

(8) All information furnished in writing to the self-regulatory organization

Securities and Exchange Commission § 240.19h-1

by the staff of the Commission for consideration by the organization in its disposition of the matter or the incorporation by reference of such information, and a statement of the organization's views thereon; and

(9) Such other matters as the organization or person deems relevant.

If the notice contains assertions of material facts not a matter of record before the self-regulatory organization, such facts shall be sworn to by affidavit of the person or organization offering such facts for Commission consideration. The notice may be accompanied by a brief.

(d) *Application to the Commission for relief from certain statutory disqualifications.* The filing of a notice pursuant to paragraph (a) of this section shall neither affect nor foreclose any action which the Commission may take with respect to such person pursuant to the provisions of section 15(b), 15B or 19(h) of the Act or any rule thereunder. Accordingly, a notice filed pursuant to paragraph (a) of this section with respect to the membership, participation, or association of any person subject to an "applicable disqualification," as defined in paragraph (f) of this section, may be accompanied by an application by or on behalf of the person concerned to the Commission for an order declaring, as applicable, that notwithstanding such disqualification, the Commission:

(1) Will not institute proceedings pursuant to section 15(b)(1)(B), 15(b)(4), 15(b)(6), 15B(a)(2), 15B(c)(2), 19(h)(2) or 19(h)(3) of the Act if such person seeks to obtain or continue registration as a broker or dealer or municipal securities dealer or association with a broker or dealer or municipal securities dealer so registered, or membership or participation in a self-regulatory organization;

(2) Will not direct otherwise, as provided in section 6(c)(2), 15A(g)(2) or 17A(b)(4)(A) of the Act; and

(3) Will deem such person qualified pursuant to Rule G-4 of the Municipal Securities Rulemaking Board under the Act.

If a Commission consent is required in order to render a proposed association lawful under section 15(b)(6) or 15B(c)(4) of the Act, an application by or on behalf of the person seeking such consent shall accompany the notice of the proposed association filed pursuant to paragraph (a) of this section. The Commission may, in its discretion and subject to such terms and conditions as it deems necessary, issue such an order and consent should the Commission determine not to object to the position of the self-regulatory organization set forth in the notice or application; *Provided, however,* That nothing herein shall foreclose the right of any person, at his election, to apply directly to the Commission for such consent, if he makes such application pursuant to the terms of an existing order of the Commission under section 15(b)(6) or 15B(c)(4) of the Act limiting his association with a broker or dealer or municipal securities dealer but explicitly granting him such a right to apply for entry or reentry at a later time.

(e) *Contents of application to the Commission.* An application to the Commission pursuant to paragraph (d) of this section shall consist of the following, as appropriate:

(1) The name of the person subject to the disqualification together with his last known place of residence or business as reflected on the records of the self-regulatory organization;

(2) A copy of the order or decision of the court, the Commission or the self-regulatory organization which adjudicated the matter giving rise to such "applicable disqualification";

(3) The nature of the relief sought and the reasons therefor;

(4) A description of the activities engaged in by the person since the disqualification arose;

(5) A description of the prospective business or employment in which the person plans to engage and the manner and extent of supervision to be exercised over and by such person. This description shall be accompanied by a written statement submitted to the self-regulatory organization by the proposed employer setting forth the terms and conditions of such employment and supervision. The description also shall include (i) the qualifications, experience, and disciplinary records of the proposed supervisors of the person and their family relationship (if any)

§ 240.19h-1

to that person; (ii) the findings and results of all examinations conducted, during the two years preceding the filing of the application, by self-regulatory organizations of the main office of the proposed employer and of the branch office(s) in which the employment will occur or be subject to supervisory controls; (iii) a copy of a completed Form U-4 with respect to the proposed association of such person and a certification by the self-regulatory organization that such person is fully qualified under all applicable requirements to engage in the proposed activities; and (iv) the name and place of employment of any other associated person of the proposed employer who is subject to a statutory disqualification (other than a disqualification specified in paragraph (a)(3)(iii) of this section);

(6) If a hearing on the matter has been held by the organization, a certified copy of the hearing record, together with copies of any exhibits introduced therein;

(7) All written submissions not included in a certified oral hearing record which were considered by the organization in its disposition of the matter;

(8) All information furnished in writing to the self-regulatory organization by the staff of the Commission for consideration by the organization in its disposition of the matter or the incorporation by reference of such information, and a statement of the organization's views thereon; and

(9) Such other matters as the organization or person deems relevant.

If the application contains assertions of material facts not a matter of record before the organization, such facts shall be sworn to by affidavit of the person or organization offering such facts for Commission consideration.

(f) *Definitions.* For purposes of this rule:

(1) The term *applicable disqualification* shall mean:

(i) Any effective order of the Commission pursuant to section 15(b) (4) or (6), 15B(c) (2) or (4) or 19(h) (2) or (3) of the Act—

(A) Revoking, suspending or placing limitations on the registration, activities, functions, or operations of a broker or dealer;

(B) Suspending, barring, or placing limitations on the association, activities, or functions of an associated person of a broker or dealer;

(C) Suspending or expelling any person from membership or participation in a self-regulatory organization; or

(D) Suspending or barring any person from being associated with a member of a national securities exchange or registered securities association;

(ii) Any conviction of injunction of a type described in section 15(b)(4) (B) or (C) of the Act; or

(iii) A failure under the provisions of Rule G-4 of the Municipal Securities Rulemaking Board under the Act, to meet qualifications standards, and such failure may be remedied by a finding or determination by the Commission pursuant to such rule(s) that the person affected nevertheless meets such standards.

(2) The term *control* shall mean the power to direct or cause the direction of the management or policies of a company whether through ownership of securities, by contract or otherwise; *Provided, however,* That

(i) Any person who, directly or indirectly, (A) has the right to vote 10 percent or more of the voting securities, (B) is entitled to receive 10 percent or more of the net profits, or (C) is a director (or person occupying a similar status or performing similar functions) of a company shall be presumed to be a person who controls such company;

(ii) Any person not covered by paragraph (i) shall be presumed not to be a person who controls such company; and

(iii) Any presumption may be rebutted on an appropriate showing.

(g) Where it deems appropriate to do so, the Commission may determine whether to (1) direct, pursuant to section 6(c)(2), 15A(g)(2) or 17A(b)(4)(A) of the Act, that a proposed admission covered by a notice filed pursuant to paragraph (a) of this section shall be denied or an order barring a proposed association issued or (2) grant or deny an application filed pursuant to paragraph (d) of this section on the basis of the notice or application filed by the self-regulatory organization, the person subject to the disqualification, or other

Securities and Exchange Commission

§ 240.21F–2

applicant (such as the proposed employer) on behalf of such person, without oral hearing. Any request for oral hearing or argument should be submitted with the notice or application.

(h) The Rules of Practice (17 CFR part 201) shall apply to proceedings under this rule to the extent that they are not inconsistent with this rule.

(15 U.S.C. 78a et seq., as amended by Pub. L. 94–29 (June 4, 1975) and by Pub. L. 98–38 (June 6, 1983), particularly secs. 11A, 15, 19 and 23 thereof (15 U.S.C. 78k–1, 78o, 78s and 78w))

[46 FR 58661, Dec. 3, 1981, as amended at 48 FR 53691, Nov. 29, 1983]

SECURITIES WHISTLEBLOWER INCENTIVES AND PROTECTIONS

SOURCE: Sections 240.21F–1 through 240.21F–17 appear at 76 FR 34363, June 13, 2011.

§ 240.21F–1 General.

Section 21F of the Securities Exchange Act of 1934 ("Exchange Act") (15 U.S.C. 78u–6), entitled "Securities Whistleblower Incentives and Protection," requires the Securities and Exchange Commission ("Commission") to pay awards, subject to certain limitations and conditions, to whistleblowers who provide the Commission with original information about violations of the Federal securities laws. These rules describe the whistleblower program that the Commission has established to implement the provisions of Section 21F, and explain the procedures you will need to follow in order to be eligible for an award. You should read these procedures carefully because the failure to take certain required steps within the time frames described in these rules may disqualify you from receiving an award for which you otherwise may be eligible. Unless expressly provided for in these rules, no person is authorized to make any offer or promise, or otherwise to bind the Commission with respect to the payment of any award or the amount thereof. The Securities and Exchange Commission's Office of the Whistleblower administers our whistleblower program. Questions about the program or these rules should be directed to the SEC Office of the Whistleblower, 100 F Street, NE., Washington, DC 20549–5631.

§ 240.21F–2 Whistleblower status, award eligibility, confidentiality, and retaliation protections.

(a) *Whistleblower status.* (1) You are a whistleblower for purposes of Section 21F of the Exchange Act (15 U.S.C. 78u–6) as of the time that, alone or jointly with others, you provide the Commission with information in writing that relates to a possible violation of the federal securities laws (including any law, rule, or regulation subject to the jurisdiction of the Commission) that has occurred, is ongoing, or is about to occur.

(2) A whistleblower must be an individual. A company or other entity is not eligible to be a whistleblower.

(b) *Award eligibility.* To be eligible for an award under Section 21F(b) of the Exchange Act (15 U.S.C. 78u–6(b)) based on any information you provide that relates to a possible violation of the federal securities laws, you must comply with the procedures and the conditions described in §§ 240.21F–4, 240.21F–8, and 240.21F–9. You should carefully review those rules before you submit any information that you may later wish to rely upon to claim an award.

(c) *Confidentiality protections.* To qualify for the confidentiality protections afforded by Section 21F(h)(2) of the Exchange Act (15 U.S.C. 78u–6(h)(2)) based on any information you provide that relates to a possible violation of the federal securities laws, you must comply with the procedures and the conditions described in Rule 21F–9(a) (§ 240.21F–9(a)).

(d) *Retaliation protections.* (1) To qualify for the retaliation protections afforded by Section 21F(h)(1) of the Exchange Act (15 U.S.C. 78u–6(h)(1)), you must satisfy all of the following criteria:

(i) You must qualify as a whistleblower under paragraph (a) of this section before experiencing the retaliation for which you seek redress;

(ii) You must reasonably believe that the information you provide to the Commission under paragraph (a) of this section relates to a possible violation of the federal securities laws; and

(iii) You must perform a lawful act that meets the following two criteria:

(A) First, the lawful act must be performed in connection with any of the

§ 240.21F-3

activities described in Section 21F(h)(1)(A)(i) through (iii) of the Exchange Act (15 U.S.C. 78u–6(h)(1)(A)(i) through (iii)); and

(B) Second, the lawful act must relate to the subject matter of your submission to the Commission under paragraph (a) of this section.

(2) To receive retaliation protection for a lawful act described in paragraph (d)(1)(iii) of this section, you do not need to qualify as a whistleblower under paragraph (a) of this section before performing the lawful act, but you must qualify as a whistleblower under paragraph (a) of this section before experiencing retaliation for the lawful act.

(3) To qualify for retaliation protection, you do not need to satisfy the procedures and conditions for award eligibility in §§ 240.21F–4, 240.21F–8, and 240.21F–9.

(4) Section 21F(h)(1) of the Exchange Act (15 U.S.C. 78u–6(h)(1)), including any rules promulgated thereunder, shall be enforceable in an action or proceeding brought by the Commission.

[85 FR 75942, Nov. 5, 2020]

§ 240.21F-3 Payment of awards.

(a) *Commission actions:* Subject to the eligibility requirements described in §§ 240.21F–2, 240.21F–8, and 240.21F–16 of this chapter, the Commission will pay an award or awards to one or more whistleblowers who:

(1) Voluntarily provide the Commission

(2) With original information

(3) That leads to the successful enforcement by the Commission of a Federal court or administrative action

(4) In which the Commission obtains monetary sanctions totaling more than $1,000,000.

NOTE TO PARAGRAPH (a): The terms *voluntarily, original information, leads to successful enforcement, action,* and *monetary sanctions* are defined in § 240.21F–4 of this chapter.

(b) *Related actions:* The Commission will also pay an award based on amounts collected in certain related actions.

(1) A *related action* is a judicial or administrative action that is brought by one of the governmental entities listed in paragraphs (b)(1)(i) through (iii) of this section or a self-regulatory organization as specified in paragraph (b)(1)(iv) of this section (collectively "governmental/SRO authority"), that yields monetary sanctions, and that is based upon information that either the whistleblower provided directly to a governmental/SRO entity or the Commission itself passed along to the governmental/SRO entity pursuant to the Commission's procedures for sharing information, and which is the same original information that the whistleblower voluntarily provided to the Commission and that led the Commission to obtain monetary sanctions totaling more than $1,000,000.

(i) The Attorney General of the United States;

(ii) An appropriate regulatory authority (as defined in § 240.21F–4); or

(iii) A state Attorney General in a criminal case; or

(iv) A self-regulatory organization (as defined in § 240.21F–4).

(2) In order for the Commission to make an award in connection with a related action, the Commission must determine that the same original information that the whistleblower gave to the Commission also led to the successful enforcement of the related action under the same criteria described in these rules for awards made in connection with Commission actions. The Commission may seek assistance and confirmation from the authority bringing the related action in making this determination. The Commission will deny an award in connection with the related action if:

(i) The Commission determines that the criteria for an award are not satisfied; or

(ii) The Commission is unable to make a determination because the Office of the Whistleblower could not obtain sufficient and reliable information that could be used as the basis for an award determination pursuant to § 240.21F–12(a) of this chapter. Additional procedures apply to the payment of awards in related actions. These procedures are described in §§ 240.21F–11 and 240.21F–14 of this chapter.

(3) The following provision shall apply where a claimant's application for a potential related action may also involve a potential recovery from a

Securities and Exchange Commission § 240.21F–3

comparable whistleblower award program (as defined in paragraph (b)(3)(iv) of this section) for that same action.

(i) Notwithstanding paragraph (b)(1) of this section, if a judicial or administrative action is subject to a separate monetary award program established by the Federal Government, a state government, or a self-regulatory organization (SRO), the action will be deemed eligible to qualify as a potential related-action only if either:

(A) The Commission finds that the maximum total award that could potentially be paid by the Commission based on the monetary sanctions imposed would not exceed $5 million; or

(B) The Commission finds (based on the facts and circumstances of the action) that the Commission's whistleblower award program has the more direct or relevant connection to that action.

(ii) In determining whether a potential related action has a more direct or relevant connection to the Commission's whistleblower program than another award program, the Commission will consider the nature, scope, and impact of the misconduct charged in the potential related action, and its relationship to the Federal securities laws. This inquiry may include consideration of, among other things:

(A) The relative extent to which the misconduct charged in the potential related action implicates the public policy interests underlying the Federal securities laws (such as investor protection) rather than other law-enforcement or regulatory interests (such as tax collection or fraud against the Federal Government);

(B) The degree to which the monetary sanctions imposed in the potential related action are attributable to conduct that also underlies the Federal securities law violations that were the subject of the Commission's enforcement action; and

(C) Whether the potential related action involves state-law claims and the extent to which the state may have a whistleblower award program that potentially applies to that type of law-enforcement action.

(iii) The conditions in paragraphs (b)(3)(iii)(A) through (C) of this section apply to a determination under paragraph (b)(3)(ii) of this section.

(A) The Commission shall not make a related-action award to a claimant (or any payment on a related-action award if the Commission has already made an award determination) if the claimant receives any payment from the other program for that action.

(B) If a claimant was denied an award by the other award program, the claimant will not be permitted to re-adjudicate any issues before the Commission that the governmental/SRO entity responsible for administering the other whistleblower award program resolved, pursuant to a final order of such government/SRO entity, against the claimant as part of the award denial.

(C) If the Commission makes an award before an award determination is finalized by the governmental/SRO entity responsible for administering the other award program, the award shall be conditioned on the claimant making an irrevocable waiver of any claim to an award from the other award program. The claimant's irrevocable waiver must be made within 60 calendar days of the claimant receiving notification of the Commission's final order.

(iv) The provisions of paragraphs (b)(3)(iv)(A) through (D) of this section apply to program comparability determinations.

(A) For purposes of paragraph (b)(3) of this section, a comparable whistleblower award program is an award program that satisfies the following criteria:

(*1*) The award program is administered by an authority or entity other than the Commission;

(*2*) The award program does not have an award range that could operate in a particular action to yield an award for a claimant that is meaningfully lower (when assessed against the maximum and minimum potential awards that program would allow) than the award range that the Commission's program could yield (*i.e.*, 10 to 30 percent of collected monetary sanctions);

(*3*) The award program does not have a cap that could operate in a particular action to yield an award for a claimant that is meaningfully lower than the maximum award the Commission could

§ 240.21F-4

grant for the action (*i.e.*, 30 percent of collected monetary sanctions in the related action); and

(*4*) The authority or entity administering the program may not in its discretion deny an award if a whistleblower satisfies the established eligibility requirements and award criteria.

(B) The Commission shall make a determination on a case-by-case basis whether an alternative award program is a comparable award program for purposes of the particular action on which the claimant is seeking a related-action award with respect to paragraphs (b)(3)(iv)(A)(*2*) through (*3*) of this section.

(C) If the Commission determines that an alternative award program is not comparable, the Commission shall condition its award on the meritorious whistleblower making within 60 calendar days of receiving notification of the Commission's final award an irrevocable waiver of any claim to an award from the other award program.

(D) A whistleblower whose related-action award application is subject to the provisions of paragraph (b)(3) of this section (including a whistleblower whose related-action award application implicates another award program that does not qualify as a comparable program as a result of paragraph (b)(3)(iv)(A) of this section) must demonstrate that the whistleblower has complied with the terms and conditions of this section regarding an irrevocable waiver. This shall include taking all steps necessary to authorize the administrators of the other program to confirm to staff in the Office of the Whistleblower (or in writing to the claimant or the Commission) that an irrevocable waiver has been made.

(v) A claimant seeking a related-action award must promptly inform the Office of the Whistleblower if the claimant applies for an award on the same action from another award program.

(vi) The Commission may deem a claimant ineligible for a related-action award if any of the conditions and requirements of paragraph (b)(3) of this section in connection with that related action are not satisfied.

[76 FR 34363, June 13, 2011, as amended at 85 FR 70943, Nov. 5, 2020; 87 FR 54150, Sept. 2, 2022]

§ 240.21F-4 Other definitions.

(a) *Voluntary submission of information.* (1) Your submission of information is made *voluntarily* within the meaning of §§ 240.21F-1 through 240.21F-17 of this chapter if you provide your submission before a request, inquiry, or demand that relates to the subject matter of your submission is directed to you or anyone representing you (such as an attorney):

(i) By the Commission;

(ii) In connection with an investigation, inspection, or examination by the Public Company Accounting Oversight Board, or any self-regulatory organization; or

(iii) In connection with an investigation by Congress, any other authority of the Federal government, or a state Attorney General or securities regulatory authority.

(2) If the Commission or any of these other authorities direct a request, inquiry, or demand as described in paragraph (a)(1) of this section to you or your representative first, your submission will not be considered voluntary, and you will not be eligible for an award, even if your response is not compelled by subpoena or other applicable law. However, your submission of information to the Commission will be considered voluntary if you voluntarily provided the same information to one of the other authorities identified above prior to receiving a request, inquiry, or demand from the Commission.

(3) In addition, your submission will not be considered voluntary if you are required to report your original information to the Commission as a result of a pre-existing legal duty, a contractual duty that is owed to the Commission or to one of the other authorities set forth in paragraph (a)(1) of this section, or a duty that arises out of a judicial or administrative order.

(b) *Original information.* (1) In order for your whistleblower submission to be considered *original information*, it must be:

(i) Derived from your independent knowledge or independent analysis;

(ii) Not already known to the Commission from any other source, unless you are the original source of the information;

(iii) Not exclusively derived from an allegation made in a judicial or administrative hearing, in a governmental report, hearing, audit, or investigation, or from the news media, unless you are a source of the information; and

(iv) Provided to the Commission for the first time after July 21, 2010 (the date of enactment of the *Dodd-Frank Wall Street Reform and Consumer Protection Act*).

(2) *Independent knowledge* means factual information in your possession that is not derived from publicly available sources. You may gain independent knowledge from your experiences, communications and observations in your business or social interactions.

(3) *Independent analysis* means your own analysis, whether done alone or in combination with others. *Analysis* means your examination and evaluation of information that may be publicly available, but which reveals information that is not generally known or available to the public.

(4) The Commission will not consider information to be derived from your independent knowledge or independent analysis in any of the following circumstances:

(i) If you obtained the information through a communication that was subject to the attorney-client privilege, unless disclosure of that information would otherwise be permitted by an attorney pursuant to § 205.3(d)(2) of this chapter, the applicable state attorney conduct rules, or otherwise;

(ii) If you obtained the information in connection with the legal representation of a client on whose behalf you or your employer or firm are providing services, and you seek to use the information to make a whistleblower submission for your own benefit, unless disclosure would otherwise be permitted by an attorney pursuant to § 205.3(d)(2) of this chapter, the applicable state attorney conduct rules, or otherwise; or

(iii) In circumstances not covered by paragraphs (b)(4)(i) or (b)(4)(ii) of this section, if you obtained the information because you were:

(A) An officer, director, trustee, or partner of an entity and another person informed you of allegations of misconduct, or you learned the information in connection with the entity's processes for identifying, reporting, and addressing possible violations of law;

(B) An employee whose principal duties involve compliance or internal audit responsibilities, or you were employed by or otherwise associated with a firm retained to perform compliance or internal audit functions for an entity;

(C) Employed by or otherwise associated with a firm retained to conduct an inquiry or investigation into possible violations of law; or

(D) An employee of, or other person associated with, a public accounting firm, if you obtained the information through the performance of an engagement required of an independent public accountant under the Federal securities laws (other than an audit subject to § 240.21F–8(c)(4) of this chapter), and that information related to a violation by the engagement client or the client's directors, officers or other employees.

(iv) If you obtained the information by a means or in a manner that is determined by a United States court to violate applicable Federal or state criminal law; or

(v) *Exceptions.* Paragraph (b)(4)(iii) of this section shall not apply if:

(A) You have a reasonable basis to believe that disclosure of the information to the Commission is necessary to prevent the relevant entity from engaging in conduct that is likely to cause substantial injury to the financial interest or property of the entity or investors;

(B) You have a reasonable basis to believe that the relevant entity is engaging in conduct that will impede an investigation of the misconduct; or

(C) At least 120 days have elapsed since you provided the information to the relevant entity's audit committee,

§ 240.21F-4

chief legal officer, chief compliance officer (or their equivalents), or your supervisor, or since you received the information, if you received it under circumstances indicating that the entity's audit committee, chief legal officer, chief compliance officer (or their equivalents), or your supervisor was already aware of the information.

(vi) If you obtained the information from a person who is subject to this section, unless the information is not excluded from that person's use pursuant to this section, or you are providing the Commission with information about possible violations involving that person.

(5) The Commission will consider you to be an *original source* of the same information that we obtain from another source if the information satisfies the definition of original information and the other source obtained the information from you or your representative. In order to be considered an original source of information that the Commission receives from Congress, any other authority of the Federal government, a state Attorney General or securities regulatory authority, any self-regulatory organization, or the Public Company Accounting Oversight Board, you must have voluntarily given such authorities the information within the meaning of these rules. You must establish your status as the original source of information to the Commission's satisfaction. In determining whether you are the original source of information, the Commission may seek assistance and confirmation from one of the other authorities described above, or from another entity (including your employer), in the event that you claim to be the original source of information that an authority or another entity provided to the Commission.

(6) If the Commission already knows some information about a matter from other sources at the time you make your submission, and you are not an original source of that information under paragraph (b)(5) of this section, the Commission will consider you an original source of any information you provide that is derived from your independent knowledge or analysis and that materially adds to the information that the Commission already possesses.

(7) If you provide information to the Congress, any other authority of the Federal government, a state Attorney General or securities regulatory authority, any self-regulatory organization, or the Public Company Accounting Oversight Board, or to an entity's internal whistleblower, legal, or compliance procedures for reporting allegations of possible violations of law, and you, within 120 days, submit the same information to the Commission pursuant to § 240.21F-9 of this chapter, as you must do in order for you to be eligible to be considered for an award, then, for purposes of evaluating your claim to an award under §§ 240.21F-10 and 240.21F-11 of this chapter, the Commission will consider that you provided information as of the date of your original disclosure, report or submission to one of these other authorities or persons. You must establish the effective date of any prior disclosure, report, or submission, to the Commission's satisfaction. The Commission may seek assistance and confirmation from the other authority or person in making this determination.

(c) *Information that leads to successful enforcement.* The Commission will consider that you provided original information that led to the successful enforcement of a judicial or administrative action in any of the following circumstances:

(1) You gave the Commission original information that was sufficiently specific, credible, and timely to cause the staff to commence an examination, open an investigation, reopen an investigation that the Commission had closed, or to inquire concerning different conduct as part of a current examination or investigation, and the Commission brought a successful judicial or administrative action based in whole or in part on conduct that was the subject of your original information; or

(2) You gave the Commission original information about conduct that was already under examination or investigation by the Commission, the Congress, any other authority of the Federal Government, a state attorney general or securities regulatory authority, any

self-regulatory organization, or the PCAOB (except in cases where you were an original source of this information as defined in paragraph (b)(5) of this section), and your submission significantly contributed to the success of the action; or

(3) You reported original information through an entity's internal whistleblower, legal, or compliance procedures for reporting allegations of possible violations of law before or at the same time you reported them to the Commission; the entity later provided your information to the Commission, or provided results of an audit or investigation initiated in whole or in part in response to information you reported to the entity; and the information the entity provided to the Commission satisfies either paragraph (c)(1) or (c)(2) of this section. Under this paragraph (c)(3), you must also submit the same information to the Commission in accordance with the procedures set forth in §240.21F–9 within 120 days of providing it to the entity.

(d) An *action* generally means a single captioned judicial or administrative proceeding brought by the Commission. Notwithstanding the foregoing:

(1) For purposes of making an award under §240.21F–10 of this chapter, the Commission will treat as a Commission action two or more administrative or judicial proceedings brought by the Commission if these proceedings arise out of the same nucleus of operative facts; or

(2) For purposes of determining the payment on an award under §240.21F–14 of this chapter, the Commission will deem as part of the Commission action upon which the award was based any subsequent Commission proceeding that, individually, results in a monetary sanction of $1,000,000 or less, and that arises out of the same nucleus of operative facts.

(3) For purposes of making an award under §§240.21F–10 and 240.21F–11, the following will be deemed to be an administrative action and any money required to be paid thereunder will be deemed a monetary sanction under §240.21F–4(e):

(i) A non-prosecution agreement or deferred prosecution agreement entered into by the U.S. Department of Justice; or

(ii) A similar settlement agreement entered into by the Commission outside of the context of a judicial or administrative proceeding to address violations of the securities laws.

(e) *Monetary sanctions* means:

(1) An order to pay money that results from a Commission action or related action and which is either:

(i) Expressly designated as a penalty, disgorgement, or interest; or

(ii) Otherwise ordered as relief for the violations that are the subject of the covered action or related action; or

(2) Any money deposited into a disgorgement fund or other fund pursuant to section 308(b) of the Sarbanes-Oxley Act of 2002 (15 U.S.C. 7246(b)), as a result of such action or any settlement of such action.

(f) *Appropriate regulatory agency* means the Commission, the Comptroller of the Currency, the Board of Governors of the Federal Reserve System, the Federal Deposit Insurance Corporation, the Office of Thrift Supervision, and any other agencies that may be defined as appropriate regulatory agencies under Section 3(a)(34) of the Exchange Act (15 U.S.C. 78c(a)(34)).

(g) *Appropriate regulatory authority* means an appropriate regulatory agency other than the Commission.

(h) *Self-regulatory organization* means any national securities exchange, registered securities association, registered clearing agency, the Municipal Securities Rulemaking Board, and any other organizations that may be defined as self-regulatory organizations under Section 3(a)(26) of the Exchange Act (15 U.S.C. 78c(a)(26)).

[76 FR 34363, June 13, 2011, as amended at 85 FR 70943, Nov. 5, 2020; 87 FR 54151, Sept. 2, 2022]

§240.21F–5 Amount of award.

(a) The determination of the amount of an award is in the discretion of the Commission.

(b) If all of the conditions are met for a whistleblower award in connection with a Commission action or a related action, the Commission will then decide the percentage amount of the award applying the criteria set forth in

§ 240.21F-6

§ 240.21F-6 of this chapter and pursuant to the procedures set forth in §§ 240.21F-10 and 240.21F-11 of this chapter. The amount will be at least 10 percent and no more than 30 percent of the monetary sanctions that the Commission and the other authorities are able to collect. The percentage awarded in connection with a Commission action may differ from the percentage awarded in connection with a related action.

(c) If the Commission makes awards to more than one whistleblower in connection with the same action or related action, the Commission will determine an individual percentage award for each whistleblower, but in no event will the total amount awarded to all whistleblowers in the aggregate be less than 10 percent or greater than 30 percent of the amount the Commission or the other authorities collect.

§ 240.21F-6 Criteria for determining amount of award.

In exercising its discretion to determine the appropriate award, the Commission may consider the following factors (and only the following factors) in relation to the facts and circumstances of each case in setting the dollar or percentage amount of the award. In the event that awards are determined for multiple whistleblowers in connection an action, these factors will be used to determine the relative allocation of awards among the whistleblowers.

(a) *Factors that may increase the amount of a whistleblower's award.* In determining whether to increase the amount of an award, the Commission will consider the following factors, which are not listed in order of importance.

(1) *Significance of the information provided by the whistleblower.* The Commission will assess the significance of the information provided by a whistleblower to the success of the Commission action or related action. In considering this factor, the Commission may take into account, among other things:

(i) The nature of the information provided by the whistleblower and how it related to the successful enforcement action, including whether the reliability and completeness of the information provided to the Commission by the whistleblower resulted in the conservation of Commission resources;

(ii) The degree to which the information provided by the whistleblower supported one or more successful claims brought in the Commission or related action.

(2) *Assistance provided by the whistleblower.* The Commission will assess the degree of assistance provided by the whistleblower and any legal representative of the whistleblower in the Commission action or related action. In considering this factor, the Commission may take into account, among other things:

(i) Whether the whistleblower provided ongoing, extensive, and timely cooperation and assistance by, for example, helping to explain complex transactions, interpreting key evidence, or identifying new and productive lines of inquiry;

(ii) The timeliness of the whistleblower's initial report to the Commission or to an internal compliance or reporting system of business organizations committing, or impacted by, the securities violations, where appropriate;

(iii) The resources conserved as a result of the whistleblower's assistance;

(iv) Whether the whistleblower appropriately encouraged or authorized others to assist the staff of the Commission who might otherwise not have participated in the investigation or related action;

(v) The efforts undertaken by the whistleblower to remediate the harm caused by the violations, including assisting the authorities in the recovery of the fruits and instrumentalities of the violations; and

(vi) Any unique hardships experienced by the whistleblower as a result of his or her reporting and assisting in the enforcement action.

(3) *Law enforcement interest.* The Commission will assess its programmatic interest in deterring violations of the securities laws by making awards to whistleblowers who provide information that leads to the successful enforcement of such laws. In considering this factor, the Commission may take into account, among other things:

Securities and Exchange Commission § 240.21F–6

(i) The degree to which an award enhances the Commission's ability to enforce the Federal securities laws and protect investors; and

(ii) The degree to which an award encourages the submission of high quality information from whistleblowers by appropriately rewarding whistleblowers' submission of significant information and assistance, even in cases where the monetary sanctions available for collection are limited or potential monetary sanctions were reduced or eliminated by the Commission because an entity self-reported a securities violation following the whistleblower's related internal disclosure, report, or submission.

(iii) Whether the subject matter of the action is a Commission priority, whether the reported misconduct involves regulated entities or fiduciaries, whether the whistleblower exposed an industry-wide practice, the type and severity of the securities violations, the age and duration of misconduct, the number of violations, and the isolated, repetitive, or ongoing nature of the violations; and

(iv) The dangers to investors or others presented by the underlying violations involved in the enforcement action, including the amount of harm or potential harm caused by the underlying violations, the type of harm resulting from or threatened by the underlying violations, and the number of individuals or entities harmed.

(4) *Participation in internal compliance systems.* The Commission will assess whether, and the extent to which, the whistleblower and any legal representative of the whistleblower participated in internal compliance systems. In considering this factor, the Commission may take into account, among other things:

(i) Whether, and the extent to which, a whistleblower reported the possible securities violations through internal whistleblower, legal or compliance procedures before, or at the same time as, reporting them to the Commission; and

(ii) Whether, and the extent to which, a whistleblower assisted any internal investigation or inquiry concerning the reported securities violations.

(b) *Factors that may decrease the amount of a whistleblower's award.* In determining whether to decrease the amount of an award, the Commission will consider the following factors, which are not listed in order of importance.

(1) *Culpability.* The Commission will assess the culpability or involvement of the whistleblower in matters associated with the Commission's action or related actions. In considering this factor, the Commission may take into account, among other things:

(i) The whistleblower's role in the securities violations;

(ii) The whistleblower's education, training, experience, and position of responsibility at the time the violations occurred;

(iii) Whether the whistleblower acted with scienter, both generally and in relation to others who participated in the violations;

(iv) Whether the whistleblower financially benefitted from the violations;

(v) Whether the whistleblower is a recidivist;

(vi) The egregiousness of the underlying fraud committed by the whistleblower; and

(vii) Whether the whistleblower knowingly interfered with the Commission's investigation of the violations or related enforcement actions.

(2) *Unreasonable reporting delay.* The Commission will assess whether the whistleblower unreasonably delayed reporting the securities violations. In considering this factor, the Commission may take into account, among other things:

(i) Whether the whistleblower was aware of the relevant facts but failed to take reasonable steps to report or prevent the violations from occurring or continuing;

(ii) Whether the whistleblower was aware of the relevant facts but only reported them after learning about a related inquiry, investigation, or enforcement action; and

(iii) Whether there was a legitimate reason for the whistleblower to delay reporting the violations.

(3) *Interference with internal compliance and reporting systems.* The Commission will assess, in cases where the whistleblower interacted with his or

805

§ 240.21F-6

her entity's internal compliance or reporting system, whether the whistleblower undermined the integrity of such system. In considering this factor, the Commission will take into account whether there is evidence provided to the Commission that the whistleblower knowingly:

(i) Interfered with an entity's established legal, compliance, or audit procedures to prevent or delay detection of the reported securities violation;

(ii) Made any material false, fictitious, or fraudulent statements or representations that hindered an entity's efforts to detect, investigate, or remediate the reported securities violations; and

(iii) Provided any false writing or document knowing the writing or document contained any false, fictitious or fraudulent statements or entries that hindered an entity's efforts to detect, investigate, or remediate the reported securities violations.

(c) *Additional considerations in connection with certain awards of $5 million or less.* (1) This subpart applies when the Commission is considering any meritorious award application where:

(i) The statutory maximum award of 30 percent of the monetary sanctions collected in any covered and related action(s), in the aggregate, is $5 million or less, and the Commission determines that it does not reasonably anticipate that future collections would cause the statutory maximum award to be paid to any whistleblower to exceed $5 million in the aggregate;

(ii) None of the negative award factors specified in paragraphs §§ 240.21F-6(b)(1) or 240.21F-6(b)(3) were found present with respect to the claimant's award application, and the award claim does not trigger § 240.21F-16 (concerning awards to whistleblowers who engage in culpable conduct);

(iii) The claimant did not engage in unreasonable reporting delay under § 240.21F-(6)(b)(2) (although the Commission, in its sole discretion, may in certain limited circumstances determine to waive this criterion if the claimant can demonstrate that doing so based on the facts and circumstances of the matter is consistent with the public interest, the promotion of investor protection, and the objectives of the whistleblower program); and

17 CFR Ch. II (4-1-23 Edition)

(iv) The Commission does not otherwise determine in its sole discretion that application of the enhancement afforded by this subpart would be inappropriate because either:

(A) The whistleblower's assistance in the covered action or related action (as assessed under § 240.21F-6(a) of this section) was, under the relevant facts and circumstances, limited; or

(B) Providing the enhancement would be inconsistent with the public interest, the promotion of investor protection, or the objectives of the whistleblower program.

(2) If the Commission determines that the criteria in § 240.21F-6(c)(1) are satisfied, the resulting payout to a claimant for the original information that the claimant provided that led to one or more successful covered or related action(s), collectively, will be the maximum allowed under the statute.

(3) Notwithstanding § 240.21F-6(c)(2), if two or more claimants qualify for an award in connection with any covered action or related action and at least one of those claimant's award applications qualifies under § 240.21F-6(c)(1), the aggregate amount awarded to all meritorious claimants will be the statutory maximum. In allocating that amount among the meritorious claimants, the Commission will consider whether an individual claimant's award application satisfies §§ 240.21F-6(c)(1)(ii) and 240.21F-6(c)(1)(iii).

(d) *Consideration of the dollar amount of an award.* When applying the award factors specified in paragraphs (a) and (b) of this section, the Commission may consider the dollar amount of a potential award for the limited purpose of increasing the award amount. The Commission shall not, however, use the dollar amount of a potential award as a basis to lower a potential award, including when applying the factors specified in paragraphs (a) and (b) of this section.

[76 FR 34363, June 13, 2011, as amended at 85 FR 70943, Nov. 5, 2020; 87 FR 54151, Sept. 2, 2022]

Securities and Exchange Commission § 240.21F-8

§ 240.21F-7 Confidentiality of submissions.

(a) Pursuant to Section 21F(h)(2) of the Exchange Act (15 U.S.C. 78u-6(h)(2)) and § 240.21F-2(c), the Commission will not disclose information that could reasonably be expected to reveal the identity of a whistleblower provided that the whistleblower has submitted information utilizing the processes specified in § 240.21F-9(a), except that the Commission may disclose such information in the following circumstances:

(1) When disclosure is required to a defendant or respondent in connection with a Federal court or administrative action that the Commission files or in another public action or proceeding that is filed by an authority to which we provide the information, as described below;

(2) When the Commission determines that it is necessary to accomplish the purposes of the Exchange Act (15 U.S.C. 78a) and to protect investors, it may provide your information to the Department of Justice, an appropriate regulatory authority, a self regulatory organization, a state attorney general in connection with a criminal investigation, any appropriate state regulatory authority, the Public Company Accounting Oversight Board, or foreign securities and law enforcement authorities. Each of these entities other than foreign securities and law enforcement authorities is subject to the confidentiality requirements set forth in Section 21F(h) of the Exchange Act (15 U.S.C. 78u-6(h)). The Commission will determine what assurances of confidentiality it deems appropriate in providing such information to foreign securities and law enforcement authorities.

(3) The Commission may make disclosures in accordance with the Privacy Act of 1974 (5 U.S.C. 552a).

(b) You may submit information to the Commission anonymously. If you do so, however, you must also do the following:

(1) You must have an attorney represent you in connection with both your submission of information and your claim for an award, and your attorney's name and contact information must be provided to the Commission at the time you submit your information;

(2) You and your attorney must follow the procedures set forth in § 240.21F-9 of this chapter for submitting original information anonymously; and

(3) Before the Commission will pay any award to you, you must disclose your identity to the Commission and your identity must be verified by the Commission as set forth in § 240.21F-10 of this chapter.

[76 FR 34363, June 13, 2011, as amended at 85 FR 70944, Nov. 5, 2020]

§ 240.21F-8 Eligibility and forms.

(a) To be eligible for a whistleblower award, you must give the Commission information in the form and manner that the Commission requires. The procedures for submitting information and making a claim for an award are described in § 240.21F-9 through § 240.21F-11 of this chapter. You should read these procedures carefully because you need to follow them in order to be eligible for an award, except that the Commission may, in its sole discretion, waive any of these procedures based upon a showing of extraordinary circumstances.

(b) In addition to any forms required by these rules, the Commission may also require that you provide certain additional information. You may be required to:

(1) Provide explanations and other assistance in order that the staff may evaluate and use the information that you submitted;

(2) Provide all additional information in your possession that is related to the subject matter of your submission in a complete and truthful manner, through follow-up meetings, or in other forms that our staff may agree to;

(3) Provide testimony or other evidence acceptable to the staff relating to whether you are eligible, or otherwise satisfy any of the conditions, for an award; and

(4) Enter into a confidentiality agreement in a form acceptable to the Office of the Whistleblower, covering any non-public information that the Commission provides to you, and including a provision that a violation of the

807

§ 240.21F-8

agreement may lead to your ineligibility to receive an award.

(c) You are not eligible to be considered for an award if you do not satisfy the requirements of paragraphs (a) and (b) of this section. In addition, you are not eligible if:

(1) You are, or were at the time you acquired the original information provided to the Commission, a member, officer, or employee of the Commission, the Department of Justice, an appropriate regulatory agency, a self-regulatory organization, the Public Company Accounting Oversight Board, or any law enforcement organization;

(2) You are, or were at the time you acquired the original information provided to the Commission, a member, officer, or employee of a foreign government, any political subdivision, department, agency, or instrumentality of a foreign government, or any other foreign financial regulatory authority as that term is defined in Section 3(a)(52) of the Exchange Act (15 U.S.C. 78c(a)(52));

(3) You are convicted of a criminal violation that is related to the Commission action or to a related action (as defined in § 240.21F-4 of this chapter) for which you otherwise could receive an award;

(4) You obtained the original information that you gave the Commission through an audit of a company's financial statements, and making a whistleblower submission would be contrary to requirements of Section 10A of the Exchange Act (15 U.S.C. 78j-a).

(5) You are the spouse, parent, child, or sibling of a member or employee of the Commission, or you reside in the same household as a member or employee of the Commission;

(6) You acquired the original information you gave the Commission from a person:

(i) Who is subject to paragraph (c)(4) of this section, unless the information is not excluded from that person's use, or you are providing the Commission with information about possible violations involving that person; or

(ii) With the intent to evade any provision of these rules; or

(7) The Commission or a court of competent jurisdiction finds that, in your whistleblower submission, your other dealings with the Commission (including your dealings beyond the whistleblower program and covered action), or your dealings with another governmental/SRO entity (as specified in § 240.21F-3(b)(1)) in connection with a related action, you knowingly and willfully made any materially false, fictitious, or fraudulent statement or representation, or used any false writing or document knowing that it contains any materially false, fictitious, or fraudulent statement or entry with intent to mislead or otherwise hinder the Commission or another governmental/SRO entity, provided that this provision should not apply if the Commission, in its discretion, finds it consistent with the public interest, the promotion of investor protection, and the objectives of the whistleblower program.

(d) The Commission may modify or revise Form TCR and Form WB-APP as provided below.

(1) The Commission will periodically designate on the Commission's web page a Form TCR (Tip, Complaint, or Referral) that individuals seeking to be eligible for an award through the process identified in § 240.21F-9(a)(2) shall use.

(2) The Commission will also periodically designate on the Commission's web page a Form WB-APP for use by individuals seeking to apply for an award in connection with a Commission-covered judicial or administrative action (15 U.S.C. 21F(a)(1)), or a related action (§ 240.21F-3(b)(1)).

(e) The Commission shall have the authority to impose a permanent bar on a claimant as provided below.

(1) *Grounds for a permanent bar.* Submissions or applications that are frivolous or fraudulent, or that would otherwise hinder the effective and efficient operation of the Whistleblower Program may result in the Commission issuing a permanent bar as part of a final order in the course of considering a whistleblower award application from you. If such a bar is issued, the Office of the Whistleblower will not accept or act on any other applications from you. A permanent bar may be issued in the following circumstances:

(i) If you make three or more award applications for Commission actions that the Commission finds to be frivolous or lacking a colorable connection between the tip (or tips) and the Commission actions for which you are seeking awards; or

(ii) If the Commission finds that you have violated paragraph (c)(7) of this section.

(2) *General procedures for issuance of a permanent bar.* The Commission will consider whether to issue a permanent bar in connection with an award application from you. In general, the Preliminary Determination or Preliminary Summary Disposition must state that a bar is being recommended, and you will then have an opportunity to respond in writing in accordance with the award processing procedures specified in §§ 240.21F–10(e)(2) and 240.21F–18(b)(3). If the basis for a bar arises or is discovered after the issuance of a Preliminary Determination or Preliminary Summary Disposition, the Office of the Whistleblower shall notify you and afford you an opportunity to submit a response before the Commission determines whether to issue a bar.

(3) *Notice and opportunity to withdraw frivolous applications.* (i) Except as provided in paragraph (e)(3)(ii) of this section, before any Preliminary Determination or Preliminary Summary Disposition is issued that may recommend a bar, the Office of the Whistleblower shall advise you of any assessment by that Office that your award application is frivolous ("frivolous application") or based on a tip that lacks a colorable connection to the action for which you have sought an award ("noncolorable application"). If you withdraw your award application within 30 days of the notification from the Office of the Whistleblower, it will not be considered by the Commission in determining whether to exercise its authority under this paragraph (e).

(ii) The notification and opportunity to withdraw provided for by paragraph (e)(3)(i) are limited to the first three applications submitted by you that are reviewed by the Office of the Whistleblower and preliminarily deemed by that Office to be either a frivolous application or a noncolorable application. After these first three award applications, you will not be provided notice or an opportunity to withdraw any other frivolous or noncolorable applications.

(iii) For purposes of determining whether a bar should be imposed under section (e) of this rule, you will not be permitted to withdraw your application:

(A) After the 30-day period to withdraw has run following notice from the Office of the Whistleblower with respect to the initial three applications assessed by that Office to be frivolous or lacking a colorable connection to the action; or

(B) After a Preliminary Determination or Preliminary Summary Disposition has issued in connection with any other such application.

(4) *Award applications pending before the effective date of paragraph (e).* (i) Paragraph (e) of this section shall apply to all award applications pending as of the effective date of paragraph (e) of this section. But with respect to any such pending award applications, the Office of the Whistleblower shall advise you, before any Preliminary Determination or Preliminary Summary Disposition is issued that may recommend a bar, of any assessment by that Office that the conditions for issuing a bar are satisfied because either:

(A) You submitted an award application prior to the effective date of this section (e) and that application is frivolous or lacking a colorable connection between the tip and the action for which you have sought an award; or

(B) You made a materially false, fictitious, or fraudulent statement or representation or used a false writing or document in violation of paragraph (c)(7) of this section prior to the effective date of this section (e).

(ii) If, within 30 calendar days of the Office of the Whistleblower providing the foregoing notification, you withdraw the relevant award application(s), the withdrawn award application(s) will not be considered by the Commission in determining whether to exercise its authority under paragraph (e) of this section.

[76 FR 34363, June 13, 2011, as amended at 85 FR 70944, Nov. 5, 2020; 87 FR 54151, Sept. 2, 2022]

§ 240.21F-9 Procedures for submitting original information.

(a) To submit information in a manner that satisfies § 240.21F-2(b) and § 240.21F-2(c) of this chapter you must submit your information to the Commission by any of these methods:

(1) Online, through the Commission's website located at *www.sec.gov*, using the Commission's electronic TCR portal (Tip, Complaint, or Referral);

(2) Mailing or faxing a Form TCR to the SEC Office of the Whistleblower at the mailing address or fax number designated on the SEC's web page for making such submissions; or

(3) By any other such method that the Commission may expressly designate on its website as a mechanism that satisfies §§ 240.21F-2(b) and 240.21F-2(c) of this chapter. For a 30-day period following the Commission's designation of any new forms by placing them on the Commission's website, the Commission shall also continue to accept submissions made using the prior version of the forms.

(b) Further, to be eligible for an award, you must declare under penalty of perjury at the time you submit your information pursuant to paragraph (a)(1), (a)(2), or (a)(3) of this section that your information is true and correct to the best of your knowledge and belief.

(c) Notwithstanding paragraphs (a) and (b) of this section, if you are providing your original information to the Commission anonymously, then your attorney must submit your information on your behalf pursuant to the procedures specified in paragraph (a) of this section. Prior to your attorney's submission, you must provide your attorney with a completed Form TCR that you have signed under penalty of perjury. When your attorney makes her submission on your behalf, your attorney will be required to certify that he or she:

(1) Has verified your identity;

(2) Has reviewed your completed and signed Form TCR for completeness and accuracy and that the information contained therein is true, correct and complete to the best of the attorney's knowledge, information and belief;

(3) Has obtained your non-waivable consent to provide the Commission with your original completed and signed Form TCR in the event that the Commission requests it due to concerns that you may have knowingly and willfully made false, fictitious, or fraudulent statements or representations, or used any false writing or document knowing that the writing or document contains any false fictitious or fraudulent statement or entry; and

(4) Consents to be legally obligated to provide the signed Form TCR within seven (7) calendar days of receiving such request from the Commission.

(d) If you submitted original information in writing to the Commission after July 21, 2010 (the date of enactment of the Dodd-Frank Wall Street Reform and Consumer Protection Act) but before the effective date of these rules, your submission will be deemed to satisfy the requirements set forth in paragraphs (a) and (b) of this section. If you were an anonymous whistleblower, however, you must provide your attorney with a completed and signed copy of Form TCR within 60 days of the effective date of these rules, your attorney must retain the signed form in his or her records, and you must provide of copy of the signed form to the Commission staff upon request by Commission staff prior to any payment of an award to you in connection with your submission. Notwithstanding the foregoing, you must follow the procedures and conditions for making a claim for a whistleblower award described in §§ 240.21F-10 and 240.21F-11 of this chapter.

(e) You must follow the procedures specified in paragraphs (a) and (b) of this section within 30 days of when you first provide the Commission with original information that you rely upon as a basis for claiming an award. If you fail to do so, then you will be deemed ineligible for an award in connection with that information (even if you later resubmit that information in accordance with paragraphs (a) and (b) of this section). Notwithstanding the foregoing, the Commission shall waive your noncompliance with paragraphs (a) and (b) of this section if:

(1) You demonstrate to the satisfaction of the Commission that you complied with the requirements of paragraphs (a) and (b) of this section within

Securities and Exchange Commission § 240.21F–10

30 days of first obtaining actual or constructive notice about those requirements (or 30 days from the date you retain counsel to represent you in connection with your submission of original information, whichever occurs first); and

(2) The Commission can readily develop an administrative record that unambiguously demonstrates that you would otherwise qualify for an award.

[76 FR 34363, June 13, 2011, as amended at 85 FR 70945, Nov. 5, 2020]

§ 240.21F–10 Procedures for making a claim for a whistleblower award in SEC actions that result in monetary sanctions in excess of $1,000,000.

(a) Whenever a Commission action results in monetary sanctions totaling more than $1,000,000, the Office of the Whistleblower will cause to be published on the Commission's Web site a "Notice of Covered Action." Such Notice will be published subsequent to the entry of a final judgment or order that alone, or collectively with other judgments or orders previously entered in the Commission action, exceeds $1,000,000; or, in the absence of such judgment or order subsequent to the deposit of monetary sanctions exceeding $1,000,000 into a disgorgement or other fund pursuant to Section 308(b) of the Sarbanes-Oxley Act of 2002. A claimant will have ninety (90) days from the date of the Notice of Covered Action to file a claim for an award based on that action, or the claim will be barred.

(b) To file a claim for a whistleblower award, you must file Form WB–APP (as specified in § 240.21F–8(d)(2). You must sign this form as the claimant and submit it to the Office of the Whistleblower by mail, email (as a PDF attachment), or fax (or any other manner that the Office permits).

(1) All claim forms, including any attachments, must be received by the Office of the Whistleblower within ninety (90) calendar days of the date of the Notice of Covered Action in order to be considered for an award.

(2) Notwithstanding paragraphs (a) and (b)(1) of this section, the time period to file an application for an award based on a Commission settlement agreement covered by § 240.21F–4(d) of this chapter shall be governed exclusively by § 240.21F–11(b)(1) of this chapter if the settlement agreement was entered into after July 21, 2010 but before the effective date of this section as amended in 2020.

(c) If you provided your original information to the Commission anonymously, you must disclose your identity on the Form WB–APP, and your identity must be verified in a form and manner that is acceptable to the Office of the Whistleblower prior to the payment of any award.

(d) Once the time for filing any appeals of the Commission's judicial or administrative action has expired, or where an appeal has been filed, after all appeals in the action have been concluded, one or more staff members designated by the Director of the Division of Enforcement ("Claims Review Staff") will evaluate all timely whistleblower award claims submitted on Form WB–APP in accordance with the criteria set forth in these rules. In connection with this process, the Office of the Whistleblower may require that you provide additional information relating to your eligibility for an award or satisfaction of any of the conditions for an award, as set forth in § 240.21F–8(b) of this chapter. Following a determination by the Claims Review Staff (and an opportunity for the Commission to review that determination), the Office of the Whistleblower will send you a Preliminary Determination setting forth a preliminary assessment as to whether the claim should be allowed or denied and, if allowed, setting forth the proposed award dollar and percentage amount, and the grounds therefore.

(e) You may contest the Preliminary Determination made by the Claims Review Staff by submitting a written response to the Office of the Whistleblower setting forth the grounds for your objection to either the denial of an award or the proposed amount of an award. The response must be in the form and manner that the Office of the Whistleblower shall require. You may also include documentation or other evidentiary support for the grounds advanced in your response. In applying the award factors and standards specified in § 240.21F–6, and determining the award dollar and percentage amounts

§ 240.21F-11

set forth in the Preliminary Determination, the award factors may be considered by the SEC staff and the Commission in dollar terms, percentage terms or some combination thereof, subject to the limitations imposed by § 240.21F-6(d). Should you choose to contest a Preliminary Determination, you may set forth the reasons for your objection to the proposed amount of an award, including the grounds therefore, in dollar terms, percentage terms or some combination thereof.

(1) Before determining whether to contest a Preliminary Determination, you may:

(i) Within 30 calendar days of the date of the Preliminary Determination, request that the Office of the Whistleblower make available for your review the materials from among those set forth in § 240.21F-12(a) that formed the basis of the Claims Review Staff's Preliminary Determination.

(ii) Within 30 calendar days of the date of the Preliminary Determination, request a meeting with the Office of the Whistleblower; however, such meetings are not required, and the office may in its sole discretion decline the request.

(2) If you decide to contest the Preliminary Determination, you must submit your written response and supporting materials within 60 calendar days of the date of the Preliminary Determination, or if a request to review materials is made pursuant to paragraph (e)(1) of this section, then within 60 calendar days of the Office of the Whistleblower making those materials available for your review.

(f) If you fail to submit a timely response pursuant to paragraph (e) of this section, then the Preliminary Determination will become the Final Order of the Commission (except where the Preliminary Determination recommended an award, in which case the Preliminary Determination will be deemed a Proposed Final Determination for purposes of paragraph (h) of this section). Your failure to submit a timely response contesting a Preliminary Determination will constitute a failure to exhaust administrative remedies, and you will be prohibited from pursuing an appeal pursuant to § 240.21F-13 of this chapter.

(g) If you submit a timely response pursuant to paragraph (e) of this section, then the Claims Review Staff will consider the issues and grounds advanced in your response, along with any supporting documentation you provided, and will make its Proposed Final Determination.

(h) The Office of the Whistleblower will then notify the Commission of each Proposed Final Determination. Within thirty 30 days thereafter, any Commissioner may request that the Proposed Final Determination be reviewed by the Commission. If no Commissioner requests such a review within the 30-day period, then the Proposed Final Determination will become the Final Order of the Commission. In the event a Commissioner requests a review, the Commission will review the record that the staff relied upon in making its determinations, including your previous submissions to the Office of the Whistleblower, and issue its Final Order.

(i) The Office of the Whistleblower will provide you with the Final Order of the Commission.

[76 FR 34363, June 13, 2011, as amended at 85 FR 70945, Nov. 5, 2020; 87 FR 54151, Sept. 2, 2022]

§ 240.21F-11 Procedures for determining awards based upon a related action.

(a) If you are eligible to receive an award following a Commission action that results in monetary sanctions totaling more than $1,000,000, you also may be eligible to receive an award in connection with a related action (as defined in § 240.21F-3(b)).

(b) You must also use Form WB-APP (as specified in § 240.21F-8(d)(2)) to submit a claim for an award in a potential related action. You must sign this form as the claimant and submit it to the Office of the Whistleblower by mail, email (as a PDF attachment), or fax (or any other manner that the Office permits) as follows:

(1) If a final order imposing monetary sanctions has been entered in a potential related action at the time you submit your claim for an award in connection with a Commission action, you must submit your claim for an award in that related action on the same

Securities and Exchange Commission § 240.21F-11

Form WB-APP that you use for the Commission action. For purposes of this paragraph and paragraph (b)(2) of this section, a final order imposing monetary sanctions is entered on the date of a court or administrative order imposing the monetary sanctions; however, with respect to any agreement covered by § 240.21F-4(d) of this chapter (such as a deferred prosecution agreement or a nonprosecution agreement entered by the Department of Justice), the Commission will deem the date of the entry of the final order to be the later of either:

(i) The effective date of this section as amended in 2020; or

(ii) The date of the earliest public availability of the instrument reflecting the arrangement if evidenced by a press release or similar dated publication notice (or otherwise, the date of the last signature necessary for the agreement).

(2) If a final order imposing monetary sanctions in a potential related action has not been entered at the time you submit your claim for an award in connection with a Commission action, you must submit your claim on Form WB-APP within ninety (90) days of the issuance of a final order imposing sanctions in the potential related action.

(c) The Office of the Whistleblower may request additional information from you in connection with your claim for an award in a related action to demonstrate that you directly (or through the Commission) voluntarily provided the governmental/SRO entity (as specified in § 240.21F-3(b)(1)) the same original information that led to the Commission's successful covered action, and that this information led to the successful enforcement of the related action. Further, the Office of the Whistleblower, in its discretion, may seek assistance and confirmation from the governmental/SRO entity in making an award determination. Additionally, if your related-action award application might implicate a second whistleblower program, the Office of the Whistleblower is authorized to request information from you or to contact any authority or entity responsible for administering that other program, including disclosing the whistleblower's identity if necessary, to ensure compliance with the terms of § 240.21F-3(b)(3).

(d) Once the time for filing any appeals of the final judgment or order in a potential related action has expired, or if an appeal has been filed, after all appeals in the action have been concluded, the Claims Review Staff (as specified in § 240.21F-10(d) of this chapter) will evaluate all timely whistleblower award claims submitted on Form WB-APP in connection with the related action. The evaluation will be undertaken pursuant to the criteria set forth in these rules. In connection with this process, the Office of the Whistleblower may require that you provide additional information relating to your eligibility for an award or satisfaction of any of the conditions for an award, as set forth in § 240.21F-(8)(b) of this chapter. Following a determination by the Claims Review Staff (and an opportunity for the Commission to review that determination), the Office of the Whistleblower will send you a Preliminary Determination setting forth a preliminary assessment as to whether the claim should be allowed or denied and, if allowed, setting forth the proposed award percentage amount.

(e) You may contest the Preliminary Determination made by the Claims Review Staff by submitting a written response to the Office of the Whistleblower setting forth the grounds for your objection to either the denial of an award or the proposed amount of an award. The response must be in the form and manner that the Office of the Whistleblower shall require. You may also include documentation or other evidentiary support for the grounds advanced in your response. In applying the award factors and standards specified in § 240.21F-6, and determining the award dollar and percentage amounts set forth in the Preliminary Determination, the award factors may be considered by the SEC staff and the Commission in dollar terms, percentage terms or some combination thereof, subject to the limitations imposed by § 240.21F-6(d). Should you choose to contest a Preliminary Determination, you may set forth the reasons for your objection to the proposed amount of an award, including the grounds therefore,

§ 240.21F-12

in dollar terms, percentage terms or some combination thereof.

(1) Before determining whether to contest a Preliminary Determination, you may:

(i) Within 30 calendar days of the date of the Preliminary Determination, request that the Office of the Whistleblower make available for your review the materials from among those set forth in § 240.21F-12(a) that formed the basis of the Claims Review Staff's Preliminary Determination.

(ii) Within 30 calendar days of the date of the Preliminary Determination, request a meeting with the Office of the Whistleblower; however, such meetings are not required, and the office may in its sole discretion decline the request.

(2) If you decide to contest the Preliminary Determination, you must submit your written response and supporting materials within 60 calendar days of the date of the Preliminary Determination, or if a request to review materials is made pursuant to paragraph (e)(1) of this section, then within 60 calendar days of the Office of the Whistleblower making those materials available for your review.

(f) If you fail to submit a timely response pursuant to paragraph (e) of this section, then the Preliminary Determination will become the Final Order of the Commission (except where the Preliminary Determination recommended an award, in which case the Preliminary Determination will be deemed a Proposed Final Determination for purposes of paragraph (h) of this section). Your failure to submit a timely response contesting a Preliminary Determination will constitute a failure to exhaust administrative remedies, and you will be prohibited from pursuing an appeal pursuant to § 240.21F-13 of this chapter.

(g) If you submit a timely response pursuant to paragraph (e) of this section, then the Claims Review Staff will consider the issues and grounds that you advanced in your response, along with any supporting documentation you provided, and will make its Proposed Final Determination.

(h) The Office of the Whistleblower will notify the Commission of each Proposed Final Determination. Within thirty 30 days thereafter, any Commissioner may request that the Proposed Final Determination be reviewed by the Commission. If no Commissioner requests such a review within the 30-day period, then the Proposed Final Determination will become the Final Order of the Commission. In the event a Commissioner requests a review, the Commission will review the record that the staff relied upon in making its determinations, including your previous submissions to the Office of the Whistleblower, and issue its Final Order.

(i) The Office of the Whistleblower will provide you with the Final Order of the Commission.

[76 FR 34363, June 13, 2011, as amended at 85 FR 70946, Nov. 5, 2020; 87 FR 54151, Sept. 2, 2022]

§ 240.21F-12 Materials that may form the basis of an award determination and that may comprise the record on appeal.

(a) The following items constitute the materials that the Commission, the Claims Review Staff (as specified in § 240.21F-10(d) of this chapter), and the Office of the Whistleblower may rely upon to make an award determination pursuant to §§ 240.21F-10, 240.21F-11, and 240.21F-18 of this chapter:

(1) Any publicly available materials from the covered action or related action, including:

(i) The complaint, notice of hearing, answers and any amendments thereto;

(ii) The final judgment, consent order, or final administrative order;

(iii) Any transcripts of the proceedings, including any exhibits;

(iv) Any items that appear on the docket; and

(v) Any appellate decisions or orders.

(2) The whistleblower's Form TCR, including attachments, and other related materials provided by the whistleblower to assist the Commission with the investigation or examination;

(3) The whistleblower's Form WB-APP, including attachments, any supplemental materials submitted by the whistleblower before the deadline to file a claim for a whistleblower award for the relevant Notice of Covered Action, and any other materials timely submitted by the whistleblower in response either

Securities and Exchange Commission § 240.21F–13

(i) To a request from the Office of the Whistleblower or the Commission; or

(ii) To the Preliminary Determination or Preliminary Summary Disposition that was provided to the claimant;

(4) Sworn declarations (including attachments) from the Commission staff regarding any matters relevant to the award determination;

(5) With respect to an award claim involving a related action, any statements or other information that the entity provides or identifies in connection with an award determination, provided the entity has authorized the Commission to share the information with the claimant. (Neither the Commission nor the Claims Review Staff may rely upon information that the entity has not authorized the Commission to share with the claimant); and

(6) Any other documents or materials from third parties (including sworn declarations) that are received or obtained by the Office of the Whistleblower to resolve the claimant's award application, including information related to the claimant's eligibility. (The Commission, the Claims Review Staff, and the Office of the Whistleblower may not rely upon information that the third party has not authorized the Commission to share with the claimant.)

(b) These rules do not entitle claimants to obtain from the Commission any materials (including any predecisional or internal deliberative process materials that are prepared exclusively to assist the Commission in deciding the claim) other than those listed in paragraph (a) of this section. Moreover, the Office of the Whistleblower may make redactions as necessary to comply with any statutory restrictions, to protect the Commission's law enforcement and regulatory functions, and to comply with requests for confidential treatment from other law enforcement and regulatory authorities. The Office of the Whistleblower may also require you to sign a confidentiality agreement, as set forth in § 240.21F–(8)(b)(4) of this chapter, before providing these materials.

[76 FR 34363, June 13, 2011, as amended at 85 FR 70947, Nov. 5, 2020]

§ 240.21F–13 Appeals.

(a) Section 21F of the Exchange Act (15 U.S.C. 78u–6) commits determinations of whether, to whom, and in what amount to make awards to the Commission's discretion. A determination of whether or to whom to make an award may be appealed within 30 days after the Commission issues its final decision to the United States Court of Appeals for the District of Columbia Circuit, or to the circuit where the aggrieved person resides or has his principal place of business. Where the Commission makes an award based on the factors set forth in § 240.21F–6 of this chapter of not less than 10 percent and not more than 30 percent of the monetary sanctions collected in the Commission or related action, the Commission's determination regarding the amount of an award (including the allocation of an award as between multiple whistleblowers, and any factual findings, legal conclusions, policy judgments, or discretionary assessments involving the Commission's consideration of the factors in § 240.21F–6 of this chapter) is not appealable.

(b) The record on appeal shall consist of the Final Order, any materials that were considered by the Commission in issuing the Final Order, and any materials that were part of the claims process leading from the Notice of Covered Action to the Final Order (including, but not limited to, the Notice of Covered Action, whistleblower award applications filed by the claimant, the Preliminary Determination or Preliminary Summary Disposition, materials that were considered by the Claims Review Staff in issuing the Preliminary Determination or that were provided to the claimant by the Office of the Whistleblower in connection with a Preliminary Summary Disposition, and materials that were timely submitted by the claimant in response to the Preliminary Determination or Preliminary Summary Disposition). The record on appeal shall not include any pre-decisional or internal deliberative process materials that are prepared exclusively to assist the Commission and the Claims Review Staff (as specified in § 240.21F–10(d) of this chapter) in deciding the claim (including the staff's Proposed Final Determination or the

815

§ 240.21F-14

Office of the Whistleblower's Proposed Final Summary Disposition, or any Draft Preliminary Determination or Draft Summary Disposition that were provided to the Commission for review). When more than one claimant has sought an award based on a single Notice of Covered Action, the Commission may exclude from the record on appeal any materials that do not relate directly to the claimant who is seeking judicial review.

[76 FR 34363, June 13, 2011, as amended at 85 FR 70947, Nov. 5, 2020]

§ 240.21F-14 Procedures applicable to the payment of awards.

(a) Any award made pursuant to these rules will be paid from the Securities and Exchange Commission Investor Protection Fund (the "Fund").

(b) A recipient of a whistleblower award is entitled to payment on the award only to the extent that a monetary sanction is collected in the Commission action or in a related action upon which the award is based.

(c) Payment of a whistleblower award for a monetary sanction collected in a Commission action or related action shall be made following the later of:

(1) The date on which the monetary sanction is collected; or

(2) The completion of the appeals process for all whistleblower award claims arising from:

(i) The Notice of Covered Action, in the case of any payment of an award for a monetary sanction collected in a Commission action; or

(ii) The related action, in the case of any payment of an award for a monetary sanction collected in a related action.

(d) If there are insufficient amounts available in the Fund to pay the entire amount of an award payment within a reasonable period of time from the time for payment specified by paragraph (c) of this section, then subject to the following terms, the balance of the payment shall be paid when amounts become available in the Fund, as follows:

(1) Where multiple whistleblowers are owed payments from the Fund based on awards that do not arise from the same Notice of Covered Action (or related action), priority in making these payments will be determined based upon the date that the collections for which the whistleblowers are owed payments occurred. If two or more of these collections occur on the same date, those whistleblowers owed payments based on these collections will be paid on a pro rata basis until sufficient amounts become available in the Fund to pay their entire payments.

(2) Where multiple whistleblowers are owed payments from the Fund based on awards that arise from the same Notice of Covered Action (or related action), they will share the same payment priority and will be paid on a pro rata basis until sufficient amounts become available in the Fund to pay their entire payments.

§ 240.21F-15 No amnesty.

The Securities Whistleblower Incentives and Protection provisions do not provide amnesty to individuals who provide information to the Commission. The fact that you may become a whistleblower and assist in Commission investigations and enforcement actions does not preclude the Commission from bringing an action against you based upon your own conduct in connection with violations of the Federal securities laws. If such an action is determined to be appropriate, however, the Commission will take your cooperation into consideration in accordance with its Policy Statement Concerning Cooperation by Individuals in Investigations and Related Enforcement Actions (17 CFR 202.12).

§ 240.21F-16 Awards to whistleblowers who engage in culpable conduct.

In determining whether the required $1,000,000 threshold has been satisfied (this threshold is further explained in § 240.21F-10 of this chapter) for purposes of making any award, the Commission will not take into account any monetary sanctions that the whistleblower is ordered to pay, or that are ordered against any entity whose liability is based substantially on conduct that the whistleblower directed, planned, or initiated. Similarly, if the Commission determines that a whistleblower is eligible for an award, any amounts that the whistleblower or such an entity

Securities and Exchange Commission § 240.21F-18

pay in sanctions as a result of the action or related actions will not be included within the calculation of the amounts collected for purposes of making payments.

§ 240.21F-17 Staff communications with individuals reporting possible securities law violations.

(a) No person may take any action to impede an individual from communicating directly with the Commission staff about a possible securities law violation, including enforcing, or threatening to enforce, a confidentiality agreement (other than agreements dealing with information covered by § 240.21F-4(b)(4)(i) and § 240.21F-4(b)(4)(ii) of this chapter related to the legal representation of a client) with respect to such communications.

(b) If you are a director, officer, member, agent, or employee of an entity that has counsel, and you have initiated communication with the Commission relating to a possible securities law violation, the staff is authorized to communicate directly with you regarding the possible securities law violation without seeking the consent of the entity's counsel.

§ 240.21F-18 Summary disposition.

(a) Notwithstanding the procedures specified in § 240.21F-10(d) through (g) and in § 240.21F-11(d) through (g) of this chapter, the Office of the Whistleblower may determine that an award application that meets any of the following conditions for denial shall be resolved through the summary disposition process described further in paragraph (b) of this section:

(1) You submitted an untimely award application;

(2) You did not comply with the requirements of § 240.21F-9 of this chapter when submitting the tip upon which your award claim is based, and you otherwise are not eligible for a waiver under either § 240.21F-9(e) or the Commission's other waiver authorities;

(3) The information that you submitted was never provided to or used by the staff handling the covered action or the underlying investigation (or examination), and those staff members otherwise had no contact with you;

(4) You did not comply with § 240.21F-8(b) of this chapter;

(5) You failed to specify in the award application the submission pursuant to § 240.21F-9(a) of this chapter upon which your claim to an award is based;

(6) Your application does not raise any novel or important legal or policy questions.

(b) The following procedures shall apply to any award application designated for summary disposition:

(1) The Office of the Whistleblower shall issue a Preliminary Summary Disposition that notifies you that your award application has been designated for resolution through the summary disposition process. The Preliminary Summary Disposition shall also state that the Office has preliminarily determined to recommend that the Commission deny the award application and identify the basis for the denial.

(2) Prior to issuing the Preliminary Summary Disposition, the Office of the Whistleblower shall prepare a staff declaration that sets forth any pertinent facts regarding the Office's recommendation to deny your application. At the same time that it provides you with the Preliminary Summary Disposition, the Office of the Whistleblower shall, in its sole discretion, either

(i) Provide you with the staff declaration; or

(ii) Notify you that a staff declaration has been prepared and advise you that you may obtain the declaration only if within fifteen (15) calendar days you sign and complete a confidentiality agreement in a form and manner acceptable to the Office of the Whistleblower pursuant to § 240.21F-8(b)(4) of this chapter. If you fail to return the signed confidentiality agreement within fifteen (15) calendar days, you will be deemed to have waived your ability to receive the staff declaration.

(3) You may reply to the Preliminary Summary Disposition by submitting a response to the Office of the Whistleblower within thirty (30) calendar days of the later of:

(i) The date of the Preliminary Summary Disposition, or

817

§ 240.24b-1

(ii) The date that the Office of the Whistleblower sends the staff declaration to you following your timely return of a signed confidentiality agreement. The response must identify the grounds for your objection to the denial (or in the case of item (a)(5) of this section, correct the defect). The response must be in the form and manner that the Office of the Whistleblower shall require. You may include documentation or other evidentiary support for the grounds advanced in your response.

(4) If you fail to submit a timely response pursuant to paragraph (b)(3) of this section, the Preliminary Summary Disposition will become the Final Order of the Commission. Your failure to submit a timely written response will constitute a failure to exhaust administrative remedies.

(5) If you submit a timely response pursuant to paragraph (b)(3) of this section, the Office of the Whistleblower will consider the issues and grounds advanced in your response, along with any supporting documentation that you provided, and will prepare a Proposed Final Summary Disposition. The Office of the Whistleblower may supplement the administrative record as appropriate. (This provision does not prevent the Office of the Whistleblower from determining that, based on your written response, the award claim is no longer appropriate for summary disposition and that it should be resolved through the claims adjudication procedures specified in either §§ 240.21F-10 or 240.21F-11 of this chapter).

(6) The Office of the Whistleblower will then notify the Commission of the Proposed Final Summary Disposition. Within thirty (30) calendar days thereafter, any Commissioner may request that the Proposed Final Summary Disposition be reviewed by the Commission. If no Commissioner requests such a review within the 30-day period, then the Proposed Final Summary Disposition will become the Final Order of the Commission. In the event a Commissioner requests a review, the Commission will consider the award application and issue a Final Order.

(7) The Office of the Whistleblower will provide you with the Final Order of the Commission.

(c) In considering an award determination pursuant to this rule, the Office of the Whistleblower and the Commission may rely upon the items specified in § 240.21F-12(a) of this chapter. Further, § 240.21F-12(b) of this chapter shall apply to summary dispositions.

[85 FR 70947, Nov. 5, 2020]

INSPECTION AND PUBLICATION OF INFORMATION FILED UNDER THE ACT

§ 240.24b-1 Documents to be kept public by exchanges.

Upon action of the Commission granting an exchange's application for registration or exemption, the exchange shall make available to public inspection at its offices during reasonable office hours a copy of the statement and exhibits filed with the Commission (including any amendments thereto) except those portions thereof to the disclosure of which the exchange shall have filed objection pursuant to § 240.24b-2 which objection shall not have been overruled by the Commission pursuant to section 24(b) of the Act.

(Sec. 24, 48 Stat. 901; 15 U.S.C. 78x)

CROSS REFERENCE: For regulations relating to registration and exemption of exchanges, see §§ 240.6a-1 to 240.6a-3.

[13 FR 8214, Dec. 22, 1948]

§ 240.24b-2 Nondisclosure of information filed with the Commission and with any exchange.

Except as otherwise provided in this rule, confidential treatment requests shall be submitted in paper format only, whether or not the filer is required to submit a filing in electronic format.

(a) Any person filing any registration statement, report, application, statement, correspondence, notice or other document (herein referred to as the material filed) pursuant to the Act may make written objection to the public disclosure of any information contained therein in accordance with the procedure set forth below. The procedure provided in this rule shall be the exclusive means of requesting confidential treatment of information required to be filed under the Act.

Securities and Exchange Commission
§ 240.24b-2

(b) Except as otherwise provided in paragraphs (g) through (i) of this section, the person shall omit from material filed the portion thereof which it desires to keep undisclosed (hereinafter called the confidential portion). In lieu thereof, it shall indicate at the appropriate place in the material filed that the confidential portion has been so omitted and filed separately with the Commission. The person shall file with the copies of the material filed with the Commission:

(1) One copy of the confidential portion, marked "Confidential Treatment," of the material filed with the Commission. The copy shall contain an appropriate identification of the item or other requirement involved and, notwithstanding that the confidential portion does not constitute the whole of the answer, the entire answer thereto; except that in the case where the confidential portion is part of a financial statement or schedule, only the particular financial statement or schedule need be included. The copy of the confidential portion shall be in the same form as the remainder of the material filed;

(2) An application making objection to the disclosure of the confidential portion. Such application shall be on a sheet or sheets separate from the confidential portion, and shall contain:

(i) An identification of the portion;

(ii) A statement of the grounds of objection referring to, and containing an analysis of, the applicable exemption(s) from disclosure under the Freedom of Information Act (5 U.S.C. 552(b)), and a justification of the period of time for which confidential treatment is sought;

(iii) A written consent to the furnishing of the confidential portion to other government agencies, offices or bodies and to the Congress; and

(iv) The name of each exchange, if any, with which the material is filed.

(3) The copy of the confidential portion and the application filed in accordance with this paragraph (b) shall be enclosed in a separate envelope marked "Confidential Treatment" and addressed to The Secretary, Securities and Exchange Commission, Washington, DC 20549.

(c) Pending a determination as to the objection filed the material for which confidential treatment has been applied will not be made available to the public.

(d)(1) If it is determined that the objection should be sustained, a notation to that effect will be made at the appropriate place in the material filed. Such a determination will not preclude reconsideration whenever appropriate, such as upon receipt of any subsequent request under the Freedom of Information Act (5 U.S.C. 552) and, if appropriate, revocation of the confidential status of all or a portion of the information in question. Where an initial determination has been made under this rule to sustain objections to disclosure, the Commission will attempt to give the person requesting confidential treatment advance notice, wherever possible, if confidential treatment is revoked.

(2) In any case where an objection to disclosure has been disallowed or where a prior grant of confidential treatment has been revoked, the person who requested such treatment will be so informed by registered or certified mail to the person or his agent for service. Pursuant to § 201.431 of this chapter, persons making objections to disclosure may petition the Commission for review of a determination by the Division disallowing objections or revoking confidential treatment.

(e) The confidential portion shall be made available to the public at the time and according to the conditions specified in paragraphs (d) (1) and (2) of this section:

(1) Upon the lapse of five days after the dispatch of notice by registered or certified mail of a determination disallowing an objection, if prior to the lapse of such five days the person shall not have communicated to the Secretary of the Commission his intention to seek review by the Commission under § 201.431 of this chapter of the determination made by the Division; or

(2) If such a petition for review shall have been filed under § 201.431 of this chapter, upon final disposition thereof adverse to the petitioner.

(f) If the confidential portion is made available to the public, one copy thereof shall be attached to each copy of the

§ 240.24b-3

material filed with the Commission and with each exchange.

(g) An SCI entity (as defined in § 242.1000 of this chapter) shall not omit the confidential portion from the material filed in electronic format on Form SCI pursuant to Regulation SCI, § 242.1000 *et. seq.*, and, in lieu of the procedures described in paragraph (b) of this section, may request confidential treatment of all information provided on Form SCI by completing Section IV of Form SCI.

(h) A security-based swap data repository shall not omit the confidential portion from the material filed in electronic format pursuant to section 13(n) of the Act (15 U.S.C. 78m(n)) and the rules and regulations thereunder. In lieu of the procedures described in paragraph (b) of this section, a security-based swap data repository shall request confidential treatment electronically for any material filed in electronic format pursuant to section 13(n) of the Act (15 U.S.C. 78m(n)) and the rules and regulations thereunder.

(i) An institutional investment manager shall omit the confidential portion from the material publicly filed in electronic format pursuant to section 13(f) of the Act (15 U.S.C. 78m(f)) and the rules and regulations thereunder. The institutional investment manager shall indicate in the appropriate place in the material publicly filed that the confidential portion has been so omitted and filed separately with the Commission. In lieu of the procedures described in paragraph (b) of this section, an institutional investment manager shall request confidential treatment electronically pursuant to section 13(f) of the Act (15 U.S.C. 78m(f)) and the rules and regulations thereunder.

[41 FR 20578, May 19, 1976, as amended at 58 FR 14685, Mar. 18, 1993; 60 FR 32825, June 23, 1995; 60 FR 47692, Sept. 14, 1995; 61 FR 30404, June 14, 1996; 79 FR 72436, Dec. 5, 2014; 80 FR 14556, Mar. 19, 2015; 84 FR 50739, Sept. 26, 2019; 87 FR 38964, June 30, 2022]

EFFECTIVE DATE NOTE: At 87 FR 78808, Dec. 22, 2022, § 240.24b-2 was amended by revising paragraph (i), effective July 1, 2024. For the convenience of the user, the revised text is set forth as follows:

§ 240.24b-2 Nondisclosure of information filed with the Commission and with any exchange.

* * * * *

(i) An institutional investment manager shall omit the confidential portion from the material publicly filed in electronic format pursuant to section 13(f) of the Act (15 U.S.C. 78m(f)) and the rules and regulations in this part and the instructions to Form N-PX (§§ 249.326 and 274.129 of this chapter). The institutional investment manager shall indicate in the appropriate place in the material publicly filed that the confidential portion has been so omitted and filed separately with the Commission. In lieu of the procedures described in paragraph (b) of this section, an institutional investment manager shall request confidential treatment electronically pursuant to section 13(f) (15 U.S.C. 78m(f)), the rules and regulations in this part, and the instructions to Form N-PX (§§ 249.326 and 274.129 of this chapter).

§ 240.24b-3 Information filed by issuers and others under sections 12, 13, 14, and 16.

(a) Except as otherwise provided in this section and in § 240.17a-6, each exchange shall keep available to the public under reasonable regulations as to the manner of inspection, during reasonable office hours, all information regarding a security registered on such exchange which is filed with it pursuant to section 12, 13, 14, or 16, or any rules or regulations thereunder. This requirement shall not apply to any information to the disclosure of which objection has been filed pursuant to § 240.24b-2, which objection shall not have been overruled by the Commission pursuant to section 24(b). The making of such information available pursuant to this section shall not be deemed a representation by any exchange as to the accuracy, completeness, or genuineness thereof.

(b) In the case of an application for registration of a security pursuant to section 12 an exchange may delay making available the information contained therein until it has certified to the Commission its approval of such security for listing and registration.

(Sec. 24, 48 Stat. 901, as amended; 15 U.S.C. 78x)

[16 FR 3109, Apr. 10, 1951]

Securities and Exchange Commission § 240.31

§ 240.24c-1 Access to nonpublic information.

(a) For purposes of this section, the term "nonpublic information" means records, as defined in Section 24(a) of the Act, and other information in the Commission's possession, which are not available for public inspection and copying.

(b) The Commission may, in its discretion and upon a showing that such information is needed, provide nonpublic information in its possession to any of the following persons if the person receiving such nonpublic information provides such assurances of confidentiality as the Commission deems appropriate:

(1) A federal, state, local or foreign government or any political subdivision, authority, agency or instrumentality of such government;

(2) A self-regulatory organization as defined in Section 3(a)(26) of the Act, or any similar organization empowered with self-regulatory responsibilities under the federal securities laws (as defined in Section 3(a)(47) of the Act, the Commodity Exchange Act (7 U.S.C. 1, et seq.), or any substantially equivalent foreign statute or regulation;

(3) A foreign financial regulatory authority as defined in Section 3(a)(51) of the Act;

(4) The Securities Investor Protection Corporation or any trustee or counsel for a trustee appointed pursuant to Section 5(b) of the Securities Investor Protection Act of 1970;

(5) A trustee in bankruptcy;

(6) A trustee, receiver, master, special counsel or other person that is appointed by a court of competent jurisdiction or as a result of an agreement between the parties in connection with litigation or an administrative proceeding involving allegations of violations of the securities laws (as defined in Section 3(a)(47) of the Act) or the Commission's Rules of Practice, 17 CFR part 201, or otherwise, where such trustee, receiver, master, special counsel or other person is specifically designated to perform particular functions with respect to, or as a result of, the litigation or proceeding or in connection with the administration and enforcement by the Commission of the federal securities laws or the Commission's Rules of Practice;

(7) A bar association, state accountancy board or other federal, state, local or foreign licensing or oversight authority, or a professional association or self-regulatory authority to the extent that it performs similar functions; or

(8) A duly authorized agent, employee or representative of any of the above persons.

(c) Nothing contained in this section shall affect:

(1) The Commission's authority or discretion to provide or refuse to provide access to, or copies of, nonpublic information in its possession in accordance with such other authority or discretion as the Commission possesses by statute, rule or regulation; or

(2) The Commission's responsibilities under the Privacy Act of 1974 (5 U.S.C. 552a), or the Right to Financial Privacy Act of 1978 (12 U.S.C. 3401–22) as limited by section 21(h) of the Act.

[58 FR 52419, Oct. 8, 1993]

§ 240.31 Section 31 transaction fees.

(a) *Definitions.* For the purpose of this section, the following definitions shall apply:

(1) *Assessment charge* means the amount owed by a covered SRO for a covered round turn transaction pursuant to section 31(d) of the Act (15 U.S.C. 78ee(d)).

(2) *Billing period* means, for a single calendar year:

(i) January 1 through August 31 ("billing period 1"); or

(ii) September 1 through December 31 ("billing period 2").

(3) *Charge date* means the date on which a covered sale or covered round turn transaction occurs for purposes of determining the liability of a covered SRO pursuant to section 31 of the Act (15 U.S.C. 78ee). The charge date is:

(i) The settlement date, with respect to any covered sale (other than a covered sale resulting from the exercise of an option settled by physical delivery or from the maturation of a security future settled by physical delivery) or covered round turn transaction that a covered SRO is required to report to the Commission based on data that the

§ 240.31

covered SRO receives from a designated clearing agency;

(ii) The exercise date, with respect to a covered sale resulting from the exercise of an option settled by physical delivery;

(iii) The maturity date, with respect to a covered sale resulting from the maturation of a security future settled by physical delivery; and

(iv) The trade date, with respect to all other covered sales and covered round turn transactions.

(4) *Covered association* means any national securities association by or through any member of which covered sales or covered round turn transactions occur otherwise than on a national securities exchange.

(5) *Covered exchange* means any national securities exchange on which covered sales or covered round turn transactions occur.

(6) *Covered sale* means a sale of a security, other than an exempt sale or a sale of a security future, occurring on a national securities exchange or by or through any member of a national securities association otherwise than on a national securities exchange.

(7) *Covered round turn transaction* means a round turn transaction in a security future, other than a round turn transaction in a future on a narrow-based security index, occurring on a national securities exchange or by or through a member of a national securities association otherwise than on a national securities exchange.

(8) *Covered SRO* means a covered exchange or covered association.

(9) *Designated clearing agency* means a clearing agency registered under section 17A of the Act (15 U.S.C. 78q-1) that clears and settles covered sales or covered round turn transactions.

(10) *Due date* means:

(i) March 15, with respect to the amounts owed by covered SROs under section 31 of the Act (15 U.S.C. 78ee) for covered sales and covered round turn transactions having a charge date in billing period 2; and

(ii) September 30, with respect to the amounts owed by covered SROs under section 31 of the Act (15 U.S.C. 78ee) for covered sales and covered round turn transactions having a charge date in billing period 1.

17 CFR Ch. II (4–1–23 Edition)

(11) *Exempt sale* means:

(i) Any sale of a security offered pursuant to an effective registration statement under the Securities Act of 1933 (except a sale of a put or call option issued by the Options Clearing Corporation) or offered in accordance with an exemption from registration afforded by section 3(a) or 3(b) of the Securities Act of 1933 (15 U.S.C. 77c(a) or 77c(b)), or a rule thereunder;

(ii) Any sale of a security by an issuer not involving any public offering within the meaning of section 4(2) of the Securities Act of 1933 (15 U.S.C. 77d(2));

(iii) Any sale of a security pursuant to and in consummation of a tender or exchange offer;

(iv) Any sale of a security upon the exercise of a warrant or right (except a put or call), or upon the conversion of a convertible security;

(v) Any sale of a security that is executed outside the United States and is not reported, or required to be reported, to a transaction reporting association as defined in § 242.600 of this chapter and any approved plan filed thereunder;

(vi) Any sale of an option on a security index (including both a narrow-based security index and a non-narrow-based security index);

(vii) Any sale of a bond, debenture, or other evidence of indebtedness; and

(viii) Any recognized riskless principal sale.

(12) *Fee rate* means the fee rate applicable to covered sales under section 31(b) or (c) of the Act (15 U.S.C. 78ee(b) or (c)), as adjusted from time to time by the Commission pursuant to section 31(j) of the Act (15 U.S.C. 78ee(j)).

(13) *Narrow-based security index* means the same as in section 3(a)(55)(B) and (C) of the Act (15 U.S.C. 78c(a)(55)(B) and (C)).

(14) *Recognized riskless principal sale* means a sale of a security where all of the following conditions are satisfied:

(i) A broker-dealer receives from a customer an order to buy (sell) a security;

(ii) The broker-dealer engages in two contemporaneous offsetting transactions as principal, one in which the broker-dealer buys (sells) the security from (to) a third party and the other in

822

Securities and Exchange Commission § 240.31

which the broker-dealer sells (buys) the security to (from) the customer; and

(iii) The Commission, pursuant to section 19(b)(2) of the Act (15 U.S.C. 78s(b)(2)), has approved a proposed rule change submitted by the covered SRO on which the second of the two contemporaneous offsetting transactions occurs that permits that transaction to be reported as riskless.

(15) *Round turn transaction in a security future* means one purchase and one sale of a contract of sale for future delivery.

(16) *Physical delivery exchange-traded option* means a securities option that is listed and registered on a national securities exchange and settled by the physical delivery of the underlying securities.

(17) *Section 31 bill* means the bill sent by the Commission to a covered SRO pursuant to section 31 of the Act (15 U.S.C. 78ee) showing the total amount due from the covered SRO for the billing period, as calculated by the Commission based on the data submitted by the covered SRO in its Form R31 (§ 249.11 of this chapter) submissions for the months of the billing period.

(18) *Trade reporting system* means an automated facility operated by a covered SRO used to collect or compare trade data.

(b) *Reporting of covered sales and covered round turn transactions.* (1) Each covered SRO shall submit a completed Form R31 (§ 249.11 of this chapter) to the Commission within ten business days after the end of each month.

(2) A covered exchange shall provide on Form R31 the following data on covered sales and covered round turn transactions occurring on that exchange and having a charge date in that month:

(i) The aggregate dollar amount of covered sales that it reported to a designated clearing agency, as reflected in the data provided by the designated clearing agency;

(ii) The aggregate dollar amount of covered sales resulting from the exercise of physical delivery exchange-traded options or from matured security futures, as reflected in the data provided by a designated clearing agency that clears and settles options or security futures;

(iii) The aggregate dollar amount of covered sales that it captured in a trade reporting system but did not report to a designated clearing agency;

(iv) The aggregate dollar amount of covered sales that it neither captured in a trade reporting system nor reported to a designated clearing agency; and

(v) The total number of covered round turn transactions that it reported to a designated clearing agency, as reflected in the data provided by the designated clearing agency.

(3) A covered association shall provide on Form R31 the following data on covered sales and covered round turn transactions occurring by or through any member of such association otherwise than on a national securities exchange and having a charge date in that month:

(i) The aggregate dollar amount of covered sales that it captured in a trade reporting system;

(ii) The aggregate dollar amount of covered sales that it did not capture in a trade reporting system; and

(iii) The total number of covered round turn transactions that it reported to a designated clearing agency, as reflected in the data provided by the designated clearing agency.

(4) *Duties of designated clearing agency.* (i) A designated clearing agency shall provide a covered SRO, upon request, the data in its possession needed by the covered SRO to complete Part I of Form R31 (§ 249.11 of this chapter).

(ii) If a covered exchange trades physical delivery exchange-traded options or security futures that settle by physical delivery of the underlying securities, the designated clearing agency that clears and settles such transactions shall provide that covered exchange with the data in its possession relating to the covered sales resulting from the exercise of such options or from the matured security futures. If, during a particular month, the designated clearing agency cannot determine the covered exchange on which the options or security futures originally were traded, the designated clearing agency shall assign covered sales resulting from exercises or maturations as follows. To provide Form R31

§ 240.31T

data to the covered exchange for a particular month, the designated clearing agency shall:

(A) Calculate the aggregate dollar amount of all covered sales in the previous calendar month resulting from exercises and maturations, respectively, occurring on all covered exchanges for which it clears and settles transactions;

(B) Calculate, for the previous calendar month, the aggregate dollar amount of covered sales of physical delivery exchange-traded options occurring on each covered exchange for which it clears and settles transactions, and the aggregate dollar amount of covered sales of physical delivery exchange-traded options occurring on all such exchanges collectively;

(C) Calculate, for the previous calendar month, the total number of covered round turn transactions in security futures that settle by physical delivery that occurred on each covered exchange for which it clears and settles transactions, and the total number of covered round turn transactions in security futures that settle by physical delivery that occurred on all such exchanges collectively;

(D) Determine for the previous calendar month each covered exchange's percentage of the total dollar volume of physical delivery exchange-traded options ("exercise percentage") and each covered exchange's percentage of the total number of covered round turn transactions in security futures that settle by physical delivery ("maturation percentage"); and

(E) In the current month, assign to each covered exchange for which it clears and settles covered sales the exercise percentage of the aggregate dollar amount of covered sales on all covered exchanges resulting from the exercise of physical delivery exchange-traded options and the maturation percentage of all covered sales on all covered exchanges resulting from the maturation of security futures that settle by physical delivery.

(5) A covered SRO shall provide in Part I of Form R31 only the data supplied to it by a designated clearing agency.

(c) *Calculation and billing of section 31 fees.* (1) The amount due from a covered SRO for a billing period, as reflected in its Section 31 bill, shall be the sum of the monthly amounts due for each month in the billing period.

(2) The monthly amount due from a covered SRO shall equal:

(i) The aggregate dollar amount of its covered sales that have a charge date in that month, times the fee rate; plus

(ii) The total number of its covered round turn transactions that have a charge date in that month, times the assessment charge.

(3) By the due date, each covered SRO shall pay the Commission, either directly or through a designated clearing agency acting as agent, the entire amount due for the billing period, as reflected in its Section 31 bill.

[69 FR 41078, July 7, 2004, as amended at 70 FR 37619, June 29, 2005]

§ 240.31T Temporary rule regarding fiscal year 2004.

(a) *Definitions.* (1) For the purpose of this section, the following definitions shall apply:

(i) *FY2004 adjustment amount* means the FY2004 recalculated amount minus the FY2004 prepayment amount.

(ii) *FY2004 prepayment amount* means the total dollar amount of fees and assessments paid by a covered SRO pursuant to the March 15, 2004, due date for covered sales and covered round turn transactions having a charge date between September 1, 2003, and December 31, 2003, inclusive.

(iii) *FY2004 recalculated amount* means the total dollar amount of fees and assessments owed by a covered SRO for covered sales and covered round turn transactions having a charge date between September 1, 2003, and December 31, 2003, inclusive, as calculated by the Commission based on the data submitted by the covered SRO in its Form R31 (§ 249.11 of this chapter) submissions for September 2003, October 2003, November 2003, and December 2003, and indicated on a Section 31 bill for these months.

(2) Any term used in this section that is defined in § 240.30(a) of this chapter shall have the same meaning as in § 240.30(a) of this chapter.

(b) By August 13, 2004, each covered SRO shall submit to the Commission a completed Form R31 for each of the months September 2003 to June 2004, inclusive.

(c) If the FY2004 adjustment amount of a covered SRO is a positive number, the covered SRO shall include the FY2004 adjustment amount with the payment for its next Section 31 bill.

(d) If the FY2004 adjustment amount is a negative number, the Commission shall credit the FY2004 adjustment amount to the covered SRO's next Section 31 bill.

(e) Notwithstanding paragraph (a)(1)(iii) of this section, any covered exchange that as of August 2003 was calculating its Section 31 fees based on the trade date of its covered sales shall not include on its September 2003 Form R31 data for any covered sale having a trade date before September 1, 2003.

(f) This temporary section shall expire on January 1, 2005.

[69 FR 41080, July 7, 2004]

§ 240.36a1-1 Exemption from Section 7 for OTC derivatives dealers.

PRELIMINARY NOTE: OTC derivatives dealers are a special class of broker-dealers that are exempt from certain broker-dealer requirements, including membership in a self-regulatory organization (§ 240.15b9–2), regular broker-dealer margin rules (§ 240.36a1–1), and application of the Securities Investor Protection Act of 1970 (§ 240.36a1–2). OTC derivative dealers are subject to special requirements, including limitations on the scope of their securities activities (§ 240.15a–1), specified internal risk management control systems (§ 240.15c3–4), recordkeeping obligations (§ 240.17a–3(a)(10)), and reporting responsibilities (§ 240.17a–12). They are also subject to alternative net capital treatment (§ 240.15c3–1(a)(5)).

(a) Except as otherwise provided in paragraph (b) of this section, transactions involving the extension of credit by an OTC derivatives dealer shall be exempt from the provisions of section 7(c) of the Act (15 U.S.C. 78g(c)), provided that the OTC derivatives dealer complies with Section 7(d) of the Act (15 U.S.C. 78g(d)).

(b) The exemption provided under paragraph (a) of this section shall not apply to extensions of credit made directly by a registered broker or dealer (other than an OTC derivatives dealer) in connection with transactions in eligible OTC derivative instruments for which an OTC derivatives dealer acts as counterparty.

[63 FR 59404, Nov. 3, 1998]

§ 240.36a1-2 Exemption from SIPA for OTC derivatives dealers.

PRELIMINARY NOTE: OTC derivatives dealers are a special class of broker-dealers that are exempt from certain broker-dealer requirements, including membership in a self-regulatory organization (§ 240.15b9–2), regular broker-dealer margin rules (§ 240.36a1–1), and application of the Securities Investor Protection Act of 1970 (§ 240.36a1–2). OTC derivative dealers are subject to special requirements, including limitations on the scope of their securities activities (§ 240.15a–1), specified internal risk management control systems (§ 240.15c3–4), recordkeeping obligations (§ 240.17a–3(a)(10)), and reporting responsibilities (§ 240.17a–12). They are also subject to alternative net capital treatment (§ 240.15c3–1(a)(5)).

OTC derivatives dealers, as defined in § 240.3b–12, shall be exempt from the provisions of the Securities Investor Protection Act of 1970 (15 U.S.C. 78aaa through 78lll).

[63 FR 59404, Nov. 3, 1998]

Subpart B—Rules and Regulations Under the Securities Investor Protection Act of 1970 [Reserved]

FINDING AIDS

A list of CFR titles, subtitles, chapters, subchapters and parts and an alphabetical list of agencies publishing in the CFR are included in the CFR Index and Finding Aids volume to the Code of Federal Regulations which is published separately and revised annually.

Table of CFR Titles and Chapters
Alphabetical List of Agencies Appearing in the CFR
Table of OMB Control Numbers
List of CFR Sections Affected

Table of CFR Titles and Chapters
(Revised as of April 1, 2023)

Title 1—General Provisions

I	Administrative Committee of the Federal Register (Parts 1—49)
II	Office of the Federal Register (Parts 50—299)
III	Administrative Conference of the United States (Parts 300—399)
IV	Miscellaneous Agencies (Parts 400—599)
VI	National Capital Planning Commission (Parts 600—699)

Title 2—Grants and Agreements

SUBTITLE A—OFFICE OF MANAGEMENT AND BUDGET GUIDANCE FOR GRANTS AND AGREEMENTS

I	Office of Management and Budget Governmentwide Guidance for Grants and Agreements (Parts 2—199)
II	Office of Management and Budget Guidance (Parts 200—299)

SUBTITLE B—FEDERAL AGENCY REGULATIONS FOR GRANTS AND AGREEMENTS

III	Department of Health and Human Services (Parts 300—399)
IV	Department of Agriculture (Parts 400—499)
VI	Department of State (Parts 600—699)
VII	Agency for International Development (Parts 700—799)
VIII	Department of Veterans Affairs (Parts 800—899)
IX	Department of Energy (Parts 900—999)
X	Department of the Treasury (Parts 1000—1099)
XI	Department of Defense (Parts 1100—1199)
XII	Department of Transportation (Parts 1200—1299)
XIII	Department of Commerce (Parts 1300—1399)
XIV	Department of the Interior (Parts 1400—1499)
XV	Environmental Protection Agency (Parts 1500—1599)
XVIII	National Aeronautics and Space Administration (Parts 1800—1899)
XX	United States Nuclear Regulatory Commission (Parts 2000—2099)
XXII	Corporation for National and Community Service (Parts 2200—2299)
XXIII	Social Security Administration (Parts 2300—2399)
XXIV	Department of Housing and Urban Development (Parts 2400—2499)
XXV	National Science Foundation (Parts 2500—2599)
XXVI	National Archives and Records Administration (Parts 2600—2699)

Title 2—Grants and Agreements—Continued

Chap.

XXVII	Small Business Administration (Parts 2700—2799)
XXVIII	Department of Justice (Parts 2800—2899)
XXIX	Department of Labor (Parts 2900—2999)
XXX	Department of Homeland Security (Parts 3000—3099)
XXXI	Institute of Museum and Library Services (Parts 3100—3199)
XXXII	National Endowment for the Arts (Parts 3200—3299)
XXXIII	National Endowment for the Humanities (Parts 3300—3399)
XXXIV	Department of Education (Parts 3400—3499)
XXXV	Export-Import Bank of the United States (Parts 3500—3599)
XXXVI	Office of National Drug Control Policy, Executive Office of the President (Parts 3600—3699)
XXXVII	Peace Corps (Parts 3700—3799)
LVIII	Election Assistance Commission (Parts 5800—5899)
LIX	Gulf Coast Ecosystem Restoration Council (Parts 5900—5999)
LX	Federal Communications Commission (Parts 6000—6099)

Title 3—The President

I	Executive Office of the President (Parts 100—199)

Title 4—Accounts

I	Government Accountability Office (Parts 1—199)

Title 5—Administrative Personnel

I	Office of Personnel Management (Parts 1—1199)
II	Merit Systems Protection Board (Parts 1200—1299)
III	Office of Management and Budget (Parts 1300—1399)
IV	Office of Personnel Management and Office of the Director of National Intelligence (Parts 1400—1499)
V	The International Organizations Employees Loyalty Board (Parts 1500—1599)
VI	Federal Retirement Thrift Investment Board (Parts 1600—1699)
VIII	Office of Special Counsel (Parts 1800—1899)
IX	Appalachian Regional Commission (Parts 1900—1999)
XI	Armed Forces Retirement Home (Parts 2100—2199)
XIV	Federal Labor Relations Authority, General Counsel of the Federal Labor Relations Authority and Federal Service Impasses Panel (Parts 2400—2499)
XVI	Office of Government Ethics (Parts 2600—2699)
XXI	Department of the Treasury (Parts 3100—3199)
XXII	Federal Deposit Insurance Corporation (Parts 3200—3299)
XXIII	Department of Energy (Parts 3300—3399)
XXIV	Federal Energy Regulatory Commission (Parts 3400—3499)
XXV	Department of the Interior (Parts 3500—3599)

Title 5—Administrative Personnel—Continued

Chap.	
XXVI	Department of Defense (Parts 3600—3699)
XXVIII	Department of Justice (Parts 3800—3899)
XXIX	Federal Communications Commission (Parts 3900—3999)
XXX	Farm Credit System Insurance Corporation (Parts 4000—4099)
XXXI	Farm Credit Administration (Parts 4100—4199)
XXXIII	U.S. International Development Finance Corporation (Parts 4300—4399)
XXXIV	Securities and Exchange Commission (Parts 4400—4499)
XXXV	Office of Personnel Management (Parts 4500—4599)
XXXVI	Department of Homeland Security (Parts 4600—4699)
XXXVII	Federal Election Commission (Parts 4700—4799)
XL	Interstate Commerce Commission (Parts 5000—5099)
XLI	Commodity Futures Trading Commission (Parts 5100—5199)
XLII	Department of Labor (Parts 5200—5299)
XLIII	National Science Foundation (Parts 5300—5399)
XLV	Department of Health and Human Services (Parts 5500—5599)
XLVI	Postal Rate Commission (Parts 5600—5699)
XLVII	Federal Trade Commission (Parts 5700—5799)
XLVIII	Nuclear Regulatory Commission (Parts 5800—5899)
XLIX	Federal Labor Relations Authority (Parts 5900—5999)
L	Department of Transportation (Parts 6000—6099)
LII	Export-Import Bank of the United States (Parts 6200—6299)
LIII	Department of Education (Parts 6300—6399)
LIV	Environmental Protection Agency (Parts 6400—6499)
LV	National Endowment for the Arts (Parts 6500—6599)
LVI	National Endowment for the Humanities (Parts 6600—6699)
LVII	General Services Administration (Parts 6700—6799)
LVIII	Board of Governors of the Federal Reserve System (Parts 6800—6899)
LIX	National Aeronautics and Space Administration (Parts 6900—6999)
LX	United States Postal Service (Parts 7000—7099)
LXI	National Labor Relations Board (Parts 7100—7199)
LXII	Equal Employment Opportunity Commission (Parts 7200—7299)
LXIII	Inter-American Foundation (Parts 7300—7399)
LXIV	Merit Systems Protection Board (Parts 7400—7499)
LXV	Department of Housing and Urban Development (Parts 7500—7599)
LXVI	National Archives and Records Administration (Parts 7600—7699)
LXVII	Institute of Museum and Library Services (Parts 7700—7799)
LXVIII	Commission on Civil Rights (Parts 7800—7899)
LXIX	Tennessee Valley Authority (Parts 7900—7999)
LXX	Court Services and Offender Supervision Agency for the District of Columbia (Parts 8000—8099)
LXXI	Consumer Product Safety Commission (Parts 8100—8199)

Title 5—Administrative Personnel—Continued

Chap.	
LXXIII	Department of Agriculture (Parts 8300—8399)
LXXIV	Federal Mine Safety and Health Review Commission (Parts 8400—8499)
LXXVI	Federal Retirement Thrift Investment Board (Parts 8600—8699)
LXXVII	Office of Management and Budget (Parts 8700—8799)
LXXX	Federal Housing Finance Agency (Parts 9000—9099)
LXXXIII	Special Inspector General for Afghanistan Reconstruction (Parts 9300—9399)
LXXXIV	Bureau of Consumer Financial Protection (Parts 9400—9499)
LXXXVI	National Credit Union Administration (Parts 9600—9699)
XCVII	Department of Homeland Security Human Resources Management System (Department of Homeland Security—Office of Personnel Management) (Parts 9700—9799)
XCVIII	Council of the Inspectors General on Integrity and Efficiency (Parts 9800—9899)
XCIX	Military Compensation and Retirement Modernization Commission (Parts 9900—9999)
C	National Council on Disability (Parts 10000—10049)
CI	National Mediation Board (Parts 10100—10199)
CII	U.S. Office of Special Counsel (Parts 10200—10299)
CIV	Office of the Intellectual Property Enforcement Coordinator (Part 10400—10499)

Title 6—Domestic Security

I	Department of Homeland Security, Office of the Secretary (Parts 1—199)
X	Privacy and Civil Liberties Oversight Board (Parts 1000—1099)

Title 7—Agriculture

SUBTITLE A—OFFICE OF THE SECRETARY OF AGRICULTURE (PARTS 0—26)

SUBTITLE B—REGULATIONS OF THE DEPARTMENT OF AGRICULTURE

I	Agricultural Marketing Service (Standards, Inspections, Marketing Practices), Department of Agriculture (Parts 27—209)
II	Food and Nutrition Service, Department of Agriculture (Parts 210—299)
III	Animal and Plant Health Inspection Service, Department of Agriculture (Parts 300—399)
IV	Federal Crop Insurance Corporation, Department of Agriculture (Parts 400—499)
V	Agricultural Research Service, Department of Agriculture (Parts 500—599)
VI	Natural Resources Conservation Service, Department of Agriculture (Parts 600—699)
VII	Farm Service Agency, Department of Agriculture (Parts 700—799)

Title 7—Agriculture—Continued

Chap.	
VIII	Agricultural Marketing Service (Federal Grain Inspection Service, Fair Trade Practices Program), Department of Agriculture (Parts 800—899)
IX	Agricultural Marketing Service (Marketing Agreements and Orders; Fruits, Vegetables, Nuts), Department of Agriculture (Parts 900—999)
X	Agricultural Marketing Service (Marketing Agreements and Orders; Milk), Department of Agriculture (Parts 1000—1199)
XI	Agricultural Marketing Service (Marketing Agreements and Orders; Miscellaneous Commodities), Department of Agriculture (Parts 1200—1299)
XIV	Commodity Credit Corporation, Department of Agriculture (Parts 1400—1499)
XV	Foreign Agricultural Service, Department of Agriculture (Parts 1500—1599)
XVI	[Reserved]
XVII	Rural Utilities Service, Department of Agriculture (Parts 1700—1799)
XVIII	Rural Housing Service, Rural Business-Cooperative Service, Rural Utilities Service, and Farm Service Agency, Department of Agriculture (Parts 1800—2099)
XX	[Reserved]
XXV	Office of Advocacy and Outreach, Department of Agriculture (Parts 2500—2599)
XXVI	Office of Inspector General, Department of Agriculture (Parts 2600—2699)
XXVII	Office of Information Resources Management, Department of Agriculture (Parts 2700—2799)
XXVIII	Office of Operations, Department of Agriculture (Parts 2800—2899)
XXIX	Office of Energy Policy and New Uses, Department of Agriculture (Parts 2900—2999)
XXX	Office of the Chief Financial Officer, Department of Agriculture (Parts 3000—3099)
XXXI	Office of Environmental Quality, Department of Agriculture (Parts 3100—3199)
XXXII	Office of Procurement and Property Management, Department of Agriculture (Parts 3200—3299)
XXXIII	Office of Transportation, Department of Agriculture (Parts 3300—3399)
XXXIV	National Institute of Food and Agriculture (Parts 3400—3499)
XXXV	Rural Housing Service, Department of Agriculture (Parts 3500—3599)
XXXVI	National Agricultural Statistics Service, Department of Agriculture (Parts 3600—3699)
XXXVII	Economic Research Service, Department of Agriculture (Parts 3700—3799)
XXXVIII	World Agricultural Outlook Board, Department of Agriculture (Parts 3800—3899)
XLI	[Reserved]

Title 7—Agriculture—Continued

Chap.

XLII Rural Business-Cooperative Service and Rural Utilities Service, Department of Agriculture (Parts 4200—4299)

L Rural Business-Cooperative Service, and Rural Utilities Service, Department of Agriculture (Parts 5000—5099)

Title 8—Aliens and Nationality

I Department of Homeland Security (Parts 1—499)

V Executive Office for Immigration Review, Department of Justice (Parts 1000—1399)

Title 9—Animals and Animal Products

I Animal and Plant Health Inspection Service, Department of Agriculture (Parts 1—199)

II Agricultural Marketing Service (Fair Trade Practices Program), Department of Agriculture (Parts 200—299)

III Food Safety and Inspection Service, Department of Agriculture (Parts 300—599)

Title 10—Energy

I Nuclear Regulatory Commission (Parts 0—199)

II Department of Energy (Parts 200—699)

III Department of Energy (Parts 700—999)

X Department of Energy (General Provisions) (Parts 1000—1099)

XIII Nuclear Waste Technical Review Board (Parts 1300—1399)

XVII Defense Nuclear Facilities Safety Board (Parts 1700—1799)

XVIII Northeast Interstate Low-Level Radioactive Waste Commission (Parts 1800—1899)

Title 11—Federal Elections

I Federal Election Commission (Parts 1—9099)

II Election Assistance Commission (Parts 9400—9499)

Title 12—Banks and Banking

I Comptroller of the Currency, Department of the Treasury (Parts 1—199)

II Federal Reserve System (Parts 200—299)

III Federal Deposit Insurance Corporation (Parts 300—399)

IV Export-Import Bank of the United States (Parts 400—499)

V [Reserved]

VI Farm Credit Administration (Parts 600—699)

VII National Credit Union Administration (Parts 700—799)

VIII Federal Financing Bank (Parts 800—899)

IX (Parts 900—999)[Reserved]

Chap. **Title 12—Banks and Banking—Continued**

- X Consumer Financial Protection Bureau (Parts 1000—1099)
- XI Federal Financial Institutions Examination Council (Parts 1100—1199)
- XII Federal Housing Finance Agency (Parts 1200—1299)
- XIII Financial Stability Oversight Council (Parts 1300—1399)
- XIV Farm Credit System Insurance Corporation (Parts 1400—1499)
- XV Department of the Treasury (Parts 1500—1599)
- XVI Office of Financial Research, Department of the Treasury (Parts 1600—1699)
- XVII Office of Federal Housing Enterprise Oversight, Department of Housing and Urban Development (Parts 1700—1799)
- XVIII Community Development Financial Institutions Fund, Department of the Treasury (Parts 1800—1899)

Title 13—Business Credit and Assistance

- I Small Business Administration (Parts 1—199)
- III Economic Development Administration, Department of Commerce (Parts 300—399)
- IV Emergency Steel Guarantee Loan Board (Parts 400—499)
- V Emergency Oil and Gas Guaranteed Loan Board (Parts 500—599)

Title 14—Aeronautics and Space

- I Federal Aviation Administration, Department of Transportation (Parts 1—199)
- II Office of the Secretary, Department of Transportation (Aviation Proceedings) (Parts 200—399)
- III Commercial Space Transportation, Federal Aviation Administration, Department of Transportation (Parts 400—1199)
- V National Aeronautics and Space Administration (Parts 1200—1299)
- VI Air Transportation System Stabilization (Parts 1300—1399)

Title 15—Commerce and Foreign Trade

SUBTITLE A—OFFICE OF THE SECRETARY OF COMMERCE (PARTS 0—29)

SUBTITLE B—REGULATIONS RELATING TO COMMERCE AND FOREIGN TRADE

- I Bureau of the Census, Department of Commerce (Parts 30—199)
- II National Institute of Standards and Technology, Department of Commerce (Parts 200—299)
- III International Trade Administration, Department of Commerce (Parts 300—399)
- IV Foreign-Trade Zones Board, Department of Commerce (Parts 400—499)
- VII Bureau of Industry and Security, Department of Commerce (Parts 700—799)

Title 15—Commerce and Foreign Trade—Continued

Chap.
- VIII — Bureau of Economic Analysis, Department of Commerce (Parts 800—899)
- IX — National Oceanic and Atmospheric Administration, Department of Commerce (Parts 900—999)
- XI — National Technical Information Service, Department of Commerce (Parts 1100—1199)
- XIII — East-West Foreign Trade Board (Parts 1300—1399)
- XIV — Minority Business Development Agency (Parts 1400—1499)
- XV — Office of the Under-Secretary for Economic Affairs, Department of Commerce (Parts 1500—1599)

SUBTITLE C—REGULATIONS RELATING TO FOREIGN TRADE AGREEMENTS

- XX — Office of the United States Trade Representative (Parts 2000—2099)

SUBTITLE D—REGULATIONS RELATING TO TELECOMMUNICATIONS AND INFORMATION

- XXIII — National Telecommunications and Information Administration, Department of Commerce (Parts 2300—2399) [Reserved]

Title 16—Commercial Practices

- I — Federal Trade Commission (Parts 0—999)
- II — Consumer Product Safety Commission (Parts 1000—1799)

Title 17—Commodity and Securities Exchanges

- I — Commodity Futures Trading Commission (Parts 1—199)
- II — Securities and Exchange Commission (Parts 200—399)
- IV — Department of the Treasury (Parts 400—499)

Title 18—Conservation of Power and Water Resources

- I — Federal Energy Regulatory Commission, Department of Energy (Parts 1—399)
- III — Delaware River Basin Commission (Parts 400—499)
- VI — Water Resources Council (Parts 700—799)
- VIII — Susquehanna River Basin Commission (Parts 800—899)
- XIII — Tennessee Valley Authority (Parts 1300—1399)

Title 19—Customs Duties

- I — U.S. Customs and Border Protection, Department of Homeland Security; Department of the Treasury (Parts 0—199)
- II — United States International Trade Commission (Parts 200—299)
- III — International Trade Administration, Department of Commerce (Parts 300—399)
- IV — U.S. Immigration and Customs Enforcement, Department of Homeland Security (Parts 400—599) [Reserved]

Chap.

Title 20—Employees' Benefits

I   Office of Workers' Compensation Programs, Department of Labor (Parts 1—199)
II   Railroad Retirement Board (Parts 200—399)
III Social Security Administration (Parts 400—499)
IV   Employees' Compensation Appeals Board, Department of Labor (Parts 500—599)
V   Employment and Training Administration, Department of Labor (Parts 600—699)
VI   Office of Workers' Compensation Programs, Department of Labor (Parts 700—799)
VII Benefits Review Board, Department of Labor (Parts 800—899)
VIII Joint Board for the Enrollment of Actuaries (Parts 900—999)
IX   Office of the Assistant Secretary for Veterans' Employment and Training Service, Department of Labor (Parts 1000—1099)

Title 21—Food and Drugs

I   Food and Drug Administration, Department of Health and Human Services (Parts 1—1299)
II   Drug Enforcement Administration, Department of Justice (Parts 1300—1399)
III Office of National Drug Control Policy (Parts 1400—1499)

Title 22—Foreign Relations

I   Department of State (Parts 1—199)
II   Agency for International Development (Parts 200—299)
III   Peace Corps (Parts 300—399)
IV   International Joint Commission, United States and Canada (Parts 400—499)
V   United States Agency for Global Media (Parts 500—599)
VII   U.S. International Development Finance Corporation (Parts 700—799)
IX   Foreign Service Grievance Board (Parts 900—999)
X   Inter-American Foundation (Parts 1000—1099)
XI   International Boundary and Water Commission, United States and Mexico, United States Section (Parts 1100—1199)
XII   United States International Development Cooperation Agency (Parts 1200—1299)
XIII Millennium Challenge Corporation (Parts 1300—1399)
XIV   Foreign Service Labor Relations Board; Federal Labor Relations Authority; General Counsel of the Federal Labor Relations Authority; and the Foreign Service Impasse Disputes Panel (Parts 1400—1499)
XV   African Development Foundation (Parts 1500—1599)
XVI   Japan-United States Friendship Commission (Parts 1600—1699)
XVII United States Institute of Peace (Parts 1700—1799)

Title 23—Highways

Chap.

I Federal Highway Administration, Department of Transportation (Parts 1—999)

II National Highway Traffic Safety Administration and Federal Highway Administration, Department of Transportation (Parts 1200—1299)

III National Highway Traffic Safety Administration, Department of Transportation (Parts 1300—1399)

Title 24—Housing and Urban Development

SUBTITLE A—OFFICE OF THE SECRETARY, DEPARTMENT OF HOUSING AND URBAN DEVELOPMENT (PARTS 0—99)

SUBTITLE B—REGULATIONS RELATING TO HOUSING AND URBAN DEVELOPMENT

I Office of Assistant Secretary for Equal Opportunity, Department of Housing and Urban Development (Parts 100—199)

II Office of Assistant Secretary for Housing-Federal Housing Commissioner, Department of Housing and Urban Development (Parts 200—299)

III Government National Mortgage Association, Department of Housing and Urban Development (Parts 300—399)

IV Office of Housing and Office of Multifamily Housing Assistance Restructuring, Department of Housing and Urban Development (Parts 400—499)

V Office of Assistant Secretary for Community Planning and Development, Department of Housing and Urban Development (Parts 500—599)

VI Office of Assistant Secretary for Community Planning and Development, Department of Housing and Urban Development (Parts 600—699) [Reserved]

VII Office of the Secretary, Department of Housing and Urban Development (Housing Assistance Programs and Public and Indian Housing Programs) (Parts 700—799)

VIII Office of the Assistant Secretary for Housing—Federal Housing Commissioner, Department of Housing and Urban Development (Section 8 Housing Assistance Programs, Section 202 Direct Loan Program, Section 202 Supportive Housing for the Elderly Program and Section 811 Supportive Housing for Persons With Disabilities Program) (Parts 800—899)

IX Office of Assistant Secretary for Public and Indian Housing, Department of Housing and Urban Development (Parts 900—1699)

X Office of Assistant Secretary for Housing—Federal Housing Commissioner, Department of Housing and Urban Development (Interstate Land Sales Registration Program) (Parts 1700—1799) [Reserved]

XII Office of Inspector General, Department of Housing and Urban Development (Parts 2000—2099)

XV Emergency Mortgage Insurance and Loan Programs, Department of Housing and Urban Development (Parts 2700—2799) [Reserved]

Title 24—Housing and Urban Development—Continued

Chap.

XX   Office of Assistant Secretary for Housing—Federal Housing Commissioner, Department of Housing and Urban Development (Parts 3200—3899)

XXIV   Board of Directors of the HOPE for Homeowners Program (Parts 4000—4099) [Reserved]

XXV   Neighborhood Reinvestment Corporation (Parts 4100—4199)

Title 25—Indians

I   Bureau of Indian Affairs, Department of the Interior (Parts 1—299)

II   Indian Arts and Crafts Board, Department of the Interior (Parts 300—399)

III   National Indian Gaming Commission, Department of the Interior (Parts 500—599)

IV   Office of Navajo and Hopi Indian Relocation (Parts 700—899)

V   Bureau of Indian Affairs, Department of the Interior, and Indian Health Service, Department of Health and Human Services (Part 900—999)

VI   Office of the Assistant Secretary, Indian Affairs, Department of the Interior (Parts 1000—1199)

VII   Office of the Special Trustee for American Indians, Department of the Interior (Parts 1200—1299)

Title 26—Internal Revenue

I   Internal Revenue Service, Department of the Treasury (Parts 1—End)

Title 27—Alcohol, Tobacco Products and Firearms

I   Alcohol and Tobacco Tax and Trade Bureau, Department of the Treasury (Parts 1—399)

II   Bureau of Alcohol, Tobacco, Firearms, and Explosives, Department of Justice (Parts 400—799)

Title 28—Judicial Administration

I   Department of Justice (Parts 0—299)

III   Federal Prison Industries, Inc., Department of Justice (Parts 300—399)

V   Bureau of Prisons, Department of Justice (Parts 500—599)

VI   Offices of Independent Counsel, Department of Justice (Parts 600—699)

VII   Office of Independent Counsel (Parts 700—799)

VIII   Court Services and Offender Supervision Agency for the District of Columbia (Parts 800—899)

IX   National Crime Prevention and Privacy Compact Council (Parts 900—999)

Chap. **Title 28—Judicial Administration—Continued**

XI Department of Justice and Department of State (Parts 1100—1199)

Title 29—Labor

SUBTITLE A—OFFICE OF THE SECRETARY OF LABOR (PARTS 0—99)
SUBTITLE B—REGULATIONS RELATING TO LABOR

I National Labor Relations Board (Parts 100—199)
II Office of Labor-Management Standards, Department of Labor (Parts 200—299)
III National Railroad Adjustment Board (Parts 300—399)
IV Office of Labor-Management Standards, Department of Labor (Parts 400—499)
V Wage and Hour Division, Department of Labor (Parts 500—899)
IX Construction Industry Collective Bargaining Commission (Parts 900—999)
X National Mediation Board (Parts 1200—1299)
XII Federal Mediation and Conciliation Service (Parts 1400—1499)
XIV Equal Employment Opportunity Commission (Parts 1600—1699)
XVII Occupational Safety and Health Administration, Department of Labor (Parts 1900—1999)
XX Occupational Safety and Health Review Commission (Parts 2200—2499)
XXV Employee Benefits Security Administration, Department of Labor (Parts 2500—2599)
XXVII Federal Mine Safety and Health Review Commission (Parts 2700—2799)
XL Pension Benefit Guaranty Corporation (Parts 4000—4999)

Title 30—Mineral Resources

I Mine Safety and Health Administration, Department of Labor (Parts 1—199)
II Bureau of Safety and Environmental Enforcement, Department of the Interior (Parts 200—299)
IV Geological Survey, Department of the Interior (Parts 400—499)
V Bureau of Ocean Energy Management, Department of the Interior (Parts 500—599)
VII Office of Surface Mining Reclamation and Enforcement, Department of the Interior (Parts 700—999)
XII Office of Natural Resources Revenue, Department of the Interior (Parts 1200—1299)

Title 31—Money and Finance: Treasury

SUBTITLE A—OFFICE OF THE SECRETARY OF THE TREASURY (PARTS 0—50)
SUBTITLE B—REGULATIONS RELATING TO MONEY AND FINANCE

Title 31—Money and Finance: Treasury—Continued

Chap.

I	Monetary Offices, Department of the Treasury (Parts 51—199)
II	Fiscal Service, Department of the Treasury (Parts 200—399)
IV	Secret Service, Department of the Treasury (Parts 400—499)
V	Office of Foreign Assets Control, Department of the Treasury (Parts 500—599)
VI	Bureau of Engraving and Printing, Department of the Treasury (Parts 600—699)
VII	Federal Law Enforcement Training Center, Department of the Treasury (Parts 700—799)
VIII	Office of Investment Security, Department of the Treasury (Parts 800—899)
IX	Federal Claims Collection Standards (Department of the Treasury—Department of Justice) (Parts 900—999)
X	Financial Crimes Enforcement Network, Department of the Treasury (Parts 1000—1099)

Title 32—National Defense

SUBTITLE A—DEPARTMENT OF DEFENSE

I	Office of the Secretary of Defense (Parts 1—399)
V	Department of the Army (Parts 400—699)
VI	Department of the Navy (Parts 700—799)
VII	Department of the Air Force (Parts 800—1099)

SUBTITLE B—OTHER REGULATIONS RELATING TO NATIONAL DEFENSE

XII	Department of Defense, Defense Logistics Agency (Parts 1200—1299)
XVI	Selective Service System (Parts 1600—1699)
XVII	Office of the Director of National Intelligence (Parts 1700—1799)
XVIII	National Counterintelligence Center (Parts 1800—1899)
XIX	Central Intelligence Agency (Parts 1900—1999)
XX	Information Security Oversight Office, National Archives and Records Administration (Parts 2000—2099)
XXI	National Security Council (Parts 2100—2199)
XXIV	Office of Science and Technology Policy (Parts 2400—2499)
XXVII	Office for Micronesian Status Negotiations (Parts 2700—2799)
XXVIII	Office of the Vice President of the United States (Parts 2800—2899)

Title 33—Navigation and Navigable Waters

I	Coast Guard, Department of Homeland Security (Parts 1—199)
II	Corps of Engineers, Department of the Army, Department of Defense (Parts 200—399)
IV	Great Lakes St. Lawrence Seaway Development Corporation, Department of Transportation (Parts 400—499)

Title 34—Education

Chap.

SUBTITLE A—OFFICE OF THE SECRETARY, DEPARTMENT OF EDUCATION (PARTS 1—99)

SUBTITLE B—REGULATIONS OF THE OFFICES OF THE DEPARTMENT OF EDUCATION

I Office for Civil Rights, Department of Education (Parts 100—199)
II Office of Elementary and Secondary Education, Department of Education (Parts 200—299)
III Office of Special Education and Rehabilitative Services, Department of Education (Parts 300—399)
IV Office of Career, Technical, and Adult Education, Department of Education (Parts 400—499)
V Office of Bilingual Education and Minority Languages Affairs, Department of Education (Parts 500—599) [Reserved]
VI Office of Postsecondary Education, Department of Education (Parts 600—699)
VII Office of Educational Research and Improvement, Department of Education (Parts 700—799) [Reserved]

SUBTITLE C—REGULATIONS RELATING TO EDUCATION

XI [Reserved]
XII National Council on Disability (Parts 1200—1299)

Title 35 [Reserved]

Title 36—Parks, Forests, and Public Property

I National Park Service, Department of the Interior (Parts 1—199)
II Forest Service, Department of Agriculture (Parts 200—299)
III Corps of Engineers, Department of the Army (Parts 300—399)
IV American Battle Monuments Commission (Parts 400—499)
V Smithsonian Institution (Parts 500—599)
VI [Reserved]
VII Library of Congress (Parts 700—799)
VIII Advisory Council on Historic Preservation (Parts 800—899)
IX Pennsylvania Avenue Development Corporation (Parts 900—999)
X Presidio Trust (Parts 1000—1099)
XI Architectural and Transportation Barriers Compliance Board (Parts 1100—1199)
XII National Archives and Records Administration (Parts 1200—1299)
XV Oklahoma City National Memorial Trust (Parts 1500—1599)
XVI Morris K. Udall Scholarship and Excellence in National Environmental Policy Foundation (Parts 1600—1699)

Title 37—Patents, Trademarks, and Copyrights

I United States Patent and Trademark Office, Department of Commerce (Parts 1—199)
II U.S. Copyright Office, Library of Congress (Parts 200—299)

Title 37—Patents, Trademarks, and Copyrights—Continued

Chap.

III   Copyright Royalty Board, Library of Congress (Parts 300—399)

IV   National Institute of Standards and Technology, Department of Commerce (Parts 400—599)

Title 38—Pensions, Bonuses, and Veterans' Relief

I   Department of Veterans Affairs (Parts 0—199)

II   Armed Forces Retirement Home (Parts 200—299)

Title 39—Postal Service

I   United States Postal Service (Parts 1—999)

III   Postal Regulatory Commission (Parts 3000—3099)

Title 40—Protection of Environment

I   Environmental Protection Agency (Parts 1—1099)

IV   Environmental Protection Agency and Department of Justice (Parts 1400—1499)

V   Council on Environmental Quality (Parts 1500—1599)

VI   Chemical Safety and Hazard Investigation Board (Parts 1600—1699)

VII   Environmental Protection Agency and Department of Defense; Uniform National Discharge Standards for Vessels of the Armed Forces (Parts 1700—1799)

VIII   Gulf Coast Ecosystem Restoration Council (Parts 1800—1899)

IX   Federal Permitting Improvement Steering Council (Part 1900)

Title 41—Public Contracts and Property Management

SUBTITLE A—FEDERAL PROCUREMENT REGULATIONS SYSTEM [NOTE]

SUBTITLE B—OTHER PROVISIONS RELATING TO PUBLIC CONTRACTS

50   Public Contracts, Department of Labor (Parts 50-1—50-999)

51   Committee for Purchase From People Who Are Blind or Severely Disabled (Parts 51-1—51-99)

60   Office of Federal Contract Compliance Programs, Equal Employment Opportunity, Department of Labor (Parts 60-1—60-999)

61   Office of the Assistant Secretary for Veterans' Employment and Training Service, Department of Labor (Parts 61-1—61-999)

62—100   [Reserved]

SUBTITLE C—FEDERAL PROPERTY MANAGEMENT REGULATIONS SYSTEM

101   Federal Property Management Regulations (Parts 101-1—101-99)

102   Federal Management Regulation (Parts 102-1—102-299)

103—104   [Reserved]

105   General Services Administration (Parts 105-1—105-999)

Title 41—Public Contracts and Property Management—Continued

Chap.

109	Department of Energy Property Management Regulations (Parts 109-1—109-99)
114	Department of the Interior (Parts 114-1—114-99)
115	Environmental Protection Agency (Parts 115-1—115-99)
128	Department of Justice (Parts 128-1—128-99)
129—200	[Reserved]

SUBTITLE D—FEDERAL ACQUISITION SUPPLY CHAIN SECURITY

201	Federal Acquisition Security Council (Parts 201-1—201-99).

SUBTITLE E [RESERVED]

SUBTITLE F—FEDERAL TRAVEL REGULATION SYSTEM

300	General (Parts 300-1—300-99)
301	Temporary Duty (TDY) Travel Allowances (Parts 301-1—301-99)
302	Relocation Allowances (Parts 302-1—302-99)
303	Payment of Expenses Connected with the Death of Certain Employees (Part 303-1—303-99)
304	Payment of Travel Expenses from a Non-Federal Source (Parts 304-1—304-99)

Title 42—Public Health

I	Public Health Service, Department of Health and Human Services (Parts 1—199)
II—III	[Reserved]
IV	Centers for Medicare & Medicaid Services, Department of Health and Human Services (Parts 400—699)
V	Office of Inspector General-Health Care, Department of Health and Human Services (Parts 1000—1099)

Title 43—Public Lands: Interior

SUBTITLE A—OFFICE OF THE SECRETARY OF THE INTERIOR (PARTS 1—199)

SUBTITLE B—REGULATIONS RELATING TO PUBLIC LANDS

I	Bureau of Reclamation, Department of the Interior (Parts 400—999)
II	Bureau of Land Management, Department of the Interior (Parts 1000—9999)
III	Utah Reclamation Mitigation and Conservation Commission (Parts 10000—10099)

Title 44—Emergency Management and Assistance

I	Federal Emergency Management Agency, Department of Homeland Security (Parts 0—399)
IV	Department of Commerce and Department of Transportation (Parts 400—499)

Title 45—Public Welfare

Chap.

SUBTITLE A—DEPARTMENT OF HEALTH AND HUMAN SERVICES (PARTS 1—199)

SUBTITLE B—REGULATIONS RELATING TO PUBLIC WELFARE

Chap.	
II	Office of Family Assistance (Assistance Programs), Administration for Children and Families, Department of Health and Human Services (Parts 200—299)
III	Office of Child Support Enforcement (Child Support Enforcement Program), Administration for Children and Families, Department of Health and Human Services (Parts 300—399)
IV	Office of Refugee Resettlement, Administration for Children and Families, Department of Health and Human Services (Parts 400—499)
V	Foreign Claims Settlement Commission of the United States, Department of Justice (Parts 500—599)
VI	National Science Foundation (Parts 600—699)
VII	Commission on Civil Rights (Parts 700—799)
VIII	Office of Personnel Management (Parts 800—899)
IX	Denali Commission (Parts 900—999)
X	Office of Community Services, Administration for Children and Families, Department of Health and Human Services (Parts 1000—1099)
XI	National Foundation on the Arts and the Humanities (Parts 1100—1199)
XII	Corporation for National and Community Service (Parts 1200—1299)
XIII	Administration for Children and Families, Department of Health and Human Services (Parts 1300—1399)
XVI	Legal Services Corporation (Parts 1600—1699)
XVII	National Commission on Libraries and Information Science (Parts 1700—1799)
XVIII	Harry S. Truman Scholarship Foundation (Parts 1800—1899)
XXI	Commission of Fine Arts (Parts 2100—2199)
XXIII	Arctic Research Commission (Parts 2300—2399)
XXIV	James Madison Memorial Fellowship Foundation (Parts 2400—2499)
XXV	Corporation for National and Community Service (Parts 2500—2599)

Title 46—Shipping

I	Coast Guard, Department of Homeland Security (Parts 1—199)
II	Maritime Administration, Department of Transportation (Parts 200—399)
III	Coast Guard (Great Lakes Pilotage), Department of Homeland Security (Parts 400—499)
IV	Federal Maritime Commission (Parts 500—599)

Title 47—Telecommunication

Chap.

I Federal Communications Commission (Parts 0—199)

II Office of Science and Technology Policy and National Security Council (Parts 200—299)

III National Telecommunications and Information Administration, Department of Commerce (Parts 300—399)

IV National Telecommunications and Information Administration, Department of Commerce, and National Highway Traffic Safety Administration, Department of Transportation (Parts 400—499)

V The First Responder Network Authority (Parts 500—599)

Title 48—Federal Acquisition Regulations System

1 Federal Acquisition Regulation (Parts 1—99)

2 Defense Acquisition Regulations System, Department of Defense (Parts 200—299)

3 Department of Health and Human Services (Parts 300—399)

4 Department of Agriculture (Parts 400—499)

5 General Services Administration (Parts 500—599)

6 Department of State (Parts 600—699)

7 Agency for International Development (Parts 700—799)

8 Department of Veterans Affairs (Parts 800—899)

9 Department of Energy (Parts 900—999)

10 Department of the Treasury (Parts 1000—1099)

12 Department of Transportation (Parts 1200—1299)

13 Department of Commerce (Parts 1300—1399)

14 Department of the Interior (Parts 1400—1499)

15 Environmental Protection Agency (Parts 1500—1599)

16 Office of Personnel Management, Federal Employees Health Benefits Acquisition Regulation (Parts 1600—1699)

17 Office of Personnel Management (Parts 1700—1799)

18 National Aeronautics and Space Administration (Parts 1800—1899)

19 Broadcasting Board of Governors (Parts 1900—1999)

20 Nuclear Regulatory Commission (Parts 2000—2099)

21 Office of Personnel Management, Federal Employees Group Life Insurance Federal Acquisition Regulation (Parts 2100—2199)

23 Social Security Administration (Parts 2300—2399)

24 Department of Housing and Urban Development (Parts 2400—2499)

25 National Science Foundation (Parts 2500—2599)

28 Department of Justice (Parts 2800—2899)

29 Department of Labor (Parts 2900—2999)

30 Department of Homeland Security, Homeland Security Acquisition Regulation (HSAR) (Parts 3000—3099)

34 Department of Education Acquisition Regulation (Parts 3400—3499)

Title 48—Federal Acquisition Regulations System—Continued

Chap.	
51	Department of the Army Acquisition Regulations (Parts 5100—5199) [Reserved]
52	Department of the Navy Acquisition Regulations (Parts 5200—5299)
53	Department of the Air Force Federal Acquisition Regulation Supplement (Parts 5300—5399) [Reserved]
54	Defense Logistics Agency, Department of Defense (Parts 5400—5499)
57	African Development Foundation (Parts 5700—5799)
61	Civilian Board of Contract Appeals, General Services Administration (Parts 6100—6199)
99	Cost Accounting Standards Board, Office of Federal Procurement Policy, Office of Management and Budget (Parts 9900—9999)

Title 49—Transportation

SUBTITLE A—OFFICE OF THE SECRETARY OF TRANSPORTATION (PARTS 1—99)

SUBTITLE B—OTHER REGULATIONS RELATING TO TRANSPORTATION

I	Pipeline and Hazardous Materials Safety Administration, Department of Transportation (Parts 100—199)
II	Federal Railroad Administration, Department of Transportation (Parts 200—299)
III	Federal Motor Carrier Safety Administration, Department of Transportation (Parts 300—399)
IV	Coast Guard, Department of Homeland Security (Parts 400—499)
V	National Highway Traffic Safety Administration, Department of Transportation (Parts 500—599)
VI	Federal Transit Administration, Department of Transportation (Parts 600—699)
VII	National Railroad Passenger Corporation (AMTRAK) (Parts 700—799)
VIII	National Transportation Safety Board (Parts 800—999)
X	Surface Transportation Board (Parts 1000—1399)
XI	Research and Innovative Technology Administration, Department of Transportation (Parts 1400—1499) [Reserved]
XII	Transportation Security Administration, Department of Homeland Security (Parts 1500—1699)

Title 50—Wildlife and Fisheries

I	United States Fish and Wildlife Service, Department of the Interior (Parts 1—199)
II	National Marine Fisheries Service, National Oceanic and Atmospheric Administration, Department of Commerce (Parts 200—299)
III	International Fishing and Related Activities (Parts 300—399)

Title 50—Wildlife and Fisheries—Continued

Chap.

IV Joint Regulations (United States Fish and Wildlife Service, Department of the Interior and National Marine Fisheries Service, National Oceanic and Atmospheric Administration, Department of Commerce); Endangered Species Committee Regulations (Parts 400—499)

V Marine Mammal Commission (Parts 500—599)

VI Fishery Conservation and Management, National Oceanic and Atmospheric Administration, Department of Commerce (Parts 600—699)

Alphabetical List of Agencies Appearing in the CFR
(Revised as of April 1, 2023)

Agency	CFR Title, Subtitle or Chapter
Administrative Conference of the United States	1, III
Advisory Council on Historic Preservation	36, VIII
Advocacy and Outreach, Office of	7, XXV
Afghanistan Reconstruction, Special Inspector General for	5, LXXXIII
African Development Foundation	22, XV
Federal Acquisition Regulation	48, 57
Agency for International Development	2, VII; 22, II
Federal Acquisition Regulation	48, 7
Agricultural Marketing Service	7, I, VIII, IX, X, XI; 9, II
Agricultural Research Service	7, V
Agriculture, Department of	2, IV; 5, LXXIII
Advocacy and Outreach, Office of	7, XXV
Agricultural Marketing Service	7, I, VIII, IX, X, XI; 9, II
Agricultural Research Service	7, V
Animal and Plant Health Inspection Service	7, III; 9, I
Chief Financial Officer, Office of	7, XXX
Commodity Credit Corporation	7, XIV
Economic Research Service	7, XXXVII
Energy Policy and New Uses, Office of	2, IX; 7, XXIX
Environmental Quality, Office of	7, XXXI
Farm Service Agency	7, VII, XVIII
Federal Acquisition Regulation	48, 4
Federal Crop Insurance Corporation	7, IV
Food and Nutrition Service	7, II
Food Safety and Inspection Service	9, III
Foreign Agricultural Service	7, XV
Forest Service	36, II
Information Resources Management, Office of	7, XXVII
Inspector General, Office of	7, XXVI
National Agricultural Library	7, XLI
National Agricultural Statistics Service	7, XXXVI
National Institute of Food and Agriculture	7, XXXIV
Natural Resources Conservation Service	7, VI
Operations, Office of	7, XXVIII
Procurement and Property Management, Office of	7, XXXII
Rural Business-Cooperative Service	7, XVIII, XLII
Rural Development Administration	7, XLII
Rural Housing Service	7, XVIII, XXXV
Rural Utilities Service	7, XVII, XVIII, XLII
Secretary of Agriculture, Office of	7, Subtitle A
Transportation, Office of	7, XXXIII
World Agricultural Outlook Board	7, XXXVIII
Air Force, Department of	32, VII
Federal Acquisition Regulation Supplement	48, 53
Air Transportation Stabilization Board	14, VI
Alcohol and Tobacco Tax and Trade Bureau	27, I
Alcohol, Tobacco, Firearms, and Explosives, Bureau of	27, II
AMTRAK	49, VII
American Battle Monuments Commission	36, IV
American Indians, Office of the Special Trustee	25, VII
Animal and Plant Health Inspection Service	7, III; 9, I
Appalachian Regional Commission	5, IX
Architectural and Transportation Barriers Compliance Board	36, XI

Agency	CFR Title, Subtitle or Chapter
Arctic Research Commission	45, XXIII
Armed Forces Retirement Home	5, XI; 38, II
Army, Department of	32, V
Engineers, Corps of	33, II; 36, III
Federal Acquisition Regulation	48, 51
Benefits Review Board	20, VII
Bilingual Education and Minority Languages Affairs, Office of	34, V
Blind or Severely Disabled, Committee for Purchase from People Who Are	41, 51
Federal Acquisition Regulation	48, 19
Career, Technical, and Adult Education, Office of	34, IV
Census Bureau	15, I
Centers for Medicare & Medicaid Services	42, IV
Central Intelligence Agency	32, XIX
Chemical Safety and Hazard Investigation Board	40, VI
Chief Financial Officer, Office of	7, XXX
Child Support Enforcement, Office of	45, III
Children and Families, Administration for	45, II, III, IV, X, XIII
Civil Rights, Commission on	5, LXVIII; 45, VII
Civil Rights, Office for	34, I
Coast Guard	33, I; 46, I; 49, IV
Coast Guard (Great Lakes Pilotage)	46, III
Commerce, Department of	2, XIII; 44, IV; 50, VI
Census Bureau	15, I
Economic Affairs, Office of the Under-Secretary for	15, XV
Economic Analysis, Bureau of	15, VIII
Economic Development Administration	13, III
Emergency Management and Assistance	44, IV
Federal Acquisition Regulation	48, 13
Foreign-Trade Zones Board	15, IV
Industry and Security, Bureau of	15, VII
International Trade Administration	15, III; 19, III
National Institute of Standards and Technology	15, II; 37, IV
National Marine Fisheries Service	50, II, IV
National Oceanic and Atmospheric Administration	15, IX; 50, II, III, IV, VI
National Technical Information Service	15, XI
National Telecommunications and Information Administration	15, XXIII; 47; III, IV
National Weather Service	15, IX
Patent and Trademark Office, United States	37, I
Secretary of Commerce, Office of	15, Subtitle A
Commercial Space Transportation	14, III
Commodity Credit Corporation	7, XIV
Commodity Futures Trading Commission	5, XLI; 17, I
Community Planning and Development, Office of Assistant Secretary for	24, V, VI
Community Services, Office of	45, X
Comptroller of the Currency	12, I
Construction Industry Collective Bargaining Commission	29, IX
Consumer Financial Protection Bureau	5, LXXXIV; 12, X
Consumer Product Safety Commission	5, LXXI; 16, II
Copyright Royalty Board	37, III
Corporation for National and Community Service	2, XXII; 45, XII, XXV
Cost Accounting Standards Board	48, 99
Council on Environmental Quality	40, V
Council of the Inspectors General on Integrity and Efficiency	5, XCVIII
Court Services and Offender Supervision Agency for the District of Columbia	5, LXX; 28, VIII
Customs and Border Protection	19, I
Defense, Department of	2, XI; 5, XXVI; 32, Subtitle A; 40, VII
Advanced Research Projects Agency	32, I
Air Force Department	32, VII
Army Department	32, V; 33, II; 36, III; 48, 51
Defense Acquisition Regulations System	48, 2
Defense Intelligence Agency	32, I

Agency	CFR Title, Subtitle or Chapter
Defense Logistics Agency	32, I, XII; 48, 54
Engineers, Corps of	33, II; 36, III
National Imagery and Mapping Agency	32, I
Navy, Department of	32, VI; 48, 52
Secretary of Defense, Office of	2, XI; 32, I
Defense Contract Audit Agency	32, I
Defense Intelligence Agency	32, I
Defense Logistics Agency	32, XII; 48, 54
Defense Nuclear Facilities Safety Board	10, XVII
Delaware River Basin Commission	18, III
Denali Commission	45, IX
Disability, National Council on	5, C; 34, XII
District of Columbia, Court Services and Offender Supervision Agency for the	5, LXX; 28, VIII
Drug Enforcement Administration	21, II
East-West Foreign Trade Board	15, XIII
Economic Affairs, Office of the Under-Secretary for	15, XV
Economic Analysis, Bureau of	15, VIII
Economic Development Administration	13, III
Economic Research Service	7, XXXVII
Education, Department of	2, XXXIV; 5, LIII
Bilingual Education and Minority Languages Affairs, Office of	34, V
Career, Technical, and Adult Education, Office of	34, IV
Civil Rights, Office for	34, I
Educational Research and Improvement, Office of	34, VII
Elementary and Secondary Education, Office of	34, II
Federal Acquisition Regulation	48, 34
Postsecondary Education, Office of	34, VI
Secretary of Education, Office of	34, Subtitle A
Special Education and Rehabilitative Services, Office of	34, III
Educational Research and Improvement, Office of	34, VII
Election Assistance Commission	2, LVIII; 11, II
Elementary and Secondary Education, Office of	34, II
Emergency Oil and Gas Guaranteed Loan Board	13, V
Emergency Steel Guarantee Loan Board	13, IV
Employee Benefits Security Administration	29, XXV
Employees' Compensation Appeals Board	20, IV
Employees Loyalty Board	5, V
Employment and Training Administration	20, V
Employment Policy, National Commission for	1, IV
Employment Standards Administration	20, VI
Endangered Species Committee	50, IV
Energy, Department of	2, IX; 5, XXIII; 10, II, III, X
Federal Acquisition Regulation	48, 9
Federal Energy Regulatory Commission	5, XXIV; 18, I
Property Management Regulations	41, 109
Energy, Office of	7, XXIX
Engineers, Corps of	33, II; 36, III
Engraving and Printing, Bureau of	31, VI
Environmental Protection Agency	2, XV; 5, LIV; 40, I, IV, VII
Federal Acquisition Regulation	48, 15
Property Management Regulations	41, 115
Environmental Quality, Office of	7, XXXI
Equal Employment Opportunity Commission	5, LXII; 29, XIV
Equal Opportunity, Office of Assistant Secretary for	24, I
Executive Office of the President	3, I
Environmental Quality, Council on	40, V
Management and Budget, Office of	2, Subtitle A; 5, III, LXXVII; 14, VI; 48, 99
National Drug Control Policy, Office of	2, XXXVI; 21, III
National Security Council	32, XXI; 47, II
Presidential Documents	3
Science and Technology Policy, Office of	32, XXIV; 47, II
Trade Representative, Office of the United States	15, XX

Agency	CFR Title, Subtitle or Chapter
Export-Import Bank of the United States	2, XXXV; 5, LII; 12, IV
Family Assistance, Office of	45, II
Farm Credit Administration	5, XXXI; 12, VI
Farm Credit System Insurance Corporation	5, XXX; 12, XIV
Farm Service Agency	7, VII, XVIII
Federal Acquisition Regulation	48, 1
Federal Acquisition Security Council	41, 201
Federal Aviation Administration	14, I
Commercial Space Transportation	14, III
Federal Claims Collection Standards	31, IX
Federal Communications Commission	2, LX; 5, XXIX; 47, I
Federal Contract Compliance Programs, Office of	41, 60
Federal Crop Insurance Corporation	7, IV
Federal Deposit Insurance Corporation	5, XXII; 12, III
Federal Election Commission	5, XXXVII; 11, I
Federal Emergency Management Agency	44, I
Federal Employees Group Life Insurance Federal Acquisition Regulation	48, 21
Federal Employees Health Benefits Acquisition Regulation	48, 16
Federal Energy Regulatory Commission	5, XXIV; 18, I
Federal Financial Institutions Examination Council	12, XI
Federal Financing Bank	12, VIII
Federal Highway Administration	23, I, II
Federal Home Loan Mortgage Corporation	1, IV
Federal Housing Enterprise Oversight Office	12, XVII
Federal Housing Finance Agency	5, LXXX; 12, XII
Federal Labor Relations Authority	5, XIV, XLIX; 22, XIV
Federal Law Enforcement Training Center	31, VII
Federal Management Regulation	41, 102
Federal Maritime Commission	46, IV
Federal Mediation and Conciliation Service	29, XII
Federal Mine Safety and Health Review Commission	5, LXXIV; 29, XXVII
Federal Motor Carrier Safety Administration	49, III
Federal Permitting Improvement Steering Council	40, IX
Federal Prison Industries, Inc.	28, III
Federal Procurement Policy Office	48, 99
Federal Property Management Regulations	41, 101
Federal Railroad Administration	49, II
Federal Register, Administrative Committee of	1, I
Federal Register, Office of	1, II
Federal Reserve System	12, II
Board of Governors	5, LVIII
Federal Retirement Thrift Investment Board	5, VI, LXXVI
Federal Service Impasses Panel	5, XIV
Federal Trade Commission	5, XLVII; 16, I
Federal Transit Administration	49, VI
Federal Travel Regulation System	41, Subtitle F
Financial Crimes Enforcement Network	31, X
Financial Research Office	12, XVI
Financial Stability Oversight Council	12, XIII
Fine Arts, Commission of	45, XXI
Fiscal Service	31, II
Fish and Wildlife Service, United States	50, I, IV
Food and Drug Administration	21, I
Food and Nutrition Service	7, II
Food Safety and Inspection Service	9, III
Foreign Agricultural Service	7, XV
Foreign Assets Control, Office of	31, V
Foreign Claims Settlement Commission of the United States	45, V
Foreign Service Grievance Board	22, IX
Foreign Service Impasse Disputes Panel	22, XIV
Foreign Service Labor Relations Board	22, XIV
Foreign-Trade Zones Board	15, IV
Forest Service	36, II
General Services Administration	5, LVII; 41, 105
Contract Appeals, Board of	48, 61
Federal Acquisition Regulation	48, 5

Agency	CFR Title, Subtitle or Chapter
Federal Management Regulation	41, 102
Federal Property Management Regulations	41, 101
Federal Travel Regulation System	41, Subtitle F
General	41, 300
Payment From a Non-Federal Source for Travel Expenses	41, 304
Payment of Expenses Connected With the Death of Certain Employees	41, 303
Relocation Allowances	41, 302
Temporary Duty (TDY) Travel Allowances	41, 301
Geological Survey	30, IV
Government Accountability Office	4, I
Government Ethics, Office of	5, XVI
Government National Mortgage Association	24, III
Grain Inspection, Packers and Stockyards Administration	7, VIII; 9, II
Great Lakes St. Lawrence Seaway Development Corporation	33, IV
Gulf Coast Ecosystem Restoration Council	2, LIX; 40, VIII
Harry S. Truman Scholarship Foundation	45, XVIII
Health and Human Services, Department of	2, III; 5, XLV; 45, Subtitle A
Centers for Medicare & Medicaid Services	42, IV
Child Support Enforcement, Office of	45, III
Children and Families, Administration for	45, II, III, IV, X, XIII
Community Services, Office of	45, X
Family Assistance, Office of	45, II
Federal Acquisition Regulation	48, 3
Food and Drug Administration	21, I
Indian Health Service	25, V
Inspector General (Health Care), Office of	42, V
Public Health Service	42, I
Refugee Resettlement, Office of	45, IV
Homeland Security, Department of	2, XXX; 5, XXXVI; 6, I; 8, I
Coast Guard	33, I; 46, I; 49, IV
Coast Guard (Great Lakes Pilotage)	46, III
Customs and Border Protection	19, I
Federal Emergency Management Agency	44, I
Human Resources Management and Labor Relations Systems	5, XCVII
Immigration and Customs Enforcement Bureau	19, IV
Transportation Security Administration	49, XII
HOPE for Homeowners Program, Board of Directors of	24, XXIV
Housing and Urban Development, Department of	2, XXIV; 5, LXV; 24, Subtitle B
Community Planning and Development, Office of Assistant Secretary for	24, V, VI
Equal Opportunity, Office of Assistant Secretary for	24, I
Federal Acquisition Regulation	48, 24
Federal Housing Enterprise Oversight, Office of	12, XVII
Government National Mortgage Association	24, III
Housing—Federal Housing Commissioner, Office of Assistant Secretary for	24, II, VIII, X, XX
Housing, Office of, and Multifamily Housing Assistance Restructuring, Office of	24, IV
Inspector General, Office of	24, XII
Public and Indian Housing, Office of Assistant Secretary for	24, IX
Secretary, Office of	24, Subtitle A, VII
Housing—Federal Housing Commissioner, Office of Assistant Secretary for	24, II, VIII, X, XX
Housing, Office of, and Multifamily Housing Assistance Restructuring, Office of	24, IV
Immigration and Customs Enforcement Bureau	19, IV
Immigration Review, Executive Office for	8, V
Independent Counsel, Office of	28, VII
Independent Counsel, Offices of	28, VI
Indian Affairs, Bureau of	25, I, V
Indian Affairs, Office of the Assistant Secretary	25, VI
Indian Arts and Crafts Board	25, II

853

Agency	CFR Title, Subtitle or Chapter
Indian Health Service	25, V
Industry and Security, Bureau of	15, VII
Information Resources Management, Office of	7, XXVII
Information Security Oversight Office, National Archives and Records Administration	32, XX
Inspector General	
Agriculture Department	7, XXVI
Health and Human Services Department	42, V
Housing and Urban Development Department	24, XII, XV
Institute of Peace, United States	22, XVII
Intellectual Property Enforcement Coordinator, Office of	5, CIV
Inter-American Foundation	5, LXIII; 22, X
Interior, Department of	2, XIV
American Indians, Office of the Special Trustee	25, VII
Endangered Species Committee	50, IV
Federal Acquisition Regulation	48, 14
Federal Property Management Regulations System	41, 114
Fish and Wildlife Service, United States	50, I, IV
Geological Survey	30, IV
Indian Affairs, Bureau of	25, I, V
Indian Affairs, Office of the Assistant Secretary	25, VI
Indian Arts and Crafts Board	25, II
Land Management, Bureau of	43, II
National Indian Gaming Commission	25, III
National Park Service	36, I
Natural Resource Revenue, Office of	30, XII
Ocean Energy Management, Bureau of	30, V
Reclamation, Bureau of	43, I
Safety and Environmental Enforcement, Bureau of	30, II
Secretary of the Interior, Office of	2, XIV; 43, Subtitle A
Surface Mining Reclamation and Enforcement, Office of	30, VII
Internal Revenue Service	26, I
International Boundary and Water Commission, United States and Mexico, United States Section	22, XI
International Development, United States Agency for	22, II
Federal Acquisition Regulation	48, 7
International Development Cooperation Agency, United States	22, XII
International Development Finance Corporation, U.S.	5, XXXIII; 22, VII
International Joint Commission, United States and Canada	22, IV
International Organizations Employees Loyalty Board	5, V
International Trade Administration	15, III; 19, III
International Trade Commission, United States	19, II
Interstate Commerce Commission	5, XL
Investment Security, Office of	31, VIII
James Madison Memorial Fellowship Foundation	45, XXIV
Japan–United States Friendship Commission	22, XVI
Joint Board for the Enrollment of Actuaries	20, VIII
Justice, Department of	2, XXVIII; 5, XXVIII; 28, I, XI; 40, IV
Alcohol, Tobacco, Firearms, and Explosives, Bureau of	27, II
Drug Enforcement Administration	21, II
Federal Acquisition Regulation	48, 28
Federal Claims Collection Standards	31, IX
Federal Prison Industries, Inc.	28, III
Foreign Claims Settlement Commission of the United States	45, V
Immigration Review, Executive Office for	8, V
Independent Counsel, Offices of	28, VI
Prisons, Bureau of	28, V
Property Management Regulations	41, 128
Labor, Department of	2, XXIX; 5, XLII
Benefits Review Board	20, VII
Employee Benefits Security Administration	29, XXV
Employees' Compensation Appeals Board	20, IV
Employment and Training Administration	20, V
Federal Acquisition Regulation	48, 29

Agency	CFR Title, Subtitle or Chapter
Federal Contract Compliance Programs, Office of	41, 60
Federal Procurement Regulations System	41, 50
Labor-Management Standards, Office of	29, II, IV
Mine Safety and Health Administration	30, I
Occupational Safety and Health Administration	29, XVII
Public Contracts	41, 50
Secretary of Labor, Office of	29, Subtitle A
Veterans' Employment and Training Service, Office of the Assistant Secretary for	41, 61; 20, IX
Wage and Hour Division	29, V
Workers' Compensation Programs, Office of	20, I, VI
Labor-Management Standards, Office of	29, II, IV
Land Management, Bureau of	43, II
Legal Services Corporation	45, XVI
Libraries and Information Science, National Commission on	45, XVII
Library of Congress	36, VII
Copyright Royalty Board	37, III
U.S. Copyright Office	37, II
Management and Budget, Office of	5, III, LXXVII; 14, VI; 48, 99
Marine Mammal Commission	50, V
Maritime Administration	46, II
Merit Systems Protection Board	5, II, LXIV
Micronesian Status Negotiations, Office for	32, XXVII
Military Compensation and Retirement Modernization Commission	5, XCIX
Millennium Challenge Corporation	22, XIII
Mine Safety and Health Administration	30, I
Minority Business Development Agency	15, XIV
Miscellaneous Agencies	1, IV
Monetary Offices	31, I
Morris K. Udall Scholarship and Excellence in National Environmental Policy Foundation	36, XVI
Museum and Library Services, Institute of	2, XXXI
National Aeronautics and Space Administration	2, XVIII; 5, LIX; 14, V
Federal Acquisition Regulation	48, 18
National Agricultural Library	7, XLI
National Agricultural Statistics Service	7, XXXVI
National and Community Service, Corporation for	2, XXII; 45, XII, XXV
National Archives and Records Administration	2, XXVI; 5, LXVI; 36, XII
Information Security Oversight Office	32, XX
National Capital Planning Commission	1, IV, VI
National Counterintelligence Center	32, XVIII
National Credit Union Administration	5, LXXXVI; 12, VII
National Crime Prevention and Privacy Compact Council	28, IX
National Drug Control Policy, Office of	2, XXXVI; 21, III
National Endowment for the Arts	2, XXXII
National Endowment for the Humanities	2, XXXIII
National Foundation on the Arts and the Humanities	45, XI
National Geospatial-Intelligence Agency	32, I
National Highway Traffic Safety Administration	23, II, III; 47, VI; 49, V
National Imagery and Mapping Agency	32, I
National Indian Gaming Commission	25, III
National Institute of Food and Agriculture	7, XXXIV
National Institute of Standards and Technology	15, II; 37, IV
National Intelligence, Office of Director of	5, IV; 32, XVII
National Labor Relations Board	5, LXI; 29, I
National Marine Fisheries Service	50, II, IV
National Mediation Board	5, CI; 29, X
National Oceanic and Atmospheric Administration	15, IX; 50, II, III, IV, VI
National Park Service	36, I
National Railroad Adjustment Board	29, III
National Railroad Passenger Corporation (AMTRAK)	49, VII
National Science Foundation	2, XXV; 5, XLIII; 45, VI
Federal Acquisition Regulation	48, 25
National Security Council	32, XXI; 47, II

Agency	CFR Title, Subtitle or Chapter
National Technical Information Service	15, XI
National Telecommunications and Information Administration	15, XXIII; 47, III, IV, V
National Transportation Safety Board	49, VIII
Natural Resource Revenue, Office of	30, XII
Natural Resources Conservation Service	7, VI
Navajo and Hopi Indian Relocation, Office of	25, IV
Navy, Department of	32, VI
Federal Acquisition Regulation	48, 52
Neighborhood Reinvestment Corporation	24, XXV
Northeast Interstate Low-Level Radioactive Waste Commission	10, XVIII
Nuclear Regulatory Commission	2, XX; 5, XLVIII; 10, I
Federal Acquisition Regulation	48, 20
Occupational Safety and Health Administration	29, XVII
Occupational Safety and Health Review Commission	29, XX
Ocean Energy Management, Bureau of	30, V
Oklahoma City National Memorial Trust	36, XV
Operations Office	7, XXVIII
Patent and Trademark Office, United States	37, I
Payment From a Non-Federal Source for Travel Expenses	41, 304
Payment of Expenses Connected With the Death of Certain Employees	41, 303
Peace Corps	2, XXXVII; 22, III
Pennsylvania Avenue Development Corporation	36, IX
Pension Benefit Guaranty Corporation	29, XL
Personnel Management, Office of	5, I, IV, XXXV; 45, VIII
Federal Acquisition Regulation	48, 17
Federal Employees Group Life Insurance Federal Acquisition Regulation	48, 21
Federal Employees Health Benefits Acquisition Regulation	48, 16
Human Resources Management and Labor Relations Systems, Department of Homeland Security	5, XCVII
Pipeline and Hazardous Materials Safety Administration	49, I
Postal Regulatory Commission	5, XLVI; 39, III
Postal Service, United States	5, LX; 39, I
Postsecondary Education, Office of	34, VI
President's Commission on White House Fellowships	1, IV
Presidential Documents	3
Presidio Trust	36, X
Prisons, Bureau of	28, V
Privacy and Civil Liberties Oversight Board	6, X
Procurement and Property Management, Office of	7, XXXII
Public and Indian Housing, Office of Assistant Secretary for	24, IX
Public Contracts, Department of Labor	41, 50
Public Health Service	42, I
Railroad Retirement Board	20, II
Reclamation, Bureau of	43, I
Refugee Resettlement, Office of	45, IV
Relocation Allowances	41, 302
Research and Innovative Technology Administration	49, XI
Rural Business-Cooperative Service	7, XVIII, XLII, L
Rural Development Administration	7, XLII
Rural Housing Service	7, XVIII, XXXV, L
Rural Utilities Service	7, XVII, XVIII, XLII, L
Safety and Environmental Enforcement, Bureau of	30, II
Science and Technology Policy, Office of	32, XXIV; 47, II
Secret Service	31, IV
Securities and Exchange Commission	5, XXXIV; 17, II
Selective Service System	32, XVI
Small Business Administration	2, XXVII; 13, I
Smithsonian Institution	36, V
Social Security Administration	2, XXIII; 20, III; 48, 23
Soldiers' and Airmen's Home, United States	5, XI
Special Counsel, Office of	5, VIII
Special Education and Rehabilitative Services, Office of	34, III
State, Department of	2, VI; 22, I; 28, XI

Agency	CFR Title, Subtitle or Chapter
Federal Acquisition Regulation	48, 6
Surface Mining Reclamation and Enforcement, Office of	30, VII
Surface Transportation Board	49, X
Susquehanna River Basin Commission	18, VIII
Tennessee Valley Authority	5, LXIX; 18, XIII
Trade Representative, United States, Office of	15, XX
Transportation, Department of	2, XII; 5, L
Commercial Space Transportation	14, III
Emergency Management and Assistance	44, IV
Federal Acquisition Regulation	48, 12
Federal Aviation Administration	14, I
Federal Highway Administration	23, I, II
Federal Motor Carrier Safety Administration	49, III
Federal Railroad Administration	49, II
Federal Transit Administration	49, VI
Great Lakes St. Lawrence Seaway Development Corporation	33, IV
Maritime Administration	46, II
National Highway Traffic Safety Administration	23, II, III; 47, IV; 49, V
Pipeline and Hazardous Materials Safety Administration	49, I
Secretary of Transportation, Office of	14, II; 49, Subtitle A
Transportation Statistics Bureau	49, XI
Transportation, Office of	7, XXXIII
Transportation Security Administration	49, XII
Transportation Statistics Bureau	49, XI
Travel Allowances, Temporary Duty (TDY)	41, 301
Treasury, Department of the	2, X; 5, XXI; 12, XV; 17, IV; 31, IX
Alcohol and Tobacco Tax and Trade Bureau	27, I
Community Development Financial Institutions Fund	12, XVIII
Comptroller of the Currency	12, I
Customs and Border Protection	19, I
Engraving and Printing, Bureau of	31, VI
Federal Acquisition Regulation	48, 10
Federal Claims Collection Standards	31, IX
Federal Law Enforcement Training Center	31, VII
Financial Crimes Enforcement Network	31, X
Fiscal Service	31, II
Foreign Assets Control, Office of	31, V
Internal Revenue Service	26, I
Investment Security, Office of	31, VIII
Monetary Offices	31, I
Secret Service	31, IV
Secretary of the Treasury, Office of	31, Subtitle A
Truman, Harry S. Scholarship Foundation	45, XVIII
United States Agency for Global Media	22, V
United States and Canada, International Joint Commission	22, IV
United States and Mexico, International Boundary and Water Commission, United States Section	22, XI
U.S. Copyright Office	37, II
U.S. Office of Special Counsel	5, CII
Utah Reclamation Mitigation and Conservation Commission	43, III
Veterans Affairs, Department of	2, VIII; 38, I
Federal Acquisition Regulation	48, 8
Veterans' Employment and Training Service, Office of the Assistant Secretary for	41, 61; 20, IX
Vice President of the United States, Office of	32, XXVIII
Wage and Hour Division	29, V
Water Resources Council	18, VI
Workers' Compensation Programs, Office of	20, I, VII
World Agricultural Outlook Board	7, XXXVIII

Table of OMB Control Numbers

The OMB control numbers for chapter II of title 17 appear in § 200.800. For the convenience of the user, § 200.800 is reprinted below.

§ 200.800 OMB control numbers assigned pursuant to the Paperwork Reduction Act.

(a) *Purpose:* This subpart collects and displays the control numbers assigned to information collection requirements of the Commission by the Office of Management and Budget pursuant to the Paperwork Reduction Act of 1980, 44 U.S.C. 3500 *et seq.* This subpart displays current OMB control numbers for those information collection requirements of the Commission that are rules and regulations and codified in 17 CFR either in full text or incorporated by reference with the approval of the Director of the Office of the Federal Register.

(b) *Display.*

Information collection requirement	17 CFR part or section where identified and described	Current OMB control No.
Regulation S-X	Part 210	3235-0009
Regulation S-B	Part 228	3235-0417
Regulation S-K	Part 229	3235-0071
Rule 154	230.154	3235-0495
Rule 155	230.155	3235-0549
Rule 236	230.236	3235-0095
Rule 237	230.237	3235-0528
Regulation A	230.251 thru 230.263	3235-0286
Regulation C	230.400 thru 230.494	3235-0074
Rule 425	230.425	3235-0521
Rule 477	230.477	3235-0550
Rule 489	230.489	3235-0411
Rule 498	230.498	3235-0488
Rule 498A	230.498A	3235-0765
Regulation D	230.500 thru 230.508	3235-0076
Regulation E	230.601 thru 230.610a	3235-0232
Rule 604	230.604	3235-0232
Rule 605	230.605	3235-0232
Rule 609	230.609	3235-0233
Rule 701	230.701	3235-0522
Regulation S	230.901 thru 230.905	3235-0357
Regulation S-T	Part 232	3235-0424
Form SB-1	239.9	3235-0423
Form SB-2	239.10	3235-0418
Form S-1	239.11	3235-0065
Form S-2	239.12	3235-0072
Form S-3	239.13	3235-0073
Form N-2	239.14	3235-0026
Form N-1A	239.15A	3235-0307
Form S-6	239.16	3235-0184
Form S-8	239.16b	3235-0066
Form N-3	239.17a	3235-0316
Form N-4	239.17b	3235-0318
Form S-11	239.18	3235-0067
Form N-14	239.23	3235-0336
Form N-5	239.24	3235-0169
Form S-4	239.25	3235-0324
Form F-1	239.31	3235-0258
Form F-2	239.32	3235-0257
Form F-3	239.33	3235-0256
Form F-4	239.34	3235-0325
Form F-6	239.36	3235-0292
Form F-7	239.37	3235-0383
Form F-8	239.38	3235-0378
Form F-10	239.40	3235-0380

§ 200.800

Information collection requirement	17 CFR part or section where identified and described	Current OMB control No.
Form F-80	239.41	3235-0404
Form F-X	239.42	3235-0379
Form F-N	239.43	3235-0411
Form ID	239.63	3235-0328
Form SE	239.64	3235-0327
Form TH	239.65	3235-0425
Form 1-A	239.90	3235-0286
Form 2-A	239.91	3235-0286
Form 144	239.144	3235-0101
Form 1-E	239.200	3235-0232
Form CB	239.800	3235-0518
Rule 6a-1	240.6a-1	3235-0017
Rule 6a-3	240.6a-3	3235-0021
Rule 6a-4	240.6a-4	3235-0554
Rule 6h-1	240.6h-1	3235-0555
Rule 8c-1	240.8c-1	3235-0514
Rule 9b-1	240.9b-1	3235-0480
Rule 10a-1	240.10a-1	3235-0475
Rule 10b-10	240.10b-10	3235-0444
Rule 10b-17	240.10b-17	3235-0476
Rule 10b-18	240.10b-18	3235-0474
Rule 10A-1	240.10A-1	3235-0468
Rule 11a1-1(T)	240.11a1-1(T)	3235-0478
Rule 12a-5	240.12a-5	3235-0079
Regulation 12B	240.12b-1 thru 240.12b-36	3235-0062
Rule 12d1-3	240.12d1-3	3235-0109
Rule 12d2-1	240.12d2-1	3235-0081
Rule 12d2-2	240.12d2-2	3235-0080
Rule 12f-1	240.12f-1	3235-0128
Rule 13a-16	240.13a-16	3235-0116
Regulation 13D/G	240.13d-1 thru 240.13d-7	3235-0145
Schedule 13D	240.13d-101	3235-0145
Schedule 13G	240.13d-102	3235-0145
Rule 13e-1	240.13e-1	3235-0305
Rule 13e-3	240.13e-3	3235-0007
Schedule 13E-3	240.13e-100	3235-0007
Schedule 13e-4F	240.13e-101	3235-0375
Regulation 14A	240.14a-1 thru 240.14a-12	3235-0059
Schedule 14A	240.14a-101	3235-0059
Regulation 14C	240.14c-1	3235-0057
Schedule 14C	240.14c-101	3235-0057
Regulation 14D	240.14d-1 thru 240.14d-9	3235-0102
Schedule TO	240.14d-100	3235-0515
Schedule 14D-1	240.14d-101	3235-0102
Schedule 14D-9	240.14d-101	3235-0102
Schedule 14D-1F	240.14d-102	3235-0376
Schedule 14D-9F	240.14d-103	3235-0382
Regulation 14E	240.14e-1 thru 240.14e-2	3235-0102
Rule 14f-1	240.14f-1	3235-0108
Rule 15a-4	240.15a-4	3235-0010
Rule 15a-6	240.15a-6	3235-0371
Rule 15b1-1	240.15b1-1	3235-0012
Rule 15b6-1(a)	240.15b6-1(a)	3235-0018
Rule 15c1-5	240.15c1-5	3235-0471
Rule 15c1-6	240.15c1-6	3235-0472
Rule 15c1-7	240.15c1-7	3235-0134
Rule 15c2-1	240.15c2-1	3235-0485
Rule 15c2-5	240.15c2-5	3235-0198
Rule 15c2-7	240.15c2-7	3235-0479
Rule 15c2-8	240.15c2-8	3235-0481
Rule 15c2-11	240.15c2-11	3235-0202
Rule 15c2-12	240.15c2-12	3235-0372
Rule 15c3-1	240.15c3-1	3235-0200
Rule 15c3-1(c)(13)	240.15c3-1(c)(13)	3235-0499
Appendix F to Rule 15c3-1	240.15c3-1f	3235-0496
Rule 15c3-3	240.15c3-3	3235-0078
Rule 15c3-4	240.15c3-4	3235-0497
Rule 15d-16	240.15d-16	3235-0116
Rule 15g-2	240.15g-2	3235-0434
Rule 15g-3	240.15g-3	3235-0392
Rule 15g-4	240.15g-4	3235-0393
Rule 15g-5	240.15g-5	3235-0394

17 CFR (4-1-23 Edition)

OMB Control Numbers § 200.800

Information collection requirement	17 CFR part or section where identified and described	Current OMB control No.
Rule 15g–6	240.15g–6	3235–0395
Rule 15g–9	240.15g–9	3235–0385
Rule 15Aj–1	240.15Aj–1	3235–0044
Rule 15Ba2–1	240.15Ba2–1	3235–0083
Rule 15Ba2–5	240.15Ba2–5	3235–0088
Rule 15Bc3–1	240.15Bc3–1	3235–0087
Rule 17a–1	240.17a–1	3235–0208
Rule 17a–2	240.17a–2	3235–0201
Rule 17a–3	240.17a–3	3235–0033
Rule 17a–3(a)(16)	240.17a–3(a)(16)	3235–0508
Rule 17a–4	240.17a–4	3235–0279
Rule 17a–4(b)(10)	240.17a–4(b)(10)	3235–0506
Rule 17a–5	240.17a–5	3235–0123
Rule 17a–5(c)	240.17a–5(c)	3235–0199
Rule 17a–6	240.17a–6	3235–0489
Rule 17a–7	240.17a–7	3235–0131
Rule 17a–8	240.17a–8	3235–0092
Rule 17a–9T	240.17a–9T	3235–0524
Rule 17a–10	240.17a–10	3235–0122
Rule 17a–11	240.17a–11	3235–0085
Rule 17a–12	240.17a–12	3235–0498
Rule 17a–13	240.17a–13	3235–0035
Rule 17a–19	240.17a–19	3235–0133
Rule 17a–22	240.17a–22	3235–0196
Rule 17a–25	240.17a–25	3235–0540
Rule 17f–1(b)	240.17f–1(b)	3235–0032
Rule 17f–1(c)	240.17f–1(c)	3235–0037
Rule 17f–1(g)	240.17f–1(g)	3235–0290
Rule 17f–2(a)	240.17f–2(a)	3235–0034
Rule 17f–2(c)	240.17f–2(c)	3235–0029
Rule 17f–2(d)	240.17f–2(d)	3235–0028
Rule 17f–2(e)	240.17f–2(e)	3235–0031
Rule 17f–5	240.17f–5	3235–0269
Rule 17h–1T	240.17h–1T	3235–0410
Rule 17h–2T	240.17h–2T	3235–0410
Rule 17Ab2–1	240.17Ab2–1(a)	3235–0195
Rule 17Ac2–1	240.17Ac2–1	3235–0084
Rule 17Ad–2(c), (d), and (h)	240.17Ad–2(c), (d) and (h)	3235–0130
Rule 17Ad–3(b)	240.17Ad–3(b)	3235–0473
Rule 17Ad–4(b) and (c)	240.17Ad–4(b) and (c)	3235–0341
Rule 17Ad–6	240.17Ad–6	3235–0291
Rule 17Ad–7	240.17Ad–7	3235–0291
Rule 17Ad–10	240.17Ad–10	3235–0273
Rule 17Ad–11	240.17Ad–11	3235–0274
Rule 17Ad–13	240.17Ad–13	3235–0275
Rule 17Ad–15	240.17Ad–15	3235–0409
Rule 17Ad–16	240.17Ad–16	3235–0413
Rule 17Ad–17	240.17Ad–17	3235–0469
Rule 19b–1	240.19b–1	3235–0354
Rule 19b–4	240.19b–4	3235–0045
Rule 19b–4(e)	240.19b–4(e)	3235–0504
Rule 19b–5	240.19b–5	3235–0507
Rule 19b–7	240.19b–7	3235–0553
Rule 19d–1	240.19d–1(b) thru 240.19d–1(i)	3235–0206
Rule 19d–2	240.19d–2	3235–0205
Rule 19d–3	240.19d–3	3235–0204
Rule 19h–1	240.19h–1(a), (c) thru (e), and (g)	3235–0259
Rule 24b–1	240.24b–1	3235–0194
Rule 101	242.101	3235–0464
Rule 102	242.102	3235–0467
Rule 103	242.103	3235–0466
Rule 104	242.104	3235–0465
Rule 301	242.301	3235–0509
Rule 302	242.302	3235–0510
Rule 303	242.303	3235–0505
Rule 604	242.604	3235–0462
Rule 605	242.605	3235–0542
Rule 606	242.606	3235–0541
Rule 607	242.607	3235–0435
Rule 608	242.608	3235–0500
Rule 609	242.609	3235–0043
Rule 611	242.611	3235–0600

§ 200.800

17 CFR (4-1-23 Edition)

Information collection requirement	17 CFR part or section where identified and described	Current OMB control No.
Regulation S-P	Part 248	3235-0537
Form 1	249.1	3235-0017
Form 1-N	249.10	3235-0554
Form 25	249.25	3235-0080
Form 26	249.26	3235-0079
Form 3	249.103	3235-0104
Form 4	249.104	3235-0287
Form 5	249.105	3235-0362
Form 8-A	249.208a	3235-0056
Form 10	249.210	3235-0064
Form 10-SB	249.210b	3235-0419
Form 18	249.218	3235-0121
Form 20-F	249.220f	3235-0288
Form 40-F	249.240f	3235-0381
Form 6-K	249.306	3235-0116
Form 8-K	249.308	3235-0060
Form 10-Q	249.308a	3235-0070
Form 10-QSB	249.308b	3235-0416
Form 10-K	249.310	3235-0063
Form 10-KSB	249.310b	3235-0420
Form 11-K	249.311	3235-0082
Form 18-K	249.318	3235-0120
Form 12B-25	249.322	3235-0058
Form 15	249.323	3235-0167
Form 13F	249.325	3235-0006
Form SE	249.444	3235-0327
Form ID	249.446	3235-0328
Form DF	249.448	3235-0482
Form BD	249.501	3235-0012
Form BDW	249.501a	3235-0018
Form BD-N	249.501b	3235-0556
Form X-17A-5	249.617	3235-0123
Form X-17A-19	249.635	3235-0133
Form ATS	249.637	3235-0509
Form ATS-R	249.638	3235-0509
Form CRS	249.640	3235-0766
Form X-15AJ-1	249.802	3235-0044
Form X-15AJ-2	249.803	3235-0044
Form 19b-4	249.819	3235-0045
Form 19b-4(e)	249.820	3235-0504
Form Pilot	249.821	3235-0507
Form SIP	249.1001	3235-0043
Form MSD	249.1100	3235-0083
Form MSDW	249.1110	3235-0087
Form X-17F-1A	249.1200	3235-0037
Form TA-1	249b.100	3235-0084
Form TA-W	249b.101	3235-0151
Form TA-2	249b.102	3235-0337
Form CA-1	249b.200	3235-0195
Rule 7a-15 thru 7a-37	260.7a-15 thru 260.7a-37	3235-0132
Form T-1	269.1	3235-0110
Form T-2	269.2	3235-0111
Form T-3	269.3	3235-0105
Form T-4	269.4	3235-0107
Form ID	269.7	3235-0328
Form SE	269.8	3235-0327
Form T-6	269.9	3235-0391
Rule 0-1	270.0-1	3235-0531
Rule 2a-7	270.2a-7	3235-0268
Rule 2a19-1	270.2a19-1	3235-0332
Rule 3a-4	270.3a-4	3235-0459
Rule 6c-7	270.6c-7	3235-0276
Rule 6e-2	270.6e-2	3235-0177
Rule 7d-1	270.7d-1	3235-0311
Rule 7d-2	270.7d-2	3235-0527
Section 8(b) of the Investment Company Act of 1940	270.8b-1 thru 270.8b-32	3235-0176
Rule 10f-3	270.10f-3	3235-0226
Rule 11a-2	270.11a-2	3235-0272
Rule 11a-3	270.11a-3	3235-0358
Rule 12b-1	270.12b-1	3235-0212
Rule 17a-7	270.17a-7	3235-0214
Rule 17a-8	270.17a-8	3235-0235

862

OMB Control Numbers § 200.800

Information collection requirement	17 CFR part or section where identified and described	Current OMB control No.
Rule 17e–1	270.17e–1	3235–0217
Rule 17f–1	270.17f–1	3235–0222
Rule 17f–2	270.17f–2	3235–0223
Rule 17f–4	270.17f–4	3235–0225
Rule 17f–6	270.17f–6	3235–0447
Rule 17f–7	270.17f–7	3235–0529
Rule 17g–1(g)	270.17g–1(g)	3235–0213
Rule 17j–1	270.17j–1	3235–0224
Rule 18f–1	270.18f–1	3235–0211
Rule 18f–3	270.18f–3	3235–0441
Rule 19a–1	270.19a–1	3235–0216
Rule 20a–1	270.20a–1	3235–0158
Rule 22d–1	270.22d–1	3235–0310
Rule 23c–1	270.23c–1	3235–0260
Rule 23c–3	270.23c–3	3235–0422
Rule 27e–1	270.27e–1	3235–0545
Rule 30b2–1	270.30b2–1	3235–0220
Rule 30d–2	270.30d–2	3235–0494
Rule 30e–1	270.30e–1	3235–0025
Rule 30e–3	270.30e–3	3235–0758
Rule 31a–1	270.31a–1	3235–0178
Rule 31a–2	270.31a–2	3235–0179
Rule 32a–4	270.32a–4	3235–0530
Rule 34b–1	270.34b–1	3235–0346
Rule 35d–1	270.35d–1	3235–0548
Form N–5	274.5	3235–0169
Form N–8A	274.10	3235–0175
Form N–2	274.11a–1	3235–0026
Form N–3	274.11b	3235–0316
Form N–4	274.11c	3235–0318
Form N–8B–2	274.12	3235–0186
Form N–6F	274.15	3235–0238
Form 24F–2	274.24	3235–0456
Form N–18F–1	274.51	3235–0211
Form N–54A	274.53	3235–0237
Form N–54C	274.54	3235–0236
Form N–CEN	274.101	3235–0729
Form N–27E–1	274.127e–1	3235–0545
Form N–27F–1	274.127f–1	3235–0546
Form N–PORT	274.150	3235–0730
Form N–17D–1	274.200	3235–0229
Form N–23C–1	274.201	3235–0230
Form N–8F	274.218	3235–0157
Form N–17F–1	274.219	3235–0359
Form N–17F–2	274.220	3235–0360
Form N–23c–3	274.221	3235–0422
Form ID	274.402	3235–0328
Form SE	274.403	3235–0327
Rule 0–2	275.0–2	3235–0240
Rule 203–3	275.203–3	3235–0538
Rule 204–2	275.204–2	3235–0278
Rule 204–3	275.204–3	3235–0047
Rule 206(3)–2	275.206(3)–2	3235–0243
Rule 206(4)–2	275.206(4)–2	3235–0241
Rule 206(4)–3	275.206(4)–3	3235–0242
Rule 206(4)–4	275.206(4)–4	3235–0345
Form ADV	279.1	3235–0049
Schedule I to Form ADV	279.1	3235–0490
Form ADV–W	279.2	3235–0313
Form ADV–H	379.3	3235–0538
Form 4–R	279.4	3235–0240
Form 5–R	279.5	3235–0240
Form 6–R	279.6	3235–0240
Form 7–R	279.7	3235–0240
Form ADV–E	279.8	3235–0361

863

§ 200.800

[67 FR 14634, Mar. 27, 2002, as amended at 70 FR 37611, June 29, 2005; 76 FR 46616, Aug. 3, 2011; 77 FR 18684, Mar. 28, 2012; 80 FR 6902, Feb. 9, 2015; 82 FR 82009, Nov. 18, 2016; 83 FR 29203, June 22, 2018; 84 FR 33629, July 12, 2019; 85 FR 26092, May 1, 2020]

List of CFR Sections Affected

All changes in this volume of the Code of Federal Regulations (CFR) that were made by documents published in the FEDERAL REGISTER since January 1, 2018 are enumerated in the following list. Entries indicate the nature of the changes effected. Page numbers refer to FEDERAL REGISTER pages. The user should consult the entries for chapters, parts and subparts as well as sections for revisions.

For changes to this volume of the CFR prior to this listing, consult the annual edition of the monthly List of CFR Sections Affected (LSA). The LSA is available at *www.govinfo.gov*. For changes to this volume of the CFR prior to 2001, see the "List of CFR Sections Affected, 1949–1963, 1964–1972, 1973–1985, and 1986–2000" published in 11 separate volumes. The "List of CFR Sections Affected 1986–2000" is available at *www.govinfo.gov*.

2018

17 CFR 83 FR Page

Chapter II
240 Policy statement 55486
240.3a1-1 revised 38911
240.3a51-1 (a)(2)(i)(A)(*3*) revised 50221
(a) introductory text amended 58427
240.10A-1 (b)(3) revised 50221
240.12b-2 Amended 32021, 50221
240.12g-3 (a)(2), (b)(2), and (c)(2) revised 50221
240.13a-10 (b) and (g)(3) revised 50221
240.13a-14 (f) revised 40878
240.13b2-2 (b)(2)(i) and (ii) revised 50222
240.13h-1 (a)(5) amended 58427
240.14a-16 (f)(2)(iii) amended 29204
240.15c2-12 (b)(5)(i)(C)(*14*) amended; (b)(5)(i)(C)(*15*), (*16*), and (f)(11) added 44742
240.15c3-1g (b)(1)(i)(A), (ii)(A), (E), (2)(i)(A), and (D) revised 50222
240.15d-2 (a) revised 50222
240.15d-10 (b) and (g)(3) revised 50222
240.15d-14 (f) revised 40878
240.17a-5 (d)(2)(i) Note 1 added 50223
240.17a-12 (b)(2) Note 1 added 50223
240.17g-3 (a)(1)(i) amended 50223
240.17h-1T (a)(1)(v) Note 1 added 50223

2019

17 CFR 84 FR Page

Chapter II
240 Authority citation amended 33491, 33629, 44041
Correction: authority citation amended 55055
Technical correction 13796, 39178
Compliance notification 18136
240.3a71-6 (d)(4) and (5) added 44041
(d)(6) added 68646
240.10A-1 (c) introductory text revised 50739
240.12b-23 Revised 12727
240.12b-32 Removed 12728
240.14a-101 Amended 2426, 12728
240.15c3-1 (a)(5) and (c)(2)(xii) redesignated as (a)(5)(i) and (c)(2)(xii)(A); (a)(5)(ii), (10) undesignated center heading and text, (c)(2)(vi)(O), (P), new (xii)(B), (xv), and (17) added; (a)(7) undesignated center heading, (i), (ii), and (c)(2)(iv)(E) revised 44042
240.15c3-1a (a)(3), (4), (b)(1)(v)(C)(*3*), and (*4*) revised; (b)(1)(v)(C)(*5*) added 44044
240.15c3-1b (a)(3)(iii)(C) amended; (b) added 44044
240.15c3-1d (b)(7), (8), (10)(ii)(B), (c)(2), and (5)(i)(B) revised 44045

17 CFR—Continued

84 FR Page

Chapter II—Continued

240.15c3-1e (c)(4)(v)(D) removed; Preliminary note, (a)(7), and (c)(4)(v)(E) through (H) redesignated as introductory text, (a)(7)(i), and (c)(4)(v)(D) through (G); new introductory text, (a) introductory text, (c)(3), and (e)(1) revised; new (a)(7)(ii), (c)(4)(v)(B)(*1*), and (*2*) added; (e) introductory text amended 44046

240.15c3-3 Introductory text and (p) added 44047

240.15c3-3b Added 44050

240.15*l*-1 Added 33491

240.15Fb6-1 Removed; eff. 4-22-19 4947

240.15Ga-2 (e) revised; (f)(i) and (ii) redesignated as (f)(1) and (2) 40258

240.16a-3 (e) removed 12728

240.17a-3 (a)(24) added 33629

Introductory text, (a)(12)(i)(I), and (25) through (30) added; (a) introductory text, (1), (3), (4)(vi), (vii), (5) through (11), (12)(i) introductory text, (A), (E) through (H), (ii), and (b) through (g) revised; (a)(12)(i) undesignated text and (h) removed; (a)(16)(ii)(A), (B), (17)(i)(A), (B)(*1*), (C), (D), (18)(i), and (19)(i) amended 68646

240.17a-4 Introductory text, (b)(8)(xvi), (xvii), (14), (15), (16), and (m)(5) added; (a), (b) introductory text, (1), (3), (4), (5), (7), (b)(8) introductory text, (i), (v) through (viii), (xii) through (xv), (9), (12), (13), (c), (d), (e) introductory text through (4), (6), (f)(3)(vii), (g), (i), (m)(1) through (4) revised; (b)(11), (e)(8), (f) introductory text, (2) introductory text, (3) introductory text, (iv)(B), (vi), (h), (j), (k)(1), and (l) amended 68649

17 CFR—Continued

84 FR Page

Chapter II—Continued

240.17a-5 Introductory text added; (a)(1) removed; (a)(2) through (7) redesignated as (a)(1) through (6); (a) heading, new (a)(1)(ii), (iii), (iv), new (a)(2) through (5), (b)(1), (c)(3), (d)(1)(i)(B), (2)(i), (ii), (iii), (3)(i)(A)(*4*), (*5*), (B), (C), (iii), (6), (e)(1)(ii), (2), (3), (4), (h) note, and (o) revised; new (a)(6), (b)(3), (4), (5), (c)(1), (2), (4)(iii), (5)(iii)(C), (d)(1)(i) introductory text, (f)(3)(v)(B), (k) introductory text, (l), (m)(1), (2), (4), and (n)(2) amended; undesignated text following (c)(4)(iii) designated as (c)(4)(iv) 68652

240.17a-11 (a) removed; (b) through (i) redesignated as (a) through (d) and (g) through (j); Introductory text and (f) added; new (a), (b) introductory text, (c), (d), and (g) through (j) revised 68655

240.17a-12 Amended 68656

240.17a-4 (e)(5) revised 33492

(e)(10) added 33629

240.17a-5 (e)(1)(i)(A) revised 27712

240.17a-14 Added 33629

240.17g-5 (a)(3)(iv) added 40258

240.17g-7 (a)(3) revised 40258

240.18a-1—240.18a-10 Undesignated center heading added 44052

240.18a-1 Added 44052

(d)(9)(iii)(A) and (B) added 68656

240.18a-1a Added 44061

240.18a-1b Added 44063

240.18a-1c Added 44065

240.18a-1d Added 44065

240.18a-2 Added 44068

240.18a-3 Added 44068

240.18a-4 Added 44071

240.18a-4a Added 44075

240.18a-5 Added 68656

240.18a-6 Added 68659

240.18a-7 Added 68662

240.18a-8 Added 68667

240.18a-9 Added 68668

240.18a-10 Added 44076

(a) introductory text, (b)(1), (2), (3), (c) introductory text, (d)(2)(ii) introductory text, and (e) revised; (b)(4) and (5) added 68668

240.24b-2 (b)(2) revised 50739

List of CFR Sections Affected

2020

17 CFR
85 FR Page

Chapter II
- 240 Technical correction...... 19884, 28484
- 240.0-13 Heading, (a), (b), and (e) revised; eff. 4-6-20 6350
- 240.3a71-3 (a)(10) through (13) and (d) added; (b)(1)(iii)(C) revised; eff. 4-6-20 6350
- 240.3a71-6 (d)(7) added; eff. 4-6-20 6412
- 240.12b-2 Amended; eff. 4-27-20 17241
- 240.12b-2 Amended 54071
- 240.12b-11 (d) revised 78229
- 240.12h-5 Revised 22006
- 240.14a-1 (1)(1)(iii) revised; (1)(2)(iii) and (iv)(C) amended; (1)(2)(v) added 55154
- 240.14a-8 (b)(1), (2), (c), and (i)(12) revised; (b)(3) added; eff. through 1-1-23 in part 70294
- 240.14a-2 (b)(9) added 55154
- 240.14a-9 Note amended................. 55155
- 240.14a-16 (f)(2)(iii) revised 26101
- 240.14a-101 Amended ... 26101, 33359, 63761
- 240.14d-1 (h) revised....................... 78229
- 240.15c2-11 Revised........................ 68203
- 240.15Fb1-1 (b) and (d) revised 78229
- 240.15Fb2-1 (d) and (e) revised; eff. 4-6-20................................... 6352
- 240.15Fi-1 Revised; eff. 4-6-20........... 6412
- 240.15Fi-3 Added; eff. 4-6-20 6413
- 240.15Fi-4 Added; eff. 4-6-20 6414
- 240.15Fi-5 Added; eff. 4-6-20 6414
- 240.15g-1 (b) and (c) revised............ 64278
- 240.16a-3 (i) revised....................... 78230
- 240.17a-3 (a)(31) added; eff. 4-6-20 6416
- 240.17a-4 (b)(1) revised; (e)(11) and (12) added; eff. 4-6-20................... 6416
- 240.17Ad-22 (a)(3), (5), and (16) revised... 28867
- 240.18a-5 (a)(10)(iii) and (b)(8)(iii) added; eff. 4-6-20........................... 6353
- (a)(18) and (b)(14) added; eff. 4-6-20 6416
- 240.18a-6 (b)(1)(i) and (2)(i) revised; (d)(4) and (5) added; eff. 4-6-20.. 6416
- 240.18a-6 (b)(1)(x) revised............... 33021
- 240.21F-2 Revised........................... 70942
- 240.21F-3 (b)(1) and (3) revised........ 70943
- 240.21F-4 (c)(2) and (e) revised; (d)(3) added................................. 70943
- 240.21F-6 Introductory text amended; (c) added................... 70943
- 240.21F-7 (a) introductory text revised.. 70944

17 CFR—Continued
85 FR Page

Chapter II—Continued
- 240.21F-8 Heading and (c)(7) revised; (d) and (e) added.............. 70944
- 240.21F-9 (a) and (b) revised; (c) introductory text, (2) through (4), and (d) amended; (e) added.. 70945
- 240.21F-10 (b) through (e) revised.. 70945
- 240.21F-11 (b) through (e) revised.. 70946
- 240.21F-12 (a) introductory text, (3), and (6) revised; (a)(2) amended................................... 70947
- 240.21F-13 (b) revised..................... 70947
- 240.21F-18 Added 70947
- 240.19b-4 (g) revised...................... 65497

2021

17 CFR
86 FR Page

Chapter II
- 240 Policy statement 11627
- 240.0-9 Revised; eff. 5-31-22............ 70251
- 240.0-11 (a)(2), (5), (b) introductory text, (c)(1) introductory text, (2) introductory text, and (d) revised.................................. 70251
- 240.3a51-1 (a) introductory text amended................................... 18809
- 240.12g5-1 (a)(2) revised; (a)(9) added 3601
- 240.12g-6 Heading and (a) introductory text revised................... 3601
- 240.13h-1 Redesignated as 240.13h-1 18809
- 240.13e-1 (a)(5) amended; (b) revised; (c) redesignated as (d); (a)(7) and new (c) added.............. 70251
- 240.13e-100 Amended 70253
- 240.13e-102 Amended 70255
- 240.13h-1 Redesignated from 240.13h-1; (a)(5) amended............ 18809
- 240.13q-1 Revised 4714
- 240.14a-2 (b) introductory text revised.. 68378
- 240.14a-3 (b)(5)(i) removed.............. 2131
- 240.14a-3 (a)(3)(i) and (ii) amended 68378
- 240.14a-4 (b), (d)(2) and (3) amended; (b)(2), (c)(5), (d)(1), and (4) revised; (b)(3) redesignated as (b)(5); new (b)(3), (4), and instruction 1 added 68378
- 240.14a-5 (c) revised; (e)(2) and (3) amended; (e)(4) added................ 68379
- 240.14a-6 (a) Note 3 revised............ 68379

867

17 CFR—Continued

86 FR Page

Chapter II—Continued
240.14a-19   Added 68380
240.14a-101   Amended..... 2131, 68381, 70257
240.14c-101   Amended 70259
240.14d-100   Amended 70259
240.14d-102   Amended 70260
240.17a-4   Correction: (a) and (l) revised....................................... 31116
240.17a-12   Correction: (i)(2) revised....................................... 31116
240.17Ad-24   Added; eff. 4-2-21 7643

2022

17 CFR

87 FR Page

Chapter II
240   Authority citation revised 73138
240.10b5-1   Preliminary note removed; (a), (b), (c)(1)(i), and (ii) revised; (c)(1)(iv) added 80429
240.10D-1   Undesignated center heading and section added 73138
240.12b-2   Amended 57398
240.12d1-3   (c) revised 35413
240.14a-2   (b)(9) revised 43196
240.14A d-1 Added; eff. 7-1-24 78808
240.14a-3   (c) revised...................... 35413
240.14a-9   (e) removed.................... 43196
240.14a-101   Amended ... 55197, 73139, 80430
240.14c-3   (b) revised..................... 35413
240.14c-101   Amended 55197
240.16a-3   (f)(1)(i)(A) and (g)(1) revised....................................... 80430

17 CFR—Continued

87 FR Page

Chapter II—Continued
240.17a-4   (f), (i), and (j) revised; (k) heading removed 66448
240.18a-6   (e) through (g) revised... 66450
240.21F-3   (b)(3) introductory text, (i), and (iii) revised; (b)(3)(iv), (v), and (vi) added 54150
240.21F-4 (c)(2) revised 54151
240.21F-6 (d) added 54151
240.21F-8 (e)(4)(ii) revised 54151
240.21F-10 (e) revised 54151
240.21F-11   (a), (c), and (e) revised....................................... 54151
240.24b-2   Note removed; introductory text and (i) added; (b) introductory text amended 38964
240.24b-2   (i) revised; eff. 7-1-24 78808

2023

(Regulations published from January 1, 2023, through April 1, 2023)

17 CFR

88 FR Page

Chapter II
240.0-2   (c) revised 12209
240.13e-100   CFR correction: Amended 18987
240.15c6-1   Revised; eff. 5-5-23 13952
240.15C6-2 Added; eff. 5-5-23 13953
240.17Ad-27 Added; eff. 5-5-23 13953

868